The Quiet Adventurers in North America

CANADA

Marion G. Turk

HERITAGE BOOKS
2020

HERITAGE BOOKS
AN IMPRINT OF HERITAGE BOOKS, INC.

Books, CDs, and more—Worldwide

For our listing of thousands of titles see our website
at
www.HeritageBooks.com

Published 2020 by
HERITAGE BOOKS, INC.
Publishing Division
5810 Ruatan Street
Berwyn Heights, Md. 20740

Heritage Books by the author:
The Quiet Adventurers in Canada
The Quiet Adventurers in North America (Canada)

International Standard Book Number
Paperbound: 978-1-55613-618-4

This book is dedicated, with great admiration, to the many women of America who have worked persistently over many decades on the records of their own and other families, to provide a permanent record for later generations.

TABLE OF CONTENTS

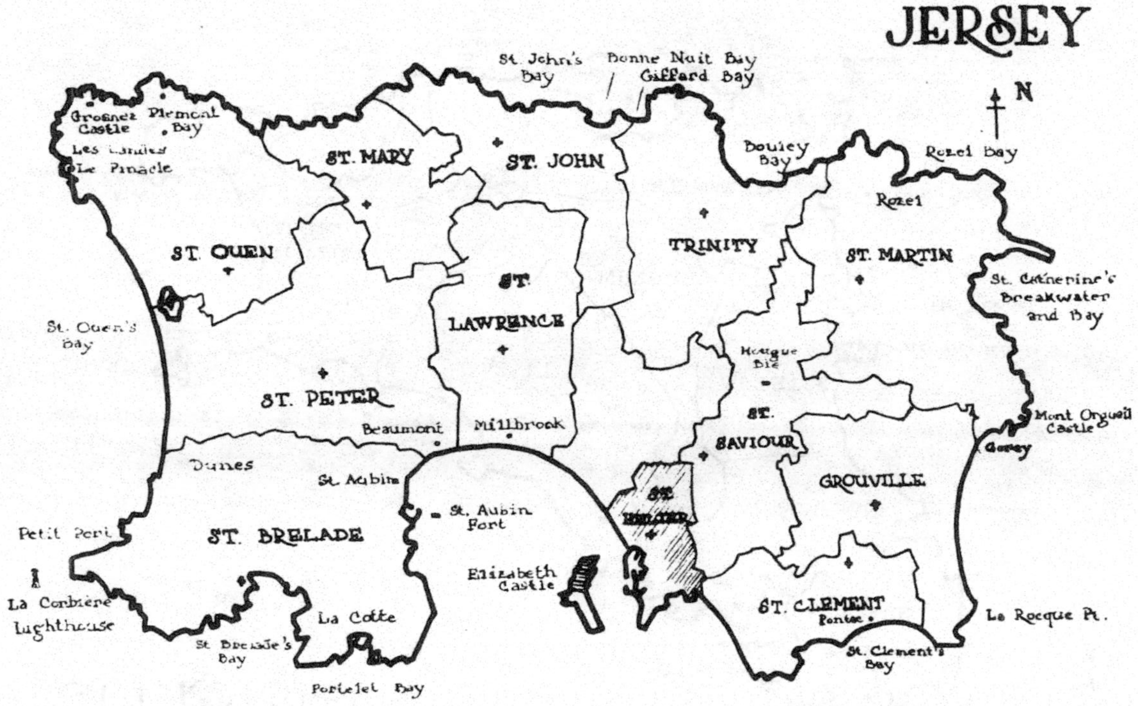

JERSEY

N

St. John's Bay
Bonne Nuit Bay
Giffard Bay
Grosnez Castle
Plemont Bay
Le Pinacle
Bouley Bay
Rozel Bay
Rozel
ST. MARY
ST. JOHN
ST. OUEN
TRINITY
ST. MARTIN
ST. LAWRENCE
St. Catherine's Breakwater and Bay
St. Ouen's Bay
Hougue Bie
ST. PETER
Beaumont
Millbrook
ST. SAVIOUR
Mont Orgueil Castle
Gorey
Dunes
St. Aubin
GROUVILLE
St. Aubin Fort
Petit Port
ST. BRELADE
Elizabeth Castle
La Corbiere Lighthouse
ST. CLEMENT
Pontac
La Rocque Pt.
La Cotte
St Brelade's Bay
St. Clement's Bay
Portelet Bay

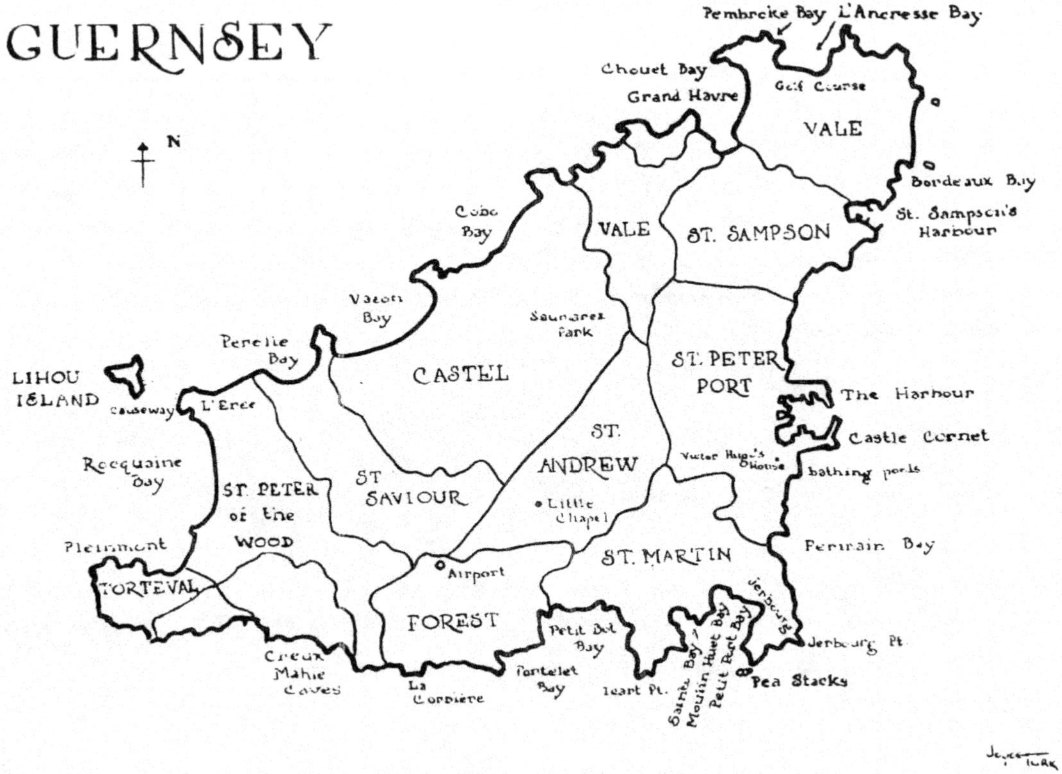

GUERNSEY

N
Pembroke Bay
L'Ancresse Bay
Chouet Bay
Grand Havre
Golf Course
VALE
Bordeaux Bay
St. Sampson's Harbour
Cobo Bay
VALE
ST. SAMPSON
Vazon Bay
Saumarez Park
Perelle Bay
ST. PETER PORT
LIHOU ISLAND
causeway
L'Eree
CASTEL
The Harbour
Castle Cornet
ST. ANDREW
Victor Hugo's House
bathing pools
Rocquaine Bay
ST. PETER of the WOOD
ST SAVIOUR
Little Chapel
Pleinmont
Fermain Bay
ST. MARTIN
Airport
TORTEVAL
Jerbourg
FOREST
Petit Bot Bay
Jerbourg Pt
Creux Mahie Caves
La Corbière
Portelet Bay
Icart Pt.
Saints Bay
Moulin Huet Bay
Petit Port Bay
Pea Stacks
Joyce Turk

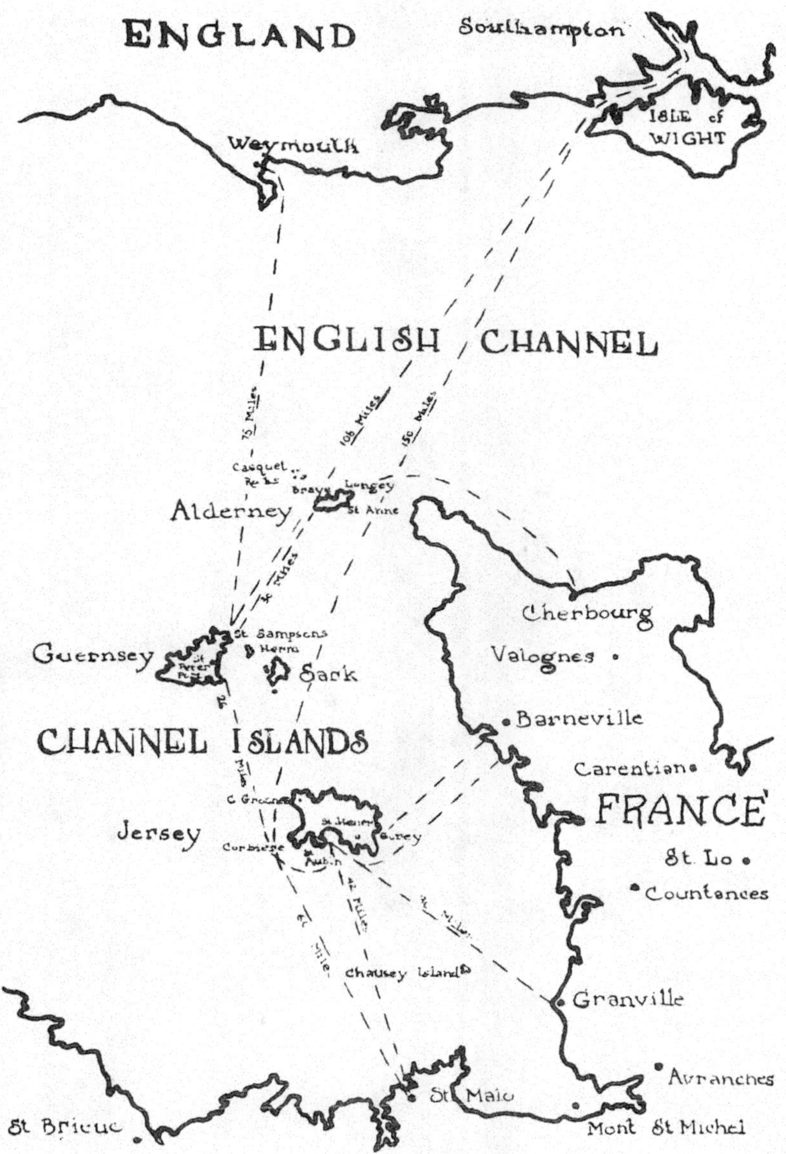

ENGLAND
Southampton
ISLE of WIGHT
Weymouth
ENGLISH CHANNEL
75 Miles
108 Miles
150 Miles
Casquet
Brays
Longey
Alderney
St Anne
Cherbourg
St Sampsons
Herm
Guernsey
Valognes
Sark
Barneville
CHANNEL ISLANDS
Carentian
C Grosnez
FRANCE
Jersey
Gorey
Corbiere
St Aubin
St. Lo
Countances
Chausey Island
Granville
Avranches
St Malo
St Brieuc
Mont St Michel

ACKNOWLEDGEMENTS

As in previous books, I would like to acknowledge my debt to the late Philip Winter Luce, newspaperman of Vancouver, BC, Canada, for the primary facts about the settlement of Channel Islanders in North America. This information came to me from Lady McKie of Ottawa, Ontario. Leads from these two sources sent me on a search for more information to be found in various parts of the continent, and led to the publication of the second and third books of this short series.

I do want to thank also Mr. A. John Jean of Jersey, who very kindly sent me information on early ship connections between the Channel Islands and the American colonies. His recent book, JERSEY SAILING SHIPS, published October 1982 in England, should prove an excellent new source for information about early American commerce. Michael Dun of Jersey, was also of help with shipping information.

I am much indebted to Marie-Louise Backhurst of Jersey for bringing me a copy of the excellent typescript by Charles Stevens of Jersey, CATALOG OF JERSEY FAMILY NAMES, a basis source book on old Island surnames. Thanks are due also to Roger Brehaut of Guernsey, who helped me compile a list of old Guernsey surnames.

For most of the family charts in this book I am deeply indebted to several thousand persons, who sent me data on their own lines and on others, as well as general information on Channel Islanders in North America. I greatly appreciate the warm cooperation of these fine people, and of the many other correspondants, who aided in compiling this book.

Thanks also to Sandra Smith-Czinger, whose typing made this book possible, and to my husband, Edward J. Turk. His patience and help were crucial to the production of this book.

LIBRARIES were a tremendous help in gathering the information in this book.

New England Historical and Genealogical Society Library, Boston, MASS.
Burton Collection, Main Library, Detroit, MICH.
Cambridge Public Library, Cambridge, Ohio

Essex Institute, Salem, MASS
Parma Library, Ridge Road, Parma, Ohio
Ohio Genealogical Society Library, Mansfield, Ohio
Fairview Park Branch of Cuyahoga County Libraries, Fairview Park, Ohio.
Western Reserve Historical Society Library, Cleveland, Ohio.

The last named Library has agreed to set up a Channel Islands Collection, which will contain books, manuscripts, letters and much miscellaneous material about the Islands and the Islanders. This should be available to the public sometime in 1984. Certain information for which there was no room in this book, such as dates, will be found in the Collection.

ERRORS AND OMISSIONS: Mistakes large and small are inherent in a work of this kind. I have done my best, but I realize that some of the information in this book may prove to be incorrect. I do apologize to the reader for this. You can help rectify this, if you will make a note of the errors you notice, correct them in your own copy of the book, and notify others who might be interested. Queries about this book will be answered by me, if your letter is accompanied by a stamped, self-addressed envelope.

Dear Reader, I do hope you will forgive the errors and remember that my intent is just to provide some information and encouragement to the thousands of amateur genealogists with Channel Island ancestors.

Marion G. Turk,
5811 Kenneth Ave.,
Parma, Ohio, USA, 44129.

Canadian researchers, you may find it helpful to join this new Society: GASPESIAN CHANNEL ISLAND SOCIETY, c/o Diane Sawyer, PO Box 841, New Richmond, Quebec, Canada. GOC 2BO

PREFACE

The misty beginnings of America's story have long beguiled the imagination of historians. Certainly Columbus was a late-comer, according to some writers, and Newfoundland may have been the first North American landing place of Europeans.

While this book is mainly family records, genealogy leans heavily on history, and an historical backdrop is very useful in clarifying the story of the Channel Islanders in America.

C.D. Howe, in NEWFOUNDLAND, AN INTRODUCTION TO CANADA'S NEW PROVINCE, says: "There is a tale that men of the Channel Islands in the latter part of the fifteenth century were blown westward off their course (to Iceland?) until they came to a strange land where the sea was full of fish." This sea of fish, the Newfoundland Banks, was a new and rich source of food for protein-hungry Europeans, and that part of the North Atlantic ocean rapidly became a mecca for any man with a ship, from the Portugal coast to the British Isles. Salted and dried codfish soon became a staple food in Europe, South America, the West Indies and the American colonies. Codfish became the standard cargo in Jersey owned vessels. (See JERSEY SAILING SHIPS, by A. John Jean.)

"There must have been a well-organized and continuous series of fishing stations along these coasts, particularly the coast of Maine before 1620." (Andrews) The buildings were mentioned by Bradford and Winthrop, and it's my belief that some of these early settlements belonged to Channel Islanders. There are no records of the arrival of most of the earliest settlers, and it seems likely that some fishing stations gradually became small coastal towns. Note that the Pilgrims came to one of these stations for food in that bad winter of 1622. They were generously treated by the rough and ready traders, who had wisely brought adequate supplies.

I also believe that some of the earliest men in New England came not directly from Europe, but had spent some time in the Newfoundland cod fisheries. Links to European families, because of this intervening time, are difficult or impossible to re-establish. There was so much of this, that the British Government published stringent laws, making it illegal to sail would-be immigrants to New England from Newfoundland. Cases are recorded where the fishermen, instead of heading back to England at the close of the season, seized the ship and headed for Maine or Boston. One year, from one Newfoundland bay alone, more than one hundred fishermen found their way to New England. A skipper, one Stout of the ship GOOD INTENT, was said to have carried six hundred men there in one year, by heading them up separately in casks, while the ship was being cleared for sea. In another case, while their ship was anchored in Chateaux Bay, Nfld., the crew seized an English ship and carried her off to Boston. (ROMANCE OF LABRADOR, by Wilfred Grenfell, NY, 1934.)

For this reason, I strongly believe that there were many more Channel Islanders settled in early America than is known by the historians. They went from the Islands to Newfoundland in great numbers, for the season, spring to fall, as many as one thousand or 1,500 each year. In the 1600s and early 1700s, New England held out great promise for these men, and what more natural than to figure out a way to avoid the backbreaking, unremunerative life of the cod fisheries?

Records of English ships are quite plentiful, but there are still thousands of early settlers whose voyages were not recorded. The Islanders had spent hundreds of years avoiding record-keepers and the Government's eye, and landing boat loads of settlers in small coves was apple pie for them. I was unable to locate records of Jersey ships landing in New England in those early years, except for two or three cases. However, A. John Jean, of Jersey, has made mention in his book, JERSEY SAILING SHIPS, (Phillimore, Sussex, England, 1982) of the many voyages that are recorded of Jersey ships going to America, and there are, no doubt, many more not recorded. It is said that only 20 percent of the immigrants, and the ships they came in, is known. Some of these anonymous ships were definitely from Jersey and Guernsey.

Note that men named Seale, Patriarche (Pedrick?), Chevalier, Janvrin, Carteret, Dean, Pipon, Lempriere, Anley, Le Bailley, Nicolle, Messervy, Marett, Maugier, Brown, Teuzell, Seward, etc., were Channel Islanders involved with the Newfoundland trade and fisheries in 1710. It is noteworthy that these names were represented in early New England. (A.C. Saunders, Societe Jersiaise, author of books about Jersey in the 16th to 19th centuries.)

Guernsey and Jerseymen settled mainly, at first, in Marblehead, Salem and Boston. Records show, however, that they were soon appearing throughout New England, and along the coasts of the Atlantic colonies. Marblehead was shared with folk from Cornwall, whose native tongue is said to closely correspond with the Channel Islander's language, an ancient form of Norman French. The Islanders had, from very early times, sailed to Cornwall to work in the mines, and were also connected by blood ties.

The Islanders came to New England from Newfoundland, from England, and directly from the Islands. Ship-building there had been an important industry from recorded times. By 1699 there were hundreds, possibly thousands, of Channel Islanders in New England. Born to the sea, most were fishermen and sailors. As land was cleared some took to farming again, as they had done throughout the centuries in the Islands. Some were tradesmen, and others, astute and ambitious, became merchant adventurers, rapidly rising from shipbuilders and ship owners to business tycoons. (See Cabot, Bertram and English.)

Coastwise shipping was vital to the colonies, as there were no interior roads. The Islanders excelled in this field, and soon changed the design of their ships to conform to the new uses demanded of coasters. The schooner quickly took the lead in the fisheries, as it was much more efficient than the previously used shallop, an undecked vessel.

The Channel Islanders fitted well into early New England life. As seamen, ship builders, carpenters, fishermen, farmers and businessmen, their talents were needed. Their "Frenchness" was a drawback in some communities, as was their predilection for legal battles. Their firm grasp of monetary possibilities and their free-thinking ways kept some of them in hot water.

They spoke their own form of French, which often alienated the predominantly British colonists. Being highly practical, many found it expedient to anglicize their Norman French surnames, or to translate them into English equivalents. Thus, LE JEUNE became Young, LE BOUTILLIER became Butler, LE BLANC became White, LE BRUN became Brown, etc. Where the name was not translated, phonetic spelling brought about many other changes in the Island surnames.

At the time of the American Revolution, some Islanders and their descendants remained deeply loyal to the British Crown, and left the colonies to settle in Canada. Hundreds were granted land in Nova Scotia, Gaspe, New Brunswick and Ontario, and thus changed the pattern of life there. Channel Island surnames appear in Loyalist lists of grants.

After the first flood of immigrants, Island emigration slacked off for a time. Perhaps the population dwindled enough to provide jobs for the young people. In any case, there are some records of Islanders who came in the early 1800s, such as those to Virginia and to Guernsey Co., Ohio.

Wisconsin drew the next settlement of Islanders, then a fair number joined the Mormon Church in Jersey and Guernsey and sailed to America, settling in Utah. There is reason to think that there were other settlements made in Iowa and possibly in the quarrying areas of New Hampshire and Vermont. California, Texas and Michigan drew other Islanders.

While ships sailed from Jersey to America directly for well over two hundred years, Mr. A. John Jean of Jersey, author of JERSEY SAILING SHIPS, provided a copy of an advertisement that ran in French in a Jersey newspaper of 1877, which reads: "ALLAN LINE, two powerful steamships of 3,000 and 4,000 tons each leave from Liverpool twice a week for Quebec, Portland and Baltimore. All classes of passengers and moderate price." Charles Durell of St. Heliers, Jersey was the agent.

Ships were being built in America for Jersey owners beginning before 1700. A long list provided by Mr. Jean shows ships built in Boston, Newbury, MA, Philadelphia and Portland in the 1700s, for Jerseymen and Jersey companies.

Many other Jersey ships were built in America, but the exact place was not recorded, only mentioned as in the British plantations. This could be Virginia, Maryland or the Carolinas, as well as New England.

An interesting sidelight on the American Civil War appears in the records of the ALABAMA, a rebel privateer ship manned in part by Channel Islanders according to A. John Jean of Jersey. "The Confederate ship named ALABAMA, which sunk off Cherbourg, France 1864 by the U.S. Gunboat KEARSARGE, (after having destroyed sixty-five vessels and ten million dollars worth of property) had several Jerseymen among her crew, one a Richardson or Robinson, a carpenter, and others. Also, another Confederate vessel, named JEDDO, and this ship might have been built in Jersey. Certainly, a steamer of this name was built by shipbuilders Esnouf and Mauger, but was not owned or registered locally. This vessel is something of a mystery at the moment, and could have been sold to the Confederate Navy." (A. John Jean; Underhill)

Looking back, the settlement of New England came at an opportune time for the Islanders. Huguenots were crowding the Islands, and the Islanders themselves must have often felt confined. No doubt they thought of the wide rich valleys and the teeming fish of the New World. Their vessels awaited only wind and tide, and then it was Westward Ho! for the fishermen-farmers of the Channel Islands.

ADDITIONS AND CORRECTIONS

Much of the data in this book has been compiled from letters sent in by persons with Channel Island ancestry. These letters and charts, plus other sources, now compose THE CHANNEL ISLANDS COLLECTION, Western Reserve Historical Society Library, 10824 East Blvd., Cleveland, OH, 44106. Phone 216-721-5722. An index of this material is available at the library.

Since publication of this book in 1983, additional data has been included in the Collection, but may not be in the Index, as yet.

If you intend to visit the Library in Cleveland from out of state, it might be wise to notify the library a day or so ahead, of the Containers and Folders you would like to see.

If you write to the CHANNEL ISLAND FAMILY HISTORY SOCIETY in St. Helier, Jersey, please note that the current address is CIFHS, P.O. Box #507, St. Helier, Jersey, Channel Is., Great Britain. Enclose with your request an International Postal Coupon. Consult the Society for other possible changes in address of CI groups. Join this fine Society.

ALEXANDER, Charles, from CI to St. Louis, MO.
ALLEY/ALLEZ, data added to CI COLL. (B.Goldsmith, MRB, MA)
ANLEY, from CI to Virginia 1635 from J
ANTHOINE, Richard and Sarah from CI to Phila.,PA 1708
APLEY/ASPLET, Charles from CI to MA mid 1800s.
ARMS, charts added to CI COLL.(June Voll, SunCityW, UT)
AUBIN, from CI to Phila. before 1874
AUBIN/OBEN, Philip, p. 659. Data added to CI COLL.
BAAL, fam from CI to Guelph, ONT 1930s
BEAUCHAMP, Jean mar Jane P.Collings in G, had at least one son, Charles Henry, mar 1880 Alice INGROUILLE, two chn, rem to Oakville, ONT (George Beauchamp,Peterborough,ONT)
BEAUCHEMIN fam from CI to UTAH, 1800s.
BIBBER/VIBERT, James.Added data (Carolyn Davis, OceansideCA)
BODRET, Michael, thought to be from CI, in ME early. (Walter Davis, Portland, ME)
BRAKE, quarry fam,of MA, data added.(H.Palmieri, Cohoes,NY)
BREHAUT, data added to CI COLL. (Mrs. Streight, Ottawa, ONT and G. Burhoe, Valrico, FLA)
BRIMAGE, John LE NORY, b 1891, son of Amelia LE NOURY, who mar 1.Richard Shepard, 2. Wm. Greening, 3.John T.Brimage. (Eliz. Duck, Toronto, ONT)
BROACHE, p.660,661. More added. This name was originally BRACHE. (Doris Miller, Mansfield, OH)
BROWN/LE BRUN?, John, b 1688 J was abducted with his brother Daniel, 2 yrs.older, and a servant lad named Duffy, ca 1698 and brought to Portsmouth, NH. See HIST. OF ROCKINGHAM & STRAFFORD COUNTIES, NH for more on this fam. (Ruth Burrell Brown)
BULLEN, Geo. was of NYCity 1690/92, mariner, bro. of Capt. James BULLEN, p. 143. (Millikin)
BURT, "My cousin, Marg.Brady found records that David Burt was son of Eli & Nancy Smith Burt, b Is. of J, to Guernsey CO.1810...Marg.Burt b G, rec'd as member M.E.Ch.Cambridge, OH 1854. (Edith Sarchet Cruce, Lubbock, TX)

ADDITIONS AND CORRECTIONS

BUSSE, Hanna, dau of Ens.Wm. BUSSE of King Wm.'s War, mar Wm. Wheeler (poss WHILEUR of CI?) 1630-1683, res Concord, MA. (Virkus II)
BUTTON, Claude, said to be of CI, in ME Early. (Walter Davis, Portland, ME)
CARRE, Thomas from France to J after 1512, and Helier CARRE, desc., rem to G, where he d 1677,of St.Peter Port.
CHAMBERLAIN, James, was Seigneur of Ald.Is. in or ca 1584, had son Wm. A Richard CHAMBERLAIN of Salem,MA 1700 was really Richard JANVRIN of Jersey Is.(NEHGS #579,p.264)
CHICK, data added to CI COLL.
CHURCH, data added to CI COLL. (Dennis Rodgers,Decatur,IL)
CLARK, shipbuilders in J 1800s, some rem to Nebraska
DE CAMP/DE CAEN fam reunion in Riley,OH 1851.Ezechiel DE CAMP or DE CAEN & wife emigrated ca 1810 to OH from CI with chn, 12boys,5girls. Sons were masons & carpenters, 9 lived Cincinnati,OH. 108 grchn, 33 grgrchn. (CIFHS bull. #34, Spring 1987)
DE CARTERET, Clement, to New England and/or Nfld. 1776.(Soc. Jers.Bulletin,#4,1880s;HIST.OF HARLEM,NY,pp 7,8,321)
DELACROIX, Peter, to ME early, from CI? (Walter Davis)
DELAREE, James & Mary Eliz. from G to US 1817.(Virginia Thomas, Amityville,NY) Note that John & James DELAREE settled WaltersFalls,ONT. (FAMILIES, ONT. GEN.SOC.)
DE MOUILPIED, Amice b 1887 CI mar Sadie B. McClennan 1891, rem to Inglis, MAN 1909,5 chn. (CIFHS #21)
DOREY, Addie to Iowa late 1800s; Joanna b 1828 J, d 1918 ORE. John DOREY b 1801 Ald Is. to Amer.West. Other data added to CI COLL.
DRAPER, Wm. H., Chief Justice of Canada, was son of a Masters/Le Maitre of Jersey Is.
DUCHEMIN, Daniel, d in Boone Co., IND age 69, native of St. Laurens, Jersey. (CIFHS #27)
DUFOUR, Hilary to Chicago, ILL 1800s from CI.
DUMARESQ, Geo., b 1649 J, to America.
DUQUEMIN, to US on TITANIC, survived and had chn in US. (Ed. Le Page, Grimsby, ONT)
DUPUY, one said to have come to Canada from CI
FERBRACHE, Daniel, ?son of Daniel P., b G 1776 had 3 chn in US: Judith b 1792, Daniel b 1794, Thomas b 1797 G. (Frances Graves & John MAHEY, Flint, MI)More-CI COLL.
FICKETT, more in CI COLL.(JoyceDavis, EllicottCt., MD)
FILLEUL, poss originates in Rouen, France.(Soc.Jers.Bull. of 1976)
FILLIATRE, Samuel, son of Francis, from J to Nfld. mar Sarah MESSERVY. (A.S.Filiatre, St. Georges, Nfld.)
FRANCIS & FERRON, 4 pp added to CI COLL.
GALLEY, LE GALLAIS?, John from J mar Florence __in Salem, MA 1635, d Beverly, MA(Hazel Hammond, Marcellus,NY)
GALLIENNE, charts added to CI COLL. (John Mahey,Flint,MI)
GOSSETT, Richard, wife LE MAISTRE, from J to ONT. (Paul Cleal, Islington, ONT)
GRUSH (DE GRUCHY?), Judith b J? d 1847 in MASS age 71.
HARKER, Kesiah, b J ca 1700 mar Bernard Stroud 1722 in Amwell,NJ. She d before 1782, when Bern.d in Salisbury PA. (Sara Burnett, Santa Cruz, CAL)

ADDITIONS AND CORRECTIONS

HERAULT, Henry from CI to New England 1679.
(Soc. Jersiaise bulletin Vol 4, 1880s)
HUBBARD/HUBERT. Early chart of this New England family:
1. Jean Hubert mar Catherine GUILLE (Source:CIFHS)
2. Edouard Hubert mar Joanne HAMON
3. Etienne Hubert mar Marie ROMERIL
4. Jean Hubert mar Elisabeth LE GALLAIS
5. Philippe HUBERT/HUBBARD b St. Sav.J, removed to Berwick, ME before 1692. Mar then Eliz. (Goodwin) Emery, dau of Dan.& Marg. (Spencer) Goodwin. Philip d ca 1723.

HUBERT, Thomas from CI was in Fayette Co,OH 1830.

JAMES, Mr. and Mrs.Alfred of Vale G, res Racine,WI 1800s.

JANVERIN, Capt. Richard of J mar at Salem, MA 30 Oct1699 (her second husb)Katherine Hutchinson, dau of Edward. Rich.changed name to CHAMBERLAIN per deed 16Feb.1703/4, "her husband of Jersey". Kath.relinquished her right of dower in estate of 1st husb., Henry Bartholomew. (BARTHOLOMEW FAM, p.65; NEHGS, Vol-1991,3579,p.264/5)

JUNE FAM, poss JEUNE?, of CI in Carolina. (Mrs. Wm.Edmund, Broken Arrow, OK)

LAFFOLEY/LAFOLLETTE, data on fam from J to NJ then to VA. (Ralph Lafollette of Indiana)

LARAWAY, more in CI COLL. (Carolyn Huyett, Westchester,PA)

LE BOUTILLIER, large chart and other data addedto CI COLL, and see HIST. OF NY STATE, by Sullivan.

LE BOURVEAU. One from Brest, Brittany, France, not a Huguenot fam.(Eliz. Bowman, Toms River, NJ)

LE BOCQ-LE HUQUET marriage in Ottawa,ONT 1870s.

LE CRAS/LE CRAW fams. Desc. Wm. Le Craw HOOPER b 1833 mar 1859 Deborah Girdler, dau of John and Eliz.1834-1907. Wm. in shoe business. 4 chn: John, Wm, Ellen Conley and Lewis. See HOOPER GENEALOGY.

LE CRAW, fam in Norcross, GA from MRB fam. (C.S. Le Craw, Falls Church, VA) LE GROW of ME, new data in CI COLL.

LE GALLEE, poss LE GALLAIS? fam of NH. Reuben LEGALLEE from G age 12. Chart, etc in CI COLL.(S.Legallee,Littleton,NH)

LE MASURIER fam from Clapham, England, but prev. from CI. Data in CI COLL. (Sandra Love, Mohave, CAL)

LE MASURIER, John Philip mar in J Ann Jane Louise BUESNEL, sister of Clement and Philip, both of whom rem to Canada. More in CI COLL. Desc. in Fresno,CA & Calgary, ALTA.

LE MASURIER, to N.Chelmsford,MA, more in CI COLL. (Harlene Palmieri, Cohoes, NY)

LE MESSURIER, John of G, b 1799 mar Eliz.ALLEZ, 3 chn, rem to Sauk Prairie, WI, to Wausau 1846, mar 1.Sol.Coulthurst, 2.Moses Turner, 3. Sol Trudeau, 4 chn by 1. and 2.

LEMPRIERE, Geo. from CI had 2 sons b Racine: Geo. Henry and Clarence Wm. Geo. had Clarence, Edna Jane & Fred. Clar. had Wm. and Clara Louise.(E.Fred Tostevin, Duarte, CAL)

LENFESTEY, data added to CI COLL.

LE PAGE, OGIER, SARCHET fams, of Guernsey Co., OH, data added to CI COLL. (Edw.Patterson, Canton, OH & others)

LE RETILLEY, see QUARTERLY REVIEW OF GUERNSEY SOC., Sum.1955

LING, Capt. Nicholas, Gov. of G, mar Cecile, dau of Thomas Andros and Eliz. DE CARTERET after 1643. (Wimbush)

ADDITIONS AND CORRECTIONS

MACHON. Current research on these N.Chelmsford, MA fams being done by Harlene Palmieri, Cohoes, NY: BRAKE, DE CARTERET, DE LA HAYE, DUMARESQ, LE MARINEL, LE MASURIER, MACHON, QUEREE, TOMS, VASSELIN, etc. See CI COLL.

MAHY, Many new charts in CI COLL. on these: FERBRACHE, GALLIENNE, MAHY, LE PAGE, OGIER, SARCHET by John Mahey, Flint, MI.

MAJOR, Eliz. and sister Mary, daus of David of G, to Newport, RI 1717. See AYLESWORTH GEN. (MarionStone, Mason City, ILL)

MACHON. Note that orig. book was incorrect on origin of Hannah, wife of Philip Machon, p. 418. Her father was John Maccoone from Scotland, and Philip was P. Gavet,qv.

MARINE, Andre of early ME, thought to be a LE MARINEL from CI. (Walter Davis, Portland, ME)

MARQUAND, Charles. See CIFHS bulletin #24, Jersey.

MARETT, John, b J ca 1766 d 1843, bur St. Andrews Ang.Ch., New Carlisle, Gaspe, QUE. Son Daniel b ca 1802 d 1875. Mar 1834 Marcia Assels, dau of James and Sarah (FLOWERS) Assels, had 8 chn, two mar Flowers.(Beverly Gilchrist, Nanaimo, BC). More in CI COLL.

MARTEL. See corrections and additions in CI COLL.

MASURY/MAJOR, Jean, son of Edward MASURY/MAJOR was in Exeter, NH 1683, soldier in 1695. Mar before 1712 Abiel widow of Wm.Morgan. Dau Jean by earlier wife. Jean mar Benj.Mason, b ca 1696, blacksmith, son of John of Hampton, and Eliz.Ward (Thomas) mar 1672. Jean had bro-in-law Joseph SWETT. Jean d by 1735, had Edw., Benj.,Fran. Mary Cath., Eliz. & Jane Mason. Benj d 1770 at Stratham. Jean/John Masury poss bro.of Wm. b 1660 J.

MOULLIN/MILLS, more data in CI COLL.

OGIER, see LE PAGE,etc. CI COLL.(John Mahey, Flint, MI)

OLIVER, Thomas, b ca 1806 G, d 1888 Independence, Iowa. (Karen Haas, Maple Lake, MINN)

ORMOND, Lt. George, Queens Rangers, b 1753 Gramont,French Flanders, mar in NY Elisabeth Smith, bur in St. Helier, J. A son Capt. George mar in J and died in G. Relatives in New Brunswick. (W.O.Adams, Vista, CAl)

PATRILL/LE PATOUREL, ten pp added to CI COLL.

PERKINS, from CI to Vancouver, BC, Canada.

POINDEXTER, Philip, b 1708, p.517, mar twice. 7 chn by 1st wife Eliz. and 6 by 2nd wife Sarah Crymes. (Barbara Safford, Darien, CT; a microfiche on this fam) See also POINGDESTRE-POINDEXTER, A NORMAN FAMILY, by John Landers.

PINEL/PENNELL, more data in CI COLL.

POLEYN/POLLAN of VA,NC,TN from CI? (Helen Hays, KS)

RENOUF and SEBIRE, data added to CI COLL, including RENOUF bulletins,records of Benj. Gaylord, Bar Harbor, ME.

ROY, some data added to CI COLL.

ROMERIL and assoc.fams. data added to CI COLL. (T. Kryssbek, Salt Lake City, UT)

SARCHET, see LE PAGE, OGIER, etc. re Ohio fams. from G. (John Mahey, Flint, MI)

SAVADE, Mrs. of Vale parish, G in Racine,WISC, 1800s/1900s.

SAVAGE/SAUVAGE, new chart from G. Finch in CI COLL.

ADDITIONS AND CORRECTIONS

SMITH, found in J and G in 1700s.

SMITH, Charles N. of G mar Jessie A. Coysh, dau of Fred., carriage maker and Jessie HILLIER, mar Bridport, England. Son Fred.L.& fam to US 1905.(Ruth Smith, Syracuse,NY)

SMITH, Fred.Cecil left J 1912, mar 1. Anderson & 2.Mary A. Morrison. Grdau Carol res Lawrenceville, NJ.

SNOW. Data added to CI COLL. Ditto SKELTON fam.chart.

STANNAGE. more in CI COLL.

STEELE, James, 1748-1807, p.606 mar Susannah KNIGHT, dau of Joseph. Orig.book calls her Sarah PUTNAM.

STEILL/STEELE/STILLE, Sir Thomas, d in J 1542.Son Robert was rector of St.Clement,J. This fam longtime in St. Martin par. as STILLE. (Soc.Jers.bulletin 1913)

STANLEY. Book mistakenly says on p.606 that STANLEY was not from CI. Some STANLEY fams did come from there to CANADA, and poss. also to US?

SWARTON/SWANTON, more data in CI COLL. (W. Branthoover, Fairport Harbor, OH)

TAYLOR, Geo. W. of G to US at age 11 with parents, 1835. (J.P. Brucken, Brecksville, OH)

THACHER, A. of Goleta, CAL is desc. of DE GRUCHY fam of St. Mary, Jersey.

TORODE. Some data pp627-630 is in error. Try original sources. Also, Nicholas, not John, built saw mill on Salt Creek,ILL ca 1845.

TOSTEVIN, more in CI COLL. Poss one fam was Huguenot.

TOUZEL, Francis of St. Clement, J res Pikesville, Baltimore, MD in 1870s.

TUCKER, M.S. mar Patricia LAMBOTTE of St. Martin,G, res Toronto, ONT.

VALPY, P.640. Note that it was Capt. Daniel Crock and not Capt. John Crocker who mar Abigail Roberts.

VALPY, Abr. mar Eliz.Fowles 1728 in Salem,MA. Same or another mar Lydia Clough. An Abr.was inSalem1790Census.

VALPY/VALPEY, Richard of Yarmouth,NS was Capt. of the INDUSTRY 1777 of Salem, MASS.(LOST IN CANADA #39,1984)

VAN COURT, Elias, b 1691 St. Andrew,G, more data with G.V. Fairfield, Pasadena,TX; Judith Stock,Van Nuys,CAL

VASSELIN, Fernand A.A., b Nehou, De La Manche, France mar Harriet Jane DE CARTERET.A son John LE CORNU VASSELIN has desc.in US. (Harlene Palmieri, Cohoes, NY)

VAUDIN, of Sark Is. in CI COLL. (Norman De Carteret, Sherman Oaks, CAL)

VERGE, VIRGEE, DU VERGEE, DES VERGES. Joseph Verge and Mary Blewett mar in Boston 1755, rem to Liverpool, NS, poss from CI. (Gloria Verge, Walla Walla, WA)

VIBBER/VIBERT, more in CI COLL. See also BIBBER.

WHITELEY, CI FAM in South Africa.

WILLIAMS, John, b ca 1761 Stepney?, G, d 1793 on Pitcairn IS. He was acting armourers mate on ship BOUNTY,mutineer.

WILSON. Fam from J to Virginia where a dau was b 1804. (Marie Stukenbroeker, Exeter, CAL)

ADDITIONS AND CORRECTIONS

A number of charts of the 1400s to the 1600s on the following CI surnames have been added to the CI COLL: BAUDAINS, BENEST, BILLOT, BISSON, BLAMPIED, BOETEL, BOUTILLIER, BROCQ, CONOFROY, CRISTIN, DE CARTERET, DUMARESQ, FALLE, GALLIE, GEYT, GIBAUT, GODFRAY, GIBAUT, HAMPTONNE, HOTTON, LANGLOIS, LARBALESTIER, LAURENS, LE BAS, LECORNU, LE CRAS, LE FEBVRE, LE GALLAIS, LE MASURIER, LEMPRIERE,LE VAVASSEUR, LUCE, MARTEL, MESSERVY, NICOLLE, NOEL, PAYNE, QUEREE, ROMERIL, ROULX, SARRE, ST. CROIX, TOUZEL, TRACHY, VALPY, VAUDIN. (T. Kryssbek, Salt Lake City, UT)

These bulletins & papers are now in the CI COLLECTION:
4 large pp 1841 St. Saviour parish, Jersey Census.
2 issues REVIEW OF THE GUERNSEY SOCIETY, 1977
3 issues QUARTERLY REVIEW OF THE GUERNSEY SOCIETY, 1960s
CHANNEL ISLANDS FAMILY HISTORY SOCIETY, Journals #6, 41,42,43.
TOURIST MAPS, PICTURES AND LITERATURES about the Islands.

Research in Channel Island Genealogy can be greatly enhanced by joining the Societies of the Islands. Especially recommended is THE CHANNEL ISLAND FAMILY HISTORY SOCIETY in St. Helier, Jersey. Past issues of their bulletins contain much data on Island families. THE SOCIETE JERSIAISE, also of St. Helier, established back in the 1800s, covers more aspects of the Islands, but many issues of their bulletins contain articles and charts on Island families. In addition, there are land records and court records, plus birth, marriage and death records of the 12 parishes of Jersey, and the 10 parishes of Guernsey.

I will answer letters that include an SASE, and I wish you family researchers the very best of luck!

Marion Turk,
5811 Kenneth Ave.,
Parma, OH, USA, 44129.
216-884-7246

ATTENTION! CANADIAN RESEARCHERS! You may not know that a new and most helpful society has now been formed: GASPESIAN CHANNEL ISLANDS SOCIETY, c/o Diane Sawyer, P.O. Box 841, New Richmond, Quebec, Canada. GOC 2BO. Write for information. Some researchers available.

JERSEY SHIPS AND THE AMERICAN COLONIES

by A. John Jean

Little early documental evidence has as yet been uncovered regarding the very first ships to reach America, but many historians now accept that the Channel Islanders were amongst the earliest, if not the earliest people to sail their ships along the coasts of North America. Certainly Jersey had the vessels and the seamen necessary to cross the Atlantic as the Islanders had ships of 40 tons or more as early as the 14th century, and although the first half of the 15th century is perhaps one of the periods of Jersey history least known, we do know that in 1420 the Island provided not only crews but also vessels for the English fleet.

The important conger exports to the English mainland were maintained only at the level it had reached by Jersey boats going ever further afield in their endeavours to continue to find the fish necessary for these exports. Their searches took the fishermen to Iceland and Greenland and also as far north as Labrador, and the rich fishing banks off Newfoundland soon became known to the Islanders. Certainly Jerseymen were eating codfish as early as the reign of King Henry VIII (1509-1547).

Some evidence of the trade between Jersey and the American colonies, although not extensive, does exist. We are allowed glimpses of this trade in the occasional references to local vessels leaving for New England, Maryland, Virginia or the Carolinas and returning to Jersey with rich cargoes. In 1715, the BONNE ESPERANCE, Capt. Edward Le Brun, was trading with New England, and later in 1737 both the sloop MARY, Capt. Thomas Balleine and the brigantine RACHEL, Capt. Jean Vincent of St. Aubin, Jersey, were trading with Virginia.

The 20th of June 1740, the vessel THOMAS AND JANE, a 60 ton brigantine, Capt. Carteret Dean, left St. Aubin for Maryland with a cargo owned by A. De Ste. Croix of Jersey. Unfortunately, the contents of this cargo were not itemized. The importation of tobacco from the American Colonies must have reached some importance, as several references to this trade are made, such as the arrival in 1750 at St. Aubin, Jersey of the snow UNITY, Capt. G. Villeneuve, from Maryland with just such a cargo. A Jersey merchant, Edward LeBreton, was importing tobacco from Virginia ca 1730, and even earlier in 1671 Philip D'Auvergne and another local merchant, Thomas Lempriere, were both bringing in tobacco from Virginia.

Thomas Pipon, a Jerseyman residing in Dartmouth, England, acted as agent for John Le Couteur of Jersey importing goods into Dartmouth from Maryland in 1731. He is recorded as importing:

A. Worsted hose from Jersey for Nicholas Patriarche,
B. Rice from South Carolina for a London merchant,
C. Staves from Maryland for George Le Feuvre of Jersey,
D. Tobacco from Maryland on a Jersey ship for himself, and
E. Exported Carolina rice to Rotterdam, Holland.

James Pipon, a Jersey shipowner based in London, was constantly engaged in shipowning, usually in the South Carolina trade, during the late 1740s and 1750s. This trade was typical of the Channel Islands at this time. Many Jersey shipowners removed to London to be nearer the source of much business, or appointed agents to act for them. The Lisbon, Mediterranean, West Indian and Carolina trades were as important to the Islanders as the Newfoundland trade. This trade persisted well into the latter half of the century, as shown by further references to vessels. The vessel named CRUISIER of 100 tons, owned and commanded by Capt. Hammond, was trading with Philadelphia in 1764 as was the PRINCESS, Capt. Nicholas Anthoine, in 1775, the owner of this vessel being Philip Winter. Nicholas Fiott and Matthew Gossett owned the 115 ton UNION, Capt. Simonet, this vessel being recorded as trading with Virginia in 1783, and Charles Robins' brig, the HOPE, of 110 tons, was in Charleston, South Carolina in 1785.

Many more Jersey seamen and shipping folk saw the opportunities that the American Colonies afforded and some settled on the coast and continued their shipping operations from Boston and Salem in particular. George Messervy was the Collector of Customs at Boston at the time of the famous Tea Party in 1773. Thomas Gruchy owned ships at Boston, and his son, Capt. Thomas James Gruchy, commanded the American privateer, QUEEN OF HUNGARY, this vessel of 120 tons.

Another privateer captain was Philip Dumaresq, master of the YOUNG EAGLE, ca 1739. Jersey vessels and Jerseymen were certainly engaged in the slave trade, but naturally, recorded details are few. Some Channel Islanders are listed as slaveholders. John Cabot, born St. Helier, Jersey, 1680, the founder of the Cabot family of America, was a slaveholder in Salem in the first half of the 18th century.

As late as 1854, the Jersey owned brigantine, NEWPORT, of 106 tons, Capt. Charles Philip Hocquard, was chased and caught by a Royal Navy anti-slaving patrol. The Jersey vessel was carrying a number of cases of muskets, knives, hachets, bells and padlocks, all goods that were used in the slave trade.

CHRONOLOGY OF CHANNEL ISLANDERS IN NORTH AMERICA

(See THE QUIET ADVENTURERS IN CANADA, 1979, for more information about settlement in Canada).

1450 "We have been endeavouring to find a source of a statement that Jerseymen were already in Newfoundland in the 15th century. In the 1933 Transactions of La Societe Guernsiaise, p. 45, it is stated that there is a tradition of the MARTIN family at Harbour Grace that an ancestor sailed from Jersey in about 1450 to fish in Icelandic waters, and was induced by an Irishman named Joyce, met in the Orkneys, to go to Newfoundland, where he became established at Harbour Grace." (Société Jersiaise Bulletin of 1979).

1504 Norman vessels crewed by Channel Islanders appeared in Newfoundland waters to catch codfish and to trade with the natives for furs. "...in the habit of visiting the coast of Newfoundland and adjacent waters from as early as 1504." (ENGLAND IN AMERICA, Tyler, Vol. 4.)

1527 Capt. John Rut, in charge of MAN-OF-WAR for King Henry VIII, arrived in St. John's Newfoundland on August 3, 1527, and found eleven sails of Normans (Jerseymen), one Breton, and two Portugese vessels, all fishing and ready to depart for Europe.

1534 Jacques Cartier of France landed on the Gaspe coast of what is now Quebec. Marguerite Syvret, in JERSEY SETTLEMENTS IN GASPE, suggests that among Cartier's crew were a few men from the Channel Islands. Guillaume de Guerneze represented that Island, and perhaps Antoine, Fleury, Olliver, Le Breton and Colas were from Jersey.

1562 Channel Island fishermen were noted on the Grand Banks, south of Newfoundland. (Chadwick, etc)

1583 Sir Humphrey Gilbert's frigate, SWALLOW, waylaid a French vessel (Jerseymen) near the entrance to Conception Bay, Nfld., heading for home. The crew of the SWALLOW were in need of clothing, and took them forcibly from the Jerseymen.

1590 By this time, many Jersey ships sailed to the Grand Banks and Newfoundland each spring, returning in the early fall in time for the autumn plowing. Nearly 1,300 men from the Islands took part each year in this commerce.

1596 Capt. Richard Clarke, who had commanded the DELIGHT in Gilbert's fleet visiting St. John's, Nfld., 1583, was in charge of his own vessel at St. John's. He was the last of the English to leave for home, there being three Norman (Jerseymen) ships left. The Islanders invited him aboard and took the captain and crew prisoners for nine days, while they pillaged the vessel.

1600 Sir Walter Raleigh became Governor of the Channel Islands in this year. His deep interest in Nfld. and Virginia were, no doubt, spurs to the Island shipping and fishing industries.

1608 Thomas Le Marchant was trading with Newfoundland from Guernsey. (OLD TIME NEWFOUNDLAND, by C.R. Fay, 1955, from papers of H.W. Le Messurier).

1621 Carvanyell is recorded in Plymouth, MA. The CARVANEL name is in Steven's book of old Jersey surnames.

1622 James Carteret is recorded in Georgia, with his wife. (LIST OF EARLY SETTLERS OF GEORGIA, by E.M. Coutler and Albert Saye).

1650 Many Channel Islanders are now settled in Marblehead, MA. Also, some have settled on the Maine and New Hampshire coasts.

1667 In the NEHGS, Vol. 40, it is stated that Marblehead inhabitants in 1667 claimed that "many came here from England, Newfoundland and elsewhere, and some were undesirable." It appears that some of the rough-and-ready settlers of the fishing-rooms of Newfoundland have begun to establish themselves in Massachusetts. Dr. Keith Matthews of Memorial University, St. John's, Nfld., has compiled a list of more than 300 Channel Islanders of early times who were engaged in some aspect or other of the Newfoundland fisheries in the years between 1660 and 1840.

1670 Philippe Langlois was born in Trinity Parish, Jersey in 1651. He emigrated as a young man to Salem, MA in 1670, inherited the estate of his wife's father, and became a very wealthy man. He is probably one good reason for the presence in Mass. of so many Jersey persons and families, as he went into a side business of bringing into the colonies hundreds of Jersey and Guernsey boys and girls, indentured to him, and bound out to others for servants, clerks, seamen and household help. He was called Philip ENGlISH in Massachusetts.

1675 Thomas Alley, servant of Daniel Chamberlain of the Isle of Jersey, apprenticed to John Pedrick of Marblehead, MA. Was Pedrick a PATRIARCHE of Jersey?

1713 John Arthur of Jersey bought land at Gloucester, MA. (PENNELL GEN by Clara Phinney, 1916.)

1731 Thomas Pipon, a Jerseyman, living in Dartmouth, England was importing goods from Maryland to England for John Le Couteur of Jersey, He brought in worsted hose from Jersey to England for Nicolas Patriarche, a Jerseyman in England. He brought rice from South Carolina for a London merchant; staves from Maryland for George Le Feuvre of Jersey; tobacco from Maryland on a Jersey ship for himself; and he was exporting Carolina rice to Rotterdam, Holland. (A. John Jean, Jersey.)

1740 Permission was granted to Peter Jeune Le Vavasseur dit Durell to pass from Jersey to Boston, MA. (Notary public book of Peter de Ste. Croix, Jersey, 1739-1744.)

1740 Capt. John Jean sailed the MARY OF JERSEY from the Channel Islands to Virginia for rice and tobacco.

1769 The ship MOLLY from Jersey, captained by Daniel Messervy, arrived at Boston. The passengers, numbering over 50, were probably business men, seamen, and indentured men and women, who had signed up to work in the colonies for from four to seven years. Most of them, from the surnames, were probably Channel Islanders. A few are foreign and British surnames. C.I. surnames: Dumaresq, Luce, Barton, Caul, Le Bourdon, Le Grand, Grandin, Gruchy, Hammon, Gallikan, Le Roy, Watton, Carell, le Masservier, Pervier, de Ste. Croix, Boucher, Colcombe (COLOMBE?), Bessin, Grautt, Pinel, Jenne, Penny. (WHITEMORE)

1806 Thomas Sarchet of Guernsey headed a group of families that sailed from St. Peter Port, Guernsey, 1806, landed in Norfolk, VA, and settled in central Ohio at a settlement consisting of two houses on Wills Creek. The county was soon called Guernsey Co., and others from the Island continued to join them until at least the 1820s.

1840 About this time there began an exodus from Guernsey to Wisconsin, possibly of 10 or 15 families, eventually.

1850s Beginning in the 1840s and continuing into the 1870s, Jersey and Guernsey families came from the Islands to UT. Some did not survive the very strenuous travel of the early years.

1877 The ALLAN LINE took many Channel Islanders from Liverpool, England to Gaspe, Quebec; Portland, ME and Baltimore, MD, about this time.

1890 In the late 1890s a group of several families left the Island of Jersey and settled in North Chelmsford, MA, where they bought quarries. This business was familiar to them in Jersey, and they brought other Jersey families to the area.

1893? "The last organized group emigration from Guernsey to America took place in the early nineties, when about thirty people went to California. Capts. Neale and Debenham were the leaders." (Philip Winter Luce, Vancouver, BC, Canada.)

There may have been other organized groups that removed from the Channel Islands to North America, as there seems to be concentrations of them in many places, such as New Jersey, Iowa, Texas, and Mercer Island, Washington. More research is needed.

The Chronology above does not include the many places of settlement of Channel Islanders in Canada. See THE QUIET ADVENTURERS IN CANADA, by Turk, 1979.

QUESTIONS AND ANSWERS

If you are reading for the first time about Channel Islanders in America, you will probably have many questions about them. Answers below will not entirely cover the subjects, but sources are given.

<u>WHAT AND WHERE ARE THE CHANNEL ISLANDS?</u> (See Channel Island Bibliography)

See the maps in the first part of the book. Then read what the Encyclopedia Brittanica has to say about the Islands. Try your local library for books about the Islands. If there are none, ask your librarian to get you some through the Inter-Library Loan.

The Islands lie in the form of a half-circle in the Bay of Mont. St. Michel, France, and are just off the west coast of the Cotentin Peninsula of Normandy, in the northern part of France. On the north is the Island of Alderney, about 2,000 acres, 1600 pop., 60 miles south of Weymouth, England. Sark is smaller, just east of Guernsey. Other small islands in the group include Herm and Jethou. There is one family in this book with Herm connections.

Guernsey is roughly triangular, about 9½ miles by 7, 24 square miles, with 55,000 pop. Agriculture, horticulture and dairying have been in the past the main occupations, as the climate is mild and sunny. In more recent years, finance, rich residents and tourism have added greatly to the income of the Islands. From 268 quarries in the 1700s and 1800s were taken thousands of tons of very durable stone for buildings and roads of England. (Robinson)

Jersey is a somewhat rectangular island about 10 miles from east to west and near six miles from north to south, about 45 square miles at high tide. Population is ca 75,000 and by 1976 only about half were of Island descent. Jersey farmers grow potatoes, tomatoes, cut flowers and broccoli. Tourism is also a prime source of income for Jersey, plus a small amount of manufacturing.

Homes in the Islands have been made of stone since time out of mind, some with walls three feet thick and always thatched in the old days. The climate is milder than in England or northern France, with a very high proportion of sunny days. The range of tides is one of the highest in the world.

The Islands are self governing, but with a Lieutenant-Governor for each Island, who represents the Sovereign. The twelve parishes of Jersey, and the ten of Guernsey each have a number of local representatives. Some parishes in Jersey date from the sixth century.

The Islands are very picturesque, with the old houses of different shades of stone, with fruit trees and water valleys, the soft-eyed cattle, the green fields, and the many striking coastal views.

The names of the parishes of Jersey and Guernsey are given in the IN SEARCH OF YOUR ANCESTORS section.

WHAT ARE THE CHANNEL ISLANDERS LIKE?

There is no easy answer to this! They are what history has made them. They are like the other Northern Europeans, but there is a difference!

Payne's ARMORIAL says, "They...are a capable, knowledgeable and hard-working people with great and proverbial powers of memory, much and genuine hospitality, an innate and Hibernianesque wit with which is curiously blended the phlegm and frugality of the canny Scot...an incurable mania for petty political intrigue and a native bravery."

In the 1600s the Governor of Cherbourg, France, was deploring the activity of the Islanders as privateers and noted their "habit of encountering the dangers of the sea renders the natives very brave...excellent marksmen...always in a state of warfare, now against the customs house officers, now against the French commercial marine. A population of this character greatly enhances the natural strength of these Islands." The fact that they were so early in the New World speaks volumes about their character and personality.

The hardships of the past, and Norse blood, perhaps, have toughened the Islanders, giving them an eager interest in travel, and molding a very sturdy ego. In addition, another strong influence on the Islanders was the heavy influx of Huguenots from France. While most of these moved on to other places in Europe and North and South America, some lingered in the Islands, promoting Protestantism, providing a tradition of being hard workers, and bringing in useful trades and abilities, as well as money and ships.

Undoubtedly other areas contributed to the genes of the Islanders, as German and Dutch names appear at times, plus Spanish, Portuguese and Italian. There was always a trickle of folk from Great Britain, which sometimes swelled to a flood, as when British Army units were stationed there, during and after the Napoleonic era. This flood continued later, when the servicemen were joined by a good many affluent Britons, who still enjoy temporary or permanent removals to the Islands. Readers should note however, that British surnames have occurred on the Islands from extremely early times.

WHICH FAMILIES AND PERSONS ARE INCLUDED IN THIS BOOK?

The Channel Islands have been home to hundreds of thousands of families since the Romans first noted them. Not all the surnames of the Islands are included in this book. More information on these interesting names can be found in the Islands, in books about the Islands, and some data in the Western Reserve Channel Islands Collection.

There are some persons and families noted in this book for which no proof can be found as to their Island origin. When there is some doubt, a question mark and/or OUTC is noted with the data. OUTC mean "origin unknown to the compiler." However, the fact that the name is included means there is some reason to think the person or family might have a Channel Island connection. The classes given below show some of the criteria used to indicate whether or not a person or family should be included in this book.

1. Families and persons of which the surname itself is uniquely associated with the Islands, and is scarce or non-existent elsewhere, within the knowledge of the compiler, except through emigration from the Islands. Such names would be, for instance, DUMARESQ, DE JERSEY, TORODE, GALLICHAN, LEMPRIERE, AHIER, PIPON, HACQUOIL, etc.

2. The family or persons said to be, thought to be, believed to be, or by tradition, from the Channel Islands.

3. The name is listed in old records of the Channel Islands, such as in the typed manuscript CATALOGUE OF JERSEY FAMILY NAMES, by Charles Stevens, 1970. (Compiler relied heavily on this excellent work.) Roger Brehaut of St. Peter Port, Guernsey, was a great help in establishing the list of old Guernsey surnames. I was not able to find a good list of Sark and Alderney surnames. These seem to have varied a great deal from century to century, as families settled there then removed elsewhere.

4. Some Huguenot families are included to a greater or lesser extent. This subject is covered in the Huguenot section, which see.

5. Families of Great Britain, of England, Ireland, Scotland, Wales, Cornwall, etc., lived in the Channel Islands, some probably from the 1500s, for a short time, or for very long periods. In most cases, marriages with the Islanders took place. The heaviest immigration into the Islands from there took place in the 1800s. The soldiers of the many regiments stationed there often married Island girls.

6. Some persons and families, settled in North America at about the same time, and in the same area where known Channel Islanders settled, and whose surnames appear in

Channel Island records, have also been included. These have a question mark or OUTC, origin unknown to compiler.

7. Some persons and families of France, settled for a short or long time in the Islands, but apparently having Island ties, will also be found in this book.

It should be noted here that Charles Stevens writes in his book about Island surnames that "Dozens of Island families... flourished in the early middle ages without betraying their existence on contemporary parchments. They are every bit as genuine Jerriais as the...people whose names sparkle in the armorials and history books." This accounts for some names of the Islands which are very common there today, but lack old records. See excellent article in CIFHS #17, by Stevens.

WHY HAVE YOU USED THIS FORM OF CHART: A,B,C, and 1,2,3?

More than 75 percent of the persons who sent information for the book are like the compiler, lately come to this field, and without training in the field of genealogy and chart making and reading. This simple chart, while it does have drawbacks, is easy enough for the newcomer in the field to understand.

WHY HAVE YOU NOT INCLUDED THE MONTH AND DAY OF RECORDS IN THIS BOOK?

The compiler greatly regrets that the problem of compressing so much detail into one book has compelled abbreviations such as this in the book. Some of this missing information will be contained in the Western Reserve Channel Island Collection and can be consulted.

HOW DID THE ISLANDERS COME TO AMERICA?

Before the middle 1800s, the Islanders often came on their own small ships, built by themselves, of 30 to 60 foot in length, undecked, open to the weather, and usually having two masts. They provided an extremely uncomfortable voyage for the one or two months of passage. See JERSEY SAILING SHIPS, by John Jean, Phillimore & Co., Sussex, England, 1982.

Later, the Islanders came on steamships from Bristol, Liverpool and London. This was a vast improvement, as the earlier passengers had to share the small ship with cargo and animals, with salt for the codfisheries, food, grain, liquor, knitwear and footwear, and dried fruit from the Mediterranean. (See records of Philip English in Essex Inst. and NEHGS, Boston, MA.)

WHY DID THE ISLANDERS COME TO AMERICA?

1. The Islands are small, and lack opportunity.

2. Laws of the Islands did not always work for the benefit of the largest number.
3. The oldest son of Island family inherits the main part of the estate, and the younger sons inevitably had to locate elsewhere. Agents in the Islands looked for likely lads and lasses to sign indentures to work in North America. In 1752 an advertisement in a Guernsey newspaper asked for Guernsey boys and girls willing to go to America.
4. Political disagreements, family quarrels, business failures, all led to some emigration.
5. Letters from America. These old letters can still be found, in which the first member of the family has settled in America, and writes glowingly of the farmland, the low taxes, the freedom and the financial opportunities. Some were exaggerated, no doubt, but conditions in the New World were often superior to those in Europe and thus a family was induced to sail westward.
6. The presence of British regiments in the Islands at times was a strong aggravation to the residents of the Islands. Also, resentment was high about the practise of the British Navy of impressment. While volunteers had served the Crown in the Navy from early times, the extremely hard life was now becoming disliked by the Island men. Most of us have read or seen the motion picture of the book, MUTINY ON THE BOUNTY, and can understand that life in America could be preferable to the servitude on a poorly run ship. (As many as 40 regiments or companies of British troops were stationed in Guernsey and Alderney in the years between 1863 and 1914-15, listed in a Guernsey PRESS directory and Almanac of the early 1900s.)
7. During the years between 1850? and 1875 the Mormon Church was proselytizing in Northern Europe, and encouraging emigration to Utah. Many of the Islanders became interested, and they sailed to America on steamships, with the fare underwritten by the Church. The cost of passage was to be reimbursed after establishment in Utah. (See Utah section.)
8. A number of separate families mentioned in their letters to the compiler that they first came to this country with cattle importations from Jersey and Guernsey. These cattle have always been greatly valued because of their high quality of milk and cream. American dairymen encouraged this importation, and Island men brought them over, often remaining to look after the herds.
9. While there is no definite evidence, the compiler suspects that a few Islanders came to America to avoid

legal and financial difficulties after having amassed a goodly fortune at privateering. (Skinner? Tupper?)

10. The Gold Rush, both in California and in Canada's Yukon, drew some Channel Islanders. One sailed around the Horn of South America, and others went overland by railroad, then by covered wagons and horses over the plains, mountains and deserts. See Personal Accounts.

MAY I EXTRACT AND USE THE INFORMATION IN THIS BOOK?

Permission is available upon receipt of your request, with information on how the data will be used, and a promise to mention the source, along with a stamped, self-addressed envelope for reply. There will be no charge for this.

IS ALL THE DATA IN THIS BOOK VERIFIED?

Definitely no!, unfortunately. Much of the information was included in letters to the compiler, uncharted, giving the source as memory of elderly relatives, the family Bible, word of mouth, etc. Therefore, if you plan an article, pamphlet or book about persons or families in this book, it will be necessary for you to personally check the sources, going back to the original records where possible. Only in this way will your work be truly valid.

WHY HAVE YOU INCLUDED DATA IN THIS BOOK THAT IS ALREADY IN PRINT?

This has happened in several cases. There are many very old books containing data, and are quoted in this book. These old books are scarce now, and it might be impossible for some researchers to locate a copy in their area. In cases where an old book is rather widely available, only the first few generations of the family are included, and the researcher will have to seek out the book for more information, or consult the Western Reserve Channel Islands Collection.

Also included in this book is the information first gathered for THE QUIET ADVENTURERS IN AMERICA, published in 1975 and now out of print. Since there were only 500 copies printed, and since the compiler has more information on many of these families, it was considered that repetition in this book would be advisable.

WHAT PROPORTION OF AMERICAN CHANNEL ISLAND EMIGRANTS IS INCLUDED IN THIS BOOK?

The compiler can only guess, but would estimate that possibly thirty or forty percent of the possible Channel Island families are recorded in this book. Researchers who wish to pursue this field might try Mercer Island, WA, Seattle, WA, Texas, especially Austin, California, Iowa, Nebraska, Maryland, Virginia, the Carolinas, Florida, etc.

HOW CAN I FIND OUT MORE ABOUT MY CHANNEL ISLAND FAMILIES?
See the section entitled IN SEARCH OF MY ANCESTORS.

WHAT IS THE WESTERN RESERVE CHANNEL ISLANDS COLLECTION?
(Sometimes abbreviated to WRCIC, and CI COLL.)
Much more data about both the Islands and their descendants in America was gathered by the compiler, more than would fit into this book. This material will be placed in the hands of the WESTERN RESERVE HISTORICAL SOCIETY LIBRARY, 10825 East Boulevard, Cleveland, Ohio 44106, after 1983, and will then be available to the public.

DID YOU KNOW?

Channel Islanders were involved in the dramatic story of the MUTINY ON THE BOUNTY in the 1700s. The first to spot the Island where the last chapter of the story was played out, was Pitcairn, who was a sailor on the ship of Capt. CARTERET of a Jersey family. On the crew of theBounty were at least two Guernsey sailors: Lawrence LE BOQUE, poss LE BROCQ?, sail-maker, and the second was a Guernsey rascal named John WILLIAMS able seaman. On Sept. 18th, 1814, appeared in the bay at Pitcairn's Island two ships, one the Navy frigate BRITTON and the other the TAGUS, Capt. PIPON, surely a Jerseyman? (MR. CHRISTIAN!, by Stanley Miller, NYCity, 1973.

Some information on the Huguenots who fled France to the Channel Islands is in THE FRENCH EXILES, by Margery Werner, London, England, 1964. "There was a large concentration in Jersey and Guernsey, the Normans and Bretons finding in the Channel Islands not only the nearest point of refuge, but also an atmosphere which resembled their own French homelands."

Daniel DUMARESQ of Jersey, 1712-1805, was a scholar and traveler. He spent 17 years at Petersburg, Russia and spoke the language fluently.

Nicholas William MOULIN of the Channel Islands served on the LONDON PACQUET ship early 1800s. This ship sailed between Virginia and Guernsey, and was taken by the French in 1806. Nicholas was still a prisoner of war in 1814.

Many old Channel Island families have Coats of Arms and Mottoes. Some of these are accepted by the English College of Arms, but others are not. See ARMORIAL OF JERSEY and HERALDRY IN GUERNSEY. Also of interest is INTERNATIONAL HERALDRY, by L.G. Pine, Rutland, VT, 1970.

PIRATES AND PRIVATEERS

"Piracy must be the third oldest profession if we give honor to the ancient craft of healing as the second." (PIRATES WHO'S WHO, by Gosse). The type of larceny known as piracy is as old as man, or nearly. While pirates have been a scourge to all races and cultures, three places on earth have suffered the most: the China seas, the Mediteranean and the North Sea.

The Vikings were so fierce that the peasants of northern Europe were wont to pray "from the fury of the Norsemen, O Lord deliver us." Air piracy is only the modern version of this old profession.

While piracy and privateering are usually lumped together in most people's minds, and at times are barely distinguishable from each other, the Channel Islanders were more notable for privateering than piracy. However, we must admit that a number of the pirates of the 1600s and 1700s were of Channel Island blood, such as Barbade LE QUESNE and Sebastien ALEXANDRE, hanged in Jersey 1550, "forced and took away with them Michael LE COUTEUR, a Jerseyman," Jersey BRIGHT, a CORBET who was wrecked on Alderney, Daniel FERRY of Guernsey who was hanged for piracy 1718 near Charlestown, SC, and many named ROBIN and ROBBINS, etc.

"Pirates and privateers on the verge of piracy named Wake, Baudains, Skinner, Smith, Blaize, Picquet, Amy and so on, were fiercely driven back to the Channel Islands by British forces in 1645." (ENGLISH SEAPOWER IN THE EARLY TUDOR PERIOD, by Fowler; GOLDEN AGE OF PIRACY, by Rankin; and several pirate books by Gosse.)

Sir George Carteret of Jersey, and of the New Jersey grant, was a Royalist, and for the ten years or so of the Commonwealth government in England, was one of those who fought the British government in many ways, successfully gambling on the Restoration of the Monarchy. One of his less applauded methods was the enlisting of pirates and privateers of any and all nations, to whom he issued Letters of Marque, official commissions to prey on English shipping. Prince Rupert, also exiled in Holland, assisted with this promotion. Cromwell, angered, called them the Jersey Pirates. Carteret is said to have made more than 60,000 pounds in this "business."

The lure of quick profits attracted the sea captains of England, France, Spain and North America in the 1600s and 1700s. England's ready excuse was protection of the widespread sea trade of the British Isles. (Societe Jersiaise Bulletin #82, 1957.)

The first known privateersman was a Guernseyman, John BRIARD, merchant, owner of the DOVE, who received a Letter of Marque from Queen Elizabeth of England, giving him permission to attack French shipping in 1578. The Tuppers of Nova Scotia had an ancestor, John Tupper, who was operating privateer ships out of Guernsey and southern England in 1667. By 1697, there were 20 Guernsey and 8 Jersey privateers in operation.

In the 1600s these were a few of the Jersey privateer ships and their captains:

BOWCOWEN, Capt. Pierre LABEY
LA DELAVARDE, Capt. Geo. MESSERVY
LA REVENGE, Capt. Charles ALEXANDRE
Philip SEWARD and a Capt. FIOTT
Other ships captained by Richard LE QUESNE
LE BURNETT, with 27 men
L'ELIZABETH, Capt. Jean ARTHUR
L'ACTIF, Capt. Jacques BALLEINE

During the Seven Years War, Jersey seized 60,000 pounds worth of privateer ships. During the American Revolution, at one time, more than 150 French prize ships were anchored in St. Aubin's Bay, Jersey. (BAILIWICK OF JERSEY, by G.R. Balleine.)

During the War of the Spanish Succession, Guernsey privateers took some 750 prize ships with a total of about one hundred thousand pounds. (GUERNSEY, by G.W.S. Robinson.) A typical Guernsey ship of that time carried only about 30 to 60 men.

Even as late as 1813, a Guernseyman, Capt. John LENFESTEY, b 1777, obtained from the Nova Scotia Admiralty Court a commission for the lugger INTREPID, which he commanded, and which was owned by Peter LE LACHEUR of Guernsey, a merchant. This small vessel of 67 tons, and 16 men, was well equipped, but no record was found by the compiler as to its success at this chancy business. (UNDER THE RED JACK, by C.H.J. Snider, London, England, 1928.) Could this have been the same John Lenfesty who showed up in Ohio in the early 1800s?

Joseph Cabot was the employer of Capt. Jonathan Haraden of Gloucester, MA. Through the influence of Cabot, and with little experience at sea, Jonathan obtained a Naval Lt.'s commission and was posted to the TYRANNICIDE 1776 under Capt. John Fisk. On the first cruise, the ship with 75 men, built at Salisbury, MA, holding a Letter of Marque, took 5 prize ships, 3 brigantines, a snow and a scow. A second cruise brought 4 more prize ships, two of which were the armed ship GLASGOW and the brig ST. JOHN. Capt. Haraden took over the TYRANNICIDE in 1777 and continued to take many prizes until the ship was lost in 1778 during involvement in the ill-fated Rhode Island Expedition. Haraden, in various ships, took a thousand canon from the British during the Revolutionary War. (TEG, May 1982.)

Another American privateering ship, the ELIZA, was captured ca 1807 between Cape Breton and Newfoundland by HMS TRIBUNE, and bought by the Nicolles of Jersey. She sailed out of Jersey until 1891, when she was reported lost on a voyage to Santos, Brazil. She is said to have been built in the year 1756, and disappeared in 1891, at the reputed age of 135 years. The usual age of a ship in those days was about 50 years.

Philip Dumaresq was born about 1695 in Jersey, second son of Elie Dumaresq, Seigneur of Augres, and of Francoise de Carteret of St. Ouen, Jersey. He emigrated to Boston, MA, and married there in the French Church Suzanne Ferry, 1716, later becoming one of the first vestrymen of Trinity Church.

About 1739 the war of the Austrian Succession broke out, and the King of England offered Letters of Marque to those who would fight the Spanish. Philip Dumaresq was Captain of the YOUNG EAGLE, out of Boston, a two-masted bilander, with 30 guns. A Michael and a William Dumaresq were part of the crew. The YOUNG EAGLE captured a Swedish ship laden with wheat and took it to Madeira. He then took other ships of various nationalities, and acted as escort to British merchantmen in hostile waters, saving then from capture. Dumaresq was badly wounded, and his place and time of death is not known. In 1744 he was believed dead. He and his wife had 5 children, Edward, Philip and 3 daughters. One daughter, Susan, mar Matthew Saumarez, and became the mother of a famous British Admiral.

A Capt. Daniel Marquand is said to have had privateer ships based in Mass. Another privateersman was Philip Bisson, Jr., bp 1760 in Marblehead, MA, who spend 60 years at sea, mostly trading with the West Indies, but often aboard a privateer ship. His first voyage was with Capt. John Stevens on the SATISFACTION, which captured four valuable prize ships. He next sailed on the FANCY, with Capt. Lee, which cruised on the Grand Banks, bringing back an English ship of 16 guns. Becoming bolder, they sailed to the English Channel and brought back to Salem a French brig, loaded with English goods.

The crew of the FANCY were caught and sent to Mill Prison, in England, but Philip survived and sailed again on a brig named NEWBURYPORT, bound for Carolina for a cargo of tobacco. They were unsuccessful, but managed to return home, and shipped out on the MONMOUTH, 20 guns, with Capt. Collier. By a series of misadventures they arrived near where George Washington himself was encamped. Their adventures were difficult for the Army officers to believe, but the men were finally released and returned home with a purse of $40.00.

Bisson soon sailed on the ship AURORA of Newburyport, with Capt. Thomas Collyer, and took several prizes, but was again caught and carried to Bermuda, then headed for Nova Scotia. A storm took them to Santo Domingo Island, where a comrade rescued him. On the next voyage they captured four English ships, and crippled a fifth.

Bisson was soon aboard another vessel for a voyage to Virginia, and from there sailed to France. Despite a fierce battle with three English privateers, they made it to France, discharged their cargo, took another, and arrived back in Boston 1783, when peace was declared.

Although Bisson made a fortune in his voyages, he was less successful as a merchant, and was compelled to go back to sea during the War of 1812, commanding several private armed vessels. He was taken by the frigate JUNIOR, but was released and landed in Manchester, MA. Another time he was captured by the BULWARD 74, and carried to Halifax, NS, being returned in a "cartel" on parole. Philip died 1836. Two sons were lost in the West Indies and another at Cape Horn. The fourth died in California. However, Philip left numerous descendants and Bissons are found in most parts of the country. (Western Reserve Channel Island Collection; Nancy Garrett, Portsmouth, VA; Mass. Hist. Soc. Proceedings, Vol. 5.) For more information on Channel Island ships see JERSEY SAILING SHIPS, by A. John Jean, Chichester, Sussex, England, 1982, and the Channel Island Bibliography in this book.

Capt. Thomas James De Gruchy, mariner, merchant, gentleman, was born in Trinity Parish, North Jersey in 1719. By 1741 he was in Boston, where he mar Mary Dumaresq, and launched a mercantile career. A son, Thomas James, Jr., was born 1743.

During the War of the Austrian Succession, Capt. Gruchy commanded a 120 ton privateer, THE QUEEN OF HUNGARY, a man-of-war with 80 in the crew. The brig was jointly owned by six Boston merchants, including Gruchy. All were officers of Christ Church, except William Bowdoin, brother of the Governor of Mass. Among prizes taken by the QUEEN OF HUNGARY were two crystal chandeliers and four gracefully carved cherubim, given to Christ Church by the vessel owners.

During the winter of 1745 Capt. Gruchy bought the Gov. Phips mansion at Salem and Chart Streets and made it the family home for 14 years. The colorful, gregarious captain was elected to several town offices by Boston Town Meetings, became trustee of a local charitable society, contributed time, money and effort toward improvements in Ward One and along the waterfront, and joined his father-in-law and other Boston merchants in various Boston shipping enterprises.

Capt. Gruchy eventually sold his Boston holdings and returned with his family to Jersey, where he also served in elected offices in Trinity, and became a leader in the Jersey Revolution of 1769. (Some data with kind permission of Clara Reeves of Boston, MA.)

NOTABLES

SIR EDMUND ANDROS, GOVERNOR OF NEW YORK, NEW ENGLAND, VIRGINIA AND GUERNSEY ISLAND

Andros, whose name figures in the history of most of the American colonies, was born in London 1637 of an old and prominent Guernsey Island family. His great-grandfather's father, John Andros, Andrewes, was an Englishman from Northampton, who settled in the Channel Islands and married in 1540 Judith de Saumarez of an ancient Guernsey family.

Andros first came to the New World as a Major in the foot regiment sent to the West Indies to protect the Islands against the Dutch. Possibly, Andros Island there is named for him. He became a landgrave of Carolina in 1672, receiving four baronies, an estate of about 48,000 acres, which he seems to have entirely ignored.

Andros served as governor of New York from 1674 to 1680. His attempt to take over the New Jersey colony was thwarted by the Carterets, said to be distant relatives, and Governor Andros was recalled to England in 1680. (See the New Jersey section.)

In 1686 Andros again appeared in Boston, aboard the KINGFISHER, as governor of New England, including Massachusetts, New Hampshire and Maine. In 1687 he took over Connecticut, although the independent citizens there would not give up their precious charter to him, hiding it in the famous Charter Oak. Between 1685 and 1688 the New England colonies, New York, and the Jerseys were combined into one vice-royalty called the Dominion of New England. Sir Edmund Andros, Bailiff of Guernsey, was given command, and ruled with a heavy hand.

Because of the accession to the English throne of the Prince of Orange, the colonists believed the power of Andros spent. They seized and imprisoned him. Andros almost escaped several times from confinement, once in women's clothing betrayed by boots showing beneath the skirt. In another attempt he reached Rhode Island before being recaptured. In 1690 he was sent back to England.

In 1692 the irrepressible Andros was appointed Governor of Virginia, where for six years he had a popular administration, in contrast to his years in New England. In THE BEGINNINGS OF NEW ENGLAND, Lady Andros was described as a sweet and gentle person. She died in 1688 and is said to be buried in King's Chapel, Boston, MA. Although Andros apparently married later a Dame Elizabeth, his will mentions "my late dear deceased wife." Her son by a previous marriage was one inheritor of the Andros estate in London.

Governor Andros returned to England 1697, and in 1704 was made Lieutenant-Governor of Guernsey Island. In 1706 he retired to London, where he died in 1714, and was buried in St. Annes, Soho, Westminster. He is thought to have died without issue. (Robotti; Clemens; Thwaites; NEHGS Vol. 42; Snow's TALES OF SEA AND SHORE.)

JOHN BERTRAM, MILLIONAIRE MERCHANT-ADVENTURER AND PHILANTHROPIST

"It is an interesting coincidence that a Jerseyman, Philip English, was the first of the great shipping merchants of that town, and another Jerseyman, John Bertram, was its last." (Perley) Between these two careers was 200 years of merchant-adventuring that saw the beginnings of the foreign trade in New England, and its ending, with the last entry being the schooner MATTIE F. from South America. After this time Salem ships still sailed, but they used the port of Boston.

John Bertram, son of John and Mary (Perchard) Bertram, was born in St. Saviour parish Jersey in 1796. In 1807 his parents brought their six children to Baltimore, Maryland. John was the only one of the family who spoke fluent English, according to Balleine. They soon left Baltimore and settled in Salem, MA, where the father opened a grocery and young John served behind the counter. The shop failed and John went to sea at age 16, serving on two American privateers, the MONKEY and the HERALD. The HERALD was captured by the British, but Bertram escaped from the prison ship. His next ship was also captured and he was sent to England as prisoner of war.

When peace was declared in 1815 he returned to Salem and then went back to sea. By 1821 he had risen to be mate and made several voyages to Java, during which time he made enough money to buy a schooner of his own. This was used in three years of successful trading on the coast of Patagonia, at the tip of South America, where, among other goods, he bought hides which he sold at a good profit. He made a last voyage as Captain to Zanzibar in the ship BLACK WARRIOR in 1830, when he bought gum-copal, a valuable and much used ingredient for varnish at that time.

In 1832 he settled down ashore, sending his clippers to the far ports of the world, but mainly to the Pacific. His brig, ELIZA, was one of the first vessels to appear on the California coast at the beginning of the Gold Rush.

Bertram was elected and re-elected to the Mass. legislature. In his old age he devoted the greater part of his large fortune to philanthropy, a home for aged seamen, endowments to the Salem Hospital, and to the Children's Friend Society. He was a non-drinker and non-smoker, unusual for that era, and once tore up a winning lottery ticket, refusing to profit from gambling.

John Bertram was married three times, to Mary Smith; to Clarissa Millett; and in 1848 to Mary Ann Ropes, who survived him. He died in 1882 and his family presented his home on Essex Street, Salem, MA to become its public library.

John Bertram's foresight and business acuity enabled him to see that American ships of the middle 1800s were losing in the race for foreign trade, and he transferred his interests to other fields, namely railroads and manufacturing.

He was an outstanding example of the American legend, poor immigrant boy to wealthy and public spirited tycoon, and no doubt was a shining example to Channel Islanders seeking their fortunes in America during the late 1800s. (BALLEINE'S BIO. DICT.; DICT. OF NATIONAL BIOGRAPHY.)

GENERAL SIR ISAAC BROCK, WHO CHANGED NORTH AMERICAN HISTORY

The first few months of the War of 1812 found Canada in serious straits. Inadequate military forces, little money to pay for military protection of the huge Great Lakes border area, and a few Canadians who sided with the American viewpoint, were just a few of the problems. This dangerous and complicated situation was quickly reversed by the actions of one man, the Hero of Upper Canada, General Sir Isaac Brock, a Guernseyman. He was born in England of a Guernsey family in 1786 and joined the British Army at the age of 15.

General Brock saw service in the West Indies, Holland, Denmark and the Baltic before coming to Canada to put down a rebellion in the forces, and in 1810 was commissioned Lt. Governor of Upper Canada, later to be called Ontario.

In 1943 Philip Luce of British Columbia wrote, "Unlike his predecessor, Sir Francis Gore, Brock was convinced war with the United States was inevitable. There was a hangover of bitterness and rancor from the Rebellion of 1776, and there were trade difficulties which the British government made no serious effort to resolve; England was too busy with Napoleon to concern herself with the affairs of the colony."

After his appointment, Brock dismissed the uncooperative Assembly, forced through the necessary money bills, proclaimed martial law, and assembled troops and supplied. In the early summer of 1812 he was in Norfolk County, Ontario, where he asked for 100 volunteers to join his regular troops. Shortly after, the small force set off by boat along Lake Erie's northern shore to Sandwich, Ontario, across from Detroit, MI. Two weeks after their arrival the men were joined by Tecumseh and his Indian troops. The combined forces crossed the Detroit River, whereupon General Hull surrendered the city of Detroit and the state of Michigan to the American government's consternation. (TECUMSEH, by Ethel Raymond, Toronto, ONT.)

This single action did a great deal to bring together the divided Canadian people, preventing any changes that the Americans had planned in the border of these two countries. Further successes by the British at Chicago, Mackinaw and Niagara Falls were good bargaining points. Government negotiations in the east soon brought the war to an end in 1814.

General Brock, after his coup in Detroit, was waging a winning skirmish in the Niagara Falls area, when he was shot by an American rifleman. Due to Brock's wide renown on both sides of the border, a truce was quickly arranged so that the General might be buried with honor at Fort George. His body was later re-interred at Queenston Heights, ONT, where a monument now stands. (Much data available on Brock which includes HISTORICAL ATLAS OF HALDIMAND AND NORFOLD COUNTIES, by H.R. Page, reprinted by Mark Cumming, Port Elgin, ONT, ca 1973; THE INVASION OF CANADA, Vol. 1, by Pierre Berton, recent.)

THE CABOTS OF BOSTON

This very notable family of Boston descends from John who emigrated from the Island of Jersey to Salem, MA, 1700. Joseph, a successful merchant and son of the immigrant, married Elizabeth Higginson. George, the seventh of their eleven children, was born in Salem 1752. He studied at Harvard and to discourage his indolent ways, was sent to sea in one of the family's vessels. This did the trick, turning the wastrel into a most successful businessman. He married his double first cousin, Elizabeth Higginson, who was a great help to him in his business and political career.

About 1777 George gave up active seafaring and was taken into his brother's firm, which during the War of Independence owned at least 40 privateer and letter of marque ships. Their armed merchantmen continued to trade with Spain, making their headquarters at Bilbao, where all the prizes taken by the firm's vessels were sold and the proceeds deposited with Gardoqui and Sons. By this means, the Cabots, unlike most privateering firms, kept their gains until peace was concluded. In 1784 two of their ships first carried the American flag to St. Petersburg, Russia.

George became director of the earliest bank in the state in 1784 and was the leading promoter of two important corporate enterprises of 1788, the Essex bridge and the Beverly cotton manufactory. He also later became a part of the nucleus of the new Federalist party, and entertained President Washington at Beverly in 1789. He was chosen senator from Massachusetts in 1791.

The Cabots have greatly prospered and have served the government on many levels. "With the exception of a very few Cabots who changed to that name from some other, all of the

Cabots in early New England and nearly all in the United States were descended from one of these brothers, John, who died in this country in 1742, and a few from a brother who returned to his birthplace." (Thomas Cabot, Boston, letter.) (See CABOT GENEALOGY.)

SIR GEORGE CARTERET, INVESTOR IN AMERICA

Sir George, Proprietor of New Jersey, was born about 1609, became an English baronet, Lieutenant-Governor, Treasurer of the British Navy, and close friend of the English Monarchy. The Carterets, for centuries, were the leading family of the Island of Jersey. One Maugier de Cartrai took part in the Battle of Hastings in 1066. The family provided at least 72 public servants to the Jersey government. Eight De Carterets are buried in Westminster Abbey. One branch dropped the "De," descendants of Elie, of St. Ouens, Jersey. Sir George was one of the De Carterets, but dropped the article, and his descendants followed his example.

Carteret was in the British Navy and received his first commission at about age 20. In the 1630s he was in command of many ships and was made Vice-Admiral of the expedition against the North African pirate stronghold of Sallee. The King of Morocco was forced to make peace and to surrender over 300 European captives.

Carteret married his cousin, Elizabeth De Carteret, in 1640, and some of their love letters survive. His political and naval manoeuvres in the 1640s saved Jersey for the Monarchial cause. He could not count on funds to carry on his war with the Interregnum, so turned to privateering with a commission from the exiled King. He was most successful in this field until 1651 when he was captured, imprisoned in the Bastille, banished from France, and joined the exiled King Charles in Holland. Upon the Restoration of the Monarchy in 1660, he was rewarded, as told in the New Jersey section.

Beside the establishment of New Jersey, Carteret had his fingers in many pies. In 1665 he obtained a license to dig for coal in Windsor Forest. In that same year he was reclaiming thousands of acres of land in Connaught, Ireland, which flooded on every tide.

In 1672 he was one of the foundation members of the Royal Africa Company, to which the King granted the whole west coast of Africa from Sallee to the Cape in return for a payment of two elephants to be made whenever he visited those domains!

Carteret was a vigorous, ambitious and able man with a thirst for new experiences and for money. Although he never came to America, he had vision enough to see its great possibilities and made sure that his colony was established in New Jersey. There is no doubt that he was one of England's Empire builders. He died in 1680, father of three sons and five daughters. (Balleine's BIOG. DICT. OF JERSEY; NEW JERSEY RECORDS; THE CARTERET FAMILY AND ITS PART IN THE EARLY HIST. OF NORTH CAROLINA, by W.P. Johnson, in NC HIST. REVIEW, 1970, Fall and Winter.)

BUFFALO BILL CODY

The story of Buffalo Bill is well known not only in America, but in many parts of the world, as the story of the American Wild West has become very appealing to adventurous minds.

Bill Cody was the descendant of Philippe LE CAUDEY of Jersey and Martha LE BROCQ of Guernsey, who married in ?St. Brelade, Jersey in 1692. The Le Caudey family had lived in Jersey at least since 1566 and may have been of Huguenot origin.

This family lived at Kipkinton, MA, where Philippe died in 1743. His name was spelled over the years in about 50 different ways. Six generations later Isaac Cody of this family, was born in Toronto Township, ONT, the sixth of nine children. When Isaac was 17, his family removed to Cleveland, OH, and had a farm near Euclid Ave and 83rd street. He married there Martha O'Connor, who died shortly after the birth of a daughter, Martha, in 1835. Isaac soon married again, to Rebecca Sumner of Medina County, south of Cleveland. She also soon died, leaving no children. In 1840 Isaac married Mary Ann Bonsell of Laycock.

This couple settled in Davenport, Iowa, in LeClaire, Iowa, then removed to Kansas, where Isaac was a first settler and prospered as an Indian trader. Their third child was born 1843, William Frederick Cody. Buffalo Bill worked on the wagon trains that were then carrying thousands of immigrants westward. The wagons were large and strongly built, loaded with six thousand pounds of freight, and drawn by several yokes of oxen in the charge of one driver. It took a big, strong physique to handle this kind of work. A train consisted of 25 wagons, all in the charge of one man who was known as the wagon-master. There were 31 men to a train, divided into messes of seven, and all were heavily armed.

From this kind of life he went to the Pony Express Line, and glamorized this service. Although it ran for just a year, it became part of the American legend. He married and had several children. There are many books about his glamorous life, and these are well worth reading.

Near the town of Cody, Wyoming, live two grandsons of Buffalo Bill, Bill and Fred Garlow. Bill has legally changed his name to Cody. He has a law degree from Harvard and served in WW2. He's married, has four sons who resemble the Cody side of the family, and operates a ranch inn that provides pack trips into Bighorn back country. (Cleveland PLAIN DEALER, May 2, 1982.)

PHILIP ENGLISH, THE FIRST AMERICAN MILLIONAIRE

Philippe LANGLOIS, ENGLISH, was born in 1651, Trinity Parish, Jersey, son of Jerseyman and possibly of a Scottish mother. (FACTS ABOUT THE LIFE OF PHILIP ENGLISH OF SALEM, by Mrs. Philip English, New Haven, CT, 1943.) In 1670 he removed to Salem, MA where a few Jerseymen had already settled. He lodged with a merchant, William Hollingsworth, whose only daughter, Mary, he married in 1675. In that same year his father-in-law died and Philip inherited the estate.

Philip soon began to build and buy ships and in "1676 revisited Jersey in his own ketch, SPEEDWELL, with a cargo of dried cod, and returned to Salem with a shipload of Jersey boys and girls as indentured apprentices. The girls were bound to him for seven years, and he let them out as domestic servants; the lads, who were bound for four years, were hired out as seamen, a usual arrangement in those days." (BALLEINE BIO. DICT.)

English prospered greatly and became very wealthy, owning at least 27 ships including ketches, schooners and a brigantine. His boats carried cargoes to Virginia and to Maryland, including rum, molasses, sugar, salt, cedar, woodenware, kegs, cider, cans, etc. From these ports they brought back wheat, Indian corn, pork, bacon, peltry, tobacco, hides, old iron, pewter and copper. His ketches fished off Newfoundland, Cape Sable and Acadie.

The fish he shipped to Barbados, or to the English West Indies Islands, and to Surinam, Spain or the Straits. Salt necessary to cure the fish was brought from Salt Island in the Virgin Islands, from St. Ubes, or from the Isle of May.

Wine was brought to the colonies from Fayal. From Barbados, he returned with drygoods, blue lining, osnaburgs and Holland duck. To the West Indies he sent lumber, shingles, whale oil, staves, barrels and hogsheads. Tobacco was sent to London. He brought staves to Ireland and probably traded with England and Holland. (Mrs. English)

The difficulties of succeeding in this business were many. Great Britain was enforcing restrictive commerce laws. The French and Indians were attacking fishing vessels. English pirates came right into Massachusetts bay and plundered vessels. Barbary and Tunisian pirates harassed the ships, and produce spoiled from being too long at sea.

Nevertheless, English prospered and built a large mansion in Salem that stood for a hundred and fifty years, called English's Great House. They had seven children, but two, William and Susanna, died young. It is said they had at least

15 Jerseymen and women working in their home.

Suddenly, charges of witchcraft were everywhere and innocent people were tried and condemned. English and his wife were charged but managed to escape to New York where they stayed for about a year. Despite their sufferings, they decided to return, and somewhat to their surprise, were warmly received by the townspeople. The town prosecutor of Salem dined with them their first evening home.

Philip English never forgave the Puritans for their actions and it is said that his wife's health failed from the accuser's treatment, resulting in her death, and this affected his mind. In 1709, twenty-one alleged witches and children of witches joined Philip English in a bold demand for restoration of their reputations and asked for cash amends. Many of these petitions were honored. Salem townsmen who had condemned many persons as witches were the only ones in witchcraft history to put it on record that they were wrong, asking forgiveness of God and mankind. On the second of March, 1712, the First Church of Salem revoked the excommunication of Rebecca Nourse, who, at the age of 92, was executed as a witch in the year 1692. (SALEM IN THE 17TH CENTURY, HISTORY OF SALEM, by Perley)

Witchcraft has bedeviled men in many places, including the Channel Islands, England and New England. In the Island of Guernsey alone, between 1563 and 1634, according to Stephen Dewar, over 75 persons were accused of witchcraft, many of whom were condemned to death or were banished from the Island. It is said that about this time there were a thousand witchcraft trials in England, and in New England 19 persons were condemned to death. The witch hunts and trials of that time are grim reminders of one of mankind's weaknesses in times of stress. Much literature on Salem and witchcraft.

DEMING JARVES AND THE SANDWICH GLASS COMPANY

Brilliant flashing color and beautiful form distinguish some early American glassware. One of the early leaders in this field was Deming Jarves, son of John and Hannah Seabury Jarves, who came from Jersey to Boston 1787. Deming was baptised in Boston 1790. At the age of 27 he was one of a group which bought the Boston Crown Glass Company of Cambridge, MASS, which produced lime-flint glass.

Secrets of good glassmaking were in the hands of the British at this time, and Jarves had to experiment to find the correct chemicals and methods needed. He was very successful and for thirty years he supplied other glass houses, and held the monopoly on galena in the United States. His firm competed with foreign firms, supplying apothecary and chemical supplies, table ware, chandeliers, vases and mantle lamps, to begin with, and soon graduated to art glass. He died in 1868 after some business reverses. His son had an interesting life--was an art collector, decorated by the King of Hawaii, and by King Humbert of Italy.

There is a good deal of information available about Sandwich Glass. See your librarian.

Barbour, Harriot B., SANDWICH, THE TOWN THAT GLASS BUILT, Boston, 1948.
Hayes-Cavanaugh, Doris, EARLY GLASS MAKING IN EAST CAMBRIDGE, MASS, Old Time New England, January 1929.
Irwin, T.T., THE STORY OF SANDWICH GLASS, 1926.
McManus, T.F., A CENTURY OF GLASS MANUFACTURE, 1818-1918.
Weeks, J.D., REPORT ON THE MANUFACTURE OF GLASS, 1883.

LILLIE LANGTRY, THE JERSEY BOMBSHELL

Even those who have not heard of the Channel Islands often know of Lillie Langtry, a red-haired, blue-eyed beauty born to the Le Breton family in St. Saviour, J 1853. Her great personal charms and good looks brought her to the attention of top personalities in Europe. However, her friends and lovers were sometimes ill-chosen, and several scandals were the result. She had natural intelligence and good business ability, which brought her financial success. Her first husband was Edward Langtry.

At one time Lillie owned a ranch near San Francisco, CA, then sold out and bought land in southern California. She was one of the first to believe in its tremendous possibilities, and disposed of her land in Los Angeles and Santa Barbara at a good profit. She was a citizen of the U.S. for about 5 years, had a daughter, Lady Malcolm, and four grandchildren. She died in 1929 on the French Riviera. An excellent TV series covered her life, and numerous books have been written about her. See the book by Noel B. Gerson, BECAUSE I LOVED HIM, 1971.

WILLIAM N. LE PAGE AND HIS FAMOUS GLUE

Any mother of a school child in the last 75 years knows about Le Page's Glue! Few know that Mr. Le Page was a descendant of a Channel Island family settled in Prince Edward Island about 1807. Elisha and his wife, Margaret DuFrecy, were the ancestors of a good many Le Pages in Canada and the U.S. William, b 1848, Prince Edward Island, removed to Gloucester, MA, where he married Ruth A. Mayo. His inventions and his strong belief in the now accepted theory of the great power of advertising, soon made him a captain of industry in New England. Other inventions were preserving processes, a holster for a pistol, and a rowlock that he sold to Admiral de Gama of Brazil for a goodly sum. Le Page died in Vancouver, BC 1919, age 70.

Le Pages seem to flourish wherever they settle. The very large and important realty firm in Toronto and other places was originated by a Le Page from the PEI family.

JOHN WESLEY MASURY AND THE PAINT BUSINESS

Mr. Masury, 1820-1895, manufacturer, inventor, was born in Salem, MA, a descendant of a Jersey or Guernsey family. We are indebted to him for the idea of ready-mixed paint in cans. Previously, the painter had mixed his own colors as he worked, a craft not easily learned by amateurs. Masury patented the metal container, and enjoyed a monopoly in the field for 21 years. He also wrote about paints and painting. He mar twice, Laura S. Carlton of Salem, MA and Grace Harkins of Brooklyn, NY. He died in New York and was buried at Center Moriches, Long Island. There is a small town in Northwestern Ohio named Masury, but no connection could be found by this compiler.

NATHANIEL MESSERVE, SHIP BUILDER

Col. Nathaniel Messerve lived in Portsmouth, NH, a descendant of Clement MESSERVY from Jersey. He was an outstanding man, of a family that has prospered in America.

In 1745 he became part of the English effort to dislodge the French from the Maritimes. Their main fort was at Louisburg, Cape Breton, which the French believed to be impregnable. Though the original thinking of Messerve, the plan to take the fort by means of crossing a supposedly impassable swamp, was very successful. Wooden sledges fifteen feet long and five feet wide were constructed and placed, the workers up to their knees in mud and water for fifteen days. The guns were brought to the desired position on a height commanding the fort, which soon surrendered. (Parkman's, A HALF CENTURY OF CONFLICT, etc.)

In 1749 he built at Portsmouth, NH the frigate AMERICA for the British government. A model of this ship is preserved in the Atheneum at Portsmouth. In 1756 a regiment of 700 men was put under his command, and he distinguished himself at Fort Edward. A testimonial of silverware was presented to him. In 1758 he and his son were at the second reduction of Louisburg, and both died of smallpox in that year. See Personal Accounts.

PAUL REVERE, AMERICAN PATRIOT

The father of Paul Revere, Apollos De Rivoire, was born in France, and sent to a relative or family friend in the Island of Guernsey while very young. From Guernsey, at the age of 13, he was apprenticed to the silversmith John Coney, in Boston, MA. Once established there, he anglicized his name to Revere. He married, and Paul was the third of 12 children, born ca 1735.

Paul learned his father's trade, and a good deal more, as a young man in Boston. Examples of his work in museums are well designed and well made. He became adept at dental devices. He designed and printed the first Continental money. He had a foundry where cannon were cast for the Continental Army, and operated one of the first rolling mills.

Paul put up 25 thousand dollars of his own money, plus 10 thousand from the government, on loan, to resheath the CONSTITUTION's bottom, then the ship, OLD IRONSIDES. The copper sheathing resisted barnacles. This was needed to make the ships speedier, to catch the Barbary Pirates, who were then very active in the Atlantic.

While his famous ride is what most people remember about him, it was vastly overrated in the poem, which he would be the first to admit. See his personal account (in Fosdick.) He married Sarah Orne 1757, had eight children, was a widower age 55, and mar Rachel Walker, who also gave him eight children.

Revere led a very useful, patriotic and honored life. Although he called himself a mechanic, he was highly skilled and had forethought and consideration for his fellow workers. He helped organize the Mass. Charitable Mechanics Association, and was its first president. He d 1818, age 83, and was buried near the State House in Boston. Many books available on Revere and his era.

HENRY DAVID THOREAU, NATURALIST AND AUTHOR

There has been a great deal written about this famous American. See your library. Thoreau was the descendant of the Thoreau and Le Gallais families of Jersey. He was born 1817 and died 1862, leaving a legacy of thought about nature and about ourselves. "His importance lies entirely in what he wrote...his seed has born flower and fruit in many alien soils." (THOREAU, by H.S. Canby, Boston, 1939.)

MONT ORGUEIL CASTLE, JERSEY. Founded on a site of a Roman fort, a good example of a Norman-Tudor fortress. (Clive Holland)

TYPICAL OLD JERSEY STONE FARMHOUSE, early 1900s. Some were built in the 1600s and 1700s. (Clive Holland)

COAT OF ARMS OF A FEW GUERNSEY FAMILIES

PERSONAL ACCOUNTS

PERSONAL ACCOUNTS: More complete records are in the Western Reserve C.I. Collection (WRCIC).

FRANCIS

Daniel Francis of Guernsey settled in Guernsey Co., OH in the early 1800s. His son, Nicholas Francis, born in Guernsey 1787, mar Thankful Phillips in 1817 in OH. This couple had four daughters: Rachel, Desier, Dorsey and Susanna. Rachel mar G.W. Pugsley in 1841, and Desier mar Thomas Wild. These families settled in Indiana, Illinois and Iowa. In March 1866 Desier and Thomas Wild went to Saline Co., KS from which place the following letter was sent. The sweet and gentle spirit of a fine frontierswoman shines through the words of the letter.

"Dear brother and sisters: I take my pen to inform you that we are all well at present, hopeing you are the sam. We arrived heere Easter Sunday. We had good roads all the way. It was pretty cold a part of the time but we got along first rate.

The nearer we got the Indian territory the less incouragement we got. He went to the land office at Junction City. They told him that people had bin driven out by the Indians. They advised us to go up the Saline river. The people told us there was some good timber on Spring Creek about six miles from anybody.

We came over heere. We like the country and stayed. There is timber enough for two or three more clames in this neighborhood. They say there is good timber on other little creeks north and west of us. Now I will describe the country as well as I can.

No timber. There is nise porarie nearly all the way after we left the Nimmehaw river, but thare was no timber and the smal streams was all dry. Thee is lime rock in abundance along the creek banks and steep side hills. Nearly all the nice buildings and a good deal of fence is made of stone.

Never saw a slew or swamp after we left the Nimehaw. We like the country in this vacinity better than any we ever saw. There is plenty of good water. Those that have no springs have good water in their wells. The Saline river water is salty.

The bottoms are rich and beautiful. The timber on the river is cottonwood and white elm. On the small creeks is ash, oak, hucklbery, wallnut, plums, goosbery and grapes.

There is plenty of rock for any purpose. Some of the springs is like the cole bank, in Ohio. I would rather live on the creeks than on the river. Thee is plenty of wind heere. We asked a Dutchman if it was very bad here. "Ono, dare ish plenty wind alway, plenty vind in de winter. De shnow fall bout six inch, de vind carry him over dare. De next day he gone"

I would like to have you come heere if this country sould sute you. I think I have told you as near how the country looks as I can.

Folks say we can rase three head of cattle hear as easy as one in Iowa. The grass is as long heer now as it is in the tenth of May up in Iowa. There is a kind of grass they call blue grass. It is about six inches long. Cattle will live on it all winter. They eat it dry. The goosbery has leaves larger than a dime.

May the 15th. I did not get a chance to send this to you so I thought I would tell you how we are getting along. We have got a house up and covered, 16 feet squair, story and half high. Have got 30 acres fenced for paster, 8 acres broke and in corn. Garden we have got potatoes, onions corn and peas up.

We have run ashore for money. [Note: This interesting use of a sea expression, in a long-time seagoing family, hundreds of miles in any direction from the ocean. Compiler] Thomas went to work out last week to raise some provision. James and Marion is brakeing porarie. Mary drops corn. I make gardin. We are living in the bend of the creek. There is just timber to shade the house. There is a good spring about 3 or 4 rods north of the house. We have got 3 cows and James has one.

It is the pretyest place I ever lived in.

We hear today there is a man coming on this creek in a few days. There is a man here now looking for a clame. If he takes the one he is looking at it is the best one. There is some timber west of us now, but it may be gone before this reaches you. James is going to work out as soon as he gets the brakeing don. I think I have told you all, so no more at present. Write us as soone as you get this. Direct to Saline country, Saline Citty, Kansas. It is about 25 miles to our postoffice.

(signed) Desier Wild"

The above letter was mailed 1866 to G.W. Pugsley, Whitesbarrow, Harrison Co., Iowa. Found many years later, the original letter was sent to Albert Wild of Barnard, KS, the only living grandchild of Desier Wild. She had 12 chn, but left five little graves along the road west. "All who are descended from this courageous woman may well be proud of their noble heritage." (Jay Pugsley of Lincoln, NEB, grandson of Rachel, Desier's sister.)

HORMAN

Francis De la Haye Horman was born in St. Heliers, Jersey in 1855 and brought to the United States in 1868 on the CONSTITUTION. He tells the story of his family's difficult journey and early settlement in Utah.

"Charles Horman and John Taylor were on a mission together in France, after President Taylor opened that mission. Father was presiding elder on the Island of Jersey for many years, and had the responsibility of arranging passage for many Saints sailing for America. His duty was to arrange their passage through the Perpetual Emigrating Fund of the L.D.S. Church. This being his responsibility, he and his family remained on the Island many years in the service of the Church until they were advised by the authorities that now was the time to move to Zion. . .

One year before leaving Jersey I was an apprentice to learn the barber trade. I got sixpence for the first six months and one shilling the balance of the year. I was supposed to work for three years to learn the trade. . .My grandmother lived with us, Mother's mother, Nancy Le Marchant De la Haye. All of our family and Grandma left the Island of Jersey for America to join the Saints in Utah the 24th of June 1868 on the sailing vessel CONSTITUTION with 457 British, Swiss and German Saints with Harvey H. Cluff in charge. I was baptized in the Atlantic ocean on the 25th of March, 1865, being 9½ years of age. Elder Cave baptized me, and father confirmed me the 27th of March 1865.

We arrived in New York August 5, 1868, and continued our journey by train to Benton, Wyoming. The freight train that our trunks and bedding were in got wrecked so we lost one trunk of clothes. We had to wait several days for our goods to reach us, and slept in what clothes we carried with us on the train for about 19 days. We left Benton on the 24th of August in Capt. John Gillespie's train of 54 wagons and about 500 immigrants, and arrived in Salt Lake City on the 15th of Sept. . .When we arrived in Toele City we were all rebaptized and confirmed in the Church of Jesus Christ of Latter-day Saints. This was done so that the ward could have a record.

One of the first houses built in Toele was occupied by my father, mother and seven children and Grandma. It was a one-room log house. We had to go to the canyon to get wood to burn. We had to make our own candles...Our benches and tables. ...The grasshoppers had been so bad that lots of people didn't have wheat. I went around town to try to buy flour for those who were sick at hom...Finally I went to a home by the name of George Atkin, who let me have about twenty-five pounds of flour. I handed him a five dollar bill to pay for it, but he would not take any pay.

That fall, Father and I dug potatoes on shares, getting every seventh bushel. We all cut peaches to dry on shares. In the winter, I went to scrape beets to make molasses. So we had bread, beet molasses as black as your hat, to eat with it, and we could also sweeten our dried peaches with the molasses. We had a little steel cut oatmeal and split peas from our rations left from aboard ship. We had no stove so we had to bake bread in the bake skillets in the fireplace. Lots of the boys and girls would go to dances in their bare feet. I had shoes to wear so I was called a tenderfoot. Father bought about fifteen acres of land on which we built a log house and planted a good orchard.

I was in charge of the garden work, as my father was working at his trade. He was a skilled worker with leather, so in Tooele he was a shoemaker and harness maker. My brother Charley was hired out. I was ordained a deacon and set apart as president of the Third Quorum of deacons...Some winters I worked in the canyon getting out sawed logs...In the early days I drove cattle to Salt Lake City with a load of tighing. I also rowed and snaked timber with the team."

Horman was ordained to the office of a priest in the Church in 1880, and in 1886 was married to Thecla Lindholm. They lived for a time in Idaho. Later, Francis and his brother, Thomas, had a lumber yard. They had a family of 12 children. (OUR PIONEER HERITAGE, by Kate B. Carter, Vol. 9.)

LE POIDEVIN

Jean LE POIDEVIN of Guernsey emigrated to Racine, Wisconsin, and shortly after gold was discovered in California, he and his brother left with a group to head for the Golden West. This account consists of several letters written to relatives in Guernsey.

"Dear Brother, according to my promise, I am going to send you some lines on the subject and progress of our enterprise. I am going to write you from time to time as we proceed, so that it will become a kind of Journal. We left Racine on April 8th. We traveled slowly until we came to the Missouri River, which is a distance of five hundred and fifty miles from Racine, and is the frontier between the Whites and the Indians. We ate and spent the night at hotels and at farmer's homes and for the greatest part of the distance, but we were obliged to camp like soldiers towards the end. We had to cross many rivers. The most important were the Mississippi and the Missouri. We stayed one week at Hainesville on the Frontier to buy the rest of our provisions and to prepare ourselves for our enterprise. ...We passed the Missouri river on the 15th of May with much difficulty, because of the large number who wanted to cross at the same time. One crosses on a flat boat, two wagons go at once, but those who have cattle take more time to get them over by boat. They then make them swim over and it is fun to see them chase a hundred bullocks and cows from a point on the main bank and make them enter the water. ...One would have said that there were a dozen of your great grand ladies about to enter a turnstile.

Until now the weather has been cold, which is why we haven't hurried, but once we had passed the Missouri River we made 30 or 35 miles of our way by day. We have found better grass on this side of the river than we expected to find. We have seen many Indians this last week, who appeared to be very savage and warlike. We have learned that they have attacked immigrants, but we ourselves, up until now, no difficulties. They are on the road and come to our camp to say How di do, How de do, and they do not stop asking for everything that they see. They ask for things to eat, for money, for clothes, etc., etc. This is curious to see them dressed as they are. One has an old hat, one has an old wesket, another a chemise, another some old handkerchiefs attached around his knees, with another one around his neck, but although most of them are only covered by buffalo skins, they are each one covered with ear rings, necklaces, medals, bells and different ornaments the like of which you have never seen.

We had the pleasure the other day in seeing three or four prepare a festival. They bought a big dog from the emigrants. They killed it, after which they lit a fire and burned off its hair. They then skinned it with a knife and boiled it all. They appeared as contented with it as though it were a large calf.

I am going to tell you how we manage our affairs. We now have a company of 8 wagons, 26 horses, seventeen men, four women and two babies. Our wagons are covered, to protect our things from the rain, then we have a tent by two or three wagons to sleep in, and eat our meals. And I sleep very well in the tent. I cannot remember having slept so well for several years, as I have since we began to camp. We have to have a watch to guard our horses and possessions, during the night. We are two men on a watch, and two watches each night. We have also a kitchen. We have superbe bread. We have good tea and coffee; meat, and if we have enough grass for our horses we expect to go far.

There are many people on the road who are going to Oregon. The government gives to each 230 acres of land free the moment they are in that country. We passed a company the other day. There were 60 wagons, five couples of bollocks and cows by each wagon. They had almost 700 head of cattle, including your beasts. Those who go to Oregon are generally families, while those who go to California are chiefly young men...

We have seen many large wolves, some deer and thousands of little animals that one calls prairie dogs. We are now in the

buffalo country. We have seen many hundreds of thousands, and there is their manure for a stretch of hundreds of miles in length, and hundreds of miles in width, thicker than I have ever seen it in any of the manure piles of Guernsey. For the lack of wood, one is obliged to burn these droppings to do one's cooking...All of our horses are in good conditions, fat as pigs. We have six that we work, two at a time on each wagon, and two that we ride and change from time to time...I prepare this letter to send to you when we get to Fort Laramie, which is a military station. ...Two of our boys went hunting the other day for buffaloes. They succeeded in killing one and they brought us a piece of it. It was extremely good. I've never eaten anything better. We have also had deer...For some time we have gotten up at half past two in the morning, we start at three, we go until seven and then we take two hours for breakfast and allow the horses to eat. From 9 to 12 we are en route again. Then we allow the horses to eat for two or three hours, then we continue on the road until six or seven o'clock. For some days we have had the most interesting view, a rock called Court House, another Chimney Rock."
(Mrs. Edward Harrison, Louisville, KY)

LE PREVOST

Capt. Le Prevost was a sea captain, born 1818 Guernsey. At an early age he was connected with the De Wolf line of steamships, and had traveled in all parts of the world, living under five flags. He was Captain of the G.L. NEWMAN, which was lost off Chicago at the time of the Great Fire, then finally settled in Mount Pleasant, WIS before 1879. He married Margaret Edmonds (Stone). His son, N. Le Prevost also came to America, and this is part of his account of his arrival in Racine.

"I left my family on the 13th [with the MANSELL family of Cleveland, OH, also of Guernsey] and proceeded to Racine... where I saw those Prairies. OH! the beautiful grounds, not a tree, and full of grass about 15 inches high, and in the lower parts 3 feet high...these prairies are not of a wet soil, but the greatest part labourable, because the ground is what is termed Voultante. In the middle of the Prairie I have a beautiful platon for hay, of which I cut myself 708 tons last week...There is about 50 vergies enclosed, the rest is not. In the middle of the farm there is a run of water that does not dry and that separates the Prairie from the woodland. The only tax we have to pay is $6 a year. May God bless Guernsey and all its slaves."

MAUGER

J.W.G. Mauger was born in Guernsey. In 1897 he travelled from Guernsey to London, to Newfoundland, New York, Chicago, Needles, and San Francisco. Below is a shortened account of his trip. (Mrs. Leland Hague, 3421 John Lee Lane, Modesto, CA)

"On Wednesday the 6th of October 1897 we left Guernsey for London via Southampton. [He mentions here Mr. Le Couteur and son George, also Guernsey folk.] We got up early, and went for a walk as far as the other side of London Bridge...then went to the Tower Bridge...open when we got there; we saw it close, then went up the stairs (only about 350) and across to the other side, came back along the level and went all over the Tower of London; then we took the underground Railway and a bus to the Zoological Garden,...came back...had a wash (you ought to have seen us, we were as black as tinkers) there had been a thick fog all day, we could hardly see across the streets...took a bus for West Kensington, saw the Big Wheel at Earl's Court Exhibition, Hyde Park and lots of other places of note. Saw the St. Paul's Colleges...went to St. Paul's Cathedral, went up to the Dome, there are only 375 steps to the Whispering Gallery. We could see all over London from there; we went down and stayed to the Service. The singing was beautiful...had something to eat and went to Mr. Ozanne's to spend the evening.

We left the hotel at half past six for Waterloo Station, took train for Southampton; got on board the S.S. PARIS, left for New York at twelve." Here he mentions fellow passengers T. Collas and M. Roussel of Guernsey.

"Monday...We got up about six, went on deck saw lots of dolphins...the first day the ship made 449 knots, and the second 485 knots." A storm left them bruised and tired, and a Mr. ALLAIRE of the Islands is mentioned as reading to the company about the Klondyke from the Strand Magazine. They were then on the Grand Banks of Newfoundland, and saw many birds and several whales.

"We passed the Hamburg American liner called the FIRST BISMARK. She is as large as this ship. We sighted Sandy Hook at nine.

Saturday...Got up soon after four, it was not daylight, had breakfast at half past five. It is the prettiest sight I have ever seen, going into New York harbour. We passed the Statue of Liberty on the left, and Brooklyn Bridge on the right. We got in dock about eight thirty. Charley was there, I hardly knew him. After we had got through customs, we went to Stephen's House...an Hotel on Broadway, the main street of New York...went to the Acquarium, then took a car to Central Park,...to the Zoological Gardens. Then we had a look at the tiptopers riding their carriages in the Park, then took the elevated Railway back.

Monday. We left the Hotel at nine and left in the train for Buffalo at ten. We went by the West Shore Line, it runs all along the west shore of the Hudson River up to Buffalo. At midnight left there about one for Chicago, got there at 6 on Tuesday. Left Chicago at ten for Kansas City, took off for NEEDLES, a small town before you come to the Mohave desert... We had to stay at Mohave. There are about a dozen houses in the place and about fifty or sixty pigs running about the streets. They have their manure heaps in the middle of the streets (it is a fine place). We left there at six o'clock on Saturday for San Francisco. Got here at eight on Sunday, only 12 hours late. JWG. Mauger"

MESSERVE

William C. Messerve wrote to the compiler in 1972: "As you surmised, I am a descendant of Clement Messervy. You have asked specifically about my involvement with the Antarctic--a connection of which I have many fond recollections. During the Antarctic summer of 1959-1960 I served as an assistant on a geologic expedition...Our field work was divided into two major segments. For a period of approximately three weeks, we man-hauled sleds along the sea ice of McMurdo Sound, studying geologic features as we went. We were principally interested in locating and measuring raised beaches, a geological feature whose existence enabled us to conclude that the ice cap in the McMurdo Sound was once considerably thicker than at present. We were the first party to extensively man-haul sleds in the Antarctic since Sir Ernest Shackleton had done so in 1915-1916, and we of course camped in tents which we carried on our sleds. One of the highlights of this field work was the discovery of a hut used by Sir Robert F. Scott's western party in 1911, together with several books and other pieces of field equipment which they had left behind.

By mid-December, since there was some danger that the sea ice which we were using as our highway would break up, our party was air-lifted by helicopter into one of the few dry valleys located in the Antarctic. These valleys receive their name from the fact that they are deglaciated, and since rock is therefore exposed, they are ideal for geological field work. Here, once again, we camped and backpacked our supplies for approximately three to four weeks and developed some evidence that multiple glaciation may have occurred in that part of the Antarctic.

There are several small valley glaciers flowing into the dry valley where we worked, and at the conclusion of the field season, one of these glaciers was named the Meserve Glacier. Through an unforeseen quirk of circumstance, this glacier has been frequently studied by subsequent geological expeditions, and a great deal of scientific literature has been published about it. Although it is not particularly large as Antarctic glaciers go, it seems to be becoming one of the more intensively studied glaciers in the world.

Oddly enough, despite my stimulating and enjoyable sojourn in the Antarctic and two other expeditions to the Arctic, I am not a geologist but am presently practising law in Boston."

PINEL

Rev. Joseph Pinel was born in Guernsey 1856, and removed later to Canada. His account of his childhood in Jersey and Guernsey will interest some readers.

"Of the eleven children born to my parents, the last four were born in Guernsey, my father who was foreman of Granite Quarries having moved there from Jersey. I was one of the four and was born 1856 in an apartment situated over a livery stable on the corner of the North Esplanade...Later, we moved to No. 8 Glatney Esplanade, a two story house with attic... facing the sea and giving a splendid view of the new harbour, and the Islands of Sark, Herm, and Jethou. At the rear of the house was a very rich garden...Here we grew quite a variety of fruits such as pears, peaches, plums, apples, cherries, gooseberries, red, black and white currants, raspberries, strawberries as well as grapes; and of course the usual vegetables common to a garden of that kind. Flowers too were much in evidence...

I distinctly recall sitting in a high-back chair in front on the fireplace, and falling forward into the fire from which I was rescued by my sister Harriet I think. Almost in front of our home was a slip used for the launching of ships from the shipyard close by; at the feet of this slip was a short ladder by which to get down to the beach, and the uprights of which were just about the height for me, probably four or five years old, to rest my hands on so as to swing my legs back and forth over the water. I evidently was swinging a little too vigorously, for I went head foremost into the water, the waves of which were seen playing with me as they willed. Fortunately a number of boys were near by, among them my brother John. They soon picked me up, and John carried me home...At La Moie in Jersey we were far removed from all educational advantages. I first went to a small private school taught by a Mrs. Marrett...later to another private school conducted by a Miss Le Boutillier. ...We were three or four miles from St. Aubin's where better school advantages were to be had, but there was no conveyances...

At La Moie (my father) had charge of a quarry known as La Rosiere not far from the Corbiere... . ...My mother kept a few of the quarrymen as boarders, sold a few groceries and baked bread for sale. Her bread was of such excellent quality that there was a great demand for it, not only in the country, but in town as well. The oven she used was enlarged so as to bake some twenty to twenty-five six pound loaves at one time. And I have known her frequently to fill the oven twice every day during the week, and indeed sometimes three times in one day, her only help being brother John who himself became quite an expert baker."

Mr. Pinel was encouraged to go to Gaspe, and he sailed there on the ship ALICE JANE 1870. See WRCIC for a copy of his account. Also see Q.A. IN CANADA.

ROBERT

Peter Robert of Guernsey Island was an early settler in Wisconsin, and his account is in a typescript held by the Wisconsin Historical Society.

"April 8th, 1842...weighted anchor and made sail at 2:30... Fine weather...April 19th, commenced with a strong gale...more than 1500 miles from Guernsey and not having any tools to repair the damages. Passed a Dutch barque...May 10: Commenced with a very strong stress of wind, with increase to a compleat gale. Split the mainsail and laid to the whole day and night, expecting every minute to carry away our mast. May 11th: Wind a hurrican, mountains high. The whole of the fore lanyards gone. Formast holding by only two shrouds. Aside and bending over the side at least 12 feet every roll...May 12th: The foretop mast with the topsail and top gallant sail is just gone over the side. The whole is in the greatest confusion on boat...6 o'clock...The whole is saved, sails and all with a great deal of exertion. May 25: More than 100 vessels passed the ship. A whale came close to the vessel. We are sailing along the shore of New Jersey for more than 30 miles at about a miles distance from shore...May 26th: At daylight was inside of Sandy Hook, and I cannot describe the beauty of the sean...Before you enter the narrows is the most splendid sight I ever beheld and with the beautiful bay crowded with ships and steamers and country seats in all directions makes me think what a fool I have been to live in Guernsey all this time."

From New York, the Roberts traveled to Albany, then Troy, where they went aboard a barge on the Erie Canal. They soon saw their first log house and first burnt forest. They bought provisions along the way: "Beef, 6 cents...Mutton 5 cents, eggs 8 cents...Fish of an unknown sort to us, but very good, 1 cent each, sugar 10 cents, coffee 16 cents."

At Buffalo, they got the very boat that they had been advised in Guernsey to take, which brought them to Fairport,

Cleveland, Amherstburg and Detroit, en route taking note of the Lake Erie Islands, which he compared roughly to Guernsey. They arrived at Racine, WISC on June 22nd, where Roberts and Ozanne looked at farmland for sale.

SWANTON, SWARTON

Hannah Hubbard, Hibbard, wife of John Swanton, Swarton, res Beverly MA and then in North Yarmouth, was captured by Indians in 1690, when her husband was killed. Her children were killed or scattered. Upon her release and return to New England in 1695, she wrote an interesting account of her captivity. See APPENDIX to Cotton Mathers, "HUMILIATIONS FOLLOWED BY DELIVERANCES," NEHGS, Vol. 11.

DID YOU KNOW?

There are many places in North America named for the Channel Islands, or for Channel Islanders who settled there: Jersey City, NJ; Jersey County, ILL; Jersey Shore, PA; Jerseyville, ILL; ILL; Jersey and Guernsey streets in Marblehead, MA; Jerseyville, NJ; Grandin Rd., Mainville, OH; Guernsey Co., OH; Guernsey in Western PA near Gettysburg, PA; Guernsey, IA; Guernsey, CAL; Guernsey, Wyoming, near the Nebraska State Line on the North Platte River, and adjoining is the Guernsey Reservation.

In 1831 Thomas Edge started making gas in his plant at St. Helier, Jersey, and began to supply gas to some of the stores in town. Later that year, 28 gaslights were put up around the harbor. To commemorate this, Jersey issued five stamps, very handsome ones. The beautiful stamps of Jersey can be obtained by writing to Jersey Post Office, P.O. Box 304 L, Postal Headquarters, St. Heliers, Jersey, Channel Islands, Grt.Britain

Many persons in the world of entertainment have Channel Island connections. Consider Rich Little, from a LE BRETON family; Karen MACHON of Calgary, ALTA; Olivia DE HAVILLAND and Joan FONTAINE, sisters who are descendants of the DE HAVILLAND FAMILY OF Guernsey, long located in southern England. Billie Burke also had Channel Island ancestors. The surnames SAVIDENT, LE MESURIER and MORANT have been noticed in screen credits, all possibly from the Channel Islands.

HUGUENOTS AND THE CHANNEL ISLANDS

The Huguenots were not the first French to emigrate to the Islands. This emigration began with the Gauls, the Celts and the Franks. Then came the Veneti, the Vaudois, the Waldensians and the Gascons. Restless seafaring merchants from all the French ports visited or settled in the Islands at various times, seeking new products and new markets. Therefore, many a French Huguenot found that he had been long preceded by others of the same surname, when he landed in Jersey or Guernsey.

The Islands, during the 1700s, were nearly inundated at times by the numbers of Huguenots fleeing from French persecution. Their welcome was in the main wholehearted, especially since most Islanders spoke Old Norman French in the home. The Islands served very well as a halfway house, when the Huguenots intended to go to more distant places.

The Islands are very small, and business opportunities few, so most of the Huguenots stayed for short lengths of time, while making their plans to go farther afield. They soon took ship for England, Ireland, Scotland, and the English colonies in North America. Others settled in Holland, Scandinavia, Germany, Switzerland, Iceland, Russia, Denmark, South Africa and South America.

It is not easy to distinguish between Huguenots and Channel Islanders among the settlers in early New England. They often arrived together on Jersey ships, and intermarried. Some Huguenots had arrived in the Islands in the 1500s, and by the late 1600s these would surely consider themselves Channel Islanders, would they not?

Marie-Louise Backhurst, in CIFHS bulletin #12, lists these families as having a Huguenot origin: AMIRAUX, POIGNAND, QUESNEL, DE FAYE, VOISIN, INGOUVILLE, GIRARD, GOSSELIN, LE TOUZEL, GOSSET, DU PARCQ and HEMERY. There were many others. See the Huguenot List.

"The baptismal, marriage and burial registers do often indicate when a person is a refugee. For example in the parish of St. Helier there are many burials of refugees, and it would be interesting if these could be extracted." (Backhurst) The author notes that information about the Huguenot refugees in Guernsey is being gathered by researchers in the Islands.

Some Huguenot family data of families that came to America is not included in this book. However, part of this data will be, by the end of 1983, in the Channel Islands Collection at Western Reserve Library, 10825 East Blvd., Cleveland, Ohio 44106.

The BLAMPIEDS of the U.S. are proud of their Huguenot tradition, and a descendant, Charles W. Blampied, wrote an account of his family origins as told to him when a boy. He was born on a farm near Mulvane, KS 1855, and died in Denver, COL 1885. A condensed version of this story is below. The compiler feels that while the details may be slightly inaccurate in some of these Huguenot tales, the stories, in general, may be true.

Jean Blampied lived in France, and joined his comrades in persecuting the small groups of Protestants who lived in his valley. On one of the raids he picked up a small Bible which had been dropped by one of the dissidents, and took it home to see what the big attraction was for these troublesome people. "Half curious and half fearing, he opened it and as he read his fear slipped away, and he read with growing zeal and interest page after page." He began to join the secret meetings and soon met with Margaret, whom he had intended to marry. Jean was disowned, and lost his position, and was caught out one night, mobbed and flogged by some of his old playmates. He fled from the area with his bride, and was able to get his wife passage on a ship going to Guernsey, but was almost caught himself. He fled the city and hid in a cave on the shore, but could not think how to join his wife in Guernsey.

One night of storm, a vessel was blown towards shore, and Jean seized the opportunity to swim out to it, and was just barely saved by the sailors. The ship was bound for England, where he found a ship heading for Guernsey. John and his wife made a home there, and raised a family. Their descendant, Elisha, was born in Guernsey in 1792, and came to Guernsey County, Ohio in 1813, a tailor. He married an Irish girl, Elizabeth Brown. Their descendants are scattered throughout the American Midwest.

There is much information on Huguenot emigration. See books by Smiles and Reaman, plus others more recent. (SOC. JERS. BULL. 1927; BALLEINE'S HIST. OR JERSEY, by Syvret and Stevens; HIST OF MODERN FRANCE, Vol. 1, by A. Cobban; HUGUENOTS IN ENGLAND, by Smiles; TRAIL OF THE HUGUENOTS, by Reaman; PROCEEDINGS OF THE HUG. SOC., London, Vol. 19, 1954; OLD CHANNEL ISLANDS SILVER, 1969, by R. Mayne, etc.) Note that K. Annett of Ste. Foy, Quebec, is gathering data on Huguenot families of Canada. See copy of the Blampied story in the Western Reserve Historical Library.

See List of Huguenot books and sources at end of Bibliography, page 670.

SOME HUGUENOT SURNAMES

Listed below are just some of the thousands of Huguenot surnames with a Channel Island connection. Some spent just a few weeks on the Islands, others became established over a century or more.

ADRIEN
ALIX
AMIRAUX
ARNAUD
AUBEL
AUBIN
AUGIER
BATISTE
BAUDOIN
BERNARD
BERTRAM
BIARD
BISSON
BLANCPIED
CHEVALIER
CLEMENT
COLLETT
COLLIER?
DALLAIN
DE FAYE
DE FEU
DE LA CLOCHE
DE LA FAYE
DE LA PLACE
DE QUETTEVILLE
DENYS, DENNIS
DE VAUMOREL
DOBREE
DU CHEMIN
DUE FRESNE
DUMONT
DURELL
DU VAL
FERREE, FERRY
FEVRIER
FOURNIER
FOYE
GAIN
GANO, GERNEAU
GARRICK
GAULTIER
GENDRON
GERMAN
GIRARD
GOSSELIN
GOSSETT
GOYON
GRANGER
GUERIN
GUERNIER
HEMERY
HERAULT
HORRY
HULIN
INGOUVILLE
JOHANNE, JOHN
JOLLYS
JUSTIN
LA GROVE
LARCOME, LACOMBE
LA RUE
LAUGA, LOUGEE
LA FALLEE
LE BAS
LE BLANC
LE COMTE
LE CORNU
LE DRU
LE DUC
LE FEBVRE
LE JEUNE
LE MARCHAND
LE MARCHEZ
LE MENUEL
LE MOYNE
LE PRINCE
LE TOUZEL
LOUGEE
MARCHAND
MASSE
MASTRE, MASTER
MAUCLERC
MERLIN
MERRIENNE
MILLET
NOEL
PAIN
PEPIN
PERRINE
PICHON
POIGNAND
POITTEVIN
POULAIN
RAMSEY
RENAUD
RICHE
RIVES
RIVOIRE
ROCHELLE
ROIGNON, RUNYON
SAUL
SEIGLE
SICHE
SIMON
SOHIER
TIFFANY
TOUCHAR
TISSUE, TISSAUD
TOURGIS
TYRELL
VALLOT
VALPY
VASSE
VAUQUELIN
VIEL
VOISIN
WALKE
WYBONE

SETTLERS AND SETTLEMENTS BY STATE

Massachusetts and Maine would appear to be the first places in this country known by the sea-faring Channel Islanders, with possibly Virginia and the Carolinas very shortly after. There were links between the new colonies and the West Indies, but this is a large subject, and was not explored by the compiler. There were also links between the Channel Islands and the West Indies, these were not researched.

The names of the Channel Islands show up in North America, in both Canada and the United States, such as Jersey Island, CAL; Jerseyville, ILL; Guernsey Co., OH; New Jersey, of course, and places named Carteret in New Jersey and the Carolinas. There is also a Guernsey in Wyoming.

The compiler has attempted to sort the Channel Island families roughly by states, but the lists following are incomplete. Also, descendants not bearing the original Channel Island surname, are included.

Some puzzling surnames might be explained by the fact that Irish, French and Cornish mercenaries were in the Channel Islands ca 1650, when 60 Poles, Swedes and Danes arrived, all being called Germans by the Islanders. In June 1651, 200 Swiss came to the Islands. (HIST. OF JERSEY, by Balleine)

ALABAMA: CARRE, COLQUITT, GALUSHA, HUBBARD, LE CRAW, LE POIDEVIN, MACHON, ROBIN

ALASKA: BALLEINE, FLOOD, LENFESTEY, SIMON

ARIZONA: DE LA MARE, FERBRACHE, GALUSHA, KERBY, LENFESTEY, LE POIDEVIN, LE SUEUR, MARETT, PALLOT, ROBBINS, TOSTEVIN

ARKANSAS: ALBO DE BERNALES, ARMS, FLOOD, GALUSHA, HALLETT, LE BOUTILLIER, MARTEL, MESSERVY, POINDEXTER, RUMRILL

CALIFORNIA: At least a hundred surnames are represented in this state. Compiler will provide a list for any interested Genealogy Society.

COLORADO: BISHOP, BOURGAIZE, BURCH, DE BRODER, DE LA MARE, DOREY, DUQUEMIN, DUCOMMUN, HALLETT, HEAUME, JANVRIN, LAINE, LE FEVRE?, LE MARCOM, LENFESTEY, LE POIDEVIN, LE ROSSIGNOL, LE VESCONTE, MESSERVY, ROBERTS, STEVENSON

CONNECTICUT: AHIER, ARMS, BALCOM, BARTRAM, BENNET, BISHOP, CORBIN?, DE JEAN, ENGLISH, FALLA, FICKETT?, FILLEUL?, FLOOD, GALUSHA, GOSSETT, GUILBERT, GUILLAUME, GUSTIN, HILL, HUBBARD, HUSE, JANVRIN, JOREY?, LAWRENCE, LE DOIT?, LE FAVOR, LLOYD, LOUGEE, MAINWARING, MARCHANT, MARINER, MARQUAND, MASTERS, MOON, MUNGER?, NICHOLS, ORNE, OZANNE, PATRILL, PERRY, PINEL, PROVOST?, PUNCHARD, QUERIPEL, QUINER?, QUITTERFIELD, RENOUF, ROBBINS, SEVERIT?, SHARP, SHELTON, STEVENSON, TOURGIS, VIBBER, VIBRANT

FLORIDA: BISHOP, BOURGAIZE, BUTT, COGLAN, DE BRODER, DEMERITT, FERBRACHE, GALLIEN, GAUDIN, GROVER, HAWKINS, HENRY, HUBBARD, LE BOUTILLIER, LE CORNU, LENFESTEY, LE POIDEVIN, LE SUEUR, LE VESCONTE, LLOYD, MARCHON, MARTEL, MESSERVY, OGIER, PERRY, PETHIC, PINEL, PUNCHARD, ROBBINS, ROBIN, TAYLER

GEORGIA: COLQUITT, GALUSHA, GOSSETT, GROVER, GUILLE, JEAN, LE CORNU, MARQUAND, MARTEL, ROBBINS, SAUL

IDAHO: CANIVET, DE LA MARE, HORMAN, LE MARQUAND, LE POIDEVIN, LE SUEUR, PENDEXTER, ROBERT

ILLINOIS: ALLES, ARMS, BISHOP, BLAMPIED, BREWER, BRICE, CARRE, DE BRODER, DUFFET, DUFOUR, FERBRACHE, FICKETT, GALLIEN, GALUSHA, GRUTT, GUILLE, GUSTIN, HALLETT, HILL, HOYLES, HUBBARD, JANVRIN, LE CORNU, LE HUQUET, LE JEUNE, LENFESTEY, LE PELLEY, LE POIDEVIN, LE VESCONTE, LING, LITTLE, MACHON, MANNING, MARQUAND, MARSH, MARTEL, MELZARD, MESSERVY, MOON, MORRELL, PITON, ROBBINS, RUMRILL, SAVORY, SYVRET, SKINNER, STEELE, TORODE

INDIANA: ARMS, BALLEINE, CARRINGTON, FICKETT?, GUSTIN, HEAUME, JANVRIN, LE FEUVRE, LE FEVRE, LENFESTEY, LE PAGE, LE SUEUR, MARQUAND, MESSERVY, PUNCHARD, SARCHET, SKINNER

(Compiler's Note: Some of the settlers in ILL, IND, IOWA, NEB and MISSOURI were descended from or related to the group that settled in Guernsey Co., OH in the early 1800s.)

IOWA: ARMS, BALLEINE, BISHOP, CAREY, CODY, DE BOURCIER, DE GRUCHY, DE PUTRON, DOREY, DURELL, DU VAL, FAUX, FRANCIS, GALUSHA, GORSCHIEL, GRUCHY, GUSTIN, HEAUME, HUNTOON, JAVRIN, LANGLOIS, LE BOUTILLIER, LE CORNU, LE HUQUET, LEIGH, LE LACHEUR, LENFESTEY, LE POIDEVIN, MARTEL, MC KINSEY, MEIZARD, MERRY?, MESSERVY, OGIER, PENDEXTER, PETHIC, PRIAULX, SALTER, SARCHET, STEELE,THOREAU, TORODE, TOUET

KANSAS: BALLEINE, BICHARD, BLAMPIED, DE CAEN, DU FRESNE, FRANCIS, GALUSHA, HUBBARD, KILNER, LE BOUTILLIER, LE CAIN, LE CORNU, LE GATE-LEGEYT?, LENFESTEY, LE PAGE, MARQUAND, MARTEL, MORRELL, PEVEAR, RENOUF, ROBBINS, SEVERY?. See LE BOUTILLIER book and PERSONAL ACCOUNTS.

KENTUCKY: AMY, BLAMPIED, BLONDEL, COLLINGS, LE FEVRE, LE PAGE?, LE PELLEY, LE SUEUR?, POINDEXTER, TAYLOR

LOUISIANA: BEDLE, BLAMPIED, BUESNEL, CARRE, DEMERITT, ESNOUF, FLOOD, GROVER, LE CRAW, LE POIDEVIN, LE SUEUR, MARTEL, POINDEXTER

MAINE: At least 85 surnames. The Compiler will provide a list for any interested Genealogy Society. There may have been a small settlement in Isles of Shoals ca 1700--needs research.

TAKEN BY THE ABENAKI! This phrase was repeated hundreds of times in the 1600s and early 1700s when men, women and children were killed or kidnapped and taken to Quebec by the Abenaki and Micmac Indians. This action was shamefully encouraged by the French in Canada. Abbe Le Loutre, missionary to the Micmacs at Shubenacadie, later Bishop of Quebec, set the price of a hundred livres for each English scalp, and paid for over a thousand scalps. When captured at long last by the English, he was sentenced to eight years in a Jersey Island prison, then was allowed to return to France.

Many Channel Island families were victims of these raids: Alexander, Carpenter?, Durell, Gallichan, Huntoon, Hammond, Lougee, Le Montais, Major?, Swarton?, Swett, Weare? and Ricker were a few names involved, and there were probably others.

Occasionally, the captives were redeemed through intermediaries and the payment of ransom. Often, the captives were tortured. Many were unable to maintain the rapid pace set by the Indians on their return through the wilderness to Canada, and were summarily killed.

Sometimes the captives refused to return to New England, preferring the way of life in Quebec. Many of the young were converted to the Catholic faith, and married into French or French-Indian families.

One captive, evidently a resourceful man, John Lougee of Jersey, resided in Exeter, NH, 1710, when he was captured by Indians. He somehow escaped after being taken to Canada, and finally returned to New Hampshire by way of England!

Although most of the captives were seized in Maine, Indians raided most of the colonies at one time or another. See sources, both in Canada and U.S.: County Histories of Maine and NH; Bell; Coleman; Gallant; Tanguay; Rutledge; NEHGS Vol 6.

MARYLAND: At least 50 surnames. The Compiler will provide a list for any interested Genealogy Society.

MASSACHUSETTS: At least 300 surnames. Compiler will provide a list for anyone interested.

Throughout this book, there are hundreds of persons and families recorded who came from the Channel Islands and settled in various places in MASS. There were more in Marblehead, but possibly nearly as many went to Salem and Boston, and some to Cape Cod. While the compiler searched hundreds of books, there are still hundreds more that were not available, and that may contain information about Channel Island families not included in this book. Libraries in New England may have a number of handwritten or typed genealogies of Channel Island Families not known to the compiler.

Ships came every year from the Islands, with at least a few settlers. The record here is one of the few that apparently survived. While all these persons came on this ship, we do not know how many were not permanent citizens here, but returned to the Islands or settled in Canada instead.

LIST OF PERSONS ABOARD THE SCHOONER MOLLY, Capt. Daniel MESSERVY, Arriving in BOSTON 1769, From JERSEY ISLAND (Whitemore)

John BARTON, Daniel BESSIN, Joseph BOUCHER, John BOURBONELL, Geo. CAUL, Thomas BINGHAM, Charles COULOMBE?, Joseph CARELL, Philip DE STE. CROIX, John DUMARESQ, Stevens DUMARESQ, Amice GRANDIN, Philip GRUCHY, Philip GRAUTT, Clement GUNNLL?, George HAMMON, John GALLICHAN, John JENNE, Francis LE ROY, Judith LE ROY, James LE ROY, William LE ROY, Charles LE MASSERVIER, John LE GRAND, P. PENNY, Peter PINEL, Elias WATTON, Capt. Joseph LUCE, John PERVIER, Charles and William LE BOURDON, BODEN, Jane FONTENAY, John BLOVEL, Magdalaine WIE, and Ann SCOBAL.

MARBLEHEAD, MASSACHUSETTS

There is information on the settlement of Marblehead, MA in the files of the Essex Inst. of Salem, MA and the NEHGS library in Boston. However, the compiler has yet to find a book about the Channel Islanders of this area. There were apparently thousands of Guernsey and Jersey folk who came to Marblehead, Salem and Boston in the late 1600s and in the 1700s. Most of them were farmers and seamen, others were carpenters, clerks and tradesmen. As early as 1634, one Marblehead merchant had 8 fishing boats constantly in use, and the Channel Islanders were probably available then as crew. In Portsmouth, NH, another had six shallops, five other fishing boats with sails and anchors, and 13 skiffs. Surely among these were fishermen from Newfoundland waters, of Channel Island origin?

While there is very little to be found on the earliest arrivals from the Islands, their surnames show up in some numbers in the second and third generations. We do not know when they came, in many cases; they were just there in the late 1600s. They kept their own counsel, raised their families, and dug in their heels when disturbed by official actions. This shows in church records and legal records. Some did not want to go to church every Sunday, a very serious fault in those days. Some did not want to be ordered about by those in charge, nearly as serious as fault as the other. What they were at heart was rebels, in many cases, and this did not endear them to officaldom. They spoke an odd language only they could understand. Their names were very French, and were written down with difficulty by the Englishmen in charge. However, they were hard workers, and none were better when it came to fishing, sailing, carpentry and shoe-making.

The Islanders were farmers, too, and food from the land was an immediate necessity. There is an early tradition in New England of seaweed being used for fertilizer. This may have come to America with the Channel Islanders, as it is there an age-old tradition bound by a number of ancient laws; and seaweed, called "vraic" or "seawrack," has always been used on the Island farms. They were sailors, and coastwise shipping was the only line of communication between the various colonies. They were fishermen, and dried cod and other fish were a source of revenue for the infant colonies.

Their names suffered many changes, such as Le Messurier to Mazury, Poingdestre to Puddester and Pindexter, Pirouet to Perreway, Le Ruez to Laraway, Augustin Jean to John Gustin, etc. Some families prospered exceedingly, such as the Cabots, the Bertrams and the Englishes, and were much in the limelight. Others prospered quietly, raised their families, and were only noted in the records of birth, death, marriage and land. They were loyal to the new government in the 1700s, and many served in the Army and at sea. Others were loyal to the British Crown, and removed to Canada in the late 1700s.

Marblehead was settled by Islanders and by the Cornish people. There have always been many links between Cornwall and the Channel Islands, including blood ties, language, and long, long before settlement in America, Channel Islanders worked in the Cornish mines. For more information on Cornish families, try the CORNISH AMERICA, 353 Ann St., N.E., Grand Rapids, MI 49505.

The Marbleheaders were "different." They were free souls right from the start, says Balitsen in ATLANTIC YACHTSMEN, May 1972. "One man went so far as to build on town property without permission. Taken into court, he was fined 10 shillings; but, it seems, the fine would be excused if he would 'cut of ye long har off his head into a sevil fram'." Marblehead had no church in the early years, as no minister wanted to come to a community with such a non-religious reputation. In 1645, it was separated from Salem, MA. When the Revolutionary War came, the town literally bankrupted itself of both men and money. The men proved invaluable to George Washington many times, especially when they rowed him across the Delaware River to surprise the British at Trenton, a defeat that shortened the war.

Jersey St. meets Guernsey St. in Marblehead, MA, called Cow Corners by the inhabitants. Today, there are thousands of tourists, sailors and boatmen who enjoy the happy surroundings. For researchers, some records are available, but others are lost, due to fires and the ravages of time.

Marbleheaders were seamen, and descendants would enjoy the book, OLD MARBLEHEAD SEA CAPTAINS AND THE SHIPS IN WHICH THEY SAILED, from the Marblehead Hist. Society, 1915, and probably a more recent reprint, available from the Essex Institute in Salem, MA. Many names in this book are of Channel Island Captains, such as BISSON, BODEN, BUBIER, FREETO, LE CRAW, LE BRITON, MESSERVY, QUINER, etc.

BIBLIOGRAPHY

RECORDS OF THE ESSEX INST., Salem, MA; MARBLEHEAD HIST. SOC. RECORDS; VITAL RECORDS: GENERAL JOHN GLOVER AND HIS MARBLEHEAD MARINERS IN AMERICAN HERITAGE, Feb. 1960; IMMIGRANTS TO NEW ENGLAND, by E. Bolton; THE CABOT FAMILY, by L.V. Briggs, 1927; THE SEAFARERS, by D.B. Cridsey, NY, 1962; HISTORY OF SALEM, MA, Salem, 1928; THE MARBLEHEAD MANUAL, by Sam Roads, Jr., 1883; OLD NAUMKEAG, by C.H. Webber, 1877; JOURNALS OF ASHLEY BOWEN, by Philip Smith, Boston, 1973; David T. Konig article in NEHGS Vol. 110, #3, 1974; GEN. HANDBOOK FOR NEW ENGLAND RESEARCH, Lynnfield Public Library, Lynnfield, MA. Much more data is available.

A list of Channel Island surnames in MASS is not included, as it would run almost as long as the name index. A list is available to interested persons and societies.

NORTH CHELMSFORD, MASSACHUSETTS

A little more than a hundred years ago a group of families came fron Jersey Island and settled in North Chelmsford, MA. A descendant of the Le Marinels of this group writes: "My grandfather, John Le Marinel, Sr., came to the United States from the Island of Jersey about 1870, accompanied by John De Carteret. They settled in North Chelmsford. They both went into the granite business and operated their own quarries for many years. My grandfather and grandmother were married by the father of Lilly Langtry, Rev. Le Breton. My father was born on the Island of Jersey and was eight years old when he came to America with his parents."

Another correspondant writes: "My ancestors on both sides were stonecutters and came to this country to work in the quarries. They were from St. John parish, Jersey. My maternal grandmother was a Queree. My grandfather's maternal grandfather, Joshua Machon, was a builder and in his young days owned sailing vessels used in the spice trade. We have a large painting of one of these boats, a two-masted schooner... THE TRUST, Philip Queree, Master, entering Malta Harbor, 1887. My husband's father sailed twice around the world on a sailing vessel. When he came to this country he worked in the quarries, and in 1913 started his own, on the same land on which my husband and his two brothers have their quarry today."

Around the turn of the century, other Jersey families came to North Chelmsford to settle, buying and operating other quarries in the neighborhood. An article about these families, in a 1969 issue of the Jersey EVENING POST, mentions the visit of the Le Masuriers to the Island, and says they were of full Jersey blood, as the group had intermarried, and some still spoke the Jersiaise language.

SOME JERSEY FAMILIES SETTLED IN AND NEAR NORTH CHELMSFORD, MA

AUDOIN, BENEST, BOUTELOUPE, BRAKE, DE CARTERET, DE LA HAYE, LE MARINEL, LE MARREC, LE MASURIER, MACHON, MALLORY, PINEL, QUEREE, SYVRET, TOMS, VASSELIN.

MICHIGAN: At least 60 surnames. The Compiler will provide a list for any interested Genealogy Society.
MINNESOTA: ARMS, ARTHUR, BISHOP, BLAMPIED, BROWN, DE BRODER, GALUSHA, LANGLOIS, LA SERRE, LE BOUTILLIER, LE BRUN, LE GALLAIS, LE MASURIER, LENFESTEY, LE POIDEVIN, LE SUEUR, MESSERVY, ROBBINS, ROBERTS, also HERIVEL.
MISSISSIPPI: LE BOUTILLIER, LE CORNU, LE POIDEVIN, POINDEXTER, ROBBINS
MISSOURI: AMY, COLQUITT, DE LA MARE, GALLICHAN?, KILNER, LE BOUTILLIER, LE FEVRE, MARQUAND, MARSH, MARTEL, MESSERVY, POINDEXTER, ROBBINS, SARCHET, SKINNER, TORODE
NEBRASKA: BISHOP, DE PUTRON, FERBRACHE, FRANCIS, FULLER, HEAUME, LE BOUTILLIER, LE GEYT, LE LACHEUR, LENFESTEY, LE PAGE, LE POIDEVIN, LE ROSSIGNOL, MESSERVY, MORRELL, OGIER, SEVERIT?, SKINNER
NEVADA: HUBBARD, KERBY, LANGLOIS, LE BOUTILLIER, OGIER, TOSTEVIN, WALTERS
NEW HAMPSHIRE: At least 85 surnames. The Compiler will provide a list for any interested Genealogy Society.

ELIZABETHTOWN, NEW JERSEY

New Jersey has a rather special relationship with Jersey Island. In 1664, Charles the Second of England granted to his brother James, the Duke of York, the district between the Connecticut River and Delaware Bay, although this land was at that time occupied by the Dutch. A small force sent to capture it was able to do so without difficulty. In that year, the Duke of York transferred the part west of the Hudson RIver, now New Jersey, to Sir George Carteret, qv, and to Lord Berkeley, who subsequently gave up his share of the grant.

Sir Philippe DE CARTERET, Seigneur of La Houge, Jersey, was born in 1639, and was a fourth cousin of Sir George CARTERET, the proprietor of New Jersey, In April 1665, Philip sailed from England in the ship, PHILIP, with a shipload of settlers said by some to be largely recruited from Jersey. The names associated with this voyage and settlement do not seem to support this belief, as they appear to be mainly French and English, so far as this compiler could tell. It seems quite possible that another voyage brought over more of the Channel Islanders, however.

After touching down in Virginia and in New York, the passengers landed in New Jersey in August. Philip is said to have marched into the settlement with a hoe over his shoulder, to show that he came as a planter, not as a conqueror.

Sir Philip named the first group of log cabins Elizabethtown, in honor of Lady Carteret, the wife of the Proprietor, George Carteret. Here, he built a large white house, with gardens and orchards around it, and surveyed off his 2,000 acres of land. The first wedding in the settlement was that of Daniel PERRIN of Jersey, and Marie Thorel, a French girl. The service was conducted by James BALLEINE, whose name now appeared as BOLLEN and BULLEN.

Sir Philip had some legal problems in the colony. A number of New Englanders had settled before he arrived, and they did not see why they should pay quit-rents to an absentee landlord who did nothing for them. Nicolls, the Duke of York's Governor, had known nothing of this alienation of his part of New Jersey from his territory, and had already confirmed many planters in possession of their land.

Troubles multiplied in the first assembly which met in 1668. In 1672, the malcontents called an assembly of their own which deposed Sir Philip, and they chose as "President" James CARTERET, a scapegrace son of Sir George.

Sir Philip sailed back to England to report to the Lords Proprietors, and they fully confirmed his authority. The Duke of York repudiated Nicolls' grants, and the King sternly ordered the rebels to submit to the Proprietary government. But, before Philip could return, the Dutch captured New Jersey and New York, and occupied them for 15 months. In 1674, peace was made, and the district was restored to English government.

In 1680, Sir Philip's right to the Governorship of New Jersey was questioned by Sir Edmund ANDROS, qv. Andros claimed a grant from the King that was to combine his governorship of New Jersey and New York with the rest of New England. Sir Philip resisted. One of his servants was corrupted, whereby Sir Philip was seized and kidnapped. He was badly treated and beaten, and injured internally, his life thereby shortened. Imprisoned for some time in New York, a jury finally, contrary to Andros' demands, declared Sir Philip not guilty of the charges. In 1681, Sir Philip was reinstated, and Andros was summoned back to England to answer charges.

In 1661, Sir Philip had married Elizabeth, dau of Richard Smith of Long Island. She was the widow of William Lawrence. They had no children, although she had children by Lawrence. Sir Philip died in 1682, at age 42. (Johnson, Smith, Balleine Biog. Dict., NJ Hist. records.)

Philip Luce of Vancouver, BC, had some interesting notes on the New Jersey Grant and the Carterets: "New Jersey...has an area about 120 times the size of the Island of Jersey. For this Sir George Carteret had to pay six pounds sterling a year to the King. (Ca $30 then.) The land remained in the possession of the De Carteret family and his heirs for 32 years, and was sold for 34,000 pounds, ca $16,000, so it is not likely that the family made much profit on the deal. The De Carterets of the day were very wealthy, much of their riches having come from privateering. In 1933, 20,000 pounds in gold was found in a secret drawer where it had been forgotten for over 275 years."

There are some discrepancies and many unanswered questions in regard to the first settlers of Elizabethtown, NJ. Some local records are missing. Rev. Hatfield's book solves one of the questions, the presence of the French settlers who came in the ship, PHILIP. "Capt. Carteret hath brought over sundry French men that know the making of salt in France." Their purpose was to set up a salt-making plant in New Jersey and also, a potash works. They discovered too late that salt was brought cheaply into the colonies in large quantities as ballast from Tortuga. Perhaps this setback was one reason for the rather rapid removal of some of the settlers to other places in the colonies, which in turn has created difficulties in tracking down the Island families that first settled in New Jersey.

Origins of all the surnames associated with the voyage of the PHILIP to New Jersey have not been verified, so far as this compiler can discover. All names on the list below are said to have been arrivals on the ship at Elizabethtown, NJ in 1665. Other accounts state that 30 persons came. Some passengers may have left the ship when it stopped in Virginia and in New York City.

BARBER, BARBOUR, BARBIER?, Claud, French?
CLOCHE, CLOCK, LA CLOCHE, CLARK, John. Carteret's mother was a La Cloche and John may have been a cousin?
DE JARDIN, John, fron C.I.?
HILL, Henry and William. HILL, a G surname, but also English.
HOUSE, HOWSE, HOWES, Erasmus, thought to be Dutch.
MICHELL, MITCHELL, Richard, from C.I. or Great Britain?
MITTINS, MITTANS, etc., John, thought to be English.
PERRINE, Daniel, b France.
PEWTINGER, PITTINGER, Richard, from Holland or England.
POULAIN, Susanna, b France.
PROU, poss PROULZ?, Ellen, b France?
ROWLAND, Dr., poss an Islander?
SEGUINE, SEGGIN, Charles, from?
SEELEY, Capt. Robert. English and C.I. surname, as SEALE.
SKINNER, Richard. See SKINNER charts. He may have been an Islander. Was he the privateer?
TAYLOR, John, from C.I. or England.
THOREL, Maria, b Rouen, France, but said to have worked in C.I. as maid, mar Daniel PERRINE, qv.
VALLOTE, Claude, poss French, but VALLOTS were in J in 1453.

VAUQUELIN, Robert, b France.
WALLIS, Robert, surname of southern England and of C.I.

Who were the other passengers on the PHILIP? It would be helpful to know, but record could not be found by the compiler.

Although Balleine, in his BIOG. DICT. OF JERSEY, states that the settlers in Elizabethtown were from Jersey, we know now that not all of them were from the Island. It is possible that Balleine confused the 1665 expedition with the aborted 1650 expedition sent from Jersey to "Smith's Island," VA. That Island was given to Sir George Carteret as a reward for his loyalty to the British Crown in the years of the Interregnum. Considering that Smith's Island was not really habitable, perhaps it is fortunate that the shipload of Jersey families "bound for Virginia with many passengers, all sorts of goods and tools for husbandry for planting an island which the Prince had given him, was taken by Capt. Green and brought to the Isle of Wight." (1650) (Whitehead's, NEW JERSEY UNDER THE PROPRIETORS.)

It is interesting to note that VAUQUELLIN, PERRINE, PROU and SEGUINE also appear as surnames of French colonists to Quebec in the 1600s. Descendants of some Elizabethtown settlers now number in the thousands. For more information, see sources.

BIBLIOGRAPHY

NEW JERSEY ARCHIVES; NEW JERSEY COLONIAL DOCUMENTS; HIST. OF ELIZABETH, NJ, by Rev. Edwin F. Hatfield; NORTHWESTERN NEW JERSEY, A HISTORY, NY City, 1927, Vol. IV; FIRST SETTLERS OF PISCATAWAY AND WOODBRIDGE, NJ, by Orra E. Monnette, 1930; NOTES, HIST. AND BIOGRAPHICAL, by Nicholas Murray, Elizabethtown, NJ, 1884; NEW JERSEY MARRIAGE RECORDS, by Wm. Nelson, Paterson, NJ, 1900; HISTORY OF NJ TO 1720, by Samuel Smith, Trenton, NJ, 1877; BIOG. DICT. OF JERSEY, by Balleine; Perrine; Murray; Soc. Jers. Bulleting of 1964.

NEW JERSEY SURNAMES: At least 60 surnames. The Compiler will provide a list for any interested Genealogy Society.
NEW YORK: At least 100 surnames. Compiler will provide list if requested.

DID YOU KNOW?

The U.S. postage stamp #1247 in the Scott Catalog issuedJune 15th, 1964 shows Sir Philip De Carteret landing at Elizabethtown, NJ, to governthe colony in behalf of his cousin George. Elizabethtown and Carteret, NJ are named for the family, and New Jersey is named for the Island of Jersey.

NORTH CAROLINA

It is possible, and even likely, that there were a great many Channel Islanders settled in early Carolina that the compiler has no information on. There is a Cape Carteret, and a Carteret county in North Carolina. It has been rumoured that several Jersey families were settlers on the Santee River and other places in Carolina, but no verification was found. James CARTERET, certainly a Jerseyman, was in Carolina in 1622.

Young Peter Carteret, nephew of Sir George, was part of a group of investors who financed a plantation to grow grapes and tobacco, and to raise hogs on Colleton-Collington Island on the Outer Banks of Carolina in the years 1664-1670. Due to repeated hurricanes at crucial times for several years, the effort was a failure, and the colonists who remained after that time resorted to commercial fishing for a livelihood. (OUTER BANKS OF NORTH CAROLINA, by David Stick, Chapel Hill, NC, 1958.) See JERSEY SAILING SHIPS, by A. John Jean.

Another Carteret of Jersey, Nicholas, was in the colony on Ashley River in 1670, and in 1677 became proprietor of 700 acres at Accabee. The next year the lands were granted to Edward May. There were Granvilles in Mecklenburg Co., NC in the 1700s. Lord Granville was a Carteret of a Jersey family. See Johnson's CARTERET GENEALOGY. Although the other proprietors of Carolina sold or relinquished their grants, John, Lord Carteret, Earl Granville, retained his share, and in 1719 became joint owner of Carolina with the King of England. He surrendered his share in 1729, and the colony was soon divided into North and South Carolina. The boundary was finally, after long dispute, settled in 1815.

Research in Carolina surnames shows a surprising number of names that could be from the Channel Islands, but just as likely in some cases to be from France and/or England. The Harliston family, of some importance in the early history of Jersey, appears in Carolina, and the Huguenot family of Gosset is noted. A list of the Palatines and Landgraves of Carolina in the last half of the 1600s includes Sir Edmund Andros of Guernsey; Thomas AMY, who may have been of a C.I. family; and the four Carterets of Jersey, John, George, James and Peter. More research needed in North and South Carolina. See CARTERET in NOTABLES section.

SOME CHANNEL ISLAND SURNAMES IN THE CAROLINAS, MANY ARE UNVERIFIED

A'COURT, ALGROVE, ARMS, BALLEINE, BULLEN, CARTERET, CLERKE, CORBETT, CORBIN, CROSSE, DEWS, ENGLISH, FLEURY, FLOOD, FLOWERS, GILES, GIRARD, GRANVILLE, GROVE, HAMON, HASKELL, JANDRON, JERSEY, LEGGE, LE GRAND, LE SUEUR, MASTERS, MESSERVY, MOTTE, NIGHTINGALE/LE ROSSIGNOL, PIPON, QUARRY/QUEREE, ROBBINS, SALTER, SEALE, SYMOND, WALTERS.

OHIO, Guernsey County

About 1800 pressures mounted in the Channel Islands, resulting in surges of emigration to Canada and to the United States. "In the years 1805/6 Napoleon Bonaparte was making preparations to invade England...(which)...for protection, stationed troops on all the Channel Islands. On the Island of Guernsey was a large force of Cossack soldiers, who made it their principal business to plunder from the small Guernsey farmers... Strict embargo laws were in force, the trade of the Island... was cut off, and the business of the Island was totally suspended. It was that depression...which caused the Colonists to leave the Island." (Sarchet)

More than fifty families from Guernsey settled in Guernsey County, Ohio between the years 1806 and 1835. "In the original party (1806) were Thomas, John, Nicholas and Peter Sarchet and their wives, their sister Judith and her husband, Daniel Ferbrache and their children, William Ogier, James Bichard, Thomas Naftel and Thomas Lenfestey and their wives and children, a total of 26 persons." (Davis)

A fishing smack took the party from St. Peter Port, Guernsey to the Island of Jersey, where a convoy was being assembled to cross the Atlantic under the protection of a man-of-war from England. "Thomas Sarchet, Jr. was forcibly taken from the ship by a press gang, but was released when his father protested energetically." (Sarchet)

"Two more Guernseymen, John Marquand and Daniel de Francis, with their families, joined the emigrants in Jersey, and the party went aboard an English ship commanded by a Capt. McCrandall, toward the middle of May. The English man-of-war left the convoy as soon as it got out of the Channel, and the next day a French cruiser gave chase. The sailors thereupon hoisted up an American flag, hung a canvas over the side with the words ELIZABETH OF BOSTON on it in large letters, and succeeded in fooling the French." (Wolfe)

A six week voyage, (they were becalmed for eight days) brought them into Norfolk, VA on June 3rd, 1806. They journeyed on to Baltimore, where they bought three large wagons and twelve horses.

"The next three hundred miles were through fairly well settled country, with ferry services across the rivers. Further on the going was tough. It was a rainy summer. There was deep mud on the lowlands. In many places brush and trees had to be cut out and spread over mud holes before the wagons could pass. Elsewhere the road was too narrow, and trees had to be chopped to clear the way. Extra horses had to be hired on the steep hills and the wagons had to be unloaded frequently." (Wolfe) What an extreme contrast to automobile travel!

David Sarchet was nine years old at the time of the trip from Guernsey to Ohio. He wrote, "started from Norfolk to

Ohio, which we reached after passing through Baltimore, crossing the Monongahela at Old Redstone and the Ohio River at Wheeling. Somewhere in the mountains we stopped one day to bury a child of Uncle Peter Sarchet. At Wheeling we came to Zane's Trace over which we continued our journey. This was a very bad wagon road...At St. Clairsville we were told of the Wills Creek Settlement further west (Cambridge) where a new town had been laid out and lots were for sale very cheap. We had intended to go much further west, Cincinnati being the place we had in mind." The party stopped at Wills Creek to rest, spent Sunday in Methodist services, and Monday in washing clothing and linen. The women of the party put their foot down, and convinced the men this was the place to settle. They erected a rough camp with brushwood huts while log cabins were built for the winter.

The women of the party were described as wearing short dresses and gowns, belted around the waist, large frilled caps, and speaking, of course, a foreign language, Guernsiaise. The men wore smock frocks and short breeches, (to which were attached long stockings) heavy shoes and white broad-brimmed wool hats. How very unfortunate that no pictures were drawn of them in those first years. Soon the clothing changed to frontier wear, homespun and calico.

Thomas Sarchet, the leader of this first group, was the only one fluent in English. He had the first store in Cambridge 1808, traveling on horseback to Pittsburgh and Philadelphia for the goods. He was the first to plant apple trees, and the first church was organized in his home. One vital necessity on the frontier was salt. Sarchet leased salt springs in Muskingum Co., OH, and manufactured salt there until about 1816. Another venture of Sarchet was the building of the ELIZA OF GUERNSEY 1826. This boat, 70 feet long, was loaded with wheat, flour and salt, and then floated down the river to Louisville, KY, where both cargo and boat were sold. (Williams; Wolfe; Sarchet; Howe)

The second group of Guernseyites came in 1807, and the list includes the following persons: James Bichard family, two William Ogier families, James Ogier family, Thomas Naftel family, Mary Hubert, a widow and her family, John Marquand family. There were also single men named Peter Langlois, John Robins, Peter Corbet, Peter Bichard, Nicholas Bichard, John Torode, Peter Torode, Paul Robert, Nicholas Plodvin (POIDEVIN), John Carlow and John De La Rue.

Other groups are said to have come from Guernsey to Ohio in 1810, 1818, the 1820s and the 1830s.

Life in the log cabins and brush huts was not easy. Meals were cooked outside when the weather was suitable, but cabins were soon fitted with iron trammels or hooks in the fireplace to hang the big kettles on. One kettle served most families to cook the tea, boil the potatoes and vegetables, or to bake the johnny cake bread. The fireplaces were built to take large logs. From the cabin ceiling joists hung the dried foods used on the frontier, the herbs, sacks of nuts, bacon and ham. Lighting was by hand-dipped candles. Get-togethers for practical purposes soon became joyful occasions, as the settlers met for soap boilings, hog killings, cabin raisings, wood choppings, quilting parties, corn huskings and paring-bees. This last was an already familiar rite to Channel Islanders. Known as black butter in the Islands, apple butter parties are still enjoyed in Ohio, the method much like that long established in Normandy, the Channel Islands and other parts of northern Europe.

There were lean years in Guernsey County, and many of the children and grandchildren sought better times elsewhere. They removed to Indiana, Illinois, Iowa, Kansas, Missouri and to the far western states. Those who stayed enjoyed a good living, in a very scenic part of Ohio, now a favorite vacation spot.

See List of Ohio Channel Island surnames.

Good news travels fast. In March 1849 Ohioans were excited about the finding of gold in California. Several men in Cambridge, OH organized a company with the purpose of going in a group to the West and mine for gold. This company was called the CAMBRIDGE-CALIFORNIA MINING CO., and eleven articles of association were drawn up and signed by 15 full members, plus others, who were apparently part members and delegates for members. Some settled as farmers in the Napa Valley, others returned to Ohio. Agreements had to do with their needs, such as rifles, shotguns and hunting knives, and their goal was to mine in California, but in a gentlemanly fashion, with no Sunday work, treating each other as brothers, no gambling and no intoxicants. This must have been difficult to maintain in the Wild West of those days! Sunnafrank appears to have been the only Channel Islander to join up in 1849, but some men in the group were husbands of Channel Island women. See typescript in Cambridge, OH Library, and in the WRCIC.

OHIO BIBLIOGRAPHY

HISTORY OF COSHOCTON CO., OHIO, by N.N. Hill, Newark, OH, 1881; MUSKINGUM CO. OHIO data; RECORDS OF THE PLEASANT HILL METHODIST CHURCH, GCO, 1888, MS, by Ferne Longsworth, 1953; GUERNSEY MILESTONES, 1798-1948, Sesqui. Celebration, Cambridge, OH, 1948, Souvenir Program; OHIO GEN. SOCIETY REPORT, a newspaper issued Feb. 1965; GEN. AND HIST. ABOUT GUERNSEY CO., OH, published through the generosity of Mrs. Robert Conners; GOLDEN GUERNSEY, by Alfred S. Campbell, New York, 1900s; PIONEER CEMETERIES OF GUERNSEY CO., OHIO; PIONEER LAND GRANTS OF

GCO: PIONEER MARRIAGES OF GCO, by E. Margaret Conner and Nola Goodpaster Eynon; Typescript about settlement in Guernsey Co., by Mrs. Albert B. Davis, who resided in Columbus, OH, 1900s; Three books by Cyrus P.B. Sarchet, b 1828 GCO, a SCRAPBOOK, edited by Mrs. Robert Conner GCO 1968, and a two volume set about HISTORY OF GCO, Indianapolis, IN, 1911; HOUSEHOLD GUIDE AND INSTRUCTOR, by T.F. Williams, 1882, Cleveland, OH, with some biographies of GCO residents; STORIES OF GCO, Cambridge, OH, 1943 and 1975. Many of these books are in the Western Reserve Library, Cleveland, OH, and in the Cambridge, OH Public Library. A fine book on Ohio research is OHIO GEN. GUIDE, by Carol Willsey Flavell, 1979, available from Ye Olde Gen. Shoppe, Ind., Indiana; another is COUNTY BY COUNTY IN OHIO GENEALOGY, from Ohio Historical Society, Columbus, Ohio.

DID YOU KNOW?

SELOUS is a Jersey name brought from England in the 1600s. The SELOUS GAME RESERVE is the largest in Africa, an area of 15,500 square miles, and probably holds the largest concentration of elephant and lion, as well as many other animals. It sits astride a complex of rivers, including the Dilombero, Ruaha and Rufigi. The vegetation is typical woodland with patches of dense hardwood forest. The reserve can be entered less than 100 miles from Dar Es Salaam in Tanzania. It is open to visitors for hunting and photographic safaris with Tanzania Wildlife Safaris, Ltd. It is named for a Selous who became a world renowned hunter. (OFFICIAL A.A. OF E.AFRICA TOURING GUIDE TO EAST AFRICA, 1968-9 edition)

A number of contributors have mentioned that their ancestor had served with Lafayette in the Rev. War. This, while unlikely, is not impossible. See these books for more information: LAFAYETTE AND HIS COMPANIONS, article by Eliz. Kite in RECORDS OF THE AMERICAN CATHOLIC HIST. SOC. OF PHILA., Vol. XLV,1934; THE PASSENGERS ON THE VICTOIRE, from LAFAYETTE COMES TO AMERICA, by Louis Gottschalk, Chicago, 1935; LES COMBATTANTS FRANCAIS DE LA GUERRE AMERICAINE, 1778-1783, published as Senate Document #77, 58th Congress, 1905. This last book is in French, is full of French names and the places where the soldiers joined up. However, it is not indexed!

SOME CHANNEL ISLAND SURNAMES IN OHIO

ALBO DE BERNALES
ALLET
AMY
ANNET
BAILHACHE
BALLEINE
BARTRAM
BERTRAND
BICHARD, BISHARD
BIRD
BISSON
BLAMPIED
BLONDEL
BOTT
BROWER, BROUARD?
BUSSE
CADORET
CARLO, CARLOW
CARRE
CORBET
DE LA RUE
DEMERITT
DE MOUILPIED
DE PUTRON
DU CHEMIN
DUMARESQ
DU SOUCHET?
FALAISE
FALLE
FERBRACHE
FRANCIS
GALLIEN
GAUDION
GIBAUT
GIBEAUT
GOSSETT
GREEN
GUERIN
GUILBERT
GUILLE
GUILLET
GUSTIN
HAWKINS?
HEADLEY?
HEAUME
HENRY
HERBERT
HERIVEL
HESKETT
HUNTOON
HUXTER
JEHAN
JERVOIS
KILNER
LABEY
LAINEY
LANGLEY
LANGLOIS
LARAWAY, LE RUEZ
LE RUE
LA SERRE
LE BOUTILLIER
LE DANE
LE FEVRE
LE GALLEE
LE GALLIENNE
LE MONTES
LENFESTEY
LE PAGE
LE PELLEY
LE POIDEVIN
LE QUESNE
LE RENDU
LE RETILLEY
LE SUEUR
MACHON
MAHY
MALLET
MANSELL
MARCHANT?
MARQUAND
MARQUIS
MARRIETTE
MARSH
MARTEL
MASTERS
MATTINGLEY?
MAUGER
MERRITT from
MARRIETTE
MESSERVY
MOSER, MOSSER
MOTTEE
MOUILPIED
NAFTEL
NICHOLS
OGIER
PATRIARCHE
PERREL?
PETHIC
PINEL
PITON
POIDEVIN
PRIAULX
PREVOST
PROVO
PROVOST
QUINER
RABEY
RETILLEY
ROBBINS
ROBERT
ROBIN
ROMERIL
ROSE
SARCHET
SARRE
SHERRARD
SIMON
SKINNER
SUNNAFRANK
TARDIF
TAYLOR
TISSUE
TOURGIS
TOUZEAU
TORODE
VARDON
VODEN
WALLER
WILLIAMS

OKLAHOMA: BLAMPIED, ESNOUF, FRANCIS, LE BOUTILLIER, LENFESTEY, MESSERVY, REMON, TORODE

OREGON: ALLEN, ARMS, DOREY, DURELL, FLOOD, FLOYD, GALLIEN, HILLMAN, JANVRIN, KELLY, LE CORNU, LENFESTEY, LE PAGE, LE VESCONTE, MARTIN, MAUGER, MESSERVY, ROBBINS, ROBERTS, STEELE

PENNSYLVANIA

AMY	DE STE. CROIX	LE DUR?	MESSERVY
ANTHONY	DU FRESNE	LE FEVRE	MORRELL
ARMS	DUVAL	LE GALLAIS	MORICE?
BAKER	GOSSETT	LE HURAY	NICHOLAS
BALCOM	GROVER	LE JENNES?	OGIER
BETTES?	GUILLE	LE MAISTRE	OLIVER
BICHARD	GUSTIN	LE PATOUREL	OQUENER
BISHOP	HELLYER	LE PELLEY	PAINTER
CARTERET	JOREY?	LE ROY	PEDDLE
CHAMPION	LAMY?	LE SUEUR	QUITTERFIELD
CHEVALIER	LANGLOIS	MACHON	RUMRILL
COLDRICK	LA SERRE	MAHY	SARCHET
DE GRUCHY	LE BOUTILLIER	MARQUAND	SKINNER
DE JEAN	LE BRETON	MARQUIS	TORODE
DE LA CROIX	LE CORNU	MASTERS	TOSTEVIN
DE LA HAYE	LE CRONIER?	MASURY	

RHODE ISLAND: ARMINGTON, BEEDE, BISHOP, BOURGAIZE, CARPENTER, CARRE, DE LA VALLEY, DURELL, GALUSHA, HAILLE?, HAVILLAND, JANVRIN, LE FAVOR, LE FEBVRE, LE GALLAIS, LENFESTEY, LLOYD, LOUGER, MACHON, OZANNE, ROBBINS, RUMRILL, TOURGIS

SOUTH CAROLINA: BAAL, BOTTILEY?, BROUGHTON?, CARTERET, CLEMENT, DARBY, DE JERSEY, DU MOULIN, FALLE, FREZELL?, GALUSHA, GILLIARD, GOSSETT, GUERIN?, JERSEY, JANDRON, LE BAS?, LEMPRIERE, LE PELLEY, MARTIN?, MIDDLETON?, MOTTE?, NICOLLE, OGIER, PIPON, PREVOST?, ROSE

TENNESSEE: ALLEY, CLEMENS?, COLQUITT, DE BRODER, DE JEAN, GALUSHA, GRANVILLE, GUILLE, GUSTIN, LAINE, LE CORNU?, LOUGEE, MESSERVY, MORRELL

TEXAS: BLAMPIED, CARTERET, DE LA MARE, GALUSHA, HEAUME, HENRY, JANVRIN, LE BOUTILLIER, LE FEUVRE, LE MAISTRE, LENFESTEY, LE PAGE, LE POIDEVIN, MARTEL, MESSERVY, NEEL, POINDEXTER, PRIAULX, REMON, ROBILLIARD, RUMRILL

UTAH

History and genealogy have a very special interest for members of the Church of Jesus Christ of the Latter Day Saints, often called Mormons. One of their important concerns is the sealing of families for eternity, including ancestors. In order to extend the rite of baptism to relatives long gone, it is necessary to find exact birth data and other details of their lives. Therefore, the Mormons have gathered enormous amounts of genealogical information. This bank of knowledge may be drawn upon by students, researchers and amateur genealogists, a truly fine and unusual service to the world in general. Millions have been assisted in their research by information from this source.

Many Channel Islanders became members of the Mormon Church through missionary work in the Islands. At least two hundred, and probably more, Islanders came to Salt Lake City shortly after its establishment in Utah. The voyage to America began usually in Liverpool, England, a short sail from the Islands. The voyage to America was partially subsidized by a fund established very early in the Church's history, called the Perpetual Emigration Fund. It was the means by which about 30,000 converts from Great Britain and Scandinavia were brought to America in the middle 1800s. The money loaned to the emigrants for the trip was to be repaid by them after settlement in Utah.

In the 1850s, the passengers usually disembarked at New Orleans, then traveled by steamer on the Mississippi River to Missouri. The later route was via New York City, then by rail to the Mississippi. The early Channel Islanders made the long, painful thousand miles from Missouri to Utah on foot, with carts and handwagons. This is some of the roughest country in midwestern America, and at times poor organization, early snows and inadequate food and shelter cost the lives of many along the way. Later, organized church trains of wagons improved and shortened the journey. Railroads reached Salt Lake City after 1869.

The number of Mormons who went to Zion by way of the historic trail is brought to mind vividly in seeing the four foot deep wagon ruts worn in soft stone near Guernsey, Wyoming.

. Ships that brought Mormon Channel Islanders to America:

OLYMPUS, 1851	GERMANICUS, 1854	ANTARTICA, 1862, 1863
KENNEBEC, 1852	MARSHFIELD, 1854	BELLE WOOD, 1865
ELLEN MARIE, 1852	CHIMBORAZO, 1855	CAROLINA, 1866
GOLCONDA, 1853	THORNTON, 1856	CONSTITUTION, 1868

Also, see PERSONAL ACCOUNTS, for settlement of the HORMAN family.

Migration of Europeans to UTAH is covered in a new book: SAINTS ON THE SEAS, A Maritime History of Mormon Migration, by Conway B. Sonne, 1983, Univ. of Utah Publication.

SOME CHANNEL ISLAND SURNAMES IN UTAH

AHIER
ALLEN
BENHAM
BERTRAND
BICHARD
BILLOT
BIRD
BOWDIDGE
BRIDGEHOOD
BUCHANT
CADORET
CANIVET
CHEVALIER
CHICK
COOK
CORBEL
CORNISH
COUTANCHE
DANIN
DE FRESNE
DE LA HAYE
DE LA MARE
DE STE. CROIX
DE ST. JEOR
DOLBEL
DU FERNOU
DU FRESNE
DU HAMEL
DURRELL
ESNOUF
FRANCHARD
GALLICHAN
GRAHAM
GRADIN
GRUCHY
HARDY
HART
HENROID
HENRY
HERAULT
HILLIKER
HOCQUARD
HORGUARD
HORMAN
HUBBARD
JEAN
JEUNE
JONES
KERBY
LABEY
LAMOUREUX
LAINE, LAYNE
LANGLOIS
LARUENS
LE BASS
LE CHEMINANT
LE CLERCQ
LE FAVOUR
LE GEYT
LE GRESLEY
LE MARQUAND
LE MARGUARD
LE MESARIER
LE MOIGNAN
LE POIDEVIN
LE SUEUR
LE VAIN
MAHY
MALET
MANLEY
MARATT
MARQUAND
MERRIT
MESSERVY
MORRIS
NOEL
OGIER
PACK
PALLOT
PERRIN
PILL
PILLING?
QUARN, QUARM
QUEREE
QUINN
QUINTON
REED
RENOUF
ROBERT
ROBERTS
ROMERIL
ROWLAND, ROULAND
ST. GEORGE
SEBRIRE
SHELTON
SMITH
SOPER
STALON
TAYLER
TAYLOR
TOURTEL
TOUZEAU
TRESEDER
VARDON
VICK, VICQ
WAKELY
WALKLEY
WALKER
WALTERS
WILLIAMS
WOLSTENHOLME
YOUNG

VERMONT: AMY, ARMINGTON, ARMS, BEEDE, CASWELL?, CROSS?, DE STE. CROIX, DE FOUR, FALLE, FLOOD, GALUSHA, GUSTIN, JANVRIN, LA GROW, LAROKE, LE GRESLEY, LE RUEZ, LARAWAY, MORRELL, PATRELL, PENDEXTER, PERRY?, PUNCHARD, ROBBINS, ROBERTS, RUMRILL, STEELE, STILLE

VIRGINIA: AMIRAUX, ANTHOINE?, BALLEINE, BLAMPIED, BALLEINE?, BRONAUGH, CARTERET, CAUDY, COLQUITT, CRAWFORD, D'AUVERGNE,

DE JEAN, DOLBEL?, EFFARD, FAVOR, FIOTT, FLORY?, GOSSETT, GUILLE, HELLYER, HESKETT, HUNTOON, JANVRIN, LANGLOIS, LE BRETON, LE CONTE, LE JEUNE?, LE MARINEL, LE MASURIER, LE POIDEVIN, LE SUEUR, LOUGEE, PAINTER, POINDEXTER, PUCKETT?, ROSE, SCOTT, SEVIREL, SEVERY, VADEN, VALLOT, WALKE, also HERIVEL.

WEST VIRGINIA: CODY, LE CAUDY, FLOOD, HUBBARD, JEHAN, MESSERVY, MOSER, MOSSER, OGIER, PARELLE?, ROBBINS

WASHINGTON: BALLEINE, BISHOP, BLAMPIED, BOURGAIZE, FERBRACHE, GALUSHA, GRAHAM, LANGLOIS, LE BOUTILLIER, LE JUENE, LEMPRIERE, LENFESTEY, LE PELLEY, LE POIDEVIN, LE ROSSIGNOL, MASTERS, MAUGER, ROBIN, ROMERIL, STEELE, TISSUE, TORODE, VAUTIER

WISCONSIN

This state was opened up to settlement in the early 1800s by the steam boat. As early as 1820 Capt. Job Fish brought passengers to Mackinac and Green Bay. By 1835 settlers were arriving by boat at Detroit, Chicago and Wisconsin ports. Very soon there were scheduled sailings every other day from Buffalo, NY to Racine, WIS, the route usually taken by the Channel Islanders. (See PERSONAL ACCOUNTS section)

Although the earliest account here of Channel Islanders in Wisconsin is in 1840, one letter on record speaks of two other Guernsey families which had previously settled in the Midwest. These were the Torodes in Illinois and the Le Messuriers of Prarie Du Sac.

Note in the diary excerpts in Personal Accounts, the very evident pleasure taken by the newcomers at the sight of the immense prairies and the quality of the soil. Only Islanders, whose farms were perhaps 9 or 10 acres in extent, could appreciate the level expanse of land spreading out to the west as far as the eye could see.

Although little is said of the women's part in the settlement, we can speculate on it, when the women were said to be "crying at our situation." No stove or furniture, totally new surroundings, continual rain at that particular time, and, no doubt, homesickness also, were part of the discouraging situation of the Le Prevost's early days in Racine. Conditions rapidly improved, and the family was soon very much pleased with their economic position in the new community. (HIST. OF RACINE, WISC, by Virginia Hooper, Santa Clara, CA, Stone.)

SOME CHANNEL ISLANDERS WHO SETTLED IN WISCONSIN

ANDERSON	GILBERT, GUILBERT	MATTHEWS
BICHARD, BISHER	GRAHAM	MAUGER
BOONE	GUNTON	MESSERVY
BREHAUT	JANVRIN	MOON

BREWER
BROWN
BULL
BULSH
BURCH
BURGESS
CARRE
CODY, LE CAUDEY
COLE
DE BORDEN
DE GARIS
DE MOUILPIED
DOREY
DUQUEMIN, DUCOMMUN
DUFFET
DU FOUR
GALLIEN, LE GALLIENNE
IBBERSON
KIMBER
LAINE
LANGLOIS, LANGLEY
LE FEUVRE
LE MARCOM, MARQUAND
LE MESSURIER
LENFESTEY
LE POIDEVIN
LE PREVOST
LE RAY
LE VESCONTE
LING
LITTLE
LUCE
MARSH
MARTEL
MOUILPIED
OZANNE
OZARD
PRIAULX
PRINCE
RAIFE
RAMIER
ROBBINS
ROBERT, ROBERTS
ROBILLIARD
ROBIN
ROISSIER
SHEPHERD
SIMON
THIELIN
TOSTEVIN
WHITE

DID YOU KNOW?

Ships of Guernsey Island have found their last resting places in several parts of North America; the seacoast of Texas, the West Indies, Virginia and the St. Lawrence River. (SHIPBUILDERS OF GUERNSEY, by E.W. Sharp, in Soc. Guernseiaise 1970 Bulletin) The Guernsey prize court was set up in 1666, and during the War of the Spanish Succession they seized some 750 prize ships. Most of the Guernsey vessels of that age were 30 to 50 tons, but one privateer ship of 4 tons! is recorded. (THE ISLANDS SERIES, GUERNSEY, by G.W.S. Robinson, North Pomfret, VT, 1977)

Channel Islanders have left traces of their voyaging in many parts of the world; Dumaresq River, Australia; Cape Carteret in the South Pacific; D'Auvergne Bay in the South Atlantic; Le Vesconte Pt. in the Arctic; and Pt. Le Mesurier in the Prince of Wales Archipelago. Philip De Carteret, 1733-1796, Seigneur of Trinity, Jersey, circumnavigated the globe, was a Rear Admiral, sailed to the South Atlantic, South Pacific, the Philippines, back across the Indian Ocean, the Cape of Good Hope, and to England. In 1777, he was in command of the ENDYMION in the West Indies. In 1781 he wrote back that he was doing very well out of his prizes, as owner of several Privateer ships.

OUR CANADIAN COUSINS

In the second part of this book, it will be noticed that many Channel Islanders who settled in Canada have descendants in the United States. Conversely, some Canadians are descendants of Channel Island families that settled first in the United States and removed to Canada as Loyalists in the 1700s. Millions of us are descendants of settlers in both countries.

Many of the Channel Island surnames in this book are also listed in THE QUIET ADVENTURERS IN CANADA, and in some cases are descendants of the same Channel Island family. If your family has Canadian connections, it may be helpful to researchers to know the lines of population movement of the Channel Islanders in North America.

1. From Newfoundland to early New England. Little information, but certainly the repetition of surnames in so many cases tells us something about this movement.

2. From Nova Scotia to New England, Carolina and Louisiana. This is the Acadian expulsion. A few Jersey folk were in Nova Scotia at the time, and some Channel Island families married into these Acadian families. (Stephen White, New Brunswick)

3. The United Empire Loyalists. These loyal British subjects removed to Canada, rather than become American citizens, before, during and after the American Revolution. Some Channel Island families, such as the Bishops, were involved in this population movement. The U.E.L.'s settled in PEI, NB and NS, and some went to Ontario and Quebec, in the late 1700s and early 1800s. See AMERICAN LOYALISTS TO CANADA, by Lorenzo Sabine, Boston, 1957, etc.

4. There was a movement between the Maritimes and the American Midwest in the years about 1840-1870, possibly as a result of the opening of the Midwest with railway transportation. The Le Huquets, and the Le Rossignols of Quebec, were a part of this movement.

5. In the 1800s there was movement between Gaspe, Quebec and New York; between Gaspe and Alpena, MI; and possibly between Gaspe and Wisconsin and Minnesota. (Piton, etc.)

6. From Utah and surrounding areas, some Channel Island families are thought to have removed to Canada in the 1800s. About this time the Mormons were forced to give up some of their tenets to maintain their religion. In consequence, some Mormon families removed to western Canada, where they were able for a time to continue their custom of plural marriages.

7. The Gold Rush in California and the Yukon Gold Rush at the turn-of-the-century drew some Channel Islanders from Gaspe and Ontario. Possibly, some of these settlers drifted north to BC, Canada, and worked in the expanding Pacific fisheries,

mining and related industries.

8. During the late 1800s, Ontarians by the hundreds, even thousands, resettled in Michigan, drawn by the availability of farmland, the growth of logging operations and the emergence of Detroit as a large industrial and waterway center. Among these Ontario families were some who originated in the Channel Islands.

9. In the war years of the 1950s many young American men removed to Canada. These so called "draft dodgers" objected to compulsory conscription for moral, ethical and legal reasons, and in general, were welcomed in Canada--unofficially, of course. Canada has a continuing need for inhabitants, and will have for some years to come. Most of the transplanted men have chosen to stay in Canada.

10. Canadians, in the thousands, annually migrate to Florida, Arizona, California, and other warm states to escape the Canadian winters. While most appear to be retirees, this does involve all age groups.

In the bulletin of LOST IN CANADA, August 1981, there is a long list of settlers noted in a Petition of 1838. These persons were living in the city of Quebec. In the list are many Channel Island surnames. Very few of these appear to have been included in the book, THE QUIET ADVENTURERS IN CANADA, regrettably. Channel Island surnames noted in the list are (there may have been others): AMIRAUX, BISSON, BOSQUET, DARBY, LE MESSURIER, MESSURIER, LE LACHEUR, LACHEUR, LA VALLEY, LE VALLEE, LA JEUNESSE, LANGLOIS, LA RUE, LE CHEMINANT, LE GALLEE, LE MOINE, LENFESTY, LA CRONIER, LE LIEVRE, MAUGER, MCCULLOUGH, MARETT, PEZET, PREVOST, PROVOST, PIKE, ROWBOTHAM, SINNOTT, and TARDIF. (Aldo Brochet, London, Ontario)

A large number of Channel Islanders settled in the Gaspe Peninsula of Quebec in the 1800s, and others settled in Prince Edward Island, Cape Breton in Nova Scotia, New Brunswick, and much earlier, many went to Newfoundland.

In the 1850s some Channel Islanders settled at Aux Gres, Trois Rivieres, Quebec and attended there the Congregational French Church. Some surnames were: HAMMOND, ROBERTS, TOURGIS, ROY, LESBIREL, and LE LACHEUR. (Therese Gravel, Montreal, QUE)

For more information on Channel Islanders in Canada, see THE QUIET ADVENTURERS IN CANADA, 1979, by M. Turk. For Quebec data write QUEBEC FAMILY HISTORY SOCIETY, P.O. Box 1026, Pt. Claire, Quebec.

In this book there are at least 216 Channel Island surnames of Canadian families. See note at the beginning of the surname index.

CANADIAN RESEARCH: Mr. D. Bisson, 47 Millar St., Hull, Quebec, will do research on Gaspe, Quebec, Canada families.

IN SEARCH OF YOUR ANCESTORS

Americans have long been interested in genealogy, and there has been a recent surge of interest lately. We all owe a great debt of gratitude to those earlier researchers who, in the 1800s, gathered tremendous quantities of data on thousands of families and printed it in county and town histories and in genealogies. We owe a more recent debt to the Mormon Church, which has gathered information on millions of persons all over the world, open to researchers in Salt Lake City, Utah.

Beginners, don't get discouraged if your first efforts have few results. This is a field where persistence wins. Too many give up before they follow through on more difficult sources, such as land, pension, church, and Army and Navy records. Get a Genealogy How-To book at your local library or buy one.

1. Use a large looseleaf notebook, in which work being done can be rearranged to suit you at each stage of your research. Take each parent, grandparent and great-grandparent in turn, and record full names, years, place of birth, death and marriage, and place of residence. Examine birth, death and marriage certificates, family Bibles, mortgage and real estate transaction papers, wills, church records, diaries, birthday books, photos, etc., for vital statistics and background information. In the case of Channel Island ancestors, it is very useful to know the parish name of birth or residence. Make an effort to find this. See parish names at end of this section.

2. The next step is to tap the memories of all of your relatives, especially the older ones in the family. A family gathering, where much discussion takes place, will reveal a good many things that are vital to your research. Sometimes there is a difference of opinion on dates, places or names. Take down both sets of information which you can later examine and verify. Do not stop at facts alone, but include the folklore, traditions, family jokes, ghosts and stories of past family events. These will be of great interest to coming generations.

3. Write the Everton Publishers, Box 368, Logan, UT, 84321, for their catalog which describes and pictures various forms of family charts for sale, or get a sampler of their charts, so you can examine them closely and see which type you need or prefer. Some libraries and bookstores also carry various types of family charts.

4. Examine city or town records, cemetery stones, state records, county histories, land transfers, probate will records, etc., for the names you have recorded.

5. Look in telephone books and directories of cities other than your own, found in most large libraries, for persons of the same surnames you are researching. Write to these persons, enclosing a stamped, self-addressed envelope, and ask if anything is known to them about their ancestors of the wanted surnames. What part of Europe did they leave to come to America? Give in return some details of your family's origin in an attempt to find common ancestry.

6. Join your local genealogical society. Take courses in genealogy at local schools or colleges. If you live in a small town, spend a day or two in the nearest large city to explore the information available there. Don't neglect the libraries of colleges and universities. See BIBLIOGRAPHY section in this book.

7. Advertise for information with queries in the GENEALOGICAL HELPER, or in the hundreds of bulletins put out in this field by societies. See these at your local large city libraries.

8. Ship passenger lists are a good source of information, not always noted by amateurs.

GOOD SOURCES OF INFORMATION IN CENTRAL AND EASTERN UNITED STATES

Send to M.W. Wiswall, c/o Lynnfield Public Library, Lynnfield, MA 01940, $4.35 for GEN. HANDBOOK OF NEW ENGLAND RESEARCH. Excellent source.

Essex Institute, Salem, MA. Very good source for Essex Co. data on early settlers.

New England Hist. and Gen. Society, Boston, MA. Largest source of New England data.

Burton Hist. Collection, Detroit Public Library, 5201 Woodward Avenue, Detroit, MI 48202.

Western Reserve Museum Gen. Library, 10825 East Blvd., Cleveland, OH 44106.

Main Library, 325 Superior, Cleveland, OH. Many old books.

Fairview Park Library, 4449 West 213 St., Fairview Park, OH. Good general library.

Newberry Library, Chicago, IL and Fort Wayne Main Library, Fort Wayne, IN.

Ohio Gen. Society Library, Mansfield, OH. Excellent Ohio collections.

Congressional Library, Washington, D.C. Largest source, outside of the Mormon holdings.

Mormon Gen. Library, Salt Lake City, UT, has more information on genealogy and family records than anywhere else in the world. Films can be borrowed and used at a local Latter Day Saints Branch Library, located in at least 54 places in the mid-west alone. Winnifred Pierce has given me this list of information in Utah of Guernsey Island records; probably duplicated for Jersey records. Probate records of wills,

1666-1798, handwritten civil records from 1204 to 1700, Land Contracts and Deeds for Guernsey from 1567 to 1900, indexed, Registers of births, deaths and marriages from 1840 to the 1960s.

SOURCES IN THE CHANNEL ISLANDS

1. Join one or more of the Island Societies (List is courtesy of Peter Johnston, Guernsey).

THE CHANNEL ISLANDS FAMILY HISTORY SOCIETY,

THE GUERNSEY SOCIETY, P.K. Johnston, Courtil a L'Herbe, Route de Bas Courtils, St. Saviour, Guernsey, Channel Islands, Great Britain

LA SOCIETE JERSIAISE, The Library, Pier Road, St. Heliers, Jersey, Channel Islands, Great Britain. This is a large society with a great deal of historical and genealogical data on hundreds of Channel Island families, not yet computerized.

THE JERSEY SOCIETY, c/o Architectural Assoc., 34 Bedford Square, London, WCI., England

THE GUERNSEY SOCIETY, Hon. Sec., M. Harwood, Fl, Plaistow Lane, Bromley, Kent, England

THE ALDERNEY SOCIETY, c/o The Museum, Alderney, Channel Islands, Great Britain

LA SOCIETE SERQUIAISE, c/o The Hon. Sec., Mrs. P. Millar, Caro Mio 11, Sark, Channel Islands

There are also other groups on the Islands having to do with conservation, wild life, stamps, coins, occupation during WWII and National Trusts to preserve the local scene.

Note that one excellent research source of information on both North America and the British Isles, including Jersey and Guernsey Islands, is the Mormon data available through FAMILY ASSOCIATIONS, 631 South 11th East, Salt Lake City, UT 84102.

2. See HOW TO TRACE YOUR ANCESTORS IN GUERNSEY, by David Wilfred Le Poidevin, a booklet, possibly available through Button's Book Store, 21 Smith St., St. Peter Port, Guernsey, or from Hilgrove Books, 22B Hilgrove St., St. Helier, Jersey.

3. Visit the Islands and check out data in the Societe Jersiaise Library in St. Heliers, Jersey, and the Guille Alles Museum Library in St. Peter Port, Guernsey, plus Public Records in both Islands. Check cemetery records and church records of the parishes where your ancestors resided.

4. Hire a Channel Islands researcher through one of the Societies.

CAUTION: Do not accept as gospel truth any information other than official legal records. Even then, some may be in error. Do your very best to verify dates, places and full names. Since it was not possible for this compiler to verify all information in this book, the reader is warned that inclusion of data in this book does not certify data on any of the families or persons included. Errors in this book may have come about through copying, and by simple misunderstanding, of either vocal or written information.

CHANNEL ISLAND PARISHES AND CHURCHES

(A more complete list of Island Churches is given in QUIET ADVENTURERS IN CANADA)

JERSEY

There are 12 parishes. Note that the records of these churches are not all complete.

1. St. Heliers, baptism records from 1596, burial and marriage records from 1663. In addition, 20 other churches of various denominations, mostly dating from the 1800s.
2. Grouville, records from 1584, plus two other churches.
3. St. Saviour, records from 1540; also Methodist churches.
4. St. Clement, records from 1623, and two other churches.
5. St. Peter, records from 1626, and other churches.
6. St. Lawrence, records from 1654, St. Mathew with records from 1840, and other churches.
7. St. Mary, records from 1647 and 1703, and Bethlehem Church.
8. St. John Church, records from 1594, plus two other churches.
9. St. Martin, records from 1593, Gouray, records from 1834, and St. Martin Methodist.
10. St. Brelade, records from ca 1560, also five churches in St. Aubin, Jersey.
11. St. Ouen, records from 1634, and other churches.
12. Trinity Parish Church, records from 1612, RC St. Thomas Church with records from 1793 and other churches.

GUERNSEY

There are 10 parishes. Alderney and Sark records are incomplete, but some Sark records from 1565.

1. St. Peter, in St. Peter Port, church dates from 1313. Some records from the 1560s.
2. St. Sampson
3. Castel, Catel, originally named in 1203, Our Lady of the Deliverance of the Castle. Records are incomplete, 1674-1714 and 1670-1796.
4. St. Saviour, church dates back to 1154. Records from 1582, some missing.
5. St. Peter-in-the-Wood, dates from 1167. Records from 1628.
6. Torteval, originally St. Philip of Torteval, dates from 1130. Some records from 1660.
7. Forest, originally St. Margaret of the Forest, church

dates from 1163. Some records from 1684.

8. St. Martin, dates from 1199, records from 1660.

9. St. Andrew, dates from 1284, records from 1573, some missing. Burials from 1728, and a census from 1788.

10. Vale, records from 1580, some missing.

(Dates of the oldest known churches from COLLECTIONS FOR THE HISTORY OF HAMPSHIRE, a very old book, 6 vols. bound in one, by Richard Warner, Cleveland Main Library, Cleveland, OH).

In addition to church records, there are in Guernsey and Jersey, records relating to property, wills and manorial data, kept at the Greffe, Royal Court House, St. Peter Port, Guernsey and in the States Offices, Registries, St. Helier, Jersey. There are Channel Island records in the care of the British government in England; Army, Navy and Civil Service. See also BIBLIOGRAPHY, CHANNEL ISLANDS in this book.

GUIDELINES AND ABBREVIATIONS

In the family charts that follow, numbers and letters have been used. Roman numerals sometimes precede the names of brothers and sisters who have removed to America from the Channel Islands. Sometimes the order of birth is not known, and the numerals are arbitrary.

The children of the immigrant to America are usually letter A, the grandchildren are letter B, great-grandchildren C, and so on. Order of birth in a family is marked by 1,2,3. However, when the birth years are missing, the order is arbitrary, as actual order is unknown.

CAPITALS. All surnames capitalized in this book have been found at one time or another in the Channel Islands. Other words capitalized in this book are names of ships, names of books used as reference, and names of states or provinces, usually abbreviated.

FRENCH SURNAMES. A very large number of Channel Island and French surnames begin with articles such as De, De La, Le, La, Du and Des. These articles are often dropped in America, or combined with the name, as in Dufour. Le Poidevin became Poidevin, De Gruchy became Gruchy and Grush, etc. Be sure to check names under both forms to avoid missing some information on your family surnames.

NAME CHANGES. Channel Island surnames suffered an excessive amount of spelling changes in early America. Some were phonetic, and some were translations of names to the English equivalent. Other surnames were changed to completely different ones, for reasons that we do not know. Here are a few examples:

BLAMPIED to BLOMPEY
GARCELON to GOSLEN
GIBEAUT to BURR
LE BAS to BARNES
L'ARBALESTIER to BALLISTER
LE HUQUET to LOUIS
LE BOURDON to BODEN
LE BOUTILLIER to BUTLER
LUCE to LEWIS
ROUGET to ROGERS
SMITH to BROWN

CHILDREN. Please keep in mind that lists of children in a family may be incomplete, and there may have been other children not recorded. Estrangement between parent and child would sometimes prevent the child's name showing in the father's will. The children of some American Channel Island families may be recorded in the Islands and not in America.

In some records, the C.I. man was first married in the Islands, and the wife died young, sometimes leaving children. The children of this first marriage might be left with relatives while the man removed to America, remarried and had other children. The connection being broken by time and distance, descendants in America are often unaware of their distant cousins in the Islands.

In regard to the plural marriages of early Utah families, it is not always clear from the records which mother had which children. (See Porter-LE GEYT family.)

ABBREVIATIONS

AKA - also known as
ALD - Alderney Island
b - born
Ch - church
ch - child, chn - children
C.I. - Channel Islands
CIFHS - Channel Islands family History Society, St. Heliers, Jersey Island
curr - current name in use within past 10 years
d - died
div - divorced
DSP - died without issue
dau - daughter
d.y. - died young
est - established
fa - father
GCO - Guernsey County, OH
G - Guernsey Island
Hug - Huguenot
J - Jersey Island
mar - married
mar (int) - marriage intention
MRB - Marblehead, MASS
NCH - North Chelmsford, MASS
NEHGS - New England Hist. and Gen. Society, Boston, MASS
NV - not verified
OUTC - origin unknown to compiler
par - parish
poss - possibly
prob - probably
pron - pronounced
qv - which see
rem - removed to another place
res - resided
TEG - Essex Co., MA. Genealogist Society Bulletin
var - variant name or names
VR - vital records of birth, marriage and death
WRCIC - Western Reserve Library and Channel Islands Collection, Cleveland, OH

STATE ABBREVIATIONS

AK-Alaska
ALA-Alabama
ARIZ-Arizona
ARK-Arkansas
CAL-California
COL-Colarado
CT and CONN-Connecticut
DC-Dist. of Columbia
DEL-Delaware
FLA-Florida
GA-Georgia
HAW-Hawaii
IDA-Idaho
ILL-Illinois
IND-Indiana
IA-Iowa
KS-Kansas
KY-Kentucky
LA-Louisiana
ME-Maine
MA, MASS-Massachusetts
MD-Maryland
MI-Michigan
MINN-Minnesota
MO-Missouri
MONT-Montana
NEB-Nebraska
NEV-Nevada
NH-New Hampshire
NJ-New Jersey
NM-New Mexico
NY-New York
NYCITY-New York City
NC-North Carolina
ND-North Dakota
OH-Ohio
OK-Oklahoma
ORE-Oregon
PA-Pennsylvania
RI-Rhode Island
SC-South Carolina
SD-South Dakota
TN-Tennessee
TX-Texas
UT-Utah and SLCITY, Salt Lake City
VT-Vermont
VA-Virginia
WA-Washington
WVA-West Virginia
WIS-Wisconsin
WY-Wyoming

CHANNEL ISLAND SURNAMES AND FAMILIES IN NORTH AMERICA

ACHARD, etc. See Underhill's SMALL GEN., p. 1200. "Samuel ACHARD of Salem, attny. to Capt. Richard MARINER, has sold to George WILLIAMS, cooper, one house and...land in Salem for five pounds...1652." Eschart, pron much like ACHARD, was in Jersey 1577. (Stevens)

ACOURT, A'COURT. From C.I. to ONT via Lancashire, England. See Q.A. IN CANADA, by Turk. This surname also noted in south Atlantic States. OUTC.

AGNES. C.I. surname. See Q.A. IN CANADA, by Turk. See Olive MAJOR.

AGNEW. A G fam to Canada, with some branches in U.S. See Q.A. IN CANADA, by Turk.

AHIER. In St. Laurens, St. Heliers and Grouville, J, 1668. In St. Saviour, Trinity, St. Martin, St. Heliers and St. Laurens, J, 1749. In G by 1300s. Curr J. Many similar sounding surnames appeared in early New England, and I have included some of them below. At this late date, it may be impossible to show connections between the New England Aires, Ayers, Ahiers, and those in England and in the C.I. Some of those listed below are known to have come from Jersey. The others are OUTC, origin unknown to compiler.

AYRES, Amy, dau of Nathaniel of Boston, mar Samuel SWASEY, qv, 1710/11. Nathaniel was son of immigrant John AYRES?, or AHIER? (A RECORD OF THE DESC OF CAPT. JOHN AYRES) OUTC.

AIRES, Edward, from J?, mar Rebecca Marshall, 1716, Boston.

AHIER, Jean/John, a sea captain, lived in and sailed from the port of Salem, MA. "His boat, the DUKE OF CUMBERLAND, sailed from Salem to Jersey in the year 1754." (D. Ahier Jaycox, Costa Mesa, CAL)

AHIER, Capt. Jean/John, was sailing the MARY OF JERSEY, under charter to Christopher Smith of London, England to Virginia in the 1740s, poss for rice and tobacco? He was hi-jacked by the ST. PETER of San Sebastion, Spain, but escaped at Bayonne, France. (Soc. Jers. vol 11)

AHIER, Capt. John, from J, master and part-owner of the MARY ANN of Boston, 90 tons, was shipwrecked 1739, but the Capt. was picked up by another vessel and returned to J. (Soc. Jers., vol. 10)

AYERS, Capt. John, res Ipswich 1648, but was of Brookfield, MA. OUTC.

AHIER, AYERS, AHIRES, John, prob from J?, taxed at Strawberry Bank, Portsmouth, NH, 1688 only.

AIRES, John, from J?, mar Rachel CASWELL, Boston, 1794.

AIRES, John and Elizabeth, res Boston, MA, a dau, Mary, b 1708. OUTC.

AYER, John. This particular John had a name that was spelled about 30 ways, and many showed a persistent "H" in the spelling, which might mean AHIER. He res Salisbury, MA, 1640, rem to Haverhill 1647, d there 1657, had a wife, Hannah, who survived him and d 1688. Chart in WRCIC, and much info available. (Essex Ant., vol 8; Manchester; Haverhill and Salem VR: Virkus; OLD FAMS OF SALISBURY AND AMESBURY, MA)

AYRES, Philip, formerly of J, late of Boston, executor in 1708 was Hannah Henley.

AHIER, Philip, of Boston, bought land 1759, widow Mary sold it in 1765.

AHIER, Capt. Philip, was trading with Virginia from J in 1737-1750. (A. John Jean, Jersey)

AHIER. A fam from J to Toronto, then to CAL, 1900s. See Philip MARRETT.

AYERS, AHIER. See info in Salt Lake City, and fams in Q.A. IN CANADA.

ALBO DE BERNALES, Lucy Maria, b 1845, St. Helier, J, dau of Emanuel Joseph de Bernales, physician, artist of Spain, and of Lucy Harriett HALLETT, b 1825, J, d 1878, London. Lucy Maria was the grandau of Wm. HALLETT, jeweler of J, and d Little Rock, ARK 1934. Lucy mar John Ross of Brooklyn, NY, 1870 (1839-1885). At least one dau, Lucy, who mar Walter Swanton, 1904. (Lucy Clark, Cleveland, OH)

ALEXANDER, ALEXANDRE. Curr J and G. ALEXANDRE in St. Clement and Grouville, J, 1668, and in St. Clement, Grouville, St. Peter and St. Brelade, J, 1749. A Capt. Charles ALEXANDRE was a privateer in J, 1756. ALEXANDERS in Topsham, ME 1719, were from Scotland to Ulster, Ireland, to Maine. C.I. research? See CIFHS #12.

ALEXANDRE, Miss A., from J, in NYCITY ca 1932.

ALEXANDRE, Arthur Herbert, b 1882, J, rem to New Zealand, then to San Francisco, CAL and finally settled in BC, Canada.

ALEXANDER, ALEXANDRE, James, a Jerseyman, in Casco Bay, ME, 1600s. A Dorothy ALEXANDER was wife of John Stebbins of ME, and was a captive in Boucherville, QUE. Her dau, Abigail, b Deerfield, ME 1684, mar in Quebec 1704, J. De Noions of Tonty's Company. (Noyes; Coleman; Virkus)

ALEXANDER, Richard, from J?, in Dover, NH 1674. The heirs of a Richard ALEXANDER are mentioned in Grouville, J 1668. ALEXANDER also in St. Clement, J, at that time.

ALEXANDRE, Francis, of a J fam in Canada, mar Beatrice Robichaud. Several of their chn b New Brunswick, Canada, rem to New England. (Q.A. IN CANADA, by Turk)

B1. Francis, b Canada, mar Elizabeth MALLETT, and rem to Orono, ME. Two chn, Harry and Helen Peters.

B2. William, mar Finn named Cullins? from Pokemouche, NB, rem to Orono, ME. B3. Vincent, b 1874 B4. James, b 1876

B5,6,7. Alice, Jane, and George, d unmar, Orono, ME

B8. Emily, b 1880, mar Denis CLEMENT of Grand Anse, NB, desc in Orono, ME B9. Emma

B10. Josephine, adopted by Phillippe McNally, mar Louis de Grace, and res MA, 13 chn

C1. Estelle, b 1905, mar J. Alfred de Grace, res Athol, MA

C12. Raymonde, b 1925, mar Charles VASSELIN, res Waltham, MA

ALGROVE, Nicholas, deposed in 1702 in Albermarle Edenton, NC that he was 49 years old, "baptized and registered in the parish of St. John, Jersey, belonging to Hampshire, England." His parents were Guillaume and Susan ALLGROW. HILGROVE and HELGROW are named in the Jersey Extente of 1668, at that time res in St. Heliers, J. HILGROVE, Clement, in J ca 1650, later rem to Southampton, England. (Soc. Jers. Vol. 4; Albemarle records)

ALLAIN, D'ALLAIN. Many ALLENS in New England, but none found definitely linked with the C.I. One line, very old, in G, 1200s. Another from Cerisy, Normandy, to J and St. Ouen, J, 1668. Huguenots in early or middle 1600s. See GOSSETT.

ALLAN, Mary, age 24, of Toronto, ONT, b J, dau of John and Sarah Allan, mar 1860 in the Congregational CH, Toronto, George A. Rawson, age 23, of Toronto, ONT. (CH records)

ALLEN. A fam from C.I. 1863, on ship ANTARCTIC, settled in UT. Catherine, George, Elizabeth, Sarah and Charles. (SLC records) ALLEN curr G and J, also Alderney Island.

ALLEN, Mr. and Mrs. W.H., from J, 1862, ship ANTARCTIC, settled in ORE. See BALLEINE, Mary Ann.

A1. Sarah A2. Jane

ALLEN. A ship builder in St. Aubin, M, 1837-1854. (Jean)

ALLES. In G 1300s on. ALLEZ, curr G.

ALLES, Josiah, from C.I. fam? Son of Wm. and Mary, was b 1651, Salem, MA, d.y. (NEHGS, vol. 36)

ALLES, Henry, res Erie Co., OH, 1860. (Census)

ALLES. Also see ALBO DE BERNALES.

ALLES, Frederick MANSELL, qv, from Forest, G to NYCITY, 1834. Later was in partnership with Daniel MAUGER, qv, and Thomas GUILLE, qv, in a decorating firm in NYCITY. Made his fortune and retired to G, where he and Guille organized the GUILLE-ALLES Library. (La Societe Guernesiaise, Guernsey) More data in WRCIC.

ALLES, Elizabeth, b 1833, G, rem to Paw Paw, MI in her teens. Mar 1856, John Matter, b 1834, Switzerland. Elizabeth d 1904, age 71, in Fisher, IL. (C.E. Butterfield, Allendale, NJ)

A1. John Matter, b 1857, Paw Paw, MI, a farmer, 2 sons. John d 1940.

A2. James Matter, b 1865, mar, div, d Champaign, IL?, 1940

A3. Mary Louise Matter, b 1866 Joliet, IL, mar Albert Butterfield, a shop owner and woodworker, killed by switch-engine in Champaign, IL, where he is bur. She d 1941. More in WRCIC.

B1. Helen Butterfield, d.y.

B2. Charles Edward Butterfield, b 1892, d 1958. Mar Bess WINTERS 1911, 1891-1964, 3 chn.

C1. Gladys Butterfield, b 1912 C2. Estelle Butterfield, b 1916

C3. Charles Butterfield, Jr., b 1928, mar Gayle Coberly 1952, res Allendale, NJ

D1. Jeffrey Butterfield, b 1953 D2. Carey J. Butterfield, b 1956

A4. Elizabeth Matter, b 1970, Champaign, IL, mar late in life, Leonard Littleton, and d 1939, age 68, in Bloomington, IL

A5. William L. Matter, b 1872, Champaign, a miner, mar a widow with six chn, and had one dau. He d 1939, Scofield, UT, age 67

B1. Jeanette Matter

ALLEZ. In St. Saviour, G, 1630. In St. Peter, G, 1639, from 1331. Curr G. ALLEY, some errors in data below!

ALLEY. Many in New England, but prob only a few from the C.I., where the name is spelled ALLES and ALLEZ, pron ALLEY, and spelled that way in early New England. Much research done by the Boothbay ALLEYS, not seen by compiler. Other researchers working on other branches by this name: Janet I. Delorey, Shrewbury, MA; Ina Harris Day, Salt Lake City, UT; Mrs. Wm. Goldsmith, MRB, MA; Mrs. James Gosling, MRB, MA; and Donald Doliber, MRB, MA. See sources: PILLSBURY GEN; JONAS HALSTEAD FAM; ESSEX ANTIQ., vol. 4; Green's HIST. OF BOOTHBAY, ME; CLEMENT GEN; SMALL GEN by Underhill; BACON GEN; Virkus; STARR GEN; MASS SOLDIERS AND SAILORS; NEHGS, vols. 27 and 38; NEW WORLD EMIGRANTS by Tepper; and EARLY SETTLERS OF ROWLEY, MA by Blodgett and Jewett.

ALLEY. CAUTION: TRIAL CHART. Not all info below is verified. Work being done in this fam by several researchers. Thomas may have been from J or G, or from England.

ALLEY, Thomas, servant to Daniel CHAMBERLAIN, qv, of Island of Jersey, was apprenticed to John PEDRICK of MRB in 1675. CHAMBERLAIN from J, ALLEY also? Thomas mar Sarah Silver, dau of Thomas of Newbury in 1670, and Mary Thomas (Wise) Silver. Sarah b 1653, Newbury, MA, d Rowley, MA 1680. Thomas mar 2. 1681, Abigail Killiam. Two chn by each wife. (NEHGS, vol. 38) (Ina H. Day, Salt Lake City, UT)

A1. Samuel, bp 1675, First Cong. CH, Rowley, MA, mar Elizabeth ____, five chn?, Dover, NH. Mrs. Day believes wife was Indian or part Indian. Res Boothbay, ME.

B1. John, b Dover, NH, d.y.?

B2. John again, ancestor of the Boothbay Alleys?

B3. Samuel, b ____, mar Judith Cenny, Kenny, b Dover, NH

C1. Anna, b 1761, mar Daniel Eastman, 1780, Alfred, ME, called Phillipsburgh
D1. Jeremiah Eastman, b 1782, mar Mercy/Mary Huff
D2. Samuel Eastman, b ca 1786, mar Polly/Mary Barnes of Cornish
D3. Timothy Eastman, b 1788 at Cornish, ME, mar Susanna KNIGHT, qv
D4. John Eastman, b 1790, mar Betsy Day
D5. Nancy Eastman, b 1797 at Cornish, mar Henry Day, son of Nathaniel and Rachel (Littlefield) Day
E1. James E. Day, b 1816, d unmar
E2. Samuel Eastman Day, b 1818, mar Aseneth Jane Thompson
E3. Nancy Jane Day, b 1824, mar Robert Reed
E4. Henry Eastman Day, b 1824, mar 1. Leah Rawlins, six chn, 2. Elizabeth Cottrell, and 3. Caroline Eugenia Augusta Nylander
F1. James Henry Day, b 1853, mar Lucy Stringfellow
F2. Joseph Elisha Day, b 1856, mar Harriet Ann Shipley
F3. Leah Jane Day, b 1858, mar James W.W. Fitzgerald
F4. Elnora A., b 1860, d.y. F5. Charles E., b 1863, d.y.
F6. Harriet Lucinda Day, b 1965, d.y.
F7. by 2nd wife, Samuel Cottrell Day, b 1864, mar Maude Evelene McGuire
F8. Nancy Catherine Day, b 1865, mar 1. Augustus Ross Ballard, and 2. Richard T. White
F9. George Addison Day, b 1867, mar 1. Florence Whittle, and 2. Myrtel E. Hughes
F10. Elias John Day, b 1869, mar 1. Olive Matilda Miller, seven chn, and 2. Christianna Eva Cottam
G1. Elias Lavern Day, b 1896, mar Gertrude Johanna VanLeeuwen
G2. Olive Marie Day, b 1898, mar George Percy Barber, both living in 1981
G3. Harmon Eastman Day, b 1901, mar Phoebe McConnell
G4. Henry Miller Day, b 1904, mar Natalie Carlquist
G5. Joseph Franklin Day, b 1905, mar Oneta Peterson
G6. Geneva Rose Day, b 1907, mar Roy A. West, both living 1981
G7. Wendell Clinton Day, b 1915, mar Ina Harris, six chn, res Salt Lake City, UT. Have 29 grandchn!
H1. Sidnee Day, b 1938, mar Donald Gelta Spencer
H2. Wendell Clinton Day, Jr., b 1939, mar 1. Franza Nadine Preator, 2. Edna Ruth Phippen, and 3. Janet Stephenson
H3. David Harris Day, b 1940, mar Susan Helene Bleyl
H4. Hannah Darlyn Day, b 1943, mar Cecil Marvette Ellisor, Jr.
H5. Inagene Day, b 1946, mar 1. Vernon Bryce Adamson, and 2. Douglas Earl Shipley
H6. LurReen Day, b 1949, mar Glen Eugene Brock, Jr.
F11. by 2nd wife, Matilda Caroline Day, b 1870, mar Jackson Rial Allen
F12. by 2nd wife, Eugenia A. Day, d.y.
F13. by 3rd wife, Andrew Jackson Day, b 1872, mar Mary Elizabeth Snow
F14. Mary Elizabeth Day, b 1874, mar Robert A. McGuire
F15. David Williams Day, b 1877, d.y.
F16. Ellen Lucretia Day, b 1879, mar Niels Anton Neilsen
F17. Rachel Ann Day, b 1881, mar Royal Garff
C2. etc. Other chn of Samuel, Jr.?
B4. Other chn of Samuel, Sr.?
A2. Sarah, b 1678, mar Daniel Pillsbury, 1704/04, Newbury, MA
A3. by 2nd wife, Thomas, b 1683 A4. Abigail, b 1687

ALLEY, Josiah, b J?, res Kennebunk, ME, d Newburyport, MA? While his ancestry is not known, his wife was a Nancy G from J. (Mrs. Wm. Goldsmith, MRB, MA)

A1. Joseph, b 1802 Kennebunk, ME, rem to Newburyport 1826. He was an excellent mechanic, built 37 organs and 10 pianos. He d 1880 leaving widow, 6 sons and 5 daus. He was a spiritualist. Mar Lucy Knowles, who d 1882 Newburyport, said to have had 23 chn.

B1. Charles Otis Alley, b 1830, d 1894, mar Elizabeth Huse JANVRIN, qv, in Newbury, MA 1855. She was b 1838 and d Lynn, MA 1915. See their fam under JANVRIN.

B2. Joseph, b 1832, d 1870 B3. George

B4. Henry, b 1836 Newburyport, res Wenham, MA, an eminent apiarist, who wrote a number of books on beekeeping and had correspondence with persons all over the world on the subject. He mar Clarissa Port, 1833-1901, and d 1908 in Wenham. (American Bee Journal, January 1959)

B5. Otis, b 1837, d 1911, mar Alvira Cook. B6. (?)

B7. Annie W., b 1841, mar Charles Warren BROWN

B8. Frank, b 1842, d 1902 Newburyport, MA

B9. Florence, b 1845, d 1919 Amesbury, MA

B10. William S., b 1847, res Haverhill,(?) MA

B11. Clara A., b 1851, mar Robert W.S. Hart

B12. Charles Adams, b 1855 B13. Jennie, 1856-1927, res Amesbury, MA

A2. Henry, plus other chn?

ALLEY. See JANVRIN.

ALLEY, Anna, mar David Boyce, ca 1712, she of Salem. OUTC.

A1. David Boyce, res Lynn and Salem MA, mar Catherine DALAND, widow of Robert NEAL of Salem, 1744. She was his wife in 1770. Note that NEAL, BOYCE and DALAND (as DESLANDES) can be of C.I. origin

ALLEY, Benjamin, mar Elizabeth ___, res Salem, MA, from J or G? OUTC. (NEHGS, vol. 6)

A1. Jacob, b 1719 A3. Elizar, b 1723 A5. Hannah, b 1728

A2. Solomon, b 1721 A4. Richard, b 1726 A6. Benjamin, b 1731

ALLEY, Benjamin, 1775-1830, res Nashville, TN. OUTC.

ALLEZ, John, b 1819 St. Brelade, J, son of Pierre and Elizabeth (LE LACHEUR) ALLEZ, thought to be from G, mar 1846, Elizabeth Esther HELLEUR, b 1823, St. Brelade, J. John d in J 1877? Other chn? (J. Robert McAdam, Sacramento, CAL)

A1. Emilie/Amelia ALLEZ, b 1856, St. Brelade, J, d 1898 St. Catharines, ONT, mar 1877 William Henry Cort NICHOLSON, b 1854, St. Heliers, J, d 1925 St. Catharines, ONT

B1. William Henry Allez Nicholson, b 1880, St. Brelade, J, mar 1903, d 1962 Vancouver, BC

ALLEY, Mary B., b 1822, dau of John and Mary ALLEY of Lynn, MA (SMALL GEN) OUTC.

ALLEY, Capt. Samuel of St. George, formerly Cushing, Lincoln Co., ME, b between 1774 and 1780, d prob between 1830/40 census. Said to be son of Samuel ALLEY, mar Sarah Wall of St. George, and were parents of 13 chn. (Research by David A. Nichols of Lincolnville, ME) OUTC.

ALLEY. Twelve fams in Lynn, MA, 1790 census, others res Sherbourne, Boston, Salem, MRB and Haverhill. Some of these prob from C.I.

ALLEY. See MRB records. Note that many ALLEYS lived in OH by 1860 Census.

ALLIE, ALIX, Pierre, came from Notre Dame de Lihou, Granville, Normandy, France. This may be another source of ALLEY fams, also noted in England. (John Dulong, Royal Oak, MI)

ALLISETT, Peter, sailmaker, mar in Boston, 1723, Ann Pitman. Cf ASLET of J, qv. (GENS AND ESTATES OF CHARLESTON, MA)

ALIX, ALLIX, Francis, built schooners in J, 1800s. ALLIX noted in colonies.

ALLO. Old name in J. See ECOBICHON.

AMIRAUX, Pierre, Peter, son of Pierre de la Galaire, dit Amiraux, from Saumur, Anjou, France, to St. Heliers, J, and his wife, Marie TIFNAU (TIFFANY), was bp 1726, St. Heliers, J. Pierre Sr. was a silversmith with many pieces in the Societe Jersiaise Museum. Mar 1. Elizabeth GODFRAY, who d 1767, mar 2. Jeanne CANIVET, in 1770, and 3. Elizabeth SOHIER. He was a Lt. in the East Reg't of the Jersey Militia, becoming adjutant in 1778. He was also Capt. of the REVENGE, 1781, and a surveyor for the parish of St. Heliers in 1791, and one of the founders of the Jersey Chamber of Commerce. He d in G, 1809, age 79? (JERSEY IN THE 18TH AND 19TH CENTURIES, BY A.C. Saunders; Richibucto records; MESSERVY records in J; OLD CHANNEL ISLANDS SILVER; Mrs. Geo. Greenwood, Arlington, VA) CAUTION: TRIAL CHART.

A1. Elizabeth mar Louis POIGNAND, a well-known Jersey watchmaker and vendor of many grandfather clocks bearing his name

A2. Delicia, mar David Poignand, also a watchmaker, bro of Louis, above, in 1764. Delicia and David rem to Boston, MA, 1787

A3. Jane, b 1767, mar John BAZIN and d in Canton, MA, 1837

A4. Matthew, b 1772, J, had a son, John, who d in Russia, age 33, in 1834, by second wife, twin?

A5. Pierre, bp 1772, rem to Kochiboguac, NB, Canada, where he d 1856, age 84. He mar 1. Magdalen PREVOST, Quebec City 1804, and 2. Patience HAINS, 1815, in Douglas, Keswick Cr. Creek Co., New Brunswick. Patience was the dau of Joseph H., and was b 1815 in Douglas. She mar 2. William McKinnon, at Richibucto, NB, 1862. Was Pierre a twin of Matthew?

B1. Matthew, b 1805, St. Anne, Quebec? B2. Timothy, b 1806

B3. Peter CANIVET, b 1808. These three born in Cornwallis Co., NB?

B4. Lemuel CANIVET Amiraux, son of the 2nd wife, b at Eel Brook Twp., Argyle, New Brunswick?, 1837, bp later that year by Rev. Snyder of Weymouth, NS, on his way to Shelburne. The birth was registered at Yarmouth, NS. Lemuel mar at Richibucto, NB, Elizabeth Handey or Handley, dau of Wm. Handley?, 1860

B5. Elias DU SORDIER, b 1838, Roberts Island, Argyle Co., NS, a tanner, d 1924, Richibucto, NB. Mar Abigail Shaddick, 1860, Richibucto, 8 chn

C1. Alice Edith Amiraux, b 1861, mar ___ Hanford

C2. Allen Coster, b 1863, mar Emma Percy, cousin of Sir James Dunn. He d 1934.

C3. George Ernest, b 1865, mar Lottie ___

C4. James Cochrane Moody, b 1868, unmar C5. Jane, b 1871

C6. Emma, b 1873, mar Horace P. Greenwood, and d 1962, Arlington, VA, bur W. Boylston, MA. Horace was the son of Robert Cameron Greenwood and Letitia SWAIN, and was b 1868, Worcester, MA. He d 1948, bur West Boylston, MA.

D1. George Donald Greenwood, mar Marion Ranton, dau of Robert Phillips and Margaret Ann (Hope) Ranton, b 1908, Niagara Falls, ONT, mar 1943. George an electronics engineer. 2 chn.

E1. Miriam J. Greenwood, b 1946, twin E2. Virginia H. Greenwood

C7. Gertrude, b 1876, mar 1948, Robert Henry Long. She d 1948.

C8. Mary/Helen, b 1880, mar George O'Leary. She d 1954, Vancouver.

D1. George O'Leary D3. Gordon O'Leary, Jr.

D2. Mark O'Leary, mar Arlys Rose Bell, res Spokane, WA

E1. Rory O'Leary, b 1940s? E2. Marsha Helen O'Leary

A6. Margaret, b 1773, mar James JEREMIE, who d 1844, in G

AMIRAUX. Noted in petition of Durham, QUE residents, 1838. (LOST IN CANADA, August 1981)

AMIRAUX. A George and Lottie said to have lived in CAL.

AMY. Common in J in the 1600s. Seventeen Heads of Families in St. Saviour, St. Clement and Grouville, J, 1607. In Grouville, St. Martin, St. Saviour and St. Clement, J, 1668, and in Trinity, Grouville, St. Saviour, St. Heliers and St. Martin, J, 1749. In G and J, 1300s. AMY shield: or, on a chief embattled sable three annulets argent.

AMY. Several in early New England, either from England, France, or the Channel Islands.

AMY, John, res Kittery, ME, late 1600s. Mar Sarah GULLISON/GALLICHAN?, prob dau of Philip and Mary Gullison. (Noyes; Virkus' Stackpole; Pope's PIONEERS OF MASS; DELAND GEN; etc.) CAUTION: TRIAL CHART.
A1. John, b 1695, d.y. A2. John, again, b 1699, mar Sarah Deering?
A3. Lawrence, b 1702, publ to Rachel DOLBE, 1724. See DOLBEL.
A4. Elizabeth?, mar Thomas PILLIAR, 1731. PELIER, PELLIER, J and French surnames.
A5. George A6. Stephen, publ to Mehitable Hodsdon 1740 in Kittery?

AMY, John, b ca 1622, ship carpenter, rem to Woburn, MA, then to Boston. Shipped on the MARY as carpenter with Capt. Trumbull for Barbados, 1657. Had bro-in-law, Edward Johnson, in 1646, who owned at that time the land first bought in Woburn, MA. John mar Mary Johnson, 1649/50. Could have mar 2. Martha ___, res Boston, had 9 chn. Mortgaged the house and land in 1691, gave deed of sale 1693, with wife named Anne, poss third wife? See WRCIC for more data and vital records in MA. Eleven chn? OUTC.

AMY, John, b 1699, related to John above?, res Andover, MA, mar 1721/22 Abigail DELAND, DALAND, qv, b 1709, d before 1732. John a wheelwright and housewright, said to be desc of Capt. Edward Johnson. See above John AMY. (Essex Antiq., vol. 4; Mrs. Herbert Kimmy, Valrico, FLA; WRCIC)

AMY. Large fams in Montevideo, Uraguay, desc from a Walter Amy of J, who settled in Uraguay in 1800s. There was also a Henry Amy, his bro, who settled in Uraguay. See WRCIC for more info on this J fam. (Ernest Amy, Beauharnois, QUE)

ANDERSON, William, from G, 1840, to Kenosha, WI, a blacksmith on Springs Rd. His wife, Mary, came from G a little later. ANDERSON curr G and J. (Ozanne)

ANDROS, in G 1600s. Compiler believes ANDROS, below, to be poss C.I. The Guernsey fam was desc from an Englishman, ANDREWS, who came early to the C.I. Much Andros data in G. ANDRESS/ANDREWS/ANDROS fams from C.I. to Nfld. ANDROS from C.I. to New Brunswick, Canada. (NEHGS, vol. 1916)

ANDROS, Sir Edmund. See NOTABLES and data in Noyes, p. 516.

ANDROS, ___, ensign on a British ship in Maine 1687. (DHSM)

ANDROS, Ames or Amice?, mar Mary Creed, 1728, Boston. OUTC.

ANDROS, Amos, Capt. appointed by Gov. Andrew, 1687, Comm. of Pemaquid Fort. (Noyes)

ANDROS. Twenty-two of this surname served in Rev. War from MA, prob including some from G. See records of Braveboat Harbor, ME, Rehoboth, MRB, Boston, Windham, ME, etc., and Underhill, Noyes, NEHGS, OLD FAMS IN SALISBURY, MA and MASS SOLDIERS AND SAILORS OF REV. WAR.

ANLEY. From J?, to America. (D. Duncan, San Mateo, CAL)

ANLEY. In J 1400s, in St. Laurens, St. Peter, J, 1668, and in St. John, St. Helier, St. Peter, St. Laurens, and St. Brelade, J, 1749. In St. Lawrence, J, 1799. Curr J.

ANLEY. See Elias DE GRUCHY from Trinity Par., J to NY 1850s.

ANNET, Philip, said to be from G, mar in Gaspe, QUE, 1859, Marie Louise Simoneau. Other ANNETTS in Gaspe, not from C.I.

ANNET. A fam in Guernsey Co., OH, 1824, poss from G?, as John ANNET, mar 1826, Lavina SUNNAFRANK, qv, and Arthur ANNETT mar Elizabeth SUNNAFRANK, 1825, in GCO, both from G fams. (Conner-Eynon)

ANQUETIL. In St. Saviour, G, 1677. This name spelled various ways, fairly common in many parts of Great Britain. ANKETIL, etc.

ANTHOINE, ANTOINE. In J, 1309. ANTHONY in G later. ANTHOINE in St. Martin, Grouville, St. Saviour, J, 1668, in St. Saviour and Grouville, J, 1749. Use CAUTION! An Anthony in Rhode Island, early, was from Hempstead, London, England.

ANTHONY, Frederick, several Jacobs, two Josephs and Michaels, and a Nicholas res in Phila. in the 1790 Census. Several other Anthonys and Antoneys also res in the district. It is thought that some of these were from the C.I. early. Others, no doubt, from England and/ or France. See ANTHOINE.

ANTHONY, Jane, mar 1815, Daniel OBER in MRB. A Jane ANTHONY mar in Boston, 1711, John Newton. (Noyes) OUTC.

ANTHOINE, John, mar Rebecca LE GROW in MRB, 1768, a dau, Anna, b 1768. Poss both from C.I.?

ANTHOINE, John, res MRB, from J?

A1. Anna, b 1756 A2. John, b 1758 A3. Rachel, b 1762

ANTHONY, John, mar 1699 at Hampton, NH, Jane Rundlett, dau of Charles and Mary (Shatswell) Rundlett. (Noyes) OUTC.

ANTHOINE, John, from C.I. to VA, settled Elizabeth City, VA?, age 23 in 1624, in the SWAN.

A1. Lucretia, b 1643, VA, mar 1. Nathaniel Powell, and 2. John COLQUITT, b ca 1636 in G

ANTHONY, John, b ca 1607, said to be of G fam, but res in Hempstead, England, came to America in the HERCULES, res Portsmouth, RI. He d 1675, age 68, leaving 5 grown chn and wife, Frances ___, who d 1692. OUTC. (NEHGS 1877; CLEVELAND GEN)

A1. ?Abraham, mar Alice Woodle, Waddell, etc., b 1650, dau of Wm. and Mary of Warwick, RI

B1. Jacob, b 1693, of Dartmouth, MA

C1. Job, mar Sarah Wing. A dau, Rhoda Anthony, mar Stephen Gifford

ANTHONY, Joseph, a silversmith in Phila., PA, 1762-1814. OUTC.

ANTHONY, Joseph, mar Salley ___, a son, Joseph, bp 1811, MRB. OUTC.

ANTHOINE, Nicholas, from J to MRB before 1750, mar Anne or Rachel HAWKES qv. Nicholas was a private in Capt. Reed's Co., McCobb Reg't., 1781. "Prob son of Richard ANTOINE of Phila., grandson of Richard ANTHOINE and wife Sarah, who came to Phila. from Isle of Jersey 1700. Nicholas mar Rachel, not Anne." (Bolton) Chn uncertain. (Amy Anthoine, Portland, ME) Nicholas mar 2. Rebecca LEGROW, qv. (MHS; Bolton)

A1. John A2. Rachel A3. Nicholas A4. Anna

ANTHONY, Nicholas, b J, mar Rachel ARMINGTON, qv, 1722, Boston, MA. (MHS; Virkus)

ANTHOINE, Nicholas, from J?, mar Anna Pattengale, 1787, in Windham, ME. (Maine Recorder)

ANTHOINE, Capt. Nicolas, in 1775 was trading with Phila. from Jersey on the ship, PRINCESS, also in 1764? The vessel was owned by Philip WINTER of J. (A. John Jean, Jersey, C.I.)

ANTHONY, Richard, of J, was in Portsmouth, NH, 1690s. (Noyes)

ANTHONY, Richard of Jersey and Portsmouth, NH, gave power of attorney, re Wm. Button's death to Clement LAMPIER, LEMPRIERE, qv, of Boston, 1697. (Noyes)

ANTHONY, William C. of J fam?, mar Hannah ___, res MRB.

A1. Rebecca Foster, bp 1838, MRB A3. William, bp 1842, MRB
A2. Hannah Cregg Hamblin, bp 1839

ANTHONY. At least 23 of this surname res in MA, 1790. (Census) Prob many from J. fams.

ANTHONY, ANTHOINE, etc. Forty-six of this surname served in Rev. War. (MASS SOLDIERS AND SAILORS)

ARCHIER, L'ARCHIER, LARCHER, COCK ARCHER, LARCHIER, AKA COK, etc. known in J, 1227-1340. See L'ARBALESTIER, poss some changed name to ARCHER as the name means Cross-Bow Archer.

ARCHER. Twenty-two served in Rev. War. (MASS SOLDIERS AND SAILORS) Poss some from J fams.

ARMINGTON. Not a C.I. surname. Poss an English fam settled for a time in G?, or French, as Armeton?

ARMINGTON, Joseph, b ca 1680 G, said to have d in England ca 1715. Rachel ___, his wife, said to be well-educated, and established a school in Roxbury, MA. More data on this fam in hands of Carl Boyer, Newhall, CAL. (Virkus; MHS; NEHGS, vol. 22; Chart by Donald Hathaway, No. Dartmouth, MA; ARMINGTON FAMILY, 39 pp, published Providence, RI, 1928, in Congressional Library; MASS SOLDIERS AND SAILORS)

A1. Rachel, mar 1722 in Boston, Nicholas ANTHONY, qv. Poss not the widow or dau, but may have been another Rachel Armington.
A2. Joseph, b 1707 G, d 1746 Rehoboth, MA. Mar there 1729, Hannah Chaffee, who d 1799. Joseph a brickmaker. (Jersey bricks were shipped to Nfld. in the 1600s. Turk)
B1. Nicholas, b 1729/30, d.y., Rehoboth, MA
B2. Joseph, b 1731, d 1817, mar (int) 1760, Esther WALKER. She may have mar 2. in 1797, Timothy Ide? A Joseph in Rehoboth 1790, fam of six. (Census)
B3. Josiah, b 1733, d 1736
B4. John, b 1735, said to have d in Waterford, VT. Mar 1. 1757, Ruth Kent, and 2. Chloe Newman of Rehoboth. Owned no real estate, but was taxed four pounds on personal property. Rem in later years to Waterford, VT. Ten chn by first wife.
C1. Sylvester, b 1757, d 1758 C4. Hannah, b 1764
C2. Joseph, b 1759 C5. Betty, b 1765
C3. Molly, b 1760 C6. Russell, b 1769
C7. Ruth, b 1771, mar Barrington, RI, 1790, E. Remington
C8. Olive, b 1773, mar 1791, Rehoboth, MA, James Peck
C9. John, b 1776. A John in Rehoboth 1790 with several chn.
C10. Prudence, b 1778, mar 1798, Oliver Chaffee
C11. by 2nd wife, Abigail, b 1789
B5. Deliverance, b 1737, d 1746 B6. Susannah, b 1739/40, d 1746
B7. Hannah, b 1742, mar (int) Rehoboth, 1763, Tom McClish
B8. Josiah, b 1744, mar 1765, Ruth Bowen
B9. William, b 1746 B10. Susannah?

ARMINGTON. See also Rhode Island and MA VRs.

ARMINGTON, Benjamin, mar 1797, Sally PAINE, Boston? OUTC?

ARMETON, Elizabeth mar Abraham LEFEVRE, 1723, Boston. OUTC.

ARMS. Not found in old surname lists of C.I. However, DUBRAS, meaning ARMS, is an old J surname. Use CAUTION, as there was more than one ARMS immigrant. By the 1790 Census, there were at least 15 fams of Arms located in MA, and others had rem to CT, RI, ME, NH, VT, NJ, NY.

ARMS. Now being researched or recorded by Eugene Stern, Las Cruces, NM. It is presumed that William, the ancestor, came from either Jersey or Guernsey. He may have been a Wm. DUBRAS, or a Wm. Arms of an English fam. He was a knitter of stockings by trade. "Would knit a pair of stockings while going to and returning from the mill at Hatfield."

This fact strengthens the idea that he came from the Islands, as knitwear was an extremely important cottage industry in the Islands in the 1600s, and knitwear made in the Islands was shipped to France, England, Spain and the Americas. So many of the Islanders became involved in this money-making project that the government in England became alarmed when agriculture was neglected for knitting.

There is said to be an ARMS cemetary in Shelburne Falls, MA. For more generations, see A GENEALOGICAL RECORD OF THE ARMS FAMILY, by Edward W. Arms, Troy, NY, 1877, a copy in Essex Institute, Salem, MA. Check also towns of Deerfield, Greenfield, Sunderland and Ashfield, MA. (Eugene Stern, Las Cruces, NM; HIST OF DEERFIELD, MA, by Geo. Sheldon; HISTORY OF SUSQUEHANNA CO., PA, by Emily C. Blackman; CENT HIST OF SUSQ. CO., by R.M. Stocker; VRs of Buckland and Deerfield, MA, and of Wilmington, VT; ARMES GEN, by Iva Armes Condreay, St. Edward, NEBR, 1933; Humboldt Co., IA Records; CLEVELAND GEN; Virkus; GEN RECORD, by Edward Arms; Jeanne Adams, Portland, OR; LaDell Zuckerman, Yonkers, NY; and Helen Riggers Anderson, Rochester, NH)

ARMS, William, from C.I.?, to MA, b 1654, mar Joanna ___, b 1653/54, dau of John and Eliz. HAWKS, qv, one of the settlers of Hadley, MA, 1677. Also res Hatfield, and rem to Deerfield ca 1684. Wm., a farm-viewer, fenceviewer and one of a committee to build a schoolhouse, also a constable and school commissioner. He was in the records of Sunderland, MA from 1714-1722, where he was called "Good Mr. Arms." Served in the Indian fight at Great Falls, now Gill, MA, 1676. He d 1731, Deerfield, bur near son Wm. and grandson Wm Arthur G. Arms wrote, "Grandfather spelled his name Harmes instead of Armes at Cody, WY, 1938." See sources for more info. Large fam chart in WRCIC.

ARMS. A fam connected with the COHU fam of Lansingburgh, NY and NY City. ARMS, Henry, mar Nancy Montgomery, 5 chn, b Lansingburgh? Nancy the dau of John and Eunice Van Buren? or Van Keuren?, Montgomery. (Susan George, Phoenix, AZ) OUTC.

A1. William, b ca 1827/28
A2. Sarah, b ca 1829/30
A3. John, b ca 1831/2
A4. Joseph, b ca 1833/4
A5. James, b ca 1845/6

ARTHUR. Curr research in C.I.? See CIFHS #9 and 12.

ARTHUR, in J from 1227, and in G a little later. In Grouville, St. Peters, St. Marys and St. John, J, 1668, in St. Peters, St. Marys, St. John and St. Ouen, J, 1749. In St. Lawrence, 1788.

ARTHUR, Capt. Jean, a privateer of J, 1756.

ARTHUR, John, from St. Mary, J, bought land at Gloucester, MA, next to Thomas PINEL, qv, 1713. (PENNELL GEN by Clara Phinney, 1916) A letter from Jean Arthur, Dewhurst, near Robertsbridge, Sussex, England, Aug. 1976, had the following information. "He must be a direct ancestor of mine, because we know that our Jean Arthur, son of Jean Arthur, son of Jean Arthur, son of Nicholas, made his wife Rachel LE COUTEUR his procuratrice in 1713, that enabled her to act legally on his behalf while he was out of the Island. We know that he travelled with Charles DU PRE of St. Laurence, and with Thomas PINEL, son of Philippe of Trinity, and of Anne LE MONTES, his wife. We did not know that Jean Arthur had bought land in Gloucester, MA, and would like very much to know where this was, and for how long he held it. He had chn b in Jersey before and after 1713. We do not know the date of his death, where or how he died. It must have been after 1724, but before 1732, when his son, also Jean, John, came of age."

ARTHUR, Jean, of St. Mary, J, is mentioned in GEN OF EDWARD SMALL, by Underwood.

ARTHUR. A petition was sent to the court at Boston, MA 1653, from the inhabitants of the Isles of Shoals, ME. They wanted a township formed to take care of their local legal problems. There were, at that time, the petition states, upwards of a hundred men, and that John Arthur, Lt., and William Seely, Ensigne, had been chosen from them to begin the service. (Noyes) ARTHUR and SEELY may have been C.I. men, but OUTC. At that time and later, there seems to have been a few C.I. surnames in the Isles of Shoals.

ARTHUR. In MD early. OUTC.

ARTHUR, Charles, age 43, and wife, Jane, age 37, both b J, res Paspebiac, QUE, 1881, with chn. (Aldo Brochet, London, ONT)
A1. Charles, Jr., b ca 1865
A2. John, b ca 1869
A3. Alfred, b ca 1874
A4. Laura, b ca 1876
A5. George, b ca 1879

ASTLETT. In G 1600s and 1700s. ASPLET in J 1668-1749, in St. Martins and Grouville, J. Curr research, see CIFHS #3,6, and 8. ASPLET of Gorey, J, a shipbuilder 1843. (Jean)

ASLETT, John, from C.I.?, mar 1657, Rebecca AYER. OUTC. (Essex Antiq; GEN AND PERSONAL MEM RELATING TO THE FAMS OF BOSTON AND EASTERN MASS, p. 194; Andover VR; Helen Herman, Jackson, MI; CLEMENT GEN) See sources for data on 6 chn.

AUDOIRE. Alderney Island surname.

AYLETT, John, mar Mary HAWKINS, 1659, Boston. OUTC. Note that ASLETT was pron close to AYLETT.

AUBERT. This is a French name, but occurs in J and G from 1300s on. This name spelled OBER in early records in J, which is close to the French sound of the name.

AUBERT, OBER, Philip, was b MRB, served in Rev. War. (SOLDIERS AND SAILORS OF MASS) OUTC.

OBER. See DUTCH UNCLES AND NEW ENGLAND COUSINS, by Wilson Ober Clough, New Orleans, LA, 1977. It is possible that some of the New England OBERS were AUBERTS from the C.I.

OBER, Daniel, mar Mrs. Jane ANTHONY, 1815, MRB (int). OUTC.

OBEAR, Ruth, dau of James Woodberry, Woodbury, and Lydia, large fam in Beverly, MA, early. OUTC.

AUBIN, from France and C.I. In J 1309, in Grouville and St. Saviour, J 1668. In St. Martin and St. Saviour, J, 1749. Curr research? See CIFHS #5. CAUTION: TRIAL CHART. SEE LATE ADDITIONS.

AUBIN, Capt. Philip, 1749-1801, from J 1767, settled in Newburyport, MA, mar 1775, Abigail Greenleaf, 1753-1801, dau of Joshua and Judith (MOODY) Greenleaf. Capt. Philip settled to West Indies ports, was commander in Rev. War of Brigantine HANCOCK. A partner in the first woollen mill in U.S., located at Byfield, MA. Owned house on Orange St., a pew in South Church, member of Mason's Lodge and Marine Society. He d of yellow fever in Guadeloupe Island 1801. Poss Capt. Philip had several sons by a previous mar before he mar Abigail? Jersey might have more on this fam. (Virkus 6; MASS SOLDIERS AND SAILORS; HISTORY OF AMESBURY, MA, by Redford; Typescript JOSHUA AUBIN, by Agnes A. Aubin, 1944; REPORT ON WOOLLEN MFG, by Joshua Aubin before 1867)
A1. a son, went to sea
A2. Solomon, went to sea
A3. Philip, went to sea
A4. (?)
A5. (?)
A6. Joshua, b 1789, Newburyport, MA, worked first in a clothing store in Newburyport, MA, later had his own business on Cornhill. He mar Mary BUSSEY Newell 1817, at West Church Boston, by Rev. Charles Lowell, father of the poet. Failed in business 1820, but was again in business next year with Amos and Abbot LAWRENCE. His firm manufactured flannels, jacquards, satinette, tweed, etc. The Amesbury Flannel Co. was valued at $100,000. In 1823 he had a power loom, first in this country, if not the world. Here,

also, cotton and wool were woven together for the first time ca 1835. He retired in 1853, an intimate friend of John Greenleaf Whittier. Mary b 1798, d 1880. The Amesbury Library was founded by Joshua.

B1. Philip John, 1822-1876, wool merchant, Boston, mar Margaret Pitts Harris, dau of Theodore Jackson Harris, a sea captain of Portsmouth, NH, and Mary MacPheadris Warner Conner. See WARNER HOUSE BIOGRAPHY, by Agnes A. Aubin, Xmas, 1945. Agnes was the dau of Dr. E.G. Tucker and Elizabeth Mary Harris.

C1. Theodore Harris Aubin, 1852-1871
C2. Philip Lawrence Aubin, 1855-1901, mar Emma Corkum, who d 1913
C3. Helen Warner, 1856-1928
C4. Margaret Harris, b 1859
C5. Mary Whipple
C6. Joshua Harris, b 1863, mar Lillian C. Loveland
C7. Agnes Aubin, b 1867

B2. Agnes Aubin
B3. Mary Newell
B4. Abigail Greenleaf Aubin, mar Rev. Charles C. Vinal

AUBIN, Solomon and Philip, poss sons of Philip, above, or another, served in Rev. War. (MASS SOLDIERS AND SAILORS)
AUBIN, as OBIN, Anne, res Newburyport, MASS 1790, (Census) alone.
AUBINS, Widow Jane of Newburyport, MASS 1769, poss Jane, dau of Philip Cole of Amesbury, MASS, and Wells, ME. (Noyes)
AUBIN, Jane, res Newburyport, MA, 1790. (Census) Two females.
AUBINS, Mary, mar John Thompson, 1742, Boston.
AUBIN, Nathaniel, res Newburyport, MA, 1790, fam of 5. (Census)
AUBIN, Philip, res Newburyport, MA, fam of 8, 1790. (Census)
AUBIN, Polly/Mary?, mar Richard George, had dau, Mary George, 1797, Haverhill, MA. (CLEMENT GEN)
AUBIN, Thomas, mar Hannah Chaple, 1725, MRB.
There is said to be an Aubin Gen., compiler did not see. See WRCIC.
OBENS, John, res Holden, MA, 1790, 2 in fam. This is prob AUBINS.
OBING. Prob AUBIN, Margaret mar John HOOPER 1736, Kings Chapel, Boston, MA.
AUDOIN, a fam from J to North Chelmsford, MA, 1870s.
AUGER. AUGAIRE and ALGARE were in J from the 1300s. (Stevens List) ALGER, at least one fam in New England said to be AUGER of J changed to ALGER. (Source not noted.) Much data on Auger in New England in SMALL GEN; PILLSBURY GEN; Essex Coll.; Virkus; and GEN by Edward Auger, Middletown, CT, 1904.
AUVERGNE. Curr research? See CIFHS #8.
AVERTY. See VERTEE.
AVERTY. In St. Clement, Grouville and Trinity, J in 1668, and in St. Clement and Grouville, J 1749. This surname often became VERTY, VERTEE in early New England. See VERTEE.
AVERTA, AVORTA, AVERTY, Susanna, Mr. Martin's Jersey maid in 1672. Her doctor bills were paid by John Thompson, a carpenter of Portsmouth, NH. (Noyes)
BAAL. In J in 1299. BAAL in St. Martin, J, 1749.
BAAL. None of those below are verified as coming from J, where the name was known in 1299. (From La Baasle, a town in Normandy). It was spelled both BAAL and BALL in 1749. Baal quickly became BALL in early New England. It is poss that other BALL fams in MA and NH were also from J. However, Ball, John, of Watertown, MA, is said by some to be from Wiltshire, England. And a Peter BAAL arrived from Rotterdam to Phila. 1741, ship Capt. being Alex THOMAS. (Rupp's COLLECTION OF 30,000 NAMES OF PERSONS TO PENNA) CAUTION: TRIAL CHARTS.
BAAL, BAALL, Sarah, dau of John, was only two in the 1630s when her father contracted to pay for her care by Richard GALE of Watertown. Sarah's mother may have died, John agreed to the terms, mortgaging

his lot to assure the payment of the pounds required. (JOHN BALL OF WATERTOWN, MA, 1630-1635, not seen by compiler) OUTC.
A1. Isaac, b 1687
B1. Jacob, bp 1708 MRB, mar Mary ___, poss mar twice?
C1. Mary, bp 1728 C2. Jacob, bp 1730
C3. Samuel, bp 1734 C4. Rachel?, bp 1742
B2. Isaac, b 1709 mar Rebecca ___
C1. Elizabeth, b 1730 C2. Isaac, b 1733, mar Hannah ___
D1. Hannah, bp 1759 D2. Sarah, bp 1763
B3. Lawrence, bp 1710,11, son of Isaac Jr. in VR
B4. Elizabeth, bp 1712
B5. Jeremiah, mar Mary ___
C1. Jeremiah Jr., b 1741 C2. Mary, bp 1743,44 bp1701
A2. Jane, bp 1690, MRB. A3. John, bp 1693 A4. Priscilla A5. Sarah/
BAAL, John mar Meriam ___, res MRB. OUTC
A1. John, bp 1754, poss mar Mary ___, a son Devereux, b 1772
A2. Jonas, bp 1756, mar Anna ___, a dau Nancy, bp 1785
A3. Miriam, b 1759 A5. Hannah, bp 1765, d.y.?
A4. Susanna, b 1763 A6. Hannah again, bp 1769
BAAL, Elias from J? d 1786, age 77 in St. John's Par., SC. In 1777 he owned many slaves in SC, and sold 140 of them to his cousin. (Troxler; SC GEN. MAG)
BALL, Peter from J?, b 1645, fisherman in Portsmouth, NH 1672, will dated 1719,23. (Noyes) OUTC
A1. Peter, mar Amy ____, 1712, d ca 1753, 6 chn
A2. Christian, mar Philip PAINE 1730
A3. Sarah, mar 1713 Robert Ward, later of Boston, a mariner.
A4. Mary, mar 1. ___JACKSON and 2. in 1716 William WHITE.
A5. Susanna, mar before 1715 John FICKETT, his widow in 1730
A6. Elizabeth, mar 1719 John Roe, a widow in 1730
A7. Margaret of Kittery, unmar 1736
BAAL, curr in Pasadena, CAL, OUTC.
BAAL, Mary, mar Peter DUSEE, DOUCET?, 1718 Boston, MA, from J or France
BALE, Edward Manwaring, Wm., Wm. Jr. and Nicholas BALE were all in early records of York, ME. Were they BAALS of Jersey? Edw. Jr. Josiah and Samuel were also in this list in Noyes.
BABBE. Curr a G surname, but not known to compiler how long in G. BABBE, Philip, signed a petition at Isle of Shoals, 1653, where some C.I. fams settled. A son of this fam was named SAMPSON. (Noyes)
BACON, not an old C.I. surname. Cf BEGHIN, pron. somewhat like BACON.
BACON. "Daniel BACON who arrived in Salem 1664 had previously gone to Jersey from MASS."(Perley) Poss because he was a ship builder, and had business with the Jersey firms? "Daniel Bacon early lived on the Isle of Jersey and came to Salem 1664". (Perley) Note that it does not say he was born in J. He mar Susannah Spenler/Spencer, and d 1720. Poss of Hug. fam? He had 7 chn, one of whom, Susanna, b 1670 mar Benjamin BOYCE, qv, 1703. BOYCE is a J and English surname.
BACON, Daniel Jr. agreed to build a ship for John BALAINE of Jersey, who was then a temp.? resident of Salem, MA, late 1600s. (Perley)
BACON, Harriet, dau of Wm. BACON, mar 1815, Azariah BULLEN (BALAINE?) of Needham, MA, and Hannah, her sister mar Ichabod BULLEN, 1814.OUTC. (BACON GEN, Michael of Dedham, 1915, Cambridge, MA, p. 230)
BACON, Nathaniel mar 1642 Hannah MAYO. Cf MAHAUT of J. OUTC
A1. Nathaniel, b 1645 A2. Samuel b 1650 A3. Jeremiah, b 1659
BACON, Mary, dau of Silas and Molly (Draper) BACON, b 1801, mar

John W. DEMERITT, qv. (BACON GEN, Michael of Dedham)

BACON, Capt. Wm., mar Abigail DEAN, dau of Jean DEAN of Dedham. Wife, Sarah, d 1727, 7 chn. (BACON AND ALLIED FAMS, Culver City, CAL, 1958) OUTC.

BADIER. In St. Martin and Grouville, J 1607, 1668, in St. Martin, J 1749, in St. Lawrence, J 1788. Curr research? See C IFHS #6. Note closeness in sound of BADIER and BADGER.

BADGER, George, "from Isle of Jersey," husbandman, b ca 1718, volunteered against the West Indies 1740. If George was a Jerseyman, perhaps his name was originally spelled BADIER, see above. A fam was in St. Martin, J 1668. Giles BADGER of early New England is said to have come from England, not Jersey.

BADGER, Mary, poss BADIER?, of J, mar 1700, John Wyatt, mariner of Arrowsic 1718. OUTC.

A1. Stephen Wyatt, mar 1723, Mary Bickham

B1. John Wyatt, bp Ports., NH B2. ____, bp Newbury, MA

BAILEY, William, age 35, of Hamilton, ONT, b G, mar 1864 in Hamilton, C. of E., Mary Devaney, dau of Jerry and Mary Devaney. William was son of Nicholas and Rachel BAILEY of G. (Wentworth Co. Marriage Register; Wm. Britnell, Mississauga, ONT)

BAILLY, LE BAILLY shield of J: Azure, a fortress argent, maconee sable.

BAILHACHE, in J 1299 and on. In St. Lawrence, J 1668 and 1788. BALLYHACK is only one of many variant spellings.

BAILHACHE, Nicholas and John of J, with John BROWNE, commissioned a ship ship to be built in Gloucester, MA in the 1600s. (Perley III; Virkus)

BALHACHET, Thomas, mar Mary MARSH, 1707, Boston. Prob from J.

BALLAST, John, in MASS SOLDIERS AND SAILORS IN REV WAR. Prob from J as BAILHACHE.

BELASH, prob BAILHACHE, Philip, prob from J, res MRB 1790 with fam of 7. (Census) Poss he was the same Philip who mar in MRB, 1763, Mary CHAMBLET? He had the admin. of his brother Francis' estate 1761. (Essex Antiq., vol. 8) Several chn, including:

A1. Mary, bp 1768. Was she the one who mar John Warren in MRB, 1790?

A2. Remember, bp 1770

A3. Philip, bp 1772

BELASH, BELSHI, Betsey, of C.I. frm?, mar Robert M. Russell, 1804, MRB. Poss ROUSSEL of J? She d 1824 and he in 1829. Dau Elizabeth Chambers Russell, b 1811.

BELSHI, Mary of Manchester, mar John SINNIT at Manchester, MA, 1755.

BELACHER, William, at Stoughton, MA during Rev. War. (MASS SOLDIERS AND SAILORS)

BAILHACHE, Nicholas, from G, mar Ruth Hurst in GCO 1825. He was the second postmaster in Cambridge, OH. Nicholas served on a committee to establish a library in Cambridge, also was editor of the Guernsey Co. TIMES, 1828-1830. He was J.P. 1833. (Wolfe)

BAKER. In J 1340, in Grouville, J 1749, and in Sark in the 1800s. Curr Sark. BAKER is also old in G.

BAKER. At least 15 came early to the colonies before 1650, one or more from J.

BAKER, Thomas, a Jerseyman, refused to be served with a warrant in Essex Co., MA 1679. He also slept through Wm. Hubbard's sermon, and was admonished by the secular authority of the county court. (Essex Hist. Coll., July 1974)

BAKER, Nicholas, poss from J?, of MRB in right of his wife Elizabeth, mar 1696, dau of Geo. BARTLETT, late of Spurwink by the land of John JACKSON...said land bought of Henry JOSLIN by Geo. Bartlett. Evidence given by Elizabeth Bryars and John BODIN before Justice LEGG. (Maine Recorder) BAKER, BARTLETT, JACKSON, JOSLIN, BRYARS (BRIARD), BODIN

(BEAUDIN) and LEGG are all names of the C.I. Nicholas was master of ketch DILIGENCE, 1684. OUTC.

BAKER, Richard BOHUN, res SC middle 1700s. He was related to the GUERIN fam of SC, qv, and poss also to the BULLINE, qv, fam of SC. BAKER poss of C.I. BOHON, DE BOHON in Stevens, J name list. BOHAN in Torteval, G 1700s. (WILL ABSTRACT BOOKS, by Caroline T. Moore)

A1. Richard Bohun, Jr.
A2. Elizabeth Elliott
A3. Mary Bonum?
A4. Harriett Bonum?
A5. Charlotte Bohun
A6. Elizabeth, d.y.?

BAKER, John, was at Charlestown, MA 1636, mar Susannah MARTIN, 12 chn. Not verified as to origin, but may have been from C.I. (Wm. Leffingwell, Wash., D.C.)

BAKER, Keith Philip, b 1945, son of Philip Stanley Baker, of Sark Island, and May ROBILLIARD BAKER, rem from Beaumont, J, to Hamilton, ONT. (P.S. Baker)

BAKER, BOULANGER, Sophia, 1800-1859, dau of Hilaire BOULANGER/BAKER of Sark Island, mar (his first wife) John DE PUTRON, qv, b 1797 G, d 1863, bur Union Bur. Grounds, Philadelphia, PA. 12 chn by Sophia.

BALCOMB, BALCAM, etc. Hug. fam settled for some time in J. In 1726, a Francois Balcam mar Anne RENOUF, qv, of St. Mary, J. In 1739, Francois and Jeanne HAMON, qv, were godparents to Elizabeth INGROUVILLE of J. By 1790, many Balcoms settled in MA and CT, but not all are part of this J fam. Balcam noted in Oxford, MA 1700s.

BALCOM, Capt. John, b ca 1697, mar 1. Sarah Jacobs, 1696-1741, dau of Joseph and Sarah (Lynzey) Jacobs, 1719. He mar 2. at Salem, MA, 1745, Hannah Proctor, who d 1753. He was in Mansfield, CT as early as 1725. In 1744, he bought land located in Salem, MA from Thomas LESBIREL, qv. Ten chn by first wife and two by second. (BALCAM FAM, by Frank W. Balcomb, Peabody, MA, 1942; Virkus; Louise Carlson, Milwaukee, WISC; Gail Nacht, Upper Darby, PA; TINGLEY, RICE AND PEABODY GENS; BALKOM FAM OF ATTLEBORO, MA; NEHGS, vol. 36; Tewkesbury, MA VR; MASS SOLDIERS AND SAILORS IN REV. WAR)

A1. Sarah, b 1720, Lynn, MA, mar at Windham, CT, 1741, Nathan SIMONS, qv
A2. Elizabeth, b 1722, d.y.?
A3. John, b 1724 Mansfield, CT, prob d at Winchester, CT, 1808. He mar 1750, Mary Gillett, poss GUILLET of J? who d in 1797, dau of Nathaniel G. of Salisbury, CT. John was grand juror at Winchester. He is listed in 1790 Census as in fam of 2 men, 3 boys and 6 females at Litchfield, CT
B1. Susanna, 1752-1825, mar 1777, Michael Grinnell, b 1752, Saybrook, CT, d 1858?
B2. Nathaniel, b 1754, soldier in Rev. War, b Mansfield, CT, d 1834, Silverlake, PA. Served at Ticonderoga 1775, rem to Wayne Co., PA ca 1813, chn b Winchester, CT.
C1. Francis C2. Nathan, b 1787, freeman of Winchester, CT 1802
C3. Jonathan, b 1791, mar Clarissa ___
C4. Silas, b 1795, mar Clarissa Webster
B3. Jonathan, b 1757, d 1790 Norwalk, CT, mar at Sharon, CT, 1779, Naomi Dickerson, b 1757. She d at Thompson, CT 1850. He served in Rev. War 1778. Chn b Winchester.
C1. John, b ca 1779, mar Mary Bixby, descendants
C2. Nathaniel, b ca 1780 C3. Keziah, b ca 1782, d unmar 1822
C4. Mary, b ca 1784, mar ___ Gates
C5. Rhoda, b ca 1786, mar Solomon Davis, b 1792, VT
C6. Irene, b ca 1788, mar Seth Goodrich
C7. Esther, b ca 1790, unmar

C8. Susannah, mar a Grinnell, a cousin?
B4. John, b 1759?, mar at Winchester, CT, 1783, Lois HUDSON. Served in Rev. War and was at Sidney, Del. Co., NY ca 1810
C1. Zilpha, b 1783
C2. Lois, b 1785, mar 1. 1810, Edward Hughes, b 1790, d at Sidney, NY 1863. Div. She mar 2. at Meredith, NH, 1841?, Albert Balch, b 1804?, d 1884, son of Abner and Lydia P. (Alden) Balch.
C3. Ebenezer C5. Una Vilda, bp 1790
C4. Elizabeth, bp 1790, had desc.
B5. Irene, b 1761
B6. Mary, b 1764, mar at East Haddam, CT 1787, Noadiah Brainard Gates of Barkhamstead, CT
B7. Keziah, b 1766 B8. Rhoda, b 1768 B8. Esther, b 1772
A4. Susannah, b 1726, d 1727
A5. Joseph, b 1728, d at Mansfield, CT ca 1810. He mar 1760, Mary KING, b 1739 Mans. and d there 1828, dau of Samuel and Mary Rose King
B1. Azariah, b 1760, mar 1. 1781, Deborah Huntington, b ca 1763, d 1814. Res Windham, CT? He mar 2. at Mansfield 1814, as her 2nd husband, Lydia (Elderkin) Fitch, dau of Joshua Booth Elderkin. Chn by 1st wife.
C1. Alpheus, b 1784, has desc
C2. Socrates, b 1786, mar Anna Brigham, desc
C3. Martin, b 1788, mar 1. Diantha Jacobs and 2. Susan Field, poss 3.?
C4. Lucius, b 1790 C5. Owen, Orrin?, b 1792, d 1798
C6. Artemesia, b 1794, mar Chester Davison
C7. Maria, b 1797, d 1814 C8. Lora Phoebe, b 1799
C9. John Adams, b 1801, d at Windham, CT 1816 or 1820?
C10. Sherman, b 1805, mar 1. Elizabeth Maxfield and 2. Louisa Almy. Desc.
B2. Elizabeth, b 1762, mar 1784, John Elijah Martin, son of Elijah Martin, Sr.
C1. Sylvia Balcom Martin, poss other chn?
B3. Uriah, b 1764, mar Lucy Webster, b 1769, d 1841
C1. Elizabeth, mar A. Gilbert
C2. Elihu, b 1796, mar Almira Gates, desc.
C3. Pamelia, b 1798, mar Andrew Sill
C4. Eli, b 1800, mar Lydia Robinson, desc
C5. Almira, b 1801
C6. Isabella, b 1803, mar Hiram Gates
C7. Webster, b 1805, mar Lucy Church
C8. Lyman, b 1807, Burlington, NY, mar Jane Kewley
C9. Lucinda, b 1809, mar Levi Thompson
C10. Marcia, b 1811, d 1837
C11. Lucia, b 1814, mar 1842, Nath. Smith
B4. Asahel, b 1766, d at Kendall, NY 1839. Mar 1788, Asenath Martin, 1769-1848, dau of Robert and Lydia Martin
C1. Gurdan, b 1791, d 1845, mar Laurana ___
C2. Lucinda, b 1793, d 1847, mar Asa Ross
C3. George, b 1795, mar Wealthy Whitney
C4. Leander, b 1798, Richfield, NY, mar Nancy Clark
C5. Daniel, b 1802, mar Lucinda Clark
C6. Vine, b 1805 Eastown, NY, mar as her 2nd husband, Maria (Munn) Merrill, and mar 2. Eliza ___
C7. Laura, b 1807 Gorham, NY, d 1890. Mar 1829, Hiram O. Northrop, b at Ridgefield, CT 1804, d Reading, MI 1868
C8. Elijah M., b 1810, d 1812
B5. Constant, b 1768 Mansfield, CT, d 1848. Mar at Mansfield,

1790, Anna Craine, b there 1766, d Hopewell, NY, 1852, dau of Hezekiah Craine

C1. Horace, b 1791, Litchfield, CT, mar Sally Lyon

D1. John Martin, res Richfield, Otsego Co., NY (Donald Harley, Kentwood, MI)

C2. Anna, b 1794, Richfield, NY, d 1870. Mar 1814, Stephen Martin, b 1788, d 1855

C3. Abner, b 1795, mar 1. Ruth Williams, 2. Philotheta Baker and 3. Philena Waring. Desc.

C4. Chester, b 1798, mar Ada Penn. Desc.

C5. Epenetas, b 1805 Gorham, NY, mar Eleanor L. McMillan. Desc.

C6. Serviah, b 1808, d 1881, mar John Lamberton, no issue.

C7. Julia Ann, b 1810 Gorham, NY, d 1858, mar 1830, Mansfield, CT, Charles Gleason?

B6. Mary, b 1771, mar Elijah Martin, Jr., son of Elijah, Sr.

C1. William Samuel Martin, b 1813, Richfield, NY, d 1892, Dayton Twp., Newago Co., MI, mar Lovilla Burr Herkimer, b 1816, Otsego, NY, d 1913 Fremont, MI

D1. Helen Louise Martin, b 1845 Otsego, NY, mar 1869, Adonijah Edd Upton, 1837-1893, b Adrian, MI, d Traverse City, MI. She d 1925, Thompsonville, MI

E1. Mary Belle Upton, b 1878 Freemont, MI, mar 1902, William Casselman. She d 1963, Milwaukee, WI

F1. Louise Casselman, mar Swen Carlson, res Milwaukee

B7. Sarah, b 1774, d 1864, mar 1. 1800, Ebenezer Gurley, b ca 1777, d 1864, son of Jacob and Hannah (Bigelow?) Gurley

B8. Francis, b 1776, Mansfield, CT, d there 1826. Mar there 1804, Eunice Lathrop, b 1776, dau of Elias and Hannah (Gurdan)Lathrop

C1. Benjamin Gorton, b 1805, mar Maria L. (Smith) White, her second husband

C2. Julia, b 1806

C3. Brigham

C4. Constant, b ca 1810

C5. Frances, b ca 1811

C6. Lois S.

C7. Francis, b ca 1819, d 1825

C8. Mary, who mar at Grafton, NH 1840, Horace Prescott

C9. Maria E., who mar 1. in 1874, Silas Stevens, and 2. James Talbert, son of Elmer F. Talbert C10. Johy Noyes

B9. Daniel, b 1779, mar at Haverhill, MA, 1804, Susan Ordway

B10. Lucinda, b 1782, mar Ebenezer Gurley. See also B7, Sarah, above, who mar Ebenezer Gurley

A6. Mary, b 1730, mar at Middletown, CT, Joseph Clark III

A7. Sarah ?, b 1732

A8. Elias, b 1733, Mansfield, CT, mar there 1754, Phoebe Foster. He was at Winchester, CT 1774. In 1776 he owned a part interest in a mill there.

B1. Sarah, b 1756, mar at Winchester, CT 1773, John DARBE, cf DARBE, qv. This surname sometimes written DERBY. DARBY in J middle 1700s.

B2. Hannah, b 1756, twin of Sarah

B3. Phoebe, b 1758, mar at New Hartford, CT 1774, Ezekiel Markham

B4. Elias CABOT, b 1760, mar at Winchester, CT 1782, Mary Dickenson

B5. Rachel, b 1762

B6. Olive, b 1766, mar at Winchester, CT 1783, Samuel Stanclift

B7. Elizabeth, b 1768, mar at Norfolk, CT 1786, Joshua MOSES, qv

B8. Jacob, b at Winchester, CT

B9. Joseph

A9. Susannah, b 1736

A10. Francis, b 1738

A11. by second wife, Samuel, b 1745

A12. Elizabeth, who mar at Mansfield, CT 1761, Benjamin Jacobs

BALCOM, Asahel. Note that this man in above chart res in NY state. Poss the Helen below belongs to this group.

BALCOM, Helen, b 1815, Charleston, NY, married into the Cone fam? This fam recorded in PORTRAIT AND BIBLIOGRAPHICAL ALBUM OF RACINE AND KENOSHA, WISC. OUTC.

BALEN. Could this be BALLEINE? Helen Balen Conklin, dau of Wm and Anna (BALEN) Conklin b 1831, NY, d 1868. She mar George Starr, his first wife. He was son of Eli Starr. Four chn. (STARR GEN)

BALL. See BAAL.

BALLAM, Thomas, b ca 1803 J?, res Cape Breton, NS, Canada in 1877. Three Ballam sisters, said to be of J, res Cape Breton. (See Q.A. IN CANADA, by Turk)

BALLUM. Is this surname in PEI of J fam? BALLUM, Alex. M. of PEI, mar Matilda Jane Beck, b 1873. She d 1943. (See BECK GEN CHART)

A1. Celena Jane, b 1894, d 1969, mar Loyial Freeman, PEI
A2. Grace, b 1896, d 1899
A3. John William, 1898-1955, mar Carol M. Gove
A4. Howard Ancil, b 1900, in Feb. d 1965, mar Anne BARTON
A5. Kenneth Erskine, b Dec. 1900, d 1958, mar Alice Frechette
A6. Lawrence Kingsley, b 1903, mar Erma Doris Beals
A7. Alex. Marfleet, b 1905, d 1947, mar Anne Barton and 2. Evelyn Leeman
A8. Albert, b 1907, d.y.
A9. Blanche Windsor, b 1909, mar Clyde H. Macdonald
A10. David Ira, b 1913, mar Mary Scriven-Niklason

BALLEINE. In J 1340, in St. Heliers, St. Brelade, and St. Peter, J, 1668. In St. Peter, St. Mary and Trinity, J in 1749. BALLEN in G early. Spelling varies from BALLEN to BULLEN, means Whalebelly, or man who played Jonah in a miracle play, or from place La Baleine, south of Coutances, Normandy, France, for La Valeine, a village in the Vale. See also BULLEN. (Stevens) Curr J. CAUTION: SOME DATA UNVERIFIED.

BALLEINE, Edward, b ca 1829 J, son of Edward, b 1791, J, and Marie (LE FEUVRE) BALLEINE. Marie was the 2nd wife, from St. Brelade, J, Edward Jrs', half-sister, Marie, b 1819, mar Daniel NORMAN of J. His bro, Francis, Frank, may have left J in the 1840s. Edward rem to CAL for the Gold Rush in 1848. He was fresh out of Oxford, England, and landed at San Francisco "when it was a wild embryo town of tents sheltering about 10,000 stampeders to the New Eldorado." He traveled east by the Santa Fe Trail in 1853 to visit his only brother, Frank, a Methodist minister at the hamlet of St. Louis, MO, and also visited the Jersey families then located in Iowa. There he mar 1854, Elizabeth LE BOUTILLIER, qv, b 1838, Trinity, J. He settled first in Louisa Co., then bought farmland in the NW part of Crawford Co., KS, after serving with the 25th Iowa Inf. in the Civil War, and being severely wounded at the battle of Vicksburg Heights. His health was badly undermined by his war wounds, and on the doctor's recommendation, the whole family left for the Puget Sound by way of the Oregon Trail, taking four months through the Indian country.

After 10 months at the Cascades, the fam returned to Walla Walla for medical care for Balleine, but he d 1882, is bur there with other Civil War veterans. In the spring of 1883, the mother filed on a homestead near Colfax, WA, where the fam of eight grew up. (Jerrold Ballaine, Bellevue, WA; Dorothy Paxton, Bettendorf, IA)

A1. Mary Ann, b 1856, mar W.H. ALLEN, qv, daus Sarah and Jane
A2. Victoria, b 1859, mar J.H. Shireman
A3. Hampton, b 1861, unmar
A4. Abraham Lincoln, b 1864, mar Flora MARSH in IA 1887. In 1900, he

res Diamond Pt., Whitman Co., WA. Flora was b 1872 in Indiana.
A5. Charles Wilford, b ca 1866?, mar Florence Drown
B1. Katherine, b 1904   B3. Olive, b 1909
B2. Horace, b 1908, mar 1930
A6. John Edmund, b 1868 Louisa Co., IA, and rem with fam to Crawford Co., KS, ca 1870, then to Puget Sound, WA. His father d when he was 13. He worked his way through school, and became a well-known newspaper-man in WA before he was 26. At 27, John was secretary to Gov. Rogers and at 29, was Adjutant-Gen. of the state, with rank of Brigadier General. He served as officer in the Philippine Insurrection. In 1902, began to promote and build the AK RR, and founded Seward as the Terminus in 1903. Former Senator George Turner of Spokane said, "John Ballaine has more varied and accurate information on more subjects, such as history, philosophy, law, geography, work conditions and the sciences, and his mind works with clear logic and precision than any man I have ever known." John mar Anna Felch, 3 chn. He d 1941.
B1. Sophronia Ballaine, b 1894, mar Albert Kalin 1919. Kalin was b 1891 and d 1944. Fam res Seattle, WA, but he is bur in Cleveland, OH. Three chn.
C1. Theodore Albert Kalin, b 1921, mar Marilyn Soul
C2. Annabelle Kalin, b 1922, mar James Truit
D1. Teresa Truit D2. Christine Truit D3. James K. Truit
C3. John Ballaine Kalin, b 1924, mar Ann Darling
B2. Florence Ballaine, b 1896, mar Dean Andrews, 3 chn
B3. Jerrold R. Ballaine, b 1906, mar Elizabeth Maxson, 2 sons
C1. Jerrold Curtis Ballaine, mar Jo Ann Heinbaugh, 2 chn
D1. Ann Theresa   D2. Peter Alexander
C2. David Allen Ballaine, mar Shelah Dunklan, 2 chn
D1. Jeffrey John Ballaine   D2. Beth Ann Ballaine
A7. Edward, poss in sanitarium in 1900
A8. Francis, mar Genevieve KNIGHT. A son, Francis, 1906-1963
A9. William Wesley, b 1874, mar Margaret Connelly, a son, Wesley, b 1907

BALLEIN, Elizabeth, res Brown Co., OH, 1860. (Census)

BALLEINE, Francis, Frank, b Trinity, J, bro of Edward, above, prob b 1820s in J, rem to Western U.S., and was located in St. Louis, MO 1850s. Not found by compiler.

BALLEINE, BALAINE, BOLLEN, etc., John. "Daniel BACON, Jr. agreed to build a ship for John BALAINE of Jersey, who was then a resident of Salem, MA," late 1600s. (Perley) See BOLLEN, BULLEN.

BALLEINE, Capt. Jacques (James), was a privateer of J in the 1700s.

BALLEIN, Peter, also noted in Brown Co., OH, 1860.

BALLINE, Samuel, mar 1672, Experience Saben, Sabine?, in Rehoboth, MA.

BALLEINE, Capt. Thomas, was trading in 1737 with VA on sloop, MARY. (A. John Jean, Jersey)

BALLEINE. Several to Canada from J. See Q.A. IN CANADA, by Turk.

BALLISTER. See LE BALLISTER, L'ARBALESTIER

BANNISTER. See LE BALLISTER.

BARBER, BARBE. Old G surname. BARBET, BARBEY in J 1668. BARBY in G.

BARBER, BARBOUR, Claude, prob a Frenchman, came with CARTERET to Elizabethtown, NJ 1665. See THE NEW JERSEY SETTLEMENT.

BARBET, John, mar Miriam Hannover, 1751, MRB. John from J? BARBET is old C.I. surname. Curr research? See CIFHS #3.
A1. Eleanor, bp 1752, MRB   A3. Miriam, bp 1756
A2. Elizabeth, bp 1754   A4. Mary, bp 1757, d.y.?

A5. Mary again, bp 1759
A6. John, bp 1761
A7. Elias, bp 1762
A8. Ann, bp 1764
A9. Samuel Scarlett, bp 1768
A10. Sarah, bp 1770

BARBET, Thomas, mar Margaret ___, res MRB. A son, Thomas, bp 1755 MRB.

BARBIER, Amice, mar Mary Ann LE ROSSIGNOL, and settled in U.S. (LE ROSSIGNOL GEN)

BARBIER, Amice, res J, mar Mary Anne COLLAS, b early 1800s, settled America. Her brother, Capt. Francis COLLAS, 1814, son of Pierre LE R. COLLAS and Esther Jeanne LE REGLE, b J, rem to Australia. Mary Ann d 1901.

BARBIER. A privateer ship captain of Jersey. (Jean)

BAREFOOT. Variant of BLAMPIED, BLAMPIED, BLANCPIED, WHITEFOOT, LIGHTFOOT. See BLAMPIED.

BARNEVILLE, Some noted in America. Poss originally BANNEVILLE? Old in G.

BARRASIN. One fam to America from C.I.

BARRETT, BARETTE. In St. John, J 1749 and in G early. Several noted in New England by compiler, but OUTC.

BARRETT, John, from G or J?, mar Sophia GREEN, 1736, King's Chapel, Boston, MA. OUTC.

BARTER, John, b England, came from Guernsey to Baltimore, MD 1828, rec'd by John Stanley. (NY NATURALIZATIONS, by Scott)

BARTLETT. A G surname. Also in J as BARTILLOT, 1607. Ship builders in J, 1800s.

BARTLETT, Elizabeth, twin of Bethia, mar Henry HOOPER, qv, 1725, MRB. Many res MRB. See also Newton's HIST OF BARNARD VT. OUTC.

BARTLETT, BARTELOT, Richard, from J?, b 1588?, to Newbury, MA 1635. (NEHGS, vol. 2) OUTC.

BARTLETT, Wm. Jr., mar Elizabeth LE CRAW, qv, 1801, MRB. OUTC, but wife is from C.I. fam.

BARTON, DE BARTONE. In J 1338, also known in G. At least two in New England from J, poss others. BARTONS also came from Grt. Britain to New England, poss also from France?

BARTON, John, of Elizabethtown, NJ, poss a Jerseyman?, mar Phoebe Bryand, a desc of James CARTERET of J. (CARTERET AND BRYANT GENEALOGY, by C. Baetjer, NY, 1887) OUTC.

A1. William Bryant, Presb. minister, stationed Woodbridge, NJ, d age 58 in 1852. He mar 1. Harriet Maria Condit of Morristown, NJ, 2. Harriet Butler Stanberry, and 3. Elizabeth Jirvis of Rome, NY
B1. Aaron Condit
B2. John Stanberry
B3. William Bryant
B4. Phoebe Marie
B5. Anna Hartley, mar Joseph Mathison Millick of Woodbridge, NJ.
C1. Anna Barton Millick, mar Willett Denike
C2. Addie Millick, mar Wethered B. Thomas
D1. Evania Thomas
C3. William Millick, d.y.
B6. Adeline Rockwell
A2. John, mar?
A3. Benjamin, went West
A4. Eliza, mar Rev. Wm. Townley, no issue
A5. Sarah Ann, mar James Paulding, bro of Commodore Paulding
B1. Julia Paulding, mar and settled in NH
B2. John, mar and settled in NH
B3. Ellen Paulding, settled in NJ
A6. Hannah Carteret, unmar
A7. Nancy, unmar

BARTON, John, of Salem, MA, a physician, mar 1676, Lydia ROBERTS, poss dau of Thomas Roberts of Boston, MA. John was a sea captain, went "home," poss to Jersey?, more than once, and d on a voyage to Bermuda.
A1. John, b 1677, d.y.
A2. John, again, b 1678, d.y.

A3. Thomas, b 1680, physician, many yrs. town clerk, Col of the Reg't, mar 1710, Mary, dau of Depty. Gov. Willoughby.
B1. John, b 1730, mar 1. Mary BUTLER and 2. Eliz. Marston and d 1772
A4. Zacheus, b 1693 A5. Elizabeth, b 1685 A6. Samuel, b 1688.
BARTON, Eli, b 1818 TN, mar Nancy KERBY, dau of Col..W. KERBY. OUTC. (Robert A. McIlvain, Fremont, CAL)
BARTON, Hannah, mar Samuel Merrifield 1817, Lancaster, MA. OUTC. (George Trigg, Brookhaven, NY)
BARTON, John, farmer, to Boston 1769 on ship MOLLY from J.(Whitmore)
BARTON, John mar Eliz. BOURGAIN, BOURGAIZE?, Boston. OUTC.
BARTON, John mar Penelope MARKOON, MARQUAND?, qv, Boston
BARTON, see many other BARTON marriages in Boston VR.
BARTON, Matthew, shoreman, b ca 1640 J?, in Salem, MA 1671, had accounts with Philip ENGLISH, qv, a Jerseyman, 1687. Matthew mar 1. Martha ___, 2. Sarah ___, before 1680, and 3. in 1694 Elizabeth Dickenson, dau of John and Eliz. (Tapley) Dickenson, desc. By Sarah he had Matthew, b 1682. See Noyes. OUTC.
BARTON, Richard, a mariner, from Grt. Britain, J?, to NY 1810. OUTC.
BARTON, Sarah, mar 1708 Daniel Rawlins, son of Nicholas of Newbury, MA. OUTC. (OLD FAMS IN SALISBURY, MA)
BARTON, note records of Oxford, MA 1700s. (B.W. Schwartz, Westfield,MA)
BARTRAM, see also BERTRAM. BARTRAM a surname of Grt. Britain, France and C.I. Some noted in New England and OH. Research on NJ BARTRAMS by Walter Winans, Carrsville, VA. OUTC.
BARTRAM, Amelia Sarah, mar 1852 Newark, NJ, Zachariah Jonathan BROUARD.
BARTRAM, Capt. Ebenezer, d 1783 Fairfield, CT, at 52, from Jersey?
BARTRAM in Nfld. "Ido know that there were two families bearing the BARTRAM family name that came from the Island of Jersey. One lived in Grafford, Jersey...had coat of arms, the other from Grouville, Jersey,...had different coat of arms...(Michael Bartram, Lethbridge, ALTA, Canada)
See BARTRAMS in MARIS GEN; Savage; Schenck's HIST OF FAIRFIELD, CT; Smith's HIST OF DELAWARE CO., PA; Todd's HIST OF REDDING, CT. A Thomas DE BARTRAM, poss from G? was in GCO before 1810. OUTC.
BASS. Poss that some in early New England were originally LE BAS? qv of J. See Samuel in Underhill's SMALL GEN, and see Noyes.
BASSETT. In J from 1299, also in G.
BASSET, Matthew from J? mar Elizabeth MALEY, MALLET? 1763, MRB, MA. See MALLET, MALEY.
BASSET, John mar Sarah DUPARR, qv, 1798 MRB.
BASTARD, LE BASTARD. In J from 1274, 1607, 1668, 1749.
BASTARD. In Norman-French has a silent "s", pron similar to BAT-TAR, BATTER. Some in early New England, as BATTER, may be from C.I., in St. Heliers, J 1600s. BASTARD was in Dorset, England in the 1500s. Curr Jersey.
BASTARD, Joseph, from J? to Fairfield, CT, mar 1685 Hannah, widow of Esbon Wakemire. (Whitmore; Virkus) OUTC.
BATTER, see BASTARD, above. See Emmerson and Green Genealogies. See also BETTIS, BATTES.
BATTER, Edmund, in Salem, MA 1635, mar twice? or poss a father and son? The first Edmund had Edmond, Mary Elizabeth and Daniel, who were under 21 in 1685. The second Edmund had Mary, b 1700, Elizabeth, Martha and Sarah, who was bp 1711 Salem, MA. Several d.y. (Essex

Coll., V8) OUTC.

BATTER, Mary, mar Rev. John, son of Rev. John Emmerson, and had at least 10 chn. OUTC.

BATTEN, from BAUDIN, BEAUDIN?, of the C.I. or even DE BARTONE? A strong tradition in Nfld. gives the C.I. as the origin of the Batten fam there, who are said to have come as early as the 1500s. It does seem poss that the Battens of New England may have come from Nfld. early, as did other fams. They were often sailors and shipmasters, which continued an old Jersey occupation. A William BATTEN mar in Saco 1655. (Noyes)

BATTIS, BETTIS, BETTES, BETTE, BETTEE, origin unknown. Compiler thinks this may be BATISTE, Hug. from Lyon, France to G and to England. None below verified, but some may have come from G to New England, or directly from France, or via England. (Essex Antiq., vol. 9; TRAIL OF THE HUGUENOTS, by G.E. Reaman; SHIPS AND SAILORS OF OLD SALEM, by Ralph Paine, Boston, 1923; PIRATES OF THE NEW ENGLAND COAST, by G.F. Dow) Research? See CIFHS #12. See also WRCIC.

BAUDAIN. In St. Martin, Grouville, St. Clement, St. John, St. Saviour, J, 1668. In St. Clement and St. John, J in 1749. In G early. This name spelled in many different ways: BAUDAINS, BAUDIN, BALDWIN, BAUDIN, BAULDEN, but is apparently the same name as BALDWIN. Since many forms are pron BODAN, BODEN, BOWDEN, it is plain that only a superhuman job would clarify the many different families of New England with names of similar sound, but immensely varied spelling.

BAUDIN. Curr G and J, also see NEHGS V 34. See also BEAUDIN, pron the same.

BAUDAINS, Capt. and BOWDEN, Capt., two partners in a privateer business of Guernsey Island in 1643. Their boldness got them into hot water, as well as compromising their leader, Sir George CARTERET of Jersey, to whom they turned over their ill-gotten ships and prisoners. They had even captured British officials through a ruse. It is quite poss that either one or both of these captains, to evade legal problems, may have settled in the American colonies.

BAUDAINS, Philip, was a thatcher in J, 1742.

BAUDIN, William, was in the Isles of Shoals, 1640s. (Noyes)

BAUDIN, dit LA GERCHE, curr research? See CIFHS #6.

BEADLE, BEDEL, BEATLE, BEDDLE, BEDELL, BEEDLE, BETELL, etc. These may not one name spelled in various ways, but several surnames of different origins. BEDEL and BEADLE were definitely in the C.I. in the 1700s. At least three seem to have a Jersey connection, but some may have been Hug., settling in the C.I. and also in England.

BEADLE, Samuel, may have come from J or France to Charlestown, MA, where he mar Susannah ___, who d 1661. Samuel d ca 1664/65, age 41, 4 chn. Most of his fam and desc are recorded in the SAMUEL BEADLE FAMILY, by Walter J. Beadle, 1970, available at NEHGS, Boston, a fine comprehensive book. According to Mr. Beadle, much research has been done on the origin of this fam, but has not resulted in a definite record of the fam in Jersey. See book.

BEADLE, John, b Salem, master mariner, mar Mercy ENGLISH in Salem. A message sent from Jersey in 1743 from a Mary LISTRIL, prob LISBEREL, to her husband, Thomas, mentioned in the postscript, "John Beadle, your mother and grandmother, sisters and brothers, desire to be remembered to you." (Konig)

BEADLE, Jonathan, wrote a letter from the Island of Jersey to someone in MA, 1700s.

BEADLE, John, res VA in the 1700s. OUTC. (Terrill Curtis, Hixon, TN)

BEDLE, Daniel, b J, mar 1797 in Natchitoches Parish, LA. (Marriage

Contracts of Natch., 1739-1803, by Edwin Adams David, 1961, pp. 91-92)
BEDEL, Elizabeth, spelled another time, BEDALL, mar John NEWELL 1745, Boston.
BEDEL, Hannah, mar John Spencer, 1730, Boston.
BEDEL, Philip, bp 1691, Salem, MA. OUTC.
BEDEL, Col., had NH Reg't in Rev. War. OUTC.
BEDEL, Sarah, mar William Bomar, 1740, Boston.
BEDEL, Thomas, mar Elizabeth ___, res MA.
A1. Thomas, b 1717 A2. Elizabeth, b 1720 A3. John, b 1723
BEDEL, Samuel, had son, Nathaniel, bp 1669, Salem, MA.
BEDEL, Thomas, mar Elizabeth Ellinwood, 1724, Boston.
BEDEL, Thomas, of Boston, mar Sarah Miller of Charlestown, 1730, Boston.
BEDELL, William, b ca 1814, NY state, also spelled BEEDLE in 1840 Census. Work in progress on this fam. (Larry Murdoch, Lafayette, IN)
More data in Essex Coll., V8; ELLSWORTH FAMILIES, by Don Tredwell, 1904; Boston, Salem and Charlestown VRs; Noyes, Hoyt's SALISBURY, etc.
BEAN, Robert, mar Mary CABOT, 1792, Boston. See CABOT.
BEAN, Remember, mar 1823, George LE MASTER in MRB. See MASTER, LE MASTER.
BEARD. Does this ever equal BIARD?, qv. John HEARL mar Mary BEARD, 1711, in Kittery, ME. (OLD KITTERY AND HER FAMILIES)
BEASFORD, Joshua F., age 24, of Louth, ONT, b Jersey, son of Joshua Beasford and Maria, his wife, mar 1864 in Hamilton, ONT, Henrietta A. Myers, age 16, of Louth, b Canada, dau of Garrett and Calia Myers. Robert A. and Mary J. Fegan of Hamilton were witnesses. (Wentworth Co., Marriage Register; Wm. Britnell, Mississauga, ONT)
BEAUCAMP. In J 1550, also in G. In Trinity, J 1736.
BEAUCHAMP. Is a surname of England, France and Jersey. An Edmund came from England to Maryland before 1666. An Edward and Mary were in Ipswich, MA by 1642. The son, John, of Isaac and Elizabeth was b in Boston 1727. The son, Peter, of John and Margaret, was b 1702, Boston. None of these are verified as from C.I. fams, but may have been.
BEAUCHAMP. Noted in Chelmsford, MA. Note QUARRY FAMILIES, in N. Chelmsford, MA.
BEAUCHEMIN. C.I. name found in Western Canada. Curr in Holyoke, MA. OUTC.
BEAUDIN. In Boston, 1975, OUTC. BEAUDIN in C.I. and curr Venice, CAL and Somerville, MA.
BEAUGIE. This name in J from 1536 spelled various ways: BEAUGY, BEAUGER, BEAUGIE. Compiler believes that some of the BODGE, BOGEE, etc., fams in early New England were quite possibly BEAUGIE from J. Curr research? See CIFHS #6.
BEAUMONT. In London, ONT, thought to be from Jersey.
BECQUET. In G 1500s, man who lives by a brook. BECQUET in J by 1309, in St. Clement and St. Brelade, J 1668, and as BECQUET?, PASQUET in St. Martin, J 1749.
BECKET. CAUTION! Francis Becket said to be b in France, settled in NY by 1834.
BECKET. This surname in early Salem, MA, may be from the C.I. OUTC. See intermar with C.I. fams and Hug fams. BECKET in Turk file from various sources. (NY ALIENS, by Scott and Conway; PEABODY GEN; BEADLE FAM; SWASEY FAM; Essex Coll., vols. 2,3,7; Salem records and Salem Cem. records)
BECKET, John Jr., mar Rebeckah BEADLE, 1738, Boston. Prob much more on these fams.
BECKET, Mary of Salem, and Joseph BROWN, res Salem, MA.
A1. Mary BROWN, mar 1831, ___ LE FAVOR (Essex Ant., vol. 13)

BECKET, Susanna, dau of San and Susannah (Fowler) Becket, mar Thomas RHUEE, prob b LE RUEZ, of J, qv. She d 1805, age 58, 3 daus and 2 sons. (Essex Coll.)

BEDEL, BEDLE. See BEADLE.

BEEDE. Not a C.I. name listed by Stevens, prob Hug? or English.

BEEDE, Eli, b 1699 J, of French and English desc, said to be Hug, rem to New England either as stowaway or cabin boy? ca age 14 to 16, spoke Jersey tongue. Eli rem to Boston, then to Hampton, NH, where he was apprenticed to a farmer. In 1720 settled Kingston, now E. Kingston, NH, and mar Mehitable Sleeper. Chn b Kingston. He was bur there June 1, 1789. Much more data, see sources and fam chart in WRCIC. (Hurd; Ruth Wood, Glastonbury, CT; Louise Brooks, Starkville, MI; Beatrice Young, New Harbor, ME; Fred Beede, Youngstown, OH; Film, THE BEEDE FAM, SLC #015498 (not seen by compiler); Merrill Beede, Alexandria, VA; Marion Rose, So. Boston, MA; Mrs. Giles Fenn, Brattleboro, VT; SAMUEL BEEDE AND HIS DESC, by Betty Bonawitz; Mrs. Don Gilham, Keyport, WA) BEEDE fam hist to be publ 1983 by Sandwich, NH Hist Soc. ((Data also from Mrs. Stuart Anson, Berlin, CT)

A1. Hezekiah, mar 1747, Hephsibah SMITH, qv, who d 1772, res Brentwood, now Fremont, NH. Hezekiah mar 2. 1772, Judith Gove. Many descendants.

A2. Judge Daniel, b 1729, mar 1750, Patience Prescott, and 2. in 1795, Dorothy Ethridge. Daniel held many public offices, and was Judge of the County Court. See HIST OF CARROLL CO., NH. Seven of his 12 chn b Brentwood, NH. Many descendants.

A3. Thomas, b 1732, d 1806, mar Elizabeth URANN/VERRINE?, but not EWING, as given in some records. Res Brentwood, NH, rem to Gilmanton, NH, 10 chn, many descendants.

A4. Jonathan, 1734-1825, mar 1. 1757, Anna Sleeper and 2. 1786, Susanna Hoag, 10 chn by Anna.

A5. Elizabeth, mar 1754, John HUNTOON, qv, 10 chn. See HUNTOON.

A6. Johannah, mar A. Davis, son of Samuel Davis?

"We have a great deal of information on the many descendants of Daniel Beede in our pamphlets." (Sandwich, NH Hist. Soc.)

BEHAN, BEHAM, BIHAN, etc. BEHAN in J 1593. BEEHAN, BIHAN in Nfld., poss from J? OUTC.

BELASH. See BAILHACHE.

BELFORD. Surname of Grt. Britain and C.I., and other places. BELFORE, some research curr, see CIFHS #3.

BELFORD, Charlotte LE SUEUR, bp 1808, St. Saviour, J, dau of Jean Belford, oarsman, HMS BRAVO, and Francoise VARDON, qv, of St. Martin, J, mar 1835 St. John's CH, Peterborough, ONT, Canada, William Hasken MARTIN, b 1812, carpenter. He d 1861, drowned at Burleigh, ONT? Charlotte was the fourth of 13 chn. (Dorothy L. Martin, Willodale ONT)

A1. John William Martin, b 1837, Peterborough, ONT

A2. Thomas Belford Martin, b 1838, mar Letitia ___

A3. William James Martin, b 1840, mar 1863, Eliza Steel Jeffrey, and d 1911, Peterborough, ONT

A4. Elizabeth Sarah Le Sueur Martin, b 1842

A5. Mary Ann Martin, b 1843, mar Aaron Comstock, d 1919 Ashbournham, near Peterboro, ONT

A6. Caroline Martin, b 1844, mar William ENGLISH

A7. Susan Martin, b 1846

A8. Richard B. Martin, b 1848, Peterborough, mar Louisa ___, and d 1893

BELIN. Occasionally a surname of the C.I. Curr research? See CIFHS #10. This name may possibly have been changed at times to BLINN, name noted in OH. BLINN, BLAIN, may also be German and/or Dutch. Some research on a CT BLIN, by Jane BLINN, Sun City, AZ.

BELL. May be at times derived from LE BELL, LE BEL of J. LE BEL, LE BELL, LE BER noted in St. Martin and Trinity, J 1607. BELL curr G & J.

BELL. "Old Guernsey surname of LA CLOCHE, often changed to BELL." (Carey-Wimbush)

BELLOT. Ship builders of Jersey, 1800s. (Jean)

BENEST, pron. BENNET, in J since 1299. In Trinity, and St. Laurens, J 1668, and in St. Brelade, St. Laurens, St. Mary, Trinity and St. Peter, J 1749. Those below are not all verified as from J, but it is likely that some were.

BENNET, Amos, poss AMICE BENEST? of J?, mar Elizabeth ___, res MRB. OUTC.
A1. Philip, bp 1787 A2. Elizabeth, bp 1790

BENEST, Benjamin, in St. Heliers, J 1832.

BENEST, C.J. and Alfred are being researched. See CIFHS #3.

BENET, David, res Salem, MA, with wife Rebecca? OUTC?
A1. David, b 1678 Salem A2. Sarah, b 1681 Salem A3. William b 1687

BENNET, Elias, mar Sarah BARNARD, 1722, Boston. OUTC.

BENEST, Francis G., son of Francis and Clara (QUEREE) BENEST, b J, rem to North Chelmsford, MA late 1800s, but returned to J. See QUARRY FAMS. (Bessie Le Mesurier, N. Chelmsford, MA) There was a BENEST in Cambridge, MA recently.
A1. Clarence, b 1884 J, rem to N. Chelmsford, mar Alice BRAKE of J, a dau, Bessie

BENNET, Philip and Thomas, members of Christ Church, Boston 1745, where a number of other C. Islanders were members. (NEHGS, vol. 58) OUTC.

BENNET, Philip, mar Elizabeth MAJOR, 1730, Boston. OUTC.

BENEST, Philip of J, res Boston 1776, and rem to Nova Scotia. His sister, Sarah, of J, mar Wm. Shirref, Deputy Quartermaster, Boston, 1776. BENEST letters to J are in the Canadian Archives, MG23, B 50.

BENNET, Rachel of Manchester, MA, mar there Edward RENOUF, qv, 1772, both prob from J.

BENNET, Stephen, mar Jane CORNEY, qv, Portsmouth, NH 1766. (NEHGS, vol. 82) OUTC.

BENNET, William, from J?, mar Susannah BRIGHT 1676, served in King Philip's War. (HIST OF STONINGTON, CT)

BENEST. Curr El Monte, CAL and Cambridge, MA.

BENFIELD. Of Alderney Island. See MACKEY.

BERNARD. In J from 1309 to 1749. Poss some from J to early New England? Name also in G.

BERRY. Hug surname in J, old in G, curr J and G. Many in GCO early 1800s, OUTC. Res Wills Twp., Liberty and Combridge Twps., GCO. (Records in Cambridge, OH Library)

BERTEAUX. See Q.A. IN CANADA, by Turk.

BERTELOT. In St. Peter, J, 1668.

BERTOLET. Do any of the early BARTOLS, BARTHOLETS, etc., in MA derive from BERTOLET of J? This surname said to have changed to BARCLAY in one case. (LE QUESNE IN NOVA SCOTIA) Curr research? See CIFHS #5.

BERTRAM. In J 1481 as BARTRAM. BERTRAM in St. Martin and St. Saviour, J 1668. In St. Martin and Grouville, J 1749. Shield: Or, an orle azure.

BERTRAM. See also BARTRAM and NOTABLES. CAUTION! TRIAL CHARTS.

BERTRAM, John, bJ, bp 1773, son of Thomas BERTRAM and Jeanne LE GROS. He mar Mary PERCHARD, qv. She had two bros. and sister, and John had one bro. In 1807, John, Mary and their six chn rem from J to Baltimore, MD on the ship ALERT. The fam rem from Baltimore to Salem, MA, where John had a store. He d 1825, age 53. Mary d 1842, age 70.

(BIO. DICT. OF JERSEY, by Balleine; Putnam; Paine; Essex Coll., vol. 2; John de Laitre, Santa Barbara, CAL)

A1. John, b 1796 St. Saviour, J, rem to U.S. 1807 with fam. See NOTABLES for more on John. He mar 1. Mary Smith, who d 1837, and 2. Clarissa (McIntyre) Millet, and in 1848, 3. Mary Ann Ropes, who survived him. He d 1882.

B1. John Henry, d 1832, age 1

B2. Ellen Augusta, d 1828, age 8, dau of Clarissa

B3. Jeannie, Mary Jane, b ca 1835, mar George R. Emmerton. She d 1888, age 53.

C1. Caroline Osgood Emmerton, b 1866

C2. Annie Bertram Emmerton, b 1868

B4. Clara, b Salem, mar David P. Kimball, res Boston, desc?

B5. Annie, b Salem, mar William G. Webb, desc?

A2. Philip, b 1797, last heard of in Cuba, 1816

A3. Mary Ann, b 1799, mar John Ashley, 1822, Boston, and d 1873

B1. Jane Bertram Ashley, bp 1833 B4. John Ashley, bp 1833

B2. Charles Henry Ashley, bp 1833 B5. Mary Ann Ashley, bp 1833

B3. Augusta Ashley, bp 1833

A4. George, b 1801, lost at sea ab 1816

A5. Elizabeth, b 1804, J, mar Elisha Sparhawk, 1823, Boston, issue?

A6. Jane, b 1807, J, mar John Lambert 1831, Boston, and d 1837

B1. John Henry Lambert, bp 1833

A7. Peter, b 1809, drowned 1813

BERTRAM, Amice, b ca 1825, J, in 1849 a laborer in Canada?, and in 1872 a merchant. Mar Elizabeth LE NEVEU of J, b ca 1825, grandau of Mlle. de Montbrun, dau of Marquis de M. (Noreen Annett, Victoria, BC) See also, SIMON. Other chn?

A1. Louisa BERTRAM, b 1849 Grouville, J, d 1926, New Westminster, BC. She mar 1872, George SIMON, 5th son of Charles SIMON of St. Brelade, J. George d 1938, Victoria, BC.

B1. Lewis Reginald SIMON, b 1878 St. Heliers, J, mar 1913, Ida Eliza SIMON in Victoria, BC, where he d 1964.

BERTRAM, George, b 1819 J, mar 1843, Maria Larrabee in MA. He was master mariner and Mason.

BERTRAM. Numerous in Boston, 1970s, but OUTC.

BERTRAND, Clarissa, in Scioto Co., OH, 1860 Census. OUTC. BERTRAND curr G and J, old in G.

BESOM, BESSOM. See BISSON.

BEST. English, but curr in G. Curr research? See CIFHS #4.

BEST, ___, mar Elizabeth Ann RABEY, qv, from G 1904 to NYCITY, had 2 daus and a son. See RABEY. (Mrs. Buttle, Columbus, OH)

BEST, Susan Elizabeth, b G?, mar Thomas John TOUZEL, qv. See desc in Q.A. IN CANADA, by Turk. Desc in Canada and U.S. (Joyce Buckland, No. Highlands, CAL)

BETTES. See BATTIS. BIARD, see CH.IS. COLLECTION

BIARD. An old G surname, a place name from Cotentin Pen. in Normandy, France. See also BYARD. Curr research? See CIFHS #12.

BIBBER. Prob VIBERT, qv, James b 1706 J, d 1773 Harpswell, ME. Rem to Dover, NH 1724/25 to learn weaving from Elizabeth Hansen? She was taken by Indians, so he went back to Jersey and returned to Dover 1728. Mar Abigail DREW, dau of John and Rebecca (Cook) Drew, settled in ME. She d 1783. (Ann Alexander, Brunswick, ME; Sinnet; Emery) Poss other chn?

A1. Abigail BIBBER, b 1727, d 1813, mar 1752, Jacob Johnson of Bailey Island, ME, b 1715, d 1803

B1. Jonathan Johnson, b 1754, mar Miriam Booker, b 1755

C1. Capt. Jonathan Johnson, b 1780, d 1854, mar 1803, Abigail Allen, res Bailey Island, ME
D1. Capt. Elisha Johnson, b 1817, d 1901, mar 1839, Almira Sprague, b 1816, d 1891
E1. Elisha C. Johnson, b 1847 of Bailey Island, ME. See D1., under James.
A2. Hannah, b ca 1731, mar Daniel Johnson, 1751
A3. Sarah, b ca 1735, mar Courtney Babbidge, 1755
A4. Rebecca, b ca 1738, mar Wm. Babbidge in 1758
A5. Susanna, b ca 1740, mar Ezra Curtis, 1768
A6. Lemuel, b ca 1750, mar Ruth Bailey, 1773
A7. Anna, b 1754
A8. James, b 1757, d 1843, mar Joanna Bailey, 1777
B1. Bailey, of Harpswell, ME, mar 1805, Dorothy Pote
C1. William Pote, b 1814, d 1873, mar 3? 1856, Mary O. Preble
D1. Gustina O., b 1858, d 1911, mar Elisha C. Johnson, b 1847, of Bailey Island, ME
E1. Florence M.E. Johnson, b 1889, of Bailey Island, mar Herbert W. Doughty, b 1887
F1. Elray R. Doughty, b 1921, mar 1941, Jean A. Allen, b 1923
G1. Ann E. Doughty, b 1944, mar 1963, Bernard W. Alexander, b 1944
H1. Mary A. Alexander, b 1970 H2. Sarah L. Alexander, b 1973
A9. Elizabeth, b ca 1758?, mar ca 1777, Jacob Curtis

BICHARD, BISHARD, etc. In J 1300s, also in G early. Curr G and J. Common in G. BICHARD in Vale, G 1821. (CIFHS #14)

BICHARD, James, b ca 1770 G, son of James and Esther (GALLIENNE) BICHARD, mar Rachel SARCHET, qv, rem to Guernsey Co., OH 1807, 9 chn? (SARCHET; Cambridge Library records; 1850 Census; Conner-Eynon Cem. records; Beverly Shephard, Cambridge, OH; Wolfe; Mrs. D.R. Dunkler, Topeka, KS; Thomas G. Bishard, Parsons, KS) See LATE ADDITIONS.
A1. Daniel, b ca 1798 G, naturalized 1824 GCO, d 1872. Mar 1819, Mary FERBRACHE, 1802-1879
B1. Daniel, b ca 1820, mar 1841, Sarah Ann MAFFETT, MOFFETT?, b ca 1824
C1. Louisa, b ca 1843, mar William McFadden
C2. Levi, b ca 1847, mar 1. Sarah J. ___, 2. ?Amanda ___, b OH, and 3. ?Bethelda ___?
D1. Cyrus, b ca 1878, d before 1925, mar Mary ___, a dau, Gladys, b 1905
D2. Stephen, b ca 1886, mar May Alice ___, son, Levi, b ca 1907
D3. Cassie, b ca 1887
C3. Thomas, b ca 1849, res KS 1875 with wife, Francis Clevenger, b ca 1851 IL, dau of Lourenzo Dow Clevenger and Eleanor McClintock. He mar 2. 1898, Jessie Connor, b ca 1858. Thomas d before 1925.
D1. Merton, b ca 1870, mar Maggie ___, had at least Willie, b 1894
D2. Theodore, b 1871, mar Augusta ___, and d 1903 in train wreck
E1. Lena, b ca 1900 E2. Lloyd, b ca 1902, d 1905
D3. Richart T., b 1873, mar Jessie N., b ca 1876, related to Braden fam.
E1. Mary L., b ca 1906 E2. Ralph W., b ca 1913
D4. Dudley, b 1878, mar Wilda ___, b ca 1886
E1. Howard, b ca 1901, mar LaDine ___
F1. Jack Dudley, b ca 1917
E2. Ray, b ca 1903
E3. Glenn, b ca 1908 Bourbon Co., KS, son Thomas

D5. Lulu, b 1881, d ca 1897
D6. ?
D7. Herschel, b 1890, mar Minnie ___
C4. Josephine, b ca 1851, mar ___ Montgomery
C5. Martha, b ca 1854, mar ___ Bish
C6. John, b ca 1856
C7. James, b ca 1859, twin, mar Ida ___, b ca 1866, 5 chn
D1. Iva, b ca 1887
D2. Alice, b ca 1889
D3. Elsie, b ca 1890
D4. Lee H., b 1892
D5. Myrtle, b ca 1897
C8. Charles, b ca 1859, twin
C9. Elizabeth, b ca 1862
C10. Rosette, b ca 1866, mar ___ Cline
B2. Mary Ann, mar Thomas MARSH, 7 chn. A Mary Ann mar Abraham Marsh in GCO 1847
C1. Dillon Marsh
C2. Thomas, mar Alice Wallace
C3. Sumner C., mar twice
C4. Grant Marsh, mar sev times
C5. Amanda, mar ___ Morrow
C6. Margaret, mar Harry SARCHET, qv
C7. Sarah, mar Joseph White SARCHET
B3. Thomas T., b ca 1827, GCO, mar Margaret SARCHET, 1851, GCO
C1. David, d unmar 1904
C2. Daniel, d unmar 1915
C3. Elizabeth Locille, b 1860, mar Charles A. Tanner 1887 (See Tanner Gen, GCO)
D1. Wellington Lee Tanner, b 1889
D2. Mignon Tanner, b 1891
D3. Carola Tanner, d.y.
D4. Kathryn Tanner, b 1894
D5. Hazel Tanner, b 1897
D6. Florence Tanner, d.y.
D7. Ruth Tanner, b 1903
C4. Emma, d age 16
B5. Rachel, b ca 1833, GCO
B6. Eliza, b ca 1845 GCO, mar 1864, John S. Boyd, 6 chn: Joe D., William H., Mary, Margaret, Amanda and Ella Boyd
B7. Henry, b ca 1848 GCO, mar Rachel A. Dessin, Dosson?, 1867
C1. James
C2. Minnie, mar ?Charles Olden
C3. Ella, mar ?David R. McCourt
C4. Alta
C5. Ollie
A2. James?, b ca 1800 G, mar 1821, Martha LE PAGE, qv
B1. Thomas, b ca 1823, mar Mary Ann BUZARD, BUZZARD, 1848
B2. Daniel, b ca 1829, mar Jane BURT, qv, d 1912
B3. Nancy, b GCO, mar Hamilton Bell, 1860s?, 6 chn: Callie, Mattie, Charles, Mary, Annie and Edward Bell
B4. Caroline, b GCO, mar Nathaniel Tolbert, 1858
B5. Peter S., b 1839 GCO, mar 1865, Catherine Gill. A Peter served in the 78th OH, Civil War. (Wolfe)
B6. Martha, b ca 1840 GCO
B7. Charles J., b ca 1843, mar 1868 GCO, Eliza Jane ROBINS, qv, 1845-1901. A Charles served in the Civil War. (Wolfe)
C1. James William, mar Elizabeth Fletcher, a son
C2. Ulysses Grant, called Grant, mar Alma Wagstaff, a son, Elmer, other chn?
C3. Homer L., mar Carrie ___, poss 2 daus, Jennie and Louise?
C4. Annabelle, b 1877?, d 1938 Jackson Twp., mar Wm. H. Wagstaff,
D1. Wayne Wagstaff, worked for PENN RR, ret to FL 1970, widow, Lola Eager
E1. Arlene Cotton, 3 daus
D2. Clyde Wagstaff, mar Peggy Craft, d Pasadena, CAL, 1969, no issue
D3. Ralph Wagstaff, mar Thelma Britlinger, worked 40 years for Ohio Fuel Gas Co., d Naples, FL, 1975
D4. Russel Wagstaff, mar Alma Spencer, ret to Ft. Lauderdale, FL,

a son, 2 daus

D5. Harold Wagstaff, mar Vivian Schwartz. He a glass cutter, d 1975, 9 grandchn

E1. Edwin Wagstaff E2. Richard Wagstaff E3. Emily Riley

D6. Robert W. Wagstaff

D7. Forest Wagstaff, mar Mary C. WALTERS, qv, res CAL, 2 chn, 6 grandchn

D8. Richard Wagstaff D9. Clifford Wagstaff

C5. Maude, mar Joseph Shackles, 3 chn. Eliza Maud b 1880,d 1938

D1. Audree Shackles D2. Jennie Shackles D3. Herman Shackles

C6. John A. C7. Charles, Jr.

C8. Minnie, mar James Oliver Clark of Coshocton. Minnie 1889-1979

D1. Ruth Clark D2. Robert Clark

A3. Rachel, b ca 1803 G, mar 1821 GCO, Peter LANGLOIS, LANGLEY

A4. Nicholas, b ca 1804?, mar 1826, Eliza/Elizabeth/Betsey BURT, qv

A5. Martha, b 1805 G, mar 1826 GCO, Moses SARCHET, d 1887 GCO

A6. John, b 1812 GCO, mar 1833 Charlotte Chambers of Chambersburg, PA fam

A7. Judith?, b ca 1810 GCO?, mar 1852, Robert Chambers

A8. Ann/Nancy, b ca 1815 GCO, mar 1839, Charles J. Albright/Albrecht

A9. Peter, b G or GCO?

BICHARD, Anne/Nancy, b 1766 G, dau of James B. and Esther GALLIENNE, sister of James above, mar 1789 in G, Thomas SARCHET, qv. She d 1849 GCO. Several of their chn came to GCO in 1806: Thomas, David, Peter D., Moses, Nancy and Rachel.

BICHARD, Martha. One Martha, according to the SARCHET GEN, mar Moses SARCHET. She was the dau of James BICHARD and Rachel DE LA RUE, qv, who settled in GCO 1807.

BICHARD, Martha. This Martha was b 1826 GCO and d there 1890, parents uncertain.

BICHARD, ___, said to be a Wells Fargo man from G. "Our family has in their possession one of his Colt pistols, half of a matched pair, silverplated, with ivory handle, with an inscription from Wells Fargo on a silver plaque on the handle," said to be used by Bichard. (David Ozanne, Toronto, ONT and Trondheim, Norway)

BICHARD, BISHER, John, from G, age 14, rem to Berryville, WISC, mid 1800s, poss relative of Alex. BURCH, qv. (Ozanne)

BICHARD, Clarence and James, served in WWI from GCO.

BICHARD, Daniel F., b ca 1827 (Cem. Stone), d 1910. Mar 1846-1850, Mary OGIER, 8 chn. (GCO BOOK, by Ohio Gen. Soc., 1979, GCO Library) This Daniel prob related to other BICHARDs of GCO.

A1. Thomas Henry, b ca ___, mar Margaret Stiles in GCO.

B1. Harry/Henry?, had at least 5 chn: Ralph, Ward, Thomas, Homer and Mildred, who mar ___ REED, and had sons

A2. David Newton, b ___, mar Clara A. Davis

BICHARD, Daniel, b 1798 G, mar Mary Ferbrache, b ca 1802 G. This is another Daniel Ferbrache fam, and compiler is not sure about these two fams. CAUTION: TRIAL CHART.

A1. Thomas, b ca 1832 A3. Eliza, b ca 1845

A2. Rachel, b ca 1833 A4. Henry, b ca 1848

BICHARD. By 1860, there were many other BISHER, BIRCHARD, BISHARD fams in counties of OH, such as GAllia, Greene and Guernsey. Some records in WRCIC.

BIDDLE, John, b Devon, England, age 31, rem from Isle of Guernsey, a butcher, with his wife, Mary, b Dorset, England, age 27, and dau, Mary Ann, age 5, b G, to New York 1821. (NY NATURALIZATIONS, by Scott) Note that this man is also listed in the book with the name BRIDLE,

same fam. BRIDEAU of the C.I. is sometimes mistakenly BRIDLE.
BILL. Noted in America. OUTC, but BIHEL, and BILLIE in J, 1528.
BILLOT, in J from 1309, in St. Lawrence, J 1788, from Lisiere, France originally. Curr research, see CIFHS #4,7,9. Cf. BELLOT.
BINET, in St. Lawrence, J 1788, in Grouville and Trinity, J 1688. Curr J. Ship builder in J.
BINET, Jean/John, b J, son of Hugh BINET, was indentured to Philip ENGLISH, qv, ca 1675 in Salem, MA. Indenture is in records of NEHGS, Boston, MA.
BINGHAM, Thomas, arrived in Boston 1769 on ship MOLLY from J, a servant. (Whitmore) This is not a C.I. surname, but prob from England. A John and Sylvia are also noted in early Boston records, OUTC.
BIRD, Frank Harold, b 1875 G, d age 52, res St. Sampson, G, mar Emma Louise TROUTEAUD, qv, dau of Eugene E. and Emma Eliza (Hancock) Trouteaud. The Bird Bros. Coal Co., G, was a fam business. (Wilfrid and Brenda Burgess, Jamestown, RI)

A1. Frank Cyril, b 1898 G, to U.S. ca 1914, but returned to serve in WWI. Res with Henry and Lene TROUTEAUD of Detroit. Mar in G, 1. Charlotte NOYON, of Vale, G, 2 daus, mar 2. Florence MARTEL of G, where Frank d 1960.

B1. Margaret Bird, widow of L. BLAMPIED, in G

B2. Carol Bird, mar H. Turner, res England

A2. Leslie Eugene, b 1901, d ca 1928 G, mar Edith MAUGER of Castel, G, no issue

A3. Stanley William, b 1903 G, rem to Detroit, MI, mar Elizabeth Maki of Upper Pen., MI, 2 chn

B1. Frank Harold Bird, b ___, mar Lana ___, res Detroit, MI, 2 chn, Sarah and Paul

B2. Mary, b ____, mar Thomas Tubbs, 3 chn, Laura, Michael and Emily

A4. Brenda Christine, b 1905 G, mar 1935 NYCITY, Wilfrid DE LISLE BURGESS of G, qv, 2 chn. The great-grandfather of Wilfrid was b in Maclesfield, England, John Gibson Burgess, b 1793. He and wife Mary, who d 1830, are bur St. Sampson, G.

B1. Bruce Robert Burgess, b 1937, mar Fredrica Lucinda Dudley 1964, and d 1972 in plane crash. Fredrica mar 2. J. Steven Rice, and res Seattle, WA.

C1. Nathaniel de Lisle Burgess, b 1967

C2. Joshua Lofton Burgess, b 1969

BIRD, Jane M., mar in MRB 1809, Thomas QUINER, qv, OUTC.
BIRD, Walter G., and son Donald from G to Los Angeles, and San Pedro, CA, 1900s.
BIRD. Also a J name occasionally. Joshua PALLOT mar in J, 1712, Mary BIRD, dau of John BIRD, by Marie GAGNEPAIN. (C.W. Bird, Calgary, Alta, Canada)
BIRD. In Boston 1641, OUTC.
BIRD, Nicholas, poss from G?, d after 1856, will date, in Coshocton, OH. BIRD also noted in Muskingum Co., OH.
BISHOP. Old in G. See Q.A. IN CANADA, by Turk. Curr G and J. Ten or 15 of this surname appeared early in the colonies, most of them from Grt. Britain. However, the kidnapped Bishop, Eleazar, and several others were apparently from the C.I. "It will be seen that four brothers came from the Island of Guernsey to Lisbon and vicinity --John, Ebenezer, Daniel and Nathaniel. The first two settled in Lisbon, one in New Haven, CT, and one near New London, CT." (Ira Bishop records) Mr. Bishop, now deceased, spent many years gathering data on desc of this surname in America, and his files are in the South Surburban Gen. and Hist. Soc. Library in South Holland, IL,and

interested readers can consult these records there. The records are mainly of non-Channel Islanders. (BISHOPS FROM ENGLAND!)

BISHOP, BISCHOPPE, Eleazar, b ca 1669 either G or J, said to have been kidnapped and taken to New London, CT ca 1676. Reports on this vary considerably. See sources. Said to have been taken with two other boys, BISSON, qv, and SHARPE, qv. Eleazar was raised by Richard Dart of CT, and mar his dau Sarah. They received several hundred acres of unimproved land at their marriage. Eleazar a wheelwright d 1755 in New London, CT. (Nova Scotia Archives; MS by W.E. Boggs and Burpee R. Bishop at Acadia Univ.; FAMILY SKETCHES IN HIST. OF KINGS CO., Nova Scotia; C. King, Jefferson, OH; Mildred Jamieson, Saint John, New Brunswick; Mrs. B. Lundbert, Glenview, ILL; and much data in South Holland, ILL Library)

A1. Eleazar, b ca 1705, d 1720, age 16. A2. Timothy, 1705-1720

A3. Peter, b 1706, d 1722

A4. John, b 1709, d 1785, mar 1. Rebecca Whipple and 2. Hannah (Allen) Comstock, dau of Samuel and Lydia (Hastings) Allen, widow of Gideon Comstock, who drowned. For part of John's family, see Q.A. IN CANADA. For more info. see WRCIC files. More work has been done on this branch of the fam by Peter Dodge, St. Paul, MINN.

B1. Col. John Jr., b 1729 New London, CT d at Gaspereau, NS 1815, age 85, mar 1. Mary (Forsythe) Avery and 2. in 1808, Mrs. Ruth Harris. At least 4 chn by 1st wife, poss 4 by 2nd wife.

C1. Amelia, b 1754, mar 1. Charles Dickson Jr. of Horton, NS and 2. Joseph McLean

C2. Hannah, b 1756 New London, CT mar 1774 Henry, son of Abel and Jean Burbidge

C3. Charles, b 1758 New London, mar 1. ?, and 2. Philander Fitch, 7 chn.

D1. Charles Jr. mar Ann Edmonds

E1. William, mar Catherine Allan

F1. Phylinda, b 1856, mar Frank Gould Gough, Goff, 2 chn

G1. Carrie Gough, b 1878, d 1950 mar Albert James Robertson, 1872-1956

G2. Alberta Gough, b 1880, d 1969, mar Archie Milburn

C4. John, b 1764, prob mar a dau of Daniel Harris

B2. Capt. William, b 1732 New London, CT, d in Horton, NS 1815, age =83. Bur Wolfville. In 1757 a Sgt. in Capt. John Latimore's Co. of the 3rd Regt. He was called out for the relief of Fort William Henry and served in the Indian Wars. In 1781 he was one of a party who under Lt. Belcher, rescued a schooner laden with provisions from Minas Basin for St. John, Nfld. that had been captured by an American privateer in the Minas Basin. After a sharp fight off Cape Split, the privateer was driven off. Capt. Bishop mar 1761 Jemima Calkin, res Greenwich, Nova Scotia.

C1. William, b 1762 mar 1788 Hannah, dau of Ezekiel and Phebe (de Wolf) Comstock, b 1771 d 1854.. Wm. d 1837

C2. Samuel Henry, b 1767 Halifax, mar 1. 1798 Anna Jacobs of Halifax and 2. 1804 Bathsheba, dau of Simon Fitch and d in Wolfville, NS 1829.

C3. Rachel, b 1763 mar 1785 Frederick, son of Ebenezer Fitch of Canaan, and his wife Lydia (Fish) Fitch. Frederick mar 2. 1810, Mary Parker, & 3. ?. Res Canaan, Horton, NS. Chn by 1st wife:

D1. Lydia Fitch, b 1787
D2. Samuel Fitch, b 1789
D3. Desire? Fitch, b 1792
D4. William Fitch, b 1794
D5. Aaron Fitch, b 1796
D6. Irene Fitch, b 1799
D7. Jemima A. Fitch, b 1801
D8. Edward Fitch, b 1803

D9. Rachel Fitch, b 1808
C4. Lucy, b 1765
C5. Eleanor, b 1770, mar 1797 Rev. Obadiah Newcomb and d 1849
C6. Joshua, b 1773 mar ___Williamson and d 1848
C7. Jemima, b 1774 mar 1794 William Best who d 1827, she in 1832
C8. Elisha, b 1777, mar 1816 Elizabeth, dau of Phineas and Abigail (Thayer) Lovett, and d Round Hill, Annapolis Co., NS 1864
C9. Hannah, b 1780, mar Enoch Forsyth, b 1774, son of Jason and Mary (Anderson) Forsyth.
C10. Sarah, b 1782, mar 1. Daniel, son of John Chipman and 2. Deacon Silas Morse of Granville, Annapolis Co., NS, son of Abner and Anna Church Morse. Sarah d 1826

BISHOP. See page 160 in Q.A. IN CANADA, by Turk. (Additional data by Peter L. Dodge, St. Paul, MINN)
B3. Peter, called Deacon Peter, b 1735 New London, CT, d Horton, NS 1826, res New Minas, NS, bur Wolfville, NS, mar 1. ___GODFREY and 2. Phebe Hamilton, dau of Jonathan & Eliz. (Strickland) Hamilton, b 1747?, 4 chn by 1st wife and 12 by 2nd wife.
C1. Simon, unmar?, conscripted 1775. C3. Lemuel
C2. Elizabeth, mar Noah Fuller 1777, 9 chn
C4. William, b 1759, mar Elizabeth Copp 1780? rem to large farm in Annapolis Co., NS 1785
D1. Elizabeth, b 1782 mar 1802 Major Chipman, d 1855
D2. Daniel, b 1783 mar Lucy Stevens
D3. Samuel, b 1788, mar Elizabeth Hutchinson
D4. William Jr., b 1790 mar Rebecca A. Morse
D5. Sherman, b 1792, unmar
D6. George, b 1794, mar Diadama LONGLEY 1817. She was b 1799, d 1868, dau of Isaac LONGLEY and Dorcas Bent. Diadama was sister of Israel Longley,(see Mary Ann BISHOP) 11 chn. George d 1873 Nictaux, NS.
E1. Maria Ann, b 1818 d 1871, mar 1836 Samuel R. Fitzrandolph
E2. Mary Eliza b 1821, d unmar 1848, d Nictaux, NS
E3. Samuel Chipman, b 1823, farmer, b Williamston, NS, d 1884, bur Lawrencetown, NS, mar 1848 Mary Robinson, 1827-1903
F1. Charlotte A., b 1849 d 1853
F2. John Henry, b 1858 near Lawrencetown, NS, d 1915. Mar 1882 Mary Florence, dau of Joseph and Charlotte (Marshall) Durling.
G1. Frederick Primrose, b 1883, res Haverhill, MA, & Lynn, MA, mar 1921 Margaret A. Fitzmaurice of Cape Breton, NS
G2. William Brown, b 1887, mar Carrie L. Banks, res Lawrencetown, NS. Carrie b 1892 dau of Beriah Spinney and Mary Isabel (Spinney) Banks, a Mayflower desc. through Bass fam.
* H1. Dorothy May, b 1913 mar Loring Arthur Dodge 1935. She d 1970. He was b 1912, d in car accident 1972, res Lawrencetown, NS.
I1. Peter Loring Dodge, b 1941 mar 1. Claudia Kutzler, no issue, and 2. Cheryl Sidlo, b 1946 in South Dakota.
J1. Susanna Rebecca Dodge, b 1981 Minneapolis, MINN.
F3. Mary Eliza, b 1867, mar 1886 William Fitzrandolph
E4. Susan Melvina, b 1825 d 1856 mar 1852 Asa Tupper Morse
E5. William, b 1828 mar Mary Ann Morse
E6. Lavinia, b 1830, d.y.
E7. Harriet Adelaide, b 1832, mar 1849 Benjamin PRINCE
E8. Dorcas Amelia, b 1834, d 1904, mar James B. Neilly
*H2. Jean Isabel, b 1914 mar Gerald BOUTILIER.

E9. Henrietta, b 1836, mar 1856 Asa Tupper Morse, her bro-in-law
E10. George Ingram, b 1836, twin of Henrietta above, mar 1. Amanda Chipman and 2. Emma FitzRandolph
E11. Lucy Caroline b 1841 d 1897 mar Adoniram Burton Neilly
D7. Elias, b 1797 mar Lovicia LONGLEY
D8. Thomas, b 1799, mar Ann FitzRandolph
D9. Rebecca, b 1803, mar Capt. John Shaffner
D10. Mary Ann, b 1806, mar 1. Israel LONGLEY and 2. Manning Morse
C5. by 2nd wife, Phebe Hamilton, Peter, b 1763, mar Amy Bowles
C6. Amy, mar George Turner
C7. Jonathan, b 1764 mar 1. ___Anderson and 2. ?
C8. John, b 1776 Wolfville, d New Minas, NS 1886, unmar
C9. Hannah, b 1768, mar James Anderson
C10. Eliphal, called Fally, b 1770, mar John Coldwell
C11. Phebe, b 1773, d 1818, mar 1. Thomas Reid & 2. David Coldwell
C12. Jeremiah, b 1775, mar Keziah Coldwell
C13. John, b 1776 Wolfville, NS, d New Minas, NS 1886, poss b 1766?
C14. Eleasar, b 1777, mar Hannah Curry
C15. Esther, b 1779, d 1840 mar John Newcomb, 8 chn
C16. James, b 1786, mar Lydia Martin of Gaspereau
C17. Harriet, d 1863 age 74, mar James Turker. See Amy above.
B4. Timothy, b 1740 New London, CT d at Greenwich, NS 1827. He mar 1. 1762, Mercy Harding, dau of Abraham and Mercy (VIBBER, qv) Harding, b 1742, 3 1783, and 2. in 1783 Mrs. Mercy (Gore) Newcomb, widow of Simon Newcomb and dau of Moses and Desire (Burns) Gore, b Preston, CT 1743, d Horton, NS 1817. By 1st wife 10 chn, and 2 by 2nd wife.
C1. Abigail, b 1763 mar Ebenezer Fitch, 9 chn
C2. Silas, b 1764 mar Anna Wells, dau of John and Ann (Bigelow)Wells
D1. Judah Wells, mar Mary Ann Strong
E1. Mary Louisa, mar Elias Bishop
E2. Anna Eliza mar John Cleveland
E3. Rachel mar James Burbidge
E4. Silas mar Frances Ann Morse, dau of Constant C. Morse
E5. Judah Wells
E6. Murilla, mar Rufus Forsyth
E7. Susanna, mar Joseph Reid
E8. Asenath mar James Fullerton
E9. Eunice, mar Comfort Healy
E10. Phoebe , d.y.
D2. Orinda, mar 1. Silas Elderkin and 2. James Burbidge
D3. Ann, mar Elisha Best of Cornwallis, NS
D4. Silas, mar Clara Davidson of Horton, NS, poss mar twice or 3 times. A son Guy.
C3. Rebecca, b 1766, mar Elijah Calkin
C4. Eunice, b 1768, mar James Prentice Harris
C5. Ezra, b 1770, mar Jerusha Newcomb
C6. Amy, b 1772, mar Oliver de Wolf (Jehiel and Phebe)
C7. Timothy, b 1774 mar Eunice Coldwell
C8. Mercy, b 1776, twin, mar Abraham Seaman
C9. Mary, b 1776, twin, mar Newton Wells
C10. Anna, b 1779, mar Samuel Cox
C11. by 2nd mar, Ebenezer, b 1784, d 1846 mar 1809 Anne, dau of Jesse and Chloe (Olney) Lewis of Parrsborough, NS, b 1790, 6chn
D1. Jesse Lewis, b 1812, mar Elizabeth Ann Johnson
D2. Augusta Maria Theresa, b 1815, mar Edward Young, LL.D.
D3. John Leander, M.D. of Phila., PA & Wash., DC, b 1820
D4. Edward Russell, b 1822
D5. Sophia, b 1825
D6. Nancy Desire, b 1828
C12. Olive, b 1789, mar 1821 George ROY of New Minas, formerly of

Edinburgh, Scotland, founder of the Roy fam of Horton, NS,5 chn.
D1. Elizabeth Ann Roy D4. Barbara Maria Roy
D2. Catherine Jane Roy D5. William Alexander Roy
D3. John George Roy
B5. James, to US. This son omitted in Q.A. IN CANADA, by Turk
A5. Samuel, b 1712, bp 1722, d 1804, mar Elizabeth ___, b 1711, d 1796, 7 chn
B1. Samuel, b 1736 B4. DAvid, b 1744 B6. Elizabeth, b 1750
B2. Elijah, b 1738 B5. Clement, b 1748 B7. Phebe, b 1752
B3. Mary, b 1742, mar Elijah Waterhouse
A6. Clement, b 1714, mariner, prob d at sea 1747. He mar Abigail ___ who mar 2. Samuel CLEMENT, qv, of Saybrook, CT.
A7. Sarah, b 1718, mar John Shaw and res NY state at Niagara Falls, lived to age 115.
A8. Mary, b 1720, mar Gilbert Forsythe of Groton, CT 1741. She and her bros. all bp the same day, July 8, 1722. Mary went with her hus= band to Horton, NS where he settled as one of the original grantees of that township. MOre info in Q.A. IN CANADA and in Nova Scotia.
A9. Nicholas, b 1723, mar 1749 Hannah Douglas, dau of Robert and Sarah (Edgecomb) Douglas. She was b Chesterfield, CT. Nicholas res Montville, CT, where he had a large farm. He took a prominent part in the Rev. War, and was 2nd Lt. at CrownPt., 1756. Was Capt. of 12th Comp., 4th Ct. Reg't in 1759, in the war between the French and English. He d New London, CT 1780, 6 chn.
B1. Sarah, b 1750 mar Edward Richards
B2. Ebenezer, b 1751, mar Sally Pierpont and d 1782
B3. Jonathan, b 1754, mar Anne Allen, d 1840.
B4. Joseph, b 1758, mar Desire Gilbert, d 1834
B5. Mary, b 1765 mar D. Congdon B6. John, b 1768 mar MaryKilburn
A10. Eleasar, b 1727, mar 1750 Susannah Whipple, dau of Silas Whipple, b 1731. Eleasar was 2nd Lt. in Comp5. of Capt. John Latimore's 3rd Reg't in 1758. Another record says Eleasar was b 1736 and d 1776. Ten chn.
B1. Susannah, b 1751 mar Comfort Davis B4. Simon, b 1757
B2. Thomas, b 1752 mar Amy Fargo 1758 B5. Rebecca, b 1759
B3. Anne, b 1754 mar Ed.Stebbins B8. Eleasor, b 1766
B6. Hannah, b 1762 mar Daniel Fargo
B7. Lydia, b 1764, mar Jonathan Noble
B9. Mary/Mercy, b 1768 mar Dan Minor
B10. George Dolbeare, b 1770 or 1760. From Ct. to Horton, NS 1760 with uncle, John Bishop and his fam. Res some years in Gasper- eau, where he bought land. Mar 1794 Jane, dau of Henry Burbidge and Hannah (Bishop) Burbidge, a dau of George's cousin Col. John Bishop. Desc of this fam res near Dorchester, NB. A book on this branch was written ca 1918.
A11. Joshua, b 1733, mar Pattie Comstock

BISHOP, Thomas, b London, England, age 44, a farmer, res OH. He brought from Guernsey Island to NYCity, 1821, his wife Elizabeth ___ of Guernsey, age 36, and son Edward Greentree, b Surrey, England, age 2. (NY NATURALIZATIONS, by Scott)

BISSON. Surname of France and the C.I., also found in England. In G and J since at least 1149. Means either BESSON, a twin, or (Latin) bissonus, a fiefless man, or Buisson, living near a thicket. BUISSON is the form used by Jerseymen in the 1300s & later, but still later the spelling appears as BISSON. BISSON in St. Laurens, St. SAviour, St. Peter, Trinity, St. John, St. Heliers, St. Mary, Grouville, St. Clement and St. Martin J 1668. In St. Laurens, St. John, Trinity,

and St. Martin J in 1749. Also seen as LE GROS BISSON. See Privateer section in this book. CAUTION: TRIAL CHARTS.
"The family of Bisson, formerly of Normandy from the most remote period, held lands and houses in the Island of Jersey. In the Archives of St. Lion, Normandy, is found a deed which shows that Geoffrey Du Bisson gave the patronage of St. Martin de Groville to the abbey of St. Trinity de Lessayon, the Vell Calend, Aug. 1149, and states that Sir Yon de Bisson, Knight, with the consent of his son Jean, recognized the right of the monks of St. Trinity de Lessay to the patronage of the aforesaid church." "Geoffrey is apparently the direct ancestor of the Bessoms who came to Marblehead, MA 1749". (Rev. Eddy N. Bisson, Berlin, NH) There are a large number of Bisson who came to America at various times, and prob. not all of them are related.

BISSON, Philip, b 1729 J, godparents at his bapt. being Jean DUMARESQ, qv, and Elizabeth de CARTERET BISSON, Jean's wife. Philip came in 1749 with his bros. He d 1797, age 66, will dated 1791. He mar1751 Sarah BUBIER, qv. He res MRB where he was a shoreman, yeoman, and owned the schooner PEACOCK. Sarah was b 1735, d 1802, dau of Christopher BUBIER and Margaret LE VALLIER, 16 chn. Below is only a small part of the great deal of info. on this fam. A complete fam. chart not found by compiler. (MRB records, MHS; Jersey records; Mrs. James Garrett, Portsmouth, VA; Mrs. E.W. Hayward, Glendale, CAL; Barker Fam. Bible; Perley's Vol 3; Barbara De Veulle,& Marie-Louise Backhurst, St. Heliers, Jersey)

A1. Ruth, bp 1752, mar 1771 William Blaney, living 1791

A2. Margaret, bp 1753, d.y.

A3. Sarah, bp 1754, mar ___Barker before 1791

A4. Margaret again, bp 1756, mar John Grant before 1791

A5. John, bp 1758, rem to NH, where he mar and left descendants. (Mrs. R.W. Swart, Nashua, NH)

A6. Philip Jr., bp 1760, prize master, privateer, owner of and part owner of many vessels. Res MRB from 1792-1820. Sailed mostly between New England and the West Indies. Active in War of 1812. Mar 1. 1779 Ruth Collyer, Collier, and in 1795 Elizabeth/Betsy Lewis, dau of Edmond Lewis and Tabitha Russel. Will dated 1818. Five chn by 1st wife and 11 by 2nd. Served in Rev. War, Capt. Abbot's Comp. of Andover; Capt. Hitchcock's Reg't of Roxbury and Dorchester. When the Britishleft, he was ordered to N.Y. Ruth Collier was dau of Capt. John C. and Ruth Blackler Collier. See Privateer section of this book.

B1. Ruth/Ruthy, b 1781, mar Samuel Stinnes 1797? Sam. b 1779, d 1816 , son of Sam. S. and Mary Card SAVAGE WIDGER, a widow, res Providence, RI. Ruth d 1855

C1. Philip, bp 1802 C2. Ruthy, bp 1805 C4. Eliz. Hill, bp 1813

C3. George Graves, bp 1807 at St. Michael's Episcopal Church

C5. Rebecca, bp 1813, at Second Cong. CH, now Unitarian

B2. Sarah, b 1794 mar Eleazar Graves 1801, son of Ebenezer and Eliz. (Andrews) Graves. Frank W. Graves is a desc.

B3. Elizabeth, b 1786, d 1817, prob mar Capt. John Tucker 1812. See Martha below.

B4. Hannah, b 1789, d 1795

B5. Martha, b 1791, mar 1818 Capt. John Tucker.

B6. by second wife, Elizabeth Lewis, Philip, b 1795, mar 1817 Rebecca Cleaves Smith, dau of James and Sarah(Pedrick) Smith. Sarah's mother was Mary BARTOL.

C1. Sarah E., b 1818, d 1907, mar George Shilleto of Cincinnati, Ohio, who d 1872
C2. Charlotte C. Woodruff, b 1820 MRB, d 1897 Richmond, VA, bur Hollywood Cem. Mar 1838 Dr. Benjamin DENNIS in Hamilton Co., OH, who was b 1816, d on steamer Wyanoke 1883. Said to be b in Richmond, but in will said he was from Bergen Co., NJ. First purchased land in Richmond 1851.
D1. Samuel Clune Dennis
D2. Marietta Jane Dennis, b 1838, d 1914, bur Richmond, VA. Mar Wm. Henry Tyler, b 1837, d 1905, bur Dennis plot in Richmond.
E1. Charlotte Woodruff Tyler, b 1861, d 1926, mar John Marshall Harwood, b 1859 Charles City Co., VA, d 1913 Richmond, VA.
F1. Russell Franklin Harwood F2. Lottie Gay, d.y.
F3. John S. Harwood Jr, b 1886, d 1917 Richmond, VA, mar Sarah/ Sadie Jefferson Wilkins, 1887-1965, dau of Thomas J. Wilkins and wife Eliz. Virginia McCoy.
G1. Saydee Jefferson Harwood, mar 1. Clay Pickett and 2. Robert Cutheriell
G2. Elizabeth Virginia Harwood, mar Lucius N. Wescoat
G3. John Stubblefield Harwood, d.y.
G4. Richard Henry Harwood, b 1916, mar 1936 Nancy Goffigon Wescoat, b 1914, dau of Wm. Henry W. and wife Harriett Spady Nottingham
H1. Nancy Wescoat Harwood, b 1937, mar 1957 James Newton Garrett Jr., in Portsmouth, VA, b 1935, son of James Newton and Ruth Marion (Pope) Garrett
I1. Gregory Rose Garrett, b 1960
I2. Melissa Pope Garrett, b 1963
I3. Amanda Marcella Garrett, b 1968
E2. Marion Gregg Tyler
E3. Arthur Melborn Tyler
E4. Bessie Grove Tyler
E5. Benjamin Maury Tyler
E6. Florence Maury Tyler
D3. Giley Dennis D4. Benj. Dennis D5. Edward Haskins Dennis
C3. Hannah Phillips, b 1822, d 1902, mar Eben. Seacomb of Salem, MA.
B7. Hannah, b 1797, d 1860, mar Capt. Thomas LYON 1820, who d at MRB 1878.
C1. James Lyon, b 1820 mar Jane FREETO, qv, at MRB 1845
C2. Elizabeth Lyon, b 1824, d 1905 Lynn, MA, mar 1846 Edward Trevett BUBIER, qv, 1826-1896
D1. Joanna Atwell Bubier, 1849-1916
D2. Sylvester Herbert Bubier, b 1856
C3. Thomas Lyon, b 1826 mar Sarah A. Smethurst, Lynn, MA
C4. William Lyon, b ca 1829 mar Lucy C. ALLEY, qv, 1854
C5. Hannah Lyon, b 1832 mar Edmund W. Morse, d 1888 Lynn, MA
C6. Edmund Lyon, b 1835 d at sea 1853
B8. Tabitha Lewis, b 1799, mar 1. John C. Cloon 1818, and 2. George W. Roundy 1828, no issue
B9. Miriam Lewis, b 1801 d 1802
B10. Miriam Lewis again, b 1802, mar Eleazer Graves, Jr., a sailmaker, ca 1818
B11. Abigail Lewis, b 1804 mar George Johnson of Norway, ME and d 1898 at Wenham, MA.
B12. Edmund Lewis, b 1815, d at sea, unmar, 1823
B13. John Russel, 1807-1810
B14. William Gray, b 1809 mar Hannah Blaney, b 1803. He d Batavia, Java, 1833.

B15. George Washington, b 1811, d unmar in California.
B16. Betsy Lewis, b 1812, d 1833 age 21
A7. Grace, b 1762 mar 1784 Joseph Nance, and d before 1791, leaving chn
A8. Joseph Browne, b 1764 mar 1786 Rebecca Chinn, who d 1837, age 77.
B1. Philip, bp 1786, mar 1. Sally Ellenwood 1827 and 2. in 1837 Jane Harris
B2. Rebecca, b 1791 mar Gamaliel Smethurst 1813
B3. Joseph, b 1794 mar 1. Annis O. Kelly 1819, who d 1820. Mar 2. Ann P. Russell 1836, who d 1844 age 32
A9. Jane, b 1765 mar 1. Francis FREETO, qv, 1785, and 2. 1802, Robert Pearce
B1. Sarah Freeto, b 1787 mar ca 1819 Capt. Samuel SWETT, qv. See Swett and Freeto.
C1. Sarah Salter Swett, mar 1834 W. H. MESSERVY
D1. Emily W. Messervy, b 1839 mar John E.C. HAMMOND
A10. Mary, b 1767 mar Samuel Chinn 1787
A11. Susanna, b 1769, d 1829 mar 1790 William Strong
A12. Elizabeth b 1771, d.y.
A13. Richard, b 1773, prob d.y. before 1791, date of father's will.
A14. Elizabeth again, b 1774, mar 1. 1792 Paul A. CAUL, CALL?, and 2. Henry P. Call, 1795. Note that a Geo. CAUL, a weaver, arrived from Jersey in Boston 1769 on ship MOLLY.
A15. Hannah, b 1776 mar 1794 Thomas Anderton
A16. William Bubier, b 1779 mar 1802 Anna M. Harris, dau of Robert and Sarah Harris, res Lynn, MA.

There are thousands more desc of the above fam in America. An interesting list of some of the grandchn, great-grandchn and grgrgrandchn about the year 1899, is included in a record named DISTRIBUTION OF AWARD BY CONGRESS, in behalf of the next of kin of Capt. Phillip Bessom, late of Marblehead, MA, who d 1839. Evidently, he was of some service to the American government and was awarded long after his death $23,180, which was divided between 65 descendants, in amounts varying between $26.65 and $639.51. The surnames involved are listed alphabetically below, with the towns where the recipients resided. Please note that while these are all descendants of the Bisson fam in Jersey, there were others not listed. (Nancy Garrett, Portsmouth, VA)

BUBIER, Lynn, MA
CASWELL, Lynn and MRB, MA
COGSWELL, Dayville, CT
COLBY, Lynn, MA
COLLYER, Lynn and Revere, MA
DENNIS, Peabody, Manchester, MA also Clayville, VA & in N.Y.
GRAVES, MRB, Allston and Lynn, MA
GREEN, in RI
HARRIS, Taunton, MA
HASKINS, Richmond, VA
HAYWARY, Middletown, CT.
HEATH, E. Douglas, MA
HOMAN, Albany, NY
HOSKINS, Cawnpore, India
HOWARD, Wilmot, NH
KNIGHT, Boston, MA
LOVEJOY, RI & Thomsonville,CT.
LYON, in Lynn, Stoneham, Ipswich, MA and St. Paul, MINN.
MAXWELL, Lynn, MA
MILLER, Baltimore, MD
PARSONS, Baltimore, MD
PLOOF, Lynn, MA
QUARLES, Richmond, VA
ROSENCRANTZ, Richmond, VA
ROUNDY, Wilcox, AZ
SECCOMB, Boston, MA
SHILLITO, Cincinnati, OH
SHUMWAY, Vassar, MI; Attleboro, MA; Dayville, CT; Evanston, ILL; Plymouth, MA; Danielson, CT
SIMONDS, Lynn, MA
STEVENS, Danielson, CT
STINNESS, RI
STOKES, Dayville, CT
TYLER, Highland Park, Richmond,VA

BISSON, ___, one of the three kidnapped boys brought from J to New London, CT, ca 1669? Name curr G and J. See BISHOP.

BISSON, BESSOM, Richard, bro of Philip above, mar Sarah GALE 1753, res MRB 1753-1798. Richard was a fisherman, coaster, truckman, yeoman. Wife living 1776. Chn bp MRB. (Essex Antiq. Vol 9)

A1. Sarah, bp 1754 MRB
A2. Jane, bp 1756, mar Peter Swains 1778
A3. Mary, bp 1758, d.y.?
A4. Richard, bp 1759, d.y.? A5. John, bp 1761, d.y.
A6. Mary again, bp 1763 mar Joseph Pedrick 1787
A7. John, bp 1765, d.y. A8. Susannah, bp 1768, d.y.
A9. John, bp 1770
A10. Susannah again, bp 1772, mar Philip Ramsdell 1792
A11. Richard, bp 1775, poss mar Hannah BOWDEN, qv, 1796 MRB. Chn:??
B1. Hannah, bp 1796 B3. Michael, bp 17999 B5. John, bp 1803
B2. Richard, bp 1797 B4. Sarah, bp 1801

BISSON, BESSOM, Nicholas, was brought to MA by Joseph BISSON, his uncle in 1766, age 11. He mar 1. Eliz. Lasky 1784. She was his wife in 1805. He mar 2. Hannah ___, res MRB, fisherman, d 1838 (Lizzie Heyward, Glendale, CAL, ca 1930)

A1. Elizabeth, bp 1785 MRB A6. Richard Hawley, bp 1796, d.y.
A2. Nicholas, bp 1788, d.y. A7. Polly, bp 1797
A3. Nicholas again, bp 1792, d.y. A8. James Laskey, bp 1800
A4. Nicholas again, bp 1792 A9. Richard Hawley again, bp 1805
A5. John, bp 1794

BESOME, Joseph, poss the one who brought over nephew Nicholas above in 1766. Mar Rebecca CHINN, 1786

A1. Philip, bp 1786 A2. Rebecca, bp 1791 A3. Joseph, bp 1794

BISSON, BESSOM, John, mar 1793 in MRB Hannah Laskey, res MRB, a coaster and truckman. Quite poss this John was also a member of the above fam of Bissons from J.

A1. Hannah, bp 1795 MRB A7. Jonas, bp 1804
A2. John, bp 1796 A8. Nicholas, bp 1806
A3. Sarah Gale, bp 1797 A9. Elizabeth, bp 1809
A4. Peggy Hawley, bp 1799 A10. Mary, bp 1811
A5. Richard, bp 1800 A11. Philip, bp 1813
A6. James Laskey, bp 1803 A12. Harriot, bp 1815

BISSON, John, res Trinity J, mar Elizabeth FALL, FALLE. He d before 1699, and Eliz. survived him. They lived and d in J. (Essex Antiq., Vols. 7 and 8)

A1. Joshua, Josue, b 1652 Trinity J, to America before 1675, a joiner, res Beverly, MA 1685. Mar 1. Martha BLACK before 1688, who d ca 1704-1710. He mar 2. 1710 Hannah, prob widow of John Sallows. She d 1726 age 63. Josue d 1750 age 98.
B1. Elizabeth, b 1688, mar Anthony Wood (DU BOIS?) of Beverly, a weaver, 1721/22, res Beverly, d 1777, as widow.
B2. Joshua, b 1690, joiner and yeoman, res Beverly, mar Hannah Sallows 1723, d 1777. She was his wife in 1738.
C1. Martha, b 1726, mar Samuel Foster 1758, living 1798
C2. Joshua, b 1728, res Beverly, mar Eunice SYMONS 1763
D1. Ann, 1763-1851 D3. Martha, 1767-1793
D2. Elizabeth, b 1765, mar Peter Glover and d 1794
D4. Eunice, b 1769, mar Peter Glover also, d 1814.
D5. Israel, b 1771, mar Molly West and d 1833
E1. Hannah, b 1801 E2. Joshua E3. Edna, b 1807
E4. Jonathan, bp 1809, poss mar Abigail BAKER?, res Beverly, MA
F1. William Gallop, b 1843

F2. Abba Baker, b 1846 F3. Ella M., b 1848
E5. Elizabeth, bp 1815 E7. Mahala, bp 1821
E6. Henry, bp 1815, but not on same day as Elizabeth
D6. Hannah, b 1774, mar Gideon Woodbury 1793. D7. Joshua?
C3. Jonathan, b 1730/31, d 1797
C4. Israel, b 1732, fisherman or mariner, mar Hannah PRIDE,(was she a PRIDEAUX?)1760, and d 1764. She res Beverly, MA 1795, 1 ch.
D1. Jonathan, b 1764, mariner, res Beverly, mar Lucy OBER 1780. He was lost at sea 1795, age 32. His widow d 1825, age 61.
E1. Israel, b 1787, d.y. E2. Jonathan, b 1788, twin, d.y.
E3. Israel again, b 1788, twin, d 1792
E4. Lucy, b 1790, mar 1808 Joseph BAKER and d 1869
E5. Israel again, b 1792, d 1794
E6. Hannah, b 1795 mar Freeborn Woodbury, and d 1833
C5. Hannah, bp 1737 prob d unmar before 1798
C6. Elizabeth, bp 1738
B3. Mary, bp 1697, d unmar age 85 in 1775. B5. John, 1703-1777
B4. Martha, bp 1687, mar 1. John Ellithorp 1719 and 2. Isaac Grey before 1749. She was his widow in 1761.
A2. Were there other chn of this fam?
BISSON. Dr. A. Bisson Frazer of Phila. PA, b 1890s, gathered info. on BISSONS but were poss not from C.I. (Soc. Jers. Bull, 1977)
BISSON, BESSIN, BISSOON. In Maryland in the 1600s, from J? (Skordas) See Capt. BESSON below.
BESSON, Capt. Thomas, b 1616 England arrived in VA ca 1640, aboard the ship ASSURANCE. There was also a BEASON fam of England that came to America. (Kenneth Rutherford, Lexington, MO)
BEZUNE, BEZUME. In old MA, poss should be BISSON?
BEZUME, John, son of John and Mary, bp 1757, MRB?
BEZUME, BEZUNE, John of MRB, published to widow Ruth Whittemore of Salem, 1775. OUTC
BEZUNE, John, publ. to Eliz. Leach, both of Salem, MA 1777
BEZUNE, Margaret, dau of John and Margaret Bezume, bp 1761 MRB. A Margaret mar in 1784 John Rogers, res MRB.
BEZUNE, Usina, a Miss of MRB, mar Samuel CRESSY, CRESEY? of Newburyport MA 1773, in MRB.
BISSON. Also a G surname. Nicolas BUISSON, BISSON DES LANDES res Vale G, where he was b 1697, mar 1716 Elizabeth HENRY. Nicolas the son of Nicolas and Eliz. Elizabeth JENRY was b 1694 Vale G, dau of Pierre HENRY and Elizabeth FLEIRL?, poss FLEURY? They had 11 chn b between 1716 and 1736. See TAYLOR and HEADLEY. See MASS. VITAL RECORDS.
BISSON, Jane, b 1806 G, d 1843 GCO, bur Old Wash. Cem., Wills Twp., GCO.
BISSON, Daniel, fisherman, farmer, b 1822/23 J, d 1899 Port Daniel, QUE. He was son of Charles a shoemaker, and Mary (HAMON) BISSON of J. Mar 1842 Shigawake, Gaspe, QUE, Mary Jane ALMOND, b 1820/21 Hope, QUE, d 1912, dau of James a seaman and Catherine (Garrett) ALMOND, res Nouvelle (Hope), QUE. (L.F. Guy, Orono, ONT; Cynthia Dow, New Richmond, QUE)
A1. Joseph, b 1844, d 1846 New Carlisle, QUE
A2. Charles, b 1846, d 1898, mar 1868 Margaret Beebe, b ca 1845, d 1884, dau of Joshua Beebe. He mar 2. 1886 St. Pauls, Paspebiac, QUE, Clara Gilker, b ca 1866, d ca 1926.
B1. Charles, b 1869 B2. James Edward, b 1871
B3. Herman, b 1874, d 1957, mar 1902 Ida Jane Young
B4. Mary Ann, b 1876, d 1960, mar Edmund Young

B5. Jos. Howard, b 1880 mar Katie WATT B6. Henry John, b 1887
B7. Percival, Percy, b 1889, mar Freda Travers (by 2nd wife)
B8. Grace agnes, b 1897
B9. Wilfred, b 1898, d 1975, mar Winnie Nelson Tenniel
B10. R. Leslie?, b 1890, d 1970, mar Bessie Hall?
A3. Daniel, b 1848 Shigawake, QUE, d 1933, farmer and fisherman. Mar 1880 St. James Angl. CH, Port Daniel, QUE, Anne Ferguson Barter, b 1859 Grand Cascapedia, Gaspe, QUE, who d 1931 or 1934 dau of Wm. Henry and Eliz. (Chatterton) Barter of Grand Cascapedia, QUE.
B1. Alexander Robert Almond, b 1882 Port Daniel, QUE, mar Ruby Barber, no issue, res Saskatoon, SASK.
B2. Milton Herbert, b 1885 Port Daniel, d 1969, well driller. Mar 1919 Bridgeville Angl. CH, Irene Hope (Pama) MacCallum, Hotel Keeper, b 1899 Bridgeville, QUE, living 1981, dau of Clarence and Emma (DE VOUGE) MAc Callum.
C1. Herbert Milton MacCallum, b 1920 Port Daniel, QUE, well driller, mar 1944 St. Mary's Angl. CH, Dalhousie, NB, Isabel Alma HUBERT, qv, b 1919, dau of Harry Jack and Alma Florien Isabel Doherty.
D1. David Charles, b 1945, bank Mgr. Port Daniel, QUE, mar 1968 Mt. Carmel, R.C. CH, Mary Ursula Dea, b 1945, dau of Charles and Minette (Nadeau) Dea. Four chn including Carla b 1973, and Josi b 1975
D2. Nancy Kathryn MacCallum, b 1951 Port Daniel, QUE, mar 1971 ___ Gormley, and 2. 1978 Peter Sherwood, author, b 1949 Nelson, New Zealand, 3 chn: Melody, Willow and Dylan, b 1970s.
C2. Eubulus Ferguson, b 1921 mar 1948 at St. James Angl. CH, Sarah Gladys Evelyn Dow, b 1923, dau of Asa and Winnifred (Robinson) Dow.
D1. Geraldine Myrna, b 1949, mar 1972 Joseph Alfred Scerba, son of Alfons and Margaret (Spingler) Scerba
C3. Clarence Orley, b 1922 Port Daniel, QUE, mar 1946 Grand Cascapedia, QUE Ethel May Gilker, b 1924, d 1971, dau of Alex. and Mae (Mc Colm) Gilker
D1. Sandra Lee, b 1947 New Richmond, QUE, mar 1969 Campbellton, NB, Terrance Howard Delaney, b 1946, son of Wm. Richard and Alexina K. (Bulmer) Delaney, 2 chn: Gregory & Tara Delaney
D2. Barry Gilker, b 1949 New Richmond, QUE, mar 1971 Hampton, NB, Mary Ann Long, b 1952, dau of Norman L. Long. Two chn: Katherine and Allison.
D3. Donna Hope, b 1950 New Richmond, QUE, mar 1977 Dale Lyle Ball, b 1947, son of Donald Arthur and Maye Leone (Clements) Ball, a son Mark G. Ball
D4. Margaret Heather, b 1952 QUE, mar 1978 Fredericton, NB, Michael Fraser Bonang
D5. Robert Milton, b 1955, mar ca 1976 New Richmond, QUE, Joy Adavilla Arseneau, b 1955, dau of Robert Benedict and Ruby Brice (McKinley) Arseneau. Two chn: Linsay Erin b 1978 and Joseph Robert, b 1980.
D6. Kimberly May, b 1964 New Richmond, QUE
C4. Alma Grace, b 1924, mar 1943 Montreal, QUE Bert Cyl MAUGER WATT, b 1921, d 1958, son of Lyle and Hilda (MAUGER) WATT.
D1. Diane Faye Watt, b 1947, mar 1971 New Carlisle, QUE, William James MIDDLETON, b 1945, son of Hugh Morton and Elizabeth F. (BARBE) MIDDLETON. Two chn: Wm. and Timothy MIDDLETON, b1970s.

D2. Cheryl Gayle Watt, b 1951 D3. Leah Dawn Watt, b 1956
D3. Katherine Lynn Watt, b 1952
C5. Luena Shirley, b 1926, d 1975, mar 1. 1048 William Pryde and 2. Russell NOEL, qv.
D1. Stuart M. Pryde, b 1949 NY, mar 1970 Oneta, NY, Johanna Kuhnemann, dau of Leonard U. Kuhemann; a son, Christopher Pryde.
D2. Collette Pryde, mar Joseph Wayman, res CAL.
D3. William Pryde, res CAL D4. Russell A. NOEL, b 1963, res CAL.
C6. Audrey Lucille, b 1927, mar 1947 Kenneth Davies
D1. Kiven B. DAvies, mar 1974 Sarnia, ONT, Carol Romo, dau of John J. Romo; 3 chn: Jason, Troy and Bretney Davies
D2. Kandyce Davies, mar 1969 Karl Basanac D3. Korie Davies
C7. Joan Alexandra, b 1930 Port DAniel, QUE, mar 1949 Ivan Malcolm Dow, b 1926 Port Daniel, son of Clare and Olive (Skede) Dow.
D1. Alanna Joy Dow, b 1950, mar 1979 Robert Allnutt
D2. William Milton Dow, b 1952 Campbellton, NB, mar 1977 New Richmond, QUE Judith Gail McInnis, accountant, b 1952, PEI, dau of Leslie A. and Eunice(LE PAGE)McInnis. See LE PAGE in Q.A. IN CANADA. Two chn: Pamela and Peter Dow.
C8. Robert Barter, b 1935, mar 1. 1959 Rockburn, QUE, Iris Elaine Waller and 2. Norma Fortier-Roach. 5 chn: Geoffrey, William C., Gregory, Deborah and Rebecca
B3. Mary Jane Elizabeth, b 1888, d ca 1890
B4. Thomas Byers, b 1891 Port Daniel, QUE, d 1956, mar Elsie BIARD, qv, b 1899, who mar 2. after death of Thomas, Lyle WATT.
C1. Stanley, b 1937 Campbellton, NB, mar Helen Cochrane, b 1943 New Richmond, QUE. A son Edward, b 1966
B5. Frederick Sydney, b 1893 Port Daniel, QUE d 1957, mar 1. Jennie ____, 1894-1919, and 2. Ena Chicoine
C1. Norma C2. Jean, by Ena C3. Bud Morel C4. Lorne C5. Mary E.
B6. Joseph Benjamin, 1894-1912
B7. Mary Eliz., 1896-1976 B8. Alma Grace, 1899-1920, unmar
B9. Emma Jane, b 1903 mar Frank Loomer, no issue
A4. John, 1850-1923, mar Martha Amelia LUCAS, 1857-1930
B1. Susanna Jane, b 1880, d 1886
B2. Edmond Fitzhughes, b 1882, mar Clara Gayle
B3. Margaret Ellen, b 1884 B4. William, 1886-1952, mar ___Black.
B5. Ellen, called Etta?, 1889-1962, mar Capt. A.J. Doran, no issue
B6. Thomas Clare, b ca 1892, d 1923 of WWI injuries, unmar
B7. Lloyd, b 1898, d.y. B8. Lloyd, b 1900 B9. Clara May, 1895-1953
A5. James Almond, b 1853, d 1938, mar Margaret Ogilvie, b 1863 Grafton, MI, d 1911 Paris, MI
B1. Bernie Daniel, b 1884, Paris, MI d there 1938, mar 1912 Mabel Wiest, b 1891 d 1933 Paris, MI
C1. Margaret, mar Ernest Knapp C2. Doris mar Leon Smith
C3. Frances, b 1928 Paris, MI mar 1950 Maurice PARROT
A6. Joseph, b 1855
A7. William, b 1857 d 1932 mar 1887 Margaret Amelia Sullivan, b 1869 d 1943 Port Daniel, QUE.
B1. Mary Jane, called Mamie, b 1889 mar Phillip Walker
B2. Annie, b 1893, unmar B3. George, d 1979, mar Annie PROVOST
B4. Timothy Valmond, b 1897, mar Gwen LE POIDEVIN, qv.
B5. Daniel, b 1899, mar Marjory Mac Callum B7. Muriel mar Ernie BIARD, qv.
B6. Gladys B., b 1902, mar an American
A8. Thomas Byers, b 1860, d 1891 Port Daniel, QUE
A9. Edward, b 1862, established E.C. BISSON COLLEGE in Michigan.

A10. Mary Catherine, b 1865, d 1869 A11. Edmond, 1868-1870

BISSON, Elizabeth, mar William Whittom, b ca 1829 res Coxtown, Bona. Co Gaspe, QUE, 1861. He was a 'colleur', age 42, and she was 46, born NB. Wm. b British Isles, Anglican, but wife was R.C. Some Whittoms have a C.I. connection.

A1. Ann Whittom, b ca 1844 A4. Ellen Whittom, b ca 1850
A2. John,Whittom, fisherman, b ca 1845 A5. Wm. Whittom, b ca 1853
A3. Mary Whittom, b ca 1847

BISSON, Philippe John, b J, see page 164 of Q.E. IN CANADA, bottom of page. This may be Philippe John BISSON, b St. Peter J, mar Mary Ann LEMPRIERE, qv. Philippe a farmer, d before 1898, son of Clement BISSON. Philippe res Gaspe, QUE 1866, 2 chn? (L.F. Guy, Orono, ONT)

A1. Mary Ann
A2. Philippe HELLEUR, b 1866 Gaspe, farmer, mar 1893 Grouville, J Elizabeth Mary Ann QUENAULT, b St. Peter J, dau of Pierre S. QUENAULT, farmer of St. Peter J.

BLACKLER. See records in Salt Lake City, UT.

BLACKLER. A South-of-England surname, but has appeared at times in the C.I. A Blackler from J visited her Jersey relatives in Montreal and in ONT. in the middle or late 1800s. It is not known to compiler if the Blacklers below were from southern England or from J. Curr J.

BLACKLER. A fam is mentioned in the HOOPER GEN., by Pope and Hooper. Capt. Francis mar Mary Ingalls Hooper, 6 chn b 1820-1835

BLACKLER, Mary mar Samuel GALE 1762 in MRB. Some Gales married into C.I. families.

BLACKLER, William, b ca 1740, was Capt. and owner of many ships. He mar 1. Mary Ingalls and 2. Rebecca Shipman, had son Wm. Jr., res MRB. (JOURNALS OF ASHLEY BOWEN) Census 1790 gives fam of 2 men, 2 boys and 9 females.

BLACKMORE, Philip, arrived in Boston from J and Falmouth 1715 on ship MARY. (Whitmore) Not known to compiler if he came from J originally. BLACKMORE is curr in J.

BLACKMORE, Lemuel, res Palmertown, MA, 1790, fam of man, 2 boys and 1 female. (Census) OUTC

BLACKMORE, Solomon, res same 1790, fam of 1 man, 2 boys and 2 females. OUTC.

BLACKMORE, David, res Greenwich, MA 1790. OUTC.

BLAMPIED. One hundred fam. groups in SLCity records. For some curr. research see CIFHS #7.

BLAMPIED, in J 1402. That line would not be Hug. Name in St. Martin, St. Peter, Trinity and St. Laurens J 1668, and in Trinity, St. John, St. Laurens and St. Martin J 1749. See Hug. section in this book. Progenitor of the line below may be Charles BLAMPIED, b 1765 either in France or Guernsey, "ordained a Methodist minister by John Wesley 1787." (Typescript)

BLAMPIED, BLANPIED, Elisha, b 1792 St. Peter Port, G, to America 1813, mar 1820 Cambridge, OH, Elizabeth BROWN, B ca 1802. Elisha d 1880 at home of dau Margaret Wilson, Newcomerstown, OH. Naturalized 1824. (Wm. Blampied, Cleveland, OH; Dorothy Gullion, Ventura, CAL; Typescript by Charles Blanpied 1913) Said to be 17 chn, but some d.y.

A1. Thomas Blanpied, b ca 1815, GCO, mar 1835 Hannah Helms. Served in Civil War and d in Danville Prison
B1. John Milton, b 1842 served in Civil War
B2. Margaret, b 1844 mar John Wilson
B3. Rachel, twin to Wm. N. below, b 1850 GCO, mar Harry Halpin of GCO?

B4. William Norman, twin, b 1850, went west as cattle and sheep herder in KS, res Belle Plaine and Mulvane. Wm. d 1917 Mulvane, 11 chn, 2 d.y.

C1. Ida Ann, b 1874 Mulvane, KS mar 1. ? and 2. Lee West

D1. Lorna May D2. Hazel West D3. Lloyd West

C2. Elmer Castor, b 1876 d 1925 Lehi, UT mar 1. Ethel Phillips and 2. in 1902 Lemma Edwards

C3. Lillian Pearl, b 1878 UT, mar Wm. Gambrill, hardware merchant in Marena, OK, his 2nd wife, 5 chn including Marie, Henry, Lucy and Sarah Gambrill.

C4. Charles Wesley, b 1885, d 1955 near Denver, COL in auto accident. He mar 1. Elsie Rising and 2. Marie ___, 4 chn by each marriage. Poss 2nd wife was Mary Angela Fanelli?

D1. Lela Lorence D2. Carol Maxine, d in Denver D3. Geo. David

D4. William Anthoine, b 1933 Rochester, NY, poss was Prof. of Pomology at Cornell Univ.? (AMERICAN MEN AND WOMEN OF SCIENCE, NY, 1976)

C5. Jesse Norman, b 1887, res Chanute, KS, d 1940s Los Angeles, CAL. His second wife was Wynona ROBBINS

C6. Elva Alvis, or Elva Avis?, b 1890, d in KS. Mar Clarence Archibald.

C7. Lloyd Emery, b 1892, d 1968 Costa Mesa, CAL. Mar 1915 Elsie Mary Oldfield, b 1896 Wichita, KS, dau of Walter S. and Nellie Alice (Varner) Oldfield, 2 chn d.y.

D1. Dorothy Nell, b 1919 Fort Worth, TX mar 1945 Los Angeles, Paul Scott Gullion, b 1919 Carrollton, KY. See GALLIEN. He was son of John Scott and Faye (Banta) Gullion.

E1. Dorothy Diane Gullion, b 1946 Los Angeles, CAL, mar 1. Thomas Burton, and 2. 1979 Robert M. Dunlap

E2. Steven Paul, b 1948 Los Angeles, CAL, mar 1976 Angela Margaret Cartwright, of TV series, MAKE ROOM FOR DADDY, etc.

F1. Rebecca M. Gullion, b 1981 Tarzana, CAL.

D2. Beverly Jane, b 1922, d.y.

D3. Lloyd Emery Jr., b 1923 Los Angeles, CAL, mar 1947 Pasadena, CAL, Orrilla Ann Daggett

C8. Elsie Bernice, b 1895 mar Gerald Hutchinson, res Mulvane, KS and d Lyons, ORE.

C9. Bernard William, b 1897 Lyons, OR, d 1975 Shreveport, LA.

A2. Margaret mar John Wilson, a dau Margaret Wilson

A3. Elizabeth B., mar Norman SMITH, res Coshocton, OH.

A4. Elisha, b 1934 Cambridge, OH, mar Isabel Demuth 1856 at Port Washington, OH, d 1911, Hutchinson, KS, bur Burrton, KS. Isabel b 1838 Gnadenhutten, OH, where she res before marr. with her bro Adolphus, and Maria, his wife. Elisha worked for the Gov!t. in Cincinnati during the Civil War. Res Newport, KY, then in Cambridge, OH.

B1. Minnie, Mary Ellen, b 1858 Guyandotte, VA, mar Robert Emmet FRAYNE qv, who d 1899 at Burrton, KS. Fraynes were a KY fam, had Frayne Furniture Co., and the Burrton Hutchinson Marble Works.

C1. Annabel Frayne, b 1883 Burrton, KS, mar Carl K. Chapin at Leavenworth, KS, Carl b 1883, 2 chn.

D1. Robert Frayne Chapin, b 1907, mar Jane Cowan

D2. Isabel Frayne Chapin, res Pasadena, CAL

B2. Elisha Adolphus, b 1860 Port Wash., OH mar Mary McFarland 1882 at Newton, KS. He d 1914 Leavenworth, KS. Mary b 1858 Mohawk Village, OH, d 1935 Topeka, KS, bur Leavenworth.

C1. Elisha Adolphus BLANPIED, b 1883 Leavenworth, KS mar Marie

Jacobson 1915. Marie b 1888, res Kansas City, MO.

C2. Lulu Blanpied, b 1885 Leavenworth, KS mar James Dale Bradfield 1904, div. 1924. He d 1934. She mar 1926 at Topeka, KS Webster Stevenson, b 1875

D1. James Dale Blampied, b 1907 Mt. Vernon, OH mar Margaret Shaw 1928 at Topeka, KS. Margaret b 1908, 2 chn: James Dale and Alice Joy Bradfield

C3. Kenneth McFarland Blampied b 1893 Leavenworth, KS mar Kathryn Johnston 1914. She was b 1893 Leavenworth. Res Wichita, KS. He was a saddle and harness maker.

D1. Kenneth McFarland Blanpied Jr., b 1917, d.y.

D2. John Kenneth Blanpied, b 1919, killed in airplane accident 1941 Wichita, KS

D3. Robert Demuth Blanpied, b 1923, ordained to the priesthood 1948 at Wichita, KS

B3. Jesse Sylvester Blanpied, b 1861 Port Wash., OH mar Hattie Bell Shepherd, dau of Rev. J.N. Shepherd, Methodist minister of Iowa. Six chn, Hattie b 1867, d 1912, Hutchinson, KS, bur Burrton, KS

C1. Jessie Wilma Blanpied, b 1888 Burrton KS, mar Victor R. Northfoss 1911 at Newton, KS, d 1949 Hollywood, CAL, bur Forest Lawn Cem. at Glendale, CAL. Victor b 1883.

D1. Harriette Jane Northfoss, b 1915 Hollywood, CAL mar Hilliard MARKS 1942 in CAL. He was b 1913. Res Sherman Oaks, CAL. A son Philip MARKS, b 1948

C2. Hazel Blanpied, b 1889, d.y.

C3. Bernice Calvert Blanpied, b 1891 Burrton, KS mar Rollin G. McLane 1912 at Hutchinson, KS. He was b 1887. Res Glendale,CAL

D1. Jeanne Calvert McLane, b 1913 Hutchinson, mar Kenneth Hunter 1931 in Glendale, CAL. He was b 1910. Three chn: Kenneth, Robert and Barbara Hunter.

D2. Robert Gladden McLane, b 1917

C4. Harry Newton Blanpied, b 1894 Burrton, KS d 1941 Topeka, bur Burrton.

C5. Violet Blanpied, b 1901 Burrton, d.y.

C6. Carl Melvin, b 1903 Bu-rton, mar Edna Tackney 1931 in CAL. She was b 1904.

D1. Russel Blanpied, b 1937

B4. John Wesley Blanpied, b 1864 Newport, KY mar Lillie May Shepherd, dau of R.H. Shepherd of Burrton. He d 1943 at Hutchinson, KS. Lillie May b 1871 Newcomerstown, OH.

C1. Blance Everal Blanpied, b 1892 Burrton, KS d 1968. Mar Fred William Camp 1915 at Hutchinson, KS, bur Burrton. He was b 1883 at Coon Rapids, IA, d 1946.

D1. Janice Everall Camp, b 1917 Hutchinson, KS mar John Harlan Callis 1948 at Somerset, KY. John was b 1920 Lexington, NY, res Pendleton, KY.

E1. Ann Everal Callis, b 1949 at Louisville, KY.

D2. Robert Wesley Camp, b 1919 Hutchinson, KS mar Helen Rose Jone, 1949 at Kansas City, MO. Helen b 1923 Warren, ARK, res Olathe, KS.

D3. Elizabeth May Camp, b 1922 Hutchinson, KS res Denver, COL.

D4. Thurlow William Camp, b 1924 KS, mar Elizabeth Helen Kennedy 1947 at Providence, RI. His wife b there 1924. Res Providence. A dau Carol Ann Camp.

D5. Joanne Eleanor Camp, b 1926 Hutchinson, KS, an Army nurse.

C2. Mildred May Blanpied, b 1908 Hutchinson, KS
B5. Harry, d.y. B6. Frank, d.y.
B7. Emma Moore, a ranch owner with partner Beatrice Cooley in Woodward, OK. Emma b 1872 Cambridge, OH.
B8. Anna Ferrar Blampied, b 1875 Cambridge, OH mar Otis Crawford 1900 at Burrton, KS. She d 1948 Los Angeles, CAL, bur there. Otis b 1875, d 1947.
C1. Beatrice Anabel Crawford, b 1901 Burrton, KS
C2. Bernard Crawford, b 1903 Burrton, KS, res Los Angeles, CAL.
C3. Dale Crawford, b 1904
C4. Lillian Claire Crawford, b 1907 Hutchinson, KS mar Earl Crewsome, 2 sons, res Tulsa, OK.
C5. Emma Crawford C6. George Crawford
B9. Bernard Blampied, b 1877 Carmbidge, OH, d 1884 Burrton KS.
A5. Wesley or John Wesley? Names of other 12 chn not found.
BLAMPIED, Judith, Virginia, Annie and Eliza Jane were sisters of Elisha and John, and came to America. Eliza Jane had been mar. but lost her husband in the 1830s in G and a bro. Michael also d in G.
BLAMPIED, Margaret, b 1790 St. Peter Port G., sister of Elisha, rem to GCO 1834. She had mar 1. in G, ___NEWMAN, 1806, and 2. F.W. Mathews 1819 in G. She mar in Cambridge, OH John BURT, and poss mar 4. John Mahaffey, had 6 chn, 4 d.y.. Margaret d 1884 at home of dau in Cambridge, OH. (Sarchet and GCO records)
A1. Elizabeth, mar 1. J.S. NICHOLAS of G? and 2. William OGIER in 1854. See OGIER.
BLAMPIED, John, b 1799 G, prob bro of Elisha and Margaret above. He left ship in Boston 1816, ran a tavern in Cambridge, MA, rem to OH 1819 as itinerant Methodist preacher?, d Delaware, OH. Poss mar Elizabeth DOLBEAR of Hancock, VT. A John H. BLAMPIED served in the Civil War. Poss other chn? (Wolf; David R. Blampied, St. Paul, MN)
A1. Benjamin, res Columbus, OH, had son John
A2. Saurin?, mar and had 2 chn, res Staten Island, NY
B1. Ralph B2. Ethel, taught French
A3. Lizzie, Elizabeth? A4. Lida A5. Mattie
A6. David, b Galena, OH, desc in MN and NH?, other chn?
B1. Fred, res NJ B3. Nelson B5. a dau?
B2. David Robert B4. a dau, res Mt. Vernon, NH?
BLAMPIED, Elijah, res Coshocton, OH 1860 census
BLAMPIED, John mar Eliza Preston 1823 in GCO. Service by D. HUBERT, J.P., qv.
BLAMPIED, Rachel A., mar in the 1830s Henry Al Healkin?, in GCO
BLAMPIED, Thomas res Washington, OH, 1860, GCO. A thomas served in the Civil War, and was bur at Danville, VA.
BLAMPIED, R.H., res Palo Alto, CAL, said to be nephew of Alton C. Blampied, prob from G fam.
BLAMPIED, Nicholas, 1803-1890, b G? , son of Nicholas and Marie COLLAS Blampied, res GCO 1800s. Mar Esther ROBIN, 1800-1871. (Frances Hale, Fort Worth, TX)
A1. Esther, b 1829 A3. Marie, b 1832
A2. Nicholas, 1831-1916, mar Rachel ROBIN, 1823-1893
B1. Nicholas, b ?, mar Rachel BICHARD of GCO?
C1. John, b 1910, d 1940 C2. Harold C3. Annette
D1. Frances Gale of TX D2. other chn?
BLAMPIED, Elizabeth, below is almost surely part of the same Guernsey County, Ohio family as above.
BLAMPIED, Elizabeth, b 1805 G, mar 1. Thomas Jean LE ROY. Widowed,she

mar 2. the Rev. Samuel Sylvester Stedman, b 1793 Harpers Ferry, who d 1860 in a Prairie schooner enroute to Leon, ILL. She was his 3rd wife, and she d 1886 in Emporia, KS. Did she have chn by LE ROY? (Ruth Coleman, Austin, TX)

A1. John Sylvester Stedman, b 1836 Cambridge, OH, d 1914 Topeka, KS, mar 1. Eleanor Emeline McDonald, and 2. Mrs. Ida May (McCrary) Mitchell.

A2. Samuel G. Stedman, b 1839 Brownsville, OH, d 1868 Leon, ILL of wounds, a Civil War vet., mar Lydia Maria Stearns.

A3. Martha Stedman, b 1842, d 1843

A4. Thomas Owen Stedman, b 1845 Brownsville, OH, d 1910 Whiteside, ILL, mar 1. Helen Cranplin, and 2. Mrs. Emma Aldrich Myers.

A5. William Rosenberry Stedman, b 1849 Wayne Co., OHd 1922 Hutchinson, KS, mar Lydia Morris Austin

The Rev. Samuel Stedman was the father of the Rev. James Henry Stedman who mar Sarah BURT, dau of John and Mary (Reed) Burt, qv. REv. James was by the 2nd wife of Rev. Samuel, Margaret Honnel, who d 1829 in VA, now West VA. (Ruth Coleman, Austin, TX)

BLAMPIED, Edmund, a Guernsey artist whose etchings particularly caught the fancy of many America. There is said to be some of his work at the Pittsburgh Art Museum. See Malcolm Salamon's book on BLAMPIED illustrations.

BLAMPIED, ___, settled in Cheticamp, in Cape Breton, Nova Scotia 1800s. (Walter Blampied, Middletown, NY)

A1. Walter Henry Blampied, b Cape Breton?, registered in ARichat, N.S. Mar Lillian Ada ____.

B1. Walter F., b 1901 First Tower, J, to US 1921, res Middletown, NY 1974.

B2. a sister, and poss other chn?

Some lines of this fam are poss Hug., perhaps coming to America via the C.I. Spellings varied in early MA records, such as: BLANCPIED, WHITEFOOT, BAREFOOT, BLOMPHE, BLOMPHEE, BLANVIT, BLAMPEY, BLAMPIED, etc. CAUTION: CHARTED FROM VITAL RECORDS.

BLAMFIT, BLAMPIED?, John mar Sarah Thonncom? (int) 1728 Boston, MA.

BLAMPIED, BLAMPIEL, Jane mar Peter Edwards 1727 Boston. (int)

BLOMPHE, BLAMPIED?, Aaron, mar Mary ___, res MRB, MA.

A1. Aaron, bp 1752 MRB A3. Sarah, bp 1757

A2. Mary, bp 1755 A4. Ann, bp 1760

Poss the Aaron above, bp 1752 MRB, was the father of fam below, and the one in the Census of 1790, of 1 man, 4 boys and 2 females in Newburyport, MA, wife Sarah.

A1. Aaron, bp 1779 A3. John HOOPER BLOMPHE, bp 1785, twin

A2. Sarah, bp 1783 A4. Thomas, bp 1785, twin

BLAMPIED, John mar 1680s Elizabeth SWASEY, qv, b 1655 in MA or in J?

BLANPIED, George David, b 1930 Ridgewood, NJ, educated Dartmouth, Cornell and MI State, Prof. of Pomology at Cornell Univ. Poss connected with fam of George Wesley in first BLAMPIED chart, qv. (AMERICAN MEN AND WOMEN OF SCIENCE, NY, 1976)

BLAMPIED, Charles, b J, mar Mary Ann GARNIER, dau of ___GARNIER and ___ CABOT. Charles rem late in life to Boston, MA, as builder and contractor, with young wife Mary Ann, age ca 35, had 5 chn. (Paul Blampied, Quincy, MA)

A1. Joshua, b ca 1870 Trinity, J, to Boston with fam, mar Lillian C. McIntosh, dau of Frank and Betsey Avis (Bowen) McIntosh.

B1. Paul Garnier, b 1903 res N. Quincy, MA.

B2. Priscilla Hopkins, b 1904 A3. Edward Wesley, b 1905

BLANCHARD, J and G surname, but also common in England and France.Curr

G and J. Note many other BLANCHARDS in early MA and NH. OUTC

BLANCHARD, Rebecca mar 1746 Nathaniel BLANCHARD, b 1718/19 Andover, MA, res Shutesburg, MA. OUTC. (SECOND BOAT, Feb. 1981)

BLANCHARD, Ebenezer, mar Mehitable Spear 1790 Boston. OUTC

BLANDY. This name and BLANDIN noted in early American records. BLANDY was in St. Heliers J 1830. OUTC.

BLENNERHASSETT. Not a C.I. name, but has C.I. connection.

BLENNERHASSETT, Herman, was b ca 1767 of Irish parents, in Hampshire, England, his mother being there on a visit. He graduated from Trinity College, Dublin, studied law, and was admitted to practice 1790. In 1797 he inherited a large fortune, mar Margaret AGNEW, dau of the Gov. of the Isle of Man. They came to America and settled in Marietta, OH on an island near Belpre, which had once belonged to George Washington. Their home became the cultural and social center for the area. In April 1805 Aaron Burr first visited this island Eden and they soon organized a very expensive project, a great western empire. The government in Wash. suspected treason and sent militia which ransacked and ruined the estate, burned down 1811. Herman and his fam went to the depths of poverty, and rem to Europe, he to die in the home of a charitable sister in Guersey, 1831. Mrs. Blennerhassett d in 1842 in a tenement in NYCity. Congress never paid the ten thousand dollars claimed against the wreck of their home by the Virginia militia. Their 3 sons apparently d without issue the youngest being killed while fighting with the rebel Army.(Howe's HIST. COLL OF OH, p.805; OHIO SCENES AND CITIZENS, by Grace Goulder)

BLONDEL. Note that a Peter BLONDEL from Ireland rem to NY 1821. (NY NATURALIZATIONS, by Scott)

BLONDEL. In J 1274, in G since 1100s. In St.Helier J 1668, 1749. In St. Saviour G 1646. Curr G. A Nicholas BLONDEL was a clock maker in G, a Quaker, 1700s.

BLONDEL, John, b 1859 Le Neuve Maison, St. Saviour G, youngest son of Abram B. and Mary (TOSTEVIN) BLONDEL. Mary b Long Frie, St. Peter in the Wood, G. John came to US on ship CELTIC from Liverpool,Eng. to NY 1885. He settled first in Delta, OH, as he had promised to deliver some silver spoons to John SIMON, qv, of Delta, who had inherited them from a relative in G. He had followed his sweetheart, Matilda Amy ROBIN, youngest of 5 chn of Daniel ROBIN and Julia TOSTEVIN of J to America. (Julia and Mary T. above were sisters.) Matilda then res with her maternal aunt, Eliz. TOSTEVIN Mutter, Mrs. James Mutter, who res Racine, WI. Matilda Amy had arrived 1884. She was b 1866 G, d 1933, 1 ch. John d 1944 Delta, OH. (Dorothy Harrison, Louisville, KY)

A1. Amy Mary, b 1889 mar Thomas H. McDonald of Detroit, MI in Delta, OH 1913. They res Detroit until 1922, then rem to Royal Oak, MI. He was Supt. of photoengraving at the Detroit TIMES. He and Amy ret. to Lake Wales, FLA after WWII, where Thomas d 1951. 2 chn.

B1. Dorothy Jeanne Adair McDonald, b 1914 Highland Park, MI, mar Edward W. Harrison, b 1914 in 1946 at Birmingham, MI. She served in Belgium with the Red Cross, and he was a Lt. with the 20th Photo. Intel., Detroit, MI.

C1. Priscilla Ann Harrison, b 1947 Indianapolis, IND mar Wm. S. Litchman 1975 at Deer Isle, ME, 1 ch.

D1. Graham Harrison Litchman, b 1981 Stamford, CT.

C2. Deborah Jeanne Harrison, b 1952, mar Gregory B. Weeter 1979 Louisville, KY, res Madisonville, LA.

C3. Julia Deane Harrison, b 1954, mar Bruce Appleton 1981 Fairfield, CT, res Stamford, CT.

C4. John Edward Harrison, b 1956 Louisville, KY mar Marla Corpus 1982 Seattle, WA, res Kent, WA.

B2. John Alexander McDonald, b 1918, d 1966, mar Kirsten Andreen, b Stockholm, Sweden. John a pilot in WWII, d a Lt. Col. at Vandenberg AF Base, CAL, 5 chn.

BLONDEL, Thomas, a mariner on sloop ADVENTURE from Nfld. to Boston 1760s, prob from G. (Whitmore)

BLONDEL. Use 3 times as a middle name in the fam of Ernest PRIAULX, qv. Poss surname of mother or grandmother.

BOALCH. Old surname of G. See LING. Curr research, see CIFHS #12

BOURDON, LE BORDON, in J 1309. In Grouville and St. Clement J 1668, also in 1749. Changed to BODEN sometimes in America.

CAUTION! Many BODENS are desc of Ambrose, who came from Yorkshire to MA early 1700s. Cf also BOUDIN, BOWDEN and BEAUDIN.

BODEN, LE BOURDON, Wm. from J 1769 on ship MOLLY of J. (Whitmore) "Edward, son of Wm. BOURDON and of Mary SOHIER, his wife, was baptised the 22nd day of Feb., 1761" St. Helier J parish church. Edward de STE. CROIX was godfather and Jane LE BOUTILLIER was godmother. Louis MALLET was the registrar. (DRIVER FAM) Edward was apparently the bro of Wm. BODEN, formerly LE BOURDON, BOURDON of J who came to New England. The first William was a mariner, but owned a large estate on J, from which he collected rents, and is said to have brought this money to America, and buried it. However, none was found in spite of much digging, and the inheritance was lost. In 1783 William BODEN, the father, bought a lot in Salem, MA and built a house, which was still standing in 1885. He served as drum Major in the Rev. Army. Mar Experience DOWNING, dau of Richard & Temperance (Derby) Downing. She d 1838 age 89. (DRIVER FAMILY,by Cooke; Elaine Moreland, Merriman, NEB; PENNA. HEADS OF FAMS; Cumberland, PA; JARVIS FAM; Rev. War Records; PARK IN AMERICA; Ancestry of Mary BAKER; Hotten; Schwenkfelder, 620; TYLER GEN; JEWETT GEN: NEW HAVEN CT FAMS; WOODSTOCK CT. GENS; Sabine's LOYALISTS; Hertman's OFFICERS)

A1. Wm. Boden, b 1775, d at sea 1820, mar 1795 Eunice Barnes, dau of Thomas Barnes of Salem, MA, b 1779, d NYCity 1845. Wm. sailed a vessel named ALERT, between Boston, England and Baltimore, MD. In 1807 he brought from J the fam of 8 of John BERTRAM, qv. In a letter to J, Wm. mentions Geo. PICOT of J, John BERTRAM, James LE GALLAIS and Elias CABOT, all four Jerseymen settled in MA. Wm. and Eunice had 11 chn b Salem, MA.

B1. William III, b 1796, d 1822 B2. Eunice 1797-1802

B3. Mary, b 1798, d 1830 mar 1827 Theodore Littlefield, son of Nathaniel and Betsy (Eldridge) Littlefield, who d 1851.

C1. Mary Elizabeth Littlefield, b 1828

C2. Theodore Augustus Littlefield, b 1830

B4. Edward, b 1800 d 1803 B6. Michael Barnes again, 1802-1804

B5. Michael Barnes, 1801-1802

B7. Edward, b 1804 d 1878, mar 1828 Martha Southwick, dau of John and Polly (Foote) Southwick, b 1806. She d of smallpox in NYCity 1865. 6 chn.

C1. Edward Sullivan C4. John Henry, b 1835

C2. Mary Foote, b 1832 C5. James Sullivan, b 1840

C3. William Aug., b 1833 C6. Michael Barnes again, b 1841

B8. Hannah Barnes, b 1806 d 1859, mar 1837 (family Bible) Thomas Ashbury Foster, son of William and Annah Choate (Knapp) Foster, 6 chn.

C1. Thomas Foster
C2. Elizabeth Boden Foster, mar 1859 Israel Safford Lee, son of William and Lois Derby (Safford) Lee
C3. Thomas A. Foster
C4. Edward A. Foster
C5. Matilda Foster
C6. Mehitable S. Foster
B9. James Sullivan, b 1810, d 1864, mar 1842 Elizabeth (Cushing) Boden, widow of Michael Barnes BODEN, bro of James. She was living in Boston, 1885, no issue.
B10. Augustus Charles, b 1813, d 1841, mar 1840 Angeline ___,no issue
B11. Michael Barnes, b 1815, d 1841 on brig. GAZELLE of Salem, while lying off the coast of Africa. Mar 1839 Elizabeth M. Cushing, no issue. She mar 2. the bro of her husband, James Sullivan Boden, see above, B9.
A2. Sally Boden, b 1778, d 1848, unmar
A3. Charles Derby, bp 1780 mar 1800 Joanna Elliot. Same or another Charles D. Boden mar 1842 Mary Knapp. A ch d 1804, and another in 1817. A charles d1837, age 51
A4. Edward, bp 1782, d at Nantucket before 1807
A5. John, b 1784, mar 1807 Elizabeth KING, dau of Wm. and Rebecca (Phippen) King. She was bp E. Church, Salem, MA 1786. William, her father, was son of Wm. and Anstis (Crowninshield) (Babbidge) King. More info. in DRIVER FAMILY.
A6. Elias Boden, d.y. A7. Elias again, b 1786, d 1801 age 15.
A8. Experience, mar ___RICH
A9. Lucy, b 1793?, mar 1815 John Mansfield, son of Joseph and Lucretia (Derby) Mansfield. (More Info in DRIVER FAMILY)
A10. Nancy, b ca 1796, d 1878, mar 1818 Thomas Hutchinson
A11. Polly, d.y. A12. Polly again, d age 18
BODEN, BOADEN. Many in colonies, but most were prob of the Ambrose Bowdoin line. See JOURNAL OF ASHLEY BOWEN, NEHGS.
BODEN, Charles, mar widow Sally STILL, qv, 1827, Salem, MA.
BODEN, Deborah, mar Ebenezer LE GROW, qv, 1767 MRB
BODEN, Edmund, mar Abigail DENNIS 1760 MRB. OUTC
BODEN, John mar Mary GIFFARD, qv, 1748 MRB.
A1. Sarah, bp 1752 was 14 in 1766. A2. Mary, bp 1754
BODEN, Capt. Samuel Jr., mar Sarah BROWN 1803 MRB. OUTC
BODEN, Sarah mar Elias LE GROW, qv, MRB, 1765
BODGE, BOAGE, etc, etc. Was this name BEAUGIE, BEAUGER from J? BEAUGIE in J and G since at least the 1500s. In St. Clement, St. Martin, St. Heliers J 1668 and in St. Heliers J 1749.
BODGE, BOGEE, BOAGE. Very common in MA and NH 1700s. See records of these places: Barrington, Gilmanton, Madbury, Lee, Poplin and Portsmouth, NH. Milltown and Windham, ME, also Boston & MRB, MA.
BOIT, BOYETT, BOYT. A Hug. Surname, to VA and Carolina colonies early, poss from France by wayof C.I., England or Ireland. (Wendy Elliott, Anaheim, CAL) See BOIT FAMILY by Robert A. Boit, Boston, 1915. This fam came from Bruchet, Normandy, France, settled first in England and then came to America. John, the progenitor was b 1774 England? The BOITS below are from an earlier arrival. Cf also the J surname BOISTE, in which the middle 's' is silent. Therefore, would prob be spelled BOIT in America. See other BOIT records. (HUGUENOT TRAILS, by the HUG. SOC. OF CANADA)
BOIT, John, res MRB 1743, from France or C.I.? mar Rebecca ___. OUTC.
A1. Rebecca, bp 1743, poss mar 1762 Abraham MULLET, qv, in MRB.
B1. Abraham MULLET Jr., b 1765
A2. George, bp 1745

BOIT, Sarah mar Rowland MAUGIER, qv, 1733 MRB. See MAUGER. Rowland poss from C.I.

BOLLEN. Often a variant spelling of J surname BALLEINE, poss an English branch? See BALLEINE & BULLEN.

BOLLEN, Capt. James. Capt. Philip DE CARTERET of J came to VA. in 1665, on his way to New Jersey, and from there he wrote a letter to John Winthrop of the Mass. Bay Colony, and a postscript goes: "Sir-if you please to doe me the favour to let me hear from you, direct your letter to Capt. James BULLAIGNE in New York. " (HISTORY OF ELIZABETH, NJ, pp 49,50). This Capt. James, later called BALLIN, BOLLEN, etc, came prob with the English fleet, and was no doubt, a member of one of the branches of the J fam of BALLEINE, though perhaps not of the St. Peter branch. Capt. Bollen joined Capt. Philip CARTERET at the new settlement in Elizabethtown, NJ, helped established the new government, became Secretary of the Province and was Justice of the Peace in 1666, performing several marriages in the colony. He wrote several volumes about the new settlement. His warm support of the De Carterets made him unpopular in town, and in 1673 he exchanged properties with John MARTIN of Woodbridge, NJ, becoming a citizen of that town.

Capt. Bollen d intestate in March, 1682/3, and admin. of the estate was granted to Samuel Moore and Nathaniel Fitzrandolph. His widow was prob. Ann Bollen. There were at least two chn: James and Anna. James mar Martha DENNIS. (NEW JERSEY WILLS, I;23; HIST. OF ELIZABETH, NJ, p. 44)

BONAMY, very old surname in both J and G, now extinct in the Islands.

BONAMIE, Peter mar Mary Johnson 1700 Boston, MA.

BOOBIER, see BUBIER.

BOODY. A puzzling surname with varied opinions as to origin. One tradition says he was French, and jumped ship at Boston, settling at Madbury, then Cocheco, and finally Dover, ME. Researcher Philip Russel thinks BOODY might be BODDIE, BODEE of Ireland, Scotland England and Holland, spelled in various ways. The French speaking tradition might mean he did come from J, where they spoke a form of Norman French in those days, and were great mariners. Some marriage and business transactions with known Channel Islanders, such as DREW and DEMERITT. Consider also surname BOUDIER.

BOSDET. A J surname pron. very similar to BOODY. Noyes says that BOODY might have been originally VODEN, VAUDIN of J. Compiler hesitates to include this fam but hopes readers will consult sources. (HIST. OF DURHAM, Clemens; BOODY ANNALS, poss some errors in it; STATE OF MAINE series, p.1468; SMALL GEN, Vol 1, p.505; NEHGS Vol 36 p.80; NEHGS Vol24; Virginia Merrill, Solon, ME; Philip RUSSELL, Wichita, KS; John R. Caverly, Placida, FLA)

BOODEY, Zechariah, b France mar a Yankee woman, name unknown, res Madbury, NH, 9 chn, all daus but the last. (ANNALS OF THE BOODEYS, John R. Caverly, Placida, FLA)

A9. Azariah, mar Bridget Bushbie of a fam that res in the Bermudas and in Boston, formerly of Norfolk, England? Poss mar 2.? and 3. ? a woman from Berwick, ME. Azariah d 1803, 7 chn. This fam included because of the DEMERITT marriage.

B1. Rev. Robert, b 1743, mar Margery Hill, Robert d 1814

B2. Zechariah, b 1745, mar Mary DEMERITT, qv, b 1743. He rem to New Durham, NH 1768 and d 1821. His wife Mary d 1835, 5 chn.

C1. Bridget, b 1769, mar Thomas Ransom of VT.

C2. Betsey mar Joseph Gilman

C3. John

C4. Daniel, d 1805

C5. Joseph, b 1773 mar Marey PIKE, 1777-1856. Joseph d 1867

BOODY. Note that several BOODYS mar into DREW fam. Not known to compiler if these were connected to the Francis DREW fam from J, or the Wm. DREW fam. which may have been from J.

BOSDET. In J since 1300s. BOSDET, Barnard came to Portsmouth, NH from London, England before 1719, when he mar Sarah Thompson. (NEHGS Vol. 24, p.13; NEHGS Vol 81) Could he be from a C.I. fam in England?

A1. Sarah, bp 1720 Portsmouth, NH. A Sarah mar1734 Jeremiah Rhodes in Boston, and /or James Collins 1740, Boston, MA.

A2. Isaac, bp 1723. An Isaac of London, England mar Mary Powell of Stratham, NH 1719. (NEHGS)

A3. Ann, bp 1725

BODIT, Peter, d before 1687 in SC, had wife Frances. OUTC. (FIRST SETTLERS OF SC, Agnes Leland)

BOSQUET. Noted in list of residents of QUE. City 1838. See LE BOSQUET (LOST IN CANADA, Aug. 1981) Four BOSQUETS were ship captains in J, 1730-1740. (A. John Jean, Jersey)

BOTT. Prob English, but some were long settled in C.I. Cf also LE BOT of J. BOTT CURR G and J. One BOTT from Sudbury England to America.

BOTT, John, b 1853 Longy, St. Anne, ALD, rem to Walkerville, ONT ca 1880, mar Jenny ___. John was son of Peter and Rachel Mary (BENEST) BOTT of Ald.

BOTT, Nicholas, bro of John above, b ALD, rem to Walkerville, ONT ca 1890. Mar Eliza Brooks, b Kent, England. Two sons, 2 daus, res Detroit, MI. (Fred Bott, Grosse Point, MI)

BOTTILEY, John, a freeman, arrived 1678 from ?, in SC (Baldwin) Poss A Le BOUTILLIER from C.I.?

BOUCHER, as LE BOUCHER, the butcher?, in J 1331. (Stevens)

BOUCHER, Joseph, arrived in Boston 1769 on ship MOLLY from J, a servant. (Whitmore)

BOUCHER, George, mar Elizabeth MAJOR, qv, 1727 Boston. (int) OUTC, but quite poss from C.I.

BOUDEN. SeeBOWDEN and BODEN. John BOUDEN a prop. in ME 1720. OUTC.

BOUGOURD. Old in G, in St. Andrews G 1754. Curr G and J. See CIFHS #9.

BOUGOURD, John, b 1890 G, son of Nicholas and Charlotte BOUGOURD, rem to North Chelmsford, MA as a young man. A son John.

BOURBONELL, John, arrived in Boston 1769 on ship MOLLY, from J, a servant. Whitmore) This is not listed as old G or J surname, poss a Huguenot?

BOURCHIER. See NEHGS Vol 112, p.169. OUTC. LE BOURCIER is old in J.

BOURGAIZE. In St. Peter G 1691, in Torteval 1706. Curr G.

BOURGAIZE, J. De Garst, of G, had large fam. Some chn came to N.A., first to Gaspe, then to Toronto and Tacoma, WA. They were born in late 1800s. (Sylvia Wilson)

A1. Basil, to Colorado
A2. George, to Los Angeles, CAL
A3. John to Rhode Island
A4. Wilfred, to Africa
A5. Hugh, to New Jersey
A6. Wallace, to Florida
A7. Edna, remained in G?
A8. Emily, mar Grauvell, res Toronto, Ontario, had issue
A9. Ida, res St. Peter Port, G.

BOURGAIZE, Nicholas of G, with the consent of his master, Capt. John HARDY, qv of G, transferred his indenture to Wm. ENGLISH of Salem, MA for four years in 1600s. He was a mariner. Witnesses were Margaret Sewell Jr., Susannah and Stephen SEWELL. (Essex Coll. Vol 2; Mrs. Philip English)

BOURGAIN, Elizabeth, mar John BARTON 1783 Boston, MA. Poss BOURGAIZE?
BOURGAIN, Joseph, mar Polly BISSON 1784 Boston, MA. OUTC.
BOUTEL, Hannah, mar Rev. Sam Bacheller, ca 1735 in Haverhill, MA. (Essex Antiq., vol. 2) Cf BOUTELOUP of J, also BOUTILLIER, LE BOUTILLIER of C.I.
BOUTELOUPE, Vincent, from J to North Chelmsford, MA early 1900s. Curr J. See section in this book about the Quarry families.
BOUTON. In St. Heliers J 1668 and in St. Helier and St. Saviour J 1749.
BOUTON, BUTTON, William, from J, was in NH 1693 and his fam on Great Island, Newcastle, NH. William drowned age 37, bur by Clement LEMPRIERE, qv. Said to have had a business on the Piscat River. A Wm. BOUTON is mentioned in St. Helier, J 1668. John BOUTON of MA 1635 was said to be from England. (Noyes) BOUTON in J 1668-1749.
BOUTON, Eleazar, mar MaryGreen 1768 in Stamford-Darien, CT. Also others. (CONN. MARRIAGES)
BOUTANG, John mar Frances Parker 1768 Boston, cf BOUTIN? of C.I. OUTC.
BOW. This name in MRB where many Channel Islanders settled early. Cf LE BOT of J. (Stevens) LE BOT is pron LE BOW. Cf also LE BEAU.
BOW, Eliezer mar Sarah WATERS 1754 MRB. OUTC.
BOW, Robert, mar Lydia CARTER of Salem 1721, MRB. OUTC.
BOW, Sarah, mar Edward SMITH 1761 MRB. OUTC.
BOW, Stephen, mar Abigail BODEN, qv, 1783 MRB.
BOWDOIN, BAUDOIN, BOUDEN, BAUDAINS, etc. There were several BOWDOIN, BEAUDOIN, etc. persons and fams in early New England and nearly all appear to be of Hug origin. However, among the many that showed up, it seems likely that a few were from the C.I. A Nicholas BOWDOIN, BOUDEN, was one of the leaders of the Calvinistic movement in J in the 1500s. Underhill mentions a bond between the BOWDOINS and the MARINER-LE MARINELS, qv. BAUDAIN and LE MARINEL are both found in St. John, J 1668. BAUDAIN curr G and J.
BOWDEN, BODEN. Many in early New England, poss that some of them being originally BAUDAINS, BAUDIN, BALDWIN, and BEAUDIN, all pron much like BODEN. We do know that a LE BOURDON fam of J, in MA, quickly began to call themselves BODEN. Therefore, it seems quite likely that several of the BOWDEN fams of the colonies may have come from the C.I.
BOWDEN, Capt., native of G, was a privateer in the 1640s for Gov. CARTERET.
BOWDEN, see also BODEN. One BOWDEN came to America from Holberton, Devon.
BOWDEN. Research on this name is very puzzling. Spelling varies considerably, even among members of the same fam. See MICHAEL BOWDEN AND SOME OF HIS DESCENDANTS, by Wm. Hammond Bowden, Wayland, MA 1960. While there is nothing to apparently connect Michael and his fam with the C.I., it is quite clear that intermar with C.I. fams took place often.
BOWDEN, Rebecca, mar Nicholas BEZUNE, BESSOM, BISSON, qv, 1725. OUTC, but prob C.I. origin.
BOWDEN, Andrew I., mar Elisabeth BESSOM, BISSON 1828, OUTC. See BISSON.
BOWDEN, Francis, b ca 1678 MRB?, mar 1707 Mary BOOBYER, BUBIER, qv. OUTC. See BUBIER.
BOWDEN, BOUDDEN?, Michael, mar Mary (Barker) LEGRO 1742 MRB. OUTC. See LEGRO.
BOWDEN, Mary, mar Benj. LE CRAW, qv. in MRB 1800, OUTC. See LE CRAW.
BOWDEN, Francis, mar Elizabeth BODEN, qv, 1768, OUTC. See BODEN.
BOWDEN, Hannah, mar 1796 Richard BESOM, BISSON Jr., OUTC. See BISSON.
BOUDEN, BOWDEN, BAUDAIN?, Francis, from C.I. to MRB, wife Marey. This might be a C.I. fam. (Underhill; MRB VR)
A1. William, b 1708 A2. Michael, b 1712

A3. Francis, b ca 1715
A4. Marey, b 1718
A5. Sarah, b 1720
A6. Joseph, b 1725
A7. Benjamin, b 1727
A8. Ebenezer, b 1728

BOWDOIN. Fams in early New England appear to have come to the Colonies from France via Ireland. There was, however, a BAUDOUIN fam in J, 1500s and 1600s. A Martha BAUDOUIN in J mar Helier FAULTRART, rector of St. Martin, J. Their dau, Jane Faultrart, 1586-1670, mar 1613 John PALLOT, whose son Daniel mar 1651 Michelle BAUDOUIN, dau of John BAUDOUIN by Martha LE PELLEY. The FAULTRART fam appeared 1607, so may have come from France a little earlier as a Hug fam. The BAUDOUIN name is old in J, 1200 and before. Some BOWDOINS of early New England may have been possibly from St. John, J, where BAUDAIN and LE MARINEL are both found in 1668.

BOWLIN, poss BALLEINE?, Peter, b ca 1745, rem to Chester Co., PA where he res until about 1800. He res Somerset Co. from 1800 till his death in 1850. He mar Nancy Blockard. He was connected with two other C.I. fams, the TISSUE and the SKINNER fams, qv. See BALLEINE. OUTC. (Joan Witt, E. Liverpool, OH)
A1. John, mar Elizabeth Barnhouse
A2. Peter, mar Susannah Ringer, dau of Adam and Margaret Ringer

BOWDEDGE, John SMITH, b 1841 St. Helier, J, son of ___ Bowdidge and Alice Smith. John mar Ann Maria MANLEY, b 1854 St. Heliers, J, 1939 Salt Lake City, UT. She was the dau of William and ___ (CHEVALIER) MANLEY of J. (Chart by Evelyn Porter, Novato, CAL)
A1. William Charles, b 1877 Salt Lake City, UT, mar 1904 Florence Mable PENNEY
A2. Elizabeth Ann, b 1879, mar 1903 Edson Abinadi Porter
A3. Richard Barrington, b 1881, mar Martha Johnson Nordstrom, div. He mar 2. Mary Larson and 3. in 1929, Thelma Ethel GROVES
A4. Edward, d.y.? A5. Augusta, b 1889
A6. Florence Pearl, b 1895 Taylorsville, UT

BOWDIDGE, Elizabeth, from G to UT 1865, ship BELLEWOOD. (SLC)
BOWDIDGE, Alice, from G to UT 1862, ship ANTARCTIC. (SLC)
BOWDEDGE, a fam from G to UT 1863, ship ANTARCTIC. (SLC)
A1. Sarah A2. Emily A3. Mary A4. Alice

BOYCE, J surname from 1309. Not common.
BOYCE, David, res Salem?, mar ca 1712 Anna ALLEY, qv. OUTC.
A1. David Boyce, b ca ___, mar Catherine DALAND, qv, widow of Robert NEAL. She was his wife in 1770.

A David Boyce was in Salem, MA 1790 with fam of 3. (Census)

BRAKE. Not old in C.I., from southern England? Curr G.
BRAKE, Elisha, Sr., b 1862 Vale, G, rem to North Chelmsford, MA 1907, mar Mary Ann HENWOOD in J. She came over 1910. Elisha d 1934, Mary Ann in 1931. See NORTH CHELMSFORD section. (Bessie Benest Le Masurier, North Chelmsford, MA)
A1. Elisha Jr., b G, mar Ada DE CARTERET, son Arthur, dau Gladys, who res Maine
A2. Alfred, b G, mar Maria TOMS, son Nelson, dau Edna, who mar ___ Howland, and d 1933
A3. Philip, b G, to N. Chelmsford 1910, unmar, d 1958
A4. Mary Ann, b G, to N. Chelmsford, mar Arthur DE CARTERET, qv. Two sons, Reginald and Clarence De Carteret.
A5. Alice, b G, mar Clarence BENEST, to N. Chelmsford, MA 1907. Alice d 1933. Two chn.
B1. Raymond BENEST B2. Bessie BENEST, mar Thomas LE MASURIER

BRAKE, Walter, b G, bro of Elisha above, mar Helena Hanley
BRAY. See Q.A. IN CANADA. BREE in J 1528, 1607. In St. Saviour

Parish, J 1668 and 1749. Variants: BREE, BRAY, may be the same fam line? Name found in NJ, MA and ME early. (Essex Coll., vol. 1, 4, 7; Underhill; Noyes; Emmerton; Stillwell's MISCELLANY, vol. 3; BRAY is in John Adams line-Burke's PRESIDENTIAL FAMILIES)

BRAY, Frederick, b 1821 J, d 1912, bur Greenwood Cem, Burlington, ONT. Mar Margaret D. Scott, b 1831 Fifeshire, Scotland, d 1912 Burlington? He was poss the bro of Henry BRAY, 1823-1908, bur same cem, with wife Margaret Donnelly, b 1832. Chn unverified.

A1. Henry Bray, 1862-1935 A2. Lavina, 1864-1946

BRAYN. Curr research in C.I. See CIFHS #11.

BREHAUT, in J 1512. In G 1100s, in St. Peter Du Bois, G 1300s. Much BREHAUT data in Danvers, MA. See also Q.A. IN CANADA, by Turk.

BREHAUT. See HAWKINS-BREHAUT fam under HAWKINS, of PEI.

BREHAUT, Henry, 1767-1845, from G to PEI 1806 with wife Elizabeth Pulham and other Guernsey fams such as LE LACHEUR, MACHON, TAUDVIN, MARQUAND, DE JERSEY and HAWKINS. See Q.A. IN CANADA, by Turk.

A1. Henry, b 1792, G, mar Frances Thorne, 10 chn A2. Daniel

A3. Thomas Smith, b 1796 G, rem to Miramichi, PEI, mar Sarah Noble, poss?, and poss 2. ? Janet Clow from Scotland, 1826-1874. (Sally Lomas, Toronto, ONT) Chn all to U.S. SEE LATE ADDITIONS.

B1. Benjamin, mar ___, res Chelsea, MA, several chn

B2. Henry, mar Margaret ___, res Dorchester, MA, no issue

B3. Elizabeth, mar ___ Southard, res Bridgewater, MA, no issue

B4. Frances, mar ___ Horton, no issue

B5. James William Brehaut, mar Annabelle HAWKINS, desc, see HAWKINS.

BREHAUT. Data below adds to and corrects data in Q.A. IN CANADA, by Turk, p. 173. (Frederick L. Church, Collinsville, CT)

BREHAUT, Henry, b ca 1767/68 G, son of Henry and Elizabeth (NICHOLAS) BREHAUT of G, mar 1791 Elizabeth PULLAM, PULHAM, etc., b 1768 England? d 1864 PEI. Henry d 1848/49 PEI, Canada.

A1. Henry, b 1792 G, d 1883 PEI, mar 1821, Murray Harbor, PEI, Frances Avard Thorne, b1801 England, d1890 Guernsey Cove, PEI

B1. Thomas, b 1821 B2. Henry, b1823 PEI, mar Maria Jane MACHON, qv

B3. Sarah, b 1825 B4. Daniel, b1827 PEI B5. Charles, b1829 PEI

B6. William John, b1831 Murray Harbor, PEI, d1886. Mar Elizabeth Hannah Brooks, who d1922 Winn, ME, b1835 White Sands, PEI.

C1. Catharine Alma, b1878 Rockland, NB, d1934 Washington, DC, mar Frederick Lewis Church, b1886 Shirley , ME, d1964 Alexandria, VA. He mar 2. 1941, Rena Mae Gaines.

D1. Ruth Elizabeth Church, b 1912 Brewer, ME, d.y.

D2. Catherine Edith Church, b1914 Bangor, ME, d1964 Bethesda, MD, mar Edward H. Porter, a Methodist minister. Dau Judith A. Porter, b1946.

D3. Frederick Lewis Church, Jr., b1915 Wash., D.C. (1980 WHO'S WHO) Mar Alma Bessie White of Cincinnati, OH.

E1. Lawrence B. Church, b1937, banker, mar ___, son Wm. F. b1964.

E2. James Frederick Church, b1947, nuclear engineer, mar Angela Tomlinson. Sons Peter T. and Nathan J. b 1970s.

C2. Artemus H. of Eagleton, WI C3. Headley J.

C4. Mrs. B.F. Wyman of Winn, ME had Harold Ivan and Ellison Wyman of Detroit, MI and Wash., D.C.

C5. G. Herbert, b ca 1873 White Sands, PEI, res Woodstock, NB, rem to Winn, ME ca 1884 where he d1929. Three sons: Stanley H., William J. and Herbert J.

B7. Anne G., b1833 B8. Maria, b1837 B9. George, b1849

BREHAUT. See p. 174, Q.A. IN CANADA. BREHAUT, Peter, Pierre, b1764 G, son of Pierre and Marie (TOSTEVIN) BREHAUT of G, mar 1792 Quebec,

Therese Bellenoy dit Le Maitre, in Trinity Cath., Quebec City. Peter was a merchant there in gen. goods, but mostly in the grain trade. His papers, 1817-1832 in Dominion Archives. He drowned 1817, and his widow mar ca 1820 Quebec, Wm. GRUT SHEPPARD, of G? Peter went to Canada ca 1788. (ARCHIVES; Stanley Ryerson, Montreal, QUE; Virginia Whitelaw, Vancouver, BC)

A1. Catherine Esther, mar Edmund Wm. Bower Antrobus. A Capt. Brehaut mar an E. Antrobus ca 1873. Antrobus was ADC of the 71st Regt. (Maple Leaves by J.M. Le Moine, QUE 1873) She d1880. Chn?

A2. Peter Percival, b1803 QUE, d1830 England, or at sea

A3. William Henry, b 1811 QUE, d1880 Trois Rivieres, QUE. He was admitted to Bar 1834 and was later a judge. Mar 1849 Esther Eliza Taylor, dau of Geo. Mortimer Taylor and Mary Ann LLOYD.

B1. Edith Mary, b1850 Montreal, mar 1875 Robert Sainte-Barbe Young, a lawyer

B2. Tessie Maria Mortimer, b 1852 Montreal, mar James Devine/ Devigne, b Ireland who d as a young man. His wife and 3 daus rem to Toronto or Newmarket, where the wife Tessie shortly died. The 3 daus were raised by their uncle Dyce Saunders & wife Amy.

C1. Ethel Devine, b ___, mar Charles Heward

D1. Effie, b ___, mar I___ Irwin, res Niagara-on-the-Lake, ONT.

C2. Edith Mary, b1878 Montreal, rem to Toronto, d unmar in 1950s?

C3. Tessie, Teddie, b ca 1883, d1965, mar Toronto, Dr. Edward Stanley Ryerson

D1. Stanley Brehaut Ryerson, b1911 Toronot, mar Mildred ___, res Montreal, QUE

D2. Donald Egerton Ryerson, b1914 Toronto, mar Edna Catherine ___, res Toronto, ONT

D3. Mary Virginia Ryerson, b1919 Toronto, mar there 1942 Dr. John Wm. Whitelaw, son of Dr. Wm. Albert Whitelaw & Eliz. Mackay

E1. David John Whitelaw, b1943 Vanc. BC, mar 1966 Ottawa, ONT, Pamela Clacken?

E2. Pamela Virginia, b1951 Vanc., mar 1973 Ronald R. Fedoruk, re Calgary, Alta., dau Daphne Fedoruk

B3. Kate Frances Elisa, b1854 Montreal, d.y.?

B4. Amy Julia Percival, b___, mar Dyce Saunders. This fam raised the chn of Tessie, her sister, and Tessie's husband John Devine/ Devigne.

A4. Mary Elizabeth, mar Capt. Wm. Crosby Hanson of the 71st Reg't, Quebec City, 1870s? JOHN BURHOE, see CH.IS.COLLECTION

BREHAUT, Henry, b1767 G, son of Henry B. & Elizabeth, also née BREHAUT. Mar 1791 Elizabeth Pulham of England. Sailed to Prince Edward Is. 1806, with about 75 other Channel Islanders to settle there. At least 9 chn. See Q.A. IN CANADA, by Turk, p. 173. See previous page.

A2. Daniel, b1795 G, d1857, res Guernsey Cove, PEI, bur Old English CH Cem. at Murray Harbor. Mar 1839 Isabel Bell, 2 daus and 5 sons. Farmer and ship builder. "While attempting to free vessel locked in winter ice, developed pneumonia and died, leaving fam of 7, from 2 to 17 yrs of age." (Amy MacNeill, Murray Harb. PEI; James V. Beck, Okemos, MI)

B1. Mary, 1840-1923 B2. Elizabeth, b1842, unmar

B3. James, b1844, d1909, mar 1873 Sarah Howe. A farmer, bur Murray Harb. Cem.

C1. Ida, 1874-1956 C3. Fred, 1880-1959

C2. William, 1877-1966 C4. Lemuel, 1888-1978

C5. Henry, 1886-1969, bur Murray Harb. Cem, mar 1909 Lena Maud Dunn A farmer, 8 chn. Sons Clarence, Elmer, Vernon and Frank, b 1909 to 1913, unmar.

D5. Sarah, b1917, mar George Serafin, Murray Harb, PEI, no issue

D6. Helen, b1920, mar George Herschfeld, Dartmouth, NS, a dau

E1. Helen Herschfeld, b1952, mar John Whitman

D7. Ethel, b1923, mar Roy Flemming, Halifax, NS

E1. Donald Flemming, b1952, mar Jane Bushett

D8. Amy, b1926, mar John MacNeill, b1919, son of Harry and Annie MacNeill, res Murray Harbour, PEI

E1. Sandra MacNeill, mar Wallace MacKay, b1944, son of Gordon and Ruth MacKay, res Beach Point, PEI. Two chn: Patty Lou and John MacKay, b 1960s.

E2. Nancy, b1952, mar Alex MacBeath, b1951, res Charlottetown PEI

E3, Jacqueline MacNeill, b1960 E4. Lena Ann MacNeill, b1964

B4. Henry Thomas, 1846-1938 B6. Joseph Watson, b1853, rem to USA

B5. Daniel, b1850, rem to USA B7. Benjamin Noble, 1855-1888 res USA

BREHAUT. Those below are part of the same Brehaut fam from G, settled in Prince Edward Island, as A2. Daniel, above. See p. 173/4 in Q.A. IN CANADA, by Turk. (Glenda Lloyd, Orangevale, CAL)

A4. Elizabeth, dau of Henry & Elizabeth BREHAUT, b1798 G, mar ca 1819 James Laird of Vernon River, PEI. At least one ch.

B1. Charlotte Elizabeth Laird, b1819 PEI, d1854 Murray Harb. PEI. She mar 1839 David Chrichton, b1805 Scotland, d1885 Murray Harb. He mar 1855, at her death, her first cousin Sarah M. Sencabaugh, also a BREHAUT desc. Seven chn by 1st wife, 6 by 2nd. Sarah b1830 England?, d1880 Murray Harbour.

C1. Alex Creighton, Crichton, b1840 Murray Harb., PEI

C2. Henry Frederick Crichton, b1842, d1885, mar Annie ___, no issue

C3. Catherine M. Crichton, b1844, mar ___, had chn Fred, Thomas, Lottie, Robert, George and Millie

C4. John Robert Chrichton, b1846 Murray Harb., PEI, mar 1873 Fairfield, CAL, Aramanda Adilue Cockern. He d1925 Redding, CAL, bur MacArthur, CAL. She was b1851 Carthage, ILL, 5 chn.

D1. Herbert Frederick Crichton, b1874 Suisun, CAL, d1964, mar 1898 Leona May Scott

D2. Cora Belle Creighton, b1877, note change in spelling. She mar 1909 Martin D. Fitzwater, she d 1960.

D3. John Henry Creighton, b1879 Glenburn, CAL, mar 1906 Minnie Grace Whipple, he d 1934.

D4. Mabel Creighton, b1882 Glenburn, CAL, mar 1905 Crawford Calvin Clarke, and d1964 Modoc Co., CAL, bur Alturas, CAL. He was son of Calvin R. Clarke & Isabella Donovan, b1868 Grass Valley, CAL. He d 1942, she in 1964.

E1. Carroll Crawford Clarke, b1910, Dixie Valley, CAL, d 1922

E2. Juanita Zoe Clarke, b1914 Glenburn, CAL, mar 1934 Reno, NEV, Glenn Raymond Gardner, b1909 Hill City, KS, d1963 Davis Creek, CAL. He was son of Charles C. Gardner & Jessie Elma Grimes

F1. Glenda Aloha Gardner, b1939, Alturas, CAL, mar Palo Alto, CAL 1972, Kenneth Harry Lloyd, b1922 Plymouth, England, son of Harry Lloyd and Agnes Penaluna, 2 chn? Glenda and Clarke Lloyd.

F2. Crawford Clarke Gardner, b1940 Alturas, CAL, mar 1963 Nancy Aileen Reed, b1941 Visalia, CAL, dau of Wm. Henry Reed and Doris H. McCallister. Two chn: Jana and Glenn.

D5. James Percy Creighton, b1888 Glenburn, CAL, mar 1. Mabel Guthrie and 2. Elizabeth ___, widow of ___ Smith, no issue. Adopted John ___.

C5. James Crichton, b1848 Murray Harb., PEI, mar Mary ___, d San Francisco, CAL, had dau Charlotte M. Meier
C6. Elizabeth Brehaut Crichton, b1850 Murray Harb PEI, d1853 age 3
C7. David Chrichton, d.y.
B2. Henry A., mar ___McKinnon
B3. John
B4. James
B5. Benj. A., mar ___ CLEMENTS, sister of Tom Clements
B6. David

BREHAUT, Peter J., of the PEI fam, mar Elizabeth C. Ferguson, b1875, d1945, res PEI. Current research: Elaine Marney, Hampton, NH.
A1. Roy, mar Ella Hanson A2. Cecil, b early 1900s?, mar J. Pack?
A3. Ethelbert, mar Jean MacWhirter A4. Leonard, mar Louise Herring

BREHAUT, Chester L., of same clan, mar Marion Beck, b1902, her 1st husb.

BREHAUT, Gladys Mildred, mar Wm. Harold Beck, b1904. Beck data from J.V. Beck, Okemos, MI

BRETON, a fam from J?, res London, ONT.

BRETON. See BRETTON and LE BRETON.

BRETON, as LE BRETON in J from 1270. In G from 1331. In St. Saviour, Grouville, Trinity, St. Clement and St. Ouen, J 1668. In Trinity, St. Saviour, Grouville, St. Heliers, St. Peter and St. Ouen, J 1749. Curr G and J, but also noted in Scotland.

The C.I. LE BRETON fams are no doubt of several different lines, coming to the Islands at various times. Many of this name and variants in early New England, but compiler does not know of any definitive work on this surname in America. See sources: Virkus; Noyes; Census; VRs and town histories. See BRETON under LE BRETON and BRITTON.

BREWER. Not an old G surname, but cf BROUARD. See also Q.A. IN CANADA.

BREWER, Charles W., b1822 G, son of Capt. Henry & Elizabeth (HAWKINS) BREWER, natives of Devonshire, England. They had rem in early life to Guernsey. Charles served an apprenticeship to the trade of CH organ and piano making. He mar in G 1852 Jane, dau of William Matthews of Guernsey. In 1853 they came to Racine, WI, where Charles began the manufacture of reed organs. He was an inventor and patented several items. Five chn b WIS. (Album, Kenosha & Racine, WIS)
A1. Charles F., a jeweler in Racine with the Elkins Jewelry Co.
A2., A3., A4. Ernest H., Emma & Laura, d.y. A5. Alice, d1890

BREWER, Alfred, b NYCity 1830, son of ___ Brewer, b J. Alfred mar Marietta Rogers, b1844 Lockport, NY, 6 chn, 3 d.y. (Bettie Francis, Fresno, CAL)
A1. Willie C., b1869 WI, mar May Yule, res Fall River, WI, 6 chn
A2. Bert A., b1871 WI, mar Mandy Bunnes, res Columbus, WI, 4 chn
A3. Fred Farnham, b1880 WI, mar Harriet L. MARTIN, res Columbus, WI and in Franklin Park, ILL, 3 chn
B1. Merrill Martin Brewer, mar ___, had dau Betty Brewer Francis

BRIANT, BRIAND, a French surname noted in J, but rare. Curr research CIFHS #9. "The French-speaking Briand group from Edmonton, Canada, claim that the name was originally BRILLIANT and was found in Bretagne, France in the 13th century. Near about that time France was in process of becoming a national state under the leadership of Isle de Paris. The Brilliant group openly resisted the aspirations of the Paris nobility. They supported a noble from Bretagne, but eventually lost the battle...Their punishment was banishment or flight. Some went to Ireland and others to the Channel Islands. Both groups, however, altered their family name's spelling to BRIAND, though to the French person the pronunciation of that name would have been practically identical to that of Brilliant." (Gary Briand, Douglastown QUE)

BRIANT. Occurs in Rehoboth, Beverly, MA: in Essex Co., NJ; in Falmouth, ME and many towns in NH and ME in the 1700s. OUTC.

BRIAND. One fam from J to NS 1700s. See Q.A. IN CANADA, by Turk.

BRIARD, in J 1299. In St. John, Trinity, St. Saviour and St. Ouen, J 1668. In St. Saviour and St. Ouen, J 1749. Name from Le Brie, East of Paris, France. Were the BRIARDS of early New England the desc of the famous John BRIARD of the DOVE? He was the first known privateersman, commissioned by Queen Elizabeth in 1578. See PIRATES AND PRIVATEERS section in this book.

Much BRIAR data in Portsmouth, NH and Kittery records, but OUTC. See WRCIC, Noyes, Stackpole, VRs of MRB, Lynn, MA, Boothbay, ME, Portsmouth, NH, Boston and Rehoboth, MA.

BRIARD, Elias, res MRB, had wife Mary Pitman. (Essex Ant., Vols 11,12) Elias may be from the C.I. CAUTION: TRIAL CHARTS. This fam also used BRYAR.

A1. Mary, bp1728 d.y. A2. Elizabeth, bp1731, d unmar age 97 in 1827
A3. Jane, bp1732/33 A5. Frances/Francis?, bp1743/44
A4. John, bp1742 d.y.
A6. Elias, bp1747, poss mar Annis/Agnes HAKE/HAWK? She d his widow in 1828, age 76.
B1. Elias, bp1773 B4. Agnes/Annis, bp1781
B2. William, bp1776 d.y. B5. Elizabeth, bp1784
B3. William again, d.y. B6. John, bp1789

BRIAR, BRIARD, Elisha, a blockmaker, d1718 Maine, age 57. Noted in 1686 and in 1695 made a coffin for "old Richard Lewis." His estate admin. to the widow Abigail DREW, qv. Mar 1689. She was living with her son-in-law 1741 in Greenland, ME. OUTC. However, note mar to DREW, qv. Many more BRIARS in ME, see records.

A1. Margaret, b1693, mar James Cate
A2. Abigail, b1695, mar 1715/16 William Cross of Biddeford, Devon
A3. Samuel, b1687, blockmaker, will admin. 1723 to widow Lucy Lewis of Kittery, ME, mar 1719. She mar 1724 Sylvanus Tripe. Two or more chn, by BRIAR or by Tripe? (Noyes; NEHGS, vol. 24)
A4. Sarah, b1700/01, mar 1. Thomas MAINWARING, qv, his 2nd wife, of Great Island, ME. Thomas had mar 1. a Kittery girl before 1715? He d1733. Sarah then mar Wm. Watson who d before 1743, 3 daus. (Noyes)
B1. Sarah, by 1st wife?, mar 1732 Ebenezer Jackson
B2. dau bp1714, d.y.?
B3. by Sarah BRIARD, John MAINWARING, who d before 1757
B4. Winchester Mainwaring, b ca 1732, d 1747 Jamaica. His guardian had been Joseph Pierce of Portsmouth, NH.
A5. Mary, b1702. Poss mar William WARNE in Boston 1727?

BRIARD, Capt. John, a Jerseyman of Portsmouth, NH from "Santel," prob St. Heliers, J before 1726. Mar that year Agnes Leby, Libby? (Bolton) John, a ship captain, had son Samuel, 1733-1788.

BRIAR, William, mar Elizabeth Weeks, dau of Nicholas and either Priscilla (Gunnison) or Ann (Adams) Hill Weeks. (Noyes)

BRIARD, poss also spelled BRIAR, BRIARS, BRYAR, etc., etc., in early New England. Some data in WRCIC. Those below are OUTC.

BRIARD, Annis, mar Wm. Cloon (int) 1809 MRB, poss dau of Elias?
BRIARD, Betsy, mar Amos GRANDY, qv, 1805 MRB.
BRIARD, Elias, mar Elizabeth ___, res MRB, dau Elizabeth bp1799 MRB.
BRIARD, Elias, mar 1771 MRB, Mrs. Mary Bavidge.
BRIARS, Joseph, mar Sarah RENEW, RENOUF?, qv, 1790 MRB.
BRIARD, Mary, of Portsmouth, NH, mar Wm. Waine of Boston 1727 (int).
BRIARS, Mehitable, mar Elizar RUMMERY 1687 MRB. See RUMMERY, ROMERIL.
BRIARD, Moses, mar Sarah Grant 1823 Lynn, MA, a son Wm. Henry b1826.
BRIARD, Moses, mar Hannah Chapman 1831 Lynn, MA.

A1. George Washington, b1831 A3. Hannah Maria, b1835
A2. John Chapman, b1834 A4. Mary S., dau of Hannah, b1845

BRIER, Robert, mar in Portsmouth, NH 1832 Olive PENDEXTER, qv.

BRIARD, Sarah, mar 1788 Benj. Viall in Rehoboth, MA.

BRIARD, Samuel, in Boothbay, ME with fam of 12, 1790. (Census)

Several BRIARD fams from J res Gaspe Peninsula in the 1800s. See Q.A. in CANADA. Some detail in that book is incomplete and some incorrect. Elias, below, was the son of John and Betsy (LE GRESLEY) BRIARD.

BRIARD, Elias, Sr., b1835 J, rem 1854 to Paspebiac, QUE age 16, mar Johanna Scott, b ca 1851. (Evelyn McLellan, Moncton, NB; Mrs. A.K. Briard-Smith, Oakville, ONT)

A1. Elias James, b1862, d1930, res Gaspe, mar Mary Ann Law, 1895, b1873, d1958. Res New Carlisle, Gaspe, QUE. Elias worked for the Robin firm as a ship carpenter.
B1. Annie Alma, b1896, d1954, mar Ogilvie McLellan 1922, b1888 d1955
C1. Leonard Alexander McLellan, b1923, mar Evelyn Pearl MAUGER 1958, b1929
D1. Sheri Lyn McLellan, b1964, adopted
B2. Lena, 1898-1976, mar 1919 Archie McKenzie, 1891-1973, a son d.y.
C2. Keith Briard McKenzie, b1922 Escuminac, QUE, d1974, mar Ada June Isabel Keays 1943, who d 1980
D1. Elizabeth Ann McKenzie, b1946, mar Danny Cochrane 1964, 4 chn: Christopher B., Elizabeth B., Patrick, and Erin J.
D2. William John McKenzie, b1949, unmar
C3. Sydney Walter McKenzie, b1926, mar Olive Munn O'Donnell 1962, res N of Keswick, NB, adopted son Kevin John, b1965
C4. Stanley Ralph McKenzie, 1928-1964, mar Sylvia K. Fyvie, 1951, 5 chn: John S., Heather S., Brian J., Grant Sidney, and Stanley R. McKenzie
C5. Gerald Wm. McKenzie, b1930, mar May Jane Waugh 1958, 4 chn: Nancy W.J., Gerald F., Stephen C. and Arthur E. McKenzie
C6. John Colin McKenzie, 1935-1936
B3. Reida Briard, b1900 Moncton, NB, mar Evelyn DE STE. CROIX 1941, b1898, d1967, no issue
B4. Mabel, b1902 Ormstown, QUE, mar Alan ENGLISH 1960, no issue
B5. Leonard, b1905 Paspebiac West, QUE, d1980, mar 1929 Dorothy Brash?, res West Hill, ONT. She was b1904, 2 chn.
C1. Everett James, Rev., b1930, mar Lorna Toohey, res West Hill, ONT, 4 chn, 2 adopted: Bruce, Mark, Joy Louise & Melanie Lynn.
C2. Marilyn, b1936, res Scarborough, ONT, missionary in Africa
B6. Stanley, b1970, res Mt. Royal, QUE, mar Isabel Hopkins
C1. Heather, 1938-1974, mar John Gibson
C2. Barbara, b1944, mar Glenn Smith C3. Donald, adopted, mar
B7. Ella, b1910, mar Otis McLellan, 1902-1974, res Panama City, FLA
C1. Elizabeth McLellan, b1941, mar Robert Stewart, res FLA
D1. James A. Stewart, b1963 D2. Brian Stewart
C2. Elaine McLellan b1945 mar Frank Romas 1967, res Idyllwild, CAL
D1. Davis Romas, b1969 D2. Bradely Romas, b1977
A2. Eliza Amelia?, 1864-1882, res New Carlisle East, QUE
A3. Annie, 1866-1886, d of measles
A4. Elvina, 1870-1927, d Paspebiac West, QUE, mar John LE GRAND, son John d.y.
A5. Walter Scott, b1872, res New Carlisle East, QUE, d1951 unmar
A6. Louisa, 1874-1947, mar Elias James LE GRAND 1892, 1873-1954, poss 18 chn?
A7. Eva Caroline, b1880, res QUE, d1957, mar 1916 George Munro, 1882-1965, no issue

A8. William, 1884-1949, res Brockville, ONT, mar 1914 Estelle Maude Ogilvie, b1890, 4 chn
B1. Lois Edna, b1915, mar Gerald McLellan 1942, b1918
C1. Sandra L. McLellan, b1944, mar 1966 Frederick Ferris, b1944
C2. Joanne B. McLellan, b1947, twin of James, mar Jim Nevin 1967
C3. James E. McLellan, twin of Joanne, b1947
C4. Faye G., b1949 C5. Walter S. McLellan, b1953
B2. Amy Kathleen, b1918, mar 1945 Douglas Smith, b1917
C1. Stephanie Ann Smith, b1949 C3. David Douglas Smith, b1953
C2. Virginia K. Smith, b1950
B3. Greta Beryl, b1920, mar 1949 Douglas Roy Draper, b191-, res Galt, ONT
C1. Lorna Jean Draper, b1951 C3. Beverly R. Draper, b1955
C2. Roy Edward Draper, b1952
B4. Earle Conrad, b1928, mar 1960 Edith Irene Bulley, b1929
C1. Paul Elaine Briard, b1962 C2. Louise Fern, b1965
A9. Annie Alma, 1896-1954, mar Ogilvie McLellan, res Caplan, and Pasp. West, QUE

BRIARD, Stanley, son of John & Ann (LE RICHE) BRIARD. He was b J 1860?, rem to Gaspe and mar Clarissa LUCE. Clarissa, 94, res recently in nursing home in St. Cartharines, ONT. (Mrs. A.K. Briard-Smith, Oakville, ONT)

BRICE. English and Guernsey surname.

BRICE, Edwin Edgar, 1878-1949, mar Jenny ___ in G, was related to LING fam, qv. (Roger Brehaut, Guernsey)
A1. Gwendolyn Brice, b G?, mar Dewey Keck A2. Edwin Brice
B1. Lores Jane Keck, mar ___ Borke, res Cupertino, CAL

BRICE, Ted, from G to Chicago, ILL early 1900s, related to DE BRODER, qv. Harriet Ann Brice mar Daniel PERRIN, qv.

BRIDEAUX. Old J surname. BRIDLE, old G surname.

BRIDEAUX, Walter PIROUET, from J to US, one of several bros and sisters in J. (Phyllis Brideaux, Sault Ste. Marie, ONT)

BRIDEAUX. See Q.A. IN CANADA, by Turk, page 176.

BRIDEAUX, Edwin Charles, b1887 St. Saviour, J, mar Phyllis Marie Chestle 1926. She was b Portsmouth, England 1905. Edwin rem to QUE, then to Sault Ste. Marie, ONT after 1910, 6 chn. (Phyllis Brideaux, Sault Ste. Marie, ONT) See Q.A. IN CANADA, by Turk.
A1. Sue Chestle, b1928, mar Charles Willet, 8 sons
B1. Jonathan C. Willett, b1949 B5. Herbert A. Willett, b1955
B2. James G. Willett, b1951 B6. Victor Willett, b1958
B3. Lorne E. Willett, b1953 B7. Edwin A. Willett, b1964
B4. Charles R. Willett, b1954 B8. Christopher R. Willett, b1964

BRIDGO. Spelled various ways, appears in MRB 1700s. Some poss BRIDEAUX from J or France, more data in MRB records. TRIAL CHARTS.

BRIDGOE, Abigail, mar 1806 Thomas MARTIN in MRB, poss 2nd wife was Sarah Vickery Pedrick, QV.

BRIDGEO, George, b J, mar Hannah HOMAN 1752 MRB.
A1. George, bp1755 A3. William, bp1760
A2. Philip, bp1758 A4. Francis, bp1762

BRIDGEO, George, of MRB, d of tuberculosis 1832, age ca 65.

BRIDGEO, George, mar Mary Porter 1788 MRB, who poss d1806 age 29 or in 1796, MRB.
A1. Mary, bp1788 d.y.? A3. Mary again, bp1792 d.y.? A5. Mary, again bp1795
A2. Abigail, bp1790 A4. Hannah, bp1794

BRIOGEO, George, fisherman of MRB, drowned on Grand Banks 1846 age 42.

BRIDGEO, George, mar Mary DENNIS 1801 MRB. OUTC.
A1. George, b1804?, mar Mary C. RUSSEL 1828 MRB.

A2. Hannah Dennis, b1806, mar 1830 John Humphries
BRIDGEO/BRIDGES?, George, mar Mrs. Nancy Redden 1807 MRB. OUTC.
A1. Mary Abigail, bp1811
A2. Elizabeth, bp1812
A3. Martha, bp1815
A4. Miriam Ball, bp1818
A5. Harriot, bp1820, poss mar 1839 Geo. M. PEDRICK
BRIDGEO, BRIDLE, Hannah, see MRB VR for some data. OUTC.
BRIDGEO, John and Mary, see MRB data for 3 fams in 1700s, also a John and Joanna Chard BRIDGEO.
BRIDGEO, Nancy B., mar Richard GIRDLER 1835 MRB, poss Nancy Barker BRIDGEO, dau of Philip? who mar Nancy ___ in MRB before 1809.
BRIDGEO, Philip, mar Hannah KNIGHT 1780, res MRB, poss lost at sea 1820, age 61-64?, poss also a son Philip, master mariner, b1782, drowned 1844, age 61.
A1. Mary, bp1784, d1805 age 20
A2. John, bp1788, poss mar Hannah DENNIS in 1809?
A3. Sarah, bp1791. Did she mar Robert B. CHINN 1816 MRB?
A4. Ruthy, bp1794, poss mar David Flint 1820 MRB?
A5. Deliverance, bp1798. Did she mar Joseph Lindsey Jr. 1821 MRB?
BRIDGEO, Philip, mariner, d1840s, age 39, of MRB.
BRIDGEO, Philip, mar 1805 Jane Goodwin in MRB.
A1. Mary, b1805, mar 1828 James B. HAWKES & 2. Samuel Sinclear 1837
A2. Jane H., b1808 d.y.? A3. Philip b1809, see Philip, mariner above
A4. William G., mariner, b1812, mar Deborah Proctor 1838 MRB, drowned on Grand Banks 1846, age 32? A dau Mary Ellen b1846.
A5. John, b1815 d.y.? A6. Jane H. again, b1816 d.y.?
A7. Jane H. again, b1818. May have mar Peter A. MARTIN 1839, his 2nd wife, as he had prob mar 1. Elizabeth Stacey in MRB 1825.
A8. John, b1821, mar ?Elizabeth Standley 1843, at least 3 chn
B1. John, b1844 B2. Philip, b1846 B3. William, b1849
BRIDGEHOOD. Fam from C.I. 1852 via ship KENNEBEC, settled UT. (SLC Records) Compiler does not know if this fam was originally BRIDEAUX. Three chn: Elizabeth, Frances S. and Virginia.
BRIGHT. Has occurred in the C.I., but compiler does not know if this is old C.I. surname. See records of Salem and Boston, MA for BRIGHT records, and also Stonington, CT.
BRINE, William, had ropewalk in J 1770 (Jean) See Q.A. IN CANADA, Turk.
BRITTON, see BRETON and LE BRETON. CAUTION: Not all LE BRETONS, BRETONS and BRETTONS came to New England from the C.I. At least one is from France, poss others from England.
BRITTON, Capt. David, prob a LE BRETON, res Boston, had sisterRachel Sowersby of Boston 1789. Poss other sisters, widow Jane Pigeon, and another in Providence, RI. William and Nathaniel Grafton were heirs 1789, and Sarah Venner. Other heirs were Mary, wife of Benjamin Carr, and Anna & Nathaniel Grafton of Newport, RI. (NEHGS)
BRETOON, John and wife from J at Machias, ME 1668, servants to J. Martell, qv. (Street)
BRITAIN, John, res MRB, mar Mary MULLET, qv, of MRB 1762, his widow in Danvers, MA 1797. OUTC. Likely to be from J. Son Thomas b1766 and dau Mary b1770.
BRETTON, Benjamin, a Jerseyman, d at Salem in house of Jon Macarter 1685. (Essex records)
BRITTON, BRETON, LE BRETON, Peter, b ca 1659 J, rem to Salem, MA 1677. (NEGHS, vol. 31) See Boston, Chelsea, Salem, and Newport, RI for more information, and WRCIC.
BROCHET. From J to Canada. See Q.A. IN CANADA and LE BOUTILLIER FAMILY.
BROCHE?, BROCHET?, Rachel, b Nov. 1808 G or J?, d1886 Richland Co., or Lima, OH, bur Lima Cem. She mar in Eng?, Edmond Orchard, b1810 Mawnan,

Redruth, Cornwall, England, son of Philip & Mary (Tregloan) Orchard. Seven chn. (Betsy Delashmitt, Mansfield, OH) See LATE ADDITIONS.

A1. William E. Orchard, b1835 England, d1883 Lima, OH, mar 1861 Lima, Martha Croft. (Arthur Orchard, Lima, OH) Martha b1843, d1915 Toledo, OH, dau of Benjamin and Mary.
B1. Charles E. Orchard, b1870 Lima, OH, mar 1890 Eschol Sawmiller
C1. Arthur Lee Orchard, 1892-1963, mar 1913 Emma B. Shaner, b1895
D1. Arthur L. Orchard, b1927 Allen Co., OH, res Lima, OH
A2. James H. Orchard, b1837 England
A3. Rachel Sophia Orchard, b1840 Illogan, Redruth, Cornwall, England, d1929 Mansfield, OH. Mar 1867 Louis NICHOLS, 1845-1978, son of John and Dinah Nichols, 2 chn
B1. Charles Melville Nichols, b1868 Nevada, OH, d1950, mar 1895 Minnie Johnson, b1872, dau of James M. & Alvira (Scott) Johnson, 4 chn.
C1. Ruby Odette Nichols, b1896, mar 1919 Orland T. Champion, b1894 Shiloh, OH, son of Rev. Tollie & Mina (White) Champion, 3 chn
D1. Robert T.R. Champion, b1920 Shelby, OH mar 1945 Wanda Yoakam
D2. Betsy Jane Champion, b1927 Sandusky, OH, mar 1955 Angela, IND Muncie Karl Delashmitt
D3. Charles I. Champion, b1927 Baden, PA, a teacher, mar 1954 Mansfield, OH Esther Neumann
C2. Robert James Nichols, b1897 Nevada, OH, twin, d1980 Mansfield, OH, mar 1927 Fremont, NEB, Barbara Jones. Robert James was an attorney and a Col., served in US Army, WWI, WWII and Korea. Barbara, b1899 Rhye, North Wales, dau of Thomas and Winefred (Morgan) Wales, 4 chn
D1. Sandra Gwen Nichols, b1934, mar James Bertz
D2. Thomas Morgan Nichols, b1936, twin, mar Judith Halstead
D3. John Richard Nichols, b1936, twin, mar Jane Hoffenhauer
D4. James Nichols, b1940, mar Patricia Sanders
C3. Russell Nichols, b1897 Nevada, OH, mar Opal Forchet?, or VORCHEE, b1902 near Canton, OH
D1. Bruce Nichols, b1924, d1975 Escondido, CAL, a school principal, mar Gloria ___
C4. Darrel Audley Nichols, b1899 OH, mar Madeline Zehner. Darrel d1958 Mansfield, OH, 2 chn
D1. Jacklyn J. Nichols, b1924 Mansfield, OH mar Harold McClellen
D2. Darrell A. Nichols Jr, b1926 Mans., OH, mar Dorothy Bartz
B2. Albert Nichols, or James Albert Nichols, b1873 Nevada, OH, d 1950 Mansfield, OH, mar 1901 Wharton, OH Mary Kauble, dau of David and Amanda (Nichols) Kauble, 2 chn
C1. Dorothy Nichols, b1903 Mansfield, OH, d1942, mar 1921 Dewey Heisz
D1. Maxwell Heisz, b1922 Cleveland or Mansfield, OH, mar 1941 Mansfield, OH, Jean Kelley
C2. Mary Adelaide Nichols, b1911 Mansfield, OH, mar 1941 Russel Porch, son of Le Moyne & Ella (Beet) Proch, 2 chn
D1. Douglas N. Porch, b1946, unmar
D2. Eric Alan Porch, b1954 Mansfield, OH, mar Vicki Humphrey
A4. Mary Jane Orchard, b1842, mar ___ White
A5. Margaret J. Orchard, b1845
A6. Hannah/Annie? Orchard, b1847 Richland Co., OH, mar Daniel Miller
A7. Poss a John Orchard? Remembered by cousins, but apparently not recorded.

BROCK, LE BROCQ, LE BROK, in C.I. since 1300s, but not always a C.I. surname in America. Has long history and much data in G. See Essex

Coll., vol. 12.

BROCK, LE BROCQ, John, b1783 G?, to Orange Co. or Chemung Co., NY. His chn b Elmira, NY. This Brock said to be second cousin to Gen. Sir Isaac Brock, qv, and prob from a C.I. fam. Some desc said to have settled Parshallville, MI. Wife, Mary Ferry. (Detroit Gen Soc Vol 2)

A1. Eleanor, b1805 A5. Matthew D, b1813 A9. Alanson Gould, b1822
A2. Mary Ann, b1806 A6. John Dester, b1815 A10. ?
A3. James, b1808 A7. Hannah Jane, b1816 A11. Maria Catherine b1827
A4. Elias b 1810 A8. William, b1820 A12. Harrison, b1829

BROCK, Gen. Sir Isaac, see NOTABLES. Many of this surname in OH & ONT.

BROCK, Andrew, mariner of Portsmouth, NH, bought land 1697, d by 1715. Widow Anna, mar James Jaffrey before 1720. (Noyes) OUTC. A Francis also res Portsmouth, NH 1686.

A1. William, Portsmouth Merchant 1720, living in 1736

BROCK, George, mar Mary FAVOR, qv, 1702 Boston, MA.

A1. George, b1705 d.y.? A4. George again, b1709
A2. Philip, b1706 A5. John, b1711
A3. Mary, b1708 A6. Peter, b1713 A7. Thomas, b1715

BROCK, John, from J in MRB 1600s.

BROCK, John, b ca 1734 entered MRB poorhouse 1794. Thought to have served in Gen. Glover's Co. #10 in 1775. (MASS HIST. RECORDS)

BROCK, John, of J, bought property from Augustin JEAN, John GUSTIN, qv, ca 1677, which GUSTIN had inherited from his parents in J. (Reading, MA records)

BROCK, John mar Mary QUINER, qv, in MRB 1758, poss both from C.I. fams.

BROCK, John, mar Eliz. LONGE? or LOUGEE?, in Boston 1730.

BROCK, Nicholas, a joiner in Newcastle, NH 1714, mar Eliz. Holden, dau of John. Nicholas from J fam? OUTC. (Noyes)

BRONAUGH, BRUNEAU?, poss Hug fam from France to VA, via C.I.?

BRONAUGH, BRUNEAU?, b ca 1650 France or C.I.?, rem to VA, prob to Jamestown in the 1600s. (Family tradition) He d ca 1692-99 in VA. (Zue MacCockley, Mansfield, OH)

A1. Jeremiah, b1672, d1749 Stafford Co., VA (Compendium of American Gen., vol. 5)

B1. David, b ca 1700, d 1774 King George Co., VA, mar Martha Moore

C1. William, b1740 VA, d1814 Mason Co., KY, mar Mary Ann GRANT, b ca 1745 in VA?, d1825 Mason Co., KY.

D1. David, b1767/69 Louisa Co., VA, mar 1787 Anna Sandidge b1769 Spotsylvania Co., VA, d1853 Louisa Co., VA

E1. Thomas, b1790 Spotsylvania Co., VA, mar 1813 Judith Hart, b 1784 Renfrew, Louisa Co., KY, dau of Malcolm & Judith (Crews) Hart

F1. Malcolm, b1816 Louisa Co., VA, mar 1841 Christian Co., KY, his cousin, Sarah Ann Bronaugh, b1815 Mason Co., KY, d1897 Honey Grove, TEX. Sarah Ann the dau of Rev. Wm. Bronaugh & Frances Carroll.

G1. Malcolm Bronaugh, Jr, b1851 Christian Co., KY, mar 1871 MO, Texana Johnson, b1855 Honey Grove, TX, d1942 Roff, OKLA. Malcolm d1927 Roff, OKLA.

H1. Volney Bronaugh, b1864 Honey Grove, TEX, d1936 Res Hugo, OKLA, mar Byrd Wilson, b1873, d1907-1915 bur Honey Grove TX

I1. Dr. Wayne Bronaugh, b1900 Honey Grove, TX, mar 1924 Kathleen P. Lowther, b1906 Orbiston, OH (Hocking Co.) who d1965 Parkersburg, W. VA.

J1. Zue Mac Bronaugh, b1926 Stockdale, OH (Pike Co.), mar 1948 Rollin Beverstock Cockley

D2. Rev. William Bronaugh, b1770 Spotsylvania Co., VA, mar 1804

Mason Co., KY, Frances Carroll, b1784 Mason Co., KY, d before 1839 Clermont Co., OH. She was the dau of Dempsy Carroll & Mary Hall.

F1. Sarah Ann Bronaugh, b1815, mar her cousin Malcolm, see F1. previous page.

BROUARD, John Guy Lowe, a shoemaker, b G? ca 1800, mar Mary Ann ___, 10 chn, some b G, rem to US. Name curr G. BROUARDS from G settled in Doster, MICH and Plainfield, NJ. (John Brouard, Orlando, FLA)

A1. Henry, poss named Zachariah Jonathan Henry, b1823 London, Eng., was a twin. The other twin died. Henry rem to America and mar 1852, Newark, NJ Amelia Sarah BARTRAM, qv.

BROUGHTON. Ususally a south-of-England surname, but has occurred in C.I. Curr G and J. "John Broughton, a sea captain and merchant of Marblehead, doubtless came as a mariner from the south of England or the Channel Isles, and possibly by way of Barbadoes, the Carolinas or Virginia...Through four generations, for over a hundred years, every male member of the family was master of a vessel, and every female member the wife of a sea captain." (Matthews) Arms: argent, a chevron between three mulletts gules. Crest: Eagles head erased sable, holding a snake argent. "A seagoing fam for over 400 years." John mar Sarah 1718, dau of John & Sarah (Maverick) NORMAN, granddau of Lt. Richard NORMAN of MRB. Sarah a widow in 1741. There was also a John Broughton from England 1615-1662 on ship THOMAS from England. (Essex Antiq., vol 12; SKETCH OF THE BROUGHTON FAM, by Henry Waite; NEHGS, vol 37, 1883; GEN NOTES OF WM JOHNSON GOLDTHWAIT AND MARY LYDIA PITMAN-GOLDTHWAITE OF MARBLEHEAD; JOURNALS OF ASHLEY BOWEN; Noyes)

A1. Ann, b1719, mar Capt. Jones DENNIS Jr., 1735

A2. Sarah, b1721, mar Capt. Richard WEBBER 1741

A3. John, b1724, d.y. A4. Norman, bp1727, d.y.

A4. Nicholas, twin, b1724, mar 1749 Sarah PEDRICK. He was a Capt. in Col. Glover's Navy, Rev. War, and was commissioned by Gen. Washington, the first in the American Navy. Sarah d1793 MRB. He d1798, age 73. Much more about him in JOURNALS OF ASHLEY BOWEN. Seven chn, most marrying into C.I. fams of MRB.

BROUGHTON, Thomas, from C.I.?, living at or near Charleston, SC as early as 1699, a representative of Lord CARTERET, qv, in 1702. (NEHGS, vol 37)

BRUER, of early MA, poss BROUARD of C.I.? BROUARD in G 1330 on, in St. Peters, G 1692, and in St. Andrews, G 1743. Curr G. See BROUARD.

BROWN, see also LE BRUN. BROWN is old in G. In J as DE BROUNE 1309, as LE BRUN, 1299, meaning brown-haired. Quite likely that most BROWNS of the colonies were from England or Scotland. Some came from J, where they res in St. Heliers, St. Peter, and St. Ouen, J, 1668. LE BRUN in St. Clement J 1749, curr research?, see CIFHS #8.

BROWNE, John, of J, was fostering trade in 1661 between Jersey and Salem, where he resided. The trade consisted of hosiery and shoes from J, wines, brandies and fruit from France, Portugal and Spain, linens from France and Holland. These were traded for fish and lumber from New England. This trade was heavy and began before 1660, continuing until the Rev. War. (Essex Coll, vol 2) "John Brown was probably John LE BRUN." (Baird, Fosdick) See JERSEY SAILING SHIPS.

BROWN, Elizabeth, b1657 J, mar John GUSTIN, qv, 1677. Her fam in Marlboro, MA. OUTC.

BROWNE, Joseph, mar Sara Cox, res Salem, MA. Sara a desc of Philip ENGLISH, qv.

A1. Sara, mar 1775 James Chever, son of Capt. James of Salem and

Mary Allin, 10 chn. See more data in Essex Coll, vol 4.

BROWN, Eli, age 24, cordwainer, son of Eli and Eleanor, mar 1845 in MRB Mary Elizabeth CASWELL age 20, dau of Richard & Sarah Caswell. OUTC. See CI COLL. for more on John Brown b 1688Jersey.

BROWN, Nicholas, a mariner and Elizabeth, his wife, res Lynn, MA 1700s, 7 chn? OUTC.

BROWN, LE BRUN, Peter, rem from J to MINN middle 1800s. He changed his name from LE BRUN to BROWN upon entering the military during the Civil War. He enlisted in the US Army at Ft. Snelling, MINN 1862, served with Co. J, 9th Minn. Vol. Inf. Discharged 1865, and home town was listed as Eagle Creek, MINN. (Mrs. Raymond Brown, St. Cloud MINN) These fams res in Wright Co., in or near St. Cloud in 1860s.

LE BRUN, John SOHIER, b1821 J, mar Susan SOHIER, b1819 J. Rem to MINN.

A1. Isabella B., b1847 J

A2. John Sohier, b1854, mar Maggie Jane ___, and 2. ?

B1. Maggie LE BRUN, b1889, dau of 1st wife

B2. Annie Le Brun, b1892

B3. James Sohier Le Brun, b1893

B4. Rose Susan Le Brun, b1895

B5. Isabelle Sohier Le Brun b1896

B6. Wilhelm Lee Le Brun, b1898

B7. Ruth Evangeline Le Brun b1899

B8. Edwin John Le Brun, b1901

B9. Albert Carlyle Le Brun, b1903

B10.Paul Winfield Le Brun, b1906

B11.Ethel Victoria Le Brun, b1908

A3. Georgiana B. Gygert, b1856

A4. Mary Jane S. McCrary, b1860

BROWN, LE BRUN, Elizabeth, b ca 1813 J, mar ___ Bitner, res Wright Co., town of Albion, MINN in 1880. (Census)

BRYANT. Shipbuilder in J 1800s, name curr J.

BUBIER, BOOBYER, etc. This name is not on the lists of old G and J surnames. The fam was poss Hug and left France in late 1500s, settling perhaps for a time in J? Other branches noted in England. Some intermar with C.I. fams and with other Hug fams. (BUBIER FAM NOTES, by Madeleine m. Bubier, Prov., RI, 1959; Mrs. Ed Weir, Bucksport, ME; Perley; Underhill; Marblehead Hist. Society; Records of Lizzie Hayward of CAL: Essex Antiquities, vol 3; Winnifred Pierce, Ann Arbor, MI; WRCIC)See LANCASTER GEN. by Josephine Ware!

BUBIER, Joseph, b ca 1645 C.I., in MRB ca 1668, mar 1. Joan Codner, b 1655 MRB, dau of Christopher & Mary (BENNET) Codner. Joan d ca 1703. Joseph mar 2. the widow Rebecca (BREEN) Pinson, Pinsent. BRINE, pron BREEN, recorded in J. (Q.A. IN CANADA, by Turk)

A1. Christopher, b ca 1675, mar 1. Jane or Jean?, and 2. Margaret PALMER, d Surinam, Dutch Basin Indies 1706, many desc, see sources.

A2. Jeanne/Jane, who mar 1703 Nicholas PICKETT, qv, many desc. (Winnifred Pierce)

A3. Mary, mar 1707 Francis BOWDEN, son of Michael and Sarah (Nourse), b ca 1678 MRB. (Essex Antiq., vols 10 and 12)

BUDDY, Nicholas, from J ca 1730 to MA. Buddy is an unlikely surname. Consider BOSDET (silent "s") and BOODY. (Bolton)

BUFFET, Mr. & Mrs. from G, settled WISC late 1800s or early 1900s.

BUESNEL, Winnifred Norah, b1906 St. Saviours, J, mar A.E. Kempster, res Edmonton, ALTA, Canada. She was dau of John BUESNEL, who is said to have had 23 chn by two wives. One son, R.G. Buesnel, rem to Louisiana, and was living some years ago at Killarney Jersey Farm, Clinton, LA. Curr research? See CIFHS #8.

BULFORD, George, b1817 Chiselborough, Somerset, England, mar Jane HALLETT, b1820 Chinnock West near the Bulfords. The fam rem to G where 4 chn were b. Two other chn b on Herm Island. While origins were English, HALLETTS have some history in the C.I. Also, the oldest son mar a Guernsey woman. The Bulfords rem to Canada in three units ca the late 1860s, settled in Farmersville/Athens, Leeds Co.,

ONT. In the Islands, George was a milkman and Jane a dressmaker. (Dave Bulford, Wawa, ONT) More data in WRCIC.

A1. George Aquilla, b1849 Hem Island, mar 1871 St. Peter Port, G, Margaret MARRIETTE, qv, 1850-1912. George d1926 Farmersville, ONT, 10 chn.

B1. Louisa, b1872 ONT, mar Daniel Wing, 1865-1906, d1957 Lyndhurst, ONT.

C1. Ada May Wing, b1895, mar Mildred Faulkner, b1909, in 1929. He d1963, 5 chn.

D1. Mildred June Wing, b1930, mar 1952 Raymond T. Radbourne, b1928, 4 chn

D2. James Leonard Wing, b1931, mar 1952 Marlene Ann Beevor, b1932, 4 chn

D3. Gertrude E. Wing, b1933, mar 1955 James L. Alexander, b1932, 3 chn

D4. Norman Daniel Wing, b1936, mar Jean Taylor, b1937, 2 chn

D5. Vivian Louise Wing, b1944, mar Jor Fahrngruben, b1933

B2. Melinda Margaret, b1874 ONT, mar 1896 John Ronald McPherson, 1871-1962, 4 chn

C1. Finnan Patrick McPherson, 1896-1965, mar 1920 Florence Mae McQuillan, 3 chn

D1. Jean Mary McPherson, 1896-1965, mar Andy Barrowman, no issue, d1973

D2. Allan McPherson, b1922, mar 1946 Joan CAREY, b1923, 3 chn

D3. John Finnan McPherson, b1934, mar 1954 Kathy Stephens, and 2. 1973 Wendy E. Phillips, b1948, 2 chn

C2. David Lawrence McPherson, b1901, mar Kathleen McDonald, 5 chn

D1. Ruth McPherson

D2. John McPherson, mar Pauline ___

D3. Donald McPherson, mar Velma Smith

D4. Christine McPherson, b 1933, mar Vern Wood

D5. James McPherson, mar Margaret ___

C3. John Bernard McPherson, b1904, mar Edna Eybel

D1. Audrey/Jo, b1927, mar Cye Verge, a dau Connie

D2. Ronald Jesse McPherson, b1930, mar 1952 Mary Facto, 6 chn

C4. Mary Margaret McPherson, b1930, mar 1942 Patrick Smith, 1899-1963, 2 daus

B3. George Marriette, b1876 ONT, mar 1902 Kate Reddick, 1875-1951

C1. Kenneth George, b1903, mar 1. 1932 Ruby Isabelle Benham, who d 1958, 2. Geneva Muir?

D1. Lorna Ethel, b1936, mar 1957 Thomas Rock, 2 chn

C2. Leonard Charles, b1903, mar 1928 Lela Judd, 3 chn

D1. Shirley Lee, b1932, mar 1952 Richard Seymour Hoyt, 3 chn

D2. Mara Lee Jane, b1941, mar 1959 John Charles Conzelmann, 2 chn

D3. Kathleen Ann, b1944, mar 1965 Bruce Sears Barden, 2 chn

C3. Beatrice Lucy, b1908, mar 1928 Oman Joseph Gardner, b1902

D1. Phyllis Jean Gardner, b1929, mar 1947 Robert Lloyd Covey, 4chn

D2. Joan Marie Gardner, b1934, mar 1956 Gerald A. Caldwell, Jr., b1935, 1 dau

D3. Leonard Oman Gardner, b1942, mar 1967 Linda M. Peterson, b1946, 3 chn

B4. Annie Jane, b1877 Farmersville, ONT, mar 1900 Frederick Miskelly, 1873-1930

C1. Eva Lillian Miskelly, b1901, mar 1934 Russell Webster, d1949, no issue

C2. Helen Irene Miskelly, b1904, mar 1930 Stanley Livingstone, who d1976, 3 chn

D1. Lynn Gary Livingstone b1937 mar 1962 Marilyn Millar b1939, 2chn

D2. Margaret Ann Livingstone b1938 mar 1957 James Dorman b1937 3chn
D3. Jean Susan Livinstone, b1947
C3. Margaret Estella Miskelly, b1906, mar 1. John Lorne Wegenast, who d1940 and 2. Peter McIntosh, who d1968. One son.
D1. John Lorne Wegenast, Jr., 1929-1977 mar Julie Budd, 2 chn
C4. Clara Winnifred Miskelly, b1908 mar James Wallace Meade, b1907,
D1. Robert James Meade, b1924, mar Dorcas ___, a son, Robert
D2. Geraldine Diane Meade, mar 1952 John Halpin, 2 chn
D3. Elizabeth Meade, b1925, mar 1950 Wendal Emms, 3 chn
B5. Lily, b1879, d.y.
B6. Harry Mariette, b1881 ONT, mar 1906 Phoebe Alberta Legacy at Hamilton, ONT. She was b1887, d1962. He d1950 at Hamilton, 5chn
C1. Harold Edward, 1906-1980, mar 1938 Ethel Gertrude Ayling, b1911
D1. David Robert b1938 mar 1966 Barbara Anne McBeth b1942, 2 chn
D2. Jane Elizabeth b1941, mar 1973 James Wilson Hislop, 2 chn
C2. Cecil Cormell, b1907, d1946, mar 1940 Jean McQueen, who mar 2. Jack Lounds
D1. Beverly Ann (Bulford) Lounds b1940 mar 1962 Terrance LANGLEY, a son
D2. Harry William (Bulford) Lounds, b1940 mar 1966 Lynda R. Ibbot, 2 chn
C3. Lilliam Albert, b1909, mar 1936 Robert Hill, 1902-1944, and 2. Macklin Barry
D1. Marilyn Roberta Hill, b1940
D2. Lorraine Joyce Hill, b1944 mar 1966 Robert Wilson b1943, a son
C4. Robert Roy, b1919, d.y. C5. Ruth Irene, b1922, d1946
B7. Stanley, b1883, d unmar 1949 at Grande Prairie, ALTA
B8. Margaret Adam, b1885, mar 1906 Frank L. Allyn at Harlem, ONT. She d 1921 Edmonton, ALTA, 5 chn
C1. Ralph Allyn, b1908, d1974, mar Helen Lambrecht, 1912-1967, 4chn
D1. Ronald Frank Allyn b1932 mar 1. ? and 2. Donna Rae Bourassa, 2 daus
D2. Robert Allyn mar Norman Bourassa, 4 chn
D3. Patricia Ann Allyn b1939 mar Paul Kelley, 5 chn
D4. Sharon Jean Allyn, b1945
C2. Irene Margaret Allyn, b1910, mar 1934 John Wm. Bush, 1905-1976
D1. Doris Jean Bush, b1936, mar 1. 1955 Albett Krueger, 3 chn, div, and mar 2. David Stallman, 1968. 3 chn by Krueger
D2. Nancy Kay Bush, b1942, mar 1961 Roger Groenewald, div 1963 and mar 2. Rick Alex. One ch by 1st and 2 by Alex.
D3. James Wm. Bush, b1944, mar 1. 1966 Linda Bass and 2. Kay Barnhill, 2 chn
C3. Lester Newton Allyn, b1911, mar 1. Sally Lilly and 2. 1948, Esther Lambrecht who d1961 and 3. in 1962 Theresa Lilly, 2 chn
D1. Sally Allyn, mar William King, 3 chn
D2. Lester Allyn, Jr., b1942
C4. Albert Lawrence Allyn, b1917, mar Gladys Black, 4 chn
D1. Larry Allyn D2. Judith Allyn D3. Linda Allyn D4. David Allyn
C5. John Ronald Allyn, b1920, mar Wilma Gene Patchett, 2 chn
D1. William Ronald Allyn b1951 D2. Valerie Irene Allyn b1958, mar
B9. Havilland, b1887 ONT mar 1915 Dukista Lopetsky in Sask b1896 5chn
C1. Irene, b1920, mar 1940 Orval Erving Nellis, b1912, 6 chn
D1. Wayne Marshall Nellis, b1941, mar 1964 Doreen Cecelia Theresa Skelly, b1943, 2 sons
D2. Shirley Ann Nellis b1943 D3. Eugene Stanley Nellis 1948-1972
D4. Donald Francis Nellis, b1949, mar 1971 Ellen Barbara Haugseth, b1951, 2 chn

D5. Philip Edgar Nellis, b1952, mar 1980 Carol Reber
C2. Harvey, twin, b1924, mar 1947 Annie Diedrich, b1922, 5 chn
D1. Lynne, b1948, mar 1968 Gerald Oe, b1938
D5. Harold, b1963
D2. Melvin, b1950, mar 1972 Marion Perry, b1955, 3 chn
D3. Grant, b1951, mar 1972 Kathleen McGreevy, b1949, 4 chn
D4. Beverly, b1957 mar 1979 Stan Tissington b1955
C3. Harry, b1924, twin, d1963, no issue
C4. Elmer, b1926, twin, mar 1947 Ann Stark, b1927, 5 chn
D1. Harry James b1948 mar 1968 Dorthea Fitzsimmons b1947, 2 chn
D2. Vernie Gene, b1950
D3. Janet, b1955 mar 1974 William Doll, b1954, 3 chn
D4. Annette Elaine, b1960
D5. Sherry Rose, b1961
C5. Elenor Bulford, b1926, twin of Elmer above, mar 1947 George Bain, b1924, 8 chn
D1. Cherly Kaye Bain, b1948, mar 1967 Murray McEwan, b1947, 2 chn
D2. Elizabeth Ann Bain b1950 mar 1969 Dennis Gubbe b1947, 2 chn
D3. Gerald Haviland Bain b1951 mar 1975 Rita Ann Henning b1953 2chn
D4. Ellen Noella Bain b1954 mar 1975 Fred McAusland, a ch Kari
D5. Donna Allison Bain b1956 mar 1972 Darryl Mayne b1955, 3 chn
D6. Cindy Irene Bain b1957 mar 1976 Keith Arlint b1956, 1 ch
D7. Elmer George Bain
D8. Brent Edwin Bain, b1965
B10. Charles Bulford, b1889 ONT, mar Mrs. Ella Dickson, late in life, no issue
A2. Edward Charles, b1852 St. Peter Port, G, mar 1878 ONT Sarah Amelia McVeigh, b1857, d1912. Edward d1907, 3 chn.
B1. George Jacob b1880 mar in Alberta, Canada and d1945. No issue?
B2. Sarah Jane, b1884, mar 1923 Edward Dowden at Farmersville, ONT, 1875-1945, d Athens, ONT. A single ch d.y.
B3. Stanley Roberts Bulford, b1891, adopted by Edward and Sarah, ch of Minnie McVeigh
C1. Hazel, b1914, mar 1934 Dan Chisamore, 1903-1978, 4 chn
A3. Melinda Elizabeth b1854 Herm Island, of unsound mind, d Kingston, ONT 1895
A4. John T., b1856 St. Martins, G, mar 1878 at Elizabethtown, ONT, Alma Jane Darling, 1858-1949, 1 ch. John T. d1879 ONT.
B1. Mae Maude 1878-1957 mar 1901 William NICHOLS 1875-1960, 4 chn
C1. Charles Clifford Nichols 1903-1959, no issue, mar twice
C2. Mable Irene Nichols b1910 mar 1931 Francis Herbert Kent, b1900
D1. Herbert Wm. Kent b1942 mar 1963 Sandra Elsie Hyland, 2 chn
D2. Francis Wilbert Kent b1943 mar 1. 1967 Marilyn Garrett and 2. in 1974 Barbara Jean Garrett, b1944, 5 chn
C3. John Arthur Nichols b1916 mar 1. Ruth Maki and 2. in 1950, Arlene Knoke, 4 chn
D1. Linda Sue Nichols b1956
D2. Donald Joseph Nichols b1960
D3. Shirley Mae Nichols b1963
D4. Howard William Nichols b1976
C4. Ivan Oswell Nichols, b1919 mar 1949 Neoma Van Luven, 13 chn
D1. Ruth Gail Nichols, b1947, mar 1. Lyle Smith and 2. Robert McCallum, 2 chn
D2. Anna Mae Nichols, b1949, mar 1. David Hyde and 2. Noel McKay, 2 chn
D3. Betty Elizabeth Nichols b1951 mar Michael Daley, 2 chn
D4. William Albert Nichols, b1952, d1968
D5. Arlene June Nichols, b1953, mar Dennis Hache, a ch
D6. Evelyn Irene Nichols, b1954, mar Terry Knapp, a ch
D7. Katherine Lynn Nichols b1955
D8. Susan Marie Nichols b1957 mar Lawrence Perkins, 3 chn
D9. Charles A. Nichols b1958
D10. Dennis Arnold Nichols b1960
D11. Paula M. Nichols b1962

D12. Barbara Jean Nichols b1964 D13. Audrey M. Nichols b1969
A5. Emily Ada, b1860 St. Martin, G, mar 1881 Noah Chant, 1855-1938, Emily d1887, 3 chn
B1. Clara Chant 1882-1966, mar 1916 Sidney C. Smith, 1881-1934
C1. Frederick Sidney Smith b1919 mar 1945 Sylvia Noreen Harbord b1920
D1. Nancy Nora Jill Smith, b1947, mar 1973 Louis Francois Courtemanche, a son
D2. Jeffrey Harborn Smith b1950 D3. Rosemary Sue Smith b1954
B2. Estella Chant, b1884, d unmar 1973
B3. George Wesley Chant, 1885-1965, mar 1920 Hilda Laurette Kinch, 1899-1965, 8 chn
C1. Lloyd Allen Chant, 1921-1930, mar 1958 Betty A. Morrison, no issue
C2. Grace Alverda Chant, b1923, mar 1945 Ronald Alexander Howard, b1924, 3 chn
D1. Rhonda Joan Howard, b1949, mar Ronald Alexander Howard, b1924, 3 chn
D2. Leslie David Howard, b1951, mar ___ Butler and 2. Heather Marshall, 3 chn D3. Dale Allan Howard, b1956
C3. Raymond Earl Chant, b1925, mar Geraldine Barrington, 2 chn
D1. Donna Chant, b1951 D2. Darlene Chant
C4. Clarie Chant, b1927, mar 1950 Irma Lamming, no issue
C5. Meredith Roy Chant, b1931, mar 1967 Nancy Mary Colleen Adair, b1944
D1. Timmy Chant, b1969 D2. Laura Chant, b1971
C6. Dorothy Estella Chant, b1932, mar John Hall, no issue
C7. Rodney Virden Chant b1936 mar 1965 Dorothy Balmer b1937, 3 chn
D1. David Wesley Chant, b1966 D3. Gerald Chant, b1969, twin,
D2. Brian Wm. Chant, b1969, twin d.y.
C8. Mavis Winona Chant b1939 mar Garnet Sands, b1938, 3 chn
D1. Terry Sands b1958 D2. Daryl Sands b1959 D3. Ricky Sands b1961
B4. Ralph Chant Smith, b1901, raised by Noah Chant, mar Hazel ___ 3chn
A6. Clara Martha b1864 St. Martins, G d unmar 1882, Farmersville, ONT

BULLEN, BOLLEN, BALLEINE, BALLAINE. One BULLEN from Norfolk, England to America. Other BULLENS appear to be orig. BALLEINE from J, poss also from G. See BALLEINE and THE JERSEY COLONY.

BALLEINE, in St. Helier, St. Brelade, St. Peter, J in 1668. In St. Peter, St. Mary and Trinity, J in 1749. BALLEN in early J ca 1340.

BULLEN, Capt. James, b ca 1630 J, qv. When the ship PHILIP brought a group of French and Channel Islanders to Elizabethtown, NJ 1665, Bullen joined the group and helped to organize the government. He became Sect. of the province, and J.P. 1665/66. Political troubles appeared and he left for Woodbridge, NJ. He d intestate 1682/83. James mar Anne VAUQUELLIN, dau of Robert (A.K.A. LA PRAIRIE) and Jeanne VAUQUELLIN, qv. Only 3 chn noted, but there may have been more. Two chn, James and Anne, selected Samuel Moore and Nathaniel Fitzrandolph as guardians. (HIST. OF ELIZ. NJ; STOUT GEN; Holman; Monette; Hatfield; Paul Millikin, Columbus, OH; Pat Sorenson, Yuba City, CAL; Jerrold Balleine, Bellevue, WASH; Bradley Ridge, NY, NY; NJ and Elizabethtown records; STOUT AND ALLIED FAMS, 2nd ed., by Herald F. Stout, San Diego, CAL, vol 1)
A1. James, b ca 1662, mar Martha Dennis
A2. Anne, b ca 1665 NY or NJ A3. Samuel ?
A4. Mary, b ca 1655?, mar Peter Stout, 1654-1703, res Middletown, NJ. He may have mar 2. Mary Bowne in 1703, just before he died. See STOUT GENS. Four chn: Mary, John, b1675, Margaret? and

Elizabeth Stout.

BOLLEN, Anna, said to be cousin or sister of above Mary BULLEN, mar 1685 Jonathan Stout, 1662-1722, large landholder with slaves in NJ, res Monmouth Co., NJ. (STOUT GEN.)

A1. Joseph Stout, 1686-1766 A6. Jonathan Stout, 1701-1768
A2. Sarah Stout, 1689-1767 A7. Anne Stout, b1704
A3. Benjamin Stout, b1691 A8. David Stout, 1706-1788
A4. Hannah Stout, 1694-1779 A9. Samuel Stout, b1709
A5. Zebulon Stout, 1699-1788, mar Charity Burrows, dau of Thomas. See Stillwell's MISCELLANY, and BURROWES OF MONMOUTH.
B1. John Stout, 1730-1798 B5. Rachel Stout
B2. Zebulon Stout, 1740-1814 B6. Mary Stout
B3. Ann Stout, mar Ichabod Leigh B7. Charity Stout
B4. Hannah Stout, d ca 1788 B8. Sarah Stout mar Abraham Skillman

BULLEN, Elisha, Ephraim, John, John, Joseph and Samuel noted in Savage I. OUTC. See also records of Dedham, Medfield and Rehoboth, MA. A Joseph was in Maine ca 1648 with 8 chn. OUTC. See HIST. OF PARSONFIELD, ME, and ANCESTORS AND DESC OF PHILIP BULLEN, by Mary and Winnifred Holman, Schenectady, NY, 1930.

BULLEN, Philip, bp1710 St. Peter, J, d in Charleston, Mid. Co., MA, between 1743-1747. He was the desc of Philip & Rachel (PAYN) BALLEINE of J. (His line was Jean, Jean, Thomas, Jean, Michel, Jean and Thomin Balleine, all of J) Philip mar before 1734 Deborah Hutchinson, who may have mar 2. after his death and before 1746, John Humphries. (ANCESTORS AND DESC OF PHILIP BULLEN, by Mary L. Holman and Winnifred Holman, Concord, NH, 1930; HIST. OF SHERBORN AND HOLLISTON, MA, Morse)

A1. Samuel, a Deacon, b1735, d Hallowell, ME 1818, age 75. Mar 1760 Anna Brown
B1. Samuel B4. Sarah Farmer B7. Abigail Marshall
B2. George B5. Anna Bullen B8. Martha Stickney
B3. Mary Lewis B6. Rebeckah Lewis B9. Persis Emerson
A2. Nathan, b1737, mar Mary Hutchinson or Mary Hirt? Poss same person?
A3. Philip, d.y.? A4. Philip again, poss d.y.

BULLEN, Mary, b Woolwich, Sag. Co., ME, mar 1779 Rev. Ebenezer Brookings, Jr. of Woolwich. She may have been a desc of Philip above. Ebenezer, 1756-1799, a soldier in the Rev. War. Mary mar 2. Henry Doe of New Milford, ME. She is bur Unity, ME. (Audrey Stone, Auburn, MA, 01501) OUTC.

A1. Hannah Brookings, mar John Costello 1819
B1. Mary Margaret Costello, mar Andrew Jackson MAINS 1841
C1. Helen Agusta Mains mar Albert DREW, ca 1864. See DREW.
D1. Georgia Anna DREW, mar Thomas Horne 1888
E1. Roland Drew Horne, mar Milicent Wilder 1925
F1. Audrey Horne, mar Howard Clifton Stone 1947, 4 chn

BULLEN, Mary, dau of Ephraim, the son of Samuel BULLEN and Mary Morse, who were mar 1641. Mary Bullen mar John Sherman, Watertown, MA, OUTC.

THE CAROLINA BULLENS. There was a grant of land 1677 to a John BULLON (Hirsch). This name was also spelled BULLEIN, and John res Oyster Pt., NC before 1677. (Baldwin) By the 1700s there were several of this name, spelled in various ways, but poss all part of the same fam. OUTC. See BALLEINE and BOLLEN.

BULLINE, BULLEIN, BULLEN, BULLON, etc., John?, first name uncertain, but apparently res in Carolina in 1600s and 1700s. (Moore's SC WILL BOOKS) <u>CAUTION: TRIAL CHARTS</u>. OUTC.

A1. John, mar and had 2 daus, Mary & Susannah, both under 21 in 1770s
A2. Ann, mar ___ Smith and had poss two sons? Thomas Smith and Christopher Peters?

A3. Alice, mar ___ Branford. See vol. 3 of the Moore Will Books for this fam, Rebecca, Susanna, William, Mary & Thomas BULLINE Branford
A4. Hester or Ester, mar ___ Glaze, at least 2 chn? including a William Glaze
A5. Mary, mar Thomas Abraham HAYN? She was a widow in 1769, a dau Susanna Hayne
A6. Thomas, res St. James Parish, SC, had dau Susannah BULLINE, under 21 in 1770s. Poss he d 1769 in Rhode Island? (SC Mag, vol 10)
A7. Poss a Francis Bulline Baker under 21, and a Thomas Baker also mentioned

BULLINE, Nathaniel, Rebecca, Deborah and Thomas, all mentioned in will of Isaac Bradwell, 1766, in SC. (Moore Will Books)

BULLEIN, Nathaniel, res Charlestown 1700s and rem to Horton, NS, a physician. Res Amelia Twp 1772, worked in the American Hospital and took an oath to the state in 1779. However, after the British took Charlestown, he was a surgeon there in their hospital for refugees. He went with the British to NYCity, and arrived in Nova Scotia Aug. 1783. He received 500 acres in Parrsborough, NS 1784, but in 1786 was living at Horton, NS. A Nathaniel Bullein in Halifax had two blacks leave his service, a slave woman and an indentured man. He offered a 20 shilling reward for them and threatened in the Halifax Gazzette, 1784, to sue anyone who should take them out of Halifax. (MIGRATION OF CAROLINA AND GEORGIA LOYALISTS TO NOVA SCOTIA AND NEW BRUNSWICK, by George W.W. Troxler, U. of NC, sent to compiler by Esther Rancier, Carson, CAL)

BULLEIN, BOLIN, John, a Sgt. in the SC Light Dragoons and the SC Royalist Dragoons in 1782, took 200 acres at Country Harbour, NS 1784. (Troxler) Related to Nathaniel above?

BULLEIN, BOLIN, James, also served in the SC Light Dragoons 1781. A James BOWLING took 100 acres in Guysborough Twp., Sydney Co., NS in 1785. (Troxler)

BULSH, Alle, from G to Racine, WIS 1842 with wife and 4 chn b in G. Not a G surname, but poss the wife was a Guernseywoman? OUTC.

BURCH, Alexander, b1810 G, son of John O. Burch of England and Mary Lewis, his wife, who was b in Bristol, England. John a civil engineer and surveyor, d1813 G, his wife in 1848, 3 chn. (RACINE AND KENOSHA ALBUM)
A1. Sarah Lewis, mar Thomas Jamieson, a Scot who d in G, after which his widow came to this country and spent her last days in Chicago, ILL
A2. Jane, mar James BENNETT. Both d and were bur in G, leaving 2 sons and a dau
A3. Alexander, carpenter, joiner, engineer, with considerable inventive talents. In 1832 he mar Jane Cargan of G, dau of James CARGAN. In 1842 they settled in Racine, WISC. Alex. supervised the building of the first wind gristmill in Somers, WISC, where he res for 5 years. He also built grain elevators, homes in Racine, and the Washingtonian Home near Chicago, ILL. Jane d 1876, 7 chn. He mar 2. in 1879 Mrs. Olive Null dau of Wm. Morgan.
B1. William b ca 1833, d1856, age 23, leaving wife and one ch
B2. Anna, b G, mar in Racine 1865 Samuel Menderson, 2 daus: Jeannie and Laura Menderson
B3. A.O., mar, had 4 chn, res Racine, WISC
B4. Jane, mar A.M. Crane of Chicago, ILL, d1862, age 23, a dau
B5. Emma, mar Richard Busustow of Racine, WISC, 2 chn
B6. Charles, of Chicago B7. George, mar, 4 chn, res Santa Rosa, CAL

BURGESS, cf BOURGAIZE

BURGESS, Wilfred DE LISLE, b 1898 St. Sampson,G, son of Arthur Leland, chemist, and Selina Jane (HUBERT) BURGESS. Apprenticed 6 yrs. to Alfred LE PATOUREL, qv, exporter of G cattle. In 1919 Mr. Burgess brought to America over 80 head of cattle for LE PATOUREL, consigned to Rundell Bros., Livingston, WISC. He later rem to Albamont Farm, Compton, NH, where Frank LE PATOUREL, son of Alfred, was herd manager. Wilfred mar in NYCity 1955 Brenda Christine BIRD, qv, of St. Sampson, G. Res Jamestown, RI. (Wilfred & Brenda Burgess,JamestownRI)

A1. Bruce Robert, b 1939 mar 1964 Frederika Dudley of Princeton, NJ,d 1972 in accident. She mar 2. J. Steven Rice, res Seattle, WA.

B1. Nathaniel De Lisle Burgess, b 1967, res Seattle, WA.

B2. Joshua L. Burgess.

A2. Marilyn Dale, b 1945, adopted, mar 1967 James Melvin Burns, res Jacksonville, NC, chn: Christina E. & David B. Burns.

BURGESS, John Gibson, b 1793, G? d 1836 St. Sampson, G. One dau to Canada. This fam from Macclesfield, England to G earlier.

BURGESS, Julia, b G, mar James P. TOSTEVIN, qv to Racine, WI. Said to have come to US 1850s. (RACINE HISTORY)

BURHOE, see BREHAUT

BURMAN, Charles, age 39, b J, and wife Ellen___, age 39, res St.Pierre de Malbay, QUE 1881 with fam. (Aldo Brochet, London, ONT)

A1. Mary b ca 1869 A3. George, b ca 1872 A4. Clara, b ca 1880

A2. Charles, b ca 1870 A4. Arthur, b ca 1878

BURR. Here is a case of a name change, from the original Jourdain GIBAUT, born ca 1800 in St. Lawrence, Jersey, a seaman, who changed his name to Richard Burr, ca 1822. Here is a rough translation of the letter to his father, Abraham GIBAUT of St. Lawrence, J, from Richard Burr, Coffee House, ship slip No. 79, New York, in 1822, but mailed from Cronstadt (Germany?) 30th July, 1822. (A.Pipon, Jersey)

Dear Mother and Father, I take this opportunity to write you to let you know the state of my health, which is good, thanks to God. I hope that the same is true of you and all our family. I am happy to have news of you. I hope you will write when you receive my letter. I am sending you (this letter) by the brig ship (and) Capt. MOURANS. I hope to leave for New York the first of August.

My dear father, I hope when you write the letter, don't mention the name of Gibaut, because I have changed my name, as I have written you before...(I expect to be sent to Bengal, East India) If God preserves me, I will come to Jersey. I am about to marry a girl of New York...15½ years old. I would like to have news of you before I leave. (I hope it is possible for me not to go to the East Indies, a country that I do not love a lot, and the voyages are too long... My dear father, would you please give my compliments to all who know me, particularly to my brothers and my sister and friends, beginning with Marie QUEREE and all her family. Nothing more, I remain your son till death, J.G.B. Richard Burr.

Researchers, note the form of the initials, J.G.B. This is Jourdain Gi Baut. This oddity is noted in several other old names of the Islands, such as Lu Cas, Lucas.

BURREN, George. "Apparently a Channel Island name." (Noyes) George res in York, ME 1665, and was apparently the same person as George BUSSE. BURREN and wife Sarah res Lower Kittery, or on the York side of Braveboat Harbor. May have rem to Falmouth, ME. Poss parents of Mary BURREN, who mar 1695 in Hampton, NH James FOGG. See BUSSY.(Noyes)

BURT, Luther, who settled in GCO ca 1807, was <u>not</u> from Jersey, but may have been b in NJ. Mary Burt of Kansas City, MO researched in PA and NJ, and found that Luther was son of Zephaniah and Hannah (Axtell) Burt, poss desc from Richard, in Plymouth colony 1639.

Compiler was long misled by a statement in the works of Sarchet, who wrote about many Channel Islanders in Guernsey Co., OH. He stated that BURT came from Jersey. This was a very common way, and is, even yet, of referring to New Jersey, whence came the Burt fam of GCO. Luther Burt was b1769 in NJ, and settled 1807 with the Guernsey Islanders in Guernsey Co., OH, and was in Cambridge 1810, where he built a brick house on 6th St. He mar Mary ___. A chart on this fam will be in the WRCIC. It was derived in part from records of Mrs. M.H. Coleman, Austin, TEX, but consult other sources listed. (HIST. COLL OF COSHOCTON, OH, by Wm. E. Hunt, 1876; Conner-Eynon Cem. List; HIST OF GCO; BIBLE RECORDS; GAR RECORDS; CENSUS; HOME GUIDE AND INSTRUCTOR-GCO, by Williams; Sarchet; PORTRAIT AND BIO RECORDS OF GCO; BURT Bible; HIST. OF NOBLE CO., OH; Mrs. Norman Clyde, Langley, WASH; Mrs. Louis Smith, Cambridge, OH; David Burt, Ryesville, OH; Mary Burt, Kansas City, MO; Mrs. Clarence Van de Kamp, Knoxville IA)

BURT. Those below are Burts who mar into C.I. fams of GCO. Quite poss there were others, also.

BURT, Glen, b1915 Noble Co., OH, mar 1945 Julia Ann SARCHET, qv, 2 chn. See SARCHET family.

A1. Judith Burt, b1946 GCO A2. James Edward Burt, b1948 GCO

BURT, Asenath, b ca 1801? mar 1820 John TORODE in GCO. See TORODE fam.

BURT, Elizabeth, sister of Asenath, b ca 1805?, mar 1825 Nicholas BICHARD from Guernsey. See BISHER, BIRCHARD, BICHARD.

BURT, John, b1795 in PA, d 1884/87, mar 2. 1835 Margaret MATTHEWS, a widow b1791 G. Poss no issue? John had chn by 1st wife Mary REED, in GCO. Margaret may have been the widow of John BLAMPIED. (Burt records) Another or the same John Burt mar Mary Fry in 1830, GCO.

BURT, Hannah, mar Peter TORODE, qv, 1820 GCO. See Asenath Burt above.

BURT. It may, or may not be relevant that BURT is noted in St. Heliers J in 1841, members of the Albion Chapel on New St. (CH. IS. FAM. HIST. SOC., Summer 1981)

BURT. "A family from England and Barbadoes rem to Guernsey ca 1807, about the same time that the TORODE bros and sisters arrived in America." (Imogene Torode Bunner, Kansas City, KS) This shows some connection with the Islands and makes it more clear why they settled in GCO.

BUSSEY, BUSSY, BUSSELL, etc. Name is old in Jersey, but not found in recent years. BUSSE was in J 1327, and BYSSE in J 1607. This last fam may be the source of the fam below. Others of the same and similar surnames in New England may be from other places in Grt. Britain. Work on these fams has been done by Laird Towle, Bowie, MD and Mrs. Charles Guittard of Dallas, TX. See also BURREN, George; HIST. OF PARSONSFIELD, ME; and MESSERVE GEN. The second volume of the BUSSEY FAM GEN was in progress 1982, by L.B. Guitard, 6245 Berryhill, Dallas, TX 75231.

BUSSELL, BUSSY, Simon?, from J?, mar 1658 Margaret Wormwood, dau of Wm. of Piscat, res Cape Porpoise, and was a witness in the years 1668 to 1681. Also mentioned in York deeds, ME. (Cape Porpoise is now Kennebunkport, ME) "Untimely death of Simon Buzie" noted in 1667, which must mean another Simon was there, poss father of Simon.

A1. John "from Jersey," "son of Simon," at Oyster River, NH between 1650 and 1694, d ca 1737. "Presumeably from the Isle of Jersey." (Noyes) Mar Sarah ___, 12 chn. (HIST. OF DURHAM; Noyes; POPE;

Savage; BUZZELL BULLETIN; Stackpole; Dolores Gutelius, Scio, ORE; Laird Towle, Bowie, MD; NEW ENGLAND GENEALOGIST, bulletin issued over several years by Mr. Towle; Wilma Regan, Exeter, NH)

B1. Martha, mar ___ Brown B2. Elizabeth, mar Benjamin BELL 1718

B3. Sarah, mar 1. ___ WILLIAMS by 1723, and by 1737 mar John ROBERTS of Madbury, b1694, d1771. She d1770, age 72, in New Durham, NH.

B4. Margaret, b1698 mar John DEMERITT, qv, his will 1770 names 10chn

B5. John, b1703, mar Sarah WIBIRD, prob VIBERT, qv, from J, at least 10 chn. Settled in Dover, NH but petitioned for boundary removal to Oyster River instead of Dover, the widow d1788 New Durham.

C1. Jacob mar Hannah ___
C2. Joseph mar Sarah Evans
C3. Benjamin, prob d.y.
C4. Hannah mar Thomas Evans
C5. Benjamin again, mar Abigail Evans
C6. Sarah mar Job DEMERITT, qv, a cousin?
C7. Abigail?
C8. Silas
C9. John mar Pheebe Evans, had large fam

D1. Deborah
D2. Robert Andrew
D3. John
D4. Abigail
D5. Lydia
D6. David
D7. Dorothy
D8. Charity
D9. Sarah
D10. Joseph
D11. Betsy
D12. Jonathan

B6. William, mar Sarah Pitman

C1. Ebenezer, mar Rachel ___
C2. Samuel, mar Lydia Evans
C3. William, mar Mary Mathes
C4. Ichabod, mar Sarah ROBERTS?
C5. Tabitha
C6. Mary
C7. Elizabeth

B7. Henry, mar 1. Abigail Daniels, 2 chn, and 2. Judith Horn, 7 chn. Henry res Barrington, NH, will dated 1764/67.

C1. Nathaniel
C2. Jane
C3. Thomas
C4. Paul
C5. Henry
C6. Abigail
C7. Margaret
C8. Mary
C9. Dorcas

B8. James, bp 1726 as adult?, mar 1733 Rachel CREDIFORD, his cousin, res Rochester, NH 1749, chn

B9. Isaac, mar Izett Hudson, dau of widow Dorcas Bradford, poss nee Dorcas Miller, and Samuel Hudson. Izett b1715, mar 2. Wm. Hunking, whose will dated 1776-82. (Noyes)

C1. Ann, mar 1753 Joseph Stevenson

B10. Mary, mar Job DEMERITT, Jr., qv. Mary bp as young adult in 1726.

B11. Hannah, bp as young girl in 1723, mar James Leighton, blacksmith, son of John. (Noyes)

B12. Ann, bp young in 1727, unmar in 1737.

A2. Rachel, mar by 1692 Joseph Credeford, res Wells, ME 1693. She was his widow in 1743. Tradition connects the Credeford fam with N. Carolina. Six chn bp Wells CH. (Noyes; Arundel & Berwick, ME records; Louisburg, NS records; Olive Schmitt, Santa Paula, CAL)

B1. Elizabeth Credeford, b1692

B2. Joseph Credeford, b1693/94, mar Esther Littlefield, settled Arundel, ME 1729, d1735, widow d1739, age 90, 6 chn bp 1723-1741

B3. Rachel Credeford, b1694/95, d.y.

B4. Benjamin Credeford, b1701/02, mar ca 1736 Jane Gypson, Jypson of Berwick, ME

B5. Josiah Credeford, b1703/04 Kittery, ME, mar ca 1734 Mary Eaton

B6. Mary Credeford, b1707, mar 1726 Ichabod Dunham

B7. Rachel Credeford again, twin, b1709, mar 1733 James BUSSEY of Dover, ME

B8. John Credeford, twin of Rachel, b1709, mar 1736 Judith Hamblen. He d1745 in Nova Scotia, poss as part of the Louisbourg Exped.?

B9. Nathaniel Credeford, b1713

A3. Dorcas, mar by 1700 Edward Evans

A4. William, mar in NH 1687 Ruth Stileman, dau of Elias. She mar 2. after 1691 Richard Tarlington. In her will of 1708, no chn mentioned. (Noyes, p. 662)
A5. Mary, age ca 12 when stolen at Cape Porpoise by "Old Doney" and associates? and yet detained in 1688. Mar 1729 Ronald McDonald?
B1. Robert McDonald, had Margaret & William bp in Oyster River 1712/14
A6. Simon? One served on coroner's jury 1685.

BUSSY, BYSSE?, George, said to be from J to ME, also res Concord, MA 1640? (Concord VR) He signed "George Burren or Bussy." Was in Kittery with wife Sarah 1764, also in Falmouth. (Noyes)
A1. ? Mary Burren mar in Hampton 1695 James Fogg. She d1750 age 80, he d1760.
B1. Mary Fogg, b1697, mar Jos. Wadleigh
B2. James Fogg, b1699, mar 1728 Elizabeth Robie, and in 1732, 2. Hannah Page. Settled Kensington, will dated 1762/67, 5 chn.
B3. John Fogg, bp 1702, d1754, mar 1729 Meribah Tilton, who d1795, 9 chn
B4. Sarah Fogg, b1705, mar Thomas Robie
B5. Enoch Fogg, bp1708, mar 1749, settled Chester, ME?
B6. Hannah Fogg, bp1713, prob mar ___ Rollins, named in will

BUSSY, BOSSY, Peter, poss related to Geo. BURREN, BUSSEY?, res MA. (Noyes)

BUSSE, BUSSEY, BUSS, in MA 1790 Census, res Lunenburgh, Sterling, Leominster, Windsor, Dedham, Stoughton, Dorchester, Salisbury, Amesbury and Bradford. OUTC.

BUSSE, BUSSEL, etc., in MA 1790 Census, res Wells, York, Conduskeeg Plantation, Eddy, Waterborough and Freeport. OUTC.

BUSS, BUZELL, etc., in NH 1790 Census, res Marlborough, Jeffrey, Concord, Loudon, Bow, Northwood, New Chester, Plymouth, Barrington, Sanborntown, New Durham and Rochester.

BYSSE, and BYSSY in Maryland 1669, also BUSSEY (Skordas) OUTC. However, these may have come fron Lincolnshire, England.(Lynn Guittard, Dallas)

BUTLER, Mary, from J, mar in Salem, MA 1675 Peter MORRELL, Jerseyman. See MORRELL, MOREL. Is BUTLER in this case a translation of J surname LE BOUTILLIER? However, BUTLER is curr G and J. (Baird; Noyes; Perley) Poss also mar Wm. DE LA RUE?, qv.

BUTLER. See LE BOUTILLIER. Note that some research has been started on BUTEL, see CIFHS #9.

BUTLIN, Thomas, b ca 1830 J, of an English fam, rem to Bonaventure Island, Gaspe, QUE, mar Elizabeth D. SAMSON ca 1859? A son George may have desc in Oswego, NY. See Q.A. IN CANADA. (Aldo Brochet, Montreal, QUE)

BUTT. This surname in Nfld. is said to be a contraction of BOUTEVILLON of J. BOUTEVILLON in J 1668 and 1749. Note that this surname was BUTTVILLON in 1607, BUTT in 1528, and BUTVILAIN in 1309.

BUTT, Roger, was in Crocker's Cove, Carboneau, Nfld. 1675-1681 (Berry's Census) In 1681 he had 6 chn. It may be that he was from Bristol, England. CAUTION: TRIAL CHARTS.

BUTT, John, thought to be from C.I., resident of Conception Bay, Nfld., 1706. (Mrs. John Butt, St. John's, Nfld.; Mary Ann Ankiewicz, Saugus, MA; Archives; VR) See FAMILY NAMES OF THE ISLAND OF NEWFOUNDLAND for other Butt fams.
A1. Elizabeth? A2. William A3. George A4. Thomas
A5. Henry, mar 1797 Elizabeth KING, both widowed, poss same as A1.?
A6. Hezekiah, a fisherman
A7. Joseph, b ca 1725?

B1. Roger, b ca 1750?
C1. Charles, bp 1781 Harbour Grace, Nfld.
C2. Jane, bp 1781 C3. Patience, bp 1781
B2. Joseph B3. Anne, mar ROWE B4. Frances, mar BAKER
B5. Jane, mar ___ Parsons

One Joseph BUTT, thought to be of above fam, mar Eliza Clarke Nov.20, 1837, res Crocker's Cove, Carbonear, Nfld. At least 4 chn b there.
E1. Esther, b 1838 E2. Robert, b 1850, d unmar
E3. Alfred, b 1854 mar Emma PENNEY 1880
F1. William Wesley, b 1881 mar Emma SHEPPARD, res Carbonear?
G1. Cyril b 1917 G2. Isabella, b 1919 G3. Margorie, b 1922
G4. Emma, b 1925
F2. Caroline, mar Augustus Bourne
G1. Hayward Bourne G2. Wm. Bourne, mar Ann, 2 sons James,Fred.
F3. Eliza
F4. Robert, b 1885, mar Sarah Clarke and/or Sarah Cole. Her step-father's name was Harry Cole. Chn b Nfld. rem to US.
G1. Irene, b 1911 mar Reginald Martin, dau Carol mar __ Temple
G2. Doris, mar Arthur Bursey, 3 chn: Arthur, Joan and Robert B.
G3. Edgar, b 1917? mar Susan Trippi, no issue
G4. Alfred, mar Gladys Powell 1940, 3 chn: Lloyd,Brenda, Alfred
G5. Sadie, mar Peterson, a son Wayne
G6. Emma Blanche, mar Edward S. Ankiewicz 1937, b 1918, res Chelsea, MA, desc.
H1. Marilyn, b 1938 H3. Robert Ankiewicz
H2. Edward, b 1942 H4. Barbara Ankiewicz b 1956
E4. Joseph, mar Catherine BUTT 1871 Nfld. Joseph d 1918, Catherine in 1921, 8 chn.
F1. David, b 1870s, mar Ann Jeffrey in Carbonear, Nfld. 1895,6 chn, see data in WRCIC
F2. William Henry, b 1872, d 1938 mar Jenny Martin and 2. Johanna Cole, chn, b Everett, MA
F3. John, b 1876, d 1950 mar Effie Oates, 5 chn b Everett, MA
F4. Edward or Edgar, b 1878 mar Lavina PEDDLE, rem to Everett,MA, 8 chn.
F5. Joseph b 1883 mar Frances Pike in Carbonear, Nfld, a son in Nfld.
F6. Michael, b 1885 d 1956, mar Diadem NOEL, 5 chn, res US.
F7. Eliza, d.y. F8. Alfred, d.y.

BUTT, John mar Maria Collyns in Mint Cove, Spaniard's Bay, Nfld. 1814 5 chn.

BUTTON, William, also spelled BOUTON, was bur in Portsmouth, NH 1693. (Noyes) BOUTON a J surname 1668, 1749.

BUTTON, poss BOUTON?, Capt. David owned the Creamer block in Salem, 1782. (Essex Coll, Vol 8)

BUTTON also noted in early CT. OUTC. See Essex Coll, Vol 46.

CABELDU, curr research in C.I., see CIFHS #3

CABOT, pron. CAH-BO, in J 1274. In St. Clement, Trinity, St. Martin, and St. John J 1749. Name is said to mean a small fish with a big head. CABOT shield: Or, three chabots haurient gules.

CABOT,Francois and wife Susanne GRUCHY, res St. Heliers J. Among their chn were three sons, Francis, George and John, who rem to America in the late 1600s. This surname in MA became so exalted and exclusive that it was said in Boston, "The Lowells speak only to the Cabots, and the Cabots speak only to God." However, in the 1800s and 1900s, this family has given many outstanding citizens to our country.

John Moore Cabot was Ambassador to five nations between 1954 and 1965, Brazil, Columbia, Finland, Poland and Sweden, and spoke Spanish and Portuguese. After retirement in 1966, he served as lecturer and consultant at Tufts Univ. and Georgetown Univ. There is a great deal in print about the Cabots. The famous Lodge family, one branch, is also desc from the Cabots. (Morrison; Foster; Balleine's BIO. DICT. OF J; STORY AND GEN OF THE CABOT FAM, by L. Vernon Briggs; MOSTLY ABOUT THE CABOTS, by Ellsworth S. Cabot, St. Louis, MO; Thomas D. Cabot, Boston, MA; Q.A. IN CANADA, by Turk; NEHGS Vol 9)

A1. Francis, b 1668 J living in 1748. Francis to America with bros. John and George below, but returned to England and mar Barbara Cooper. He became Mayor, Southampton, England 1725, res near Dover, Eng. His son Francis was Sheriff of Southampton 1733.

A2. George, b ca 1677 J, to America ca 1700 with his bros. and d 1717 in Boston. He mar Abigail Marston, 2 chn.

B1. Rev. Marston Cabot, b 1706, d 1756, mar Mary Dwight ca 1731. Had 14 chn between 1732 and 1756. "Descendants to the Wild West, farming families." (Balleine) See book by Ellsworth Cabot.

B2. Abigail, b 1704, d.y.

A3. John, b 1680 J, to MA 1700, d 1742 Salem, MA. Mar Anna Orne 1702 Salem. Was well-to-do, had slaves in Salem in early 1700s, 11 chn, with many notable descendants.

CABOT, noted in Anticosti, QUE 1900, OUTC. (Aldo Brochet, London, ONT)

CADORET, noted in Grosse Pointe, MI and Cleveland, OH, but poss French? Sometimes spelled CARDRY in Utah records. Noted in Alderney & Jersey

CADORET, Daniel, a miller, was christened 1793 St. Saviour J, son of Jean and Eliz. (RENOUF) CADORET. Daniel mar 1814 St. Heliers J, Eliz. RENOUF, qv. A Daniel and Mary came from J to UT 1855, via ship CHIMBORAZO. Note use of CARDRY in records.

A1. Daniel bp 1815 St. Saviour J d 1852 UT.

A2. Nancy, bp 1822 St. Saviour J mar 1849 Elie Jean LAURENS, qv.

A3. Mary CARDRY, bp 1831 J, d 1882 UT? Mar 1. James/Jacques Phillip DERFRESNE, DU FRESNE, and 2. David NICHOLAS, prob in UT. See Du Fresne and Nicholas.

CAIN, and LE CAIN noted in New England. Not known to this compiler if these persons and/or fams came directly from J as LE QUESNE, qv, or were from Canadian LE QUESNE/LE CAIN fam. See Q.A. IN CANADA. Consider also DE CAEN, for CAIN in J 1749, sometimes as DE CAIN.

CAIN, Arthur, early in MA mar 1675 Sarah Gold, poss from Isle of Man?

CANE, John, b 1706, mar Judith ___, and 2. Mary FAVOUR, qv, in Kittery, ME 1735. OUTC. For CANN, see DE CAEN, & J.LANGLOIS.

CALLEY noted in early New England. Was this CAILLET, in St. Lawrence, J 1788? See MRB records. CALLEY, Benj. commanded schooner MOLLY, sailing between MRB and Jersey. (JOURNALS OF ASHLEY BOWEN). Note Richard of Newburyport, MA 1790. OUTC. See also Jean book, JERSEY SAILING SHIPS.

CALLEY, Sally mar Richard BESSOM, BISSON 1802 MRB, also Tabitha, who mar Benj. BODEN 1769. See BODEN, and BISSON.

CANIVET, in St. Saviour J 1607, 1668. Curr research, see CIFHS #3. In St. Lawrence J 1788.

CANIVET, Elisabeth Esther, b 1822 Grouville, J d 1912 Clark, ID. Dau of Philip and Sarah (MORRIS, MAURICE) CANIVET. She mar Josias YOUNG, qv. Note that some Canivets came from St. Prive, Yonne, France. (SLC records) CANIVET curr in J.

CAREY, sommon G surname, but also in South of England. Noted in MA ear early. A Geo. CAREY was of J 1741.

CAREY, John, b J, was living with the LE BOUTILLIER fam in Iowa 1860.

CAREY, Peter, owned the Guernsey privateership FRIGATE.

CARLO, CARLOW, John from G to GCO 1807. See Ohio section. Rem to Zanesville, OH ca 1820? Mar Rachel LENFESTEY, qv, a dau Harriett. (Sarchet Scrapbook)

CARLO. Jacob and Elizabeth with fam settled in Dresden, ME early. A Hug. fam. (HIST. OF DRESDEN, ME, by Charles Allen)

CARPENTER, LE CHARPENTIER in J 1528. CHARPENTIER a G surname in late 1600s. Cf TOURGIS called CARPENTER in J (Stevens) In J 1200s, through 1500s and later. CARPENTER curr G and J.

CARPENTER, Elizabeth, see ORVIS

CARPENTER, Philip of J, fisherman in Cape Eliz., ME, 1688 had 20 acres on Isles of Shaols 1702, bought Lewis plantation on Smuttynose Is. and settled his fam in Kittery, but was killed by Indians at Spruce Creek with wife and one ch 1707. Survivor dau Mary, bp 1715, mar1. before 1721 John Deering, and 2. in 1729 Capt. Stephen SEAVEY. Son John Seavey mar Eunice Spinney, res Saco and Paris, ME. Dau Margery Seavey mar Googins, Gookins. (Noyes)

CARPENTER, Elisha and Lydia GREENE mar 1767 No. Kingstown, RI, OUTC.

CARPENTER, Dinah and Joshua GREENE mar 1746 No. Kingsgown, RI, OUTC. Note that TOURGIS fam settled same town. Cf TOURGIS called CARPENTER, surname of J. See TOURGIS. (THE EPISTLE, July 1979)

CARPENTER, many in Rehoboth, MA records including

CARPENTER, Wm., 1605-1659 mar Abigail ___, who d 1687. (Virkus II)

A1. Samuel, b ca 1644 d ca 1683?, mar 1666 Sarah READAWAY, dau of James of Rehoboth. Cf Hug surname RIDOUET, = READAWAY? See Virkus.

CARRE, in G since 1331, curr G. See also DE PUTRON. Some CARRE fams were Hug. Original CARRE of some lines was Helier, b J, rem to G, d 1677 at Blanque G, had son Helier, 1658-1727.

CARRE, John, with wife Susan DE JERSEY, res La Blanque, St. Peter Port, G. (George Thompson, Hollywood, CAL) CAUTION: TRIAL CHART

A1. Henry, wine merchant, rem to US 1818, bringing goods from France to D.H. Holmes in Alabama. He mar Amelia Wingate in Fort Clairborne, Monroe Co., AL ca 1822. Her fam had earlier rem from NC. Res Gainesville, MISS on the Pearl River, 4 chn. Henry drowned in Bay St. Louis, MISS 1829. Henri had cousin John NAFTEL, qv, who mar Henri's only sister Susan. Henri's bro, either John or Thomas, inherited family home in G, La Roussailerie.

B1. Henry? B2. Susan B3. Robert

B4. Walter William, b 1829 res New Orleans, operated the W.W.Carre Lumber Co. Mar 1862 Elvira Adams Beach, had 4 sons that survived,and other chn.

C1. Walter Wingate C3. Henry Beach C4. Tudor Beach

C2. Darwin Beach, d 1928, mar Leila M. Had chn D. Morey and Benita Carre.

A2. Susan, mar John NAFTAL, her first cousin, who also came to America 1818, at least one ch: John Naftal.

A3. John res G, and mar there.

B1. John, b 1810, lived to 90, mar Mary Ann PAGE or LE PAGE in G. His son John res Millmount, G.

Desc. of above fam inclue a Mrs. Anne Curson of Los Angeles, CAL and T. Barry Gotham of Barberton, OH, or were related through DE PUTRON fam.

CARRE in New York, 1618, Hug fam? Curr Princeton, NJ. OUTC, & in OHIO.

CARRE, Anne, b 1799 G, mar Daniel DE PUTRON, qv, 1822. She d in ILL 1872. She was said to be related to John and Susan(DE JERSEY)CARRE above.

CARRE, Anne and Ellen mar DE CARTERET bros. See CARTERET, DE CARTERET.

CARRE, Ezekiel rem to Kingstown, RI 1686, OUTC. (Savage I)

CARRE, Ellen J., b J, mar Walter DE CARTERET, qv, rem to North Chelmsford, MA late 1800s.
CARRE, John, rigger and stevedore, settled in NY by 1825, alien. (NY ALIENS, by Scott& Conway) OUTC.
CARREE, Louis, Lewis, son of Lewis, plus others in NJ GENESIS, 1956
CARRE, Louise, from G to Racine, WI 1842 with the OZANNE group, qv. She mar Sanford S. Strong. See WISCONSIN section.(Ozanne; Stone)
CARRE, Thomas, res Scioto Co., OH 1860 census. OUTC.
CARRELL in J 1402, 1528, in St. Brelade J 1749, in St. Lawrence J 1788. Also in St. Ouen J 1607, when name appeared as QUARELL. CARRELL also found in England. Poss some in New England from J. One CARRELL was a ship owner in J 1800s. (A. John Jean, Jersey)
CARYL, Edward and wife Elizabeth res Salem, MA. (Essex Coll) A son Samuel bp 1723. OUTC.
CARRELL, CARRYL, Hannah, from J? mar Isaac LE CAUDEY, qv, in MA 1720s. Prob both from J. See Salem and MRB, MA records for much more.
CARRELL, Capt. John, master of a ship that brought many immigrants to New England ca 1736, poss some from C.I.
CARRELL, Joseph arrived 1769 on ship MOLLY from J, as indentured servant. Another or same Joseph had fam of 3 in 1790. A Joseph Jr. was also part of a fam of 3 in same census. (WHITMORE)
CARRILL, William mar Sarah BEADLE bp 1739 Salem, MA. (SAM. BEADLE FAM)
CARRELL and WESTAWAY, both J surnames at that time, had land in Georgetown, PEI, early 1800s. OUTC. (Old map)
CARRELL in Maryland 1600s, poss from J? (Skordas)
CARRINGTON, Stanley, b G, res Fort Myers, FLA 1900s. Relatives in St. Peter Port G.
CARRINGTON, Jack, b G, res Le Pave, Castel G, rem to Indiana, a Guernsey cattle breeder, 1900s.
CARTEE, Philip, mar 1668 Elizabeth York, dau of Richard of Dover, ME. (Noyes) Was this a CARTER, or CARTIER of J? CARTIER old in J and G, also current.
CARTER, John son of John, bp 1706 Salem, MA. (Essex Coll Vol 8) OUTC.
CARTER, Mary/Maria b 1869 J, d 1951 Montreal, QUE. Mar Walter K. Rowcliffe, qv.
CARTER, Margaret, b ca 1810 St. Peter Port G, d 1886 B.C., Canada. See John MOLLET.
CARTERET, see NOTABLES and NEW JERSEY section. See DE CARTERET.
CARTERET in J before 1156, also early in G. DE CARTERET in St. Laurens, St. Ouen, Trinity, St. Brelade, St. Heliers, Grouville, St. Saviours and St. John J between 1668-1749. Curr J. DE CARTERET shield: gules, four fusils in fess argent. See CIFHS #3.
CARTERET is one of the most distinguished surnames of the C.I., and the roster includes many notable men. Some branches can be traced to 1186 in J. Much more info. in Balleine's BIO. DICT OF J; W.P. Johnson Ed., NORTH CAROLINA HIST. REVIEW, Raleigh, NC 1970 Fall & Winter Bull. NEHGS Vols 82,86,88,100, etc. More info. in Jersey.
CARTERET, Capt. Philip, b ca 1703 J? mariner of Boston, mar 1727 Elizabeth Dunster, b ca 1699. Res Medford, Menotomy, and Charlestown, MA. Later res Arlington, MA. Wife was a woman of ability, and ran their business for her husband while he was overseas on many voyages. She was called by relatives Aunt CARTERET and Aunt Cartwright. Capt. Philip d 1767 age 64. She survived him 20 yrs. (MA records and DUNSTER GEN)
A1. Mary Carteret, b 1730, d 1751
A2. Ruth, b 1736 d 1754 A3. Elizabeth, b 1737, d 1751

A4. Abigail, b ca 1739/40 mar 1758 William Whittemore, son of Samuel and Elizabeth (Spring) Whittemore. Abigail d 1809 age 70, and Wm. d 1818 W. Cambridge, MA age 86.
B1. Elizabeth Carteret Whittemore, b 1763, d.y.
B2. Elizabeth again, b 1764 mar 1. Moses ROBBINS, and 2. John Frost, his second wife. Chn by Moses?
C1. William Whittemore Frost, bp 1803.
B3. Philip Carteret Whittemore, bp 1766, mar Lydia Phelps.
B4. William Whittemore, bp 1769, d 1771 age 2.
B5. William again, Whittemore, bp 1772 mar 1796 Anna Cutter, dau of Samuel and Rebecca (Hill) Cutter of Menotomy. She was b 1771. He a farmer, d Chelsea, MA 1854. She d 1849. 7 chn.
C1. Ann Whittemore, bp 1799, mar 1822 Samuel Adams, b 1790 W. Cambr. rem to Lexington, MA 1827. He d 1866, she in 1862. 4 chn. See DUNSTER GEN for more.
C2. Eleanor Whittemore, b 1801 d 1805
C3. William Augustus Whittemore, b 1804, mar Abigail C. Tuffts 1838. He d Arlington, MA 1867, 6 chn. See DUNSTER GEN.
C4. Susan Francis Whittemore, b 1807 mar Pascal Sprague of W. Cambr. MA in 1832, and 1850. 4 chn.
C5. Eleanor Sophia Whittemore, b 1809 mar John P. Daniels 1832 d1868, 4 chn.
C6. Geo. Washington Whittemore, b 1812 mar Cynthia Richardson and d 1870. Had Wilde's Hotel in Boston, 6 chn.
C7. Thomas Whittemore, b 1815, mar Clara RICHARDSON of Fitchburg,MA, 1837, 2 chn.
B6. Abigail Whittemore, bp 1776 mar John Davenport of Cambridge, OH, prob the keeper of the Davenport Tavern. There was a John Davenport in Belmont Co., OH 1826. A John owned land in Madison Twp., GCO 1840. (Wolfe) See sources for much more info. on desc.

CARTERET, Philip, said to be son of the above Capt. Philip by an earlier marriage, was also a sea captain out of Boston, and mar there 1740 Rebecca Stone. He was living in 1787? (TINGLEY GEN) This fam poss related to the MARRETTS? (Suffolk Estates)
A1. Philip, b 1741 A4. Richard, b 1746/7
A2. Rebecca, b 1743 A5. Hannah, bp 1748/9 Boston
A3. John, b 1745 mar Mary Crosby 1768 Boston, was enlisted soldier 1779.

CARTERET, Rebecca of Boston? mar 1797 John Vinton. See VINTON GEN.
CARTERET, DE CARTERET, Richard mar Lydia Pierce 1768 Boston, MA
DE CARTERET data, see BULLEN FAM HIST. by Holman.
CARTERET, CARTWRIGHT, ---, Chaisemaker, mar Sarah GALE 1800 Boston.
CARTERET, Wm. d in Philadelphia, PA 1838
CARTERET, curr Los Angeles, CAL and in TX

CARTERET, James, b 1600s, d 1682, called the New Jersey Rebel, raised in France and sent to sea as a young man, poss in a privateer ship. He later left the Navy and in 1671 was one of the Lords Proprietors of Carolina, with a barony of 12,00 acres, near the head of Cooper River. In that same year he was in New York and in 1672 in New Jersey, where his father was a Lord Proprietor. He promoted dissension in the NJ govt. and the tax payers revolt fizzled out, upon which he left. In April 1673 he mar Frances, dau of Thomas DE LA VAL, Mayor of New York. He and wife set out for the Carolinas, but the ship was captured by the Dutch, and they were set ashore in VA. By 1676 they were back in NY and he was leading a dissolute life. He was disinherited by his father, and returned to J to plead his case, and died there 1682. Three years later his wife and 2 small chn, George and Elizabeth, came to Jersey Island. She d in 1688, and when George, the son came of age, he went to NY in 1702 to try to recover the property which his grandfather settled on his mother at the time of her marriage. However, George was killed in an accident while in London, England. Elizabeth, his sister, mar 1. Philippe DE CARTERET, Seigneur of Rozel, Jersey, and 2. Philippe PIPON, Seigneur of Noirmont, J. She returned to New York, a widow. (A. Pipon, St. Lawrence, J)

DE CARTERET, John Dumaresq, b 1855 St. John J, son of Isidore and Jeanne (LE CORNU) DE CARTERET. He mar 1. Mary LE MASURIER, b 1854 St. Ouen J, d in J., dau of Jean LE MASURIER and Rachel VAUTIER, 6 chn. John mar 2. Mary Jane Ellis, 3 chn, and 3. Annie QUEREE MACHON, qv, widow with 8 chn by previous mar. John res North Chelmsford, MA 1873. (Edith Hainsworth, N. Chelmsford, MA; Phyllis Perreault, Hubbardston, MA)

A1. John Alpheus, b 1873 on ship coming over, mar Eugenie Gagne Vaillan-court 1924, no issue.

A2. Alfred, b 1874, mar Ada Swanwick, 1897, d 1953 N. Chelmsford, MA, 4 sons, 3 daus.

A3. Arthur, b 1875 mar Anne CARRE, qv, d at childbirth, a son. Arthur mar 2. Mary Ann BRAKE, qv, 2 sons, 1 d.y.

A4. Walter, mar Ellen J. CARRE, qv, sister of Anne above. Walter d 1919, 3 daus.

A5. Mary Dithia, b 1880 mar Silas Josiah ROBERTS, qv, 1900. Mary d 1968 bur N. Chelmsford, MA, 2 sons and 4 daus.

A6. Ada, b J, mar Elisha BRAKE, qv, bro of Arthur's wife Mary, 1904. One son, one dau. Ada mar 2. Charles Griswold of ME, a son.

A7. by 2nd wife, Harriet, b 1889 St. Ouen J, mar Theophilus MACHON, qv, no issue.

A8. Sidney DUMARESQ, d.y.

A9. Ethel Mary, mar 1. Harold Sanders, 3 sons and a dau. She mar 2. ___Erickson, no issue.

CARTERET, Ames, poss Amice?, mar Mary BUTLER 1729 Boston, MA.

DE CARTERET, Charles arrived in Boston from J 1715 on ship MARY from J. (Whitemore)

DE CARTERET, Clement of C.I. mar 1880 at Orillia, ONT, Cora V. Pearn of Bowmanville, ONT. (Orillia PACKET; Gary French, Elmvale, ONT)

CARTERET, Edward, b J, arrived in Nantucket, MA with son Nicholas from Isles of Shoals, ME ca 1763. He d Nantucket 1705 leaving issue. He is said to have gone there to teach the natives the art of catching and curing codfish.! If not a joke, this may mean that he had been with the Newfoundland codfisheries previously. (Letter of Arthur Goff from C. Langton, Granville, Bagot, Jersey, C.I. 1931) There were possibly two other Edward CARTERET/CARTWRIGHTS res in MA as early as 1662. One res Martha's Vineyard toward 1700s. OUTC. (Boston Transcript, Aug. 1908)

A1. Sampson, b 1678 A2. Susanna, b 1681 A3. Edward, b 1683.

A4. Mary, b 1687

CARTERET, Hannah of Boston mar Marston Chappell. (NEHGS Vols 82,88,100)

CARTERET, Hugh, ensign and cooper, arrived from J with wife Ann 1671, d before 1693. He was in Owen's Parliament 1670. Res Old Charles-town, Lot 18. (Baldwin) Anne later mar Daniel Bullman. SC records.

CARTERET, James, recorded in GA 1622, with wife. (LIST OF EARLY SETTL-ERS OF GEORGIA, by Coulter and Saye.

CARTERET, John mar Hannah ALLEY 1781 Boston

CARTERET, John of Jersey and England, later Lord Granville, son of Sir George, was Secty. of State in England, linguist, ambassador, etc, and joint owner of Carolina with the King of England. He surrendered his share in 1729. (SCHS)

DE CARTERET, John, b 1745 Charlestown, SC, d 1821 Boston, MA, an artificer in the Commissary Dept. of the US Army. Mar Nancy Smith, his third wife in Boston? A dau Mrs. Rebecca Pratt, b 1816 Boston. (DAR, Vol 22)

DE CARTERET, John mar Mary Crosby 1768 Boston, MA

CARTERET, Mary, mar Robert Jackson 1799 Boston, MA.

CARTERET, Nicholas and fam res Ickerby, SC 1672, with 5 servants, from England in the first Fleet of the CAROLINA. Poss res Charlestown, ca 1700. (SCHS)

CARTERET, Peter, from J, in Virginia by 1664, was manager of an experimental farm on the Carolina Outer Banks. Peter was a nephew of Sir George, and was part of a group of investors who financed a plantation to grow grapes and tobacco, and to raise hogs on Colleton-Collington Island. Due to repeated hurricanes at crucial times for several years, the effort was a failure, and the colonists who remained after that time resorted to commercial fishing for a livelihood. (Stock) See Carolina section.

DE CARTERET, Peyton, son of Sir Philip DE CARTERET, 1584-1643 and of Rachel POULET, grandson of Helier DE CARTERET, and was b in Sark. Peyton drowned with Prince Maurice off the West Indies in 1652.

CARTERET, Peter of Jersey came to VA 1664, kinsman of Sir George, and left in 1673.

CARTERET, DE CARTERET, Philip, son of Helier and Rachel(DE LA CLOCHE) DE CARTERET of J, sailed from England in the ship PHILIP in April 1665 with settlers from J and France, possibly from England also? Philip was b 1639 J. The ship is said to have first landed in VA, then in NY, and finally sailed to NJ in August, making a settlement there named ELizabethtown. Philip mar 1681 Elizabeth Smith LAWRENCE, and d there 1682, no issue. (NJ HIST. RECORDS; NJ GENESIS, 1956) Philip was named Gov. of New Jersey.

CARTERET, Philip, 1733-1796, Seigneur of Trinity J, served in British Navy becoming Rear Admiral. He went twice around the world, 1764 and 1769, discovered Pitcairn Island, famous now through story and movie MUTINY ON THE BOUNTY. He privateered very successfully from the West Indies and took some American ships in the Rev. War. BALLEINE'S BIO. DICT. OF JERSEY; CARTERET'S VOYAGES AROUND THE WORLD, by Helen Wallis, England, for Hackluyt Soc.)

CARTERET, CARTWRIGHT, Sampson mar in Boston Bethia Pratt, who d 1741. Was he a son of Edward above?

CARVANYELL appeared in Plymouth, MA 1621. CARVANELL was in J 1516. (PLANTERS OF THE COMMONWEALTH by Banks; HIST AND GEN OF THE MAYFLOWER PLANTERS, by L.C. Hills.)

CASELL, CASTEL, Robert, a Pequot soldier from Ipswich, MA 1637. (Noyes) CASTEL a J surname 1291-1668.

CASSIDY, Margaret, age 32 of Toronto, ONT b J, dau of Thomas and Mary, mar 1862 Toronto by Rev. Isaac Brock Howard, Meth., Christopher Anderson, age 35 of Toronto, b England, son of Christopher and Annie. (Wm. Britnell, Mississauga, ONT)

CASWELL, many in early New England. "We have found a Caswell family who came from the Island of Guernsey around 1704-1714". MRB Hist.Soc. Compiler could find nothing more on this fam. Some Caswells came from Somerset, England to MASS.

CASWELL, Simon, res MRB, from G? with wife Ann. Other chn?

A1. Grace, bp 1728 A2. Thomas, bp 1730

CASWELL, John res MRB, mar Elizabeth SAVAGE, OUTC. 10 chn: Simon, bp 1744 MRB, John, Samuel, Tabitha, Richard, Tabitha, Hannah, Grace, William and Richard Savage, bp 1764.

CASWELL, John mar Elizabeth SEAVERY, poss SYVRET, qv, 1767, res MRB, a son John bp 1767. OUTC.

CASWELL, Samuel mar Hannah LE GROW, qv, 1779 MRB, poss son of John?
A1. Anna, bp 1780 A3. Samuel, bp 1784 A5. Philip, bp 1789
A2. Thomas, bp 1783 A4. John, bp 1787 A6. William, bp 1791

CASWELL, more data in Mass. Vrs; Barnard, VT; ANNALS OF OXFORD, ME; N Noyes; Lynn, MA; Essex Antiq, Vol3; Barre, VT; TINGLEY GEN, Vol 1; Rehoboth and MRB VR; NEHGS Vol 9; HOOPER GEN; PIERCE GEN; Skordas Maryland records; etc.

CAUDY, see CODY, LE CAUDEY

CAUDY, David and James have wills in Book 2, of EARLY RECORDS OF HAMPSHIRE CO, VA, now West VA, by Clara Sage and Laura Jones, Balt,1976. CAUDY may easily be LE CAUDEY. See book for more data.

CAUL, also spelled CALL, or COLE? Prob Hug surname.

CAUL, George a weaver arrived from J Boston 1769 on ship MOLLY. (Whitmore)

CALL, Paul A. mar Elizabeth BESSOM, BISSON in MRB? 1792. She mar 2. Henry P. Call 1795.

CAUX, see COW and LE CAUX. LE CAUX in J 1668-1749.

CAVE, CAVET, Thomas from C.I.? to Salem, MA ca 1700? Sons Thomas and Sylvester, bp in Salem 1715, 1717. Consider also GAVET. (Salem VR) CAVEY and CAVE curr G and J. CAVET, CAVEY noted in Stevens list of Old Jersey Surnames. Curr research? See CIFHS #7.

CAVE, Mary see MARQUAND and HORMAN. Patty CAVE mar George Kreider 1835 in Coshocton, OH. OUTC.

CEVERNE, Janette, John Pickering's Jersey servant was in court 1673. (Noyes)

CHAMBERLAIN. There is a Chamberlain Fam Assoc. in US, Box 1494, Edgartown, MA. It appears that one Capt. Chamberlain was said to have come to America from J in the 1600s. See DUNSTER GEN; NEHGS Vol 132; Koehler; Census; Westboro, Oxford, Woburn, Billerica, MA records.

CHAMBERLAIN, Ebenezer arrived in Boston from NC 1715 on sloop MARTHA, OUTC, but poss a Jerseyman? (Whitmore)

CHAMBERLAYNE, Abram, said to be French Hug. in NJ. (Koehler)

CHAMBERLAIN, Daniel and Eli from J? Rev. hero of Westboro, MA. (Boston TRANSCRIPT, Feb. 1917)

CHAMBERLAYNE in J 1607, spelled earlier--CHAMBELLANS.

CHAMPION, found early in both J and G, but also in Isle of Wight and other parts of England, also in France. (Myra Champion, Ashville,NC)

CHAMPION, Mary Ann, b ca 1853 J, d 1910 US. She mar Elias FALLE, qv, in St. Saviour J, rem to Lansingburgh, NY, 3 chn. Mary Ann was dau of Abraham, b Bristol, England and Jane b England, res J. Their other chn were b J. (Betty Wickham, Loveland, COL)

CHERRY, James from G? to GCO, mar there Jane HANNAH 1819.

CHEVALIER in J since at least 1274, in St. Helier and St. John parishes by 1668. (Stevens) Translated at times in America to KNIGHT.

CHEVALIER, Edward, b J, d in Salem, MA 1700s age 55

CHEVALIER, Jacques/James, a J apprentice in New England 1676, engaged by Philip ENGLISH, qv. (NEHGS)

CHEVALIER, J.A. in Wash. Co., OH 1810; John in NY 1810; John in Phila. 1782. OUTC.

CHEVARLY, Mary and Richard, chn of M. Chevarly bp Salem, MA 1691. OUTC (Essex Coll, Vol 8)

CHEVARLY, Mary in Philadelphia, PA 1790. (Census) OUTC

CHEVALIER, Marie, b 1823 Trinity J, mar Philip DE LA MARE, qv, rem to UT 1852, via ship KENNEBEC. D 1884 Tooele, UT. She was dau of Daniel Matthew CHEVALIER. (Prudence Fyffe, Central, AZ)

CHEVALIER, Nicholas from J to MA late 1600s. (Fosdick)
CHEVALIER, Philip and Richard, bp Salem, MA 1692. OUTC
CHEVALIER, Thomas and John arrived in Boston on sloop ADVENTURER 1760s from Nfld., mariners. These men were prob from J fams. (Whitmore)
CHICK, surname of G and of southern England, Devon? Name curr G.
CHICK, CHEEK?, fam from C.I. to UT 1852 on ship ELLEN MARIE. A family, George, Mahala, George and Barnabas. Prob English.
CHICK, fam from Devon, England connected by marriage to the PENDEXTER fam, qv, through the Kennard fam. (Janet Ward,Gardiner, ME)
CHINN, old J surname (Stevens), however, also in southern England. Noted in US but not traced.
CHINN, John, from C.I. or Devon? to MRB, wife Hannah. See BISSON fam. 9 chn: Mary, b 1727, John, George, John, Hannah, Samuel, Rebecca, Sarah, and Elizabeth, bp 1746.
CHURCH, George Dalimore, b J?mar Elizabeth JERVOIS (JARVIS? GERVAISE?) dau of Benj. JERVOIS, 1828 in G. (Dennis B. Rodgers, Decatur, ILL)
A1. Richard Howard, b 1846 J, brought to Columbus, OH 1852 by parents, with 3 siblings. Richard rem to Cincinnati, OH ca 1862/64 then to Indianapolis, IND where he d 1914.
A2. Joseph H. A3. Henry A4. Frank A5. Eva A6. others?
CLARK, ship builders in J 1800s. (A. John Jean, Jersey)
CLAVELL, some curr research in J? See CIFHS #6. A Clavell was author of SHOGUN, and other excellent historical fiction of 1980s.
CLEMENTS. Most of this surname in early New England were probably from England. However, CLEMENT was in St. Peter J 1607, and it's possible that several came to the colonies from J. Richard CLEMENTS, deputy-surveyor of Gov. Andros may have been from the Islands.
CLEMENT, John of J res Burgeo Nfld. 1865
CLEMENT, Seivery (prob SYVRET of J) mar Hannah Dodd 1758 in MRB.
CLEMENTS, Capt.John, 1715-1805, from J? res MRB then rem to Nova Scotia shortly after 1776. OUTC. (Robert J. Frost, Victoria, BC)
CLEMENT, Henry was in SC 1675 (Baldwin) Poss from J? See Clement data in NEHGS Vol 74, etc; Noyes; Essex Coll; and Haverhill, MA records.
CLEMENTS, Job res Dover, ME with wife Betty Rollins. OUTC. 10 chn. (NEHGS Vol 74)
CLEMENT, Capt.Peter was trading with Antigua and South Carolina in the J ship NONPAREIL 1770. (A. John Jean, Jersey)
CLEMONS. The orig. form of this was probably CLEMENT, and it has not been verified that John below originated in G. "Tradition of the origin of the family was that two brothers from G were kidnapped and carried to sea, brought to America, one of them to Danvers, MA." (Hon. Llewellyn A. Wadsworth, Hiram, ME. Historian) "While on their way to school on the Island of Guernsey, two little boys, Isaac and Jacob Clemons, were stolen or kidnapped, placed on a British Man-of-War, (perhaps as cabin boys?) and brought to America. They landed at Salem, MA. This was probably during the early part of the 18th Century." (Mrs. Mary Newton Clarke, grandau of John Clemons Jr. of Sandusky, OH) See book, THE CLEMONS FAMILY OF HIRAM, MAINE, by Hubert Clemons and Ruth Clemons Murphy, with much info. on this large family. Some data unverified.
CLEMONS, CLEMENT?, Isaac, from G to Salem, mar ___?
A1. Edward A2. Jonathan, who d ca 1799
A3. John. The book deals mostly with his desc. He was b at Danvers, MA before 1743, was a colonial soldier 1755. Rem to Saco Valley 1779 with wife and 6 chn. He mar Abigail Southwick, dau of Jonathan or John Southwick III, Quaker. Desc of this fam owned for several generations potteries and a tannery at Danvers.

John and Abigail are said to have left 164 desc. when she d at age 104. 8 chn, see book.

CLEAR, CLERE, CLERK, CLERCQ, all poss LE CLERCQ of J, where fam res in St. Clement and St. Saviour parishes 1668. Researcher should consider origin in J if no other source is found. Records of CLERKE noted in MA and NH early. See VRs of Beverly, MA; Portsmouth and Goffstown, NH, 1700s. Also see NEHGS Vol 82.

CLOCK, CLOCHE, CLARK, John from J with CARTERET, qv, on ship PHILIP to Elizabethtown, NJ, 1665. Poss he was related to Philip CARTERET, who whose mother was a LA CLOCHE. Surname CLOCHE, DE LA CLOCHE, DE LA CLOSE, was in St. Saviour and St. Helier J 1668. CLOCHE curr J. (NJ Colonial Documents; Monette)

CLOCK, Peter, a DE LA CLOCHE?, son of Peter and Hannah (BALDWIN) CLOCK, mar in Smithtown, LI, NY, 1789 Nancy AKER. (CT NUTMEGGER, Mar,1981)

CLOCHE, DE LA CLOCHE, DE LA CLOSE, etc, Rachel, from J to Salem, MA 1600s, mar Peter BALDWIN, poss BAULDIN of J? in Salem 1672. See above Peter CLOCK. (Noyes; Fosdick, Savage, etc.)

CLOCK, J.M. on ship CHESTER 1851 at San FRancisco, CAL (Rasmussen) OUTC

COADY, see CODY and LE CAUDEY, CAUDY.

COCK, Thomas mar Abigail Cock 1740 Boston. Could this be LE COCQ of J?

CODY, LE CAUDEY, Buffalo Bill, was the direct desc. of Philip LE CAUDEY b 1668 J, variously spelled LE CODY, LAGEDY, MC CODY, CODIE, CODY, COADY, etc, etc, who came from St. Peter J to MA. In 1698 Philip bought a home at Beverly, MA, where he farmed 6 acres, and res for 25 years. He and wife Martha LE BROCQ, from G, were members of the First Church of Beverly, and 5 of his chn were bp there. Philip and Martha were said to be married in St. Brelade J 1692, but record not found. In 1720 Philip acquired land at Kipkinton?, MA rem there, and d 1743. His will spells the name COADY. At least 4 thousand desc of this fam today. See the many books about Buffalo Bill, esp. LIVES AND LEGENDS OF BUFFALO BILL, by Don Russel. Below is just one of hundreds of lines of this Jersey family. (Margaret Swanson, Vandenberg A.F. Base, CAL)

A1. John, b ca 1695, had 8 chn

A2. Joseph, b 1700, will probated 1756, res Beverly and Hopkinton,MA, mar 1722 Mary MARTIN.

B1. Philip, b 1729 Worcester Co., MA mar 1754 Abigail Emerson. D 1808

C1. Philip b 1770, d 1850 Cleveland, OH mar Lydia MARTIN, 1764-1846

D1. Philip b 1816 d 1846, physician in Sheboygan, WI, mar Harriet M. Sherwin, 1820-1854.

E1. Lindus Cody, 1840-1926, mar Sarah Amelia Farnsworth, 1843-1928, res Cleveland, OH, 10 chn.

F1. Harriet Eliza, 1862-1904, mar 1880 Andrew Marsh, b 1857 Goshen OH, 3 chn

G1. Lindus Cody Marsh, b 1883 Cleveland, OH mar 1909 Eleanor Blake, b 1884, div, dau of Charles Blake of St. Louis, MO, & mar 2. in 1923 Ann Barraud CLOCKE, Bermo Bluff, VA, 2 chn.

G2. Roy Parker Marsh, b 1885 E. Cleveland, OH res Willoby, OH

G3. Edith Marsh, mar C.E. Murray

F2. Lydia Sarah Cody, b 1863 E. Cleveland, OH, res Willoughby,OH

F3. Henry Bissell Cody, b 1866

F4. Frank Lindus Cody, b 1867 mar Ida R. Baker

F5. Mary Amelia, b 1871 F6. Leonard F. Cody, d.y.

F7. Arthur Philip Cody, b 1875 mar Marie Davis

F8. Jane Ethelind, mar 1904 Samuel Higginbottom

F9. Grace Isabel Cody, b 1882

F10. Gertrude Louise Cody, b 1885, mar Wm. H. Wheaton.

D6. Isaac, b 1811, Toronto, ONT, fam rem to Cleveland, OH. Isaac mar Martha Miranda O'Connor, 2. REbecca Sumner of Medina, OH, and 3. in 1840, Mary Ann Bonsell Laycock of a Derby, PA fam from England 1690. See Russel book and others for much more interesting data on this branch which includes Buffalo Bill.

A3. Abraham, b 1701, d.y.

A4. Isaac, b 1703/4 Beverly, MA, d Hopkinton, MA 1737, mar 1733 Hannah CARRYL, qv, b 1706.

B1. Joseph, b 1736 Beverly, MA, d 1787 Milford, mar Mary Parmenter,b 1737. (Margaret Swanson, Van.AF Base, CAL)

C1. Mary Cody, b 1760 mar Thomas Hiscock C2. Martha b 1761

C3. Sarah, b 1763 mar Richard Hiscock

D1. Luther Hiscock, b 1801 Pompey, NY, d 1879 Jackson, MI, mar Persis Higbee, b 1805, d 1896 Morley, MI.

E1. Sarah Hiscock, b 1838, mar Wm. Henry Bush 1859.

F1. Emma Rosette Bush/Rose Bush, b 1864 Pompey, NY, d Spokane,WA 1950. Mar 1887 Robert Kellogg , b 1861 Salem, ILL, d 1932 Grand Rapids, MI.

G1. Alice Eliz. Kellogg, b 1904 Grand Rapids, MI, mar 1928 Fred. Martin Phelps, b 1903 Newark, NY.

C4. Anna, b 1765 mar James Hiscock C6. Joseph, b 1769

C5. Hannah, b 1767, d.y. C7. Hannah again, b 1771

A5. Thomas, b 1707, poss another Thomas b a little later?

A6. Mary, b1710.

LE COUDEY, LE CODEY,Lucy, dau of John and Allis, b 1723 Beverly? MA. OUTC.

COADY, James mar Sarah BEADLE, qv, dau of Thomas of Salem, MA, widow of Stephen Welcome of Salem, tailor 1739. James Coady was a baker 1783. See James CAUDEY. OUTC.

CODY noted in Pres. Jefferson's line, but OUTC.

CODIE, Susanna, dau of John and Alice bp 1726 Beverly, MA. OUTC. See Lucy LE COUDEY above.

COGLAN, Wm. and wife, Lillian DE BRODER, qv, b G, to Canada then to WI 1964. Rem to Hialeah, FLA. COGLAN curr in J, but prob Irish?

COHU, old in G and J. In Castel G 1676, curr in G.

COHU, Thomas Ashburn, b 1850 Martin House, St. Sampson, G, son of Nicholas and Marie (LE POIDEVIN) COHU. Thomas rem to Phila. ca 1869, then to NEBR? settling finally in MO. (Willis Cohu, Ouray, COL)

A1. William Edward, b 1879 Granby, MO d 1962, mar 1901 Ella May Clark.

B1. Crystal Leona, b 1906 Diamond, MO, mar 1921 (Wm.) Lewis England, b 1901 Granby, MO, d 1970 Denver, COL son of Charles L. England and Martha C. Black.

C1. John Clifford England, b 1922 La Junta, COL d 1974, mar Lola ___.

C2. Naomi Darline England, b 1927 Shawnee, OK mar 1946 Barton Ahlberg, and 2. Chester Lewis Pittser, 7 chn.

D1. Glen B. Ahlberg, b 1947 D5. Linda D. Ahlberg, b 1953 marJohnson

D2. Wm. M. Ahlberg, b 1949 D6. Debbie Ahlberg, b 1955 mar Peters

D3. Thomas O. Ahlberg, b 1951 d 1970

D4. Jerry L. Ahlberg, b 1952 D7. Patricia L. Pittser, b 1961

C3. Bonnie Lucille England, b 1929 Tulsa, OK, mar Walter Southall

B2. Bonnie Marie, b 1909 mar 1926 Charles E. Stoffel

C1. Waltrina Joan Stoffel, b 1927 La Junta, COL mar Daryl K. Baker.

B3. Willis Leon, b 1913 Diamond, MO mar ca 1935 Edith Mallard, and 2. Elizabeth Marie Hinty, b 1920 West Branch, IA.

C1. Willis Jr, b 1935 Col. Srings, COL.

C2. Melvin Douglas, b 1936 mar Terry Montgomery

C3. Gary Denis, b 1938 mar 1972 Nancy Jo Weber

C4. by 2nd wife, Clifford David, b 1946 West Branch, IA
C5. Charles Edward, b 1948 Denver, mar 1969 Nancy Belden
C6. Susan Elizabeth, b 1949 Denver, mar 1982 John A. McCormick
B4. Donald RaChell mar 1938 Elizabeth Teats, b1919 RockyFord, COL.
C1. Catherine Elaine, b 1938 mar 1958 Charles E. Hays, and 2. Glen Fulton. chn: Rachelle Hays, Betty Ann, Charles K. Fulton
C2. Donald Sherwood, b 1941 Alamosa, CAL mar Linda G. Kilgore, 2 chn: Kirsten S. b 1968 and 2. Michael Sean, b 1970.
A2. Maurice Bert, b 1880 Granby, MO d 1972 Neosho, MO, mar 1905 Lona Dell McFadden, b 1889.
B1. Lila June, b 1906 Granby, mar 1926 Mark Everhard, 6 chn.
C1. Malbyrn Everhard, b 1926 mar Elza Winter, 3 chn: Tom, Alice and Mark Winter.
C2. Patsy Ruth Everhard, b 1928 mar Bill Spillman
C3. Janice Marie Everhard, b 1930 mar John Leslie Jr.
C4. Bertha Anne Everhard, b 1933 mar Jack Sexton
C5. Kathleen Everhard, b 1937 mar Melvin Carothers
C6. Paul Richard Everhard, b 1941 mar Linda Jackson
B2. Wilford Merle, b 1910 mar 1930 Zorada Ann Peebles
C1. Merle D. b 1931 Granby, MO mar Dorothy ___, 3 married daus.
C2. Tandy Win, mar Diane ___
C3. Torchy Linn, b 1949 GrandviewWa, mar Karen ___, 2 chn.
C4. Randy Fred, b 1954 WA, mar Laurel ___.
B3. Fred Lenwood, b 1907 Diamond, MO mar 1935 Ercel Rawlinson
B4. Carl Loyd, b 1912 Granby, d 1978, mar 1939 Eva Kinney and 2. Martha Rutherford 1953.
C1. Steven Glen, b 1944 mar 1966 Barbara Ann Haseltine, sons Jeffery and Erick K.
C2. Alvin Dale, b 1949 mar Linda Schudel, son Clifford Scott
C3. Dana Joy, b 1941, d.y.
B5. Mack Fadden, b 1914 Granby, mar 1936 Helen Smith
C1. Sandra LeAnne, b 1941 Granby, mar 1965 Dale John Billam, 2 sons Dale J. and David J. Billam
C2. Gary Wayne, b 1945 mar 1965 Glenda Lee Colvin
C3. Dick Edwin, b 1952 mar 1973 Ruth Meador, 2 daus
C4. Janelle Elaine, b 1956 mar 1973 Bobby Dean Peters, son Robert.
B6. Maurice Jr., b Diamond MO, mar 2. 1960 Mary Creason, 3 chn by 1st wife, 4 by 2nd: Scott, Sandy, Gregg, d.y., David, Debbie, Gregg again and Mike.
A3. Nicholas Rochelle, b 1882 Granby, MO mar 1911 Mary/May Boehning, b 1883 d 1970 MO.
A4. Winona, b 1886 mar 1909 George Jones. She d 1981 Hood River,OR. He d 1944 Commerce, OK. Chn: Berle Jones, Mike Jones and a dau.
A5. Neftal Arabella, b 1888 Granby, MO, d 1982, mar 1915 Frank Sitler.
B1. Robert Thomas Sitler, b 1917 mar 1963 Letha Martin, 2 daus: Barbara and Betty Stiler, b 1960s
B2. Norma Nadine Sitler, b 1920 Granby, mar 1945 Alex Rolek
C1. Jeannette Ann Rolek b1946 mar Junior Lee Jarvis 1971, sons Paul and Alex C.
C2. John Alex. Rolek, b 1950 mar 1975 Kim Denise Mabe, dau Molly D.
B3. George Frank Sitler, b 1924 mar Johnnie Bower.
A6. Herbert David, b 1892 Granby, MO mar 1916 Blanche M. Holley, b1897
B1. Glen Roger, b 1917 La Junta, COL mar 1937 Una C. Gillmore,6 chn.
C1. Loyd Wayne, b 1938 C2. Roger Dale b 1939
C3. Tommie Lee, b 1942 mar 1976 Inez F. Renberg, 3 chn: Rollin, Sherri and Camille
C4. Janet Louise, b 1943 Neosho, MO mar 1962 Robert Kyle Sitton, a

Daughter Janelle

C5. Patty Lou, b 1946 Yakima, WA mar Wayne L. Ross, 2 daus, Katherine and Krista Ross.

C6. Roger Lenn, b 1950 mar Mary E. Love, 2 daus, Heather and Jennifer

B2. Juanita Marie, b 1924 La Junta, mar 1946 Grady Thomas Justice, b 1924 Rockwood, TX.

C1. Steven T. Justice, b 1949 Ft. Walton, FLA

C2. Jetta Marie Justice b 1953 Cocoa FLA, mar 1973 Jack Brown, dau Carli Brown

C3. Mike Allen Justice, b 1955 Germany, mar 1978 Terri Sue Yoden

B3. Orval Leon, b 1932 Neosho, MO mar 1956 Evelyn Lois Wilson, 2 chn.

C1. Pamela Lynn, b 1961 Yakima, WA, ar 1982 Blake McCoach.

C2. Debra Lois, b 1962

A7. Orval Leon, b 1895 d 1907. A8. Rachel?

COHU, Peter, b G, mar Lansingburgh, NY, Judith __, from G?, b ca 1765? Judith poss living in NYCity 1840 with Elliot. (Susan George, Phoenix, AZ)

A1. Susan, b ca 1788 bp at the 'English Church', in G?, mar ca 1814 John LONEY sr., poss LAUNAY, DE LAUNEY of G? She mar 2. Wm. Mansbandle. One ch by Loney and 3 by Mansbandle.

B1. John Loney Jr., b 1815 NYCity, mar in Lansingburgh, NY, 1835 Sarah Ann Montgomery, dau of John and Eunice (Van Keuren? Van Buren?) Montgomery. John d 1845, 4 chn. Susan mar 2. 1852, Aaron B. Myers, bur 1890 NJ, 3 chn.

C1. Joseph Loney, b 1837 NY, d.y. C2. Charles Elliott Loney,1838-56.

C3. Susan Harriet Loney, b 1841 NYCity, mar William Ferris Hueston, Sr. son of James and Eliza (McDonald)Hueston, b 1837 NYCity, d 1933 Brooklyn, NY, bur Plainfield, NJ, 9 chn. Susan d 1902 in Brooklyn, bur Evergreen Cem., Brooklyn.

D1. Sarah Myer Hueston, b 1866 NY, d 1954, mar 1901 William Henry Rogers. See ROUGET/ROGERS.

E1. William Henry Rogers Jr, b 1903 d NJ unmar.

E2. Eunice Van Buren Rogers, b 1904 d 1906

E3. Lois Kathryn Rogers, b 1906 NJ, mar 1930 Robert Garfield Palmatier, 3 chn.

F1. Robert Henry Palmatier, b 1939 Pine Plains, NY, unmar

F2. Andrea Lois Palmatier, b 1940 mar 1960 Harold Wilson, 2 chn. Mar 2. ___Cervasio, 2 chn: Peter W. and Frances L., b 1961/2.

F3. William Palmatier, mar and div.

E4. Margaret Elsa Rogers, b 1908 mar 1931 Harry Charles Marsh.

F1. Anne V. Marsh, b 1936 TX, mar 1962 John G. Heonig, 2 chn: Anne E. b 1963 and John G b 1966.

F2. Sarah Rogers Marsh, b 1940 mar 1965 Donald I. Dussing, Jr. 3 chn: Elizabeth M., Sarah Anne and James A. Dussing.

D2. Eliza Irene (Lida) Hueston, b 1868, NY d 1955, unmar

D3. Thomas Heuston, b 1869 NY, d.y.

D4. Susan Loney Hueston, b 1871 d 1958 unmar

D5. William Ferris Hueston Jr, b 1872 d 1924 unmar

D6. Margaret Louise Hueston, b 1874 d 1955 unmar

D7. Frank Montgomery Hueston, b 1876 d 1941 Mar 1915 in Phoenix, AZ, Cuba Sanders, b 1886 New Castle, IND, dau of Wm. A. and Jenette (Good) Sanders. Frank d Scotch Plains, NJ 1941, and Cuba in Ariz. 1977.

E1. Susan Jeannette Heuston, b 1916 Phoenix,AZ, mar 1937 Wm. S. George, b 1913 Bkln, son of C.R. and Fanny V. (Burgess)George.

F1. Susan Eliz. George, b 1939 Brooklyn, NY mar 1959 Robert Ernest Drescher, 3 chn: Donna S., Linda L. and Paul K.

F2. Margaret Jeannette George, b 1941 Bkln, NY, unmar
E2. William Ferris Hueston, III, b 1920 Phoenix, AZ mar 1949 Elsie Mae Sanders, b 1922 Curtis, ALA, dau of John F. and Mary L. (Kennedy) Sanders, 3 chn.
F1. Marian Elaine Hueston, b 1951 Birmingham, ALA, mar 1975 Kent EdwardJohnson, a dau Emily Erin Johnson.
F2. William Frank Hueston, b 1954 Brownsville, TX mar 1981 Maria Hurt, a son Anthony Hueston.
F3. Robert Allan Hueston, b 1956 Phoenix, AZ
D8. Howard Russell Hueston, b 1879 NY, d 1962 unmar
D9. Charles Elliott?, b 1882 NY, d 1946, mar Ione West, no issue
C4. Julia Hester LONEY, b 1845 mar 1867 John Mackey, d 1919, 7 chn.
D1. Charles Mackey, b 1868 d 1949 mar ca 1888 Lillie Pfleuger
E1. Paul Fleuger Mackey, mar Blanche ___
D2. Sarah E., b 1870, d 1941, unmar
D3. Edwin Mayer Mackey, b 1873 d 1919, mar Margaret Hale MacLean, 1872-1947.
E1. Edwin B. Mackey, b 1902 d 1975, mar 1. Mary Jensen, 1903-1931 and 2. Betty ___, 1 ch.
F1. Edwin Albert Mackey, b 192- F2. Beatrice Mackey, b 1925
F3, by 2nd wife, Gregory Mackey, b 1942
E2. Vaughn Mackey, b 1910 mar Rita Kathryn Rae, b 1914, 4 chn.
F1. Patricia Rae Mackey, b 1940 mar Robert T. Taylor
F2. Wade Clark Mackey b 1945 mar 1969 Bonnie Watson
F3. Martha Boyd Mackey, b 1949 mar Charles de Montpellier
F4. Vaughn Jr. Mackey, b 1951
D4. Ellen Josephine, b 1877 d 1943 mar 1906 Charles Homer Wilson, 1878-1939.
E1. Helen Mackey Wilson, b 1911 mar 1939 Willard G. Dobler
E2. Charles Homer Wilson Jr, b 1913 d 1982, mar 1947 Louise Lubkert had dau, and mar 2. 1964 Lois Cron.
D5. Julia Mackey, b 1879 d 1939 unmar D6. Anna L. Mackey1881-1939
D7. Sidney A. Mackey, b 1888 d 1961, mar 1924 Grace Smith
C5. Margaret Myers, b 1853, by 2nd husband, not a C.I. desc. d 1911. Mar 1877 John R. MARSH. 4 chn: Josephine, Mary, Edith and Lilian
C6. Josephine Myers, mar John Johnson, poss 3 chn?
C7. John Myers, d.y.
B2. by 2nd husband, Harriet Mansbandle, b ca 1820, mar Daniel LUCAS, qv, 1 ch?
B3. William Mansbandle, b ca 1822, unmar?
B4. Mary Mansbandle, mar Gideon RICKARD, qv.
C1. Nelson, adopted?
C2. Henry RICKARD, b?, d 1970, mar Anna ___2 chn: Nelson & Margaret.
A2. Elliot, b ca 1803
A3. John, b ca 1805? mar ___
B1. Mary E., b ca 1835/40 mar Benjamin Moore.
C1. Emily Moore mar Virgil P. CORBET, a son Wm. Corbet
B2. Julia, mar Abraham Meyers, daus Fannie and Tillie Meyers
A4. William, b ca 1807? mar Eliza ___, b ca 1810-20, 5 chn
B1. Sarah, b ca 1830 mar --Clitz B4. Hannah, b ca 1837 mar J.Waglom?
B2. Eliza b ca 1832? mar ___White B5. Silas, d out West.
B3. Mary, b ca 1835 mar Dr. Monnell
A5. Betsy, mar Samuel Large. Dau Mary Large and dau Josephine Large, who mar Dr. Cadmus, a dau Bessie Cadmus, d.y.
A6. Judith, mar James ROUGET, qv, 5 chn
B1. Peter ROUGET B2. James ROUGET

B3. Nicholas ROUGET, changed name to ROGERS from ROUGET, mar Jane Parker.
C1. James Rogers mar Fanny Brown C3. Daniel Rogers
C2. Henry Rogers C4. May Rogers mar James Deering
B4. Thomas ROUGET mar ___, 4 chn: Thomas, John, Jane and Mary Ann
B5. Kate ROUGET mar John Poole
A7. dau, mar ___Husson, a son James Husson
COHU, John, b ca 1805, wife a little younger, had a small girl under 5, a man in his twenties, woman in her 40s, plus a black servant in the 12th Ward, NYCity in 1840 census.
COHU, Moses, b ca 1790-1800, wife, boy and girl under 10., lived in12 the Ward, NYCity, 1840 census.
COHU, Paul from C.I.? in Salem, MA 1762 had at least 2 daus.
A1. Elizabeth, bp 1762 A2. Susanna, bp 1771
COHU, Peter, B G, mar ___, res NYCity 1812 and 1817. (Ency. of Amer. Quaker Gen.)
A1. Henry, b 1821 d 1883
A2. Joseph S., b ca 1820, d 1887 age 67, mar Eliz. J. WILLIAMS, who d 1882 age 62.
B1. Aaron B., b 1842/3 d 1904 age 61, mar 1866 Eugenie Lecordier TOUSSAINT, from G? who d 1889 age 42. A son William d 1885, 11.
B2. Anna S., b 1846 d 1926 White Plains, NY
B3. Henry M., b ca 1850 mar 1891 Annabell Turck, living 1908
C1. La Motte b 1895 C2. Henry Wallace, b 1897
B4. Elizabeth, b 1853 d 1861
B5. Lydia L., b 1856 mar 1886 Robert W. Hull. B6. William, d.y.
COHU, William, wooden ware storekeeper, from GB, recommended by James ROUGET, qv, mariner, and Wm. Ketcham, Attny, 1831. (EARLY NY NATURALIZATIONS, by Scottand Conway)
COHU, William, recorded 1821-1834 (Quaker Ency) Res NYCity, 14th Ward, in 1840 census.
A1. Rachel, b 1830s Long Island, NY, mar Lowerre, poss Lowry?
A2. William,, A3. Harriet, and Julia, d.y.
COIGNARD, COIGNERT, etc, see QUINER and COONIER.
COLDRICK, noted in Q.A. IN CANADA in conn. with C.I. fam, and also in connection with LE MUNYON fam in PA. OUTC.
COLE, curr G and J. A John COLE said to have come from G 1800s and settled in Racine, WI, where other G fams settled. See also CAUL, pronounced COLE.
COLLAS in J from 1528 at least, in G 1331. Curr in Vale Parish G. Research? see CIFHS #7.
COLLAS, curr in Pacific Palisades, CAL and in Boston, MA. OUTC.
COLLAS, Harry from J to Montreal and BC early 1900s. (Joan Stevens,J)
COLLENETTE in St. Andrews G 1816. Several thought to be in US and Can.
COLLEY, several noted in Colonies, some poss from C.I. COLET, COLLET, curr G and J, in J 1461-1600s. Pron. COLLEY. Poss Hug?
COLLIE, William, photographer in J 1840s. (PHOTODISCOVERY, by Bruce Bernard, 1980)
COLLEY, Benj. of J? mar 1756 Hannah LE CRAW, qv, in MRB.
COLLEY, CALLEY, COLE?, Thomas mar 1748 Anne HOOPER, b 1722, dau of Greenfield HOOPER, son of Robert H. and of Alice Tucker.(HOOPER GEN)
COLLETT in MD 1600s, poss from J? (Skordas)
COLLIER, COLLYER, prob Hug surname. John, a baker, went first to Boston from either the C.I., Grt. Brit. or from France, later rem to MRB before 1705. Not an old C.I. surname, but poss came to America on a Jersey vessel, and was closely assoc. with the Jersey and Hug. fams of early New England. He d before 1751/2. He mar 1705 at MRB

Elizabeth WITCHALL, poss VINCHELEZ/Winchell of C.I. or southern England. The French form of the surname lingered from 1300s to1600s in J as de Vinchelez. Joseph ROUNDY was Collier's attny. Philip HOOKER, poss LE HUQUET?, was one of his associates. Elizabeth BESSOM, BISSON and Margaret BESSOM were mentioned in his will, as was John PUNCHARD, a Jerseyman of Salem. The Putnams in his will were also closely assoc. with Channel Islanders. This information from small file collected by Lizzie Heyward of Glendale, CAL ca 1930. (WRCIC) Also see MRB VR, Salem VR, Perley vols., COLLIER GEN, and JOURNALS OF ASHLEY BOWEN, at NEHGS.

COLLIER, Elizabeth b 1709 dau of John COLLIER the immigrant mar 1727 Joseph SINGCROSS, STE. CROIX, of J? See SINGCROSS. Eliz, 2nd of 8.

COLLIER, Sarah, mar 1743 John MAIN, LE MAIN?, poss of J fam? Sarah was the sister of Elizabeth above.

COLLINS, prob from England to G early. Curr G and J.

COLLINGS, large fam of G, still current there. OUR KIN, by De Guerin, states that the first one of this fam to change the surname from Collins to Collings was Edward, b 1712, res G, son of Thomas of St. Brelade J, a surgeon, and wife Jane JORET. See JOREY. This fam had 4 sons and 3 daus. COLLINGS appeared in Boston 1693, however, when Daniel COLLINGS mar Rebecca CLEMENS. OUTC. Nehemiah COLLINGS was a privateer captain of Jersey in 1649.

COLLINS, COLLINGS identified with the whaling fleets from Truro, Cape Cod, etc, which sailed to the Falkland Is. on whaling voyages in the 1700s. Prob most were from England and Ireland, but poss some from G? The surname COLLING was in Cornwall England 1620. (Mrs. Glen Hackman, Indianapolis, IND; Wm. M. Murphy, Denver, COL; Patricia Johnston, Portland, OR; Francis Collings, Chevy Chase, MD; COLLINGS, RICHEYS and VARIOUS ACCOUNTS OF THE PIGEON ROOST MASSACRE from Mrs. Kenneth R. Scott, 917 Ramblin Rd., Greenwood, IND)

COLLINGS, Dr. Felix Benj., b 1808 Spencer Co., KY may have been from a C.I. fam. He mar in Spencer Co., 1836 Adelia E.R. LE PAGE, qv, also from a G fam. 7 chn. (Wm. Murphy, Denver, COL; Mrs. Glen Hackman,IND)

A1. John Eberley, b 1836 d 1839
A2. Caroline Sarah, b 1838
A3. George Felix, b 1839
A4. Clara Emma, b 1840 d 1843
A5. Adelia Elminia, b ca 1840?
A6. Mary Eliz., b 1844 mar Capt. Steven Franklin Crabb, b 1842 Henry Co., KY, 10 chn. He d 1917, bur Taylorsville, KY. She d 1911.
B1. Adelia Mary Crabb, b 1865 d 1957 age 92, mar 1891 James William Pittenger, qv.
B2. Myrtle Harper Crabb, b 1867 d unmar 1955
B3. William Samuel Crabb, b1869, mar Amy Rogers, d 1938
B4. Carrie/Caroline Thorne Crabb, b 1870, mar 1894 Charles Francis Pittenger, qv, and d 1950.
B5. Sarah/Sally Lela Crabb, b 1872 Elk Creek, Spencer, KY mar 1896 1. Leonard Rozel Pittenger, and 2. 1921 Robert J. Paden, and 3. Adams
B6. Collings Benj. Crabb, b 1874 d 1935, mar 1899 Ella Bland Jewell, b 1876 d 1950, dau of A.J. Jewell & Sarah F. Read.
C1. Jewell Mae Crabb, b 1900, mar 1919 Mortie Walker Hundley in Jeffersonville, IND.
C2. Wm. Benj. Crabb, b 1903 d 1938 mar 1. 1925 Vera Rice, and 2. Louise Simms.
C3. Collings Clifton Crabb, b 1912 mar 1936 Thelma Humphrey
B7. Charles Bethuel Crabb b 1876 d 1909 unmar B8. Alex. Crabb, d.y.
B9. Richard Moody Crabb, b 1880 d 1965 mar1918 Oma J. Polk.
B10. Lewis Lemuel Ellis Crabb, b 1882 mar Meda ___ of Canada?
B11. Edward LE PAGE Crabb, 1885-1959, mar Julia Stoker, res L'ville,KY

A7. Charles Algernon, b 1846

COLLINGS, Caroline, 1775-1852, res G, mar 1798 Daniel NAFTEL, b 1771, son of Thomas and Mary L'Etac NAFTEL. At least 5 chn, of whom Abraham Naftel, b 1814, mar Elizabeth Stonehouse and had 2 sons and a dau, all of whom settled in Canada. Caroline's son, John NAFTEL also settled in Canada with wife Caroline Slocomb. (OUR KIN by De Guerin) See also CARRE.

COLLINGS, Francis D'Auvergne, rem from G to Kingston, ONT 1953, then to Washington, DC, brother of Philip below.

COLLINGS, Philip D'Auvergne, rem from G to Vancouver, BC, Canada 1955.

COLLINGS, Wm. Frederick was Seigneur of Sark Island 1882. He mar Sophia Moffat, dau of George and Mary (Ridge) Moffat of Canada. Sophia was later Dame of Sark.

COLQUITT, work now being done on this fam by Charles Nicholson, Hampton, VA. Note that Colquitts also settled in Cornwall, England, and some in America may be from Cornwall. See OLD NORTHWEST, Vol II.

COLQUITT, John, b ca 1513 in St. Sampson, G, d 1579, at least 5 chn. There is an arms and crest.

COLQUITT, CALCOAT, CALKETT, COCKET, CORKET, etc, etc, at least 40 variants of this surname. One went to England from Normandy with William the Conqueror in 1066. One branch res Hull Parish, Yorkshire, England and others live Cornwall and Guernsey. (OF WHOM I CAME;FROM WHENCE I CAME, by Zelma Wells Price, Greenville, MISS) More info in book, available Virginia State Library, Richmond, VA.

COLQUITT, John, b ca 1611 St. Sampson G, d ca 1668 Isle of Wight Co., VA, mar ca 1633 in england. He was son of Henry Colquitt and Dorothy Willcocke. He and bros Henry, James, Robert and Samuel rem to Virginia. No info found on the brothers.

A1. Henry, b ca 1634 St. Sampson G A3. James, b 1638, d 1688 VA,mar.

A2. John b ca 1636 St. Sampson, G d ca 1693 VA, mar 1678 Lucretia ANTHONIE, qv, dau of John, b ca 1643 VA, d ca 1689. She may have been prev. mar to Nathaniel Powell of VA.

B1. John, b 1682 Isle of Wight Co.,VA d 1769 Cumberland Co., VA,bur there. Mar 1709 Essex Co., VA, Anne Hawes, b 1692 Halifax Co,VA, d 1761 Cumberland Co., VA.

C1. Anthony, b 1710 Essex Co., VA d 1774 mar 1752 King Wm. Co. Christian Terry, who d 1801.

D1. Permenas, b ca 1753 d 1812, mar Lucy Davenport, 7 chn: Christian Sally, Anthony, Henry, Davenport, Fanny & John

D2. Achilles, b ca 1755 mar 1795, her 2nd husband, Mary __Franklin, no issue by Achilles. Stepdau Eliz. mar Thomas COLQUITT.

D3. John Terry Colquitt, b 1757 d after 1813 in Hancock Co., Georgia mar 1786, her 2nd husband, Alice (Townes) Dickie. Poss others?

E1. Thomas, b 1787 Halifax Co., VA d 1865 Russell, ALA, mar 1808 Ogle. Co, GA Eliz. Franklin, 1793-1848, bur ALA. Thomas served with Andres Jackson in the Ala. Indian Wars.

E2. Achilles Booker, b 1804 GA d 1881, mar 1842 Meriewether Co,GA Margaret Harris Sewell, dau of James and Margaret.

D4. Henry, b 1759 VA d 1920 GA, mar 1796 Nancy Singleton Holt, dau of Simon and Sarah (Hines) Holt, b 1781 VA. Henry d in GA and Nancy mar 2. 1823 Andrew Tarver.

E1. Sarah/Sally, b 1797 VA d 1852 GA, mar 1. 1814 Edmund H. Randle son of James and Rosanna. She mar 2. ___Watts. Res near Atlanta, GA. Desc named Randle-Watts in Bradley, ARK.

E2. Walter Terry, b 1799 VA, d 1855 Macon, GA, bur Columbus, GA. Mar 1. Anna Nancy Hill Lane, dau of Jos. & Eliz. He mar 2. 1841, Alphia Fountleroy, who shortly died and 3. 1842

Harriet M. Ross, dau of Luke. Walter a Judge and Senator.
E3. John Henry Holt, b 1801 VA, mar 1823 Martha H. Eley, said to have desc in Louisiana. Refer to Chas. Nicholson, Hampton,VA for more on this branch.
D5. Walter Evans, b ca 1767 d 1810 VA, mar 1803 VA Catherine Wooding, dau of John, issue. Catherine mar 2. 1811 Henry Kent.
D6. Sarah/Sally, b ca 1769 VA, d in GA, mar 1792 Hartwell Carter.
C2. Henry, b VA, d.y. C3. Hezekiah C5. Lucretia
C4. Ann, b VA mar ____Scruggs, had John and Sarah Scruggs
C6. James, b 1720 Essex Co., VA d there 1774, mar 1748 Sarah Coghill 1723-1784.
D1. Sarah, mar before 1774 ___Gibson
D2. Ann, b VA mar ___Garnett
D3. William Samuel b before 1758 Essex Co., VA mar 1795 Pitts Co., VA Rachel Richards. Wm. called CORKITT & COTTERALL
D4. James Wales, b 1761 VA d 1841 Oglethorpe Co., GA, mar 1785 Margaret Temperance Susan Hampton dau of Thomas and Sarah,b 1768.
E1. dau, mar ___Wilson, poss res Hamilton Co., TN or nearby.
E2. James, b 1795 VA d 1835 GA, mar 1825 Mary Ann Wise, no issue
E3. Jonathan, b 1798 VA, d 1867 Upson Co., GA mar 1. 1823 Sarah Susan Banks, b 1803 VA, d 1848 GA, issue. Jonathan mar 2. in GA Mary/Polly Miranda Stephens, b 1815, d 1889, no issue. 6 sons by 1st wife served in Confed. Army, and 3 survived.
E4. Mary E5. Martha E6. Sarah
D5. John Hawes b ca 1763 Essex Co., VA d after 1830 Cumberland Co. mar 1795 VA Judith Hobson, who d after 1910 in VA. Order of these chn unknown.
E1. Catherine mar 1813 Cumberland Co, VA Nathaniel A. Crenshaw
E2. Louisa or Lucy, d 1829 unmar E3. John H. mar R. Davenport
E4. William L. E5. Joseph E6. Thomas E7. Caleb
E8. Mary/Polly, b VA mar 1827 Josiah Thompson
E9. Janet H., b VA E10. Judith H., b VA
D6. Phoebe? b Essex Co., VA.
C7. Hawes, more on him in records.
C8. Jonathan, b 1724/5, d 1801 mar 1749 Tabitha Ransome,1732-ca1800.
D1. Ransome, b VA mar 1785 Susannah Baker, a dau Christian
D2. Frederick, b VA d 1798, mar 1. 1786 Eliz. Bolt or BOTT, qv. Mar 2. 1788 Mary Stubblefield, dau of George and Keziah.
D3. Elizabeth mar 1781 Jesse Spradling
D4. Nancy, b VA mar 1788 Obadiah Bostick
D5. Sarah/Sally, mar 1795 John Baynes, a son Fred. Baynes
C9. John, b 1726/7, d 1800 Oglethorpe Co., GA, bur there. Mar 1753 Eliz. Hendrick, b 1732 King Wm. Co,VA, d 1809, prob dau of Wm.
D1. Mary Ann Hawes poss d in her teens, b 1755.
D2. Robert, b 1759 d 1834 GA, mar 1785 Susanna HUBBARD, 1764-1831
E1. Judith, b 1786 VA d 1921 GA, mar 1815 Wm. Andrews, issue. Wm. mar 2. Patsy Guthrey, 1st cousin of his 1st wife, Judith.
E2. John Anthony, b 1788 VA d 1848 GA, mar 1813 Sarah Watts Smith, 1798-1870. She mar 2. 1851, his 2nd wife, Benj.F.H. Lindsay.
E3. Henry, b 1794, d 1796.
E4. William Henrick, b 1797 d 1871 GA mar 1820 Zilpha Kidd, 1801-1851. All 8 of their sons served in Confed. Army.
E5. Cynthia Hubbard, b 1801 GA, d 1876, mar 1821 Sherwood Wise, son of Jos. and Margaret (Patton) Wise, 1796-1845.
E6. Henry Parker, b 1802 GA d there 1847, mar 1824 Mildred Pinson.
E7. Joseph E. b 1806 GA, mar 1834 Ava Annie Lee, cousin of Gen.Lee
D3. Samuel, b 1762 VA d 1834 Franklin Co., TN, mar 1788 Martha

Mollie Woodruff, 1766-1835 TN.
E1. John Hawes, b 1789 VA mar before 1820, res TN, issue
E2. Mary Ann, b 1791 VA.
E3. Nancy Elizabeth, b 1793 VA d 1835 Franklin Co., ALA, mar 1815 his first wife, John NORMAN, b 1789 NC, d 1862 ALA.
E4. Hannah Jane, b 1795 GA E5. Sarah Frances, b 1796
E6. Reuben Henry b 1798, d 1830 TN, mar, had issue.
E7. Martha Woodruff, b 1800 GA
E8. James Robert, b 1802 GA, mar before 1830 res TN and ALA.
E9. William Lewis, b 1804 E10. Samuel Green b 1806 GA
E11. Hendrick Bostick, b 1808 TN
E12. Catherine Lucretia/Lucy, b 1809 Franklin Co., TN mar Middleton Upshaw, issue. Res ALA and Oregon Co., MO 1880s.
D4. William, b 1767 VA, d GA, said to have been 'afflicted'.
D5. Hannah, b 1771 VA, d GA, poss mar Robert Smith of GA?
D6. Sarah, b 1773 VA d GA, mar 1793 Beverly Guthrey, b VA, d GA.
E1. Nancy Guthrey, b GA mar 1813 William COLLINS
E2. Elizabeth Guthrey, b GA mar 1816 Andrew Turner
E3. Martha Glenn Guthrey, mar 1822 Kimbrell Summer.
E4. Patsy Guthrey, b GA mar1822 GA, 2nd wife, Wm. 'Buck' Andrews, son of Garnett Andrews. She was first cousin of Judith Colquitt, her husband's first wife.
E5. Nehemiah Guthrey, b GA mar 1828 in GA Nancy B. Turner.
A3. James, b ca 1638 G, d ca 1688 VA, mar ca 1660.
COLQUITT, see book for more info.
COLOMBE in J from 1274. In St. Laurens J 1788. See LE SEELEUR.
COLOMBE, Charles arrived in Boston 1769 on ship MOLLY from J. His name in Whitmore is spelled COLCOMBE. COLOMBE means DOVE, and might be the origin of several of the many DOVES in early MA. (WHITMORE)
COLUMBE, Joseph R. mar Ruth MESSERVE in MA. OUTC.
A1. Raymond Columbe b 1939 mar Penelope Foster. A2. Romayne, b 1943
CULLUM, poss COLOMBE?, Daniel mar Abigail Waters, 1717 Boston. OUTC
CULLAM, John, poss COLOMBE? mar Lydia Young 1738 Boston. OUTC. 7 chn b 1739-1751: Lydia, Amy, Sarah, John, Joan, David and Ann.
CALLUM, poss COLOMBE?, Eliz. mar 1738 in MA John Webb, son of Perez. OUTC. (Perley III)
CONROY, Susan, b 1832 G, rem to US. (Essex GEN., May 1981)
COOK, Ann, from C.I. 1863, via ship ANTARCTIC, settled in UT. COOK is curr G and J. (SLC)
[COOPER, JBR, b 1798 Alderney, rem to CAL, ½bro.to T.O.Larkin, Consul.]
COONIER, see QUINER.
COOPER, Catherine, see TAYLOR. COOPER curr G and J.
CORBEL in J 1668 in St. Saviour parish, and in St. Lawrence J 1788. In J since 1274. Curr J.
CORBEL, Lucy res Cuya. Co., OH 1860 census. OUTC.
CORBEL, Nancy, b ca 1804 St. Laurens J. See Abraham ESNOUF.
CORBET, as CORBEY in J 1331. CORBET in J 1607, in St. Saviour and St. Brelade J 1749. In St. Saviour G 1716. CORBET in St. Heliers J 1668 CORBET curr G. CORBETT curr J. This name also of southern England.
CORBET, Abraham in New England 1674, poss from J? (Underhill) OUTC
CORBETT, Eliza, b 1838 G? d 1874 GCO. An Eliz. CORBET b 1836 mar Isaac Westley b 1831 GCO. OUTC. (Conner-Eynon)
CORBET, Elizabeth, 1804-1880 res GCO, bur Founder's Cem, Cambridge,OH.
CORBETT, Michael mar Hannah SEVERY, SYVRET?, 1791 MRB.(CLEMENS) OUTC.
CORBET, Peter from G to GCO ca 1820 there in 1840, had fam of 7 in1830. (Census; Sarchet; Wolfe; Conner-Eynon Cem.Books; GCO records)
CORBIT, CORBET:, Robert mar Susanna Fuller 1818 GCO. (Conner-Eynon)
CORBIN in J 1299. In St. Peters G 1642.

CORBIN, noted in GCO 1840, and a firm named Hutchison & Corbin (Wolfe)
CORBIN, Clement b 1626 England or C.I.? d 1696 New England. Was in America 1637 or between 1640-50. "Strong tradition in several branches suggest...were of French Huguenot origin." While Clement was a favored first name in C.I. it was also popular in southern England and Wales. See HIST. AND GEN. OF DESC OF CLEMENT CORBIN of Muddy River, MA, by Virginia Corbin Flowers, Littleton, COL, At least 8 chn. A grandau Eliz., dau of James, mar Samuel HUNTOON, qv.
CORBIN, John mar Abigail CABOT 1761 in CT. See CABOT. (Ct Marriages)
CORNE, CORNEY, surname of England. CORNU, LE CORNU, surname of C.I. LE CORNU in J 1309. CORNET, pron. CORNEY was in St. Martin, St. Clement and Trinity J 1668, and in St. Clement J 1749.
CORNE, John, Susannah and Thomas res Portsmouth, NH early 1700s, poss from J? See Noyes for more info. (NEHGS Vol 81)
CORNISH, at times a C.I. surname. Curr G and J.
CORNISH, Joshua res Boston 1790 with fam of 4. (Census) OUTC
CORSE, COURSER, poss DE COURCY of J or Franc? James CORSE in Deerfield early. (NEHGS Vol 42)
COURSER, Wm. of Maine. (HOOPER GEN)
COSTER in colonies. COSTARD old J surname. See NEHGS Vols 81,82,100
COTEREL, John mar Ann Remick, dau of Joshua of Kittery early. (Noyes) COTREL a J surname.
COTILLARD, curr research? See CIFHS #7.
COUES, Samuel Elliott, b 1842 Portsmouth, NH, d Baltimore, MD 1899. A formost ornithologist of his day, mar 1. Jane A. McKinney 1867 and 2. in 1887 Mary Emily Bates. He wrote several books, and was a leader in reducing species to varieties. Wrote lucidly with charming style, also worked on Central and South American and British ornnithology. (SCIENCE ENCY) "Coues, like Thoreau, is descended from a native of the Island of Jersey, who came to America before the Revolution" (SPEAKING FOR NATURE, by Paul Brooks) See COUS below.
COURT, said to have come from the Channel Islands to Somerset, England very early. Desc to America. Cf DE LA COURT, A'COURT, qv, and COURT Antoine, a Hug., 1696-1760, from Nimes, France.
COURTIER, see CIFHS #9, curr research?
COUS. Note this name under COWES in Noyes, p. 166. Joseph, Mary and Sarah res in Falmouth and Portsmouth, NH. See COUES above. This may be Coues' family. COUE in J, also LES COUEZ in 1381.
COUSIN in G 1700s. Several COUSIN fams to early America. OUTC.
COUTANCHE in J 1528. In St. John J 1667 and in St. Laurens J 1788.In St. John and St. Laurens J 1749. See files on this name in SLCity, UT. COUTANCHE shield: azure, two bars argent between 6 bezants.
COTONCE, prob COUTANCHE?, Clement and Jane Armstrong were mar 1730 in Boston, MA. OUTC. (NEHGS Vol 100)
COUNTER, Edward from J? in Salem, MA 1668. OUTC. See LE COUTEUR.Note that an Abraham COUTEUR, a Huguenot, res in Leicester, England, long time resident in 1600s.
COUTANCE, Elias mar Eliz. Crown 1717 Boston, MA.
COUTANCH, Jane from C.I. on ship CHIMBORAZO, to UT 1855. (SLC record)
CATTANCE, COUTANCE, John, son of Elias and Mary b 1754 Boston, MA.OUTC.
COUTANCHE, John, b 1805 Trinity J, may have rem to UT, or was ancestor of a UT fam. He mar Mary Eliz. ___, b 1811 St. Martin J. 7 chn. (SLC records; Mrs. A. Christofferson, Lehi, UT)
A1. John, b1831 Trinity J A2. Mary Ann b 1833 A3. Philip b 1839 J
A4. Jane, b 1841 A5. Charles b 1845 A6. George, b 1848.A7. Eliz,b1849
COUTANCHE, Capt. Joshua was in 1742 master of the WILLIAM OF JERSEY, and sailed from Cape Fair, NC with a cargo of tar and turpentine for

Dartmouth, England. In a bad storm the cargo was jettisoned, but the ship finally arrived in J. (Soc. Jers. Bull, Vol 11)

COTONCH, Malicah was in Beaufort Co., Newbern Dist. 1790 with fam of 2 boys and 3 females. (Census)

COUTANCHE, Michael, settled in BAthtown, Beaufort Co., NC, d there 1762, left a small estate in St. John, J. (J.P. Landers, Wash., TX)

COX, see Noyes book. Poss that one or more of these early COX fams poss were CAUX, LE CAUX from J, there 1668, 1749. Cf also LE COCQ.

COW, COWE, consider CAUX, DE CAUX, COUS and COHU as orig. spellings.

COW, COWE, Peter of St. Peter J mar Mary Long in Portsmouth, NH 1735. LE CAUX surname in St. Peter J 1749. Several others in fam in NH? Some DE CAUX in America were Hug. (Smiles) COX curr G and J. See NEHGS Vol 81.

COWE, Esther, rec'd into Ch.1720, Portsmouth, NH

COWE, John, had son Thomas bp 1746 Portsmouth, NH

COWLEY, Richard B., b Gloucester, England, rem from G, a storekeeper, to NY in 1819. (NY NATURALIZATIONS by Scott & Conway.)

CRAFFORD, see CRAWFORD.

CRAPO. Pierre seems to have been the first of this name in New England and may have been shipwrecked on the coast. (CERTAIN COMEOVERERS, by Henry Howland Crapo) Cf CRAPAUD, pron. CRAPO, is a common slang word for a Jerseyman, used long ago by Channel Islanders. Some research done on this fam by Harold Everitt, Saugus, MA.

CRAWFORD, CRAFFORD, SArah, b J? wife of Thomas POINDEXTER, qv, b 1666 d Louisa Co., VA 1752. OUTC.

CRAWFORD, CRAFFORD, Stephen from J? in ME 1642, partner of Wm. SEVEY, poss SYVRET? in a fishery firm. Mar Margaret and d before 1647. (Noyes) OUTC. A dau Sarah survived?

CREDEFORD, noted in colonies. CREDIFORD, RAchel, mar 1733 James BUSSY, qv, in NH. She was his cousin. OUTC. (Noyes)

CREFORD, Mordecai of Salem, MA bought 1/4 of the barque MARY from John BROWN, LE BRUN of J in 1661.(Perley)

CROSS, LA CROSS, LE CROIX, LA CROIX, etc, etc. Very difficult to distinguish at times between LE CROSS, LE CROIX AND LE CRAW/LE CRAS. See also DE STE. CROIX, a Hug surname.

CROIX, LA CROIX, DE LA CROIX in J 1508. CROSS curr G and J. Note that one CROSS in early MA came from Ipswich, England to New England. (Noyes) The CANNELL-CROSS fam came from the Isle of Man. See info in Boston TRANSCRIPT, 1908, on CROSS fams.

Five CROSS men said to have come to Vassalboro, ME ca 1778, from C.I.?

William, poss mar before arrival? James, noted as living alone in 1790 census. Moses Jr. who mar 1778 Mary GRAY of Clinton, ME. CABOT who mar 1784 Judith HOOPER. Benjamin, mar 1785 Sarah Lampson. Sons of the above men are thought to have been named Caleb, Jonathan, Zebedee, Simeon, Simon, John and David. Note that these all show up in Cross fams of Methuen, MA. See data of Plaistow and Atkinson, NH. (Carolyn Nelson, Vassalboro, ME)

LE CROIX, CROSS, Dr. Abraham, from J or G? mar 1700 in MRB Martha Beal, b 1667, d 1750, widow of Capt. John Beal. She mar 3. John Waldron 1729. 2 chn. OUTC.

A1. Ann, b 1702 mar 1721 Thomas Dyer in MRB. A2. Martha, b 1704.

CAUTION: TRIAL CHARTS.

CROSS, Ephraim of Salem, mar 1767 in MRB. Eliz. ANDREWS, b1749, dau of John Andrews and Mary SAVORY. Cf ANDROS of G and SYVRET of C.I. A son Wm. b 1768. OUTC.

LE CROSS, John, poss LA CROIX? of C.I.? mar Sarah ___, res MRB. OUTC This may be a Hug. fam, poss from France by way of C.I.?

A1. Isaac, b 1741
A2. David, b 1743, mar Mary Dulap 1764
B1. Ann, b 1764 B3. Sarah, d.y. B4. Isaac b 1769
B2. Mary, b 1766 mar John NORTHEY, qv, 1784
B5. Sarah, b 1772 B6. Margaret, b 1774

CROSS, John, mar 1762 in MRB Mary Dodd, 11 chn, small chart in WRCIC.

CROSS, Michael, bur 1728, Michael mar 1762 Elizabeth Gilbert, and Philip, all three of MRB, small charts in WRCIC, OUTC.

LE CROIX, Elush, prob Elisha?, served in Rev. War. (MASS SOLDIERS AND SAILORS) OUTC.

LE CRAS, LE CROSS, Hannah mar Robert Black 1740 Boston. OUTC.

CROSS, John II, mar Hannah MARTIN 1833 MRB. NOte MARTINS in LE CRAS family. OUTC.

A1. George CROSS or LE CRAS?, b 1842 A2. Mary, bp 1844.

CROSS, Thomas D. mar Rachel PAINE, qv, 1793 MRB. OUTC

LE CROIX?, Wm. mar Lydia Ireson 1819 MRB. Note ROSS in LE CRAW fams. This may be a LE CRAS fam of J.

A1. William, b 1821 A2. David ROSS, b 1824.

CROSS, Wm., mar Mary FAVOL, poss FAUVEL of J?, 1706 near Methuen, MA.

CROSS, William, mar 1716 Portsmouth, NH Abigail BRIARD, qv. (Noyes)

CROSS, See STARR GEN for CROY, which may be CROIX, also records of Plymouth, VT, Plattsburg NY and book, JOHN FRANCIS CROSS, by Lilian Cross, Oakland, CAL 1933. Also see data of Evelyn Cross, Nobleboro, Maine.

CUNNINGHAM, from C.I. to Canada? (L.F. Guy, Orono, ONT, Canada)

CURNOW, CURNEW, CURNOE, CURNEY, etc. Consider that these may be forms of two C.I. surnames; LE CORNU andQUENAULT. CURNEW in Nfld. may be anglicizing of C.I. surname QUENAULT, qv. See also LE CURNAH. (Rev. Hammond, Bell Island, Nfld.)

CUTTER. 39 heads of housholds in MA 1790. (Census) Among these poss a few may have been LE COUTEUR of the C.I. See LE COUTEUR.

DAIN, see LE DAIN and DEAN.

DANIN, August and Nancy, from C.I. to UT via ship CHIMBORAZO 1855. SLC RECORDS)

DARBY in J 1700s, but primarily an English surname from several west. counties of England. A DARBY was in SC before 1680, also noted in Elizabethtown, NJ. (See NJ section) A Col. Darby was with Roger's Rangers. OUTC. (LOST IN CANADA, Aug. 1981; Underhill; UPPER CANADA GAZETTE microfilm, 1798-1807; Mrs. K.H. Darby, CAmden, TN; Smithsonian Bulletin, July 1979; Troxler; STARR GEN; Virkus V. 5; Baldwin; CT Marriages; etc.)

DARBY, James of J fam? mar Florence E. Sencabaugh, b 1881 PEI, Canada. (BECK GEN, Jim Beck, Okemos, MI)

DARBY, John mar Rebecca PUNCHARD, res Andover, MA 1700s. See PUNCHARD

DARBY, Joseph, b 1787 J settled in Halifax, NS 1863, where he d. Desc. (Terence Punch, Nova Scotia Hist. Soc., Halifax, NS)

DARBY, Joseph in South River, Ann ARundel Co., MD 1703 with wife Rebecca and 4 chn. OUTC.

DARBY, Wm and wife Elizabeth sold house to John Blanchard in Eliz. NJ 1701. OUTC. (E. Jersey Deeds, Liber C, p. 236)

DARLING, poss some in early New England were DALLAIN, of J, there in the 1400s through the 1700s. Much more data in New England. Note that DALLING was also in England 1409. DALLAIN in St. Law. J 1788.

D'AUVERGNE of France has interesting connections with Jersey Island. See BIOG. DICT. OF JERSEY by Balleine.

D'AUVERGNE, Philip, a j merchant, was importing tobacco from VA to J and to England ca 1671. (A. John Jean, Jersey)

DAUVERNE, Philip, mar 1670 in MA Mary RICART. (Stileman's Court Files)

DAVEE, could be either DAVEY or DAVIS, noted in Annals of Oxford, ME. DAVIS in J early.

DAVEY, John of ALD, bur Goodwood Cem., Uxbridge Twp, ONT 1893, age 72, mar Anna GAUVAIN of C.I. who d 1888, age 83, chn? (William Britnell, Mississauga, ONT) John above.

DAVEY, Charles H. son of James and Mary A. Davey, d 1875, bur with /

DAVEY, Maj. Christ. was one of a pair of balloonists who flew a helium balloon from Nfld. to Ireland ca 1978. DAVEY, 34, was from Jersey. His companion was Don Cameron, 39, of Bristol, England. DAVIS surname in J 1607.

DAVIS, DAVISSON?, David mar Susanna SMITH, poss LE FEUVRE? of J. Davis came from Wales to Casco Bay 1640. Susanna was b 1660 and they had a grant ca 1688 at Lubberland, ME 1694. David was killed by Indians 1696. Susanna mar 2. James Durgin. Poss more chn by Durgin? (HIST OF DURHAM, NH by E. Stackpole; Elaine Adjutant, Ossipee, NH; Noyes; DURGIN SCROLL; fam records)

A1. Abagail Davis, b ca 1687 about age 16 in 1703.

A2. David, b ca 1688 in 1756 sold 14 acres of his father's 40 acres. Res Packer's Falls, NH? mar Eliz. THOMAS, 5 chn.

A3. Elizabeth DAVIS or Durgin, b ca 1690, bp 1719.

A4. Francis Durgin, b ca 1700 mar Susan DURRELL, 9 chn

A5. William Durgin, mar Margaret Crommett, 5 chn.

A6. Jonathan, mar Judith Edgerly, 9 chn A7. James Jr. mar D. Edgerly.

A8. Truworthy, mar Mary DURRELL, 7 chn

A9. Susannah, mar James Goodwin of Newmarket, NH, 3 chn.

DAVIS, Dennis, b J, mar at Kinderhook, NY 1775 Geeje Moor, b Claverak, in Ireland? (MAR. RECORDS OF KINDERHOOK, at Coshocton, OH)

DAVIS, Elizabeth mar 1. Moses DAVIS and 2. John DEMERITT, qv, after death of Moses ca 1769 in Salisbury, MA. OUTC (OLD FAMS OF SALIS)

DEAN in J 1299-1700s. A DEAN-LEMPRIERE mar took place in Bath,England ca 1860. (NEHGS Vol 42)

DEAN, Capt. Carteret, traded with Maryland from J in 1737 on the ship THOMAS AND JANE, 60 tons. Was in River St. Mary, Potomack, MD 1740 for tobacco. (A. John Jean, Jersey)

DEAN, Thomas, res Salem, MA 1701, mar Elizabeth Drake BEADLE. She was Mrs. Dean 1729. OUTC. (SAMUEL BEADLE FAMILY)

DE BARTRAM, see BARTRAM and BERTRAM.

DE BEAUVOIR, old in C.I. See CIFHS #9

DEBENHAM, DE BENHAM? "one of a group of Guernsey folk who settled in CAL in the 1890s." (Philip Luce, Vancouver, BC)

DE BLOIS, Stephen, b France? to US in ship SEAHORSE, Capt. Philip DUMARESQ, 1720 in retinue of Gov. Wm. Burnet. A desc of De Blois mar a desc of Philip DUMARESQ ca 1836, Boston. (NEHGS Vol 67)

DE BOURCIER, of C.I. One said to have rem to Iowa. A Peter from J res Cape Breton, NS, Canada 1767.

DE BRODER, George Peter, b 1861 Vale, G, mar Philippa Louisa GAUDIN, qv, b 1860 J. This fam was orig. from Nantes, Frances to J.(Linda Romeril, RAcine, WI; Gladys De Broder, Denver, COL; Lena Orchard, St. Martin, G)

A1. Philippa Georgina, b 1885 J, d 1965 Madison, WI mar George Prince in Vale, G. d.y.

B1. Phyllis Maud Prince, b 1909 mar Clarence Knudsen, a dau Clarisse/

B2. Nellie Gaudin Prince, b 1916

A2. George Philip, b 1891 J mar in US Laura ___, who d COL 1972.

A3. Frederick John, b 1893 J mar 1. Ethel Budge, who d 1927 Chicago, leaving dau Jean. He mar 2. 1929 Gladys PERRIN, qv, b Vale, G. Widow Gladys res Denver, where F.J. d ca 1972.
B1. Jean, b 1927 mar Orville Hanneman
C1. Deborah Hanneman, mar __, 2 chn, Shannon and Ryan
C2. Gordon Hanneman, unmar, choir director, res Denver, COL
C3. Glendon George Hanneman, Capt. in Navy, mar __, sons John & Mark
C4. Gladys Hanneman, twin of Gloria, d.y.
C5. Gloria, mar Robert Whitfield, res Arvida, COL, 3 sons, Robert, Daniel and James Bryan Whitfield.
C6. Caryl Hanneman, mar Gilbert SALTER, res Arvida, COL, 2 sons, Kevin and Philip.
C7. Charles Hanneman, twin to Caryl, chiropractor, mar Jeanne CARROLL 2 CHN: Charles and Lynn.
A4. Elise Marie Louise b 1894 Vale G, to Toronto, ONT ca 1916, then to Racine, WIS to care for sister Philippa who later d. Elise mar Lawrence Moffatt. Res Racine & Milwaukee, 10 chn, of whom 1 d.y. Moffatt was of the Campbell clan.
B1. June Moffatt, b 1922 mar Edw. Wm. DAVIS 1939, 13 chn.
C1. Alfred Wm. Davis, b 1941, unmar
C2. Jack Russell Davis, b 1945 mar Mary Agnes Hurley, 4 chn: Jack, Tracy, Matthew and Melissa
C3. Lawrence Edw. Davis, b 1947 mar Jo Anne Breber, 3 chn: Brett, Laurie and Kelly.
C4. Richard Francis Davis, b 1948 d 1961
C5. Sharon Lorraine Davis, b 1949 mar 1968 Thomas A. Kennedy, 3 chn: Donna, Thomas and Jake Edward Kennedy.
C6. Cynthia Ann Davis, b 1951 mar Gilbert J. Beech, res Vancouver,BC
C7. Douglas Allen Davis, b 1952 mar Bobbie Breber, 3 chn: Theresa, Anthony and Patricia.
C8. William Ronald Davis, b 1953 mar Mary Dutkiewisc, son Jason.
C9. Marietta Ellen Davis, b 1954 mar Randall C. Maze, 3 chn: Tanya, Nadine, Michelle Maze.
C10. Betty Kay DAvis, b 1956 mar 1973 David P. Knutson, 2 chn: Julie and Paul Knutson.
C11. Nancy Jean Davis, b 1958 mar Dale A. Schneider, son Jesse Lee S.
C12. Cyril John Davis, b 1961, d.y. C13. Lisa Joy Davis b 1963.
B2. Lorraine Moffatt, b 1923 mar 1. Robert N. Callahan 1945, 2 chn, a and 2. Louis R. Stuff, 2 chn. Res Malta, MONT.
C1. Colleen Ruth Callahan, b 1946 C3. Lu Anne Stuff, b 1958
C2. Timothy N. Callahan, b 1950 C4. Ronald Stuff, b 1958,notTwins.
B3. Pearl Moffatt, b 1924 mar Howard R. Graves, 4 chn.
C1. Karleen Sue Graves, b 1944 mar Robert Bjorkland, 2 chn, Kirsten and Ian Bjorkland.
C2.Judith Marie Graves, b 1946 mar Gary O'Neal, 2 chn:Brent, and Bret O'Neal.
C3. Gene Howard Graves, b 1951 mar Beverly Siedner, dau Dawn Marie
C4. Peggy Ellen Graves, b 1960
B4. Virginia Moffatt, b 1925, d.y.
B5. Francis Moffatt, b 1927 d 1962, mar Marcella Opperman, 3 chn
C1. Sandra Jean Moffatt, b 1950 mar Paul Radmer, 2 chn: Michelle and Brian Radmer.
C2. Robert Moffatt, b 1954 mar Rosemary Connerton, son Francis R. Moffatt
C3. Darlene Dawn Moffatt, b 1960
B6. Douglas Moffatt, b 1929 mar 1950 Joyce Mulholland, 2 chn
C1. Roxanne Moffatt, b 1951, mar 1972 Leonard Daemrich.

C2. Laura Moffatt, b 1954 mar 1975 Richard Bartz
B7. Richard Moffatt, b 1921 mar 1. Delores Fleischman, 5 chn, and 2. Dee ___, 1 ch.
C1. John J. Moffatt, b 1953 mar 1976 Linda Deymar
C2. Denise Marie Moffatt, b 1954 mar 1973 Guy Davis, 2 daus: Alicia and Yvonne Davis
C3. Jane Renee Moffatt, b 1956 mar 1972 Gilberto Buenrostro, 2 daus: Gliberta and Mia Buenrostro.
C4. James N. Moffatt, b 1957 C5. Donna N. Moffatt, b 1962
C6. Derek Moffatt, b 1975
B8. May Moffatt, b 1934, d.y.
B9. Ronald Moffatt, b 1935, mar Alida Karpus, 6 chn: Mark, Lou Anne, Pamela, Karen, Gary and Paul Moffatt.
A5. Lillian Maud b 1895 G, mar Wm. Coghlan of G in Canada, res Racine, Chicago and Hialeah, FLA. Wm. d 1977.
B1. Robert Goghlan, res FLA
B2. Dorothy Coghlan mar ___Walsh, 2 chn, res Cordova, TN
B3. Colleen Coghland, mar ___Maxwell, res Miami, FLA, 2 daus: Kathleen Rainey and Patricia ___.
A6. May Gaudin, b 1900 Vale G, mar ___Steel, and now a widow in G.
A7. Linda Lucy, b 1901 Vale G, mar Edwin ROMERIL, qv, at St. James, G, rem to NY 1947 with 2 sons.
B1. Allan Brian ROMERIL, b 1932 Fort George, NY, forester at ParkFalls, Wisconsin.
B2. Robert Francis Philip ROMERIL, b 1936 St. Peter Port G, served with with US Army abroad. Mar Jackie Skull of Kent, England in Racine WIS 1958, 5 chn: Catherine, Mark, Bruce, Paul and Jennifer ROMERIL
A8. Lena Maude b 1907 Vale G, mar 1. Gerald Chalfont, div, a son Roy. Lena mar 2. Algernon Orchard in England, now a widow, res G.
B1. Roy Chalfont, b 1930 G, to US 1947, mar in Chicago Betty Merkle, res Rolling Meadows, ILL, 2 sons: Gary and David Chalfont.

DE CAEN in J since at least 1528. Others of this name may have come from France in the 1800s. In St. Laurens J 1607, and in St. Ouen J 1749. (Roland de Caen, Calgary, ALTA)

DE CAEN, see Q.A. IN CANADA. Curr research? See CIFHS #6. Curr in Beverly Hills and Los Angeles, CAL. OUTC.

DE CAEN,Lady Ann from J mar Thomas Nelson Palmer, res Galway, IRE, and rem to Nfld. Ann was dau of Jean and Esther (BALLEINE) DE CAEN, mar Thomas ca 1845 St. Saviour J. Note: Some desc use PALMER and some use Nelson-Palmer. Thomas was a merchant, and had the T.N.P. Flour Mills on Nun's Island, Galway, Ireland. He may have been a desc of Lord Horation Nelson and Lady Emma Hamilton, whose maiden name was Lyon, poss related to the Dowager Queen of England, Elizabeth Bowes-Lyon. (Lorraine Aleong, Montreal, QUE)
A1. Harry Nelson-Palmer, b Ireland mar ___, d ca 1973. Wife was poss Maisie ___, a widow.
B1. Valda Nelson-Palmer, b Galway, IRE.
B2. Anna Palmer B3. Pat Palmer.
A2. Frank Thomas Nelson-Palmer, b 1886 Galway or Dublin, IRE, d 1927 Topeka, KS. To Canada 1923, to BC, then to Eastport, ID 1925. A citizen 1940, mar 1923 Winnipeg, MAN, Canada, Eveline Wade, b 1890 Darlington, Durham, England. She d 1964 Topeka, KS.
B1. Peter Robert, b 1924 Winnipeg, MAN, mar 1946 Janice Rutherford, b 1925 Lawrence, KS.
C1. Michael Ken. Nelson-Palmer, b 1949 Topeka, KS mar Cynthia Mitchell 1979 in Augusta, GA.
C2. Sharon Royce Nelson-Palmer, b 1950 KS mar 1975 Stephen C.Keating.

C3. Kim Nelson-Palmer, b 1958 Topeka, KS DE CAMP FAMILY, se
B2. a dau, d in childbirth C.I. COLLECTION.
B3. Frank Terrance Nelson-Palmer, b 1930 mar 1953Betty Jean PERRIN, qv in Topeka, KS
C1. Steven Nelson-Palmer, b 1957 St.LOuis, MO.
C2. Patricia Ann Nelson-Palmer, b 1960 C3. Scott Nelson-Palmer,1962
A3. John Charles Nelson-Palmer, b 1888 Galway, Ireland, d 1966 Vancouver, BC, mar Nora Marjorie Christie 1910 Dublin, IRE.
B1. Frank Geoffrey Nelson-Palmer, b 1911 mar 1944 Madeline Rose Duncombe, b 1920.
C1. Stanley Wilson Palmer, b 1947 mar Beverley Joan Wash, b 1948. 3 sons: Kyle, Brock and Creig Palmer, b 1970s.
C2. Geoffrey Charles Palmer, b 1950
B2. Charles Henry Nelson-Palmer, b 1912 Winnipeg, MAN mar Annie M. Howe, b 1913, 3 chn.
C1. Ralph K. Nelson-Palmer, b 1940 Winnipeg, mar Annette Crowder, sons Sean and Trevor.
C2. Terrance C. Palmer, b 1948 mar Darlene Ward, sons Michael and Todd Royan Palmer.
C3. Wayne Kevin Nelson-Palmer, b 1955 Fort Churchill, MAN, Canada.
B3. Ronald George N. Palmer, b 1915 Winnipeg, mar 1938 Donna G. Smith.
C1. Paul R.B. Palmer, b 1939 mar Carol Fidler, b 1942, 4 chn: Karen, Keith, Bryan and Janice Palmer, b 1960s, 1970s.
C2. David William Palmer, b 1942 mar Elaine Lewis, 3 chn: Kelly, Lisa and David Palmer.
C3. Lorraine G. Palmer, b 1947 mar Conrad Aleong, b 1946, Port of Spain, Trinidad. 2 chn: Brigette C. and Andrea L. Aleong.
B4. Blanche Valerie Palmer, b 1922 mar 1952 Wm. M. Bowie, b 1916
C1. Brenda Joy Bowie, b 1953 mar 1972 Wayne A. Foster, 3 chn: Shannon, Shawn and Marcy, b 1970s.
C2. David Blaine C. Bowie, b 1955 C3. Michael Wm. Bowie, b 1962
B5. Ralph B. Nelson-Palmer, b 1916, d WWII, mar Iva Nelson.
C1. John Barry Nelson-Palmer, b 1942 mar Ellen Christine ___, b 1945 3 chn: Colleen, Ryan and Robyn Nelson-Palmer.

CAEN, poss DE CAEN?, John mar Jane ENGLISH qv, 1726 MRB. ENGLISH poss LANGLOIS. See ENGLISH.

DE CAEN, Frank, b 1897 J to Canada ca 1914, worked for Robin, Jones & Whitman Co., in Gaspe, QUE, mar Dalila Poirier from Magpie, QUE, 3 chn. Dalila was 74 in 1982. Frank's sister Rose remained in J. (Irene De Caen, Montreal, QUE)
A1. Elsie, b 1928 mar Wm. Poirier, son Gordon Poirier mar, has daughter Melanie. A2. Irene, b 1930
A3. Gordon, b 1932 mar Micheline ROUSSEL from Mont-Louis, QUE, owns Lafayette Hotel at St. Flavie, QUE, 2 chn: Richard and Shirley.

DE COENE, Fred, a shoe mfr. res Salem, was in Masonic Lodge there 1848. Poss a misreading for DE CAEN? Another Fred. res QUE, 1800s.

DE CARTERET, see CARTERET.

DE CAUX, DE COX, COX, etc. from Payes du Caux, France. "Our ancestors, Huguenots, fled from France at the time of the French Revolution. We know there were ancestors that went to Jersey, and our relatives are in England." (Gregory Lynn De Caux. See also COW, COWE.

DE COSTER, DA COSTA, ___"was prob a native of the Channel Islands, and in his early years...stationed at Annapolis Royal, NS, 1738"..."Da Costa was in Boston, MA for the preparations for the second reduction of Louisbourg in 1758, and later was in Halifax." (Can. Masonic Research Assoc., Halifax, in letters to Richard E. Spurr of Arlington, VA, 1965) In spite of this info. there appears to be only the mention of the De Costa, De Coster fams being Huguenots in New England. At least one was in Plymouth, MA 1623. See more data in HIST OF BUCKFIELD, ME: Congressional Library; ANNALS OF OXFORD, ME; Beverly Newton, Pittsfield, ME; BICKNELL GEN; etc. Poss no direct Jersey link.

DE COSTER, John mar Sarah PAIN, qv, 1757 Boston. OUTC.

DE COURSEY curr Los Angeles, CAL, from C.I.?

DE GARIS in Vale G 1821. See CIFHS #4,14,15. In St. Peter G 1663, name curr in G.

DE GARIS, Thomas and George, from G to Racine, WI ca 1860?

DE GARIS, DE GARIE, Charles, b 1819 G, a mason, mar Annie BURDIN, BAUDIN?, 1856, res Mt. Pleasant, WI, 5 chn. (Leach; RACINE HIST)

DE GAREY, __ of a C.I. fam res FLA 1980s.

DE GREAVES, John, b 1833 J, mate on schooner GENERAL WOLFORD, chartered for a cruise in the South Seas by Lola MONTEZ, entertainer. John was a Board of Health employee in Honolulu 1878. D Molokai 1910. (Cf MONTEZ in ROMERIL fam.) John was at one time a Hawaiian Gov't immigration agent cruising on the brig POMARE on a labor-recruiting expedition to the New Hebrides and other Pacific Islands, 1881. (JOHN CAMERON's ODYSSEY, New York, 1928, pp 163,206; Haw. ARchives)

GRUCHY, DE GRUCHY in J 1089, from a hamlet in the Cotentin Peninsula, Normandy, France. DE GRUCHY, GRUCHY in Trinity, J, St. Clement, St. Martin, St. Saviour, Grouville, St. John, St. Ouen and St. Laurens, J, 1668, and in Trinity, St. Laurens, Grouville, St. John and St. Ouen J 1749.

"Family settled in Jersey for over 800 years, prob from village and Seigneurie of GROUCY near Caen, Normandy, France and desc. probably from Hugo DE GRUCHY, a farmer of J in 1080 under the Duke of Normandy. Ralph, the probably ancestor of many DE GRUCHY families was born ca 1440, d sometime before 1524, res Trinity or St. John Jersey, having land in both parishes. Much research done on past generations of this family."..." Two first cousins DE GRUCHY in 1580-1650 produced 12 sons, most of whom left a numerous descent...by 1848 there were some 40 farming families of J called GRUCHY and DE GRUCHY, many in Trinity Parish." (Guy Dixon, Pickering, Yorks,England) (John De Gruchy, Fresno, CAL)

GROUCHY, Marshall was a Frenchman who fled from France for political reasons, and settled for a short time in G, where he took the name M. Gautier. His full name was Emmanuel de Grouchy, 2nd Marquis de Gruchy, Marshall of France 1815. He later in 1821 returned to France, and left issue there. "In regard to De Gruchy of Jersey, they belong to the same family, therefore we ought to have the same coat of arms." (Gen. Victor De Grouchy to the Count of Malortie) "I have heard my father say the two branches of our family were forced to emigrate after the conquest of Normandy by Philippe Auguste. (1202-1214) One took refuge in Jersey and became a tradesman. The other went to England and again were forced to emigrate, coming to America at the time of the Cromwell Protectorate (ca1650)"

GRUCHY, see GRUSH, and records in WRCIC. Check sources.

DE GRUCHY, David, b 1822 St. John J, rem to Arichat, NS, Canada, 1836, mar Jane Catherine Robertson JEAN, qv. 5 chn. See Q.A. IN CANADA for JEAN fam. (Allan G. Gruchy, College Park, MD)

A1. John P., b 1849 D'Escousse, Cape Breton, NS, rem later to Vancouver, BC, mar Henrietta Helen Weeks of Sidney Mines, NS.

B1. Lewis B2. Frederick

B3. David, b 1876, Petit de Grat, Cape Breton, settled Vancouver, BC, mar Sadie Ann SAMPSON, qv. of Cape Breton, 4 chn.

C1. Seymour C2. John C3. Robert
C4. Allan Garfield, b 1906 Vancouver, mar Florence K. Schumacher of Batesville, IND 1937, rem to College Park, MD.
D1. Allan Garfield, b 1942 D2. Katherine Anne
B4. Roy B5. Jenny B6. Mary
A2. Philip
A3. Henrietta, mar Dr. H.C. FIXOTT of Arichat, NS, Canada. See Q.A. IN CANADA, by Turk, and a few records in WRCIC.
A4. Peter, b ca 1839 mar Sophia McClean.
B1. Elizabeth, mar ___FIOTT, rem to US, a son Eric Fiott.
B2. Aubrey, b ca 1868 B3. William, b ca 1869
A5. David Jr., mar Eva ___
B1. Irene Mildred, 1890-1968, res with aunt Mrs. FIXOTT, mar Geo.Rice of Liverpool, NS.
C1. Howard Rice, res Liverpool, NS C2. Wm. Rice, res Saint John,NB.
C3. Helen Rice, mar Edward MacKinnon, res Brooklyn, New York.

DE GRUCHY, Elias, b 1831 Trinity, J son of Elias and Susan (PICOT) DE GRUCHY, mar 1. 1850 Ann Hepburn, a ch b Trinity, J. He then rem to NYcity 1852. His two bros are said to have come at the same time, John and Thomas. Thomas settled in PA? Elias was a carpenter, and served in the NYState National Guard 1863-1890, as Sgt. Elias mar 2.? Rachel Jane Anley, ca 1856/1861? Two chn by 1st wife.
A1. Ann, b 1851 Trinity J.
A2. Edwin P.J., b 1855 NYork, carpenter, mar by 1880 Hannah ___, 2 chn
B1. Elias, d.y. B2. Edwin, res Suffern, NY.
A3. Susan Rachel, b 1862 NY, mar Walter Thompson, 2 sons, Dewitt and Elmer Thompson.
A4. Elias John, b 1864 NY, mar 1892 Emma Taber, a son. His wife died soon, and Elias John, his father, and his son, res NYCity, then rem to Rutherford, NJ late 1890s. The fam later res Passaic, NJ, ca 1906/7.
B1. Frank Savory DE GRUCHY, b 1893 served in Navy, WWI. Mar Eleanor Marie Ackerman of Passaic, NJ 1922. Rem to Ridgewood, NJ, and later to NYCity.
C1. Kenneth Ackerman, b 1923 mar Jean Perdue of Ridgewood, NJ, 2 chn: Kenneth and Cheryl.
C2. Donald C., b 1930 Ridgewood, NJ mar Betty Jane Tate in Oneco, FLA, 1962, res Wash., DC and Monte Sereno, CAL, sons Donald & Daniel DE GRUCHY.
A5. Mary Marguerite, b 1866.

DE GRUCHY, James Gwyer, b 1871 La Profond Rue, Trinity, J, mar Mary BALL from Northumberland, England, rem to US 1890s. (Dr. James H. B. De GRuchy, Kowa, OK)

DE GRUCHY, GRUCHY, John, b 1826 J, d 1899. (John De Gruchy, Fresno,CAL)
A1. Walter John, b 1857 J, d 1944/46 in US? Mar ___
B1. Richard, b 1885 d 1975, no sons, poss daus. He was 14th in line from Ralph Gruchy of J in the 1400s.
B2. John, had no sons. b4. Rita B5. Molly
B3. Francis William, d 1936 in US, mar ___.
C1. Peter, b 1928 res Glendora, CAL, had son Andrew and adopted son Philip.
C2. Michael, b 1930 had 3 sons and 1 dau, res Bundaberg, Queensland, Australia.
D1. Timothy D2. James D3. Michael D4. Jane
C3. John Francis, d 1936 US? mar ___.
D1. John Francis Jr., b 1925, res Coarsegold, CAL.
E1. Vivienne E2. Julie E3. Susan E4. Simon, b 1956.

DE GRUCHY, David, b 1854, son of John T. and Jane Elizabeth (VALPY) DE GRUCHY, rem to Baltimore, MD age 18 in 1872, mar Grace Blakely. David was b Ramsgate, England of a J fam from Trinity, J. (Muriel Howard, Baltimore, MD)

DE GRUCHY, Edward, b 1850 J, d 1926 Bishop's Crossing, QUE. He was active in the Methodist Church of Jersey, even in his teens, rem to Canada 1868, ordained 1876 in QUE. Served in St. Theodore, and in Montreal. Mar Celina Racicot, 5 chn, 2 d.y. Wrote JOURNEY THROUGH 19 CENTURIES OF THE CHRISTIAN CHURCH, publ. Montreal. (Mrs. John Harriman, Melbourne, QUE)

A1. Mrs. Eva R. Moore of Montreal, QUE.

A2. E.F. DE GRUCHY of New York A3. E. Douglas of Chicago, ILL.

A4. Sarah Allard, adopted?, b ca 1880? mar 1900 Frank RENAUD, who d 1907. A son d.y. She mar 2. Placide Demerd, had dau & 2 sons.

DE GRUCHY, Elias res NYCity 1790 with fam of 6 men, 1 boy and 1 female (Census)

DE GRUCHY, George, res Coxackie, NY, son of John, who came from Jersey to New York via St. John's, Nfld., said to be related to other fams of Gruchy and De Gruchy in US. (Donald De Gruchy, Monte Sereno, CAL)

A1. Evelyn mar Stanley Blanchard of Essex Falls, NJ.

DE GRUCHY, Capt. Frederick son of John and Caroline (DE QUETTEVILLE) DE GRUCHY of Jersey, rem to south Africa 1890s. Caroline was sister of Jurate Clement Nicolle DE QUETTEVILLE, qv. Capt. Frederick was master of a square rigged ship, and removed toSouth Africa where he carried on for 50 years an importing business, bringing South African goods to England. He received an OBE for his service to the Ministry of Shipping, which he worked for in WWI. He d 1960 leaving 4 sons and 4 daus, all in South Africa. (Guy Dixon, England)

DE GRUCHY, Capt. George, was master of a sailing ship, and retired from the sea to St. Peters, J. Capt. George was grandson of Philip, of La Piece Mauger, Trinity, J. Had sons Francis, Edward and Thomas, said to have emigrated to Canada.

DE GRUCHY, George John, settled in Canada ca 1870, killed in RR accident on his own land. (Guy Dixon, England)

DE GRUCHY, Henry Eustace Sligh, b 1897 England of J fam, was officer in Shropshire Light Inf., rem to Burma 1920, mar an American, Barbara Beanke, rem to Maine, US. Became a citizen. (Guy Dixon)

DE GRUCHY, James, b 1871, son of Jean and Elizabeth(Gwyer) De Gruchy, of La Chase, J, rem to USA. (DE GRUCHY chart)

DE GRUCHY, Jeanne Marie, b 1857 J, sister of David above, mar J.Bromfield Hine in J, and rem to Baltimore, MD 1913, 7 chn. Note also the HINE name in GRUSH fam. (Muriel Howard, Baltimore, MD)

DE GRUCHY, John, to Nfld. and then to US. Bro of Elias above.

DE GRUCHY, John Walter, b J, mar ___, rem to Montreal, QUE, res there ca 1900. (Douglas H. De Gruchy, Montreal, QUE)

A1. Steward Noel, res Montreal? had son and dau? A2. John Walter

A3. Douglas Herbert, res Montreal, had sons Douglas E. and James F.

GRUCHE, John of Bow, NH 1793. (CLEMENT GEN)

GRUSH, John, also spelled LE GRUCHA, LA BRUCHA, LA GRUCHE, LE GRUCHE, etc, etc, res MA 1740. See this fam under GRUSH.

DE GRUSHE, John mar Eunice ___, res Woburn, MA.

A1. Mary b 1734 Woburn, MA. A2. John, b 1743

DE GRUSHE, John was in NYCity 1790 with fam of 5, res North Ward.

GRUCHE, Joshua on Ketch AMERICA 1684 in ME and NH with Capt. John JACKSON.

DE GRUCHY, Matthew, a Jersey banker, b 1789 St. Saviours J mar 1811 Francoise LE CAPPELAIN of J. Rem to VA 1825. She was a cousin of

Jean LE CAPPELAIN, artist of J. Matthew was bro of Abraham DE GRUCHY merchant of St. Heliers J, and they were sons of Philip of Trinity,J and Maufant J. The mother was Eliz. LE GEYT of Les Pigneaux, St. Saviour J. (Guy Dixon, Pickering, Yorks, England)
A1. William A2. Marie Anne? A3. Matthew
DE GRUCHY, Muriel, b 1892 J rem to Baltimore, MD, 1907, mar ___Howard. A dau Jane Susan Howard. (Muriel Howard, Baltimore, MD)
GROUCHY, Matthew from J rem to Osceola, IA 1870s. A RR foreman. (LE BOUTILLIER-BUTLER GEN, by Brechtel, IA, 1980)
DE GRUCHY, Paul, prof. of Sherbrooke, QUE, desc of J fam of Gaspe.
DE GRUCHY, Philip, from J to US 1798/99. (Guy Dixon, England)
DE GRUCHY, Philip, to US 1776.
DE GRUCHY, Philip, from J to US 1769 on ship MOLLY from J, indentured man. (Whitmore)
DE GRUCHY, Philip, res Montreal, b ca 1850 J, cousin of Edward above. Living in 1926.
DE GRUCHY, Philip J., merchant of London, England, son of Philip Peter DE GRUCHY of J and London, of the DE GRUCHY, LE BRETON & CO. firm. Later was partner in FIOTT, DE GRUCHY & CO. Philip got over his depth financially, and fled to America ca 1798 to avoid creditors. He mar in America. (Guy Dixon, England)
DE GRUCHY. "the brothers Philip, b 1789; Moses, b 1791; Abraham, b 1793; and Jean/John b 1795/6, all emigrated from St. Saviour J as young men, initially to Canada", poss some to US. (Guy Dixon)
DE GRUCHY, Philip, b 1812 St. Heliers J, uncle of George above, was a senior partner in DE GRUCHY, RENOUF, CLEMENT AND CO, of Burgeo, NFLD and Jersey. By the 1870s they were operating some 25 sailing vessels in connection with the trade. (Guy Dixon, England)
DE GRUCHY, Raoul, res Rochester, NY. In 1975 he paddled a kayak from Rochester via Muskingum, OH, Kanawaha, New and Tennessee rivers to Guntersville, ALA, where he planned to settle. A carpenter, his customized fiber glass kayak could carry 250 pounds of equipment. His parents res Akron, OH, and he attended Barberton High School. Poss son of Dr. Charles D. De Gruchy of Akron, there 1970s. A Leon De Gruchy also res Akron, OH in the 1970s.
GRUSH, Sarah mar Jonathan CLEMENTS of Haverhill, MA 1745/6. He was the son of Nathaniel Clements. She was b Bradford, MA and d before 1826, dau of John and Sarah GRUSHE. John, her father d ca 1754, and Sarah, her mother, in 1760. (CLEMENT GEN)
DE GRUCHY, Thomas James, b J, merchant adventurer of Boston, had a large business as privateer and ship owner. Mar 1741 Mary DUMARESQ, qv, of Boston, and retired to J on the death of his father there. He planned and led a Rebellion, the nearest thing to a Revolution known in J. See NOTABLES. (A. John Jean, Jersey; MA Archives)
DE GRUCHY, DE GRUSHE, Thomas res with 1 female in Mamaronek, NY 1790. He may have been the bro of Elias above.
GRUCHY, Thomas mar Mary Edwards 1749 MRB.
GRUSH, Willard P. of Lexington, MA was doing much research on the DE GRUCHY and GRUSH fams in the 1960s and 1970s. Where is his work?
DE GRUCHY, William, b ca 1854 J rem to Mount Holly, VA 1870s. He was part of the Abraham DE GRUCHY fam of St. Heliers J.(Guy Dixon)
DE GRUCHY, William, res Phila., PA from a J fam, d before 1945. "We found a letter from Col. Alphonse De Gruchy, who went to meet his parents in the USA, dated Northumberland, England, 1817, addressed to his mother. By a lucky accident I met a gentleman of our name in this country, a Monsieur de Grouchy who came from England to settle in America."

DE GRUCHY, ___, emigrant from C.I. in CAL 1900s.
DE GRUCHY, Mrs. res Culver City, CAL, another in Dorchester, MA 1970s, and one in Lancaster, PA.
DE HAVILLAND in G 1331, many res in St. Andrews and St. Peter Port, G. See A CHRONICLE OF THE NORMAN FAM. OF DE HAVILLAND, by John Von Sonntag De Havilland, St. Louis, MO 1895, not seen by compiler.
DE HAVILLAND, Olivia, and sister Joan Fontaine, both movie stars, are desc of Capt. Sir Geoffrey De Havilland, b G, and founder of the De Havilland Aircraft Co. of England.
DE JARDIN, John, from J? in 1665 with Carteret to NJ. See NJ section. DE JARDIN noted in G. Poss JARDINE is a variant spelling.
DE JEAN curr Los Angeles, CAL. See also JEAN, in J 1274. In Vale, G, 1300s. In St. Ouen and St. Heliers J 1668, in St. Ouen J 1749. Not known to compiler if JEAN and DE JEAN are the same.
DE JEAN. Capt of a group of ships voyaging to SC in the 1700s. "Convoy of DE JEAN...DE JEAN's next return". (SC GEN. & HIST. MAG, vols 3,4)
DE JEAN, DE JERSEY, Elizabeth, b ca 1703 J? mar 1724 Samuel Starr, son of Joseph and Comfort Starr, b 1703/4 in Middletown, CT. "Tradition says that she and her sister were the only chn of a French nobleman, prop. of a large estate in Jersey...left orphans at an early age, and placed under the care of an uncle, to whom the estate would revert in the case of their decease. He, under the pretense of sending them to England to be educated,put them on board a ship bound for America. On arriving in New York the captain sold them for their passage money. They were brought to Middletown, CT and given the surname DE JERSEY. The elder was about 10." After many years it is said the uncle in remorse wrote and begged them to return. The letters remained unanswered. Note that many romanticized tales of the early settlers were woven out of whole cloth; others were true. Another record says their name was FARRIE, poss FERREE?, Hug? Eliz. d 1768 age 65. 9 chn. (STARR GEN: THE STOW STARR FAM, by Bernice Wiltshire, Parma, OH; Elizabeth Lof, Omaha, NEB; NUTMEGGER, June 1982 WRCIC) DE JAUSSERAND, from J to ONT and BC, CANADA

A1. Samuel Starr, b 1725 seaman, ashore in 1755/60 when he was elected to office in Middletown, CT. Sailed from New London, CT for the West Indies in company with bro Capt. Timothy Starr in another vessell. Capt. Samuel's ship was lost in a storm. Samuel mar 1748 Chloe, dau of Dr. Daniel and Patience Cruttenden of Chatham, CT, 1728-1801.
B1. Samuel Starr, b 1751 d 1756.
B2. Patience Starr, b 1757 d 1825, mar 1784 Jacob, son of Jacob and Susannah (White) Hall, b 1756 Middletown, CT.
C1. Jacob Hall, 1785-1806 C3. Leonard Hall, b 1789 d 1849
C2. Lucy Hall, b 1787 mar Samuel PATTEN, who d 1848. Lucy d 1832
C4. Elizabeth Hall, b 1791 C5. Henry Hall, b 1796
B3. Elizabeth Starr, b 1761 mar Wm. Starr, res Greenfield, MA and rem in 1804 to Deerfield, MA, where Wm. was Supt. of the StebbinsMills He d 1831, Vet. of 1776.
C1. Esther Southmayd Starr, b 1782 d 1912, unmar C4. Samuel,1786-1843
C2. William Starr, b 1783, desc C5. Seth Starr, b 1789
C3. Elizabeth Starr, b 1785, d.y. C6. Oliver Starr, b 1791
C7. Lucy Starr, b 1793 d 1843 mar 1824 Capt. John Chapman, b NH, res Sullivan, NY, contractor for Chenango Canal, d 1850 Binghamton, New York, a son John F. Chapman.
C8. Elizabeth again, b 1798 d 1813. C9. Beverly Starr, b 1801, d.y.
B4. Lucy Starr, b 1762 d 1840 Plymouth, PA, mar1. Samuel, son of Wm. and Tryphena (Jones) LUCAS, b 1754, who d 1819. Lucy mar 2.

1820, his 2nd wife, Calvin Wadhams.
B5. Hannah Starr, b 1764 B6. Samuel again Starr, b 1766
A2. Benj. Starr, b 1726, prob d.y.
A3. Mary Starr, b 1728 d 1811, mar1. 1748/9 Stephen, son of Robert and Isabel (Whitmore) Warner of Middleton, CT, b 1722. He d 1752 Bay of Honduras, per account from Capt. Giles Hall. She mar 2. 1761, Stephen Van Overwyk, who d 1764. 3 daus, more data in book.
A4. Timothy Starr, b 1730, sea captain, absent on voyage when 1st wife died, later became a businessman in Middletown, CT, d 1802. He mar 1. Eunice Parsons, and 2. 1770, Abigail Talcott, widow of Christopher Hamlin, who d 1804 age 67. More data in book.
A5. Elizabeth Starr, bp 1733/4 mar 1755 William Redfield, of Killingworth, CT, 1727-1813, res Middletown. See REDFIELD GEN, 10 chn.
A6. Elihu, b 1735/6, merchant, active in Rev. War, treas. of Middletown, CT, mar 1756 Mary Birdseye, 13 chn, many desc.
A7. Ruth Starr, b 1738 mar Robert Fairchild, res New Haven, CT and Pawling, NY ca 1789.
A8. Grace Starr, b 1739/40 mar 1774, his 1st wife, Col. Return Jonathan of Middletown, CT. Rem 1788 to Marietta, OH, d 1823, 3 chn.
A9. James Starr, b 1742, d 1781 mar 1768 Anna, dau of John and Eliz. (Foster) Kent of Middletown, 4 chn, desc.

DE JERSEY in J 1274, in Vale G very early. In St. Peters G 1679. In St. Saviour G 1672. Hilary and Peter DE JERSEY in G 1750.

DE JERSEY, A.F. was member of the SC Hist. Soc. in 1899, in Charleston, SC. (Vol. 1 of SC Mag)

DE JERSEY, John mar Margaret Parker, 1743 Boston, MA, dau Mary b 1746.

DE JERSEY, Peter and Mary res Boston, MA, 2 or more chn.
A1. Henry, b 1734 A2. Mary, b 1738

DE JERSEY, Arthur Francis, b 1856 G, son of Carey BROCK DE JERSEY of G mar Isabella Huger/Hewgee in Charleston, SC. Both bur Magnolia Cem. Charleston, SC. (R.E. Babb Jr., Charleston, SC)

DE JERSEY, John mar Elizabeth Briscomb 1755 Boston, MA.

DE LA COUR, see Jane ROBERT. DE LA COUR curr in J. In G 1315 in St. Peter of the Wood.

DE LA COURT in G 1588. DE LA COUR in St. Lawrence J 1788.

DE LA COURT, Pierre of G had dau Agnes who mar 1393 Pierre BERNARD. See this Bernard Gen. in Tingley.

DE LA CLOCHE, Rachel, mar in Salem, MA Pierre BAUDOIN, of Rochelle, France, a Hug who first fled to Ireland and then to MA. (Perley 3) Gov. Andros gave him 100 acres in Casco Bay, ME 1687, but he rem ca 1689 to Boston, where he d 1706. He mar Elizabeth ___, who d 1720 age 77, by whom he had several chn. Prob none by Rachel of Jersey, who may also have been a Hug. Cf BELL. Sometimes DE LA CLOCHE is translated as CLOCK, qv.

DE LA CROIX, see also LE CROSS, CROSS, LE CROY, LA CROY. In J 1309, 1528, etc.

DE LA CROIX, Peter was in ME 1659, and sued Thomas NICKOLS in court. (Noyes) OUTC.

DE LA CROIX, this name noted in Phila. deaths in the 1800s. OUTC

DE LA CROIX, F., was on the ship TEPIC fromQueen Charlotte Islands, BC, Canada to San Francisco, CAL 1852. OUTC, poss from C.I.?

DE LA HAYE in J ca 1160. DE LA HAYE in St. Martin and Grouville, J 1668, and in St. Martin J 1749. Name in G 1331, curr G. Noted in Fremont, CAL, etc.

DE LA HAYE noted in many places in America, and in early Maryland records, some by 1637. (Skordas) Poss from J, as ships from J were stopping in the West Indies, Virginia and Maryland at this time..

DE LA HAYE in Phila. death records 1800s. OUTC

DE LA HAYE, HAY, HAYES in Norfolk and Yorkshire England 1600s. (Bardsley)

DE LA HAYE, Bertram James, b 1898 J, d 1953 US, son of J fam. Bertram mar Evelyn Grace Macon, b 1901 J, dau of Normandy French fam. (Lawrence De la Haye, Victoria, BC)

A1. Doreen, b 1920 J mar ___Barlow A3. John, b 1926 J, res Sussex,Eng

A2. Rosene?, b 1922 J B4. Brian, b 1929 J

A5. Lawrence, b 1938 St. Saviour J mar Carole May TRACHY, qv, b Weymouth, England, dau of Eric Charles TRACHY of St. Peter Port G, and Gwendoline Mary Dearing.

B1. Suzanne, b 1961 B2. Paul b 1963

DE LA HAY, John from J? in Isles of Shoals, ME 1706. (Noyes)

DE LA HAYE, Eliza, dau of Joseph mar ___Stephenson 1822 in QUE, at the Garrison Prot. Ch. OUTC, but poss. C.I., as others were there also.

DE LA HAYE, Elias Francis, son of Philip, was one of 12 chn, 7 boys and 5 girls, res J. One sister also came to America. Elias Francis b 1866 J, rem to Lowell, MA 1896. Mar Louisa PINEL, qv, next to youngest in fam of 8 chn, dau of Philippe PINEL, with quarry and farm, and wife, who was also a DE LA HAYE. Louisa brought with her to America her aunt, a Mrs. BISSON, 2 sons and a dau. She d ca 1952 age 83. Elias in America was a stone and brick mason, and built mills, bridges and dams. Desc in Fallon, MO. (G. Ulrich, Sudbury,MA)

A1. Charles A2. Elias Jr., b J d ca 1952 A3. Hilda Louise, d ca 1942

A4. George, b N. Chelmsford, MA, res Lowell, MA.

A5. Edith Mary, mar ___STEELE, qv, res Middleton, MA. She was b 1898.

DELAWAY, Henry and Abigail res Boston. OUTC, was this DE LA HAYE? A dau Mary was b 1723, other chn?

DE LA HAYE, John, merchant in Barbadoes 1639/40. Daniel DE LA HAYE sent to him a seaman named DE LA HAYE. In book mentioned there are 3 entries from Jersey and Guernsey, but names omitted. (AMERICAN COLONISTS IN ENGLISH RECORDS, by Sherwood)

DE LA HAYE, Margaret, b 1828 J, mar Charles HORMAN, qv, d UT 1906.

DE LA HAYE, Nancy, mother of Margaret, from J to UT 1868, via ship CONSTITUTION, returned to Jersey later. (SLCity records)

DE LA HA, Philip in Cascataqua 1697 (Noyes) From J? OUTC.

DILLEHAY, Thomas mar Hannah GAVETT 1740 Boston. Both from J fams? See GAVETT, GAVEY.

DE LE HAY, DILLAHAH, DE LA HAYE?, Thomas mar Mary Smiter? or SMITH? 1734 Boston. OUTC.

DE LA HAYE, William, E.B., midshipman, retired 1866, d 1892, served in US Navy. (Callahan List)

DE LA HAYE, ___ mar Mrs. Jesse Gill of N. Chelmsford, MA, b J.1800s.

DE LA HAYE, James, b ca 1883 St. Peter? J, a tenant farmer, to US as livestockman, with a herd of Jersey cows ordered by a NJ gentleman farmer. Mar Ada MICHEL, dau of MICHEL and MARQUAND, and niece of George DE LA HAYE of the North Chelmsford, MA fams. To America 1926 via ship OLYMPIC. (Henry Ulrich, Sudbury, MA)

A1. Marguerite mar Albert Woodhull of NJ, settled Lexington, MA.

A2. Joyce, d ca 1952 A3. Georgiana,unmar, res Morristown, NJ

A4. Ada Blanche, b 1918 mar Henry T. Ulrich, res Morristown, NJ

B1. Henry T. Ulrich III of Weston, MA B2. Joyce Laura Ulrich

DE LA MARE in Torteval G 1600s. In St. Peters G 1741. In J by 1180 in G by mid 1500s, poss from name DE LA MARE DE LA LANDE, and DE LA MARE DE CRESENVILLE of Normandy, France. There is a Hug. Wagner pedigree of the DE LA MARE fam in England. Name curr G. (Barry W. De La Mare, CIFHS #9)

DE LA MARE, Philip, b 1823 Grouville J, son of Francois and Jeanne (AHIER) DE LA MARE. To US 1852 via ship KENNEBEC, then to UT. Philip was 4th of 14 chn of Francois. He mar 1. Mary Ann Parkin b England, 3 chn b J. Mary Ann d 1896. Philip later mar 2. Marie CHEVALIER, bp 1823 Trinity J, dau of Daniel M. CHEVALIER. Marie d 1884, 7 chn. Philip mar 3. Jennette Mickeljohn of a Scottish fam. 8 chn. At least 5 chn d.y. of this Plural marriage. Most have desc. This fam is traced at least back to Jean and Lorance(RENOUF) DE LA MARE in 1687. Much more data in SLC records. (CARTER; UTAH GEN. MAG, Vols 20,23,26,27; HIST. OF TOOELE CO; Prudence Fyffe, Central, AZ; SLC and UT records) See also WRCIC.

A1. Mary Jane, b 1847 J d 1852 St. Louis, MO.
A2. Philip Francois, b 1849 J mar Elvina MALLET, qv, 5 chn
A3. Theophilus, b 1851 J d 1854 UT.
A4. Elizabeth, b 1854 mar before 1875 John W. Tate, 14 chn.
A5. Esther Jane, b 1855 Tooele, UT mar 1873 Charles John WALTERS, b 1842 J who d 1919. Esther d 1920. See WALTERS
A6. Sophia, b 1857 mar 1875 John McLaws, 13 chn, 2 d.y.
A7. John Chevalier, b 1859 UT mar 1. Agnes McKindrick, 11 chn, and 2 Agnes M. Ellison. 5 chn d.y.
A8. Joseph William, b 1859 Tooele, UT mar 1.Alice Atkins 1884 and 2. Caroline GREENE. 3 chn by Alice, none by Caroline.
A9. Mary Eliza, b 1861 mar 1880 Alvin J. McCuistion, d 1890, 4 chn
A10. Thomas, b 1864 mar 1885 Ann Loretta McKendrick, res Tooele, UT 12 chn.
A11. Alice Ann, b 1867 mar 1885 James Gowans, 10 chn.
A12. Lydia, a nurse, b 1864
A13. Josephine, b 1869 mar1891 Wm. H. Boyce, res Ft. Smith, ARK,3 chn.
A14. Franklin Mickeljohn, b 1871 Tooele mar 1902 Ellen Holstein,2 daus
A15. Collin M., b 1873 mar 1892 Caroline GREEN, 2 chn.
A16. Ann Jennette, b 1875 mar 1898 Henry Droubay, 4 chn.
A17. Clarence Philip, b 1884

DE LA MARE in J, see CIFHS #9.

DE LA MARE, Rev. Francois, Francis, b 1821 Grouville J, son of Francois and Jean, brother of Philip above, mar 1. Marguerite GAVEY, b 1819 St. Clement J, d 1845. He mar 2. Charlotte DE MOUILPIED, B 1821 G, d ca 1909. The Rev. Francis was minister at Gaspe, QUE; on Mauritius Island off Africa and in South Africa, and other places. He drowned in an accident 1869. 2 chn by GAVEY and 3. by Charlotte DE MOUILPIED. (UTAH GEN. MAG, Vol 21)

A1. Francis, b 1843
A2. Lydia, 1845-1892
A3. Jemima, b ca 1847 G, d 1927
A4. Alpheus, b 1849 J mar 1870s NYCity.
A5. Clarence, b 1862 d 1884.

DE LA MARE, Philip MOURANT, b 1856 St. Helier J, son of Abraham and Eliz. (MOURANT) DE LA MARE, mar Louisa Jane Waddington, b 1863. She d at ST. Heliers J 1912. He then rem to BC Canada, and to Los Angeles, CAL, where he d 1916, leaving widow, Mrs. Cora DE LA MARE, who had by prev. mar. 2 grown sons, names not known. 4 chn by 1st wife. (UTAH GEN. MAG)

A1. Philip Waddington, b 1889 res BC Canada.
A2. Winifred Eva, b 1891 St. Helier J d 1922 Mission City, BC, 2 chn.
A3. Wilfred Gerald b ca 1893, d.y.
A4. Nita Louisa, b 1900 St. Heliers, rem to Los Angeles, mar --Adams.

DE LA MARE, Edgar Naftel with wife and 3 sons sailed from St. Peter Port G early 1900s in packet ALBERTA to Southampton, England and from there to NYork on liner CITY OF PHILA. REM TO Chicago, ILL, then to Los Angeles, CAL, where Edgar had a bro. On their way, they visited Edward LE PELLEY of Chicago, from G. Edgar was related to the ROBILLIARD and LE PELLEY fams of Guernsey through his mother. (UTAH GEN. MAG)

A1. Alan, son of Edgar, res Los Angeles, CAL, mar ___.

DE LA MARE, Francis in Beaufort Co., NC in March 1741 left will. His wife was Susannah ___, sons Thomas and Francis. OUTC. (WILLS OF NC, by Moore; Mrs. F. Borchers, Omahan, NEB)

DE LA MARE, one involved in the 1900s in a gold mine in Reno, NEV.

DE LA MARE, Julia left G ca 1857 to live in Canada with her G-born uncle, Thomas Naftel DE LA MARE, and his Alderney-born wife, nee Eliz. BOTT. Julia mar a Canadian, Henry Grimsell of Strathroy, ONT, who soon died, and she returned to G, where she d 1912. (GUERNSEY SOC. BULL. Winter, 1952)

Note that DE LA MARE was in London, 1717, in Clerkenwell, England 1675 and in Yorkshire, England 1584, 1612 and 1665.

DELANCEY, Capt. ___, res North WArd of NYCity 1790, where some Channel Islanders settled. OUTC. 5 in fam. DELANCEY, DE LANCEY old G name.

DELAND, DALAND. There is nothing to definitely connect the DELAND fam in NA to the Channel Islands, except the statement in the GEN that the orig. name was DE LONDES, and they had fled from France to the Islands of Man and Jersey, and later rem to Holland before coming to America ca 1636, landing at Portsmouth, NH? There was also a DES LANDES fam long in the C.I., and at times the name was spelled DELON, which is similar to the pron. of the name in the Islands. Note that AMY is also a C.I. surname, but found in France and England also. (THE DELAND FAM IN AMERICA; Mary Belle KImmy, Valrico, FLA) Much more data in WRCIC, but not included, as connection with C.I. is unverified. See AMY.

DELAND, Abigail b 1709 MA d before 1732, mar in Boxford, MA 1721/2 John AMY, qv, of Andover, MA b 1699, wheelwright, carpenter. OUTC.

A1. Abigail Amy, b 1722/23 Boxford, MA

A2. Micah Amy b 1726 mar in Haverhill, MA 1757 Eliz. MIDDLETON, rem 1775 and was elected first town treas. of Guildhall, VT 1783. Note that MIDDLETON was also a J surname, as well as English.

DE LA PERELLE in St. John, St. Peter, St. Mary, St. Ouen J 1668, and in St. Ouen, St. John, St. Brelade and St. Peter J 1749.

DE LA PERELLE, see PEARL and PERREL. Also see Q.A. IN CANADA.

DE LA PERELLE, Capt. E. of the GASPE, a J owned ship, repulsed the US privateer ship DI(MEDE in the Gulf of St. Lawrence, off QUE, 1814. (JERSEY IN THE 18TH AND 19TH CENTURIES, by Saunders)

DE LA PLACE. Cf PLACE surname in early New England.

DE LA PLACE, in Trinity and St. Martin J 1668, and in Trinity and St. Brelade J 1749. HUG?

DE LA PLACE, Thomas mar Prudence Keeling 1736 in Boston, King's Chapel. OUTC, but other Channel Islanders were mar there.

A1. Susanna, b 1739 Boston, MA.

DE LA ROCQUE in St. Heliers and Trinity J 1668, and in St. Heliers, St. Peter and St. John J 1749. DE LA ROCQUE, and EDMONDS AKA ROCK in J before 1607. See LAROKE and LEAROCK

DILLOROCK, Eliz. mar John Hutchins 1712 Boston. Same or another Eliz. mar Alex. Grimes 1719 Boston, MA. OUTC.

DILLOROCK, Philip, had wife Eliz. and a son William b 1701, Boston, MA.

LA ROKE, LAROKE, Ellener, from J age 15 to Salem, MA 1677. She was indentured to Philip ENGLISH, qv. (NEHGS Vol.31)

DE LA RUE. Note that this name is fairly common in Europe, and DE LA RUE and LA RUE are not all from the Channel Islands.

Note that DE RUE of the Channel Islands became in one case DREW, qv.

DE LA RUE in G 1331, in St. Peter G 1827
DE LA RUE, Elias in GCO 1860. Prob from G.
DE LA RUE, Elias mar Sarah Parker 1747 Boston, MA (int). OUTC.
DE LA RUE, Eliz. mar Geo. Conner 1785 Boston, MA. OUTC
DE LA RUE, John of G rem to GCO early 1800s. See also LA RUE.
DE LA RUE, Philip mar Sarah Parker 1747, res Boston, MA. (NEHGS Vol 100)
A1. Elizabeth, bp 1764 Christ Church, Boston. Did she mar Geo. Conner 1785? A2. SArah.
DE LA RUE, Rachel from G mar James BICHARD in GCO early 1800s. See Moses SARCHET, and BICHARD.
DE LA RUE, Thomas of St. Peter Port G, mar 1814 in Devon, Jane Warren, an instance of the many marriages between South-of-Englanders and Channel Islanders.
DE LA REW, Thomas mar Eunice ___, res Boston. OUTC
A1. Eunice, b 1732 Boston, poss mar Geo. BRIGHT?, qv, 1750.
A2. Thomas, b 1733 A3. Ann, b 1738 Boston.
DE LA RUE, Thomas and Catherine res Boston. OUTC
A1. William, b 1766, twin A2. Elizabeth b 1766, twin.
DE LA REW, William mar Mary BUTLER 1764 Boston. Same or another mar 1765 Catharine BRYANT, in Boston. OUTC
DELAUNEY, Pierre A. from C.I.? to NY 1838 (NATURALIZATIONS IN NY, by Scott) See LONEY. OUTC.
DE LA TASTE, Jean of Jersey, of a Hug fam? had considerable trade with VA, and other parts of the coast. From VA tobacco was imported directly to the C.I. and manufactured there for use of the Islanders. (A. John Jean, Jersey)
DE LAUNE curr G, in J 1299. Noted in Fremont, CAL. See LONEY. OUTC
DE LA VALLEY, John and Nicholas were in Maryland 1657. (Skordas) LE VALLEY curr in G.
LE VALLEY, Pierre, Peter, "believed to have been born in the Channel Islands and to have landed at Marblehead ca 1700, moved in Warwick, RI 1727. He had at least 6 chn, and was the ancestor of the LEVALLEY fam of Warwick and Coventry." (Loughrey) A Hug fam? Pierre mar Eliz. Yabsley. (MHS; MRB VR; NEHGS Vol 37) Chn: Peter and Mary.
DELEREE, James H., age 22. of Holland ONT, b G, son of Peter and Rachel DELEREE, mar 1858 in Arran, ONT, M.A. Smith age 17 of Holland. (Huron Co., ONT Marriage Reg; Wm. Britnell, Missauga, ONT)
DE LISLE in G 1331, curr G and J.
DE LISLE, Alfred Henry, b 1863 London, England son of Alfred T. DELISLE a Guernseyman, b 1822 in Paris, France, d 1884 England, wife Catherine Messiter Burnard, b and d England, 1836-1904. Alfred Sr. was a banker in London, and his father had been a Guernseyman, a banker in Paris. These Paris, London and Guernsey banks were apparently family owned. Alfred Henry d 1934 in CAL, traveled to FLA and Canada before 1890. Settled in CAL 1892/3 where he was a civil engineer and RR surveyor for the Northwestern Pacific and for Southern Pacific RR. He mar in Victoria, BC 1892 Anna Young Fraser, b 1873 Scotland, d 1956 CAL. Desc res CAL. (Joan De Lisle Myers, San Jose)
DE LISLE, Daniel son of Daniel D. and Eliza (Tear) De Lisle rem to America from G in 1800s.
DE LISLE curr Fremont, CAL. DE LISLE, see THOMAS SARCHET.
DELON, Ann and Mark were in NC 1781. Note that DES LANDES of J were also called DELON. (QUAKER ENCY, V.1, p. 138) OUTC. The fam chart of Nicholas BISSON includes surname DELON. See DES LANDES, DALAND.
DE LOUCHE, also at times, DE LUCE?, old name in J. (Stevens) Curr J. Means dweller at house with enclosed garden.
DE LOUCHE, Joseph Charles, b J ca 1825/30, poss uncle or father of

Joseph below?, was mar 1827 in Presb. CH, Quebec City, to June/Jane ROSIER, qv. (Ch records) More data on fam below in WRCIC.

DE LOUCHE, Joseph Charles, b 1846 J, rem to Indian Head, near Stephenville, Nfld., a fisherman and mail carrier, d 1923 Port-o-Port, Nfld. Was also a layreader of Angl. CH at Port-au-Port, and church Warden. Mar Hannah Hunt, 1840-1923, dau of Wm. Hunt. (Greta De Louche, Boswarlos, Nfld.) Other chn than John William?

A1. John William, b 1868 Nfld. d 1914 mar 1889 Jane Ann Legge, qv, 1858-1926, 6 chn.

B1. Kesiah Jane, b 1890 mar 1. Henry Hines/Hynes and 2. 1916, Joseph H. Sherwood, 5 chn by Hynes, 6 by sherwood.

C1. Wm. Henry Hynes, b 1909, mar Helen Nicolson, 3 chn: Linda, Judy and Norma.

C2. Leah Gertrude Hynes, b 1911, d 1945, mar Harold Percy Lordly, 7 chn: Helen L. Harold, Elizabeth, Mary Louise, Josephine and Winston Lordly, 5 mar with chn.

C3. Chester Joseph Hynes, mar Mary MARMO, see Q.A. IN CANADA. 7 chn. Evan, Desmond, Shirley, Sonny, Robert, Carol and Stewart Hines.

C4. and C5. two chn d.y.

C6. by 2nd husband, Joseph Jr., b 1918 mar Hazel A. McCormick, 7 chn: Nancy P., Geraldine, Roy Douglas, Margret, Phyllis, William and Gail Marie Sherwood.

C7. David Sherwood, b 1920, d.y. C8. Ruby P. Sherwood, b 1921

C9. Douglas Sherwood, b 1922 mar 1. Ruth Mackley, 3 chn: John, Louise and Paul Sherwood.

C10. Gerald Sherwood, b 1925 d 1942

C11. Melvin Richard Sherwood b 1929 mar 1950 Geraldine Chaddock, 2 chn:David and Ardith.

B2. Winslow Buchanan, b 1891 Nfld, d 1972, mar 1919 Florence S. MARTIN 7 chn. Winslow a WWI veteran.

C1. Phoebe, b 1920 mar Cater Hoskins, and 2. 1960 Lloyd Eddy, 7 chn by #1, and 3 by Eddy: Marie Harvey, Laura Abbott, Ivy Thistle, Patsey Abbott, Michael, Raymond, Eric, Beverly Eddy, Carol Eddy and Karon Eddy.

C2. Laura, b 1921 mar 1944 Edward Hoskins, 8 chn: Bessie Cluney, Barbara Eddy, Cecil, Joseph, Brian, Thomas, Edith Childs and Edwin Hoskins.

C3. Gertrude, b 1923 mar Joseph Hynes, 8 chn: Percy De Louche, Theresa, Clayton, Isabel Kendall, Wilhemina Gaudet, Kathleen Godin, Florence Kendall and Wilfred Hynes.

C4. Wilhemina, b 1924

C5. Winslow Jr., b 1925 mar Theresa Gladys Doucette, b 1929, 6 chn: Doreen, Charles, Florence Ann, Daniel, Thomas and Derek.

C6. Joseph Charles, b 1927 mar Greta Lily Janes, 6 chn: Randy Joseph, Heather, Iris, Harold, Scott and Fraser Arthur.

C7. DAvid Nathaniel b 1930 mar Ellen (Hoskins) MARTIN.

B3. Joseph Charles, 1893-1912

B4. Hannah Elfreda Gertrude, b 1895 d 1981 Halifax, NS, mar Horatio P. Chaddock, 7 chn: John, Lionel, Reginald, Raymond, Beverley, Geraldine and Ruth Chaddock.

B5. John Henry Lerish (LE RICH?) b 1896 Port-au-Port, Nfld., d 1978 Georgetown, ONT. Mar 1930 Gladys Moore, 3 chn: Thelma Boutcher Hann, Percy, and Reginald.

B6. Mary Matilda, b 1901, d 1974, mar John H. Hynes, who d 1973, 6chn: Douglas, Olive Shears, Gordon, Marie Hunt, Brenda ROBERTS and Patricia Hynes Bard.

DE MERITT, DE MERIET, MERRITT, MERHET, MERIT, MERIOTT, DEMRY, etc. In 1607 Richard MERIOTT was a partner in the Great Mill of St. Heliers J. There are so many variants in the spelling of this surname of J that much more research is needed to distinguish the families involved, in early New England. Poss that MERIOTT, DEMERITT and MERIT were interchangeable? MERHET, MERIT, in J 1749 in Grouville Parish, and both names pron. much like MERRY.

DEMERITT, Eli settled in Durham, NH, said to be from J. Mar ca 1695. Eli had town grant in Dover, NH 1694, and the fam in the early 1800s split into three groups. One part to VT, settled in Montpelier-Stow area. A second part went to Maine, settled Liberty then Dover area. The third group stayed in the Dover-Durham area of NH. There is an old DE MERITT home in Madbury, NH near Durham, which was in the fam from the early 1700s to about 1934. It is believed that there is a great deal more information on this fam in the hands of desc. and researchers. (Stearn's NH GENS;,Vol 4; Greenfield's SOMERSETSHIRE MERIET GEN; Stackpole's HIST OF DURHAM, NH; GREELEY GEN; GRANITE MONTHLY #9; DOVER HIST. COLL, Vol 1; Scale's HIST OF DOVER, NH, Vol 1; Rev. John PIke's JOURNAL; NEHGS Vols 25,29,87,6,41,31; RUNNELS, REYNOLDS GEN; JOHN HAYES OF DOVER, by Richmond; CATES FAM OF AMERICA Noyes; Dwight Demeritt, Brooklyn, NY; Mrs. Myron L. De Meritt, Drain OR; Mrs. Wm. E. Williams, Tampa, FLA)

A1. Eli, res Dover, NH 1736-1753, mar by 1723 TAbitha Pitman, and later had a mill in Madbury, d 1774
B1. Capt. Samuel, b 1723 mar Eliz. RANDALL, served in Col. Army, Elizabeth bp 1728, dau of Nathaniel and Mary (Hodgdon) Randall. (Noyes, p. 576)
C1. Major John Demeritt, a soldier in the Col Army, carried powder at battle of Bunker Hill, was b Madbury, NH
D1. Paul, res Madbury, NH mar Betsy DAVIS of Lee, NH. Poss name was Paul David, or David Paul? There was a Paul in Rochester, NH 1790.
E4. the 4th ch said to be Mark, b 1792 Farmington, NH. Unver. data
D2. Davis, b 1786
B2. Ebenezer, b 1726, mar Hannah Thompson. One Eben. res Madbury, 1790 with fam. (Census)
B3. Sarah, b 1736 mar 1764 Daniel MESSERVE, qv.
A2. John, b 1698 mar 1724/5 Margret BUZZELL, qv, 1698-1777
B1. Elizabeth, bp 1727, mar Benj. DREW? qv.
B2. Deborah, bp 1734, mar William DREW?, qv.
B3. Paul, bp 1737
B4. Joseph, bp 1741 mar Susan RENNELS, REYNOLDS, qv. A Joseph res Northwood, NH 1790, with a fam.
B5. John, b 1728 mar Eliz. Cate. Two Johns were in Madbury, NH 1790 with fams. (Census) See CATE, CATES GEN. John d 1826.(DAR #43)
C1. Major? JOhn mar Lois Davis
D1. Davis, b 1786 mar 1805 Abigail, dau of Sol. and Eliz.(Smith) Emerson, rem to Montpelier, VT
E1. Samuel mar Maria Knapp
F1. Olive, mar Ed Everett Sheldon
G1. Winafred Sheldon, b Ft. Atkinson, WI, mar ___CASWELL.
B6. Mary, mar Ebenezer Tasker B7. Sarah, mar Solomon Emerson
A3. Job, b 1705 mar Mary BUZZELL, qv, d 1772
B1. Job, bp 1735 mar Sarah BUZZELL, qv, 4 chn
B2. Eli, bp 1738 mar ___Marshall of Dover, NH, 8 chn
B3. Abigail, bp 1741, unmar

B4. Mary, b 1743 mar Zechariah BOODY, qv, res New Durham, NH 1790, with fam of 1 man, 3 boys and 3 females. (Census) .
B5. Solomon, mar Annie DEMERITT B6. James mar Betsy DEMERITT.
DEMERITT, Abbie J. mar Joseph Porter Batchelder, b 1835, son of Joseph and Hannah (Hill) Batchelder. (BATCHELDER GEN)
A1. Alfred Porter Bachelder, other chn also?
DEMERITT, Ann, mar ___JARVIS, early New England.
DEMERITT, Charles from J? in Boston 1700. (Stackpole) A Charles DEMERY mar Eliz. Eades 1707 Boston, MA.
DEMERRY, Charles and Sarah res Boston, same as Charles above?
A1. Sarah, b 1700 Boston. A2. Samuel b 1702 Boston.
DEMERITT, Daniel mar 1823 Libby?, ME Eliza G. Longfellow. He was son of Capt. Daniel and Sarah (Hays) DEMERITT. Eliza d 1853 Dover, ME, he in 1862. (GREELEY GEN)
A1. Daniel H. b 1824 mar Lucinda Macomber, who d 1860, 4 chn
B1. Augustus Hayes, b 1848 B2. Sarah Eliz., b 1851, d.y.
B3. Henry Lycurgus, b 1854 mar Stephana Sprague, res Minneapolis,MN
B4. Leslie Oscar, b 1858, mar Mary L. Burgess, res Saugerville, ME?
C1. Eva L., b 1882 C2. John L.
A2. Stephen L., b 1825 d 1853 A4. Nathan B. b 1829 d 1853
A3. Eben G. b 1827, d 1858 A5. Charles P., b 1832 d 1857
A6. Jonathan C., b 1835 mar 1876 Mrs. Lizzie B. DEMERITT, widow of his bro Daniel H. Jonathan d 1891. A dau Carrie b 1878.
A7. Sarah A., b 1838 mar Albion K.P. Merrill, res Blue Spgs., NEBR.
A8. Geo. D. b 1840 mar 1879 Louise A. Burgess, d Saugerville, ME 1881.
A9. Susan E., b 1843, d.y. A10. William S., b 1845, d.y.
A11. Edwin M., b 1848 mar 1883 Louise A. DEMERITT, widow of his bro Geo. D., res Dover, ME.
DEMERITT, Deborah, deposed with Eli in 1702, NH. (Noyes)
DEMERITT, Dorcas, mar John Batchelder, b 1793, son of John B., who d Northwood, NH 1812. (BACHELDER GEN)
DE MERRITT, Eliz. Anne, first wife of Albion Samuel CLEMENT. She was b 1856 Ossippee, NH, dau of James M. and Albina C. DEMERITT. Albion mar 2. after 1891 Edith E. Daniels. 2 chn by DEMERITT. (CLEMENT GEN)
A1. Merton Wallace Clement, b 1879 Palmyra, ME
A2. Albina Melinda b 1891 Dorchester, MA mar 1917 Frank Augustus Wright
B1. Marcellus Morton Wright, b 1918 Worcester, MA.
DEMERIT, George mar Hannah MOLEY, prob MOLLET, qv, 1749 Boston, MA
DE MERRY, Hannah mar John Hill 1756 Boston, MA
DEMERITT, Hannah mar Wm. Batchelder, b 1770s? son of John, b 1741 and Sarah (Murray) Batchelder. John d 1809. Wm. res Nottingham, NH had 7 chn. (BATCHELDER GEN)
DEMERITT, Israel, res Durham, NH 1790 with son and 6 females. (Census)
DEMERITT, John W. mar Mary Bacon, b 1801, dau of Silas and Molly (Draper) Bacon. (BACON GEN, Michael of Dedham)
DEMERITT, J.H., served in the Navy 1815-1817, and was a paymaster 1863. (Callahan List)
DEMERITT, John b 1811 Ossipee, NH, son of David? and Betsey, both b New Durham, NH. John mar Sara S. Ireland, dau of John and Mercy (Carlton) Ireland, d 1879 Boston. John d 1886 New Canaan, CT, bur Jamaica Plain, MA. John was Pres. of Eliot Nat. Bank. (Louise Williams, Tampa, FLA)
A1. Louise Demeritt, mar Paul Sauve, res New Orleans, LA and Jefferson Par., LA. A dau, had a dau SAra Louise Sauve, mar Wm. Williams.
DEMERIT, John mar DEborah MESERVE, dau of Ebenezer and Eunice (Tarr) MESSERVE. Deborah b prob in 1770s. (MESSERVE GEN)

DEMERY, John and Sarah res Boston, prob a DE MERIT of J, or desc.
A1. John, b 1710, d.y.? A3. Sarah, b 1713, d.y.? A5. Sarah, b 1721
A2. John again, b 1712 A4. Charles, b 1716
DEMERIT, Sarah mar Daniel MESERVE, b 1734, son of Daniel and Abigail
A1. Thomas Meserve, b 1769, no issue
A2. Daniel Meserve, b 1777, mar Sarah PENDEXTER, qv.
A3. Lydia Meserve, b 1767, no issue A4. Betty Meserve, 1771-1857
A5. Mary Meserve, b 1775, mar 1. John Ham and 2. Paul Gerrish.
DEMERY, Thomas and Hannah res Boston, chn: Hannah b 1715, & Charles.
DE MERRY, Thomas in MD before 1665. OUTC. (Skordas)
DE MERRY, Thomas of Boston mar Abi Richardson of Woburn 1736. OUTC
DE MERRY, William mar Abigail Pitman early NH. (Noyes)
DEMERITT noted in OH 1860 census. See also Virkus Vol 3.
Many DEMERITTS in 1790 census in NH, and also in MA.
DE MOUILPIED, old in J and G. In G 1300s. Curr G and J. In St. Andrews G 1627.
DE MOUILPIED, Nicholas b 1819 G, rem to Mt. Pleasant, WIS 1840s. Mar Ann Hosmer 1848. He d 1875 age 56. (RACINE HIST)
A1. Eliza A2. Mary. A3. Martin A4. Thomas A5. Laura A6. John.
DE MOUILPIED noted in Ohio 1860 census.
DE MOUNT noted in Boston 1729, 1837. DU MONT in J 1168-1528, and DES MONTS in J 1668.
DEMOUNT, John from J? mar Dorcas Mason 1729 Boston. See also LE MONTAIS, and LE MONTES.
DEMOUNT, John mar Rebekah SAMPSON 1738 Boston. OUTC.
DENNIS in J 1254 as DIONIS, DENNYS, DENISE. In G 1300s, later in St. Saviour G. DENNIS in London, Eng. 1717 (Bardsley) See Boston and MRB VRS. Many of this name
DENNISE, Eliz. of Boston mar there Gamaliel CLARK 1710 Boston. OUTC
DENNIS, DENNISE, DENNIZE, Ebenezer and Damaris res Boston. He mar 2.? Susanna ___? OUTC. 6 chn: Damaris, b 1701 Boston, stillborn in 1707, Susanna, 1708, Mary, 1710, Ebenezer 1713, & Michaėl 1715.OUTC.
DE PUTRON in G 1331, noted in 1770 and curr. See QUARTERLY REVIEW OF THE GUERNSEY SOCIETY, Winter, 1958. Americans of this surname are prob desc of Jean, who had 2 sons: Daniel, 1795-1865 and Jacob. CAUTION: TRIAL CHARTS. There may be more info. in NEBR. & IOWA. Some confusion of names in this chart, as first names were repeated.
DE PUTRON, Daniel b 1795 G or 1789?, son of Jean and RAchel (TARDIF) DE PUTRON. Mar 1822 in St. Peter Port G, Anne CARRE, dau of Thomas. This is sometimes written CORRE in US. Anne b 1799, d 1872. Daniel was a Methodist, settled first in ?, then rem to Cleveland, OH and later went to Pittsburgh, PA, where he was employed as a Chamberts glass mixer in a glass factory. Daniel traveled to OH with a 'Bell team', 10 or 12 horses pulling long wagons. He left the glass factory, rem to Sewickley, PA, and bought the Fleming estate there, was well-to-do and sent money home to his fam in G. "Finest man that walked Sewickley Valley" said Judge White. Ann d age 73 in Wheeling, WVA. Daniel d age 70 in Effingham, ILL. (Thomas B. Gotham, Akron,OH; George Thompson, Hollywood, CAL).
A1. Ann Carre, b 1824 G d 1896 PA. Mar Hugh Linn 1839. (OH GEN. SOC. REPORT, Vol 12, #1) Hugh b 1813 d 1895, son of Robert and Rebecca (Lytle) Linn.
B1. William Marcus Linn, b 1856 d 1911 mar 1879 Mary V. Gibb,1861-1936
C1. Anne De Putron Linn, b 1881 d 1913 PA, mar Thomas Barry Gotham Sr. 1875-1941.
D1. Thomas Barry Gotham Jr., b 1901 mar June Viola Hardesty.
B2. Mary M. Linn B3. Daniel D. Linn, mar Virginia Beisinger?

A2. John Carre, b ?, of Sewickley, PA d Lincoln, ILL 1908.
B1. Daniel E. B2. Ray L. B3. Mary M. Desc in Effingham, ILL.
Other desc of above fam may be Eunice O'Riley, Louise Bailey, Thomas, Wilson, George and Fanny McLelland.

DE PUTRON, John, b 1797 G, d 1863, bur Union burial grounds, Phila. PA. Came to Phila. in 1834, was shoe merchant on Market St., Phila. He was prob the son of Jean and Rachel above, and bro of Daniel, but not proved. John mar 1. Sophia BOULANGER or BAKER, 1800-1859, and 2. Julia Anne CARRE?, who d 1912. No issue by 2nd wife.
A1. William d 1906, had 12 chn of whom 6 d.y., res Phila. PA. Chn: Edward, Alexander, Charles, Joseph, J. Fred, and Frank, b 1881
A2. Jacob Coleman, b 1843 d 1925, attny. at Wash. DC mar Mary Elizabeth Sherwood, 1848-1923. Jacob was Commonwealth Attny for Fairfax Co, VA 1868-1870. 6 chn.
B1. Eustace Coleman, b 1868
B2. Louis Sherwood, 1871-1914
B3. Edith Sophia b 1874
B4. Lillian C., b 1877 mar Leonard P. Daniel, b Falls Church,VA, res Sherwood and E. Falls Ch.
C5. Maurice Bentley, b 1879
C6. Marianne Beatrice, b 1883, mar ___ Carlston?, res St. Louis, MO.
A3. Claire R. Muckleston, 4 chn: Charles H., Wm. H. Louise H. and Sarah Muckleston.
A4. Sophia Wade, 2 chn: George Wade, fire chief of Camden, NJ & Frank.
A5. Mary Louise Erven, 4 chn: Mary H., Edna, Samuel R. and John Erven.

DE PUTRON, Catherine, b G, mar Walter King and res OH. (Mrs. Herivel, Cleveland, OH)
A1. Melvin, b ca 1895 res Richmond, VA
B1. Rita King Wylee, 2 sons
A2. Walter King, res Berea, OH, 2 chn
A3. Herbert King, res Kansas City, no issue.
A4. Gertrude, mar Walter Penrod, no issue
A5. Frances, mar Arnold Sauer of Standard Oil,several chn, inc. twins.

DE PUTRON, Mary b 1824, youngest dau of John and wife Ann CARRE/CORRE. Mary mar in Pittsburgh, PA Samuel Wilson Little, b 1818 Old Harmony, PA. He learned his trade of glassblowing in Pittsburgh, spent some time in Keene, NH, was a steam boater on Ohio and Miss. rivers, sold merchandise from a ship on the rivers for some years. They res Wheeling, Cincinnati, Greencastle, IND, Effingham, ILL, Catlettsburg KY, and in CAL. Settled in Lincoln, NEB 1871 where he was a partner in several businesses, such as milling, land and bldg. operations. He was Mayor of Lincoln, NEB 1874. He was also in business with J.C. de Putron. (Geo. Thompson, Hollywood, CAL)
A1. Wilson De Putron Little, b 1846, d.y. in Wheeling, WVA.
A2. Ann Frances Little, b 1848 d 1932 Los Angeles. Mar 1867 Elijah Curson of Clarksburg, WVA, b 1845, d 1902. Cursons res Whittier CAL in 1916.
B1. Samuel T. Curson, mar Josephine ___, no issue
B2. Albert E. Curson, mar Cora ___, 2 sons, other chn?
A3. Mary Mazena Little, b 1850 Greencastle, IND mar 1869 Dr. Wesley Thompson, b 1844? ILL, who d in CAL 1917. 6 chn.
B1. Mary K. Thompson, mar ___Knapp B2. Victor L. Thompson, mar Nettie?
B3. Anna R. Thompson, b 1881 mar ___Harris of Laskey Films, d 1972
B4. Jennie R. Thompson, b 1882, mar Fredrick Spencer, attny.
B5. Ada F. Thompson, b 1885, mar Dolson Held?, dau Edith Held, b 1913
B6. Emma J. Thompson
A4. Virginia Little, b 1852 d.y.
A5. Samuel Miller Little, b 1854 Clarksburg, KY,mar Delfena Osborn 1880 in Lincoln, NEBR.
B1. Samuel Wilson Little, had dau Dona Dewey Little.

A6. Emma Jane Little, b 1859 d 1890 Los Angeles, CAL. Mar Dr. Nathan Hay West 1888.
B1. Mary De Putron West, b 1889 Homestead, PA mar Perry Ferguson,
C1. Louis Perry Ferguson, 1908-1922.
A7. Lulu May, b 1866 Effingham, ILL d 1944 Los Angeles, CAL. Mar 1893 Charles Henry Shaffner in Los Angeles, and 2. in 1965 Geo. E. Thompson, b 1877 from Mt. Pleasant, IA, d Santa Monica, CAL. Charles had mar 1. F. Probasco, 2 chn.
B1. Samuel Wilson Little Shaffner, b 1894 mar Dora? Campbell,CAL,1918
C1. Donald Campbell Shaffner, b 1920, res Pasadena, CAL
B2. George E. Thompson Jr, b 1907 Venice, CAL.
DE PUTRON, curr Austin, TX. OUTC
DE PUTRON, Richard C. and Walter C. are in NYTimes of 1969.
DE PUTRON. Another Daniel came to America from G, prob related to above fam.
DE PUTRON, Dan, had bro John, res G early 1800s. DATA UNVERIFIED.
A1. Daniel John, mar ___, had several chn.
B1. Daniel, no issue B2. Rosa, no issue
B3. Ada, mar ---Taylor, had 5 boys and 5 girls
B4. Estelle Luscombe, had dau Phedora
B5. Edwin Norton, of La Fontaine, Clifton, G, 3 chn: Irene, Dorothy and Edwin.
B6. Emeline DE LA RUE, had dau Rose DE LA RUE, prob res G?
A2. Peter, had at least 2 chn, Peter and Martha
A3. poss a Mary LE LIEVRE, who had 5 chn.
DE PUTRIN, Marilla of Ware, MA mar Joseph Peel, Andover, MA (int) 1843
DE RIVOIRE, see REVERE
DE RUE, see DE LA RUE and DREW.
DE RUE, Lucas and wife Jane AUBIN res St. Saviour J 1700. See DREW
DE RUE, Betsy mar Joseph Ruggles 1775 Boston, MA
DE RUE, George mar Mary RUSSEL 1747 Boston, MA. A dau Mary b 1748 Boston, may have been the Mary ROUSSEL, relative of John D'Lisle ROUSSEL, who d 1729 Ipswich, MA. Mary and George were mar by Rev. Andrew LE MERCIER, Hug. (George Russell, Middletown, MD)
DE RUE, Mary mar John Minot 1771 Boston, MA. OUTC
DE RUE, Mary mar James SHEPARD 1763 Boston, as Mary DREW.
DE SAUSMAREZ. There are two branches of this old and noted family of G. One of St. Martin, Sausmarez Manor, and the other of Catel, G. The latter branch spells name without middle 's', res Saumarez Park. Several fams in America, but none found by compiler.
DE SHEAY, Janet. While not totally relevant, this item was in the records of St. Botolph, Aldgate, London, England. "Didyer, Didier, Michael, born Marseilles in Provence, a pilot under Mr. Cavendish in his voyages to the South Endyes, mar 1588 Janet Desheay, a maiden born in Jersey."
DESBOROUGH has occurred in C.I.
DES BROSS, James mar Mary Ann GUIONOW, prob GUIGNION?, qv, of C.I. in MA 1700s. OUTC.
DESBOROW, Mary was in MD 1600s. (Skordas, p. 132) OUTC
DISBROW, Samuel mar Ann Sutphen. OUTC. (SECOND BOAT, Feb. 1981)
A1. Mary DISBROW, b1789 mar 1808 Christopher Bergen of Cranbury NeckNJ.
DISBOR, etc. noted in Stillwells MISC. IV. OUTC.
DISBEROE, Isaak in court records, Salem, MA 1638. (Essex Coll, Vol 8)
DISBROW, Lydia, mar Henry Beach LYON, b 1816, son of Peter Starr's dau Lucy and Phil LYON. OUTC.
DESCHAMPS, Thomas arrived in Shelburne, NS 1783, from C.I.? mar Hannah SYMONDS, qv. OUTC. A son mar Polly Ames of Boston.

DES CHAMPS, Arthur and a bro? rem to US from the C.I. 1900s?
DES LANDES in St. Laurens J 1788. In St. John J 1668, in St. Heliers and St. John J 1749. In J by 1309, and also in G very early. See CIFHS #3.
DES LANDES, Geo. builder of over 100 ships in J in the early 1800s.
DES LANDES, some to Canada from C.I. See Q.A. IN CANADA, by Turk
DES LANDES, Capt of the barque ROYAL SOVEREIGN from Cardiff, Wales to San Francisco, CAL 1851. During the passage, William Williams of Martha, Wales; John Melley of France, and Philip BAKER of J died. Peter LE MAISTRE was also a passenger. (Rasmussen)
DESLAND, Mrs. Maud (Blair) res Granby, QUE, 1900s. Some early settlers from the C.I. were in Drummondville, QUE. See HERIOT in Q.A.IN CANADA
DESLANDES is sometimes written DELON, DALON.
DESPERQUES, curr G.
DESPERQUES, Myra, b 1900 G, dau of Edwin James, a postman, b 1856 England and Ellen Goman, b 1861 Alderney. Myra came to MI, mar 1. Thomas Pate, and 2. Glen Dotson. (Cathleen Hollingshead, Battle Creek MI) This fam related to the OZANNE fam of G.
A1. Kenneth Dotson, b 1930 Detroit, MI mar Joanna Frances Kiraly, b 1931 Detroit, dau of Joseph and Anna (Kratz) Kiraly. 4 chn
B1. Eric Robert Dotson, b 1949
B2. Lee Ann Dotson, b 1950
B3. Cathleen Dotson, b 1952 Highland Park, MI.
B4. Craig Wm. Dotson, b 1956 Royal Oak, MI.
DESPERQUES, Edwin, bro of Myra above, b G, d ca 1945. Others in G fam were Ellen, Grace and Stephen.
DESPRES, a fam from C.I. to Canada, possibly to Gaspe.? Christine D. Despres mar Elias DUMARESQ 1857 in Fox River, Gaspe. This surname noted in Alpena, MI ca 1905, where a number of Gaspe/CI fams settled.
DE STE. CROIX, see SINECROSS. Research in C.I.? See CIFHS #3.
DE STE. CROIX, in J from 1528, poss Hug. However, there were prob more than one group of this surname that came from France to J in the 1600s and 1700s. Moyse DE STE. CROIX was in New Rochelle, NY from France 1751, res a period of time in J? His wife was Marie GAURE, prob b France. Their son was b J. There were ten heads of fams with this name in J by 1607, mostly in St. Clement, St. Helier and St. Laurens parishes, Jersey. Some DE STE. CROIX fams to Canada. See Q.A. IN CANADA, by Turk. DE STE. CROIX in St. Lawrence J 1788. Aaron DE STE. CROIX in St. Clement J 1809.
DE STE. CROIX, Joshua Temple, b 1734 J, of Hug fam. Was in NYcity before 1783 mar 1759 Leah Gallaudet. Joshua d 1803 Bridgetown, Annapolis, N.S., Canada. See sources for more info. (Q.A. IN CANADA; Noes; CALNEK; Savary; Trudy Mann, Mississauga, ONT; Syvret; Morse; Gilroy ; Noyes; HIST. OF ANNAPOLIS CO., NS)
DE STE. CROIX, Capt. Andrew, a privateersman in J 1709.
DE STE. CROIX, Ann, apprenticed servant who came from J 1772 to Isaac LObdell of Phila., term 7 yrs., pay-17 pounds. (RECORD OF INDENTURES, by Gibson and Fisher)
DE STE. CROIX, Benjamin, druggist in NY 1829, alien. (Scott and Conway)
DE STE. CROIX, Nicholas France from C.I. to Gaspe ca 1888 to work as apprentice for Wm. Fruing & Co. at Pte. Alexandre-LE GOULET, later a manager at Caraquet, NB. (Blanche De Ste. Croix, Montreal, QUE)
DE STE. CROIX, Philippe, at Bellows Falls, VT late 1800s, uncle of Nicholas above.
DE STE. CROIX, Philip, servant, arrived in Boston 1769 on ship MOLLY from J. (Whitmore)
DE STE. CROIX, William, age 26, b J, son of Alan and Agnes Louise DE STE. CROIX mar 1860 in Toronto ONT, Ellison Kerr, age 21.(CH record)

DE STE. CROIX, A. of J owned a brigantine THOMAS AND JANE, 60 tons, which operated in 1740 between Jersey and Maryland. Capt. Carteret DEAN was master and part owner. The cargo went to John Clark in River St. Mary, Potomac, MD, the return cargo being tobacco. (A. John Jean, Jersey)

DE STE. CROIX, Thomas DUMARESQ, and his bro John prob settled in New Brunswick or Gaspe Canada in early 1800s from C.I. Thomas mar Mary FAIRSERVICE (BECHERVAISE?) She was b 1854, d 1945. (Mrs. L.A. McLellan, Moncton, NB)

A1. James, b 1876 d 1965 mar ? A6. Austin, 1887-1968, mar ?
A2. Lillian, b 1878 d 1969, mar John Campbell, dau Sybil Campbell
A3. Howard, 1879-1967 mar ? A7. Mabel McGee, 1889-1926
A4. Robena b 1882 d 1969, mar Cleveland MAJOR, qv.
A5. Alice, b 1884, d 1957 mar Weston Howatson. A8. Wilson, 1894-1970
A9. John Evelyn, b 1898 d 1967 mar Reida BRIARD 1941, no issue.

DE ST. JEOR, not found in C.I. However, St. GEORGE in J by 1149. DE ST. GEORGES in G early.

DE ST. JEOR, Francis F., b J, with wife Elizabeth Jena or Jones rem to UT 1855, ship CHIMBORAZO. Poss other chn b J or UT. Note that St. JORE, DE ST. JORE is mentioned in CIFHS #12. Much more data in UT.

A1. Eliza?
A2. Francis John, b 1846 J, d 1908 Clover, UT, mar Inger Larsen, b 1843 Denmark, d 1937 Ogden, UT, dau of Lars and Caroline Larsen.
B1. Ephraim Francis, b 1874 UT mar 1901 Salina GREEN
B2. ARchie John, b 1876 d 1935, mar 1908 Susan Jane GREEN
B3. Caroline Eliz., b 1879 mar 1921 Peter Kranenburg
B4. Walter Christopher, b 1882 d 1945 mar 1910 Annie GREEN
B5. Josephine, b 1885 mar 1906 David Moroni GREEN
B6. Selina Mary, b 1888 mar 1910 Ernest Edward Ahlstrom
B7. Ada, b 1893, d 1917, unmar?
A3. Louisa
A4. Ephraim, b 1857 Clover, UT, d 1934 Provo, UT, mar 1875 Mary Garner, b 1855 Kensworth, england. Mary d 1927
B1. William Ephraim, b 1875 UT d 1937, mar Marie E. Olson
B2. Mary, 1877-1891
B3. Sarah Emma, b 1880 d 1951 mar 1900 David Cook Strasburg
B4. Elizabeth, b 1882 d 1925, mar 1902 Lester N. Thompson
B5. Teresa May, b 1884 d 1947 mar 1901 Amos Davis
B6. Newel Hansen, b 1886 d 1946, mar 1911 Hannah Laurinda Peterson
B7. Wallace, 1888-1905 B8. Albertb 1890?
B9. Della Lucy, b 1892 mar 1914 Charles W. BERRY
B10. Afton Francis, b 1895 mar 1916 1. Vera Peck, & 2. Helen ___.

DEVEREUX. While several items in various places connect Devereux and the Channel Islands, there seems to be no definited connection, except through marriages to Channel Islanders in New England. The line below is included because of the BIBBER fam, qv. See DEVEREUX sources: HIST. OF SALEM: BLETHEN GEN: ANTHONY MORSE GEN: MUNSEY HOPKINS GEN: JOHNSON GEN by Rev. Chas. N. Sennett; NEWELL GEN, by Emery; MRB VR; GORHAM ME. HIST by McLellan; BIBBER GEN,by Sinnett; JOHNSON GEN, by Sinnett.

DEVEREUX, John b ca 1614 was in MRB 1630, poss from France by way of Ireland, a fisherman. Mar Ann ___. See BIBBER. (Ann Alexander, Cuddy's Harbour, ME)

A1. Hannah Devereax mar Peter Greenfield of MRB
B1. Hannah Greenfield mar 1688 Wm. Pote, b ca 1640 MRB.
C1. Capt. Wm. Pote, mar 1715 Dorothy Getchel of MRB
D1. Capt. Greenfield Pote, mar 1758 Jane Grant of Freeport, ME.

E1. Dorothy Pote, prob dau of Capt. Pote, mar 1805 Bailey BIBBER of Harpswell, ME.

F1. Wm. Pote Bibber, mar 3rd, 1856 Mary O. Preble of Haskells Is.

G1. Gustina O. Bibber, b 1858 d 1911, mar 1875 Elisha C. Johnson, b 1847, of Bailey Is., ME.

H1. Florence Johnson, b 1889 d 1975, mar Herbert W. Doughty of Bailey Is., b 1887, d 1974

I1. Elroy F. Doughty, b 1921 mar 1941 Jean Ann Annen of B.Is.

J1. Ann E. Doughty, b 1944 mar 1963 Bernard W. Alexander, b 1944 of Cundy's Harb., ME.

K1. Mary E. Alexander, b 1970 D2. Sarah L. Alexander, b 1973

DEVEREUX, John, b ca 1627? d ca 1695, res MRB 1637 and Lynn, MA 1659. Connected with the HIBBERT, HUBERT fam. OUTC. (Virkus 2 and 4)

DE VEULLE, Henry, age 33 from J was in Paspebiac, QUE 1881, agent for a fishery firm with Abel BRADFORD, 37, cook, Thomas LE CRAS, qv, and Francis LE CORNU, qv, clerks. (Aldo Brochet, Montreal, QUE)

DE VOUGE, from Paris, France in early 1800s to either Gaspe directly or by way of the C.I. "My grandfather Peter De Vouge and grandmother Jane Frances Boulier...settled at Pt. St. Peter and my father James lived with them...I am Lima, his dau" Mrs. Adolphus Le Gresley, Verdun, QUE) See also Q.A. IN CANADA. This fam included because of the many marriages with C.I. fams. in QUE. (BOULIER poss BOULET at times?)

A1. James, mar Martha Jane GIRARD. James b middle 1800s?

B1. Alfred and B2. Mary, d.y. B5. Bertha mar Elias Buckley

B3. Emma, mar Clarence McCullam B6. Winnifred mar Hedley HOTTON

B4. Anorah, mar Wm. SYVRET B7. Gladys mar James LUCAS

B8. Horace mar Florence LE PAGE, had sons Cecil, Melvin, Boyd, Alva and Austin.

B9. Raymond mar Edith GIRARD, had 2 sons, Laurence and Rodney

B10. Lima mar Adolphus LE GRESLEY, res Verdun, QUE has chn in Bougainville, Gaspe, Prescott, ONT and Montreal, QUE.

DE VOUGE, Thomas, Francis and James also res Gaspe 1800s.

DE VOUGE, Emiline Myra, 1897-1943, dau of George DE VOUGES and Alvina INGERVILLE, INGROUVILLE, qv, res Gaspe. She mar Wm. Herbert LE GRESLEY, qv. (Edith McKitterick, Pte. aux Trembles, QUE)

DEWS. "In Memory of Thomas Dews Jr., b St. Peter Port G, 1808, d 1838 age 30 yrs., 2 mos and 25 days." (Gravestone in Rutherfordton, NC)

DILLEY, fam in OH said to be desc from a Hug fam that settled in J, then rem to England and later to America. Poss connecting relationship to the OH Dilleys through Hannah Perry Dilley, relative of Commodore Perry. (Sarchet; DAB)

DISPOSE, Jennet, "Jerseywoman and child" in Portsmouth, NH 1676. Cf DESPRES, qv, and DESBOROUGH, qv. OUTC. (Noyes; Smiles)

DISPAW, Henry, from J in Lynn, MA d 1676. (Savage) Cf also DESPART?

DOBREE, curr research, see CIFHS #9.

DOLBEL in J 1299. In St. Saviour, St. Mary, Grouville, St. John and ST. Martin J 1668, and in St. Heliers, St. Saviour, St. John and St. Martin J 1749.

DOLBEL, Philip, b 1796 G, d 1882 UT? He was son of Jean and Esther (GRUCHY) DOLBEL of J. He mar 1823 Susan ESNOUF, b J, bp 1800, dau of Thomas ESNOUF and Ann QUEREE. Philip rem mid1800s to UT? See more in SLCity records.

A1. Philippe, bp 1824 St. John J, d 1825 A7. Marie Dolbel,1836-1848

A2. Philippe, bp 1825 J A8. Richard, bp 1838 J d 1854

A3. Charles, bp 1828 and Susanne, bp 1831, d.y.

A5. Jean, John, bp 1832 J A9. Jane, bp 1841 J

A6. Eliza A., b 1834 J d 1908, mar 1856 Christopher L.Riding, of UT.

DOLBE, Edward, shoemaker, Portsmouth, NH, drowned 1701. (Noyes) OUTC
DOLBEL, Joshua arrived from Nfld. on schooner NANCY 1763 in Boston, Capt. John PELE, LE PELLEY? (Whitmore) Both poss from J fams.
DOLBE, Nicholas in ME before 1700, mar in Hampton Falls, NH 1713 Sarah SMITH, qv. Desc in HIST. OF RYE, NH, pp 333/4 (Noyes) See also Dow's HAMPTON, Vol 2, p. 675. OUTC
DOLBE, Rachel mar Lawrence AMY, qv, in Kittery, ME ca 1724. OUTC
DOBEL, DOBLE, DOLBEL?, Thomas mar Mrs. Abigail Jones 1789 in MRB, mar 1775 Hannah Hye, and a Lucy Sargent in 1783. More than one Thomas?
DOBELL, DUBELE, DOLBEL?, Henry, to VA from London on the ABRAHAM 1635, age 20. See Boston TRANSCRIPT, Dec. 1930.
DOLBEL, Susan and Elizabeth/Eliza? of the large fam above? rem from J to UT 1855, via ship CHIMBORAZO.
DOMAILLE in Vale G 1821. See CIFHS #14.
DOUBLARD, DOUBLE and DOUBLEL in J, latter in 1331-1528. See also DOLBEL above. DOUBLARD is curr in G.
DOREY in St. Saviour and St. Helier J 1668, and in St. Helier 1749. Means golden-haired, or is short for Theodore. Name in Torteval G 1783, and earlier. Curr G and J.
DOREY, see Q.A. IN CANADA NEW DATA IN CH.IS. COLLECTION!
DOREY, John, b 1801 Alderney rem to US where he d after 1885, place unknown. Mar Harriet Winsey, b 1803 G. To US late 1850/51, settled Bridgeport, CT. (Winifred Dunham, Woodburn, OR)
A1. Harriet Louise, b 1823 G, to US late 1850s?
A2. Addie, later res Atlantic, IA, mar ___Woodward.
A3. Johanna, b 1828 J, d 1918 Albany, OR. She mar Capt. Wm. DOREY, a relative, who was lost at sea, had son William. She mar 2. 1855 Bridgeport, CT William LEIGH, b England, d 1891 Shelby, IA.
B1. William DOREY B6. Alfred Leigh, b 1865, d 1932 CAL.
B2. Thomas Dorey Leigh, b 1857 Lone Tree, IA, d 1932 Albany, OR
B3. Jestina Leigh, b 1859, d IA B7. Ada Eliza Leigh, 1866-1931, OR
B4. Drolinda Leigh, b 1861 d 1864 B8. Drucilla Leigh, 1867-1869,IA
B5. Herbert Leigh, b 1863 d 1864
DOREY, fam in MI and OH from C.I.? (Census 1860, Butler, Cuy., Hardin and Hamilton Counties)
DOREY, ___, mar Rita TOSTEVIN, qv. San Leandro, CAL
DOREY, Alice, wife of ___TAYLER, qv, age 87 in 1966. See TAYLER.
DORE, DOREY, Joanna, widow of David Cane, mar John BOURNE of Portsmouth NH. Widowed again, Joanna was paid by town of Portsmouth for keeping Roger ANDROS. Had 5 chn bp 1715. She mar 3? 1716/7 Stephen Knowles, Nole, from Lahant, Cornwall, England. (Noyes) OUTC. Ch by Knowles??
A1. ch by Cane? A3. Benj. Bourne A4. Wm. Bourne A5. Eliz. Bourne
A2. Mary Bourne, mar 1715 John Gardner from Glouc. England. She d 1788
DOREY, Philip, b 1799 J, d 1863 Arichat, NS, Canada. Mar 1829 Margaret Leete, b 1809, in Ireland? (Leander Dorey, Huntington Beach, CAL) This surname spelled DORÉ on cem. stone.
A1. George Wingate, bp 1831 Arichat, NS
A2. Caroline Ann DOREY, b 1836 Guysborough, NS, d 1900. Mar 1861 Michael BRYNE, 1828-1885.
B1. Andrew Willis Bryne, b 1862 Truro, MA mar Annie BARRETT
B2. Thomas Howard Bryne, b 1863 d 1951
B3. Willard Beecher Bryne, b 1866 d 1941, mar Catherine HILLIARD and 2. Emma Edwards.
B4. Etta Dora Bryne, b 1867 Truro, MA, d 1868.
B5. George Milton Bryne, b 1869 Truro mar Blanche Louise Bruce
B6. Edward Bonner Bryne, b 1871, d.y.
B7. James Lewellen Bryne, b 1873 d 1952, mar Ella Whidden

B8. Estella Dora Bryne, b 1875 d 1958 Boston, MA, mar Daniel A.DOREY, see fam below under A6.
B9. John Dorey Bryne, b 1877 Wellfleet, MA d 1905.
B10. Louise W. Bryne, b 1879 d 1884
A3. Julia T. A4. Louise B5. Elizabeth, b 1843
A6. John James, b 1845 mar Celia Barrett, b 1852. Other chn?
B1. Daniel Aloysius, b 1874 mar 1896 Estella Dora Bryne, 1875-1958, see above, B8.
C1. Hazel Miriam, b 1897 d 1979 C2. Evelyn Hamilton, b 1899 d 1900
C3. Ruth Caroline, b 1900 d 1920
C4. Daniel Dorey, b 1902 d 1978, mar Gladys F. Hajos, 1908-1967
D1. Peter Malcolm, b 1934 D2. Caroline L., b 1936 d ca 1941
D3. David Conrad, b 1938 mar Ellen Tarr Lassard.
E1. David Daniel Lassard Dorey
D4. Stephen Willard, b 1942
C5. Leander Elmore, b 1908 mar 1942 Marion Gray Clirehugh, b 1921
D1. Susan Jane, b 1944 mar 1. James Leland Codding Jr, 1963 and 2. in 1974 Steven Dillon. Dau Yvonne C. Codding b 1965
D2. Martha Louise, b 1947, mar 1975 Paul J. Bakonyi
C6. Marion Cecelia, b 1910 mar 1924 Harold A. Carlsen, 1905-1968
C7. Estella Elizabeth b 1913 mar Claude William Stuck, a son David Neil Dorey Stuck b 1951.
A7. Andre, b 1848 d.y. A8. Henriette, b 1848? A9. Cyrus, 1853-1913
DORE, DOREY?, Philip, from J? of Portsmouth, NH, in Exeter 1715, in Newington, NH 1717, and in 1735 Philip of Dover, NH gave land to Philip Jr. in Rochester. Res Dover 1743, mar 1708 Sarah Child, his widow of Lebanon in 1761. Of chn below, only Wm. and Sarah are his with certainty. Was Philip related to Joanna above? (Noyes)
A1. William, res Rochester, NH 1737. A Wm. Dore of Cocheco mar 1740 Mary Wallingford of Newington, d 1785 age 78. Widow Dore d 1799 Dover, ME.
A2. Sarah, mar 1730 Richard Child
A3.? Philip bp 1730 mar Lydia ___, 6 chn bp Rochester, 1755, otherchn?
A4.? Henry, res Rochester, with wife Mary 1761, chn.
A5.? Elizabeth A7.? John, bp 1730
A6.? Frances, bp with Henry and Eliz. 1727 Newington, mar Abijah Stevens, d 1804.
DORE, Richard, related to above fam. (Noyes)
DORELL, DORILL, DORRILL, etc. noted in records of MD 1600s. (Skordas) Also in Christchurch, SC 1765, poss variant of DURELL? OUTC.
DOWNER, surname of England and J. See Donald LUCE
DOWNS, DOWNES in J, the latter in 1607. Many in New England early,OUTC
DOWNING, sometimes in C.I. John and Richard in NH 1721. OUTC
DREW, Francis, b ca 1700 J, son of Lucas DE RUE and Jane AUBIN of St. Saviour J. Note that his correct name was DE RUE, changed to DREW in New England. CAUTION: there were many other Drew fams in early New England, not from C.I. Compiler did not find a Francis DREW genealogy. Francis may have arrived from J 1715 in Boston, ship MARY of J. (Whitmore) He mar 1726/7 Sarah HUCKINS, poss HOQUIN? His will proved 1746 in Portsmouth, NH, 9 chn. See also DE RUE. (NH State papers; Bolton; Underhill; Noyes; NEHGS Vols 81,82)
A1. Agnis, bp 1728, d.y.? A3. Sarah, bp 1731 A5. Hannah, bp 1735
A2. Jane, bp 1730 A4. James, bp 1733 A6. Mary, bp 1738/9
A7. Ann, bp 1741 mar 1761 Henry SEAWARD, SEWARD, qv, who d 1785 age 48
A8. Agnis again, bp 1744 A9. a ch, bp 1745, poss Dennis?
DREW. 34 interments of DREWS in Pine Grove Cem, Barrington, NH, OUTC. (John Caverly, Cape Haze, Placida, FLA)

DREW, many in Noyes, see, also in BICKNELL GEN: Underhill; NEHGS V.24; MORRILL GEN; and many town histories of ME and NH.

DREW. At least 45 men of this surname in NH 1790, heads of fams, res Durham, Middleton, Barrington, Madbury, Dover, Ossipee, Gilmanton. A Clement res Loudon, a Joshua in Nottingham, NH, from C.I.?

DREW, Benj. mar Eliz. DEMERITT, QV, bp 1727 Madbury, NH

DREW, William mar Deborah DEMERITT, bp 1734 Madbury, NH

DREW, Charles of St. Saviour J mar Mary Montgomery, NH 1738. (Jean A. Sargent, Laurel, MD; NEHGS Vol 26)

DREW. The class of 1957 of Oakfield, ME High School published a two volume Hist. of the town as a combination English and typing project. A Carolyn Drew gathered some Drew History, but OUTC. Much data is not dated. (Hilda Clough Lincoln, Gainesville, MO)

DREW, William, b 1627 in C.I.? d ca 1669, mar ca 1650 Eliz. MATTHEWS, b 1623. OUTC. See DEVEREUX. (Ann Alexander, Brunswick, ME)

A1. Sargent John Drew, b ca 1651, d 1723 Dover, ME,mar 1720 Rebecca Cook. Harpswell, ME

B1. Abigail, mar James BIBBER, prob VIBERT, qv, b 1706 J, d 1773 7

C1. Abigail Bibber, b 1727/1737? d 1813, mar 1752 Jacob Johnson of Bailey Island, ME. See DEVEREUX, AND BIBBER.

DREW, William, in Oyster River NH 1648-1669. Spelled name DRUE at times, poss from C.I. as DE RUE? Poss son of Wm. above?

DUBOIS, DU BOIS in St. Laurens and St. Heliers J 1668, and in Grouville, J 1749. Many DU BOIS in America, but none traced by compiler. Note that DU BOIS sometimes equals Wood and Forest.

DUBRAS. Old in J. (Stevens) See ARMES, ARMS.

DUBRAS, Maurice of St. Heliers J, res Cambridge, ONT with wife Anne English, 3 sons. To Canada ca 1965. (Elaine Hall, Toronto, ONT)

DUCEE, DUCIE, DUSEE, Mary mar Joseph BEDUNA 1747 Boston. OUTC. DOUCET old in J. Does BEDUNA equal BAUDIN?

DUSEE, Peter mar Mary BAAL, qv, 1718 Boston, MA, prob from J or France

DU CHEMIN in J since 1309, in Trinity J 1668, and in St. Laurens C 1788. DU CHEMIN more often DUQUEMIN in G. In St. Saviour G 1772. See CIFHS #9.

DUCOMMUN, prob DUQUEMIN, Herman A., bur Riverside Cem WWI, Ladysmith, WI. OUTC, but sev fams from G settled in WIS. Also in Fremont, CAL.

DU FEU/DE FEU in Trinity J 1668, and in 1749. FEW, DU FEW noted in colonies, but OUTC.

DEFEW, Rachel of Boston mar Wm. FAVOR of France or C.I.? 1717 in Boston, MA. See CIFHS #3.

DUFFET, Wm. Edmund, b ca 1821 England, but lived early in G, d 1889 age 68 in Chicago, bur Graceland Cem. Mar 1? 1856 Johanna Henrietta BARRETT, b ca 1840 G? dau of Edmund and Mary McCarthy Barrett, to US age about 18. Duffett's siblings also to America? DUFFETT bur Prot. Cem. and his wife in R.C. cem. Not clear that chn belowwere his, poss his siblings? (Jeanette Loring-Gelbach, Oak Lawn, ILL)

A1. Rosie, mar Wm. Hemmings, to US ca 1854? d 1914 Chicago?

A2. Babette

A3. Guillaume-Edmond, or William Edmund, b 1868 Chcago, mar 1892 Isabella Gertrude Loring, b 1870 Worcester, MA, d 1951 Long Beach, CAL.

B1. John F. Duffett, changed name to Loring, known as Jack Loring.

C1. Florence Jeannette Loring, b CHI, mar 1947 Edward M. Lorbach, res Oak Lawn, ILL.

DUFFETT, Mr. and Mrs. res 8th St. Superior, WISC. She was Lillian Kimber, schooled in G. (DE BRODER fam records)

DU FOUR, old in J and G. Curr J.

DU FOUR, several chn of one fam of C.I. rem to NY late 1800s or early 1900s. OUTC. (Josephine Du Four, Brooklyn, NY)

DU FOUR, Josephine from G? mar David T. RABEY, from G, several chn b 1900s. See RABEY

DU FOUR, Elizabeth GILBERT, b G, whose husband Hilary DU FOUR d in G 1851, a blacksmith. Eliz brought 3 sons and a dau to Racine, WIS ca 1854. (Racine ALBUM; Leach; RACINE HISTORY)

A1. Joseph, b 1836 G, to NY for 19 months, then to Racine in 1855. Mar Amelia C. Peterson, nee Foemel, b Hesse Castle, Germany. 6chn. Amelia had 2 chn by 1st mar: Edward N. and Julia.

B1. Walter G. B3. Arthur G. B5. Laura

B2. Charles W. B4. Lizzie A. B6. Herbert.

A2. Mary, b 1839 G, mar William Bull, b Orange Co., NY, d Racine 1878. A dau mar Geo. Jagers.

A3. Hilary, b 1841 G, to US 1854, to Racine ca 1857, Civil War Veteran. D Chicago, ILL 1909.

A4. Peter C., b 1842 G, to Racine ca 1853, res Fair Oaks, CAL.

DU FOUR, Peter, b 1826 St. Peter in the Wood G, to Racine 1844, mar Catherine PALMER of Canada. He was a blacksmith, and prob the father-in-law of Elizabeth Gilbert DUFOUR above.

DU FOUR, noted in Detroit MI where many G and Ald. fams settled.

DUFUR, Hepzibeth, b 1808, poss in NH? mar 1830 Wm. N. Miltimore in Rich ford, VT, res later in Glen Sutton, QUE, 1775-1850. Res also in NY? (Patsy Becick, Sacramento, CAL)

DU FRESNE curr G, pron. DU FRAYNE.

DU FRESNE, Dr. Samuel of Lancaster, PA d 1835, age 43, poss from G?

DU FRESNE, fam in Detroit MI area is thought to have come from C.I.

DU FRESNE, James Philip, b 1800 St. John J, d 1858 J or UT. Mar 1. Mary REMON, qv, and 2. Mary CADORET, qv. Mary REMON DU FRESNE rem to SLCity, UT 1854, via ship MARSHFIELD, with chn below. A1-5.

A1. Mary Ann A4. Peter C. A5. Jane Mary

A2. Elizabeth I. A6. James Philip, b 1856 UT, d 1871 (By Cadoret?)

A3. John P. A7. Mary Ann, b ca 1858, d.y.

DU FRAYNE, DU FRESNE?, FRAYNE, Robert, connected to above fam? mar Mary Ellen BLAMPIED, qv, near Barrton, KS 1882, d 1899.

DUGUE. Fam of this name res J early 1800s. Desc of Sarah Jane DUGUE was Richard Elliott, Englewood, NJ 1970s.

DU HAMEL in St.Heliers J 1668, 1749. Curr J.

DU HAMEL, John, b ca 1816 J mar ca 1840 Mary LE GRESLEY, qv, who d 1877 Kamas, UT. He d ca 1851 J. Chn of this fam to UT 1851, ship OLYMPUS. Mary was dau of Philip and Judith (MARQUAND) LE GRESLEY, and mar 2. Philip MERRIT. See DE MERITT. (SLCity records)

A1. John, b 1841 J mar Sarah Pilling

A2. Mary A3. John, relative? not sibling, who came with them?

A4. Julia, b 1844 J, mar James Woolstenholme. A5. Leah.

DU HAMEL, from J? to GCO 1800s. A Benj. DU HAMEL mar Ann Schoonover 1830 in Guernsey Co., OH. Several others are bur there.

DU HAMEL, noted in 1860 OH census

DU HAMEL, HAMMEL, Jonathan and Rachel res Coshocton, OH. Jonathan d 1862 age 48. RAchel d 1895 age 78. OUTC. (COSH. CEM. RECORDS)

DUMARESQ shield, gules three escallops or.

DUMARESQ in J since 1291. Name in St. Martin, St. Ouen, Grouville, St. Brelade, St. Saviour, St. Clement, St. Heliers, Trinity and St. Laurens J 1668, much the same 1749. Curr G, where it was known 1331. An illustrious Jersey name, very scarce now, but with many desc. widely scattered. (Soc. Jers. files; Margaret Le Breton, Belleville, ONT; James Dumaresq, Halifax, NS; Donat Robichaud,

Beresford, NB; Rev. Albert Dumaresq, Caraquet, NB; Emery Dumaresq, Gaspe, QUE; Census of Gaspe, QUE 1861; JERRI JADIS, by Geo. LE FEUVRE; BIO. DICT. OF J by G.R. Balleine; NEHGS Vol 17; LE COUTEUR PAPERS; by Joan Stevens, J; Nicolas Denys Soc., Vol 1,#5; SOC. JERS. BULLETIN #11; HIST OF HUG EMIGRANTS TO AMERICA by C.W. Baird; A SKETCH OF THE FAM OF DUMARESQ, by August T. Perkins, Albany, NY.1863)

DUMARESQ, Capt. Philip, b 1695, 2nd son of Elias D., Seigneur of Augres, J, and wife Frances, dau of Sir Francis DE CARTERET, qv. Capt. Philip to Doston before 1716, res Summer St., was one of the first vestrymen of Trinity Ch, Boston. Mar there 1716 Susanne FERRY, dau of Capt. Henri Ferry of Boston, a Hug. of Havre de Grace, France. It is said that Philip brought over several ship loads of Hugeunots. He d ca 1741 leaving his widow guardian of 3 youngest chn. (NEHGS Vols 17, 67, 82; Pickering Gen, p. 844)

A1. Edward, mar 1743 Mary, dau of Stephen Boutineau, Hug., by whom he had had 2 chn.
B1. Stephen, b 1744, no issue. B2. Anne, b 1746 mar Wm. Turner 1761.
A2. Philip, d 1721
A3. Susan, mar 1741 Trinity Ch, Mathew SAUMAREZ, qv of J, and d 1743. By 2nd wife Saumarez became father of Admiral Lord de Saumarez.
A4. Elizabeth b 1730
A5. Douce, b 1743, mar Geo. BANDINEL of J, 2nd wife? Res there?
A6. Anne, b 1736 mar Nicholas MALLETT of J, res there?
A7. Philip, b 1737 mar 1763 Rebecca Gardiner, dau of Sylvester Gardiner of Boston, a Loyalist, who rem to Halifax, and was later Customs Collector at the port of Nassau, BWI, where he d. 10 chn of whom 5 d.y. He mar 2. ?
B1. Anne, bp 1765 mar John Ferguson, son of Sir John F. of Ayrshire, Scotland, and 2. Charles Gow, Esq.
B2. Sylvester, bp 1766 d.y. B3. Rebecca, bp 1768 B4. Susan, d.y. 1771
B5. James, bp 1772, served in Royal Navy, then studied law with his uncle John Gardiner of Boston. He mar 1797 Sarah, dau of Eben Farwell of Vassalboro, ME, res Swan Island there, 4 chn
C1. Jane Frances Rebecca, b 1799 Vassalboro, mar in Boston 1820 Lt. Col. Thomas Handasyde Perkins, officer of the Liberal Army of Columbia, Chief of Staff to Major-Gen. Devereaux. 6 chn. Perkins d 1851, his wife in 1856.
D1. Thomas Handasyde Perkins, b 1823 mar Eliz. J. Chadwick
D2. Augustus Thorndike Perkins, b 1827 mar Susan, dau of Henry Timmins.
D3. Philip Dumaresq Perkins, b 1829
D4. Francis Codman Perkins, b 1830 d 1842
D5. Louisa Dumaresq Perkins, b 1831 mar Wm. Morris Hunt.
C2. Louisa b 1802 mar 1843 Hon. John Rice Blake, Senator of VT.
C3. Philip, b 1804 educated a Gardiner, ME entered merchant service was Capt. at 20, and for over 30 yrs. was a skilled and successful merchant Captain. He mar 1836 Margarita Mary, dau of Francis Gilbert DEBLOIS and wife Millicent. His wife and eldest dau were drowned 1855, and he returned to sea, being the first to commence traffic with the Japanese. He was lost overboard in Long Island Sound 1861, bur Forest Hills Cem.
D1. Margarita, b 1837 d 1849
D2. Frances Perkins, b 1840 drowned 1855 with mother
D3. Philip Kearney b at Macao, China, and bp 1842 on board ship CONSTELLATION.
D4. Florence Saumarez, b 1843 D7. Herbert, b 1851
D5. Sarah, d.y. D6. James, b 1848 D8. Francis, b 1854.

B6. Philip, bp 1772 B9. Abigail, bp 1776, d.y.
B7. Francis, bp 1774, d.y. B10. Dr. Francis of Jamaica, BWI. His
B8. Hannah, bp 1775 2 chn d without issue.
The other chn of Elias and Frances (DE CARTERET) DUMARESQ were:
1. Rev. Elias, res Boston 6. Caroline Alice
2. Philip, Capt. of the Royal Navy 7. Douce
3. Anne, mar Elias LE MAISTRE, Seigneur de Quetivel in J.
4. Frances, mar Edward LE CRAS of J 8. Elizabeth
5. Magdalen, b 1695, mar at Boston 1722 THomas Wroe from Yorkshire, England. 3 chn: Mathew, Anne and Thomas Wroe.

DUMARESQ, Edward, b ca 1695 J son of Rev. Dumaresq, rem to Boston ca 1717, mar Mary BRITTON, qv. Edward d 1767, his wife in 1744. (NEHGS Vol 17; BIO. DICT. OF JERSEY, by Balleine)
A1. Mary, b 1720 A4. Edward, 1730-1753
A2. Catherine, but in Doston 1723 A5. Charlss b 1729
A3. Jane, b 1728 mar John PIGEON 1752 Boston. A6. Elizabeth, b 1732.

DUMARESQ, Ann, mar1767 Wm. Turner in Boston. (NEHGS Vol 100)

DEMORSQUE, Mrs. Betsy, spinster from New London, CT, to Boston 1767. See Rachel from CT? who mar Hyatt.

DUMARESQ. E., res Brecksville, OH, res on 114 acre farm 1852. (Land Index Map)

DUMARESQ, Ebenezer, res Palmertown, MA 1790 with fam of 5. Ebenezer in 1780 was 19, bp Boston, served in Rev. War. (Census; MASS SOLDIER)

DUMARESQ, Edward, Lt. of H.M. ship LIZARD, 1699/1700, res Barbadoes. (NEHGS Vol 67) Had nephew Philip, bro John, sister Jane Berry, to whom he left a part of the ship SUSANNA of London, and also left funds to Trinity Parish, Jersey. Will proved 1701.

DUMARESQ. George W., mar Florence Wheatland and res Boston. A dau Florence b 1870 Boston mar 1889 Jacob Crowninshield Rogers Peabody, b 1866 Danvers, MA. (PEABODY GEN)

DUMARESQ, Henrietta, res Liberty Center, Henry Co., OH 1860. (Census)

DUMARESQ, John mar Rachel BRITTON, qv, 1719 Boston, MA.

DUMARESQ, John mar Margaret McKay in Cleveland, OH 1837

DUMARESQ, John arrived in Boston 1769 on ship MOLLY from J. (Whitmore)

DUMARESQ, John, b 1914 St. Martin G, rem to New York, patent lawyer. He mar Eleanor ___, 3 chn. Res Long Island. (G. WEEKLY PRESS, 7/21/64)
A1. a son b 1947 A2. a son b 1949 A3. a son b 1956

DUMARESQ, spelled DE MARSQUALL, Lewis res Dracut, MA 1790, fam of 12.

DUMARESQ, Michael and William sailed with Capt. Philip DUMARESQ on the American privateer ship YOUNG EAGLE. See Pirate-Privateer section. (NEHGS Vol 100)

DUMARESQ, Rachel, sister of Edward above, b ca1800? to Boston, mar John Sowersby.

DUMARESQ, Rachel, b Hackensack, NJ, dau of John mar 1702 Tammes Heyet, Thomas Hyatt of MA or of CT. OUTC. See also Betsy above. (Dutch Reformed Church Records)

DUMARESQ, Sarah was in Dresden, ME 1814, where she was bp as adult.

DUMARESQ, Sarah, sister of Edward above, b J, to Boston, mar __Venner

DUMARESQ, Steven arrived in Boston 1769 on ship MOLLY from J. (Whitmore)

DUMARESQ, Thomas from Jto Salem, MA 1685 wife Marie LE BROCQ, qv. (Soc. Jers. Bulletin of 1905)

DUMARESQ in Lenawee Co., MI 1850. See also Q.A. IN CANADA by Turk.

DUMARESQ. A Macdonald fam in Agincourt, ONT said to be DUMARESQ desc.

DUMESNIL, Anthony mar Polly Cunningham 1798 Boston, MA. MESNIL in J 1583.

DU MOULIN, Augustine, d 1810 on schooner TWO BROTHERS from Senegal, Africa to SC. DU MOULIN in J 1309. OUTC. (SC GEN. MAG)

DUNDAS, Amelia Sophia, b C.I. mar Edwin J. O'Reilly of Hamilton,ONT. at St. Mary's, ONT 1862. (Ted Rowcliffe, St. Mary's ONT)

DUNSTAN, Wm. mar Helen Mary DOREY, qv, 1909 in St. Peter Port, G, and rem to Toronto, ONT 1920. Celebrated 70th wedding anniversary in 1979. (GUERNSEY EVE. PRESS, June 2, 1979)

DUPAH, DUPAR, DUPARR noted in early MA. Was this DU PARC of J? there in 1607 as LE PARKE, of the park, which could mean cattle pen, tournament lists or skittle alleys! (Stevens) DU PARC in Grouville, J 1607, 1668 and 1749. See PARK and YOUNG, also CIFHS #8.

PARCQ, DU PARCQ, shield: azure, three mullets of six points pierced or.

DUPAR, DUPARR, Elias M. mar Sally or Polly McElroy of Salem, MA 1797.

DUPARR, Elias and Mary res Boston. Note that Mary equals POLLY.

A1. William, bp 1803   A2. Sally, bp 1805

DUPARR, Mary mar Ezekiel RUSSELL (int) 1802 MRB.

DUPAH, Ann, d 1834 MRB, age 49, from C.I.?

DUPAH, DUPARK, DUPARR, Mary mar Geo. WEBBER? 1825 MRB.

DUPARR, Sarah mar John BASSET 1798 MRB. OUTC

DUPAR, Samuel age 22, cordwainer, son of Elias and Ann, mar Annis Shirley Cloutman, age 19, dau of Jacob C. and Abigail, 1849 MRB.

DU PLAYN, old Alderney surname, now spelled DUPLAIN.

DU PORT, curr G, some to US?

DU PRE, curr G. DU PRE in St. Heliers J 1668, and in St. Laurens, St. Mary, and St. Clement J 1749. DU PRE in St. Laurens J 1788. See CIFHS #12.

DU PRE, Charles from St. Laurens J bought land near Thomas PINEL, qv, 1713 on Cape Cod.

DU PRE, several ship captains in J 1700s-1800s. (A. John Jean, Jersey)

DU PUIS. This often spelled DUPEE in early New England. Prob Hug? However, DU PUY is noted in Stevens list of old J surnames. CIFHS#9.

DURANT, a privateer Captain of Jersey 1703-1711. Common in US.

DURELL, in J 1607. LE VAVASSEUR dit DURELL in J 1651. DURELL in St. Saviour and St. Heliers J 1668 and 1749. DURELLS in early America said to have come from Guernsey.

DURELL, DURRELL, Philippe, 1707-1766, Vice Admiral. In 1745 was on the ELTHAM, which took part in the expedition against the Louisbourg fortress on Cape Breton, NS. Nathaniel MESSERVY, of a J fam in NH also served in the hxpedition. Adm. Durrell passed 7 ships up the St. Lawrence River to near Quebec City, in the face of much difficulty, helping to win Canada for the British. He d at sea, and was bur in Halifax, NS. He was the 2nd son of Jean DURRELL and Eliz. CORBET of J. More in BIO. DICT. OF J by Balleine.

DURRELL, Thomas, 1685-1741, Capt. of the Royal Navy, sonof Jurat Jean DURELL and Anne, dau of Elie DUMARESQ, qv, Seigneur of Augres. Thomas was b St. Heliers J, joined the Brit. Navy, and served in command of the sloop SWIFT later in command of the SEAHORSE, 20 guns. In 1 1724 he was in charge of trial for captured pirates in Boston, MA. See BIO. DICT. OF JERSEY, by Balleine.

DURELL, DURIN, Susanna, mar John Best 1670, b ca 1742, a currier in Salem, MA 1670-1711. He mar 2. Edith Hull 1692/3, his widow in 1748 Chn b Salem. He may have been from Canterbury, England. Poss Susanna was an indentured servant from J or G? OUTC.

A1. John Best, b 1671, living 1704

A2. Susannah Best, b 1673 mar John Messinger of RI, of Long Island1712

A3. Wiliam Best, mariner, res Newport, RI d 1712, prob unmar. His will 1711 devised all to his cousin John Best of Salem.

A4. Jonathan Best of Salem, sailor on ship ESSEX, d unmar? ca 1700.

A5. Benj. Best, under age in 1700 living 1704.

A6. by 2nd wife, Mary Best, twin, b 1693 living 1704
A7. Judith Best, twin b 1693
A8. David Best, b 1694/5, currier, res Salem, mar Lydia Kimball of Wenham, MA, 1719/20, d 1730
B1. John, living 1703 B3. Lydia living 1730
B2. Elizabeth, mar Stephen Webb of Salem 1746
B4. Mary, mar Nathaniel Nurse of Salem 1754
A9. Mary Best, b 1696, d age 10. A10. Sarah Best, b 1698, living 1704
DURIN, Jane, mar early 1700s John Elwel, poss related to Susanna above. (Marjorie Drisko, Boothbay Harbor, ME)
DURELL, DUDAY, DUBY, DUDY, DURIN, Philip, b ca 1665 G, res Exeter, NH, mar ___. The Purinton woman is said to have not mar this Philip, but mar the son of Philip, "an older son of his". (Dorothy Whitney, Seaside, OR) Philip Sr. d in Kennebunkport, ME ca 1745/6. His wife was twice captured by Indians, the first time in 1703, when Mrs. Durell, her two daus Susan and Rachel, and two sons, one of them an infant, were captured. One son drowned? in Saco River, but the baby son and Mrs. Durell were allowed to return home. The two daus were taken to Canada and there married Frenchmen. In the second raid in 1726 Mrs. Durell and Mrs. Baxter, her dau, and Mrs. Baxter's chn were killed. John, the 12 yr old son, lived among the Indians for two years and was then exchanged. He lived much like an Indian for the rest of his life. (DURRELL GEN, by Harold C. Durrell, Cambridge, MA, 1918; Dorothy Whitney, Seaside, OR; Mrs. Robert Miles, O'Neill, NEB; Carolyn Nelson, Vassalboro, ME; Library, Astoria, OR; etc)
A1. Joseph, b ca 1685 mar Rebecca Adams before 1711, dau of Charles Adams, JR, b 1660 Lexington, MA and wife Temperance Benmore, dau of Philip and Rebecca (Tibbetts) Benmore of Dover, NH. See NH & ME records for much more on these Durells.
B1. Benmore, bp 1717 mar Elizabeth ___
B2. Susanna, bp 1717, mar Francis, son of James Durgin
B3. Joseph Jr., bp 1718, mar Hannah ___. He d fairly young, leaving 3 minor chn: David, Eliphalet and Mary. He was innkeeper at Durham 1749. His widow mar 2. Nathan Keniston of Newmarket, NH, & had at least 2 other chn: Rebecca Stevens and Eliz. K. by Durell.
B4. Mary, mar Truworthy, son of James Durgin, b 1714, who d 1787. Mary d 1800.
B5. Temperance, bp 1726
B6. Ebenezer Dudey, alis DURRELL, bp 1728/9, a tradition that he was killed fairly young by Indians.
B7. Nicholas, b ca 1730 mar 1752 Rachel Wakefield of Wells, ME, and 2. Abigail MESERVE, qv. of Durham. (Dorothy Whitney, Seaside, OR)
C1. ? Nicholas, b ca 1752 Lee, NH, d 1788 Embden, ME, mar Judith Keniston of Exeter, NH.
D1. Joseph, b 1793 Nottingham, NH, d 1882 Embden, ME, mar 1816 Olive Thompson, b 1796 d 1878.
E1. John, b 1818 Solon, ME d 1902 Pilot Mound, IA, mar 1843 Mary PAINE, b 1820 Embden, ME d 1895 Ogden, IA.
F1. Isabel P. Durrell, b 1851 Monroe, WI, d 1947 Corvallis, OR. Mar Charles Whitney, b 1838 Scriba, NY, d 1907
G1. Charles S. Whitney, b 1870 Dayton ,IA d 1957 Joplin, MO. Mar Mary F. Durrell, 1892, b 1870 IA, d 1963 OR.
H1. Dorothy Whitney, b 1894 Parkersburg, IA
B8. Zebulon, b ca 1732 Durham, NH, mar ___.
C1. Abigail C2. Zebulon C3. Joseph
C4. Betsey, mar Benning Swart C5. Temperance, mar John Edgerly.
C6. Susanna, b ca 1775 Newmarket, NH d 1857 Windsor, ME, mar 1794

in Parsonsfield, ME John Thurston, b 1772 Exeter, NH d 1853. Res also in Monmouth and Dixmont before settling in Windsor, ME.
D1.Abigail Thurston, mar ca 1815 Simon DAVIS of Hallowell, ME
D2. Caleb Thurston, mar ca 1818 Olive CROSS, qv. He was b 1797 Windsor, ME d 1875 China, ME. Olive b 1801 d 1867 China, ME dau of Samuel CROSS.
D3. Deborah Thurston, mar Enoch JOSLYN D4. Susan mar William Adams.
D5. Mary Thurston mar Rev. Wm. Dunningham of Litchfield, ME
D6. Emily Thurston mar Waterman Reed.
A2. a dau who mar Joshua Purinton? (D. Whitney)
A3. Susan, b ca 1687, taken to Canada by Indians, and married there.
A4. Rachel, b ca 1689, ditto
A5. Benjamin, b ca 1691, taken by Indians 1703 and drowned in Saco Riv.
A6. Philip Jr., b ca 1701, mar Keziah Wakefield.
A7. Mary, b ca 1703 Arundel, ME, mar at Wells, ME 1719 James Wakefield.
A8. Sarah, b ca 1705, mar ca 1724. She and baby son killed by Indians.
A9. Elizabeth, b 1707 ME, mar 1724 John Wakefield
A10. Benjamin, b ca 1711 mar Judith Perkins
A11. Lydia, b ca 1712, mar 1728 Stephen Larribee
A12. John, b 1714 mar Lydia (Hutchins) Jellison.
DURRELL, Joseph, b 1769, d 1842 St. Armand, QUE, mar Mary Campbell, b 1775 d 1858, 9 chn. The ancestors of this man have not been verified, but it's poss. that this was the Joseph noted as son of David, b Lee, NH 1746, desc of Philip. David had 9 chn, the first being Joseph, called the grandson of Benj. Meeds Lord. Joseph disappeared, poss to Canada? (Mrs. C. McArthur, Toronto, ONT) OUTC.
A1. William, b 1806, d 1841 St. Armand, QUE mar 1835 Agnes Jardine, b 1810 d 1888, Pembroke, ONT, dau of James and Catherine (Johnston) Jardine. Widow Agnes mar 1844 James S. Johnson.
B1. James Jardine Durell, b 1836 Pembroke, ONT d 1911 mar 1. Mary E. Snowden, and 2. Mary Caroline McChesney, 1858.
C1. Margaret b 1869 Westmeath, ONT mar Charles Heman Howe, 1866-1951
B2. William, b 1838 d 1928 mar Amelia Kennedy. B3. Henry, 1840-1864
A2. Eliza Jane, b 1796 mar 1840 Joseph Hillman
A3. Jane, b 1796, twin of Eliza Jane
A4. Emeline Sophia, b 1811, mar 1834 James Wells Abbee
A5. Suzy, mar 1822 Jacob Titemore A7. Thomas, mar Jane Ostrom 1827
A6. Ephrem A8. Dolly A9. John Nelson
DURRELL, Moses, also called DUDAY and DURIN in various deeds in late 1600s, prob came from J or G ca 1660? and was employed by Robert Elwell of Gloucester, MA. Served under Capt. Joseph Gardner in the Narraganset War, and was in RI with the company in 1675. In 1676 he was at the Garrison at Hadley, MA. He was granted land in Glouc. in 1679 which he sold in 1680. Rem to Salem, MA until ca 1690, when he returned to Gloucester. Moses mar 1686 at Scarboro, ME Sarah, dau of John and Sarah (Pease) SAMPSON, who d ca 1736. He d 1753 and his son Benj. admin. the estate. (Typescript at NEHGS, dated 1928) See sources for more info.
A1. Nathaniel, bp 1703 mar Hannah, da of Robert and Sarah (Gardner) Elwell, b 1694, mar 1716 at Glouc. Rem ca 1726 to Biddeford, ME. In 1730 he was paid for making bricks for the blockhouse on the Saco River. In 1734 he had 25 acres on the east side of the Saco, which he sold in 1740. There were a couple of bad years ca 1762, caused by drouth and a fire, which caused many of the settlers to move away from Brixton, ME then called Narragansett #1. 7 chn. His widow poss mar 2. Walter Murch 1749 at Biddeford, ME.
B1. Nathaniel, b 1718 Gloucester, MA B3. Moses, b 1723 Glouc.

B2. Hannah, b 1720 Clouc., mar (int) at Biddeford, ME 1739 James Sands
B4. Jonathan, b 1725 Glouc mar Mary Donnell. He d ca 1748. His widow had a ch in 1750.
B5. Benjamin, b ca 1728 Saco, ME mar ca 1755 Mary Sillea, dau of John and Hannah (Seavey) Sillea. Served at Saco under Lt. Jonathan Be Bean, and was a private under Capt. Tristram Jordan 1757. Fought in the Rev. War. and was pensioned in 1819 by Govt.
C1. Mary, bp 1757 C2. John Glidden, bp 1759
C3. Hannah, bp 1763 mar 1786 John Grace of Scarboro,ME.
C4. Moses, bp 1765, drowned near Little Falls 1787
C5. Theophilus, bp 1767, mar Melissa Wing
C6. Nathaniel, bp 1769 mar Dorcas Gould. Theo. and Nath. settled as young men in Stewartstown, NH. Dorcas d Kingfield, ME 1848, and Nathaniel d in Freeman, ME 1863. A son d.y.
D1. Mary May mar Abijah Usher?
E1. Mary Ann Usher mar John PULLEN, jr.
E2. Robert Usher, had sons: Silas, Charles, James and Nathaniel
D2. John Gould, b 1797 mar 1. Hannah Parent, 2. Jane SAVAGE, and 3. Harriet PULLEN, cf POULAIN of C.I.
D3. Reuben, b 1799 mar Dorcas Blethen, see Blethen, and MARQUAND.
D4. Ann, b 1800 Leeds, ME mar 1. 1817 Lewis Brewster, d 1827. She mar 2. 1830, John Adams PULLEN, b 1798. She d Portland, ME 1870, and he d Turner, ME 1880
E1. Stephen John Brewster, mar Mary T. Blanchard, who d at Winona, MINN 1905. He d 1912
E2. Elbridge G. Brewster, b 1820 mar Nashua, NH, Edie Butterfield, b 1824. Res Amboy, ILL, where she d 1903, he in 1906.
E3. Loren Brewster, b 1823, d 1825
E4. Dorcas Brewster, b 1825 mar Joseph BROWN
E5. Nancy Dinsmore Brewster, b 1827 mar Samuel Starbird
E6. Albany Clinton Pullen, b 1831 mar Henrietta Brooks
E7. Celia Ann Pullen, b 1836 mar David N. Coffin, whodied Dorchester, MA 1893.
E8. Emily Butterfield Pullen b 1844 mar 1862 Sullivan Kilbraith, who d Lewiston, ME 1915.
D5. Dorcas, b 1802, mar George Washington PULLEN, b 1798, who d 1873. She d 1878, 6 chn.
E1. Julia Ann Witham? E2. Olive Mitchell
E3. G.W. Pullen, b 1825 mar Mary Ann Usher
E4. John Adams Pullen, b 1827 mar Roxana Perham
E5. Hiram Durrell Pullen, mar 1878 Fannie Cooper
D6. Eunice, b 1804 mar G.W. Peterson, 8 chn: Rufus, George, Eliza, Lewis, Ira, Nelson, Orrin, Lovisa
D7. Benjamin, b 1806 mar twice, Tracy and Richards
D8. Noah, b 1809, mar twice, Rose and Knapp
D9. Ira Gould, b 1811 mar Lucy Fessenden
D10. Moses, b 1812, mar 1. Hannah Abbot and 2. Ruby Morse
D11. Eliza Dennett, b 1812 mar Hull Abbott, 6 chn: Eliza, Edwin, Hattie, Hull, John Wesley, Maria P. Abbott.
D12. Nathaniel, mar Betsy Keeble
B6. Mary, b ca 1732 mar at Saco, ME 1754 Jonathan, son of Edward and Sarah (DURRELL) RUMERY, prob ROMERIL from J. A son.
B7. Abigail, b ca 1734, mar at Biddeford, ME 1756 Solomon Ross.
A2. Jonathan, b 1702 d ca 1725.
A3. Sarah, bp 1703 mar 1. at Cloucester, MA 1717/18 Thomas PENNELL, qv He d 1723 age 34, 3 chn. She mar 2. Edward RUMERY, ROMERIL, qv, of Biddeford, ME, 4 sons. She d 1776 age 86.

B1. Sarah Pennell, b 1718
B2. Thomas Pennell, b 1719/20 mar 1743 Biddeford, ME Hannah Brooks.
B3. Rachel Pennell, b 1721 mar (int) 1736/7 Richard Clay
B4. Edward Rumery, b 1730 mar 1760 at Biddeford, Eliz. HOOPER, qv.
B5. Jonathan Rumery, b 1731 mar at Biddeford 1754 Mary, dau of Nathaniel and Hannah (Elwell) DURRELL, b ca 1732
B6. Thomas Rumery, b 1733 mar at Biddeford 1758 Charity, dau of Robert and Sarah (Elwell) Edgecomb, b 1735 Saco, ME. He d before 1807
B7. William Rumery, b 1737 mar 1758 Rebecca Austin. He d 1764.
A4. Lydia, b ?, d 1723 Glouc. MA ca age 14.
A5. Elizabeth, mar 1731/2 John, son of Robert and Sarah (Gardner) Elwell, b Glouc., MA 1708.
B1. Sarah Elwell, bp 1742 Biddeford, ME.
B2. Rhoda Elwell, bp 1745 mar 1768 Gibbins, son of Thomas and Sarah (Fletcher) Edgecomb, b 1743. She d 1822.
A6. Moses? Poss fits in here, who d Boston 1730 age 24. (Noyes)
DURRELL ADDENDA from Dorothy Whitney, Seaside, OR.
"The Durell family was prolific and tough enough to make its way throu many hardships...I know there are now many Durrell descendants in California, as three of my great uncles went there from Iowa, but I know little about them now. Through two cousin marriages I have an extra proportion of Durrell blood...My cousins in the eastern states now put the accent on the last syllable, but our main line accented the first syllable, and I'm told that the Canadian Durrells also accent the first...A cousin Donald Durrell, son of my mother's brother Will Durrell, until his retirement, was a professor at Boston Univ. and author of several books on teaching retarded readers, now res Durham, NH...I have a proved supplemental in COLONIAL DAMES, 17th Century, from Philip DURRELL...John Harvey Durrel, my mother's brother, was for many years one of the Vice Presidents of the National City Bank of NY, in charge of foreign affairs...He has told us interesting stories of other lands...My great-grandfather John Durrell, on his farm in Boone Co., IA used to look with pride on his children and grandchildren assembled for Sunday dinner after church, and say... "I wish I had a hundred children, and a table big enough to seat them all.".
DURRELL, Peter JEUNE LE VAVASSEUR dit DURELL, native of J, worked in Boston, MA 1700s for John Henry Bastide, a carpenter.
Poss DURELL sources: Dracut and Woburn, MA records; HIST. OF LEXINGTON, MA; ANNALS OF OXFORD, ME; Noyes; MASS. SOLDIERS AND SAILORS and many, many other books on early New England.
DURELL, Francis arrived in Boston 1715 on ship MARY from J (Whitmore)
DU SOUCHET, see SARCHET. DE SOUCHES in St. Lawrence J 1788.
DU SOUCHET, Francis, said to be b in France, was the admin. of the estate of Peter TORODE, qv, 1823 in GCO. It is an oddity that DU SOUCHET was said to be the original form of the surname SARCHET, qv, and also odd that DU SOUCHET should turn up in the area where the SARCHETS resided, Guernsey Co., OH. Francis was naturalized 1824, had fam of 8 in 1830, not found by compiler, a mason in GCO 1833.
DUTOT, surname of France and C.I. See CIFHS #3.
DUVAL, common in many countries of Europe. In J 1299, in G 1200s. Does not appear in Extentes of J 1607,1668, 1749, but may have lived in St. Heliers J and were not farmers. Book by Ida Duval, Peterborough, ONT is now in progress. See also Q.A. in CANADA, by Turk.
DUVAL, Philippe, b ca 1807 J res Paspebiac, QUE 1861, mar Jane Scott, b ca 1808. At least 2 chn.
A1. Philip Jr. b ca 1840 A2. Sarah Ann, b ca 1838? mar Philip GALLIE.

Of a DUVAL fam of C.I. one settled Australia, Fred res Fiji, and had a bro who lived in Southampton, England. Some DUVALs b Penang, Malaysia. Their father mar Emily HARDOUIN, whose bro was French Consul-General in Penang, Malaysia.

DUVAL, Capt. __, of J, was a privateersman, sailing around Bermuda, but settled early 1800s in Gaspe, QUE, on Bonaventure Island.

DUVAL, Prof. Errol of Sherbrooke, QUE, is from a J fam in Gaspe, desc of Francois DUVAL.

DUVAL, Susannah mar Henry Styles 1801 Boston, MA. OUTC.

DUVAL, Philippe, b ca 1771 J, son of Daniel and Marie (REDMAN) DUVAL of of J. Capt of ship ESTHER 1810, res in New Brunswick for some time? Mar Marie HUELIN, qv. (THE DUVAL FAMILY by John LE Rossignol, in LE ROSSIGNOL GEN; Mrs. Harold Dolling, Ames, IA; Ida Duval, Peterborough, ONT; LE BOUTILLIER-BUTLER FAM HIST. by Gladys Brechtel,1980)

A1. Mary Anne, bp 1798 A2. Elizabeth, bp 1800, mar Henry MAYNARD

A3. Anne.

A4. Jeanne, bp 1802, mar Edward LE BOUTILLIER, b 1814 J, son of Edouard and Elizabeth (VIBERT) LE BOUTILLIER in St. Ouen J, 4 chn. See book for more data on this fam.

A5. Nicholas, bp 1807 J, d 1891 mar Marguerite LEIGH of J, dau of Leigh and QUERIPEL. See book.

A6. Anne, bp 1810

A7. Philippe, bp 1813 J, d 1862, mar Jeanne/Jane ROUET, b ca 1814 Gran'mere, QUE, see part of this fam in Q.A. IN CANADA.

A8. Amice, bp 1815 mar Esther ROUET. A son Capt. John d in Liverpool.

A9. Nancy Eliz., bp 1818, d.y. A10 Pierre-Jean, bp 1821 died Australia

DYER, British? However, DYERE in G 1300s. DOYRE noted in early J.

DYER curr G and J. A Capt. Wm. Dyer sailed to Azores and West Indies in Middle 1600s.

DYER, Anthony from ?, settled onFox Islands, on Crockett and CABOT farm, poss from J? (Underhill)

DYER, John DUMARESQUE, mar Mary Jasper 1792, Boston, MA. OUTC.

EAYRES, see AHIER

ECOBICHON, Edward, b 1910 St. Peter J, son of Mathurin Francois and Victorine Marie (ALLO) ECOBICHON, a farm fam. Ca 1930 brought cattle to the McMonnies Farm in Florham Park, NJ, then returned to J. Rem to US 1932, settled NJ, mar 1941 Thelma Frances Decker of Elizabeth, NJ, one ch. Edward a carpenter, d 1954. His widow mar 2. ___Jenkins. (Alice Ecobichon, Fords, NJ)

A1. Alec Edward, b 1944 mar Margaret Ann D'antico, b 1945, 2 chn

B1. Christopher Edward, b 1972 B2. Jeffrey Alec, b 1976.

ECOBICHON, relatives of above fam are in Q.A. IN CANADA.

EDMONDS, several early fams in America, but OUTC. EDMONDS curr J and G. EDMONDS alias ROCK in J 1607. Cf ROCK, LAROKE. EDMONDS in G from 1331. See Essex Coll, Vol 6.

EFFARD in St. Saviour J 1668, 1749. A small EFFARD chart is in WRCIC. See EFFORD, EFFARD in DAR PATRIOTS. OUTC.

EFFARD, EFFORD, Peter, a cousin of the POINDEXTER fam of VA, son of Rev. Effard of G and J, rem to York Co., VA 1657. He had 900 acres there in 1660. (VHM, Vol 13; Frances Speer, Arlington, VA)

A1. Nicholas, d.y.

A2. Sarah, mar Samuel Weldon, J.P. for James City Co., VA, there 1675.

B1. Samuel Weldon Jr., mar 1725 Elizabeth ALLEN of York Co. VA, at least 4 chn, some of whom served in Rev. War.

EFFORD, Peter, in DAR Patriot Index. (Mrs. Donald Speer, Arlington,VA)

EFFORD, Abigail, from C.I.? mar Simpson BOWDOIN 1758 MRB. He was bp

1732 in MRB, a shoreman. She was living 1771. (Underhill) OUTC

EFFARD, Elizabeth, b 1597 was the mother of George POINDEXTER of Swan Farm, Jersey, who rem to Gloucester Co., VA. See POINDEXTER.

ELLIS, some in early New England and also in G early.

ELLIS, Eleanor mar John EARES, poss AHIER?, qv, 1734 Boston, MA. OUTC

ELLIS, ___, mar Philip ENGLISH, qv, b 1684, Salem, MA. Poss from C.I.

ELSBURY, ELLSBURY. "The records show us to be a Guernsey family of peasant stock going back very many generations...my own grandfather married an Austin, and they left Guernsey in the latter part of the 1800s. My father was born in London. A sister of my father is in New Zealand. (S.M. Elsbury, Shrewsbury, England) "In the early records mention is made of the hereditary water boat franchise, which seems to have been held in the family. The right to sell water to returning vessels, many of which would not have made landfall for weeks or even months, was quite jealously safeguarded. Probably a good deal of blood was shed over it, because it was undoubtedly a reasonably lucrative monopoly, if it could be preserved as such." (ibid)

An Elsbury rem to Somerset, England, and his desc came to America. John Elsbury, b 1792 Somerset, England, was said to be one of the guards of Napoleon on St. Helena, rem to Skaneatles, NY in 1832. Mar Elizabeth Gould of England, and they brought 5 chn with them. Other chn were b in US. Order of chn is uncertain. John d 1867 in Tower City, ND, bur St. Charles, MN. Elizabeth d 1882. (Mrs. B. Ward Phelps, San Luis Obispo, CAL) CAUTION: TRIAL CHART

A1. Mary Ann A2. John, farmer and blacksmith A4. Nancy.

A3. Harriet, mar ___CORNELL, a cabinet-maker, res Tower City, ND

A5. Charles E. b England, mar 1855, Phoebe Adelaide Wright, b 1835 ONT, Canada, d 1904 St. Charles, MN.

B1. Lyman Henry, b 1854 Skaneatles, NY, d 1934 Spearfish, SD, mar Elizabeth West. At least 1 ch.

A6. Dinah, mar James Kibby, a blacksmith, res Troy, NY on a farm. He d quite young and she rem to St. Charles, MN. From there she and family, and her nieces husband, Peter Smith, rem to ND 1881, by box car and team. Some chn d.y.

A7. Cornelia A8. George A9. Sarah mar ___Messenger A10. James.

ENEVOLDSEN, Clifford, b Talbot Valley G, to America 1928, res Bernardsville, NJ. Name curr J, but prob. Scandinavian. (Guernsey PRESS, July, 1964)

ENGLISH, see NOTABLES and LANGLOIS. CAUTION: TRIAL CHARTS

Please note that while Philip ENGLISH below was originally Philippe L'ANGLOIS of Jersey, there were also people named ENGLISH living in St. Peter Du Bois, Guernsey in middle 1800s, and possibly before.

ENGLISH, Philip, b 1651 J, son of Jean LANGLOIS. He became the first American millionaire? mostly through shipping and related business in the American colonies in the late 1600s and early 1700s. See A SKETCH OF PHILIP ENGLISH, 1670-1734, by George F. Chever. CAUTION, there was at least one other Philip English/Langlois from J who settled in MA early. See more data in WRCIC. (Perley; Savage; BIO. DICT. OF JERSEY, by Balleine; FACTS ABOUT THE LIFE OF PHILIP ENGLISH OF SALEM, coll. by Mrs. Philip English, New Haven, CT, 1943, booklet; Blanche Dickover, Tenmile, OR.) Philip mar 1. Mary Hollingsworth, and 2. Sara Ingersoll 1698? CAUTION; CHN NOT ALL VERIFIED. See also data in SLCity records.

A1. William, d.y. A6. Susannah again, b 1686, mar John TOUZEL, qv1720

A2. Mary, b ca 1676, mar Wm. BROWN, or WM. LE BRUN? from J?

A3. William again, b 1679 A7. William, d 1689?

A4. Susannah, b 1682, d.y. A8. Ebenezer, b 1694
A5. Philip, b 1684, tavern owner in Salem, mar Mary Ellis, d 1750
A9. John, mariner, living in 1746, mar 1731 Hannah SWASEY, qv, b 1702. This son is by the 2nd wife.
ENGLISH, Clement, said to be bro or cousin of Philip above, from J to Salem, MA 1600s. One Clement mar Mary Waters in MA 1667. (Essex Coll, Vol2; TUTTLE FAM; BULKLEY GEN by Jacobs; DOOLITTLE FAM IN AMERICA; Salt Lake City records) CAUTION: TRIAL CHART
A1. Mary, b 1668 A2. Elizabeth, b 1670
A3. Joseph, b 1672 mar 1693 Mary SEARL, qv.
B1. Mary Searl B2. Mary again?, b 1701
B3. Mercy, b 1704 Salem, poss mar John BEADLE 1722 Salem, MA
A4. Benjamin, b 1676, d.y.? A5. Abigail, b 1680/81, d 1697
A6. Clement, b 1682/3 poss mar Susanna ___, res Salem, MA, more chn?
B1. Susanna, bp 1714 B3. Abigail, bp 1719
B2. Clement b 1715 B4. Mary, b 1723 B5. Elizabeth, bp 1727
A7. Benjamin again, b 1705 New Haven, CT. (Chart of Eva Hill, Payson, UTAH) Note number of years between 1st ch in this fam, and this son Benjamin. OUTC. Is there a generation skipped?
B1. Sarah, b 1738 New Haven CT, d 1794, mar 1757 Wm. Pluymert
B2. Abigail, b 1741 d 1815, mar Nathaniel Spencer
B3. Benjamin, b 1742, called Capt. Benjamin, d 1809 in NH. Mar 1768 Abigail Doolittle, b 1749 New Haven, d 1794 Wallingford, CT, dau of Isaac and Sarah (Todd) Doolittle.
C1. Benjamin, b 1770 CT, d 1809, mar 1793 Mary White
C2. Sarah, b 1771 d 1843. C3. John Todd, b 1773 d 1801
C4. Abigail, b 1776 d 1834 mar 1802 Immanuel Hopkinson
C5. Mary, b 1778 d 1845 mar 1799 Roswell BROWN
C6. Hannah Rebecca, b 1780 d 1807, mar 1799 Bethuel Tuttle
C7. Isaac, b 1782 d 1826, mar 1807 Catherine Ross
C8. James, b 1784 d 1850 mar 1807 Nancy Griswold
C9. Aaron, b 1786 d 1839 mar 1822 Sarah Haynes, b 1802
D1. Hannah Rebecca b 1824 D3. Frederick Nathan, b 1829
D2. Charles Haynes, b 1826 d 1837 D4. Sarah E, b 1831 mar David B. Mansfield.
C10. Eli, b 1789 mar 1821 Emily Stocking.
C11. Nathan Frederick, b 1792 d 1814.
B4. Mary, b 1744 d 1794, mar 1771 David Phipps
B5. Hannah, b 1749 d 1829 mar 1770 Daniel BROWN.
ENGLISH, Benjamin, from same fam as above, or another LANGLOIS fam from J? OUTC. Mar Rebecca BROWN. (SLCity records)
A1. Clement, b 1720 New Haven, CT, mar Ruth Wisebury, b ca 1731 in D Derby, CT, 8 chn.
B1. Naomi, b 1753 Derby, CT B2. Ruth, b 1754 d 1799
B3. Clement, b 1756 mar Sarah ___, b ca 1770? Oxford, CT.
C1. Daniel b 1794 Oxford C3. Stephen Bennet, b 1801
C2. Amzi, b 1798 C4. Sarah R., b 1806
B4. Henry, b 1757 B5. Benjamin, b 1760, d.y.
B6. Benjamin again, b 1761 d 1827 mar Lois Smith
C1. Polly, b ca 1795 mar Andrew S. Graham
C2. Abel, b ca 1797 d 1859. C3. Benjmin, b ca 1801 d 1860, mar Mary?
B7. David, b 1765 Derby, CT mar Jerusha ___, b 1770 Oxford, CT, 6 chn
C1. Willis, b 1793 C3. Joel, b 1799 C5. Sally G, b 1804
C2. Anna, b 1796 C4. Minerva, b 1802
C6. Albert B., b 1807/8 d 1872, mar 1830 Acenith Kingsberry White
B8. Abraham, bp 1767
ENGLISH, Clement, mar Margaret ___ in Salem, MA, a dau Margaret, b1736
ENGLISH, Elizabeth mar Jonathan MESSERVY, qv. 1751 Salem, MA

ENGLISH, Jane, niece of Philip ENGLISH from J in Salem 1719. Was she the Jane who mar John CAEN, see DE CAEN, 1726 MRB?
ENGLISH, Elizabeth b 1670 MA, da of S. English. OUTC.
ENGLISH, Joseph mar 1735 Salem, MA, Mary Phippen. OUTC.
ENGLISH, Philip mar 1814 Rebecca BRIANT, res Beverly, MA. OUTC.
A1. William Groves, b 1815 A5. Lydia Ober, b 1821 A9. Philip A.b 1830
A2. James Briant, b 1816 A6. Lydia, b 1823 A10. Susan I., b 1832
A3. John Wilson, b 1818,d.y. A7. Rebecca B, b 1826 A11. Philip, 1834
A4. John Wilson, b 1819 A8. Elizabeth b 1828 A12. Philip, b 1838.
ENGLISH, Philip mar 1760 in Salem, MA Eunice GOURDON.
ENGLISH/LANGLOIS, Rachel b 1764 G? d 1846 GCO. OUTC. Conner-Eynon of GCO lists James, Hugh, John, Rachel and Nancy, poss from G fams.
EREAUT, Lemuel of a C.I. fam, res earlier in Montreal, QUE.
ESNOUF in J 1528 from Frankish Eanwulf. In St. Heliers, St. John and St. Peter J 1668, 1749. Curr J. See Q.A. IN CANADA for others. ESNOUF and MAUGER were ship builders in J 1700s. ESNOUF, ENOUF noted in St. Lawrence J 1668 and 1788.
ENOW, AYNOW, prob ESNOUF, ENOUF, Elizabeth mar 1721 in Boston, MA, John SOUSMATE, prob SAUSMAREZ, qv.
ESNOUF, Abraham, bp St. John J 1804, son of Thomas and Jeanne (QUEREE) ESNOUF, mar Nancy CORBEL, b ca 1804 St. Laurens J. Desc of this fam were sealed to parents (Mormon Church) in both LA and OK. Abraham Elizabeth and Thomas came from J to UT 1855, via ship CHIMBORAZO. (George Riding, Calif)
A1. Abraham Isaac Esnouf, bp 1824 St. John J A4. Nancy, bp 1829
A2. Jean, bp 1827 J A5. Philippe, bp 1833 St. Mary J
A3. Joseph, b 1829 J A6. Thomas, bp 1836 J.
A7. Joseph again, bp 1839 St. John J.
ESNOUF, Susan, sister of Abraham above, b ca 1800 J, d Santa Clara, UT. She mar Philip DOLBEL, qv. (SLC) 9 chn. See DOLBEL.
ESTIENNE in G 1331. This name often translated to Stephen, Stevens in both C.I. and in US.
FAINTON, Capt., ?,was sailing between Gaspe, QUE and Jersey in 1774, also to MA? FAINTON poss equals FANTON? FENTON? in America? See CT and MA records.
FAIRSERVICE noted in New England. Robert, John and Mary res Boston late 1700s. Noted by compiler that this is a rough translation of old name BECHERVAISE of the C.I. Name also noted in QUE early. See Q.A. IN CANADA.
FALAISE, FALLAIZE, etc. Judith, b G, wife of John SARCHET, qv, to GCO 1806. (Sarchet)
FALLA and FALLE are two different C.I. surnames. Some curr research? See CIFHS #8,9. FALLA is old in J and G.
FALLA, Nicholas, b 1857 Vale, G, son of Jean FALLA and Anne NOEL, mar Harriet Ann RENOUF, dau of Joseph and Harriet(LANE) RENOUF. Harriet b 1857 St. Sampson G, rem to Weymouth, MA with husband1908, then to Milford, MA. Nicholas d 1938 Holbrook, MA. The 3 oldest chn remained in G and England. Name curr G and J. (John Falla, Tenant's Harb., ME; H.T. Falla, Agincourt, ONT)
A1. John Nicholas, b G mar, and res Weston-super-Mare, England
A2. Walter, b ca 1879, unmar res G then England, was 90 in 1970.
A3. Eugene, b ca 1883 G, mar Aldine B., d 1968
A4. Emile Albin, b 1884 Vale G, to MA 1905, mar 1912 Eugenia Rose Paradis. Rem to Milford, NH then to Tenants Harb. ME 1933, where he d 1938. Widow mar Robert G. Wood, d Camden, ME 1968, bur Thomaston.
B1. Vivian Eugenia, b 1924 mar Donald C. York, son of Henry F. York and Grace Elwell. Donald a fisherman, Vivian had bookstore.

C1. Michael Henry York, b 1947 Rockland, ME C2. Janine D.York, b1950
C3. Peter Emil York, b 1960 B4. Rebecca Jane York, b 1968
B2. Richard Henry, b 1926 Milford, NH mar 1949 Phyllis Morrill Johnson b 1918 Waltham, MA, dau of Elmer M. and Eliz. (Buckle) Johnson. Richard a lobster fisherman, Phyllis taught school, Tenant's Harb.
C1. David Richard, b 1950 mar 1969 Brenda J. Vose, dau of Leroy Vose and Beatrice Miller, res Lubec, ME. Son Michael David.
C2. Jeffrey Robert b 1953 C3. John Morrill b 1954
A5. Hedley, b 1887 La Mielle G, reg. at St. Sampson, mar 1912 Milford, NH, Dora Vigneault. Hedley d 1947, bur S. Merrimack, NH.
B1. Ivy Dorothy, b 1914 Milford, mar George Hilton Jr. and d 1953. George the son of Dr. George L. and Ethel Hilton. Ivy bur S. Merrimack. George remar. One ch, adopted, Geo. L. III, b 1947.
B2. Lorraine Doris, b 1922 Milford, mar 1947 Tyngsboro, MA, Joseph M. Demers, son of John and Alma (Pelletier) Demers, b 1916.
C1. Hedley John Demers, b 1948 Nashua, NH
C2. Nathan Joseph Demers, b 1955 C3. Alison Julia Demers, b 1959
A6. Daisy Harriet, b 1889 G, mar Richard Purchase, d 1962, bur Holbrook, MASS. One son.
B1. Richard Emile Purchase, b 1911 Stoughton, MA mar 1935 Providence, RI Carolyn Snell, b 1908 Brooklyn, NY. Richard was pastor at Saxonville Bapt. Ch.
C1. Richard Thomas Purchase, b 1937 Guilford, CT mar Eliz. HILLYER, 1958 at Woodbury, NJ. 3 chn: Carole, Lynn, Wendy Purchase.
B2. Albin Francis Purchase, b 1915 Brookville, MA mar 1937 Northampton MA Helen Golash, dau of John G. and Mary Kowloski, b 1913
C1. Patricia Frances Purchase, b 1939 Brockton, MA mar Edward Gagnon
C2. Gail May Purchase, b 1951
B3. Robert Fremont Purchase, b 1925 Brookville, MA mar 1946 Holbrook, Ruth Lucille Chandler, dau of Horace and Susan (Howard) Chandler.
C1. Robert Elmer, b 1946 mar Dayle Ann Bearse 1970 Portsmouth, NH A son Robert Elmer Jr.
C2. Carolyn Ruth Purchase, b 1949 mar Richard Osborne 1968, a son Richard Wayne Osborn
C3. Richard Wayne Purchase, b 1951
A7. Albin, b 1896 G, mar 1918 Lila BelleDrake, res TEnants Harb. ME.
B1. Gerald Wilbur b 1919 Milford, d 1920
B2. Arlene Ruth, b 1921 mar 1942 Douglas Auld, son of Gilbert Stuart Auld and Ethel C. Black. Douglas b 1920 Milford, NH, pastor at First Bapt. CH, Weymouth, MA. Arlene a C.E. Director.
C1. Corrinne Lee Auld, b 1945 Bangor, ME C2. Douglas G. Auld,b 1950
B3. Harold Robert, b 1927, mar Katharine Hall
B4. Beverly Lucille b 1936 Ten. Harb. ME mar Robert Daniel Faustini, 1955, son of John Sr. and Josephine Paridis, res St. George, ME.
C1. Robert John Faustini, b 1956 C2. Rachel Anne Faustini, b 1960
FALLA, Judith b 1809 G, mar J. LE POIDEVIN, qv, bur Somers, WI.
FALLA curr Brighton, MA, Chelmsford, MA and Essex, MD. OUTC.
FALLE in J 1274. In G 1331. In St. Saviour, Grouville and St. Martin J 1668. In St. Saviour, Grouville, St. Martin, St. Peter and St. Clement J 1749. Curr G and J. FALLE shield: argent, on a chevron between three martlets sable, as many fleurs de lis of the field.
FALL, Philip, b ca 1649? in J, mar in ME poss Eliz. Basson, mother of Joshua Basson of Beverly, MA. Philip a J mariner, in Portsmouth, NH 1669/70. (Noyes; Maine Wills; Roger Easton, Olympia, WA; EARLY SETTLERS OF ESSEX AND OLD NORFOLK) Much more data. Some proof lacking in this record.
A1. John, b ? mar 1710 Judith HEARD, qv, dau of Samuel. John d ca

1745, 10 chn?

B1. John, b 1711 mar Lydia ___, 4 chn: Eliz., Lydia, Thomas, Judith.

B2. Tristram, b 1713/14 mar Abigail __, or Martha PRAY?, bp 1739, dau of John and Experience Pray. Poss another Tristram?

C1. Tristram C2. Stephen

C3. Ebenezer, b 1747-1809, mar Mary McCrellis 1751-1819, res where?

D1. Tristram, b 1775 D4. Mary, b 1783

D2. Otis, b 1777 D5. Nabby/Abigail, b 1786

D3. Ebenezer, b 1780 D6. Daniel, b 1790 D7. Betty, b 1793

D8. John, b 1798/99?, d 1839 mar Sally ___, 1798-1851, 7 chn

E1. Alexander H., b 1821 d 1902 Racine, WI mar Frances Abbott, 1820-1876 Racine, 2 chn.

F1. Isabel, b 1848

F2. John W. 1851-1891, mar Nellie Hughes, 18601896, 2 chn

G1. William Alex., 1885-1922, desc

G2. John William, 1890-1977, mar Jane Evans, desc.

E2. Mary, b 1824 E5. Lorenzo b 1831

E3. John, b 1826 E6. Elizabeth b 1833

E4. Sarah, b 1829 E7. Daniel b 1836

C4. Eunice C5. Dorcas C6. John

B3. Lebedee B4. Philip

B5. Samuel. It seems poss that the two men below, C1. and C2. may be sons of this Samuel.

C1. Samuel? b 1760, served in Rev. War, res Pepperellborough, Topsfield, Ticonderoga and Berwick, NH. He was 5 ft. 9, light compl. b Berwick, ME, discharged 1783. Had bounty land warrant 1795. He and Aaron below, said to be his bro, were jailed in Lincoln Co., MA for debt in 1793.

C2. Aaron Sr., b 1761 Lebanon, NH, and closely assoc. with Samuel in various ways and places, but Aaron was not listed as a son of Samuel in any records. He enlisted and served in REv. War. Was allowed pension on his application 1832, while res Homer or Marion Twp., Athens Co., OH, and d 1851. Mar Joanna Bickford 1786. Uncertain as to chn, but prob a Moses and Aaron at least.

D1. MOses

D2. Aaron, noted in 1820 census, poss mar Charity Rood, 1817 Wash. Co., OH. Served in MA Militia in War of 1812.

E1. ? Elijah b 1819 OH res near Aaron Fall Sr. in Athens Co., OH. Mar Lucinda Wood, dau of Benj. and Lavina(Lees) Wood, res Athens, OH, 11 chn.

F1. Lavina Fall, b 1842 d 1881 mar ___Ridgely

F2. Aaron, b 1844, d 1846 F3. Franklin, b 1846

F4. Alvin B., b 1849 mar Phebe

F5. Robert S., b 1851 F6. Sarah E., b 1856

F7. George M., b 1860 d 1864 F8. Wm. J., b 1862 mar Rachel A.__

F9. Oscar B., b 1864 Morgan Co., OH mar Frederica McClelland in Polk Co., IA 1895, d 1942 Olympia, WA. More data by Easton in WRCIC and with Easton.

G1. Bertha E., b 1896 IA mar John Edw. Mayes, d 1969 Olympia,WA

G2. Dora Irene, b 1898 mar Robert Scott 1919

G3. Cecile H., b 1899 mar Wm. H. Miller

G4. Ada Collins, b 1901 mar Peter Cutshall in Lacy, WA

G5. Agnes, b 1903 Rolf, IA mar Stanley Ames, and 2. Ted PAYNE

G6. Oscar B., b 1905 d.y.

G7. Elsie Lucinda b 1907 MI, mar Roy Easton 1935, had mar 1. Maurice Lachman. 2 chn: Roger Easton b 1937, & Hollie Easton

F10. Alice Ann, b 1867 F11. Bertha Ellen, d.y.

B6. Susannah, b 1716
B7. Judith, b 1719 mar Richard Hodsdon. She admin. the estate 1804.
C1. Margaret Hodsdon, bp 1745 mar Jeremiah Hodsdon 1771
C2. David Hodsdon, bp 1745, mar Sarah ___, made will 1807
C3. William Hodsdon, bp 1746/7, mar Anna or Amy Nason 1772
D1. Richard Hosdson, b 1774 mar 1. Lydia Cooper and 2. Eunice Lord at Berwick, ME, dau of Richard and Mary (Gerrish) Lord. Eunice b 1791 d 1862. Richard d 1851
E1. William Hodsdon, b 1796, d.y.
E2. Martha Hodsdon, b 1799 mar Sam. Pierce, d 1842
E3. Lois Hodsdon, b 1800 mar John Thompson
E4. John Hodsdon, b 1802 mar 1825 Lydia Thurston
E5. Mary Hodsdon, b 1804 mar Ebenezer FALL, d 1882
E6. SAbina Hodsdon, b 1806
E7. Sarah Hodsdon, b 1808 mar Ellis Aspinwall, and d 1889
E8. Ephraim Hodsdon, b 1811, d.y. E9. Almira Hodsdon, 1813-1826
E10. Wm. Hodsdon, b 1816 E11. Matilda Hodsdon, 1818-1838
E12. by 2nd mar, Ephraim Hodsdon, 1820-1823
E13. Richard Lord Hodsdon, b 1825 mar Maria Eunice Wellington
E14. Ephraim Hodsdon again, b 1827 mar Judith H. Foote
E15. Lydia Sabina Hodsdon, b 1828 mar 1853 John B. Varney, d 1880
E16. Elizabeth Ann Hodsdon, b 1831 mar William Tibbitts.
D2. Benjamin Hodsdon, mar Sally Cooper D4. Judith H. mar Amos Pray
D3. Robert Hodsdon mar 1803 Fanny Wadleigh
D5. Keziah Hodsdon mar Moses RICKER, qv, of Lebanon, ME.
C4. Robert Hodsdon, res Berwick, ME 1810. C5. Andrew, ditto.
B8. Mary? B9. Margaret?

FALLE. This fam often uses FALLEY, and is said to belong to the Maufant branch of the FALLE family in J.

FALLE, Richard, bp 1672 J, mar ca 1700, rem to Nfld. and later to George's River Dist, ME. Rem later to Westfield, MA, where he prob died. At least 2 chn, prob others. Much data. (CLEVELAND GEN; BUSH GEN by Arthur J. Goff, 1924; Sir Bertram G. Falle of J; SOC. JERS. BULLETIN, 1906; DAR Lineage books; Westfield, MA VR; Mrs. Eugene Baldwin; NEHGS Vols 11, 21, 40, 46; Mrs. Richard Kramer, Weston, CT; WRCIC) Pres. Cleveland is a desc of this fam.
A1. William ?
A2. Richard, b ca 1711? mar ca 1739 Anna Lamb, dau of Richard of Comb, Ireland, who settled in Westfield, MA. Richard d there 1756 when his son was 16.
B1. Richard, b 1740, George's River, ME, d 1808 Westfield, MA. At age 16 a soldier in the French and Indian War, captured at Ft. Edward on the Hudson. Later commanded a company at Bunker Hill. Mar Westfield 1761/2 Margaret Hitchcock, b 1741, dau of Samuel and Ruth (Stebbins) Hitchcock. She d Volney, now Fulton, NY 1820. Mrs. Richard Kramer, has more data on Lovisa's desc. 11 chn: Louisa, Frederick, Margaret, Richard, Russell, Daniel, Daniel, Ruth, Lewis, Samuel and Alexander.
B2. Rachel, b ca 1742 ME, d Pittsfield, MA 1828, mar Daniel HUBBARD, at least 5 chn: Anna, Naomi, Daniel, Molly and Daniel again.
B3. Elizabeth, b ca 1743, d 1812 Benson, VT, mar-1767 Westfield, MA William Ford, who d 1816 at 78, bur Middletown, VT. 7 chn: Wm., Molly, John, Oliver, Betty, Electa and Charlotte Ford.
B4. Mary, b 1744 Concord, MA d Lewis Co.,NY 1822. (NEHGS Vol 21) Mar 1764 Zachariah Bush, 1742-1811, 7 chn: Oliver, Enoch, Oliver, Edward, Walter, Charles chaney and Polly Bush.
B5. Samuel, b 1746 Concord, MA B7. Frederick b ca 1752, d ca 1753.

B6. Sarah, b ca 1750 Ware River, MA, d unmar 1801

FALLE, Joshua, from C.I. fam? mar Betsey Higgins (int) 1787 Pittston, ME. (Mrs. R. Johnson, Austin, TX)

A1. Lydia, b 1792 Orono, ME, d 1836, mar Elijah Livermore Norcross 1808. Other chn?

FALLE, Thomas, b 1804 St. Saviour J, shoemaker, d 1849 J, mar Susan Jane LE SUEUR, b 1802 St. John J, d 1871 Lansingburgh, NY. (Betty Falle Wickham, Loveland, COL)

A1. Thomas, b 1827 St. SAviour J, shoemaker, mar Helen Ellnora/Elinore LE FEBVRE, b ca 1838 J, d 1916 Rens. Co., NY.

B1. Elinora R.M., b ca 1861 J, d same day as mother.

B2. Thomas, b ca 1868 J d 1885 Troy, NY.

A2. Susannah, b ca 1830 St. Saviour J d 1848 there

A3. Henriette, b 1831 St. Saviour J

A4. Philippe, b 1833 J, d 1862, bur at sea on voyage from Australia.

A5. Mary Ann, b 1835 St. Saviour J, d 1893 Troy, NY. Mar 1. Philippe LE SUEUR, b 1828 J, d 1866 Rens. Co., NY. She mar 2. Nathaniel B. Gardner, who d by 1886 Troy, NY.

B1. Philip LE SUEUR, b ca 1865 J, d 1906 Troy, NY

A6. Jane, b ca 1837 J to Ottawa, ONT, where she mar ___Fraser. Chn?

A7. Elias, b 1839 St. Saviour J, a tailor, d 1904 Troy, NY, mar 1871 Mary Ann CHAMPION, qv. b 1853 Melbourne, AUST. Mary Ann was dau of John and Elizabeth (GREENE) CHAMPION, d 1910.

B1. Elias Thomas Marche?, b 1871 St. SAviour J, d 1960 Troy,NY,unmar

B2. Elizabeth May, b 1875 Troy, NY mar William Bissel

C1. Harold Bissel res Troy, NY

B3. William Champion, b ca 1877 Troy, NY d 1941 age 58, no issue. Mar 3 times, first wife being Catherine J. He was a Capt. in WWI , had feed store with bro Elias in Troy,and retired to FLA, d 1956

B4. Albert Henry, b 1882 Troy, NY, machinist, d 1940 Tusla, OK. Mar 1. Elizabeth Dixon Schermerhorn, 2 chn, and mar 2. Louise May Cook, b 1890 Lansingburgh, NY. Louise d 1979 Troy, NY.

B5. John Edward, b 1886 Troy, NY d Syracuse, NY mar Sarah/Sally See, 3 chn. He d 1968. Chn: Leone, Alma N. and John Edward Jr.

A8. Rachel b 1841 St. Saviour J, milliner, bur Oakwood Cem. Troy, NY, mar Julius Pfau, 4 chn.

B1. Ida J. Pfau, b ca 1865 Canada B3. Maude R., b ca 1874 New York

B2. Viola Pfau, b 1870 Troy, NY B4. Julius Pfau, b ca 1878 NY.

A9. Annie H., b 1843 St. Saviour J d 1921 Troy, NY, mar John F. Parrett b 1830 England, d 1893 Troy, no issue. Cem Marker reads BARRETT.

FALLE, those below prob belong to same family as Thomas above.

FALLE, John age 32 in 1870 res Troy, NY, mar Frances ___(NYCensus) Chn: Ella, John, Laura, Eugene, b ca 1870.

FALLE, Ira, b 1865 d 1924 Troy, NY-FALLE, May? b 1874 d 1905.

FALLE, from various sources.

FALL, FALLE, Aaron, attny in J, mentioned in Suffolk deeds, Boston, liber 17, had property in J.

FALLE, Alice mar Archie LE MESURIER in Gaspe, QUE early 1900s. See LE MESURIER and Q.A. IN CANADA.

FALL, Daniel mar Margaret CRAWFORD 1797 Augusta Co., VA. OUTC. (Amanda Forbes, Silver Springs, MD)

FALL, Jane from J? mar George SIRY, poss SYVRET?, qv, 1697 Boston, MA.

FALLE, Joshua, b 1817 J to Gaspe ca 1840, after a shipwreck off Cap des Rosiers, Gaspe, QUE. (Vera Patterson, Gaspe, QUE)

FALL, Mary mar 1813 Daniel Goodwin in MA. (NEHGS Vol 69)

FALL, Matthew arrived in boston 1715 on ship MARY from J and Falmouth, England. (Whitmore)

FALLE, Pearl, mar Wharrel G. LE MESURIER of Gaspe, QUE early 1900s. See LE MESURIER.

FALL, Philip, poss same as another Philip above? Officer of ship SUCCESS at Exeter, NH 1684.

FALLEY, Samuel res Lennoxtown, MA 1790 with fam of 9. (Census)

FALLE, Thomas, b 1678 J, rem to New England ca 1699. (FALLE GEN)

FALLU, in J 1309. In St. Peter J 1668 and in St. John and St. Ouen J 1749.

FALLU, Irene Gladys from St. Mary J? stepdau of John Philip LEMPRIERE, b ca 1888 St. Mary J, came with or after the fam of LEMPRIERE, and settled in Edmonton, ALTA. John's wife was Eva HUBERT, who d 1964 age 83 in Edmonton. She may have been the mother of Irene and of Monica below. Irene mar ___Knowles, settled CAL.

FALLU, Monica Maude, sister of Irene, went first to Canada, settled in CAL, mar Voss.

FARNHAM, Augustus, see PILL. FARNHAM is old in G, and curr G and J.

FAUVEL in J 1309, means with tawny hair; a fallow deer; or a chestnut horse that tricked people! (Stevens). FAUVEL in Grouville, St. Martin, and St. Clement J 1668, also in St. Saviour and St. Laurens J 1749. Curr J. Also noted in Dracut, MA.

FAUVEL, FAVILL, John from J? to MA early. OUTC.

FAVOL, poss FAUVEL?, Mary mar Wm. CROSS 1706 near Methuen, MA. OUTC

FOWEL, FOVEL, poss FAUVEL?, John at York, ME, a bro-in-law of Sam. Johnson, mar 1727 Anna BURRILL, 6 chn recorded. OUTC. (Noyes)

FAUX, Cassaline?, b J, age 17 in 1860 was living with the LE BOUTILLIER fam in IA at that time. See LE BOUTILLIER-BUTLER book by Brechtel.

FAVOR, see LE FAVOR, LE FEVRE, LE FEUVRE, LE FEBVRE.

FAWNE, George, sonof George F. Fawne of Guernsey, woolcomber, at age 10 was bound to John BARE (LE BER?) for 12 years in Jamaica, BWI, 1685. FAWNE does not appear in lists of old surnames, but does appear in England. For more FAWNE data see Essex Ant., Vol 3; Savage; Chase's HIST OF HAVERHILL; OLD FAMS OF SALISBURY AND AMESBRY BY Hoyt; Virkus #4. A Thomas FAWNE left a will in VA dated 1651.

FELLOW, FELLOWS, English surname. However, cf FALLU, FILLEUL of C.I. Joseph and Samuel FELLOWS res ME 1790. OUTC.

FELLOW, poss FILLEUL? or FALLU?, Abraham from J? in Casco Bay, ME1658. (Underhill) See new FERBRACHE data in C.I. COLLECTION.

FERBRACHE in J 1309. In St. Peter Port G 1700s to at least 1871. Name means iron-arm. Note FURBISH, FURBUSH of early ME and NH. Could they be derived from FERBRACHE? CAUTION, TRIAL CHARTS.

FERBRACHE, FURBUSH, FURBRUSH, Daniel P., b G, "when a boy in his teens came as a volunteer in the Army of Lafayette to aid Gen. Washington. returned to America with wife and 7 chn in 1802". (Not verified) Settled in GCO, then some of fam left for the West. (Dorothy Ferbrache, Hermosa Beach, CAL; GCO records; Evelyn Penberthy, San Jose, CAL; Mrs. J. Lusby, Lebanon, OR; Stark Co., ILL records)

A1. Thomas R.

A2. Peter T., b 1797 G, used FURBRUSHE, mar Eliz. Hall. A record in DOCUMENTS AND BIOGRAPHY PERTAINING TO THE SETTLEMENT AND PROGRESS OF STARK CO., ILL by M.A. Leeson, 1887, reports a Peter b 1797 G, to OH with parents, mar 1818 Elizabeth Frum, native of VA. He resided Preble Co., OH, then Stark Co., ILL ca 1854, where Peter d 1855. His widow d ca 1875. 7 chn, 4 alive in 1880s. Not know to compiler if Eliz. Hall and Eliz. Frum were the same person. Poss mar twice? (Ted Rowcliffe, St. Mary's ONT)

B1. Judith, b 1820 GCO mar 1841 David John who was b ca 1816 in VA. Ca 1846 they rem to Butler Co., ILL? res Valley Twp. He d 1879.
C1. Elizabeth A. John, d.y.? C5. Geo. L. John rem to COL
C2. John A. John, res KS C6. Clara L. John taught in Stark Co.
C3. Mary E. John mar H. MARTIN, res Castleton, ILL
C4. Emma S. John mar A. Schanck, res Stark Co., ILL
C7. Nellie E. John res Stark Co., ILL.
B2. Elizabeth M. Furbrushe B4. Susannah B. Furbrushe B6. ?
B3. Daniel D. Furbrushe B5. Peter A. Furbrushe B7. ?
A3. Daniel D., mar 1848 Angelina E. Foreman, 1826-1866
B1. Elizabeth mar 1868 T.H. Crawford, and d 1878. A son Frank d.y.
B2. Harriet, poss oldest?, mar 1879 Jas. T. Roney, 3 chn
C1. James D. Roney, mar res Chicago, ILL
C2. Helen S. Roney, ditto C3. Paul F. Roney, mar, res Minn., MN.
B3. Harvey, mar 1879 Eva M. Stone, or Mary Eva Stone, 2 chn
C1. Rieve S. mar 1912 Charles T. MORRELL, dau Frances Morrell b 1913
C2. Converse H., mar 1906 Edna MAIN, and d 1920.
D1. Harvey b 1914 D2. Donald b 1916
B4. Chester Fremond, mar 1890 Sarah E. RICKER, 5 chn. Settled Chadron, NEB and in Grand Junction, COL 1901.
C1. Jessie Evelyn, b 1891 mar R.H. Pemberthy, 3 chn
C2. Chester Miles, b1893 mar Mabel Shellenberger 1915. Chester d ca/1965
D1. Barbara Ann, b 1928 res Sacramento, CAL
C3. Warren Neal, b 1895 mar Dorothy Shellenberger 1924. He d ca 1965
D1. SArah Mary b 1932 res CAL? D3. Susan d.y.
D2. Martha Leona, b 1941 D4. Peter Warren, b 1944
C4. Irving Treese, b 1897 mar widow with 3 chn, had dau Sadie Marie. One stepdau. named Billie Lushby.
C5. Marjorie b 1901 mar J. Earl Smith, had dau and son, both mar, res CAL.
B5. Peter S. mar 1884 Mary Quayles, and d 1920, 3 chn. Settled east of Seattle, WA.
C1. Daniel C2. Hetty, mar Fred Radike, res Centralia, WA.
C3. Maud, mar Dr. P.C. West, res Seattle, WA, poss also San Fran,CAL
A4. Nathaniel A4. Andrew N. A6. Solomon T. A7. Susan M.A8. CarolineJ.

FERBRACHE, Daniel, b 1772 St. SAmpson,G, son of Pierre and Marie (NICHOL) FERBRACHE, rem to GCO 1806. Mar Judith SARCHET, qv, b 1774 He d before 1821, 9 chn. (DAILY JEFFERSONIAN, Cambridge, OH, 6/1/1963; Alice Behner, Brecksville, OH; Margaret Estep, Cambridge, OH)
A1. Daniel, b 1794 G, d 1806 at sea on voyage to America.
A2. Judith, b G, mar William OGIER, qv, 1819 GCO
A3. Mary, b G, mar Daniel BICHARD 1819 GCO
A4. Thomas, b 1795 G, d 1879 GCO, unmar, res Knox Twp., GCO? 1840.
A5. John, b 1804 G, d 1883 GCO, at least 9 chn. Poss mar Johanna ___, 1806-1886.
B1. John B4. Martha, mar John P. OGIER, qv, 1848
B2. Daniel, mar Nancy Law? 1861 B5. Mary, poss mar Sylvanus Wharton/1859?
B3. Thomas B6. Elizabeth. Poss mar John Smock 1858?
A6. James, b 1806 d 1896 GCO? mar 1. 1830 Cassandra Shriver, 2 sons. Mar 2. 1835, Mahala Shriver, 1818-1848, 6 chn. Mar 3. 1851 Eliz. Hopper, 5 chn. Many in this fam rem to West and Midwest.
B1. David, unmar B2. Solomon, unmar, res Cambridge, OH.
B3. Ruth S., mar James or John W. Bowdle?
B4. Elijah mar Harriet Moore, 5 daus and a son. B5. Adam, mar Laura?
B6. John, poss the one who was a prisoner in the Civil War?
B7. Sarah, mar J.G. MacGregor, a son Harold MacGregor b in 1850s?

B8. Thomas, 1847-1923, mar Mary Watson, 4 chn
C1. David, 1897-1934 C2. Ruth Wood C3. Alice Behner
C4. Dr. D. Ferbrache
B9. Lizzie, mar ___Black B10. Lena C., mar Sam. P. Thomas 1840s.
B11. Belle, mar ___McConnell B12. Reuben B13. James
A7. Jacob N., b 1808 GCO, d 1884 OH. First male ch b Cambridge, OH. Mar 1828 Eliz. Underhill, b1809 PA, dau of John and Jane Underhill Jacob mar 2. Mary Estep, b 1817, 9 chn. Jacob had 120 acres in Knox Twp., GCO 1840. (Wolfe) Chn: Thomas, Elizabeth, Jane, James, Daniel, John, David, Sarah E. and: (Sarah E. by 2nd wife)
B3. Jacob G., mar 1858 Hannah Barber
B11. George W., poss mar Ann Thomas? res Jefferson Twp., GCO, had dau Kathy Nora, b 1879.
B12. William A., d.y.? B13. Edmund B14. Rachel A. B15. Nancy mar Rob't Watson?
B16. Martha, poss mar Daniel D. Stout?
C1. Ralph Stout mar Carrie Alberta McCourt 1900
D1. Margaret Stout mar Clarence Hammond. She d 1942, 4 chn.
E1. Alberta Brown Hammond E3. James Hammond, had dau Zelma Warrell
E2. Ralph Hammond E4. Elaine King
D2. James Stout mar Ruby Fairchild D3. Lucille Stout mar Ch. Moffat.
B17. William G. B18. David again.
A8. Nancy, b 1809 GCO mar William WALTERS, b 1808 PA.
B1. Judith Ann Walters
B2. David F. Walters, b 1825 Knox Twp., GCO, served in Civil War. Mar 1866 Mary Ann Patterson, dau of James and Laurice (Gray) Patterson, b 1839 Center Twp., GCO. David d 1912, bur Cambridge.
C1. Charles W. Walters, d.y.? C4. Lerna Blanche Walters
C2. Milton C. Walters C5. Mary M. Walters
C3. Leroy S. Walters C6. John F. Walters.
B3. May Rebecca Walters B4. John F. Walters
B5. William W. Walters, b 1842 mar Eliz. Davis 1870, b 1847 Ham.Co./ ILL.
C1. Dora May Walters, 1840-1858 C4. Alva Garfield Walters
C2. Harry Davis Walters
C3. Stella D. Walters C5. Edward Irving Walters, 1877-1879
B6. Hannah M. Walters.
A9. Dr. David, b 1812 GCO, d 1884, mar1833 Rachel OGIER, 1814-1870, 4 chn, some bur Bethel Cem. Valley Twp., GCO. A David res in Senecaville, OH.
B1. Carrie, mar ___West B3. Anne J. mar Abr. Smock 1859
B2. Mary S. mar Samuel S. Carnes 1862 B4. Eliz. d age 24,prob unmar
FERBRACHE, Gilbert, res GCO 1800s.
A1. Roland Gilbert res Cambridge, OH rem to Phoenix, AZ
B1. Richard Robert, res Cambridge, OH rem to Massillon, OH
C1. Deborah, mar ___LA RUE, qv, res Ft. Lauderdale, FLA.
FERBRACHE, Thomas, several of this name. One mar Christina F. Alexander, poss dau of Thomas Alexander, b 1815 GCO, and wife Barbara Frederick. This may have been Thomas R., who had a son Charles Francis b 1871 GCO.
FERBRACHE, W?, mar 1904 Nancy Harriet Marlatt, b 1882 GCO, d 1952. (Sarchet Scrapbook)
A1. a dau who mar Earl Willey. A2. Wilbur Ferbrache.
FERBRACHE. Those below res Guernsey Co.,OH 1800s, prob of fam above.
Daniel P. mar 1858 Russia A. Stone, res Senecaville, OH. A Daniel F. was a doctor before 1850.
Code, res Cambridge, OH late 1800s-Eliz. Smock, wife of Dr. FERBRACHE
Eliz., b 1780 d 1815, prob sister or mother of an early FERBRACHE
Amanda, mar David F. Shelton 1800s GCO

Elizabeth Ann mar Wm. Kirkpatrick-Elizabeth, res GCO 1824-1906
E., mar Katie Moore 1800s-John W. mar Nancy M. Kimball early 1800s
Ernest mar Minnie Mulligan 1800s-Mary Jane mar Geo. Hutchinson 1854
Edward A. mar Sarah E. Mahama? 1800s-Mary A. mar Alex Speer 1800s
George mar Alma Thomas 1800s-May mar Sylvester Wharton 1859
Isaac manufactured salt ca 1870-Nancy mar James Lent 1843 GCO
Johanna, b 1806 d 1886 res GCO-Rachel, 1814-1870 res GCO
James D. mar Rebecca Patterson 1800s-John mar Catherine Zimmerman 1820?

FERRAN, noted in US. In J 1270, in St. Clement J 1607, in St. Martin J 1668.

FEREY old in J, also Hug. Susanna FERRY, a Hug from J, mar Capt. Philip DUMARESQ, qv in Boston 1716

FEVERYEAR, FEVRIER, FEBRUARY, Edward, Edmund, said to be Hug from J in Boston by 1664, mar Tabitha Pittman. (Essex Coll Vol 2) CAUTION: TRIAL CHART!

A1. Priscilla, b 1665, d.y.
A2. Elizabeth, b 1666
A3. Edmond, d.y.
A4. John, b 1670
A5. Abraham b 1672
A6. Mary, b 1673
A7. Isaac, b 1674, twin
A8. Rebecca, b 1674, twin.
A9. Edmond or Edward, not clear if he was the one who mar Mary Hardy Grafton. See records in Perley and Fosdick, etc.

FEW. Not certain if this name in US was orig. DE FEU of C.I. or France

FICHET, of Normandy, France 1080, in England from 1166

FICKETT, in J 1461, in St. Clement and St. Helier J 1607 and 1668. A Thomas Ficquet res in J 1668. This is a puzzling fam in early New England with no definite origin so far as this compiler could find. John in late life signed his name Jean, which is French for John, and would imply that he came either from France or from the C.I. Tradition though says he spent time in Scotland and Ireland. Said to be b ca 1645, granted land in Scarboro, ME, was a hunter, farmer and fisherman, also served as a soldier in King Philip's War, as did many Channel Island men. Mar Abigail Libby, dau of John. Poss that he had other chn than those listed here. In the division of the land, the wife's share went to Thomas Fickett and Sam. Snell. Thomas had bought from his bro John and from their aunt, Rebecca GUY. More info in sources. (Noyes; Joyce Davis, ElctCy, MD, Freeman Morgan, Takoma Park, MD; STATE OF MAINE by Little; SMALL GEN by Underhill; WRCIC)

A1. John b ca 1675? mar Susanna BALL, qv, his widow 1730. Bought land with his father or uncles 1690, 1708. Had at least 6 chn: Thomas, John, Margaret, Abigail, Sarah and poss Rebecca FOSKETT?
A2. Rebecca, mar at MRB 1707/8 Henry GUY, widow in 1744, had 4+ chn.
A3. Mary, mar Samuel Snell or Snelling of Portsmouth, NH, where they were bp with 7 chn, 2 of them adults in 1724.

FILLIATRE, see PHILATER, LE FILLATRE, curr J.

FILLEUL, in J 1528 meaning godson. See Q.A. IN CANADA. In Grouville, St. Clement and St. Heliers J 1668, and in Grouville and St. Clement J 1749. Fam fromROuen,France.See SOC.JERS.bull. 1976.

FILLEUL, see p. 241, Q.A. IN CANADA, fam of Philip Thomas, b 1887 J, d 1965. (Yvonne Kleisinger, Aberdeen, Scotland)

A8. Yvonne, b 1931 mar Ralph Kleisinger, 5 chn
B1. Donald Kleisinger, b 1953, mar Doreen Kontros, 2 chn:Tracy, Kevin.
B2. Denise K., b 1954 mar Harry Chupik, 2 chn: Jason & Yvonne
B3. Rita/Angela K., mar Alex. Chupik, no issue
B4. Martin Kleisinger, unmar B5. Leonard Kleisinger, unmar.

FIGHTLIN, Mrs. Jane of Chevy Chase, MD, said to be from J early 1900s

FILION, see PITON.

FINDLAY, Ann Maria, b ca 1838 C.I. mar 1858 in Hamilton, ONT, John Hancock, age 23, b England son of Wm. and Rebecca Hancock. (Wentworth Co. Mar. Reg; Wm. Britnell, Mississauga, ONT)

FIOTT, in St. Helier J 1668. Arms: Azure on a chevron between iij lozenges or, an anchor sable. Some Fiotts Huguenots?

FIOTT, Capt. a privateer master in J 1758. FIOTT in St. Lawrence J 1788.

FIOTT, Nicholas and Matthew GOSSETT, qv of J owned the 115 ton UNION, Capt. SIMONET, a ship trading with VA in 1783. (A. John Jean, Jersey)

FIOTT, A Capt. Peter of the sloop ADVENTURE is listed in J 1737.

FISHER, Margaret Emily, b ca 1857 J, d 1902 US, mar Albert NEEL, qv. FISHER is curr G and J.

FLEURY in J 1185, as FLORIE in St. Helier J 1668, and in St. John J 1749. Cf FLORENCE of early New England. While FLEURY was in J 1600s and 1700s, it was also in London 1680, 1682. (Tepper's NEW WORLD IMMIGRANTS, Vol 1) Were some FLEURYS in New England and the Carolinas from C.I.? (GEN. by Wm. M. Clemons, NYCity, 1917, Vol 7; MASS SOLDIERS AND SAILORS; MA, VA, OH, Phila.and Easton, PA records; also Cowan Co., NC; Hirsch; CIFHS #6)

FLEURY, Charles from C.I. before 1725 mar Mary Handcock in MRB, had at least these chn: John, Charles, Jane, Henry and David. Another, in 1760s had Charles, John and Lydia, bp MRB.

FLOOD, in Grt. Britain and C.I. FLOOD in G 1700s. In St. Martin J 1607 and 1668.

FLOOD, Philip, said to be from G, poss with Lord CARTERET in 1665 to Elizabethtown, NJ. See NJ section. Flood rem to Newbury, MA ca 1680, mar Mary ___, who d 1742 age 80. Philip d 1717 leaving 12chn. The youngest, Samuel, was 10 when his father d. There is thought to be a wealth of FLOOD data somewhere, but not found by compiler. (Andover Hist. Soc; Savage; SOME DESC OF PHILIP FLOOD, by E.F. Maloney and Norton Bagley, MS, no date; OLD HANCOCK CO. FAMS, by Wm. Pierce; THE ELLESWORTH, SURRY AND BLUEHILL REG , 1908; Maine State Library at Orono, ME; HIST. OF EAST SURRY, by Sam. Wasson;TENNY-FLOYD FAM by Leonard F. Tibbetts and Clarence H. Drisko; Elizabeth Wescott, Bluehill, ME; Papers of Dr. Albert Hill, in Blue Hill, ME Hist. Soc; Sally Guadagni, Derby, VT;Farmer; Donald Stevens, Delmar, NY; THE DOWNERS OF AMERICA) Please note that some desc use FLOOD and others use FLOYD. Also some FLOYDS came from Oxford, England to Scituate, MA early. CAUTION: TRIAL CHART!

A1. Joseph, b 1684 mar Martha Acres (int) 1705, dau of Henry and Hannah (Silver) Acres. See Silver also in early FICKET fam.

B1. Joseph, b 1705 Newbury, MA mar 1. Hannah __, and 2. Keziah?, who prob d 1756 Oxford, MA.

C1. Enoch?, b 1728, poss either a son of Joseph, or a bro?, since an Enoch bro of Joseph d 1722. In any case it is likely that this Enoch belongs to the fam. Enoch mar 1758 Mary Goodridge, and 2. in 1771 widow Grace Mackerley. Enoch d 1810 age 85 Newbury, MA.

D1. Joseph, b 1753 mar Martha ___, who d 1843 age 83 at Georgetown, MA. Joseph d 1847 age 95. Other chn than Michael?

E1. Michael b 1802 d 1847 age 57? bur Georgetown, MA mar Betsy Woods at Atkinson, NH 1827.

F1. Joseph, b 1828 Salem, NH

F2. Martha Jane, b 1829 mar Luther P. Gould 1845, chn: Ruth, John

F3. Hannah, b 1832 F4. Andrew, b 1835? d 1837

D2. Hannah, b 1755, mar ca 1775 (int) Gideon Rogers, son of Wm. and Judith (Downer) Rogers.

E1. Rebecca Rogers, mar Nathaniel Pearson

F1. Susan Pierson mar Lorenzo Dow Stevens
G1. Geo. Nichols Stevens mar Lizzie KNIGHT
H1. Orrin Belmont Stevens mar Ella F. Bent
I1. Donald Belmont Stevens
D3. Israel, b 1759 D4. Bethiel, b 1760, d Newbury, MA 1810
C2. Eunice, b 1741 Newbury, MA C3. Sarah, b 1756
C4. Enoch, b 1758 Newbury, MA. This third Enoch given in Maloney MS.
B2. Hannah, b 1706, d.y.
B3. Elizabeth b 1708 mar Eliphaz Dow of Salisbury, MA 1729. He was hanged at Portsmouth, NH 1755 for kiling Peter Clough of Salisbury MA in self defense.
B4. Daniel, b 1710 mar 1. Sarah Laboree? 1735/6, and 2. Eliz. Hutchens 1755 at Plaistow, NH. Said to have been at Ticonderoga in 1757 with Capt. John Hazen's Co.
C1. Mary, b 1736 Newbury, MA
C2. Silas b 1738, prob the one on master roll of Capt. Hazen's Co1757
C3. Daniel, b 1741 d 1805 age 67, Warner, NH mar Rachel Annis, dau of Daniel and Hannah Annis. (See AGNES, ANEZ, of C.I.) Rachel d 1829 age 84. This was Capt. Daniel Flood of Rev. War fame.
D1. Nathaniel, b 1765 Warner, NH mar Rhoda Kendrick
E1. Benj., b 1793 NH d 1879 E2. Polly, b 1797
D2. Achsah, b 1768 mar Jonathan Rowell of Sutton,NH- D4. Rachel, b 1778
D3. Eliz., b 1773 mar Robert Smith JR, d before 1805
D5. Dorcas, spelled Duchers! in will, b 1785, unmar in will 1805.
D6. Daniel, b 1788 Warner, NH d Franklin NH 1828, drowned. Mar Sarah or Sally.
E1. Arnold, b 1806 Warner, NH, prob d Ossipee 1885.
E2. Clementina, b 1808 Warner. E3. Emily?, b 1815
C4. Elizabeth, b 1743 Plaistow, NH C5. Lydia b 1747
C6. Richard, b 1749 res Warner with his bros Amos and Daniel
C7. Sarah, b 1751 C8. Amos, b 1753, d 1755
C9. Amos again, b 1757 d 1834 at Day, Saratoga Co.,NY, mar 1. Hannah Kimball 1780 at Warner,NH, who d 1791? Mar 2. Polly Wallis or Witcher 1793 at Croyden, NH. She d 1863. Amos served in Rev.War in Capt. Watt's Co, rem to NY and changed surname officially to FLOYD.
D1. Daniel Floyd, b 1782 d 1867, bur E. Derry, NH mar Esther Asby 1806 at Salem, MA. Esther was b there 1778, bur E. Derry, NH 1874. Will prob at Exeter, NH 1867 gives some gen. data.
E1. Caroline, b 1804 Salem, MA d 1827
E2. Eliza Bartlett, b 1806 Salem, d 1828 Warner, NH
E3. Daniel, b 1808 Warner, NH mar Susan Bushey 1835 at Salem
E4. James Madison, b 1810 Warner, NH d 1896 age 86, at Londonderry, NH, bur Lawrence, MA, where most of his fam is buried. Mar Sarah KARR, b 1813 New Chester, NH (now Hill), dau of James and Sarah (HUSE) Karr. Sarah d 1891. They were mar 1834 at Lyndeboro, NH.
F1. Eliza Bartlett, b 1835 Warner, NH d 1921, unmar
F2. James Karr FLOYD, b 1837 Lowell, MA d 1898 Franklin, NH. Mar Harriet E. Crowell, dau of Sam. and Sarah (Smithurst) Crowell, 1865. She was b 1830 d 1915 Franklin, NH
G1. Sarah Hattie Floyd, b 1867 Methuen, MA d 1892 unmar
G2. Charles Lang Floyd, b 1869 Londonderry, NH d 1892, unmar
G3. James Bartlett, 1872-1875
F3. Daniel, b 1839 Lowell, MA d 1891 NH, mar Eliza Ann Buffum 1862 at Lawrence, MA, b 1842, bur Grafton, MA.
G1. Sarah Maud, b 1863 d 1944 BC, Canada. She mar1. George

Stevens, div, and mar 2. Arthur Sanborn, who d 1936 in BC.
G2. William Claud, b 1865 d 1941 Derry, NH, mar Ada Belle Wells, dau of Frank and Isabella (Andrews) Wells of Auburn, NH 1888.
H1. Henry Claud, b 1889 Londonderry, d 1955 Lowell, MA
H2. Estella May, b 1891 Derry, res there 1967
H3. Sarah Adeline, b 1893 d 1964 Fayetteville, NC
H4. William West, b 1895 d Derry 1942-H5. George M., b 1897, d.y.
H6. Eliz. Viola, b 1900 res Derry H7. Carl Daniel, 1904-1960
H8. Caroline Marilla b 1913 res CT 1968
G3. Lizzie Blanche, b 1867 Lawrence, MA d 1957 Glouc.,MA mar 1. 1888 Frank Allen Cram, who soon d. Mar 2. George Allen Jones 1895 in NYCity.
H1. Addie Serena, b 1889,d.y. H2. Floyd Jones, b 1896, d 1953
G4. Daniel Carl, b 1877 Lawrence, MA d 1957 Derry, NH, mar Gertrude E. Simson, b 1885 Plymouth, MA d 1954 Portsmouth, NH.
H1. Madison Simpson, b 1905 Lowell, MA res NH
H2. May Eliza b 1907 Derry NH living 1967
H3. Elmer Stanley, b 1910, living 1967 in Maine.
H4. Inez Ruth, b 1919 Manchester, NH res 1967 in Alaska.
G5. Lulu Ruth, b 1883 Lawrence, MA living 1968 Santa Fe, NM, unmar, teaching missionary to Indians in OK and NM.
E5. Lucy Asby, b 1812 Warner, NH, d 1892 Derry, NH, mar Isaac Colby b 1807 d 1866, bur E. Derry, NH
E6. Wm. Scott FLOYD, b 1813 d 1862 Claremont, NH mar ca 1836 Mary BURHOE, qv, dau of Joseph A. of Northport, ME. She d 1861, MA
F1. Lavinia, b 1840 Woburn, MA d 1881 Derry, NH. Mar George Parsh-ley of Derry, who was b Charlestown, MA. Geo. remar.
G1. Mary Parshley, b 1876 d 1883
F2. John
E7. Charles Oliver FLOYD b 1816 d 1884 Galena, IND mar Caroline Taggart 1839 at Hillsboro, NH
E8. Esther Ashby, b 1817 d 1841 at Contoocookville, NH
E9. Thomas White b 1819 d 1870 Lawrence, MA
E10. Ira Gay, b 1820 d 1883 National City, CAL
E11. Harriet Wheeler, b 1822 d 1853 Conto'ville, NH mar George K. Kimball. A dau Hannah Jane Kimball.
B5. John, b 1712 mar Abigail Laboree, ca 1741 Newbury, MA
B6. Ebenezer FLOOD, b 1714 mar Margaret Courser, (int) ca 1737 Newbury.
C1. Ebenezer, poss res Newbury 1790 with fam of 4. (Census)
C2. John, b 1743 C3. Wm., b 1745 d 1821 Newbury, mar, 3 chn d.y.
C4. Nathan, b1748 mar Eunice DAVIS 1770. "He took the said Eunice naked, and so would not be obliged to pay any of her prior husband's debts." She d 1785 Newbury, MA.
D1. Sarah, bp 1770 D2. Ebenezer, bp 1772 D3. Nathan, bp 1774
D4. Ebenezer/Eben, bp 1777, mar Anna ___, d 1848. She prob d 1835 age 52.
E1. Nathan, b 1804 Newbury, MA
E2. Ebenezer FLOOD, b 1812 d 1881 Georgetown, MA mar 1833 Lois Pulsifer of Rowley, MA, b 1805 d 1875.
F1. Ebenezer M., 1834-1859 F3. Caroline Barbour, bp 1838
F2. Elizabeth, bp 1835 F4. Harlan Page, bp 1844, d 1920 G'town,MA.
E3. Ann, b ca 1819 mar Silas FLOYD, qv, 1847 at Newburyport, MA
E4. Eunice, b 1820 Newbury E5. Lois, b 1823 Newbury
D5. Levi, bp 1779, d.y. D7. Joanna, bp 1784
D6. Levi again, bp 1781 Newbury, prob mar Eliz. SMITH 1802
C5. Moses, b 1751 Newbury, prob mar Hannah Flanders (int) 1772

B7. Moses Flood, b 1716, mar Mary Harris of Dover, NH 1738 at Newbury, MA.
B8. Mark, b 1718 mar Catherine Laboree 1741 at Newbury, served in Rev War. Admin of his estate granted to Jos. Flood of Cambridge, VT 1798. NOTE: some data incomplete and uncertain below. (Sally F. Guadagni, Derby, VT)
C1. Peter, b 1742 Newbury, MA C3. Elizabeth, bp 1745/6 Haverhill
C2. Mark, bp 1743/44 Haverhill, MA C4. Moses, bp 1747 Haverhill.
C5. Joseph, uncertain, but thought by desc that he belongs in this fam, poss mar a Judith ROOD?, res Cambridge, VT.
D1. Mark, mar Anne Perkins, 1804 Cambridge, VT prob d Underhill,VT
E1. John B., b 1812 d 1884 Fairfield, VT age 72. Mar Adelia/Delia
F1. Olivia F., mar David Grindle of Fairfield, CT 1868 age 38.
F2. John B., b 1838 Fairfield, VT d there 1891. Mar Salina??
G1. Augusta, b 1857 d 1864 G5. Helen, b 1862, twin
G2. John B., b 1855 d 1859 G6. Holmes, b 1866
G3. Solon, b 1860 Fairfield G7. Selina, Celina, b 1870
G4. Henry, b 1862, d.y.
G8. Pearl b 1873 mar Vanner Chase 1894 at age 21
E2. Fanny, d 1805 Underhill, VT.

E3. Joseph, b VT mar Betsy Niles? or Betsy Miller, b VT, or both?
F1. Orrin, b 1843 Bakersfield, VT d Essex Jct.,VT 1908, mar Mary Ann Tracy 1867, age 21 at Franklin, VT.
G1. Armanda, mar John Copeland 1884, at age 16, Montgomery, VT
G2. Clara, b Bakersfield, VT mar 1885 age 17 Albert Lumbra
G3. Calista, b 1872 Enosberg, VT
G4. Adelbert, b 1881 Fairfield, VT mar Inez Niles 1908
G5. Dexter Benj., b 1883 mar Nina King at Essex, VT 1903
G6. Josepine b 1885 mar 1904 John B. FLOOD
G7. Jennie b 1888 mar at Eden, VT 1902 Edw. Shotney.
G8. Godey, b 1892 Craftsbury, VT. G9. Hayden, b 1895
G10. Lottie May, mar 1907 Essex VT Arthur Fred Thompson.
F2. Mortimer, b 1851 Bakersfield, VT mar Flora E. Smith 1872
G1. Albert S. FLOOD mar Christina Condie
H1. Donald R. mar Lena Tift
I1. Sally Flood, mar ___Guadagni, res Derby, VT.
G2. Eunice, b 1876 mar James Whalen at Essex VT 1894
G3. Edward, age 21 mar Genevieve Tatro, Essex 1897 1896
G4. female, b 1877 Essex, VT G5. Adda, age 17 mar Jordan A.Ogle/
G6. Nellie May, b 1884 d.y. G8. HiramC., b 1888
G7. John B., b 1886 mar Josephine FLOOD, qv, 1904
G9. Edwin, b 1890 Essex G10. Margaret, 1893-1894
F3. Flora?
D2. Isaac, b 1787 Weare, NH d 1861 Fletcher, VT, mar 1813 Phebe Meacham. Other chn?
E1. Alonzo, b Holland Purchase, NY mar 1. Martha Reynolds, dau of Wm and Ellen, b ME, who d 1881 age 57.
F1. Freeman, b 1846 d 1895 Fletcher, VT. Mar Almira or Cynthia Thompson at Fletcher 1868.11? chn, and others who d.y.
G1. Adona E., d 1894 age 22 G4. Levi b 1880-G11. Gordon,b1893
G2. Lucretia Ellen, 1873-1888 G5. female, b 1882
G3. George, 1877-1893 G6. Benjamin, b 1886, d.y.
F2. Silas, b 1847, d 1897 age 50 mar Lucy Whitney 1878, dau of Alonzo and Mahala(Dyke) Whitney. Lucy mar 2. Emerson Meacham 1901.
G1. Harris b 1879 Bakersfield, VT G2. Deforest, b 1880

G3. Alice, b 1882 mar Harland Barnes of Bakersfield, VT.
G4. Herbert S, d.y. G5. Judson, b 1886 G6. Arthur, d 1906
G7. female b 1895 G8. Luther, b 1893 d 1907 Vergennes, VT.
F3. Levi, d 1870 age 19 at Fletcher, VT
F4. Eliza Ann, b ca 1853 mar 1870 Benj. Wood at age 17
F5. Daniel, b ca 1856 d 1899, mar Mary A. Cummings 1882. She prob mar 2. Deforest FLOOD 1901 at St. Albans, VT.
G1. Norman or Nelson, b 1883 G2. Homer, b 1885 VT
G3. Hattie b 1887 Bakersfield, VT mar Geo. Cummings 1905, VT
F6. Charles, b 1857 Fletcher, VT F7. Clarie, b1860
F8. Anna, b 1863 mar Ranson Davis at Belvidere, VT 1881
E2. Phebe mar Henry Thompson 1848 at Fletcher, VT.
E3. Otis, b Bethany, NY d 1902 Fletcher, VT age 78. Mar Polly Flanders, dau of Alpheus and Sally. Polly d 1901 age 86. Otis mar 2. Ellen ___.
F1. George b 1844
F2. Allen, b 1847 Fletcher, VT mar Marley, Mary or Melissa Carlin at Waterville, VT.
G1. Edwin, b 1870 d 1892 G4. Ethan, b 1879 VT
G2. Cora, b 1872 mar Willie Brill at Waterville 1891
G3. Lucy, b 1878 mar Charles Jerome at Northfield, CT 1898
G5. Myrtle, b 1879? mar George HUNTOON at St. Johnsbury, VT
G6. Ely, b 1880 G7. Merta Melissa b 1882
G8. Erwin Otis, b 1885 G9. Agnes, d 1908 Morristown, VT
F3. Sally, b 1849 mar Monroe Taylor 1867
F4. Cyrus, d Fletcher 1908 age 52, mar Myrtle Lapan, b Stanstead, QUE 1892
G1. Harris Arthur FLOOD b 1893 Camb., VT G2. Pearly C., b1895
F5. Anna, b 1856 mar Nathan Aldrich 1874 at Fletcher, VT
F6. Persis, b 1863 mar Joseph Lowell 1885
E4. Isaac, mar Ann Eliza Glines? who d 1835 age 28 at Derby, VT.
D3. Moses, mar Susanna Page 1806 at Cambridge, VT.
B9. George, b 1721 mar prob Mary Pin, 1767 B10. Enoch, b 1722,d.y.
B11. Martha, b 1724, mar Israel Gardiner 1755 Newbury, MA.
B12. Mary, twin of Martha, 1724-1736
A2. Hester, Esther, b 1686 mar 1710 Ebenezer BARTON, qv, son of Wm., mariner. (Noyes)
B1. Chelb Barton, b 1742 B3. Penewell Barton, b 1712
B2. Ebenezer Barton, b 1711, d.y. B4. Sarah Barton, b 1714 Newbury,MA
B5. Ebenezer Barton again, b 1718 Newbury, mar 1741 Margaret Hunt.
A3. Mary, b 1688, d 1736 Newbury, MA
A4. Henry, b 1689 mar 1710 (int) Mary Stevens, b 1689 Amesbury, MA, dau of John STEVENS and Mary Gimpson? Jamison?, 5 sons, 5 daus. Henry rem ca 1710 from Newbury to Amesbury, MA. There is said to be more data in Hill Papers, in ME? (Eliz. Wescott, Bluehill, ME)
B1. Anne, b 1710/11 B3. John, b 1715 B5. Henry, b 1720
B2. Susanna, b 1713, d.y. B4. Stephen, b ca 1718 B6. Mary, 1723-1727
B7. Andrew, b 1726 d Surrey, ME after 1809 mar 1753 Bradford, MA Sarah Hopkinson, b 1732, d Surry before 1806, dau of John and Sarah (Carlton) Hopkinson. In or before 1774 rem to Surry, ME coming from Newbury, MA or Cheshire, NH. Built log cabin on shore of E. Surry, sold out to Stephen Strong, bought land in Surry from Matthew PATTEN. Juror in 1791, at Castine. Chn not all proved.
C1. Sarah, b 1754 C3. Molly, bp 1759, d before 1790
C2. Hannah, b 1756 Amesbury, MA, bp Bradford 1756, d Stetson, ME 1818 Mar in Surry James PATTEN.

C4. Dominicus, b 1762 Cheshire, NH d 1845. Mar 1. Elizabeth/Betsy SMITH, and 2. in 1816 Betsey (Brown) Young, widow of James Young, b 1783 Surry. She d 1874 age 91 (cemstone) dau of Philip BROWN and Betsy SEAVY.

D1. Andrew, b 1787 d 1855 mar Phebe J. Lord, dau of Jacob and Lucy (Morgan) Lord. Mar 2. 1818 Surry, Lorana Morgan, b 1799, d1821 dau of Benj. Morgan and Polly. Mar 3. 1822 Surry, Phebe Wormwood, b ca 1796 d 1829 age 33?, prob dau of Capt. Jos. Wormwood and Mary Hall. Mar 4. 1830 Miranda C. Milliken, b 1809, d 1891 age 79, dau of John Milliken and Mehitable Wormwood.

E1. Sally, b 1815 mar 1836 Jotham S. Billington. (by 1st wife)

E2. Lewis, b 1819 d 1845 age 26 (stone), mother of E2. and E3.was called Susanna in VRs.

E3. Benjamin, b 1820 d 1883 mar 1844 Charlotte P. Watts, b 1823

E4. by 4th wife, Phebe Ann, b 1832, d 1915 age 83 (stone), mar 1855 (Surry records) Leonard L. Wood, b 1825, d 1896, age 69 (stone)

E5. Aphia E., b 1833 d 1904, mar 2. Jonathan Dow, b 1825, d 1899 Surry age 73. He mar 1. Sarah Flye.

E6. Sewell J., b 1835/6 d 1877 age 40. Mar (int) 1869 Sophia E. McFarland, prob b 1830.

E7. Algernon S., b 1838 lost at sea 1872 age 33

E8. Georgianna, b 1840 d 1872 E9. Lydia A., b 1843 d 1861

E10. Albertine Frost, b 1845, d 1848 E11. Lewis E., b 1848 d 1869

D2. Charity, b 1789 d 1829 (Hill Papers) mar (int) 1825 Cyrus Buker

D3. Sally, b 1791

D4. Dominicus, b 1792 d 1865 Surry, mar Nancy Wormwood 1832, 1812-1896, d in Drummond, Montana, prob dau of Capt. Jos. Wormwood.

E1. May Eliz., b 1833 mar 1848 James M. Gaspar, b 1825 Surry, d 1864 Baltimore, MD, sonof Francis Mancel Gaspar and Susan Meador.

E2. Sarah Frances, b 1835 mar Edw. Jarvis Milliken, b 1834, son of Philip J. Milliken and Phebe W. Ray.

E3. Emery Newell, b 1839

E4. William Henry b 1842/52 mar Rosa Watkins.

D5. Betsey FLOOD, b 1794 d 1846

D6. Asa, b 1796 d before 1851, mar Betsy Townsend.

D7. Jonathan Smith FLOOD, b 1798 d 1874 age 76, mar 1828 Mary Haney who d in San Francisco, CAL 1884 age 84. She was dau of Edw. Haney and Patty (Collery?)

E1. Samuel b 1829 d 1864 age 35

E2. Wm. H. E3. Josiah E4. Morris E5. Alvin Thurstin

E6. Alvah Hatch FLOOD, b 1841 d 1936, mar Grace Austine, and res Burlingame, CAL.

D8. Affee, b 1800 d 1834 D9. John C., b 1803, d 1804

D10. Amasa Bryant FLOOD, b 1817 d 1893 KS. Mar 1844 Surry, Lydia Amarintha Milliken.

D11. Simon or Simeon, Wright FLOOD, b 1819 d 1913, mar 1. Adaline P. Norris and 2. Nancy W. Bickford, and 3. Sarah Almira/Myra Pert, b 1833 d 1905, dau of Capt. Allen C. and Phebe (Carter) Pert.

E1. Ashbel, a son, b 1846 d.y. Other chn?

E2. Elsie, mar ___West of E. Bucksport, ME.

D12. Heman Nickerson FLOOD, b 1825 d 1871

D13. Sarah Jane, b 1825 d 1909, mar 1842 Sam. Newell Treforgy?

C5. Capt. Bartholomew, d 1828. Mar 1. Margaret Smith, who d 1817 Surry, ME. Mar 2. 1817, Lydia (Fernald) Greene, b 1779, Gouldsboro, who d 1843 Surry. She was widow of Capt. Asa GREENE, dau

dau of Clement and Dorcas (Tucker) Fernald
D1. Eunice, b 1790 d 1815 D9. Charlotte, b 1804
D2. Jesse, b 1791 d 1812 D10. Anson, b 1807, mar 1. Mary ___
D3. Lydia, b 1793 d 1812 and 2. Ruth Fullerton
D4. Jane, b 1795 D5. Margaret, b 1797, d 1817
D6. Nahum, b 1798 d 1828 D7. Temperance, b 1800 D8. Polly, b1802
D11. Belinda, b 1809 D12. Jesse D13, Clarinda,mar E.Pinkham
D14. Thomas Nelson, b 1819 d 1850 mar 1849 Phebe J. Hopkins, who mar 2. John W. Palmer of Brewer, ME 1858.
C6. Susan, b Surry, d there 1830, mar Benj. SMITH
C7. Rev. John Hopkinson FLOYD, b 1768 d 1828 Centerville, ME. Mar 1790 Surry, Phebe SWETT, b 1777 Waterboro, ME, and 2. Jemima or Jerusha Wormwood, res Waterville, ME.
D1. Joseph S. b 1798 mar Elizabeth A. Tenny
D2. Hannah, b 1799 mar Wm. Callaghan
D3. John Hopkinson FLOYD Jr. b 1801 d 1867. Mar 1. Brittany Tenny (Wasson) and 2. Rosilla WEBBER, b 1812 Brookville, d 1896 Surry dau of Joseph WEBBER Jr. and Polly Varnum. Rem from Centerville to Surry. Widow there in 1853. Son-in-law Philip Stinson res there later.
E1. by 1st wife, Charles T., b 1836, mar 1858 his cousin Abigail Archer, b 1837 d 186-. She was dau of David Cobb Archer and PhebeFLOYD.
E2. Thomas, b 1840 Centerville, rem to Oregon.

For more info. on Conary, Stinson, Haskell, etc, see HIST. SKETCH OF DEER ISLE, ME, by Hosmer.

E3. Dorothy Ann, b 1842 d 1918, mar Jesse L. Conary, b 1834 Surry, d 1891 age 56, son of Stephen Conary and Abigail Billings. Chn: Jesse, Wm., Clara A., Leovan, Rosaella, and Levi Conary.
E4. William, b 1844 or 1854, d 1862 New Orleans, LA
E5. Mary Susan, b 1848 Penobscot or Centerville, ME mar 1. Forrester Mark WEBBER, b 1846 Castine, ME d 1874 Surry. She mar 2. (his 3rd wife) Capt. Philip Stinson, b 1838, d 1921 Surry, son of Wm. Stinson and Hannah Crockett. He had mar 1. Mary Susan Cole and 2. Rose Haskell. Chn: Harry E. and Capt. Arthur Webber; Susan, Annie, Martha, Flor, Rose G. and Sarah? Stinson
E6. John Ashbell, b 1850 Surry.
D4. Susannah, b 1803 d 1889 Penobscot, mar Reuben Grindell
D5. Phebe, b 1805, mar (int) 1828 David Cobb Archer, see above
D6. Abigail, b 1806 d age 12.
D7. David Swett FLOOD or FLOYD, b 1809 d 1874, mar Huldah Sinclair, 1810-1876, dau of Thomas and Dolley (Allen) Sinclair.
D8. Belinda/Linda, b 1811 d age 17
D9. Briggs Curtis, b 1813 (Bible) mar Mary Anne Stone
D10. Jesse Lee?, b 1815 of Ellsworth, mar 1. Lavinia Saunders, Mar 2. ? and 3. ?
D11. Jeremiah, rem to CAL, mar prob his cousin Nancy Ann Archer, b 1836. Res also in Seattle, WA.
D12. Eunice B., mar Rev. E.P. Kirkland, res Los Angeles, CAL.
C8. Jesse, b Surry C9. Eunice C10 other chn?
B8. Mary, b 1728 B9. Susie, b 1731 B10. Jonathan, b 1735
A5. John, b 1693 mar 1714 Lydia Kenna, prob d 1796 Newbury, MA.
B1. John, b 1715 Newbury, MA.
A6. Richard FLOOD, b 1696 mar 1729 Mary Connaway of Ipswich, MA. Rich a propr. of Boscawen, NH, going there in 1734, and said to have rem to Concord, NH. No record of his death found.

B1. Richard, b ca 1739 mar Abigail Farnum of Concord, NH. He d Boscawen, NH 1815, age 76. Abigail d there 1834 age 82.Other chn?
C1. Esther, b 1783 Boscawen, NH C4. Abigail, 1789-1812
C2. Simon, b 1785 d 1846 age 60 C5. Hannah, b 1792
C3. Mary, b 1787 d 1823 age 29
A7. Rachel, b 1697 mar Wm. Danforth of Concord, NH 1733/34
A8. Philip, b 1700 mar Sarah Poor 1721 Newbury, MA. Other chn?
B1. Seth, b 1722 mar Hannah Evins 1744
C1. James, b 1745 Newbury, MA d 1825 age 80. Mar Sarah __,d 1824,70.
C2. Sarah, b 1747 Newbury, MA. C3. Anne, b 1748 Newbury.
A9. Ann, b 1702 mar Samuel Johnson 1727
A10. Benjamin, b 1705 mar Mrs. Eliz. Morey 1741 in Newbury, MA
A11. Samuel, b 1707 res Andover, MA? Mar 1. Joanna Lewis ca 1738, a dau b 1738, and mar 2. Tryphena Powers, dau of Ephraim, in Groton CT ca 1742. 7 chn.
B1. Mary b 1742 B2. Martha b1746 B3. Samuel b 1749 B4. Timothy b1751
A William FLOOD of Andover, MA mar 1798 Lydia Dame of Reading, MA. OUTC
FLOYD, Ebenezer, b 1756 d 1809 age 53, mar 1791 Susanna (BROWN) Hinckley, 1758-1821. Eben was an officer in Rev. War, town clerk at Bluehill, ME before 1790, selectman. Note many Ebenezers in basic fam. (Burial Yards, by Wm. P. Hinckley, 1976) OUTC.
A1. Delia, b 1792 d 1820
A2. Sophia, b 1795 d 1838, mar 1825 Jeremiah Faulkner, b 1796 d 1845, son of Daniel Faulkner and Mehitable Peters. Faulkner res Bluehill
A3. Horatio, b1798 d 1820
A4. Betsy Atkins, b 1801 mar (his 2nd wife) Jeremiah Faulkner, her sister's widower.
B1. Enoch Floyd Faulkner, b 1840 B2. Wm. Peters Floyd, b 1842
FLOOD, Isaac, b ca 1824 MA rem to Green Co., WISC mar Eliz. Lazar 1849 Eliz. b VT, her father in MA. (JoLynn S. Alford, Milpitas, CAL) This Isaac may be part of basic FLOOD fam. Desc in CAL. OUTC.
A1. James Addison, b 1850 WISC A3. Homer Isaac b 1857
A2. George Hiram, b 1855 San Luis Obispo Co., CAL
A4. Alice M., b 1862 A5. Emma J., b 1864
FLOOD, James of Fletcher, is prob part of the preceding FLOOD fam. (SOME DESC OF PHILIP FLOOD) OUTC. See D2. Isaac FLOOD above.
A1. Ellen b 1870 mar Alfred Ramey 1885 at age 15
A2. Charles, b 1873 Fletcher, VT prob mar Julie Ann Meacham 1902
A3. Lydia b 1875 Fletcher, VT mar Frank B. Decell 1895.
A4. Earl William, b 1878 mar Annie Thayer at Bakersfield, VT
B1. Harold W., b 1903 Montpelier, VT
B2. Ruel Earl, b 1906 B3. Morton Gay, b 1900 Bakersfield, VT
A5. George, b ca 1881 mar Julia McKinney at Bakersfield 1904, 3 chn born before 1907.
A6. a son b 1883 A7. Emily, b 1886 mar Richard Carleton 1902
A8. Rosetta, b 1889 A9. Howard, b 1891 A10. Mabel b 1894 A11.Grace,dy.
FLOOD, James W. of Clinton, ME d Monmouth, ME 1873, also part of above fam? Mar (int) Mary Dearborn Blake, b Epping, NH 1811, dau of Dearborn Blake and Betsy Chase of Monmouth. Chn: Sarah Judkins,Ann Maria, Henry Lincoln, James Warren, Geo. W., Aug. Leverett, Kibby Blake, all b between 1839-1851. (DESC OF JASPER BLAKE, by C.E.Blake, 1980)
FLOOD, James, res Falmouth, ME 1700s. OUTC.
A1. ch b 1752 A3. ch b 1759 A5. Morris, b 1769
A2. son b 1755 A4. Hannah, b 1767 A6. Abigail/Nabby b 1774
FLOOD, John in WVA 1821-1828 at least had 10 chn. See EARLY RECORDS OF HAMPSHIRE CO., VA BY Clara Sage and Laura Jones, Balt., 1976.

FLOYD, Morris of Gorham, ME, see HIST. OF GORHAM by K.B. Lewis, 1903.
FLOOD, Wm., mar Hannah LOUGEE at Glover, VT 1827. She d there 1886, age 81, dau of John LOUGEE, qv, and Hannah.
A1. William P., b Albany VT mar Abigail, 3 chn: son, Isabell & Harry
A2. John, b 1832 mar Lydia GRAY 1860 at Wheelock, VT. He d there 1867 age 35. She mar 2. Robert Coleman 1868. She was dau of Samuel and Elvira GRAY.
A3. Melissa, b ca 1835 mar Ezra Clark at Glover, VT 1858
A4.Loren?, b 1842 mar Jennie Wilson at Glover 1864
A5. Lois, mar Samuel Wheeler 1868 at age 21.
FLOOD, Benj. and Mary res Boston. OUTC.
A1. Benj. b 1703 A2. Hannah, b 1713/14
FLOOD, Flan?, mar Mary LARANCE 1742 Boston. LAURENS of CI,also FLOOD?
FLOYD, FLOOD?, Geo. and Abigail res Beverly, MA. OUTC.
A1. Geo. Augustus, b 1830 Bev. A3. Mary Abba b 1839 b 1847.
A2. Joseph MASURY, qv, b 1834 A4. Stephen, b 1841 A5. Georgianna,/
FLOOD, Hannah, mar Josua Mesack?, 1747 Boston. (int) OUTC
FLOOD, Mary, mar ca 1749 in Kings Chapel, Boston, MA, DARBE LINGEWAI. Lingewai is likely to be LANGLOIS. See also DARBEY.
FLOOD, see data in Beverly, MA records; C.H. Batchelder records; FIRST MAINE HEAVY ARTILLERY, by Charles J. House 1903; Salisbury, MA records Noyes; SOME DESC OF PHILIP FLOOD; Records of Bluehill, ME: NEHGS Vol 63; DESC OF JASPER BLAKE; Records of: Strafford, VT; Marlboro, NH; Bolton, MA; Derry, NH; Walpole, NH. Note that FLOODS came early from England also. (Tepper, Vol 1)
FLORENCE. Thought by some that the FLEURY, FLORIE and FLORENCE surnames of early colonies may be variants of the same name. See FLEURY.
FLORENCE, Henry, Capt.of several ships from MRB in 1700s. OUTC. See JOURNALS OF ASHLEY BOWEN, in NEHGS.
FOLIE noted in New England. LAFFOLEY, LE AFFOLIE, meaning the crazed man. In J 1340, in St. Saviour J 1668, 1749. FOLLET is pronounced FOLEY. Other variants: FOLLETT, LA FOLLETT, LAFFOLLEY, LAFLEY, etc. FOLEY, LAFFOLEY curr J. An Osmondville LE FOLLIOTT was living 1011 AD
FOLLET, Philip from J? b ca 1730 mar 1752 at MRB, MA, Miriam PICKETT, poss PICOT of J?, qv. She was bp 1732 MRB, dau of John and Miriam. (Robert Worthington, Natick, MA) OUTC.
A1. Philip bp 1753 mar 1778 Sarah SMITH A5. John Picket, bp 1762 MRB
A2. Meriam, bp 1755 A6. Hannah Picket, bp 1766 mar 1787 Geo.Oakes.
A3. Damaris, bp 1757 mar 1775 John PATTIN
A4. Elizabeth Picket, bp 1760 A7. George, bp 1770 MRB.
FOLLEY, were the fams of Corinth, ME originally LAFFOLEY?
FOLLETT, Thomas, b J, d by 1739, mar 1730 Susanna Coolbroth, Portsmouth NH. She mar 2. Joseph Rollins. At least one son, Thomas, bp 1739 MRB. (NEHGS Vol 25; Noyes; Bolton)
More FOLLETT info: Noyes; Underhill; Perley; FOLLETT-DEWEY-FASSETT-SAFF ORD ANCESTRY, by War; OLD NORTHWEST, Vol 1; Marjorie Locke, Tucson, AZ; Lucy Leseman, Eveleth, N; Katherine Follett, Largo, FLA; Stackpoles KITTERY; Holmes DIRECTORY OF HEADS OF FAMS; Boston VRS; Pope.
FOLLETT, Johanna, b J, second wife of Sam. MITCHEL mar 1761. Res 1762 North Yarmouth, ME. (Underhill; Perley)
FONDAN in J 1180. In St. Ouen, St. Laurens and St. Peter J 1668 and in St. Peter J 1749. Curr research? See CIFHS #12.
FONTAINE, FONDAN. "In 1686 Pierre FONDAN rem (from J) to New England, and was renamed FONTAINE. Another Peter FONDAN res 1762 in MRB, MA. (Soc. Jers. Bull of 1905)
FONTENAY, Jane arrived on ship MOLLY from J at Boston, MA, servant. (Whitmore)

FOSSE, old in J and G. FOSSEY in G early. See CIFHS #12.
FOSS, Susanna mar in Greenland, NH 1723 Joseph GRANT, 8 chn bp there 1724-1744. (Noyes) OUTC.
FOSS, Maria W., mar (int) Geo. T. BROWN 1847 MRB. OUTC.
FOSKET, fam in Palmer MA 1720-1790, 17 chn. OUTC, but cf FICQUET and FOUQUET of J.
FOURNIER, old in J and G. This name noted in Canada and New England.
FOYE, many in early New England, and not all from C.I. This is prob a Hug fam, of which a branch lingered in G for some time after rem. from France. Some material gathered, but see in WRCIC, and sources noted here. Since this is not a long-time C.I. fam, only a few items are included.
FOYE, James, res Kittery, ME early 1700s. He and wife Grace deeded land to their son-in-law Nathaniel Hicks, 1711/12. (OLD KITTERY AND HER FAMILIES, by Stackpole) OUTC. James, a fisherman, b ca 1658, was 53 in 1710, res Braveboat Harbor 1686. Wife Grace there in 1712, wife Martha in 1715. (Noyes) CAUTION: TRIAL CHARTS
A1. Richard, ship carpenter and Mariner, mar Naomi Blake, d ca 1745? had son James.
A2. Martha, mar 1711 Nathaniel Hicks
A3. Robert, b 1691 mar Hannah McKenny, d before 1724. Wife mar 2. Wm. GROVES, and rem to Wiscasset, ME. 5 chn by Robert, poss 6?
A4. Joseph, bp 1691, twin mar Susannah Jenkins 1729, at least 3 chn.
A5. Charles, b 1702 mar ca 1728 Elizabeth SEAVEY of Rye, NH or poss Hepzibah Seavey? (Noyes) dau of Benj. and Mary (Wallis) Seavey. Living 1762. At least 7 chn.
A6. James, b 1704/5
FOYE, James and John, mariners and sea-captains. John in Boston 1670s, master of the DOLPHIN to London 1687. A John was in Kittery, ME ca 1630. (Kate Berocht, Charlottetown, PEI) John Foye, 1609-1684.
FOYE, Abigail mar Peter MARTIN 1746 MRB. OUTC.
FOYE, Susannah from J? mar 1775 Wm. MITCHELL. (Underhill) OUTC.
FOYE, William, b ca 1745 J? or G? d 1825 Salem, MA, bur Old Point, Salem, MA. Mar 1. 1776 Elizabeth MASURY, qv, b ca 1755 Danvers or Salem, and d 1794 age 39 in Salem, dau of Thomas and Mary LE GRO Matthews MASURY. Wm. owned or managed a ropewalk at the neck gate Salem. It was later run by Tuttle and Foye, until it was burned in 1811. Some question as to number of chn by MASURY, but all are given. Foye mar Mary Collins, dau of James and Sarah (THOMAS) COLLINS in 1798. At least 3 chn. He mar 3. ?Polly Estes?, widow of Prince or Peirce?, b ca 1765 d 1849, Salem, dau of Nathaniel?, poss no issue? (Danvers and Salem records; Essex Coll, Vols 72,74; DIARY of WM. BENTLEY; Perley, Vol 3; Churchrecords of East Church, Salem; Eleanor Conary, Bethel, ME)
A1. Elizabeth, b Salem mar 1797 Edward Tuttle
A2. Dorothy, b ca 1779 Salem d 1858, mar 1801 Joshua Safford
A3. William Jr b Salem mar 1806 Hannah Chapell
A4. Henry, b Salem mar 1805 Mary Ledbetter, res Portland, ME, in twine and rope business, d 1851, had son Wm. H.
A5. Esther, bp 1786 Salem, mar 1809 Samuel Fairfield.
A6. ?Sally/Sarah, bp 1787 d 1875 Salem, mar 1812 Thomas SAUL, qv.
A7. John, bp 1791 Salem A8. Martha, bp 1791 mar 1824 John SAUL, qv.
A9. another ch? A10. by Mary Collins, a dau d.y.
A11. James Collins, 1801-1806 A12. Edw. Tuttle, b 1805 d.y.
FOYE, Joshua and wife Ester res Salem, MA 1791 (Emmerton records) Poss from G? OUTC.
A1. Joshua d.y. A2. Joseph, bp 1791 A3. Lucy, bp 1791

A4. Hannah, bp 1792 A5. Patty bp 1794 A6. Sally, bp 1801

FOY, Jeffery, from C.I., Hug?, in Boston MA 1676, mariner. "Jeffrey and John...were probably from Guernsey". (Baird)

FOY, John, 1609-1684, mariner. "Perhaps these mariners were from Guernsey or other Channel Islands." (Savage) In Boston 1671. By wife Dorothy at least 9 chn. (Underhill; Douglas; Savage; Noyes)

A1. Elizabeth, b 1672 A4. Benjamin, twin, A7. Joseph, b 1685
A2. John, b 1674 A5. William A8. Samuel, b 1688,d.y.
A3. Joseph, twin, d.y.? A6. Hannah, b 1683 A9. Samuel, b 1689

FRANCIS, LE FRANCEYS in G 1300s. While the FRANCIS fam below orig. in G, some desc believe the point of origin was France. This is prob. due to the fact that they spoke French, and Guernsey is just off the French coast. "It had come down by word of mouth from Thomas Francis to his grandson, my grandfather Albert Francis, that he came from France as a young boy, and at one time had lived for a while in Canada, and one day getting lost. In this history in Daniel Francis diary he tells about living in Niagara for three years...Thomas was nine years old when he left for America with his parents and bros. and sisters." (Hilah Wilkinson, Robinson, ILL)

FRANCIS, Daniel, b 1759 G, d age 93, 1850 in Logan, OH. He is said to have come from a fam of ship builders and ship chandlers in G. Rachel LE MESSURIER, qv, his wife, b 1756 prob in G. Seven of their 9 chn were part of the first Ohio group to arrive in GCO 1806. They left the group from the Channel Islands in Baltimore, MD, settled for some time in Brooklyn, NY, then rem to upper NY state. (This may be when they lived for a time in Canada) Then rem to Athens Co., OH, where some desc still live. A gradau Desier Wild, pioneered in KS. See in PERSONAL ACCOUNTS. (Walden; Atha Brace, El Campo, TX; Jay Pugsley, Lincoln, NEB; Patricia Surface, Tazewell, OH; Hilah Wilkinson, Robinson, IL; Mary Hammingsen, Elwood, NEB)

A1. Rachel Francis, b 1782 G, prob mar and remained there A2. Susanna?

A3. Nicholas, b 1787 G mar Thankful Philipps of Amesville, OH 1817. She had 3 chn and d before 1831. He mar 2. Marcy Rathbun, 1802-1891?, b VA, 7 chn. Nicholas d 1863, res Logan, OH, but is bur in Harrison Co., IA.

B1. Rachel Francis, b 1821 mar G.W. Pugsley, rem to Woodbine, IA, 8 chn

C1. Marcellus Pugsley, b 1842/3 Ohio

C2. Marcella Pugsley, b 1844, d 1915, mar 1869 H. Kinton Peckenpaugh.

C3. Georgiana Pugsley, b 1846 OH C6. Charles Pugsley, b 1852, OH
C4. Francis C. Pugsley, b 1848 C7. Laura Pugsley, b 1856 IA
C5. George Pugsley, b 1850 C8. James R. Pugsley, b 1859 IA

B2. Desire, b 1825, d 1912 Stillwater, OK mar 1843 Thomas Wilds, Wile or Wild, b 1820 England, d 1891, bur Beverly, KS. Also res Wash. Co., IND. Ca 1855 rem to Harrison Co., IA, then later to Saline Co., KS. 13 chn, but several d.y.

C1. James Wilds, b 1845 OH C3. George Wilds, b 1860 IA
C2. Maria F. Wilds, b 1851 OH C4. Mary Wilds, b 1856, IA
C5. through C9: Lucy, Sarah, Grant, etc., d.y.
C10. Marion Wilds C11. Ellen Wilds C12. Charles Wilds C13. JohnWild

B3. Dorsey, d.y. B4. Susanna, d.y.

B5. by 2nd wife, Thankful, b 1832 mar 1852 Johnson Coe, son of James, desc of Robert Coe from England 1634 to MA. Johnson b 1826 d1890. Thankful d 1858 leaving 2 small sons.

C1. J. Gaston Coe, b 1853 d 1915 farmer near Nelsonville, OH, mar 1877 Isabella Martin, b 1853, dau of Peter F. Martin, 2 chn.

D1. Celia Coe mar John T. Hope Jr, see page 43, HOPE LINEAGE

D2. Letty, mar Hintz, no issue
C2. George Coe, b ca 1857 res near Chauncey, OH mar Della Shaffer.
D1. Olive Gertrude Coe, mar Charles Daughterty, chn.
B6. Laura Francis, d.y. B8. Augusta Frances, d.y.
B7. Gideon Francis, b 1835 mar Sarah Watson Tyndall, rem to OK, and d at McAlester, OK. Chn, but only one, Benjamin, is known.
B9. Lucy U., b 1840 mar ca 1859 Frank J. Porter, b 1837 Canada, res Woodbine, IA.
C1. Emma Porter, b 1860 C4. Edgar Porter, b 1867 C7. Ada Porter
C2. Francis/Frances? b 1862 C5. Georgia Porter b 1870
C3. William Porter, b 1865 C6. Kate Porter C8. Inez C9. Harry
B10. Louisa Lucina b 1841 mar Amos Lawson and res Red Oak, IA, said to have had 15 chn.
B11. Foster, b 1845 mar Emma Stevens, res Woodbine, IA, 5 chn, including one named Joseph
B12. possibly a Franklin F. Francis also?, b OH?
A4. Elizabeth, b 1789 G, d 1854, came with parents to America, and poss mar in New York? ___Brickley. No record found, but perhaps mar in MD? She mar 2. 1822 Ethan Beebe in Athens Co., OH, but he soon died. She mar 3. William Six, 1824, young widower near Athens, OH, noissue? A niece, Charlotte Francis, res with her for several years and was mar from Elizabeth's home. Eliz. is bur near Kimberly, OH, Boyles Cem.
A5. Jean/John, b 1790 G, d 1870, res Cayuga Co.,NY mar 1920 Owasco,NY Nancy Van Houten. In the census of 1860 and in his will, his wife's name is Lydia, so he prob mar twice. There may be other chn than those below.
B1. Rachel Ann, b 1826 mar Daniel N. Curtis, res Moravia, Cayuga Co., NY. A son Frank S. Curtis, d 1936 unmar
B2. Nancy, mar ___Marshall of Locke, NY. B3. John, res Chicago, ILL.
B4. Hiram S., mar and res in NYCity? A son Judson F.?
A6. Judith, b 1793 St. Andrews G, res Cayuga, NY, mar Rev. Moses Osborn, several chn. Judith d 1878 Greene Co., ILL. Moses was b 1782 CT, mar 1808 Kings Co.,NY and d 1862 Greene Co., ILL. He was son of Josiah Osborn and Dolly. Mar 1. ? Anna Lyons?
B1. Josiah Osborn, b 1809 NY, poss d.y.?
B2. David Osborn, b 1814 NY, d 1873 Mowcaquid?, ILL, mar Susan ___.
B3. Francis Osborn, b 1818 Athens, OH d in ILL, mar Martha ___
B4. Isaac Osborn, b 1820 Athens, OH
B5. Alanson Osborn, b 1822 Athens Co., OH d 1895 Shelby Co., ILL. Mar Carrollton, ILL Sarah Pruitt, dau of James and Mahala (Ambrose) Pruitt. Sarah b 1836 d 1925, bur ILL, 8 chn.
C1. James A. Osborn, b 1851 Fidelity, ILL d 1937. Mar 1871 Alice Coater, dau of Francis and Adaline Coater, who d 1924? James mar 2. Idella Brown. Was Alice a LE COUTEUR?
C2. Richard Francis Osborn, b 1854 Fidelity, ILL d 1944 Scotts Bluff, NEB, mar1. Lumina COATER and 2. Mary WINTER. Richard an inventor, farmer, realtor and Judge, and 32nd deg. Mason.
D1. Victor Francis Osborn, b 1875
D2. Adeline Osborn, b 1879 ILL, d 1970 IND. Mar Waldo Remy, 1885-1971, 2 daus.
D3. Richard E. Osborn, b 1883 ILL mar Hilda Schelm, 1839-1916,4chn
D4. Luminia Osborn, b 1886 d 1887 ILL D5. Effie May, 1889-1902
D6. Oscar Francis Osborn, b 1885 d 1965 WA. Mar 1. Lena Finney, 1885-1919, 2 chn, and 2. Rose Tenold, issue?
E1. Helen Osborn E2. Howard Osborn
D7. Grace Osborn, b 1892 ILL d 1970 COL, mar Roscoe Haworth, 2 chn.

E1. Robert Haworth E2. Virginia Haworth
D8. Edith Osborn, b 1895 mar Rev. Lavern Hicks, 1 dau, with chn.
D9. Nelle Osborn, b 1897 ILL, mar Wm. A. Kent, 1892-1969, no issue
D10. Raymond Martin Osborn, b 1903 ILL mar Mildred M. Rucker 1925. Mildred b 1907, 5 chn. She the dau of James and Rose (Sanford) Rucker.
E1. Mardele Osborn, b 1925 Denver, COL mar 1. Eugene Shaul, a son. Mar 2. Robert Moody, a son and dau. Mar 3. Donald E. Coble, adopted Cindy.
F1. Craig Eugene Coble, b 1945 mar Harriet Wieher, 2 daus, Toni Dee and Wendy Sue Coble
F2. Roger N. Moody, b 1948 Ainsworth, NEB, mar and div.
F3. Jerrie L. MOody, b 1949 mar 1968 James Schurr, 2 chn: Sean R. and Jill Schurr.
E2. Staley E. Osborn, b 1926 mar Verna Fowler in WY.
F1. Bradley G. Osborn, b 1950 mar Sandra Geiger in Vinton, IA
F2. Vickie Lou Osborn, b 1950s F3. Curtis W. Osborn, b 1962
E3. James Richard Osborn, b 1935, mar 1. Sally Tarza and 2. Trudy.
F1. Joyce Lynn Osborn, b 1960 F3. Julie Ann Osborn, b 1965
F2. Jackie M. Osborn b 1962 F4. Joni M. Osborn b 1967
E4. Mary L. Osborn, b 1937 Ainsworth, NEB mar R. Swett, 2 adopted chn: Tim and Nancy. Mar 2. Allen Hemmingsen, res Elwood, NEB.
F1. Louise Hemmingsen, b 1970 North Platte, NEB. Also Milton, Royce, Timothy and Wanda Hemmingsen.
E5. Glenn D. Osborn, plumber, b 1938, mar Virginia Skinner, b Germany, 5 chn: Glenda, Mart Ray, James D., Thomas R. & Charles.
D11. Glen Osborn, b 1905 d 1969 WA. Mar 1. Doris Sisson, 2. Blondi Clark, and 3. Ethel ___, 2 chn
E1. Brett Osborn, b 1955 E2. Diana Osborn, b 1963
C3. Lewis Osborn, b 1856 Fidelity, ILL d 1921 Ainsworth, NE mar Margaret English, who d 1931.
C4. Luther Osborn, b 1863 d 1947, mar Anna Zeitz, 1867-1949, ILL.
C5. Mary Elizabeth, mar Rev. Isaac Haverfield
C6. Jeannette Osborn, mar 1. Wm. Manley and 2. J. Dorman
C7. and C8. Amanda and Oscar, d.y.
A7. Daniel, b 1796 G, mar 1818 Martha Phillips, dau of Daniel Phillips of Amesville, Athens Co., OH. Daniel and farmer, and Martha, sold their land in Athens in 1832 and moved West. No more known.
A8. Alexander Thomas, b 1797 G, d 1856, filed citizenship papers 1823, was mason and builder. Marshall in Athens 1832, councilman 1834. Mar 1. 1819 Polly Fulton, who d ca 1825, 3 chn. Mar 2. 1828 Mrs. Mary Eliz. (Baker) GRAY, b 1801 MA, widow of Combs GRAY, and dau of Isaiah BAKER. Thomas d in RR bridge accident. Eliz.d 1886 Both bur West State St. Cem., Athens, OH.
B1. Alexander, b ca 1820, served in Mexican War, in 2nd OH Inf. under Capt. Robert McLean, and in Capt. Earhart's Co., for which he received a grant of land. Mar ca 1839 Nancy ___, b 1818 MD. He d ca 1850, and his widow and chn rem to IA in 1856.
C1. Lucy, b 1840 C3. Charles b 1844
C2. Julia, b 1842 C4. Melissa, b 1846 C5. Mary Ann, b 1848
B2. Daniel, b ca 1822 mar 1842 Eliza B. Conner, and in 1860 res Summit Co., OH.
B3. Charles, b ca 1824, res Fairfield Co., OH, 1860.
B4. Charlotte, by 2nd wife, b 1827, mar 1. 1843 Martin Boyles, and res near Nelsonville, OH. Rem to ILL soon after their mar, but returned to OH. In 1849 they went to ILL, where he d ca 1850. She came back to OH, and mar 1855 Elisha BENJAMIN, b 1817.

C1. Mary E. Boyles, b 1844 ILL C4. Martin Boyles, b 1850 ILL
C2. Minerva Boyles, b 1846 d 1861 C5. Charlotte Benjamin, b 1856 OH
C3. Charles A. Boyles, b 1848 OH C6. Jessie Fl. Benjamin, b 1858 OH.
B5. Minerva, b 1831 d 1909. Mar 1849 Athens Co., OH Joseph B. Eckley, 1828-1902.
C1. Elizabeth Eckley, b 1852 mar ___Garnett, and res Kansas.
C2. Robert W. Eckley, b 1853 mar ___Hawk
C3. Joseph Hadley Eckley, b 1856 res Council Grove, KS
C4. Nettie Eckley, b 1861, no issue C5. Elma Eckley, rem to KS
B6. Robert B., b 1833, d.y.
B7. Thomas Jefferson, b 1835, d 1919 Clark Co., ILL mar 1. Eliz.Bosman a son William. Mar 2. Mary Frances Edwards, b 1841 ILL, d 1910.
C1. William Forest, b 1864 d 1918
C2. Albert Edwards, b 1872 Grundy, where?, d 1944, mar 1895 Sarah Amanda Canaday. Albert a farmer, bur Clark, ILL. Sarah b 1869, d 1941, dau of Wm. H. and Susan E. (Evans) Canaday, 3 chn.
D1. Mary Esther, b 1897 ILL, d 1979 Crawford, ILL, mar 1918 LeRoy Wheeler, son of Reason and Dolly (Hand) Wheeler. Mary mar 2. Wm. Leasure.
D2. Iva Ethel, b 1899 Hutsonville, ILL d 1971 Robinson, ILL mar Noah Joseph Willard, son of Joseph and Add (Lindley) Willard. Noah b 1900 d 1971.
E1. Hilah May, b 1928 Robinson, ILL mar 1952 Herbert Lawrence, son of Paul and Lola (Russell) Wilkinson, 2 chn. Herbert a Vet,WW2.
D3. Emery Voorhees, b 1907 Melrose Twp., ILL, d 1957 Findley, OH, mar 1934 Pauline Gibler.
C3. Windfield S., b 1875 d 1947,? unmar.
C4. Emma C., b 1876 d 1896 unmar C5. Eda Mae, b 1879 d 1951 unmar
C6. Mary A., b 1886 Grundy, mar 1908 Jacob Beck. A Mrs. Mary Beck res Paris, ILL. Some records in Marshall, ILL?
B8. Eben F., b 1837
B9. Edward N. b 1838 mar 1861 Athens, OH Sarah Walker, b 1839 Athens.
C1. Forrester, b 1863 mar Eliza Vore, no surviving issue
C2. Ethel mar Harry Campbell, no issue
B10. Mary A., b 1840 mar 1858 J.C. Walker. B11. John Q., b 1842
B12. Wm. Blackstone, b 1844 served in Civil War. Mar 1. 1869?Sarah Ann Buchanan. He was 50 yrs. an engineer on the Hocking Valley RR, mar 2. in Athens, OH Isabel ___.
C1. Warren, mar, with dau Isabelle. C2. Mildred, mar L.V. Brown.
A9. Peter, Pierre, b 1799 G, mar in Athens Co., OH 1823 Edith or Faith Cambe, Camby. Peter bought land in Athens 1830 but sold it in 1832 and is said to have rem West.

A FRANCIS fam is noted in HIST. OF CLERMONT CO., OH, a Rev.War soldier with the Jerseytroops. Had son Joseph who mar Sarah Clifton. OUTC.

See Athens Co., Summit Co, and census records for many more Francis.

FRANCIS, fam in Beverly, MA 1700s with a Judith and an Ebenezer, poss from C.I.?

FRANCY is the pron. of FRANCIS in French. Poss fam below, bur in Madison Twp., GCO may have been FRANCIS from G. (PIONEER CEMS OF GCO, p. 51, by Conner-Eynon)

FRANCY, Wm., b 1798 d 1881. Jane, 1810-1884, his wife? Martha B. poss a dau, 1845-1918, and Jennie, 1887-1903, a grdau. Wm. John, 1850-1927, a son? Sarah Jane and Ida Ethel also listed.

FRANCOIS in J 1214, in St. Laurens J 1607. Common in C.I. as FRANCIS. See CIFHS #6.

FRAZER, Caroline, age 21, b J, dau of John and Sarah, mar 1865 in Toronto, ONT, James Breckon, 26, b Scarboro. (St. Paul's records)

FRECKER, surname of Grt. Britain and sometimes in C.I.
FRECKER, George, b ca 1850 J? mar Harriet NORMAN b G. (Robert L. Scheurman, Sarnia, ONT)
A1. a dau who was b ca 1868, d Brooklyn, NY 1934 age 66.
FRECKER, Noel, a seaman of J 1741 was captured by the French, taken to France and escaped. (Saunders)
FREEMAN, old name in G. A Freeman from G rem to ONT. (L.F.GUY,Orono, Ontario)
FREETO. "The FREETOS in this area, I believe, did come from the Ch. Islands, not France, as did many settlers in Marblehead." (Peggy Gayron, Lynn, MA) Note that some FRITOTS also came from France to America in 1803. FREETO was prob from J, as Stevens lists FRITOT as an old Jersey surname. Difficult to sort branches of this fam without more info. Note FRETEAU in John LE FAVOR fam. (Noreen Pramberg, Newburyport, MA)
FREETO, Francis and wife __, res MRB, a son John bp 1715
FREETO, Francis, mar Jane BESSOM, BISSON 1785, res MRB, at least 7 chn.
A1. Jane, b 1786 A5.Mary/Polly, b 1793 mar Francis SWETT 1817?
A2. Sarah, b 1787, see BISSON chart
A3. James, b 1789 A4. Francis, b 1791
A6. Grace, b 1797 mar Mark. H. MESSERVY, qv, 1827
A7. John, b 1798 res MRB mar Mary BROWN. See also John & Mary below.
B1. Philip, b 1831 A3. Rachel F., b 1836
B2. Frank, b 1834 A4. Thomas A., b 1841
B5. Sarah Ellen, b 1843 MRB d 1911 mar John Henry HASKELL, b 1837 MRB, d 1905, his 3rd wife. Much more data on Haskells available.
C1. Nellie Florence Haskell, b 1872 MRB d 1954 Salem, mar Axel W. Pramberg, b 1862 Sweden, d 1936 MRB.
D1. John Haskell Pramberg, b 1909 Lexington, MA d 1973, mar Bessie Webster, 1907-1972.
E1. John Haskell Pramberg, Jr, b 1929 mar 1953 in TX, Noreen Cook.
FREETO, Francis mar 1817 Eliz. D. Crowninshield,res MRB. Dau Mary Jane b 1825.
FREETO, James mar 1731 Mary GRANT, res MRB. OUTC.
A1. James, bp 1732, d.y.A3. John, bp 1736 A5. Patience, bp 1744
A2. Mary, bp 1734 A4. Elizabeth, bp 1741
A6. Francis, bp 1746 A7. William, bp 1750
FREETO, James mar Hannah CHINN 1750. Hannah d 1795 MRB.
FREETO, James mar 1754 Sarah Pittman, res MRB.
A1. James, bp 1756 A4. Francis, bp 1761 A7. Philip BISSON, b 1799d.y.
A2. John, bp 1757 A5. William, bp 1764 A8. Philip again, b 1801
A3. Mary, bp 1759 A6. Sarah, bp1765
FREETO, James, mar 1815 Grace Blancey, res MRB.
A1. Grace, bp 1817
A2. Jane BESOM, bp 1818, mar 1845 James LYON, age 24, son of Thomas and Mary LYON, qv.
A3. James Jr. b 1822 mar age 25 in 1847 Sarah E. Russell, dau of Ezekiel and Sarah RUSSELL, qv.
A4. William Blaney, bp 1825, mar the same or another Sarah RUSSELL?
A5. Mary, b ca 1829 mar John H. RUSSELL, b ca 1828, son of John and Sarah RUSSELL, in 1848.
FREETO, John and Mary res MRB. Note John and Mary above, in fam of Francis and Jane FREETO.
A1. Hannah Brown, b 1813. A Hannah age 22 mar in 1847 John O. Chapman, son of Nathaniel and Martha.
A2. Mary Elizabeth b 1819 A5. Sarah Rebeckah, b 1827, d.y.
A3. Jane Bessom, b 1821 poss mar 1836 Alex Standley Jr.

A4. John, b 1825 A6. Sarah Rebecca again, b 1829.
FREETO, Mrs. Jane mar 1802 Robert Pierce of MRB. She was b 1765.
A1. Robert Pierce III, b 1803 mar 1823 Mary Ann DAVIS, 1812-1847. (Peggy Gayron, Lynn, MA)
FREETO, John mar Sarah Giles of Danvers, MA 1757
FREETO, John d very old 1807, b J?
FREETO, Manuel mar Mary BROCHETT, BROCHET? of J? 1776, MRB.
FREETO, Mary mar Benj. White 1756 MRB
FREETO, Mary E. mar Benj. GALE Jr 1841 MRB.
FREETO, Ruth H. mar Geo. W. Standley 1843 MRB.
FREETO, Sarah mar 1787 Clement SEVERY, prob SYVRET, MRB.
FREETO, Sarah mar Sam. SWETT Jr. 1813 MRB.
FRENCH, see FRANCOIS and FRANCIS.
FREZELL, Daniel, a freeman, to SC 1671 on ship BLESSING. (Baldwin) FRIZELL in J ca 1340.
FROST, several b St. Helier J 1830s, from southern England? Thomas Evan, bp 1834 and Edwin, b 1836. (M.L. Backhurst, Jersey)
FULLER. See Q.A. IN CANADA for John F. Fuller of NS who mar a girl from Guernsey. FULLER is curr in G. Some said to have come from J to New England in the 1600s or 1700s. A Thomas FULLER mar Abigail GUSTIN, qv, in Lynn, MA 1693. Another FULLER was in Concord, MA 1641. OUTC. (Concord VR)
FULLER, Frederick, b J after 1853, son of Joseph, b 1815 England. Frederick rem to what became Fullerton, NEB, then rem to Vancouver, BC. A grandau res NEBR. (Arthur Fuller, Los Osos, CAL)
FULLER, Joseph, father of Fred. above, b 1815 England rem to J ca 1853, had 4 daus and a son Fred. The daus remained in J. (Arthur Fuller, Los Osos, CAL; Mrs. Falla, Guernsey, 1975)
FUREY, noted in CAL and elsewhere. This is said to be a variant(very!) of LE HURAY, qv, and one fam settled in Conception Bay, Nfld. ca 1750 has desc in N.A. Said to be from J. (G.W. LE MESURIER; Lady McKie)
FURNACE in New England. Cf FURNEAUX, French and C.I. surname. See Q.A. IN CANADA.
FURRY, Lydia, d 1826 Phila. PA age 84. (Quaker Ency, Vol2) OUTC.

GABRIEL. Poss that some Gabriels in America were GABOUREL, in St. Ouen J 1668, and in St. Peter J 1749.
GALE, GAILLE, GALLE, GALLEZ? GALES settled early in New England. Some mar into C.I. fams. In the Essex Inst. are 3 pages of a personal or Bible record, about the Gales of Salem, MA, dated 1765-1845, donated by Charles F. Townes 1937. GALE in Alderney Is., 1800s, curr G. GALLES curr J. Other Gales no doubt from England.
GALE, Ann, b ca 1850 ALD, mar ___PALMER, qv, to Toronto, ONT, d Detroit MI 1935.
GALE, Benj. from C.I.? to MRB. Wife Lydia, unver. OUTC.
A1. Mary b 1677 A4. Elizabeth, b 1685 A7. Benjamin, b 1694
A2. John, b 1679 A5. Deliverance, bp 1688, d.y.? A8. Samuel, b 1699
A3. Ambrose, b 1683 A6. Deliverance again, b 1690.
GALE, Eliz., mar Elias BRYARS 1799 MRB. See BRIAR, BRIARD
GALE, Edmund, coaster of Beverly and MRB, bought land 1678/9 Falmouth, ME, mar Sarah Dixey, dau of Capt. Wm. of Bev. Ten chn bp Salem and Bev. of whom Azor claimed the ME lands, his heirs selling in 1731. (Noyes) OUTC.
GALE, Abigail, b ca 1681, dau of Edmund above, d 1769 Manchester, MA. Mar Wm. HOOPER, son of Wm., b 1673 Beverly, MA ca 1703/4. He was a blacksmith, d Manchester 1755 age 81. More. (HOOPER GEN).
GALE, Sarah, from C.I.? wife of Richard BISSON 1756 in MA.

GALLEY, GALLIE, John b ca 1783 MA, poss of C.I. fam there? His grandmother may have been Margaret DAVIS GALLEY, who d on Mt. Desert Is. 1821, dau of Joseph Warwell. Margaret said to be b 1723. John was on Mt. Desert Is. by 1810, res Tremont, mar 1. ca 1809 Hannah ___.He mar 2. another Hannah, b prob 1794, who was his widow 1851, liv. 12 chn. Curr research. (ME Census records; Cem. Inscriptions; Hancock Co., VR; Probate records; Mrs. Rebecca Dow Burnham, Wilton, ME; Emery W. De Beck, Melrose, MA; Elizabeth C. Westcott, Blue Hill, ME; Phila. Hist. Soc; Hazel E. Hammond, Marcellus, NY; WRCIC)

GALLEE, John, ca 78 in 1683, will dated 1683. Res Essex Co., MA, OUTC. Was John a GALLEZ or LE GALLAIS from C.I? Note that GALLEY may be Irish, German or English as well as C.I.

GALLICHAN, see also GALLISON, GALUSHA, GALEUTIA.

GALLICHAN in G 1331, in J 1240. GALLICHAN in St. Martin, St. Brelade, and Trinity J 1668, and in St. Martin and Trinity J 1749. Curr G.

GALLICHAN, Walter M., author of WOMEN UNDER POLYGAMY, Dodd Mead, NY 1915. OUTC.

GALLICHAN, Abigail mar James Bragg 1774 in Gloucester, MA. (Essex Ant)

GALLISHAN, Abigail mar Joseph Burpee, res Sheffield, NB (Perley Fam, by M.B.V. Perley, Salem, MA 1906) Poss other chn? OUTC.

A1. Mary Gallishan Burpee, b 1801 mar 1. ___, and 2. Thomas Perley, b 1778, Maugerville, NB, Canada. He d 1838 French Lake NB, she in Sheffield, NB 1887. 9 chn

B1. Janet Bean, Charity Eliza and Martha Harrison Perley, by 1st wife

B4. Mary, b 1826 by Abigail Gallichan Burpee Perley, mar 1848 Charles Burpee, b 1817, son of Jeremiah and Betsy (Stickney) Burpee of Sheffield, NB, no issue

B5. Caroline Perley, b 1829 Sheffield, mar 1852 Charles Benj. Barker, b 1827, son of Benj. and Mary(Coburn) Barker.

C1. Charles Woodville Barker
C2. Thomas Benj. Barker, b 1855
C3. Harriet Atwood Perley Barker, b 1856
C4. Fred. C. Barker, b 1860, twin
C5. Thomas P.Barker, twin, d.y.
C6. Clara L.Barker, b 1864

B6. Charles Perley, b 1853 mar 1878 Harcourt, NB Marilla Eliza Dunn, b Chipman, NB 1854, dau of Andrew and Jane (Paine-Quint) Dunn.

C1. Wm. Harrison Perley, b 1880

B7. Fred C. Perley, b 1860 mar 1898 Gibson NB, Laura A. Frandsham, no issue.

GALLICHAN, Hannah, 2nd wife of Samuel Peabody, who mar 1. 1773 Molly Hilldrick, b Boxford, NH. Rem to Maugerville, NB. (PEABODY GEN) Not known to compiler which chn were those by Hannah, and which by Molly. OUTC, but prob Hannah was from C.I. fam.

A1. Francis Peabody, b ca 1774, called Capt. Francis of Chatham, NB.
A2. Rhoda Peabody, b ca 1776 mar Thomas Perley
A3. George Peabody, b 1778, desc
A4. Hannah Peabody, b 1780
A5. Stephen Peabody, b 1782, desc
A6. Samuel Peabody, 1784-1809, unmar
A7. James Peabody, 1787-1848,unmar.
A8. Francis Peabody, 1789-1827, unar.
A9. Maria, b 1791 mar Adam B. Sharp of Woodstock, NB in 1822
A10. Hepzibah Peabody, b 1793,unmar.
A11. John Peabody, b 1795, desc.
A12. Rebecca Peabody, b 1797, mar Thomas Gill./
A13. Isaac

A13. Isaac Peabody, b 1799 mar Eliz. Ann Huntington of Devon, England and d 1828 on a voyage to the East Indies.

GALLICHAN, John, arrived in Boston 1769 on ship MOLLY from J.(Whitmore)

GALLICHAN, Mary dau of Thomas G. and Elizabeth VARDON, qv, of J, mar Charles HORMAN, qv.

GALLIE in St. Saviour and St. Martin J 1668 and in St. Saviour J 1749. Curr G and J.

GALLIE, Francis, b 1762 J d 1824, bur St. Peter's Cem, Paspebiac, QUE.

(Loretta Gallie, Lapeer, MI)

A1. John Francis, b 1790 J, d 1874 mar Anna Maria Scott, dau of James Sr. and Johanna Brotherstone Scott, b 1800 d 1863, 7 chn.
B1. Joanna, mar Thomas Brock Munro
B2. Margaret, b 1819 QUE mar Wm. Munro, b 1802, 7 chn
C1. Johnston Munro, b 1838
C2. William George Munro, b 1839
C3. Mary Ann Munro, b 1842
C4. Albert Munro, b 1844
C5. Ann Munro b 1846
C6. Robert Munro, b 1848
C7. Frederick Munro, b 1851
B3. Mary, b 1823, d 1889 mar John HOCQUARD, qv, b 1816 J?
C1. John Hocquard, b 1841 Gaspe, QUE d 1912
C2. Philip HOCQUARD, 1843-1869 C3. Ann Elizabeth Hocquard, b 1846
C4. Francis Hocquard, 1848-1919 C5. Susan M. Hocquard, 1850-1922
C6. George, Hocquard, b 1852, d 1915
C7. Charles Hocquard, b 1858 d 1921 mar 1891 Rachel Ann MICHEL, qv, 1848-1924.
D1. Mary Louisa Hocquard, b 1892, also Frederick, Mona, George, Charles, Mabel, Stella and Rachel.
D9. Wilfred Hocquard, b 1905 d 1968, mar 1930 Muriel Sullivan
E1. Wilfred Hocquard, res Paspebiac, QUE.
B4. John Francis, b 1824 Paspebiac, QUE mar 1846 Elizabeth Whittom, 1825, 1908. John d 1899, bur St. Peters, Pasp., Gaspe, QUE.
C1. Susan, b 1847 C2. John, b 1850,d.y. C3. Elizabeth, b 1852
C4. Ann, b 1854 C5. Jane, b 1857
C6.Francis, b 1859 mar 1888 Elizabeth Law, b 1862. Rem to Ludington, MI to work in the lumber mills. He d 1927 and she in 1906.4chn
D1. Mabel, b 1889 d 1938
D2. Fred Edwin, b 1893 d 1906
D3. Lloyd, b 1895 d 1964
D4. Roy Richard, b 1897 mar Ann Griswold, res Lansing, MI.
C7. John b 1862
C8. Edward, b 1862, twin of John? in Paspebiac, QUE mar Susan A. MICHEL, qv, b 1866. He d 1934, she in 1946
D1. John, 1899-1920 D2. Harold, 1900-1962
D3. Percy, b 1901 mar Mae Brooks, res McAdam, NB, dau Suzanne.
D4. Clifford, b 1903 mar 1935 Ida McColm, res Howick, QUE
D5. Eva, b 1905 d 1978 D6. Arnold, b 1907, d.y.
D7. Frederick, b 1908 mar Ena LE GRAND, qv, he d 1976 Montreal,QUE
D8. Reginald, b 1909 mar Claire ___, res Verdun, QUE
C9. Frederick James, b 1867 rem to Ludington, MI 1887, mar 1892 Ella McDole, b 1872 d 1954. Fred d 1928
D1. Harold, b 1893 mar 1915 Ellen Nelson, b 1894. He d 1953. She res Ludington, MI.
E1. Russell Francis, b 1916 mar Betty Marie Conrad 1939, res Muskegon, MI. 3 chn.
F1. Sandra Lee, b 1940 mar 1960 Joseph Bandock, and 2. Wm. Goloversic. 4 Bandock chn.
F2. Larry Russell, b 1942 mar 1969 Karen Wentzloff, res Musk.3chn
F3. James Frederick b 1946 mar 1970 Loretta Pickering, res Lapeer, MI, 2 chn.
E2. Donald Percy, b 1918 mar 1938 Irene Thompson, res Ludington.
F1. Thomas Donald, b 1940 mar Susan Gordon, res Eaton Rapids, MI 3 chn.
F2. Jack Leroy, b 1942 mar Marilyn Herin, 2 daus, and 2. Arlene LACerra, a dau.
F3. Linda Kay, b 1944, mar Barry Schrader, and 2. ___Kipham, res FLA. 3 chn by 1st husband?
E3. Doreen Ellen, b 1923 mar 1942 Jerome Van Aelst, b 1919 d 1978
F1. Jerome David Van Aelst, b 1943 mar Phyllis A. Murray and 2.

Margaret SAli, 2 chn.
F2. David Allen Van Aelst, b 1947 mar Christine Ann Beaune, 3 chn
F3. Elizabeth Ellen Van Aelst, b 1957 mar 1980 Lewis E.Smith.
E4. Delores Emily, b 1930 mar 1950 Andrew Di Piazza, res Los Angeles, CAL.
F1. Kathy Ellen Di Piazza b 1954
F2. Susan Andrea Di Piazza b 1957 F3. David A. Di Piazza b 1965
D2. Eva Elizabeth, b 1894 mar Charles Willhoite, res FLA
D3. Percival, b 1896 mar Henrietta ___, a dau Beatrice?
D4. Ella Verbena, b 1898 d 1906
D5. Fern Genette, b 1901 d 1904 D6. Frank Fred. b 1906 d.y.
D7. Marjorie, mar Leonard Case, res Detroit, MI
D8. Frederick, mar Dora Sonn, a dau Joyce b 1934
C10. Rosalie, b 1871 Paspebiac, QUE mar Ray Oswald
B5. Jane, b 1829 mar John LE MASURIER, b 1826, d 1901, at least 3 chn.
C1. Emily LE MASURIER, b 1858 C2. Ann Mary LE MASURIER, b 1864
C3. Susan Jane LE MASURIER, b 1869
B6. Ann Marie, b 1832, d.y.
B7. Philip, b 1834, mar Sarah DUVAL, dau of Philip D. and Jane Scott, b 1838 d 1899. He d 1906, bur Pasp. 6 chn. (Aldo Brochet,London)
C1. Sarah Ann b ca 1863 C3. Edith Bertha b ca 1868 C5. Margaret,1869
C2. John Francis, b 1865 C4. Philip R. b ca 1869 C6. Susan I.,b 1873

GALLIE, Susan Isabel, last ch above? mar Adolphus GRANDIN, qv, and d 1894 Paspebiac, QUE age 22.

GALLIE, John b ca 1789 J, d 1874 St. Peters, Paspebiac, Gaspe, QUE

GALLIE, Francis, b ca 1768 J d 1924, bur Paspebiac.

Sponsors at above marriages and baptisms were WINTER, AHIER, LE BRUN and LE DAIN, all of J fams.

GALLIEN, GALLIENNE, LE GALLIENNE, in J 1309, and very old in G. Means from a galleon, nautical. In St. Peters G 1647, in Torteval G 1720 and in other parishes.

GALLIENNE, Eva LE GALLIENNE, a very famous actress of England, Canada and US, b ca 1900, living in 1983 in NY. Her father once said that he came of a long line of Guernsey sailors. She was dau of Richard and Julie LE GALLIENNE.

GALLIENNE, many in Canada. See Q.A. IN CANADA by Turk.

GALLIEN, JOhn, b ca 1812 G, son of John and Rachel (LANGLOIS) LE GALLIENNE, mar Rachel ___, rem to NY then to GCO where he farmed 80 acres in Adams Twp., GCO 1840. One farm was sold to James Mahaffey in 1837 and another part was sold to John PRIAULX 1839. They rem to Racine, WIS ca 1848, where John became a contractor and builder. At one time he had partners James P. CORSE and Joseph MOON. John d 1871 Racine, age 62. Rachel d 1883 in MI, age 71 (GCO RECORDS)

A1. John b 1836 or 1840 in G, mar Martha Tinker, dau of James Tinker, b 1843 WIS. John served on Great Lakes ships and became captain and owner of several ships. He sailed on the brig HOMICAN age 14, later on the ONTARIO, his father's vessel, becoming master 1858. He sailed on schooner ROANOKE, in which he owned an interest, and then on the HENRY R. SEYMOUR. For 7 years he commanded the LONE STAR, but lost heavily on the sailing schooner NEWSBOY. In 1891 he commanded the SAVELAND in the Lake Superior trade, one of the largest vessels on the lake. He was said never to have met with a collision, lost a vessel, had one ashore or dismasted, or lost a man overboard! (RACINE PORTRAIT AND BIO. ALBUM; Racine VR)
B1. Cora, b 1867 WI mar William Hood
B2. John, b 1869 WI worked for Racine Hardware Mfg. Co.
B3. Lela, a Leila res Racine 1894 with two J. Galliens, on Racine St.

A2. Peter, b 1837 OH A4. Julia, b ca 1842 GCO d 1929 Racine, WI
A3. Mary b 1840 OH A5. Ellen, b 1845 GCO
A6. James, b 1848 GCO mar Mary ___, b WI. He was a RR worker.
B1. Amelia R., b 1871, d.y. Poss other chn?
A7. Clara, b 1849, d 1851
GALLIEN below may be connected with the above fam. (City Directory)
GALLIEN, Jacob A., currier, res Racine, WI 1882 and 1894
GALLIEN, John L., lake Capt., res Racine 1882, 1894
GALLIEN, John T., clerk, res Racine 1882, 1894
GALLIEN, James, laborer res Racine 1882, also a painter named James.
GALLIENNE, Mathieu mar Fanny GAUDRON, res Pte. aux Esquimaux, QUE. (Aldo Brochet, Montreal, QUE and London, ONT) OUTC, poss French?
A1. Francois, mar 1870 Bibianne Cummings in QUE.
GALLIEN, Nettie, wife of Nicholas?, or sister?, b ca 1808 G, res Racine WI 1870.
GALLIEN, Nicholas, b ca 1808 G, mason, with a boy age 8, b WI in Racine.
GALLIEN, Rachel, dressmaker res Racine, 1882
GALLIEN, Rachel, widow of John, res Racine, same or another Rachel
GALLIENNE, Joseph, res Huntington, LI, NY 1970s. OUTC.
GALLIEN, Abraham, Abram, b ca 1812/13 G, mar NYCity Amelia or Emily Fowler b between 1806 and 1813 NY. Abram res GCO, in Adams Twp. 1850. Rem to RAcine, WI 1853. Abram d 1886 and Amelia 1858, both bur Mound Cem., Racine. (Mrs. John Martin, Chesterton, IND)
A1. Rachel b ca 1838 d 1886 unmar, a seamstress
A2. Abram Joseph, b 1842 GCO mar 1868 Racine, Mary Roche, dau of Wm. Roche, b Ireland and Margaret Dorothy. Mary was b Canada 1845, d Racine 1912. In 1860 Abram was a tinner's apprentice in OH, but was a currier in Racine 1870.
B1. Charles, b 1870
A3. Susan M., b 1845 GCO, d 1915 Denver, COL. Mar Racine 1866 Henry Irish, son of George and L. (Parker) Irish. Henry a Civil War Vet, b 1839 Ogdensburg, NY.
B1. Laura A., b 1867 Racine, d 1954, mar 1889 Thomas Culloton, Racine
B2. Jessie Emily, b 1868 Racine, d 1932 Denver COL mar Emil Thorney in 1910.
B3. George Abraham, b 1872 Racine, d 1940. Mar 1904 Chicago, ILL, Eva Evans, b 1882 Paris, ONT, d 1928 Chicago, ILL, bur Rosehill Cem. She the dau of John and Mary Louise (Gilliard) Evans.
C1. Myron Knapp Irish, b 1905 Chicago, ILL d there 1943. Mar Mary E. Weiland, 1929, Evanston, ILL, res Skokie, ILL, 3 chn.
D1. Mary Jane Irish, b 1930 Evanston, ILL mar John A. Martin 1950, son of John James and Margaret M. (Devine) Martin. WW@ Vet.
E1. Evelyn Eliz. Martin, b 1951 Valparaiso, IND.
E2. Thomas Edw. Martin, b 1953 mar 1974 Lynne S. Johnson
E3. Gregory J. Martin, b 1954 E6. Katherine A. Martin, b 1963
E4. Steven James Martin b 1956 E7. Patricia M. Martin, b 1964
E5. William Myron Martin, b 1961
D2. James Evans Irish, b 1935 mar Marilyn Mitchell 1956 Skokie, ILL.
D3. Nancy Joan Irish, b 1943 Evanston, ILL mar Gregory Schmidt 1962 in Crown Pt., IND.
C2. John Parker, b 1915 Chicago, mar Frances Gill, res St. Aug., FLA.
C3. Grace, b 1919 Chicago, d 1970 Portland, OR, unmar
B4. Myron Knapp Irish, b 1874 Racine, d 1901 unmar
B5. Hattie, Harriet G., b 1876 Racine, d 1906 unmar
GALLIEN, W.D. res Hamilton Co., OH 1860, from G?
GALLION, D.R. ? mar 1907 Julia CABOT, qv, Coshocton, OH. OUTC
GALLION, Edwin mar 1918 Mary WILLIAMS, Cosh., OH. OUTC.

GULLIAN, Ann, 1875-1907, res CGO, from G?
GULLIAN, Henry, 1874-1941, res GCO (Conner-Eynon Cem. book)
GALIAN, Philip mar Mary Dolby 1736 in Boston. (int) OUTC
GALLIENNE in Annapolis, MD 1970s, in Balt., MD, and in Huntington, LI, New York. OUTC.
GALLIEN, Gloria mar 1949 Joseph Philip Flood, b 1928, son of Ralph West Flood of NH. (SOME DESC OF PHILIP FLOOD, by Mrs. Estella Maloney & Norton R. Bagley, MS)
GALLIEN, Nicholas, b 1808 G, also Christian Peter, b 1830, Mary b 1809, Mary b 1846, Martha b 1834 and Maud b 1877 in G, all to US?
GALLIEN, William, 23 in 1870, RR clerk, b ILL, his father of foreign birth, res town of Holland, P.O. New Amsterdam, near city of LaCross WIS. OUTC. (Census 1870)
GALLIER, a Hug. fam with some connection to the large LE BOUTILLIER fam of Jersey and US. See note in WRCIC and chart.
GALLISON, GALLISHON, poss GALLICHAN, Vincent, from C.I.? d Essex Co., MA 1678, poss father of Joseph below? (Essex Inst. Vol 58) Also father of John below?
GALLISON, John, said by T.A. Lee to have come from either G or England, bro of Joseph below.
GALLISON, GALLICHAN? Joseph b ca 1674 in G? mar Jeanne or Jane MICHELL/MITCHELL, qv, 1698 MRB. Ahomeowner 1706, d 1754. In will mentions wife Jane, grandson John and 2 grandaus, Elizabeth Stacey and Sarah Ashton. Also Mary Girdler, widow of MRB, Gradau Eliz. Grist, wife of John, a fisherman of MRB. See book for much more info.

(THE GALLISONS OF MARBLEHEAD, by Thomas A. Lee; MHS; COLONIAL FAMS; Essex Inst. Vol 58; Ruth Gray, Old Town, ME; Winifred Pierce, Ann Arbor, MI)

A1. Sarah, bp 1699 MRB d before 1754 A2. Joseph, 1702-1719
A3. John, b 1701 mar Agnes Stacey, who mar 2. 1744 Joshua Orne Jr. John d 1736 age 34, merchant. 6 chn by John. See book.
A4. Elizabeth bp 1707 MRB d before 1754, mar Samuel Nicholson
B1. Elizabeth Nicholson mar ___Stacey
A5. Jane, bp 1709 MRB, d 1727 MRB, mar 1726 Philip Ashton, son of Philip and Sarah (HENRY) Ashton. Philip mar 2. 1729 Sarah Bartlett Philip Ashton Jr., Janes husband, kept a sea journal, 1722-1725, see in NEHGS. A dau Sarah bp 1727 by Jane.
A6. Mary, bp 1712 MRB, mar 1732 Francis Girdler, son of Francis and Mary(Gifford)Girdler. Francis d 1750 age 39. Or Francis Girdler was son of Robert and Eliz. (Gale) Girdler of MRB. (Pierce)
B1. Deborah Girdler, b 1747 MRB mar 1765 Capt. John Selman, son of Arch. Selman and Elizabeth BLACKLER of MRB.
C1. Elizabeth Selman, b 1772 MRB mar 1789 Benj. KNIGHT, son of Wm. Knight and Mary CHINN of MRB. Eliz. d 1841 MRB.
D1. Franklin Knight, bp 1806 MRB mar 1831 Jane QUINER, dau of Capt. Thomas QUINER, qv, and Jane Miller BIRD of MRB. Franklin d 1839 at Amherst, NH.
E1. Jane Miller Knight, b 1832 MRB mar 1854 Lewis Girdler SWETT, son of Capt. Woodbury Swett and Sarah (Girdler) Brown. She d 1868 Lynn, MA.
F1. Helen Woodbury Swett, b 1864 Lynn, MA mar 1888 Orville Gram Poland, son of John Smith Poland Jr. and Elvira Cram of Waitsfield, VT. Helen d 1943 Reading, MA
G1. Burdette Kerkhoff Poland, b 1902 Niagara Falls, NY mar 1. 1922 Georgiana Belle Crawford, dau of Frank E. and Winifred (MIDDLETON) of Emberton, PA. Durdette d 1976, MA.

H1. Georgiana Winnifred Poland, b 1924 Phila., mar 1947 Roy Pierce, son of Roy A. Pierce and Eliz. Scott of NYCity.

See GALLISON records in MRB, Barnstable, Glouc., Charlestown, Beverly, MA records. Also in Kittery, ME and in WEYMOUTH FAM HIST. by Ruth Weymouth; Noyes; ME HIST AND GEN RECORDER, Vol 9; PIERCE GEN, etc.

GALLISON, Eliz. mar John BATTIS, qv, int, 1776 MA.

GALLISON, Thomas mar Frances TOOZEL 1794. See TOUZEL

GALLON, Jane in NY 1844, alien, poss GALLIEN? See GALLON in Q.A. IN CANADA, by Turk.

GALLOUPE, Wm. also as GALLOP?, noted in New England by 1630. See Topsfield, Boston and Beverly records. GALOUPIN in J 1299

GALPIN, old in G. Adah Smith, Athens, MI has data on Lucy GALPIN, OUTC

GALPIN, Nathaniel mar Susannah BILL 1731 Boston (int) OUTC.

GALUSHA, GALEUCIA, etc, origin is puzzling, despite much work by desc. Janet Helgemoe, Lynette Komarek and others. In 1706 Daniel Galluccia, b 1652 Isle of Jersey, was captured by Indians and taken to Montreal, QUE where it is said he d 1710. Fam legend has it that the family was French, fled to the Netherlands, and then to Jersey. There is another legend that he came from Wales, and was sent or brought by his parents or guardian to Plymouth Colony ca 1630, when he was about 8 yrs. old. This conflicts in timing with the other report. It is said the first immigrant had sons Jacob and Daniel. Daniel settled in Salisbury, CT, having 3 sons, Jacob, Daniel and Jonas. Jacob Jr. had 16 chn, and rem to Shaftsbury, VT. There may some truth in all the rumours but early info. is lacking. They appear to be all related, according to known documents. Daniel of the 4th gen. in Lynn, MA was clearly traced to Daniel the first.

A branch in Maine, arriving shortly before 1800 seems to have no known connection with other Galushas in America. Elijah and his 7 bros settled in Litchfield, ME. Elijah mar Ann Fisher of Durham, Dec1800. They later rem to Bowdoin, then to Clinton in 1827. Elijah's father d 1838. The men of the fam were hunters and trappers. Few records available on this fam, and they stayed in Maine until recent generations.

The surname is said to be French Huguenot from the Auvergne area of France. Variants are GALLUCIA, GALUSHA, GULETIA, GALICHET, GALICHON, of Anjou and Brittany; GALLUCCIO of Naples and GALUSCHKA of Bavaria. Galichat is a term of leather processing, and leather goods, especially boots and shoes, was an important business in the Island of J. in the 1600s. (Town Records; Savage; Court records of MA; Ancestral Heads; COMPENDIUM by Penhallow; Journal of Rev. John Pike; BOSTON TRANSCRIPT; GOULD FAM HIST; Virkus 2 and 3; AMERICAN ANCESTRY, Vol Z; Shaftsbury VR, Norwich, VR, Salisbury, CT VR; CONTINENTAL ARMY REG. by Heitman; Rev. War Rolls; Arlington Nat. Cem. Records; Shaftsbury Hist. Soc., VT; ANCESTRY & DESC OF CHAUNCEY AND ANN ROOD HOWARD, and THE GALUSHA FAM, by L. Komarek, Cedar City, UT; GALUSHA-GALEUCIA FAM. by Janet G. Helgemoe, Bow, NH; Mrs. Stanley Swanson, Lompoc, CAL)

GALUSHA, Daniel, poss Jacob? b ca 1652 J or Wales?, served in King Philip's War 1676, mar Hannah GOULD of Chelmsford, MA that year. Hannah b 1655 at Braintree, MA, dau of Francis and Rose GOOLE, GOULD. After Francis d 1676,Hannah and Daniel res Robin's Hill, outside Chelmsford, MA, house built 1673 as lookout post to warn of approaching Indians, being one room, 16x8 ft, having one window. In 1696 rem to Dunstable. Their home at Salmon Brook used as garrison during Queen Anne's War. 8 chn b Chelmsford, MA.

A1. Hannah, b 1677

A2. Jacob, b 1680 Chelmsford, MA mar 1707 or 1710 Sarah Read. He was a soldier in Queen Ann's War, and defended the garrison when the Indians attacked in 1706. In 1734, he was warned out of Chelmsford and rem to Rehoboth, MA.

B1. Jacob, b 1712 Chelmsford, mar Martha Norton 1741, who was b 1719 Newport, RI and d 1787 S. Kingston, RI. Jacob d Norton, MA 1802, cordwainer.

C1. Daniel b 1740 Norton, MA d 1825/6 Lynn, MA, mar 1. 1768 Hannah Lindsey, and 2. 1782 Eliz. Lindsey, and 3. 1810 Eunice Field, and 4. 1812, Eliz. Tarbox THOMAS.

C2. Sarah, b 1743 Norton, mar 1764 John Pratt, res Thompsonville,CT.

C3. Charity, b 1746 mar 1773 Elihu Daggett of Attleboro, MA,d 1823

C4. Martha, b 1750 d in Swansea, MA 1820 mar 1772 Constant SMITH of Rehoboth, son of Ephraim and Abigail Bowen Smith.

D1. Charles Smith, b 1773, d 1793 at sea

D2. Rachel, b 1774 mar Daniel GRANT

D3. Hannah, b 1777 mar Gardner Mason

D4. Jonathan SMITH, b 1779 mar Abigail Bowen

D5. Betsy Smith b 1782 mar Reuben Franklin

D6. Martha Galusha Smith, b 1784 mar Mason Barnby

D7. Elisha Galusha Smith, b 1788 mar Abby Carpenter

D8. Eleazer Smith, b 1790 mar Experience Barney D9. ?

D10. Davis Smith, b 1793 d 1838 Mobile, ALA, unmar?

C5. Hannah, mar 1775 Jacob Graves of Lynn, MA

C6. Anna, b 1757 mar 1786 Jacob Shaw

C7. Rebecca, b 1752 mar Dr. Adam Johnson of Attleboro, MA, who came from Norton, MA 1799. He was first physician in Danby, VT, d 1806 age 54.

B2. Hannah, b 1713 d 1788, mar 1735 Rev. John Hix, Hicks of Rehoboth Chn: John, Jacob, Nathaniel, Josiah, Daniel, Sarah, Hannah and Anne Hicks, Hix.

B3. Mary, b 1714 mar in Rehoboth 1735/6 Ephraim Hix and d 1749

B4. Charity, b 1716, d in Rehoboth 1736, mar there 1734 Edward Thurber, son of Joseph.

B5. Samuel, mar Esther ___. They were apparently warned from settling in Concord and Chelmsford, and from Watertown 1743/44. Samuel took part in the Louisburg Expedition, with 9th Regt. MA, 1745. At least 3 sons, poss other chn.

C1. Nathaniel, b 1741 Chelmsford, d there 1745

C2. Elijah, b 1743 Chelmsford, d 1756 in campaign against Quebec.

C3. Joseph, b 1747 Billerica, MA. Another, or same Joseph, an early settler in Pittison, ME, but prob not the same branch.

A3. Rachel, b 1683 d 1706 in Indian raid on garrison in Dunstable, MA

A4. Daniel, b 1686/7, d.y.

A5. Daniel b 1688 Chelmsford, MA mar 1710 Sarah Warren at Watertown, MA, dau of Daniel and Eliz. (Whitney) Warren. Sarah b 1701 Watertown, res Weston, MA where Daniel was carpenter, farmer, had much land in Weston. Later res Colchester, CT 1716, and still later East Lyme, CT.

B1. Daniel, b 1711 Weston, d.y. B2. Dinah, b 1713, mar Daniel Stanton

B3. Daniel, b 1716, fam untraced. At least these chn? David, Jacob, Timothy, Samuel, Mary, who mar David Chandler, and poss Thomas?

B4. Elizabeth, b 1719 Colchester, CT.

B5. Jacob, b 1720/21, d 1792 Shaftsbury, VT, mar 1. 1745 Lydia Huntington, 2. widow Thankful (?) King; 3. Desire (Andros? Andrews) Metcalf, and 4. Abigail (Foster) Porter. Lydia b 1728 d 1764 at b birth of Anna. She was related to Gov. Sam. Huntington. More.

C1. Mary, b 1746 mar in Norwich, CT 1764 Elijah Willoughby.
C2. David, b 1748 d 1804, mar 1. 1773 Charity Lathrop/Luther and 2. 1779, Rhoda Galusha, his cousin, b 1760, dau of Jonas and Anne Galusha in Sheffield, MA. David was Capt. in Rev. War, served with Green Mountain Boys, repr. in Legis. 1779, and sheriff of Bennington, VT.
D1. Gershom, b 1774 Shaftsbury, VT d ca 1806 VA, mar Ann ___.
D2. Mary, b 1776
D3. Henry, by Rhoda, b 1780 Shaftsbury, mar Sally BARBOUR, d 1865 Arlington, VT.
D4. Charity, b 1782 d 1836 mar 1805 Abraham COLE, had 6 chn.
D5. Semantha, b 1785 Shaftsbury, mar 1808 Jonathan Howlett, d 1848
D6. Rhoda, b 1788 mar Benajah Furlong, d 1867 OH. D7. Maria,b1793
D8. David, b 1795 mar 1824 Marilla HICKS, b ca 1799, a cousin. He d 1880 Newton, IA. Marilla b Sunderland, VT, rem from there to Perrysburg, NY between 1831 and 1834. In 1836 res Sodus,NY then in Buffalo, NY, Mt. Vernon, OH, Marion and Newton, IA. 7 chn. Much more data available on this branch, see sources.
C3. Jacob, b 1750, mar 1765 Pathenia Hard, res Shaftsbury, VT, where he was town clerk for 40 yrs. He was b Norwich, CT, d Shaftsbury VT 1834. Parthania was b ca 1755 Arlington,VT d 1846. (DAR records of Mrs. Karl Colson, Delmar, NY)
D1. Aurelia, b 1779 VT, d 1862 mar 1799 Elias Huntington. More in HUNTINGTON GEN. MEMOIRS
C4. Jonas, b 1753 d 1834, mar Mary, dau of Gov. Thomas and Eliz. Meigs Chittenden, 1778. Capt. in battle of Benninton, 1777, sheriff of the county, Judge of the Supreme Court, Pres. Elector 4 times, Gov. of VT, 1809-1812, and 1815-1819, bur Shaftsbury Cem. Mar 2.Martha Sammons 3. Abigail Ward, 4. Abigail Atwater Beach 1818, 9 chn. Five sons were Green Mt. Boys.
C5. Amos, b 1755, d 1839, Capt. in the Rev. War, mar 1788 Mary Clark
C6. Elijah, b 1757 Norwich, mar Beulah Chittenden, sis. of Mary above Died in sawmill accident Arlington, VT 1783, age 25
C7. Olive, b 1759 Norwich, mar 1780 David Stanton, b 1758
C8. Lydia b 1762 d 1802, mar 1786 Asa Hutchinson
C9. Anna, b 1764, mar 1787/8 Salisbury, Conn Ebenezer Wright, son of Amaziah and Zerviah (Fitch) Wright of Mansfield, CT, 8 chn.
C10. Lucy, by thankful, b 1765 Norwich, CT.
C11. Daniel, by Desire, mar 1765/66.
C12. Benjamin, b 1770 CT, d 1854, mar 1790 Mary Trowbridge. (data from Mrs. Stanley R. Swanson, Lompoc, CAL. More info available.)
C13. Ezra, mar Mable Barney 1799 d 1853 Warrensville, ILL.
C14. Desire, b 1771/2 CT, mar1791 John Parks
C15. Sarah, b 1774 CT, d 1813, mar 1795 John F. Bacon.
C16. Elias, b 1775, mar 1796 Susan Sears.
B6. Jonas, b 1723/4 Lyme, CT, d between 1802 and 1813. Mar 1. Sarah D Doolittle, div 1757, and mar 2. Anne ___. His name is miswritten Jonah on many records, and has also been confused with Jacob, his bro. In 1756 he was with Capt. Elisha Noble's Co. of Sheffield,MA.
C1. Nathaniel, b 1743 Kent, CT, d MA 1817?
C2. Oliver, b 1744/5 Kent, served in VT Militia in War of 1812.
C3. Anna, b 1747 Kent, CT.
C4. Hulda, b 1758 Sheffield, MA, by 2nd wife C5. a son d.y.
C6. Rhoda, b 1760 d 1835 mar David GALUSHA, her cousin. C7. Anna,1762
C8. David, b 1765 d 1854 Shaftsbury, VT mar Ruth Osborn
C9. Electra, Lecter, b 1767, mar 1785 Abraham Harrington
C10. Jonas, b 1769 res Rupert, VT.

B7. Sarah, b 1726 Lyme, CT.
A6. Nathaniel, b 1691 Chelmsford, MA mar Anna ___, res Sudbury, MA then in Rutland, VT, may have d between 1720 and 1723.
B1. Jacob b 1715 Sudbury, MA B2. Nathaniel b 1719 Rutland
B3. Rachel b 1720 Rutland, mar poss Eleazer Corey of Chelmsford, MA 1742.
A7. Dinah, b 1695/6 Chelmsford, MA
A8. Richard, b 1696, recorded as son of Hannah, but which Hannah, mother or dau? Poss Richard was father of Ebenezer, who enlisted in 1760 age 17 for the reduction of Canada, and Elijah, servant to Samuel Sureen of Capt. Aaron Willard's Co., who was killed 1761. Richard's wife may have been the widow Galusha bur 1790 age ca 79 at First Cong. CH in Chelmsford, MA.

GALUSHA, GALUCIA, and others noted in CLARK GEN. by Robert F. Gould; PEABODY GEN; Middleton, West Stockbridge, MRB, Beverly and DAnvers MA records; Census, Shaftsbury, VT records, and in Edgewood, MD.OUTC.

GANO, GERNEAUX, Hug fam from France, said to have come to America by way of Guernsey, settled at New Rochelle 1661. "A Boston attorney was engaged many years ago to settle a Gano estate on Jersey." (Howard Le Master, Waggoner, ILL) See sources: NEW JERSEY GENESIS; THE GANO FAM; by H.M. Gano, Carlinsville, ILL 1970; New York Gen. Record; Virkus; GAN FAM HIST, by Howard M. Lemaster, Waggoner, ILL, 1974? (a copy in Akron Hug. Library).

GARCELON. "The Garcelons are of French origin. Peter Garcelon was an R.C. priest b Clermont, France, who became a Protestant refugee. On account of religious disturbances in that country, he removed to the Island of Guernsey and became an Episcopal minister, married and raised a family. James...second child of seven offspring...His father was rector of the Church known as St. Peter of the Wood, in the years around 1730. ...My greatgrandfather was Mark, son of James, who settled in Lewiston, ME 1776.. One of his sons was named Asa, who married Sophia Frye. My father was William F., for whom I am named. I was born in 1868 and have two children, one a sophmore at Harvard College and the other a girl of eighteen who is in school at Troy, NY. I am a lawyer, graduated from Bates in 1890, and from Harvard Law School in 1895. I have served in the MASS. Legislature three years, have been Graduate-Treasurer of Harvard Athletics for five years, and notwithstanding my great age, still insist on being active." (Wm. F. Garcelon, Boston 1923) Much data available, including writings of Garcelon in Bowdoin,College, Brunswick, ME. Data in WRCIC includes fams of Dr. Alonzo, James, Lydia Ann and Moses. A GARCELON was Gov. of Maine. (Mildred McBride, San Clement, CAL; PEABODY GEN)

GARDE, poss from DE LA GARDE, Jean, in Grouville and Philip in Grouville and St. Ouen J 1668.

GARIS, see DE GARIS. Cf Howard R. Garis, author of the old children's favorites, the Uncle Wiggley stories, res E. Orange, NJ. OUTC.

GARNER, Philip, from J? before 1718 mar (int) Hannah BALL, poss BAAL? of J 1718. (Bolton) Surname GASNIER (silent s) in St. Mary and St. Ouen J 1749. In J since 1550.

GARNER, Thomas, res MRB 1790 with fam of 7. OUTC.

GARNEY, Thomas mar 1777 at MRB Margaret Tewksbury, bp 1757, dau of Sarah GRUSH Tewksbury, and James T.

GAUDIN, in J 1528, in St.Heliers, St. Martin and St. Peter J 1668, and in St. Heliers and St. Martin J 1749. Also in G. Curr Dorchester MA and Austin TX. Curr J. This fam has shield: azure, a chevron between three eagles argent, a chief glues fretty of the second.

GAUDIN, Hedley of a Gaudin fam settled in QUE and ONT from J, mar Lizzie Breen, who d 1926, res Plymouth, NH, fam of 3 sons and 3 daus. (Vera McAuslan, Charlesburg, ONT) See other GAUDIN fams in Q.A. IN CANADA by Turk.

A1. Vera Evangeline, b 1888 mar ___MCAuslan, 2 daus mar, res Toronto,O.
A2. Lenora Elizabeth, b 1890 res Toronto, ONT, unmar
A3. Errol Francis, b 1892, res Toronto, mar, served in WWI
A4. Valentine Adelaide, b 1896 res Toronto, ONT, married.
A5. Esdale Little, called Pat, b 1899, res Ft. Lauderdale, FLA, mar.

GAUDEN, Henry, Capt. of the Abigail, from Weymouth, England 1628 to Naumkeag, MA and again in 1635. Prob from a GAUDIN fam of C.I.? (Perley II)

GAUDIN, Philip, b J, son of Amice GAUDIN, rem to Salem MA as young man in 1675. Indentured to Philip ENGLISH, qv, for 4½ yrs. Papers witnessed in J by LE RICHE and LANGLOIS. See Indenture in NEHGS,Boston.

GAUDION, common to G and J but mostly in G, where it is current. See CIFHS #6. At times this has been an Alderney Island surname.

GAUDION, Wm. Thomas, b 1881 ALD, son of John Richard and Mary (SIMON) GAUDION, rem to Detroit MI 1906, then to Rochester, NY 1910. Mar Orpha Gascoyne 1911. (Donald Gaudion, Rochester, NY)

A1. Donald A., b 1913 Rochester, mar Gertrude McKie 1940, 3 chn.
B1. Sharon M. mar Robert Sanford, res Southboro, MA 1976
B2. Jacquelyn E. mar George McClelland, res Southboro also
B3. Donald A., res Rochester, NY.
A2. Harold W., b 1917 mar 1941 Jean Reid, res Reston, VA, 3 chn: Karen, Patricia, and Peter
A3. Richard H. b 1925, mar Betty Byrnes 1950, 5 chn, res Kettering, OH. Chn: Thomas, John, Anne, Mary Beth and ?.

GAUDION, Louisa Martha Nancy, sister of Wm. Thomas above, 2nd of 8 chn. Mar Wm. Edward KNIGHT, qv. Louisa d 1930 age 72, bur Detroit, MI.

GAUDION, others to Canada. See Q.A. IN CANADA.

GAVET, GAVEY in J 1400s. In St. Saviour J 1668, and in St. Laurens and St. Saviour J 1749. In G 1744 and before. In St. Saviour G 1819. Philip and Thomas GAVEY of J built small cutters and other vessels. Curr research in J, CIFHS #6. (A. John Jean, Jersey)

GAVEY, GAVET, Philip, b 1631 J settled in Salem, MA, mar ca 1655, who? Poss 2 or more chn: Katharine, who mar 1677 Job Pillsbury, b1643, and John who mar Sarah ___, res Newport, RI 1699, when their first ch, a dau, was born.

GAVEY, GAVET, Philip, b 1651 J, prob the son of Martin and Eliz. GAVET of St. Saviours J. See NEHGS Vols 77, 88, etc, for excellent coverage of this fam in J by Joseph Gavit of Albany,NY.

A1. Elizabeth, b 1682, bp 1696, prob mar in Boston 1723 Mathew DELAWAY, DELLAWAY, etc. possibly DE LA HAYE of C.I.?
A2. Ezekiel, b 1683 MRB, bp 1696, yeoman, deacon, d ca 1753, mar 1704 Hannah Wilcox, dau of Edward. Ezekiel rem to Westerly, RI ca 1700 became a Presbyterian, and was well-to-do. 8 chn. See source.
A3. Samuel, bp 1696 Salem, MA A4. Philip bp Salem 1696
A5. John, bp Salem 1696, living 1754, mar 1716 Mary CARTER, dau of John and Sarah. Desc.
A6. Hannah, bp Salem 1696, poss mar Thomas DILLEHAY. See Elizabeth.
A7. Joseph, b 1699 Salem d after 1764, mar 1. 1725 Mary WILLIAMS, b 1699, d 1743, dau of Isaac and Mary (Endicot) Williams and 2. 1746 Susannah Carwick, widow who prob d 1779. 5 chn by 1st wife and 2 by second.

GAVEY, Daniel b 1782 G, d there 1835. At least one and poss more of his chn rem to Gaspe, Canada. See also p. 257, Q.A. IN CANADA.

(Shirley O'Neil, Newport Beach, CAL)
A1. John, b ca 1819 G, rem to Gaspe, mar there Laura Isobel Price of an English fam with Guernsey ties. John d 1869 Gaspe? age 50.
B1. Abraham mar Esther Rachel LE HUQUET 1867 Gaspe. He d 1927.
B2. Daniel, b 1844? d 1926? Poss mar Jemima LE HUQUET, res Grand Greve Gaspe, QUE. Dau Lucy Ada?
B3. Caroline
B4. Amelia, b 1853? d 1932, bur Grand Greve, Gaspe. Mar Charles P. Bartlett, 1850-1928. (GLF)
B5. Elias, b 1854 Gaspe, mar Priscilla SIMON, qv, b 1862, who d 1926 Rem later to North Vancouver, BC, where Elias d 1941.
C1. Gertrude, b 1885 Gaspe?, unmar d 1905 C3. Norman, 1889-1914
C2. John, b 1887 mar Mable Jeffries, and d 1975
C4. Hollie, b 1892, d 1947 mar Mervyn Wallace, 2 chn.
C5. Amy, b 1895 mar Harry C. Hilts, res Los Angeles, CAL.
D1. Shirley Hilts, b 1927 mar Wm. O'Neil, 2 chn, res Newport Beach.
E1. Richard O'Neil, b 1947 E2. Mark O'Neil, b 1968
C6. Violet, b 1901 mar John Fisher, res San Francisco, a son Harold
B6. John, d 1886 B7. Lizzie, 1878-1882 B8. Joseph, d 1936
A2. George, b G, in Douglastown, Gaspe, QUE 1861 (census)
A3. Frederick A4. Martha A5. Charlotte A6. Ezekiel, all b G.

GEAR, George, from J to Boston before 1720, mar (int) Mary MURRINER, MARINER, LE MARINEL? 1720. (Boston records, Vol 28, p.99) GEAR is said to be variant of DE GUERRE, a warrior. (E. Warr, Willowdale, ON) A Thomas GEER went from England to CT early 1700s. There is a GEER Assoc., Mrs. I. Geer, Ledyard, CT.

GEE, appears in two forms in J where a Peter GEE/GOE lived in 1607. GOE in St. Peter and St. Clement J 1607, and in St. Peter and St. Heliers J 1668. Curr research? see CIFHS #3

GEE/GOE, Peter from J?, signed the Isles of Shoals Petition 1653 in ME. (Noyes)

GEE, Nancy mar John CROSS Jr., she of Gloucester, MA 1835

GEE, Joshua and Eliz. had dau Ann 1711/12 in Boston, MA.

GEFFORD, Robert mar 1754 Eliz. HOOPER in MRB, MA. See GIFFARD.

GENDRON, see JANDRON. GENDRON in St. Laurens J 1788.

GERARD in J 1309, 1528, and later. None verified in US. Curr J.

GERMAINE, GERMAN in J 1381. GERMAYNE in St. Clement J 1607. GERMAINE curr J. Curr research? See CIFHS #3.

GERMAN, John was with Wm. COCK (LE COCQ?) getting fishing supplies from Philip ENGLISH, qv, 1684 in Salem, MA. (Noyes) OUTC.

GERMAN, John a surgeon, found 9 badly wounded men at Casco Fort 1703, and cured all! (Noyes) OUTC

GERMAN, JERMAN, Wm. of MRB? a soldier from York Co., ME 1722. (Noyes)

GERVAISE, see JARVES

GIBEAUT, GIBAUT, in J 1497, in G in 1600s, in St. Laurens J 1668, 1749. See CIFHS #8.

GIBAUT, in GCO early 1800s, but the fams dispersed throughout the Midwest and info difficult to find.

GIBAUT, in GCO. "Anyhow, Sophia behaved like a lady." This unusual story was published in a Columbus, OH newspaper some years back, not seen by compiler. "She died in Cambridge, OH May 1865, and is buried in Cambridge City Cemetery. After her death, it was learned that she was a he, but no fuss made. He had arrived on a west-bound stage coach about 25 years earlier, a tall well-dressed blond, had remained and worked for people, an excellent nurse, even a midwife. All the information he gave was that he had been born on the Island of Guernsey 1812. Some thought Sophia was a French pirate, with a price on on his head, others that he was a political refugee...the name inscribed on his tombstone was GIBAUT". (Florence Larrick, Santa Barbara, CAL)

GIBAUT. "All of my aunts as well as mother, married Jerseymen and just to keep up the good work, I went to Jersey in 1912 and managed to pick up a Jersey girl for my wife. We have two American cousins, Edward VALPY, a son of Drucilla, American by adoption, res Poughkeepsie, NY, and Marion DE QUETTEVILLE, res Port Jervis, NY, a teacher." (Francis Gibaut)

GIBAUT, Edward, b 1728 G, d 1803 Salem, MA. He res corner of Essex and Walnut. He mar 1758 Sarah Crowninshield, b 1730, dau of John and Anstis (WILLIAMS) Crowninshield. He mar 2. Abigail, widow of James Whittemore, and dau of ___Yell. 3 chn by Abigail, and poss 5? by first wife? He was Tax Collector under the Jefferson Admin., from Gloucester, MA. Info not clear on this fam. (DRIVER GEN; Essex Coll, Vol 4; prob other data not found by compiler)

A1. Sarah A2. Edward

A3. John, who d unmar at Glouc., MA 1805. Customs Coll. at Glouc.

GIBEAUT, Joseph from G? mar Arabella COLLEY, from G? res GCO. (David Griffin, Cameron, MO) More data in WRCIC.

A1. Cordelia mar Henry Steer, at least 2 chn.

A2. Julia, mar ___White, res CAL, bur Restlawn Mem. Park, CAL.

A3. (Florence) May, b 1858 GCO mar Luther Whitney of NY, son of Edgar. Juther had run away from home at age 9. He d 1912, and May in1921.

B1. Edgar Whitney, b 1875 d 1935 mar Lillian Casselberry

C1. Gordon Whitney C2. Eileen Whitney

B2. Edna Whitney, b 1878 d 1955 mar Charles Rosenbaum

C1. Glen Rosenbaum, mar 1. Winifred HOOPER, 2 daus and 2. Dorothy ___

C2. Ethel Rosenbaum, mar 1. __Bryant and 2. Pat McDonald, adopted son Michael.

C3. Margaret Mae Rosenbaum, mar Kenneth Pankey, a son Jake Weaver Pankey?

B3. Joseph Whitney, b 1883 d 1969, mar Tressa Ritcherson

C1. Kenneth Whitney, mar Frances Klingensmith, 7 chn: Mary Louise, Betty, Harold, Joe Frank, Huey Donald, Judy and Sue Whitney.

C2. Charles Whitney mar Ethel Jackson, 3 chn: Terry Joe, Linda and Thomas Whitney.

C3. Frances Whitney, mar Gerald Harris, 3 chn: Marilyn, Marvel Sue and Mildred Harris.

C4. Florence/Flossie Whitney mar Chester Tate, 2 chn: Jerry and Carolyn Hanks.

C5. L.H. Whitney, mar Maxine Rosenbaum, 3 chn: Ronnie, Roger and Nila Whitney

C6. Erma Whitney mar Homer Blackburn and 2. Oren Hildebrand, a ch by each.

C7. Joseph Gene Whitney mar Mary McClain, 2 chn: Eddie and Sheryl Kay Whitney.

C8. Harry Dale Whitney mar Helen Duncan, 3 chn: Darrell, Virginia and Christine Whitney.

B4. Luther Whitney, b 1886 d 1960, mar Frances Metcalf, 4 chn.

C1. Luther E. Whitney mar Farrell Brummitt, 3 chn: Donald, Dianna and Larry Whitney

C2. Mary Whitney mar Dennis Maxey, 4 chn: David, Stephen, Daniel and Ann Maxey.

C3. Patricia Whitney mar Junior Griffin, 3 chn: Christopher, David and Dwight Griffin.

C4. Julia Whitney mar Evelyn Whorton and 2. Elma Metsker, several chn d.y.. A son Buford Whitney.

B6. Aaron Whitney, b 1891 d 1968, mar Gladys CARTER, 5 chn.

C1. Donald Whitney mar Oneida ___

C2. Dorothy Whitney mar Leo Schuster, 4 chn:Leo, Elaine, Tommy and Tammy Schuster

C3. Jimmy Whitney mar Avis McCulley, 3 chn: Greg, Cindy, Rick Whitney

C4. Margaret Whitney mar Kenneth Sutton, 2 chn: Delvin & Sharon "

C5. Stuart Whitney mar Ruth Baugher, a dau Pam Whitney

GIBAUT, see Mary BILLOT

GIBAUT, Abraham and Mary, prob from G or J, res Boston, dau Mary b 1739

GIBEAUT, Alanson A. mar Maggie Canaday in GCO.

A1. Franklin A., b 1871 A2. James D.

GIBEAUT, Charles J. appears in Muskingum Wills Book 1, OH.

GIBEAUT, George M., 1860-1935, bur Old City Cem., Cambridge, OH.

GIBEAUT, Hilda M., 1872-1937, ditto

GIBEAUT, Howard C., 1897-1950, ditto. Ch Joseph, b 1932, d.y.

GIVAUT, Elizabeth, see Francois ROMERIL

GIBAUT, John had ship BORNEO built for him in MA, and was Capt. of this ship 1799, res Salem, MA? Dee DRIVER, WHITTAKER, WHITTEMORE, DE HAVILLAND and CHESEBOROUGH GENS.

GIBEAUT, Jourdain, b ca 1800 St. Lawrence J, son of Abraham, was a mariner and wrote to his father in Jersey from Cronstadt, Germany, while on a voyage, that he had decided to change his name to Richard Burr, res in or near NY, and intended to marry a young girl there. See Burr.

GIBEAUT, Lance, mar Mary Canady in GCO, a son James W. b 1876. See Alanson above.

GIBEAUT, Peter Sr. appears in Muskingum, OH book 5; Mary in book 4, named Kirkpatrick; Sarah in Book 2. and Wm. in Book 3. (Muskingum Court House records, OH)

GIBEAUT, GIVEAUT, Rachel, was first wife of Peter SARCHET, qv. She was b 1778 G, rem to GCO 1806. Some GIBEAUTS listed in Spencer TWP., GCO in 1800s.

GIBEAU, Robert Narcisse/Nelson mar 1846 in St. Jean Chrysostome, Chateauguay Co., QUE, Margaret Adeline Parent. He was son of Pierre Gibeau and Josette BISSON. She was dau of Joseph Bisson and Louise JARVIS. OUTC. (Fern Gibeau, Springfield, MA)

GIBAUT, William, 1843-1964, bur McQuade's Cem., Wills Twp., GCP. OUTC

GIBEAUT, Capt. ___, head of the Washington Union Rifle Co., from GCO in the Civil War. (Wolfe)

GIFFARD in J 1528. In St. Helier, Trinity and St. Mary J 1668. In Grouville, Trinity, St. Mary and St. Martin J 1749. IN G 1100s. Also many of this surname res England in 1600s. Means open-handed, the giver. Many distinguished members of the Jersey fams served as officers and engineers in Egypt, India, Iraq, France, etc. There is also a French family long established in Canada. GIFFARD noted curr. in Toronto, poss from J? See Q.A. IN CANADA. by Turk (Henry A. Giffard, Toronto, ONT)

GIFFARD noted in colonies, but OUTC.

GIFFARD, GIFFORD. "In Marblehead at the end of the 17th century, there was a group of GIFFORDS having the names Nicholas, Robert, John, Peter and William." Others were in Sandwich, MA and Norwich, CT. "Gifford is written Giffert, Gilford and Giffard, the original Norman spelling, which survived among probably Burlington Co., NJ desc. as late as 1884." (NEHGS Vol 128) A Norman spelling might mean a Jersey Giffard fam.

GIFFARD, Florence Mary, b 1872 J, mar 1. George Francis LE FEUVRE, qv,

6 chn, see Q.A. IN CANADA. She mar 2. William Henry Keys b England. She d Ottawa, ONT 1934, and Keys d 1949. (G.F. Le Feuvre, Trenton,MI)

A1. Elsie Ann Keys, b 1908 Ottawa, rem to Wyandotte, MI 1929. Mar John Mercer Trowbridge of Montreal,QUE. He d 1964 Montreal. She rem to Ottawa, d there 1970, no issue.

A2. William Henry Keys, b 1910 Ottawa, rem to Wyandotte, MI 1929, mar Pearl Matteson, res Detroit, MI.

B1. James, mar and res CAL B4. June mar Stan. Bartnicki, res MI

B2. Frank, a Marine B5. Elsie mar Alex Vlad, res Allen Park, MI.

B3. Edward, mar res Detroit, MI. B6. Beverly, res Detroit, MI.

GIFFARD, Walter LE MONTAIS, b 1856 J son of John and Eliz. (BISSON) GIFFARD, DESC OF John GIFFARD B IN J 1475. He began as clerk and cashier, went to Honolulu 1875 for the Waterhouse firm, soon became V.P., and officer of 12 corporations. He was acting Chancellor of the French Legation, Consul General for Portugal, member of the Privy council at the time of the overthrow of the Monarchy, chairman of Hawaiian Sugar Planters Assoc., organized an experimental station, etc, etc. Enthusiast in Horticulture and Forestry. (John Wm. Siddals, MEN OF HAWAII) He mar 1. ___, and 2. Mattie Peter Brickwood. (M.Lee, Bernice Bishop Museum, Honolulu, HAW)

A1. Walter Dudoit, by 1st wife. A2. Jane

A3. Harold B., b 1884, mar Julia Damon 1908, a son Walter.

GIFFARD, Deborah mar Philip Brimblecome 1727 MRB. OUTC

GIFFARD, Jane mar Nicholas MERRITT 1724 MRB. OUTC.

GIFFARD, Mary mar John BODEN, qv, 1748 MRB. OUTC, but all likely C.I.

GILBERT, early in G? In J 1299, later spelled GUILBERT, GUIBERT, etc. See also GUILBERT.

GILBERT, Elizabeth, b G, mar Hilary DU FOUR, qv, in G, but widowed, then rem to Racine, WIS, with 3 sons and a dau after 1855. (ALBUM; Leach)

GILBERT, Eliz. mar Michael CROSS, qv, 1762 MRB. OUTC.

GILBERT, Sophia, from G, see MOON

GILBERT, John mar Rebekah BODEN 1772 MRB. OUTC.

GILE, GILES, GILLES in J 1607, in St. Laurens, St. Peter and St. Ouen J 1668, and in St. Ouen J 1749. GILES also in G early. See GUILLE.

GILES, Eli was in Salem, MA 1600s, poss from C.I.? CAUTION:TRIAL CHART

A1. Abigail, bp 1685 Salem A3. Edward, bp 1689

A2. Ruth, bp 1687 A4. James, bp 1690

A5. Samuel, bp 1694, poss mar Susanna ___, had dau Eliz. b 1724?

A6. Eleazor, bp 1698 A7. Mehitable, bp 1702

GILES, Lydia mar Thomas LE MARSTERS 1810 MRB. See LE MASTER & MASTERS

GILES, Samuel mar at Salem, MA 1762 Lydia DE COASTER, qv. She may have mar John CLARK in 1777 in MRB. OUTC.

See also GILES in Noyes; Essex Coll; A GILES MEMORIAL; 1864, in FOUNDERS OF EARLY AMERICAN FAMILIES by Meredith Colket of Cleveland,Ohio. See also OLD FAMS IN SALISBURY, MA.

GILL, Mrs. Jesse, b J, to North Chelmsford, MA ca 1890 with parents. She was née DE LA HAYE, qv. GILL curr G and J.

GILLAM, see GUILLAUME and WILLIAMS

GILLAM, sometimes originated as GUILLAUME, qv, WILLIAM in French.

GILLAM, Zachariah, master of ship VISITATION, 100 tons, in 1663 was authorized to carry Wm. Hollingsworth of Salem, MA to 1. Plymouth, England; 2. to the Island of Jersey for 4 days; then to 3. any one port in Holland. Capt. GILLAM also involved in the Hudson Bay fur enterprise promoted by Sir George CARTERET, qv. of Jersey and England. Was GILLAM of J fam? His wife Ann came in the ship ABIGAIL 1635, at least 5 chn. (Perley II; Nute)

A1. Benjamin, b 1634, mar 1660 Hannah SAVAGE, at least 5 chn
A2. a son A4. Ann, b 1638, d.y. A6. Elizabeth, bp 1642
A3. Zachary, bp 1636 A5. Ann again, bp 1640 A7. Joseph, bp 1644
A Capt. Gillam drowned in Hudson Bay, Nelson's River, 1683. His 14 year old son was captured by Radisson, who had reverted to French interests, after having sold out his rights to the England. The son was afterward released and returned to Boston. (Andrews, NARRATIVES OF THE INSURRECTIONS)
GILLET, GUILLET?, Mathew, a Jerseyman, was indentured to George WILLIAMS, qv, in Salem, MA 1641, in MRB 1646. See GUILLET. (Perley)
GILLEY, William and wife Hannah LURVEY?, res Baker's Island ME 1806. Gilley's father came from Grt. Britain, poss C.I.? See GUILLET. (JOHN GILLEY, by Chris. Eliot, 1904)
GILLIE, GILLEY, poss same as GUILLET in some cases. Those below appear to have mar into C.I. fams. Silent 't' in this French surname.
GILLIE, William mar Sarah LE CRAW 1807, res MRB. (CAUTION!TRIAL CHART)
A1. William, bp 1807, poss mar Betsy GOSS 1833 MRB?
A2. John b 1809 A3. Ebenezer, bp 1812, poss mar Sarah ROBERTS 1837?
GILLIE, Thomas mar Sally (LE CRAW?) res MRB.
A1. Sally Rebecca LE CRAW, bp 1818, prob mar Lewis R. Power 1837
A2. Esther QUINER, qv, bp 1825
A3. Elizabeth Abigail, bp 1818, poss mar Thom. Pedrick 1834 MRB.
Note that Sarah and Sally above may have been same person, mar bros?
GILLEY, Esther, age 27, dau of Wm. and Sally mar Michael P. CARROLL, age 27, cordwainer, son of John and Tabitha CARROLL 1849 MRB.
GILLEY, John mar Esther QUINER, 1813 MRB.
GILLEY, Wm., mar Eliz. FLORANCE 1780 MRB. Could he have been father of Thomas and William GILLIE above?
GILLYARD, Peter from G to Portsmouth, NH before 1733, mar Ann ROBERTS of Newcastle, ME in Ports. 1733. (NEHGS Vol 25) Note that GUILLARD AND GUILLIARD were in J 1309, and curr G and J.
GILLMAN, Mary dau of Henry, b 1796 G? mar Major G.F. Westcot, had 5 chn, and d 1851 in G. There are still Gillmans in G, poss of this fam, originally from Ireland.
GIRARD, curr and common in G, none traced in US, but some may have settled here, from the Islands. GIRARD in St. Saviour J 1821. A Normandy fam came to America by way of the C.I., settled in Sacramento, CAL. (Mrs. Joseph Girard, W. Sacramento, CAL)
GIRARD, Syvret, almost certainly from C.I., res Toronto, ONT 1970s.
GIRAUT, GIRAUD. Andrew F. GIRAUD, passenger on the WISCONSIN, from NY to CAL in 1850. (Rasmussen) Curr in Bakersfield, CAL.
GIRAUT, Sophia, 1812-1863, res Cambridge, OH. Note GIBAUT also.
GIRAUT, Emily, 1820-1877, and Jane, 1849-1921, also res GCO. (Conner-Eynon book)
GIRAUT, Cornelia, 1842-1877, mar ___Wills?, res Cambridge, OH. See under GIBAUT.
GIRDLER, not a C.I. surname, in spite of the fact that one was called 'a Jersey rogue' in MRB. However, Girdlers often mar into C.I. fams in MRB because of propinquity. Thus, several charts included.
GIRDLER, Francis res MRB, wife? (Essex Coll, Vol 7)
A1. George, bp 1678 A4. Benjamin, bp 1678 A7. John, bp 1684
A2. Francis, bp 1678 A5. Mary, bp 1678
A3. Hannah, bp 1678 A6. Ann, bp 1680
GIRDLER, Richard mar Sarah/Sally Candage, Cavendish, res Boston, MA. (Sprague's JOURNAL OF ME. HIST., Vol 4)
A1. Maria Theresa, b 1823, mar 1846 Wm. Henry HOOPER, son of John. She d a widow 1885, 4 chn.

B1. Wm. Henry HOOPER, b 1849   B3. Harry Hooper, res Alameda, CAL1902
B2. John Glover Hooper, b 1849? B4. Maria T., 1853-1870 Medford, MA.
GIRDLER, John and Eliz. res MRB.
A1. Deborah, 1834-1907, mar 1859 Wm. LE CRAW HOOPER, who had shoe bus.
B1. John G. Hooper, b 1862, d.y. B4. Lewis Bowden Hooper,b 1876
B2. William Le Craw Hooper, b 1866
B3. Ellen Bowdoin Hooper, b 1870 mar 1895 Frank Edward Conley.
C1. William Hooper Conley, b 1899.

GLASGOW, Ezekiel, b G, was in Charles Co., MD before 1713. His second son Jeremiah, b G 1713. Jeremiah a tanner, who mar 1737 Patricia BALL, qv, b 1717, 2nd wife? 5 chn. While Ezekiel may have been b in G, it seems likely they came from Scotland or Ireland. James Glasgow and wife Mary came from Antrim, IRE ca 1770 with chn. An Arthur Glasgow had acreage in Guernsey Co., OH 1840s. (Wolfe). (Diane Pheneger, Granville, OH; Robert Glasgow Jr., Adamsville, ALA)

GLENN, see OLIVER

GLYN, Elinor, famous author, said to have grown up in Channel Islands.

GODDEN, George Henry, b 1874 J, mar Dorcas Jessup THOUMINE, qv of G, rem to NYCity 1907, d Bronx, NY 1956. GODDEN curr J. Note close resemblance of GODDEN to GAUDIN of C.I. See THOUMINE. (George GODDEN, Hartford, CT.)
A1. George Augustus, b 1899 G, to NY 1907, res Hartford, CT
A2. William Alfred, b 1900 G, d Bronx, NY 1924
A3. Dorcas Florence, b 1913 NY? mar George Fanning, 2 chn: Wm. and Dorcas Fanning.

GODDEN, Jonathan, res Medford, MA 1790 with fam of 6. Poss GAUDIN of C.I.? See also Q.A. IN CANADA.

GODFREY, GODFRAY in J 1200, in St. Clement, St. Saviour, St. Mary and Trinity J 1668. In St. Clement, St. Saviour, St. Mary and Grouville J 1749. The GODFRAY shield is Argent, a griffon segreant sable between eight bezants.

GODFREY, noted in SC before 1680. OUTC. (Baldwin)

GODFREY, John, son of John and Susannah bp 1764 Boston, MA. Godfathers were John PULLEN (POULAIN?), Mr. CARRELL and Mrs. MAXWELL. OUTC. (NEHGS Vol. 100)

GODFREY, Sarah mar 1728 John Redman, b 1701 son of John of Hampton, NH. (Noyes) OUTC.

GODFREY, Elizabeth mar James BOLEN 1699 in NY. See BOLLEN, BALLEINE.

GOE, see GEE

GOODWIN, Eliz., b 1687, had bro Zachariah, b 1690, res Berwick?, ME. GOODWIN noted in G 1750, poss before. See Noyes.

GORGES, Thomas in G 1274. Cf famous explorer of England. (NEHGS V 19)

GORSCHIEL, Mary dressmaker from J to IA in 1870s. Not an old C.I. name

GORY, Sarah mar 1700 in Boston, MA John SELLEY. GOREY poss was GOUREY, in J 1607, 1668, 1749, from the 1200s. If GORY from J poss also SELLEY, as SEALE or SEELEUR?

GOSS, curr J and G. GOSSE in G 1300s.

GOSS being researched by Georgia Curtis, Eugene, OR. One, Deliverance mar Benj. HUNTOON 1764. Also see Boston TRANSCRIPT, Dec. 1930; Underhill; MRB VRS; JOHN LAWRENCE GEN; Noyes; Sprague's JOURNAL OF ME HISTORY, Vol 4.

GOSSELIN, some confusion owing to mispellings of surnames GARCELON, GOSSELIN, JOCELYN, ETC.

GOSSELIN, Helier, in G before 1541, ancestor of all the G. GOSSELINS. The name was in G by 1200s. They were first a G fam, rem to J 1506-1524, then returned to G. In St. Peter G 1865. Another GOSSELIN line was in J 1331, in St. Heliers J 1607 and 1668.

There may have been other GOSSELIN lines from Normandy in the 1600s and 1700s to the C.I. Several different branches came to America. Name curr G and J.

GAZLIN, GOSLEN?, data in YANKEE HERITAGE MAGAZINE, OUTC. (Barbara Haskell, Gansevoort, NY) One page of data in WRCIC from Mrs.Haskell.

GOSSELIN, John T. Sr., b 1814 St. Heliers ? J, d 1880 Monroe Co., NY. Naturalized 1872, mar Mary MULLEY, MOLLET?, b ca 1815 J. John to US in or ca 1864. See Thomas RENOUF for other desc. Poss Mary MULLEY was dau of Peter and Mary MOLLET? (Margaret Beatty, Rochester, NY)

A1. John T. Jr., b 1839 J d 1908 Rochester, NY bur Riverside Cem. Carpenter and Methodist. Mar Hannah M. ___b 1840 England, d 1908,2chn

B1. Alfred, b 1862 Rochester, d 1950, mar Lillian Hall who d 1950

B2. Minnie M., b 1865 mar 1. Charles Losey and 2. ___Brooks

C1. Mildred J. Losey b 1890 Rochester, NY

A2. Jane K. or Jane Mary?, b ca 1845 J mar Thomas RENOUF, b J, d ca 1871-1874, when Jane brought her fam to US. 3 chn, but only 2here. See Thomas RENOUF. Jane d 1880?

B1. May Jane RENOUF, b 1865 J d 1896 Monroe Co., NY mar 1894 Peter G. Vandevate, 1853-1935. See RENOUF, 4 chn.

B2. William F., b 1871 J, d 1926 Rochester, NY, mar C.K. Wagner.

A3. Frank G., b 1852 J, mar 1875 Mary ___, b 1851 J, in Rochester, NY.

B1. Sydney, b 1876 Rochester, NY mar Lillian Davis

B2. Arthur F., b 1878 Rochester, mar Lillian A. Baker. ARthur d 1955 Rochester, NY, bur Mt. Hope Cem.

A4. Philip b J, res Sydney, Australia

A5. Mary, b J, mar ___Allen, res Southampton, England

A6. Elizabeth, b J, res there, mar ___Merriman.

GOSSELIN, John mar Catharine GRANT 1813 St. Andrews Presb. CH, Quebec City, Canada. OUTC.

GOSSELIN, Clement, a Canadian who fought for the American side in the Rev. War. Had an intelligence network, raised a company of men in 1775. Mar 2. at Longeuil, QUE, Charlotte Ouimet? Mar 3. Marie Catherine MONTY (poss MONTAIS?) before a J.P. (LOST IN CANADA, 1980-1981)

RESEARCHERS: Note many GOSSELIN-GAZLIN in Vassalboro, ME records 1786 on, but OUTC.

GOSLIN, Sarah mar Butler Wood, b 1793 d 1873 Union, ME. OUTC. Sarah d 1880. Butler may have been b in NH. (Eliz. Mello, Hazelwood, MO)

A1. Benjamin, b 1830 Vassalboro, ME d 1914, mar Mary Eliz. Wing.

A2. Samuel, mar 1861 Sarah Johnson A3. Manuel, mar Emeline Preble

A4. Mary, mar ___Turner B5. Consuella mar 1860 Warren Waterhouse.

A6. Viola mar 1844 Noah Wentworth.

GOSSELIN, Charles and Corbet, b G, ca 1780, d in Trinidad 1803.

GOSSETT is a form of GOSSELIN, qv. Jean GOSSETT, a Huguenot, b and mar in France, rem to J 1685. He was b 1618 near St. SAuveur, Normandy, and d 1912 in Bagot Manor, Jersey. See Hug. section. Chn of this fam were b in France. See Sources: Chart by contributors in WRCIC; HIST. OF SC: AMERICAN HIST. SOC., NY 1934; Library of Congress; LE MASTER, USA; LITTLEJOHN GEN; LIPSCOMB GEN; Wallace's HIST OF SC; Virkus; WRCIC; Edna Greer and Mrs. Raymond Brooks, Spartanburg, NC; FAMILY OF GOSSETT, by E. Newcomer, Pico, CAL 1954, not seen by compiler.

GOSSETT, Matthew and Nicolas FIOTT of J were owners of the 115 ton ship UNION, Capt. SIMONET, a ship trading with Virginia 1783. (A.John Jean)

GOSSETT, one group said to have left France and settled temp. in Holland, men named John or Jacques, Jacob and Philip. Rev. T.M. Gossard, Presb. minister. John GOSSERT said to be 2nd Lt. in Gen. Washington's

Army, owned a farm in Antrim Twp., Franklin Co., PA, is bur there, near Waynesboro, PA. (Weltha LInville, Kendallville, IND)

GOSSETT, Charles mar Ann ROWELL, REVALL (int) 1768 MRB. OUTC.

GOSSETT, Jean, John, son of Jean the Huguenot, was b 1649 France, educated England, d 1730 J, mar in J. Susan D'ALLAIN, b Cerisy, Normandy, France, of a Hug fam that also fled to J. 6 sons, poss some daus?

I. John, b 1699 J, d 1735 Cumberland Co., PA

II. Abraham, b 1701 J, d 1785 J, mar Jane White, dau of John, in J.

III. Jacob, b 1703 J d 1788 London, England.

IV. Peter, b 1705 J, d 1765 Chester Co., PA, mar Catherine DU FOUR, DU FORE, b 1705 Normandy, France, who d after 1765 in Chester Co., PA. Peter and Catherine and 5 chn came to America between 1650-1660. Res VA and PA.

V. Gideon, b 1707 J, d 1785 London,England. Mary Ann ___, who d 1761. Both are bur in Ma-thew Gossett's tomb at St. Marylebone Cem., London, with others of family.

VI. Isaac, b 1713 J, d 1797 London, although one record says 1799. Mar ___BOSQUET, of J? Very talented artist, who modeled in wax. One of his works was exhibited in VA, where the POINDEXTERS and other J folk settled.

GOSSETTS in VA 1782-1790: Thomas, Philip, James, John, Shadrick in Henry and Pitts Co.

GOSSETTS in SC 1790 Census: Isaac, John, James, Gabriel, Elijah, Pickney, Asbury, Major, Abram,Joseph, Nicholas, Thomas, Tilman and J. or S. in 1800, 1810, 1820.

IV. Peter above, b 1705 J. Skeleton chart of this family below. Since this is not strictly a C.I. fam, all info has not been included. More data is in WRCIC, from Edna Greer and Mrs. Raymond Brooks of Spartanburg, NC. Peter mar Catherine DU FOUR, desc rem from VA to South Carolina.

A1. John, b 1731 J d 1818 Spartanburg Dist., SC, mar Martha Groom 1752 in London, England.

B1. John, b 1766 J, d 1844 SC, mar Anna LEMASTER 1816 in VA.

C1. John, b 1797, d 1869 SC

D1. Eliza Ellen, b 1820

D2. Pleasant Tollison, b 1826, 10 chn: Martha Jane Stone, Nancy Z. Kirby, Emma Eliz., John Gideon, James Pleasant, Wm. G., Thomas Henry, Edgar Converse, Edward Bobo and Emma again.

D3. John Wesley Calvin, b 1828 mar Isabella Bryant, 10 chn: Eli J., Robert C., Sarah Madore, George Huggins, Jane George, Hester Easler, Martha Turner, Cosciden, Nan Littlejohn, Alfred Bryant and Alonzo Rolen.

D4. R.W. Pinckney, b 1822 d 1899, mar Anna Tollison, 14 chn, bur SC

D5. L. Frank D6. Martha, b 1833 D7. Marcus M., b 1839

D8. George W., b 1839, twin? d 1948, 6 chn in will.

D9. Elmira, b 1830 mar John N. LEMASTER, b 1818, bur White Stone, SC

D10. Missouri, b 1831 mar Sam. Sherbert

D12. James, b ?, mar Caroline Smith b 1836?

C2. Lucy, mar John Harmon C3. Sallie, mar ___Hendley

B2. Major, b 1768 England d 1862 SC, bur Pacolet, SC. Mar 1799 Anne Tollison, 8 chn.

C1. James, b 1800 C5. Fielder, b 1810, d 1887 Greenville, SC

C2. Joel, b 1802 C6. Loving, b 1810

C3. Mannington, b 1804 C7. William Washington, b 1819.

C4. John Tollison, b 1807 C8. Pinckney, b 1821

B3. Elijah, b 1773 J, d 1833 age 60, mar Lucy LEMASTER, dau of Wm.
C1. Melissa, b 1822, d unmar ca 80 C2. Martha
C3. Louisa, b 1835-40, mar Houston Foster
D1. Melissa Foster mar Edward Mason, 4 chn: Nellie, Lettie, Annie and Howard Mason.
D2. Poss a Wilson Gossett belongs in this fam? and a Sarah?
B4. Gabriel, b 1779 England, d 1835 Spartanburg, SC, mar 1799 Fannie LEMASTER, 9 chn.
C1. Ephraim, 1800-1816 C2. David, 1801-1816
C3. Moses M., b1803, mar Nancy White, dau of John White, 10 chn.
D1. Henry also Thomas, Caroline, Nancy and Jane.
D6. Lucy, mar A.W. Hazelwood D9. Mary mar ___Foster
D7. Leonard C. D8. Joanna, mar __Willard-D10. Martha mar __Hyatt
C4. Martha W., 1804-1853 C6. Mary, 1808-1866
C5. William, b1806 mar 1830 'Jiney' Hendley, 2 chn
D1. Walter C., b 1831 d 1840 D2. Martha B., b 1836?
C7. Matthew P., b 1809 d 1872, mar Sarah Hendley 1830. 1 ch, more?
D1. Alfred Clark, b 1831 Spartanburg, SC, wounded in Civil War, d 1862, mar 1858 Julia Smith, a son Alfred Clark Jr.
C8. Elihu Marion, b 1836 d in Civil War. Mar Rose Anna Wingo, a son Elihu M. Jr.
C9. Sara Frances, b 1842 d 1927, mar1861 Eli Hood, 6 chn: Anna Harmon, Maude Hendley, Zula K., Oscar, Edward and Clay Hood.
B5. Abraham, mar Polly LEMASTER
B6. Richard, b 1775 mar Judah LEMASTER, res Floyd Co., GA 1839
B7. Mary b 1799, mar Abraham LEMASTER. Richard and Mary were b in Frederick Co., VA.
A2. Matthew A3. Jane, b J, mar Abraham D'ALLAIN 1750 in J?
A4. Esther, b J or England.
A5. Mary, b 1743 J, d 1817 VA, mar 1761 Rev. Morgan Morgan Jr. in Leesburg, VA, an Episcopal minister, youngest ch of Col. Morgan Morgan, and of Catherine Garretson of Charlestown, WVA. He was b 1737, d 1797 at Bunker Hill. 7 chn
B1. Phebe, b 1762 B4. Mary, b 1768, mar Thomas Lewis Rebeckah 1782
B2. William, b 1764 B5. Morgan III, b 1771
B3. Eli, b 1766, d.y. B6. Catherine, b 1773 mar Josiah Hedges
B7. Zackquill, b 1776 rem to Tyler, later Wetzel Co., OH.
GOSSETT, one or more fams of GOSSETTS settled in and around Marietta, OH in either the late 1700s or early 1800s, but not known to compiler if they were from the early French GOSSETT fam, or came later from J. (OLD NORTHWEST, Vol 5; Wills of Wash. Co., OH)
GOSSETT, John Jr. res Marietta, OH 1810, fam of 3 men, 1 boy, 3 females and wife of one of the two younger men. (Wills)
GOSSETT, these mentioned in Wash.Co.,OH: John Harriet, Betsy, Margaret, (poss Mrs. Wm. Riley in 1813?) Giles, Mary Ann and Matilda, wife of Robert Miller.
See sources: HIST. OF MARIETTA AND WASH. CO., OH by Andrews, OLD NORTHWEST Vols; THE LEFFINGWELL RECORD, 1897; Martha Priest, Holden, MA; R.N. Wiseman, Jackson, OH, etc.
GOSSARD, GOSSERT, John, "My ancestors came from Guernsey Island. John GOSSERT...served in the Rev. War, res in Penna."
GOSSERT, another spelling of GOSSETT? Shield: Argent three owls gules, a free quarter azure. Crest: A hand couped at the wrist, erect, holding a dagger in pale. (Weltha Linville)
GOULD, early in G. Many noted in colonies, some mar to C.Islanders, but none researched by compiler. Name curr G and J.
GOURDEN noted in early New England, cf similar names of J and G.

GOURDEN noted in early New England, and similar names in G and J. Cf GOURDEN, JORDAN, etc.

GOURDEN, Mary mar Thomas MARTIN 1746 MRB. OUTC.

GRAHAM, Frederick, b 1832 G, son of Peter GRAHAM and Mary LE HURAY,qv. Peter's ancestors were Scottish, and the family in G was notably long lived. Frederick, a mason, rem to Racine, WIS 1854, and in 1855 became a contractor and builder. Worked both in Racine and in Chicago. After the great fire in Chicago 1871 he did a great deal of re-building there. He was instrumental in building the Belle City Opera House. He mar 1856 Matilda LE MESSURIER, dau of Abraham and Mary(LE PREVOST)LE MESSURIER, b G. 6 chn. (RACINE BIOG.ALBUM)

A1. Eleanor Matilda, mar James Cuzner of Racine. A5. Ada Lisle

A2. Frederick William, carpenter A6. Verna Belle

A3. Henry Edmund, cabinet maker, rem to Washington State

A4. Lillian Grace, mar Edward H. Hanson and res Fond du Lac, WIS.

GRAHAM, Eliza, Elizabeth, mar 1855, a plural marriage, Robert Hamill Porter of UT, see Porter fam. 3 chn? (LE GEYT ASSOC; S. Rizzuto)

A1. Georgianna Porter, b 1856, mar 1873 Conrad Hamil Staley, 19 chn b Upton, UT. (STALEY FAM HISTORY)

A2. James Hamil Porter, b 1858 in Skull Valley, Tooele Co., UT

A3. Mary Geneva, b ca 1865, d.y.?

GRANDIN in J 1528. In St. Martin, Grouville and Trinity J 1607. In Grouville and Trinity J 1668. In St. Ouen and Trinity J 1749. Many in America, spelled GRANDY, GRANDIN, etc, but compiler unable to locate sources of info. Curr in J. See CIFHS #8.

GRANDIN, may be orig. form of some early New England surnames such as GRENTE, GRANDY, GRUNDY, GRINDLE, GRANDE, etc. GRANDAY noted in JOURNAL OF ASHLEY BOWEN, of MRB. also in Upper Freehold, NJ. OUTC. (Stillwell's MISCELLANY) Cf also LE GRAND.

GRANDIN, Daniel, b 1695 J? d 1742 NJ. Prob son of Daniel and Rachel (LE BROCQ)GRANDIN of C.I. (LE BOUTILLIER CHART) Was Judith, age 20 in 1743, a dau of Daniel?

A1. Philip, b 1731, d 1791 mar 1753 Eleanor Forman, dau of Capt. John Forman, who was b 1701 and John's second wife, Jane Wykoff.

B1. Dr. John F. Grandin, b 1760 d 1811 mar Mary NEWELL, bp 1756

C1. Philip, b 1794 d 1858 mar 1816 Hannah C. Piatt, 1789-1884

D1. Lucy A., b 1827 d 1888, mar 1847 Wm. A. Goodman, b 1822

E1. Fannie Goodman, b 1849 d 1925, mar 1873 John GALLIER LE BOUTILLIER, qv.

GRANDY, Abigail, widow of Capt. Francis, d 1807 MRB. LE GRAND? OUTC.

GRANDAY, Amos, note AMICE below, one or more of this name active on ship and ashore at MRB area last half of 1700s. A Capt. Amos GRANDAY res MRB, and was captain of schooner SALLY 1765, SUSANNA 1775, brig WOLFE 1771, sailed from Lisbon, Portugal in the 1760s, captured at Bayonne Castle 1761. Another Amos Granday served on privateer ships THORN 1780 and UNION 1780 also. Heights given in records are different, one tall, one short! A John GRANDAY commanded the schooner KINGFISHER 1753 from MRB. Same or another was tarred and feathered at MRB for stealing. An Amos, son of Capt. Amos, d 1814, a prisoner in England age 24.

GRANDIN, Amice arrived in Boston 1769 on ship MOLLY from J. Poss a father and son, as one was a passenger, the other a mariner. Amice, James and Philip res about this time in Trinity and St. Ouen J. One Grandin in J built a screw steamer there 1872. (John Jean)

GRANDIN, Eliz. wife of Amice? also on this voyage.

GRANDIN, Helen, arrived in America 1825, from J? OUTC.

GRANDIN, John res Lebanon, Hunterdon Co., NJ 1790 was in NJ Militia.

GRANDINE, John res Roxbury, Mid. Co., NJ 1790, was in NJ Militia.OUTC.
GRANDIN, Lillian Mary, 1876-1924, missionary doctor, dau of Francis Philip and Anne (BENEST) GRANDIN of St. Helier, J. She was the 1st Jerseywoman to obtain a medical degree, took special courses in dentistry and midwifery in Dublin, eye problem courses in Moorfield, England and Tropical Diseases in London. In Jan. 1906 she sailed for Shanghai, and settled in Yunan province, the only qualified doctor in an area as large as France. She started a leper colony, and in 1912 mar Edwin J. Dingle, author of ACROSS CHINA ON FOOT, and THE CHINESE REVOLUTION. Lillian later worked in Hankow, Wenchow and Shanghai. She worked in London during WWI, returned to Yunan, China and d in 1924. Her life was fictionalized and was filmed as INN OF THE SEVENTH HAPPINESS? starring Ingrid Bergman.
GRANDY, Mary res Boston 1790 with fam of 3. More in Boston records.
GRANDINE, Samuel and William were in NJ Militia 1790.
GRANDY, Susanna mar Wm. DOVE 1752 MRB. See COULOMBE, COLOMBE. OUTC.
GRANDIN, some settled 30 miles north of Fargo, ND 1800s, said to be from Tidioute, PA. They had 40,000 acres, and in 1878 were breeding purebred shorthorns. (FOLLOWING THE FRONTIER, by Freeman Tilden, NY, 1964) OUTC.(More in CI COLL. Dawn Byro, MO)
GRANT in J 1309, and many noted in colonies, but none traced by compiler. Note that several GRANTS mar C.I. women in early New England.
GRANVILLE, poss that some of this surname were desc of Lord Granville, who was a CARTERET of Jersey. "The first settler of this name was a desc. of Lord Granville of England." (HIST OF PARSONSFIELD) He had 2 chn: Joseph and Nancy. Said Joseph (or a son by that name) was b in Newburyport, MA 1762, entered the army at 16, came to Parsonsfield 1783, built first saw mill in town, had 8 chn, 4 sons and 4 daus. One settled in Parsonsfield, and had one son Rufus, living in 1888. Said Rufus married and has several chn. One of the Granvilles settled in Effingham, NH, and had sons Thomas and John and daus." (HIST. OF PARSONSFIELD) John CARTERET, son of George CARTERET (who was the first Lord Carteret) and of Lady Grace Granville, became Earl Granville, 1690-1763, a very outstanding statesman of England. Chn of Rufus? Thomas, John, a dau who mar Elijah Taylor, Hannah, Sophronia who mar Cyrus Champion, a dau who mar a GRUSH of Brooklin, MA, and Mary, who d 1861. See DE GRUCHY, GRUSH.
GRANVILLE, ___, mar Rueben Edwards, raised a large fam in the 1700s. (HIST. OF PARSONSFIELD, ME)
GRANVILLE, Joseph, res Durham, ME with wife Molly 1783, and mar 2. another Molly. 6 chn by 1st wife. OUTC. Trial Chart!
A1. Molly
A2. Nancy, mar Jonathan Kimball, 12 chn, res Parsonsfield, ME. Chn: John, Joseph, Polly, Daniel, David, McHenry, Mercy, Thomas, Alvah, Nancy, James and John G. Kimball, b 1791 to ca 1813.
A3. to A12: Hannah, Thomas, Stephen, Mercy, Joseph, Sally (by 2nd wife) Lydia, Fanny, Elizabeth, George.
A13. Joseph, b 1762 Newburyport, MA to Parsonsfield, ME 1783, mar, had 8 chn, 4 sons and 4 daus.
GRANVILLE, Ursula, d ca 1820 Bedford Co., TN. She and husband Samuel Bigham Sr. had previously owned land in Mecklenburg Co., NC, from which co. he had served in Rev. War. Trad. in this fam is that Ursula was a niece or grt-niece of Lord Granville, of the CARTERET family, Seigneurs of Sark Island. (Mrs. Ralph Bigham, AlbuquerqueNM.)
GREY in J 1226. GREY in St. Saviour J 1607 and 1668. GRAY in J 1584. In St. Martin J 1607. See in Noyes.
GRAY, George of J mar Mary MURRINER (MARINER? LE MARINEL?) 1720 Boston.

GREY, Mary Jane, age 21, of Toronto, ONT, b G, dau of Samuel and Eliz. mar 1867 in Toronto, William Brannigan, age 30, b US, at the Baptist CH. Witness John Moorhead of Toronto, ONT. (CH RECORDS)

GREELEY. While the GREELEY GEN. by G. H. Greeley, Boston 1905, has no mention of a C.I. connection, it has been said by other researchers that there might be a link to the LE GRESLEY fam. In LE GRESLEY, the 's' is not pronounced by Islanders. Andrew, b ca 1617, d 1697, said to come from England ca 1638, was prop. at Salisbury, ME, at Haverhill, MA, 1669, mar Mary dau of Joseph MYSE, poss MOYSE? of J?

GREELEY, LE GRESLEY, Thomas, from J, tanner in Portsmouth, NH. Will of 1723 names wife Rebecca and chn, leaving estate in J to son Peter LE GRESLEY in St. Ouen J 1668. (Noyes)

A1. Peter, mar ___Phipps, 4 chn A2. John.
A3. Thomas, bp 1710, mar ESter WOODEN, WOOTEN or VAUDIN? of C.I.?
A4. Samuel bp 1716 A5. Sarah A6. Hannah

GREEN, common, but note that some in colonies may have come from C.I.

GREEN, Eliz. mar William DENNIS 1771, and/or Thomas DENNIS 1790, MRB.

GREEN. Note many listed in GCO early 1800s.

GREENSLAD, GRINSLATE, GREENSLET, GREENSAQUE, etc. This puzzling surname found in J records 1607, and also occurs in Devon, England, OUTC. Note that the widow below mar a Jerseyman, Jacob PUDEATOR, PUDESTOR, POINDEXTER, which might mean the fam was from J.

GREENSLAD, etc, ___, had wife Ann, who mar 2. Jacob PUDEATOR, POINDEXTER of Salem. Ann hanged as witch 1692. Will named chn GREENSLADE. (Noyes) OUTC.

A1. John, mariner, gone by 1689, mar Abigail Curtice of Salem 1693, who mar 2. Thomas Mason, and 3.? in 1733 Samuel CARREL. See CLEMENTS and CARREL. (CLEMENS FAM CHRONICLES by Sam. Clemens, 1914) John's chn? from another mar?
B1. Ann, mar in Topsfield 1710? B2. Ruth, in Salem 1724
B3. Sarah in Wenham 1724?
A2. Thomas, a mariner, b ca 1652, Cleeve's servant in 1666, in 1678 was in Salem from the Barbadoes, named in Philip English's records 1692. With his mother when she was hanged.
A3. Ruth, mar in Ipswich 1677 Josiah Bridges.
A4. Samuel at Falmouth 1675/6
A5. James in 1690 had left Salem since 1689. In 1692 sued for stepfather's legacy.
A6. Sarah??, fined in Essex court 1673, not named in PUDEATOR will.

GREENSLET, GRINSLETT, GREENSALDE?, James b J? or poss son of fam above? in Salem, MA 1711 when he mar Rebecca Stearns. OUTC. (Perley)

A1. Rebecca, b 1711/12 A3. Elizabeth, bp 1720 A5. Mary, bp 1722
A2. Abigail, b 1714 A4. James, bp 1720 A6. Hannah, bp 1723.

GREFFARD, Joseph Josue, son of Josue and Catherine (GAUDIN) GREFFARD of St. Heliers J, mar 1786 Marie Amable Milot in Yamachichi, QUE. (Lucille Rock, Woonsocket, RI)

GREGORY in J 1309.

GREGORY, John, b J, d at Paspebiac, QUE 1858 age 37.

GREGORY, Hannah mar Nathaniel Brimblecome Jr. 1824 MRB. OUTC.

GREGORY, many in Boston area 1700s, but OUTC. A Joseph GREGORY mar Hannah HOOPER, qv, dau of Hannah SIGNCROSS, qv.

GRELLIER, a ship builder in J early 1800s. (A. John Jean, Jersey)

GRIFFITH in southern England and C.I. Some research in J? See CIFHS8.

GROS, GROSSE, LE GROS, etc. "There was an early migration to New England from the Norman-English families of the Channel Islands of Jersey and Guernsey, etc...Among these colonists settling on the shore of Massachusetts Bay were some of the name of LE GRO, LE GROS and

LE GROW, or so they are written...about 30 marriages recorded in Marblehead, MA before 1800 of ...these families, the earliest in 1684." (JOHN LE GROW OF IPSWICH, by Davis) Confused history of these fams. is mostly due to the extremely varied spelling. See LE GROS, LEGROW. LE GROS curr J. GROVES curr G. See LA GROVES.

CAUTION! Isaac GROSSE came to Salem from Cornwall, England ca 1637. Also Jacob GROSS came from Mayence, Germany, on the Rhine, to the US and some desc res Ontario. A GROSS fam noted in early Windham, CT may have been from C.I. See sources: MRB VR; Truro, Lancaster, Provincetown, Boston, Wellfleet, Scituate, Petersham, Beverly, Ware and Newburyport records in MA.

GROSSEE, GROSS, LE GROS?, John from J? to MRB. Mar Elizabeth ___ See also PERRY.

A1. John, bp 1736 A2. Thomas, bp 1736 A3. Elizabeth, bp 1738

GROUARD noted in MRB, Boston and Portsmouth, but OUTC. See also NEHGS Vol. 81.

GROUT curr G. See also GRUTT.

GROUT, GRAUTT, Philip from J to Boston 1769 on ship MOLLY. GREULT in J 1340. GRAULT in St. Martin, St. Mary, St. Clement and St. Helier J 1668, and in St. Mary J 1749.

GROUT, Capt. John was at Watertown, a prop. there 1642, rem to Sudbury, then to Cambridge, MA. A book about him, by Eliz. Boice Jones, 1922, not seen by compiler.

GROUT, also said to have come from So. Trent, Devon, England. (Noyes)

GROUT, many in MA 1790, see Census

GRAUT, Gabriel, partner of Wm. Williams in Portsmouth, NH and Williams admin. his estate there in 1707. (Noyes) OUTC. Gabriel is often a Hug. first name.

GROVER, not an old name in G, but there before 1798.

GROVER, May b 1798 G, dau of John and Marie (MOLLET) GROVER. See MOLLET. Marie MOLLET was dau of John and Marie (ROBIN) MOLLET of St. Sampson G. Mary mar 1824 in G. Major Joseph Antony Beard of Manchester, England. He was b 1804 Portsmouth, England, emigrated with wife and 2 chn to Atlanta, GA, 1830, then rem to NEw Orleans, LA 1836, where he d 1857. He was later Aide-de-Camp to the Commanding Gen. of the LA Militia, and an auctioneer in New Orleans 1845. (Timothy F. Beard, New York, NY)

A1. Joseph Robert Beard, b 1825 St. Peter Port G, living in 1859, mar twice. A son Charles Calhoun Beard. Other chn?

A2. Dr. Cornelius Collins Beard, b 1828 G, d 1906. He mar 1. 1852 Philadelphia Stuart-Menteth, 1834-1881, of Canandaigua Lake, NY. Dr. C. studied in Baton Rouge, Paris and Vienna, and fought in the Mexican War. He was one of the founders of the School of Med. of the LA Univ. Res New Orleans, Biloxi and NY. Mar 2. 1881 Anais Bonnabel, dau of Dr. Henri Bonnabel of New Orleans, LA.

B1. Maire Stuart Beard, 1853-1912, mar Dr. Henry Stewart, no issue

B2. Joseph Menteth Beard, 1854-1856

B3. Philadelphia Beard, 1857-1892, mar Dr. Robert Walmsley of N.O., re res Canadaigua, NY.

C1. Gratia Walmsley, mar Elbert Harral, and d 1951

D1. Elbert Harral, mar 1949 Dorothy A. Larson

D2. Com. Brooks Harral, USN, Rear Admiral, mar Sally Muma, 4 chn: Sally McQuillan, Brooks, Martha Ahrens, and John M. Harral.

D3. Robert Harral, mar Ruth Northen?, div 1959, 2 chn: Rob't & Sandra

D4. Margaret Harral, mar Harry Gilman, res Islip, NY, 2 chn: Patricia and Margaret Gilman

D5. Gratia Harral, mar Dr. Fred Dexter of Albany, NY, 4 chn:

4 chn: Gay, Fred, Andrew and Judith(Ahern) Dexter
B4. Alice Emma Beard, 1859-1860
B5. Maximilien Cornelius Beard, b 1864 d 1924. Mar 1888 Gertrude F. Finley, 1864-1941.
C1. Maximilien Beard, d 1891 C2. Philadelphia Isabella Beard
C3. Stuart Menteth Beard II, b 1893, d 1955, mar 1921 Natalie Delores Sudler Turner, b 1890
D1. Stuart Menteth Beard III, b 1922 d 197-. Mar Alice Hopkins Warner
D2. Henry Sudler Beard, b 1924 mar Frith? Johnson
D3. Timothy Field Beard, b 1930
B6. Stuart Menteth Beard I, 1867-1941, mar Lila Palmerlee
C1. Catherine Beard, mar Edgar G. Wilson, res Boca Raton, FLA
D1. Leila May Wilson, mar 1950 West Point, Lt. Rob't R. Werner
E1. Jacqueline Werner, b 1954 E2. Robert Rehm Werner Jr.
B7. Consuelo Beard, by 2nd wife, b 1882 mar Wm. Kimball Smith.
C1. Celeste Smith, b 1911 mar 1947 Robert Candee Texido
B8. Bonnie Belle Beard, mar 1908 George D. Smith
C1. Cornelius Beard Smith C2. Bonnie Belle, mar Dr. Theodore Sack
B9. Col.Cornelius Beard, b 1886 mar Amy Lansing, dau of Jos. of Great Barrington, MA.

GROVES, LA GROVES, ALGROVE, HILGROVE, HELGROW, etc, etc. The spelling of these names is also confused in old J records, as the same fam appears as HILGROVE, HELGROW and ALLGROW in 1668 in St. Heliers, J. Possseveral different fams? (SOC. JERS. BULL, Vol 4)

ALGROVE, Nicholas, "deposed in 1702 ...in NC that he was 49...born... parish of St. John, Jersey, belonging to Hampshire, England." His parents were William and Susan ALLGROW. Note that name also appeared in New England, and that LE BOSQUET means GROVE. Some GROVES of New England may have been ALGROVE or LE BOSQUET.

GROVES, LA GROVE, Nicholas, b ca 1654 Francos of a Hug fam later temp. settled in J. Rem from J to Salem, MA before 1668. Mar 1671 Hannah Sallows, b 1654, res Beverly, MA. At least 6 chn. See GEN for more details, and see other sources. (GROVES GEN; NE HEADS OF FAMS;Savage; Boston TRANSCRIPT for Jan.Mar, Apr. and July 1908; GROVES FAM IN AMERICA, by W.T. Groves, Ann Arbor, MI, 1915; WRCIC)

GROVES, see HIST OF BRIMFIELD, MA; JOHN GROW OF IPSWICH: NEHGS Vol 51; Boston records; Noyes; Provi, RI and Glouc. records for more on GROW and GROVES.

GRUNDY, see GRANDIN, and sources such as Virkus; M. Drisko, Boothbay Harbor, ME.

GRUSH, DE GRUCHY, qv. GRUSH in America is apparently one variant spelling of surname DE GRUCHY, qv, old name of the C.I. and France. However, at least one GRUSH came from Germany. Much research done on this fam by Henry GRUSH, connected at one time with the American Embassy in Berne, Switzerland. Compiler was unable to find these records, or Mr. Grush. (Guy Dixon, Cheltenham, England)

GRUSH, Philip and Judith res Beverly, MA. Was he the Philip who came to MA on the MOLLY from J in 1769? (Whitmore)
A1. Nabby, Abigail, b 1798
A2. Philip, b 1800, poss mar Lydia ___?
B1. Lydia Pinder, b 1823 B2. Benj. Green, b 1825
A3. Francis Woodberry b 1802 A4. Isaiah, b 1804
A5. John Roberson, b 1808, d 1849 Bev., MA age 41, mar Louisa S. Edwards, res Beverly, MA.
B1. Reuben E., b 1838 Wenham, MA B3. Francis W. b 1842
B2. Louisa Ellen, b 1840, d.y.? B4. Addison E., b 1844

B5. Louisa Ellen Grush, b 1846 B6. Martha Jane Grush, b 1849
A6. Judith b 1810 A8. Nathan Woodberry, b 1815
A7. Else Bridges, b 1812 A9. Samuel Woodberry, b 1818
GRUSH, GRUCHE, LE GRUCHE, etc, John, d in MRB MA 1738. "John Gruchie and others, all of Guernsey, owners of ship WILLIAM AND MARY, 70 tons built at Boston 1700". (MASS Archives) John and Sarah GROSSE had 3 chn in MRB. (Willard Grush, LExington, MA)
A1. Sarah, bp 1729, d 1815, mar 1750 MRB James Tewkesbury bp 1727/8 MRB son of Henry and Greace Tewksbury. Chn b MRB.
B1. Sarah Tewksbury, bp 1751 B4. Margaret Tewksberry, bp 1757, mar
B2. Grace Tewksbury, bp 1753,d.y.?-Thomas GARNEY MRB 1777
B3. Grace again, bp 1755, mar Frederick Roach 1773 MRB, a son John Grush Roach.
B5. James Tewksbury, bp 1760 d 1812, mar Nancy Goodwin, b ca 1764 d 1835. Both bur OLD BURYING HILL, 3 chn.
C1. Sarah Grush Tewksbury, bp 1800 mar 1816 John Thompson III
C2. Jane Bridges Tewksbury, bp 1803 mar 1828 Andrew Mattison
C3. Grush Tewksbury, bp 1805 d at Manila 1825
B6. Jean bp 1764 B7. John Grush Tewksbury, bp 1767
B8. Hannah Tewksbury, bp 1770, mar 1790 Isaac Mansfield.
A2. John, bp 1732, d 1787 MRB. Mar 1. 1757 Hannah Collyer, bp 1741, d 1760, dau of Sam. and Eliz. (Bennett) Collyer. John mar 2. 1767 Widow Sarah Cahill. After his death she mar 1790 Burrill Devereux, at MRB. 3 chn by 1st mar, poss none by 2nd. Much info on Capt. John Grush referring to cargoes and ships going out of MRB to Bilbao, St. Kitts, Barbadoes, Guadaloupe, Anguilla, Turk's Island, Monte Cristo, etc, etc.
B1. Mary, b 1758 d 1812 a widow. Mar 1774 Nathaniel Raynolds, b 1751, son of John and Judith RAYNOLDS, qv, 7 chn b MRB. More on fam.
C1. Mary Raynolds, bp 1783 mar 1809 Wm. Cruff
C2. Sarah Raynolds, bp 1785, mar 1801 Wm. Goodwin
C3. Thomas, bp 1787, prob d.y.
C4. Joseph Raynolds, bp 1789 poss mar 1838 Rebecca Wooldridge?
C5. Martha Raynolds, bp 1791 mar 1809 Knott MARTIN IV, qv.
C6. Thomas Raynolds again, bp 1793 C7. Abigail Raynolds, bp 1796
B2. Thomas Grush, b 1759 MRB, d 1820 or 1821? Mar 1784 Eliz. NORE? NOURY? at MRB. He mar 2. 1785 widow Margaret (Wooldridge) JACKSON and 3. 1800, Esther Trask, b 1774 MRB, dau of Job and Martha (GRAY) Trask, who d 1815 MRB. Thomas a cordwainer, res corner of Crocker Place and Front St. at MRB. He had 16 chn, one by 1st wife, 8 by 2nd and 7 by 3rd, all b MRB.
C1. Elizabeth, b 1784
C2. Thomas, b 1786, d 1855 MRB. Mar 1811 Eliz. VICKERY, qv, b 1781, dau of Wm. and Eliz. VICKERY. Thomas was made prisoner by the British at Dartmoor Prison during War of 1812, poss no issue
C3. Robert Wooldridge b 1788, d at sea
C4. Margaret Pitman, b 1790, d 1880, desc.
C5. Joseph Pitman, b 1792 d at Amsterdam, Holland, a shipcaptain.
C6. Sarah Woodridge, b 1794, d.y. C7. Sarah again, b 1796, desc.
C8. John Pitman, twin, b 1798, d.y. C9. Mary, b 1798, twin, d ca 1871
C10. Job Trask, b 1800 d 1889 Danvers, MA, desc.
C11. Martha Gray, b 1802, d 1888, desc. C14. Richard T., b 1805,d d/ at sea
C12. and C13. twins, b 1804, d.y.
C15. Benjamin, b 1810 d at sea 1833-C16. Elizabeth, b 1812, d 1816.
B3. Michael, res Boston 1790, mar Hannah HINE, qv.
C1. John Hine, b 1784, d 1855 Boston. Mar 1808 Hannah SALTER, qv in MRB. She d 1849.

D1. Elizabeth, b ca 1810, d 1860 Roxbury, MA mar 1833 John Calvin Pillsbury, a builder, in Boston, b 1805 Rowley, MA. He d 1900 9 chn. (JEWETT GEN)

E1. John Hale Pillsbury, b 1834 mar Evelina J. Dame. He d age 35.

E2. Edward Payson Pillsbury, b 1836, d 1838

E3. Martha Eliz. Pillsbury, b 1838 d ca 1875 Boston.?

E4. Hannah Maria Pillsbury, b 1841 d 1878

E5. Joseph Hopkins Pillsbury, b 1842, d.y.

E6. Sarah Jewett Pillsbury, b 1843 mar Henry Lee Shepherd, desc.

E7. Geo. E. Pillsbury, b 1845, d.y. also E.8. George.

E9. Emma Mary Pillsbury, b 1852 Reading, MA. Desc. Mar 1881 Charles Edmund Merchant of Troy, NY, son of Geo. W. and Mary A. (Wallington) Merchant.

F1. Lawrence Hale Merchant ,b 1882, mar 1906 Jenny Mae Thomas, res Malden, MA.

D2. Other chn of John Hine GRUSH?

C2. Polly, bp 1786 d 1825 MRB. Christened May Scudder Grush. Mar Edward BROWN 1808 MRB. Desc.

C3. Hannah, b 1788 d.y. at Boston C5. Benjamin, b 1792, lost at sea.

C4. Michael, b 1790, drowned in Baltic Sea 1823

C6. Hannah, b 1795, descendants

C7. Nathaniel b 1797, lost at sea

C8. Sally, b 1800, d at MRB. Mar 1819 Thomas Tindley, desc.

A3. Elias, bp 1736, prob d.y.?

GRUSH, Charles Henry, b ca 1848 Roxbury, MA. (Amy Grush Johnson, West Chicago, ILL)

GRUSH, Elizabeth mar Joel Eby, oldest son of Benj. and Salome Baer Eby. Rem to ILL 1847. She d Piatt Co., ILL in her 86th year. 18 chn, 12 sons, including George, William, John, Solomon, Philip, Benjamin, Joel and David. Joel, on of the sons, had a Civil War record. He was b Huntington Co., and entered the service in ILL. In later yrs. res in Old Soldiers home and 1930. CAUTION: This may be a GermanFam.

GRUSH researchers: Mrs. Vuille Stewart, Huntington, PA; Mrs. Nolan R. Deets, Jr., Sterling, ILL.

GRUSH, John, selectman and overseer of the poor in MRB 1778-1780, commanded many ships, including SALLY, UNION, DOVE, SWALLOW, privateer brigantines BELLONA and GENERAL GATES. D 1787 age 54. (JOURNALS OF ASHLEY BOWEN, NEHGS)

GRUSH, John, prisoner at Dartmoor, England, War of 1812, living in 1853

GRUSH, Michael res Boston, MA 1790 with fam of 5. (Census)

GRUSH, Philip, cordwainer, prob from J mar Mary ___, res Beverly, MA.

A1. Mary Eliza Ober, b 1846, plus a son and dau b 1849, twins.

GRUSH, Philip Jr. mar Mary B., a 2nd wife, same as above?

A1. Joseph, b 1843 Beverly, MA.

GRUSH, Philip, son of Philip, bp 1785 Beverly, MA.

GRUSH, Sarah mar Jonathan CLEMENTS of Haverhill, MA 1745/6. He was son of Nathaniel. She was b Bradford, MA and d before 1826, dau of John and Sarah GRUSHE. John d ca 1754, and her mother Sarah in 1760. (CLEMENTS GEN)

GRUTE, fam from C.I. living in Windsor, ONT. (Aldo Brochet,London, ONT) See also GROUT.

GRUT. In G 1700s, curr G. This fam assoc. with the MARQUAND fam in G, being sponsors to their chn 1750. Noted in OH 1800s and in ILL.

GRUTT, Benjamin, "A native of the Island of Guernsey, Mr. B. Grutt read the Episcopal service in Albion, ILL, set apart for the Public Library." (Flower) GRUTT and LA SERRE, qv, had a sawmill east of Albion, ILL at Bonpas Bridge ca 1820, an early English settlement.

GUERIN, meaning gamekeeper, in G and J very early. There was also a Hug fam, one or more, with desc in early America. Some GUERINS desc from Jean, a native of Clairac, Agenois, Guienne, France. His son Daniel escaped from France during the Revocation ca late 1500s, by way of the Pyrenees Mts., Spain, Lisbon and a Guernsey ship in Lisbon Bay, skippered by Capt. Peter Marten of G. GUERIN mar the refugee Marie BACON. Many marriages of this fam with prominent fams of G. GUERINS of Devon, England were originally from Guernsey. The Guerins of Somerset Co., England are from Champagne, Isle de France and from Auvergne, Grance. Note that some GUERIN fams names changed over the years to GEARING and GARING, etc. (Smiles; OUR KIN by W.C. LE GUERIN, 1873; Charlotte Stupek of the GEURIN, GUERIN FAM BULLETIN, Santa Cruz, CAL; SC records; SC WILL BOOKS by Caroline T. Moore, 1969, etc, Columbia, SC; Muskingum Co. records by Chamberlain, book 7)

GUERIN, Susannah mar Peter MARTAIN, MARTIN 1808 Boston, prob from G?

GURRIN, William and Mary had dau named Mary, bp 1714 Boston, from G?

GUERIN, in CT. See AMERICAN GEN., CT, Vols 9 and 10.

GUERNSEY, GARNSEY, LE GUERNSIEIS. The latter name appeared in J 1309. However, the fam has long been gone from the Island, apparently, and it occurs in the 1200s in southern England, and in the 1385-1467 records of Early Chancery Proceedings, edited by Clarude Walmsley, London, 1927. Since the early Channel Islanders were sailors, it seems highly likely that some of them turned up in England, and called themselves 'of Guernsey'. The only other instance noted by compiler was one Guillaume DE GUERNEZE, WHO WAS A CREWMAN ON Cartier's 1534 voyage to Canada, possibly more data in England? A fine new edition of the GARNSEY-GUERNSEY GENEALOGY can be obtained from Judith Young-Thayer, 2044 Crawford Dr., Walla Walla, WA, 99362.

GUERNSEY, Joseph G., settled in Guernseytown, now part of WAterbury, CT, ca 1730, with wife Rachel MARCHANT, from G? OUTC.

GUERNSEY sources: Holmes; Bronson, DAR Hist. of Waterbury 1907; Lucille Nunn, Glendale, CAL; Sara Velder, Lincoln, NEB.

GUIBERT noted in MD 1600s (Skordas) poss GUILBERT of C.I. or France?

GUIGNION in G 1700, in St. Andrews parish.

GUIGNION, Nicholas Sr. b 1811 G, with wife Harriet Mary ROSE, b 1821, came from G 1842 to Gaspe, QUE. (K.H. Annett; Mrs. Hazen Stanley, Mesa AZ; Eunice Stanley, Traverse City, MI; Robert A. Guignion, Montreal, QUE; Inez Cosgrove, Thomatasassa, FLA)

A1. Nicholas, b 1843 Gaspe? d 1926 mar Hilaria LE MESSURIER, qv, b 1844 d 1924.
- B1. James, b 1865 mar Julia SIMON, qv, dau of Wm. and Mary SIMON
  - C1. Lena mar E. Scrimger C2. Raymond, mar ___Lee, no issue.
- B2. Isaac, b 1866 d.y. B3. Phyllis, b 1868, d.y.
- B4. Drusilla, b 1869 mar Nicholas SIMON, qv, poss b 1874, d 1947? 7 chn: Earnest, Ada, Bertha, Mary, Wallace, Flossie and Watson SIMON
- B5. Moses, b 1871 mar Nellie Stanley
  - C1. Esther, mar Frank McWilliams
  - C2. Ethel, mar John Stickney, 4 chn: Bobbie, Dale, Donnie & Heather
  - C3. Winnie C4. Goldie C5. Dorothy
  - C6. Gladys, mar James Paige, 2 chn C7. George
  - C8. Frances mar Bruce McWilliams. Chn: John, Paul, Gloria, etc?
- B6. Nelson, b 1872, d.y.
- B7. Clarissa, b 1875 mar George LE TOUZEL, qv. Another record says he mar Charlotte Rose RABEY. See Q.A. IN CANADA. Poss 2 wives?
- B8. Wilson, b 1876 mar Emily Miller, 2 sons, Louis and Percy.
- B9. Jacob, b 1877 mar Grace Patterson, res Western Canada? Chn: Elizabeth, John, James and Harvey

B10. William, b 1881 mar 1914 Rachel Matilda ROSE, Tillie, dau of Elias Rose and Clara Stanley, b 1888, d 1964.
C1. Helen Rose, b 1915 mar Thomas MacKenzie, 2 chn: Susan & Sharon
C2. Eunice Grace, b 1917 mar Hazen Stanley, 2 chn: Terrence and Linda Stanley
C3. Joan, b 1919, unmar
C4. William John called Jack, b 1921 mar Sheila Simpson, 3 chn: Maurice, Sharon and Milton GUIGNION
B11. Julia, b 1882 mar John ROSE. Julia d in childbirth
B12. Arthur, b 1884, mar Eliz. Patterson, res Western Canada. 2 chn: Evelyn and Grace, who mar Harvey Goode
B13. Felicia, b 1885 d.y.
B14. Wesley, b 1888 mar Charlotte Barnes from Montreal, res Western Canada, 5 chn: Hope, William, Ruth, John and Berwyn
B15. Lester, b 1890 mar Caroline Elizabeth Hannaway, b Ireland, and 2. Lillian Limon. Chn from 1st mar.
C1. Nelson, b 1917 mar Lulu Stanley b 1923, dau of Clifton Stanley and of Gertrude GUIGNION, dau of Abr. and Mary GUIGNION.
D1. Patricia b 1944 mar Reynold Kelly, 2 chn: Clayton, Clint Kelly
D2. Roy, b 1948 mar Donna Nelson
D3. Carolyn b 1955 mar Ronald Clark, a ch, Kerin Clark
C2. Cecil, b 1918 mar Margaret Brownsburger
D1. Judith Gayle mar Ray Chappel, 4 chn: Dawn, Paul, Kelly and Marci Chappel.
D2. Gayle D3. David
C3. Roy, 1919-1924
A2. Susan, b 1846 A3. James, b 1849 A4. Benj. I, b 1851 A5. Eliza / b 1855
A6. Elias, b 1857 d 1942 mar Elvina, Alvina Stanley, 1862-1935, mar ca 1880, 11 chn.
B1. Bert, b 1881 d 1917, killed in action, WWI, unmar
B2. Frederick, b 1884 d 1941 mar Susan Amelia West, 1889-1970, mar 1913. Fred d in Montreal, QUE
C1. Stanley Wesley, b 1913, d 1933 unmar C2. William E., 1914-16
C3. Greta Opal, b 1916 d 1971 mar Thomas S. Wylie, no issue
C4. Rhoda Lillian, b 1919 d 1954, mar James N. Young, no issue
C5. Herbert Norman, b 1921 mar Cecile Boyer, b 1924 mar 1953, res Ottawa, ONT, 4 chn: Fred. Herbert b 1954, Edward A., Eric David and Carl Stanley, b 1962
C6. Florence Faye, b 1925 mar Jean Paul DUPUIS, no issue.
C7. Robert Albert, b 1925, mar Alice M. Elliott, 1949, b 1929, res Montreal, QUE. A dau Linda Faye b 1950
C8. Eileen, b 1928, d.y.
C9. Alfred John, b 1932 mar Sheelagh Maureen Stevenson 1960, res Brantford, ONT, 2 chn: Alan John and Sheelagh Kathryn
B3. John, b 1892, d 1916 killed in action, unmar
B4. Gordon Albert, b 1901 d 1969, mar Muriel Blanche LENFESTY,no issue
B5. Jessie, mar Dawson Davis, res near Gaspetown, QUE
B6. Hilda, mar Reg. Simpson, raised a large family.
B7. Alma, mar Frank Stevens, Stephens, mar and d in Montreal, 1 ch.
B8. Jennie, mar Reg. James RABEY, qv. See Q.A. and Q.A. IN CANADA. At least 4 chn.
B9. Felicia, b 1883 d 1939 mar James Phillip Robinson, raised a fam, d in Gaspe, QUE
B10. Lillian mar Gordon RABEY, see Q.A. IN CANADA and Q.A., by Turk. She d 1979, 4 chn.
B11. Phyllis Muriel, b 1906 d 1967, mar George Mayer
A7. Alma, b 1859 mar Thomas GARDINER and res PEI

B1. Hazard Gardiner, mar Bessie Bramhall, 8 chn, including: Wayne, Sheldon, Jessie, Gerald, Alvin Gardiner
B2. Frame Gardiner, mar Ethel Campbell, and/or ___Taylor, 3 chn: Wesley, Jennie and Isabel, res Toronto, ONT
B3. Muncey Gardiner, mar Mae MacKinnon, 3 chn: Alma, Mary and Belle
B4. Leonard Gardiner, mar Hazel MacDonald, 4 chn: Verna, George, Harry and Dorothy Gardiner
B5. George, mar Esther Crooks B6. Harry, unmar B7. Dorothy, unmar
B8. Wilton Gardiner mar ___, 2 chn, res Toronto?
A8. Eva, b 1861 mar George MacWilliams, res PEI, at least 6 chn.
B1. Hattie MacWilliams, mar Willard Leard, res Borden, PEI, chn: Urville, Ralph who mar Millie Bearsto and Grace, who mar __Currie.
B2. Jack MacWilliams mar Mable MacKay, 5 chn:
C1. Claud MacWilliams
C2. Helen, mar Melville Bell, sev chn including Dianna & Lois
C3. Winnie, mar George Strang, a dau Nancy Strang
C4. Frank MacWilliams mar Esther GUIGNION, dau of Moses GUIGNION, qv. 4 chn: including Bobbie, Dale, Donnie and Heather.
C5. Bruce MacWilliams, mar Frances GUIGNION, sister of Esther above. 2 chn: Gloria and John MacWilliams res Cape Traverse, PEI.
C6. Eldon MacWilliams mar Anna Howatt, 2 or 3 chn?
B3. Lester MacWilliams mar Emma Dixon. Chn: Olga Rodd, Lillian Cutcliffe.
B4. Gordon MacWilliams, mar Mable Howatt, chn: Lloyd and Marion MacWilliams, and Gordon poss mar 2. Rita ___?
B5. Mildred MacWilliams, mar Elmer Francis, chn: Arnold and Winston Francis
B6. Leeman MacWilliams, mar Eileen MacInnis. Chn: George, Shirley and Jean MacWilliams.
A9. Abraham/Abram, b 1865 d 1944, mar Mary ROSE, 1874-1945, res Gaspe.
B1. Melinda May, 1891-1973, unmar
B2. Hazel, b 1893 d 1979 mar Garnet LE LACHEUR, qv.
C1. Weston Le Lacheur mar Thora FALLE, 2 chn: Gaile and Dale Le Lacheur, twins.
C2. Gladys Le Lacheur mar David Russell, 3 chn: Gary, Carol & Joyce Russell.
C3. Truman Le Lacheur, mar Pauline ___, 2 chn: Linda & Diane Le / Lacheur
B3. Sybil, b 1896 mar Herbert Miller and 2. Wallace Whitlock.
B4. Daisy, b 1898 d 1939 mar James Coldrick, qv
C1. Audrey Coldrick, mar Wesley PULLING, 3 chn: Donald, Wesley and Sandra Pulling.
B5. Norman John, b 1901 d 1968 mar Eva Pitman, 5 chn, mar & res? Ont.
C1. William John b 1924 mar Kathleen Tremblay 1945 and 2. in 1970 Joan Heuchan, 3 chn: Gillie Ann, Graham W. & Samantha.
C2. Robert Norman, b 1926 mar Doreen Cecile 1948, 2 chn: Shelly and Michael
C3. Erma Fay, b 1930 mar Garth Rumble, 3 chn: Robert, Donald and Douglas Rumble.
C4. Betty, b 1931, unmar
C5. Sharon b 1948 mar Douglas Ladore 1966, 3 chn: Monique, Shaun, and Lee Ann Ladore.
B6. Gertrude, b 1903 d 1979, mar Clifton Stanley
C1. Lulu Stanley, b 1923 mar Nelson GUIGNION
C2. Leonard Stanley, b 1926 mar Emily BARTON, a dau Sharon Stanley
C3. Silvia Stanley b 1927 mar Gary Howell and 2. Raymond Sinnett, 7 chn: Carol, Judy, Samuel, Thomas, Elaine, Linda, Todd Sinett.
C4. Lorna Stanley, b 1929 mar Leo Nish, 2 chn: Clifton & Maureen

C5. Rhoda Stanley, b 1930 mar Stanley Hamilton, res BC. 5 chn: Ronald Diane, Debra, Richard, and Stanley Hamilton.
C6. Vera Stanley, b 1932 mar Raymond Stanley and 2. Harry Suiskins, 3 chn: Lana, Glenn and Gertrude Stanley
C7. Vida Stanley, b 1933 mar Maynard Mullin, 3 chn: Kenneth, Shirley and Kerry Mullin.
C8. Marjorie Stanley, b 1934 mar Wilson LE MESURIER, a dau Lisbeth.
C9. Murray Stanley, b 1935 mar Ruth Peters, 3 chn: Betty, Carol and Wayne Peters Stanley
C10. Lois Stanley, b 1939 mar Irvin Phillips and 2. Allan ROBERTS, 2 chn: Gary and Lynne Phillips.
B7. Effie b 1905 d 1970, mar Harris McAfee, fam res Gaspe and Que.City.
C1. Daisy McAfee, b 1924 d 1940
C2. Ronald McAfee, mar Madeline McKenna, 6 chn: Sharon, Rosemarie, Marion, Arthur, Ronald and Michael McAfee
C3. Mildred McAfee, mar Lester Assels, 4 chn: Glenn, Philip, Robert, and Linda Assels.
C4. Charles McAfee, mar Jean Gunn, 5 chn: Wm., Charles, Richard, James and Charlene McAfee.
C5. Dorothy McAfee mar Guy Mullin, 5 chn: Judy, Joyce, Andrew, Sean and Gordon Mullin
C6. Wendell McAfee mar Lorraine Morris, 8 chn: Wayne, Carol, Shirley Linda, Jennifer, Debra, Clayton and Beverly McAfee.
C7. Arthur, unmar
C8. Margaret, mar Weston Hackett, 7 chn: Holly, Rose, (twins), Ronald, Carl, Allan, Noreen and Johnny or Tabby Hackett.
B8. Edna, b 1908 d 1964, mar Albert RABEY, res Gaspe. See Q.A.IN CAN.
C1. Ruby Rabey mar Elmer Mullin, chn: Brenda, Jean and Judy (twins), and Ronald Mullin.
B9. Lloyd, b 1911 mar Mabel Annett, res Gaspe, 4 chn.
C1. Garth mar 1. Gladys BECHERVAISE and 2. Valerie Piercey, 3 chn: Dane Lynn, Delora and Loretta
C2. Daryl, mar Joanne Reid and 2. Margot Gillis, 3 chn: Geoffrey, Susanne, and Daryl
C3. Sandra, mar Arden Adams, 3 chn: Rhonda, Craig and Cory Adams
C4. Marlene, mar Maurice COADY
B10. Leeman, b 1913 d 1944 WWII, mar Elva Simpson, 2 chn: Raymond and Beryl.
B11. Lorna, b 1918 d 1921.
A10. Amelia, b 1869 mar Howatt Dawson, res PEI. She mar 2. Con Campbell, 2 chn by Dawson, and one by Campbell.
B1. Mamie Dawson, mar Philip Saunders, Philip d 1981 Hamilton, ONT.
C1. Daniel Campbell Saunders, b ca 1923 mar Christine MacMillan, res PEI, 5 chn: Marylyn, Barbara, Judy, Philip and Jeff Saunders.
C2. Kay Saunders mar Ira E. Barlow, res Boston, MA
C3. Isabel Saunders, res Boston, mar Fred Pierce.
C4. Mary Saunders res Boston.
C5. Margaret Saunders, mar Allison Gills, res Charlottetown, PEI.
C6. Irene Saunders, mar Russell MacNeill, res PEI
C7. Martha Saunders, mar Archie Vickerson, res PEI
C8. Philip Saunders, res Charlottetown, PEI
B2. Reggie Dawson, had dau who mar 1. MacWilliams, had son Horace.
B3. James Campbell, mar and with chn.
A11. Mary Louise mar Capt. Edward Adams, res Fontenelle, GAspe, QUE.
B1. Dora Ann Adams, b 1862 Fontenelle, Gaspe, QUE d 1950, mar Robert MacWilliams, 1860-1937, bur Cape Traverse, PEI.

C1. Edwin MacWilliams, b 1886 d 1978 mar Edith Jane Stanley, 1882-1959, dau of John Stanley and Louise ROSE. 5 chn: Raymond R., Norman S., Wendell Earl, Hazen H. and Inez Bouyer MacWilliams, 4 having issue, many desc. See record in WRCIC.

B2. Sarah, Sally?, mar Arthur Stanley

B3. Julia Adams, mar ___Brown, res Colma, CAL

B4. Esther or Emmeline? mar 1. Henry Stanley, res Gaspe, his 2nd wife. He had mar 1. Edith Stanley, dau of John and Louise ROSE Stanley. Esther mar 2. Willie Miles Stanley, had son Vincent Stanley.

C1. Henry Stanley Jr., mar ___, 4 chn: Allan, Delie, William and Laura Stanley

B5. Stephen? Adams B6. Allan Adams? B7. Frank Adams.

GUIGNION, Simon, from C.I. to Gaspe early 1800s.

GUIGNION?, spelled GUIONOW?, Mary Ann, mar James DESBROSS, poss DESBOROUGH in MA 1700s. This appears to be a mar of 2 from C.I. OUTC.

GUILBERT in G 1331, curr G. Early in Vale G. GUILBERT in J 1331-1607. Curr but scarce in J. See CIFHS #8. GUILBERT curr in Chicago, OUTC.

GUILBERT, Arthur, mar in late 1800s Bessie, dau of Frank K. Bull. See BULL. Bessie b 1850s. Res Spring Prairie, Walworth Co., WIS. (COMMEM. BIOG. RECORD OF PROM. AND REPR. MEN OF RACINE, 1906, Chicago)

GUILBERT, James, b G, to RAcine, WI ca 1850. James poss a ship captain. The last two chn from a 2nd mar? Or poss grchn of James? (1860 census) See Elizabeth GUILBERT.

A1. Albert b ca 1807 G A3. Jane, b ca 1812 G Guernsey.

A2. Alexander, b ca 1810 G A4. Jane, b ca 1838 G. A5. Anne, b/ca 1839

GUILBERT, John, d 1673 New Haven, CT. He mad will mentioning wife, sons Matthew and Samuel, daus Mary AUGER, Hannah Parker and grandson John GUILBERT, also a cousin Sarah How. OUTC.

GUILBERT, Judith, 2nd wife of Peter PRIAULX, qv, desc. She was dau of James and Elizabeth GUILBERT, rem to GCO early 1800s. See PRIAULX.

GUILBERT, Marguerite mar Daniel ROSE, res Muskingum Co., OH early 1800s. from G.

GUILBERT, Martha, b G, mar James COCKRAYNE, res OH? from G.

GUILBERT, Rachel, b G, to OH, mar ___ROSE, qv.

GUILD, GUILE, GUILL, GUILLE, etc. Sometimes "of Scottish origin, the records showing the surname as early as 1449, when one Alexander Guilde owned property at Sterling, Scotland. In the 16th century we find the family in Dundee, and in the 17th at Forfarshire and Perth. This Scottish family may have desc from the GUILLE family of the Isle of Guernsey, the original seat of which was on the Bay called Saint in the parish of St. Martin, Guernsey. According to tradition, they were there before or at the time of the Norman Conquest. At the dedication of the St. Pierre Du Bois Church in 1167, John GUILLE is mentioned as one of the honorable gentlemen present. The surname is said to be Norman and is probably the Norman form of the Latin Aegidium (Giles in English). The coat of arms of the Scotch Guilds resembles closely that of the Guernsey family. The American families of Guild and Guile are descendants from two brothers John...and Samuel, who with their sister Ann arrived in MASS ca 1636, and settled in Dedham. They were probably quite young when they came...Ann about 20, John about 18 and Samuel 16. Ann mar 1638 James Allen, and in 1645 settled in Medfield. Samuel went to Newbury, MA 1640, and then to Haverhill." (GEN. AND FAM. HIST. OF CONN, by Cutter, Vol 1.; Pope; GUILD, GUILE AND GILE FAMILY, by Charles Burleigh, Portland, ME 1887)

GUILE, Joshua in NH 1700s, desc to Ont. Co., NY, and to Indiana. (Bernice Clayton, Shattuck, OK)

GUILLARD, GUILLIARD in J 1309. Orig. form of GAYLORD

GUILLAUME in J 1190. In St. Heliers and St. Mary J1668 & 1749. Sometimes spelled GILLAM, and sometimes translated to WILLIAM,WILLIAMS. See Soc. Jers. Bull. 1977.

GUILLAUME, GILLAM, Charles b 1671 G, d 1727, rem ca 1690 to Saybrook, CT with two CARTERET bros. and wrote his name, GILLAM. Charles d unmar. He was an excellent joiner, and produced a beautiful tulipwood chest of drawers, which has been proved to be Gillam's work, and is now at the Henry Francis Du Pont Winterthur Museum in Delaware. (CABINET MAKERS OF AMERICA, by E.H. Bejerkoe, 1951) His estate went to his nephew James.

GUILLAUME, Jacques, James, bro of Charles, mar Douce LA CLOCHE, qv, dau of the Rev. Estien, Stephen LA CLOCHE in 1667, J. They had 5 chn, including two sons who rem to America. Jacques, a man of some standing, and godparents for these chn were three Seigneurs of J.

GUILLAUME, Carteret, 1668-1714, b J, emigrated to Saybrook, CT ca 1690 and anglicized his name to GILLAM. Carteret mar Mary Arnold 1691. (1749 EXT. of J; Soc. Jers. Bull. 1977)

A1. Arnold Gillam A4. Benjamin, a natural son A5. Anne Gillam
A2. James Gillam, inherited estate from his uncle, Charles GUILLAUME.
A3. Charles Gillam A6. Mary Gillam.

GUILLIAMS fam in Coshocton, OH middle 1800s. OUTC. (Cem. Stones)

GUILLE in G 1300s, in Sark 1500s. In St. Martin and CAstel G 1600. In St. Andrews G 1750. Curr and common in G. Scarce in J. See CIFHS #4. Name formerly in St. Ouen J.

GUILLE, Joseph Francis Nicholas, b 1776, either in G or Spain, son of Nicholas GUILLE, a G merchant established in Barcelona, Spain, b G. Joseph served in the Royal Navy? then rem to Philadelpia, PA ca 1810, where he mar 1813 Anna Margretta Von Ficke, dau of Henry Augustus of Prussia and of Anna Catherine. Anna Jr. was b Phila. 8 chn. (Margaret Guille, Wooster, OH; Marian Guille, Ooltewah, TN; Amy Sylar, Ooltewah, TN; OLD NORTHWEST, Vol 4; Henry Henegar Jr., Chattanooga, TN; Mrs. Robert Sloan, Ft. Worth, TX)

A1. Francoise CARRE A3. Napoleon A5. Josephine A8. St. George.
A2. Carnot A4. Vardinique A6. Elizabeth DE LISLE
A7. Andros, b 1832 Zanesville, OH, d 1910 age 78. Served in 97th OH, wounded, and served in battle at foot of Lookout Mt., TN, in the Civil War. Res Zanesville, OH. Mar 1854 Augusta Caroline Fleck, 1839-1904. Her parents d at sea on way to America, and she was raised by John Zockman.
B1. William Andros, b 1855 McLean Co., ILL, mar Florence? Plant
C1. Katherine, b 1905 mar Wm. Everhart, 2 chn: James and Rosalind Savard.
C2. Leslie mar Inez ___, a son Sherred L. Guille was Commander of the Naval Oceans System Center, San Diego, CAL.
B2. Amelia, b 1857 res Putnam, OH mar 1879 Zanesville, OH James Milligan from Lancaster, OH. A James Milligan of OH was b 1790, PA. (GCO Library, Cambridge, OH)
C1. William Vincent Milligan C2. Sherred Milligan C3. Max Milligan
C4. Carnot Milligan, mar __, 2 chn: Sarah HOOPER & Fred Milligan of TN
C5. Dana Milligan C6. Amelia Milligan
B3. Edward, b 1859 Zanesville, OH, called Ned, mar Henrietta Plant
C1. Joseph Francis Nicholas, b 1908 mar Sara Watts, res Ooltewah, TN, rural mail carrier, 2 chn: Margaret Poe and Jane
C2. Dixie mar James RUE. Dau Phyllis Rue. Cf LA RUE, DE LA RUE.
B4. Frank, b 1861 Putnam, OH, Presb. minister mar Margaret DavisBAKER dau of Robert PERRY and Mollie E. (Sensabaugh) Baker. Margaret b

1873 ILL, 4 daus.

C1. Elizabeth Augusta, b 1901 Harriman, TN d 1946. Mar Eugene Mc Williams, 3 chn: Eugene, Francis Blais & Betty Freeman,res SC.

C2. Katharine Louise, b 1901 Watseka, ILL

C3. Frances Vernon, b 1908 Atlanta GA, twin.

C4. Margaret Baker, b 1908, twin of Frances, res Wooster, OH.

B5. Harry Leslie, b 1866 Putnam, OH mar 1902 Stella Bell.

C1. Amy Bell Guille, b 1904 mar 1926 Luther W. Sylar, res Ooltewah, TN, 3 chn: Kathryn Echerd, Stella Sylar and Lewis H. Sylar.

C2. George Edward/Ned mar Annabel Morgan, no issue

C3. Marian Guille, unmar, res Ooltewah, TN

B6. Katherine, b 1870, mar Robert Fielding Sloan, res Charlevois, MI. This data uncertain. 2 chn bur Chattanooga, TN, d.y.

C1. Robert F. Sloan III, res Alvarado, TX mar Martha ___ of Muskegon, MI, 3 chn: Mary Martha, Katherine Amelia and Robert F. Sloan IV.

C2. Mary Katherine Sloan, called Sally, res Grand Haven, MI, 1925-1979.

C3. Paul Stewart Sloan, M.D., res Houghton, MI mar Laverne, 4 chn.

C4. Suzanne, b 1935 mar H. Scott, res Lawton, OK, 2 chn, Anne and Robert Scott.

C5. Dorothy Evelyn?, mar William Walter Rowe, widower, in Ft. Worth, TX. Dorothy b ca 1929 Battle Creek, MI, 2 chn: Wm. & Peggy, adopted?

B7. Dr. George, b 1873 Zanesville, OH mar Mae Gettys. First Pres. of Wm. J. Bryan Univ. in Dayton, TN, res Athens, TN, 2 chn.

C1. Emily Egerton, b 1902 Athens, TN mar Henry A. Henegar 1933, 3 sons: George Guille, Edward A. II, and Henry Alexander, two mar, and with chn.

C2. Wilberforce Gettys Guille, b 1900 d 1970 Athens, TN, mar Alice Alater Cannon, b 1927 Salisbury, NC, res NC.

B8. Charles, b 1873, twin of George above, mar Lela Taylor, no issue, res Chattanooga, TN.

GUILLE data in MS owned by Mrs. Chetmell of Bosqville, G, dated 1898, not seen by compiler.

GUILLE, Andrew, from G? in Muskingum Co., OH 1860 (CENSUS)

GUILLE, James Philippe, b 1867 G, to US early 1900s, res VA, 4 chn. (Guernsey STAR, 1979). Had bro. Walter, see below.

A1. Arthur LE PAGE GUILLE, b 1892 G, mar ___, a dau Jeanne who mar Alan Seigfried.

GUILLE, Julie Marie, sister of above Walter and James, res G? or US?

GUILLE, Noah of G? mar Sarah Brikendine, res Boston. Widowed, she mar 2. 1712, John Parker, widower of Sary Vering, who d Boston 1711. Sarah Guille Parker, d 1750, age ca 81. Parker d 1744, age ca 80. 7 chn in Boston b 1695-1707, by GUILLE but not found by compiler. Poss name was changed to GILE, GILES? GILLE or similar, or the chn took name of stepfather? (ARMORIAL OF JERSEY; Boston VR)

A1. Sarah, b 1702 A2. Katherine, b 1703.

GUILLE, Walter Peter, b 1865 G, to US? Bro of Julie and James. His chn were named Walter Peter Jr. and Ida Evelyn Guille.

GUILLE noted in CT marriages, poss from G? See Mary GUILLE MESSERVY.

GUILLE, Thomas from Forest G, to NYCity ca 1834. Painter-decorator. Made a good size fortune and retired to G, where he and ALLES, his partner, qv, organized the GUILLE-ALLES Library. (Warren)

GUILLET in J 1461, 1607, 1664, 1691. Curr J. Curr TEXAS, but OUTC.

GUILLET, Walter John, first of the four chn of John GUILLET by 2nd wife Charlotte PAYNE. (See Q.A. IN CANADA, by Turk) Walter ran away from home 1850 to Brazil, where he operated a store that sold ornaments, curios and naturalists supplies. Carried on a trade in exotic insects, corals, sponges and feathers, with scientists, travelers and sailors his customers. His partner ruined the business, and he rem to London, where he preached in Hyde Park. Later visited in Canada and in Virginia, US. (GUILLET-THOREAU GEN, by Edwin Guillet, Toronto, ONT, 1971)

GUILLET, a fam in Akron, OH until the 1970s was desc from the above Guillet fam of Jersey and Ontario, Canada.

GULLET, Peter, a boatmaster at Richmond Island, ME 1636, poss a GUILLET of J?

If no other origin can be found, it's possible that some of the GULLEY, GULLET and GILLETT fams of early New England were GUILLETS of J.

GUILLON, noted in Steven's list of Old Jersey surnames as LE GUILLON.

GUILLON, spelled many different ways, GEULLOW, GEULO, GUILLOW, GULLO, GULLON, etc., Francis, of Bristol Co., MA or RI mar Phebe Bassett in Norton? MA? 1787. Poss son of Francis and Molle (DERBEY, DARBY?) GUELO, mar in Norton 1761. (Judith Peterson, Acton, MA)

GUISE, Jeannette, dau of a J fam, rem to Whitby, ONT, Canada ca 1967, mar Raymond Etter, a Swiss. (Elaine Hall, Toronto, ONT)

GULLY, GULLEY curr in G. GULICH, OUTC, but appeared in G before 1814

GUNO, Francis, mar Sarah Belchar 1730 in Boston. Was this GERNEAU, GANO, or GUENO? GUENO is old in J.

GUNNLL, Clement arrived in Boston 1769 on ship MOLLY from J. (Whitmore) Unlikely surname. Cf MATTHEW GUNNIEL or GERNEAU?, mar Mary Coharan, or Cochran 1773 Boston. Note also that Gunnels res in TN early 1800s. (TENN. CEM BOOK) Cf also GUENO, GUNO, above.

GUNTON, curr research in J? (CIFHS #8)

GUNTON, this fam from J to Vittoria, ONT ca 1860. The original fam in J came from Matishall, Norfolk Co., England, to J in 1700s. Ernest, son of John and Eliza, was b 1842 J and d 1862 ONT. Other GUNTONS of J rem to WISC, Montreal and CAL. Name curr in J.

GUNTON, John Russell, b 1839 J rem to Vittoria, ONT, mar 1859 Eliza JARVIS. John a carpenter and joiner. Another Jersey fam or two had preceded him to Vittoria, MACHON and LE LIEVRE, see Q.A. IN CANADA. (Booklet, HIST OF FAM OF ISAIAH JARVIS AND OLIVE R. FLEWELLING by Robert E. Gunton, 1933; Diane Gibson, Guelph, ONT; David Avery, 18 Dutch Myrtle Way, Don Mills, ONT, M3B 3K8, new Gunton book available in 1983) A little more info. in WRCIC.

A1. Ellen Elizabeth, 1860-1937, mar Edward Anson Buchner, 1858-1941, 5 chn, see book.
A2. Robert Edwin Gunton 1863-1935, mar Annie Perry Austin, 1863-1948
A3. Walter John, or John Walter, 1864-1937 mar Margaret Lindsay King, 1881-1920.
A4. Ernest, 1867-1869
A5. Rev. WM. Arthur, 1870-1935, mar Joanna/Jean Ross, 1875-1959
A6. Lucy Harriet, 1873-1953, mar Thomas Harrop, no issue
A7. Charles Alonzo, 1876-1877
A8. Louis Alfred, 1879-1962, mar Annie Horneblower, 10 chn.
A9. David Duncan, 1881-1971 mar Margaret Emma Church, 1885-1976
A10. Ruth Eliza, 1885-1977 mar Frank A. Schafer

GUNTON, Joseph Robert, b 1842 J? d 1919 in ONT, mar Mary Ann ___, 1851-1890. OUTC, but quite likely to be from J. (Judy Congdon, London, ONT.)

A1. Arthur Joseph, b 1869 d 1956 ONT
A2. Robert William, b 1871, d.y.
A3. Emma Jane, b 1872 d 1958
A7. Jane, b 1878
A8. Lillian Mary, b 1880 d 1967
A9. Ernest Robert, b 1882 d 1919

A4. Robert William again, b 1874
A5. Alice Joanna, b 1876
A6. Charles Frederick, b 1877
A10. Ethel Maud, b 1885 d 1975
A11. Rosa Louisa, b 1887, d 1966, mar Brickham, dau Doris Brickham

GUPPY. Surname of southern England, but also occurred in C.I. Two names are poss originals of this name. LE GOUPIL, the fox, was in J 1255. In St. Brelade and St. Mary J 1668. The other surname, LE GOUPILLOT was in G early. Some data on this surname in WRCIC, gathered from Vital Records; THE HOOPER GEN; Noyes; the Essex Coll, vol 2; NY Aliens, by Scott and Conway; MESSERVY and GALE records. The English surname GUPPY may have another origin.

GUPTIL. Origin not clarified. GOUPTEILLE was early in Island of G. (Wm. Guptil of NY) The surname GOBTEL was in G from the 1100s to the 1500s at least. There is a Guphill genealogy, claiming an origin in Wiltshire, England. (Harleean MS) Others said to come from the Isle of Man. Marion Rogers of Berkeley, CAL has done some work on this surname, but her records were not found by compiler. It is likely that the first one settled in ME, poss shipwrecked as tradition has it. At least one branch rem to Grand Manan Island, where Wm. and Mary Gubtail are listed in 1821 census with 9 chn. (BURIAL BOOKS OF JOHN GRAHAM, GRAND MANAN ISLAND, to 1974, film; Evelyn Cross, Nobleboro, ME; Robert D. Metcalfe, North Palm Beach, FLA; OLD KITTERY AND HER FAMILIES; CLEMENT GEN; CAVERLY GEN; Noyes; Underhill) See WRCIC for a few items on this fam. Note there were a number of marriages with C.I. persons.

GUBTILE, GUPTILL in MD in 1600s. (Skordas) And in SC, see Vol 7, SC Magazine. Note also GUPTILL name in Lake and Cuyahoga Cos., OH.

GURDAN, Hannah, mar Elias Lathrop. Their dau Eunice Lathrop, b 1776, mar 1804 Francis BALCOM, qv. of Mansfield, CT. Francis was the grt. grandson of Capt. John Balcom, qv, who is said to have been born in J ca 1697. The surname GURDAN sounds very close to GUERDAIN, known in J since 1300s to at least 1749. GUERDAIN in J assoc. with the HERAULTS, qv, and the DE CARTERET, qv, in St. Heliers 1749, when the name disappears. GURDON in Salem, MA 1970. OUTC.

GUSTIN. This very large fam has been traced back to Augustine JEAN, b 1647 Jersey. He d in Portland, Falmouth, ME 1719. Between these two dates he led a very full life. Jean was a desc of several Hug. fams in J for a long time. His father was Edmond JEAN, b 1579 at L'Etacq, St. Ouen parish. His mother was Esther LE ROSSIGNOL, Nightingale. Both fams were seafaring, and both were land owners in the Island. It is said that the ROSSIGNOLS were traders with the natives of Acadia as early as 1604, and Lake Rossignol in NovaScotia may possibly be named for an early trapper there, from France or J.

One account of Gustin says that at the age of 28, he and three friends, named ARSENAULT, BAYER and LE BRETON came to America in their own small ship, arriving just in time to take part in King Phillip's War. Some of the men in the outfit were killed, but Jean survived. He met Elizabeth BROWN (Scottish) of Boston, they mar, and later rem to Portland, ME. They had 10 chn. The GUSTINE COMPENDIUM explains the change in surname thusly: His last name was anglicized to John, and he became Augustine John. AUGUSTINE was whittled down to GUSTIN, and in military and land records the name was turned around to John GUSTIN. On his deathbed, however, he circled the AU of AUGUSTINE, to clarify his real name.

"From what I understand, LE ROSSIGNOLS were old families in Jersey, but the JEANS were Huguenots that escaped from France and settled in Jersey, where some stayed for a time, but not permanently." (Winifred (H. Harden, Tallahassee, FLA)

There is a great deal of information on this fam. Therefore only a small portion is included here. See sources. (Mrs. Zelona Chinn, Indianola, NEB; Mrs. Leslie Jasperson, Galesburg, ILL; Byrle Cosner, Woodhull, ILL; G.L. Woughter, Milford, MI; Julie Bearden, Escalon, CAL; Mrs. Cecil Gustin, Waterville, OH; Mrs. Charles Reen, Ottawa, ONT; Betty Holmes, Long Beach, CAL; Mrs. R. Glen Jones, Casa Grande, AZ; THE GUSTINE COMPENDIUM, etc, etc.)

A1. Sarah, b 1679 Falmouth, ME mar 1704 Salem, MA Jonathan Bly, Bleigh
A2. Mary, b 1677/8, mar 1697 Boston Richard Ward and 2. in 1710, John Bushnell, 5 chn.
A3. Samuel, b ca 1680 Falmouth, ME mar 1712 Stonington, CT Abigail Shaw, by Rev. James Noyes, 6 chn. (Betty Holmes, Long Beach, CAL)
B1. Lemuel Gustine, b 1724 Saybrook, CT mar ?. CAUTION: NOT VERIFIED.
C1. John Gustine Sr., b 1760, d 1858 Richmond, OH, mar Mary Blair, 1759-1848.
D1. John Gustine Jr., b 1790 PA. (1850 census)
E1. Lemuel Gustine, b 1822 OH, d 1904 Storm Lake, IA, mar Eliz.___ b 1820 OH, d 1898 Storm Lake, IA
F1. Bishop Simpson Gustine, b 1857 Richmond, OH mar 1881 Mary Kruckenberg, b 1860 Germany, d 1936 Galva, IA. He d 1934
G1. Mildred Iola Gustine, b 1900 IA, mar Wm. Jordan Holmes.
A4. William, bca 1687, mar Abigail Thayer, d quite young.
A5. Elizabeth, b 1687 mar 1708 Boston, MA, James Towle, rem to Frankford, NJ.
A6. John, b 1691 Lynn, MA. (GL Woughter, Milford, MI)
B1. Eliphalet, b 1724 Stonington, CT, d 1778 on a trip into Canada from Susex Co., NJ.
C1. Eliphalet Jr, b 1766 Sussex Co., NJ d 1860 Burlington Twp., Bradford Co., PA, mar 1. Jemima Horton, a son John mar 2.no chn.
D1. John, b 1796 Sussex Co. NJ mar Fannie Smith
E1. Charles, b 1828 d 1898, mar 1. Abi. J. Meade, and 2. no issue.
F1. John H. b 1853 d 1915 mar Orley G. Bennett, res Luther'sMills
G1. Fannie Lorinda Gustin, b 1889 Granville Center, PA, mar Louis A. Woughter, both liv 1979, res Binghamton, NY.
H1. Gerald Louis Woughter, b 1922 Johnson City, NY mar Lou Ellen Rooch of Mentone, IND.
I1. John B. Woughter, b 1958 Dayton, TN
I2. Frederick R. L. Woughter, b 1962
A7. Abigail, b 1693 Lynn, MA mar Thomas Fuller.
A8. Ebenezer, b 1696 Lynn, settled in Phippsburg, ME.
A9. Thomas, b 1698/9 Lynn, MA mar 1722 Sarah Holmes, and d 1765 Colchester, CT. Sarah was b ca 1702 Stow, MA, d ca 1763 Colchester, dau of John and Eliz (Gates) Holmes. (Zelona Chinn, Indianola,NEB)
B1. Thomas Gustin, b 1725 Colchester, CT mar 1746 Hannah Griswold.
C1. David, b 1747 New London, CT d 1750
C2. Sarah, b 1749 C3. Walter, b 1751 C4. Ezra C5. Thomas
C6. Edward, b 1758 served 14 mos. in Rev. War, res Hinsdale, NH, mar Elizabeth ___. Bur 1845 near Brodhead, WIS. See Gov't data.
C7. Elizabeth, b 1760 Colchester, CT mar 1786 Ephraim Derrick
D1. Polly Derick, b 1787 Claremont, NH mar 1806 James Mills
D2. Morris Ames Derrick, b 1788
D3. Elizabeth Derick, b 1791 mar 1809 Elisha Kellogg, & d 1832
D4. Rodolphus Derrick, b 1793 mar 1817 Loranda Sheldo, d 1860
D5. Bybie Luke Derick, b 1795 Bethel, VT, mar 1821 Statira Felton.
D6. Sophia Derick, b 1797 Bethel, VT.-D7. Eben C. b 1799 VT.
C8. Ebenezer, b 1762 Colchester, CT.

C9. Amos?, mar1778 Lydia Gardiner of Gardiner's Island, where she was b 1751. Amos b 1755?
B2. Samuel B3. John B4. Josiah, b 1749 B5. Stephen
A10. David, b ca 1703 Lynn, MA.
One GUSTIN fam desc from John, lived first in Portland, ME, rem to CT, to NJ, to PA, to OH, near Dayton, OH. (Winifred Harden, Tallahassee, FLA.)
GUY, French and English surname, old in J. Curr G and J.
GUY, Leonard Frank, b 1936 St. Helier J, computer auditor. Mar 1956 in St. Heliers J, Dorothea May Freeman, b 1933 St. Heliers. He was son of Ernest Frank Guy, b 1913 Sussex, England and Annie Rachel LE MARINEL, b 1913 St. Helier J. Dorothea the dau of Frederick Charles FREEMAN, b 1892 St. Helier J, soldier and Florence Mary Spratt, b 1894 J. Leonard rem to ONT by 1957, and res Oshawa, Whitby, Windsor and Orono, ONT. 5 chn. (L.F. Guy, Orono, ONT)
A1. Gillian Dawn, b 1957 St.Helier J, d in accident 1959 Oshawa,ONT.
A2. Keith Leonard, b 1959 Oshawa, ONT.
A3. Mark Bradley, b 1961 A4. Karen Joy Gillian b 1964
A5. Christopher Michael b 1965 Windsor, ONT.
GUY, Henry mar Rebecca FIGGET, FICKET, FICQUET?, 1707/8 MRB. See FICKETT. OUTC.
A1. Abigail, bp 1717 A3. Elizabeth, bp 1724, twin
A2. Rebeckah, bp 1720 A4. Henry, bp 1724, twin.
GUY, John mar Frances NEAL 1660 Falmouth, OUTC. (Noyes)
GUY, William in New England 1634, prob from Hampshire, England. (Booklet in Cong. Library) Note that the Channel Islands were said by ALGROVE to be a part of Hampshire, Engl. in 17th Cent.
GYLES, GILES, GUILLE?, Mathew from C.I.? in Isles of Shaolas, ME 1653. See also GUILLE, and GUILD. (Underhill)
GYLES, John from C.I.? res Beverly, MA, mar Eliz. GALLY, qv, widow of Osmond TRASH, TRASK, poss TRACHY?, qv, 1679. 11 chn. (Perley)
HACQUOIL, Oswald Xavier, from J to Canada 1805/6 (Norma Pookanen)
HACKING in J 1800s, poss English or Irish surname?
HACKING, John Thomas, shoemaker, b J, mar Sarah ___ 1792 in MRB?, settled New York? (Kathleen Killeen, Richmond,Hill, NY)
A1. John Thomas, b 1833 St. Heliers J
A2. William, b 1835 J A3. Mary, b 1837 J, d.y.
A4. Mary again, b 1841 St. Heliers J mar 1859 William Henry WOLFREYS, b J. See WOLFREYS. Mary to US.
HAILES, HAILE, old in J, appearing in many different spellings from 1274. HALE, HALES, HALEY curr in C.I. but not HAILE. HELLES in J 1331, 1607, 1668 in St. Clement and St. John J.
HAILES, Abigail mar Capt. Joseph Selman. A dau Abigail mar John CROSS 1792 in MRB? OUTC.
HAILE, James b 1745 Warren, RI d 1808 Putney, VT. He mar Hannah HICKS, J fam? b 1740 Rehoboth, MA, dau of Hezekiah, 1719-1788, and Desire CARPENTER, b 1716 Rehoboth. Poss that both Hicks and Carpenter were from C.I. fams? OUTC. (Reetha Clancy, Bonsall, CAL)
A1. Richard, b 1769 Putney, VT A4. Nathan, b 1774 Putney, VT
A2. Hezekiah b 1770 A5. Desire, b 1775 d 1777
A3. Mary, b 1774 mar Reuben Noble Jr. 1796 A6. Hannah, b 1776
A7. Anna, b 1778 d 1856 Fowler, NY mar Simeon Hazelton, Jr.
A8. John, b 1781 Putney, VT mar Eunice HENRY, b 1781
A9. James Jr., b 1782 d 1861 mar Tabitha Johnson, 1784-1857
HAILES, John mar Ann LE CRAW 1766 MRB. See LE CRAW
HAINES in J 1340. In Trinity J 1607. Not researched by compiler. See Noyes.

HAKE, Thomas mar Sarah Hoskins 1747 Boston. (Int). Poss that HAKE is French, and early HAWKS in NE said to have spelled their name HAKE ?
HALE, Caroline, Carolyn, b G, mar Charles TURNER, qv, to NY ca 1855. HALE curr G and J.
HALLETT, name of southern England. At least one branch settled C.I. Other HALLETS came to New England from Dorset to MA. "One of the oldest names on the Cape". (AND THIS IS CAPE COD, by E. Early)
HALLETT, see New York Gen. Record, vols 6 & 7, not seen by compiler.
HALLETT, see ALBO DE BERNALES
HALLETT, Jane, b 1820 Chinnock West, Somerset, England, rem to Herm Island, C.I. with husband George BULFORD, qv. Two chn b Herm, then fam rem to Guernsey Is. 3 chn b St. Martin G, and one at St. Peter Port G. (Dave Bulford, Wawa, ONT) See BULFORD.
HALLETT, two sisters of Jane above married and rem to Leeds, ONT. One mar CHICK of G and the other mar PATTEMORE or CHANT. (D. Bulford)
HALLETT, Lydia, b 1788 Barnstable, MA, dau of James and Susanna (TAYLOR) HALLETT, mar ca 1830s Sylvanus Gorham, son of Sylvanus and Ann Gorham. Note that this fam was connected with the jewelers trade. (John Chadbourne, Rochester, NY) OUTC.
A1. Lydia Allen Gorham, b 1832 adopted by Gorham. She was natural dau of Lucy Hallett, and mar 1853 Edwin Pinkham, sailmaker of Boston.
HALLETT, William, jeweler of J, mar ___. Note persistence of name Lucy.
A1. Lucy Harriet Hallett, b 1825 J, d 1878 London, England- mar Emanuel Joseph de Bernales, physician and artist b Spain. (Lucy Clark, Cleveland, OH)
B1. Lucy Maria de Bernales, b 1845 St. Heliers J, d in Little Rock, ARK 1934. She mar John Ross, 1839-1885 of Brooklyn, NY 1870.
C1. Lucy Ross, b ca 1880 mar Walter Swanton 1904
D1. Lucy Swanton, b early 1900s mar ___Clark, res Cleveland, OH.
HAMEL, old in J. See CIFHS #3
HAMEL, DU HAMMEL?, Amos res Oxford Twp., GCO 1840. OUTC. (Wolfe)
HAMELIN, in Vale G 1821. (CIFHS #14) See also CIFHS #5
HAMMON, HAMON, HAMMOND in J 1156. In Trinity, Grouville, St. Ouen, St. John, St. Laurens and St. Mary J 1668. In St. Martin, St. Peter, St. Brelade, St. Ouen, St. John, St. Saviour, St. Laurens and Trinity J 1749. Names spelled variously, in the Islands, in Canada and in the colonies. HAMON in G 1300s, in Sark Island 1500s. HAMON and HAMMOND both curr G and J. HAMON research, see CIFHS #4.
HAMMOND, Abigail mar 1713 Benj. BEADLE, b 1687, cordwainer, in MA, son of Thomas, a sea captain, was in 1886 trading with Barbadoes. Wife of Thomas was Elizabeth DRAKE. 6 chn. OUTC. (Typescript on HAMON, HAMMOND)
WALTERS AND HAMMOND, small firm in GCO early 1800s. (Wolfe) OUTC.
HAMMONS, Edmund of Kittery, ME there in 1673, age about 32 in 1683/4. Res Spruce Creek. His wife was Jane MONTESSE, quite likely to be MONTAIS of J, widow in 1704. In 1719 living with Nathaniel Keene fam complaining that son Benj. would not care for her. She was d in 1733. Note that there were prob. 2 Edmunds, father and son, one b 1651. The son had a grant 1694, but was dead by 1705. At least 5chn. Data not found by compiler. See sources and ME and MA records. (Noyes; York deeds; OLD KITTERY AND HER FAMILIES; BEADLE GEN) OUTC.
A1. Benjamin, b ca 1681 mar 1731 Eliz. GROVER of York ME, liv 1760.
A2. Patience, captive in Canada March 1711, in Boston 1719, mar Daniel Jones and rem to New York, d there ca 1731. NO issue.
A3. Elizabeth mar Stephen ROSE, widow 1719, living 1745
A4. Margaret, mar Paul WILLIAMS 1716, and 2. Wm. Dealing, see D'ALLAIN.
A5. Abigail mar Benj. BEADLE, res Salem, MA 1734. A6. Jane, d 1728.

HAMMONS, Benj. mar 1722 Sarah BRIAR, BRIARD? in ME?, prob widow of Wm. BRIAR, qv.
HAMMOND, Edward, mar Mary MULLY, qv, 1732 MRB. MULLY may be MOLLET, qv
HAMON, Elie from J to MRB 1730
HAMON, Elizabeth, dau of Wm., b 1661 Rehoboth, MA. OUTC.
HAMMOND, George arrived in Boston on ship MOLLY 1769 from J.(Whitmore)
HAMMOND, John, 1643-1707 from Isle of Wight England to Annapolis, MD. 1685. (VirkusII)
HAMON, Martha of Boston mar Andrew Willitt 1719 Boston. OUTC
HAMMON, Mary mar Robert Newman 1790 Boston. OUTC.
HAMON, Nicolas, son of Elie above, was b 1733 America, returned to J, married and res St. Helier J. His oldest son went back to America, when?, follow career of"Barreau" 1785. Nicolas and Jacques, his bro divided the father's property. The oldest took over the American property. Nicolas has American descendants, but not found by compiler.
HAMMON, Philip from J? and Mehitable res Beverly, MA. OUTC.
A1. Mehitable b 1792 A2. Hannah, b 1799 A3. Philip b 1805
HAMMOND, D. Sarre, res Saint John East, NB, Canada, poss of C.I. origin.
HAMON, Thomas H. of San Jose, CAL, desc of J fam.
HAMMOND, Capt. on vessel named CRUISER, 100 tons, was trading with Philadelphia, PA 1764.A Jersey owned vessel named CRUISER was captained by a LE FEUVRE of J in 1787. (JERSEY SAILING SHIPS by A.John Jean)
HAMONS, a Hug fam to Ireland.
HAMPTONNE, one from Southampton, England settled in J by 1340. Old in G. HAMPTONNE in St. Clement, St. Laurens and St. Ouen J 1668, and in St. Ouen and St. Laurens J 1749. In St. Laurens 1788. Poss some from C.I. in America?
HANNAH, Jane from G? mar James CHERRY GCO 1819. Curr G and J.
HANNAH, Mary from G? mar Isaac Fox, GCO 1816. (Conner-Eynon books)
HARDING, Philip from C.I.? mar Susannah HAVILLAND, qv, a widow 1659 in Boston, MA.
HARDY, LE HARDIE, LE HARDY, Clement of the year 1360, founded the J Hardy line, which has may illustrious descendants, including Thomas HARDY the writer, Sir Charles Hardy, Admiral of the Brit. Navy, Sir Thomas Masterman, Sir Thomas Duffus, etc. (THE HARDY FAM ASSOC. of America, RFD #1, Box 327 A., Manchester, NH 03104; HARDY & HARDIE, PAST AND PRESENT; MAINE RECORDER; Essex Coll, Vols 1 to 4, and 8)
Much HARDY data available, but none found with direct C.I. origin. Most prob from England. HARDY, LE HARDY in J 1299. In St. Martin, St. Saviour, Grouville and St. Heliers J 1668. In St. Martin, Grouville, St. Heliers and St. Laurens J 1749. Curr G and J.
LE HARDY shield, sable on a chevron between three escalops or as many griffin's heads of the field.
HARDY, Joseph in Salem ca 1700, ship builder, from J? Poss also another Joseph, in Essex Co., had chn b 1658-1674. OUTC.
HARDY, fam from C.I. on ship CHIMBORAZO 1855, to UT. Elizabeth, Anne and William. (SLC records)
Note that in HARDY AND HARDIE, PAST AND PRESENT, there are many Hardys that may have come from C.I. such as those named Amos (Amice?), Ebenezer, Francis, Gideon, Joshua and Noah. OUTC.
HARLISTON, an English fam connected with the C.I. by 1467. Later res Sussex, England. Some of this name in SC by 1669, ship CAROLINA.
HART, James H. and Emily, from C.I. 1854 via ship GERMANICUS, to UT. HART is curr in G and J. See CIFHS #7.
HARVEY in J 1528, in St. Heliers J 1607. Curr G and J.

HARVEY, William, age 45 in 1823, was b England, but came from G to Baltimore, MD 1818. (NEW WORLD IMMIGRANTS, Vol ii, By Tepper)
HARVEY, from C.I.? to SC before 1680. (Baldwin) OUTC
HARVIE, Clement in Greenland, NH, was a MESSERVY from the C.I., the name being mangled in Nfld. to MESHARVY at first.
HARVEY, Peter, had wife Sarah and son Samuel in Weymouth, MA1696.OUTC.
HARVEY, a Capt. Thomas res Portsmouth, NH 1663. OUTC. (Noyes)
HASKELL of England. HASCOUL, HACCOUL, HACOUL, HACQUOIL, etc were French and C.I. variants of Frankish AESCWULF. HASCOUL & HACQUOIL in J 1331, in St. Ouen J 1607, 1668. Some data below from YOUR YANKEE HERITAGE.
HASCALL, Norman French, in Salem 1637. (ANCESTRAL HEADS by Frank Holes)
HASKELL, James Bowdoin, 1803-1860, of China, ME. OUTC.
HASKELL, Eliza Foster, dau of Nathaniel Haskell Jr., cordwainer. She was adopted by Israel LE FAVOUR upon death of her mother, her name being changed to LE FAVOUR 1845. (Essex Co. records)
HACKERIL, HACQUOIL?, Hannah mar Wm. Speakman 1719 Boston, MA. OUTC
HACQUOIL, James Clement of J, deserted from the Royal Navy, and settled in Turnip Cove, Nfld. as Jim Clement. After his death, a search for him as beneficiary of a J will revealed the facts and the family thereafter used the correct name HACQUOIL. (E.R. Seary, Nfld.)
HARQUAIL, G.M. of a J fam, res North York, ONT, 1900s.
HARQUAIL, John Albert, b 1875 Dalhousie, NB mar Edna Hattie CLEMENT, b 1880, dau of Eben Crosby Clement of Winterport, ME and Hattie Ann Vinal. OUTC. (Rasmussen)
A1. Avis Pearl Harquail, b 1904 Winterport, ME.
HECKEW, John mar Rachel Welsh 1741 Boston. Poss HASCOUL of J?(silentS)
HESKEW, Philip mar Eliz. Cox 1716 Boston. Poss HASCOUL of J and CAUX, LE CAUX of J. A son John, b 1717/8 Boston.
HATCH, HACHE, Hug fam to Ireland from France. (Grace Lawless Lee) Note BAILHACHE. OUTC. Much data on this fam, no record of C.I. connection.
Note that Noyes suggests that HATCH was not from C.I. However, while first officer of ship SUCCESS, he was in company with Philip FALL, qv, also James & Simon MOUNTES, poss LE MONTAIS, LE MOUNTS, qv, of J. Other HATCH fams from Kent, England to Barnstable, MA.
HATCH, John, said to be from J, was in Portsmouth, NH before 1684, a mariner. Mar Sarah ___, who d before 1712? He was first officer of the SHUTTROSS, Capt. Mathew Estes, and first officer of the gun ketch AMERICA. Purchased of Sam. Cutt the house and land adjoining the house commonly called the Great House, and bounded on the south side by the Highway. This house was prob on Jefferson St., Portsmouth,NH. He also had a wharf, bought from Sam. Rhynes. At death, inventory of his personal estate included a watch, two rings, a quadrant, scale, two foot rule, a Bible, pair of compasses, silver headed cane, and 34 oz. of silver plate? He signed the NH petition 1689, and supported the Protestant Succession. A member of the Gen. Assembly held at Newcastle 1696. Left 3 chn. (Underhill; Noyes; Doris Smale, Santa Rosa, CAL; RAMBLES ABOUT GREENLAND: Mary Hatch, Salisbury, MA; WALKERS YESTERDAY, by E.G. Walker, 1937; BICKNELL GEN; CHADBOURNE GEN; Bowdoin, Concord and Durham, NH records)
A1. Samuel, Capt. Samuel in some deeds. In Jan.1712 conveyed 46 acres of land in Portsmouth, NH, rec'd from his father. Also owned a wharf wharf & warehouse near wharf of Robt. Walker. Had pew in South Meetinghouse. Mar Eliz. ___, who after his death mar Thomas Greenough of Newcastle. D 1716 leaving 2 chn.
B1. Thomas, hatter and felt maker, parishioner at Queen's Chapel. Mar 1. Mary ___,2 daus. Mar 2. Alice KNIGHT/CHEVALIER, qv of

Newington, NH, sister of John KNIGHT. 8 chn.
C1. Deborah C2. Sarah mar John GREGORY, poss d 1845 in ME?
C3. Mary, b 1754, unmar C4. Thomas, b 1757, set. Bethlehem, NH 1790
C5. Samuel, b 1759 mar Mary Pickering, dau of Joshua 1783. Res in his youth with his uncle John KNIGHT at Bloody Pt., Newington. His uncle left property to both Samuel and to John KNIGHT Hatch.
D1. John Knight, b 1784 mar Ann Simms Johnson 1816. Was in Legis. 1830s and State Senator 1840-1845.
E1. Albert Ruyter, b 1817 grad. from Bowdoin, ME 1837, admitted to bar 1841, mar Margaret Rooksby Harris, dau of Thomas Aston Harris, Speaker in 1874. Albert d 1882.
F1. John, mar 1873 Alice Caroline, dau of Rev. Geo. Benton.
G1. Margaret Harris, b 1875 G2. John Knight, b 1877
G3. Caroline Benton, b 1878 G6. Samuel Fink, b 1884
G4. Mary Aston, b 1880 G7. Alice Spencer, b 1886
G5. Albert Ruyter, b 1882
F2. Francis March of Honolulu, HAW, mar Alicia Haws of San Fran.
G1. Harriet G2. Alexander Gilchrist
F3. Annie Miller, mar James K. Cogswell, USNavy, who served in Battle of Santiago.
G1. Bianca Cogswell G2. Francis Cogswell G3. James K. Cogswell
F4. Mary Aston, unmar
E2. Mary Ann, b 1819 mar Hosea? or Moses F. Hoit, d 1848
E3. Caroline Hannah, b 1823 mar T.W.T.,Curtis d 1859
E4. Sarah Augusta, b 1833 d 1852. E5. Ann Simms, b 1838 d 1854
D2. Mary b 1787 mar John George of Concord, and had one son, celebrated railroad lawyer of Concord, MA.
D3. Samuel, b 1789 mar Nancy Wiggin, 5 chn
E1. Elizabeth, mar Oliver BERRY E4. Sarah Ann mar Charles Seavey
E2. Charles W. mar Mary C. Hall E5. Harriet, mar ___Clough
E3. Samuel Augustus, mar ___Adams.
F1. dau, mar John Pottle F2. Dau, mar Ernest Holmes
F3. George, rem to Klondike and d there.
F4. John, mar and res Elliott, ME.
D4. Sarah P., mar Sims Frink of Newington, NH, who succeeded Deacon Bailey in his tavern at Greenland.
E1. Samuel Frink, d.y. E3. Mary Abby, who d unmar
E2. John Samuel Hatch Frink, mar Lucretia M. Pickering, dau of Wm. Pickering. A son Wm. P. Frink.
E4. Sarah Olivia Frink, who mar Joseph Simpson
C6. Polly, b 1761 C9. William, 1766-1854
C7. Elizabeth, b 1764 mar ___Henderson C10. Alice, mar ___Currier of Portsmouth, NH
C8. John, emigrated to OH 1815.
B2. Sarah, b 1717, first wife of Wm. Odiorne of Portsmouth, NH &Durham
A2. Sarah, mar 1. 1709 Josiah Downing Jr. farmer of Kittery, ME, who d 1712. She mar 2. 1713 James Chadbourne, b 1684.
A3. Ann, b ca 1700 mar Samuel Small 1716/17 in Kittery, ME son of Samuel and Eliz. (Heard) Chadbourne Small. See Underhill and Noyes, more.

HAWTHORNE, English surname. However, Ebenezer Hawthorne, Hathorne, son of John and Susanna (Herbert) was a desc of Philip ENGLISH, qv of J. As young man Eben. went to sea, then to the western states and MEXICO early 1800s. Returned to MA, worked in customs house, and settled at Salem Neck, MA. Mar Catherine Peace and d 1858. (Essex Coll,Vol 6)

HATHORNE, Wm. and Mary res Salem, MA. Wm. a desc of Philip ENGLISH, qv, of J and Salem. Note TOUZEL, qv. CAUTION: TRIAL CHART.
A1. Mary bp 1743 A5. Sarah, bp 1750 A9. John TOUZEL, bp1763
A2. William, bp 1743 A6. Ruth, bp 1753 A10. Ann, bp 1766

A3. Joseph, bp 1745 A7. Nathaniel, bp 1755
A4. Ebenezer, bp 1747 A8. Susanna, bp 1759

HAVILLAND, DE HAVILLAND very old in G. One branch from G to England ca 1540. Desc to Newport, RI and to Flushing, LI, NY 1653, 1688. (Frost). HAVILLAND, DE HAVILLAND, Christopher, son of James of G, 1517-1540, is the ancestor of the HAVILLANDS in Montreal and in Prince Edward Island, Canada. See DE HAVILLAND.

HAVILLAND, Jane of G, second wife of Capt. Wm. Torrey, b Bristol, Eng. of a G fam in 1612. Torrey brought their sons to New England after her death ca 1640. Jane was a desc of Sir Thomas DE HAVILLAND of G, as are many English fams of this name. Torrey mar 3 times. It is said that most of the Torreys in America are desc of this family, a proportion of them being also desc of Jane DE HAVILLAND of G. (Mrs. Gilbert Fike, St. Petersburg, FLA)

A1. Samuel Torrey, b ca 1632 England, mar 1. Ray Rawson and 2. Mary Symmes. Samuel was pastor of Weymouth, MA church in 1664, d age 75, left desc.

A2. William Torrey, b England ca 1638, mar Deborah Greare in America.

For more info. see HAVILLAND GEN by Josephine C. Frost, NYCity 1914; CHRON. OF THE HAVILLANDS by A.W. Havilland and Charles H. McKeel, St. Louis, MO, 1893; TORREY FAMS OF AMERICA by Fred Torrey, 1924; PIONEERS OF MASS by Pope; ANCESTRAL ROOTS OF 60 NEW England Colonists by Fred Lewis Weis.

HAVILLAND, Susannah, widow, mar Philip HARDING 1659 Boston. OUTC. (Clemens)

HAWKINS, English surname, in G 1700s, some being Quakers. Noted also in Wills of Essex Co., NJ 1800s from England or G. Note that old J surname HOCQUIN, 1330-1749, pron. very like HOWKIN. HAWKINS curr G and J. CAUTION: TRIAL CHARTS

HAWKINS, Giles, b G? d 1839 PEI mar Susannah Chessell, 5 sons and 3 daus. This fam said to have come to PEI with the Guernsey group. See Q.A. IN CANADA by Turk. See Matthias below. 1806/ (Sally Lomas, Toronto, ONT; James V. Beck, Okemos, MI)

A1. Giles Nicholas, b 1799 G? d 1875 PEI, mar Harriet Norcum LE LACHEUR, qv, 1798-1883, 3 sons and 5 daus.

B1. Susanna Maria, b 1820s? mar ___ Jenkins

B2. Charles Augustus, 1829-1913 mar Charlotte Simpson, 1827-1901. Charles rem from PEI to Newport Landing 1855, and later to Halifax, NS ca 1873, 4 sons and 2 daus.

C1. Elisha, 1856-1859

C2. Anna belle, b 1859 d 1942, mar James William BREHAUT, qv, 1863-1928, son of Thomas Smith BREHAUT and Janet Clow, a Scot. See BREHAUT fams in Q.A. IN CANADA by Turk

D1. Wilfred Hawkins Brehaut, 1895-1958 mar Olive Johnson PAYNE

E1. Mary Charlotte Brehaut, b 1920 mar Richard Lee Treat, 3 chn

F1. Richard Lee Treat Jr, b 1948 mar Catherine A. Lloyd, div. 3 chn: Margaret, Richard and Doris Marie Treat

F2. Mary Ellen Treat, b 1950 d.y.

F3. Donald James Treat, b 1952 mar Anne Susan Ziegler

E2. Wilfred Hawkins Brehaut Jr., b 1923 mar Gloria Gillis, 2chn. Jill and Joy Brehaut, both mar.

D2. Ellerton James Brehaut, b 1897 mar Catherine Hortense Farrell.

E1. Elaine Janet Brehaut, b 1927 mar Hubert H. Marney, 2 daus

F1. Susan Janet, b 1956 mar R. GALVIN, chn: Valerie, Matthew

F2. Mary Catherine, b 1958 mar Wm. Herbert Standen

C3. Arthur Charles, b 1861 d 1926, doctor, res Halifax, NS, mar Caroline McLellan Spike 1890.

D1. Gertrude May, 1891-1971, mar Allan M. Butler, 4 chn
E1. Allan Butler, b 1923 mar Helen ___, 2 chn,Allan and Jane
E2. David Butler, b 1925 mar Mary Gidney, 2 sons: David, Brian
E3. Carolyn Butler, b 1929 mar Warren Jennings, dau Carol Ann
E4. Arthur Butler, b 1931 mar Alice ___, 4 chn: Allan, Arthur, Debby and _____ Butler
D2. Rupert Clarence Giles, 1892-1960, unmar
D3. Charlotte Dorothy, 1895-1980, mar C. Russell Johnson, a dau
E1. Mary Kaye Johnson, b 1923 mar Dr. John Francis L. Woodbury, 3 chn: Susan, Mary Gail and Frank
D4. Arthur Cowie, 1898-1971, mar Eunice Read, no issue
D5. Mary Caroline, 1903-1975, mar Henry Leamon Roper, 2 chn
E1. Sarah Ann, b 1932 mar 1. Manfred Richter, 2 daus, div 1976, mar 2. Alex Lomas.
F1. Kirsten Maria Richter, b 1962 F2.Heidi Richter, b 1968
E2. James Cecil, b 1904 mar Jean MacLeod, res Halifax, NS, no issue
C4. Giles Nicholas Chessell, 1863-1925, mar Rachel Entwistle, 7 chn: Lucille, Robert, Raeburn, Lionel, Horace, Elizabeth, Tait.
C5. Ella Maude Simpson, 1866-1925 C6. John Gesner, 1868-1871
B3. Jane Winsor, mar Wm. Beck, 1827-1913, who mar 2. Jane LE LACHEUR, qv, 6 plus 3 chn.
C1. Selina Eliz. Beck, 1854-1867
C2. Elisha Hawkins Beck, 1856-1941 mar Annie McKinnon
C3. Vere Beck, 1858-1925 mar Jennie Ida Chase/Chace?
C4. David Beck, 1860-1904
C5. Louisa Elizabeth Beck, b 1864 mar Charles Matthews
C6. William Windsor Beck, b 1868 d 1930 C8. Peter Beck, 1871-1890
C7. Bart. John Beck, b 1869 d 1950 mar Jane Mackay
C9. Matilda Jane Beck, 1873-1943, mar Alexander M. Ballum
C10. Selina Beck again, 1877-1952, unmar
B4. Elisha lost at sea, 1832-1856
B5. Mary Margaret, mar Thomas Marfleet Beck, 1830-1914, see large fam recorded in WRCIC.
C1. Wm. Mitchell Hawkins Beck, 1862-1938 mar Katie Jane Cameron
C2. Alice M. LE MESSURIER Beck, 1864-1953, mar Wm. D. Irving
C3. Harriet Eliz. Beck, b 1865 mar W. Forbes Cameron
C4. Charles Aug. Beck, 1867-1905, mar Mary Murray
C5. Elisha Thomas Beck, 1869-1944 mar 1. Margaret J. LE LACHEUR and 2. Mae Lyens.
C6. Mary Jane Ellen Beck, b 1872-1947, mar Thomas M. Annear
C7. Albert Henry Clark Beck, 1873-1874
C8. George Ira Beck, 1875-1943, mar Annie Rosella Campbell
C9. Alfred E. LE PAGE Beck, 1877-1878
B6. Elizabeth, 1835-1858
B7. Louisa Chessell, 1837-1932, mar Wm. Simpson, 1835-1909
B8. John LE LACHEUR Hawkins, 1839-1923, mar 1. Maria Jane BREHAUT, 1837-1874, and 2. Hannah McNeill, 1846-1918, b Cavendish, PEI, dau of Daniel and Sarah (Poole) McNeil.
C1. Elisha M., contractor of New York, NY.
C2. Charlotte, res Prov., RI C3. Eliza M., res Prov., RI
C4. by 2nd wife, Maria J. C5. John H. C6. Earnest A. C7.Charles W.

HAWKINS, Matthias, b 1804 G, mar Nancy Ann MACHON, qv, 1810, dau of Daniel MACHON and Frances PULLEM, PULHAM? of Murray Harb., PEI, from G also. (Marilyn Cahill, Cherry Hill, NJ; Fam Bible; Vital Records, PEI; and VR in MA also; Q.A. IN CANADA, by Turk)
A1. William, b Murray River, PEI mar Sarah McLeod, res Murray River.

B1. David Hawkins, mar Annie McLeod B3. Albert, unmar
B2. Louise, mar Gavin MacLeod
A2. Elizabeth, unmar A5. Charlotte, unmar, res Boston, MA
A3. Eleanor Mary, b 1835 PEI A6. Ann Maria, b 1839
A4. Susannah Frances, b 1838
A7. Maria A., b 1839 mar Thomas ROBERTS, qv, d 1932, res Boston, MA, no issue
A8. Priscilla Jane, b 1843 Murray River, PEI mar Henry Alline Bears 1866, res Gladstone, PEI. He was b 1841 Canso, NS, d 1909 M.Riv. She d 1926, 9 chn.
B1. Eleanor Lavinia Bears, b 1867 Gladstone, PEI mar 1888 Peter Van Iderstine, b 1827?, a cousin, son of Alex. Van Iderstine and Elizabeth MACHON.
C1. Gladys Van Iderstine C3. Myra Van Iderstine
C2. Morris Van Iderstine C4. Ralph Van Iderstine
B2. Elizabeth Ann Bears, b 1869, twin, mar 1888 Ezra Matthew HENRY, qv of G fam, res Boston, MA. 6 chn. See HENRY
B3. David Matthias Bears, b 1869, twin, d.y.
B4. Alexandra Louisa Ally Bears, b 1871 mar Charles Graham, d 1921
C1. Charles Leroy Graham, b 1905, mar Vera Wensell, d 1975
B5. Cyrus Wilfred Bears, b 1875, mar 1905 Olivia Nicholson, dau of John and Thankful (Stewart) Nicholson, 3 chn, res Boston, MA.
C1. Daniel Ernest Bears, b 1906, d 1929, unmar
C2. Allin Chessel Bears, b 1908 Gladstone, PEI mar 1942 Verne Makin.
C3. Jennie Thankful Bears, b 1909, mar 1939 Wm. Elliott Whalen, d 1961, no issue.
B6. Elsie Gertrude Bears, b 1878 d 1885, unmar
B7. Sydney, mar Della Jordon, res Gladstone, PEI
B8. Ralph Rosco Bears, b 1883 mar 1907 Cassie May Hume and d 1939. Bur Evergreen Cem, Brighton, MA. Cassie the dau of Samuel and Damaris (Watts) MacLeod Hume. She mar 2. Louis George THERRIAN, res Boston, MA.
C1. Inez Bears, b 1908 mar 1930 Douglas E. Smith, b 1907 Chelsea,MA, son of Frank B. and Cora W. (Stone) Smith, res Quincy, MA, 3 chn.
D1. Barry Smith, b 1932 D2. Jan Smith, b 1934 D3. Wayne, adopted.
C2. William Russell Bears, b 1910 Gladstone, PEI mar 1. Kay Ford, and 2. Bernice Hoty, no issue
C3. Amy L. Bears, b 1912 Somerville, MA mar Robert A. Shillady, Jr.
D1. Robert Shillady, b 1949, adopted.
C4. Violet Gertrude Bears, b 1914 Somerville, MA mar 1939 Maynard W. ALLARD, 4 chn: David, Susan, Peter and Ralph Allard.
C5. Ralph Hume Bears, b 1931 Boston, MA mar 1959 Anne Louise Clark, b 1940 Boston, dau of Arthur T. and Margaret(Connelly) Clark. 4 chn: Kevin, Lisa, Amy and Joseph Bears
B8. Sidney Whitfield Bears, b 1887 PEI mar Della Beatrice Jordan, b 1889, Sussex, NB, dau of Edward and Jane (Buell) Jordan. She mar 2. Aubrey James Crocker, b Halifax, NS and d Miami Shores, FLA 1974. Sidney d 1918 bur Murray Harb. Cem., PEI, res Gladstone,PEI
C1. Hazel Wilemina Bears, b 1913 PEI mar 1937 Fraser Lee, and 2 in 1967, Clyde McNeil. Lee d 1942, no issue.
C2. Rita Louise Bears, b 1914 mar 1931 John A. Grieves, div, no issue
B9. Henry Alline Bears, b 1890 Wilmot, PEI mar 1. Florence Woodward 1913, b 1892 Charlestown, MA, d 1965 Woburn, MA, bur Everett, MA. Dau of Fred. and Esther (Donaldson) Woodward, 5 chn. Henry mar 2. 1959 Mary P. Moran Poor.
C1. George Wendell Bears, b 1914 Somerville, MA mar 1935 Elsie V. Thompson, dau of Harry and Edith (Howard) Thompson.

C2. Warren Allen Bears, b 1915 mar 1935 Catherine Edna Pettee, a son Warren Jr. mar 1968 Leona May Ernst.
C3. Harry Alline Bears II, b 1919 Medford, MA mar 1947 Ann Mary McQuilkin, dau of John and Margaret (Clifford) McQuilkin.
C4. Alfred Lincoln Bears, b 1923 Medford, MA mar 1. ? and 2. Pauline E. Waterman, and d 1950, no issue
C5. Dorothy Priscilla Bears, b 1928 Boston mar 1946 Arthur Ross Smith, and 2. Paul ___.

HAWKINS, Charlotte, b 1852 Murray River, PEI, unmar.
CAUTION: Most named HAWKINS came directly from England.
HEADLEY, English surname found at times in C.I. See BISSON
HEADLEY, susan, b G, dau of Brian HEADLEY of St. Peter Port, G, mar there 1902 Samuel M. Taylor of Boston, MA. See TAYLOR.
HEADLEY, John, b G? 1808, d GCO 1873. (Conner-Eynon)
HEARD, prob from England, but curr G and J. Found in Suffolk, England. Poss at times variant spelling of HERAUD, HERAULD of C.I.? in J by 1299. See Q.A. IN CANADA.
HEARD, Capt. Benj., poss spelled at times HURD?, b G, was in NJ 1690. A Benj. Heard mar Eliz. ROBERTS, qv, res Cochechoc, ME 1674. Mar 2. Ruth Eastman 1690. (Underhill; Noyes)
A1. Benjamin A2. James who had chn between 1715-1730.
A3. Lydia A4. Rebecca mar ___Gorton A5. Sarah mar Simon French
A6. Ann, b 1681, captured by Indians, said to have mar at age 24 Sebastian Cholet in Quebec, Canada. (Coleman, Olivier)
HEARD, Capt. John, from G also? or from England? in ME 1660s, another in Salem, MA 1633 from Devon? Another John, bp Dorset, England, 1608. (Evelyn Wright, San Diego, CAL)
HEARD, Judith from G? mar Philip FALL, qv.
See sources: Noyes; Underhill; OLD KITTERY AND HER FAMS, by Stackpole, York Deeds #9; Mrs. Glen Cambridge, Weskan, KS; CHADBOURNE GEN; LORD GEN.
HEARL of Kittery, ME. Cf HUREL, curr G and L'HERAULT from J to Gaspe, QUE and HERAULT from Isle d'Oleron, France, to Ireland. Wm. Hearl was in the FORTUNE 1638.
HEARL, said by Noyes to be peculiar to Cornwall, England, still poss variant of HERAULT?
HEAUME, DU HEAUME, pron. DUYOME in G. In J 1528 from Paye de Houlme, south of Falaise, France. In St. Heliers, St. Peter and St. Ouen, J 1668. In St. Heliers and St. Ouen J 1749. See CIFHS #12. Curr G and J. (Sarchet, Vol 2, p.528; Conner-Eynon; Secrest; SPAID GEN; Florence Larrick, Santa Barbara, CAL; HOWE HIST. OF GCO, with pictures of HEAUME homestead, and som fam data; Quarterly Review of the Guernsey Soc., Summer, 1960, pp 34,35)
There are at least two separate lines of HEAUME in G, those of Candie, Castel, and those of Friquet de Haut, both in G. Some Heaumes from Le Becquet Farm, St. Martin, G. "Pierre Heaume of Le Becket, G, was dead by 1808 leaving a son, Pierre, who inherited the house and garden, also the furze brake and meadow, while a dau Judith, b 1784, wife of Pierre BOURGAIZE, inherited the field Courtil des Landes on Vertes Rue...Pierre bought from Samuel LE PAGE the house and garden called La Ruette, and the field Courtil Simonne that belonged to Nicholas MAUGER 1780, and to Jean MARTIN ...1666...also the house and garden that belonged to Josue MAINDONAL 1666...mar Judith HEAUME" ...not known if related. In 1832 they rem to USA, but did not dispose of Le Becquet until 1836...when on Sept. 24th, Jean LE CLERC, holding a Power of Attorney under the seal of the Clerk of Common Pleas in Muskingum Co., OH, sold on behalf of Pierre HEAUME, senior,

native of the Parish of St. Martin, but resident in Ohio, the house, barn, stable, carthouse, hard and Garden to Thomas MARTIN, son of Jean MARTIN...many changes and improvements made to the property." (Quarterly Review of the Guernsey Soc., Summer 1960, p.34,35)

HEAUME, Pierre Jr., b 1781 G, d 1859 OH, youngest son of Pierre and Elizabeth HEAUME. Mar Judith HEAUME, 13 chn. Mar 2. Anna Groves HELLYER. Judith, b 1781 or 1788 G, d 1852 GCO.

A1. Pierre, b 1814, lost at sea as a young man?

A2. John, b 1816 Vale or St. Martin G, to US 1831, mar 1847 Rachel PRIAULX, qv, 3 sons, 2 d.y. John d 1894 GCO, bur Valley Twp. One son d in Civil War.

B1. Thomas Corwin, b and d 1848 B3. Geo. Washington, b 1853, d1854.

B2. William Edward, b 1850 near Buffalo, GCO, d 1929. Mar 1873 Amanda Salladay, 1854-1926, res near Pleasant City, GCO then in Springfield, OH. Wm. had property and hotel.

C1. Minola Millicent, b 1874 d 1942, mar 1903 Rev. Charles U. Larrick 1868-1927. Larricks were Hug. DE LA ROCQUES, who came to America from France via Holland. Minola educ. Wittenberg Coll, OH.2 chn

D1. Florence Larrick, b 1904 res Santa Barbara, CAL, unmar

D2. Victor Heaume Larrick, b 1910 mar Fern Malherbe, b 1914. Victor was Adv. Dir. of the JEFFERSONIAN, newspaper in Cambridge, OH, 4 chn.

E1. John Victor Larrick, b 1947, mar 1974 Linda Suzanne Keeler, b 1950, a son Jared B. Larrick b 1978

E2. ? E3. ? E4. ?

C2. John Salladay, b 1876 mar Julia D. Moler, b 1883

D1. Marjorie Amelia b 1905 mar 1927 Paul Baylor

E1. Nancy Baylor, b 1930 mar Thor Ronemus, div, res OH, 4 sons: Eric, Michael, Andrew and Kyle Ronemus.

D2. Mary Catherine, b 1909 mar 1937 R. Shewalter, no issue.

D3. John Douglas, b 1911 mar 1939 Bette Nichols, no issue.

C3. Oella Joyce, b 1878 d 1920 mar 1903 Onan B. Drake, 1874-1928, 2 chn, res Arvada, COL.

D1. Roberta C. Drake, b 1907, d.y.

D2. John Heaume Drake, b 1908 res COL. A dau Marianne.

C4. Amy Alberta, b 1881 GCO mar 1906 Jasper Emmett Secrest, D.D.S. 1876-1955, dentist in Cambridge, OH, 4 chn

D1. Robert Heaume Secrest b 1907 mar 1930 M. Wishart, b 1907. Robert d 1981 at Salt Fork Lodge, GCO, had res Maitland, FLA. Served in US Navy Dental Corps for 30 yrs.

E1. Carolyn Mae Secrest, 1933-1964, mar1955 James Walker Storey Jr, b 1934, 3 chn, res Dover, MA.

F1. Elizabeth Jane Storey, b 1958

F2. Wm. Walker Storey, b 1960 F3. Margaret A. Storey, b 1963

E2. Robert Secrest Jr., b 1940 d.y.

E3. David Emmett Heaume Secrest, b 1943 mar 1967 Christie Patricia Bell, b 1944, 4 chn. David a Comm. in US Navy, based in HAW. 4 chn: Rachel, Christie, Helen and David R. Secrest

D2. Harriet Eliz. Secrest, b 1911 mar 1932 Robert L. Mock, b 1905, res New Concord, OH.

E1. Charles Emmett Mock, b 1937 mar 1969 Barbara Knicely, b 1941, a son Duane Mock

D3. RobertaM. Secrest, b 1913, mar 1947 Wm. Kenneth Cantrill?, res El Paso, TX, no issue

D4. Sarah Rachel Secrest, b 1917, mar 1941 Wm. Russell ROSE, b 1918 res Indianapolis, IND.

E1. Wm. Russell Rose, Jr, b 1948 mar 1972 Mary Catherine Jones.

2 chn: Eric and Kathleen Rose.
A3. Nicholas, b 1818 changed name to HUME and res Brighton, ILL, has desc. Bessie McNeel.
A4. Judith, b1821 mar 1841 Martin E. ROBBINS, 6 chn. See ROBBINS, ROBINS, John of GCO.
A5. Betsy, b 1823, d 1824. A6. Charlotte, b 1827 G A7. Daniel, b 1828
A8. Joseph, b 1829 d 1830. Another Joseph came to US, data unknown.
A9. Mary Ann, b 1834 GCO, d 1863, age 28, bur Buffalo Twp., GCO.
A10. David, b 1836 US, killed or missing in Battle of the Wilderness, Civil War.
HEAUME, Ann, b 1795 G, d 1866 GCO, poss sister of Peter.
HEAUME, Thomas, b 1845 d 1848 HEAUME, Mary, 1835-1863
HEAUME, George, b 1854, d.y. HEAUME, Peter, b 1788, d 1865 GCO
HEAUME, Judith, b 1792 G, d 1852 GCO HEAUME, RAchel, b 1821 d 1892 GCO
HEAUME, John, half bro of John above, b G, rem to OH, but returned to G in 1836, where he mar 1837 Elizabeth BAILLEUL.
HEAUME, Nicholas, also half bro of said John, b G, rem to OH, but ret. to G, and mar there Rachel PRIAULX of Candie, Castel, G.
HEDLEY, see HEADLEY, BISSON and TAYLOR.
HELLEUR, see ALLEZ and NICHOLSON. HELLIER in J 1299 as HELIER, also early in G.
HELLEUR, from French HELER, to hail, to annouce, poss a 'crier'? See CIFHS #14, for tree. This fam in J related to DE GRUCHY, JOURNEAUX, DE STE. CROIX, GIBAUT, ROMERIL, LE BOUTILLIER, BISSON, HUELIN, SALMON, BENEST, AMY, LE FEUVRE, PIPON, HAMON, LE GROS, MARTEL, etc,etc. HELLEUR poss as HELLER? in America.
HELLEUR, Stanley from C.I. rem to BC, had bros Sidney and Clarence. (Eva Luce, Vancouver, BC)
HELLYER, Robert from England or C.I.? mar Elza DAVIS, res Hampshire Co. VA, rem to Noble Co., OH where he was first Recorder. (GUERNSEY CO., publ. 1978) OUTC.
A1. Rachel, b 1816 d 1906, mar Daniel Snider, Snyder, b 1813, d 1866
HELLYER, Bernard, b Barnhill, Wales, England of J fam (tradition) rem to Phila., PA early 1700s then rem to Winchester, VA. Said to have mar ___ Barr or Dunbar. Said also to have been one of 5 sons and dau Jenny of immigrant HELLYERS. Some data in WRCIC. (Hampton, NH by Dow; Harriet Gettman, Modesto, CAL; Mary Hellyer Evans, Carlsbad, NM; WENTWORTH GEN) See CIFHS #4.
HENROID, Henry David, b 1830 Havre, France, mar 1853 in St. Heliers J Elizabeth Susan McBride of St. Heliers. Henry also mar Sarah Allen of J? Part or all of fam rem to UT 1862.
A1. Elizabeth Henriette, b 1853 St. Heliers J mar Farmer Sanford.
A2. Emily Julia, b 1855 St. Saviour J, d.y.?
A3. Leah Rose, b 1857 St. Helier J d 1937, mar 1876 UT? Ralph Lowe Bassett.
A4. Henry A. Thomas, b 1859 St. Saviour J.
HENROID, William John, of above fam? mar 1909 in UT? Martha HORMAN, qv.
HENRY, in J 1286. In G 1392. In Sark 1900s. HENRY in Vale G 1821. See CIFHS #3 and #14.
HENRY, Thomas S., b 1815 G son of ? Jean HENRY of St. Peter Port G. and Elizabeth ROBIN? Rem to PEI and mar there in Murray Harb. 1842 Margaret NICHOLLE, qv, b 1822, dau of John Thomas and Elizabeth (MACHON) NICHOLLE of a G fam. Thomas S. was bur 1899 United CH Cem. Georgetown, PEI. Eliz bur 1902 same, 10 chn. (Marilyn Cahill, Cherry Hill, NJ)
A1. Elizabeth, b 1845 PEI A3. Charles Cupp, b 1849
A2. Thomas S. Jr, b 1847 PEI mar Kate Maria Hadley, who d 1887 in

Georgetown, PEI. Thomas d there 1835, 2 chn d.y., Albert, Calveny.

A4. Elkanah James, b 1851 mar Mary Porter. He d 1935, she in 1921.

B1. Bessie

B2. Maud, b 1875 mar Wm. Hobbs, 4 chn: Robert, Eleanor, Arnold and Wm.

B3. Clara Medlar, b 1875, not a twin, mar Andrew Lavers, 5 chn: Bert, David, Harold, Bessie and Elsie Lavers.

B4. Ida, d 1910 B5. Winnie, mar Wm. Hobbs, sons Louis and HowardHobbs

B6. Percy, mar Agnes Solomon, 5 chn: Marina, Mary Lou Walsh, who had 6 chn, Roma, Larry and Percy.

B7. Sullivan, mar Lillian Publicover, 7 chn: Bessie, Gary, Charles, Lillian, Watson, Sullivan and James W., the latter b 1933.

A5. Margaret Ann, b 1853 PEI mar Josiah ROBERTS, see Q.A. IN CANADA.

A6. Benjamin, b 1855

A7. Mark Watson, b 1857 PEI d 1939 Beverly, MA. Mar Eva Hadley, b 1859 Nova Scotia, dau of Thomas and Jane (Kenton) Hadley. Eva d 1926 Beverly, MA.

B1. dau? B2. Edgar Stanley, b 1888 Georgetown, PEI

B3. Thomas Arthur Herdman, b 1898 PEI mar Jane L. Murphy, b 1899.

C1. Arthur Robert, b 1923 Bev., MA. C2. Norman Fred. b 1929 Salem,MA

A8. William Nicholle, b 1859 PEI

A9. Ezra Matthew, b 1862 PEI mar 1888 Charlottetown, PEI Eliz. Ann Bears, dau of Henry Alline Bears and Priscilla Jane HAWKINS, qv. 6 chn. Ezra d 1950 Boston, MA.

B1. Chester, b 1889 PEI mar 1920 Sarah Cora BEADLE, qv. He d 1962, bur Swampscott, MA. Sarah b 1892 dau of Wm. H. BEADLE of Long Island, NY and Blanche Harding, b Saint Johns, NB, Canada,1 ch.

C1. Lila Blanche, b 1925 mar 1951 Paul Francis Hennessey, son of Dr. Thomas F. and Gertrude R. (Miller) Hennessey, no issue.

B2. Elsie Louise b 1892 PEI mar 1912 Arthur Joseph HARDY, Sr., a twin. Both bur Forest Hills, Jamaica Plain, Boston, MA.

C1. Arthur J. Hardy Jr. b 1914 Malden, MA mar 1939 Dorothy K. Walsh, dau of James E. and Helen (Hefferan) Walsh. A dau Marion Hardy, b 1941 mar 1966 Arthur Henry Ross JR, 2 chn: Nina, Christopher.

C2. Frank Vincent Hardy, b 1918 Boston mar 1950 Pauline MacDonald, b 1920 Sidney, NS, has son Joseph A. Hardy, who mar A. Norton.

C3. Evelyn Virginia Hardy, b 1922 mar 1941 Herbert F. Dugan, div.

B3. Mary Inez, b 1893 PEI, unmar

B4. Frank Irving, b 1895 PEI mar 1913 Boston, Bertha Wandelear, dau of Louis and Lena, div. Ch was raised by Wandelear grparents, and took their name. Frank mar 2. Lulu May (Dewar) MacDonald.

C1. Frank Louis Henry Wandelear, mar 1. Lydia Johnson and 2. 1939 Winnifred May Rowe. 4 chn: Carol Ann by Lydia, Leslie Frank, Judy Bertha Bogen, and Lynne Marion Roach.

C2. Stewart Matthew Henry, b 1927 Malden, MA mar 1951 Irene L. Lindstrom, of Swedish parents, 2 daus, Linnea Horine and Dianne Weincek Ouellette.

B5. Harold Alline, b 1898 E. Boston, MA mar 1925 Clara Eunice Farrar, b 1906 d 1979.

C1. Charles Alline, b 1928 d 1934

C2. Shirley Ann, b 1931 mar 1955 Everett R. Redden, b 1930 Boston, 3 chn: Lorna, Scott and Jenny Louise Redden.

C3. Gail Elizabeth, b 1935 Brockton, MA, unmar

B6. Vinton Carl, b 1900 S. Boston, mar 1930 Annie C. Suirane, b 1910 Pictou, NS dau of Fred. and Mary Ella (Hume) Suirane, 3 chn?

C1. Douglas Frank, b 1932 mar 1957 Joan Frances Crockett, b 1934 Boston, 3 chn: Matthew, Kurt and Alyson, b Norwood, MA.

C2. Marilyn Ann b 1936 mar 1955 Francis C. Cahill, res Cherry Hill,

NJ, son of Francis E. and Ruth (Tetz) Cahill. Two chn: Mark Douglas Cahill b 1958 mar Jane E. Davies, and Meredith Diane Cahill,b 1965
C3.
A10. Mary Ella Jane, b 1865 mar Capt. John MacDonald of PEI
B1. Edna MacDonald, b 1897 Georgetown, PEI
B2. Vivian Margaret MacDonald, b 1907 mar Elmer McDonald of PEI
HENRY, some are bur in GCO, but compiler is not certain they came from C.I. See records of Wills Twp., Wash. Twp., Madison and Oxford Townships in Guernsey Co., OH.
HENRY, Elizabeth, b 1783 St. Peter Port G, d 1855 Mormon Grove, UT, dau of Thomas and Rachel (LE CHEMINANT) HENRY of J. Mar John PILL, qv. (SLCity records) See LE CHEMINANT.
HENRY, sailmaker in J 1800s. (A. John Jean, Jersey)
HENRY, Jean mar Elizabeth ROBIN. (Mormon Records in Weston, MA Libr.) Not known if this fam or desc rem to America.
A1. Mary Ann, b 1811 St. Peter Port G
A2. Thomas, b 1814
A3. Susanna, b 1816
A4. Pierre, b 1818.
HENWOOD, Mary Ann, rem to North Chelmsford, MA from J, wife of Elisha BRAKE, qv. Curr J. This is an English surname.
HERBERT, John and William were named as part of a GCO group settling in OH 1807. Not found. It is likely that this HERBERT was HUBERT.
HERIVEL, in G 1600s. In J 1515, in St. Ouen parish J 1607. Curr G and J. See CIFHS #6,38. (Somtimes spelled HARIVEL)
HERIVEL, some res Trinity Parish J, artisans, Methodists, town folk, and quite musical.
HERIVEL, Capt. John Richard Philip, b 1846 mar Jane LUCAS of G, 1845-1879. (A. Sweetman, Qu'Appelle, SASK, Canada)
A1. John Lucas, b 1874, went to sea at 14, not heard of again.
A2. Winter Richard, b 1876, d 1971 owned Herivels Wallpaper and Paint Store in St. Heliers J, 7 chn.
B3. Rev. Helier John mar Estelle LE BRUN, Meth. minister, St. Heliers
C1. Simonne Estelle, mar J. Bailey, had 2 sons, res New Guinea.
C2. Antoinette Esme, b 1943, mar 1968 Harry Sweetman, res SASK 1967 as teacher. 4 chn, including twin sons.
B5. Leonard, a J musician, mar, 2 sons in England have chn.
B7. Edward, mar ___, had 2 daus, one a folk singer in AUstralia.
HERIVEL, Clarence Sears, mar Violet ___, res Cleveland, OH. Clarence was son of a G fam settled in OH, son of a first wife. The second wife may have been a DE PUTRON, qv. 3 sons. (Mrs. Violet Herivel, Cleveland, OH)
A1. ?
A2. David, res Lander Rd., Cleveland Hts., early 1970s.
A3. Donald, res FLA
HERIVEL, Three boys of this fam to US from St. Anne's parish, Alderney ca 1913, settled Detroit, MI. (Richard Herivel, Detroit, MI)
HERIVEL, Alfred, d 1973, had wife Muriel, and 2 chn.
A1. Ronald, b Detroit?, mar ___ res Minnesota, 3 chn
A2. Elaine, b Detroit? mar ___, res Virginia, 5 chn.
HERIVEL, William, the 3rd bro, res Alderney Is., age 67 in 1975.
HERIVEL, Richard, b ca 1895 G, res Detroit 1975, mar Grace May NICHOLS, b ca 1901, mar 57 yrs. in 1975. 4 chn, 1 d.y. Richard a lithographer and printer. HERIVEL curr in Detroit, MI, 16 grchildren.
A1. William, b ca 1919 mar Dorothy ___, 9 chn, res Everett, WA.
A2. Robert, b ca 1925 has at least two sons, Richard and Robert and 2 daus, Janet and Barbara.
A3. Janice, b ca 1930 mar Roy ___, 3 chn, Roy, Jeannie and Karen.
HERIVEL, from C.I. to Ontario. (int forbid by Clark in MA 1710)
HERIVEL, Nicholas of Chester, MA mar/Eliza Kammon, HAMON? /

HERO, noted in Canada and US, poss HERAULT of J?, there in 1274. In St. Clement, St. Saviour, St. John and St. Brelade J 1607, and in St. Clement, St. Heliers and St. Peter J 1668. Pron. much like HERO.
HERO in Plaisance, Acadia, NS early 1700s, prob French?
HERO, Samuel, bp 1767 Salem, MA, son of Lawrence. OUTC.
HEARRO, Jane mar Lewis Cronier 1747 Boston, MA. OUTC
HEAIRO, Peter mar Jane Alden 1739 King's Chapel, Boston. This church attended by Channel Islanders and others. OUTC. OUTC
HERO, Willard Daniels mar 1856 Hannah Eliz. Peabody, b 1834/Mason, NH.
HESKETT, "About 1750 three brothers by that name came to Virginia from Guernsey Island. One later went to Pennsylvania and one to Florida, but one stayed in Loudoun Co., VA". (Alice Gougan, Bolivar, OH) Name curr in J. Researcher, note that there were many of this surname settled in GCO, especially in Richland and Valley Twps. 1800s. See also NEHGS Vol 42, and Conner-Eynon Cem. Book of GCO. A George HESKETT was b 1690 in Boston, d 1747. This is an English surname. (Mrs. W.G. Clothier, London, ONT; Wm. O. Goss Jr., Ipswich, MA)
HEWES, SEE HUES and HUGHES.
HEWITT, from C.I.? to SC before 1680. (Baldwin) OUTC.
HEWITT, Thomas mar 1710 in St. Sampson G, Jane COLQUITT. See COLQUITT
HICKS, HICQUES in J 1331. In St. Martin J 1607, 1668. Curr G and J.
HICKS, Hezekiah b ca 1719, prob in Rehoboth, MA, d 1788. Mar 1738 Desire CARPENTER, b 1716, Rehoboth. OUTC. However, CARPENTER might be TOURGIS called CARPENTER, of N. Kingston, RI. Desire is likely to be a Hug. first name. See HAILE. Note that HICKS is a Devon and Cornish surname of England. (Reetha Clancy, Bonsall, CAL)
A1. Hannah, b 1740 Rehoboth, MA d 1812 Putney, VT mar James HAILE, qv.
A2. James, b 1742 Rehoboth A4. Mary, b 1740?
A3. Hezekiah Jr., b 1744 A5. Desire, b 1750
A6. Gideon, twin to Desire. (Gideon-French Hug. first name)
A7. Jotham Hicks, b 1752, mar Chloe Wheeler. Cf WHILEUR/WHEELER.
HICKS, Thomas from J? mar 1706 Abigail BLETHEN, whose mother was a Guernsey girl. See LE MARCOM.
HICKS, Josua and Martha had son John bp 1721 Salem, MA. OUTC. (Essex Coll, Vol 8)
HICKS, Eli, b 1793 d 1868, mar in Fred. Co., VA, Charity Anderson, 1794-1863. OUTC. Eli a popular J first name.
HICKS, see MRB records, also those of Plymouth and Scituate. See Pope, under HIX, Savage, Underhill and Dean's SCITUATE.
HIER, see AHIER.
HIGH, John and Elizabeth, poss MAHY of C.I.?
A1. Rebecca S., b ca 1823 mar Samuel Cox MULLET, poss MOLLET? of C.I. See MULLEY and MOLLET.
HILL, English surname. Curr G and J. Some from Bristol and Lincolnshire to America.
HILL, Emanuel mar 1843 in J Elizabeth MOON, rem to US 1850. Res New London, CT, Rockford, ILL 1854. Poss rem to MI? 3 chn. (Rose Vincent, Belleville, MI)
A1. Rosalia Mary, b 1844 J A2. Emanuel, b 1847 J A3. John, b 1849 J/
HILL, Clement, went to MD with Lord Baltimore 1662, d 1708. OUTC.
HILL, Zebulon mar Elizabeth ___, res Salem, MA. OUTC. (Essex Coll,V2)
A1. John, b 1659 A2. Philip b 1662 A3. Zebulon, b 1666
A4. Eliza b 1664 A5. Mary, b 1667 A6. Abigail b 1670 A7, Sarah,1675
HILL, William and Henry from J on ship PHILIP in 1665 with CARTERET to NJ. HILL now more common in G. See JOURDAIN. (NJ Documents)
HILL, Samuel, from G or J? had land in or near Kittery, ME 1653.(Noyes)

HILLIARD, HILLER, HILLIER, HILYARD, etc., Edward, b J to MRB ca 1736, wife Mary Boyle. At least 7 chn. HELLER, HELLES in J before 1528. See HELLIER and HELLEUR. (Perley; MRB VR)
A1. Edward, b 1765 A4. Edward, b 1788 A7. Mary HILLYARD, bp1796
A2. Francis, bp 1771 A5. Benjamin Hendly, bp 1790
A3. Molly, b 1780 A6. George HILLER, bp 1793
HILLIAR, Nicholas, from C.I.? to Boston before 1712 mar (int) Mary Drumer? 1712. (Perley III)
HILLIARD, Philip, a Jerseyman in MA late 1600s. (Perley III)
HILLIARD, Capt. Edward, b ca 1628 J? master mariner, mar Martha, d1706 (Perley III) OUTC.
A1. Elizabeth, b 1658 mar Gilbert PETERS
A2. Mary, b 1659 A5. David, b 1665 mar Priscilla? 1689 in MA?
A3. Edward, b 1660 d ca 1702 A6. Jonathan, b ca 1668, d before 1706
A4. Sarah, b 1662 mar John CARTER A7. Joseph, b 1673/4
HILLIER, HILLYER, Lydia from J? mar Daniel WEARE, qv, in Boston 1698.
HILLIARD, Joseph, poss son of Capt. Edward above? mar Rachel ALLEN 1694. He d ca 1745 MA. (Perley III) OUTC.
A1. Martha, mar Clifford Crowninshield 1721
A2. Rachel, b 1690s mar Paul KIMBALL
A3. Elizabeth, b 1690s mar Nathaniel MASSEY, qv, ca 1730
A4. Joseph, b 1700, mar Hannah BACON, qv, 1722
A5. Edward, b ca 1701 mar 1. Esther Loverin 1723 and 2. Elizabeth MASSEY, qv, rem to Oxford, MA.
A6. David, a ropemaker, mar Mary SWASEY, qv, 1738.
HILLIARD, HILLYER, HELYER, HELLYER, OUTC. Curr research on these surnames. See DRIVER GEN: DALAND FAM data; Helena McBridge, Long Beach, CAL; Joseph Dow, Summersworth, NH; AYER FAM data; Noyes; Virkus; Hingham, Boston, Salem MA VRS; Essex Coll. Vol 2; Cutter's NEW ENGLAND FAMS; Rhode Island data; THE RECORD, OH Gen.Soc., Spring 1974, etc.
HILLIKER, Mary E., from C.I. 1852 via ship KENNEBEC, to UT. Some Hilliker data in SLCity records. This is said to be a Dutch surname.
HINE, not an old C.I. surname, but some HINE fams res J and G.
HINE, Rev. James Samuel res G, and mar Sarah Hornbuckle. A son George Augustus HINE was b 1825 Wirksworth, Derby, England, a second son, who mar Marianna Robson, 4th dau of James Woodhouse, b 1836 London. A dau Edith Frances Hine, 1866-1913. Geo. A. to Toronto, ONT 1852 where he d 1900. Other HINES from C.I. to Australia. (CIFHS #15)
HINE, note those in MRB, MA, 1700s, some marrying C.I. persons.
HINE, Hannah, wife of Michael GRUCHY, b 1760, d 1823 MRB, 8 chn.
HINE, John Bromfield of J, mar Jeanne Marie DE GRUCHY, b 1857 J, sister of David, who also came to America. See. HINE and DE GRUCHY to Balt. MD 1913, 7 chn: John, Muriel who mar Charles Howard,(a dau Jane Howard), Mildred, Grace, Arthur, Marcius/Marcus?, and Nesta.
HINET, B., a Channel Islander removed to Nova Scotia. (Lorway)
HOCQUARD in J 1528, in Trinity J 1668 and 1749. Curr J. Also as HO-CART in G. See CIFHS #3. See fam chart of Francis GALLIE for a HOCQUARD fam in QUE.
HOCARD, Elizabeth mar Geo. Monk 1712 Boston, MA. (int) also spelled HOCERD, HOEARD.
HOCQUARD, Francis, b 1790 St. Brelade J d 1865 Alpine, UT. He was the son of John and Marie (BICHARD) HOCQUARD. Francis mar Elizabeth JEUNE, qv, dau of Clement and Elizabeth (HERAULT) JEUNE. (Sylvia Wilson, Medina, WA)
A1. Francis b 1821 St. Brelade J.
A2. John, poss John Churchill?, b 1823 J mar 1865 Jane HALL, d 1899.

The same or another John had wife Elizabeth, res UT 1854, came to US on ship MARSHFIELD. John C. d 1897 SLcity, UT. Poss other chn?

B1. Francis B2. Thomas

B3. Alice, d 1927 SLCity, UT mar Arthur Clare.

A3. Philip, b 1825 J, d at sea

A4. Elizabeth, b 1827 d 1917 Mar 1857 John Carlisle in UT, descendants An Eliz. HORGUARD came to America 1855, via ship CHIMBORAZO, settled UT.

A5. Frances Sophia, b 1829 J d 1922 UT. Mar 1852 Thomas Fields Carlisle in UT.

A6. Charles b 1831 J, d at sea.

HOCQUARD, Capt. Charles Philip of the J brigantine NEWPORT, 106 tons, was chased and caught by the Royal Navy anti-slaving patrol. The ship carried a number of slave goods, such as muskets, padlocks, etc. (Saunders) Does HOOKER equal HOCQUARD sometimes?

HODEL, old J surname, one settled in Australia, some to America? (CIFHS #6)

HODGDON, HODSDON. A large fam figures in early New England records, but origin not seen by compiler. While Hodson occurs in St. Clement parish J 1668, the HODSDONS were prob from England. However, many mar into C.I. fams such as RICKER, GALLISON, MORRELL, MESSERVY, etc. See sources: OLD KITTERY AND HER FAMILIES: WEYMOUTH FAM HIST, by Ruth Weymouth; GALLISON GEN.

HOMAN, common in early New England, esp. in MRB. OUTC. Poss that this may be variant of HORMAN? later found in Grouville, St. Saviour, St. Peter, St. Laurens, and St. Martin J, 1668, 1749.

HOMER, English surname of Warwickshire and southern England, Wales, and in C.I. HOMAR, HOMMART in St. Heliers J 1668, in St. Clement J 1607. Curr in G, prob from England? See Boston, MA and Barrington, NS rec.

HOOKEY, see LE HUQUET.

HOOPER. There may be several names involved as the original surname of the HOOPERS in early New England. Some are admittedly from the C.I., and others were no doubt English. Compiler is not able to distinguish and verify which were HOUPER, HUPPER, HOOPER and HUBERT, all four of which may be original forms of some HOOPERS in New England.

HOOPER in J 1607, in Grouville, St. Saviour and St. Martin J 1668, sometimes spelled HOUPER. In Grouville J 1749. Curr G. Origin of HUPPER may be either HUBERT or HOUPER?

HOOPER ISLAND, off New England coast, ..."originally called HUPPER ISLAND, the Hupper family being natives of the Channel Islands." (ISLANDS OF NEW ENGLAND, by Hazel Young, 1949, Boston, MA)

HOOPER GEN., by Charles Henry Pope and Thomas Hooper, publ. 1908 Boston gives a number of fams in early New England, those of Reading, Marblehead, Beverly, and what they call the MAINE family. The latter is said to have come from the Channel Islands, and a partial chart is given in this book. The Marblehead and Maine fams. mar many times into C.I. fams. This is also true of the Beverly fams.

HOOPERS were in Maine before 1642, in which year a John HOOPER, cordwainer, made a pair of boots for a Capt. WINTER. The name given then was HUPPER. The original name might also have been HUBERT, qv. Consider that the HUBBARD family of this book also began as HUBERT from J. The business of hundreds of Islanders over a long period was the manufacture of shoes and boots, and an Islander might be likely to be a cordwainer. Notice the many other cordwainers in this book, coming from the C.I. in the 1600s and 1700s.

HOOPER, William, b 1673 Beverly, MA, mar ca 1703/4 Abigail GALE, dau of Edmund of Beverly, MA. Wm. may or may not have been a Jerseyman, but many of his desc mar Channel Islanders. A blacksmith, res Manchester, MA, near the Gloucester line 1711 on. He d there 1755 age 81. (HOOPER GEN) CAUTION: TRIAL CHART.

A1. William, bp 1705 mar Lydia ALLEN, d before 1739
 B1. Lydia, b 1731/2, mar (int) 1748 Edward DE QUETTEVILLE, called here KITFIELD, qv, from J, son of Abraham?
 B2. Abigail, b 1733
 B3. William, b 1735/6 mar at MRB 1757 Mary Sallins. He was a shoemaker, and served as Capt. in a company raised for coastal defense in Rev. War. 7 chn, some with desc.
 B4. and B5. d.y. B6. Asa, bp 1740, in Col. Bagley's Regt. 1759.
A2. Andrew, b ca 1706
 B1. Andrew, b 1730 mar 1751 Hannah Foster, dau of Jacob and Abigail. Widowed, she mar 2. Samuel Burnham 1765. He left chn Hannah, b 1753 and Abigail, who mar Isaac Morgan.
 B2. Mary, b 1732, mar 1754 Joseph MARSTERS, see LE MASTER, MASTERS.
 B3. Edward, b 1735 mar 1759 Mary, dau of John and Abigail Edwards, b 1737, 9 chn, many with desc: Edward, Andrew, Patty, Molly, Nathaniel, Israel, Abigail, Daniel and Wm., who d.y.
 B4. Rachel, b 1737/8, mar 1760 Isaac LEE B5. William, d.y.
 B6. William again, b 1742 mar Abigail GILBERT, dau of Jonathan and A. (Rogers) GILBERT, b 1744, who d 1827 age 83. 7 chn: Betsey, Wm., Jonathan, John, Andrew, Abigail and Molly, some with desc.
 B7. David, bp 1745 mar Rachel Story, who d age 91 in 1842. David res Freeport, ME, served in Rev. War and d 1835. 6 chn: David, Nehemiah, Rachel, Miriam, Story and Sally Cushing, some with desc.
A3. Abigail, mar 1727 John Edwards A5. Lydia, mar 1735/6 (int)A.Allen
A4. Elizabeth, mar 1729 (int) John Bishop Jr.
A6. Sarah, b 1717 mar 1735 Benj. Searls.
A7. Jacob, bp 1722, mar 1747 Anna LEE, who d 1794 age 64. He mar 1796 Lydia Badcock, who d a widow 1808 age 59. Jacob d 1801.
 B1. Jacob, b 1749/50, mar Mary OBEAR of Beverly. A son Abraham HOOPER bp 1774, and dau Anna, b at Manchester 1774, d 1794.
 B2. Anna, b 1752 d 1755 B4. Thomas, b 1756
 B3. Elizabeth, b 1754 B5. Anna, b 1758 d 1759
 B6. Joseph, b 1761 mar Nabby/Abigail CRAFT, dau of Eleazar and Eliz., b 1767, had chn: Joseph, b 1786, Nabby, Jacob & Eleazar, desc.
A8. Priscilla, mar 1739/40 Malachi ALLEN
A9. Judith or Juda?, bp 1725, mar 1747 (int) John RONELS, REYNOLDS, RENAULT?

HOOPER, Thomas, res Kittery, ME and mar 1693 Eliz. Small. OUTC. In 1738 Eliz. was a widow and res at Biddeford, ME. 6 chn, including Nathaniel and Joshua, who left desc. (Underhill)

HOOPER, John, believed to be member of same HOOPER fam as above Thomas, was a shoemaker in Kittery, ME 1701, and was prob a desc of the HOOPER who provided boots for Capt. Winter in 1642. Mar Charity ___. (HOOPER GEN)

A1. John, b 1701/2 at Berwick, ME mar Mary ___. Called HUPER and HUPPER, shoemaker, rem to Nason's Mills in Kennebunkport ca 1756. Said to have lived to at least 102, and to have made a pair of shoes after that birthday. 10 chn. More info. in Gen.
A2. Charity, b 1706/7, mar John KEY
A3. Samuel, b 1709 mar Eliz., widow of Josiah Plumer of N. Yarmouth, ME, a shoemaker, res Arundel/Kennebunkport, ME 1763, served at Louisburg NS 1745 with Major Cutts. More in HOOPER GEN.

A4. Mary, b 1711 mar Thomas SHOREY, cf CHORET
A5. Joseph, b 1712, not noted in will, no record
A6. William, bp 1719 Berwick, ME mar Eliz. Emery. Wm. a bootmaker, tanner, sometimes wrote his name HUPPER, as in a deed in 1761. Widow d 1812. More in HOOPER GEN.
A7. Benjamin, bp 1720/21 Berwick, ME mar at Biddeford, ME 1734 Lydia, dau of Capt. Daniel and Rebecca SMITH, qv. Lydia d 1806 age 79. Benj. was first postmaster of Biddeford, d 1902 age 82. See GEN.
A8. Solomon, bp 1723, mar 1. Bridget, and 2. Abigail. Solomon a shoemaker at Berwick, ME, d ca 1787, 5 chn.
A9. Love, mar ___Sprague.

The following HOOPERS mar into C.I. fams. See also BRIGHT.
Eli, res MRB 1790 with fam of 11 (Census) OUTC
Elizabeth mar Daniel MALLEY, MALLET of J?, 1720 MRB.
HOOPER, Eliz., mar Henry BUBIER 1786 MRB
HOOPER, Lydia mar Capt. Benj. BODEN 1778 MRB.
HOOPER, Mary mar Peter BUBIER 1761 MRB
HOOPER, John, bp 1744 son of John, mar Hannah SIGNCROSS, STE. CROSS, 1766 MRB. John, fisherman, d before 1772 (JOURNALS OF ASHLEY BOWEN)
HOOPER, John, bp 1741, son of Joseph, 1701-1743, soldier in Wm. Hooper's company 1766, also crewed on several privateer ships: MASSACHUSETTS 1776; TYRANNICIDE 1777; TRUE BLUE, 1776; FREEDOM, 1777; WILLIAM AND ANN, and PILGRIM, in 1778. Caught and imprisoned from prize ship WILLIAM AND ANN, served in Halfiax, NS.
HOOPER, Martha, b 1682, dau of Benj. and Eleanor (Clark) HOOPER, mar John PUNCHARD, qv, son of Wm. PUNCHARD from J, of Salem?, MA.
Note MRB marriages of HOOPER and LE CRAW. See LE CRAW and BRIGHT.
HOOPER, Frank, b J, rem to Nfld. and sailed from there as a mariner/ fisherman. His work took him to the French Islands of St. Pierre and Miquelon, the only remnants of the huge French settlements in early North America. There he met FrancoisAntoine, native of Dijon, France who had several chn. One, dau Fanny, was born on PEI. She mar Frank HOOPER the Jerseyman, and they settled in Nfld. Frank may have later rem to Montreal. Of 4 chn, 1 survived. (Roger Gauthier, Montreal, QUE; LA PATRIE, Sept. 12, 1948)
A1. Ernest, b 1871 Burin, Nfld. rem to Montreal 1898, had lived some time with his grandfather in St. Pierre Islands, as his father d while young. Ernest converted to Catholicism, and mar Josephine Biseuil, dau of a fisherman and his Basque wife, who had come to St. Pierre Island from either Hendaye, France or from Portugal. 7 chn, 6 survived.
B1. Francis, d WWI 1918
B2. Edouard, CPR repres. in Chicago, ILL.
B3. Andre, permit inspector, Montreal
B4. Arthur, greffier
B5. Ernest, a civic official
B6. Joseph, mar Benoit ROBILLIARD of Bell, QUE
B7. Malette, remained with parents.

Also of this fam was a girl who mar Andre PATUREL of St. Pierre Is., had 10 chn and a bro assoc. with Anglo-Amer. telephone, who mar a Spanish girl, and had 3 chn, res Montreal, QUE.
HOPIN, HOPEN, HOPPIN, HOUPIN of J and/or HORPIN of G, now appear as AUPIN in QUE. HOPPIN noted in BACON GEN, Michael of Dedham, Camb., MA 1915. See also Q.A. IN CANADA.
HORMAN in J 1164, few in G now, but some curr in J.
HORMAN,Charles b 1825 St. Saviour J, son of Charles and Mary (GALLICHAN) HORMAN. See GALLICHAN. Charles mar 1. Eliza COOK?, and 2. Margaret(DE LA HAYE) POWELL, widow. Charles was a sailor, baker, farmer, towncrier and carpenter. Fam to UT 1868 via ship CONSTITUTION. They walked from St. Joseph, MO to SLCity with John Gillespie

Company, assigned to Tooele by Brigham Young. Charles joined the Mormon Church in J 1849, and wife Margaret joined in 1853. (HIST. OF TOOELE CO; Lucile Gagne, Seattle, WA; OUR PIONEER HERITAGE, by Kate Carter, Vol 9) See UTAH section and PERSONAL ACCOUNTS.
A1. Charles, b 1854 J d 1920 unmar A3. John, b 1857 J, d.y.
A2. Francis, b 1855 J mar Thecla Lindholm, and d 1940 ID, 12 chn. He mar 2. Martha Lindholm, who d 1940 Idaho Falls, ID.
B1. Francis, b 1887 Tooele, UT, d 1888
B2. Clara, b 1889 mar 1907 Joseph Moss B3. Albert, 1891-1892
B4. Lula, b 1893 mar 1920 John Miller, d 1965
B5. Maud, b 1895 mar 1916 Jacob Goodson
B6. Ross, b 1898 mar 1927 Mary E. Willyard. B7. Charles, b 1900,d.y.
B8. Johanna, b 1901 mar 1924 Clifford Scoresby
B9. Martha, b 1903 Iona, UT mar 1925 Leslie J. Lingren
B10. Phyllis, 1906-1908 B11. Merrill, b 1908 mar 1934 Melila Torash
A4. Mary, b 1859 J mar Arnold Cunon, and d 1883
A5. Edmund D., b 1860 St. Heliers J, settled UT mar 1885 Martha Spiers Smith.
B1. Martha, b 1886 Tooele, mar 1909 William John HENROID, qv, and 2. i in 1911 Samuel Potts. She mar 3. in 1918 Philip Jackson BARTON.
B2. Edmund, b 1888 mar 1. 1923 Clara E. Long and 2. 1926 Ella May Wildfang.
B3. William, b 1890 SLCity, d 1899 B5. James, b 1893 d 1899
B4. Mary Ann, b 1892, mar 1913 Stephen Leetham. B6. Lillias
B6. Lillias, b 1895 mar Wm. J. Holt
B7. Charles, b 1897 mar 1921 Catherine Haggen. B8. Margaret, d.y.
B9. Joseph, b 1900 mar 1922 Johanna Noorda. Jos. a twin of Hyrum below.
B10. Hyrum, b 1900, twin, mar 1922 Lillian RUSSELL and 2. in 1949, Margaret BLANK, LE BLANC?
B11. Agnes, b 1903, mar 1. 1922 Warren Smith? and 2. in 1945 John Webb She mar 3. Clarence Wible.
A6. George, b 1863 J, mar Florenda Vowles 1890. She was dau of Wm. V. and Isabella Hardwick. Florenda b at Bitten, Glouc., England.7 chn
B1. George W., b 1891 Tooele, UT mar 1. 1917 Ruby Peters and 2. in 1943 Katherine McKenzie.
B2. Florinda Pearl, b 1893, d.y.
B3. Elsie V., b 1894 mar 1917 Wm. Hesse, d 1948
B4. Herbert, b 1896 mar 1. 1918 Alvena Bloecklinger and 2. Margaret Shumaker. A dau Lucile b 1920, Seattle, WA, mar Ralph D. Gagne.
B5. Ernest, b 1898 mar 2. Fair Todd, and 3. 1936 Joyce Bowen
B6. Florence, b 1901, mar 1920 Erwin Gilbert Murphy
B7. Lillian Margaret, b 1904 mar 1922 Oswald Howick, and 2. Joseph Rothaus.
A7. Alfred, b 1865 J, d.y.
A8. Ann, b 1866 J, mar Edward B. GREEN, d 1886. A9. William, b 1870dy.
A10. Thomas De La Haye, b 1871 UT, a bldr. and contractor in SLCity, mar Sarah Ann Vowles. Thomas d 1891.
HORMAN, John, d in Orange Co., CAL and his estate of more than 50,000 dollars prob went to the state, as he was listed with no heirs, 1970s.
HORMAN, note that a German fam named HORMAN res Hamilton Co., OH 1860.
HORMAN, curr Detroit, MI, from C.I.? or Germany.
HORMAN, see HOMAN.
HOTTON, in J from Houghton or Hutton, England? In St. John J 1668,1749. HOTTON also in G early. Curr G and J.
HOTTON, Nicholas, farmer in G, mar Eliz. CARREL, qv. Their chn to Canada, and to US. (Mrs. Beverly Hotton, Exton, PA) See Q.A. IN CANADA.
A1. Nicholas

A2. William Philip, b 1873 Les Prevosts, G, in St. Saviour par. Wm. d 1962 in Salisbury, MD. He rem ca 1909 to Mission, BC, then res Vancouver, SASK and ONT, rem to MD ca 1921. Mar Henrietta Eliz. GIRARD, b 1879 Marcherie, St. Martin?, G. Henrietta d 1966 Salisbury, MD, bur Parson's Cem. She was dau of Jean Guillaume GIRARD and Mary LE TISSIER.

B1. Percy Philip, b 1903 G mar Louise Williams and d 1958 MD.

B2. Francis Bevan, b 1905 G, mar Louse TOADVINE, TOSTEVIN of G.

B3. Cecil George, b 1906 G mar Henrietta Carruthers

B4. William Arthur, b 1907 G mar Irene HARRELL, HUREL? of G?

B5. Lawrence Girard, b 1908 G, mar Gertrude Farlow

B6. Daphne Henrietta, b 1912 Chilliwack, BC, mar Charles JACKSON, res Ocean City, MD.

B7. Della Elizabeth, b 1920 Peterborough, ONT mar Jesse Warner

B8. Theodore, d.y. B9. Evie, d.y. age 7.

A3. Walter, A4. Minnie, mar Wm. TONERI, see Q.A. IN CANADA for TONERI

HOUGARD, see HOCQUARD

HOUSE, HOWSE, HOWES, Erasmus, came with CARTERET, qv, to NJ 1655. This is likely to be a Dutchman, not from C.I.

HOWS, James res in Upper Pens Neck, Sale Co., NJ 1790. OUTC.

HOWARD, old name in J. Some from C.I.? Not researched by compiler.

HOYLES of J, but prob from England 1700s?

HOYLES, fam in St. Clement J early 1800s. Eliz. Hoyles McWhinney, bur Montreal, QUE, from J fam. Jane HOYLES FALLE, rem to Montreal, where J desc still live. (Q.A. and Q.A. IN CANADA) Mary Ann HOYLES LE CORNU, from J to Gaspe, then to Alpena, MI, some desc. Nancy Ann HOYLES, to ONT, Canada, some desc. (Q.A., Q.A. IN AMERICA: Q.A. IN CANADA, by Turk)

HOYLES, James, bro of Hoyles girls above, b ca 1845 St. Clement J, mar Elvina ___ in J, rem to Chicago, where name is written HOILES in Census of 1880. Record says b England, but was b J.

A1. William George, b ca 1868 A3. Albert, b ca 1875 A5. Mary

A2. Alice, b ca 1872, mar __Gundlach? A4. John, b ca 1878

HOILES, fam of 3 bros said to first res in NJ, there in 1786, Joshua, Levi and Nicholas. Joshua b ca 1786 in NJ mar Rachel Hess, and a son William Penn Hoils b 1912 in Phila., PA. OUTC. Rem to Columbiana Co., OH, later to Alliance, OH. From J? (Linda R. Timpe, Toledo, OH)

HOYLE, HOILE, from J? to MRB ca 1669, 1687. HOYLE in St. Clement J 1800s, curr J.

HUBBARD. Some HUBBARD fams in America originated in J as HUBERT, qv. HUBERT in J 1299. In St. Martin, Grouville, St. Saviour and St. Laurens J 1668. In St. Martin, St. Clement, St. SAviour and Trinity J 1607. In St. Martin J 1749. Curr G and J as HUBERT.

HUBBARD, note that most Hubbards in early New England came from MEndelsham, Suffolk Co., England. James who came in 1637 from Langham,England, settled on Long Island, etc. Many sources: OLD KITTERY AND HER FAMS; Underhill, Vol 1; ONE THOUSAND YRS. OF HUBBARD HIST; SACO VALLEY SETTLEMENTS; GREELEY GEN; Charles VARNEY and Rachel Parker of Berwick, ME by Ruth V. Held; WENTWORTH GEN; WEYMOUTH GEN; HIST. OF LIMINGTON, ME by R. Taylor; ANCESTRAL LINE OF CORA L. CLEMONS;BIOGRAPHICAL REVIEW, 1897; HIST. OF BROWNFIELD, ME by Dr. Wm. TEG, 1968; THE CLEMENT FAM by Percival W. Clement, 1927; HUBBARD NEWS LETTER; OLD NORTHWEST, Vol 8; DESC OF SIDENY TANNER by De Brouwer; FAM RECORDS of Ella Clemons Butterfield; Hira, S. Gorham, and Biddeford records; Evie Hanson's Diary, 1910-1936; Records of Guy P. Wakefield, Lodi, CAL; DIARY OF MONROE BOYNTON, 1890; Gloria B. Lloyd,

Orlando, FLA; Reels of film and 14 books in SLCity Archives; Maine Archives; Census; Civil War pension records; Vermont records; Mrs. Robert Emerson, Kaneohe, HAW; Leslie Hubbard, Lompoc, CAL; Donald Stevens, Delmar, NY; Elizabeth de Brouwer, Modesto, CAL, Mrs. Mary Jennings, Woodland Hills, CAL. Part of above list courtesy of Hubert Clemons, Hiram, ME.

HUBBARD, HUBERT, Philip b St. Saviour J, son of Jean H. and Elizabeth LE GALLAIS of St. Heliers J, rem to Berwick, ME before 1692. His bro Josue, called Joseph, d in ME 1701/2, unmar. Philip was an educated Jerseyman, and was several times selectman and treasurer of the parish. He mar 1692 Elizabeth (Goodwin) Emery, dau of Daniel and Margaret (Spencer) Goodwin. He d ca 1723? Some of the sources listed above for this fam were not seen by compiler. Much data available. See sources.

A1. Philip, b 1693 mar ca 1718 Elizabeth ROBERTS, dau of Joseph and Elizabeth of Dover, NH. He was prob killed by Indians in 1723. His widow mar Capt. John Gage of Dover. She was b 1697, had at least 3 chn by Philip HUBBARD, HUBERT.

B1. Capt. Philip, b 1718 mar ca 1740 Hannah Plummer? He held many town offices and was Captain in the Rev. Army, d ca 1792. Hannah the dau of Daniel and Sarah (Wentworth) Plummer.

C1. Benjamin, bp 1747 mar 1771 Abigail HEARD, or HEARL, rem to Shapleigh.

C2. Elizabeth, bp 1747, mar 1765 John NEAL of Kittery, son of Andrew and Catherine (Furbish) NEAL.

C3. John, bp 1747 mar 1777 Sarah Nason, d at Berwick, ME ca 1793

D1. Moses, b ca 1781 mar 1. 1810 Sally, dau of Nathaniel and Patience (NOWELL) Hobbs and 2. Almira Hayes of S. Berwick, ME.

E1. John, a lawyer

E2. Nathaniel, lawyer in Winterport, ME

E3. Sarah

E4. William P. of Bangor, ME.

E5. Emily H.

E6. Almira H.

E7. a dau

D2. Mary, b 1779 mar 1800 Joseph Emery, d 1814.

D3. Lois

D4. Philip, b 1792, d 1830, to Cornish, ME from Berwick. He was Postmaster at Cornish from 1824 to 1830. Mar Nancy Barker, 1796-1852.

E1. John, Hon. John Philip, b 1817, d 1875, settled Hiram, ME 1841 Business man and merchant, town official, served in ME Legis. Built Mt. Cutler House in Hiram. Mar 1. Mary A. Sargent, 1823-1852, and 2. Lusannah Wadsworth, 1840-1908, related to Henry Wadsworth Longfellow.

E2. Hon. Noah B. Hubbard, 1824-1884, settled in Hiram and was Postmaster there for 27 years, in bus. with bro., town officer and repr. in LEgis. Mar Emeline Kimball, 1824-1887

C4. Hannah, bp 1748/9 mar John Hodgdon

C5. Abigail, bp 1750, mar 1. 1771 Ebenezer Goodwin of Berwick,d 1828. (See VARNEY-PARKER book)

C6. Moses, bp 1753, unmar, lost at sea in privateer in Rev. War.

C7. Aaron, bp 1753, mar 1779 Martha Nason, rem to Shapleigh d 1814

C8. Sarah, bp 1756, mar 1787 Aaron Goodwin of Berwick, ME

C9. Richard, bp 1760, rem to Shapleigh.

C10. Jonathan, bp 1762 Berwick, ME mar Frances Parsons 1791/2 at First Church, Berwick. He d 1845 Acton or Shapleigh, ME, bur Acton. Vet of Rev.War. Frances the dau of Dr. John and Mary (Wise) Parsons.

D1. Stephen, b 1791 mar Lydia Coffin-D2. John, b 1798 mar Mary G. Hemmingway.

D3. Maria, b 1799 mar 1. Moses Hemmingway and 2. Clement Parker
D4. Martha, mar Capt. Guy HUBBARD
D5. Jonathan, bp 1803 Shapleigh, mar 1. Mrs. Nancy Shapley 1824, and 2. 1827 Keziah Lord, b 1810 d 1864, dau of Andrew and Priscilla (Corson) Lord, bur Maple Grove Cem., Acton.
E1. Frances H. Hubbard, b 1827 Acton, ME d 1904 Newburyport, MA, bur Oakhill Cem. Mar 1847 Augustus Safford, b 1824 Newbypt.
F1. William Hills Safford, b 1850 Manchester, MA mar 1. Lucy A. Perkins, who d 1880. He mar 2. later in 1880 Lucy M.H. Stevens, in either Newbury or Newburyport, MA. He d Daytona, FLA 1909, bur Newburyport.
G1. William Johnson Safford, b 1879 d 1880 with mother.
G2. Arthur, b 1881, mar Martha D. Home had chn.
G3. John Lunt Safford, b 1883 mar 1909 Salisbury, MA, Martha E. ROWE, 1887-1978, dau of Gustavus and Ida (Rowe) Rowe. Died 1933, bur Belleville Cem., Newburyport, MA.
H1. Priscilla Bartlett Safford, b 1911 mar 1938 Donald Stevens, son of Orrin and Ella (Bent) Stevens. Sons John B. and Peter B. Stevens have desc.
G4. William Hills, Jr, b 1884 mar Bessie M. Davis, 2 chn: William Hills Safford and Nancy Safford
G5. Deloid Safford b 1886 d 1950 mar Mabel A. Peabody, son Donald P. Safford, b 1911 has dau Helen Safford
F2. Charles N. Safford, b 1853 Newburyport, mar Addy? Olive Pierce Alvah, res Newburyport, MA
F3. Edward Augustus Safford, b 1862 mar Eliz. Eldridge Marston, res Waltham, MA.
F4. Fred Hubbard Safford, b 1864 mar Minnie Mable Gordon Mason, res Boston, MA.
D6. Fanny, mar ___Loud D7. Mary, d.y.
C11. Eben, bp 1765, d.y.
C12. Ichabod, b 1769 mar 1794 Sally, dau of John Hodgdon. Ichabod d 1807 Berwick, ME.
D1. Hannah Plummer, b 1796 mar Hope Nason
D2. Nancy, b 1798, d Eutaw, ALA, unmar
D3. John Philip, b 1800 mar 1. Hannah Chadbourne, dau of Wentworth and Sally (Butler) Chadbourne, had 2 sons who d.y. He mar 2. 1827 Lovey (Butler) Marsh, dau of Moses and Abigail (Pugsley) Butler, widow of Daniel MARSH. She was b 1808. John Philip d 1852 Mobile, ALA.
E1. Mary Eliz., b 1828 mar 1851 John Simpson, d 1892
E2. Richard, b 1830, d unmar
E3. Abigail E., b 1832, mar Wm. P. Bradford
E4. Moses, b 1834 rem to Evanston, WY.
E5. Albert, b 1836, d 1863 in Civil War, 7th Kansas Cavalry.
E6. Sarah Ann, b 1840, d 1866 unmar
E7. George Henry, b 1845, unmar, d 1861 served in ME Infantry.
D4. Sarah Holly, b 1802, d ca 1822 unmar
D5. Moses, b 1806, mar 1. Sarah Dunlap, and 2. Rebecca Bell, rem to E. Eutaw, ALA.
C13. Stephen, b ca 1770, lost at sea.
B2. Joseph, bp 1721 mar ca 1746 Sarah, dau of Daniel and Mary (Hodgdon) Emery, res Berwick, ME. D after March 1794. She d 1795.10chn
C1. Mary, b 1745 mar 1770 Job Emery, d 1812.
C2. Joseph, b 1748/9 mar 1770 Honor ROBERTS, 3 chn
D1. James, b 1777 mar Sarah Tibbetts of Rochester, NH
D2. Sarah, mar Paul Ellis D3. Ruth mar James ANDREWS

C3. Samuel, bp 1751 mar 1778 Eliz. Nason, d 1816
C4. Daniel, bp 1753 mar 1777 Lucy RICKER, rem to Shapleigh
D1. Daniel, mar Fannie Day
E1. Daniel mar Jane Clark
F1. George M. Hubbard, mar Eliz. Seivwright
G1. ? H1. Edward Hubbard, Milwaukee, WIS.
C5. Philip, bp 1755, mar 1777 Mehitable Underwood, rem to Shapleigh
C6. William, bp 1758, unknown
C7. Sarah, bp 1761 mar 1780 William LEAVER, poss LE LIEVRE? of C.I., she d 1810.
C8. Thomas, bp 1763 mar 1790 Lydia Goodwin, d before 1810
D1. John, b ca 1795
C9. Elizabeth, bp 1766, mar 1788 John Goodwin
C10. Timothy, bp 1769 mar 1789 Jane Pike, d 1810.
B3. Elizabeth, bp 1723, mar Timothy Weymouth of Kittery, ME. He prob d 1772 and she later than husband. See WEYMOUTH GEN. for more.
A2. John, b 1696 d unmar after 1735
A3. Elizabeth, b 1697 mar 1719 Jacob Redington of Topsfield, ME, cooper, son of Daniel and Eliz. Redington. At least 7 chn.
B1. Ch, prob d.y. B3. Daniel Redington, bp 1726/7
B2. Dorcas, bp 1724, d.y. B4. Jacob Redington, bp 1729
B5. Dorcas again Redington, bp 1732 B7. Eliphalet Redington, bp1738
B6. Phoebe Redington, bp 1735 Topsfield, MA d 1770? Tolland CT. Mar at Tolland Jacob Fellows, b ca 1734 of Tolland, d 1803 at 69 in Chester, MA.
C1. Parker Fellows, b 1762 Woodstock, CT, d 1820 age 58 near Chester, Geauga Co., OH. Mar 1793 in Middlefield, MA Dorcas Meacham, b 1772 Enfield, CT, d 1813, age 41 Middlefield, MA.
D1. Abigail Fellows, b 1799 Middlefield, MA d 1831 age 32, near St. Charles, MO. Mar 1821 Chester, OH John Mathias Burk, b 1793 German Flats, Herk. Co., NY, d 1853 Ogden, UT.
E1. Charles Allen Burk, Sr., b 1823 Kirtland, OH, d 1888 Minersville, UT. Mar 1850 Littlecottonwood, UT, Lydia Tanner, b1832 Bolton, NY, d 1910 Minersville, UT.

Charles Allen Burk and Lydia Tanner lived in Kirtland, OH, and were recruited to accompany Brigham Young on the first trek to the Salt Lake Valley in 1847. They then joined a group to establish a Mormon Colony in southern CAL, and their first ch was born after crossing the Mohave desert, the first white ch b in San Bernardino Co.,CAL, near present Barstow. The fam was recalled to UT, and res in Minersville, where Charles d 1888. 11 chn. (Elizabeth De Brouwer, Modesto, CAL)

F1. Louisa Abigail Burk, b 1851 Mhave River, CAL, d 1943 Provo,UT. Mar 1870 UT John Horace Lightner, b 1847 Galena, ILL, d 1923. (More data with source, and in WRCIC)
G1. Ada Caroline Lightner, b 1870 UT, d.y. G2. another ch?
G3. Mary Abigail Lightner, b 1891 UT mar 1910 James Earl Mc Farlane, b 1881 Nephi, UT, d 1954 Caliente, NEV.
H1. Thora MacFarland, b 1911 Nephi, UT H2. Marie MacFarland/ b 1914
H3. James Lightner MacFarlane, b 1916, mar Marie Robertson,3chn.
H4. Elizabeth L. MacFarlane, b 1923 mar 1943 San Fran.CALWalter William Brouwer, b 1911 Kansas, a dau d.y.
F2. John Sidney Burk, b 1853 San Bern. CAL
F3. Mary Ellen Burk, b 1856
F4. Charles Allen Burk Jr. b 1859 Parowan, UT. ??
F5. Charles Conley Burk b 1861 Minersville, UT d 1895 unmar
F6. Algernon Gilbert Burk, b 1864, d 1865.

F7. Lydia Salina Burk, b 1866 d 1891, unmar
F8. Elizabeth Keziah Burk, b 1868
F9. Nellie May, b 1870 F10. Laura Pearl Burk, b 1873
F11. James Edmund Burk, b 1876 UT, d 1915 unmar
A4. Moses, b 1700 mar 1723 Abigail HEARD, b 1702, dau of Capt. John and Jane (Cole-Littlefield) Heard, res Berwick, and Eliot, ME, d 1757?
B1. Jane, b 1726 mar 1749 Hugh Tucker, Jr. of Kittery, ME
C1. Dorcas Tucker, bp 1757 C2. Abigail Tucker, bp 1757
B2. James, b 1728 mar 1752 Mary Bean of York, rem to Kennebunk, a Capt. in Rev. War. Killed at Cambr. MA 1775
B3. Mary?, b 1724, 1734?, mar ___Davis
B4. Warwick, b 1731 mar 1757 Mary Littlefield of Wells, ME, d 1792.
B5. John Heard, bp 1735 Wells, ME pub. 1748 to Hannah NEAL, b 1727, dau of Andrew and Dorcas (Johnson) NEAL, res Wells, ME. John a tanner, Rev. soldier and Indian fighter, prom. citizen of Wells.
C1. Abigail, bp 1756 Wells, ME mar 1770 Obediah Emmons
C2. Dorcas, bp 1756 mar ___Buffum
C3. Hannah, bp 1756 mar 1775 Simeon Hussey, and d before 1790.
C4. Mary Heard, bp 1756 mar (int) 1776 Joshua Gillpatrick, and d before 1790.
C5. Eunice, bp 1757 mar 1783 Benjamin Cheney
C6. Jane, bp 1760 mar 1778 Andrew NEAL, b 1742 Berwick,? ME.
C7. Heard, b 1760, d 1826, mar Ruth Allen, b ca 1769, d 1845 Hiram,ME Mar 1792 Cornish, ME, dau of Solomon and Catherine (NEAL) Allen. Ruth and Heard were Quakers, rem to Limington 1796.
D1. Hannah, b 1792 Cornish, ME d 1862 Parsonsfield, ME, mar 1818 James Fogg, b Ossipee, NH
D2. Allen, b 1795 d 1877 Hiram, ME. Mar 1820 Sarah Bradbury Lord, res Hiram, and bur there. Allen was Capt. in Militia, and in 1847 was Repr. in Maine Legis.
E1. John Allen, b 1820 mar 1842 Hannah (Hubbard) Pike, b Fryeburg ? Maine, John d 1893.
E2. Hannah Fogg, b 1821 mar 1846 Samuel Boothby
E3. Thomas Lord, b 1823 Hiram, ME d 1871. Mar Mary Jane Mason, 1823-1877.
F1. Clinton P., M.D., b 1849 Hiram, ME, res Lovell, ME many yrs. D 1934, mar Esther J. Wentworth, b 1851.
G1. Fannie L., b 1871 Hiram, ME
G2. Carrie E., b 1877 G3. Elwin T., b 1879
F2. Elwin T., M.D., b 1854, d 1894 Rochester, NH, mar Nellie Churchill, b Madison, NH?, no issue.?
F3. Lansing H. b 1859 Hiram, d 1925, mar Iza M. Fessenden, b 1865, d 1957 Vernon, CT.
G1. Leman H. b 1890 Brownfield, ME mar Edith ___
H1. Hope, mar ___CARPENTER.
E4. Simeon Pease, M.D., b 1827 mar 1850 Harriet A. Barrett, who d 1883
E5. Mary Pease, b 1830 d 1831 E6. Erastus, b 1832 mar J.Abbott
E7. Daniel Brockett, b 1835 d 1908 Grafton, MA, mar 1.ADelaide Wilcox, and 2. 1892 Louisa Grommes.
E8. Henry Hyde, b 1838, d 1839
E9. William Henry, b 1840, d 1863 on ship USS ALABAMA,CivilWar.
D3. Ephraim, b 1798 Limington ME d 1880, mar Sarah Durgin, b1801
D4. Dorcas, b 1800 d 1803
D5. Dorcas again, b 1803 d 1853 Gorham, ME mar Artemas Richardson, b 1805 Hiram, ME d 1887.

D6. Nancy, b 1805 d 1881 Brownfield, ME mar Joshua Durgin, Jr., b 1804, son of Joshua and Sally (Folsom) Durgin, a fam from Kent, England.

E1. Henry J. Durgin, b 1829 Limington, ME d 1905, mar M. Day.

E2. Sarah E. Durgin, b 1831 d 1914 mar Marshall Day 1851

E3. Cyrus L., b 1833 mar 1863 Mary G. Libby, b 1834 Porter, ME. He d 1919 and she in 1903, both in Brownfield, ME

E4. Lydia A. Durgin, b 1838 mar (int) 1856 Nicholas Peterson, Jr.

E5. Andrew J. Durgin, b 1840 d 1925, mar Marie Hanscom 1862, b 1841, and d 1915.

E6. Simeon, b 1842 d 1862

E7. Ruth A. Durgin, b 1843, mar 1865 Joseph CLEMENT, qv, b 1836 Brownfield, ME, who disappeared ca 1871, while bringing the payroll from Portland to Brownfield. His horse, wagon & hat were found at Hiram Falls. The horse had been shot. No trace ever found of Mr. Clement.

F1. Jennie F. Clement, b 1866 Brownfield, ME d 1943 Concord, NH. Mar before 1880 William Butterfield, b 1852 d 1916. He was son of John and Eunice (Wentworth) Butterfield. They res Burnt Meadow Pond, Brownfield, until Wm.died. Jennie mar 2. 1919 Fred Miller.

G1. Grace Butterfield, b 1881 Brownfield, ME d 1935 Hiram. Mar 1898 Nelson Sanborn, b 1877 Baldwin, ME d 1953 Morrisville,VT

G2. a son, d.y.

G3. Harold C., b 1884, d 1978 Bridgeton, ME, mar 1905 Ella F. Clemons, b 1888 d 1974 Hiram, ME.

G4. Florence Butterfield, b 1888 d 1922 Hiram , ME mar 1903 Herbert Flint, b 1884 d 1932 Hiram.

G5. Almon E. Butterfield, b 1891 d 1892

G6. Leola Butterfield, b 1895 d 1973 Lexington, MA, mar 1919 Alvin Newton Day, b 1893 Cornish, ME d 1960

G7. Merlin Butterfield, b 1901 d 1963, unmar, Cambridge, MA.

G8. Carroll Butterfield, b 1905 d 1935 Portland, ME, mar 1928 Edna Thompson, b 1911.

F2. Almon W. CLEMENT, b 1869 d 1954 Orlando, FLA, mar Nashua,NH ca 1900 Sarah E. Burchell, b 1871 Lancs, England d FLA.

G1. Evelyn R. Clement, b 1902 Pepperell, MA mar Clinton H.Bouton

G2. Sylvia Clement, b 1904 mar Alfred A. Baldwin

G3. Joseph Clement, b 1906 d.y. G4. Natalie Clement, 1908-1975

G5. Roger Clement, b 1910 d 1973 Orlando, FLA, murdered.

F3. Joseph E. Clement Jr., b 1872 ME d 1950. Mar 1898 Florence Bartlett, b 1880 d 1966 Fryeburg, ME.

G1. Bernice Clement, b 1900, d 1962 Bridgton ME, unmar

G2. Wallace, b 1902, d 1920, unmar

G3. Nellie Clement, b 1904, d 1928 Portland, ME, mar Clayton Eaton, b 1892 d 1969

G4. Evelyn R. Clement, b 1907 mar Ralph Eaton, a son Wallace.

E8. Hannah F. Durgin, b 1845 Brownfield, ME E9. Mary F. Durgin

E10. Stillman Joshua Durgin, b 1850 d 1923 ME, mar 1880 Ellen M. Peary, b 1854 Fryeburg, ME d 1941 Brownfield, ME

E11. Margaret Durgin, b 1852 d 1855

D7. Eunice, b 1807, d 1831 Limington, ME

D8. Ruth Allen, b 1809 Limington, ME d 1880 Hiram, ME, mar Walter F. Watson 1834, b 1811 Hiram, d there 1880.

E1. Francis Watson, b ca 1835 Hiram, d ca 1837

E2. Frank L. Watson, b 1837 Hiram, d 1915. Mar 1856 Charlotte Evans, b 1835, d 1900 Hiram. She the dau of Oliver and Mary

(Locke) Evans. Frank mar 2. 1909 Ella S. Bradbury Howard.

F1. Cora A. Watson, b 1857 d 1893, mar George R. Clemons, b 1853 d 1937, son of Caleb C. and Hannah Boynton Clemons.

G1. Louise A. Clemons, b 1880 d 1953 Portland, ME mar 1898 Henry N. Burbank, 1863-1948

G2. Mamie Clemons, b 1883 d 1975 Alamonte, FLA. Mar 1903 Wilbur Martin, b 1880 Sebago, ME, d 1963 Portland, ME.

G3. Walter Clemons, b 1885 d 1965, mar 1909 Ethel Douglass, b 1892 Lynn, MA.

G4. Ella Fie Clemons, b 1888, d 1974 Hiram, ME mar 1905 Harold C. Butterfield, b 1884 ME, 4 chn: Louise Wentworth, Philip, Kenneth and Celia Morrison.

F2. Mary E., Mamie Watson, b 1858 d 1945 Stockton, CAL. Mar Charles F. Wakefield, b 1851 ME, d 1924 CAL. A son Guy Wakefield was b Hiram, d 1921 Lockeford, CAL.

F3. Charles W. Watson, b 1865, d.y. F4. Charles, 1867-1884

F5. John F. Watson, b 1869, d 1934 CAL, mar 1899 Maude A. Davis, b 1879 Bartlett, NH.

F6. Eunice Belle Watson, b 1871, d 1892.

E3. Zilpah B. Watson, b 1839 Hiram, d 1909 Gorham, ME, mar 1861 Charles W. Deering, b 1837 Scarboro, ME d 1932.

E4. Arabella S. Watson, b 1842 d 1902 Biddeford, ME mar (int) 1862 Edwin Woodman, b 1838 d 1907.

D9. John Allen, b 1812 Limington, ME d 1816

C8. Noah, bp 1764 Wells, ME d before 1823, mar 1790 Maribah Littlefield, b 1767

C9. Asa, bp 1766 d 1805 mar 1792 Lydia Cheney

B6. ?

B7. Joseph, b 1741 mar ca 1764 Ann Gowan, rem to Wells, ME. He was a Colonel in the Rev. War, d 1819.

B8. Joshua, b ca 1744 mar 1770 Dorcas Shapleigh, d 1809 Kittery, ME. His wife d 1818. A dau Abigail b 1770 mar Dr.Benj.Chickering.

A5. Aaron, b 1702, d 1751 mar 1733 Mary Curtis Howe. Aaron a tanner.

B1. Mary, b 1734 mar 1753 William Hood of Topsfield. B2. Lydia, d.y.

B3. Elnathan, b 1740 mar 1763 Mary Redington, who d 1773. He mar 2. Mary ___, 1748-1799. 1780-1818

C1. Mehitable, bp 1773 C2. Wm., b 1779, Lt.?, mar1804 Rebecca/Gould

B4. John, b 1743 B5. Joseph

A6. Patience, b 1704 mar 1723 Ensign Wm. Card of York, ME, and 2. 1733 Daniel Farnham of York, ME. She d Georgetown, ME 1751.

A7. Mary, b 1705 Kittery, d 1744, mar 1725 John Bean, of York, ME.

HUBBARD, Joseph, John and Philip of J, 1701. See Noyes.

HUBBARD, Philip, b 1787, thought to be of J fam, res Maine. Was shoemaker 1850, age 63, in Palmyra, ME. Philip mar Mary ___, and d in Palmyra, ME, 2 chn known. (ME Archives; Census; Civil War Pension records; Vermont records; fam. records; Shirley Emerson, Kaneohe, HAW)

A1. Philip Jr., b 1810 ME, mar Keziah Murray 1831, d Palmyra?, 9 chn

B1. William Henry, b 1832 Waterville, ME d 1906, mar 1. Eliz. N. Thompson 1855 Auburn, ME. and 2. Nettie L. Eagleton 1901 in Lowell MA. Chn below by 1st wife.

C1. Blanchetta, b 1856, d before 1876

C2. Rosalind, b 1858 d 1936 Amherst, NH. Mar 1. Wm. Frederick Burton 1875 in Charleston, VT and 2. ___Flanders ca 1892, and 3. Aaron Watson Emerson ca 1898 Framingham, MA, 2 chn.

D1. Cloiva Burton, b 1876 Danville, VT, mar 1. Ellison Aaron Emerson 1899, d 1958 Townsend, VT, bur Upton, MA, 2 chn.

E1. Lester Ellison Emerson, b 1900, mar Mildred Ellen Warren 1926

in Hopkinton, MA, d 1972 Dunbarton, NH
F1. Dorothy Priscilla Emerson, b 1928 Framingham, mar Geo. T. Appleton 1947 Toledo, OH, 2 chn: David, Dorothy Appleton.
F2. John Arthur Emerson, b 1930 Milford, MA, unmar
F3. Margery Frances Emerson, b 1931 mar Fred. Heading Sr., 1953 in Hopkinton, MA, 2 chn: Barbara and Donald Heading.
F4. Judith Ann Emerson, b 1944 Upton, MA mar 1. Richard Marecaux a son & dau. Mar 2. Ralph Jones
E2. Robert Edward Emerson, b 1920 Hopkinton, MA mar Shirley L. Young 1941 Salem, NH.
F1. Robert Norman Emerson, b 1942 mar Isadora Dacallos 1963 in Subic Bay, Philippines, 2 chn: Albert and Vivian Emerson.
F2. Jeannette Emerson, b 1943 Marlboro, MA mar Richard I. Mitobe 1966. A dau Antoinette Mitobe
F3. Lewis Ellison Emerson, b 1949, VT, unmar
D2. Arthur Morello Burton, b 1878 d 1888
C3. Emma Hubbard
C4. Georgianna Hubbard, b 1863 Palmyra, ME mar Mark Watson, Nashua, NH, d Nashua.
D1. Rena Watson D2. Roland Watson D3. Harold Watson
B2. Mary J., b 1834
B3. Charles H., b 1836
B4. Caroline E., b 1838
B5. Philip H. b 1840
B6. Oremand M., b 1842
B7. Georgiannah, b 1844
B8. George B., b 1846
B9. Ellen F., b 1849
A2. other chn of Philip Sr., one b 1787?
HUBERT in J 1299. In Vale G 1821. In St. Martin, Grouville and St. Saviour J 1668? Curr G. See CIFHS #14.
HUBERT, John of Boston, rem to Roxbury after 1670. Was poss related to Philip HUBBARD, qv, above. He had prob been in Capt. Isaac Johnson's Co., in King Philip Indian Wars, 1675/6. Mar Rebecca Wells?, who was bp 1683. Quite likely a J fam, not verified. OUTC.
A1. Rachel, bp 1684, mar 1690 John Holmes of Woodstock.
A2. Rebecca, bp 1684 mar 1701/2 David BISHOP of Woodstock
A3. Sarah, bp 1684, mar 1707 Josiah Bugbee of Woodstock.
A4. Mary, bp 1686 of Mashamequet, d Pomfret 1724. Mar 1711 Capt. Leicester Grosvenor, b 1676 Roxbury, MA, son of John and Esther (Clarke) Grosvenor.
B1. Jerusha B. Grosvenor B3. Anna B. Grosvenor
B2. Mary B. Grosvenor B4. Zeruiah Grosvenor B5. Sarah Grosvenor
A5. John, b 1689 Woodstock, d after 1731, mar Elizabeth ___
B1. Benjamin, a great many desc. See ONE THOUSAND YEARS OF HUB. HIST.
B2. Joseph, res Salisbury, MA ca 1781, a Tory, had at least 5 chn: Luther, Jesse, Olive who mar Ethel Reed, Sybil, who mar Joseph Whitney, and Parley who mar Anna Catlin.
B3. Jonas, res Canterbury, and Brooklyn, CT.
B4. Elizabeth, d 1754 B5. Timothy, d 1758
HUBERT, Johannah/Hannah, wife of John SWARTON/SWANTON, res No. Yarmouth ME. See SWARTON.
HUBERT, Ann mar John PERRIN, sr., d MA 1600s. (WINEINGER, Haddam, KS)
HIBBERT, HUBERT, Jeremiah mar Mrs. Patty of Manchester, MA 1776. OUTC
HUBERT, Daniel and George arrived in Phila. from Rotterdam on ship FRIENDSHIP 1741, master-Capt. Alex. THOMAS. OUTC.
HIBBERT, HUBERT?, Joseph, shipmaster in Essex Co., MA 1752-1773, commanded the HANNAH, DOLPHIN, BETSY, AURORA, WILLIAM, ABIGAIL, LISBON, MERRILL, YARMOUTH. His wife d 1779. (JOURNALS OF ASHLEY BOWEN)
HUBERT, from G to OH:
Andrew in GCO 1860, res Liberty Twp., GCO, served in Civil War.(Wolfe)

Catherine, b G, mar 1812 in GCO Thomas LENFESTEY, qv. (Sarchet)
Jane, a widow from G, settled in GCO 1830, with 4 daus under 20, and 2 young women. (Sarchet; GCO records)
Jane, and others res Butler Co., OH 1860. OUTC
Daniel, a candidate inelections in GCO ca 1824. (Wolfe)
Mary, b 1787 G mar 1810 John ROBBINS, qv. Mary d 1845. (Sarchet)
HUBERT, a fam from G to CAL in the 1800s.
HUELIN, HULLYN, HULEN, etc, etc, in J ca 1340. In St. Peter and St. Laurens J 1668. In St. Peter J 1749, in St. Lawrence J 1788. Curr G and J. A group of HUELIN companies based in J. Many resided in Boston, Salem and MRB MA in the 1700s and 1800s.
CAUTION: HULING fams in RI apparently from England. HULING, HULINGS and HEWLINGS in PA are of Swedish origin. Carolina HULIN, HULEN fams were prob French. (Ray Green Huling, Fitchburg, MA)
"HULEN-UNION-. There is found in Marblehead a remarkable case of variation of surname among descendants in the male line from a common ancestor. On the second book of records of the First Parish in that town occur the births, deaths and marriages of two groups of persons of the family in question, each group consisting of father, children grandchildren, etc, the fathers appear to have been brothers. In the first group the surname occurs 27 times between 1762 and 1829, being written HULION once, UNION nine times, HULING four times and HULEN 13 times; modern representatives of this group use the form last mentioned. In the second group the surname is mentioned eleven times between 1779 and 1833, being written HULING six times and UNION five times; the living members of this group bear the latter name. It is hard to determine from these records which is the earliest form of the name. Elias HULION married Feb. 7, 1762 Elizabeth Selman. His children, baptized between 1762 and 1777 are all called "children of Elias and Elizabeth Union." Two of them at marriage are called HULING, and three HULEN. The family according to tradition had its origin in the Isle of Guernsey. Perhaps it was the difficulty of preserving the French pronounciation of the name, together with an infrequent use of the pen by the early members, wich occasioned the present variation. The name seems to have been at first HULIN, as it is now found in Normandy and in Paris. " (Ray Green Huling)
See records in Essex Co., MA for much more data on this family. (NEHGS Vol40; MHS; MRB VR; Emmerton; Census; Essex Coll; Clemens; name curr in Roslindale, MA; BICKNELL GEN)
HULIN, Abraham, drowned near Cape Cod 1822 age 40.
HULEN, ARchibald, res MRB 1810. An Archibald S. mar 1807 Sarah, Mrs. C.R. Leach, in MRB, MA. An Archibald lost on Grand Banks 1811, wife Sarah d 1805, age 32. Chn?
HULEN, HUELIN, Elias, b 1733 G, d 1809 MRB. Wrecked off Nfld. 1751? saved by Capt. Selman in a MRB fishing boat. Carried back to MA, he mar Elizabeth Selman 1762, poss had 2nd wife? An Elias, son of Capt. Elias and Polly, d 1822, age 25.
A1. Capt. Elias HULEN and other chn? Elias mar 1820 in MRB Olive Putnam, d 1827 MRB?
HULEN, Elizabeth res MRB 1810. Elizabeth wife of Elias d 1815 age 70.
HULEN, Francis mar Susannah NICHOLAS in NY 1696, poss from C.I.?
HULIN, Jacob, b Fayette Co., PA 1780, mar Nancy Saddler, res Wills Twp., GCO, then in Cumberland Twp. OUTC. See Cambr. Library, GCO.
HULIN, Louisa J, mar Benj. DENNIS 1825 MRB. OUTC.
HULEN, Mary Elizabeth, dau of Capt. Elias and Polly, d 1797 MRB.
HULEN, Sarah mar Nicholas GALE 1799 MRB.

HUGH, HUGHES in J1309. In St. Mary and St. Laurens J 1607, and in St. Heliers J 1749. Curr research on Peter HUGHES b 1821 J, see CIFHS #4, #6.

HUE, HUGH, HUGHES. "The HEWS, HEWES, HUGHES fams of Boston are particularly difficult to trace.". (Underhill) This may be because some of them were from Jersey and the name variations were not realized as being the same name. Jersey origin for some of these families has not been explored, so far as compiler knows. HUGH and HUGHES are south-of-England surnames, often Welsh.

HUGHES, Clement, poss from C.I.? A witness for the will of John KNIGHT, qv, 1721 in Newington, NH, and in Portsmouth 1720 for will of John JANVRIN, qv., both from Jersey.

HUES, Mary from J? a widow in Boston 1720, friend of MAHIER, qv, from J

HUGHES, Peter, b 1820 J, desc in Australia.

HEWS, Philip in ME 1666, OUTC. (Noyes)

HUSE, Sarah mar John 1700s and res Thompson, CT. OUTC. (STARR GEN)

A1. Jonas Huse Wilson mar Mary Starr, dau of Eben. Starr. Jonas a shoe maker, who d 1841 age 57. See DE JEAN and DE JERSEY, re Starr fam.

HULET, HULLETT, HOWLETT, George, came with CARTERET on ship PHILIP to NJ 1665. HOWLETT is now curr in C.I., but not listed by Stevens. Note HULET in Shrewsbury, NJ Militia 1790, also John, Robert, Samuel and William, the latter in Upper Freehold Comp. OUTC.

HULIT, Daniel and John in NJ Militia 1790. OUTC

HULETT, HEWLETT in OLD FAMS OF SALISBURY. OUTC.

HUNKING, HUNKINS, etc noted in early New England. The varied spellings might suggest that some were orig. HOCQUIN of J, pron. close to Hoken, in J 1668 and 1749.

HUNTER, Patricia, b 1900s, G, evacuated with her sister Jean from G in WWII, to England, trained as teacher and returned to G to teach at Amherst. Later, she and sister Jean, a nurse, settled in Toronto, ONT. Their bro Alan teaches at Elizabeth College, C.I. Patricia mar ___Murphy. (GUERNSEY PRESS, Dec. 5, 1979)

HUNTER, John, age 27 of Harrisburgh, ONT, b J, son of John and Eliz. (CAREY) HUNTER, mar 1866 Geraldina AUGER, age 52 of Harrisburg, ONT, b Dumfries, dau of ___Vrooman and R. Coleman.

HUNTOON, Philip, b ca 1664? d 1752 very ancient, said to have come from Jersey. However, HUNTOON is not, according to what info compiler has, an old C.I. surname. Poss that he was a son of Wm. Hunton of England. Perhaps came to America on a Jersey ship? This surname in Wiltshire, Hampshire, Cambridgeshire, Yorkshire and Berkshire, England. Compiler suggests fam may have res for a short time in J. Much data on this fam available; booklet, 33 pp on HUNTOON FAM; Belknap's HIST; Penhallow's INDIAN WARS; Virkus; PHILIP HUNTOON AND HIS DESC by Daniel Huntoon, Canton, MA 1881; GREELEY GEN; MASS SOLDIERS AND SAILORS; Morley Library, Painesville, OH; Adj. Gen. Report for NH, Vol 2; HIST OF BARNARD VT; Noyes; Painesville and Concord, OH Cems; SOME DESC OF PHILIP FLOOD OF NEWBURY, MA; TYLER GEN, Vol 1; SWETT GEN; Census; MAINE RECORDER; PEABODY GEN; Cleveland, OH VR; WASHINGTON CO., OH MARRIAGES; Cutter, Vol 4; Mrs. Gregory Smith, Webster, IND; Mrs. Lois Blake, Caldwell, OH; Marion Rose, So. Moston, MA; Walter Welch, Peabody, MA; Georgia Curtis, Eugene, OR; E.M. Huntoon, Cleveland, OH; Batchelder Gen; Michael I. Killy, Evanston, ILL; Larry A. Severns, Citrus Hts., CAL; Dearborn's HIST OF SALISBURY, NH; Dow's HAMPTON, NH Wheeler's HIST OF NEWPORT, NH; Rasmussen; OHIO GEN. SOC. REPORT, 1873 1976; Eastman's HIST OF ANDROVER, NH; HIST OF LITTLETON, NH, by Jackson; HIST. OF CANTERBURY, NH; ANCESTRY AND DESC OF THE IOWA HUNTOONS, by Joe C. Huntoon Jr., 1971; Chase Coll., in Wiscasset, ME Library.

HUNTOON. Some data on desc in WRCIC. Philip mar 1. Betsy Hall, and 2. Hannah ___. See sources, and WRCIC.
A1. Samuel, b ca 1689 Exeter, NH
A2. Philip b ca 1694 Exeter, d 1780, mar 1. Ann Eastman and 2. ?Elliot?
A3. John, b 1696, mar Mary Rundlett, many, many desc.
A4. Sarah, b 1703 Exeter or Kingston, NH, d.y.
A5. Elizabeth b Kingston, mar 1725 Deacon Joseph Elkins
A6. Sarah again, b Kingston, mar 1729 Darby Kelly.
A7. Nathaniel, b 1724, estate settled 1793. Mar 1742 Anna Dearborn, and 2. Martha Judkins. Connection with this fam in some doubt.
HUPPER. "HOOPER ISLAND...was originally named HUPPER ISLAND, the Hupper family being natives of the Channel Islands." (ISLANDS OF NEW ENGLAND, by Hazel Young, 1945, p. 96) Poss this name was HUBERT? See HOOPER and HUBBARD.
HUPPER, John Jr. of St. George, ME was part owner of the ELIZA HUPPER of Machias, ME 1841. (Ship Registers of Machias, 1780-1930, Pt.1)
HUPPER to US from the Channel Islands. (Lady McKie, Ottawa, ONT) Roscoe Hupper, marine lawyer in New York. His widow res in Tenant's Harbor, ME in the summer.
HUQUET, Claude in Boston 1800. Was this a LE HUQUET of C.I.?
HUREL, HURREL, etc, noted in US. Some may be HUREL of G, curr G. Note that some settled in GCO middle 1800s, where other G folk lived. (Conner-Eynon Cem. Book)
HUXTER, Wm., b Yorkshire, ngland, grain importer and exporter, res G. (Kimberlee Perkins, Woodland, CAL)
A1. Elizabeth, b 1862 Elizabeth, NJ d 1925 Los Angeles, CAL. Mar Oliver Brentnall DAWSON.
B1. Brentnall Oliver Dawson Jr., b 1894 Caldwell, NJ mar 1920 El Paso, TX, Adella Alma De Berry, b 1895 Gonzales, TX. Brentnall d 1957.
C1. Elizabeth Catherine Dawson, b 1921 San Diego, CAL
D1. Kimberlee S. Dawson, b 1948 Washington, DC mar 1971 in Davis, CAL Frederick C. Perkins, b 1948 Mokelumne Hill, CAL.
HYER, HIER, noted in NJ and MA records. Poss that some began as AHIER? of C.I.? (Cambridge and Boston records; Stillwell's MISCELLANY)
IBBERSON, George of England, mar Mary Ann Storor?, dau of Abraham and Elizabeth in G? and rem to Stewartville, MN. This is not an old C.I. surname, but IBBITSON is curr in G. They res 1870 in Racine, WIS. Mary Ann d 1897 age 78. (Mrs. Lloyd Cole, Colville, WA)
A1. George b ca 1841 in England or C.I.
A2. Ernest, b ca 1844 WIS
A3. Frances, b ca 1844 WIS.
A4. Mary Ann, b ca 1845 WIS.
A5. Charlotte, b ca 1849 WIS.
A6. Thomas, b ca 1852 WIS.
IBBERSON, Elizabeth, b ca 1819 J, poss sister of above George? rem to MN, mar 1846Abner De Graff in Racine, WIS. (Mrs. Lloyd Cole, WA)
A1. Abner De Graff Jr., b ca 1848 ILL, mar Eliz. __, who d 1884 Dexter, MN, age 37.
B1. Bertha De Graff, b ca 1870 MN
B2. William A. De Graff, b ca 1872
B3. Arthur J. De Graff, b ca 1874
B4. George De Graff, b ca 1878
B5. Lunrae B. De Graff, b ca 1880
B6. Bin James De Graff, b 1882.
INGRAM, fam in Detroit, MI area ca 1900 from G. INGRAM is a Scottish and English surname, curr in G and J.
INGROUVILLE, INGOUVILLE in G since 1200s. See Q.A. IN CANADA.
INGERVILLE, INGROUVILLE, Alvina of Gaspe, QUE mar Geo. DE VOUGES, qv.
INMAN, noted in CT with several C.I. fams, but none found by compiler with C.I. links. However, INMAN is curr in J.

JACKSON, old G surname, curr G and J.
JACKSON, Capt.Clement in Portsmouth, NH 1694, mar 1700 Sarah Hall. She

admin. estate in 1708, taxed as widow 1708-1715. Mar 2. after 1717 Joseph HUBBARD, living in Boston, MA 1738. (Noyes) OUTC. See Noyes for other Jacksons, OUTC, but poss that some were from C.I. See also NEHGS Vol 39.

JACKSON, early in GCO, poss connected with the Guernsey Islanders who settled there early 1800s and later. OUTC.

JACKSON, Eliz. 1745-1824, of Jackson Twp., GCO.

JACKSON, Rachel, 1794-1876, of GCO JACKSON, Henry, 1770-1838, of GCO

JACKSON, John, from C.I.? in Salem, MA with wife Margaret and son John b ca 1634. Some Jackson fams res Gloucester, MA very early. (NEHGS Vol 6)

JACKSON, John early at Blue Pt., ME, d ca 1663 leaving widow Eleanor, who later mar Jonas BAILEY, qv of same place, having son John. (NEHGS Vol. 39/41)

These JACKSON marriages took place in Portsmouth, NH middle 1700s. Note that spouses were poss from C.I. fams. (NEHGS Vol 82)

JACKSON Martha mar John PENDEXTER, qv, 1774 Portsmouth, NH.

JACKSON, Rachel mar Joseph LOWE, QV, Ports. Samuel mar Sarah LOW 1760.

JACQUES, JAMES, old in J. Many in colonial America, but none verified that compiler could find, as from C.I.

JACQUES, Henry, carpenter, b 1620, settled Newbury, MA, freeman in 1669, mar Anna KNIGHT, qv, in Newbury, and d 1687. If Anna KNIGHT was formerly Anna CHEVALIER, then Henry may also have been from C.I. OUTC. (NJ GENESIS, 1956)

JACOB, curr G and J. Not researched by compiler.

JAMES in J 1528 and 1607. Old in G, both as James and JACQUES.

JAMES, Francis, b ca 1634 C.I.? a seaman and baker in Hampton, NH, 1670, mar Hannah Swain. (HIST OF HAMPTON, NH) OUTC.

JANDRON, JEANDRON, old in J and curr. Cf also GENDRON, old French name.

JANDRON, Jean to SC early (Filby) In Manikintown, VA 1659. OUTC

JANDRON, Francis Lyster, b ca 1850 J, educated there, res Gaspe, QUE, then Ontario, Detroit MI and Boston MA. Served from 1921-1964 the FIRST CHURCH OF CHRIST SCIENTIST in Boston, as practitioner, teacher, committeeman, trustee and Director. He d 1968? Boston. (Q.A. IN CANADA: GENEALOGIE DES FAMILIES LE MOIGNAN, of Gaspe; Christian Science Monitor and Church records, Boston, MA)

JANVRIN in J 1607 as VALPY DIT JANVRIN earlier. VALPY in J very early.

JANVRIN in St. Peter, St. Heliers and St. Brelade J 1668. JANVRIN recorded in SLCity as coming to America from Manche, France; St. Lawrence Jersey and St. Heliers Jersey. One, unverified as yet, report says three Janvrin bros. came from J to New England, settling in 3 towns, Seabrook, NY, Newbury, MA and Salisbury, MA early in 1800s. These late arrivals are said to be desc of the same John JANVRIN who fathered John and George of Seabrook and Boston, who came to America in the 1600s. The later settlers were not researched by compiler. CAUTION: TRIAL CHARTS.

JANVRIN, Jean/John, b 1671 J under surname of VALPY dit JANVRIN, mar Elizabeth LE COUTEUR, qv of J. This fam may be desc from Nicholas VALPY dit Janvrin, in St. Brelade J 1624. The fam legally dropped the VALPY in the English court early 1700s. In the 1500s this fam had ships and traded with the English and Welsh ports. One branch settled in Southampton, England 1560, where they prospered. A royal pardon was granted one member of the family, who had been a privateersman, verging on piracy.

JANVRIN, Jean, son of the above Jean and Elizabeth, came to Portsmouth, NH in the late 1600s. He mar Elizabeth KNIGHT/CHEVALIER, qv, in 1706 She was the dau of Richard KNIGHT/CHEVALIER of J, and Mary Sherburne

Sloper of Portsmouth, NH. Widowed, she mar 2. 1720 Joseph Adams, son of Joseph of Newington, NH. There is much data in records of NH, and also some data in J, and in Southampton, England. RESEARCHER: Please note that MS by Marguerite SYVRET of J gives different parents for the immigrant John JANVRIN. JANVRIN desc were in Revere, Everett, Stoneham, Wakefield, Groveland, Merrimack, Bradford, Rowley, Newburyport, Salisbury, Amesbury, MA and some in Plaistow and Seabrook, NH. It is poss that some of these fams are not of this line, but of another line of JANVRINS, also emigrants to America from J. (Noyes; Savage II, III; Pope, 155,248,300,340; Boston VR; NEHGS Vols. 81, 82, and 88; Seabrook, NH Cem. Stones; Dover, NH HIST. SOC; NH Gen. Records Court, Church, Estate & Army records; Eben Putnam's MS in Salem, MA; Essex Co. records; JANVRIN GEN, not found by compiler; PICKERING GEN; BRACKETT GEN; KINGSBURY GEN; SHANNON GEN; FISHER GEN; HIST. OF HAMPTON FALLS, NH by Warren Brown; Hurd's HIST OF ROCKINGHAM; PORTSMOUTH FAMS by Bartlett; Mrs. Malcolm Loring, Portland, OR; Donald Pitcher, No. Haven, CT; John Herlihy, Silver Spring, MD; Mary Hatch, Salisbury, MA; Mrs. William Goldsmith, Marblehead, MA; Mrs. Charles Carroll, Marblehead, MA.)

A1. John, bp 1709, schoolmaster in Kittery 1732, after grad from Harvard 1728. He mar Elizabeth Stickney, b 1722 Newbury, MA, d at Seabrook, NH 1809 age 87. They res Berwick, ME 1743, and Newington, NH 1751. At least 4 chn.

B1. John, b 1754 Seabrook, NH mar Olive Griffith

B2. William, b 1756? d 1839 age 79, mar Abigail Adams, dau of ?Dr. J. Adams, who died at Barnstead 1799. Chn b Seabrook, NJ. (HIST. OF BARNSTEAD, NH)

C1. Joseph Adams b 1786? mar at Exeter, NH Lydia A. Colcord, and mar 2. 1809, Newbury, MA, Joanna Thurlow, b 1890? dau of Joseph and Joanna (Chase) Thurlow

D1. Betsy Adams, b 1809, mar 1. John SCribner 1828, ? and 2.? a Pike of Salisbury, MA.

D2. Joseph, b 1811, mar 1833 Elizabeth Ladd b 1813, of Newburyport, MA, d 1894 in LYnn, MA, dau of Capt. Daniel Ladd of Newburyport and Elizabeth HUSE, qv.

E1. Joseph A., b 1835 E2. Mary Ann Ladd b 1837

E3. Elizabeth Chase, sometimes written Elizabeth HUSE JANVRIN, b 1838, Newbury, MA, d LYnn, MA 1915. Mar Charles Otis ALLEY, qv b 1830 Newbury, d 1894 Lynn, MA.

F1. Lizzie M. ALLEY, b 1855 d 1924 Lynn, MA, mar George H. RENO, see RENOUF, who d 1930.

G1. Elsie Reno, b 1892, who mar Everet B. Stacey, no issue

F2. Lucy Alley, b 1857, prob d.y.

F3. Jennie Kelton Alley, b 1859 d 1936, mar William Sproul, who d 1940.

G1. Lulu Gertrude Sproul, b 1883, d 1979 MRB, MA.

F4. Lulu B. Alley, b 1860, d 1922 mar Henry J. BARTON, who d 1929

G1. Alice Beatrice Barton, 1884-1980

F5. Ida H. Alley, b 1863 d 1913, mar Frank G. Olin, 1861-1928

F6. Charles A. Alley, b 1868 d 1915, mar Lynn, MA 1915 Florence Aborn

F7. Frank B. Alley, 1870-1919, unmar

F8. Lillian Mable Alley, b 1874 Lynn, MA, d1951 Utica, NY, mar in Lynn Elmer R. LEGRO, qv, b 1871 d 1937 Utica, NY.

G1. Brainard LEGRO, b 1894 Lynn, d 1972 Utica, NY, mar Frances E. Sheehan, 1895-1931.

H1. Robert LEGRO, b 1926, mar Janet Wenner, NY, b 1926, 4 chn: Bonnie, Sherrie, Richard and Jeffrey LEGRO.
H2. Richard H. LEGRO, b 1930, mar in NY, Hilda S. Brady, b 1932 2 chn: Brady and Hilda LEGRO.
G2. Lillian LEGRO, b 1909 Pittsfield, MA mar Andrew W. Lewis, b 1909 PA, d 1961
F9. Joseph Adams Janvrin Alley, b 1875 mar 1. Alice Prince?, had dau Marion, and mar 2. Frieda WEBBER.
F10. Lotta Alley, b 1878, d 1908, mar Charles Wallace Marsh, b 1872 Cheslea, MA, d 1942 MRB.
G1. Beatrice Marsh, b 1903 Lynn, MA, mar 1944 William Martin Goldsmith, b 1894 MRB, d 1977
G2. Dorothy Lillian Marsh, b 1907 Lynn, mar 1934 Dr. Adelbert Parrott, b 1910 Lynn, MA.
H1. Jane Parrott, b 1936 mar 1961 Rev. Ira Gregg Carter, b1929 2 chn: Catherine and Scott Carter
H2. Marcia Parrott, b 1938, mar 1964 Alexander Akerholm, d 1968
F11. Ernest Linwood Alley, b 1879 Lynn, MA d 1948, mar Annie Thurber.
G1. Lotta ALLEY, b 1908 Lynn, MA mar Edward K. Hempel, b 1903 Attleboro, MA, son of Carl and Grace.
H1. Edward King Hempel, Jr., b 1932 mar 1. Margaret Perham, 4 chn, and 2. Linda Johnston. Chn: Marcia, Karen Goldsmith and Lynn Mulligan.
G2. Doris Louise Alley, b 1911 mar Charles Carroll, res MRB.
H1. Paul Dana Carroll, b 1939 Salem, MA mar Sue Belles Parker 1970, res Glendale, AZ, 2 chn: Sheri and Christy Carroll.
H2. Richard Dexter Carroll, b 1943 mar Judith Henderson 1965, res E. Sandwich, Cape Cod, MA, 3 chn: Elizabeth, Steven, and Deborah Carroll.
E4. George Albert, b 1846 E5. Charles A., b 1847
E6. Helen M., b 1853, d 1923, mar Nelson Christopher, 1844-1907.
E7. Jennie, mar ___Kelton.
F1. Edme Kelton, mar June ___, b Ireland.
G1. Pert Kelton, the noted stage, TV and movie actress, 1903-1968, mar Ralph Bell. 2 sons: Brian and Stephen Bell
G2. Gladys Kelton, b ca 1899.
E8. other chn? Perhaps a Fred. Janvrin belongs here?
D3. Joanna Thurlow, b 1813, mar 1830 Jonathan D. Eaton and 2. 1833 Lorenzo D. Ross. Chn?
D4. John, b 1816, clerk in Newburyport, MA mar 1842 Eliz. Chase.
E1. Cynthia, b 1844 E2. Fidelia, b 1846 E3. John Quincy, b 1848
D5. George, b 1818 mar Mary Chase, 1839 and res Newbury, MA. 1848
E1. George, b 1840 E2. Dennis A., b 1842 E3. Myron Fillmore,b/
D6. Hiram Gilman, b 1820 mar 1843 Emeline Felch, Newbury, MA, poss 7 chn? (Pitcher records) A son Hiram b 1845
D7. Jane, poss 2 Janes?, one in 1822 and one in 1823. Jane SWETT mar Geo. A. George of Newburyport, or George Jefferson?
D8. Mary Ann, b 1825, d.y.?
D9. William Swett/Small, b 1827, mar either Pratt Revere, or Revere Pratt??
D10. Mary Elizabeth, b 1829 mar 1849 Robert J. Torrey, b 1827, son of Joseph and Ruth, d 1895. More data available?
E1. Roland Torrey, b 1850, unmar
E2. Mary Torrey, b 1852 mar George Osgood 1879, Newburyport,3 chn.
F1. Jessie Eloise Osgood, b 1882 F2. George R. Osgood, b 1885
F3. Mary H. Osgood, b 1893 mar __Pitcher, a son Don in NewHaven,CT

D11. Ruth Ann, b 1832 mar Albert Randall or Geo. Randall 1849
D12. Frank/Francis Andrew, b 1834 Newbury, MA.
C2. other chn?
B3. James, b 1758? mar 1786 Mary/Polly Chase, b 1765?, dau of Dr. Joshua Chase of Hampton Falls, NH. James paid taxes in H.F. 1812 to 1822, had 4 chn. Mary d 1839 age 74? James d 1822 age 64.
C1. Eliza?
C2. David, had the homestead, mar Mary Towle of Hampton, NH. He d 1878.
D1. Edwin, repr. in 1883, built house in Hampton Falls 1867, mar Sally ___.
E1. Bertram T., b 1869 was in lumber business with father, mar Mary Brown, dau of Charles T.
E2. Charles, b 1868 Hampton Falls, NH
E3. Fred, b 1855? E4. Frank, b 1865
C3. Joshua, mar dau of Nathaniel Hubbard Dodge, and d 1875. His wife d 1888 age 92.
D1. James D. D2,3,4, daus including Louise who mar John A. Merrill.
C4. Mary, b 1787, d 1871. Mar 1807 Capt. Nathaniel Perkins, b 1771 in Hampton Falls, NH, d 1848
B4. George, bp 1762 Hampton Falls, NH, inherited the homestead, mar Dolly Lovering, Kensington, NH, who was b 1763, d 1848 age 79. George d 1841 age 79.
C1. Sally, b 1790 poss mar Levi Veasy? KIngston First CH, 1811.
C2. Dolly, b 1792 Seabrook, NH, a Dolly d 1864 age 72.
C3. George, b 1794 C4. Lorany, Loreana, b 1797 C5. Ruth
C6. Bertha Lampre, b 1798 C7. Fanny, b 1801.
C8. Jefferson, b 1803 Seabrook, NH, inherited the homestead and in 1840 mar Mary Wadleigh of Meredith. Rem to Hampton Falls 1853. Jefferson was in the State Assembly.
D1. Miranda, mar Henry McDevitt, had son Wm. Henry McDevitt
D2. Eliza, mar Joseph T. Sanborn, had dau Fanny Ward Sanborn
D3. Geo. Albert, b ca 1846, din Washington, DC, in Civil War.
C9. Miranda, b 1805 d 1837 age 32.
C10. Eliza. One Eliza Janvrin, b 1808 Seabrook, wife of Nathan Brown late of Southampton, was dead 1893 in Seabrook, NH.
B5. Elizabeth, b ca 1764 mar Wm. Sweet or SWETT.
A2. Elizabeth, b 1711 admitted to Newington Church 1727
A3. George, bp 1713, d 1789, age 77, of Portsmouth, a mariner, mar 1774 Abigail (Pickering) Patterson, widow, dau of Thomas and D Dorothy Pickering. She d 1832, age 100. He was active in civil life and in maritime affairs.
B1. Mendum, bp 1746/7, mar at Newington 1772 Mrs. Katherine Lange, age 53 in 1804, a widow. Mendum was a mariner, and served as Officer in Capt. Pierce Long's Co. at Janvrin's Island 1776. Will proved 1783. Mar 2. Martha Marshall. (NEHGS Vol 82)
C1. Thomas, bp 1776 C3. Martha Moulton, b 1780 /
C2. Mary, bp 1777 C4. Abigail/Nabby, b 1782
B2. John, mariner, mar at Newington, NH 1772 Katherine Lange. See above.
C1. Elizabeth Mendum, bp 1775, mar Capt. Pierce Long, son George.
C2. George C3. Thomas, inherited house and wharves,in will.
A4. Mary, bp 1715?, mar 1743 at Newington, Thomas Pickering, 1703-1786, son of Thomas. He had mar 1. 1726/7 Mary Downing, and had 8 chn?
JANVRIN, John, b ca 1769, either part of above fam, or came from C.I. He was son of John JANVRIN, and mar Sarah Locke, dau of Thomas and Elizabeth (Collins) Locke, 1773-1844. 5 chn. (SLCITY RECORDS)
A1. Belinda, b 1801 Seabrook, NH, d 1872 mar Edmond PILLING.

A2. Denis, b ca 1803 mar Sarah ___, a dau Helen mar Fred. W. Sargent in Chelsea, MA

A3. John, b ca 1805 A4. Sally, b ca 1807 A5. Olive G., b ca 1809.

JANVRIN, Joshua N. belongs to one of above fams, b ca 1776, lost at sea 1817 age 41. Mar Mary French. He was called grandson of emigrant John, 5 chn: Susan, Joshua b 1802 Seabrook, NH, Matilda, Mary J. and Salley.

JANVRIN, William, b 1799 Seabrook, NH d 1853, mar Mary Walton, 1805-1898, and/or Rebecca Walton 1823 Mary was dau of Jonathan and Polly (Brown) Walton. (SLCITY records)

A1. John A., b 1822 Seabrook, d 1849 A3. Emma H, 1841-1859

A2. Wallace, 1832-1854 A4. Sarah E., 1845-1872 A5. Frank, 1846-1892

JANVRIN, George, bro of first John above, b ca 1682?, son of Jean and Elizabeth LE COUTEUR, LE COSTEUR, JANVRIN of J, rem to Boston and mar there 1719 Susanna MONTEIR?, poss MONTAIS? LE MONTAIS of J? He d ca 1735. Susanna remar by 1738. One ch by Janvrin? (Mrs. E.M. Loring, Portland, OR)

A1. Mary, b 1727 Boston, d 1761 Needham, MA, mar Nathaniel Fisher, b 1723 Dedham, MA, who d 1807. He mar 2.? He was son of John and Elizabeth (Hunting) Fisher of Dedham. 6 chn by Mary.

B1. Susanna Fisher, b 1747, d 1765, mar Oliver Mills 1764

B2. Rebecca Fisher, b 1750 Needham, d 1810 Dover, NH. Mar 1777 Ebenezer Tebbets, b 1747 Rochester, NH d 1804 Dover, NH, son of Edw. and Mary. Other chn?

C1. Mary Tebbets, b 1778 Rochester, NH d 1821 Saco, ME, mar Richard Cutts Shannon 1801 in Dover. (See SHANNON GEN, by Hodgdon)

D1. Caroline Shannon, b 1802, d 1803

D2. Charles Tebbets Shannon, b 1803 mar Jane Randall Stanwood.

D3. Abigail Shannon, b 1805/6 mar Calvin Locke

D4. Richard Shannon b 1807/8 d 1809

D5. Mary Barker Shannon, b 1810 mar Edwin Jennison

D6. Samuel Tebbets Shannon, b 1812, d.y.

D7. Samuel Tebbets Shannon again, b 1814 mar 1. Rebecca Scammon and 2. Martha Ann Prentice Stevens.

D8. James, b 1816 mar Lucy Newcomb Saville and 2. Sarah H. Hawes.

D9. Caroline Shannon again, b 1819 Saco, ME, mar Cyrus Kingsbury Goodale, as Caroline FEchem Shannon in 1845. She d 1881 Lancaster, MA, and he in 1880. He was son of Paul Jr. and Azubah (Newton) Goodale. 4 chn.

E1. Clara Louise Goodale, b 1846 Worcester, MA d 1914 W. Boylston, MA, mar 1875 Lancaster, Harlan Wm. Kingsbury, b 1847 in Chester, VT, d 1914, bur Sterling, MA, 4 chn

F1. Helen Shannon Kingsbury, b 1876 Sterling, MA, d 1960 N. Waterford, ME, mar 1. 1909, Charles Frank Newell, his 2nd wife, and 2. Alley L. Harrington 1926, no issue

F2. Carrie Blake Kingsbury, b 1878 d 1958 N. Waterford, ME. Mar 1905 Charles Alvin Hersey, b 1878 Waterford, mar in Sterling, MA d 1966 Rumford Center, ME, son of Ezra and Mary Hersey.7chn

G1. Louise Laurestine Hersey b 1907 N. Waterford, ME mar 1930 John Malcolm Loring, b 1906 Bath, ME, son of John Mason and Priscilla Jane BALLEM Loring, the latter of Mt. Albion, PEI, Canada. 3 chn.

H1. Priscilla Louise Loring, b 1931 Col. Spgs., COL mar Vernon H. Leach 1952 Okanogan, WA, 4 chn: Barbara, Richard, Glenn and Douglas Leach

H2. John Malcolm Loring Jr, b 1934 Mancos, COL mar Rose Marie Verzal 1953 in UT, dau of Frank and Eva (Groh) Verzal of of Croatia, 3 chn: Margaret Rose, Catherine Lynn and Jacquel-ine Anne Loring.

H3. Janet Carole Loring, b 1938 Denver, COL mar Lawrence F. Coleman, b Coos Bay, OR, 3 chn: Carolyn, Frederick and Susan Coleman

G2. Leroy Harlan Hersey, b 1908 N. Waterford, ME mar 1934 MD. Laura G. Knighton.

H1. Paul Kinsbury Hersey, b 1945, adopted, mar Joyce Sisson, 2 chn: Paul and Todd Hersey

G3. Alfred Ezra Hersey, b 1911, ME, mar 1937 Kingston, RI, Eleanor Streeter, 3 chn.

H1. Harry H. Hersey, b 1938 Prov., RI mar Jane Hummerstone, 2 chn: Laura and Karen Hersey

H2. Hope Hersey, b 1939 mar 1962 Donald T. Lester, 2 chn: Naomi and Jeffrey Lester, b Madison, WIS

H3. Harlan S. Hersey, b 1940 Prov., RI mar Nancy Dadekhian 1971

G4. Mary Caroline Hersey, b 1913 Waterford, ME mar Harold A.Hil-key, b 1912 Denver, 2 chn.

H1. John Charles Hilkey, b 1943 COL, mar Alice Joyce Williams of England, 2 sons: Jason and James Hilkey

H2. Michael H. Hilkey, b 1948 COL, mar Gloria Cummings in IND. 3 chn: Tracey, Dustin and Anthony Hilkey.

G5. Alvin K. Hersey, b 1916 ME, mar 1938 Margaret E. Murray, b 1918 Chatham, NB, Canada, 4 chn:

H1. Margaret Julia Hersey, b 1938 MD, mar Vincent Robert Wills of ME, 3 chn: Sharon, Deborah and Jennifer Wills.

H2. Albany K. Hersey II, b 1940 Annapolis, MD mar Paula Alma M Morin, b ME, 5 chn, div, mar 2. Roberta Thomas 1977 Auburn, ME, 2 chn: Kenneth, Scott, John, Brenda, Paul, Brian, Joline Lynn Hersey.

H3. Barbara Jean Hersey, b 1942 Annapolis, MD mar Amos A. Mc Callum, 2 sons: Patrick and Christopher McCallum

H4. Elizabeth Carole Hersey, b 1943 Old Town, ME mar Harold Hale Bartley Jr., a dau Bethany Bartley

G6. Mabelle Helena Hersey, b 1917 Waterford, ME mar 1938 Belmont, MA Warren E. Colburn, 3 chn.

H1. Lois C. Colburn, b 1945 mar W. Carson, adopted dau.

H2. Warren Colburn Jr, mar Leslie Blizard

H3. Kenneth H. Colburn, b 1952, mar A. Armitage, div.

G7. Charles Wm. Hersey, b 1924 ME, mar Jean F. Howard, 4 chn

H1. James C. Hersey, b ME, mar Linda/Laura Herwerth, 3 chn.

H2. Jane M. Hersey, b 1950 mar James Chandler, a dau

H3. David W. Hersey II, b 1952, mar Vickie Eden, 2 chn

H4. Ralph Edwin Hersey, b 1955 Conway, NH mar Robin (Clark) Baillargeon, Brunswick, ME.

F3. Mabel Louise Kingsbury, b 1879 Sterling, d 1936 CT.

F4. William Goodale Kingsbury, b 1881 mar 1911 Helen F. Wheeler.

G1. Francis C. Kingsbury, b 1912 d.y.

G2. Doris Kingsbury, b 1914 Sterling, MS, unmar, res Boston

G3. Helen Kingsbury, b 1915, unmar

G4. Frank Wm. Kingsbury, b 1916 mar Mary Alice Leathers, b 1920 Fargo, ND, 4 chn.

H1. Wm. Leathers Kingsbury, b 1947 Boston, MA

H2. Daniel Frank Kingsbury, b 1949 Clinton, MA

H3. Lawrence J. Kingsbury, b 1950 mar Alice Maddox

E2. Mary S. Goodale, b 1849 d 1870, unmar d 1893 unmar

E3. Henry J. Goodale, 1853-1870 E4. Charles F. Goodale, b 1863/

B3. Mary Fisher, b 1753 mar Rev. Joseph Haven of Rochester, NH 1776. See HAVEN GEN.
B4. Nathaniel Fisher, b 1754, Rev. War soldier.
B5. Janvrin Fisher, b 1758 rem to Dover, NH. Poss d of yellow fever 1798 in Durham, NH. Had mar at Rochester, NH?Sarah Gage, b 1764 dau of Capt. John Gage. Poss a son Silas Fisher?
B6. Lucy Fisher, by 2nd wife, b 1764, d 1836, mar 1784 James How, M.D. of Rochester, NH
B7. George Fisher, b 1765 mar Elizabeth Ellis of Dedham 1789
B8. Susanna Fisher, b 1774, mar Joseph Richards, Jr. of Roxbury, MA 1808. See RICHARDS GEN by Morse.

Note: A Janvrin Fisher Pinkham mar in MA? 1832 Lozette Knox. (NEHGS 69)
Much more info. available on this fam, some not seen by compiler. See records of Salisbury, Newbury, Chelsea, Methuen in MA, and records of Hampton, Seabrook, Rockingham, Kingston, Portsmouth, Exeter, Great Falls, etc, in NH.
JANVRIN,"Capt. Daniel of the Island of Jersey, now resident in New England, 1681" (Perley 2)
JANVRIN, Florence, b J, sister of the Seigneur of La Haule, J, mar in 1800s? a Mr. Armstrong and went to Ottawa, ONT. (Lady McKie,Ottawa)
JANVRIN, John, arrived in Boston 1715 on ship KING GEORGE from Surinam, with Philip Reason, Nicholas Arthur Marr, and Richard Sprague, a cooper. (Whitemore)
JANVRIN, John of Saybrook, mar Jane SWETT, b 1752, d 1833 age 81, sister of the Wm. Swett who mar Elizabeth JANVRIN. John d 1837, age 83.
JANVRIN, John and John Lord were in Falmouth 1643. (Underhill)
JANVRIN, James Monroe of Salisbury, MA was the great grandson of a JANVRIN from Jersey. (Alice Janvrin, Salisbury, MA)
JANVRIN, Thomas from J, in ME 1648. (Underhill)
JANVRIN, Abigail, mar ca 1840 Samuel BROWN. (Sarah Moore, Amesbury,MA)
A1. Abbie A. Brown, mar Amos Brown, b 1843 Kensington, NH, son of Stephen and Dolly (Batchelder) Brown. Amos served from NH in the Civil War, and later res Illini, ILL, and Warrensburg, ILL.
B1. James Emery Brown, b 1868 Illini, ILL mar 1892 Katherine M. Batchelder, 6 chn
B2. John Amos Brown, b 1871 d 1955, mar 1898 Mabel C. Ingham, 2 chn
B3. Alice Myrtle Brown, b 1876, unmar B5. Arthur Brown, b 1884, d.y.
B4. Mary Helen Brown, b 1878, d 1945 unmar B6. a son d.y. 1885.
JARVES, see C.I. NOTABLES
JARVIS, old in G and curr there. JARVES, from French GERVAISE. One fam rem to J from France, and John Jackson Jarves was said to be b in J. He and wife Hannah Seabury, dau of the American Loyalist Sea bury, res London, where John advertised as a cabinet maker, chair & clockmaker. They rem to Boston 1787. The son Deming was b prob in J 1790, although exact place not known. He was bp Boston that year. Henshaw and Jarves was a crockery firm in Boston 1812. Deming mar 1815 Ann Smith Stutson, and had 9 chn, including 6 sons. Deming was the originator of the very famous SANDWICH GLASS. The story of this early American craft and business is told in some very interesting books. Deming d 1869. (SANDWICH, THE TOWN THAT GLASS BUILT, by H.B. Barbour, Boston 1948; EARLY GLASS-MAKING IN EAST CAMBRIDGE, MA, Camb., 1929; etc.)
A1. James Jackson, b 1818, d 1888, editor of the first newspaper publ. in the Hawaiian Islands, author, critic, pioneer art collector, b Boston, MA, d Switzerland, bur Rome. He published a dozen books, served as US consul at Florence, Italy ca 1880. Under financial stress he sold a collection to Liberty Holden of Cleveland, and

the collection later became part of the Cleveland Art Museum's holdings. James mar 1. Eliz. Russell Swain at New Bedford, MA 1838, and 2. in 1862 at Boston, Isabel Kast Hayden. He survived both and four of his 6 chn.

A2. George A4. Billy A6. MAria A8. Isabella
A3. Jon A5. Ann A7. Mary A9. Deming Jr.

JARVIS, note that a number of this name married into C.I. fams in early New England, but OUTC.
JARVIS, Isaac mar in Boston 1698 Abigail VODEN
JARVIS, Hannah mar John BUBIER 1784 MRB
JARVIS, John mar Elizabeth BODEN 1788 MRB.
JARVIS, Elias mar Mary Sunderland, 1715 Boston.
JARVIS, John res Boston 1790 with fam of 4. (Census)
JARVIS, Thomas mar 1778 in Boston Ann DEMERY, prob DEMERIT, qv.
JEAN, curr research in C.I.? See CIFHS #12. Were some John, Johns fams of America originally JEAN or DE JEAN?
JEAN, JEANNE curr J. JEAN curr G. JEAN in St. Ouen and St. Heliers J 1668, and in St. Ouen J 1749. JEANNE in J as early as 1461, JEAN in St. Lawrence J 1788.
JEAN, Britton in Heard Co., GA 1840. OUTC. (Opal Boyett, Ft. Worth, TX)
JEAN, from J to Canada 1700s. (See Q.A. IN CANADA) Curr Boston, OUTC.
JEAN, Augustine, this is the correct name of John GUSTIN, qv.
JEANDRON, John Edward, b 1839 St. John J, d 1924. Mar 1865 St. Genevieve, QUE, Ann Hall, b Ireland. JEANDRONS related to the CABOT fam of J. See Q.A. IN CANADA. (Florence Waugh, Toronto, ONT; John Withrow, MN)
A1. William John, b 1866, mar Ada Rutledge, from NJ, res E. Orange, NJ, 3 chn. He d 1930.
A2. Arthur Edward, b 1867 mar Bertha Sharp of Toronto, 3 chn. He d 1936.
A3. Herbert Henderson, b 1869, d.y. A4. Charles F, 1871-1894, unmar
A5. Eda Gertrude, b 1874 mar John A. Withrow 1890, d 1942, bur Toronto.
JEFFREY, JEFFREYS curr G. JEFFERY curr J.
JEFFREY in St. Clement J 1668. Many of this name in early New England but none traced by compiler.
JEFFERDS, John and Joanna res Salem, MA. Could this have been a GIFFARD of J? OUTC. (Essex Coll, Vol 6)
A1. Elizabeth, b 1690 A4. Dau b 1700 A7. Joseph, b 1706
A2. Sarah, b 1693 A5. John b 1702 A8. Benjamin b 1714
A3. Tabitha, b 1696 A6. Abigail, b 1704
JEHAN, curr and common in G, curr J. In Torteval G 1774.
JEHAN, Capt of the JERSEY PACKET, 1755-1765, in J.
JEHAN, Lucy, b 1830 G, rem to Hocking Co., OH, poss with her sister? ca 1846, res near Nelsonville, OH. They had an aunt from G who res in OH, but name not known. Lucy mar 1848 Henry Barrows Baker of Hocking Co., an engineer. She d 1859 Logan, OH, and Henry mar 2. Martha McCollister, 1836-1910, in 1861. 5 chn by Lucy and 2 by Martha. (Patricia Surface, Taxewell, VA; Wm. F. Baker, Nelsonville, OH; Mrs. A.T. Cheon, Moundsville, WVA)
A1. Lucinda Baker, b 1849 Chauncy, OH, mar Hezekiah Boyers Williams 1867. She d 1935 Dodderidge Co., WVA. Hezekiah, 1842-1916.
B1. Luella, b 1868 mar Mark Smith 1888
B2. William Henry Williams, b 1870, mar 1. Minnie O'Dell Dotson 1896 who d 1909. He mar 1910 Temperance Genevra Garner. 3 chn by 1st.
C1. Bessie Williams, b 1897 mar George Robert Watson 1918
C2. Goldie Williams, b 1901 mar 1923 Howard Elifritz
C3. Fredie Williams, b 1905 mar 1924 Clifton Shepler
C4. William Boyers Williams, b 1921 mar 1933 Madge Massar
C5. Edgar Dale Williams, b 1914 mar Agnes Samples

C6. Arvilla Lee Williams, b 1917 mar 1938 Johnson Fleming
C7. Madaline May Williams, b 1919 mar 1934 George KNIGHT
B3. Charles Franklin Williams, b 1872 d 1928 mar 1898 Florence Calhoun
C1. Beulah Myrtle Williams, b 1899 mar 1917 George R. McCullough
C2. Elsie Leona Williams, b 1902 mar 1925 Cleus R. Swick
C3. James Franklin, b 1905 d.y.
C4. Waldie OwenWilliams, b 1907 mar 1935 Opal White
C5. Charles Freel Williams b 1910 mar 1932 Lucy McIntyre
C6. Wanita Madge williams, b 1915 mar 1939 Delbert Wilson
C7. Madaline Virginia Williams, b 1918 mar 1937 Charles J. Kerr
B4. Clara Williams, b 1875 d 1917, mar 1911 Thomas Mills
B5. James Boyd Williams, b 1878 d 1931 mar 1908 Annie Laurie Welsh
C1. Margaret Williams, b 1911 mar 1932 Thornton Irwin Boileau
D1. Margo Donna Boileau, b 1936 mar David E. Hamil 1958
D2. Linda Ann Boileau, b 1939 mar Fred L. Dupre 1963
C2. Patricia Williams b 1925 mar Henry Shelton Surface Jr 1951. She was b Columbus, OH.
D1. Laura Eleanor Surface b 1954 D3. Jennifer L. Surface, b 1957
D2. Julia Karen Surface, b 1955 mar 1977 DAvid Harmon Fox.
B6. Homer Clinton Williams, b 1881 mar 1904 Ellen Isabelle Johnson
B7. Loris Harrold Williams, b 1887 mar 1915 Lucy Estella Johnson, who d 1922, and mar 2. Gertrude Leona Holcraft.
B8. Vivian Ralph Williams, b 1896, d.y.
A2. Louisa Baker, b 1851, d 1908 mar Barnum Compton
A3. Lovina Baker, b 1853, d 1895 mar Albert Postel, b 1832
A4. Charles H. Baker, b 1856 mar Ida Varner, d 1907
A5. Ida Lucy Baker, b 1858 Logan, OH mar Solomon Douglas
A6. by 2nd wife, Dora Baker, b 1864 mar John NICHOLS, 1888. She d 1910
A7. William Franklin Baker, b 1873 unmar d ca 1957 Nelsonville, OH.

JELLISON, see GALLISON, GALLICHAN. JENKINS in J&G, 1600s,1700s.

JENNE, in J 1528, in St. Clement J 1668, and in St. Lawrence J 1788, written JENNER.

JENNE, John arrived in Boston 1769 on ship MOLLY from J, servant. (Whitmore)

JENNE, man in MA 1790, mostly in New Bedford, MA. First names included Abner, Caleb, Eliz., Henry, Israel, Jabez, Jethro, Job, Jonathan, Levi, Nathaniel, Reuben and Seth.

JENNE, Jennys?, Prince mar Polly Murick, Merrick? 1802 Boston. OUTC

JENNES in St. Martin and Grouville J 1668. Cf also JEUNAIX, LA JEUNESS, DE GENNES.

SHENNES, Geo. res Boston 1790, fam of 2. (Census) OUTC.

JENNES, Richard and Sarah res Boston, son Richard b 1771. OUTC

JENNES, Simon and Samuel from J? res York Co., ME 1700s. OUTC

JENNEE, mentioned in CLEVELAND GEN, OUTC, from Canada to Royalton,VT.

JENNES, Francis mar in ME 1600s Hannah SWAIN. (Noyes; NEHGS Vol 31)

JENNINGS, Nicholas, of MA was identified in SAvage as 'prob a Suffolk man', but was a Jerseyman according to Konig, in article about the 'French' in early New England. His name was spelled JENNESS and JENNINGS. Note Solomon JENNINGS also, poss JENNES? See Noyes, and Essex Coll, Vol 110, #3, 1974.

JENNINGS, Solomon and Ann res Boston, son Solomon b 1733. OUTC.

JENT, John and Abigail res Boston. JENNETT, old J surname. A dau Elizabeth JENT b 1718.

JEPSON in G before 1814, but not traced by compiler, ditto for JEREMIE.

JERMAN, from J? in Salem, MA 1692. (Perley) See also GERMAN.

JERMAN, Mary mar Sam. BLAMPIED, qv, of Salem, MA. She d 1790 age 103. (Perley; Swasey; Noyes)

JEREE, DE JERSEY?? JERSEY, DE JERSEY in G 1600s, in J 1274. Curr G.

JEREE, Peter from J to Boston before 1716, mar Ann Foosheron 1716. Peter came with Capt. THOMAS. (Noyes)

JARSEY, Peter mar Mary LEER 1733 Boston

JERSIE, Mary, servant of Mr. Jose in NH (Noyes)

JERSIE, William taxed in Portsmouth, NH 1731/2

JERSEY, Frank/Francis d 1914 Romeo, MI. Mar and had at least one dau, b ca 1908, who mar ___Eastway, and had dau Jeanne Eastway. Frank had two bros. OUTC. (Mrs. Norman Thome, Belding, MI)

JERSEY, Henry A., mar Mary A. Madden of Greenville, MI, res Romeo, MI, a lawyer, b 1850, poss son of Peter H. Jersey, 1826-1900. Henry had bros? Edgar W., b 1852 NY, d 1931, and Albert A., b 1854, d 1881. One son was a marble cutter. (Mrs. Norman Thome, Belding, MI) OUTC.

JERVOIS, Benjamin from J 1835 with his 3rd wife and 3 chn to Buffalo, NY, and then to Columbus, OH, where he d 1850. (B. Rodgers Dennis, Decatur, ILL)

A1. Emma

A2. Harriet, mar 2. Robert George, a grocer in Columbus, OH, 2 chn by Mr. George.

B1. Harriet George, b 1849 B3. George George, b ca 1843

B2. Clara George, b 1850, d.y. B4. Albert George, b ca 1845

JESSUP, Dorcas Fannie, b 1854 G, mar ___THOUMINE, qv, and d 1922 Bronx, New York. Name curr G.

JEUNE, in G 1300s and in J 1299. Curr J. See LE JEUNE and YOUNG

JEUNE, Elizabeth, b 1793 St. Brelade, J, dau of Clement and Elizabeth (HERAULT) JEUNE, d 1864 Alpine, UT.

JEUNE, four bros b J, 3 of whom rem to BC Canada before 1886. The fourth bro, William settled in Boston, MA. They were sons of a sea captain. See Q.A. IN CANADA for more info. (Wallace Jeune, Sidney, BC, Canada)

JEUNE, Francois of Les Vaux, St. Aubin, J furnished a shed in his yard for meetings of the then new-in-Jersey Methodists. He and wife were later missionaries to the French-speaking natives of Granada in the Windward Isles, West Indies. (Balleine's BIOG. DICT. OF JERSEY)

JEUNE, Julia from C.I. 1855 on ship CHIMBORAZO, settled UT.

JEUNE, Philip, from C.I. 1852, via ship KENNEBEC, with wife Fanny and Chn to UT.

A1. Philip A2. Fanny E. A3. Julia M., dau or sister?

JEUN, LE JEUNE, RAchel from C.I. 1851 via ship OLYMPUS to US, to UT.

JOGUET, Peter and Rebecca res Boston, from C.I.? JOUGUET old name in J. A son Peter b 1714.

JOINER, JOYNER, Edward, said to be from Wales or J, was in Sudbury, MA ca 1740, also res other towns. OUTC. (Carolyn Flagg, Novato, CAL; Bolton) Chn: Edward, Elizabeth, William who d 1796 Deerfield,MA.

JOLLY, see BERTRAND. JOLLY curr G and J.

JONES in G. See CIFHS #14. Also two Captains of this name in J, but the name is prob. Welsh. (A. John Jean, Jersey)

JORDAN, JOURDAIN, Ignatius of Exeter, England was b G, will in England dated 1635. His grandson was Joseph HILL of New England. (NEHGS Vol 49) JORDAN, JOURDAN in J 1309, and current. JORDAIN old in G, JORDAN curr G and J. See also JOURDAINE.

JORDAINE, Thomas mar Easter Hall in REhoboth, MA 1674. OUTC

JORDAIN, Mary of Falmouth mar Jacob Parker of Boston 1731 (int). OUTC

JORY, old G surname, spelled also JORET. Cf SHOREY, CHORET

JORET, Jane of G mar Dr. THomas COLLINGS of St. Brelade J 1700s. Their son Edward was said to be the one changed the spelling from COLLINS to COLLINGS. See OUR KIN, by De Guerin in Congressional Library.

JOREY, John in PA 172-. Mar Rachel Hudson. OUTC. (PA Arch.S2,V8)
JOREY, Joseph in Wethersfield, CT, also Martha, Mary and Wm., 1700s. OUTC. Also noted in MD.
JOSEPH, curr G and J, in St.Heliers J 1834, not researched by compiler.
JOSSELYN, JOCELYN, GOSSELIN, qv, from England to New England. However, JOCELYN, JOSLIN are old J surnames. Some in New England may have originated in C.I.
JOUAN, JOUANNY curr J. JOUHNING curr G. See Q.A. IN CANADA.
JOURDAIN old in G, JORDAN curr G.
JOURDAN & JORDAN in J 1309, curr J. John JOURDAIN was an early English trader-explorer to the East Indies and the coast of East Africa. A Joh John JOURDAIN res Plymouth, MA 1643. Was he from a C.I. fam of England? See JORDAIN above. See also Jehosabeth JOURDAINE, dau of John mar John ROBBINS, son of Nicholas ROBBINS, qv, 1665 in MA. ROBBINS was from G.
JOURNEAU, JOURNEAUX in J 1515. In Grouville, St. Mary and St. Heliers J 1668, and in St. Clement, Trinity, St. Mary, St. Heliers and St. John J 1749. Curr J. See Q.A. IN CANADA. JOURNEAUX research curr in J? See CIFHS #3.
JOURNEAULX, John bur 1729 MRB. One said to have settled in Wallkill,NY 1850. OUTC.
JOURNEAULX, Mary, bp 1728 MRB, no parents given.
JOY, Capt. Melzar mar Mary Eliot 1800s Boston. See MALZARD, MELZARD. OUTC. Joy noted in C.I.
JUSTICE in Grouville J 1607, and noted in colonies. OUTC.

KAHO noted in GCO. KEYHO, pron. KAHO, an Irish surname KEOGH, was in G since middle 1700s. See Q.A. IN CANADA. Not known to compiler if KAHO below were part of the influx of Guernsey folk to Guernsey Co.,OH in early 1800s.
KAHO, Mary Thompson, 1847-1919, res Richland Twp., near Cambridge, OH.
KAHO, James, Rebecca Ann, George Sidney, res GCO 1846-1934.
KAHO, James of GCO 1894-1900, county commissioner, GCO (Wolfe)
KAINES, in G before 1814, and curr. None ver as from G in America.
KEEPING, curr J. Noted in some N.A. C.I. fams.
KELINECK, Hannah, mar Samuel Frankling 1719 Boston, MA. Undoubtedly a QUELENEC from France or Jersey.
KELLING, Roy Thomas, b 1927 St. Martin G, mar Elizabeth Anne Church TAYLOR, b 1929 St. Peter Port G, mar 1955. He was a postmaster and merchant in ONT. (Roy Kelling, Laurel, ONT)
A1. Matthew John Russell, b 1962 St. Peter Port G.
A2. Clarie Margaret, b 1963 G.
KELLY, not an old C.I. surname, but Cf KELLET, in J 1668, pron. KELLY. KELLY is curr G and J.
KELLY, William, bp 1830 St. Helier J, son of John KELLY b Cornwall, England and Elizabeth Woodley, also b Cornwall, mar 1951 St. SAmpson, G, Betsy Marguerite HILLMAN, b 1832 St. Sampson, G, dau of John HILLMAN, b Somerset, England and Judith MARTIN, b G? Chn b St. Peter Port, G. Poss other chn to N.A.? (Mrs. P. Elliott, Woodland,CAL)
A1. Rachel Kelly, b 1852 Longstore, St. Peter Port G, res NewLondon,CT
A2. Elizabeth Emma, b 1853 St. Peter Port
A3. Rosina Jane Kelly, b 1854 St. Peter Port, G d 1917, England. Mar 1878 Thomas John ROBERTS, qv, a fam raised in US
A4. Mary Ann, b 1857 A5. Louisa A. Hillman, b 1859, d 1939, mar 1878 James Eastland
A6. William James, bp 1862, d.y.
A7. Mary Ann/Polly, b 1863 d 1943, mar Charles W. Munday
A8. Emelina Hillman, b 1866 d 1900, unmar

A9. Ada Ann Hillman, b 1868 St. Peter Port G d 1938 mar James Hannah.

KEMPSTER, Albert Enslin, b 1901 St. Clement J, son of Sgt. Major Kempster of the J Militia, being one of 12 chn. Mar Winifred Norah BUESNEL, b 1906 St. Saviour J, d 1969, also of a large fam. See in Q.A. IN CANADA. Rem from J to Canada 1926. (A.E. Kempster, Edmonton, Alta, Canada)

A1. Kenneth Albert, b 1932, res Edmonton, ALTA. 4 chn

A2. Constance Winifred, b 1934 Canada, mar Doland Colpitts, div, 3 chn, res King City, CAL.

B1. Cathy Colpitts, b ca 1959

B2. Dean Colpitts, b ca 1961 B3. Janye Colpitts, b ca 1963

A3. Shirley Ann, b 1936 Canada, mar John YOUNG of Penticton, BC, res Surrey, BC, 2 chn.

KENNELLS, Robert, taxed at Strawberry Bank, Portsmouth, NH 1671. Was he he a QUESNEL, pron. KENEL, of J. Name in J 1300s, 1771, etc.

KERBY, fam in J 1700s, assoc. with several old J fams. Also a name of Grt. Britain.

KERBY, Henry in Blue Point ME? 1676-1685, then in Boston 1713. (Noyes)

KIRBY, John age 26, b G, son of Wm. and Mary Kirby, mar 1860 in Toronto ONT, Elizabeth Campbell, age 18, b Kingston, ONT, dau of John and Eliza Campbell. Witnesses Edward and Mary Harrison of Toronto. (St. James records)

KERBY, Jean, master of the CORBET of J, a ship built in Boston 1774. (A. John Jean, Jersey)

KERBY, Francis Jr., b 1825 St. Helier J, son of Francis and Jane (GUILLEAUME) KERBY, mar 1845 Mary LE CORNU, b 1826 J, dau of John & Mary (RENOUF) LE CORNU. Francis and Mary rem from J ca 1850 to US, poss went directly to UT or AR? (Mrs. Erlene Stewart, Las Vegas, NV; Mrs. Thomas Price, Arlington, TX) Other chn?

A1. Mary Jane, b 1850 J, d 1931 Showlow, AZ, mar 1866 Edward Stock, b 1822 Melchbourne, Beds, England, d 1906 Linden, AZ.

B1. Francis Moroni Stock, b 1871 Bingham, UT, d 1942 Tucson, AZ, mar 1891 Olive Maria Huff, b 1875 Upton, UT, d 1921 Tucson, AZ

C1. Francis Stock, b 1894 Pinedale, AZ, d 1951 Tucson, AZ mar 1921 Florence Matilda Farr, b 1903 Colonia, Dublan, Mexico, d 1971.

D1. Erlene Stock, b 1924 Tucson, AZ, mar 1946 Harold Press Stewart b 1923 Alamo, NEV, 4 sons.

KILNER, Francis George, photographer-artist of J, rem with his fam to Topsham, England and then returned to J. Mar 1861 at St. Saviours J, Mary Ann RENOUF, b St. Helier J 1842, dau of Nicholas RENOUF and Ann Mary MAUGER. Francis was bp St. Andrews, Plymouth, England 1836. (Edith Thompson, Manhattan, KS; Gerald Deney's book, KILNERS OF LONDON)

A1. Edmund, b 1869 J d 1951 Manhattan, KS, mar KC, MO 1916 Julia Bell Rouch, 1896-1962, dau of Greenvarry Rouch and Martha Ellen Reed. Had restaurant and farmed.

B1. Vivian, b 1917 Garrison, KS mar Wallace Dibble, son of George D. and Louise (Paulson) Dibble. Two sons, George & Norman Dibble.

B2. George, b 1920 mar Annie Mae ROBERTS, a dau Ann

B3. Elsie, b 1921 mar James Mitchem, son of Peter and Eula (Robinson) Mitchem. 2 chn: Doulgas and Joni Mitchem

B4. Lloyd, b 1923, d 1945 Freising, Germany, in WWII

B5. Edith, b 1926 mar Martin Thompson, son of Martin and Lavon (Dowhower) Thompson

B6. Ralph, b 1928 d 1950 in Korea. B7. Lawrence, b 1931, unmar

B8. Donna, b 1935 Garrison, KS mar Alvin James Lovgren, son of John Peter and Agnes (HUBERT) Lovgren. See HUBERT.

B9. Wayne, b 1937 mar Rita Brockish, dau of Oscar F. and Mary J. (Sable) Brockish. 2 sons, David, b ca 1960 and Gary.
A2. Fred, to Kansas City, MO at 19, worked in restaurant, and farmed in Pot. Co., KS.
A3. Philip went to Australia, and d there of typhoid
A4. Florence, left J during WWII, and res Suffolk Co., England, d there
A5. Francis, rem to New Zealand. A6. Mary, A7. Kate, to Devon, England
A8. Ralph, res Ghana, Africa, and Jamaica, BWI.
KILNER, Emily, and others res Cleveland, OH, bur in Erie St. Cem. in the 1800s. OUTC.
KITFIELD, is really the French and C.I.surname DE QUETTEVILLE, much mangled in America, to Kuetfield, Ketville, Quitafield, etc, etc. DE QUETTEVILLE in J since 1299. However, others came from france at later dates and settled in the Islands, often from Quetteville, a town in Normandy. Abraham de QUETTEVILLE was a mariner, who made voyages between Jersey and MRB, and settled in MRB before 1681, when hehad litigation with Andrew Tucker. The KITFIELDS below may or may not be his descendants. See also QUITAFIELD and DE QUETTEVILLE. (HOOPER GEN; Essex Hist. Coll, 1974)
KITFIELD, Edward, b 1728? of Gloucester, MA, d abroad 1778, age ca 50? Mar 1748 Lydia HOOPER, qv. She was b ca 1732, d 1825 age 93, dau of Jacob and Anna Lee HOOPER.
A1. Lydia, b 1749, poss mar 1770 William Badcock?
A2. Capt. Edward, b ca 1751 mar Elizabeth HOOPER, both d 1798, she at 44,he at 47.
B1. Edward, b 1777 d age 17 B5. Lydia, bp 1786
B2. Elizabeth, bp 1779 poss mar 1801 Nehemiah Goldsmith? Res Manchester, MASS?
B3. Thomas Hooper, bp 1783 mar Anna KITFIELD, widow in 1823
C1. Thomas Hooper, b 1823 C2. Eliz. Ann, b 1826 C3. ?, d 1829
B4. Asa, b ca 1785 d 1835 age ca 50?, mar 1812 Elizabeth LEE.
C1. Elizabeth b 1813 poss mar 1834 Albert E. LOW? C2. Henry
C3. Thomas Hooper, b 1818 mar 1839 Harriet C. BAKER
D1. George Hooper, 1841-1847 D3. Harriet, 1845-1846
D2. Josephine C., b 1847 D4. Harriet again, b 1849
C4. Nancy Norwood, b 1820 mar 1839 Isaac S. West (int)
C5. Mary Abigail, b 1923 mar Daniel Leache Jr, age 23, cabinetmaker, son of Daniel and Deborah Leach.
C6. Asa Edward, b 1826. His journals are in Essex Inst., Salem,MA.
C7. Emily Augusta b 1828 C8. Lydia Hooper, b 1830
A3. Jemima Davis, b 1754, poss mar 1781 Solomon LEE
A4. Nabby/Abigail, b 1762 d 1849?
A5. Sarah, b 1767 poss mar 1788 Hooper Allen.
A6. Betsy, b 1771 poss mar 1792 Israel HOOPER, son of Edward.
B1. Betsy HOOPER, b 1794 mar Jacob HOOPER.
KITFIELD, Asa E., C6 above, son of Asa and Elizabeth, was a member of a company that voyaged to CAL 1849 in ship LA GRANGE. Four journals of this voyage survived, unpublished, in Essex Inst., Salem, MA. Asa left a wife and 2 chn. There is a model of the ship in the Peabody Museum, Salem. (Essex Bull., April 1979)
KITFIELD, Benjamin mar Lydia Kitfield1811, who d 1841 age ca 53.
A1. Benj. Jr. b 1817, cabinet Maker, mar 1843 Ester M.P. Miller
B1. Lydia Augusta, b 1844 Also other chn?
A2. William, b 1819, d 1941 age 22
A3. Harriet, b 1821 mar age 24 in 1846, Geo. Hartley, age 31, cabinet maker, son of Samuel and Elizabeth Hartley.

KITFIELD, Edward B. mar Alla A.___. (HOOPER GEN)
A1. Helen P., b 1871 Manchester, MA d 1897. She mar 1894 Carrol I. HOOPER, b 1870, So. Paris, ME. A dau Helen Hooper, b 1897
KITFIELD, Edward res Manchester, MA 1790 with fam of 9. (census)
KITFIELD, Jacob, b ca 1781, mar Anna Kellaham 1805 Manchester, MA. He d 1814 age 33.
A1. Jacob b 1807 A4. William H. b 1813, d 1841 age 33
A2. Edward, b 1809 d 1835 age 26 A5. a ch, d 1814
A3. William Kellaham, b 1811, prob d.y.?
KITFIELD, ___, of Manchester, MA mar Simeon SWETT, had 7 chn. Few descendants. (An insert in the TYLER GEN)
A1. Fred Kitfield Swett, had son Fred Jr. res Manchester, MA.
A7. Herman, mar Ethel Stanley.
KNIGHT curr G and J. CHEVALIER curr J.
KNIGHT, as CHEVALIER in J 1274. CHEVALIERS in St. Helier, Trinity, and St. John J 1668. This fam translated their name to KNIGHT very early in MA, etc. Prob a number of Knight fams in New England came from England, not from the Islands, such as Wm. Knight who came from Chelmsford, england to New England in 1635.
KNIGHT, John, formerly John CHEVALIER, b 1659 J, mar 1684 Portsmouth, NH Bridget Sloper, dau of Richard. He may have been the same person as John CHEVALIER of Martinique, West Indies. He was taxed in Ports. 1681 as merchant, and owned much property in Ports. and Newington, NH. He d Newington 1721. Briget d ca 1740. (Underhill's SMALL GEN; Noyes; HIST. OF PARSONSFIELD, ME; HIST. OF HAMPTON FALLS, NH; OXFORD MAINE ANNALS; Essex Coll; Essex Antiq; PICKERING GEN; KNIGHT FAM in HIST OF WINDHAM, NH, by Leonard Morrison, not seen by compiler; Stackpole; NH records of wills; Evelyn Wright, San Diego, CAL; Jane Nielsen, Danville, ILL)
A1. Capt. John, b 1684/5, mar Elizabeth Shapleigh, dau of John, who was still living in 1769. Capt. John res Portsmouth, served as Moderator, selectman and Repr.
B1. John, mar 1743 Patience SMITH of Durham, and 2. 1759 Temperance Pickering, who d ca 1770 leaving highly genealogical will, researcher should locate this.
B2. Nicholas, mar 1744 Sarah Thompson, 4 chn
B3. Mary, bp 1717, d.y. B4. Daniel, bp 1720, d.y.?
B5. Bridget, bp 1721, mar 1. 1740 James Chadbourne and 2. before 1769 ___ALLEN.
B6. Alice, bp 1723 mar Thomas HATCH, qv.
B7. Susannah, bp 1727/8, not in will
B8. Mary again, bp 1729, not in will, but poss mar 1757 Jonathan HILL of Durham, NH?
B9. George, bp 1732, mar 1. Mary, grdau of Samuel Penhallow, and 2. Susannah Chesley. His will dated 1785, 9 chn.
B10. Deborah, bp 1735, mar Nathaniel Adams, and d before her father.
B11. Elizabeth mar Richard SALTER, by 1743, a son Richard Knight SALTER, bp 1744 Portsmouth, NH
B12. Sarah, mar 1. ___Norwood, and 2. 1758 Samuel Brewster of Barrington, NH.
A2. Elizabeth, b 1687 mar 1706 John JANVRIN of J, whose estate she admin. in 1720. She mar 2. 1720 Rev. Joseph Adams, 1689-1783, son of Joseph and Hannah (Bass) Adams, uncle of President John Adams. Rev. Joseph mar 2. 1760 Elizabeth Brackett of Greenland, NH. See record of Elizabeth's JANVRIN chn under JANVRIN.
B1. John Janvrin B2. Mary Janvrin B3. Eliz. Adams Janvrin, d.y.

B4. Joseph Adams b 1723, physician, mar Joanna Gilman, dau of Ezekiel of Exeter, 7 sons and 2 daus. Res Newington and Barnstead, NH. (GEN. MS by Eben Putnam, Salem, MA, 1896)
C1. Ezekiel G. Adams C2. Ebenezer Adams C3. Joseph Adams
C4. Dudley Adams
C5. John Adams, b 1759 Newington, NH mar Abigail Coleman of Newington and had 2 chn. Abigal the dau of Phineas Coleman and __Huntress. John d at Newington 1831 age 72.
D1. Elizabeth J. Adams
D2. Reformation John Adams, b 1791 Newington, d Newmarket, NH 1850 age 59. Mar Sarah Sanderson of Waterford, ME, 7 chn.
E1. John Adams of Durham, NH E4. Sarah E. Adams, d.y.
E2. Enoch George Adams E5. Mary A. Adams of Durham, NH
E3. Charles W. Adams, d.y. E6. Joseph Martin Adams of Durham.
C6. Benjamin Adams C7. Nathaniel Adams C8. Elizabeth Adams
C9. Abigail Adams, mar her cousin Wm. JANVRIN, qv, son of John, and was grandmother of Dr. J.E. Janvrin.
This Adams family is desc from John Alden and Priscilla Mullen, and is related also to the Presidents named Adams. (Jane Nielsen, Danville, Illinois, 1978)
B5. Eben?, b 1726 d 1767 B6. Benjamin Adams, b 1728 d 1803
A3. William, mar 1722 in North Church, Deborah Penhallow, who admin. his estate in 1730 when he was 37.
B1. William B2. Temple B3. Deborah mar Henry CARTER, of Gosport.
A4. Mary, mar Capt. John Cox, Boston merchant, whose will she admin in 1733, 2 daus.
A5. Temple, mariner, taxed in Portsmouth 1722, 1724, no issue.
KNIGHT, Mary, b ca 1770 G, mar ca 1790 at St. Peter Port G, John NICOLL b ca 1760 Dundee, Scotland, a Capt. in the Fourth Royal Vet. Batt. of the British Army. He d 1839 Perth, ONT. See page 441. Q.A. IN Canada. (A.D. MacDonald, Sydney, NS; Stella Brown, Halifax, NS; Donald M. Stacey, Sudbury, MA) This corrects & adds to data in Q.A. IN CANADA.
A1. John Nicoll, b ca 1792 A2. Alexander Nicoll, b ca 1795
A3. James Nicoll, b 1798 St. Peter Port G, rem to NS, Canada and d 1877 in Bagarus, NS. He was in the Brit. Army and was stationed in Cape Breton ca 1820? Mar a Sydney NS girl, Lucy Morley, 1794-1875, dau of George and Mary Morley of Sydney, NS. 8 chn b Sydney River, NS.
B1. Mary Nicoll, b 1817 d 1902 age 85, mar 1834 Edward HARDY, b 1805
B2. Lucy Nicoll, b 1819 d 1899 age 80, mar ca 1838 Charles Stacey, b 1817 Irish Brook, Gabarus, NS, d there 1884, son of Thomas and Frances (Hardy) Stacey. 13 chn.
C1. Harriet, b 1839 d 1920 mar 1. ca 1862 Joseph Bagnell, a son Russell. She mar 2. 1868 Wm. Henry Bagnell, son Charles Bagnell
C2. Ann Stacey, b 1842 d 1918 mar ca 1862 John W. Cann, 1839-1905, 5 chn.
C3. Matilda Stacey, b 1844 d 1868 unmar C6. Margaret, d.y.
C4. Oscar Stacey, b ca 1845, d.y. C5. Charles Stacey, d.y.
C7. Mary Jane Stacey, b ca 1851
C8. Maria Stacey, b 1853 mar 1873 Charles Ormiston, b 1851, 6 chn
C9. Alexander Stacey, b 1855 d 1938 mar 1880 Helena Cann, 2 chn.
C10. Ross Stacey, b 1857 d 1921 mar 1879 Susan Alma Bagnell, b 1858 d 1929, 9 chn. Ross d 1921 at Cambridge, MA.
D1. Clifford Leslie Stacey, b 1880 Gabarus, NS d 1954, mar 1900 Edna I. Munday, b 1884, 13 chn.

D2. Catherine Serna Stacey, b 1883 d 1936 mar 1. 1902 Walter Belyea, 7 chn, and 2. Fred. Belyea
D3. Charles Heber Stacey, b 1885 d 1902 age 17.
D4. Howard Ephraim Stacey, b 1887 d 1967 mar 1908 Sarah Mae Clark, b 1886, 6 chn.
D5. George F. Stacey, b 1892 d.y.
D6. Herbert Osborn, b 1894 Cambridge, MA d 1962 Medford, MA mar 1917 Edith Mae Stimpson, b 1897 Cambridge, d 1975, dau of Geo. and Mary (Smith)Stimpson. 4 chn b Cambridge, MA.
E1. Edward Herbert Stacey, b 1921, mar 1941 Dora COLLOMB, b 1917, 3 chn.
E2. Donald Milton Stacey, b 1923, mar 1946 F. Pearl Minty, b 1927 Belmont, MA, dau of Robert and Beatrice (Fisher) Minty. 7 chn, most b Waltham, MA: Carolyn L., Kenneth Paul, James Donald, Nancy Schimp, Sandra, Donna and Scott Stacey
E3. Marion Elsie Stacey, b 1927, unmar.
E4. Norman Richard Stacey, b 1933, d 1975, mar 1961 Lois A. Jackson, b 1939. 2 chn.
D7. George Frederick Stacey II, b 1898, d 1901 D9. Oliver, d.y.
D8. Alma Adell Stacey, b 1900 d 1969, mar 1923 Wm. P. Prouty, b 1897, 3 sons.
B3. John Nicoll, b 1822, d 1909 age 87, mar 1.. ca 1845 Susan Mann, b 1827, d 1860 age 33. 5 chn b Louisbourg, CB, NS. John mar 2. ca 1865 Esther L. Spencer, b 1827, no issue.
B4. Alexander Nicoll, b 1825 mar Lucy Ann ___, 5 chn.
B5. Ann Nicoll, b 1827 d 1906, mar ca 1846 Abraham/Abram HARDY, b 1823 son of Charles Hardy of Greenwich, England, 5 chn.
C1. Samuel Hardy C2. Charles Hardy C3. James Hardy, 1850-1906
C4. Elizabeth Hardy, b 1852 mar Joseph Brown, a dau Stella mar Michael Brown.
C5. Leah M. Hardy b 1855 mar James W. Grant from Ohio, US, rem to NB.
C6. Alexander Hardy, b 1856 d 1937, mar Margaret Bagnell, 1843-1938.
D1. Annie E. Hardy, b 1882 d 1972, mar Charles Lyman Smart
D2. Leah F. Hardy, b 1889 mar Dr. D. MacDonald, 1886-1965.
E1. Alexander D. MacDonald, b 1922 mar Minnie A. O'Hara, b 1930, 5 chn: Daniel, Donna, Eldon, Karen and Noel MacDonald. 1975
E2. Christina M.R. MAcDonald, b 1927 mar John U. McIntyre, 1923-/
B6. James E. Nicoll, b 1831 d 1907, mar ca 1850 Mary Ellen Hardy, b 1831, 9 chn. 5 chn.
B7. William George Nicoll, b 1833, mar ca 1854 Jane J. Stacey, b 1829/
B8. David Edward Nicoll, b 1837 d 1913 age 77. Mar 1. 1862 Caroline M. Kendall, 1838-1877, 4 daus. Mar 2. Ruth M. ARmstrong, 1838-1900, no issue.

KNIGHT, William Edward, b ca 1857 G, raised on Alderney Is., mar there Louise GAUDION, qv, rem to Detroit, MI 1910. Their chn came to Amer ica before them. Wm. was son of George Knight and Fanny Elliot of Dorset, England, bp St. Martin, G. Louisa was dau of J. R. and Mary (SIMON) GAUDION.
A1. Frances Mary res FLA. A2. William John? b ca 1857, d 1935 Detroit
A3. Louise, b ca 1858 G d 1930 Detroit, MI
A4. George Elliot A5. John Oliver.

KNIGHT, William, master of the coasting schooner MIRIAM, and a fisherman out of MRB 1779. Constable in MRB 1766. D 1799 age 77. OUTC. (JOURNALS OF ASHLEY BOWEN)

There is much info. on KNIGHTS scattered in Noyes, but it is not known to compiler which ones are desc of KNIGHT fams from J. See 1790 Census.

KNIGHT, Susannah Putnam, widow in 1772 mar James STEELE, STEALL, STILLE B Milford, NH, 11 chn. See A5. James Steele.
KNIGHT, Franklin mar Jane QUINER, MRB. 1831. See QUINER.
KNIGHT researchers may subscribe to KNIGHT LETTER, 2108 Grace St., Fort Worth, TX.

LABEY, L'ABBEE in J 1528, in St. Martin and St. Saviour J 1668. In St. Saviour, Grouville and St. Clement J 1749. Curr J. Also early in G. Note that MRB records give LIBBY as variant spelling, possibly, for LABBEE, LABBY, LABEY. Capt. Pierre LABEY was a privateersman of J 1756. See LABEY, etc, records in SLCity. (Mrs. Roberta Palmer, Salt Lake City, UT)
LABEY, LABEA, LABBEE records, many in early Boston, MA. OUTC.
LABBY, Martha mar John JEPSON 1751 Boston. (int). OUTC. Note that JEPSON was in G before 1814.
LABEY, Philip and Mary, S.F., from C.I. 1854, via ship MARSHFIELD, rem to UT. (SLCITY records)
LA BLOND, James and Ann res Boston, MA, a son Philip b 1704. OUTC, but this old name in J, as well as French surname.
LABORNE, Henry, surgeon at Portsmouth, NH ca 1700 sued Philip PAYNE that year, when Margaret Bond ca 69 and Sarah FOLLETT ca 22, testified that they lived in the same house as Dr. L. and wife. (Noyes) Was this surname poss LA BORGNE of J? PAYNE, and FOLLETT also recorded in C.I. BORNEY, in St. Clement J 1607. DE BOURNE in G 1668. LE BORGNE curr in J.
LACELLS, George, in Salem, MA 1790 with fam of 6. (Census) Cf LESCELLES of England, and LAYZELL of J.
LACEY curr G, not researched by compiler.
LACHEUR, see LE LACHEUR, LASHURE, LASHER. Curr G, many variants.
LA CLOCHE, curr J. See DE LA CLOCHE, in early New England, means Bell. Poss some Bells were orig. LA CLOCHE? DE LA CLOCHE? Curr research, see CIFHS #3. See also CLOCK.
LA COMBE, see LARCOMBE
LA COUTEUR, see LE COUTEUR
LA CORNU, see LE CORNU
LA CROIX of early New England was poss LA CROIX, ST. CROIX, DE STE. CROIX of J or France, poss Hug.? See DE STE. CROIX, also in Q.A. IN CANADA, by Turk. See also CROSS.
LA CROIX, Sarah from J? mar 1732 in MRB. Joseph SINECROSS, DE STE. CROIX of J, or poss a Hug.
LA CROIX, Pierre, from C.I. or France?, in Kittery, ME 1659. (NEHGS Vol 39, 40)
LA CROSS, noted in LIST OF CONVICTS, by Coldham, NAT. GEN. SOC. QUARTERLY, Dec. 1972
LA CROW, LACROW, Abraham, at Monhegan, ME 1672. "Poss a clue to the origin of Abraham CROSS, who mar Martha Beale 20 Sept. 1700, in MRB they being called Abraham LA CROIX, physician, and wife Martha in 1701." (Noyes)
LA CROIX, ___, b early 1900s, whose father had come from Jersey and settled in MA. (Ernest Gustin, Arlington, MA)
LAELL, LYALL, see LISLE.
LA FETRA, Edmond, a Hug from C.I. to Salem, MA 1666, then to NJ, where he bought land and settled in Shrewsbury, NJ. Later a part of the fam rem to Harveysburg, OH. Edmond said to have mar a widow named Frances West, and d 1687 leaving widow and son Edmund, and a dau Elizabeth, who mar John West. (Mrs. Richard L. Schmidt, Stamford, CT; NJ GEN SOC. BULLETIN 1956)

LA FETRA. Another record says that La Fetra came from France to NY 1640, first settling on Long Island, NY. (NAT. CYCLO. OF AMER.BIOG) Edmund Jr. mar Hannah ALLEN, who may have been from the Islands? Work being done on this line. (Marion Mizenko, Levitttown, PA; QUAKER ENCY; PERLEY GEN; Salem, MA, 1906; Boston TRANSCRIPT, Aug.1904)

LA FEVRE, see LE FEVRE, etc.

LAFFOLEY, means the demented one, in J 1274. In St. Martin and St. Saviour J 1668. In St. Martin, St. Saviour, St. Heliers and St. Ouen J 1749. In St. Lawrence J 1788. Several of this name settled in New Brunswick, Canada from J, such as Philip below. LAFFOLEY curr J.

LAFFOLEY, Philip b J, rem to Quebec ca 1812 and mar ___ DE VERE. This is said to be a Hug. fam, but this is in doubt if they were an old Jersey family. "Philip came to Canada in a boat he designed and built. Later in Boston, he made wood vestibules for the trolley system. He was also a violin maker, made hundreds of them. " (Paul Laffoley, Boston, MA.

A1. Edmond A2. Frederick A3. Percival A4. Reginald A5. Alice.

LAFLY, LAFFOLLEY, James from J? witness with Henry LAMPREY, LEMPRIERE? qv, 1667 in Portsmouth, NH. (Concord File 2,153; Noyes) See also FOLLETT, LA FOLLET.

LAFFOLEY, from C.I. to NB, Gaspe, Quebec City, Montreal and Grand Manan Island, as wella s NS. See Q.A. IN CANADA. (Mrs. Ivan Laffoley, Mrs. Claude Ellis, Gales Ferry, CT)

LA FLOWER, LA FLEUR, FLEURES, FLEURY, qv, ____, and wife, St. Robin's granddau, res Eggemoggin Reach, ME 1688. FLEURY in J 1668. (Noyes)

LA FONTAINE in St. Martin J 1668. Curr J 1970s. Many FONTAINES in early America, Huguenot? Cf also FONDAN, FONTAINE.

LA GROO, LA GROU, see GROUT, GRUT.

LA GROW, LA GROO, LE GROS, LE GROW, LA GROVE, see GROS, GROSSE, LE GROW

LA GROVES, Nicholas, b ca 1654 France, a Hug., rem to J, then to Salem, MA before 1668. See GROVES.

LA HAYE, see DE LA HAYE. In MD 1600s, OUTC. Note LA HA, etc in early New England records. OUTC.

LA HAH, DE LA HAYE?, Jane and Abraham res Isles of Shoals, ME 1713-1722, where other C.I. folk also settled at times. OUTC. (NEHGS V66)

L'AINEE in Vale, G 1821. Was this same as LAINE?

LAINE, LAISNE in J 1607, 1668, from 1331. Common and curr in G. In St. Lawrence J 1788.

LAINE, Sarah b Rehoboth, MA 1764, dau of Amos (Amice?) and Lois. OUTC.

LAINE, James DE BEAUCHAMP, b 1824 G, and wife Rachel MAHY, rem to Racine, WI 1847. James was a partner in firm of LANGLOIS & LAINE Co. He d 1856. (G.SOC. BULL, Spring 1973; Elvira Belden, Racine, WIS)

LAINE, LAISNE, William John from G mar F. DE GARIS, qv, res Memphis,TN

LAINE, Julia HAMELIN, of Les Houges, Vale, G mar Henry LE PELLEY, qv, res UT, but returned to G. Some desc rem to Ontario, Canada, 1900s.

LAINE, James and Rachel (MASSEY) res or visited in NYCity and WI 1847, but returned to G. (G.SOC. BULL, Spring 1973)

LAING, ship owner in J 1839. (A. John Jean, Jersey)

LAISNE, LAINE, Alfred, son of Jean and Marie (COLLAS) LAINE of G, rem ca 1840 to US. (Charles Nitka, Col. Spgs., COL)

A1. Ernest, d in G.

A2. Alfred mar Florence Shafer, res Ogden, UT

B1. Ernest Harvey, d 1937 Los Angeles CAL in car accident.

B2. Ruth Nellie, b 1925 Ogden, UT, mar Charles Benj. Nitka, b 1923 Chicago, ILL, 3 chn.

C1. Ernest Edward Nitka, b 1954 COL. C2. Jessica A. Nitka, B COL.

C3. Alfred Charles Nitka, b 1952 Simla, COL mar Susan Tafoya.

A3. Marie, mar Morris Brandon of Memphis, TN
B1. Valerie Brandon B2. Daniel Brandon of New Orleans
B3. Gail Brandon B4. Gilbert Brandon of Memphis, TN

LA JEUNESSE noted in QUE Petition 1838. (LOST IN CANADA) OUTC

LA JOIE, LA JOY, Old and curr in G. Poss some fams named JOY from G?

LAKEMAN, English surname curr in J. See CIFHS #6

LAMBERT, old in G, curr G and J. See also TRESEDER

LAMBERT, John, b 1715 England? a political prisoner, banished to G, later rem to Elizabethtown, NJ. Said to have had 10 chn, some b G. One ch mar a Capt. Blackburn. A dau Mary mar Charles, son of Lord Hatton. See book, THINGS SEEN IN THE CHANNEL ISLANDS, by Holland. (Lloyd Rieck, La Junta, COL)

LA MONTAGNE, said by a Canadian to be old surname in C.I. Noted in Holyoke, MA. OUTC.

LAMOUREAUX, Andrew L., from C.I. 1855 via ship CHIMBORAZO, res UT. (SLCITY records)

LAMPREY, see LEMPRIERE

L'AMY, AMY in J 1309-1749. AMY in G 1300s, see. Curr research, see CIFHS #3. LAMEY curr J.

LAMY, Anthony escaped jail in York, ME 1673. (Noyes)

L'AMY, James a lawyer res Edinburg, PA 1836. OUTC. A Mrs. Mary L'Amy died there, the sister of Mrs. Joseph B. Lapsley of Phila. Some Channel Islanders settled in Phila.

LANDES, see DES LANDES. LANDES, Abraham bur Seemsville, PA 1902. OUTC. (OGS cardfile)

LANFESTEY, see LENFESTY.

LANGLEY, see LANGLOIS and ENGLISH. LANGLEY and ENGLISH often are from LANGLOIS of France and C.I.

LANGLOIS in J 1299, in St. Laurens and St. Ouen J 1668, 1749. In St. Laurens J 1788. In G 1300s, in Torteval G, 1738; in St. Peters G, 1764, curr G and J.

LANGLEY, LANGLOIS, Peter from G mar Rachel BICHARD, qv, in GCO 1821. (Conner-Eynon). He was b ca 1795 G, d GCO 1875. He mar 2. Mary ___ See also ROBBINS.

A1. Peter b 1826 d 1909, mar Rachel Fishel, 1832-1919
A2. Thomas, b 1829, d 1871 A3. John, b 1833 d 1906
A4. James, b 1839 d 1880? Mar Christina Robinson 1859
A5. Elizabeth, b 1842 d 1884
A6. Christenia, 1842-1929, mar Joseph B. Schofield?

These LANGLEYS of Guernsey Co., OH may be desc of Peter LANGLEY/LANGLOIS above. (Conner-Eynon) Middle and late 1800s.

John, mar Elizabeth BARTON Rachel mar Aaron STEVENS
Mary Ellen mar Hugh S. Downey Lena mar J.C. Dilley
John mar Elizabeth K. STEELE Myrtle mar Charles F. Danford
Kate mar Geo. W. Enos Emma J. mar John BUTLER
Sarah mar John W. Spaid. See HEAUME in SPAID GEN. in GCO and WRCIC
LIZZIE A. mar J.A. Cowgill.

Many LANGLEYS in early New England, most from England but some may have been LANGLOIS from C.I. See Essex Coll, Vols 3 & 4, & Noyes.

LANGLE, LANGLEE, Lemuel was on the TYRANNOCIDE ship in 1700s, with many other C.I. names. (MASS SOLDIERS AND SAILORS) OUTC.

LANGLOIS, James Mowbray, said to be itinerant preacher on J, and a labourer in Rochester, NY, said to have bro named Philip and sister Martha residing in Rochester, also. James, b 1830 J, son of Amos, Amice and Judith(Mowbray) LANGLOIS, to US ca 1869, div first wife,Mary Ann 1872 in Rochester, NY. Mary Ann had remained in J. He mar 2. Ellen Jane Van Houten, dau of John and Orilla(HULING) Van

Van Houten, in 1873, became citizen 1892, and d there 1912. 2 chn by 2nd wife. 6? chn by 1st wife? (Mrs. Walter Andrus, Rochester, NY) The first 6 chn may have emigrated between 1861 and 1869 to US.

A1. James M., mar Mary Ann ___ A3. Philip

A2. Elizabeth M., mar Thomas Tamblingson

A4. Anna/Hannah mar John T. GOSSELIN

A5. Martha M., mar Thomas LE ROSE or LE ROSS? A6. Henry Charles

A7. Orilla Huling, by 2nd wife, b 1873 d 1934 mar George Edwin Foster 1896, 3 chn.

B1. Luella Grace Foster, b 1898, mar Walker Allen Pierce 1916

C1. George Albert Pierce, b 1917 mar Margery Hill, who d 1978

D1. Donald Pierce, d.y.

D2. Nancy Pierce b 1946 mar Wm. Thomas, 2 chn, Kristin and Wm. Thomas

C2. Raymond Elmer Pierce, b 1919 mar Frances Kluth 1942

C3. Evelyn Esther Pierce, b 1922 mar 1951 Norman Leshley, who d 1963, 3 chn: Beverly, Myra and Blake Leshley

C4. Milton Allen Pierce, b 1924, mar 1947 Martha Hutton, 3 sons: William, Lawrence and Jeffrey Pierce.

B2. Elmer Francis Foster, b 1901 mar Betty ___, 2 sons: George and Richard Foster

B3. Milton George Foster, b 1905 mar Myra Stiffler 1937, 3 chn: Anne, Heather and Dawn Foster.

A8. Harriet Eliza Langlois, b 1886 d 1970, mar Robert Fernald Farnham 1913, 5 chn.

B1. Marion Grace Farnham, b 1915 mar Owen Rood Jr, 1937

C1. Owen Stephen Rood III, b 1939 mar 1964 Carol Baser in WIS. 3 chn Jason, Jeffrey and Michelle Rood

C2. Nancy Jean Rood, b 1942 mar 1965 Joseph Kress in Rochester, NY, 2 chn: Eric and Amy Jo Kress.

C3. Susan Jane Rood, b 1946 mar 1966 Robert Trox, Rochester, NY, 2 chn: Cynthia and Michael Trox.

B2. Robert James Farnham, b 1918 mar Marion Donner, a dau Judy adopted

B3. Doris Jean Farnham, b 1924 mar Walter E. Andrus 1943

C1. Barbara Jean Andrus, b 1945 mar 1965 David Postles, 2 chn: Jill E., b Cleveland, OH and Jeffrey David Postles, b NC.

C2. Kenneth Robert Andrus, b 1948 mar 1970 Williamsport, PA, Diane Caschera, 2 chn: Lisa Maria and Kimberly Jean Andrus

B4. David Donald Farnham, b 1929 d 1963, mar Mary Farren, 2 sons: Richard and Kevin Farnham.

B5. Dolores Margaret Farnham, b 1929, twin, mar David Carson, 2 chn: Lori and Mark, adopted.

LANGLOIS, Thomas, b ca 1794 G, mar ca 1829 Rachel Rose in G. She was b there 1810. Rem to Gaspe, where Thomas was a carpenter, Fisherman and preacher. Six chn b Gaspe Bay North. By 1874 most of the fam had rem to the Port Hope, ONT area, then in about 1876, rem to Hamilton, ONt, and later to Beaverton, ONT, where Thomas d 1878. Rachel res in Stratford, ONT 1881 with dau Mary Jane, and d 1892 Toronto, at Mary Jane's home, poss bur Prospect Cem., Toronto. This fam changed their name to Langley in Ontario, and only two branches retained the name LANGLOIS: Thomas T. son of Nicholas and Jane, and William, last ch of Thomas and Rachel. Some dates in this chart are not verified. Work still proceeding. (Mrs. G. Langlois, Toronto, ONT and Mrs. Edward Marshall, dundas, ONT) See LE MESSURIER.

A1. Rachel, b ca 1834 Gaspe, mar Peter LE MESSURIER, b ca 1834 Gaspe, QUE. Both prob d in Detroit, MI. Peter a carpenter, res next door to Nicholas L. in Port Hope, ONT 1871 census. Rem to Detroit, where a son Joseph started a business called La Measure Bros., INC.

Launderers and Dry Cleaners, in early 1900s. See LE MESSURIER.

A2. Nicholas, b ca 1844 Gaspe, mar Jane Emery, b 1852 Gaspe. Both d in Port Hope, ONT, in 1873, withing 3 weeks of each other, of TB. Nicholas had a flourishing carpentry and joining business in Port Hope. The 1871 census shows that he hired 10 men, and had 18 thousand dollars worth of oak and pine lumber. Said to have built some of the churches in the Port Hope area. At least 4 chn, 2d.y.

B1. Thomas Tolton, b 1867 Gaspe, d 1937 Westmoreland, CAL mar 1892 Dia Diana Baker Hall, a widow b 1862 Orangeville, ONT, d 1943 El Cajon, CAL. Thomas was raised by his aunt Mary Jane and his grand mother Rachel.

C1. Albert Wm. Langlois, b 1894 Toronto, d 1979 Hemet, CAL mar 1917 1. Flora Marion Winstel, b 1898 d 1925, mar 2. ca 1930 Sybil Nablett.

D1. Alan Winstel, b 1918 Los Angeles, mar 1943 Reno, NEV Gail GRAY.

E1. Lynn Diane, b 1944 Seattle, mar 1. 1970 Pasadena, CAL Lawrence Russel Alesio, div 1973, and mar 2. Bruce Nye 1978 Arcadia,CAL A dau Alysia Gail Nye, b 1979

E2. Richard William, b 1947 Inglewood, CAL mar Janet Ann Rooney, 2 chn b NEV and CAL, Thomas and Scott.

E3. James Alan, b 1949 Inglewood, CAL mar Sally S. Moore in CAL, 3 chn: Jeffrey Alan, Adam and Brian

D2. Donald Robert b 1920 Los Angeles, mar 1948 Barbara Leona Patrick

E1. Laura Lee, b 1950 CAl mar Terry D. Conway, son Michael Conway

E2. Leslie Lorraine, b 1953 mar Paul D. Gustafson, a son Paul

E3. Luanne Louise, b 1954 CAL, mar Gary Philip Levin, a son Brandon Lane Levin.

E4. Lonnie Linda, b 1958 Anaheim, CAL.

C2. Muriel Gwendolyn, b 1905 Staff., England adopted by Thomas LANGLOIS in England 1909, single, res El Cajon, CAL

B2. Anne, b 1870 Port Hope, ONT, d.y.

A3. James Langley, b Gaspe, poss d in Toronto?

B1. Arthur James Langley, b ca 1877 d 1929 Toronto, ONT, mar Flora CARTER.

B2. Pearl Langley, mar ___Lindsay, res Toronto, ONT.

A4. John, b ca 1842 Gaspe. A John aged 27 was living with Mary Jane in Stratford, ONT 1881, and a John 28 was living 1871 in Gaspe with Rachel and Thomas.

A5. Mary Jane, b 1851 Perce, QUE, d 1930 Vancouver, BC, mar 1873 ? in Port Hope, ONT? Edmund Samuel/Ned Roberts, b 1849 Wales, d 1880 Stratford, ONT, a cabinetmaker. Ned d of TB, age 31, leaving 4 chn. Mary Jane mar 2. 1886 Stratford, ONT, Alex. George Morrison, b 1851, d 1930 Vancouver, BC, 4 chn.

B1. Amos Alfred Roberts, b 1874 Port Hope ONT, d 1947 Toronto, ONT. Mar 1896 Lily Maud Pinkham, b Toronto?

C1. Margaret May Roberts, b 1897 Toronto, d 1979, mar Wm. McArthur, who d 1942. 10 grchn, 24 grgrchn, 3 grgrgrchn!

D1. Evelyn McArthur mar A. Fleming D2. James Wm. McArthur

C2. Wm. Edmund G. Roberts, b 1903 Toronto C3. Joseph A. b 1905

C4. Thomas Alfred Roberts, b 1907 Toronto

C5. Annie Vera Roberts, b 1914 Toronto mar 1937 Harold DAVEY,Toronto.

D1. Patricia DAVEY, b 1946 Toronto mar A. Kausch, 2 chn: Cathy and Chris. Kausch.

B2. Amelia Florence Roberts, b 1876 mar 1912 Vancouver, BC Herman Herolz, d 1957, no issue

B3. Edmund Samuel Roberts, b 1878 Beaverton, ONT, d 1892 Toronto, ONT

B4. Frederick Wm. Roberts, b 1880 Stratford, ONT, d 1944 Toronto. Mar 1900 Detroit, MI Leavy Morrison, b ca 1880 MI, and 2. Violet ___ in MI, and 3. SAdie McArthur in Toronto, ONT.
C1. Edmund Frederick Roberts, b 1901 Detroit, MI, d 1964 Vancouver, BC. Mar 1926 there Jane Ann Affleck, b 1906 Scotland.
D1. Geraldine Eliz. Roberts, b 1928 Vancouver, mar 1946 Dundas, ONT Edward T. Marshall, b 1926 Greensville, ONT, 4 chn: Gaye Ann, Nancy, Deborah and Randall Marshall.
D2. Joyce Virginia Mary Roberts, b 1929 Vancouver, BC mar 1947 Waldemar Siemens, b 1926 Russia. 6 chn: Susan Joy, Jill Ann, Michael E., Daniel, Paul and Elizabeth Siemens.
D3. Richard Edmund Roberts, b 1933 Vancouver, mar 1954 Shirley Stelps 2 chn: Christopher and Stephen J. Roberts.
D4. Paul Ainslie Roberts, called Teddy, b 1935 d 1979 White Rock, BC Mar Helen Browne, 3 chn: Judith M., Laurie A. & Lonnie Roberts.
B5. by Morrison, Lillian Ann Morrison, b 1888, d Trail, BC?
B6. Josephine May Morrison, b 1890, d Vanc., BC, mar Albert V. ROBINS in Detroit ca 1910. 2 chn: Margaret and Phillis ROBINS.
B7. Mary Rosabella Morrison, b 1892 Toronto, d 1894
B8. Alma Rachel Morrison, b 1894 Toronto, d Vancouver? Mar Dr. Stanley Sievenpiper, 3 chn: Joan, Peter and William Sievenpiper.
A6. William LANGLOIS, b 1855 Gaspe, QUE mar Jennie Whitecross GRAY.
B1. Mabel, b 1889 mar Norman Carter B4. Pearl, b 1898 mar Monte Griffin
B2. Mary, b 1893 mar Milton Lovering B5. Gordon, b1900,mar G.Booth
B3. Isabella, b 1895 mar Hubert Dundas B6. Evelyn, mar Ed Radke.
LANGLOIS, Amos, res Rochester, NY 1861. (SLCity records)
LANGLOIS, Daniel, mariner of C.I. was in Boston MA 1689, from St.Ouen,J?
LANGLOIS, D.R. of SLCity, UT is a desc of a Guernsey LANGLOIS-TOSTEVIN family.
LANGLOIS, James, b 1816 G, to America 1832, settled Richmond, VA? See John below. Rem to RAcine, WI before 1840. Mar 2. in G. Margaret LE PREVOST, dau of Nicholas in 1845. Farmed in Somers and Mt. Pleasant, WIS. (Racine Album)
LANGLOIS, Jane from J, niece of Philip ENGLISH, qv, was in Salem, MA 1720. Mar John CANN 1731 MRB,res Yarmouth,NS.(Gottwald)
LANGLOIS, John, from J, in Hingham, MA 1666. See ENGLISH.
LANGLOIS, John, b 1815 G, son of John and Elizabeth (LANGLOIS) LANGLOIS. The father was b 1798 G, and Elizabeth was his first cousin. John was the 2nd son, another son being Nicholas, who res in Jersey. At age 11, John boarded ship JOHN F. PATTON, and rem to Richmond, VA where an uncle lived. Retruning later to G, he farmed, and mar Sophia SIMON, qv, and had 3 chn. In 1856 John brought his fam to Racine, WI and in 1860 was in partnership with Peter ROBILLIARD, qv, a paint and wallpaper business, becoming in 1869 sole prop., when the partner died. The firm continued under name of LANGLOIS & SON. John's wife d 1889. He lived at least age 77. (Racine ALBUM)
A1. George, d.y.
A2. John Jr, b 1846 in business with his father, mar 1875 Ellen Dutton
B1. Alfred, b 1877 B2. John E. B3. Harold
A3. George, b 1854 G, a farmer in Greenville, Caly Co., IA, and in Placerville, CAL, still living at age 92.
LANGLOIS, John age 45 in 1881 and wife Mary age 41, res Cap des Rosiers, Gaspe, QUE. (Census; Aldo Brochet,Montreal, QUE and London, ONT)
A1. Thomas J., b ca 1865 A3. Amelia J. b 1870 A5. Henry, b ca 1875
A2. Peter, b ca 1867 A4. George, b ca 1872 A6. John, b ca 1878
LANGLOIS, Mary age 26, of Hamilton, ONT, b G, dau of Thomas and Mary LANGLOIS, mar 1863 in Ch of England, Hamilton, ONT, Thomas Styles.

Thomas, b England, age 30, was son of James and Mary Styles. Witnesses included D. LE MERCIER & Julia LANGLOIS (Wentworth Mar.Reg.)

LANGLOIS, Marie of Caraquet, NB mar Francois Josse. Their son, Jean Marie Josse mar 1771 at Isle Madame, NS, Anne SAMSON. SAMSON and LANGLOIS were prob of C.I., as the Islanders settled here in some numbers in the 1700s, but OUTC.

LANGLOIS, Martha, b J, sister of Philip, came to US 1800s. (Mrs. Andrus Rochester, NY)

LANGLOIS, Nicholas, b 1834 G, son of James LANGLOIS, rem to Somers, WI 1843, mar Elizabeth GILLETT, poss GUILLET?, 1866, 4 chn. Nicholas d 1877. (HIST. OF RACINE, WIS)

A1. Flroence, b 1867 A3. B. Etta, b 1871

A2. Mabel E., b 1870 A4. Archie, b 1878

LANGLOIS, Peter, see Peter LANGLEY.

LANGLOIS, Pierre, Peter, b QUE, Methodist, from C.I. fam, age 47, 1881 res Cap des Rosiers, Gaspe, QUE with fam. Wife Mary age 41. See Peter LANGLOIS of Shiphead, Gaspe, in Q.A. IN CANADA. (Aldo Brochet)

A1. John, b ca 1863 A3. Nicholas, b ca 1867

A2. Louise, b ca 1866 A4. Rachel, b ca 1871 A5. William, b ca 1874

LANGLOIS, Philip of J imported Jersey stockings to Salem, MA 1670, had 2 vessels. (A. John Jean, Jersey)

LANGLOIS, Philip, b J to US 1800s. (Mrs. Walter Andrus, Rochester, NY)

LANGLOIS, RAchel b G, mar Jacob Near of Racine, WI ca 1850. (Racine ALBUM; Virginia Hooper, Santa Clara, CAL)

LANGLOIS, Richard G., b 1926 San Diego, CAL, mar 1946 Vivian Dolores Portner, b 1928 Minneapolis, MN. He was the son of Irving Charles LANGLOIS b 1903 and Delvina COLE, b 1904 Clark, SD. OUTC.

LANGLOIS, Samuel b 1796 St. Sampson G mar 1831 St. Heliers J, Maria Ann LE MARGUARD, qv. He d 1875 Ogden, UT, was son of Thomas L. and Elizabeth (LE POIDEVIN) LANGLOIS. He mar 1. Elizabeth OGIER, 2. Judith SEBIRE, LESBIREL, qv, 3. Mary Ann BUCHANT, BUCANT, and 4. Maria Anne LE MARGUARD. At least 10 chn. Some chn came with him from J on ship CHIMBORAZO, THEN REM TO UT. Desc in UT. (SLCITY records)

A1. Mary Marguerite, b 1832 St. John J, d 1864, mar Daniel THOMAS

A2. Nancy, b 1833 St. John J, mar ___Sizemore.

A3. George, b 1837 d 1911 UT? mar 1865 Mary C. Ohlason

A4. Elizabeth, b 1839 A8. Eliz. Ann, b 1846 mar Charles M. GROW

A5. Victore, b 1841 A9. Henriette/Harriet b 1850 mar ___Coffin

A6. Samuel, b 1842 A10. Pierre, b 1852, d.y.

A7. Samuel again, b 1844, d.y.

Please note: If this was a plural marriage, there may be other chn.

LANGLOIS curr Willimansett, MA. OUTC

LANGLOIS, anumber of fams in Racine, WI, poss desc of the fam from G? Name noted also in Cem. records of Wisconsin Rapids, WI. OUTC

LANGAWAY, prob LANGLOIS, Jeremiah, res Salem, MA 1790. The Gaspe people of the 1900s pronounced LANGLOIS very similar to this, as LONGLAWAY. OUTC.

LONGAWAY, Ann, prob LANGLOIS, in Salem, MA 1790, fam of 3. (Census) LONGLEY in MA 1810. OUTC.

LANGTRY, Lillie LE BRETON, the Jersey Lilly, b 1853 J. LANGTRY an English surname. Curr research. See NOTABLES, and CIFHS #3.

LANYON, noted in US. LANYON is an old name in G, curr G and J.

LARAWAY. Some data on this name, not included in book, will be in WRCIC, as origin was uncertain.

LARAWAY, name in some cases in America derives from LE RUEZ, which name was in J 1461, in St. Ouen J 1668 and 1749.

Note that many LARAWAY, LARROWAY fams in and around NY state did not originate in the C.I., but are desc of a Dutch fam. LE RUEZ, qv, curr J.

LARAWAY, LE RUEZ, Philip, b 1757 J, son of Elias LE REUZ, "came from the Island of Jersey" (Underhill) Philip mar 1784 in West Stockbridge, MA Ruth Smalley, b 1764, dau of Benj. and Rebecca (Snow) Smalley. Ruth d 1848. Philip d 1844, bur Poultney, VT. He had served in the 7th MASS Volunteers in Rev. War. Note that his desc? in Geauga Co., OH also served in various wars of the US. Philip said to have had 13 chn, but compiler was unable to find complete records of this fam. (Alice Brinson, Knoxville, TN; Underhill's SMALL GEN; Vivian Kill, Sharon, VT; Charles Laraway, Cleveland, OH; Violet Warren, Middlefield, OH; WRCIC)

A1. Stephen Van Rennselaer, b 1791 Philipstown, NY, d 1866 age 75. More on this fam in WRCIC. Are the Geauga Co., OH people his desc?

A2. Philip, b 1796

A3. Lucy, b 1800, mar 1815 Benj. Farewell, d 1863. Is it poss that this same Lucy mar John Gould? b 1783 Groton, MA, 6 chn b Poultney, VT. (Vivian V. Kill, Sharon, VT)

B1. Benj. F. Gould, b 1816 B3. Charlotte Gould, b 1827

B2. Dan Pond Gould, b 1822 B4. Lucy Gould, b 1829

B5. Fonrose Gould, b 1831 B5. Laura Gould, b 1834

A4. Elias, twin, b ca 1806. An Elias res Geauga Co., OH 1840, mar Esther Stebbins 1828.

B1. Adelia, b ca 1833, d 1835 B2. George Henry, d 1852 age 4.

A5. Elijah, twin, b ca 1806 A6. Ira, b ca 1808.

LARAWAY, Frank, Francis, b ca 1810-1820, where? mar Mary Gorzey. Was he a son of Philip above? (Etwalla Thompson, W. Townsend, MA.)OUTC.

A1. Frank, Francis, b 1837 St. Mary's, QUE, Canada, d 1910 age ca 73. Mar 1855 Franklin, VT Melinda Jacobs, b 1839 d 1915 Waterville, VT res 1861 Johnson Twp., La Moille Co., VT.

B1. Frank Wilbur, b 1858 Waterville, VT d 1907, mar 1883 Flora Balch Flora mar 2. Frank Jacobs 1911 at age 47. 12 chn, mostly b VT.

B2. Delia Mary or Adelia, b 1859 VT, d 1930 mar 1880 Adelbert Charles David Stockwell, son of Azro Buck Stockwell and Sarah Morgan Griffith, 4 chn, res VT.

B3. Abraham L., b 1860 Waterville, VT mar 1887 Aline A. Green Anderson

B4. Alfred, b 1861 B5. several daus named Lucettie, d.y.

B6. Willie, d.y. B7. Nellie, d.y.

B8. Ella/Ellen Mary, b 1873 d 1950, mar 1889 George Morrison, 1867-1939.

B9. Thomas J, b 1875 d 1957, mar 1896 Hattie Aline Green, 1876-1939, dau of Henry Green and Susan Larabel or Larway?

B10. Harry B11. Fred B12. Idelia, d.y. B13. Eddie, d.y.

A2. Leander, b 1840 Canada, d 1922 A4. Albert, 1850-1931, mar Esther Balt.

A3. John, b 1845 Canada d 1921 Johnson, VT

A5. Alexander, b 1844 d 1937 mar Ida E. Putnam

LARAWAY. There is data in Slcity on the LARROWA fam of New York State of Dutch origin, and some desc. There is also data on another LARAWAY fam, OUTC, who were settled in Marietta, OH 1849, Peter Byron and Susannah (Starting) LARAWAY. OUTC. They were later in Glenwood MIlls, IA. Others res in NYCity, Montana and CAL, but OUTC. In the UT records are also names of some LE RUEZ of the C.I.

These VT Laraway fams may be desc of Philip above:

Alexander and Mary res Orleans Co., Barton Twp., a son Charles,b 1868

Francis and Edna res Johnson Twp, VT, dau Hattie M b 1866, LaM. Co.VT

LARAWAY, Frank and Melinda res Johnson Twp., La Moille Co., VT.
A1. Alfred, b 1861 A2. Frank b 1864 A3. Frank b 1865
Francis and Mary res Barton Twp., Orleans Co., VT, dau Anna b 1869
Hiram and Ellen res Berkshire Twp., VT, poss Ellen Rice?
A1. Homer E., b 1858 A2. Willie b 1860 A3. Lester, b 1864
James and Philory? ___, dau Elannie b 1869 Orleans Co., VT
Joseph and Celeste ___, a son Joseph b 1867
Joseph and Sally Cabinaw, a son Albert b 1869 Johnson Twp., VT.
Philip and Nellie___, res Morristown, VT, son Willie b 1869.

L'ARBALESTIER, crossbowman, old J surname. See BALLISTER, BALISTER. One Joseph L'ARBALESTIER, BALLISTER res Boston early 1800s. See under E4. Benj. PUNCHARD.

LARCHER, John in early New England. Was this L'ARCHER, or L'ARBALESTIER, meaning Archer?

LARCOM, Mordicai, b ca 1629 C.I. but prob of Hug. fam? mar ca 1652 Elizabeth, ___, widow of William Clarke. Mordicai d 1712/13 in Beverly, MA, had also res Ipswich, MA 1658. There is much info. on this fam but it is clear that they originated prob in Italy, rem to the Languedoc area of France, then to Isle of Wight, England, from which a branch prob settled for a short time in Jersey or Guernsey. See sources for more info. A John Larcume from Bristol, England settled 1663-1679 in VA. (Bristol Records) Only the chn of Mordicai are included, as this was really a Hug fam, not a C.I. fam, and it is not known if his wife was from the Channel Islands. (Gerald Fuller, Okla City, OK; Essex Coll, Vols 40-58, etc; ANCESTORS OF GUILFORD SOLON TINGLEY; Rutland VT records; GEN OF THE LARCOM FAM, by Wm. F.Abbot) Note that a G.A. Lewis of Phila. worked on this fam, and his records may be available there. Note also that a number of Larcoms, and desc. mar into C.I. fams. such as HOOPER, MASURY, LE GROVE. See ABBOT, DANE AND HALE Gens, etc.

A1. Thomas, b ca 1651 Ipswich, MA d 1710 Beverly, MA, fisherman and farmer. Mar 1. 1674 Hannah, dau of John and Elizabeth (Allen) Kettle of Salem, MA, 1665-1697. Thomas mar 2. Abigail, widow of Thomas Woodbury, Jr, who had a ch by John Ford of Beverly in 1700. 7 chn by 1st wife.

A2. Cornelius, b 1653, d 1747 Beverly, MA age 94. Mar 1. 1680 Abigail dau of Benj. and Sarah (Gardner) Balch of Salem, b 1663, d 1706 Beverly. Mar 2. 1707 Margaret LOW, d 1756 age 85.

A3. Mordicai, b 1658 Ipswich, MA d 1717 Wenham, MA. Mar 1681 Abigail, dau of John Solart of Wenham, MA, b 1664- d 1741, 9 chn.

A4. Elizabeth b ca 1660 Ipswich, MA d 1747, mar Isaac Whittier of Man chester, MA, no issue.

A5. Daniel b ca 1663/4 MA d 1750 Beverly, MA age 87. Mar 1693 Phebe, dau of Nathaniel and Sarah Stone of Salem, MA, bp 1672, d 1756,85.

A6. Rebecca, b 1665/70 Beverly, d 1734. Mar 1699 John Stanley of Beverly, MA, who d 1758 age 86. 5/6 chn.

LAROKE, see ROCK, LEAROCK and LARRICK.

LAROKE, LA ROCQUE, DE LA ROCQUE, LEROCK, etc, variants of French and C.I. surnames, many in G a long time, some from 1300s. ROCHE and ROCK are curr in G. See also DE LA ROCQUE. See CIFHS #3.

LA ROCQUE, LAROKE arms; Argent, a fesse between 3 trefoils slipped and couped, sable.

LA ROCQUE, "fam of ancient settlement in Jersey." (NEHGS Vol 31)

LAROKE, John age 27, from "France', in MA. Note that several were said to be from France, when they were from C.I., as they spoke Norman French. (MASS SOLDIERS AND SAILORS)

LAROCK, David and Mary, had son Benj. who d 1848 Bakersfield, VT,3mos.

LAROCK, Francis and Margaret, had son Isaac in MA, who d 1849.
LAROCK, Zebulon and Mary had Rosa Ann, who d.y. 1867 (NEHGS Vol 82).
LEAROCK, LAROCQUE, John b ca 1734 G, rem to Boston, MA where he mar Mary Gold, Gould, dau of James and Margaret of England. He d 1821, age 87 of TB, bur Pickering Hill, Salem. Was Cordwainer and laborer. Served as private in Rev. War, Col John Nixon's Rgt., Capt. Winship's Co., to end of 1776. In 1780 served on brigantine GRIFFIN, out of Salem, MA. (MASS SOLDIERS AND SAILORS; Pension List; Gazette 1821; First Ch records, Salem; Thelma Janney, Danvers, MA)
A1. Mary Learock, b 1766 Salem, mar 1786 James NICHOLS Jr, b 1765 Salem who d 1846 age 88, bur Salem. (UPHAM GEN;, South CH records)
B1. Polly/Mary Nichols, bp 1787, mar Joshua Upham
B2. Elizabeth Nichols, bp 1797 mar Benj. Gardner, 1815
B3. James Nichols, bp 1798, d.y.
B4. Benj. Nichols, bp 1797 B5. Sally Nichols, bp 1797
B6. Lydia Nichols, bp 1799, mar 1. 1821 Jacob Ellsworth, seaman, who d 1827, and 2. Charles Briggs, mariner, b Wales. 2 chn by 1st H?
C1. Frances Todd Ellsworth, d 1824
C2. William Ellsworth, b ca 1822 teamster, mar Nancy ___.
D1. Mary Ellsworth, b 1844 Lynn, MA.
C3. Joseph Brown Briggs, b 1833, mar 1. Julia A. Emerson, 2 chn, and 2. 1827, Hellen Frances Maria (Nevills) Larrabee, b 1839 Sedgewick, MA. Helen d 1883 in Salem. A ch by Julia d.y.
D1. Julia Briggs, b ca 1856 Salem, MA mar 1876 George E. Dodge,d1881
D2. William Larrabee, b ca 1856 ch of Helen Frances.
D3. Edward Larrabee, b ca 1857 D4. Alice M. Larrabee, b 1861
D5. Joseph Francis Briggs, b 1870 Salem, mar Caroline A. Price of Danvers, MA 1897.
E1. Kenneth F. Briggs, b 1897 Salem E4. Dudley T. Briggs b 1914
E2. Philip B. Briggs, b 1901 Salem E5. Sidney C. Briggs, a girl,
E3. Thelma Helene Briggs, b 1904. b 1923 Danvers, MA.
D6. Bertha L. Briggs, b 1872 d 1878 D7. Harry E. Briggs, b 1874
B7. James Nichols, b 1802 mar Margaret Shannon 1824
C1. Elizabeth G. Nichols mar Jonathan Shove SYMONDS 1849
B8. John Nichols, b 1805 mar Mary Ann Waters 1831
B9. Samuel Barker Nichols, b 1809 mar Betsey L. Frye 1832
A2. John Jr., mar Hannah Breed 1806
A3. Margaret mar Samuel Barker 1791, d 1846 TB. Capt. Sam. Barker d 1816, age 47?
A4. Nancy, mar Philip SAUNDERS, SANDERS, 1792 Salem, MA.
A5. Sally, mar William DALAND, qv, 1792 and 2. Andrew MILLET 1798.
LEAROCK in Salem records, poss related to above fam.
LA ROCK, Ebenezer mar Katy Brown 1797. An Eben b 1884 Salem. Another Eben was master of brig TRIAL in 1810.
LEAROCK, John Jr. mar Katy Brown 1806
LEAROCK, John M. mar 1841 Sarah E. Treadwell. John M. b 1820 Salem.
LEAROCK, Sarah M., mar 1832 William L. MILLET
LARROCK, Mary mar 1818 Isaac Goodhue
LEAROCK, Sally mar 1795 (int) Michael Bridgden of Charlestown, MA.
LEAROCK, Hannah B. mar 1837 Benj. Lang.
LEAROCK, Sarah E. mar John M. SEAMAN Salem, MA.
A1. Caroline A. Seaman, b 1843 A2. Anna M. Seaman, b 1849.
LA RUE, DE LA RUE, RUE. It is very difficult to distinguish between desc of these fams in America. LA RUE to America from England in the PRIMROSE 1635. LA RUE and DE LA RUE were both used by Guernsey Islanders in Guernsey Co. and other counties in Ohio. The 'De' was often dropped.

LA RUE, DE LA RUE, John, listed by Sarchet as coming to OH from G., and a John LA RUE, had 161 acres in Wills Twp., GCO 1840. (Wolfe) Others noted in Richland Twp., GCO. John LA RUE b 1801 Loudoun Co., VA, came with his parents to Richland Twp., 1808. Did this fam come from G? His chn are listed, but OUTC. (Camb. OH Library)
A1. James A4. La Van A7. Mary M. A9. Judson
A2. Stephen B. A5. John S. A8. Elizabeth A10. Eli J.
A3. Hamilton A6. Samuel R., b 1842
LA RUE, DE LA RUE, John, to GCO with the Sarchet group 1806. Was he same John as the one above, with family?
DE LA RUE, RAchel, wife of James BICHARD from G.
DE LA RUE, Elias res GCO 1860. Those below mar in GCO middle 1800s:
LA RUE, Eliza Ellen mar John QUEEN, QUINN? James mar Catherine Ann Foreacre, James mar Melinda Dennison 1836; John B. mar Sonora LA RUE, and John DE LA RUE mar Nancy Scott 1861, the minister being named Elias DE LA RUE. This fam chart needs much work.
LA RUE, Margaret and LA RUE, Laban were both over 76 in 1876, in GCO, Richland Twp.
LE RUE, Thomas, res and d in Coshocton, OH 1800s. (Sarchet) OUTC.
See sources: Burial records of Richland, Jackson and Cambridge, in Cam. OH; County records, Cambridge, OH; Wolfe; OLD NORTHWEST Vol 4; TINGLEY GEN; Sarchet books; Williams; Conner-Eynon; WRCIC; GCO COLL. OF HIST. SKETCHES AND FAM HISTORIES, 1979, GCO Gen. Soc., Dallas, TX.
LA SERRE, Octave, b 1801 G, son of John and Mary (LE PELLEY) LA SERRE. Mary was dau of the Seigneur of Sark. Octave, desc of Jean Pierre, Vicomte de la Serre de Villemaine, near Cette, Languedoc, France, who fled to G in 1685. Octave rem to OH where he d at Roscoe, 1849. He mar 1825 Elizabeth Tillard GILES, Ohio Co., WVA, was naturalized 1840 in Zanesville, OH. 6 chn. (NORTHWEST GEN. QUARTERLY, Vols 3,8)
A1. Frederick John, b 1834, d 1898, mar Mary Almack?
B1. Charles Frederick, res Minneapolis, MN 1900.
LA SERRE, Charles, b G, rem to Phila. PA, where he mar and had 3 chn, one named James. Charles was bro of Octave above.
LA SERRE, Catherine, dau of J.S. and Jane LA SERRE, d 1867 age 28. (OLD NORTHWEST, Vol 8)
LA SERRE, Martha, b 1786, sister of above Charles and Octave, res G, where she mar Rev. Peter CAREY, dean of Guernsey. Other sisters were Sophia, Marie Ann, and Julia, unmar.
LA SERRE, William W. mar 1899 Lizzie Leavengood, in Coshocton, OH.
LASERE, Fred mar 1860 Cynthia? Chapman
LA SERRE, or LE SERRE, Mrs. Mary mar J.L. DAVIS 1899 Coshocton, OH.
LASERE, Cora mar Hulbert Kitchen 1890 Coshocton, OH
LASERE curr Minn. and Hopkins, MN. OUTC.
LASHER. This surname apparently comes mostly from the descendants of Francois Lessieur, a Hug. from Scalmeny or Chalmenil near Dieppe, France. He mar Jannet Hildebrandts 1659, and settled in Kingston, NY. Most LASHEURS will prob be his desc. However it is poss that some LASHERS are desc of a C.I. LE SUEUR, or LE LACHEUR. There is a LASHER GEN, publ. 1904, not seen by compiler.
LASH, Nicolas, poss LACHEUR, LE LACHEUR?, res Saco and Scarboro, ME 1664/7, res Boston, MA 1679. Had wife Gertrude 1672, living 1676. (Noyes) Had son Robert and desc. OUTC.
LASH, also a Wm. and John res Boston 1600s. OUTC.
LASHURE, LE LACHEUR, George N. b 1863 of G fam in Cape Breton, NS, Canada, d Danvers, MA 1955, son of Rachel HELIER, qv of G. See also LE LACHEUR and Q.A. IN CANADA. (Wm. Goss, Ipswich, MA)
LASHURE, William b G, to GCO early 1800s. (Sarchet) Name curr J.

LASHURE, LACHEUR?, Susan mar Nathaniel LE PAGE, qv, in GCO 1800s.
LAUGIER, see LOUGEE
LAULY noted in early colonies. LAULY in J 1607
LAURENS, LAWRENCE in J 1515. In St. Martin, St. Peter and St. Laurens J 1668. In St. Martin and St. Laurens J 1749. In St. Laurens J 1788. LAURENCE from C.I. to Nfld. 1676. A LAURENS had a rope walk in J 1790-1860. LAURENS curr in J. see also LAWRENCE.
LAURENS, Henry, b J? in slave traffic Charleston, SC 1769. (A.John Jean, Jersey)
LAURENS, Elie, b C.I.? See CADORET, Nancy.
LA VALLEE, ___res Alderney Island, mar ___GALE. See Thomas PALMER. LA VALLEE and GALE rem to London,England and then to Chatham, ONT. (Mildred Chase, Montague, MA)
A1. Thomas, b Ald? A2. Henry, b ALD had fam early 1900s in Chatham,ONT
LA VALLEY, said to be Hug fam from France to the C.I. to MRB, MA,1700s. LA VALLEY to GA and Carolinas 1740. OUTC. (Coulter & Saye)
LA VALLEY b Canada to Chippewa Valley, WI. OUTC.
LA VALLEE, Esther mar 1827 John Wm. PEZET, at St. Andrews Presb. CH, City of Quebec. (LOST IN CANADA, Aug 1981)
LA VALLEE, Elizabeth mar James MAUGER 1828 at St. Andrews Presb. Ch, City of Quebec.
LA VALLEY, DE LA VALLEY, John and Nicholas in MD 1657. (Skordas) OUTC Poss Hug or from C.I.
LA VIRES, named as immigrant from G to GCO by Sarchet in his book. Probably mispelled or misread in publishing, should be LE LIEVRE?
LAWRENCE, Capt. John of J, b 1682, rem to Boston, where he mar 1. Marian BEAUCHAMP 1713. Some question of a 2nd wife, Dorothy Sastero? His widow mar 2. Capt. John Keith, b Scotland in Hartford, CT. Dorothy had Mary and Benjamin, any by Capt. Keith? (Bolton; Boston VR; CLEVELAND GEN; Hartford records) CAUTION: TRIAL CHART
A1. Marian
A2. Hon. John LAWRENCE, b 1719 appointed Treasurer of the CT colony, and served over 20 years. D Hartford, CT 1802, mar 1748 Margaret Chenevard, of a Swiss fam.
B1. William, b 1751 d 1821. Mar Alice Adams, who d Hartford, CT 1845, age 89.
C1. Sarah Lawrence
C2. Alicia Lawrence, d 1864, mar Charles Sheldon, who d 1855/6. Chn b early 1800s: Alicia, Elizabeth, Jane S., Charles Henry, Wm. Larence, Edward, Henry, Catherine and George Sheldon.
C3. William Henry Lawrence, b ca 1790
C4. Roderick, mar 1. 1823, Mrs. Hester (Molieres) Sickle of Phila.,PA b ca 1796, d 1830 age 34. Mar 2. Eliz. L. Lowndes of NY, 1807-1837, bur NY. He mar 3. 1850 Calarinda Chevers of NY. One son by 1st wife.
D1. William Roderick D2. John Beauchamp D3. Cecelia Roderika
See Boston VR for many more Lawrence fams. See also MRB records.
LAWRENCE, Joseph mar Ann MARKS, qv, 1742 Boston. See MARKUM
LARANCE, Mary mar Flan FLOOD 1742 Boston. See FLOOD
LAWRENCE, David, see Noyes, p. 659.
LAWRENCE,John and Nicolas in ME early, spelled name LAURANC, from C.I.?
LAYNE, see LAISNE and Walters, G.W.
LAYZELL in American colonies as LACELLS, etc. LAYZELL, old in J.
LEALE, LISLE?, Capt. ___, b G, master of a ferry in San Fran., CAL. 1800s. (Luce)
LEAVER in early New England. Were some of these LE LIEVRE of C.I.?
LE BAILLIF, LE BAILLEY in J 1668, 1749. Curr J. Some to US? CIFHS #7.

LE BALLISTER of early MA was no doubt L'ARBALESTIER of J, meaning cross-bow-man. In J 1309, in St. Heliers J 1607. Also see BALESTIERS OF BEECHWOOD, by Gordon Ireland, Wash., DC, 1948, which deals with a Balestier from France? to Martinique. Joseph believed b1788 France, but origin not proved, mar Maria REVERE, Col Paul Revere's 15th child, before 1816. Balestier a temp. Consul on Island of St. Thomas, Danish West Indies, then merchant in New York, with poss an interest in Balestier Tanneries in York, PA. This fam may be from C.I. See CIFHS #3. Note that Paul Revere had C.I. ties. CAUTION TRIAL CHARTS.

LE BALLISTER, Joseph from J to MRB, wife Sarah Gatchell 1728.
A1. Sarah, bp 1728 A2. Joseph, bp 1730, d.y.
A3. Joseph again, bp 1732, one Joseph mar Eleanor Hanover 1787 MRB.
A4. Jeremiah, bp 1734, poss mar Mary Twisden 1760 MRB, name written LE BANNISTER.
B1. Mary, bp 1762 MRB. B3. Sarah, bp 1769
B2. Joseph, bp 1766. Poss had firm in Boston early 1800s? Were these his chn?
C1. Molly Twisden, bp 1787 C2. Eleanor, bp 1789 C3. Joseph, bp 1793
A5. Philip bp 1737 A6. Ann, bp 1739, d.y.? A7. Samuel, bp 1744
A8. Charles, bp 1746 poss mar 1769 in MRB Hannah MARTIN?
B1. Sarah, bp 1772 MRB. B3. William, bp 1779
B2. Thomas, bp 1775 B4. Hannah, bp 1782
A9. William, bp 1748 MRB, mar Sarah VICKERY 1771 MRB.
B1. Sarah, bp 1771 MRB B2. Hannah, bp 1774
A10. Ann, bp 1751

LE BALLISTER, L'ARBALESTIER was pronounced BANSTER in MRB., therefore sometimes changed to BANNISTER. (JOURNALS OF ASHLEY BOWEN)

LA BALISTER, Elizabeth, age 18, of Toronto, ONT b J, dau of John and Elizabeth, mar 1868 in Toronto John Maddocks, age 21. Witness, James Thompson. (C OF E records, Toronto)

LE BALASTER, Hannah, mar Jacob Dockindorf, Jr., 1797 Boston, MA.

BALLISTER, Jeremiah, son of Joseph, shipmaster of MRB, commanded the schooner POLLY, 1763/4, and the PATTY, ca 1766/68, also brig PATTY, 1769/73. (JOURNALS OF ASHLEY BOWEN) See Jeremiah in chart above.

LE BALISTER, John mar Mary Adams of Salem, MA 1768 in MRB.

BALESTER, BANESTER, Sally mar William BODEN, qv, 1788 MRB.

LE BALLISTER, BANNISTER records in Longmeadow, Medford, Conway, MA and Histories of Goshen, Framingham, Marlboro, Medway, MA. See also HIST. OF BARNARD, VT, and HIST. OF N. BROOKFIELD, MA. See records of BANNISTERS in Boston.

LE BARGY, from G to Canada, curr G. Many in NY State, and bur Rush Co WIS, but OUTC. Amelia Bargy mar Charles Bordeaux 1800s, Canada. (James Lalone, Lansing, MI)

LE BAS in St. Brelade and Grouville, J 1668 and in St. Brelade J 1749. Curr J. Some from J settled in Gaspe QUE and Nfld., Canada. See Q.A. IN CANADA. It is poss that some named BASS in early New England were LE BAS, either from C.I. or from England.

LE BAS, James, merchant, called Frenchman, had warrant for 1000 acres of land 1683 in SC. See LE BAS data in Boston TRANSCRIPT, Nov. 1923.

LE BAS, Anne and Elizabeth, sisters, b St. Heliers J ca 1820, daus of Francis LE BAS and Mary DURELL, were wives of Peter ROMERIL, qv, and rem rem to UT middle 1800s. (SLC records)

LE BAS noted in Geauga Co., OH, 1900s.

LEBBEE, cf L'ABBEE, and LABEY of C.I. See Portsmouth, NH records and NEHGS Vols 24,81. OUTC.

LE BLANC, LE BLANCQ in J 1309, in St. Mary and St. Ouen J 1668.

LE BLANCQ in St. Peter and St. Mary J 1749. Curr G and J. Means whitehaired. Those in America from varied origins.

LE BLANC, LE BLAM, Philip arrived in Boston 1715 on ship MARY from J and Falmouth, England. (Filby)

LE BLANC, Peter was with Capt. Isaiah Boudreau's Co. of Frenchmen, sworn sworn to in Machias, ME. (Noyes)

LE BLANC, Philip, Zachariah and John came from J to Salem 1678 and in 1720 Philip died without heirs in America. His bro in J inherited 1745.

LE BLANC, Zachariah, mariner from Salem ,bought at Back Cove in 1682, was in Falmouth, ME and also in Casco Bay. A nephew, Philip WHITE, LE BLANC, sold both lots in 1729. There are prob desc of Philip White, but prob none of Zach.

LE BLANCQ, of a C.I. fam settled in Lower Sackville, Nova Scotia, Canada.

LE BLOND curr G and J., noted in MA 1600s. (Savage) and in PA. 1700s.

LE BOEUF, Hug surname said by some to have rem to the C.I. from France, and later to the Canadian Maritimes. (Wayne Willett, New Richmond,QUE)

LE BOEUF in St. Heliers J 1668.

LE BOSQUET in J 1437, means GROVE. Cf Bosky dell! See GROVE and LA GROVES, etc. LE BOSQUET in St. Mary J 1668. See CLEVELAND GEN.

LE BOSQUET, Henry, mar Lydia Scottow in Charlestown, MA 1731, taxed 1756. OUTC. (GENS & ESTATES OF CHARLESTOWN, by Wyman)

A1. John, bp 1737 mar Sarah Brooks, 4 chn

B1. John, bp 1761 B2. Henry, b 1763 B3. Caleb Brooks, b 1764

B4. Sarah, b 1765

A2. Henry, bp 1739

A3. Lydia, bp 1741 poss mar John WAY, b ca 1770, d as young man? She mar 2. ___Milliken in Lynn, MA. Dau Eliz. d unmar, and dau Sarah mar ___Dow.

LE BOSQUET, Caleb B. res Haverhill, MA 1810. (Census) OUTC

LE BOSQUET, Ebenezer, had dau who d 1833 Concord, NH. (NEHGS Vol 67)

LE BOSQUET, Henry and John res Medford, MA early 1800s. OUTC.

LE BOURDON in Grouville and St. Clement J 1668 and 1749. See BODEN.

LE BOURDON, Wm. and Charles rem to Boston from J on ship MOLLY, 1769.

LE BOURVEAU, ___, b France, Hug minister, became a Col. in Rev. War. Curr research. (Charles Le Bourveau Sr., HISTORY OF EATON; Eliz. Bowman, Toms River, NJ, and others)

LE BOUTILLIER in J 1309 or before. In St. Laurens, St. Saviour, Trinity, and St. Peter J 1668. In St. Laurens, St. Saviour, St. John, St. Helier, St. Brelade and St. Peter J 1749. Curr G and J. LE BOUTILLIER shield: azure, 7 chevronels argent, in base a stag trippant of the second. These Channel Island fams have become well distributed throught the world. Many settled in US and Canada. CAUTION: These fams do not all have a common origin. Some came to the C.I. from France very early, while one fam in America claims to be Huguenot. No verification. (Lawton)

LE BOUTILLIER, see BUTLER.

LE BOUTILLIER-BUTLER fam in Mid-West America. Much research, fine book published, THE LE BOUTILLIER-BUTLER FAM HIST, by Gladys Brechtel and Betty Jean Dolling, 2009 Kellogg Ave., Ames, IA, 50010. The four fams below are partial excerpts from this book, with permission. See book for much more info.

These three LE BOUTILLIERS were the chn of Edward, a shoemaker, b St. Ouen J 1815, and wife Jane DUVAL, qv, b St. Peter J. Edward had a bro Philip, a carpenter, b St. Ouen 1833, and sister Jane, a dressmaker, b St. Ouen 1812, plus other siblings. See Philip of Hawaii.

I. LE BOUTILLIER, Heloise Jane or Jane Heloisa, a dressmaker, b 1837 St. Ouen J, rem to Osceola, IA 1897, where she mar 1898 George W. Robinson. She d 1908. (Dolling)

II. LE BOUTILLIER, Edward John, b 1840 J, d there 1897. (Brechtel book)

III. LE BOUTILLIER, Jane Elizabeth, b 1842 St. Ouen J. She mar 1. Elias LE SUEUR. They had son Elias, who d in IA as a youth in a hunting accident. Elias Sr. d at sea, and Jane then married John LE BOUTILLIER below, on condition he not remain a sailor. They settled in IA. See Johns chart below.

LE BOUTILLIER, Jean/John, b 1838 St. Peter J, carpenter's apprentice 1851, sailor 1853-1869. He was son of Francois and Betsey (DE GRUCHY) LE BOUTILLIER. He mar 1870 Jane Elizabeth LE BOUTILLIER LE SUEUR, as noted above,a widow. The couple emigrated to US on their honeymoon, changed name to BUTLER and settled in IA. He d 1912 Osceola,IA 7 chn. See book.

A1. Jane Eliz. BUTLER, b 1870 Osceola, IA d 1934, mar 1. 1896 Chauncey Monroe Dunbar, who d.young, and 2. 1912, August R. Becker, 2 chn.

A2. John Walter, b 1871 d 1947 mar Lydia Merbah Wilson, 12 chn, desc.

A3. Florence Heloise, b 1874, mar Orla Guy LE HEW, 1 ch, with desc

A4. Alfred George, b 1876 d 1907, mar Viola Frances Valentin, 7 chn

A5. Frances Duval, b 1878, d 1928, mar Letha A. Newlin, 2 chn

A6. Lillian Alice, b 1880, d 1911, mar Charles Joseph McDonald

A7. Philip Edward, b 1884 d 1915, mar Myrtle Catherine Hacker

LE BOUTILLIER, Alfred, b ca 1847, d 1892, rem from J to Scotland, where he mar Catherine McKay. Their five chn: Alfred, John, Elizabeth, Donald and Hugh McKay. (Brechtel-Dolling book)

A1. Hugh, b Glasgow, mar Margaret Boyle Beattie 1903, and rem to Newport News, VA, retired to Ormond Beach, FLA.

B1. Ann Jane, b 1904 B2. Alfred Butler, b 1907

B3. Georgina Butler, b 1911 in Scotland

B4. Harry Boyle Butler, b 1920 Newport News, VA, res CAL?

LE BOUTILLIER/BUTLER, Charles, b prob 1804 J, d 1876 Parsons, KS. Mar 1830 Anne LE SUEUR in Trinity Par, J. She was bp 1809, dau of Jean LE SUEUR and Anne HUBERT. She d 1880 Parsons, KS. Charles was a colorful figure, said to be well-educated, listed 1841 in J as a carpenter. Fam rem to Louisa Co., IA ca 1851, where he was granted much land, but lost some of it for non-payment of taxes. In 1856 he became a citizen. In 1868 they rem to Osage Twp., Labette Co., KS, where he was listed 1870 as a physician, and also said to have a drug store which he ran in connection withhis practise. Charles and Anne are bur in Pleasant Hill Cem., located 1 mi. south of Dennis, KS. The inscription on the stone differs from info. above by a couple of years for both Charles and Anne. Could there have been two Charles born close to same time in J? (Some data from John Balleine, Seattle, WA; Brechtel-Dolling Book)

A1. Ann, bp 1831 Trinity J, poss d. there?

A2. Charles, bp 1833 Trinity J, mar in Louisa Co., IA, 1854, Sarah Ann Smith. She was b 1826, dau of James and Sarah (Hill) Smith. They rem to MINN, where Charles Jr. practised medicine in St. Anthony, where they were living 1855. He enlisted in 9th Regt, also served a term in MINN 7th Legis. Charles d of scarlet fever 1863, bur St. Peter, MN. Sarah Ann and her three chn returned to Louisa Co., IA, then lived with her mother in Morning Sun, IA. Sarah Ann d 1894, bur Morning Sun. (John Balleine, Seattle, WA)

B1. Ella Pauline, b 1856 St. Anthony, MN, mar 1875 Charles Fassett,IA. Charles, a machinist, b NY,4 chn, res Hannibal, MO.

C1. Elizabeth Fasset, b 1879 MO, mar ___GILLE.

C2. Helen Fassett, b 1883 SD, mar ___Herrin
C3. Edna Fassett, b 1891 MN C4. Raymond Fasset, b 1895 MN
B2. Charles Victor, b 1859 Hennepin Co, MN mar Kitty Koponstall 1881 and 2. Emily or Esther ___. Charles res Burlington, IA 1915,3chn
C1. Mary S.,b 1893, d.y.? C2. Charles W., b 1896, in 1915 Census
C3. Sarah M., b 1898 Iowa
B3. Alice Mary Le B. was b 1862 Minn. and d 1917 Hannibal, MO while visiting her sister, Ella Fasset. Alice unmar, a dressmaker.
A3. Mary Le B., bp 1835 Trinity J, to Iowa with fam. Mar there 1854 Francis Abraham or Abram Booth Smith, son of James and Sarah Hill Smith. The Smiths were from England to Iowa 1844. Smith d 1900, bur Parsons, KS. 1900 Census states that they had 9 chn, 8 living.
B1. Frank Smith b 1855 IA, M.D., d of TB in CAL 1894. His widow rem to Indiana, mar there. Frank bur Parsons, KS.
B2. Mary E. Smith, b 1860 Louisa Co., IA mar Donald Stewart, rem to OR, where she d. Her oldest dau Ella res with Nora and Flor.Smith
C1. Ella Stewart, b 1884 C2. Florence Stewart, b 1886
C3. Charles Stewart, b 1889
B3. Sarah Smith, b 1861 IA, d 1931 Edna, KS mar Dr. E. Dobson, 3 chn
C1. Marie Dobson, b 1901 mar E. Olson, res Joplin, MO
C2. Lenore Dobson, res Tulsa, OK. C3. Francis Dobson, of Tulsa, OK.
B4. Elizabeth Smith, b 1862 Louisa Co., IA, d Parsons 1948, mar 1884 age 21., Harry Condit Taylor, b ILL, 2 chn.
C1. Francis Glenn Taylor, b 1886 KS, mar Anna Evans 1920, d in MISS 1946, and wife in 1970. 3 chn
D1. Francis Abraham Taylor, b 1921 mar Janis Dow, 4 chn
E1. Michael, b 1946 mar Linda Martin, 2 chn: Michael and Tatum
E2. Janis Eliz. Taylor, b 1948 mar 2. 1974 Wm. Weidner, 2 chn: William and Janis
E3. Frank Glenn Taylor, b 1949
E4. Jetson Stuart Taylor, b 1952 mar Cynthia Townsend, 2 chn: Jetson and Hayley Taylor.
D2. Douglas Evans Taylor, b 1923 served in WWII, mar 1949 Dell Evans and 2. Jesse E. Conner. Taylor a prof. golfer, 3 chn: Douglas, Nicolle and Leigh Taylor
D3. Elizabeth Ann Taylor, b 1925, mar Dr. J.P. Tatum
C2. Crystal Fae Taylor, b 1889 Southmound, KS, d 1954, bur Parsons,KS
B5. Charles Smith, b 1865 d 1943. Bur Parsons, conductor for "Katy"RR Thrifty, left estate valued at $100,000.
B6. William Hulbert Smith, b 1868, d 1964
B7. Nora Edith Smith, b 1871 d 1950, teacher
B8. Florence Smith, b 1874, d 1954, unmar, kept house for siblings.
B9. John Smith, b 1876 Kansas, d 1943.
A4. Elizabeth Le B., b 1838 J, mar in IA at age 16 to Edward BALLEINE, qv, also of J in 1854. See BALLEINE fam.
A5. Philip Le B., b 1840 J, in Louisa Co. 1856/1860
A6. Rachel LE B., b 1843 J, 7 when fam came to IA. Mar Robert Smith after 1860, as Robert was with his parents in 1860 Census, res Crawford Co., KS 1880.
B1. Fannie Smith, b 1862 Louisa Co., IA, teacher in Crawford Co,KS1880
B2. Ulyssus G. Smith, b 1864
B3. James W. Smith, b 1865 d 1941, bur KS. Mar and had dau who mar Charles STEELE, qv.
B4. Lillie A. Smith, b 1868 mar ___Venable. A son Welsh Venable
B5. Daniel H. Smith, b 1870 KS. B6. Alice P. Smith, b 1872
B7. Olive A. Smith, b 1875 mar ___Fitzgerald, d 1943, bur Parsons, KS
B8. Sarah E. Smith, b 1877

B9. Charles W. Smith, b 1879 KS, d 1920, bur in Parsons, KS
A7. John, b 1847 J, farmer, mar Mattie ___, res KS 1880. Mattie b OH.
B1. Walter Botillier, b 1873 KS B2. Charles, b 1876 B3. David,b 1879
A8. Esther Le B., b 1848 J, about 20 when her parents rem from IA to KS She mar there 1870 John B. Oliphant who was b 1847 MO. a farmer. Esther d 1922.
B1. William J. Oliphant b 1871 KS, farm laborer & RR worker.
B2. Frank L. Oliphant b 1872, miner of zinc
B3. Silvia B. Oliphant b 1875, teacher, mar Plunket, later a widow. Had dau Hazel, b 1894
B4. Alma A. Oliphant, b 1877--B7. Charles Oliphant, b 1883
B5. Maggie C. Oliphant, b 1880-KS B8. Ruby Oliphant, b 1888
B6. Olive M. Oliphant, b 1885 KS
A9. William Boutillier, b 1852 Louisa Co., IA, mar Mary ___. They were prob living in Blue Jacket, OK 1894.
A10. Harriet Le Boutillier was b 1854 in IA, mar ___Becker?
LE BOUTILLIER, Philip, b 1840 St. Peter J, bro of John above, mar Eliz. Blaisdale, 1852-1910, 3 chn. (Brechtel) See book
A1. Lillian Butler, b 1870 Honolulu, HAW, d 1950 Santa Rosa, CAL, mar Albert Lock
A2. William Butler, b 1882 Hawaii, d 1957 Santa Rosa, CAL, mar Kate Elizabeth De Bolt.
A3. John Walter Butler, b 1884 San Francisco, CAL d 1962 Santa Rosa, mar Dama Helen Tuller.
LE BOUTILLIER, George, b 1783 Trinity J, son of Jean and Rachel LE GEYT, mar Elizabeth LE MAISTRE, qv. Astute business man and politician in C.I. but overextended in promoting a business arcade in G. To recoup his fortunes, came to America and established a draper shop in Cincy, OH 1838. It prospered, and he soon had branches in Phila. and NYCity. He returned to J in 1864, but some desc remained in America settling in the Mid and far West, and in Washington, D.C. The Guernsey Gazette called Le Boutillier, "a man of novel ideas and vast undertakings..." His sons served in the Civil War. (Cincinnati Library; Balleine Bio. Dict. of Jersey; Harlow; Florence Pinkham, Sarasota, FLA; Philip Le Boutillier, Toledo, OH)
A1. Elizabeth b 1809
A2. Charles, b 1811, d 1890, mar 1839 Charlotte ROBERTS, 1815-1895.
B1. Charles, b 1841 d 1852 B2. George, 1844-1848
B3. Edward, 1845-1847 B4. Edward, b 1847 d 1918, mar 1871 Frances/Homer
B5. Robert b 1850 d 1931, mar 1875 Jennie W. Howell, who d 1886. He mar 2. 1893, Minnie C. Woods, 1857-1931.
B6. Charlotte, b 1856 d 1932, mar 1877 Thomas B. Homer.
B7. Elizabeth ?
A3. George, b 1813 d 1829
A4. James, b 1814 G, d 1906, mar 1843 Mary Gallier, b 1824
B1. Margaret b 1847 mar 1870 John J. O'Connell
B2. James, b 1850 d 1912 mar 1872 Lucy C. Goodman, who soon died.
B3. Charles A., b 1852 d 1913, mar 1879 Ella Ingoldsby.
A5. Thomas, b 1816, d 1880, mar 1845 Margaret Gallier, 1825-1910. The GALLIERS were of Scotland and London, England.
B1. John b 1846 d 1907 mar 1873 Fanny Goodman, 1849-1925
C1. Margaret G., b 187-, d 1905, mar 1895 Benj. Strong, 1872-1928
D1. Benjamin Strong, b 1896 mar 1924 Laura Pratt
E1. Benj. Strong, b 1925 E2. Jone E. Strong, b 1931
E3. Laura G. Strong.
D2. Margaret Strong, b 1898, d 1906 D3. Philip G. Strong
D4. Katherine Strong, b 1904 mar 1924 Walter S. Humphrey

E1. Philip S. Humphrey, b 1926
E2. Watts S. Humphrey, b 1927 E3. Wm. H. Humphrey, b 1928
C2. John A., b 1875 d 1925, mar 1920 Gertrude Bovee?
C3. Thomas, 1879-1924, mar 1909 Florence S. Stevenson, 1882-1945
D1. Florence S., b 1910 mar 1940 Edward W. Pinkham Jr, b 1911
E1. Patricia Pinkham, b 1941 E2. Edward III, b 1944
D2. Thomas, b 1913 mar 1937 Ann Foster, 2 sons David and Thomas Jr.
D3. Marjorie, b 1916 mar 1938 Stuart Inglehart, and 2. in 1948 David B. McElroy. A son Stuart Jr. b 1940.
C4. Philip b 1880 mar 1. 1909 Gertude H. Tifft and 2. in 1944 Florence Higby Bachman.
D1. Margaret b 1910 mar 1936 Bronson Williams, 2 sons
E1. Galen Williams, b 1938 E2. Peter Williams b 1939
D2. Philip, b 1916 mar 1941 Felia? Ford, 2 sons, Philip & George
D3. Gertrude, b 1919 mar 1940 Wm. A. Wood. 2 sons, Wm. & Michael
D4. Peter b 1923, mar 1945 Mary A. Poulois, son C. Peter Philip.
C5. William A.G., b 1888, mar 1913 Stella Woods, son Wm. G.
B2. Thomas, 1848-1930 B5. George, 1850-1936, mar Isabel Groshon?
B3. Elizabeth, 1852-1908 B6. Charles, 1855-1939, mar Sarah Martin
B4. Mary G., 1854-1856 B7. Mary, 1857-1944
B8. William G., 1859-1923
B9. Clement, 1858-1944, mar 1887 Carrie Austin, 1862-1917
C1. Austin, b 1891 mar 1920 Isabel Exton
A6. Marie, b 1818, d 1884
A7. Anne, b 1823, mar 1848 Charles J. ROBERTS, b 1816
B1. Charles Roberts, b 1849 d 1878, mar Mary Berrill
C1. Edith Roberts, b 1873 mar Lewis Rees, a son Berrill Rees
C2. Charles W. Roberts, b 1875, mar Eliza Marcus
D1. Mary A. Roberts D2. Charles W. Roberts
B2. Edith M. Roberts, b 1851 d 1938 B4. George Le M. Roberts,1859/60
B3. Mary Roberts, b 1858 d 1936 B5. ___Roberts.
B6. John M. Roberts, b 1856 d 1901, mar Eliz. K. Hyde, who d 1887?
C1. Ella F. Roberts, b 1876 mar Ralph GODFREY
D1. Mildred Godfrey.

The following LE BOUTILLIERS res Cincinnati, OH 1850 (Census) prob from Channel Islands.
Elizabeth age 42 Margaret b 1848 Ann, b 1828
James b 1824 Mary b 1792 England or Jersey
Mary b 1823 Charles, b 1818 Charles b 1848

LE BOUTILLIER, George, b 1876 Cincinnati, OH, son of James and Lucy Goodman Le Boutillier, grandosn of James and Mary Gallier Le B., came from G 1827 to Cincinnati. George became Supt. of and later Mgr. of the New York Zone of the Pensy. RR, was also connected with many other firms, and an incorporator of the World's Fair at NY, 1939. He mar 1907 NYCity, Ilse Margaret, dau of John Crawford, no issue.

LE BOUTILLIER, see Q.A. IN CANADA, pp 308,9.

LE BOUTILLIER, Philip Henry, b ca 1865 J, rem to England, mar and poss returned to J for a short time. At least 4 sons and a dau. (Jack Boutillier, Victoria, BC)
A1. Philip Henry, b Liverpool, England rem to Gaspe, then to Minneapolis, MN, where he died.
B1. Edward, d age 12 in Minneapolis.
B2. Thomas Henry, b 1891 Paspebiac, QUE mar Hyla Stanforth, res MN
C1. Philip George, b 1920 mar Irene Stanton?, res Stillwater, MN,a son Marc b 1947
C2. Joan, b 1922, mar Merril Fox, res Washington, DC

C3. Gordon, b 1928 mar Patricia Leeper, res Rock Rapids, IA, 4 chn
D1. Linda, b 1952 D2. Cynthia, b 1954 D3. Steven, b 1955,Paul-1957
C4. Jean, b 1931 mar Kenneth Anderson, res MN
C5. John E., b 1931 Montreal, mar Barbara Anderson, 5 chn: Kent b 1952, Scott, Lynn, Jeffrey and Renee, b 1963.
A2. Thomas C., b St. Malo, France, d Montreal, QUE, sons Wm. & Jack,BC
A3. Madeline, b France, and d Paris, France.
A4. Ernest, b St. Malo France, d Minneapolis, MN, mar Lillian ___, res New Brighton, MN
A5. Frank, b St. Malo France, d in concentration camp, France, WWII.
LE BOUTILLIER, Charles C. to Phila., PA c 1844 from J. (Filby)
LE BOUTILLIER, Charles from St. Lawrence J, b 1888, rem to Canada? Mar Florence RENOUF, qv, was in Montreal 1913. Poss also other chn? (Ivy O'Reilly, S. Portland, ME)
A1. Florence V.I., b 1909 St. Aubin, J, mar 1931 JOhn V. O'Reilly, to Canada 1920, rem to NJ 1924, then to ME 1928. More data in Q.A. IN CANADA.
B1. Charles O'Reilly, b 1932, mar Norman McGlinn, 3 chn
B2. Patricia A., b 1936 mar Marvin A. Clifford, res Topsham, ME,2 chn
B3. John R. O'Reilly, b 1950, div, a dau Stephanie, b 1972
LE BOUTILLIER, fam from J to PA, settled in Wayne, PA 1800s. (A.P. Le Boutillier, Schenectady, NY)
LE BOUTILLIER, Emma-Jan, b 1844 J, d Seguin, TX 1878. Mar Samuel NEEL See NEEL fam.
LE BOUTILLIER, Mrs. ___ of G, res NYCity June 1847. (G. SOC. BULL, Spring 1973)
LE BOUTILLIER, Jane, b J, mar NEEL, qv, rem to Seguin, TX 1860s. (Lola Eubank, Ballinger, TX)
LE BOUTILLIER, Oliver Colin of a J fam in East Orange, NJ, was a US airman trained in Canada, and was an eyewitness of the shooting down of the Red Baron, Von Richthofen, of Germany, in WWI. He was in business more recently in Las Vegas, NEV. (R.J. Anderson, Can.Press staff writer, a clipping, source unknown)
LE BOUTILLIER noted in a number of places in US, including TX.
LE BOUTON, see BOUTON, in J 1668 and 1749. Noted Geauga Co., OH, 1900s
LE BRAS, Charles mar Eliz. RICH 1722 Boston. OUTC.
LE BRETTON, LE BRETON in J 1274. In St. Saviour, Grouville, Trinity, St. Clement and St. Ouen J 1668. In Trinity, St. Saviour, Grouville, St. Heliers, St. Peter and St. Ouen J 1749. Curr G and J. In G 1330, in St. Peter G 1812.
At times this name is very difficult, as variants are spelled in many different ways such as BRETON, BRITTON, LE BRETTON, BRINTON, BRETOON, BRITTAINE, etc. Note that LE BRETONS and BRITONS, etc, came to America from France, England and the Channel Islands. At least 12 fams in MA 1790, prob some of C.I. origin. (Census)
LE BRETON, Charles William, b 1886 J, rem to Pittsburgh, PA 1903, mar there Mary Catherine McGovern, b 1885, dau of Thomas and Eliz. E. (Doyle) McGovern, b Beaver, PA.(Rebecca L. Wain, W. Homestead,PA)
A1. Lillian E. b 1908 Braddock, PA mar Oral Ullom, b 1904 WVA, 1921.
B1. Lillian Lucille Ullom, b 1933 Munhall, PA mar Dr. John Charles Wain, b 1928 Homestead, PA, in Munhall 1956. 3 chn: Rebecca L., Dr. John Charles and Esther Ruth Wain ERRORS IN THIS CHART,
B2. Oral Arles Ullom, b 1938 Munhall, PA SEE CH.IS.COLLECTION.
B3. Mary Ruth Ullom, b 1929 mar 1948 Edw. G. Burgess, b 1928
A2. Charles John, b 1909 A6. Jean Willis, b 1918 mar __Calhoun
A3. Mabel Maud, b 1910, mar __Leitzell A7. Robert Harold, b 1920
A4. Edwin Thomas, b 1914 A8. Raymond Richard, b 1922

A5. Howard William LE BRETON, b 1916 A9. Duane Dean Le Breton b 1925

LE BRETON, BRITTON, BRINTON, Philip from J to Falmouth, ME with Peter Bowdoin early 1700s, and was therewhen town was devastated. and Philip MORRILL was taken prisoner. Philip LE BRETON returned to Boston, where he and wife Eliz. deeded their land in Falmouth, 1715/6 to dau Elizabeth, wife of John YOUNG of Salem, mar Boston 1713.Philip was living in Boston 1734, age 74. Will dated 1737, signed as BRITTAINE. See Noyes.

A1. Elizabeth mar 1713 John YOUNG of Salem, MA, a joiner. Was he a JEUNE of Jersey? A5. Mary, mar 1717 Edw. DUMARESQ

A2. Philip, d 1721 leaving widow Lois A6. Rachel, mar 1719 JohnDUMARESQ

A3. Peter A4. David, b 1707 Boston A7. Sarah, mar 1724 HenryVenner.

A8. Jane A9. Ann.

LE BRETON, Charles of Dover, ME drowned 1695. (Noyes)

LE BRITON, Charles and Elizabeth had son Charles b 1728 Boston, MA

LE BRETON, Clement rem from J to Brazil where he mar and raised a family, 1800s.

LE BRETON, Edward was importing to Jersey tobacco from VA ca 1730. (A. John Jean, Jersey)

LE BRETON, Eliza Margaret b 1803 mar 1842 Edward K.S. Butler of Martock Nova Scotia, Canada. OUTC.

LE BRETON, Harriet had will in Essex Co., NJ 1826. (NJ INDEX, Vol 1)

LE BRETON, James P., from France? 1803 to NY. (NY NATURALIZATIONS)

LE BRETON, John, b J, in Wicomico, VA 1664. (VHM, Vol 10; Stanard; Northumberland, VA records)

LE BRITTON, Peter in Boston 1790 with fam of 6, wife Elizabeth. (Census)

LE BRETON, Capt. Peter Jr., mar Tabby Lewis 1800 (int) He res Newburyport, MA. OUTC

LE BRETON, Stephen and Felicity res CT. 1800s? (CT. MARRIAGES)

LE BRETON, Thomas from J to Washington, DC, 1900.

LE BRETON, Trevor Alex., a Lt. of the Royal Marines, son of the Very Rev. Dean of Jersey, d 1870, and was bur St. James Cem., Toronto.

LE BRETON, curr CAL and Austin, TX. OUTC.

LE BRETON, some listed in Filby, including one in RI 1686, A. to NY 1820; Aimé to Phila, PA 1798; two to MISS and LA 1820, and one to Phila. 1798. OUTC.

LE BROCQ in J 1309, means badger. In St. Mary, St. Laurens, St. Brelade, St. Ouen and St. Peter J 1668, and in all but St. Laurens J 1749. Curr and common in J.

LE BROCQ, see BROCK, and Sir Isaac BROCK.

LE BROCQ, George, son of Philippe LE BROCQ of J was at Boston, MA. 1727. (Rev. J.A. Messervy)

LEBROK, John arrived in Boston 1760s on sloop ADVENTURER FROM Nfld., a mariner. (Whitmore) OUTC.

LE BROCQ, Marie, wife of Thomas DUMARESQ in New England 1698, both from J? See DUMARESQ.

LE BROCQ, BROCK, Martha, b G, in Bev. MA 1698, mar Philip LE CAUDEY, CODY, at St. Brelade J? 1692. To America 1698? See LE CAUDEY,CODY.

LE BROCQ, Pierre of Newport, RI 1711, was son and heir of Peter LE BROCQ of St. Brelade, J.

LE BROKE from Paris, France. (Laphams PARIS, ME, p. 660) Note that this name was also in England early, as DEL BROK of Essex Co., LE BROK of Devon Co. and DE LA BROK of Kent and Glouc., England.

LE BROCQ, E., Capt of the JENNY, a ship built Boston, MA 1764, owned by GOSSETT, see. (A. John Jean, Jersey)

LE BRUN, see also BROWN

LE BRUN in J 1299, meaning brown-haired. In St. Martin, St. Heliers, St. Ouen, St. Peter and St. Brelade J 1668, and in Grouville, St. Peter and St. Saviour J 1749. In St. Laurens J 1788. Curr G & J. See CIFHS #3.

LE BRUN, Jean/John, b 1799 St. Peter J, son of Jean and Marie, mar Elizabeth THELLAND, qv, 1812, in St. Peter J. She was dau of Wm. and Esther (LUCE) LE BRUN. Jean d 1845 St. Peter J. Eliz. d 1846 J, 7 chn. At least 3 of their chn below settled in Quebec, two at Havre St. Pierre and another at Riviere-au-Tonnerre, Thunder River, QUE. See THELLAND. (Lucille Roy, Malartic, QUE)

A1. Esther, bp 1826 A4. Charles Henry, bp 1835
A2. Jean, bp 1828 A5. Philip John, bp 1838
A3. James, bp 1831 A6. Jane Adelle, bp 1841 A7. William John, b1843

LE BRUN, two bros., poss John and Peter, b J, rem to MINN. Peter changed his name to BROWN upon entering the military during the Civil War. He enlisted in US Army at Ft. Snelling, MN 1862. Served with Co. J, 9th MN. Was discharged Aug. 24, 1865, his home town being listed as Eagle Creek, MN. (Mrs. Raymond Brown, St. Cloud, MN) Residing with the LE BRUNS below was Eliz. Bitner, a sister-in-law of the emigrant. She was b ca 1813 in J.

LE BRUN, Susan b 1819 J, to MN.

LE BRUN, John, b ca 1821 J, mar Susan SOHIER, who was b 1819 J, at least 4 chn, res MINN. See SOHIER.

A1. Isabella B., b 1847 A2. Georgianna B. Dygert, b 1856
A3. John, b 1854 mar ___
B1. Annie, b 1892 B4. Wilhelm Lee b 1898
B2. Rose Swoon, b 1895 B5. Ruth Evangeline, b 1899
B3. Isabelle Sohier, b 1896 B6. Edwin John, b 1901
B7. Albert Carlyle, b 1903 B8. Paul W. b 1906 B9. Ethel V. b 1908

LE BRUN, others in Albion, Wright Co., MN 1880, in St. Cloud,MN 1900s.

LE BRUN, John S., b ca 1857 in MN, parents b J.

LE BRUN, John age 59 in 1880, res MN

LE BRUN, Susan, 61 in 1880, b J, res MN.

LE BRUN, poss as BRAWN? in ME 1600s. (Noyes) OUTC.

LE BRUN, see Mary Elizabeth MALLET

LE BRUN, W. in J, mar Adele VAUTIER, who had 3 sisters. One desc is of the REIS-ROMERIL fam of Toronto. See ROMERIL. (A. Sweetman, SASK)

LE BRUN, Capt. Edward was trading in 1715 from Jersey to New England on ship BONNE ESPERANCE, GOOD HOPE. (A. John Jean, Jersey)

LE BRUN noted in Canada, NY, VA, NH and MA, curr. OUTC.

LE BRUN, BROWNE, Moses from J was in New England 1686. (Perley)

LE BRUN curr in Dundalk, MD. OUTC.

LE CAIN, LE QUESNE. A fam of this name from J is in Q.A. IN CANADA. Richard S. Le Cain of Bridgewater, Nova Scotia has traced this fam back to Thomas and Elizabeth (HAMON or HORMAN) LE QUESNE b 1570s J. LE QUESNE is pronounced LE CAIN.

LE CAIN, Benj. b Union, ME, mar Zulina Patch RICHARDSON. (Richard A. LE CAIN, Enfield, CAL) Poss other chn?

A1. Joseph J., b 1849 Union, ME mar 1875 Waldeboro, ME Mary Almeda Cummings, b 1853, dau of Andrew and Mary Ann (Nash) Cummings. Joseph d 1921.
B1. Sylvester A., b 1877 Evanston, WY B4. Leo Leroy, b 1887 Phillipsburg, KS.
B2. Joseph M. b 1879 ditto
B3. Levi A., b 1881 Green River, WY mar 1903 W. Somersville, MA Caroline Mifflin, b 1877 Bona Vista, NFLD, dau of James and Jane (MANUEL) Mifflin. Levi d 1954 Somersville, MA. More data on this family, some in WRCIC.

CAIN, CANE, LE QUESNE?, John b 1706 mar Judith ___, and 2. Mary FAVOUR qv, in Kittery, ME 1735. OUTC. See sources for more info: VR of Sedgewick by Grace Limburner; Blue Hill ME Library; FAMS OF EARLY SETTLERS IN BLUE HILL, MAINE, Vol5; Marjorie Deal, Soquel, CAL. See other LE CAIN data in Boston and Dorchester, MA records and Q.A. IN CANADA, by Turk.

LE CAPPELAIN in J 1331-1799. Several fams in Canada. CAPPELEN noted in ID, from J? Desc of this name noted in ONT, Canada; Detroit,MI; and Bloomfield, NJ, also in CAL.

LE CAPPELAIN, George, b 1850 St. Peter J, mar 1880 at Alice Twp., ONT Susan WHITE. Geo. d 1935 at North Bay, ONT. Other chn? (Richard Le Cappelain, Pasadena, CAL)

A1. Samuel Jacob, b 1889 Papineau, ONT, d 1964 North Bay, ONT, mar 1917 Eidth G. Saunders, b 1897 Forest Gate, Essex, England.
B1. Gertrude Florence, b 1918 North Bay, mar Harold Ross Alcorn 1939
B2. Constance Victoria, b 1920 North Bay, ONT mar Aubrey Lasalle, and 2. Lou Bachelor at Toronto, ONT.
B3. Haroldine Rebecca, b 1921 mar Wm. ARthur KNIGHT 1945 at Toronto.
B4. John Milton, b 1924 mar Theresa PEPIN, and 2. Alice Ferris 1964
B5. Albert Howard, b 1926, mar Rhoda Vaughan, 1949 at North Bay.
B6. Richard Samuel, b 1929 mar Mary Jean QUINN, 1952 in Brockville, ONT. Mary b 1930 Montreal, QUE
C1. Elizabeth Irene, b 1953 North Bay mar Bradley Gordon Beach 1975 at Houghton, NY.
C2. Linda Rose b 1955 mar Park Benj. Smith, Jr at Patterson, NJ.
C3. Mark Richard, b 1957 New Rochelle, NY mar Amy Vanek 1980 at Denver, COL, res Cleveland, OH, a son Joshua Raymond b 1981.
C4. Kenneth James, b 1961 New Rochelle, NY
C5. Sandra Jean, b 1962 Phila., PA.
B7. Dorothy Edith, b 1931 North Bay, ONT, mar William Snoddon
A2. Albert Eska, b 1895 Papineau, ONT d 1962 North Bay, mar Betsy V. MacBeth, b 1902 Widdifield Twp., ONT, res North Bay, 3 chn.
B1. George Duncan, b 1927 mar Christina Hastings, res Sudbury, ONT.
B2. Alton MacBeth, b 1929 mar Marie Simms, res North Bay
B3. Beth Florence, b 1932 North Bay, mar Ellard Mousseau.

LE CARRY, noted in MASS SOLDIERS AND SAILORS. This may be LE QUERÉE of J, pron. LE CARRY.

LE CARPENTIER, old in G. See CARPENTER.

LE CAUDEY, the orig. surname of the Philip CODY fam, from J in 1600s to America, the ancestor of Buffalo Bill Cody. See data under CODY. This name variously spelled as LAGODY, MCCODY, CODIE, COADY, etc, etc LE CAUDEY is curr in J.

COUDE, COODE, John of Maryland in 1676. In 1689 John gathered men on the Potomac, and captured St. Mary's, the capitol of the province. They had control for 2 yrs. COODE mar dau of Thomas GERARD. OUTC.

LE CAUX, John, merchant in Boston MA from J 1700s. (A. John Jean,of J)

LE CERF, old in G, and in J 1299. In St. Ouen J 1668, in St. Mary J 1749. Noted in NC early, but OUTC

LE CHAIR, old in J and curr.

LE CHEMINANT in J 1607, in St. Laurens J 1668. Curr and common in G. See also PILL. LE CHEMINANT curr Los Angeles. Poss more info in UT.

LE CHEMINANT, Sara Farr, b 1816 Somerset, England, dau of Capt. Edward Farr, and Mary Ann Durham. Sara raised in G, mar there Peter LE CHEMINANT 1839. They had 5 chn, but Peter d 1853, and Sarah followed through with his intention to settle in America. They landed at New Orleans and took steamboat to St. Louis, then to Westport, KS, where chn took cholera, but survived. They went overland with a Wm.

Empy wagon train, encountering bad weather for the latter part of the 7 month treck, arriving in SLCity Oct. 1854. Sarah mar Robert Porter, prob in early 1855, res Clover and Fairfield, UT. Sarah d 1901. See PORTER. (Shirley Rizzuto, Sandy, UT)

A1. Elizabeth A2. Peter A3. Osmond A4. Edmond A5. Agnes, all bp 1851 G. Prob other chn by Robert Porter.

LE CHEMINANT, noted in Quebec City, 1838 Petition. (LOST IN CANADA, Aug. 1981)

LE CHEMINANT, John, b C.I. rem to Weston, MA 1900s.

LE CHEMINANT, LE SHEMINAW, Robert in UT 1850s, prob from C.I.

LE CHEMINANT. For the first time in 400 years, the Lt. Gov. of Guernsey was a Guernseyman, Air Chief Marshall Sir Peter LE CHEMINANT, in the 1900s.

LE CLERCQ in G 1331, in St. Saviour G 1738. In J 1331, in St. Saviour and St. Clement J 1668 and 1749, pron. LE CLAIR and LE CLERK. Curr G and J. See SLCity files.

LE CLERE, LE CLEAR data in NY GENS vol. 60, but OUTC.

LE CLERCQ, Marion res CAL, dau of Mary Frances and James R. Mitchell of Glendale, CAL, 1900s. See Q.A. IN CANADA, bu Turk.

LE CLERC, John, a will in Essex Co., NJ 1899. OUTC.

LE CLERC, in Boston 1970s from France, Canada or C.I.?

LE CLERCQ, CLERK?, George from C.I. 1863, via ship ANTARCTIC, set. UT.

LE CLERCQ, Henrietta and Jane from C.I. 1862, via ship ANTARCTIC, to UTAH.

LE CLERCQ, Mary and Jane from C.I. 1854, via ship MARSHFIELD, to UT.

LE COKE, ___, mar Abigail Moulton, res Exeter, NH 1697. OUTC. She was a widow in 1705. (Noyes) Was he a LE COCQ from C.I.?

LE COCQ, in J 1309-1528 at least. Variants of this surname are COCK, COOK and LEACOCK. Check LEACOCK in PA archives, not seen by compiler. Curr research? See CIFHS #3,4.

LE COCQUE, Philip, had land in PEI near Fairchild's Pt. in early 1800s (PEI Map) Poss from C.I. as other Channel Islanders rem to PEI late 1700s and early 1800s. See Q.A. IN CANADA, bu Turk. OUTC.

LEACOCK, Stephen, the humorist, said to have come of a LE COCQ fam.

LE COCQ, see LE MASURIER

LE COCQ, COCK, Wm. from C.I.? mar Elizabeth SAUNDERS in New England 1688. See LE CURNEE, John in Clemens book, OUTC.

LE COE, Charles mar Mary COLLIS 1736, Kings Chapel, Boston. Was he a LE CAUX, pron. LE COE? LE CAUX in St. Peter and St. Mary J 1668, and in St. Peter J 1749. Curr G and J.

LE CONTE noted in G, and curr there. Research? See CIFHS #3, #12.

LE CONTE noted in Culver City, CAL and Los Angeles, CAL, but OUTC

LE CONTE, Clara Elizabeth, b 1866 G, to US ca 1910 after her husband, Benj. LE CONTE, a cousin, had died. She d 1930, age 74 in Lynnhaven VA, bur Virginia Beach, VA. (David O. Le Conte, St. Peter Port, G)

A1. Harold Benj. or Harold BLONDEL? preceded her to US, but soon died.

LE COUNTE, James of Rowley, MA mar 1735/6 Mary DAVIS of Newbury, MA.

LE CONTE, John E., had will in Essex Co., NJ 1822, not seen by comp.

LE CONTE, Peter, physician of Shrewsbury, NJ 1734. OUTC. NJ GENS, 1956)

LE CORNU, see also CORNEY. LE CORNU Derives from LE CORNUAILLE, the Welshman, name given to an immigrant from Wales who settled in the C.I. at an early date. CORNUELE appeared 1203 in J. Cf English surname CORNWELL.

CAUTION: CORNU, Peter arrived from France? in NY 1730s and then settled in Schectady area, many desc. (CORNU BIBLE)

Note that CORNEY was also an English surname.

CURNEY, CURNE settled in MA 1790, one in Glouc., one in Cummington,MA.

CURNE, LE CURNE in Winthrop, ME 1790, James. OUTC.

LE CORNU in J 1203, curr G and J. In St. Brelade and St. Ouen J 1668 and in St. Brelade and St. Laurens J 1749. Many in early records may be LE CURNU or CORNET of C.I., and others from Grt. Britain.

LE CURNAH, CURNOW, CORNEW, Catherine, accused in Kittery court with Mark ROBERTS 1680. In 1684 she was accused with Paul WILLIAMS of Kittery, and married him. In 1682 was servant of Mr. Hookes? She was Paul's first wife. He mar 2. after 1690 Joanna (Crocker) Gaskin. Paul was living 1715, prob d 1732/3. He had poss one ch by Catherine, named Magdalene, who mar Nathaniel Leach. (Noyes) He had other chn by 2nd wife. Many WILLIAMS in early records. Was Paul also from from G? See WILLIAMS. (Noyes)

LE CORNEE, Elizabeth, 178-, in PA Archives, Vol 8, S2, from C.I. fam?

LE CORNE, Amy and a Jeremiah res in Harris Co., GA early. OUTC.

LE CORNEE, Joanna, formerly Joanna Whittemore, widow of Capt. Peletiah Whittemore, who d 1741. Noyes) OUTC.

A1. Peletiah, bp 1728 Kittery, mar Eliz. Walker

A2. Ebenezer, bp 1730 A3. Joanna, bp 1735

LE CORNEE, John, mariner from J, mar before 1742 Joanna Moore, her second husband. chn?

LE CORNU, John, b Trinity J, 1798, son of Philip and Eliz. (HAMON) LE CORNU, mar 1823 J Mary RENOUF, qv, b 1804 Trinity J, dau of John and Eliz. RENOUF. This couple to UT with dau? or dau went alone? (LeNeta Simmons Foy, SLCity, UT)

A1. Mary LE CORNU, b 1823 J, d 1893 Wallsburg, UT, wife of Francis KERBY, qv.

LA CORNEY, John, age 48 in 1870 census, res Louise Co., IA, b J. (Darlene Paxton, IA)

LA CORNU, Rev. J., age 51, and Margaret JARVIS, age 57, stated that they had known the widow of Edward BALLEINE for many years. (Pension record of Edw. Ballaine) In WRCIC is a Grand Army of the Republic certificate, Gettysburg Post, OR, dated 1888, certifying that a John LE CORNU, clergyman and soldier, was discharged from an Iowa Regt. 1865, b 1835 Jersey. (Cert. from Joan Little, Pomeroy, WA)

LE CORNU, Philip, age 33, b ca 1837 J, res Neosho Twp., Labette Co., KS with wife Mary C., age 27, b Indiana, and 4 chn. (Census) A Jarvis connected with this fam. See above, Margaret Jarvis.

A1. Ann C., b ca 1864 IA A3. John B., b ca 1868 IA

A2. Ida R., b ca 1865 IA A4. Ellen M., b 1870 KS.

LE CORNUE, Peter, b early 1800s J, to Alpena, MI ca 1860, mar Mary Ann HOYLES, from a St. Clement J fam. See Q.A. IN CANADA, by Turk.

A1. Ann, b ca 1845? mar Francois Napoleon GEZEQUEL, 3 chn, res MI.

A2. Frank, b 1842, res Alpena, MI, at least 8 chn.

LE CORNU, a large fam is noted in TN and KY. There is no reason to believe they came from C.I., but also there seems to be no strong French connection, from first names given. See good fam charts in WRCIC, from Mrs. Sam. B. LE CORNU, Jackson, TN.

LE CORNU, John Alexander, b 1824 Paris? or near Paris, France, d 1889 KY. He mar 1. 1845 KY, Mary Jane Fields, b there 1825, d 1872, 9 chn. He mar 2. Middie Mann, his niece by mar., 18 yrs. his junior, sister of his son-in-law. Middie d 1883 and he mar 3., no issue, S.E. Blalock, 1884.

A1. A.A. b 1846, drowned in Civil War, with Confed. Army.

A2. Wm. Francis, b 1848 mar 1874 Georgiana Roach, 11 chn.

A3. Gideon F., b 1850, mar 1870 Midda C. Enoch, 3 chn.

A5. Mary Lee, b 1854, d.y. Also A6. and A8.
A7. Ada Dora, b 1860 d 1919, mar Marshall Mann, 9 chn
A9. Peter N. b 1865 mar M.S. Milner
A10. Stephen E., b 1874 d 1944 Greenfield, TN A12. Levi, d.y.
A11. Ida, b 1875 mar 1893 Marcus Traughber, and d 1918 Tiptonville, TN
A13. Hugh B., b 1879 mar 1903 Lillie Mae Duncan and d 1971 Fulton, NY
He mar 2. Alpha Connie Chadwick, b 1883. Lillie Mae d 1904.
A14. Earnest, b 1880 mar 1902 Cora Lee Conner, and d 1950, bur TN

LE CORNU, Francis, from J fam? clerk for fishery firm in Paspebiac, Gaspe, QUE, 1881. (Aldo Brochet, London, ONT)

LE CORNU, noted in Bakersfield, CAL, but OUTC

LE COUTEUR, old in J, in many parishes 1668, 1749, some to Canada. See Q.A. IN CANADA. One fam changed name to CUTLER in Nova Scotia. (Lady McKie, Ottawa, ONT)

LE COUTEUR in J 1299 meaning church sacristan. In St. Heliers, St. Peter, St. Mary, St. Martin and St. Saviour J 1668. In St. Peter, St. Martin and St. SAviour J 1749. In Sark Island 1500s. Curr G and J. There were also late comers of this surname from France to the C.I. in 1700s and 1800s, some Huguenot.

COUTEUR, Abraham, a Hug.,was a long time resident in Leicester, England in the 1600s.

LE COUTEUR, E., master of the GEORGE of Jersey, which was built in Philadelphia 1769, owned by PIPON, qv, of J. (A. John Jean, Jersey)

LE COUTEUR, LA COUTEUR, LA COOTER, John, poss b J? mar Elizabeth MARINER, LE MARINEL? early 1700s, res Boston. John d before 1713. Poss his son John mar Eleanor BISSEL in Boston 1730. OUTC. (Underhill; NEHGS Vol 100)

LE COUTER in Boston TRANSCRIPT, Oct. 1915. Curr Salem, MA.

COUNTER, LE COUTEUR, Edward from J? in Salem, MA 1668. (Holmes; Underhill)

LE COUTEUR, noted in Detroit and Taylor, MI, and in Spokane, WA. OUTC

CUTTER in early New England. Were some of them LE COUTEURS?

LE COURTOIS, a G surname. See CIFHS #9.

LE CRAS, LE CRAW in early New England. See also LA CROIX and CROSS

LE CRAS in J 1299. In St. Mary and St. PEter J 1668. In St. Laurens, Trinity, St. Brelade, St. Heliers and St. Mary J. 1749. In St. Saviour G 1676. Some data found in Essex Coll; Essex Ant.; and TINGLEY GEN; MASS SOLDIERS AND SAILORS: LITTLE GEN, etc. CAUTION: TRIAL CHARTS.

Note that some of these LE CRAW, LE CRAS fams also appear under CROSS in the records. Compiler has tried to separate, but much care must be taken in research. Note also that early LE CRAS persons and fams may have come to New England from the C.I. via Nfld.

LE CRAW, Wm., b LE CRAS? in J, mar 1728/9 in MRB Sarah Goodall? (Donald Doliber, MRB, MA) (also David LeCraw,Norcross, GA)
A1. John, b 1731, d.y.? A2. William, 1732-1735
A3. Capt. William, b 1736 d 1902, mar 1766 Hannah MARTIN, dau of Knott MARTIN and Sarah Arnold.
B1. John, b 1767, d 1818, mar 1792 Rebecca Ross, who d 1840 age 71.
C1. Rebecca, bp 1792 mar Samuel RUSSELL Jr., 1820. C2. John, b 1794
C3. William, b 1796 mar 1819 Lydia Dennis Ireson
C4. Hannah, b 1798 d 1867 mar John Conway Jr., 1822. C5. David, d.y.
C6. David Ross again, bp 1801. Capt. David Ross LE CRAW mar 1835 Hannah R. Girdler in MRB.
D1. Wm. Lewis, bp 1837, twin D3. Charles Henry bp 1838
D2. David Ross, bp 1837, twin D4. Rebecca Ross, bp 1841
C7. Knott Martin, bp 1803, d.y. C8. Knott M. again, bp 1809, sick.

B2. Hannah b 1769, d.y. B3. Hannah again, b 1770
B4. Abigail, b 1774, mar 1799 John HOOPER, b 1774, son of John. (HOOPER GEN) Abigail d 1846 age 72, John d 1850.
C1. John Lee Hooper, b 1800 became a planter in LA, where he d unmar
C2. Wm. LE CRAW HOOPER, bp 1804 mar 1832 Mary Cloutman, dau of Joseph and Ruth (BOWDEN) Cloutman, bp 1807. Wm. a fisherman, drowned off Grand Banks from schooner ZELA 1846. Widow d 1881.
D1. Wm. Le Craw Hooper, b 1833
D2. Mary Ellen Hooper, b 1835 mar 1855 Wm. H. Powers
D3. Abigail Hooper, b 1838 mar 1872 Geo. W. SHEPARD Jr, qv, b 1835. Abigail d 1876
D4. Ruth Ann Hooper, b 1840 mar 1882 Geo. W. SHEPARD, res MRB.
D5. Joseph Bowden Hooper, b 1843
C3. Abigail Hooper, bp 1807 mar 1829 Andrew Leavitt
C4. Ebenezer LE CRAW HOOPER, bp 1813 MRB, mar 1845 Elizabeth, dau of Joseph and Eliz. RUSSELL, age 27. Ebenezer a Master Mariner, who later farmed at Boxford, MA and d ca 1893.
D1. John Lee Hooper, b 1846 mar Christine Fraser, b Nova Scotia.
E1. Mabel Hooper, b 1876 Prairie Bluff, ALA
E2. John Ebenezer Hooper, b 1879 Boxford, MA
D2. Ebenezer Leavitt Hooper, b 1847 MRB, mar Addith Smith
D3. Sarah E. Hooper, b 1852 D4. Caroline Hooper, 1856-1881
D5. Joseph Russell Hooper, b 1857 mar Ida (Furbush) Davis.
D6. Edgar Hooper
C5. Knott Lee Hooper, b 1816 MRB, mar 1839 Tabitha Stone, who d 1905. Knott was mariner and merchant, d 1864, 8 chn.
D1. Sarah Hooper, b 1842 mar 1864 Philip L. Humphrey
D2. Abaigil, b 1843
D3. Mary E. Hooper, b 1846 mar 1867 Edward T. Humphrey
D4. Knott H. Hooper, b 1847 d unmar 1868
D5. John Joseph Hooper, b 1850 MRB, mar 1880 Hannah Stacey, age 21.
E1. Mary Stacey Hooper, b 1880 E2. Hannah M. Hooper, b 1883
D6. Hannah Maria Hooper, b 1851 mar 1874 Geo. H. Sherry Jr.
D7. Wm. F. Hooper, b 1852 D8. Henry B. Hooper b 1857
B5. William, b 1786 d 1799, drowned on passage to New Orleans with Capt. Silver of Salem, MA. Poss another Wm. of this fam d 1810 in MRB.
B6. Ebenezer, b 1789 d 1845, mar 1810 Elizabeth ROUNDY
C1. Eliza bp 1811 C2. William, bp 1812 A Capt. Wm. d 1840 age 28.
C3. Hannah, bp 1814 C4. Jane Roundy, bp 1818
C5. Ebenezer, b ca 1816, drowned on Grand Banks 1846 age 30?
C6. Mary R. bp 1823 mar 1847 Sam. B. Crowninshield, age 26, seaman, son of Edward and Sally.
C7. Michael R.?, son of Ebenezer, d 1839 age 6

LE CRAS, John mar Margaret Hawkesworth 1729 Boston, MA. A Margaret LE CRASS mar James Griffin 1744 Boston, her 2nd mar?
A1. Elizabeth b 1731 Boston A2. Margaret b 1733 Boston.

CRAY, poss CRAW, or LE CRAS?, John mar Susanna Witham 1777 MRB. OUTC.

CRAW, LE CRAW, John, d 1807 at sea, lost off Cape Cod with Philip LE CRAW, all perished. Mar Hannah WIDGER.
A1. Alice, b 1771 mar 1790 Nathaniel Thayer
A2. Hannah, b 1781 mar Nicholas MALEY, MALET, MALLET, 1808. See MALLET.
A3. Sarah, b 1783 d 1833, mar1807 Wm. GILLEY, GUILLET of J?, qv.

LE CRAW, LE CROIX?, John, d before 1734, mar 1701 Miriam Woodley.
A1. John, b 1703 A2. William, 1705-1740 A5. Mary, b 1712, mar Joseph
A3. Miriam, b 1706 mar 1725 Charles Whiden. Andrews, 1731
A4. Samuel, b 1709 res Newport, RI. A6. John b1714 A7. Richard b1716.

LE CRAW, poss LE CROIX, CROSS?, John mar Hannah ___, who poss mar 2. Benj. CALLEY or COLLETT?
A1. John b 1742 A2. Mercy, b 1744 mar Joseph NORTHEY, qv, 1762
A3. Mary, b 1746
LE CRAW, John mar 1756 Sarah Roads, widow of John Roads in MRB.
LE CRAS, Philip from J? mar 1726 Alice Tucker, bp 1703, dau of Nicholas and Priscilla Bickford.
A1. Benjamin, b 1729
A2. Alice, b 1734, mar Lawrence Grace 1766 MRB. A3. Charity, b 1743
A4. Philip, b 1745, d 1807, lost off Cape Cod. Mar Elizabeth CLARKE. She was b 1752, dau of George CLARKE and Martha Goldsmith, 12 chn.
B1.Elizabeth b 1771 mar 1801 Wm. BARTLETT jr. (int)
B2. Benjamin, b 1773 d 1809, froze to death in open boat. Mar Mary BOWDEN 1800, b 1777, dau of Francis and Sarah (BROWN) BOWDEN.
C1. Mary, b 1804 C2. Abigail Harris, b 1806
B3. Martha, b 1775 d 1846, mar Jacob Thorner 1804. B8. Alice, d.y.
B4. Philip b 1777 B5. George Clark, b 1780, d.y.
B6. Miriam, b 1784 B7. Mary, b 1787 mar 1807 David Newell
B9. Alice, b 1792 mar Daniel C. Watts of Lynn, MA 1814, twin
B10. Tabitha, b 1792, d 1824, twin, poss mar a BARTLETT?
B11. George Clarke, b 1794 d 1799. B12. William, b 1809
LE CRAW, also CRAW, Philip mar 1767 MRB, Sarah Smith, bp 1751, dau of Robert Smith and Susannah Hatlett, 2 chn
A1. Mary, b 1767 A2. Mary Peach, b 1769
LE CRAW, Philip, mar 1779 Mrs. Mary Laskey, b 1736/7, prob dau of Cornelius and Eliz. Allen and widow of Benj. Laskin/Laskey
A1. Susannah, b 1768 d 1847, mar 1795 Cornelius Phillips Dodd
A2. Ann, bp 1770 A3. Philip, b 1780 A4. John, b 1782
LE CRAW, Richard, mar 1720 in MRB. Priscilla Tucker, bp 1697, dau of Nicholas and Priscilla (Bickford) Tucker. See Philip & Alice above.
A1. Mary, bp 1728 mar 1753 Wm. Parsons, and d 1819. A2. Richard,bp1731.
LE CRAW, Richard, mar Deliverance ___, res MRB, poss 2nd wife of above Richard?
A1. SArah, b 1733. A Deliverance LE CRAW mar John Hills and res No. Bolton, MA, where 13 chn were born. See NEHGS Vol 36.
LE CRAW, Peter mar Margaret ___, who poss mar 2. John Stanley 1756 MRB.
A1. Mary, d 1736 A4. Sarah, 1745-1746 A5. Peter, b 1747
A2. Mary again, b 1741 mar 1760 John VOLPEE, VALPY, qv.
A3. Ann, b 1743 mar John HAILES 1760-1766. See HAILES
A6. Elias, bp 1749, as CRAW. A7. Grace, b 1757 mar John Powsland 1776.
LE CRAS noted in MA records. See much more in NEHGS and Essex Inst.
Elizabeth mar Eleazar Johnson 1758 Boston, MA.
James, sea Captain, bought the CHARMING BETSEY in J 1741
John, mariner, arrived in Boston 1760s on sloop ADVENTURER from Nfld.
John, from J? to Boston 1716. (Filby)
John of MRB mar Ann Griffin of Boston in MRB 1717
LEYCROS, Peter in Salem early. (Essex Coll, vol 110, #3; Konig)
LE CRAW noted in MA.
Abigail mar John Lancey 1842 MRB
Alice mar Lawrence Grace 1766 MRB. Same or another mar 1790 Nathaniel Thayer in MRB.
Edward mar 1757 Sarah McColley
Hannah mar John Conway Jr. 1822 MRB. Hanah mar Caleb Prentiss Jr. 1835
Jane R. mar Philip T. Woodfin 1838 MA.
Peter B., b G, went first to Brazil, a mariner, then settled NYCity1822
Philip, fisherman, served in Wm. Hooper's Co. of MRB 1775/6
Capt. William of the schooner SUCCESS, 1772/1775; privateer BLACK SNAKE

1777; privateer schooner NECESSITY 1776. Poss was also master of the MORNING STAR 1780, age 35, five foot ten, dark compl. (JOURNALS OF ASHLEY BOWEN)

LE CRONIER in J 1331-1768, noted in US. A Capt. LE CRONIER of J was a privateersman. He captured 9 prize ships in 1757.

LE CUIROT, common and curr in G, old in J. This name means SKINNER in French. Cf with the many SKINNERS in early America, some said to have come from C.I. Is it poss that their orig. surname was LE CUIROT, and was rapidly changed to SKINNER in America?

LE CURRIL noted in MASS SOLDIERS AND SAILORS. Cf LE CUIROT and LE CARREL, CARRELL of France and C.I.

LE DAIN in St. Peter J 1668, in St. Laurens J 1788. See also DAIN, and DEAN.

LE DANE, George and Mary had fam in Boston, OUTC.

A1. George b 1729 A2. Mary b 1731

LE DAIN, Prof. Gerald from J fam, of the faculty of Law at McGill Univ. Canada, was a close friend of Sam Pollard, and was much interested in the famous trial of Wilbert Coffin, hanged in 1953 for the murder of Eugene and Robert Lindsey and Frederick Claar of PA, in the back country of Gaspe, QUE.

DAIN, poss LE DAIN?, John b ca 1724, prob mar 1750s, d Durham or Lisbon, ME 1817. Had chn. One dau mar John Balke curr 1780 in New Gloucester, ME. OUTC. (SECOND BOAT, May 1981; Mrs. Warren Campbell, Old Orchard Beach, ME)

DAIN, Isaac, mar 1814 Margaret Foreacres in Muskingum Co., OH. OUTC.

LE DREW, see DREW, DE RUE, DE LA RUE, and DRIEU is old in J.

LE DRU noted in PA and NY, OUTC.

LE DREW, said to be from J settled in Change Islands, Nfld. (Seary)

LE DREW, Robert, res Deer Lake, Nfld., said to be from J, and to have come from Change Island to Port de Grave, where he mar Jemima Dawe, and then rem to Cupids, Nfld. They were mar 1871 in Brigus, by John Peach, witnesses John ROWE and George GUSHUE. See Q.A. IN CANADA. One document says his father was Robert George LE DREW. Jemima d 1925 Cupids, Nfld. age 77. (Merle Mortimer, Toronto, ONT)

A1. Naomi, b ca 1873 mar John Alfred Stephens of Brigus, and d there 1906.

B1. Annie May Stephens, b 1892 mar Joseph Mortimer

B2. Alvina Stephen, b 1894 d 1971 unmar B4. Geo. A. Stephens, b 1898

B3. Miriam Stephens, b 1895 mar. Wm. Long. mar D. Marwick.

B5. Molly Stephens, b 1900, d.y.

LE DROW, said to be originally LE DROIT of J, in Nfld. LE DROIT old in J, and current there. The name mans 'law'.

LE DROS, William had land in Conception Bay, Nfld. 1804, from 1762. (Plantation Book, 1804)

LE DROS, Mary had land in Conc. Bay also, neighbor of George, one stage, one flake, three houses, two gardens, one meadow, date of entry 1762.

LE DROS, George, Nicholas, Richard and John all in Nfld. early 1800s.

LE DROW, John of Cupids mar 1827 Eliz. SMITH of Cupids. witnesses being Abraham and Susannah LE DROW.

A1. Ann Eliza, b 1841 A3. James John, b 1853, twin

A2. Robert John, b 1843 A4. Naomi, b 1853, twin.

LE DROW, Ester, of Cupids, mar 1846 at Brigus, Nfld. Jonathan TAYLOR.

LEE, in J 1441. See Q.A. IN CANADA, curr G and J.

LEE, John b ca 1825 J, drowned in Toronto Harbor as young man. At least two sons, with desc in Canada and US. For more see Q.A. IN CANADA.

B7. Arthur Lee, b 1887, d 1957, bur Pomona, CAL, mar ___Dyce.
C1. Arthur E. Lee, b 1911, d 1970 San Clemente, CAL, mar 1. --Weinman, and 2. ___Dauks.
D1. Doris Jean Lee, b 1941 mar __West, res Burbank, CAL
D2. Larry Dean Lee, b 1943 mar __Glawenwhite, res Visalia, CAL
E1. Bryan Lee, b 1964 E2. Dean Arthur Lee, b 1966
C2. Helen Amy, b 1916 d 1964, mar ___McWherter, bur Pomona, CAL
C3. A. Howard Lee, b 1916, twin mar ___Patterson, res Visalia, CAL
D1. Robert A. Lee, b 1939, mar ___Harmon, res Visalia, CAL, 3 chn: Kari, Shari and Robert Lee b 1960s, CAL.
D2. Charles H. Lee, b 1939, twin of Robert mar __Dewlaney
D3. James Marvin Lee b 1945, d 1961, bur Pomona, CAL

LEE, Abraham from J? in Dover, NH ca 1680. "His wife Esther, widow of Henry Ellins and dau of Major Richard Waldron, upon his death mar Richard Jose, Sheriff of the Province, outlived him and d on the Isle of Jersey. "(Savage)

LE FAVOR. "I have material on the ORNE and LEFAVOR families of Jersey and Guernsey." Not seen by compiler. (Mrs. Wm. Boyer, PinellaPK,FLA)

LE FEVRE, LE FEUVRE, LE FEBVRE are French and C.I. surnames. LE FEVRE in Vale G early. LE FAVER, LE FABER in J 1306, meaning the smith. FEVRE, LE FEVRE and LE FEUVRE curr J. LE FEUVRE and LE FEVRE curr G. LE FEUVRE in G 1331. LE FEUVRE is now the commonest form in the C.I. LE FEUVRE dit FILLATRE in St. Lawrence J 1788. See FILLATRE and LE FEUVRE.

It is possible that in early America all three of these surnames may have been mispelled FAVOR, FAVOUR, LE FAVOUR, which makes it most difficult to distinguish between different lines. To complicate matters, some were prob. Huguenots, while others were long-time residents of the C.I. Still others may have been Norman families from England.

A further complication is mentioned in the correspondence of Wm. Stubbs of Sherbrooke, QUE, a LE FAVOR descendant, in which he says about the LE FAVOURE of Salem, MA (Source not found)"..at some time in France, some provincial or national aspirant to a position of some power had been aided and supported in his struggle...by a local family, and upon eventually acquiring the sought-after-position had issued a decree...to the effect that henceforth and in perpetuity this family and its ensuing members should be named LES FAVOURES DE LOUIS? or whichever king he was." If an old written record could be found which had an accent over the "E" in FAVOURÉ, this suggestion would be greatly strengthened.

Mr. Stubbs further says: "My mother also said that family tradition had it that there were three original Le Favoure brothers who built their own sailing vessel, hence they must have lived ...near the sea-coast or on an Island, probably the Channel Islands." Mr. Stubbs goes on to say that Brittany was thought to be the origin of this family, who lived in Salem, MA, and one Le Favour operated the music store. (Hayward's HANCOCK, NH; New England HEADS OF FAMILIES; RHODE ISLAND HEADS OF FAM, Vol 10; Rev. War Records; BALDWIN GEN; THATCHER GEN; DRIVER FAM; BOSTON TRANSCRIPT, Sept. 1907; PA. AND RI records; MISSOURI PIONEER FAMS, p. 199; HUGUENOT EMIG, Vol 2, p. 191; AMERICAN ANCESTRY: Bolton's WESTCHESTER CO., NY, 16-744; Sylvester's HIST OF ULSTER NY; Lapham's HIST OF NORWAY, ME; GREELEY GEN; Little's HIST OF WEARE, NH) Please note that some of the sources are about Hug. fams. Also see long list of LE FEUVRE Sea Captains in book: JERSEY SAILING SHIPS by A. John Jean of Jersey.

LE FEVRE, also res Crowland, Lincolnshire, England 1793. (MHS;Fosdick;

Perley; NEHGS Vol 41)
LE FAVOUR, Amos and Ann, res Beverly, MA. Anna b 1750? Amos b 1745?
A fam of 9 in 1790 census. OUTC. CAUTION: TRIAL CHART
A1. Amos, poss AMICE originally?, b 1771 poss mar Abigail Dodge 1798, res Beverly, MA, fam of 4 in 1790.
B1. Amos Jr., b 1799 poss mar Mary OBER, AUBERT?, qv, 1825 Beverly. Mar 2. Nancy LOVETT, qv, 1834. Amos a shipmaster by 1848
C1. Nancy Lovett, b 1837 C3. Mary, b 1841 C5. Georgianna, b 1849
C2. Amos, b 1838 C4. Charles b 1846
B2. Israel, b 1801 mar Betsy LARCOM, qv, 1827 B3. Joseph, b 1803
B4. David, b 1805 mar poss Nancy Foster? 1827, 4 chn
C1. Nancy Wallis, b 1828 C3. Joseph, b 1836
C2. David, b 1832, d.y. C4. David Thomas, b 1840
B5. John, b 1807, poss mar Nancy Woodbury, 1832
C1. John Henry, b 1834 C4. Israel, b 1839 C7. Nancy A., b 1848
C2. Mary Obear b 1836 C5. Charles Porter, b 1842
C3. Elizabeth Gallop b 1837 C6. Woodbury Prince, b 1845
B6. Anna, b 1812 B8. Issachar, b 1816
B7. Lydia b 1815, poss mar 1841 Jewett Tasker of New Market, NH?
B9. Thomas, b 1819 A Thomas II mar 1844 Lydia Dodge, he a cordwainer
A2. Mary, b 1773, d.y.? A6. Elizabeth b 1780
A3. Polly/Mary b 1774, poss mar Jonathan Dodge 1801?
A4. Nabby, b 1775 A7. Anna b 1780 A9. John, b 1784
A5. Lydia, b 1776 A8. Thomas, b 1782, d.y.? A10. Thomas b 1787
LE FAVOUR, LE FAVOR, Anna of C.I.? mar Stephen Parker, res Warren, MA. OUTC. 7 chn b 1760s to 1781: James, Josiah, Pheny, Farenton, twin, Nathan, twin, Levi, twin, and Simeon, twin, Parker.
LE FAVOUR, John, b ca 1717 G or J, bur Topsfield, MA 1798. Mar Mary Cook of MRB 1743, 1723-1797, dau of Augustine and Anna, poss from C.I.? 14 chn, but a number d.y.: John, Thomas, Lydia, William, Sarah and Amos. (Charts by Paul Lefevor in WRCIC. He res Salt Lake City, UT; Susan Kraus, New Hartford, CT; Wm. STubbs, Sherbrooke, QUE; Stewart Sheedy, Syosset, Long Island, NY) On Mary's tombstone is the following:

READER, PASS ON, NE'ER WASTE YOUR TIME
ON (BAD) BIOGRAPHY AND BITTER RHYME.
FOR WHAT I AM, THIS CUMBROUS CLAY ENSURES
AND WHAT IWAS IS NO AFFAIR OF YOURS.

Erected by
Amos Le Favour.

A1. Mary, b 1744 Topsfield, MA mar Philip THOMAS
A2. Rachel, b 1745 mar 1799 Joseph Goodhue
A3. John, b 1748 mar 1773 Abigail LAKEMAN, d 1834. 6 chn. Many desc in Pawtucket, RI.
B1. Amos, b 1795 B3. Thomas, b 1797, poss mar Isabella Hill 1816
B2. Lucy, b 1796 B4. Lucy again, b 1799, twin of David below.

B5. DAvid, b 1799, mar1824 Mary Ann Baldwin, b 1798 Brimfield, MA,chn
C1. Edward b 1827, d 1874 Detroit, MI, mar 1. Mary Drown Read, only ch of Gen. John B. Read of Pawtucket, RI. A son John, then Mary d 1858. John mar 2. 1886 Martha Walker Hutchison of Bay City,MI
D1. John E. mar Jennie Rawson Smith, mar 1909, d 1910.
D2. Helen Hutchison b 1869, by 2nd wife.
D3. David, b 1873 d 1910, mar 1901 Amsterdam, NY, Helen MacLaren Kline. 1895
E1. David Edward, b 1904, twin, mar Catherine Louise LE FEVRE, b.
F1. Susan Le Favour, b 1931 mar John Scott Repass, and 2. Franz Kraus 1963. 2 sons use Kraus name
G1. Scott Douglas Kraus, b 1953 mar Megan Godfrey 1977

G2. David Bruce Kraus, b 1956
E2. William Bruce, b 1904, twin of David, mar Harriet Walden, b 1910, 2 chn.
F1. Bruce, b 1934, mar ___, 2 daus, Nicole and ___.
F2. Sidney, female, b 1941
C2. Horace, b 1830 d 1832 C4. Heber, b 1837, d 1878 Pawtucket, RI
C3. Mary, b 1833 d 1857 Pawtucket, RI
C5. Latimer, b 1841, d 1870 Jacksonville, FLA.
B6. Sarah G., b 1801
A4. Anne, or Hannah, b 1749 mar 1780 John Norfolk
A5. Robert, b 1751 mar 1773 Elizabeth Whittel/Whitting?, at least 8 chn A Robert res Salem, MA 1790 with fam of 11.
B1. Polly, bp 1780 B4. Sally, bp 1780 B7. Samuel, bp 1788
B2. Betsy B5. Lydia, bp 1783 B8. Lydia again, bp 1791
B3. Nathaniel, bp 1780 B6. Robert, bp 1784
A6. Ruth, b 1759 Topsfield, MA mar 1781 John Perkins
A7. Joseph, b 1764 d 1838 mar 1785 Susanna Dike, 1764-1846, dau of Wm. and Eunice (Gallup) Dike. Fam res Beverly, Ipswich & Salem, MA.
B1. Nathaniel, b 1785 mar 1814 Hannah Fowler Jenness
B2. Lydia, b 1790 mar 1809 Jonathan SYMONDS and d 1877.
B3. William Dike b 1797 Salem, d 1834, mar 1821 Elizabeth Tarbox
B4. Thomas, b 1799 Salem, mar1822 Sally Morgan Howe, dau of Daniel Howe and Lucy Morgan. Sally b 1803 d 1866, 7 chn. Fam rem to Athens, OH ca 1830.
C1. Daniel, b 1830, d 1902, mar 1862 Mary Ellen Parker in Union Star, Dekalb, MO. Mary Ellen b 1838 ME, d 1872 MO. She was dau of Wm. Parker and Mary Hoyt. Daniel mar 2. Matilda Sisk 1874, in MO. 6 chn by 1st wife and 3 by 2nd.
D1. Martha Emma b 1864 MO, mar 1881 Frank Snuffer and d 1903
D2. Sarah Ellen, b 1865 d 1943, mar Patton Price Miller
D3. William Thomas, b 1866 MO, d 1953, mar 1891 Annie Haigh in Salt Lake City, UT, dau of Wm. John Haigh and Sarah Kershaw. She was b England, widow of Wm. T. Donelson, 5 chn.
E1. Alfred, b 1892 SLCity, d 1940, mar 1915 Rachel Miller BIRD
F1. Gene Elizabeth, b 1920 SLCity, d 1974, mar 1937 Gover James Monsen.
F2. Alfred Melvin, b 1923 mar 1948 Thelma Jean ROSE, div.
F3. Paul Harold, b 1930 mar 1959 Doris Jean Armstrong, dau of Albert and Virgie (Ethington) Armstrong.
G1. Paul Harold b 1961 mar 1982 Kristen Sue Vincent
G2. Gary Kent, b 1962 G3. Laurie A, b 1963 G4. Kimberly, b 1967
E2. William Thomas, b 1895 d 1953 mar 1915 Ruth Cherrington
E3. Warren Leslie, b 1899, d 1962, mar Eleanor Crockett
E4. Vern Raymond, b 1902, d.y. E5. Helen, b 1906, d.y.
D4. Charles Arthur, b 1868, d.y.?
D5. Lucy Ann, b 1870, mar Frank St. John D6. Joseph, d.y.
D7. by 2nd wife, Daniel Franklin, b 1874, mar Ruth Flanagan
D8. Roscoe Paskel, b 1875, mar Matilda Jane Flanagan
D9. Minnie Mae, b 1877, mar Charlie Flanagan
C2. Susanna, b 1833 Athens, OH mar Jud A. Simpson?
C3. Lucy Ann, b 1836, d.y.? C5. William, b 1841, d.y.
C4. Joseph, b 1839, d 1917, mar 1861 Laura Ann Parker
C6. Helen/Ellen, b 1842 mar 1859 James Bunting
C7. Lydia, b 1845 Athens, OH d 1917, mar 1895 John Brimm.
B5. Susanna, b 1802 Salem, MA, d 1871, mar 1835 Moses Edmester
B6. Mary Ann, bp 1804, mar John WILLIAMS.

Although the record above shows that Amos of the orig. family d.y., it is apparent that an Amos survived, and provided the tombstone for the mother of the above family. He must somehow be related, if not a son.

LE FAVOUR, Amos, b 1766, poss mar Betsy ___, res Salem, MA, had several chn. Note there was another Amos, res Beverly 1810, also John Jr., Joshua O. and Philip. (Census) Likely related to above large family.

A1. Betsey, bp 1789 d.y. B4. Susanna B7. Harriet, bp 1800
A2. Nancy, bp 1791 B5. Andrew Preston?, bp1795 Poss as many as 11-
A3. Sophia, bp 1793 B6. Betsey again, bp 1798 (-14 chn in this fam?

LE FAVOR, John Jr. mar 1804 Jane FREETO, qv. A John res MRB 1790, fam of 7. (Census)

A1. John, bp 1804 A3. James Freteau, bp 1806 A5. Jane BESOME, bp1812
A2. Francis Freteau, bp 1805 A4. Mary Jane, bp 1808
A6. Lydia ORNE, bp 1811

LE FAVOUR, John mar Lydia ORNE 1775 MRB. 2 chn: Thomas, bp 1788, Mary bp 1792. OUTC.

Many more listed in Boston and MRB Vrs; GENS AND ESTATES OF CHARLES-TOWN, MA; OLD FAMS OF SALISBURY, MA; Census; Noyes; Essex Coll, Vol 8; HOOPER GEN; NEHGS Vols 17,100; Bolton; York, ME records.

LE FAVOR, Amos mar Anna DELLEWARE, French woman, 1768 MRB

LE FAVOR, Amos res Beverly, MA 1810. Cf AMICE, a C.I. first name.

LE FAVRE, Dolly Newhall, wife of Joshua ORNE, d 1833 Stoneham, MA,at17.

LE FAVOUR, Francis, cordwainer, mar Eliz., a son b 1846, MRB. OUTC

LE FAVOUR, James mar Ann BESSOM, BISSON, qv, 1836, MRB.

LE FAVOR, FAVOR, Sarah of Meredith, NH mar Jacob Tenney, b 1808, 3 daus (TENNEY FAM, by M.J. Tenney, 1891 Boston) OUTC.

LE FAVOUR, Thomas, b 1797 son of John, b 1748, who was son of John and Mary (COOK) LE FAVOUR, qv., poss mar Isabella Hill 1816 in Beverly, MA. Note large family above. Unverified.

A1. Isabella, b 1817, d.y. A2. Thomas, b 1821, d.y.?
A3. Isabella again, b 1824, mar 1849 at age 25 Robert G. BENNETT, cashier, age 28, son of Cotton and Mary Ann BENNETT at Newton, MA.
A4. Thomas, b 1826 A7. Anna Elizabeth b 1834
A5. John William, b 1829, d.y.? A8. James again, b 1838, d.y.?
A6. James Hill, b 1831, d.y.? A9. James Walker, b 1840

LE FAVOUR, Thomas II, cordwainer, mar Lydia Dodge 1844, res Beverly, MA See large fam above.

A1. Lydia b 1846 A2. Thomas, b 1847 A3. Azor Dodge, b 1849

LE FAVOUR, Thomas A., b 1826 Beverly, MA mar 1859 Susan O. Batchelder, b 1828, dau of Col. Ezra Batchelder. Thomas d 1895. OUTC. (BATCHELDER GEN)

A1. Fred Gardiner LE FAVOUR, b 1859, res Beverly mar 1886 Laura Greenwood Davenport.
A2. Susan Batchelder LE FAVOUR, b 1862 mar 1888 Stephen MASURY Gordon, res Fall River, MA.

FAVOUR, FAVOR, Thomas and Mary res Boston, OUTC.

A1. Amos, bp 1746
A2. John, bp 1753, poss mar Anna, and 2. Annice? CAUTION!
B1. Anna, bp 1769 B2. Amos, bp 1771 B3. Mary, bp 1-73

LE FAVOUR, Thorndyke, b 1852 Salem, MA. (Wm.O. Stubbs, Sherbrooke, QUE)

A1. Maybelle, b 1877 Salem, MA mar ___Stubbs, rem to Canada.
B1. William O. Stubbs
A2. Herbert Thorndyke, a son Herbert Jr. b early 1900s, rem to CAL.

LE FAVOUR, Timothy mar Hannah/Anna Willard in Boston 1707. She mar 2. 1718 John Bosworth as Timothy's widow. She d 1747. (Boston TRANSCRIPT, Sept. 1907)

A1. Timothy Jr. mar 1731 Elizabeth Bosworth, b 1711, who d 1748.

Timothy d Bristol, RI, age 33. Elizabeth the dau of John and Eliz., the first wife. 5 chn, many desc.

B1. Timothy, b 1732, d.y. B3. Anna b 1736 b4. Sarah, b 1738
B2. Daniel, b 1733, d 1797 age 64 B5. Elizabeth b 1741

LE FAVOUR, William C., cordwainer, age 20, son of John and Jane, mar 1846 Sally J. Phumphreys, age 20, dau of Edward and Sally. A dau b 1847, and son Wm. bp 1849. OUTC.

LE FAVOUR, William, served in Rev. War. (MASS SOLDIERS AND SAILORS)

FAVOR, William, from France or C.I. before 1717, mar (int) Rachel DE FEW, qv. (Bolton; Boston Records, Vol 28) OUTC.

LE FEBVRE, see also LE FAVOR, etc.

LE FEBVRE, Marie, b G, dau of Daniel LE FEBVRE de Guarnare, and widow of Jean HARDY, Sieur de la Touche, mar 2. at St. Malo, France 1696 Augustin LUCAS from La Rochelle. Rem to Newport, RI, and poss before that, had res NY? Marie d 1698, RI? Prob a Hug. fam. More on this fam in TWO HUGUENOT FAMILIES, DE BLOIS-LUCAS, by Frank Fox, Cambridge, MA, 1949.

LE FEBVRE, Elinor M., b 1831 J, mar T. FALLE, qv, res Troy, NY

LE FEBVRE curr in CAL and other places. OUTC.

LE FEUVRE curr G and J. In St. Clement, Grouville, St. Heliers, St. Laurens, St. Peter, St. John, St. Brelade, St. Martin and St. Savior J 1668. In St. Clement, St. Peter, Grouville, St. John, St. Heliers and St. Martin J 1749. LE FEYVRE in G 1393. LE FEVRE and LE FEUVRE curr G and J. See CIFHS #3 for LE FEUVRE dit FILLASTRE.

LE FEUVRE shield; argent, a chevron gules between three mullets pierced sable.

LE FEUVRE, several to New Orleans, LA 1823, from J? or G? Or were these the LE FAVOURS noted above in the large family group?

LE FEUVRE, Capt. Robert in 1741 bought the JOHN AND MARY, of J.

LE FEUVRE, Rev. Clement FALLE, son of Rev. George LE FEUVRE, one time Chaplain to the British Embassy in Paris. Rev. LE FEUVRE settled in WIS shortly after the Napoleonic War, in which as a young man, he had served as officer in the Marines. Ordained in the Anglican CH after the war, he became disenchanted with his calling, and emig. to WIS, where he became a backwoods farmer. He had a large family with several sons, one of whom mar the dau of the Gov. of the state, Gov. Beale. He had descendants, but these were not traced by compiler. (Guy Dixon, England)

LE FEUVRE, Daniel of Jersey, was witness to will of John KNIGHT/ CHEVALIER, qv, from J also, in Newington, NH 1770. (NH WILLS)

LE FEUVRE, George Francis, b 1869 J, mar Florence Mary GIFFARD 1877, and rem with some of his fam to Gaspe, QUE then to Ottawa, ONT. Many desc in US and Canada, including San Antonio, TX; Lubbock, TX; Ottawa, ONT; Brampton, ONT; Waterloo, ONT; Coquitlam, BC; Amherstburg, ONT; Kirkland, QUE; Trenton, MI; Wyandotte, MI; Utica and Detroit, MI; Indianapolis, IND; Scarborough, ONT; Aylmer, QUE, etc.

LE FEUVRE, George Francis, son of the immigrant, was a well-known writer and commentator, who did much to preserve the ancient language of Jersey, called Jersiaise, said to be almost the same as the original language of the Norman French, spoken by William the Conqueror in 1066. See Q.A. IN CANADA.

LE FEVRE, LE FEAVER. Please note that many came to America from places other than the Channel Islands.

LE FEVRE, Abraham, d 1807 Wayne Co., KY, mar Catherine ___. OUTC. (Laurel Stockton, Sebastopol, CAL)

A1. Elizabeth, b 1776 VA, mar Reuben Ard, d 1842 Morgan Co., MO.
A2. Sarah, b ca 1777? mar ___ A3. Catharine, b 1780-1785?

LE FEVRE, Clement Fall, b 1797 Herts, England, son of Rev. Geo. and Phoebe (Bayley) LE FEVRE of a J fam, rem 1817 to NYCity where he taught French, then took studies for the ministry in Kingston, ONT. Ordained 1821 in England, at the Soc. for the Propagation of the Gospel in Foreign Parts. Appointed to Sherbrooke, QUE, but left to join the Universalist Ch. in Troy NY, 1829, then rem to NYCity. Later served in Hudson, NY and Wilwaukee, WI 1844. Mar 1822 Mary, dau of Joseph and Hannah (Van Wyck) Clowes of Hempstead, LI, NY. He d 1882 in Milwaukee, WI, 3 chn.

A1. William A2. George A3. Ellen, mar John Crapser Coleman.

LE FEVRE, Elias res Salem Twp., Shelby Co., OH, was 70 in 1880. OUTC.

LE FEVERE, John, silver and goldsmith in Phila. PA 1806. OUTC

LE FILLIATRE, LE FILLATRE, FILLATRE, etc. LE FILLIATRE, meaning step-son, in J 1309. In St. Laurens J 1668. Note there was also LE FEUVRE dit FILLATRE in St. Brelade J 1700s. (ALLEZ records, J.R. McAdam, Sacremento, CAL) FILLASTRE curr J and Nfld.

LE FILLIATRE, PHALATER, Abraham, a Jerseyman, met in ME waters by John Josslyn, noted in his TWO VOYAGES TO NEW ENGLAND.

LE FLOCQ, from France to J 1800s? See Q.A. IN CANADA. Noted recently in CAL and Boston, MA.

LE GALLAIS in J 1226, in G 1200s. In St. Heliers and St. Laurens J 1668. In Grouville, St. Laurens, St. Heliers and St. Saviour J 1749. In St. Laurens J 1788. Curr J. LE GALLAIS and GALLEY, GALLIE are not necessarily the same surname. Found separately in J since 1528.

LE GALLAIS, Capt. David, b ca 1697 J, settled in MRB and mar Hannah BROWNE 1727. He mar 2. Sarah Wanton? of Newport, RI 1753, and d 1755. No surviving issue? Records of his fam not found. His widow Sarah mar Wm. ___, had 4 daus, desc from 3. David was very rich, owned ships named DUKE OF CUMBERLAND, JERSEY, ELIZABETH, CHARMING SALLY, and SEAFLOWER. SEAFLOWER was the name of many J ships. See Q.A. IN CANADA. (JOURNALS OF ASHLEY BOWEN; Essex Antiq. Vol 12; NEHGS Vol 118; PEABODY GEN, etc)

LE GALLAIS, ___, rem from J to NH 1700s, when he tried to persuade Elizabeth WEBBER to return with him to her fam in J. (FAM. TRAD) She refused, so he married her and both remained in Portsmouth, NH. He soon died, and she mar 2. a Corliss? LE GALLEE had son Thomas? (David H. Le Gallee, Parma, OH)

A1. Thomas, b 1786 d 1852, mar Sally Everett, nee BAKER, qv.

B1. Charles B2. David B3. John B4. Ellis

LE GALLAIS, Philip, carpenter, b J, age 72 in 1861, res Paspebiac, QUE, mar Mary Holmes, age 63 in 1871. Thomas COLLETTE, a servant res with them, b England, age 25. (Census)

A1. Francis, b ca 1832, mar Marguerite ___, b ca 1835.

B1. Mary Jane, b ca 1859 B3. Emma, b ca 1866

B2. Celina, b ca 1864 B4. Adelise, b ca 1868 B5. Francis, b1870?

LE GALLAIS, Edmund, b Quebec ca 1837, farmer in Gaspe, QUE 1871, had wife Mary Ann, age 28, and 3 chn: William 5, Mary Ann 3, and Edmund age 1.. (Census)

LE GALLAIS, Philip, carpenter, b Quebec, ca 1827, with wife b ca 1835, poss Rebecca Smith? Mary LE GALLAIS b J ca 1795, res with them in 1871. See Philip above.

A1. John, b ca 1858 A4. Charles, b ca 1862 A7. Edmond, b ca 1868

A2. Philip, b ca 1859 A5. Annabella, b ca 1864 A8. Mary, b ca 1870

A3. Jane, b ca 1860 A6. William, b ca 1866

LE GALLAIS noted in Phila. Archives #9301. Richard poss to PA 1880? (Filby)

LE GALLY, J., res Hampshire Co., MA 1810 census

LE GALLY, Thomas res Roxbury, MA 1810 census
GALLAIS, Mary and Steven Vallou mar in NYCity 1692. (Clemens)
GALLEY, Thomas, res Salem, MA 1790, fam of 4. (Census) Not certain if this was GALLEZ of C.I. or LE GALLAIS of C.I.
GALLEY, GALLIE, Mary res Salem, MA 1790
LE GALLEE noted in Quebec City resident Petition 1838. (LOST IN CANADA Aug. 1981)
LE GALLEZ, curr and common in G. Not in Stevens book of old J surnames Poss came from France to G in 1800s? or is same as GALLEZ?
LE GALLEZ in Detroit MI 1970s, prob from C.I., as other Channel Islanders settled there from G and Alderney in 1800s & 1900s.
LE GALLEY, curr Bowling Green, OH, OUTC
LE GALLIENNE, see also GALLIEN
LE GALLIENNE, Eva, b 1899 England? dau of Richard Le G. and wife Julie Norregaard, educated London and Paris, on stage from 1914 to 1980. Many honorary degrees from the US, and special awards . Author and translator, res Weston, CT. Richard, her father, 1866-1947, was quoted in England: "I know little of my name, except that it came to us from the Channel Islands, all my father's ancestors being Guernsey sailors." Richard res many years in US. Eva living 1983.
LE GEYT in J 1274. In St. Heliers, Grouville, St. Saviour and Trinity J 1668. In St. Heliers and St. Saviours J 1749. Curr J. See Q.A. IN CANADA. Mostly pronounced LE JET, sometimes LE GATE.
LE GEYT, Daniel b 1844 St. Saviour J d at Omaha, NEB 1894, bur 1895 J. He mar 1872 Fannie Julia Crossley, who d 1900. One dau, Fannie Julia b 1873 d at Omahan, NEB, bur J.
LE GEYT, LIDGET, LE GATE, LEGGETT, Peter from J?, merchant in Boston, age 38 in 1667, mar Elizabeth SEAMMON 1677, a dau Elizabeth, a son Charles. (Noyes) See also SOC. JERS. BULL. 1904.
LE GETTE, LE GEYT?, some from J to San Remo, CAL ca 1900, poss with the Debenham group?
LEGATE, James, res Leavenworth, KS 1888. OUTC. (NEHGS Vol 42)
LEGATE in MD 1652. OUTC. (Skordas)
LE GEYT, fam in America with origin in England. This fam was located in Dartford, Kent and Middlesex, England in 1600s, later in Suffolk London, etc. It is not known to compiler if the fam originally came from C.I. or was directly from France, possibly with the Conqueror? John LE GEYT, who came from England, settled in Hartford, CT, and one of his daus mar Robert Hamil PORTER, qv. This Porter also mar 3 women from C.I. fams settled in UT, so his fam is included in this book. Much work was done on the CT fam. See sources. (Dorothy Le Geyt, E. Hartland, CT; SLCity records; WRCIC)
LE GEYT, Capt. George from J was trading with Virginia 1787. (A. John Jean, Jersey)
LEGG, old in J and curr in G and J.
LEGG, Elizabeth mar John BROWNE of Exeter, England in MA 1686. OUTC.
LEGO, LE GAULT?, see Filby and Q.A. IN CANADA. OUTC.
LE GRAND, see Q.A. IN CANADA, curr Los Angeles, CAL, but OUTC.
GRAND, LE GRAND, old in J, in St. Lawrence J 1788.
LE GRAND, John arrived in Boston, MA 1769 on ship MOLLY from J.(Whit/more)
LE GRAND, noted in Green's KENTUCKY FAMS, and curr Chicago, OUTC
LE GRAND, Philip, age 22 of Carranbrook, ONT, b J, son of Philip and Jane, mar 1864 in St. James, Toronto, ONT, Jane DU HEAUME, age 24, also of Carronbrook, b J, dau of Philip DU HEAUME and Jane. Witnesses: Henrietta Grasett of Toronto, and Wm. DU HEAUME of Brampton, ONT.

LEGREE, LE GROW?, John mar ___, res Salem, MA. OUTC. (Essex Coll,#8)
A1. Hezekiah, bp 1715 A2. Mercy, bp 1717 Salem, MA.

LEGRESLEY in J 1607, meaning slim. In St. Ouen J 1668, in St. Ouen, St. Heliers and St. John J 1749, curr G and J. Islanders pronounce this name LE GRAYLEY. "Sir Roger de Toeny, living in the year 1000, came from France with William the Conqueror. His son William took the name of De Gresley from Castel Gresley. Men of the Norman nobles of that time took the name of their estates, and dropped their family names...one Lord Le Gresley,Baron, Knight of the Bath under Edward II, living about 1285. There is no doubt that they came from England to Jersey...Sir Robert Gresley of Drakelow is 24th in direct descent from Robert de Gresley, grandson of Nigel, who was a kinsman of the Conqueror. Nigel's son William built and lived in Castel Gresley in Derbyshire. After three centuries the family moved to Drakelow in the same estate, which has been their seat since the time of the Conqueror." (Sophia R. Le Gresley, via C.E.B. Le Gresley, Toronto, ONT)

LE GRESLEY, see Q..A. IN CANADA. See also PILL.

LE GRESLEY, four bros. to Gaspe QUE from J. Two settled in New Carlisle, QUE. Poss Frank of St. Ouen J was one of these. He became Sheriff at New Carlisle, QUE, and also a county Judge, mar Queenie Cook. The two who settled at Bougainville, QUE were Philip and John. Another report says they settled at Belle Anse, QUE. CAUTION: TRIAL CHART. (Lima De V. Le Gresley, Verdun, QUE; Edith McKitterick, Pte. aux Trembles, QUE)

LE GRESLEY, John, from J ca 1840? mar ___?
A1. Edward, mar Marianne LUCAS, a son Lloyd, unmar
A2. Frank, b 1840?, mar Isabel GIRARD, GERARD, qv.
B1. Frank Jr. mar Lena VARDON, qv. B4. Liza, had chn
C1. Eva C2. Ava C3. Milton, b ca 1916
B2. John mar Ina Girard
B3. Ida, mar ?, had chn. B5. Mary Ann, mar A. McCallum
A3. Philip, b 1853, of Belle Anse, GAspe, QUE mar Eliza Hotton of Malbaie, QUE.
B1. William Herbert, b 1885, d 1935, mar Emiline Myra DE VOUGES, qv, b 1897 Bougainville, QUE.
C1. Sylvia, b 1916, mar Charles Burton ofNew Richmond, QUE, no issue
C2. Elias, b 1917, mar Ada Hotton of Belle Anse, 2 chn.
D1. William, b 1942 mar Patricia McCrea of Montreal, 2 sons, Randy and Robert
D2. Mary, b 1943, mar Andre Arneault of PEI, 3 chn: Valeria, Richard and Roger Arneault.
C3. Grace, b 1918 mar Allan Hotton, res Brantford, ONT, 3 chn
D1. William Hotton, b 1942 mar Mona O'Brien, 2 chn: Leigh & Corey
D2. Linda Hotton, b 1945 mar Robert Gaylor, 2 chn: Darren, Darlene
D3. James Hotton, b 1949, unmar, res Montreal.
C4. Theresa, b 1919 mar Stewart McColm of New Richmond, QUE, 2 daus, Heather and Holly McColm.
C5. Edith, b 1922 mar Thomas McKitterick of Montreal, 5 chn
D1. Keith McKitterick, b 1948 mar Rachel Desmarchais of Montreal.
D2. Sharon McKitterick, b 1949
D3. Timothy McKitterick, b 1950, mar Huguette Paquin of Montreal, 2 daus, Shannon and Samantha McKitterick.
D4. Bryne McKitterick b 1952 D5. Francine McKitterick, b 1953
C6. Rena, b 1924, mar Thomas LUCAS of Bougainville, Gaspe, QUE, res Prescott, QUE.
D1. Darlene Lucas, b 1951 mar Wally Kolodziechuk of Cardinal, ONT,

who had 2 chn from prev. mar.
D2. Melissa, a son Jonathan
C7. Herbert, b 1926 mar Pierette Duguay of New Richmond, QUE, no chn.
C8. Wanda, b 1928 mar John TISSIER of Montreal, QUE, 4 chn.
D1. John Tissier, b 1952 D3. Ricky Tissier, b 1957
D2. Wendy Tissier, b 1953 D4. Marlene Tissier, b 1962
C9. and C10. Other chn?
C11. James, b 1934 mar Patricia Ryan of Nfld., 2 daus, res Calgary.
D1. Debbie D2. Lillian b 1962
B2. Philip B3. Walter
B4. Elsie mar Arthur GERARD, res Belle Anse, Gaspe, QUE, 10 chn: Leslie, Myrtle, Howard, Lottie, Ina, Richard, Effie, Harvey, Herbert, and Harold GERARD.
A4. Elias, mar Dorcas LUCAS.
B1. Adolphus, b 1890 Bougainville, QUE d 1966, mar Lima DE VOUGE, b 1885 Belle Anse, QUE.
C1. Ewart, b 1914, mar Myrtle Chicoine, and d 1971
D1. Lima, b 1943 D2. Lena, b 1945 D3. Lorna, b 1947
C2. Stanley, b 1917 mar Exilda Chiasson, res Prescott, ONT, a son Vernon b 1953
C3. Alvin, b 1920 mar Pauline Estey, res Two Mts., QUE, 5 chn.
D1. Patricia, b 1944 D3. Arlene, b 1949
D2. John, b 1946 D4. Donna, b 1955 D5. Rodney, b 1961
C4. Raymond, b 1922 res Verdun, QUE
C5. Una, b 1925, mar Lionel Hodgins, res Verdun, QUE
D1. Evelyn Hodgins, b 1943 D2. Lynda Hodgins, b 1947
D3. Gary Hodgins b 1953
A5. ? A6. Isabella Victoria, b 1859 d 1927
A7. Alphonse,? 1862-1921, mar Edith Hotton
B1. Laura, mar Allan LEGGO, 6 chn: Emmett, Mansel, Wilton, Beulah, vera and Thelma Leggo.
A8. Edith Emily, 1871-1945, mar John James LE GROS, qv, 1868-1923
LE GRESLEY, John, merchant at Pt. St. Peter, QUE, 1829-1877
LE GRESLEY, Philip, b 1785 St. Ouen J, d 1866 UT? He was son of Philip and Elizabeth (GRANDIN) LE GRESLEY of St. Ouen J. He mar 1805 Judith MARQUAND b 1788 Vale G, dau of Jean and Caroline (LANGLOIS) MARQUAND of G. She d 1860. Caution: Compiler was not able to tell from the chart prepared by John P. Le Sueur of Mesa, AZ if this couple and chn came to UT. Other LE GRESLEYS to UT, also. (SLCity records)
A1. Philip, b 1807 St. Ouen J mar Ann Johnson
A2. Betsy, b 1810 St. Ouen J, d 1891, mar Elias BRIARD, qv.
A3. John b 1812 J, mar Mary Boyle and d 1892
A4. Caroline, b 1814 Ville Baget, St. Ouen J mar John LE SUEUR.
A5. Mary, b 1816 J, mar 1840 John DU HAMEL, and 2. Philip MARIT, MARETT qv. Mary d 1877 Kamas, UT.
A6. Edward, b 1818 St. Ouen J d 1859
A7. Francis, b 1821 St. Ouen J d 1852, mar Rebecca BALLON
A8. Rachel b 1823 J? d 1863, mar Peter HACQUOIL, mispelled HALQUOIL in record. A9. Jensy, b 1826.
LE GRESLEY, John Walter, b 1859 St. Brelade J, d there 1947 age 88. He mar Lilian Elsie Brown, b 1868 England, d J 1947 age 79. They came to America but returned to J. (J. Diane Le Gresley, New Carlisle,QUE)
A1. Lasco A2. Glen A3. Howard
A4. Francis John, b J, rem to New Carlisle, QUE before WWII. Served in France, returned to New Carlisle, where he was a general merchant. Mar Mary Florence Cook, 4 chn.

B1. John, merchant in New Carlisle, QUE, mar 1. Diane Sawyer, b 1931 in J, div.
C1. Faye, b 1951 mar 1975 William Griffiths, dau Sara M. Griffiths.
C2. Gary, b 1952 mar 1976 Manon Chouinard, 2 chn: Julie C. and Alain Francis.
C3. Bryan, b 1956 C4. Karen, b 1960
B2. Peter, b 1931 mar Renate Knippleholz, b 1931 Germany, 3 chn: Lisa Mark and John
A5. Norris, b US?, res Rutland, VT mar Grace Hastings, 2 daus, Mary and Mildred
A6. Arthur, b US, to J, then to Canada, mar 1. Sybil Frazer in J, div, and mar 2. Dolly ROMERIL. This couple recently d in J.
LE GRESLEY, from C.I. to CAL early 1900s. (Luce)
LE GRESLEY, John and Elizabeth from C.I. 1855, via ship CHIMBORAZO, settled UT. (SLC RECORDS)
LE GRESLEY, Emilie, b 1842, from J to North Chelmsford, MA, ca 1870 with husband John LE MARINEL, qv. LE GRESLEY curr J.
LE GRESLEY, see LE SUEUR, John and PILL, Alfred.
LE GRESLEY, GRIZLEY, John mar Mary Sadler 1740 Boston, MA.
LE GRESLEY in Duplessis Co., QUE late 1800s. OUTC. (Aldo Brochet)
LE GROS in J 1100s. In Trinity, St. Laurens, St. Martin, Grouville, and St. Saviour J 1668. In St. Mary, St. Laurens, St. Brelade, St. Saviour, Grouville and St. Clement J 1749. LE GROS in Sark 1700s Curr J. A Hug. LE GROS fam in England directly from France appears as GROS, GROW, GROSSE, etc. in the colonies. One LE GROS shield is azure, three lions rampant or. LE GROS crest; a dexter arm, embowed ppr vested gules, holding by the blade a sword, point downwards, hilted or. Motto; In Deo Confido. Many, many spelling variants.
By 1790 there were 21 heads of fams in New England with names spelled LE GROS, LE GROW, LE GRO, LE GROUE, LE GROO, LE GROSS and LE GROSE, some of which, but not all, were likely from the C.I. Compiler has not been able to take the amount of time necessary to sort all of these, and will leave it to desc. See NEHGS Vol 31; ANCESTORS OF GUILFORD SOLON TINGLEY; Davis; MRB VR; Groves; Perley, etc.
LE GROW, from C.I. to Newfoundland, to Canada and US. See Q.A. IN CANADA, by Turk. (Susan Squires, Newburyport, MA)
LE GROSS, Francis, b ca 1764 J, d 1809 Concord, MA, mar 1787 Dolly Barker, d 1795. Francis served in Capt. Wm. Park's Co., Col.Tupper Regt, 1781, MA line. A desc Mary LE GROSS Bulmer Barber was b Lowell, MA. (DAR Vol 69) CAUTION: TRIAL CHARTS
LE GROW, Elias mar Elizabeth Dodd 1761 MRB MORE IN CI COLLECTION.
A1. Elias, bp 1763 MRB, d.y. A3. Elias again, bp 1767 MRB
A2. Elizabeth, bp 1765 MRB A4. Joseph, bp 1769 A5. Rebeckah, bp 1772
LE GROW, Elias mar 1765 Sarah BODEN, qv, res MRB.
A1. Jane, bp 1766 A2. Elias bp 1767 A3. Sarah, bp 1769
LE GROW, Elias, 1755-1815, d Windham, ME, mar ___BAKER. OUTC.(DAR#43)
LE GROSS, John and Sarah res MRB, a son John bp 1733
LE GROE, Joseph killed by lightning in Salem Harbor 1729
LE GROW, Joseph mar Ann Thorn 1759 MRB, 3 chn. Note: 3 Josephs then!
A1. Rebeckah, bp 1760 A2. Hannah, bp 1762 A3. Ann, bp 1766
LE GROW, Joseph, mar Rebecca ALLEN 1734 MRB, mar 1759 Ann Thorn.
A1. Joseph, bp 1735, d.y. A2. Jane, bp 1737
A3. Joseph again, bp 1739 mar Lydia Dodd 1757? 3 chn
B1. Joseph, bp 1751 B2. Lydia bp 1758 B3. Wm. Dodd, bp 1765
A4. Elias, bp 1741 poss mar Elizabeth Dodd? 1761 MRB.
A5. Rebecca, bp 1743 MRB, poss mar 1768 John ANTHOINE?, qv.

A6. Ebenezer, bp 1744, poss mar Deborah BODEN, BOWDEN, 1765 MRB. Did he mar 2. Alice Riddan, who d 1827 MRB age 82. His chn?
B1. Ebenezer, bp 1768 B3. Alice, bp 1773
B2. Rebecca, bp 1771 B4. Hannah, bp 1773

LE GROW, Nathaniel mar Elizabeth Hines 1769 MRB. Same or another mar Elizabeth Pritchard 1775 in MRB. Nathaniel res there 1790 with fam of 6. OUTC.
A1. John Hinds, bp 1771 A3. Mary Cruff, Croft?, bp 1776
A2. James, bp 1773 A4. James, bp 1779 MRB, mar? Tabitha CLARKE 1807.
A5. Betsy, bp 1781 A6. Molly Cruff, Croft?, bp 1783

LE GROW, Philip mar Mary Wills 1777 MRB
A1. Jane, bp 1778 A3. George, bp 1786
A2. Philip, bp 1783 A4. Betsy, bp 1788 A5. John, bp 1793 MRB

LE GROE, LE GROW, Philip mar Ann SAUNDERS 1739 MRB.
A1. Mary, bp 1745, d.y.? A4. Hannah, bp 1752 A7. Miriam, bp 1764
A2. Mary again bp 1746, d.y.? A5. Mary again, bp 1755
A3. Philip, bp 1750 A6. Sarah, bp 1757 A8. Philip again, bp 1774

LE GROO, Philip, b ca 1671, J, to Salem MA ca 167. (NEHGS Vol 31)

LE GROW, Philip mar Anna ___. An Anna LE GROW d 1799 MRB.
A1. Anna, bp 1740 MRB. A3. Mary, bp 1760
A2. Elizabeth, bp 1742 A4. Thomas, bp 1761

LA GROW, Thomas L., 1851-1912 mar Edna Cassavant, b 1854. (Gravestone, Bakersfield, VT; NEHGS Vol 82) A family which included a Howard, Norman, Florence and Adelbert, etc.

See Portland, Kittery, Salem and Ipswich Vital Records for much more info on LE GROW, LE GROS fams. See also NEHGS Vol 42.

LE GROS, James from J to Los Angeles, CAL before 1960. (E. G. Morrissey, Toronto, ONT)

LE GROS, Charles in Clermont or Columbiana Co., OH 1860s. (Census)OUTC

LE GROSS, Francis from J? res Concord, MA 1790 with fam of 5. (Census)

LE GROW, Hannah, mar Samuel CASWELL 1779 MRB. OUTC.

LE GROW, John mar Jane QUINER in MRB 1776 (Int) OUTC

LE GROUE, LE GROW, Mary mar Walter WILLIAMS 1685 MRB.

LE GROW, Louisa of Danvers, MA ca age 22 mar Wm. C. Martin, age ca 22, 1845. He was son of Knott and Sally MARTIN. See Knott elsewhere.

LE GRO, Mary mar 1. MATHEWS and 2. Thomas LE MASURIER in MA. (Tingley)
A1. Elizabeth MASURY, LE MASURIER, b ca 1755 Danvers or Salem, MA, mar ca 1795 William FOYE, qv, 9 chn. Foye mar 2. Mary Collins, w widow of David Ledbetter, and dau of James COLLINS and Sarah THOMAS

LE GRO, LE GROS, Christian from J? mar 1. ___GREY, qv, from C.I.?and 2. John SWASEY, qv, 1695 in Salem, MA. (Swasey)

LE GROE, John from J? res Salem, MA 1674, rem to MRB 1677, living in 1682, fisherman, with wife Dinah.

LE GROS, fam from C.I. to Chicago, ILL.

LE GUEDARD, see page 347 in Q.A. IN CANADA.

LE GUEDARD, John Sr., from J to Gaspe 1907 age 16, d age 58. Mar B1 Blanche COULOMBE of Gaspe, who was living at 80, 1976. John was son of Eustache Le G. and Anne-Marie Thermin. (Mme. F. Turcotte, Ste. Foy, Quebec)
A1. Roland, b 1920 mar Rose-Aimee Cote, res Ancienne-Lorette, QUE.
B1. Clermont, b 1946 B3. Murielle, b 1950 B5. Denis, b 1955
B2. Blanche, b 1948 B4. Linda, b 1953 B6. Carole, b 1956
A2. Julien, b 1924, mar Gaetane Chicoine, res Cloridorme, Gaspe, QUE
B1. Gaetan, b 1947 B3. Rejean, b 1950 B5. B5. Gerald, b 1952 B7.Alain b 1958
B2. Claude, b 1948 B4. Rejeane, b 1950 B6. Leger, b 1954
A3. Clement, b 1925, mar Antoinette Froment, res Repentigny, QUE
B1. Sylvie, b 1958 B2. Helene, b 1960 B3. Lucie b 1963

B4. Jean, b 1965 B5. Guy, b 1969
A4. Florian, b 1928, mar Jeanne Ouellet, res Murdochville, QUE.
A5. Francoise, b 1921 mar F.L.G. Turcotte, who sailed on freight ships for 18 yrs. then was store Mgr. for Hyman and Son in Cloridorme,QUE
LE GUEDARD, Marguerite-Francoise, res St. John J, d 1971, mar George RENAULT. She was sister of John Sr. above. A son Francis RENAULT mar and res St. John, Jersey.
LE HARDY, see HARDY.
LE HUILLIER, noted in Racine, WI and in Gaspe, QUE, but OUTC.
LE HUQUET. Note that one Canadian fam changed this surname to HAWKEY.
LE HUQUET, old in J, curr G and J. LE HUQUET in St. Lawrence J 1788. One branch was a shipbuilding fam in J. One fam changed this surname to Louis. See CIFHS #3.
LE HUQUET, Walter of J mar an American woman, but div. The wife returned to MA with 2 chn b J?, Naomi and Freda, the latter an artist. Frederick, bro of Walter, d ca 1973 J. (P. Le Huquet, Herts, England)
LE HUQUET, William b 1935 J, rem to Canada 1968, mar Ruth Huish, b J, in J. Res Toronto, ONT. (P. Le Huquet, Herts, England)
LE HUQUET, William, a RR worker, b J, rem to IA 1800s. (Brechtel and Dolling book)
LE HOCKEY noted in Chicago, poss a variant spelling? OUTC
LE HUKEY, Roy, res Jarrettsville, MD 1900s. Variant spelling? OUTC
LE HUQUET, Francis, b ca 1800 J, mar Elizabeth Susan HAMON, qv, before 1828. Res Chariton, IA 1905. Widow later mar John BOURGAIZE, qv. At least 2 chn by 1st husband. (Sylvia Wilson, Medina, WA)
A1. Wm. John, b 1833 QUE. A2. Francis Philip, b 1857 mar IA 1884.
LE HUQUET, Thomas, bro of John and of Capt. Philip, b Les Champs, St. Martin J 1820, rem to San Francisco, CAL. A son John, and grandson John, b 1874. (Sylvia Wilson, Medina, WA)
HOOKEY, John and Patience McArthur of Saco, ME mar 1811. Was this a LE HUQUET? (Doris Smith, Haverhill, MA) OUTC.
A1. Martha Harris, b 1812 A2. Mary Edgecombe, b 1814.
LE HURAY, from the Norman French 'hatter', in G 1300s, curr J. Curr and common in G. In St. Peter Port G 1635. See GRAHAM
LE HURAY, John of Alderney or J, mar Mary ROBERGE, dau of Wm. and ___ (DE GORGY) ROBERGE. John was one of 7 chn, rem to ONT? (Stephen Le Huray, Middletown, NY)
A1. John, b Alderney, mar Winnifred Spencer, b Chatham, ONT.
B1. Stephen, d ca 1932, no issue B2. Mary, b 1868, no issue
B3. Spencer, b 1887, mar Sadie Bartlett, and d 1948
C1. Robert, b 1915 mar Norma Berwick, 2 chn, res Dartmouth, NS
D1. Sandra, b 1941 mar W. Clark D2. Carol, b 1944
E1. Laura E2. Alan
C2. Stephen, b 1918 mar Mona Dunne, 5 chn, res Middletown, NY
D1. Stephen, b 1942 mar LydiaAaron D4. Brian Spencer, b 1955
D2. Marilyn, b 1943 mar Sam Spisso D5. James Neil, b 1961
D3. Anne Patricia, b 1952
B4. Olive, b 1890 mar Reginald BRAY, no issue
B5. Blossom, b 1893 mar Geo. Smith
C1. Donald Smith, d.y. C2. Winifred mar A. Pugh C3. Sandra
A2. Malinda, mar Fred PALMER, qv, res Chatham and Windsor , ONT.
LE HURAY, Herbert St. John, b 1853 or 1862 J? d San Fran.,CAL 1885.
LE HURAY, one in NY d after WWII, had a fam tree. Desc?
LE HURAY, Wm. Fowler, b 1894 Torteval, G, mar ___, had 3 daus, res BC, Canada.
LE HURAY, Nicholas Jr., res Phila. PA early 1800s. (DEATH NOTICES)
A1. Charles, res Phila. and d age 23 in 1830s

A2. Nicholas Jr., res Frankford Rd., near Hart Tavern in Phila., PA in 1830s.
A3. Harriet, b early 1800s, res Phila., mar ___Goodrick, d 1830s, , Phila., had 3 chn.
LE HURAY in Nfld. is changed to FUREY!
LE HURAY in NY 1940s, in Middletown, NY and Dartmouth, NS.
LEIGH, a ship builder in St. Aubin J 1834-1845. (A. John Jean, Jersey)
LEIGH in Grouville J 1668. Some Leigh fams in the C.I. from England. Curr G and J. Note this occurs in several C.I. fams such as Le Boutillier and Dorey, qv.
LEIGHTON, old in G, curr G and J. Note old LIGHTON records in Rowley, MA. OUTC.
LE JENNES, as JENNES in St. Martin and Grouville J 1668. See JENNES
LE JENNES, Jacob in Phila. 1749. OUTC. See also JEUNE
LE JEUNE in J 1299, more recently on Sark Island. LE JEUNE in St. Clement J 1668. In G 1300s, later in Vale G. LE JEUNE curr J.
LE JEUNE to MD 1763 from? OUTC
LE JEUNE, Gregoire to VA 1621 with wife and 4 chn. OUTC. (Filby)
LE JEUNE, see Q.A. IN CANADA. Eliz. LE JEUNE, see John MOLLET
LE JEUNE curr Chicago, ILL and Spokane, WA. OUTC
LE JEUNE, William of J settled in Boston, MA 1880s, not found.
LE JEUNE, Lucq, from J sent to John Netherway in Nevis, St. Kitts, BWI Was an indentured boy in 1684. (Ghirelli)
LE LACHEUR in G 1300s, in St. Saviour G 1680. Curr G. See Q.A. IN CANADA. Curr in France. Many in Canada of G origin. Many desc in Iowa and Nebraska.
LE LACHEUR, LACHEUR noted in Petition of 1838 in Quebec City. (LOST IN CANADA, Aug. 1981)
LE LACHEUR, ___, mar Wm. Hugh of Murray Harbour, PEI 1800s. (Pat Sinclair, Charlottesville, VA)
A1. Edith Hugh A2. Marion Hugh, b early 1900s PEI
LE LACHEUR, Angus, mar Laurette Ada Ferguson of the Beck line. Laurette b 1883, d 1937, res PEI. (BECK GEN. CHART by J. Beck, Okemos, MI)
A1. Harold, b 1901 d 1908 A4. Thomas Ernest, b 1911 mar Rita Crugliano
A2. Kenneth James, b 1903 d 1977 mar Mabel Elwood Turner
A3. Angus Guild, b 1907 mar Mae Nyross A5. Lauretta Adam, b 1916,unmar
LE LACHEUR, Bartholomew, mar Stella Margaret ROBERTS, 1882-1955, res PEI. (BECK CHART)
A1. Ethel, b 1907 marEdmund Morahan A2. Robert, b 1909
LE LACHEUR, Dr. Gustavus, b G, son of Isaac LE LACHEUR. Gustavus mar Mary Louise Brewster 1892 in Brooklyn, NY. A dau Faith Brewster Vaudin Le Lacheur b 1897.
LE LACHEUR, Jane of PEI mar Wm. Beck, b 1827, d 1913, his 2nd wife. Wm. had 6 chn by 1st wife, Jane Windsor HAWKINS, qv, and 4 by Jane. More in WRCIC. (J. Beck, Okemos, MI)
A1. Selina Elizabeth Beck, 1854-1867 A4. David Beck, 1860-1904.
A2. Elisha Hawkins Beck, 1856-1941, mar Annie MacKinnon
A3. Vere, b 1858 d 1925 mar Jennie and Ida Chace
A5. Bartholomew John Beck, b 1860 d 1950, mar Jane Mackay, 8 chn
A6. Louisa Eliz. Beck, b 1864 mar Charles Matthews
A7. William Windsor Beck, b 1868 d 1930, no issue
A8. Peter Beck, 1871-1890, no issue
A9. Matilda Jane Beck, b 1873 d 1943, mar Alexander M. BALLUM, chn. See Q.A. IN CANADA.
A10. Selina Elizabeth Beck, 1877-1957, unmar.
LE LACHEUR, Jane, dau of John LE LACHEUR of G, who rem to PEI 1806. Jane was b ca 1800 G, and Mar Thomas ROBIN, qv, 1836. He was b 1804

in G, and had rem with his parents either to WISC or to Gaspe, not clear. They then moved west to Castlerock, WA. See Thomas ROBIN. (More in WRCIC)

LE LACHEUR, Peter, b C.I. ca 1807, d 1889 QUE. Mar 1. Jane LA RUE ca 1825, who d ca 1851. He mar 2. 1852 Marion McLean, 2 chn: Colin and Marion, and mar 3. 1865 in Ship Harbor, Cape Breton, NS Christina McKinnon, no issue. Poss 10 chn, but only 6 in this chart. (Wm. O. Goss, Ipswich, MA; Eleanor Spiller, Glencliff, NH) Some data uncert.

A1. Peter, b 1826, d 1906, mar 1852 in Poulamont, CB, NS, Rachel Judith Helier, b ca 1830 G, d 1890 NS, dau of Mathew and Rachel HELIER, 6 siblings. (Arichat records)

B1. Peter Matthew Joseph, b 1852 d 1935 NS, mar 1. 1878 M.A.M. and 2. Victoria A. MAUGER, qv, b 1873 d 1953, 2 chn by 2nd wife.

C1. Ida mar Lennox MAUGER, dau Genevieve Mauger mar Connelly, a dau Pearl Connelly.

C2. Lilly, b 1897 mar Edward James MAUGER, 1891-1963, a dau mar Gordon MAUGER.

B2. George N., b 1854, d.y.

B3. Matthew Mark Luke John, b 1856 d 1935, mar 1884 Louise Grant.

C1. Ada C2. Wm. C3. Clyde, d 1958, mar Bernice?, a son Glendon

B4. Rachel Jane, b 1858 d 1922 mar 1886 J. Hurst

B5. Judith Louise, b 1860 d 1947 mar 1882 John NICOLL, 1855-1919

C1. Florence Nicoll, b 1884 d 1962, mar Collin Diggdon, 1855-1919.

B6. Ellen Elizabeth, b 1863 d 1895, mar 1890 E.G.

B7. John James, b 1867 d 1951, mar 1889 L.G.

B8. Josephine Annie, b 1870 d 1895

B9. Henry William, b 1865 d 1955, mar 1892 Mary ___, who d 1950s.

C1. Ernest Stacy, b 1892 C3. Edna Lavinia, b 1898 C5. Josephine b 1905

C2. Henry Melvin, b 1895 C4. Albert Alex. b 1901

B10. George Nicholas, b 1873 Arichat, CB, NS, left NS 1890, and rem to Salem, then to Danvers, MA. He d 1955. Mar 1. 1895 in CB, Margaret Mary Thomas, 1869-1906, and 2. in Salem 1910, Sarah Barbara Joudrie, d 1970 Danvers, MA. 4 chn by 1st, and 2 chn by 2nd wife.

C1. Harold Raymond, b 1896, d.y. C2. Ivan George, b 1897 d 1913

C3. Harold Raymond again, b 1901, d 1975, mar Mrs. Hilda ___,no issue

C4. Lillian Rosalie, b 1900 Salem, d 1974 Danvers, MA mar 1927 Victor Harland Spiller, 4 chn

D1. Eleanor Virginia, b 1928

D2. Allison Parham, b 1930, d 1931 D3. Barbara Louise, b 1936, d.y.

D4. Richard Wayne, b 1931 mar 1955 Violet ALLEY, b 1926, son Richard

D5. Elmer Ivan, b 1910 Danvers mar Etheline Monro, 2 chn: Florence and Nancy.

D6. Diana Barbara, b 1912 d 1979 mar Daniel Wayne Woodman, 1915-1973

E1. Daniel Wayne Woodman, mar Joanne Pizzo, 2 daus, Debra, Adeen

E2. Tracy Friend III, 1946-1982, mar Debra Pouliot, 2 chn

E3. Allen George, d.y.

A2. James, b 1830 d 1881 A5. Henry J., ? b 1845 Arichat, NS d 1920 MA.

A3. Caroline, bp 1843 A6. to A10. other chn.

A4. William, bp 1843

LE LACHEUR, Kimball F., mar Florence Harriet Gossbee, b 1923 PEI(Chart)

LE LACHEUR, Margaret J., mar Elisha Thomas Beck, b 1869 d 1955, res PEI. He mar 2. May Lyens. 4 chn by Margaret. (BECK CHART)

LE LACHEUR noted in Warren and Dearborn, MI, In Royal Oak, MI, Great Falls, MONT and Wyomissing, PA. OUTC.

LE LIEVRE, see DUVAL in Q.A. IN CANADA. Curr research? See CIFHS #7

LE LIEVRE, in J 1309, means 'hare'. In Grouville J 1607, 1668. Also in Grouville J 1800s.

LE LIEVRE, Daniel b ca 1766, d 1845 Grand Riviere, Gaspe, QUE, said to be from C.I. Poss was orig. a DUVAL?, and name changed by Daniel's father? (Aldo Brochet, London, ONT) ca 1725. Daniel mar 1. Genevieve Becker/Blondin/Baker, of a German? fam, and 2. Felicity Stiber?, widow of Jean Laneup? Rockford, dau of Philip Henri and Felicite H Huret. Not certain that Daniel is from C.I. fam, but see Q.A. IN CANADA for other LE LIEVRE fams from C.I. More on this fam in WRCIC.

A1. Jean/John, b 1790 Grand Riviere, QUE

A2. Daniel, b 1792, mar 1816 Grand Riv., Gaspe, Sophie Beliveau, bp 1799, dau of Joseph Beliveau and Anne BEAUDIN, qv. Daniel mar 2. ____, in 1843.

B1. Appoline, b 1817 Gaspe mar 1. 1835 Jean B. Couture

B2. George, d 1822

B3. Daniel, b 1821 mar 1847 Eliz. Couture

B4. Joseph, b 1823 mar 1847 Appoline Couture

B5. Olivier, b 1825, mar 1850 Marie Anne Couture, dau of Pierre and Sally (Cimaid) Couture. More on this family in WRCIC

B6. Louis, b 1827 mar 1848 Sophie Falardeau

B7. Charles, b 1832, d.y.

B8. Isidore, b 1834

B9. Jean B., b 1836

B10. Maria, b 1839

B11. Periatue?, b 1841

B12. Philippe b 1842

A3. Francoise, b 1793

A4. Louis Daniel b 1795, mar 1819 Rosalie Grenier

A5. Thomas, b 1797

A6. Angelique, b 1799, D.Y.

A7. Elizabeth, b 1815, mar 1834 Simon BEAUDIN

A8. John, b 1816 mar 1842 Julie BEAUDIN

A9. Nicolas, b 1821

A10. Pierre, b 1822 mar 1849 Madeline Rousey

A11. Julienne, 1825-1832

A12. Angelique, b 1828

LE LIEVRE, Louise mar 1821 St. Andrews Presb. Ch, City of QUE, George Morrison. (LOST IN CANADA, Aug. 1981)

LE LIEVRE in QUE City 1838.

LAVIRES, John, prob. LE LIEVRE from G, farmer in Valley Twp., GCO 1811. (Sarchet)

LE MAIN, MAINE, MAYNE old in J. (Stevens) Curr J.

LE MAINE, MAINE, several in colonies but not verified as from C.I.

LE MAIN, John and Mary res Boston, had son John, b 1760. OUTC.

LE MAIN, John mar Lydia BOWDEN, qv, res MRB, dau Sarah bp 1774. OUTC

LE MAIN, Sally of MRB, mar Robert Pearce 1826. OUTC.

LE MAIRE, Francis mar Elizabeth Moore 1783 Boston. OUTC.

LE MAISTRE, LE MAITRE, LE MASTER, MASTER. LE MAITRE in Vale G 1821. See CIFHS #14.

LE MAISTRE in G and J 1331. In St. Saviour G 1829. In St. Martin, St. John, St. Peter, St. Heliers, St. Ouen and St. Saviour J 1668. In St. Peter, St. Martin, Grouville and St. Mary J 1749. In St. Laurens J 1788. Curr G and J. LE MAISTRE usually the spelling in Jersey. LE MAITRE curr G. See also MASTERS & LE BOUTILLIER.

LE MAISTRE, MASTERS, etc, Thomas b 1754 J, son of George LE MASTER and MAdeleine HAMON, rem to MRB 1700s. Mar Jane ___.

LE MAISTRE, Rachel from G to Cooperstown, NY 1900s. Mar __Raubacher.

LE MAISTRE fam from J to Canada 1870s. A son Frederick John res Ridley Park, PA 1900s.

LE MAITRE, LE MASTER, Abraham, b 1639 St. Mary J, son of John and Sarah res Maryland 1662. (Martha Wolf, Gaithersburg, MD)

LE MAISTRE, Philip and wife Rachel res Saint John, NB, had son John who d 1830, age 10.

LE MAISTRE, Francis, an orig. settler in Monmouth, NJ, 1667, but soon changed name to MASTERS. (NJ GEN. SOC. BULL, 1956) OUTC, but note that other C.I. fams came to NJ in 1600s.

LE MAISTRE, Peter, from J? a passenger from Cardiff, Wales to San Francisco, CAL on barque ROYAL SOVEREIGN 1851. Another Jerseyman, Philip BAKER of J, d on same voyage. Capt. DES LANDES, prob of J fam was master of the ship. See DESLANDES. (Rasmussen's SAN FRAN. SHIP PASSENGERS, Comal, CAL, 1965)

LE MASTER, see HEADS OF FAMS, SOUTH CAROLINA, p. 87.

LE MAISTRE, Edward, d 1751, mar Rachel DURELL. (LE BOUTILLIER Chart) They or their ancestors came from J to US.

A1. Edward, d 1793, mar Eliz. MARETT, 1727-1812

B1. Edward, b 1751 d 1838, mar Sarah GALLICHAN, qv, dau of Thomas and Elizabeth (BAILHACHE) GALLICHAN.

LE MAISTRE, fam in Canada from C.I. (Mrs. F. Wm. Long, N. Falls, ONT.)

LE MAISTRE, curr Los Angeles, CAL, and LE MAITRE curr Boston, MA.OUTC.

LE MATRE, poss LE MAITRE?, Rachel Mary Steen, b ca 1829 J, mar Edward Lye, b 1829 Somerset, England. He d Toronto, ONT 1919. She d 1908, age 79, bur St. James, Toronto, ONT. Desc. include Rachel Louise Gearing, 1870-1956 and Carl Wm. House, 1902-1973.

LE MIST, LE MAISTRE?, John was in Dorchester, MA 1810.(Census) OUTC

LE MAISTRE in Phila, PA 1860: Frederick, Henry, John, Peter and Thomas. (Filby) OUTC

LE MAISTRE curr Austin, TX, OUTC. LE MAISTRE from CI to Winnipeg, MAN.

LE MAITRE, Philip, mar Elizabeth GIRARD 1889 Anticosti, QUE, from the C.I. (Aldo Brochet, London, ONT)

LE MARCHAND, Nicholas, from St. Lawrence J ca 1795,d in Montreal, QUE 1867. A Nicholas res Gaspe, QUE 1820, when he signed a Petition. (Q.A. IN CANADA; CIFHS #14)

LE MARCHANT, LE MARCHAND in J 1200. Both forms old in G from 1200s. In Catel G 1700s. In St. Brelade and St. Heliers J 1668, and in St. Laurens J 1749, 1788. LE MARCHANT curr J.

LE MARCHANT, Johanna, b 1842 G, to NY where she mar Wm. Francis Fee, b NY. (Mrs. Irene Fee, Eugene, OR)

LE MARCOM, Jane, a 'Jersey Maid', mar John Blethen 1676 Salem, MA. See LE MARQUAND, and MARKS.

LE MARGUARD, Maria Ann, b 1810 J or G, d 1900 UT. Dau of Philip or Francis LE MARGUARD and Jeanne HATTAN, HOTTON? Mar Samuel LANGLOIS, QV, 1831 St. Helier J. See HOTTON in Q.A. in CANADA. LE MARQUARDT and similar names in early Ohio may be German in origin.

LE MARINEL in J from 1400. In St. John J 1668 and 1749. Curr J and G. Noted in Pacific Palisades, CAL and other places.

LE MARINEL, John Sr., b 1840 St. John J, mar 1861 Emelie LE GRESLEY, qv. Fam to North Chelmsford, MA 1873, with John DE CARTERET, qv. The mother of John, Aurelia ___, of J. (Lillian Marinel Browne, Chesapeake VA; Joyce Petterson, N. Chelmsford, MA; Thelma Marinel Welch, N. Chelmsford, MA; George Byan, Nashua, NH)

A1. John Jr., b 1862 St. Brelade J, mar Ada Alice SHEPHERD 1890s, b ca 1865 Preston, England.

B1. Amelia Beatrice, b 1889 d 1961 Carlisle, MA, bur S. Chelmsford. Mar Arnold Adams Byam, b 1882, d Chelmsford, MA 1950.

C1. dau, stillborn 1908 C2. Marjorie Estelle Byam, 1911-1944

C3. Barbara Althea Byam, b 1912 mar 1. 1933 Hooksett, NH, Charles H. Currier, div, and mar 2. Wm. Burt Foston 1936, 1901-1981.

D1. Jane Byam Foster, b 1937 Quincy, MA mar Douglas Allen Mohns,div.

D2. Wm. B. Foster Jr., b 1940 Lowell, MA.

C4. Arnold Adams Byam Jr., b 1914 d 1971, mar 1. Julia E. Jenkins, b 1937, div 1954, 2 chn.

D1. Sondra Ruth Byam, b 1938 D2. Linda Pauline Byam b 1942

D3. Julia Elizabeth Kiberd, b 1965, by wife's 2nd husband Richard.

C5. a son, b 1915, d.y.
C6. Paul Wellington Byam, b 1917 res S. Chelmsford, MA, unmar
C7. George Alan Byam, b 1919, mar 1946 Ruth Estabrook Jenkins, b1920 Res 1982 in Nashua,NH. .
D1. Nancy Ellen Byam, b 1948 mar N. Albert Moussa, Lowell, MA 1977, Wayland, MA.
D2. Martha Ann Byam, b 1953 mar Gary W. Fincke in Lowell, MA 1979, res Newmarket, NH.
C8. Robert Spaulding Byam, b 1921 Lowell, MA mar 1. 1947 Mt. Vernon, NH Doris Ann Palm, b 1927 Yonkers, NH, div 1968, mar 2. Frances Louise Stanley, res Acton, ME.
C9. Amelia Beatrice Byam, b 1924 MA mar 1. James Burgoyne Judge 1946, div, and mar 2. Charles Duston, res 1982 in Honduras.
D1. Peter Judge D2. James B. Judge Jr., b 1948 Boston, MA
D3. Peter Judge again, b 1951 D4. Stephen Adams Judge, b 1952
C10. David Amos Byam, b 1930 Lowell, MA mar 1961 in Dracut, Carolyn Diane Lombari, div.
D1. Carolyn Beth Byam, b 1963 D3. David Amos Byam II, b 1966
D2. Marjorie Ann Byam, b 1965 D4. Wm. Arnold Byam, b 1969 Lowell
B2. Lillian mar 1. Everett Field, 2. ___Pushie, and 3. __Browne.
B3. George, b 1894 d 1980, mar Lillian Mattson 1915.
C1. Phyllis June b 1916 mar Daniel E. Walker, 1937, 2 chn
D1. Daniel B. Walker, b 1937 mar Patricia Keating 1964, div, 5 chn: Daniel E., Keith, Kurth, (twins), Kelly and Kimberly Walker.
D2. Carolyn J., b 1943 mar Austin Raus, 1965, 2 chn: John and Christine Raus.
C2. Lillian Thelma, b 1917 mar 1940 Roger P. Welch, 3 chn.
D1. Roger J. Welch, b 1941 and Emily Dean
D2. Sharon Welch, b 1943, mar Ronald Dean 1966, 2 chn: Michael /
D3. Sheila E.Welch, b 1945 mar Wm. J. Gilet, 2 chn: Wm. J. & Karen Gilet.
A2. Emilie Ann, b 1865? St. Heliers J d 1866.
A3. Theodore, b 1867 St. Brelade J, mar NellieMay Brown,1892, Tyngsboro, MA, a desc Brian LE MARINEL/MARINEL
A4. Amelia, b 1875 mar Thomas E. Mitchell, res Irwin, CAL, had 2 sons
A5. Cecelia, b 1877, mar David Frank Small, killed in a CAL flood.
A6. Walter, b 1879 mar Amelia SYVRET 1915. See SYVRET.
B1. Joyce B2. Alix B3. Linda B4. Donald, b 1922
LE MARINEL, curr Los Angeles, CAL.
LE MARQUAND in J 1515. In St. Laurens, St. Brelade, St. Peter and St. Ouen J 1668. In St. Peter and St. Brelade J 1749. In G 1513. Curr G and J. This name usually without the LE in Guernsey. See also MARQUAND, and LE MARCHANT. See CIFHS Bull. #15 for more info. and fam chart of Jean MARQUAND, of Vale G, who settled in J ca 1800.
LE MARCOM, LE MARCUM, MARKS, prob LE MARQUAND, Jane of Jersey, in Salem, MA, b 1653 J, "a Jarzey maid". She came from J to New England 1659 age 6?, d 1704. Mar 1674 John Blethen. (Lillian Seebohm, Winter Park, FLA; Ann Alexander, Brunswick, ME; Sinnett; Helen Herman, Jackson, MI; HIST. OF SALEM, by Perley, Vol 1)
A1. John Blethen Jr., b 1676 Salem, mar 1701 Mary ___
B1. John Blethen III, mar Hannah Kane of Georgetown, ME
C1. Sarah Blethen, mar Francis Wyman, b 1728
D1. Mary Wyman, b 1756, d 1830, mar at Georgetown, ME Daniel Morse, 1750-1848.
E1. Jane Morse, b 1784, d 1831, mar 1803 Jethro Sprague, b 1775, d 1848.
F1. Almira Sprague, 1816-1891, mar Capt. Elisha A.Johnson 1839

G1. Elisha C. Johnson, b 1847 mar Gustina O. Johnson, 1858-1911, of Bailey Is. ME. See James BIBBER.

C2. James Blethen, mar 1757 Miriam Day, bp 1739, d 1836

D1. Rhoda Blethen b 1758 d 1851, mar 1778 Wm. Wallace, 1753-1846

E1. Jesse B. Wallace, b 1797, d 1880, mar Hannah Wallis, b 1779

F1. Almira Wallace, b 1817, d 1896, mar 1835 Capt. David Doughty, 1808-1896

G1. Jesse W. Doughty, b 1852 d 1922, of Bailey Is., ME, mar Julia E. Sinnett, b 1855, d 1927.

H1. Herbert W. Doughty, b 1887 d 1974, of Bailey Is., ME.

I1. Elroy Doughty, mar Jean A. Allen. See James BIBBER.

A2. Jane Blethin, b 1678 Salem, MA.

A3. Elizabeth Blethin, b 1680, d 1719 Swansea, MA, mar 1704/5 Isaac Chase. 5 chn: James, Waitstill, Isaac, Wm. and Eliz. Chase.

A4. Hannah Blethen A5. Sarah Blethen, b 1684 Salem, MA.

A6. Abigail Blethen, b 1685, mar 1706 Thomas HICKS, HIX.

BLETHEN, Mary, mar 1. ___Fish, 2. Ezekiel Emerson, b 1763, Georgetown, ME, and 3. ___Whitney. (Mrs. James H. Groves, Rockland, ME)

LE MARQUAND, John, b ca 1818 J, rem to Nfld., then to Cape Breton, NS, and settled later at New Carlisle, QUE. Mar there Marie E. Castillon and had at least 11 chn. (Mary Sullens McEwan, Salt Lake City, UT) Most of this fam uses the name MARQUAND.

A1. John, b ca 1846 New Carlisle, QUE A3. Mary Jane, b ca 1850

A2. Frank, b ca 1849 A4. Philip, b ca 1853 A5. Marie, b ca 1855

A6. Elizabeth, b ca 1857 mar Stanley McCoubrey, b 1859 QUE, d 1932 Spokane, WA, son of Richard McCoubrey of Nfld. and Matilda COLE. Rem to Clocquet, MINN where they became parents of 6 chn. Later rem to Spokane, WA, where they are buried.

B1. Ethel McCoubrey, mar Arthur Leon Earin

C1. Dorothy Eliz. Earin, b 1913 Spirit Lake, ID, mar George Henry Sonnichsen, b 1913 Coeur d'Alene, ID, son of George Wm.

D1. Richard Charles Sonnichsen, b 1939 ID, mar 1965 in BALT. Mary Sarah Shipley

D2. David Paul Sonnichsen, b 1941 mar 1964 Lewiston, ID Janet Wagner

D3. Amy Kathleen Sonnichsen, b 1946 mar Richard R. Gehring, 1969

D4. Barbara Jean Sonnichsen, b 1950, mar 1969 Edw. J. Kposszynski

C2. Mary Jeanette Earin, b 1914 ID mar 1935 Wm. Howard Kilborn, Osteo-pathic Physician, ID, son of Fred. Nicholas and Mary R.Kilborn

D1. Wm. D. Kilborn, b 1936 ID mar 1964 Barbara Zornes

D2. Robert H. Kilborn, b 1940

D3. Mary Katherine Kilborn, b 1948 San Francisco, CAL mar 1966 Roger F. Tanner

C3. Arthur Douglas Earin, b 1917 ID, mar Virginia Fuller

D1. James, mar Ida Gayle

D2. Michael mar in Heyburn, ID 1971 Jolene ___.

C4. Robert J. Earin, b 1921 mar 1. ID Ossie Carlson, and 2. 1970, V. Blanche Taylor, b 1919, dau of V. Taylor & Rose Young.

C5. Barbara Ann Earin, b 1928 ID, mar Harold S. Alexander of USPOST. Serv., son of Wm. Alexander and Elizabeth.

D1. John Alexander, b 1955 D3. Donald Alexander, b 1960

D2. Thomas Alexander, b 1958 D4. David Alexander, b 1965

B2. Alice Ann McCoubrey, d.y. 1888

B3. Edward McCoubrey, mar Susan Bridget, b 1888 LaCrosse, WIS? dau of Charles Weston and Agnes Murphy. No issue

B4. Bertha Alice McCoubrey, b 1891 Cloquet, MINN mar 1914 Frank C. Weston, b 1889, d 1961 Denver, COL, 6 chn. Bertha d 1967, Frank in 1961.

C1. William Roger Weston, b 1915 Denver
C2. Alice Louise Weston b 1918 mar Martin Chadwick, dau Alice Ann b 1945 Denver, COL.
C3. Elizabeth Agnes Weston, b 1921 Denver, mar George Harold Sullens, res Napa, CAL.
D1. Elizabeth Marie Sullens, mar 1958 Don G. Honey, 2 chn: Don and Paige Honey, b 1959 and 1964 Sacramento, CAL.
D2. Mary Joanne Sullens, b 1943, mar 1962 John Shirl McEwan, 7 chn
E1. John Bromley McEwan, b 1963 Provo, UT
E2. Haley Gwen McEwan, b 1966-E5. HeidiE. McEwan, b 1972, d.y.
E3. Hilary L. McEwan, b 1968 E6. James S. McEwan, b 1974
E4. George T. McEwan, b 1970 E7. Martha E. McEwan, b 1977
D3. George Grant Sullens, b 1955 CAL mar Ruby Chavez, div.
E1. George Grant Sullens, b 1974 CAL.
C4. Robert Charles Weston, b 1923 Denver, mar Norma __, twin daus and a son.
C5. Jane Weston, b ca 1924 mar ___Lindsey, no issue
C6. Rosemary Weston, b 1925 Denver, mar Curt Anderson, 2 chn: John and Carol Anderson
B5. Charles McCoubrey B6. Loretta McCoubrey
A7. Peter b ca 1859
A8. Edward, b ca 1862 New Carlisle, QUE, farmer, mar 1890 Ludington, MI, Mary Bertha Keson, b 1869, MI d 1945. She was dau of Fred of Germany, and Caroline Grassa. Edward d 1944 Scottville, MI.
B1. Caroline, b 1891 Ludington, MI mar 1913 Amber, MI Herman Hansen
B2. Ruth E., b 1897 MI B4. Raymond, b 1903
B3. Gertrude, b 1900 B5. Kenneth W., b 1905 Amber, MI.
Much more on this fam in records of Mason Co., MI.
A9. Anne Louise, b 1863 A10. Amelia b 1867 A11. Susan, b 1869
LE MARQUAND, from J to ONT. (L.F. Guy, Orono, ONT)
LE MARQUAND, Charles P., b 1882 St. Peters J, d 1926 Seven Islands,QUE (A marker raised by firm of Robin, Jones and Whitman)
LE MARQUANT in Duplessis Co., QUE late 1800s, but OUTC. (Aldo Brochet)
LE MASTER, SEE LE MAITRE and LE MAISTRE. See MRB records & GOSSET fam.
LE MASTER, George mar 1924 Mrs. Mary Oliver? Valentine in MRB. OUTC
A1. George, bp 1833 A3. Mary Oliver, bp 1835
A2. Thomas, d 1841 age 9 A4. Sarah Jane, bp 1837,
LE MASTER, Jane mar Wm. H WKES Jr. 1819 MRB.
LE MASTER, Thomas mar Mrs. Jane Sawins 1781 MRB. She d 1828?
A1. Thomas, bp 1782, d.y. A4. Mary, bp 1787 A7. George, bp 1793
A2. Thomas, bp 1784, d 1822 age 39 A5. Sarah, bp 1789, d.y.?
A3. Jenny, bp 1786 A6. Sarah again, bp 1791 A8. Tabby, bp 1800
LE MASTER, Thomas res MRB 1790 with fam of 5
LE MASTER, Thomas mar Tabitha Homan 1765 MRB.
LE MARSTERS, Thomas mar Lydia GILES ca 1810 MRB. Some chn d.y.
LE MASTER, noted in TN Cem. listings.
LE MASURIER, see LE MESURIER, and LE MESSURIER under MAJOR.
LE MASURIER in J 1299. In Trinity J 1668 and 1749. Curr G and J. Not all LE MASURIERS are from J, as eleven fams of this surname are said to have left France after the Revocation of the Edict of Nantes. See also LE MESURIER, and LE MESSURIER, 3 different surnames, al-they are said to have been once the same family. One tradition says that differences among 3 members of a family resulted in 3 different lines.
LE MASURIER, Thomas, b 1881 Trinity J, son of Thomas and Mary Ann (LE COCQ) LE MASURIER, settled in North Chelmsford, MA, among the quarry folk. Mar there Christine MACHON, b 1883 Trinity J, in 1907.

Christine inherited the quarry from her father, d 1923 leaving the quarry to her 3 chn. Thomas mar 2. Bella Hamilton and had several chn.

A1. Thomas George, b 1913 mar Bessie BENEST, qv, 2 chn
B1. Eunice b 1942 B2. Elsie Ruth b 1946
A2. Joshua, b 1915 mar Gladys Smith, b 1918
B1. Roy R., b 1942 mar a schoolteacher
B2. Christine, b 1940 mar Lloyd Crockett, 3 chn: Gary, Dawn Marie and Steven, b 1960s.
A3. Theodore, b 1919, d.y.
A4. John Blampied, b 1922, mar Catherine Fisher, b 1922, 7 chn: Elaine, Catherine A., Linda M., John L., Richard J., Thomas D. and Stephen R., b 1965.

LE MASSERVIER, Charles arrived in Boston 1769 on ship MOLLY from J. (Whitmore) This prob. was LE MESSURIER

LE MASURIER, Charles Garnet, b J, rem to MA, but returned to Jersey after about 15yrs., early 1900s.

LE MASURIER, George, b 1883 J, d 1949 MA, had bro Thomas John who res Mass.

LE MASURIER, John T., b J, husband of Jane E. GALLIE, d at Paspebiac, QUE, 1901 age 75.

LE MASURIER, Josue Elie, b 1820 J, to America 1847, settled Richmond, VA. He brought with him a 3yrs old son, Amedee Ernes Pierre Lionel, b 1844 Granville, Normandy, France, where his father was for many years a Prof. of English in the college SUR LE ROC, Granville. Both Josue and Amedee served in the Confed. Army in the Civil War, and later Josue was Consular Agent in Richmond and Norfolk VA. A son Joseph b Richmond, VA. (J. Le Masurier, Fairfax, VA)

LE MASURIER, Mary Ann, 1868-1951, res Gaspe, QUE.

LE MASURIER, Philip from C.I. had desc in St. Vin , MINN near Mpls. (Murray Le Masurier)

LE MASURIER, Thomas mar Mary LE GRO MATHEWS, res Salem or Danvers, MA.
A1. Elizabeth, b ca 1755 Danvers or Salem mar Wm. FOYE, qv, b ca 1745, d 1825 Salem, MA, at least 9 chn.

LE MAY, noted in early America. LE MEE, pron. LE MAY, is old in J.

LE MAY, noted in petition of QUE. City residents 1838. OUTC. (LOST IN CANADA, Aug. 1981)

LE MEE, Francis to Phila., PA 1807, OUTC. Poss from J? (Filby)

LE MERCIER, old name of J but also French. One from St. Malo, France to MASS early. (NEHGS Vol 5)

LE MERCIER, Mary mar Earl Sturtevant in Boston, 1801. OUTC.

LE MESSURIER old in J. In St. Peter of the Wood G, 1300s. See LE MESSURIER family under MAJOR, also under MASURY.

LE MESSURIER, Thomas of G, mar in GAspe, QUE Elizabeth LENFESTY. At least 10 chn. (Esther LE Messurier, Honeoye, NY)
A1. Jean/John b 1827 Gaspe or G? A2. William, b 1829 A3. Daniel,b1832
A4. Pierre, b 1834 Gaspe, mar Rachel LANGLOIS, qv. Peter a carpenter, res Port Hope, ONT 1871, rem to Detroit, MI where his son began a firm called La Measure Bros., launderers and dry cleaners in early 1900s. (Mrs. G. Langlois, Toronto, ONT; Mrs. Edward Marshall, Dundas, ONT; Shirley O'Neil, Newport Beach, CAL) See also LANGLOIS
B1. George, b 1861 Gaspe, QUE
B2. Clarissa, b 1863 Gaspe, poss as Clara Alicia?, poss mar __ROSE?
B3. Joseph Tallman, b 1868 Hamilton, ONT mar 1891 Christina W. Sartor of Alma, MI. 2 chn: Lawrence? and Vida Rachel
B4. Dorcas E., b 1870 ONT.
A5. Thomas, mar Charity Gunby 1863. Thomas d 1923, Charity 1924.

B1. William John, b 1867 mar Margaret Campbell 1894. William d 1942 and Margaret in 1934
C1. Clyde, b 1895 mar Esther Bentley 1921
D1. Robert b 1924 mar Esther Hollon 1946, 3 chn
E1. Suzanne, b 1947 mar David Lippert, a son Keith Lippert b 1969
E2. Barbara b 1948 mar Thomas Walker 1973, ch b 1975?
E3. Matthew b 1963
D2. Bruce, b 1926 mar Jean Klein 1949, 4 chn
E1. Carol b 1952 mar 1974 Robert Marryman
E2. Nancy, mar 1975
E3. Sandra
E4. Scott, b 1956
A6. Marie, b 1838 Indian Cove, QUE mar Wm. P. SIMON. Marie d 1907 Grand Greve, Gaspe, QUE. A dau Priscilla SIMON mar Elias GAVEY, qv.
A7. Caroline b 1839 A8. Abraham b 1840 A9. Enoch b 1842
A10. Hilaria, b 1844 d 1924, mar Nicholas GUIGNION, see, 1843-1926.
LE MESSURIER, Abraham mar in G. Mary LE PREVOST and had at least 3 daus Abraham d in G at 39, and widow Mary came to RAcine, WI 1847, where she mar 2. William GRAHAM, qv, who had been a soldier in the Mexican War. He was a ships carpenter, and res at Racine, WI, dying at ca age 79. Mary LE PREVOST LE MESSURIER d age 75,1886. Chn by Abram.
A1. Margaret, mar Thomas LE POIDEVIN, qv.
A2. Mary Ann, mar Peter OZANNE, qv, middle 1800s, res Somers, WIS.
A3. Matilda, mar Fred GRAHAM, qv, res Racine, WIS, 6 chn. See GRAHAM.
LE MESSURIER, Mary, Minister of Culture recently for Prov. of Alberta.
LE MESSURIER ASSOCIATES/SCI, of Cambridge, MA, eminent engineering firm firm, work including MED. MUTUAL CENTER in Cleveland, OH.
LE MESURIER, the third of these three similar surnames. One LE MESURIER was Lord Mayor of London, England, and others were Governors of the Island of Alderney. LE MESURIER bros. owned the ship RESOLUTION of the C.I. with 20 guns, and in 1770 captured three ships.
LE MESURIER arms: a chevron between 3 dexter hands gules, later argent on a chevron between 3 dexter hands gules, as many bezants. Crest: a hawk proper, wings extended or.
LE MESURIER, Alfred, b 1874 Rosebridge, Gaspe, QUE, Canada, son of Joseph and Susan (GUIGNION) LE MESURIER. See GUIGNION. Alfred mar Mary E. Mullin, prob in Gaspe? See Q.A. IN CANADA. (Merle Wagenaar, Dutton, ONT)
A1. Leonard Gordon, b 1900 res Montreal, mar Mabel Coffin of L'Anse aux Cousins, who d 1966, Gaspe, a son Robert who had 2 daus Linda and Lisa
A2. Russell John, b 1902 marGreta Annett, both bur Peninsula, QUE, a son Desmond res USA.
A3. Eva Gladys, b 1904 mar George Willis, bur Thassalon, ONT, 3 daus: Mildred, Barbara and ? Mildred has 3 chn, Barbara has 4.
A4. Raymond Philip, b 1905, mar Dorothy LE TOUZEL, res Rose Bridge, Gaspe, QUE, later in Windsor , ONT, no issue
A5. Phyllis Audrey, b 1907 mar Max Sykes, res West Lorne, ONT, 3 chn
B1. Philip Sykes, res Dawson Creek, BC, 3 chn
B2. Grant Sykes, bur Dawson Creek, BC, mar ___, 3 chn
B3. Clifford Sykes, res Mossley, ONT mar ___, 2 chn: Jennifer,Jeffrey
A6. Lewis Harris, b 1909 mar Alice Patterson, res Farewell Cove, Gaspe 3 chn: Rodger, Sandra and Susan
A7. Helen Cora, b 1910, mar Whitney Trenholm, res Wallace, NS, 6 chn: Robert of Eastern Passage, NS; Nancy, Whitney; Marianne MacMillan of Pictou, NS; Sally; and Helen Trenholm.
A8. Archie Howard, b 1912 mar 1. ? and 2. Alice FALLE, res Wallaceburg, ONT, 3 chn: Garry, mar Jean LE LACHEUR, Barbara and Brenda.
A9. Lloyd Alfred, b 1915 mar Carol VARDON, qv, called KAY? res Fremont,

Gaspe, QUE, wife bur Peninsula, QUE.

B1. Shirley, mar Dominique Lavoie, res Fontenelle, QUE, 3 chn: Michael, Sandra and Carol.

B2. Nancy, mar Calvin ROBERTS, res Cambridge, ONT, 2 sons, Terry and Chris.

A10. Vivian Mary, b 1917 mar Henry Wright, a son and mar 2. ___,no chn.

A11. Merle Arden, b 1919 mar Richard Wagenaar, res Chatham, ONT and Dutton, ONT, 2 sons

B1. Floyd William Wagenaar, b 1944 mar ___, 2 chn: Wayne & Lisa

B2. Richard Alfred, b 1947 d 1968, bur Harwich Twp. Ont.

A12. Wharrel George b 1921 mar Pearl FALLE, 3 chn: Connie, Perry, Karen

A13. Francis Arthur, b 1924 mar Dorothy Annett, res Peninsula, Gaspe. Francis d 1964, bur Pen. Dorothy mar 2., res US, 3 chn by Francis: Donald, David and Melody.

A14. Wilson Carol, b 1925, mar Marjorie Stanley, res Wainfleet, ONT, a dau Elizabeth?

LE MESURIER, Wm. Fraser, b 1831 St. George Cove, Gaspe, QUE, by 1855 was a grocer in Quebec City, on his own, and later as partner of a Mr. BROUARD, qv, until about 1871. Wm. d 1884 Que. City. Mar Eliza Sewell, b 1829 Devon, England, d 1874 QUE, one ch. (Gary French, Elmvale, ONT)

A1. Louisa Jane Nile, b 1860 QUE City d 1955, mar 1883 Alex. James Learmouth, b 1829, d 1925 QUE City, 9 chn.

B1. Florence Isabel Learmouth, b 1884 Buffalo, NY d 1970, mar Gilbert H. Henderson, 2 sons, Gilbert and Stuart Henderson of Chicoutimi.

B2. Wm. Fraser Learmouth, b 1886 QUE, d 1957?

B3. Janet Pearl Learmouth, b 1888 d 1979?

B4. Elsie Grace Learmouth, b 1890 d 1964, mar James G. Stenhouse, who d 1960.

B5. Marjorie Nile Learmouth, b 1892 d 1970

B6. Mildred Viola Learmouth, b 1895 d 1978, mar 1918 Frederick Harold Andrews, who d 1974

B7. Alexander Gordon Borvier? Learmouth, b 1897 QUE City, d 1966. Mar Ella Frances Blondin in Montreal 1929.

B8. Allan Montague Learmouth, b 1899 d 1966, mar Simonne Paquette 1942

B9. Kenneth Robert Learmouth, b 1901 d 1961 mar Lily Eliz. Pugh, 1929

LE MESURIER, Jean/John in the grocery and tobacco business in QUE City from about 1854 to at least 1871, poss bro. of above Wm. Fraser? (Gary French, Elmvale, ONT)

LE MESURIER, LE MESARIER, Harriet from C.I. to UT 1863 via ship ANTARCTIC. (SLCity records)

LE MESURIER, see page 365 in Q.A. IN CANADA. This fam desc from Henry LE MESURIER, b 1791 G, son of Haviland LE. M. A great grandson was Charles Stuart of Montreal, who mar 1919 Beatrice Mary Ross, dau of James and Beatrice (Graham) Ross. (WHO'S WHO IN CANADA, 1975)

D1. Marguerite D2. Andrew D4. Mary.

D3. James Ross, b 1923 Montreal, QUE mar Elizabeth Anne Murray, dau of William J. Murray. James an investment dealer in Toronto, and director of many firms, Harvard grad. and lawyer, served in WWII, 4 chn: Stuart, James, Lesley and Lynn.

LE MESURIER, noted in petition of QUE City residents 1838. (LOST IN CANADA, Aug. 1981)

LE MESURIER, John, d in Salem, MA 1735.

LE MOIGNAN in J from 1300s, means stump of amputated limb. Poss several fams, related and unrelated, came from England, France and C.I. to America. In spite of much research by the LE MUNYON desc. a connection has not yet been found with the C.I. Since no strong link was established, only a small part of known info. has been included in this book. Some in WRCIC, more in hands of T.L. McAdam, Warren, MI and A.G. Teague of Detroit, MI.

MUNYON, Edmund mar Mercy Wood of Reading, MA 1727, 5 chn. (Reading VR)

MUNYON, LE MUNYON, Judah mar Joseph MAJERY, qv, 1694 Salem. See MASURY, MAJERY, MAZURY. More data may be available in MA.

MUNYON, LA MUNYON, Philip mar Elizabeth MASURY 1778 Salem, MA.

LA MUNYON, Joseph and Edward are said to have come to MA ca 1717 from "the Isle of Jersey". Settled first in Salem, MA, later rem to Thompson, CT. The name became Munyon. Joseph mar Sarah JOSLIN, who was b 1741. (Uncertain) Edward mar Sarah Proctor 1700 in Salem, who was b 1676, dau of John and Eliz. (BASSETT) Proctor. Sarah was Edward's third wife. He was executed as a witch or wizard, and Sarah was also accused but released. Edward said to be a weaver, with a wife, son and 2 daus. The son Joseph had a house in Salem 1739.

LE MUNYON, Samuel, 1728-1800, a weaver. Samuel res Tiverton, RI formerly Dartmouth, MA. The New Paltz, NY group may have been desc. of Samuel's bro John. Other Munyon sources: Rev. Tim Goldrick, New Bedford, MA; Maxwell Emerson, Memphis, TN; BASSETT FAM, by Chandler; ANNALS OF LYNN, MA by Lewis and Newhall; VR, Lynn, MA; Sidney Perley 's SALEM, Vol 2; WINDHAM, CT, Vol 1; Salt Lake City ARchives; PENN-YAN records; New Paltz records; Tiverton and Killingly, CT records; Dorset, England records, 1544; THE FRENCHTOWN SETTLEMENT, by Elisha R. Potter (LE MOINE); R.I. LAND EVIDENCES, 1648-1696 (Minnion); Westport, MA records; Bristol Co., MA records; PIERCE PAPERS, New Bedford, MA Library; Notebook 61 (KING-LE MUNYON); Tiverton records.

LE MOINE, LE MOIGNE, the monk, in G early, sometimes changed to Monk. In J 1299, in St. Heliers and St. Laurens J 1668, in St. Martin and St. Heliers J 1749. Curr J. LE MOIGNE curr G. MOINE also noted in Ireland, Devon and Cornwall, GB. See Holmes; Fosdick.

LE MOINE, John Charles, b 1816 J, of parents from St. Malo, France, rem to Nfld. 1835 where he mar 1840 Ann Poole of Fortune Bay, Nfld. Chn b Channel, Nfld. (Charles P. Smith, Fairbanks, AK)

A1. George, b 1843, wire man for telegrapher A4. Francis T., b 1854
A2. Julia, b 1845, mar Nathaniel Smith a telegrapher
A3. John Charles Jr., b 1847, worked for Dominion Coal Co.
A5. Nathaniel, b 1858, Church of England minister
A6. Alexander W., b 1863 went down 1894 on ship MAUD GILLAM, from Channel, Nfld.

LEMMON, LE MOINE?, Hannah, mar 1668 Samuel BEADLE, qv, res Salem. He d before 1706, 12 chn. (SAM. BEADLE FAM, 1979) OUTC. Note Robert and Peter in Salem, MA 1637, Hug? or from C.I.?

LEMINE, LE MOINE?, John mar Mary Derbey 1757 Boston. DARBY was a J surname in 1700s. OUTC.

LEMMON, Nancy mar Wm. T. Gerts 1836. Note GERTS, was this LA GERCHE of C.I.? OUTC.

MAWNEY, corruption of LE MOINE, Mary, mar Brig. Gen. James Angell, son of John. OUTC. Angells in MA very early. (DRIVER GEN, 1889)

A1. Abigail Angell
A2. Deborah Angell, mar ___Smith
 B1. Martha Smith mar ___BROWN
  C1. Amey Brown mar Capt. Benoni Cooke
   D1. Charles Dexter Cooke, mar Mary Anna King.
    E1. Henry Charles Cook, mar Harriet Ruth Waters, comp. of DRIVERGen.

LE MOINE noted in Petition of QUE City residents 1838. (LOST IN CANADA)

LEMON, LEMMON, Hundreds in colonies, mostly from England? but poss some were from C.I., such as John & Susan (LE CRAW) LEMONEE,mar 1711.

LE MOIGNE curr Brighton, MA. OUTC.

LE MOINE, see PENN. MAG., Vol 5.

LE MOINE, Henry, son of Anne CENNETTE of G, res J, then rem to London, England. (DAB)

LE MONTAIS, LE MONTEZ in J 1461. In St. Heliers, St. Ouen, St. Peter and St. Laurens J 1668. In St. Peter and St. Ouen J 1749. Curr J. Shield: sable, four fusils in fesse or.

LE MONTAIS, Clement of J, was CARTERET's bro-in-law, and disposed of prize ships, paid crews and victualled the ships of the Privateersmen in Jersey in the 1600s. (A. John Jean, Jersey)

LE MOTAIS in St. Laurens J 1788, poss LE MONTAIS?

LE MONTAIS, Jane called Jane MONTESS, wife of Edmund HAMMOND, living in Kittery, ME 1707. Noyes:" MONTESSE, Jeanne (Jane) wife..A French version of some English name, but what one?" Most likely LE MONTAIS. Edmond was prob. HAMON of J, often changed to Hammond. The dau of Edmond and Jane, Patience, was an Indian captive in 1705, but was in Boston by 1719. See HAMMOND, Edmund. (Noyes; Coleman)

MONTASE, Philippe, also in captivity 1710 in Canada, bro of Jeanne?

LE MONTES, LE MONTAIS, John, b J, to NYork before 1686 when he mar Helena, dau of Simon and Anneken (Vincent) Fell. His will dated 1692, at which time he had no chn living. However, 2 chn were b before he d in 1693. Helen, his widow, 1660-1727, bp under name Magdaleen, mar 2. Robert Griggs, who d before 1700. She mar 3. Caleb Cooper, and had chn by him. (Noyes; Coleman; Elmer Jacobs, Lakewood, OH; Mrs. R.H. Horn, Blacklick, OH: OLD NORTHWEST, Vol 8; Records of Reformed Ch in New York) John LE MONTES had cousin James in Jersey.

A1. Anneken and A. 2. Johannes, d.y.

A3. Jean/Jan/John, bp 1692 bur 1735, mar 1727 Aelfje, dau of Johannes and Henrickje (TenEyk) Van Norden, bp 1705, bur 1744.

B1. Rachel, bp 1728, bur 1731 B2. Johannes, bp 1730 B4. Helen, b1733

B3. Rachel again, bp 1731, mar 1751 Asher NOE, d before 1765

A4. Rachel, bp 1693 mar before 1720 Dugald Campbell, d 1726-33.

B1. Janett Campbell, bp 1720 d 1796, mar 1740 Tobias, son of Johannes Van Norden, bp 1715, d 1800. Other chn?

C1. Rachel Van Norden mar John Boudinot. Other chn?

D1. Elias Boudinot D2. Jane Boudinot

B2. John Campbell.

LE MOTTEE in J 1541, in St. Heliers J 1668, old in G. Curr J. Sometimes changed to MOODY?, qv.

LE MOTE, George mar Eliz. Messenger 1725 Boston, MA, from J?

LE MOTE, LE MOTTEE?, Matthew from J? mar 1728 Marcy Billington, b1704, res Plymouth, MA. (Underhill)

LE MOTTEE curr Los Angeles, CAL, and noted in S. Weymouth, MA, said to be from C.I.

LEMPRIERE, see TOSTEVIN

LEMPRIERE, in J at least by 1180. In all parishes of J except Trinity, Grouville and St. Peter by 1668. In ten parishes by 1749, curr J. This is one of the most notable names in the C.I., with many historical figures. Strongly involved in sea-going, both in commercial vessels and in the British Navy. Thomas of Jersey was shipping tobacco from Virginia to Jersey by 1671. A LEMPRIERE firm was in Nfld. at least by 1717, and probably before. Clement apopular first name, and one Clement drew a map of Bermuda in 1738.

LEMPRIERE, Capt. Clement mar Elizabeth VARNOR or VERNON? in Christ Church Parish, Charleston, SC 1744/45. (SC GEN. AND HIST. MAG) This was prob. the Clement who was the delegate for Christ Church to the Continental Congress in Phila., PA 1775. (SC Mag. Vol 7) He settled in Charleston, but sailed to many other ports. He was in command of the COMMERCE during the Rev. War, and captured a large amount of powder held by the English patriots on an English ship in St. Augustine, FLA. This he sold to the rebels in SC. A number of letters about this are in the SC Mag. His wife in 1749 was Anne, and had dau Anne. A Mrs. Lempriere d 1767, wife of Clement. Poss his third wife was Sarah, who was his widow 1784 at Charleston, SC. Not known to compiler if there were other chn than Anne.

A1. Anne, b 1749 Charlestown, SC, mar 1763 Lt. PRINCE. (Clemens)

LAMPRELL, John was in the boat when Wm. Button drowned 1693 on the Piscataway River in ME. Poss that this was a LEMPRIERE, or a DE LA PERELLE?, as LA PERELLE sounds much like LAMPRELL.

LAMPERELL, Simon, res MRB, mar Eleanor ___. A Capt Simon d 1824, age 50. OUTC.

A1. Margaret, b ca 1806, d 1812

A2. Benjamin? A Benj. d MRB 1837 age 26.

LEMPRIERE, Brian M. of a J fam in Canada, res Mercer IS., WA, curr.

LEMPRIERE fam. to Racine, WI.(E.Fred Tostevin,Duarte,CAL)

LEMPRIERE, Lt. ARthur Reid, b 1835 Ewell, Surry, England, 9th of 13 chn, son of Capt. R.C. LEMPRIERE, desc of the Lemprieres of the Manor of Roselle, Jersey. The Seigneur was a patron of MILLAIS, the famous artist of Jersey and England, who did sketches of the family, and painted Arthur Reid Lempriere as the YOUNG HUGUENOT. See picture. LEMPRIERE served in BC, Canada from 1859-1860, as Royal Engineer, serving from 1850 to 1882. He d Camberley, England 1927. It is possible that Lempriere Bank, Lempriere Station, and Lempriere Creek in BC were named for him, but his short term of service makes one wonder. Other Lemprieres of the past were noted as explorers, etc. Lt. Lempriere had 3-4 daus, and some desc in England, poss in Canada? (Frances Woodward, Spec. Coll., U. of BC, Vancouver, BC)

LEMPRIERE, see MONOGRAPH ON THE HOUSE OF LEMPRIERE, London, England, 1862 by J.B. Payne.

LEMPRIERE, John Philip, b ca 1888 St. Mary J, son of George L., mar 1. ___, and 2. Eva HUBERT, qv. John rem to Edmonton, Alta., Canada, served in WWI, returned to Canada 1919. He was a shoemaker, retired 1951, d 1954. Eva HUBERT Lempriere d 1964, almost 84, bur Edmonton, ALTA. (G. Lempriere) Two of John's stepdaus, Irene FALLU and Monica Maude FALLU, qv, came to Canada with the Lemprieres and settled in CAL.

LIMBREY, Capt. Philip, res Surry Co., VA 1668, and mar that year Mary Barker, dau of Capt. Wm. Barker of Charles City, VA, sea Capt. and Burgess. LIMBREY may be LEMPRIERE and for that reason is included here. Edmonia C. Wilkins, b 1865 Warren Co., NC was a desc of that fam. OUTC. See source for more data. (Virkus VII, pp 467,468)

LAMPRIERE, note that many of this name rem to England from the Islands.

LEMPREY, Etienne, was in New Rochelle, NY 1698, OUTC. (Koehler)

LE NEVEU, in St. Clement and Grouville J 1668. Curr J

LE NEVEU, David, from C.I., in CAL 1851, rem to Victoria, BC

LE NEVEU, see Amice BERTRAM.

LENFESTY, LENFESTEY, in J 1700s, but usually a G surname. In G 1305, in St. Peter Port G 1636, in Torteval G 1714, also early in St. Saviour Parish G. Curr and common in G. See Q.A. IN CANADA by Turk.

"It is clear from the extensive local records in existence, that the family name of LENFESTEY is of Guernsey origin, being locally recorded from the early 14th century, from 1305 onwards in the parishes of St. Pierre-du-Bois, St. SAviour and Torteval. It is of simple peasant origin, most probably meaning L'Enfete, the Festive, which would suggest regular inebriation, etc." (J. H. Lenfesty, G, 1973)

"My Husband's sister told me years ago that three brothers came to America, one to New York, one to Canada, and one to New Orleans, and he was the pirate LaFitte." (Mrs. E.M. Bourquin, Santa Clara, CAL) This last is somewhat doubtful, as compiler was told there is documentation on background of the pirate LaFitte. However, the names are very similar.

LENFESTY, see page 377, top of page, in QUIET ADVENTURERS IN CANADA, by Turk, for place in Lenfesty chart for family below.

B6. William LENFESTY, b 1853 Perce, QUE. He was the son of Charles, b 1814 Perce, QUE, and grandson of James, b 1786 Guernsey, and Susanne (MAUGER) Dobson. Wm. mar Anna Young, b 1857, d 1914 Delia, ALTA. Wm. d 1943, bur Delia. They res 1895 in Orillia, ONT. Some desc to Michigan. Others to BC. Wm. said to have left home at age 11, and said to be second youngest in fam of 8. He was first a stonecutter, drove a food wagon during the Riel Rebellion, was shot in the forehead by an Indian arrow, worked as steam-shovel operator for the CPRR, brought his fam west in 1902, homesteading at Shepard, ALTA, which is now part of Calgary, ALTA. In 1910 the fam rem to the Hand Hills area, and homesteaded there. Charles Douglas and Mark Arthur, both grandsons of Wm., farm the original homesteads. (Corrine Lenfesty, Criagmyle, ALTA, Canada)

C1. Charles, ran away from home at age 15, no record

C2. Henry, d 1957, mar Maggie ___, poss Miss Michigan of 1919?,9 chn

D1. Mamie Mary, b 1903, mar ___Quinlan 7? chn, res London, ONT.

D2. Cecil Charles, b 1906, d 1955

D3. Laura Ann, b 1908 mar ___Leadbetter

D4. Dorothy Margaret, b 1910 mar ___MCCartney, 7? chn

D5. Verne Veronica, b 1912 mar ___Iiecia?

D6. Stella Nonnie, b 1916 mar ___Lipka

D7. William, b 1918 mar 1. Martha ___, div, and 2. Shirley ___, 8 chn: Lorne, Mary Jane, Ken, Linda, William, Faye, Raymond and Lenore.

D8. Lorne Joseph, b 1920 res Prince George, BC, mar 1. Irene LENFESTEY, his cousin, div, and mar 2. Goldie ___, 13 chn: Herma W., Daniel, b Alberta, Garth, Lorel, Judy, Faye, Cheri, Carol, Wendy, Lorne, Tim, Robin and Matthew

D9. Ruby Rose (Ruth) Lenfesty, b 1924 mar ___Hornbeck. She was Miss Michigan of 1946. See Magazine US, p. 45, Sept.4, 1979.

C3. Mark ARthur, b 1884 North Bay, ONT, d 1970, bur Hanna, ALTA.

C4. Sterrie Hunt, b 1885 Detroit, MI d 1949 bur Hanna, ALTA, mar Dulcie W. Ringrose, b 1894 England, d 1974 Edmonton. 3 chn

D1. Raymond Sterrie, b 1919 Lawsonburg, ALTA, mar Barbara MacDougall

E1. Lillian Dulcie, b 1950 Merritt, BC, mar Ken Parsons, dau Diana

D2. Charles Douglas, b 1920 Craigmyle, ALTA, mar Julia M. Turkosz

E1. Wayne Douglas, b 1947 mar Joan Clark, 2 chn: Angela & Jody

E2. Corrine B., b 1949 ALTA res Craigmyle, ALTA

E3. Theresa Elaine, b 1955, d.y.

D3. Irene Dulcie Ada b 1923, mar 1. Lorne LENFESTY, div, and 2. Nick Chaykowski, b 1930. Her chn by Lorne L. are above.

C5. Roy Day, b 1894 North Bay, ONT d 1958 Hanna, ALTA, mar Maggie Preston, b 1904 Cartmel, Lancs, England, 4 chn.

D1. William Day, b 1931 ALTA, d 1947 in horse accident

D2. Joan Margaret, b 1933 mar Don Jones, res Olds, ALTA, 5 chn

E1. Nancy Cecile Jones, b 1955 mar Terry Rinas, 2 chn: Greg and Robin Rinas.

E2. Sandra Diane Jones, b 1956 Calgary mar Dave Kruger
E3. Don Jones Jr., b 1958 ALTA E4. Carolyn Faye Jones, b 1961
E5. Bonnie Elaine Jones, b 1963 Red Deer, ALTA.
D3. Roy Day, b 1942 d 1943, drowned
D4. Mark Arthur, b 1938 mar Rosanna Wiens, b 1937, res Craigmyle, AlTA. 5 chn: Roy, Faye, Donna, Diane & Timothy, b ca 1960s
C6. Elsie Annie, b 1896 North Bay, ONT d 1964 ALTA, mar Martin Martin b 1891 PEI, d 1976, bur Drumheller, ALTA, 3 chn
D1. Wm. Phillip Martin, b 1921 ALTA, unmar, res Walsh, ALTA
D2. Anna Martin, b 1922 mar Ivan Rosin, b 1916. She d 1966, he in 1978, Grande Prairie, ALTA, 4 chn.
E1. Shirley Rosin, b 1948 mar Dennis Ponto, 2 chn: Gaylene, Jason
E2. James Allen Martin Rosin b 1949
E3. Joyce Rosin, b 1960 E4. Joy Rosin, b 1960, twin
D3. James Henry Martin, b 1925 d 1966 train collison, mar Edna Wilkinson, 2 chn
E1. Gregory Dale Martin, b 1947 mar 1. Linda Branum, div. and 2. Colleen Albert, res Calgary, ALTA.
E2. Rex Lee Martin, b 1949 mar Noreen Landon, res Drumheller, ALTA, 2 chn: Gregory and Darren Martin, b 1970s
C7. Stella Eliza/Babe, b 1900 North Bay, ONT mar Laurence Ringrose, b 1888 Nottingham, England, res Drumheller, ALTA, 3 chn
D1. Muriel Stella Ringrose, b 1920 mar Frank Charney, 1916-1963, res Burnaby, BC, 2 chn
E1. Cheryl Charney, b 1946 Vancouver area, mar Vince Henthorne, div 2 chn: Annette and Colin Henthorne, b 1960s.
E2. Daryl Charney, b 1951 mar Judy ___, a son Shawn b 1972
D2. Agnes Annie Ringrose, b 1922 ALTA mar Don Nottell, res Calgary
E1. Hazel Nottell, b 1947 mar Grant Baker, res Fort MacLeod, ALTA, a ch Jody Lynn Baker, b 1974
E2. Gordon Nottell, b 1952 mar April York, res Calgary.
D3. Ella Josephine Ringrose, b 1925 mar Lloyd Bixby, b 1920, 3chn.
E1. Eileen Bixby, b 1943 mar Jim MacDonald, 3 chn: Debbie, Cindy and Jim Brian MacDonald, b 1960s
E2. Alma Diane Bixby, b 1946 mar Daryl Gray, res Sherwood Park, ALTA, 2 chn: Duane and Vicki Gray, b 68 and 77.
E3. Garry Laurence Bixby, b 1952 mar Marlene Volb.

LENFESTEY, Peter James, b 1850 Perce, QUE (P. 377, Q.A. IN CANADA) Desc of this fam res in Eau Claire, WI; Superior, WI; Okla City, OK; Baraga, MI; Kettering, OH; Camden, NJ; Hoquiam, WA & San Francisco, CAL. (Claudette Maroldo, Cherry Hill, NJ)

LENFESTY, Peter b 1739 G, son of John and Judith L., bur St. Peter in the Wood G. Peter rem to Maine, and mar there in New Gloucester, Lydia Harris, b 1755 Dracut, MA. He d 1820, she in 1829, both at Lewiston, ME. (Typescript by Bertram A. Lenfest dated 1931 in Library of Congress; NEHGS Vol 63; Claudette Maroldo, Cherry Hill, NJ; Nathiel Kramer, Oregon City, OR)
A1. Judith b 1775, d.y. A2. Peter, b 1776, d.y. A3. John, b 1778 ??
A4. Thomas, b 1779, mar Abigail Coburn of Dracut, MA. She d Methuen, MA 1860. Thomas d 1863 Lawrence, MA. At least 9 chn: Rebecca, Martha A., Lydia who mar John Getchell, Abigail R., James, Mary A., Maria, Thomas and
B7. Caroline, b 1823, Charlestown, MA, mar Jess Town of Methuen, and died there 1902.
A5. Lydia, b 1781 d 1863 Lawrence, MA mar John Getchell?
A6. Rebecca, b 1783 Lisbon, ME mar 1813 Israel Glidden of Alma, ME. Rebecca d 1849.

B1. Peter L. Glidden, b 1815 Lewiston, ME
B2. Lydia H. Glidden, 1817-1839 B3. Eunice Glidden, b 1820
B4. Joseph H. Glidden, b 1824 d 1826 Lewiston, ME.
A7. Peter again, b 1785 mar 1815 Margaret Campbell of Bowdoin, ME, dau of Daniel and Abigail (Hall) Campbell. Margaret was b 1799 and d 1815 New Sharon, ME. Peter d 1849 Washington, ME.
B1. Daniel, b 1816 Wash., ME, mar 1844 1. Lucy Thompson, d 1878 Edgar, NEB. Lucy d 1857. Daniel mar 2. Eliza Gowen, Cowen 1859, who d 1909 Ong, NEB, 4 chn, 2 by each wife.
C1. Elvira T., b 1845 Liberty, ME mar 1879 Mpls, MN, John Pemberton, b 1850 Leistershire, England. Elvira d 1927 St. Paul, MN. John remar, but his 2nd wife soon died. 3 chn by John.
D1. John Lenfest Pemberton, b 1880 Mpls, MN, mar 1907 St. Paul, Lucy Finney, b 1880 Big Stone City, MN, 1 ch, Virginia, b 1911
D2. Joseph Gould Pemberton, b 1882 mar 1910 Lucia E. Carr, b 1885, 1 ch, Nan Yvonne, b 1918 Mpls, MN.
D3. Lee Randall Pemberton, b 1884 mar 1917 Margaret Johnson, 1 ch: Randall Stewart Pemberton, b 1917 Marshall, MN.
C2. Chessman E., b 1848 Liberty, ME mar 1882 Fairfield, NEB Mary Stone, b 1851 Bainbridge, OH, 3 chn
D1. Grace E., b 1883 Fairfield, NEBR
D2. Roy E., b 1889 d 1927 Winter Park, FLA, mar there 1912 Hazel Frances Coffin, 2 chn: Eugene, b 1918, Carol b 1923
C3. Lee Randall b 1860, by 2nd wife, in Appleton, ME, mar 1883 Edgar NEB Lillian Edith Slawson, b 1861 Howard, ILL, 6 chn
D1. Blossom Edith, b 1884 mar 1913 San Jose, CAL Lavergne Gardner Graves, b 1886 Chester, NY, 3 chn
E1. Herbert Ray Graves, b 1914 E2. Alvin Lee Graves b 1916
E3. Henry Lavergne Graves, b 1919 San Jose, CAL
D2. Calvin Ray, b 1886 Edgar, NEB.
D3. Nellie May, b 1888 mar 1914 Sam. L. Worsley, b1889 Newark, ILL. 3 chn b Prov. RI: Alice Edith, 1915; Charles S., 1920, and Ruth Edna Worsley, b 1923
D4. Bessie Lea, b 1895 NEB.
D5. Jasper Daniel, b 1898 mar 1926 San Diego, CAL Marian Gamble, b 1906 Wessington, SD, 2 chn b Reedley, CAL: Eliz. H. & Lois M.
D6. Dora Lucille, b 1901 Lake Charles, LA, mar 1924 San Jose, CAL Wilbert J. Jones, b 1902 Morrlan, KS, a son John Daniel Jones, b Morgan Hill, CAL.
C4. Lucy E., b 1864 Appleton, ME.
B2. Abigail, b 1817 Wash., ME mar 1842 Palermo, ME Samuel Turner, who was b 1814, d 1889. Abigail d 1896, 7 chn.
C1. Viola Cross Turner, b 1845, mar 1861 Cushman Jones, b 1835 Wash., ME. Mar 2. John Rufus Lamson, b 1842 Liberty, ME, who d 1924.
D1. Alvra Cushman Jones, b 1862 mar 1887 Liberty, ME Alice Mabell Hisler, b 1866 Centre Palermo, ME, 2 chn
E1. Lulu Imogene Jones, b 1889 mar 1907 Burleigh Turner, b 1884
F1. Varal Alvra Turner, b 1909 F3. Lois A. Turner b 1914
F2. Leta Maxine Turner, b 1910 F4. Joyce A. Turner, b 1919
D2. Cora Jones, b 1863 mar 1884 Pawtucket, RI David McComb, b 1853 Carbondale, PA.
D3. Letitia Jones, b 1865 mar 1888 Springfield, MA, Clinton B. Thayer b 1862 Blackstone, MA, 2 chn
E1. Ruth M. Thayer, b 1896 RI E2. Arthur Thayer, b 1900 Cumberland, RI.
D4. Prince Albert Jones, b 1867 ME mar Central Falls, RI 1889 Margaret Willoughby, b 1869, 2 chn
E1. Ethel Mabel Jones, b 1893 Central Falls, RI

E2. Cora Willoughby Jones, b 1902 Prov., RI
D5. Jennie Abigail Jones, b 1870 E. Palermo, ME
D6. Elden Burkett Jones, b 1872?, d 1910. Mar 1901 Adelaide Neil, b 1874 Pawtucket, RI, and 2. in 1912 Isabel Campbell, b 1870 at Attleboro, MA.
D7. Walter Scott Jones, b 1874, ME mar 1896 Central Falls, RI Eva Ione Ingalls, b 1873, 2 chn
E1. Lloyd Walter Jones, b 1899, d.y.
E2. Doris Mae Jones, b 1900, mar 1920 Franklin Davenport Snow, b 1898, 2 chn
F1. Franklin D. Snow, Jr. b 1922 F2. Priscilla B. Snow, b 1926
C2. Orissa, b 1849 Palermo, ME mar 1869 Liberty ME Vinal Turner, b 1847 Liberty, ME.
D1. Clinton Turner, b 1870 d 1893
D2. Azelle Turner, b 1871 mar 1892 Prov., RI Edgar M. Lenfest, b 1866, 2 chn
E1. Marjorie Lenfest, b 1897 Manchester, ME. E2. Donald b 1906
D3. Estella Turner, b 1873 mar 1902 Fred E. Spratt, b 1863, d 1920. She mar 2. 1924 Fred H. Howard, b 1859 Wash., ME, who d 1926. 2 chn: Melissa Spratt and Elmer Howard
D4. Rose Turner, b 1875 mar Miles Earnest Creamer, b 1870, 1ch
E1. Clinton Creamer, b 1898 mar 1. Mary Burgess, b 1902, d 1921 He mar 2. Gladys Keene by 1903, Boston, MA, 2 chn.
F1. Burgess Creamer, b 1921 F2. Lola Creamer, b 1923
D5. Sylvia Turner, b 1880 mar 1900 Boston, Oscar Johnston, b 1873 Bremen, ME, 1 ch: Millway Johnston, b 1901 Portland, ME
D6. Burleigh Turner, b 1883 mar 1907 Augusta, ME Lulu Imogene Jones, b 1889, 4 chn. See Lulu Jones Turner above, for chn.
D7. Elvin Turner, b 1883 mar 1909 Palermo, ME Elsie Belle Glidden, b 1888, 2 chn: Max E. Turner, b 1909, Harland G. b 1916
C3. Samuel Turner Jr, b 1851 d 1863 C4. Cora Ella Turner, b 1855
C5. Letitia Lowell Turner, b 1857, d 1865 d.y.
C6. Roland Jacob Turner, b 1860 mar 1889 Elzona Turner, b 1867
D1. Ralph Turner, b 1889
D2. Carl L. Turner, b 1892 d 1914 Montville, ME mar Lucy Fuller, b 1894 Montville.
E1. Ruth Turner, b 1914 E3. Louise Turner, b 1921
E2. Dorothy Turner, b 1919 E4. Evelyn A. Turner, b 1925
D3. Earl Turner, b 1903 d 1918 D5. Biney?, 1904-1917
D4. Hazel Turner, b 1903 mar 1924 Winthrop, ME Walter B.Griffin, b 1902 Norwell, MA. Dau Laura Arlene Griffin b 1926
D6. Virgie Turner, b 1906 mar 1927 ME, Everett F. McDonald, b 1906 Washington, ME.
B3. Adeline, b 1819 mar 1846 Bowdoin ME Cyrus Campbell, b 1817. Adeline d 1893 New Sharon, ME, and Cyrus d 1887, preacher,5chn.
C1. Courtney Campbell, b 1847 Bowdoinham, ME, d.y.
C2. Margaret Campbell, b 1848 mar 1871 Granville Brown, b 1849 Industry, ME who d 1877, 4 chn. She mar 2. Geo. A. Hatch, b 1858 Skowhegan, ME, d 1920 Seattle, WA, 1 ch
D1. William Cyrus Brown, b 1872 New Sharon, ME
D2. Ida Gertrude Brown, b 1874 mar 1895 Dixfield, ME Charles D. Holman, b 1864 d 1911, 2 chn. One son d.y.
E2. Elsie Margaret Holman, b 1898 mar 1925 Richmond, ME Waldo B. Gould, b 1899 Wilton, ME.
D3. Blanche Adeline Brown, b 1875 mar 1897 Redfalls, MN, Adelbert Richard Lyman, b 1869, 4 chn, a son d.y. 1908
E1. Keith Adelbert Lyman, b 1899 Mazeppa, MN mar 1922 Anna B.

Lyman, b 1897 Tabor, IA, 1 ch

F1. Keith Winston Lyman, b 1924 Bremerton, WA.

E2. Harold Dwight Lyman, b 1900 Morton, MN mar 1924 Yamhill, OR, Evelyn Content DeMoss, b 1902 Cove, OR.

E3. Marjorie Lyman, b 1903 Inkster, ND, mar 1925 Salem, OR, Roy South, a son d.y.

D4. Granville Brown, b 1877 mar 1921 Tacoma, WA, Carrie Alice Jenkins, b Freeport, ILL, who d 1930 Puyallup, WA.

D5. Effie May Hatch, b 1885, mar Frank N. Fisher, b WIS, 4 chn, Myrtle, Howard, Walter and Frank S. Fisher, res WA and AK.

C3. Marth J. Campbell, b 1851 d 1853

C4. Sarah Etta Campbell, b 1853 mar 1878 Noyes H. Williamson, 1 ch. See sources for more data on fams below.

C5. Anne Eliza Campbell, b 1855 Phippsburg, ME mar 1879 Edwin O. Andrews, 3 chn

B4. Elcy Jane, b 1821 Wash., ME mar 1857 Foster Lee Randall, b 1820 Lewiston, ME, 3 chn

B5. Lois S. Lenfest, b 1823 ME mar 1849 Oliver Boynton, who d 1897 Wilton, IA, 4 chn

B6. Margaret R., b 1825 mar 1850 Montville, ME Joel Clark, b 1823. He d 1904 Athol, KS, and she 1882 in Manhattan, KS. 4 chn

B7. Lavinia, b 1827 Wash., ME d 1912 Conrad, IA, mar Orris T.Walker.

B8. George Lenfest, b 1829 mar ME Bertha Turner, b 1835. Res MA & ME.

B9. Elbridge, b 1831 ME mar 1869 Arabell Glidden, b 1843, who d 1914 in Berkeley, CAL. 2 chn

B10. Peter Lincoln, b 1834, miner near Pike's Peak, disappeared.

B11. Helen Matilda, b 1837 ME mar Joab Boynton, 2 chn

B12. Sylvia Ann, b 1839 mar 1863 Simon E. Daggett, b 1838. She d 1915 Conrad, IA, 8 chn.

B13. Solomon Augustus Lenfest, b 1841 mar 1865 Lowell, MA Jennie Adelaide Churchill, b 1844 Newmarket, NH. He d 1928 Melrose, MA. 7 chn, several stillborn.

A8. James, b 1786/7 mar 1. 1813 ME Eunice Gillpatrick, b 1795. He d 1868 Palermo, ME, 11 chn.

B1. William P., b 1814 mar 1. 1865? ___Howard, and 2. widow of John Lenfesty in 1870.

B2. Nicholas N., b 1813 B7. Peter M., b 1829

B3. Rosannah P., ? b 1819, d.y. B8. Charles P., 1832-1919, d ME.

B4. Eunice P., b 1822, d 1904 Lowell, MA? B9. Lydia J, b 1835

B5. Hannah R., b 1825 B10. Lizzie A., b 1836

B6. James N., b 1827 d 1869 Palermo, ME B11. Harriet O., b 1838

A9. Judith again, b 1789 Lewiston, ME mar 1812 Samuel Getchell, son of Robert, b 1783 Durham, ME, 8 chn.

B1. Nathan Hall Getchell, b 1813 Gorham, ME mar 1843, d ME

B2. Robert Getchell, b 1817 Brooks, ME mar Stillwater?, ME

B3. Lydia Lenfest Getchell, b 1819 mar Pittsfield, ME d Mpls., MN

B4. Solomon L. Getchell, b 1821 d 1846

B5. Moses Whittier Getchell, b 1824, mar 1855 St. Anthony, MN, d CAL

B6. Samuel Getchell, b 1826 Unity, ME mar Pittsfield, ME,d 1858

B7. Judith L. Getchell, b 1829? mar New York, d 1869 Osage, IA

B8. Rebekah Ann Getchell, b 1831 mar 1839 Bangor, ME.

A10. Abraham, b 1791 Palmyra, ME mar 1839 Almyra Robinson, who d 1880?

B1. John Fairchild, b 1839 ME B4. Daniel R., b 1845

B2. Thomas H. Benton, b 1840 d 1864, Civil War? B5. Sarah A.,1847-1850

B3. Josephine R., b 1843, mar in Palmyra, ME 1871

A11. Nicholas, b 1792/3, mar 1. 1820 in Wash., ME Hannah Gove, who d insane ca 1834, 6 chn, and 2. Betsy Gentner.

B1. John Gove, b 1821 Wash., ME mar 1848 Lavinia Hills. John was a rebel prisoner in 1863. Other chn? (Sibley A. Lenfest, Malden,MA)
C1. John Leslie Lenfest, had son Sibley A., who had son Richard S. and son Leslie W., who had son Charles
B2. Abraham, b 1823, d 1850 San Fran, CAL B5. Mary G, b 1829
B3. Martha, b 1825 d 1848 B6. Maderson?, b 1832
B4. Harris, b 1827 B7. Isaac by 2nd wife, b 1835
A12. Solomon, b 1795 Lewiston, ME mar 1823/5 Boston, Mary Ann Hancock, b 1799 Leominster, MA who d 1858 Cambridge, MA. Solomon d 1858.
B1. Louise Chamberlin, d 1893 Cambridge, MA
LENFESTEY, William Peter, b NYCity 1835-1837 mar Elizabeth GRAY of Scotland, b 1835, d 1917. William hit and killed by a streetcar in San Francisco, CAL 1920. (Marjorie Adams, Glenridge, NJ)
A1. Wm. Gray Lenfesty, b 1866 NY or Brooklyn, d 1950 Berkeley, CAL mar Clara Louise Crosby of Rocksville, CT, in Curry Co., OR 1869. She d Berkeley CAL 1938, 4 chn. NOTE! ERRORS IN THIS CHART!
B1. George Crosby, b 1890 OR, mar Dorothy SEARLE 1915, and d 1957,3chn
C1. Dorothy Elizabeth b 1917, d.y. ((Wm.Lenfestey,Hayward, CAL)
C2. Alan Searle, b 1920 killed in WWII 1944 (See CH.IS.COLL.)
C3. George Crosby Jr, b 1926 Berkeley, mar Antoinette Grosnez 1950, res Moraga, CAL, 6 chn
D1. Theresa, b 1951 mar James Steinwandt 1971, ch Gretchen Steinwandt.
D2. Catherine b 1953 D5. George Alan b 1962
D3. Jacqueline mar Peter Barone 1976 D6. Robert Craig, b 1964
D4. Christina, b 1959
B2. Marjorie, b 1893 mar Russel Brown Adams, 1921, who d 195-, 3 chn
C? Russell Brown Adams Jr, b 1924 Berkeley, mar Janet Watson, 3 chn
D1. Ellen Leslie Adams, b 1956 D2. Paul T. Adams, b 1958
B3. Claire Louise b 1900 San Fran., mar Edward Hatton Gallup Jr. of Boston, MA 1924, who d 1969 Mt. Lebanon, PA, 2 chn
C1. Edward Hatton Gallup III, b 1926 res Gibson, PA, mar Celeste Van Sickle 1950
D1. Anne Gallup, b 1954 D3. Richard Gallup b 1960
D2. David Gallup b 1956 D4. Daniel Crosby Gallup b 1962
C2. Marion, b 1931 mar Robert H. Drummond 1954, res Oberlin, OH, 3chn
D1. Paul Frederick Drummond, b 1956
D2. Stephen Drummond, b 1959 D3. Jean Louise Drummond, b 1963
B4. William Robert b 1903 San Fran., mar Beauton Krops, 2 chn
C1. Wm. Robert res Hayward, CAL
C2. Howard b 1934 mar 1963, 2 chn: Scott Kenneth, b 1964 and Glenn, adopted Navaho Indian
A2. Helen, mar Robert R. Vail, 3 chn
B1. Alida, mar George Forsyth, res Winter Park, FLA
B2. Elizabeth mar Herbert NOWELL, no issue
B3. Robert Brittain, b 1900, mar, div, remar, res San Mateo, CAL,chn
A3. Mary/Mame, mar Frank Bell, 3 chn: Helen Barns, Emily McVicker, and Frank Bell, res Honolulu.
A4. Percy Ernest, mar, div, mar 2. Marjorie Hutchinson, of New England
A5. George, d 1890 Oregon.
LENFESTY, Robert, reportedly arrived in US 1770, and res Philadelphia, was Capt. of a privateer in War of 1812, captured by the British and hanged as a pirate! (Claudette Maroldo, Cherry Hill, NJ) A desc, Robert H., b 1809, mar Priscilla Ballenger 1831, rem to Grant Co., IND 1835/6. Robert d 1860 and Priscilla in 1879, both bur IOOF Cem. Marion, IND. This fam called LENFESTY.
A1. Henry A2. Edward
A3. Robert Don, called Don, mar Elizabeth LUCAS, and 2. Mary Dunn.

2 chn by 1st wife. 9 chn: Alvin, Hillary, Harry/Jack, Lewis/Cy, Burr, George and:
B7. Eva, mar Ernest Ogburn, res Saginaw, MI, at least 2 chn.
B8. Edward, mar, had at least 2 daus, Gertrude and Anna
B9. Charles, rem to Walla Walla, WA ca 1900, 2 chn
C1. Philip, mar Florence ___, d ca 1975, 4 chn
D1. Joan mar Richard James D3. Lois mar Michael Springer, res IA.
D2. Martha, mar Richard Zobl, res Cedar Rapids, IA
D4. Charles D., mar Lois ___, res Yakima, WA
C2. Robert G., mar ___, res Seattle, WA, had 2 adopted daus.
A4. Elizabeth mar Isaiah Cox, a dau.
B1. Hattie Cox, mar ___Price, a son Isaiah Price had ch, Pennel Price
A5. Sarah d age 4
A6. Charles, mar Sarah Vantilburgh, 2? chn
B1. Lenora, mar Curtis C. Hiatt, 3 chn: Leah H. Sturgis, Mary Warfel and Anna Moore. no issue
B2. Frank Charles mar Florence Abbot, a son Franklin A./mar R.Campbell
A7. William L., mar Sarah Coggeshall
B1. Alice mar Tony Lupo B3. Elizabeth, unmar
B2. Lucy, mar John White, had 2 chn: Wilfred and a dau?
B4. Mildred, mar Louis De Wolfe, son Francis/Louis and a dau?
B5. Jessie, d in her teens B6. a dau B7. a dau
B8. Nathan C., b 1890 Marion, IND, rem to Boston, then to NY 1917. Mar 1919 Jeannette Hazen Ricketts in NY, d 1954 Summit, NJ, 4 chn
C1. William R., b 1919 mar Brinton M., res Riverside, CT, 3 chn: Wm. Jr., Gail B. mar a Frenchman?, and Lynn G., unmar
C2. Virginia, mar ___Knouse, res Pittsfield, MA, 3 daus, Penelope, GIgi and Diana Knouse.
C3. Janet, mar Paul Gadebusch, res New Canaan, CT, 2 chn: Paul and Bradford Gadebusch.
C4. John Francis, mar Katherine S., b 1920, res Toledo, OH, 2 chn: Hazen and Marion

LENFESTEY, Abraham Alfred, III, b 1848 G, d 1914 Jonesport, ME. (Chester E. Lenfestey, N. Whitefield, ME)
A1. Ewart Gladstone, b 1898 Jonesport, ME, res Beals, ME
B1. Chester Ernol, b 1925 res Jonesport, ME
C1. Chester Ernol, b 1949 Addison, ME res N. Whitefield, ME
D1. Ralph Willis, b 1972 Calais, ME.

LENFESTEY, John from G ca 1876, mar Elizabeth Brill, who was b 1865, d 1927. John d 1937 Toledo, OH age 82? He was son of Fred. and Julia DU MAUIER?) LENFESTEY of G. He worked an Ohio farm on shares with John BLONDEL, qv, in Fulton Co., OH before rem to Toledo area. (Mrs. Arthur Jordan, Toledo, OH)
A1. John mar Ethel Miely A2. Cora A3. Harry, d.y. A4. Arthur, d.y.
A5. Mary, mar Garfield Mock, 5 chn: Hazel, Melba, Doris, Violet and Dale Mock
A6. Ben, mar Lucille HAWKINS, qv, adopted son Robert. Ben d 1976.
A7. Margaret Julia mar Clarence T. Jordan, res Swanton, OH
B1. Virginia Mae Jordan, res Toledo
B2. Wayne, res FLA B3. Ruth Jordan, res FLA
A8. Frank, mar Hazel ___. Frank d early 1960s
A9. Ruby Mae mar Arthur Harry Jordon 1925
B1. Phyllis Joanne, b 1929 mar Robert M. Elkins, b 1928, 3 chn
C1. Carolyn Joanne, b 1950, twin, mar 1. David Davies, div. and mar 2. Farooz ___, res Knoxville, TN
C2. Marilyn Suzanne, b 1950, twin, mar Ronald R. Yarbrough 1965, 2. John Blenkinsop, and 3. J.N. Triplett Jr. 1981

D1. David Yarbrough res Huntsville, ALA
C3. Robert Mathew Elkins Jr, b 1955 mar Elaine F. Coward 1974, div, res NJ, a son Robert Mathew III, b 1975
B2. John Edward, res Toledo, OH B3. Carolyn Mae
A10. Martin, b 1925, mar Alice Wagoner
B1. Beverly, res MI B2. Joan, res MI B3. Joyce res Toledo, OH
A11. Lawrence, res Wauseon, OH mar Meredith Turpening, 2 chn. Poss also res Delta, OH?
B1. Brenda Louise res FLA B2. Elizabeth Ann res NJ.
LENFESTEY, William, related to above fam?, 1829-1896, bur Madison Twp., Guernsey Co., OH. See John below.
LENFESTEY, some from G to Ireland, and from there to America.
LENFESTY, Thomas a miller, res Chicago, ILL late 1800s?
LENFESTY, John, cooper of Pittsburgh, had a house and land there, plus other property, including land in Cambrdige, OH, where the other Guernsey folk settled. 6 chn. He d ca 1837. (Will in GCO courthouse)
A1. Harriott, mar ___MCWilliams A5. Keziah
A2. John A3. Sarah A4. Matilda A6. Thomas M., minor in 1830
LENFEST, Martha A. mar Enoch Whittier (int) 1836 Dracut, MA
LENFEST, Rebecca, dau of Thomas and Abigail, b 1809 Dracut, MA
LENFEST, Thomas, son of ditto, b 1829? Dracut, MA.
LENFESTEE, LENFESTY, noted in Petition of Quebec City residents 1838. (LOST IN CANADA, Aug. 1981)
LENFESTY, Carterette HUBERT, b 1788 G, d 1878 GCO. See HUBERT, curr G.
LENFESTEY, Harriet, b G or poss Pittsburgh?, see John above, mar Benj. Edenburn 1826 GCO, and 2. Wm. Noble 1827. (Conner-Eynon)
LENFESTEY, John, b G, to OH before 1860 worked a farm on shares with John BLONDEL, qv, in Fulton Co., OH.
A1. William,?, 1829-1896
LENFESTEY, Mary mar Isaac P. Gillette late 1800s, GCO
LENFESTEY, Nacy, b G, mar Charles MARQUAND, qv, 1815, GCO.
LENFESTEY, Thomas, b 1788 G, to GCO 1806, mar 1812 Catherine HUBERT, qv D Winchester, OH 1847.
LENFESTEY, Thomas M., clerk of court in GCO 1858-1864. Poss son of John of Pittsburgh?
LENFESTY, John b 1868 QUE of G fam? to Mt. Clemens, MI.
LENFESTEY, see page 378 in Q.A. IN CANADA, by Turk. Please add from Mrs. Eugene Morse, Chippewa Falls, WI:
E2. Donald E. Erickson, b 1941, twin, mar Susan O'Donahue 1974, 3 chn: Brian, Martina and Nolan Erickson, b 1970s.
See same, line 28 in book, E1. Eugene Pierre Morse, b 1946, mar 1974 Julie Thur. 2 chn: Heidi and Erin.
LENFEST curr Texas and in Fremont, CAL.
LINFESTYS in Denver, COL and in Bakersfield, CAL.
LENFIT. "Eliz. Lenfit, my great grandmother, was born 1846 in Ottawa Co., of Perth, ONT. Her father was John LENFIT/LINFOOT/LINDFAST, who according to record...was born in England." Note that in Gaspe, QUE the name was often written L'ENFETE. (Robert Gustafson, Rochester, New York)
LENFESTEY, James of St. Saviour G, to Vancouver, BC 1860s. James L. of Torteval founded the Lenfestey Broom Corp., run in 1970s by his grandchildren in FLA. Desc. in Oregon.
LENFESTEY, Peter, from G to US 1870? (J. H. Lenfestey)
LENFESTEY in Seattle, pres. of a large corp. (J.H. Lenfestey, Guernsey)
LE NORMAND, a G surname in 1619. Curr J. NORMAN in J from 1331, variously LE NORMANT, NORMAN, etc. In St. Laurens J 1788. Poss some NORMAN fams of early New England were from J?, not researched.

LE NOURY, NOURY in J 1309, curr and common in G. The NOURSE fam of Salem, MA has a name very close to this, but compiler found no record to connect them with the C.I.

LE NOURY, from G to CAL 1920s

LEONARD, in J 1528, in St. Clement and Grouville J 1668. Curr G and J. Origin of Leonards in early New England not researched by compiler.

LEONARD, Sarah from J? wife of John WHITE, qv, 1660s, MA. OUTC

LEONARD, Uruiah mar Eliz. CASWELL in Taunton NJ, 1685. OUTC

LE PAGE in J 1299-1528. In Forest G 1700s. In Sark Island 1800s. Common and curr in G. CAUTION: TRIAL CHARTS

LE PAGE, Thomas, b 1809 G, rem to GCO 1818, mar 1829 Rachel SARCHET, qv 1810-1845. Mar 2. Margaret Cullen Ramsey, widow with 6 chn. Thomas an orig. stockholder of the National Bank of Cambridge, OH, and res there. He d 1876 age 66. The father of Thomas, and his sister, Martha LE PAGE BICHARD, qv, owned commercial sailing vessels and was lost at sea. The chn were brought to GCO 1818 by an aunt, when Thomas was 10 and Martha 7 yrs. old. Six LE PAGES are said to have come about this time, relatives of Thomas and Martha. Prob more data in GCO. (Sarchet; Williams; Conner-Eynon; Mrs. Frank Le Page, Lake Worth, FLA; STORY OF GUERNSEY CO.)

A1. Simon, d as young man, but said to have left chn?

A2. Peter, mar Mary Ann Rollinson 1850. He served in Civil War, resGCO

B1. Rev. John, b ca 1886 rem to Boston, where he mar 1913 Irene Lowden and poss d 1926?

B2. Rev. Samuel Maynard, b ca 1885, mar 1912 Rosetta Pearl Jones of S. Hamilton, MA, was minister in Rowley, MA 1930s.

A3. Cyrus, mar Elizabeth Rollinson, Rollingstone? 1857

A4. Cornelius, served in 197th OH in the Civil War. Mar 1. Nancy Myers and 2. Mary Jane Miller.

A5. Adam, b 1839 mar Elizabeth Jane/Jennie Smith 1865, dau of John and Isabel (Riggs) Smith, b 1838 Antrim, Ireland, to OH ca 1840. Adam served in Civil War. One record says he rem to WI, and chn are not verified: John Smith, Lilly Ann, b 1867, Myrtle F., Ida M., Lute A., Thomas M., Rebecca Alice, mar Daniel Rankin?, Malinda W, Mary Jane.

A6. Martha, called Mattie mar James Burnsworth, 2 sons, Le Page and James Burnsworth served in Civil War.

A7. Mary Jane, mar John Campbell of a Scotch-Irish fam, 14 chn: Thomas, Margaret Ann, James, John, Andrew, Mattie, Amanda, William, Cornelius, Charles, Nathaniel, Mary and Samuel Campbell. Dates may be available in County Court House, Cambridge, OH.

A8. Rachel mar Jesse Buzzard and rem to KS.

A9. Nathaniel McCoy Campbell Le Page, b 1841 mar 1. Susan Lavina Lasure b 1844, mar 1861, d 1864, 2 daus. He mar 2. 1864 Mary Eliz. ROSE, b 1847, d 1881. Mar 3. Mary Ellen McVicker, 1883, no issue, d 1907 9 chn by 2 wives.

B1. Lilly Maybell, b 1862, eloped to NYCity. B2. Floretta b 1864,d.y.

B3. Charles Abram, b 1866, mar 1. Charlotta Bozman 1890, who d 1931, 2 chn. Mar 2. Bessie Gwinn 1934, who d 1950. Charles d 1962.

C1. Ada, b 1892 mar Charles Clark BIRD, 1894-1954

D1. Betty Jean Bird, b 1925 mar ___Bryant

C2. Frank Bozman, mar 1922 Ethel Albright, 3 chn: Robert Arch, Frances, and Rev.? Frank A. LE PAGE.

B4. Leona Ann, b 1868 d 1946, mar 1. John Wm. Chester and 2. Judson Silvester Milhone in 1932

B5. Cora Isadora, b 1871 mar Wm. Elmore Smith, b 1867 in 1891.

C1. Leona Ann Smith b 1891 C2. Bessie C. Smith, b 1894

C3. Mary Irene Smith, b 1896

B6. Thomas Franklin, b 1873 Richland Twp., GCO
B7. William Bert, b 1876 d 1945 B8. Mary Adelia, b 1879 d 1887
A10. Thomas, mar Mary Ferguson in GCO, Nathaniel Edmond, b 1867
A11. Mary A12. a ch d.y.
LE PAGE, Martha, sister of above Thomas, mar James BICHARD, 7 chn. See family under BICHARD.
There is a large LE PAGE family in book, Q.A. IN CANADA, p. 384,385, which is partly in error, and below is a chart to correct the fam of Elisha Jr. (Lola Le Page, Southbury, CT)
LE PAGE, Elisha, 1764-1813, from G to Charlottetown, PEI, Canada. He is bur there in Elm St. Cem. Mar Margaret Dufrecy.
A1. Elisha, 1787-1813, bur Elm St. Cem, mar Elizabeth ___.
B1. Elisha Columbus, 1808-1885, mar Maria Blatch, 1804-1865. At least 5 chn: Louisa, Elizabeth, Eliza and Emma, who mar Buntain and
C5. Elisha Christopher, 1845-1928, mar Millicent Woolner
D1. Oliver Cromwell, 1874-1942, mar Amelia Bell MacMillan,1875-1954
D2. Wm. Bradford, 1876-1958, mar Harriet E. Christie, 1875-1961
D3. Clara Woolner, 1878-1948, mar ___Dupee
D4. Elisha Chester, 1878-1948, mar Bessie MacKenzie, 1884-1960
D5. Emma May, d.y. D6. James F., b 1892, mar Lucy MacKenzie
D7. Garfield, 1881-1962, mar Martha Bulman, 1883-1937
B2. Alfred, 1810-1883, mar Emma Spratt, 1814-1890
C1. Frederick, 1838-1910 mar Eliz. Passmore, 1841-1907
D1. Annie Louisa, 1867-1933 mar Charles Black, D2. Bessie E. d.y.
D3. Arthur Fred., 1870-1954 mar Agnes Caw Smith, 1877-1970
D4. Fannie Laura, 1872-1953 D5. Frank C., 1873-1898
D6. Aubrey Johnson, 1875-1942 mar Florence M. Armstrong, 1880-1944
D7. Mary Passmore, 1878-1928 D8. Elsie E, b1880 mar Gladstone Mac-
D9. Ella Georgina, 1882-1953 D10. Abbie E.1884-1950. Donald
C2. Lemuel, 1840-1914, mar Mary Snelgrove, 1842-1906
D1. Connie, 1868-1937 mar ___MacNamara
D2. Ethel Lucretia, 1869-1956 mar Herbert Wheeler
D3. William Morley mar Jessie Broatch D5. Mary, d 1938
D4. James Harold, 1885-1944 mar Nellie Rushworth
C3. William, 1849-1919 mar Ruth Abbie Mayo, 1854-1923
D1. Nelson Spratt, 1876-1950, mar Ellen Mabel Le Page,b1876
D2. Willie Havelock, d.y. D3. Earnest B., b 1878, d.y.
D4. Wilbur E., b 1879, d.y. D5. Ethel b 1881
D6. Alfred Wolseley, 1883-1956, mar Madge A. Blackman, b 1904
C4. Alfred, b 1842 d 1916, mar Helen Taylor
D1. Alfred, b 1870, mar ___ D2. Emma Jane, b 1872
D3. Hattie L., 1874-1909 D6. Eva Ernestine, 1881-1887
D4. Ellen Mable, 1876-1940, mar Nelson Spratt, see above
D5. John Taylor, 1878-1965, mar Minnie Ethel Burtt, d 1959
D7. Martin Lemont, 1883-1884 D8. Charles Spratt, b 1887
C5. Henry, 1854-1943, mar Margaret A. Moore, 1866-1939
D1. Albert Edward, 1887-1968 mar 1. Louisa Arnott, 1887-1936, and 2. Florence Johnston, b 1892
D2. Bessie Louise, b 1888 d 1956 mar Norman COLLETT, 1887-1946, some COLLETT data in JOHN HEMSTREET, by W.M. Rosewarne, Ottawa,O.
D3. Herbert Moore, 1891-1898 D7. Anna Emma, b 1900
D4. Dorothy M., 1892-1923, mar Douglas Chrighton, 1891-1954
D5. Harry Aylesworth, 1894-1922 mar Marjorie Bickel, b 1897
D6. Lillian Irene, b 1896 mar 1. Cecil Brydon Wood, 1892-1922 and 2. Walter Twigg, 1889-1927.
D8. George Morley, b 1902 mar Evelyn Carter, b 1902

C6. Emma Lucretia, b 1844 d 1934, mar John D'Orsey, 1835-1884
D1. Alfred D'Orsey D2. Fred D'Orsey D3. Hensley D'Orsey
D4. John Ezra James D'Orsey, 1880-1956 mar Olive Ann Shaw,1904-1958
C7. Elizabeth, 1845-1922 mar C.M. Atwood C8. Julia, 1852-1921
C9. Ellie, mar ___Dawson, 7 chn: Fred, Beatrice, Erna, Will, Glendon Ernest and Laurie Dawson
C10. Louisa, 1836-1859
A2. John Nicholas, 1792-1824, bur Elm St. Cem., Charlottetown, PEI
A3. Margaret, 1793-1848, mar Richard Rollings, 1775-1852, bur So. Rustico Cem., PEI. See Q.A. IN CANADA for more on this fam.
A4.? Octavius, 1808-1878 A5.? Napoleon, some doubt on these two.
LE PAGE. "My grandparents...came from St. Peter Port G to this country ca mid 1800s. They were mar 1871 Eastchester, NY,(later incorp. with Mount Vernon, NY)...had a greenhouse in Mt. Vernon, and "at least two children." (Mildred B. Bishop, Lakehurst, NJ)
A1. Nicholas mar and had 3 chn: Wilbur, Hillary and Lois
A2. John mar Sophie De Voe LE RAY, 1871, 4 chn
B1. Amy Beatrice, b 1876 d 1916, mar Arthur F. Babcock 1903
C1. Mildred M. Babcock, mar Wm. H. Bishop Jr. 1930, 3 chn
D1. Marjorie Dale Bishop, b 1932 mar Everet F. Hier 1955, 2 chn
E1. Shirley Ann Hier, b 1956 E2. Gordon Bruce Hier
D2. Wesley E. Bishop mar Elizabeth J. Cotterill 1958, 3 chn
E1. Scott Wesley Bishop b 1959
E2. Gregg Mitchell Bishop b 1961 E3. Jonathan D. Bishop, b 1965
D3. Donald S. Bishop, mar Louise E. Salva 1966, 2 chn
E1. Glenn Peter Bishop b 1967 E2. Jill Karen Bishop, b 1968
B2. John DE GARIS, mar Jennie L. Beck, a dau.
C1. Helen Louise mar Wm. H. Chamberlain 1926, a du.
D1. Joan Le Page Chamberlain b 1932 mar Ralph G. Engelsman Jr.
E1. Marc Wm. Englesman E2. Daniel Garis Engelsman
B3. Marion Harriet, unmar B4. Gertrude Sophia, unmar
LE PAGE, see also COLLINGS.
LE PAGE, Samuel b ca 1740-45 G, son of ___LE PAGE and Esther DE JERSEY, qv, and grandson of Samuel LE PAGE. Esther DE JERSEY was dau of Susan LE PERNE? Samuel mar 1769 NYCity, Susan DE GRAY, said to be of a Hug. fam. Samuel d 1805 in Baltimore, MD. This fam was involved in a real estate settlement in G, middle 1800s, the lawyer in G being John OZANNE, qv. (Wm. Murphy, Denver, COL; Mrs. Robert Johnston, Portland, OR; SUMNER GEN; Henrietta Sollers; Rose Hutton, Columbia, MD; WRCIC; HIST. OF ST. JOSEPH CO., MI; NATL. CYCLO. OF AMER. BIOG, Vol 10; GILES MEMORIAL by J.A. Vinton; Fam Bible and records; Jan Lamb, Beaumont, TX)
A1. Samuel, b 1770s? 1780s? rem to OH, had at least 3 chn. Poss mar Hannah Johnson?
B1. Adelia, b 1804 Baltimore, MD mar 1836 Dr. Felix Benj. COLLINGS in Spencer Co., KY. He was b there 1808. She d 1866.
C1. John Eberley Collings, b 1836 d 1839
C2. Caroline Sarah Collings, b 1838 d 1913 mar 1855 Dr. E.F. McCammon
C3. George Felix Collings, b 1839 d 1974 Terre Haute, IND, mar Mary Ann M. MARTIN
C4. Clara Emma Collings, b 1840 d 1843
C5. Adelia Elmira Collings, b 1842 mar 1862 Dr. S.I. Bell, d 1886
C6. Mary Eliz. Collings, b 1844 mar 1864 Capt. Steven Franklin Crabb
D1. Adelia Mary Crabb, b 1865 d 1957, age 92, mar 1891 James Wm. Pittenger.
D2. Myrtle Harper Crabb, b 1867, d 1955 unmar
D3. Wm. Samuel Crabb, b 1869 d 1938, mar Amy Rogers

D4. Carrie/Caroline Thorne Crabb, b 1870 mar 1894 Charles Francis Pittenger, and d 1950
D5. Sarah/Sally Lela Crabb b 1872 Elk Creek, Spencer, KY, d 1958 Roswell,NM, mar 1. 1896 Leonard Rozell Pittenger, Sr. and 2. Robert J. Paden 1921. Mar 3. ___Adams in 1921.
D6. Collings Benj. Crabb, b 1874 Spencer Co., KY d 1935, mar 1899 Ella Bland Jewell, b 1876 d 1950. Collings d 1935, 11 chn. Ella the dau of Andrew Jackson and Sarah F. (Read) Jewell.
E1. Jewell Mae Crabb, b 1900 mar 1919 Mortie Walker Hundley
E2. Wm. Benj. Crabb, b 1903, d 1938 mar 1. 1925 Vera Rice, and 2. Louise Simms.
E3. Collings Clifton Crabb, b 1912 mar 1926 Thelma Humphrey
D7. Charles Bethuel Crabb, b 1876 d 1909 unmar
D8. Alexander Crabb, b 1877, d.y.
D9. Richard Moody Crabb, b 1880 d 1965 mar 1918 Oma James Polk
D10. Lewis or Lemuel Ellis Crabb b 1882 mar Meda ___, res Canada?
D11. Edward/Ned Le Page Crabb, b 1885 d 1959, mar 1906 Julia Eliz. Stoker, res Louisville, KY.
C7. Charles Algernon Collings, b 1846 KY d 1906, mar 1865 Florence B. Crume
B2. George Robert? Baptist minister, 1806-1872, mar 1835 Sarah A. COLLINGS, b 1806 Shelby Co., KY, d 1872, bur Bullet Co., KY, dau of Benj. COLLINGS and Sarah McGraw or McGrew. Sarah was sister of Dr. F.B. Collings.
B3. Elizabeth? mar Denmarks Shelburn in Spencer Co., KY.
A2. Hester/Ester, b 1770 NYCity mar Wm. Welling 1794, chairman of First NY Assembly.
B1. Mary Ann Welling, b 1795 d 1883, mar John Cronmiller Sr., MD, 1814 b 1793 d 1875. Of 9 chn, Isabel and Thomas, d.y. Eliza Jane, 1819-1866 and Susan Roberts, b 1822, d unmar. 1850
C5. William Welling Cronmiller, b 1825 d 1908, mar Mary Jane/Champayne
C6. Thomas Le Page Cronmiller, b 1827 d 1864, Howard Co., MD, mar Joshuaine Gardner, 1832-1915, 3 chn. D2.not found.
D1. Le Page Cronmiller, b 1861 d 1937 mar Susan Boyer Bansemer 1880
E1. Honora Selby Cronmiller, b 1887 d 1977, mar 1911 Haskett Lynch Conner, M.D.
F1. Haskett L. Conner Jr., Col USArmy b 1916, mar Sybil W. Parslow of England 1950, dau Sheila Conner mar in Dublin, Ireland to Hilary LE QUESNE Stuart Williams, son of a C.I. fam. Son Owen Lynch Conner b 1961 Carmel, CAL.
E2. Eliza Gardner Cronmiller, b 1888 d 1955 mar Ogle Marbury 1915 in Laurel, MD, a dau Anne b 1916 mar David E. Oberweiser of WIS 1943, had son Edward b 1947
E3. Susan Le Page Cronmiller, 1890-1952, mar Geo. Steiger, no issue
E4. Joseph Cronmiller, b 1898 d 1957, not married
E5. Le Page Cronmiller Jr., b 1900 Laurel MD, bur Arlington Cem. Mar 1930 Jeanne Gravatte
F1. Jeanne Woodward Cronmiller b 1933 mar Payton Lamb of Beaumont, TX, 4 chn: Jeanne E., Susan P., Margaret L. and Gloria M. Lamb, b 1959-1966 in Beaumont, TX
D2. ? D3. Thomas Cronmiller b 1864 d 1903 MD. Mar 1900 Josephine Dean Smith of Baltimore, MD, 1 ch.
E1. Rosalva Gillet Cronmiller, b 1902 Laurel, MD mar 1924 Balt. Ulric O. Hutton of Montgomery Co., MD.
F1. Thomas Watkins Hutton b 1927 mar 1954 Barbara Ann Brooks of NY Res Doylestown, PA, 3 chn: Janney, Geo. and Janet Hutton

F2. Mary Brook Hutton, b 1930 mar 1961 Michael D. Papagiannis, res Lexington, MA, 2 chn: Demetrios and Christina
C7. Catherine Cronmiller, b 1829, d ca 1912 Laurel, MD
C8. Dr. John Cronmiller, b 1832 mar Laura Jane Heath 1868
C9. Hester Welling Cronmiller, b 1835, d 1920 Baltimore, MD, mar 1887 Alfred Cole.
B2. Eliza Welling mar Rev. Bart McCreagh, 2 chn: Fidelia and Anthony
B3. Samuel Le Page Welling mar Hannah Hussey
C1. Hester Ann Welling mar Watson Sumner 1841 at Mottville, MI.
D1. George Watson Sumner, b 1841 Constantine, MI, d 1924 Patchogue, NY, served in Navy in Civil War, Comm. Rear-Admiral 1899. Mar 1. Henrietta Eliza Ruan, b 1850 St. Croix, Virgin Islands, dau of John and Henrietta (Kraus) Ruan, 6 chn. She d 1885. He mar 2. Maudethild, dau of Wm. H. and Joanna (White) Willis. The last ch of this fam d.y., Henrietta.
E1. Florence Watson Sumner, b 1869 Brooklyn, NY d 1913 Wilsonville, NEB, mar Walter N. Giles, see fam below.
E2. Alice Blythe Sumner, b 1872 mar Clay John Halverson 1899 in Wash., DC, and d 1905. Dau Henrietta R. mar Allan A. Sollers 1933 Laurel, MD.
E3. George Watson Sumner, b 1874 d 1964 Brooklyn, NY
E4. John Saxton Sumner, b 1876 Wash., DC d 1971, mar 1904 Eloise Peckham.
E5. Georgine/Helen L. Sumner, b Wash., DC mar Sidney Weber Brewster
D2. Mary Elizabeth Sumner, b 1844 d 1845 MI.
D3. Jeannette Judson Sumner, physician, b 1846, d 1906 Wash., DC.
C2. Margaret H. Welling,d unmar.
C3. Elizabeth Fulton Welling, b 1835 Cold Water, MI, adoptedby her cousin, Mrs. Hannah Ireland in NYCity when her parents died. Eliz. mar Walter H. Giles, missionary in Turkey, where he d 1867
D1. Walter Newell Giles, b 1866 Cappadocia, Turkey, mar Florence Sumner, see her fam above.
E1. Elizabeth Welling Giles, b 1895 NEB, mar 1915 Chalmers Lee Johnston in Wilsonville, NEB.
F1. Donald Sumner Johnston, b 1917 Bridgeport, NEB, RR Engineer, mar 1947 Dorothy Nicholson, R.N., b 1920 Laporte, IND, dau of Arthur and Alma (Snyder) Nicholson, 2 chn: Cheryll Argall and Wm. Donald Johnston.
F2. Helen Irene Johnston, b 1921 NEB, mar 1941 Eldon Elery Lincoln b 1920 Bayard, NEB son of Elery R. and Nellie (Whitman) Lincoln. 3 chn: Kenneth R., Richard K. & Michael Lee Lincoln
F3. Robert Giles Johnston, b 1924 Bridgeport, NEB, served in WWII, mar Patricia Ann Gansneder, R.N., b 1925 Portland, OR, dau of Fred J. and Margaret, 3 chn: Christopher, Fred. and Teresa.
E2. George Herbert Giles, b 1892 Culbertson, NEB mar Elsie __ no chn
E3. John Howard Giles, b 1903 twin, mar Lucille CARTER, 3 chn.
F1. Shirley Ann Giles b 1942 mar John H. Quella, a son Chad Quella
F2. James Walter Giles, b 1945 mar Karon Irene De Buhr, 2 chn: Tiffany Lynn and Lindsay Leigh Giles
F3. Florence Alice Giles, b 1950 mar Wm. A. Owen, 3 chn: Kimberlee, Kevin and Elizabeth Owen, b NEB.
E4. Gilbert Sumner Giles, b 1903, twin, mar Edwina, no issue
C4. Col. George R. Welling, served in KY Union Cav. Civil War.
D1. Edith Welling, res Louisville, KY during 1890s
C5. William Mitchell Welling C6. Edward Le Page Welling
B4. Susan Welling mar Harry Moore.
C1. Col Henry Moore, servd in Civil War under Gen. Geo. McClellan

C2. William Welling Moore, some members res Mamaroneck, NY
C3. Thomas M. Moore C4. Mary Moore C5. Elizabeth Moore
A3. Jane, mar Phillip Vanderlip of NY A4. Margaret mar Samuel GALE
A5. Susannah Morel, b 1781 Albany, NY mar Geo. ROBERTS 1797, b 1766 Easton MD.

Many LE PAGES recorded in the Conner-Eynon Cem. book, of Guernsey Co., OHIO, and others in Muskingum Co., OHIO. See List in WRCIC.

LE PAGE, Nathan was in Shelby Co., KY 1810, 3 sons and 2 daus. OUTC

LE PAGE, Nicholas, b G, son of Thomas BLONDEL LE PAGE, to US 1800s. His mother was Mary Ann DE GARIS. He was a cousin of John, Thomas and Norman , noted below. (Edw. Le Page, Grimsby, ONT)

LE PAGE, Rowland, mar in Salisbury, MA 1733/34 Hannah, prob dau of Samuel Winch of York, ME. OUTC. (Noyes)

LE PAGE, Peter, B G, age 26, of Hamilton, ONT, son of John and Mary (Saunders) LE PAGE, mar 1859 in St. Mary's RC Church, Hamilton, ONT, Honora Kennedy, age 22 of Hamilton, b Ireland, dau of Michael and Honora (Sealey) Kennedy. (Wentworth Co. Mar. Reg; Wm. Britnell)

LE PAGE, Samuel mar Charlotte Correll in GCO, a dau Eliza E, b1879.

LE PAIGE, Susanna mar 1738 in Boston MA, Robert Fouracres, OUTC.

LE PAGE, Thomas, John and Norman, sons of Thomas DE GARIS LE PAGE and Emma HOCART, HOCQUARD?, rem to US in the 1800s. (Edw. Le Page, Grimsby, ONT)

LE PAGE, Thomas, b 1813 G, d 1869, bur Adams Twp., GCO

LE PAGE, Thomas, b 1817 G, d 1889 GCO, mar Mary OGIER, 1829-1901.

LE PAGE, William, mar Hattie Lowry, dau of James and Adeline (Eaton) Lowry of Knox Twp., GCO.

LE PATOUREL in St. Martin G 1700, curr in G. See also PATRILL, etc.

LE PATOMAL, Elias James, age 24, b G, son of Thomas and Julia LE PATOUREL?, mar Margaret LANGLOIS 1859 in Hamilton, ONT. Margaret was age 23, dau of Thomas and Margaret LANGLOIS of G. (Wm. Britnell)

LE PATOUREL, Arthur James, b 1881 St. Peter Port G, d 1962 Cayley, ALTA, Canada. J. Lewis Le Patourel, his bro, also rem to Alberta. See Q.A. IN CANADA, by Turk.

LE PATOUREL, Alfred, b G, mar Emily GAUDION, qv, rem to Allentown, PA 1886 for 18 mos., returned to G, where other chn were born. (Eliz. Powell, West Grove, PA)

A1. Marcus, b ca 1887? PA.
A2. Francis, Frank, b 1889 La Ramee, G, to New Hampshire 1909/1910, then to PA. Mar in G, Miriam Flere BISSON OGIER, qv, b 1893 La Vrangue, G, dau of John and Emma Flere (Bisson) OGIER. He brought G cattle to America, exported by his father Alfred LE PATOUREL. They settled at La Ramee, a farm ouside of West Grove, PA.
B1. Elizabeth Ogier, b 1928 mar 1950 J. Lewis Powell, son of Jeremiah Ware Powell and Amy Hanna Pusey Powell of Avondale, PA, from Hancock's Bridge, NJ.
C1. Jeremiah Ware Powell II, b 1952
C2. Frank Le Patourel Powell, b 1954, mar 1981 Lynne Ann Benson,b1957
C3. Elizabeth Flere Powell, b 1956 C4. Wm. P. Powell, b 1958

LE PATOUREL, Anthony from G to PA 1900s.

LE PATOUREL, Ada Maud, d in Australia in her late 90s. Mar Charles Gay ROWCLIFFE, qv, of a G fam. She lived most of her life in G. (Irene Rowcliffe, St. Lambert, QUE)

LE PELLEY in G 1331, in St. Saviour G 1647, in Sark Island 1700s. Cf LE PELLETIER of J, and PELIER, PELLIER of G. Curr G. See Q.A. IN CANADA. See also LA SERRE.

PELLEY is a surname of Poole and Dorsetshire, england and poss of other English counties. Some data below is unverified. CAUTION!

PELLEYS of Nfld. are thought to have come both from C.I. and from England. Those of Nova Scotia, who removed to New England, not verified as from G to date. Some research done by Mary Ann Gallup of Swampscott, MA.

LE PELLEY, Alfred from G to US before 1910, b 1883 G, d 1969 US. Lumberjack and surveyor. (Mable Le Pelley, Guernsey)

LE PELLEY, Charles, a plumber in Cleveland, OH 1901. OUTC

LE PELLEY, Edward, from G to Chicago, ILL late 1800s.

LE PELLEY, Edward from Le Manoir, St. Stephen G, to US. His grandson was Guernsey LE PELLEY, noted Christian Science Monitor cartoonist.

LE PELLEY, Ella CARRE, mar in Cohasset, MA 1928, prob from G or NS,Can.

LE PELLEY, Ernest, b 1892 d 1926 Phila., PA. (GEN. SOC. OF PA, Vol 12)

LE PELLEY, Gladys, from from G or Nova Scotia mar Bernard S. Toothaker 1929 Boston, MA. OUTC

LE PELLEY, Harold 21, res Saugus, MA mar 1925 Sarah McCormack, age 19, dau of Wm. H. and Mary E. Kenney. Harold b Halifax, NS, son of John and Amelia.

LE PELLEY, Henry, b G, to Ogden, UT ca 1891, mar Julia Hamelin LAISNE, qv, qv, also b G. One ch: Gordelia DE GARIS LAISNE LE PELLEY. Henry d, and widow and ch returned to G. Gordelia/Delia mar there Emile MAHY, qv, of Vale, G. (C. Nitka, Col. Spgs., COL)

LE PELLEY, James d in Prince George, MD 1747. OUTC.

LE PELLEY, John B G, age 30 in 1806, Capt of the brig FLYING FISH, was 5'4", dark comp, certified 1806 in Charleston, SC as being an American citizen. This may have been a form of protection against privateers of of the time, whose countries were waging admitted and unadmitted actions against the British at sea. (Article in GUERNSEY WEEKLY PRESS, July 15, 1976)

LE PELLEY, John of Boston, b Nova Scotia, son of John and Amelia LE PELLEY, mar 1934 Margaret MacPhee, 23, b Brockton, MA, dau of James or Joseph MacPhee and Hannah Lyons in Boston, MA. See Harold above, a brother. (Mary Ann Gallup, Swampscott, MA)

LE PELLEY, John, son of John and Marie, d Boston 1927, b Eng. or C.I.

LE PELLEY, John F., d 1964 Saugus, MA age 33, mar Barbara Tailieri. He was son of Wm. and Margaret (Lewis) LE PELLEY, b Nova Scotia.

LE PELLEY, Margaret from N.S. fam? mar Robert Gillespie, who d 1975, age 48, in Saugus, MA, 3 chn: Sharlon L., Robin M. & Wm. Gillespie.

LE PELLEY, Philip mar 1926 in Palmer, MA.

LE PELLEY, Richard, arrived in MD 1664, some desc to KY. OUTC

LE PELLEY, Wilfred, unmar b 1879 G, d Los Angeles, CAL, bro of Alfred above. (Mabel Le Pelley, Guernsey)

LE PELLEY, Wm. C., 19, res E. Boston, b Halifax, NS, son of John and Millie Earl. He mar 1925 in Chelsea, MA.

LE PELLEY, William G., a carpenter in Cleveland, OH.1901 OUTC

LE PELLEY, William R., paperhanger, res Cleveland, OH 1901. OUTC

LE PELLEY, curr in Tacoma, WA. There is said to be a LE PELLEY from G in most states of the Union. (MAbel Le Pelley, G)

LE PELLEY, several from G to Chicago, To CT, OH, MA, GA, etc.

LE PELLEY, some res for generations on Sark Island, and are said to be the descendants of the Viking Prince Harry. (G. LE PELLEY, Sharon, CT)

LE PEVEAU, see PEAVEAR

LE POIDEVIN in G 1331. In Vale G 1821. CIFHS #6, #14. Current and common in G. LE PETEVIN dit LE ROUX in St. Lawrence J 1788. LE POIDEVIN in St. Brelade and St. Peter J 1668, in St. Peter J 1749.

Note that PEDVIN, in various forms occurs in Mid-West America. OUTC. Note also that letters from Guernsey spoke of a LE POIDEVIN fam as PEDVIN.

LE POIDEVIN, Jean/John, b 1819 G, d 1896. He and bro Thomas came to Racine, WI and from there went to CAL 1842. He returned to G and wrote about his trip in French. This was translated into English by a cousin in Jersey, Jean Le Poidevin, a musician, who later lived in England until about 1970. See PERSONAL ACCOUNT. (Mrs. Richard L. Le Poidevin, Rockford, ILL)

LE POIDEVIN, Thomas, bro of Jean above, went on the trip to CAL, was b 1816 G, d 1876 Racine, WIS.

LE POIDEVIN, Walter, poss a son of Thomas?, b 1857 Racine, d there 1927, mar Lucy REMON, qv, b 1863 G? d 1947. A dau Olive d.y.

A2. Elsie Maude, b 1885 mar 1909 James Arthur Hanson, b 1883, exec. with Eisendroth Tannery in Racine, WIS, d 1969 Racine.

B1. Everett Arthur Hanson, b 1910 mar Helen Coe 1935, res Eagle River, WIS, and North Redington Beach, FLA in winter, 3 chn

C1. James Coe Hanson, b 1939 mar Mary Ann Foertch 1961, 3 chn: James, Elizabeth and Catherine Hanson.

C2. Linda Karen Hanson, b 1941 mar John Huenink 1963. 3 chn: James, Brenda and John L. Huenink

C3. Sharon Elizabeth Hanson, b 1946 mar Donald Schroeder, 4 chn: Scott, Erick, Ian and Tad James Schroeder.

B2. Roy K. Hanson, mar Ann Donaldson Smiles, res Beloit, WIS, 5 chn: Suzanne, Stephen, William, Sally and Robert Hanson

A3. Walter William b 1889 Racine, d 1968 Silver City, NM. Mar Frances Louise Mahler 1921 in WA. Worked for Western Union for 50 yrs. Rode in US Cav. at the Mexican border, served in communications, WWI. Louise b WA 1898. A son Walter d.y.

B2. Frances Andrea, b 1924 Seattle, WA mar 1945 John Paul Schumaker, of USNavy, res Mesa, AZ

C1. John Steven Schumaker, b 1949 d 1974

C2. Frances Ann Schumaker, b 1945 mar 1967 Kenneth Murray, 2 chn: Elena and Kelley John Murray.

B3. Leigh Wade, b 1925 Seattle, WA mar 1974 Monika Steiniger in Port Elizabeth, South Africa. Res St. Charles, LA.

B4. Lucy Jane, b 1927 mar 1948 Robert Wynkoop, res Lake Havasu, AZ.

C1. Nancy Ann Wynkoop, b 1955 mar 1976 Robert Repp, res Snohomish, WA, a dau.

B5. Nancy Louise, b 1930 Seattle, mar Donald Maxwell, dentist, 1952, res Silver City, NM.

C1. Denise Michele Maxwell, b 1956 res Houston, TX, mar Rex West

C2. Donald Scott Maxwell, b 1958

B6. Richard Louis, b 1930, twin of Nancy, mar 1956 Catherine Wood, Moline, ILL, 4 chn: Laura Jane b 1957, Richard W., Dana Michael, and Roy Thomas, b 1968.

A4. Harry R., b 1896 Racine, WIS d 1979, mar 1. Eda? and 2. Nora, poss 3. Eleanor? Served in WWI Navy, was Racine publisher.

B1. Dr. Jean of Waterloo, IA, pediatrician

B2. Gwyn Carol, b 1923 Racine, mar 1946 LaVerne T. Laustsen, b 1921, Beresford, SD, res Aberdeen, SD, 2 chn

C1. David Scott Laustsen, b 1947 Racine, mar in CT Jean Barnum, b NJ. 2 chn: Sacha and Darren

C2. Judith Jean Laustsen, b 1950 mar 1972 Scott V. Kernon, b TX. A dau Ann Meredith Kernon.

B3. Jack S. of Racine, mar Pat ___, 3 chn: Dean, Linda J. & Gail.

LE POIDEVIN, Michael GOUDION or GAUDIAN, b 1849 G, son of Michael G. and Elizabeth(DE SAUMAREZ) LE POIDEVIN. Michael, the father, was b in G, but the mother was born in Paris, France. Michael left home very young, and finally settled in Pensacola, FLA where he d 1912.

Michael mar Sena Brown 1876, who shortly died. He mar 2. 1877 Savine Brown. Michael returned with a small fam to G, ca 1878 or 1880, where the next ch was born 1882. Michael returned to FLA, where he worked on the Revenue Cutter PENROSE as a lighterman, on ships such as the lighter LOUISIANA, taking cargo to larger ships that anchored in the Pensacola Bay. The cargo was mostly lumber. This fam is related to the ROBIN and OZARD fams of G. (Regina Walker, Pensacola, FLA)

A1. Elizabeth Ann, b 1870s Trout Bayou, Santa Rose Co., FLA mar 1897 in Pensacola, FLA Carl Ropke, 8 chn: Hilda, Mildred, Gladys, Elizabeth Anne, Carl, Robert and Albert Ropke.
A2. Michael Alexander, b 1882 G, d age 4 mos.
A3. Nora, b 1880s, mar 1901 Pensacola, mar Wilmer Walker.
B1. Ethel Frances Walker, b 1902 mar Wilmer Richard Hall, 1900-1976.
C1. Wilmer Richard Hall Jr., b 1926 Pensacola, FLA
C2. John Edward Hall, b 1933 Miami, FLA
B2. William Douglas Walker, b 1904 mar Thelma Louise Arnold, b 1906, and 2. Hazel F. De Freitas.
C1. Joanne Walker, b 1930 Pensacola, mar ___Russell
C2. Carolyn Louise Walker, b 1933 mar ___Soltys
C3. William Douglas Walker, b 1935, d 1979
C4. James Arnold Walker, b 1948 C5. and C6. by 2nd wife.
C5. Denise, b 1954 Georgetown, Guyana, SA, mar Rosenbloom.
C6. Allison, b 1955 S.A. mar ___Purser.
B3. Wilmer Walker, b 1906 mar Alma J. Brewton, b 1908, no issue.
B4. Lois Walker, b 1908 mar John James Murphy, b 1907 Kirkland, ALA
C1. Donald E. Murphy, b 1931 C2. John Richard Murphy, b 1936
B5. Catherine Mae Walker, b 1910 mar Joseph Michael Williams, b Beaumont, TX, 2 chn, and 2. Joe Davis Altman, 1 ch.
C1. Joseph Terrence Williams, b 1937 d 1979
C2. Patricia Ann Williams, b 1935 mar ___Margeson
C3. Linda Susan Altman, mar 1. __Holifield, and 2. ___Bray, b 1947.
B6. Oliver Raburn Walker, b 1912 d 1980 Pensacola, mar Wilma Aleene Huggins, b 1916 Bluff Springs, FLA, 2 chn.
C1. Wilma Janet Walker, b 1951 mar ___Cherry.
C2. Joyce Olivia Walker, b 1951, twin, mar 1. ___Hardy, 2. __Elliot, and 3. ___Knowles.
B7. Maurice Franklin Walker, b 1918 FLA mar 1. Clara Lee Boone, and 2. Mary Katherine Harry, b 1912 Fort William, Canada, d 1961 FLA. Maurice mar 3. Regina Higgins Knight, b 1918 Sardis, MISS. Regina has 3 chn by first husband; Harry, Shirley Blake & Sandra Mandel.
A4. Azeal Leo, b 1885 FLA mar Nina Parise, 3 chn: Azeal Leo, Virginia and Ferrel.
A5. Clifford, mar 1. Mary J. Brassel 1913, and 2. in 1917 Mary Eliza Grimes, 5 chn: Dani C., Thelma L, Kenneth G., Mary & James W.
A6. Enos Eldridge, mar 1923 Dora Mixon, 3 chn. He mar 2. Louise MAJORS no issue, and 3. in 1949 Martha Rebecca Zellena. Chn: Enos, Dorothy and James.

LE POIDEVIN, Thomas, b 1781 G, mar Elizabeth ___. (Noel Conger, Brookings, SD)

A1. Elizabeth b 1815 G A2. Marie b 1816 G
A3. Thomas, b 1817 G, d 1883 Est Martina, G, mar ___, a son Thomas. The wife of Thomas d 1896 at Boull, Vale, G.
B1. Thomas, who d in G? 1890. B2. Julia, mar John A. OGIER,son & dau.
B3. ___, a dau, mar Thomas A. HENRY, 3 chn: Ernest, Edith & Lilly.
A4. Daniel, b 1820 G, d 1906 Les Villets, Forest, G. Mar ca 1850 Jane Moore, b 1828 London, England d June 1878 Riverdale Twp., Watonwan

County, MINN, bur there. Daniel was a farmer, came to US ca 1852, res NYCity, then rem to St. Peter, Nicolette Co., MN then to Watonwan, MN. After the death of his wife Jane, Daniel returned to G, where he mar 2. a "French Lady". They made one visit to Minn. and Nebr. after their marriage,in 1899.

B1. Daniel PEDVIN, Jr, b 1852 NYCity, d 1906 unmar

B2. Jane PEDVIN, b 1855 NYCity, d 1929 St. James, MINN, unmar

B3. Thomas PEDVIN, b 1857 Belgrade Co., MN, d 1895 CAL. Bur Madelia, MN. Mar Luella Melick 1882 at St. James. She was b 1862 Putnam Co., ILL d 1945, dau of Nicholas A. Melick and Phebe Bradford, who was a desc of Wm. Bradford of the MAYFLOWER. Thomas was a grocer.

C1. Ada Blanche Pedvin, b 1884 Madelia, MN d 1965 Little Rock, CAL Mar 1906 Willard Leory MARTIN, b 1871 St. Charles, MN d 1941 Mpls, bur there. Son of Dr. Joshua MARTIN.

D1. Donald Leroy Martin, b 1906 Mpls, mar Ruth Thomas, b Bluffton, IND, dau of Ralph Thomas and Carol Stream.

E1. Ralph Thomas Martin, b 1930 Ripon, WI

E2. Peter Martin, b 1941 Ripon, WI

D2. Rodney Burnham Martin, b 1908 Mpls, MN mar 1933 Orpha Jane Jones b Bangor, WI, dau of Eben Jones and Albra Thomas, res LaCrosse.

E1. Jean Orpha Martin, b 1934 mar 1954 Stanley ROBERTS

E2. Rodney Douglas Martin, b 1936 mar 1958 Sally Koula

E3. Mary Albra Martin, b 1940 Whitehall, WI mar 1967 Barry Hast.

E4. Willard Burnham Martin, b 1942 LaCrosse, WI mar 1969 Kathleen Linton.

D3. Roger Frederick Martin, b 1910 Minneapolis, d there 1975. Mar 1935 Adeline Williams, b MN, dau of Ray & Elizabeth.

E1. Susan Martin, b 1941 mar 1966 Robert Fellers.

E2. Steven Martin, adopted b 1947 Mpls.

C2. Luella Mae Pedvin, b 1885 Madelia, MN mar 1913 John E. Larson

C3. Roscoe Thomas Pedvin, b 1888 Madelia d 1962 mar 1924 Eda W. Gaw.

C4. Jessie Melick Pedvin, b 1890 d 1965 Vernon Center, Blue Earth Co. MN, mar 1916 Luther J. Austin, b 1892

D1. Jean Austin, b 1918, d.y.

D2. Margaret Luella Austin, b 1922 mar Vernon Center 1942 Thomas H. MacKenzie, b 1918 MN, son of Delbert L and Jessie Marie, res COL

E1. Thomas Austin MacKenzie, b 1945 Key West, FLA mar 1976 Karen Hoagland

E2. Claudia Jean MacKenzie, b 1947 Lubbock, TX, mar 1972 Raymond A. Schemm. A son Thomas Andrew b 1977.

E3. Douglas Leroy MacKenzie, b 1953 Mpls.

E4. Mary Elizabeth MacKenzie, b 1956 Peoria, ILL.

D3. Mary Etta Austin, b 1925 Madelia, MN mar 1945 Bruce Edgar Hansen b 1922 MN d 1975, son of Christian P. and Glayds (Wyman) Hansen.

E1. Susan Diane Hansen, b 1946 mar 1966 Larry S. Cumming, 3 chn: Todd, Laura and Allison Cumming, b MN.

E2. Joel Bruce Hansen, b 1949 mar 1971 Ruth Louise Geistfield, 2 chn: Andrea and Christy b Coralville, IA.

E3. Jon Christian Hansen, b 1952 Vernon Center, MN.

E4. Jeffrey David Hansen, b 1956

D4. Ruth Harriet Austin, b 1927 mar 1946 Robert R. Bennett, b 1926 Garden City, MN, son of Ray John Bennett.

E1. Robert Mark Bennett, b 1948 Mankato, MN

E2. Diane Rae Bennett, b 1952 mar 1977 Dr. Bradley R. Nelson

E3. Alan Wayne Bennett, b 1955

C5. Hazel Belle Pedvin, b 1892 Madelia, d 1961, mar 1910 Arthur J. Jacobson, b 1892, d 1951 Brainard, MN on fishing trip.
D1. Hollis Jacobson, b 1911 mar 1937 Catherine Reynolds, b 1913, dau of James T. and Bessie (Yates) Reynolds. Hollis a grocer.
E1. Betty Jo Jacobson, b 1940 mar 1963 Dale Barrett, 3 chn: David, Jennifer and James Barrett.
E2. Patricia Catherine Jacobson, b 1943 Madelia, mar 1965 Lynn Abraham, 2 chn: Lisa and Tracy Abraham
E3. Christine Lucille Jacobson, b 1946 mar 1974 Roy McCabe, a dau Denise McCabe.
D2. Phyllis Jacobson, b 1916 d 1972 Rochester, MN. Mar 1935 Paul Harris Tatman, b 1915 WI, d 1968 bur Ft. Snelling Nat. Cem.,MN.
E1. Marcia Catherine Tatman, b 1936 d 1977, mar1. __Rice, and 2. Waldon Laverne Zoellmer, b 1937, son of Henry. A son David Rice d 1975
E2. Gary Arthur Tatman, b 1937 mar 1958 Sylvia Carol Gerske, 3 chn: Thomas, Linda and Christine Tatman.
E3. Robert Tatman, b 1939 Mankato, MN mar 1973 Linda May Bilgen
E4. James Dorance tatman, b 1947 mar Christine Audrey Olson, div, a dau Marisa Clair, b 1963
E5. Barbara Marie Tatman, b 1941 mar 1. 1959 Charles Lee Evenson, killed in accident 1962, mar 2. 1965 Richard A. Blackstad, b 1930. 4 chn, 2 by each husband: Brian, Kevin, Jeffrey & Rick.
D3. Ardelle Jacobson, b 1922 mar 1943 Fairmont, MN Fritz Krumholz, b 1908 WA, d 1971 Blythe, CAL. Ardelle a teacher.
E1. David Wm. Krumholz, b 1944 MN, mar 1967 Shiloy Speilman, div, a son Thomas, b 1967
E2. Susan Marie Krumholz, b 1945 mar 1968 Joseph Watkins, div, a dau Stephanie Watkins, b 1970.
E3. Margaret Ann Krumholz, b 1946 E4. Thomas, b 1948, d.y.
E5. Peter Krumholz b 1950
E6. Jean Eliz. Krumholz, b 1951 mar 1970 Rodney Sewell, div, 2 sons: Jeffrey and Mark Sewall
E7. Ann Marie Krumholz, b 1957 E8. Paul Francis Krumholz, b 1959
C6. Rodney Daniel Pedvin, b 1894 Madelia, d 1967. Mar 1930 Melva Aamodt, b 1905 MN, now retired school teacher. Res Mesa, AZ
B4. Rachel Pedvin, b 1859 Nicollet Co., d 1949 Seattle, WA. Mar 1878 MN, John Murphy b 1842 Ireland d 1908 Blue Earth, MN, son of Patrick Murphy and Bridget Pepper.
C1. Lulu May Murphy, b 1880 MN d 1964 Whittier, CAL, mar 1897 John Colvin Conger, b 1874 MN d 1954 Oroville, CAL. Div. Mar 2. 1907 John's bro. Wm. Farr Conger.
D1. Olive Arlina Conger, b 1898 De Graff, MN d 1918, mar Roy Godfrey son of Ralph and Nettie (Farr) Godfrey. (2nd cousins)
E1. Ralph Otis Godfrey, b 1918 mar Violet Mae Englund, res Mpls.
F1. Ramona F2. Sharlynn F3. Bonita F4. Julia Ann Godfrey
D2. Colvin De Witt Conger, b 1901 Lake Crystal, MN d 1955 WA, mar 1. 1926 Goldie Lena Morris, div and mar 2. 1936Violett Mae Hamm, 5 chn.
E1. Gordon Dean Conger, b 1926 CAL d 1974 Seattle, WA, mar 1950 Paula H. Laurie, b 1929, res Seattle, WA
F1. Marilyn Louise Conger, b 1951 mar 1971 Dan Warwick, and 2. James Howshall, 2 chn: Noel and Kathryn
F2. Carolyn Marie Conger, b 1951 Seattle, mar 1971 Paul Johnson, 3 chn: Seth, Jared and Tara Johnson
F3. Gordon Dean Conger, Jr, b 1953 Bremerton, WA
F4. Robert D. Conger, b 1956 mar Dan. F. Treichel, a son Daniel

F5. Paul Morris Conger, b 1958
F6. Edward Noel Conger, b 1960 F7. Ronald Alan Conger, b 1962
E2. Elizabeth Louise Conger, b 1937, by 2nd wife, Portland, OR, mar 1956 Richard Roll, b 1934, res Auburn, WA, 5 chn: Richard, Mark, Debra, Patricia and Michael Roll.
E3. Wilford Howard Conger, b 1938, d.y. 1943
E4. David Michael Conger, b 1941 mar 1960, div, mar 2. 1972, 2 chn: David and Justin Conger.
E5. John Colvin Conger, b 1946 Auburn, WA mar 1966 Coeur d'Alene, ID, Vicky Louise Lord, b 1945, dau of Geo. Robert Lord and Eliz. Louise Dionne. Res Houston, TX, 2 chn: John & Lesley Conger.
D3. Winifred Lucille Conger, b 1909, MN by second husband Wm. Farr Conger, mar 1935 Howard Stensrud, b 1909 Mpls, MN. No issue
D4. Noel Wm. Conger, b 1913 Olivia, MN mar 1938 Brookings, SD, Nellie Virginia McCormick, b 1914 Brookings, dau of Alex and Dora (Larson) McCormick, res Brookings, SD.
E1. William McCormick Conger, b 1938 Los Angeles, CAL, mar 1. 1961 Norma Brannock, in MD, who was b 1940, 3 sons: William, Kevin and Michael Conger.
E2. Sylvia Winifred Conger, b 1946 mar 1. 1964 Jerry Nelson, div, mar 2. 1971 Marlen Enser, div, mar 3. 1979 James Stoen,no issue.
C2. Kittie Olive Murphy, b 1884 MN d 1908, mar 1906 Samuel Smith, no issue.
C3. Wynn Mary Murphy, b 1888 d 1957 Seattle, WA, mar 1918 Benj. Randall, b 1876 Phila., PA, no issue
B5. Elizabeth Pedvin, b 1861 MN d 1948, mar 1882 Charles Edwin Fuller, b 1855 St. Lawrence Co., NY d 1939 St. James, MN, son of Edwin Fuller and Sarah Metcalf. Claim desc. from Sam.Fuller, MAYFLOWER.
C1. Edna Marion Fuller, b 1884 d 1974 mar 1906 John Roland Schoffman, b 1882, a dau Ann b 1915 d 1965, unmar
C2. Frederick Daniel Fuller, b 1885 MN d 1939 mar Hilvie Johnson, b 1886, d 1956, dau of John O. Johnson.
D1. Paul Loren Fuller, b 1908 mar 1938 Alma Anne Munsterman, b 1905, St. James, MN dau of August and Vinnie (Vohs) Munsterman.
E1. Joann Margaret Fuller, b 1940 St. James, mar 1961 Darwin Soderman, b 1935 St. James, 3 chn: Deborah, May Jo & James Soderman
E2. Loren Paul Fuller, b 1945 mar Judith Theneman, b 1946, no issue
D2. Irwin C. fuller, b 1910 MN d 1976, mar 1930 Erna Malwitz, b 1908 MN, dau of Charles Malwitz and Bertha Petsch.
E1. Irwin C. Fuller, Jr, b 1931 mar 1954, and div. Joan Mae Schiller, 4 chn: Rick, Mhana, Scott and Mark Fuller
E2. Marlitt Jane Fuller, b 1933 mar 1952 Robert Fihner, 4 daus: Ann Finhalt, Sue and Beth Fihner and Kim Stulc.
E3. Laurel Jean Fuller, b 1934 mar 1955 Donald Leroy Oseth, 3 chn: Jull, Tim and Kirsten Oseth.
E4. Terry Wayne Fuller, b 1940 MN mar 1960 Eilene Ethel Olson, 3 chn: Todd, Karin and Linda Fuller.
D3. John Charles Fuller, b 1919, MN mar 1941 Evaline Meyer, b 1923 Red Lake Falls, MN, dau of Bernard Meyer and Hulda Malwitz, res St. Paul, MN.
E1. Jane Eliz. Fuller, b 1942 mar 1969 Michael Twiest
E2. Kaethe Rae Fuller, b 1946 mar 1969 John Bisek
E3. Deborah Jean Fuller, b 1951 mar 1972 James Fikiowich
E4. John Thomas Fuller, b 1954 St. Paul E5. Kristine K. Fuller,1961
C3. Grace Mary Fuller, b 1887 St. James, MN d 1962, mar 1914 Hugo Stumm, b 1880 Avoca, MN d 1976, son of Franz Stumm and Anonia Peltzel.

D1. Robert Hugo Stumm, b 1916 mar 1943 Marion Jackson, b 1916 Dawson, MN, dau of Wm. T. Jackson & Nellie Wedge, res.St. Paul.
E1. Robert Jackson Stumm, b 1948 Newport News, VA.
D2. James Edwin Stumm, b 1919, mar 1954 Marian Louise Davis, b 1917 Beatrice, NEB, d 1966 Hopkins, MN, no issue. James and Marian were 3rd cousins, she being grgrandau of Nicholas LE POIDEVIN.
C4. Nina Gladys Fuller, b 1891 St. James, d 1970, Cleveland, OH. Mar 1910 Carl Wm. Johnson, b 1886 Red Wing, MN, d 1956 Detroit, MI.
D1. Catherine Vera Johnson, b 1911 MN mar 1. 1934 John G. Baehr, and 2. 1961, Harold H. Cook, res Scottsdale, AZ
D2. Alice Marion Johnson, b 1812/14 St. James, MN d 1942, mar 1930s Ralston Fox Smith
D3. Laura Gladys Johnson, b 1920 Cleveland, mar 1942 Wm. David Cameron Jr., b 1917 Chicago, ILL, res Chagrin Falls, OH. Chn b Detroit, MI.
E1. Lynn Eliz. Cameron, b 1946, mar 1967 Michael V. Dawes
E2. David Phillip Cameron, b 1948 mar 1970 Suzanne Myerholtz
E3. Carl Johnson Cameron, b 1953 mar 1977 Katerine Plummer.
E4. Catherine Alice Cameron, b 1953, twin, mar 1975 Robt.Anderson.
C5. Harry Edwin Fuller, b 1895 d 1946 Cleveland, OH mar 1922 Marie Fullerton b 1900 Joliet, ILL, dau of Richard T. Fullerton and Kathryn Roach.
D1. Bette Fuller, b 1922 Cleveland, mar 1. 1940 Robert A. Irish, an and 2. 1950 Raymond M. Bittence, b 1922 Cleveland, res AZ.
E1. Joyce K. Irish, b 1941 E. Cleveland, OH mar 1960 Donald H.AMY.
E2. Robert A. Irish, b 1943
E3. Judith A. Irish, b 1946 mar 1965 William Cook.
D2. Marjorie Fuller, b 1924 Cleveland, mar 1. 1945 Thomas Brenner, and 2. 1977 Charles R. Adams, res Manchester, CT.
E1. Lynn Marie Brenner, b 1946 E2. Christine D. Brenner, b 1948
E3. Wendy Fuller Brenner, b 1949 Euclid, OH.
C6. Grant Leo Fuller, b 1901 St. James, MN mar 1921 Mpls, MN, Mona Guge, b 1901 Story Co., IA, res Glendale, AZ
D1. Elaine Ruth Fuller, b 1923 Cleveland, mar 1944 Charles E. Anthony, div 1971.
E1. Peter Grant Anthony, b 1948 Cleveland, mar 1971 Sharon T. Vespie
E2. Jeffrey C. Anthony, b 1957 Euclid, OH
D2. Joan Gladys Fuller, b 1928 OH mar 1948 Peter Malvern Sterrie, b 1922 St. James, MN, res Fairhope, ALA
E1. Richard Grant Sterrie b 1956 E2. Kristine Elaine Sterrie, b/1961
E3. Jane Ellen Sterrie, b 1964 Mankato, MN
B6. John Pedvin, b 1863 St. Peter, MN d 1928 Sioux City, IA, mar 1. 1884 Carrie Oleson, b 1866 Cottage Grove, MN d 1919. Mar 2. 1922 Mrs. Jeannette Durlin, b 1875 d 1944 IA. John a RR man.
C1. Esta Luella Pedvin, b 1885 MN d 1887
C2. Laura Isabelle Pedvin b 1891 d 1967 Mpls, mar 1918 Lester H. Taylor, b 1896 IA, d 1969 Mpls, son of Jacob A. Taylor and Amelia Ayers.
D1. John/Jack Elliot Taylor, b 1921 St. James, MN mar 1947 Virginia Harrington, b 1924 Lincoln, NEB dau of Lewis A. and Alberta Mae (Iler) Harrington, res Mpls.
E1. Marilyn DeMaris Taylor b 1949 St. Paul, MN mar 1970 Albert L. Shopper, 2 chn: Emily and Sally Shopper, b Columbia, MO.
E2. Marc Elliot Taylor b 1951 Mpls, MN
E3. John Allen Taylor b 1954 E4. Jean Mari Taylor, b 1956

B7. Julia Ann Pedvin, b 1866 Watonwan Co., MN d 1896 mar Frank H. Newell. A dau Cora A. Newell, 1890-1901, Sioux City, IA
B8. Frederick William Pedvin, b 1868 Watonwan Co., MN d 1906/7 CAL. Mar Geneva Elnora Parmelee, who d 1954 Pasadena, CAL
C1. Bernard? Arnold Pedvin b 1896 IA mar Mollie? Florine?
D1. Melvin A. Pedvin b 1920 mar Ruth Elaine Madden 1942 Houston, TX
D2. Mildred B. Pedvin, mar 1942 Clarence W. Janke, Kingman, AZ.
D3. Fred.
C2. Veda Marion Pedvin, b 1899 mar 1. Curtis Underwood and 2. 1941 Howard Sheets.
D1. Roland Underwood, b 1926 mar Doris___, a dau Debra M. b 1956
B9. Evelyn/ Carrie? b 1870 MN d 1943 St. James, MN, mar Fulton,no chn.
A5. Marthe, b 1822 Guernsey
A6. Nicholas, b 1823 G, d 1891 Beatrice, NEB, mar Julia A. ___, b 1827, d 1911 Beatrice, used name LE POIDEVIN, not PEDVIN.
B1. Charles Nicholas, b 1848, d 1870 Beatrice, unmar
B2. Elizabeth b 1850, d 1923 Beatrice, mar Ezra Buswell, b 1844,d1906
B3. Louisa Le Poidevin, b 1854 Beatrice d 1928 Cobble Hill, B.C. bur Beatrice. Mar John Scribner, b 1845 d 1928.
C1. John Scribner, b ?, d 1951 Cobble Hill, BC, Canada, mar Marion_?
B4. Emma Le Poidevin, b 1858 Beatrice d 1909, mar Junius/Jude Wallace, 1855-1925.
C1. Will Wallace, d 1946 Sheridan, OR
C2. Charles E. Wallace, b 1886, d 1942, son Charles d.y.
C3. Earl Wallace, d 1954 Portland, OR bur Sheridan, OR, mar Hattie ___, who d 1951 Portland, bur Omaha, NEB
C4. Edith Wallace mar Art Elfeldt.
C5. Julia Wallace mar Ira Davis and rem to Portland, OR
D1. Marion Davis, b 1917 Beatrice d 1966 Hopkins,MN, mar James Edwin Stumm, grgrandson of Daniel PEDVIN.
C6. Pearl Wallace, b 1899 d 1914.
A7. Pierre, b 1826 A9. Rachel b 1829 G
A8. John/Jean LE POIDEVIN, b 1827 G, d 1902 Beatrice, NEB, mar Axie___, b 1844 d 1935 Beatrice, NEB.
B1. Elizabeth, d 1959, unmar
LE POIDEVIN, Job mar Rachel COLIN in G. Som of their chn came to US.
I. Thomas J., b 1840 St. Sampson G, ca 1863, came with bro John to Racine, WI where they farmed. In 1866 rem to NEB, where John farmed near Odell, mar Teanna Henrietta Tanner, 1847-1936, b Switzerland. Chn b Gage Co., NEBR. (Neil Conger, Brookings, SD; Marie Le Poidevin, Rockford, ILL) More data below.
II. Alfred, b 1840s G, mar Emma __, res Flushing, Long Island, NY, very wealthy.
A1. Ida, mar ___Walsh. She d 1963. (HIST. OF GAGE CO., NEBR)
B1. Donald Walsh, mar Dorothy ___, and res with Ida.
III. John, b 1842 G, rem to Beatrice, NEB 1868, mar 1873 Aphelia A. Martin, b 1855 in essex, NY, d 1916. 10 chn: Lillie B., Alfred, Clem, Phebe A. Zugmeir, Etta, Bertha R., Herbert, Job E., Grace, who mar O. Martin of Lincoln, NEB, and another ch?
IV. Joseph, b G, rem to NYCity 1800s, mar Hattie ___. Joseph a shipwright, at least 3 chn: Frank, Joseph and ?, res Manhattan, & CAL.
V. Alice, mar Martin ROBBIN, res G.
VI. Amelia, mar Nicholas MAHY, res G?
VII. Rachel, res G, had dau Lydia who lived to at least age of 90.
LE POIDEVIN, Thomas J, b 1840 St. Sampson, G, see above, 1st ch. (Marie Le Poidevin, Rockford, ILL; Neil Conger, Brookings, SD)
A1. Adelia Elvira, b 1869 d 1925, mar Lincoln A. Thornburg,1865-1956.

B1. Clifford T. Thornburg, mar Ruth Ellinger who d 1963 age 65
C1. Kenneth Thornburg, mar Viola, a son Keith mar and had Eugene, Keith, Dale, Jane and Kevin
C2. Oda, mar George Moore, no issue
C3. Howard L. Thornburg, unmar C4. Ruth Thornburg, unmar
C5. Vern Thornburg, mar Arlene, 3 chn: David, Betty & Michael
B2. Guy Thornburg, mar Grace ___
C1. Lowell Keith mar Vetta ___, res Denver, dau Denise R. Thornburg
C2. Donald Thornburg mar Elizabeth Thornburg, res Napa, ID, 2 chn: Dwayne and Patricia Thornburg
C3. Norman Thornburg mar Barbara ___, res UT, mar 2. Esther Brown. Curtis, by 1st wife, Tisha Marie, adopted, Farris, and Thelma.
A2. Amelia, or Alamede Louise, b 1870 d 1932, mar Edward Essam, b 1870
B1. Bernice, mar Earl Harris, no issue
B2. Gladys, mar Lloyd Bledsaw, 3 chn: Harold, Leonora who mar __Sapp, and Ralph Bledsaw.
A3. John Thomas, b 1872 d 1956, mar Lottie Kettering, 1878-1958
B1. Hazel
B2. Loree, mar Clarence Larsen, 4 chn: Marvin, Wayne, Ralph and Ruby, who mar Roland Hardin, all with desc.
B3. Verna mar Rankin Busboom. A dau Lois mar Clark Tinkner
A4. Bertha A5. Job A6 Jabel
A7. Ezra, b 1880 Midland Twp., NEB d 1966, mar 1909 Bessie Essam, 1889-1977, dau of Jacob and Mollie (BARTRAM) Essam. 2 daus, Irma b 1912 and Irene, b 1913.
A8. Charles Clinton, b 1882 d 1960 mar 1907 Mary BArnard, b KY, dau of George.
B1. Velma, b 1907, mar Wayne Cooper B4. Sandy, mar Gay Jacobson
B2. Lucille/Kay? b 1914 mar Kurt Jacobson, who d 1963
B3. Thomas, b 1918? mar Zillah Cooper, who d 1963
A9. Marie Alice, b 1884, living in 1977
A10. Josepine Inez, b 1886, d 1959 A11. Seba Jay, b 1889 d 1977

LE POIDEVIN, Willis Thomas, from G as a youth, to Racine, WI, mar Margaret Pheleger, rem to ID, bur 1924 Mountain Home, ID. Margaret d 1935 at Anaconda, MT. 4 chn.
A1. Elva Maude, b 1885 d at Bonner Ferry, ID 1972
A2. Kate Tina, b 1889 mar Cornell Segar, Bowbells, ND, d 1960s, 6 chn.
A3. Willis Thomas II, Bill, b 1891, mar Margaret Keely. He d 1960 at Bonner's Ferry, ID, 3 chn: Jean Marie, Willis III & Kenneth.
A4. Floyd Frederick, b1900 Pipestone, MN, rem to Bowbelles, ND then the two boys and the mother homesteaded in Rosebud Co., MONT. Floyd mar Christel B. Klar, Miles City, MONT 1934, 5 chn.
B1. Floyd William, b 1935 mar Mary Curl, Edgemont, SD 1960, res Broadus, MONT, 3 sons: Bert Floyd, Reed William & Cord Barnet.
B2. Harold Dell, b 1938 mar Joanne Snodderly 1960, res Spokane, WA, a son Errol Ray.
B3. Larry L., b 1943 mar Ruthadell Nokelby at Cando, ND 1964, Pastor at Albert Leo, MN, 2 daus: Lori Lynn and LaRae Dawn LE POIDEVIN
B4. Bonita Marie b 1944 mar 1966 Rev. Floyd O'Bryan, Rapid City, SD, res Rochester, MN, 2 sons: Stephen Jay & Allan Lee O'Bryan.
B5. Raymond Gene, b 1946 mar Cherly Horine 1970 res Spokane, WA, 4 chn: Rae Gene, Nicole, Joshua and Jeremy Lyle.

LE POIDEVIN, Ezekiel, res Essex Co., NJ, recorded 1884, prob from G. (STATE OF NJ WILLS AND INVENTORIES, Vol 1, 1912)

LE POIDEVIN, J., b 1809 G, d 1872, bur Oakwood Cem., Somers, WI, mar Judith FALLA, qv, b 1809 G, d 1874, bur Somers, WI.

POTVIN, John b 1798 Boston. OUTC. (NEHGS Vol 41)

LE POIDEVIN, Nicholas b 1798 G, d 1846 GCO. Nicholas a cousin of James BICHARD, qv, and poss the bro of John who went to Racine, WIS. A Nicholas PEDVENT mar Nancy O'Haver or O'Hara in GCO 1821. 1 ch? (Conner-Eynon)

A1. Sarah, mar James P. WILLIAMS, res Jackson Twp., GCO (Sarchet)

PEDWIN, Nicholas, poss same as above, had 160 acres in Jackson Twp., GCO in 1840. A J. H. Potwin & Co., was a Cambridge OH firm, 1800s.

LE PREVOST in J 1299. In St. Clement and St. Heliers J 1668 and 1749. Common and curr in G, there from 1331. Note that PREVOST and PROVOST may sometimes be confused. See Stevens book, OLD JERSEY FAMILY NAMES PROVOST and PREVOST both noted in early America.

PREVOST, Capt. N.M., ex sea Captain, b 1818 G, was at an early age Mate on one of the Cunard steamers, was also connected with the De Wolf line of steamships. Had traveled in all parts of the world, lived under five flags, captain of the bark G.L. NEWMAN, lost off Chicago at the time of the great fire. Res Mt. Pleasant, WI, a farmer in 1879. Mar Margaret Edmonds 1874. (RACINE HIST; Stone)

LE PREVOST, Louisa, from G to WI ca 1847, also her sister Mary. Poss just visitors, not settlers. (G. SOC. BULL, Spring 1973)

LE PREVOST, Mansell, mentioned as visitor or settler in WI 1800s.

LE PREVOST, Deborah, from G to WIS, engaged to a Rev. Oliver there in 1847. He was a widower with 2 sons.

LE PREVOST, noted in Geauga Co., OH middle 1800s. OUTC.

LE QUELENEC, see QUELENEC.

KALLINACK, Philip, mar in Boston Hannah CHAMBERLYNE. Both from C.I.? KALLINACK, LE QUELENEC poss a Breton surname in C.I.

LE QUESNE, see LE CAIN and CAIN.

LE QUESNE, LE CAIN, as LE QUESNE in J 1528, meaning 'lived by an oak'. LE QUESNE in St. John J 1668 and 1749. Curr and common in J, curr G.

LE QUESNE, called LE CAIN, a very large fam in Nova Scotia that originated in J, and has spread throughout North America. See Q.A. IN CANADA.

LE QUESNE, Annis, widow of Francis, res Cleveland, OH 1901. (City Dir)

LE QUESNE, A.K.; A.E. St. Elmo, a musician; A.W. Sydenham; Dr. Daniel; Fred R.; Honory J.N., a clerk; Susan E., a widow, all res Cleveland, OH 1901, but no desc found.

LE QUESNE, Richard, son of Clement of J was apprenticed to Benj. Swinnerton of Marblehead, MA 1740. (Soc. Jers. Bull, Vol 10)

LE RAY, see also LE ROY. See CIFHS #6, #9.

LE RAY curr G. In St. Martin and Grouville J 1668, in St. Martin 1749

LE RAY, see under LE PAGE, Sophie De Voe LE RAY.

LE RAY, Peter, b 1822 G, to Racine, WIS 1850s, carpenter, joiner and fanning mill operator, also manufacturer. Mar Margaret TOSTEVIN, qv, b G, 2 chn.

LE REGLE, John from 'Toin', Jersey, prob St. Ouen, J, before 1752, a mariner, settled in Boston. REGLE in OH 1800s. LE REGLE, LE REIGLE res in St. Ouen on the fief Haubert, and owned in 1724 a field on the Mont Vautier, and one at Val de la Mare. (LE ROSSIGNOL GEN) Note that LERIGAL was in early MA, poss a phonetic LE REGLE?

LE RENDU, Alexander, in Cleveland, OH 1901. (City Directory) Curr and old name in J.

LE RETILLEY, noted in Militia records of G 1750.

LE RETILLEY, RETILLEY, James Sr., b ca 1788 G (or as one record has it, Scotland?) rem to Roscoe, Coshocton Co., OH ca 1825. A merchant there until he d 1850. Mar 2? dau of T. Emerson of Keene, NH (Hunt) Mar 1.? 1816, Elizabeth Taylor, dau of Wm. Taylor of VA. (Hunt; Hill; Sarchet) See family under RETILLEY.

LE REVEREND, LE RIVEREND, a Cuban fam rem to US in recent years. Ancestor said to have settled in Cuba early 1800s poss from C.I.? LE REVEREND in Canada, poss from G? Name curr in G. See Q.A. IN CANADA.

LE RICHE, in J ca 1340, in Trinity and/or St. Heliers J 1668, 1749. In St. Laurens J 1788. Curr G and J. See CIFHS #4.

RICH, Jonathan from J? to MRB, MA mar Phebe BRIDGES, BRIDGEO?, qv,1727 3 chn. OUTC.

RICH, LE RICHE, Thomas from Trinity J d 1702 Salem, MA. See RICH FAM. ASSOC., Wellfleet, MA.

LE RICHE, to Carolina 1679, from France or C.I.? OUTC.

LE ROSSIGNOL, the Nightingale, or the chatterer. ROSSIGNOLL in J 1607. LE ROSSIGNOL in St. Ouen J 1668, and in St. Laurens J 1749. Curr J. This name also in England and France.

LE ROSSIGNOL, see GUSTIN. "The JEANS and LE ROSSIGNOLS were both fams of great antiquity on the Island (Jersey, and both were followers of the sea; one of the latter traded with the natives of Arcadia as early as 1604. There is a lake in Nova Scotia today called Lake Rossignol, named for a trapper who lived there in the 17th century." (GUSTIN COMPENDIUM) The mother of John Gustin was a LE ROSSIGNOL.

Variant spellings of this name include: RUSSNEL, RUSENALL, RACIGNAL. Not necessarily of C.I. fams. (Elsie Nemchick, Vancouver, WA)

LE ROSSIGNOL, Peter from J, in early life a sailor, prospered, became a ship captain and owner. Traded between England, Jersey, Italy and Quebec. Left the sea trade and became a merchant in Quebec City and Levis, QUE. (Q.A. IN CANADA, by Turk; Mrs. Helen Dvoracek; Mrs. D. L. Loetterle, Vancouver, WA)

LE ROSSIGNOL. Note that in the Q.A. IN CANADA book, an error was made on page 394 and 397. The family of Leda LE ROSSIGNOL, p. 397, Wilfred, Laureanne and Violet Matte, should have been placed as B9., near bottom of page 394, under B8. Francois/Francis. Sorry! M.Turk. (Gabrielle Slotsve, Estevan, SASK)

LE ROSSIGNOL, Peter, b 1826 St. Mary? J, son of Edouard and wife Eliz. ESNOUF, a cousin. Peter mar in Canada Mary Gillespie, b 1840 near QUE. City, who d 1935 Montreal. Peter d 1874 Levis, QUE, 5 chn. (Mrs. Helen Dvoracek, Lincoln, NEB; Mrs. J.D. Ketchum, Toronto, ONT; LE ROSSIGNOL FAM IN JERSEY by S.E. LE Rossignol) Mary Gillespie mar 2. poss Rev. Henderson? (Eleanor Butterfield, Englewood, COL) The following info. is in addition to, and corrects data in Q.A. IN CANADA, pp 394,5,6,7.

A1. Peter, d in his 20s.

A2. Annie Elizabeth, b 1864 d 1944, res where?

A3. James Edward, b Little River, just outside QUE City 1866, mar 1898 Jessie Catherine Ross of Montreal. James d 1959, and Jessie in 1953, 2 chn.

B1. Edward Ross, b 1902 Denver, COL mar Blanche Simmons 1925, 5 chn

C1. James Edward, b 1926 d 1978 mar Beverly Borgen of Billings, MONT 1949. James in Newspaper bus, in Lincoln, NEB. 3 chn: Curtis of Denver, Cadis of Carlsbad, NM, and Carin of Omaha, NEB.

C2. Jean, b 1928, M.D., unmar, res Lincoln, NEB

C3. Nancy, b 1931 mar Carlos Hansen, 2 sons and a dau. Nancy mar 2. Robert Godsey, had dau, res Palo Alto, CAL

C4. Patricia, b 1935, mar Donald Loetterle, b 1932, son of Harry L. and Virginia, res Vancouver, WA, 3 chn: Janmarie b 1957, Margaret b 1960 and Teresa b 1962.

C5. Helen b 1941 mar Richard Maxwell, 2 sons and a dau, res Englewood, COL.

B2. Helen, b ca 1909 mar Carl Dvoracek, Lincoln, NEB, no issue
A4. Dr. Walter J., b ca 1870 d 1954, mar Laura Maberry.
B1. Annie Elizabeth b 1903 mar Vernon Duke and res Rockville Centre, NY NY, then rem to Denver, COL
C1. Annie Elizabeth Duke, b 1929 Schenectady, NY mar Dr. Duane B. Butterfield, res Englewood, COL, 3 chn: Gregg, Carol Hall and David Butterfield.
C2. Mary Anne Duke, b 1931 Denver, mar James D. McKibben, res Newark, DEL, 3 chn: Molly S., Sarah L., and Jeffrey J. McKibben
C3. Vernon Leslie Duke, b 1932 Denver, COL mar Ida Lee Enyor, res Albuquerque, NM, 2 chn: Elizabeth and Janet Duke
C4. Laura Louise Duke, b 1934 Denver, mar Robert Determan, res Denver 2 chn: Wayne B. and John C. Determan
C5. Walter Clifford Duke, b 1936 Denver, mar Eleanor J. White, 2 chn: Heather and Christopher Duke.
B2. Mary Alice, b ca 1899
A5. Mary, b 1872, d 1958 mar Arthur O. Dawson, res Montreal, QUE, 7 chn
B1. Ruth Dawson, 1894-1972, mar A.S. Bruneau, Mont., 1893-1979,4 chn.
C1. Mary Bruneau, mar and had 4 chn
C2. Ida Bruneau, mar res near Montreal
C3. Arthur Bruneau, mar, had 3 sons, res Montreal
C4. Evelyn, mar Wm. K. Ross, & res Calgary, ALTA, 4 chn.
B2. Howard Le Rossignol Dawson, mar has 3 sons
C1. Arthur, b 1934, res La Jolla, CAL, 3 daus
C2. John, b 1935, mar and has 3 sons and 2 daus.
C3. Douglas, mar, res Montreal, 2 daus.
B3. Anna, 1899-1913
B4. Katherine, b 1903, mar J.D. Ketchum, res Toronto, ONT.
C1. Margaret, b 1935, mar L. Catto, res Toronto, 3 chn
C2. Edward, b 1940, mar P. Wake, Ottawa, ONT, 4 sons: David, Michael, Christopher and Stephen A. Le Rossignol Ketchum.
B5. Arthur, b 1907, d 1912?
B6. Isabel, b 1912 mar D.L. Gales in Montreal, 4 chn, 3 with desc.
B7. Olive, b 1914, Montreal, mar M.T. Sinclair, 4 chn, 3 with desc.
LE ROSSIGNOL, Edward, b 1817 J? mar Elizabeth COLLAS, qv, settled in Canada, has desc.
LE ROSSIGNOL, Mary Anne, sister of Capt. Francis Collas Le Rossignol, who was b 1814 J, mar Amice BARBIER and settled in America. Mary and bro Francis were chn of Pierre Le R. and wife Esther Jeanne LE REGLE of J. (LE ROSSIGNOL GEN)
LE ROSSIGNOL curr in Malibu, Culver City, CAL and many other places.
LE ROUX, the red-head, in J 1331. In St. Clement, St. Saviour, St. Heliers and St. Brelade J 1668, and in St. Clement and St. Heliers J 1749. Some to America as ROW? or ROWE?
LE ROY in J 1331, in St. Martin J 1607. In St. Saviour G 1738, now often as LE RAY. Curr G and J.
LE ROY, Sophie, b G, mar John LE PAGE, qv.
LE ROY, William, bro of Sophie above, from G to US 1800s.
LE ROY, ___, to Philadelphia 1769 from C.I.? (Filby) OUTC
LE ROY, Judith arrived with Wm., Francis and James on the MOLLY from J in 1769. (Whitmore)
LE ROY, Marien mar Elizabeth Lane 1798 Boston. OUTC
LE ROY, Peter mar Anna Gates, or Gete, 1806 Boston. LE GEYT?
LE ROY, Simeon, a soldier of the Rev. War d 1855. OUTC. (GLAZIER fam Bible, Vol 81, NEHGS)
A1. Phebe mar Asher SHEPHERD
B1. Aurilla SHEPHERD, mar Rodney WEBBER
C1. Loretta Jane WEBBER mar Ezra Bruce Glacier.

LE ROY, Elizabeth, Francis Jr. and Sr., John, John, Michael, Peter, Robert, Simon, Simon and Teunis res Fishkill, Poughkeepsie, NY 1790. (Census) OUTC. Could be also German or Dutch.
LE ROY, res Marion, NY 1800s and in Geauga Co., OH. OUTC.
LE ROY, see STILLWELLS MISCELLANY.
LE RUE, see LA RUE.
LE RUEZ, see LARAWAY. Philip LE RUEZ of J, NY state and VT, changed his name to Laraway.
LE RUEZ in J 1461, in St Ouen J 1668 and 1749, a seafaring family. Also in St. Ouen J 1795, and in St. Laurens J 1788. Curr J. (LE BOUTILLIER CHART)
LE RHUEE, Abraham and Mary res Salem, MA.
A1. Susanna, bp 1743 First Church, Salem, MA.
LE RHUEE, Thomas mar Susanna BECKET, qv, dau of Wm. and Susanna (Fowler) BECKET in Ma. Susanna d 1805 age 59, 3 daus and 2 sons. (Essex Coll). See BECKET
REHEWEE, Thomas, res Salem, MA 1790 with fam of 10. (Census)
RUEE, Thomas, first mate of the BRUTUS, wrecked on Cape Cod, MA 1802, having sailed from Salem shortly before. The ship BRUTUS, along with the ULYSSES and the VOLUSIA were East Indiamen, full rigged sailing ships. (IT'S AN OLD CAPE COD CUSTOM, by Edwin V. Mitchell, NY, 1949)
RUEE, William and Molly res Salem, MA, a dau Molly bp 1781.
LE SAGE, curr J. LE SAGE, Claude, arrived in Boston 1760s on sloop ADVENTURE from Nfld., a mariner, poss a Jerseyman? (Whitmore)
LE SAINT, old and curr in J.
LE SAUTEUR, curr research, see CIFHS #3.
LE SAUVAGE, in J 1309, old in Torteval G. Curr Los Angeles, CAL,OUTC.
LE SAUVAGE, ___, b G 1883, has grandson in ONT. (Susan Le Sauvage, Thunder Bay, ONT)
LESBIREL, LE SEVIREL, SEBRILL, LE SIBERELL, LE SIBBEREL, etc, etc.
LE SEBIRELL, SIBERELL in J 1515 in Grouville, St. John and St. Peter J 1668 and 1749. LESBIREL curr G and J.
LE SIBERREL, Thomas to Boston from J 1766, also Elias. (Filby)
LISBIREL, Daniel mar Sarah BROUGHTON 1769 MA. (BROUGHTON FAM)
LESBIREL, LE SEBIREL, Thomas of St. John J to Salem, MA 1718. Indentured to Philip English, qv. Mar and had at least one son by 1733. Two letters of this fam and an indenture dated 1718 are in the Essex Inst. Library.
LESBRILL, Daniel from J mar Hannah ___ in MRB. Son Daniel bp 1748/9
LE SEELEUR, see Q.A. IN CANADA.
LE SEELLEUR, LE SCELLEUR, etc, the tumbler, leaper, in J 1734 or earlier. (CIFHS #6) In St. Martin J 1749. Curr J.
LE SEELLEUR, Charles Josue, b 1847 J, son of Charles and Sophie Esther (JANDRON) Le Seeleur of J, one of four chn, rem to Gaspe, QUE and m mar 1876 Josepine Caron, who d 1927. 13 chn, 6 of whom d.y.: Marie, George, Marcelline, George, b 1887, Philippe and Joseph.
A1. Charles Raymon, b ca 1877 mar Nancy Ann TRACHY A2. Willy, mar Ida Jalbert
A3. Joseph, mar 1. Emilie COULOMBE, qv, and 2. Maria C.
A4. John, b 1879 mar Leda Hemet
A5. Edward/Eddy mar Blanche Bernard
B1. Emile, b 1920 mar 1. Lucille Dunn, 6 chn and 2. Ann Marie Cotton
B2, 3, 4, other sons. B5, 6, 7, three daus.
A6. Sophie mar Octave GIRARD A7. Eva May, unmar
LE SELEUR, George of J, mar Mary Hichcock? of Lymington, Hants, England in 1747. (Records of Boldre, Hampshire, England)
LE SERRE, see GRUTT. SARRE curr G and J.

LE SIEUR, P., a banker, b ca 1849 J, Methodist, res St. John's, QUE. His wife M---, b England ca 1853. 4 chn. (Gary French, Elmvale,ONT)

A1. M., b ca 1883 A2. H.J. b ca 1884 A3. R.J. b ca 1887 A4. F,b1889?

LE SUEUR, the shoemaker, in J 1309. In St. Heliers and Trinity J 1668, and in Trinity, St. Heliers, St. John and St. Laurens J 1749. In St. Laurens J 1788. Curr and common in J. Crest: azure, a chevron between two crescents in chief and a rose in base or. CAUTION! Some LE SUEUR directly from France to America, some from France to Canada, then to US.

LE SUEUR, shipowners and builders of ships in J 1800s. (A. John Jean,J)

LE SUEUR, John, b 1813 St. Saviour J, son of Jean and Marguerite (LE VAIN) LE SUEUR, mar 1836 in St. Ouen J, Caroline LE GRESLEY, b 1814, dau of Philippe and Julia or Judith (LE MARQUAND) LE GRESLEY. The first seven chn were b J, and rem to Bountiful, UT where an 8th ch was born, Wm. Francis. They came via ship CHIMBORAZO, joining a shipload of Mormons at Liverpool, England, 70 of whom were from the Channel Islands. They traveled by boat to Phila. then by train to Pittsburgh, where they boarded a steamship named the AMAZON, to St. Louis, arriving there June 2nd. Then rem to Atchison, KS where they began their wagon-train journey across the plains. This difficult trip took four and a half months, arriving in Salt Lake City, Oct. 1855. John LE GRESLEY, their uncle, had assisted them in making their trip possible, but he died when they had been there just 2 wks. John LE SUEUR, the husband, d at 49 in 1862, and was bur at Woods Cross, UT. Caroline and her husband's aunt Eliza raised the chn, leasing out the farm. They rem to Mesa, AZ, where the dau Caroline Mallory d, along with her newborn dau. They then rem to San Juan, COL. The Mallorys rem to ID, and the Warners to Layton, AZ. The mother Caroline d 1898 St. John's, AZ age 84. (Waldo and Louise B. Le Sueur; Lenore G. Merrill, Mesa, AZ; James W. Le Sueur of Scottsdale, AZ; Virginia Fackrell, San Fran., CAL; Charles A. Bernau, English Genealogist; Vera Le Sueur, Mesa, AZ; FIRST FAMS OF AMERICA, Vol.5; Virkus; plus more data in SLCity)

A1. A son d.y.

A2. Mary Ann, b 1838 St. Peters J, mar 1856 in UT James Fackrell, farmer, b 1829 Moriah, NY, d 1892 Boutiful, UT, son of James and Amy (Crumb) Fackrell.

B1. Mary Caroline Fackrell, b 1857 UT, d.y.

B2. John L. Fackrell, b 1859 d 1943 mar 1887 Christie Eldredge

B3. Ella Jane Fackrell, b 1860 d 1942, mar1882 John E. Ingles

B4. Angeline Fackrell, b 1862 d 1882. B5. Aurelia Fackrell, 1864-1878

B6. Seymour Fackrell, b 1867 d 1952 mar 1890 Priscilla E. Sparks

B7. Willard Fackrell, b 1869 Eden, UT d 1929

B8. Alexander Fackrell, b 1871 Bountiful, UT d 1871

B9. Annie Independence Fackrell, b 1872 Eden, UT d 1957. She mar 1919 Henry Wilson

B10. Christina Fackrell, b 1876 mar 1897 Charles Abraham Brunson

B11. James Leory Fackrell, b 1878 d 1950, mar 1902 Thirza McBride.

A3. Jean Philippe, b 1840 St. Helier J d 1845

A4. Jane Caroline, b 1842 St. Helier J, d 1926 Blackfoot, UT. She mar 1860 John Davis of Stoke Abbott, Dorset, England, son of Wm. and Lucy Davis. 8 chn.

B1. John William Davis, b 1860 Bountiful, UT d 1866

B2. Jane Caroline Davis, b 1863? UT d 1907, mar John White.

B3. Nofear Davis, b 1866 Montpelier, ID d 1935, mar 1891 Signe Aurora Jacobsen.

B4. Harriet Ann Davis, b 1869 ID, d 1945, mar 1887 Welcome Chapman

B5. Alma Davis, b 1871 ID d 1856, mar 1895 Annie Johanna Peterson.
B6. Lucy Ellen Davis, b 1874 ID d 1949, mar1919 Oscar Leonard Rider.
A5. Caroline Mary Turner, b 1847 St. Heliers J d 1878 US. Mar 1866 Charles Mallory.
A6. Harriet Ellen, b 1850 St. Heliers J d 1933. Mar 1867 Charles Alma Warner, b 1840 Homer, MI, d 1911 Layton, AZ, son of Luther and Permelia (Stanton) Warner, 11 chn. Much more on this branch. (Lenore Merrill, Mesa, AZ)
B1. Caroline Permelia Warner, b 1868 Montpelier, ID d 1868
B2. Charles Alma Warner, b 1869 North Ogden, UT d 1873
B3. John Luther Warner, b 1872 Montpelier, ID, d.y.
B4. William Taylor Warner, b 1873 Montpelier, ID, d 1874
B5. Alvin Warner, b 1875 ID d 1944, mar1901 Caroline Josephine Chesser
B6. Mary Jane Warner, b 1877 ID, d 1938, mar 1905 John Rich. Davidson.
B7. Perhelion Warner, b 1881 St. Johns, AZ mar1905 Estella Morris
B8. Sylvia Warner, b 1884 Layton, AZ, d 1966, mar 1902 James Albert GALE, b 1880 Beaver, UT d 1954 Los Angeles, CAL, son of James and Sarah Ann (Thompson) Gale, a carpenter.
C1. James Otho Gale, b 1903 Franklin, AZ d 1911
C2. Gerald Gale, b 1904 d 1960 mar Florence Bricker, 3 chn: Phyllis, Jerry and Patricia Gale.
C3. Harriet Lenore Gale, b 1906 Clifton, AZ mar 1922 Charles Sibley Merrill, electrician, Santa Ana, CAL, bur San Pedro, CAL, son of Charles Mower Merrill and Daisy May (Kaulback) Merrill. Chas.d1968
D1. Charles J. Merrill b 1923 Los Angeles, CAL mar1942 June Wallbank He served in US Navy, and d off New Guinea in WWII
D2. Donna-Mae Merrill, b 1927 Southgate, CAL mar1944 Eldon Magnusson, b 1920 Mesa, AZ, son of Peter and Lettie (McAlister) Magnusson, 7 chn.
D3. Marvin Gale Merrill, b 1930 CAL mar 1953 Fukoko (Kim) Okabe,4 chn
D4. Joan Merrill, b 1933, d.y.
D5. Paul Allen Merrill, b 1936 Glendale, CAL mar 1957 Ludean Lockhart, 8 chn
D6. Norman James Merrill, b 1938 mar 1964 Helen Wallence Lawler,4/chn
C4. Charles Sheldon Gale, b 1909 Franklin, AZ d 1910
C5. Paul Jay Gale, b 1913 Clifton, AZ d 1979, mar 2. Maxine Crook,/2 chn
C6. Marjoire Gale, b 1922 Safford, AZ mar Lloyd Lane, 3 sons.
B9. Derius Warner, b 1887 Layton, AZ, d.y.
B10. James Cyrus Warner, b 1888 Layton, AZ d 1965, mar 1. Mabel __div., and mar 2. 1936 Stella Frances Singer Bridge, a widow.
B11. Lillie Thompson, b 1894 AZ mar Jay Fredricks.
A7. John Taylor, b 1852 St. Heliers J d 1945, mar 1875 Geneva Casto, b 1857 Ogden, UT, d 1927 Mesa, AZ, dau of James and Sarah (Odekirk) Casto, 12 chn. (Virkus)
B1. John William, b 1876 ID, d.y.
B2. James Warren, b 1878 Montpelier, ID d 1948, mar 1902 Anna Marie Anderson, b 1881 Grantsville, UT d 1958 Mesa, AZ, dau of Charles P. and Anna Louisa Anderson, 8 chn.
C1. Leola, b 1903 St. Johns, AZ mar 1927 Renz L. Jennings of Taylor, AZ, 2 daus, Juliene and Joyce Jennings.
C2. Frank, b 1905 AZ d 1959, mar 1926 Vivian Schultz and 2. Della Cox Mar 3. Evelyn Joos.
C3. Charles Marlow, b 1908 Mesa, AZ mar 1. Marlene White and 2. ? Kathryn Davies.
C4. Nellie Josepine, b 1910 mar 1931 Olen Fox of Phoenix, AZ
C5. Nadeen, b 1912 mar 1938 Richard Gordon Johnson
C6. Ann Louise, b 1914 mar 1937 Willis Howard Gaylord

C7. Margaret Lenore, b 1920 AZ mar 1941 Jose Marla Hernandez, and 2. 1937, R. Stafford
C8. James Kay, b 1921 mar 1949 Maxine Claudin
B3. Frank, b 1880 St. Johns, AZ d 1900 mar Jennie Kemp
B4. Alice Geneva, b 1882 AZ d 1956, mar 1904 John Alma Crosby and 2. George Wilhelm
B5. Charles Taylor, b 1884 d 1949 mar 1908 Helen Graham and 2. 1913, Velda Jean Hunsaker
B6. Nelle, b 1887 d 1959, mar 1909 Wallace Arid MacDonald
B7. Ray, b 1890 d 1958 mar 1910 Vera Bell Richins
B8. Leo, b 1893 d 1933 mar Jessie L. Robertson
B9. Karl Casto, b 1895 d 1968, mar 1. Alberta Pederson and 2. 1920, Merle Skousen
B10. Paul Harry, b 1896 d 1948 mar 1. Stella Harton, 2. Georgia Hurley
B11. Walter Bryant, b 1898 mar1924 Viola Blood
B12. Harvey Ross, b 1901 AZ, mar 1924 Phyllis Ruth Brizzee and 2. Eileen Kelliber
A8. William Francis, merchant and rancher, b 1856 UT d 1941 Eagar, AZ, mar 1. Anner Mari Bingham, b 1860 Hyrum, UT d 1910 Springville, AZ dau of Calvin and Eliz. Lucretia (Thorn) Bingham, 12 chn. Mar 2. 1913, Elna I.N. Hansen, b 1883 Denmark, 3 chn.
B1. William Calvin, b 1879 d 1913 unmar
B2. LeRoy LeGrand, b 1882 Brigham, AZ d 1921 mar 1904 Mary E. Nielson
B3. Ella, b 1883 AZ, d 1948 mar 1903 Graham Hamblin
B4. John Perry, b 1885 d 1973, mar 1909 Emma Lee Ennis, div, mar 2. 1917, Hannah Manila Maxwell.
B5. Geneva Jane, b 1887, d.y. B7. Twin of Rulon, b 1888, stillborn
B6. Rulon, twin, b 1888, d 1947, mar 1933 Elizabeth Schuster Lunds.
B8. Emeline, b 1891 mar 1. 1936 Fred Lee Sauls, and 2. 1948 James L./
B9. Elizabeth Lucretia, b 1891 B10. dau stillborn 1892
B11. Caroline, b 1894 Springerville, AZ d 1894
B12. Grover Bruce, b 1895 AZ mar 1917 Ila Pearson
B13. Elna's ch, Carl Gordon, b 1915 Eagar, AZ, mar 1952 Mary E.Terhune
B14. Woodrow Francis, b 1917 mar 1940 Mary Hall, and 2. 1974 June Shuller Jamison, widow.
B15. Genevieve, b 1924, d.y.

LE SUEUR, Peter b 1849 J, son of Peter and Mary Ann (DAVISON) LE SUEUR. Mary Ann was from an Aberdeen- Scotland fam. Peter was in 1905 a retired toy merchant. This fam said to be desc from Jean LE SUEUR, who d 1681 J, author of L'HISTOIRE DE L' EGLISE ET L'EMPIRE, who is said to have had a son who emigrated to America, where he was a planter, data not found by compiler. Mary Ann d 1934 age 82. (Mrs. J.H. Le Sueur, Meadville, PA)

A1. Peter, b 1871 J "had long and distinguished career in the realm of music". A child prodigy, at 9 was organist of the Acquila Rd. CH in J, then organist of the Victoria St. Cong. CH at 16, winner of a medal from the Cardiff, England WESTERN DAILY MAIL, for orig. comp. Went to New College, Oxford 1892, and became music master at Methodist College, St. John's, Nfld. Taught piano, organ, voice & theoretical branches of music. Founder of the St. John's Choral & Orchestral Soc. Rem to Erie, PA 1905 as organist and choirmaster of St. Paul's Episcopal Church. Opened the Erie Conservatory of Music with his bros., Charles and Percival, which functioned until 1960. Peter mar 1905 Muriel Hunter-Watters, in London, England, who d 1958 Erie, PA.
B1. John Hunter, b 1912 Erie, PA mar Virginia Clementine Tucker 1939 at St. Paul's Cathedral, Erie, PA. 2 chn.

C1. Jill Richey, b 1943 Erie, PA, res Bel Air, MD, with Red Cross.
C2. John Hunter, Jr., b 1947 New Haven, CT, res Raleigh, NC.
A2. Florence, b 1872 Charing Cross, St. Heliers J, d during German Occupation ca 1940s.
A3. Mabel, b J, mar Jack LE MOTTEE, and 2. John Wellman? d 1945
A4. Maude Blanche b J, mar 1897 Herbert Woodington at St. Heliers J, d 1917 Bristol, England.
B1. Violet Woodington b 1898 Bristol, res there 1979
B2. Olive, b 1902, d 1963 Bristol, teacher of cello, studied with Casals.
A5. Charles, b 1880 J, mar Winifred Knightly, and d 1948 Erie, PA.
B1. Hardress Norman, b 1905 Hastings, England mar Lola MacArthur 1946 Erie, PA. Mar 2. Dorothy___.
A6. Percival, b 1882 J, mar Betty ___ ca 1914, a dau Jeanne b ca 1915.

LE SUEUR, Joshua, bro of the Peter above, b 1849 J, remained in J, and has desc there.

LE SUEUR, Arthur, first cousin of Lester LE VESCONTE, qv, rem to MINN was a lawyer from J. His dau Meridel was a writer. (LE VESCONTE CHART)

LE SUEUR, Caroline, b 1831 J, mar __LE VESCONTE, to US 1872 from J, res MINN and FLA.

LE SUER, LE SUEUR?, Cassandra, from J fam? mar 1791 Samuel Lewis of MD rem to NC, then to VA. OUTC. (Melvin Ricks, La Canada, CAL)

LE SUEUR, Hubert from C.I.? in New England 1633. (DAB)

LE SUEUR, Gilbert, age 19, b J, res with the LE BOUTILLIER FAM from J in IA 1860. (Gladys Brechtel)

LE SUEUR, Nicholas, to LA 1756, but OUTC. (Filby)

LE SUEUR, LESURE, LASHURE, etc., Philip b C.I. mar in Mendon, MA, Temperance ___. (Perley; Mendon, MA VRS) Sarah White
A1. Tamar, b 1712 Mendon A3. Abigail, b 1717 A6. John b 1723 mar/
A2. Margaret, b 1714 A5. Isaiah, b 1721 mar Rachel Allen A7.David?
A4. Philip, b 1719 mar Abigail Benham, d 1811 Mendon, MA, 13 chn.

LE SUEUR, Philip, b 1828 J, d 1866 Lansingburgh, NY, mar Marianne FALLE qv, 1835-1893. (Frances Broderick, Lansingburgh, NY)

LE SURE, ___, poss desc of Philip and Temperance above?, res Uxbridge, Grafton, Upton, Mendon and Rehoboth, MA 1810 census. OUTC.

LE SUEUR, Susan, b ca 1805 St. John J, mar Thomas FALLE, rem to US, 9 chn. See FALLE.

LE SURE fam in Barnard CT and in Winchester, NH early. Some also in Royalton, VT, Orange, Warwick, Fitchburg and Springfield, MA; Keene, NH and Leicester, NY. OUTC.

LE SUER in Bedford Co, VA, late 1700s. OUTC.

LE SUEUR, rather dispersed fam from J in US and Canada. The emigrant came from J in early or middle 1800s and desc are found in Sherwood Forest, MD; Barrie, ONT; Delta, OH; Poland, IND; Deerfield Beach, FLA; Toledo, OH and Boca Raton, FLA. (Robert Le Sueur, MD)

LE SUIRE noted in St. Ann Co., MD, OUTC. (Skordas)

LE SUEUR, Peter, son of Abraham in VA 1700s. OUTC. (Mrs. Paul Roberts, Urbana, ILL)

LE SUEUR, in Jessamine Co., KY ca 1820. OUTC. (O. Caruthers, Cedar Rapids, IA)

LE SUEUR records in Salt Lake City of fams in Pte. aus Trembles, QUE and St. Francois,Isle Jesus, QUE; Isle d'Orleans, QUE; and QUE.City, some from Jersey.

LE SUEUR in NJ. See NJ GENESIS, 1956. OUTC. Curr Los Angeles, CAL.

LE SUEUR, in Baie St. Paul, Duplessis Co., QUE 1906. OUTC. (Aldo Brochet, London, ONT.

LE TELLIER, Henri, b 1905 J, res Grouville J, d 1979 Montreal, QUE. Res also St. Lambert, QUE, mar Alice Lanoue. Henri son of Fleurimond LE TELLIER, b Baubigny, France, 4 chn. (Maurice Le Tellier, Longueuil, Quebec)

A1. Maurice mar 1. ? and 2. ?, 2 chn by 1st mar, 1 by 2nd.
B1. Mylene, b 1965 B2. Lisanne, b 1966 B3. Sandrine, b 1978
A2. Roger A4. Henriette, b 1945
A3. Madeleine, b 1943, a dau Isabelle Leduc, b 1966.

LE TISSIER, old G surname, curr and common in G. This surname said to be changed to THISTLE in Nfld. Note that some Thistles are recorded in Amer. colonies, but OUTC. Some research? See CIFHS #8.

LE TOCQ, in J 1331, common in G. Could some of the Tuck fams of early New England have been TOCQUE, OR LE TOCQ of J or G? Note Nancy TUKEY in the PENNELL fam.

LE TEMPLIER in J may be Hug. TEMPLE and TEMPLIER curr J. LE TEMPLIER, prob Hug? In J 1607, and in St. Clement J 1668. Note TEMPLE in early Boston. OUTC.

LE TOUZELL, the stripling, in J 1309. In St. Clement J 1668, in St. H Helier, Grouville, St. Clement and St. Brelade 1749. Cf TOUZEAU of G Curr J. Also as TOUZEL.

LE TOUZEL, George of J fam in Gaspe, mar Clarissa GUIGNION, qv, b 1875, 4 chn. See Q.A. IN CANADA, p. 401. (Eunice Stanley, Mesa, AZ)

A1. Louis, res Gaspe, mar Beatrice GALLIARD, 2 chn? Layland, who d.y. and Anita, unmar A3. Francis, to Toronto
A2. Mildred mar Wm. Markwick, no issue A4. Otis, res Gaspe.

LE TOUZEL, Dorothy mar Raymond P. LE MESURIER of Rosebridge, Gaspe, 1800s.

LE TUBELIN, old in J, see CIFHS #5.

LE VALLEY, LE VALAIS in J 1331. In G 1200s. Curr G. Cf LE VALLIER in J 1528.

LE VALLEE, Pierre/Peter, believed to have been born in the C.I. of a Hug. fam, and said to have landed at MRB ca 1700, rem to Warwick, RI 1727. At least 6 chn, and was ancestor of the fams of Warwick and Coventry. (Loughrey; NEHGS Vol 37; MHS; MRB VR) Peter mar Elizabeth Yabsley.

A1. Peter, bp 1728 A2. Mary, bp 1730

LE VALLEY, Elizabeth mar 1739 Andrew LEE in MRB. OUTC

LE VALLEE, Mary, widow of Thomas Westget in 1749 (Noyes) OUTC

A1. Thomas Westgate of Berwick mar Margaret DAVIS 1745

LE VALLIER, Margaret mar Christopher BUBIER, qv, b ca 1706. She d 1782 age 73, prob from a Hug fam. OUTC.

LE VAVASSEUR, noted in C.I. and in Yorkshire, England early. Named in some Presidential Lines. (Burke)
LE VAVASSEUR dit DURELL, dit MARTINER and dit NOEL were in St. Helier J 1668. Prob the 'dit' names took over, as the name is scarce. A Paul LE VAVASSEUR res in Salem, MA recently, but OUTC. Compiler has seen somewhere that VASSAR took its name from this old surname.

LEVERIT, not listed by Stevens as old J surname. Cf LE LIEVRE

LEVERIT, Somon, from parish of 'Sanua', prob St. Ouens J? before 174-. Mar Eliz. Hepworth 1740s. Res Portsmouth, NH, a dau Anna? (NEHGS, vol 27; Bolton)

LEVERITT, Ann mar Joshua JACKSON, qv, 1761 Portsmouth, NH. (NEHGS Vol 27) OUTC.

LE VESCONTE in J 1299. In St. Ouen and St. Peter J 1668. In St. Ouen, Trinity and St. Brelade J 1749. Curr J. See Q.A. IN CANADA by Turk.

LE VESCONTE, Daniel built ships for foreign trade in the 1700s in J. See JERSEY SAILING SHIPS, by A. John Jean of Jersey.

VISCONTE, BISCON, LE VESCONTE?, Isaac mar Ann Brooks, Boston, MA 1690. (Clemons) A son John b 1700, poss other chn?

LE VESCONTE, Charles, b 1830 Grouville, J, son of ?, at age 13 lost his father, his uncle, 3 cousins and 9 neighbors in a shipwreck off the coast of Jersey. This left Charles, his mother and his sister, age 17. About age 21 Charles mar 1. Margaret Mackay, the dau of David Mackay, a mason of Bermuda. Later Charles had a contract to build a seawall at St. Catherines Bay, Jersey. His work was destroyed by a big storm, leaving him bankrupt. Charles and Margaret then, with son Charles, rem to Tasmania as a carpenter on barracks for an English prison camp. Dau Margaret was born there. Wife Margaret d in England or Jersey, upon their return, and Charles mar 2. 1861 in St. Saviour parish, Caroline LE SUEUR, dau of Philip LE SUEUR, a farmer, b 1831 St. John, J. In 1861 they res St. Peter, J. After 11 years and 7 chn, they rem from La Rigondaine for America, settling in Hastings, MN 1872 with 9 chn. Caroline d 1913 at Prior Lake, MN. (Lester Le Vesconte, Elmhurst, ILL)

A1. Charles, b 1854 J, mar 1880 Orael Poor, res MN, d 1912 Hastings.
 B1. Sadie Marian, b 1883, unmar, d 1941
 B2. Ira, b 1885, mar 1911 ___.
  C1. Edward, b 1913 mar 1. 1938 Margaret ___, no issue and 2. Gail___ 2 chn: Theodore, b 1954 and Ronald b 1958
  C2. Jeanne, b 1920 mar 1941 Donald T. Knutson. Jeanne d 1976, 4 chn, including Donald and Bruce Knutson.
A2. Margaret, b 1856 Tasmania, mar 1881 Neil Livingstone, res Montana, MN and CAL. D ca 1928.
 B1. Robert Livingstone, res Los Angeles, CAL
 B2. Helen Livingstone, res Hollywood, CAL
A3. by 2nd wife, John, b 1862 St. Martin J, mar 1893 Ramsey Co., MN, Lillie Belle Gibbs, b 1865, res Prior Lake, MN. John d 1945 and Lillie in 1945 also.
 B1. Harold John, b 1894 mar 1922 in MN Ethel Joseph, b 1892? res ILL, CAL, and Medford, OR. D 1971.
  C1. Norman Eileen, b 1923 Chicago, ILL mar 1947 Abram Goldstein
   D1. Marianne Goldstein, b 1947 Chicago, ILL. D3. Joanne Goldstein b 1954
   D2. Michael Jacob Goldstein, b 1950?, mar ___.
  C2. Harold John, b 1925 mar 1949 Shirley Woodrick, b 1929, res ILL and OH. 3 chn
   D1. Kathryn Ann, b 1950 mar in OR 1979 Edward Moore
   D2. Steven Michael, b 1953 of OH. D3. Thalia Lynn,b 1959, res OR.
 B2. Amy Marie, b 1898, teacher of Austin, TX.
 B3. Lillian Ruth, b 1901 mar 1927 James Ira Dickson, missionary in Taiwan, where James d 1967
  C1. Jeanne Naomi, b 1929 C4. Dolly Bi-Lian
  C2. Ronald James, b 1930 mar 1951 Lois Forry, no issue, res Taiwan.
  C3. Marilyn Ruth, b 1932 mar 1958 Taiwan, Vernon W. Tank, 4 adopted chn: David, Michelle, Lori and Sheryl
 B4. Lester Burton, b 1903 mar 1927 Faith Reynolds, res PA and Elmhurst ILL, 2 chn
  C1. Ruth Marie, b 1929 mar 1953 Philip L. Phipps, res St. Paul, MN 4 chn: Alan, David, Brian and Karen Phipps.
  C2. Carolyn Kay, b 1932, adopted, mar Jack B. Tathwell, res MO., MI and La Brea, CAL. 4 chn: Denise, Judith, Tamara Sue & Todd Charles Tathwell.
A4. Carrie/Caroline, b 1863 St. Martin J mar 1892 James Robertson, res MINN and CAL. Carrie d Glendale, CAL 1938. Chn: Jean and Grace Robertson.

A5. George, b 1865 Grouville, J went to the Klondike Gold Rush as a porter in 1896, mar 1900 Lucille Gilman, res MN, rem to Yakima, WA 1908. Lucille d 1943, and George d 1964 in IA. 1967
B1. Gilman Robert b 1901 mar 1928 Grace V. Large, res WA, Grace d/
C1. Grace Marie, b 1933 mar 1955 Richard B. Kaylor, res Seattle, WA 3 chn: George W., Judith Ann and John Thomas Kaylor, b 1964
C2. Vera Elizabeth b 1935 mar 1962 John Keith McDonald, res Portland OR, 2 chn: Brian and Daniel J. McDonald, b 1960s.
B2. Philip, 1903-1905
B3. Elizabeth, b 1903, twin, mar 1926 in WA, Richard F. Howerton, res Chicago, ILL, Davenport, IA, and Estes Park, COL.
C1. John Kent Howerton, b 1941 adopted
C2. Nancy Beth Howerton, b 1944 adopted, mar T.K. Kessinger, 3 chn
B4. Ruth Caroline b 1909 mar 1939 Robert Emmet McMahan, res CAL. Ruth mar 2. 1967, Arthur F. Klos, res Seattle, WA.
C1. Robert George McMahon, b 1943, mar 1978 Laurie Mason Boyce, a stepdau Heidi.
A6. Henry, b 1867 Grouville J, res Prior Lake, MN, unmar d 1943
A7. Alfred, b 1868 mar 1894 Jean Pierson, res Tampa, FLA, 2 sons: Frank and Edward
A8. Emile, b 1871 J, mar 1895 Laura Camp in MN. A9. Ernest, 1872-1875
LEWIS, a south-of-England surname, curr G and J, some prob long time resident in the Islands.
LEWIS, Noel Lawson, res Cleveland, OH 1936, had C.I. connection.
LEWIS, note that a LUCE fam was sometimes known as LEWIS.
LEWIS, see WARREN.
L'HERAULT, curr Austin, TX, OUTC. HERAULT in J 1299, 1607, 1668,1749.
L'HERAULT,Octave, b 1868 France, raised in J, mar 1903 Eveline MACHON, qv, of J, rem 1903 to North Chelmsford, MA. He d 1962. (Eveline Gray, Barstown, CAL; Irene Lherault, Lowell, MA)
A1. Reginald Joshua, b 1904 mar Irene Profio of Lowell, MA 1944, a son Reginald John b 1946
A2. Eveline, b 1907 mar 1927 Wayne L. Gray from Vermont.
B1. Wayne Gray, b 1933 mar 1958 Mary Radcliffe of Lowell, MA.
LIBBY, see LABEY
LIGHT, John of Jersey mar Sarah Camis 1793 in St. Michael's, Winchester, Hampshire, England. This name noted in G records. Cf also LIOT of J. One in G currently.
LIGHT, Peter, b 1741 to Waldeboro, ME. OUTC. A son George b 1764, mar mar 1794 Mrs. Hannah MESSERVY, b 1771 Bristol, ME.
LIGHT, John mar Dorothy Pike, whose first husband was Joshua Pierce, whom she mar 1668. Res Portsmouth, NH. (Noyes) OUTC.
LIGHT, Hannah, b early 1700s, mar Jonathan Lord. OUTC. See A.6. Edmund and A8. Elizabeth LOUGEE.
LIGHTFOOT, in some cases this is a translation of BLANCPIED, BLANPIED, BLAMPIED, from the C.I. in MRB, MA. Some LIGHTFOOTS are English. Cf also WHITEFOOT and BAREFOOT.
LIGHTFOOT, John from J res MRB, mar Elizabeth Fortune 1692 in MRB.
A1. William, bp 1695
A2. John, bp 1696, poss mar Mary Elkins? 1722, a son Wm. bp 1723 MRB
A3. Mary, bp 1699 MRB, poss mar Thomas Pimer? 1727 MRB.
LIGHTFOOT, John mar Eliz. SWASEY in Salem, MA, 1680. OUTC. Other chn?
A1. Joseph, b 1681 A2. Samuel b 1683
LIHOU, old and common in G. Cf Lihou Island, C.I. Curr G and J.
LIHOU, several from G or ALD to ONT, then to Detroit, MI early 1900s? Assoc. surnames were SMITH, LE COCQ, latter said to be also from ALD

LIHOU, James, Adele and Louise from Alderney Is. to Detroit, MI 1913. Louise res NY state. (Richard Herivel, Detroit, MI)
LIHOU, Jose, Josephine?, mar Wm. M. Stockdale, res Burnaby, BC, 1981. STOCKDALE also found in G.
LILLY, LILLIE, LILLE, old in G. LILLY curr G and J.
LILLY, George, wounded in ME 1691. (Noyes) OUTC
LING, in G very early, from a sp of heather? Curr G and J.
LING, Edgar Alfred, b 1865 G? mar Elizabeth Rachel LITTLE of G or J, dau of Abraham LITTLE and Rachel LE TOCQ. LING was son of Frederick and Esther LING of G? Edgar rem to US ca 1906. (Roger Brehaut, G)
A1. Esther, mar ___ BOALCH
B1. Edna May Boalch mar Don Oldfield, res Northbrook, ILL
C1. Alice or Aline Oldfield, mar Wayne Longhorst, a son Douglas Longhorst.
C2. Janice Oldfield
A2. Edgar Frederick Ling, b 1892 mar Clarinda Ling in G? b 1890, res Chicago, ILL.
B1. Doris Ling, mar Leo Misiaszek, res Wauwautosa, WI, dau Diane.
LING, Emma Alice, b 1857 mar Edwin BRICE. Emma was sister of Edgar above, and rem to US.
A1. Edwin Edgar Brice, b 1878 d 1949, res US, mar Jenny ___
B1. Gwendoline Brice mar Dewey Keck, a dau Lores Jane Keck mar ?Borke.
LION, old and curr J. In St. Laurens J 1788. Note name in CT marriages, but OUTC.
LIRON, old and curr in J.
LISLE, see DE LISLE
LISLE, LAELL, LYALL, LOYAL, Francis from J? in Boston 1637. LISLE in St. Mary,St. Clement, and St. Saviour J 1607. LYLE, LISLE curr G.
LLOYD, Welsh surname, old in G and curr G and J.
LLOYD, Philip, b 1831 J, mar 1. 1852 Chatham, NB, Helen Christian or Christie, b 1830 Aberdeen, Scotland, d 1879 Chatham, NB, dau of Charles Christian and Mary, his wife. Philip mar 2. 1877 Margaret Williston, b 1849 Escuminac, d 1928, dau of Alex MacDonald. Philip d 1906 Escuminac, NB. (Robert Haggett, Lexington, MA)
A1. Mary Coy, b 1853, Escuminac, NB mar 1872 Chatham, NB, Robert MacLean, 1846-1921, b Chatham, son of John MacLean and Janet McColl. Mary d 1954 Ottawa, ONT.
B1. William G. MacLean, b 1875
B2. Ada MacLean, b 1876 Escuminac
B3. Gordon James MacLean, b 1878
B4. Alex. Robert MacLean, b 1880
B5. Walter W. MacLean, b 1882
B6. Lillian L. MacLean, b 1884
B7. Burton F. MacLean, b 1885
B8. Margaret H. MacLean, b 1887
B9. Bertha Jane MacLean, b 1893
B10. Bessie Pallen MacLean, b 1898
A2. George James Lloyd, b 1858 NB mar Margaret ___, adopted ch Goldie
A3. William Lawlor, b 1862 NB d 1945 Somerville, MA, mar 1890 Portland ME, Margaret Ann Rigley, b Portland, d Miami, FLA. Dau of Benj.
B1. William James b 1892 Dorchester, MA mar Bridgeport, CT, Mary Alice Bump, b 1893 d 1970 Enfield, CT ,dau of Franklin & Stella.
B2. Ethel Marion, b 1895 Dorchester mar Andrew Lawson Jr, b 1893 Dover, NJ, d 1933 Bridgeport, CT, son of Andrew & ___Rudine.
C1. Robert Lloyd Lawson, b 1916
C2. Edward Wm. Lawson, b 1918
C3. Elinor Marie Lawson, b 1920
C4. Thomas James Lawson, b 1930
B3. Marguerite Phyllis b 1898 Malden, MA mar Austin Raymond Morse, b 1900 Milford, CT, son of Wm. Austin and Minerva (Keyes)Morse
C1. Austin Raymond Morse Jr, b 1925
C2. William Allen Morse, b 1927
C3. Robert Earl Morse b 1928
B4. Robert Earl, b 1900 Pawtucket, RI d 1965 Miami, FLA mar Marion Reilly at Bridgeport, CT dau of John Henry and K.(O'Brien)Reilly.
C1. Marguerite Phyllis b 1925
C3. Ileen Marie, b 1928

C2. Elizabeth L. b 1928 C4. Robert Earl Jr, b 1935
A4. Elizabeth Vance, b 1863 Escuminac, NB d 1901 Portland, ME, mar 1889 Portland, David McNeill.
A5. Margaret, b 1865 or 1866, mar 1885 Portland, ME Robert Headley, b Scotland, d Prov., RI, 5 chn: Helen, Winnifred, Robert, Wm. and John Headley.
A6. Jessie Alecta, b 1870 Escuminac, NB d 1965. Mar 1888 Portland, ME, James Frederick Albert Comber.
B1. Georgia Eliz. Comber, b 1888 d 1936 Oakland, CAL, mar 1918 San Francisco, CAL,Charles A. Stork, b 1884 SF, d 1951 Hayward, CAL
B2. Philip Michael Comber, b 1890 Portland, ME mar 1917 CAL Amelia Barbara Rohrbach, b 1895 Oakland, CAL, dau of Joseph Philip and Augusta (Schuler) Rohrbach.
C1. Phyllis Jane Rohrbach Comber, b 1926 mar George Doherty, a son
D1. Dennis Michael Doherty b 1946
B3. a son, b 1892, d.y. B4. ?
B5. James F.A. Comber Jr, b 1897 mar 1932 Alameda, CAL, Undine Mona Rehfuss, b 1906 San Fran., dau of Herman and Elizabeth Ann (Ward) Rehfuss.
C1. Undine Jessie Comber, b 1935 C2. Patricia Ann Comber, b 1937
B6. Helen Margaret Comber, b 1899 MA, mar 1923 Los Angeles, CAL, Albert Leonard Johnson, b 1900 NEB, son of Carl Johnson.
C1. Georgia Helen Johnson, b 1920 mar Edward A. Davis. 4 chn: Sharon Ann, Nancy Lee, b 1944, Judith C. and Edward A. Davis.
C2. Alberta Winifred Johnson, mar Ben Furman Wilkes, res CAL. 3 chn: Edward H., Sandra Nan, Deborah Sue Wilkes
C3. Leonard T. Johnson mar Juanita Stewart C4. Eugene M. Johnson
C5. Grace Madeline Johnson mar Gerald Arlen Beam, 2 chn: Randal A. and Donna Jean Beam.
C6. William Clinton Johnson C7. Richard Paul Johnson, b 1934
B7. Grace Madeline Comber, b 1901 mar 1918 San Fran., CAL, Benne La Vergne Slimmer, b 1898 KS, son of Oliver and Aimee (Wood)Slimmer.
C1. George Lloyd Slimmer, mar Gertrude Sue NICHOLAS
D1. Nicholas L. Slimmer, b 1946 D2. Lyndell S. Slimmer, b 1947
C2. Aimee Lynette Slimmer, mar Harry D. Brown III.
D1. Lynn Ardith Brown, b 1941 D2. Robert Douglas Brown, b 1942
C3. Oliver Comber Slimmer, mar Wanda Willey
D1. Tracy Joe Slimmer, b 1947 San Diego, CAL.
A7. Ellemina b 1875
A8. Isabella Jane by 2nd wife, b 1878 Escuminac, NB d 1969. Mar 1.1899 Portland, ME,John Hiram Fletcher, b 1871 Delphos, OH, son of Charlesand Elizabeth (Towle) Fletcher.
B1. Charles Lloyd Fletcher, b 1900 Portland B2. Harold Lloyd, b 1901
A9. Ellen Louisa, b 1880 NB d 1968 New Bedford, MA, mar Donald Angus McLean, who d 1934?
B1. Leithwood Lloyd McLean, b 1909 mar Carol Thomas, 2 chn: Janet and Edwin McLean
B2. Mary Thelma McLean, b1910 Loggieville, NB mar Raymond Eva, b 1909.
C1. Mary Elizabeth Eva, b 1936 mar Paul R. Daniels, b 1933, 2 chn: Donna and Joan Daniels.
C2. Raymond Donald Eva, b 1942
B3. Philip Augustine, b 1912
A10. Phyllis Alvina, b 1884 NB, d 1922 Greenwood Mt., ME, mar in Westbrook, ME, George Delaney, b Trenton, NJ, d 1921, son of John Delaney and Catherine Campbell.
B1. Margaret Delaney, b 1910 Chatham, NB mar 1929 Westbrook, ME, Hugh Francis Kennedy, b 1897 Pawtucket, RI, son of John Kennedy and

and Mary Cosgrove. twin

C1. Mary Margaret Kennedy, b 1930 C6. Hugh Francis Kennedy, b 1939,
C2. stillborn, 1931 C7. Phyllis Eliz. Kennedy, b 1941
C3. Maureen Rita Kennedy, b 1932 C8. Sharon Ann Kennedy, b 1945, twin
C4. Patricia Ann Kennedy, b 1935 C9. Sheila Kennedy, b 1945, twin
C5. Sue Frances Kennedy, b 1939, twin.

A11. John Alexander, b 1887 NB mar Mary Matilda MacRae/McGraw?, dau of Gregory MacRae and Annie Nowlan, 10 chn

B1. Marion Helena, b 1909 NB, mar Earnest Jenkins, son of George.

C1. Lola Jenkins C3. George Jenkins
C2. Lora Ann Jenkins C4. Marilyn Ann Jenkins

B2. John Roy, b 1911 NB mar Delilah MacIntire, dau of Robert.

C1. Sharon Ann, b 1944 C2. Bryan, b 1946

B3. Arthur Donald, b 1913 NB mar Lydia MARTIN, dau of Charles MARTIN and ___HACHEY

C1. Claude, b 1935 Dalhousie, NB C2. Leola C3. Donald Arthur

B4. Philip Earl, b 1914 mar Myra Martin, dau of Benj. and Grace Martin 2 chn b Chatham, NB, Belinda and Wesley

B5. Pearl Mary, b 1917 mar Albert Savoy, a son Lloyd Savoy b 1941

B6. Doris Ann, b 1919 mar Allen Ross in Toronto, ONT

B7. Gerald Raphael, b 1925 mar Bernetta Jenkins

B8. Cecil William, b 1928 mar Orine Martin, 1948 Toronto, ONT.

B9. Aloysius George, b 1930 B10. Noreen Ann, b 1936

A12. Donald Edrick b 1889 NB mar 1. Ella Nowland, dau of John and Ellen Nowland, and 2. Stella Thiboudeault

B1. Eldon, b NB mar Emilda Tebo, at least 4 chn: Marvin, Donald, Leonard, Irene, etc.

B2. Alfred, mar Mona O'Leary, dau of Florez and Minnie (Bransfield) O'Leary, res Chatham, NB?

B3. Reginald, mar Audrey Jimmeau, dau of Edmond.

B4. Phyllis, mar Harold Preston, son of Edmond and Clara (Jimmeau) Preston.

B5. Hollis B6. Edric

LLOYD, some in early New England, in MRB, etc, a few from J?

LOARING old in G and current. None verified in US by compiler.

LONGE, this appears in some records instead of correct name LOUGEE.

LOGGEE, LOGGIE, in J 1377, note LOGGIEVILLE in NB. Not researched.

LONEY, not in this form a C.I. surname. However, it appears in conjunction with C.I.Fam in America. Poss that this is a phonetic spelling of LAUNAY, curr G, or LE LAUNE, old in J, both pron. much like LONEY.

LONEY, John Sr., b G? mar Susan COHU, qv, b G, dau of Peter and Judith. He soon d, 1800s, and Susan mar 2. Wm. Mansbandle. See COHU. (Susan George, Pheonix, AZ)

A1. John Jr., b 1815 NY, mar 1835 Sarah Ann Montgomery. John d 1845.

LONGLEY, see LANGLOIS.

LONGLEY, Robert and Anna of Bolton, MA. OUTC. Note Eli, often in C.I. (STATE OF MAINE, by Little, Vol 3, see for more data)

A1. Eli, b 1762, mar 1784 Mary Whitcomb, dau of John W. of Bolton, MA. Eli became member of Gen. Court of MA, built first hotel and store and was first postmaster in Waterford, ME. His tavern, Eli Longley's Inn, in 1797 Raymond, ME.

B1. Rebecca, b 1802 Waterford, d Casco, ME 1879. Mar John SAWYER, b 1800 Standish, ME d 1870 Casco, ME, farmed & kept Longley's Inn. 6 chn.

LONSDALE, Frederick, English Dramatist, b 1881 J? said to be pseudonym of Fred. Leaonard Seaman of J. He was author of several famous plays such as THE LAST OF MRS. CHENEY, and PRIVATE LIFE OF DON JUAN. The surname SEAMMEN is curr in J.

LOUGEE, LOGEE, LOUGIER, not listed by Stevens as old J surname. Poss Huguenot? However, LOGGE was in J 1377. Note that LAUGEE was in J 1692. More work needed on origin.

There is much LOUGEE data in various places, but compiler does not know if these fams are part of the original fam, or came from Europe at other times, from other places than Jersey Island. See records of Rhode Island for LOGEE, records of Loudon, VT and Canterbury, VT. A fam in Oakfield, ME is thought to be part of the C.I. LOUGEE fam, poss connected with the Limerick, ME branch.

LOUGEE, John b ca 1682 or 1695 J? mar ca 1718 Exeter, NH Ann Gilman, dau of Moses and Ann (Heard) Gilman. John d 1759? age 77. Ann d in Exeter, NH 1771. One fam tradition says John arrived ca 1702 on vessel FOUR FRIENDS, owned and captained by Jean JANVRIN, qv. of J, who also settled there. John was captured by Indians, but survived, and returned to New England, 9 chn. There is much more on this fam. See sources. (Dearborn; Swasey; Savage; Coleman; Noyes; NEHGS Vol 118; MS by Winifred Holman; HIST. OF GILMANTON; Runnells HIST. OF SANBORNTON, NH, Vol 2; HIST OF CANTERBURY, VT; STARR GEN; FLOOD GEN; BICKNELL GEN; Essex Coll, Vol 2; HIST. OF PARSONSFIELD, ME; HIST OF EXETER; HIST OF LITTLETON, NH; HIST. OF BARNSTEAD; Merrills HIST. AND GEN OF BARNSTEAD EARLY FAMS; HIST OF ROCHESTER, NH; SAMUEL FOGG, His Ancestors and descendants; NH TOWN PAPERS, comp. by Isaac W. Hammond; 1883; Smith Cem., Gilmanton; War Memorials, Gilmanton; Microfilms fr from Mormon Archives; Mrs. Eda St. John's paper dated 1974; Grave stones in Prot. Cem., Compton, QUE; Church records, Sherbrooke, QUE; Stearns NH GEN, Vol 4; JOHN LOUGEE AND SOME OF HIS DESC IN NEHGS, 1964?; THOMAS MUDGETT AND SOME OF HIS DESC OF SALISBURY, MA; GILMANS OF HINGHAM, England; EDGERLY AND ALLIED FAMS; John Herlihy, Silver Spgs., MD; Rose Morrison, Needham, MA; Hilda Lincoln, Gainesville,MO; Charlotte Nicely, Pensacola, FLA; Prescott Brown, Tolland, CT, etc)

A1. John, Clothier, trader, innkeeper, Baptist, b ca 1719, prob in Exeter, NH mar 1. ca 1744, prob at Exeter, Molly Leavitt, who d ca 1761. Mar 2. ca 1762 Susan Hull, and 3. in 1789 Gilmanton, NH, Judith, widow of ___JACKSON, Thomas Chattle and Thomas Beale. Judith d 1836 age 97. 9 chn plus 6 chn, none by 3rd wife.

B1. Sarah/Sally, b ca 1745 Exeter, mar Jotham Gilman 1770, 1747-1819, son of Jonathan Gilman. They res Gilmanton after 1773. Sarahd1820

C1. Polly Gilman C3. Joseph Gilman C5. Betsy Gilman C7. Abigail Gilman
C2. Cotton Gilman C4. Sally Gilman C6. Alice Gilman

B2. John, cordwainer, b ca 1747, mar Anna Avery, dau of Samuel. John later had a fulling mill and store.

B3. Nehemiah, b ca 1749 mar ca 1768 Mary MARSH. He d 1833 age 73, was in Gilmanton, NH 1776

C1. Nehemiah C2. Lucy C3. Nancy C4. Isaac

C5. John, b 1771, soldier in War of 1812, wounded, hatter by trade, mar 1801 Betsey, dau of Joseph MARSH, b 1781 Gilmanton, d 1867.

D1. Leavitt, b 1801 D 3. Eliza, mar Frank MARTIN.

D2. Olive, b ___, mar Timothy BARNARD in the West.

D4. John, b 1806, mar 1831 Rebecca, dau of David Edgerly. John d/1893

E1. George, d.y. E2. Laura, mar Charles H. Thompson

E3. Julia A., mar Horace Edgerly, 2 chn: Albert C. & Annie M.

E4. George, d.y. E5. Clara, d.y. E6. Emma, d.y.

E7. Dudley E8. Betsey

D5. Joseph, b 1810, d.y. D8. Jacob Moody, b 1820, d as young man

D6. Charles b 1819 mar Mary Ross
D7. Hazen, poss mar 1836 Mrs. Susanna B. Packard Bicknell, QuincyMA
D9. Merill, b 1825 mar Susan Wheeler
D10. Joseph b 1826 mar Mary Ann Sargent
B4. Joseph Leavitt, b 1751 Exeter, NH d 1845 age 94, Gilmanton, NH mar 1. Apphia SWAZEY, who d ca 1780. He mar 2. 1780 Miriam Fogg, b 1757, dau of John and Betty (Dearborn) Fogg, who d 1849,13 chn.
C1. Elisha, b 1772 Exeter, mar 1794 Nancy Lord, dau of Robert, d1860 Elisha d 1843. Poss other chn?
D1. Joseph, mar Sally Cram, a dau Elmira mar Franklyn R. Osgood
D2. Charles, b 1794 mar 1816 Hannah, dau of Jonathan C. Sanborn, b 1794, res Littleton, NH, 1823-1836, farmer, served in War of 1812, d 1863 Sheffield, VT.
E1. Darius, b 1816 Sanbornton, mar 1857 Eliza T. Marsh, who d 1862 at Danville, VT.
E2. Jonathan S., b 1818 mar 1847 Mary Pierce. Jonathan a carpenter res St. Johnsbury, VT.
E3. Mary S., b 1820 mar 1847 Allen Higgins
E4. John L. b 1822, mar 1850 Mary Somerville, served in Civil War, d 1865.
E5. Judith Ann, b 1826 Littleton, NH mar 1. 1859 Joseph Hoyt, farmer, who d Lyndon, VT. She mar 2. 1870 Decatur C. Hoyt of VT.
E6. Hannah, b 1828 mar 1860 D.W. Fisher of Lyndon, VT
E7. Chastina, b 1832, d 1842
E8. George C., b 1836, merchant in Turner's Falls, MA mar 1864 Sophia Bickford.
C2. Polly, b ca 1774, d.y. C4. Polly, b ca 1781 mar Abel Dudley
C3. Apphia, b ca 1776 mar Dudley Swazey C5. Sally, b ca 1783, d.y.
C6. Sally again, b ca 1785 mar Asa Page
C7. John Fogg, b 1787 mar Anna Smith, dau of Dr. Wm. Smith of Gilmanton. John d 1880 age 93 at Rochester, NH. A Dr. Isaac Williams appears in this branch.
D1. Joseph, d at age 25, other chn?
C8. Anna, b ca 1789 Exeter, NH mar Moses STEPHENS
C9. Joseph, b ca 1791 mar Mary Greeley Smith, rem to Compton, QUE. Poss other chn? Mary apparently mar 2. ___Woodward, and had 4 chn by him: Josephine, Georgina, Mary Jane (who mar Hon. Joseph G. Robertson of Sherbrooke, QUE) and James Robertson Woodward, of Sherbrooke. Joseph d 1878 at Compton, QUE.
D1. Charles Frederick, mar Jane B. ___, who was a widow 1900. Charles d 1898. 4 daus.
E1. Mary E., mar Charles C. Davis of NYCity
E2. Jennie R., mar Dalton Fallon of Brookline, MA
E3. Josephine, mar John H. Fallon of Salem, MA.
E4. Susan C., an attorney! acted on behalf of her fam 1900.
D2. Mary Greeley
D3. Noah Smith, who d after 1872 (will date) mar Harriet Julia MARTIN, a son Martin M. res Sherbrooke, QUE. Other chn?
D4. Poss a son Francis Claude?
C10. Seth, b ca 1792 Exeter, mar 1. 1819 Gilmanton, NH, Joanna Kimball, who d 1841 at Compton, QUE. Mar 2. Asenath VINCENT, 1802-1874. Seth d 1871, all bur Prot. Cem. at Compton, QUE.
D1. Darius D2. Lucinda, b 1819, d 1904 Compton, QUE, unmar
D3. Julia Ann, b 1818 Gilmanton, NH mar Benj. Davis, b VT, d Oswego, NY? Julia d 1908 Compton, QUE
E1. Hannah Maria Davis, b ca 1845 QUE, unmar
E2. Edwin Seth Davis, b 1850 Whitehall, NY d 1893 Lowell, MA.

E3. Sarah Lucinda Davis, b 1851 Whitehall, NY, mar 1876 in QUE Charles Napier Brown, b 1854 QUE, son of John and Margaret Annis (Wilson) Brown. Both d QUE, she in 1914, he in 1912.

F1. Francis Lee Brown, b 1879 Compton, mar 1908 Louise Violet Baird. Francis d 1931 Winnipeg, MAN. Louise b 1880 Woodstock, NB, d 1943. Francis a pharmacist, Montreal & Winnipeg.

G1. Mabel Louise Brown, b 1911 Winnipeg, mar 1933 John Reginald McMillen, son of George A. and Mary. He was exec. with CNR and res Victoria, BC

H1. Frank Donald McMillan, b 1933 mar 1955 Barbara G. Munro, 4 chn: Barbara, Susan, Catherine & John McMillen

H2. Mary Lou McMillan

H3. Marion Jerrine McMillan, b 1938, mar 1962 Leland L. Hansen of Westwood Village, CAL, 3 chn: Nancy, Frank, Gregory

G2. Robert Asquith Brown, b 1915 Winnipeg, mar 1941 Elizabeth E. Smith, b Vivian, MAN, worked for CNR, no issue

F2. Harry Raymond Brown, b 1883 Compton, QUE mar 1915 in MA, Minnie M. Libbey, b 1891 Beaufort, SC, dau of C.F. and Ida (Blodgett) Libbey. Harry d 1953 Hartford, CT, she in 1977

G1. Prescott Libbey Brown, b 1916 Compton, QUE mar 1938 Mendham, NJ, Yvonne S. Crilly, b 1915 Hartford, dau of John A. and Eleanor (Stephen) Crilly.

H1. Eleanor Madge Brown, b 1939 Hartford, mar 1. 1959 Tolland, CT, Raymond J. Caldwell and 2. Clifton G. Drew, 2 chn by each: Cheryl-Ann, Wm. D. Caldwell; Scott A. and Chris.C. Drew

H2. Doris Ruth Brown, b 1946 mar 1968 James Peter Stamos, a dau Christina K. Stamos.

G2. Charles Davis Brown, b 1918 Lennoxville, QUE mar 1943 Natalie M. Pattelkan. CHarles d 1944, RCAF flyer in Germany.

G3. Phyllis Brown, b 1920 G4. Frederick Brown, b 1922, d.y.

G5. Ida Elizabeth Brown, b 1925 Hartford, CT mar 1952 Alphonso Genovese, who d 1979, 2 sons: John Peter and Patrick Genovese

G6. Mildred Brown, b 1927 mar Charles M.D. Rarus, dau Wendy

G7. Barbara Brown, b 1935 mar 1957 John Joseph Shea, 4 chn: Cynthia, Pamela, Jeffrey and David Shea.

F3. Mabel E. Brown, b 1891 Compton, QUE d there 1908.

E4. Eliza Lovilla Davis, b 1854 Oswego, NY mar 1874 Marquis Lafayette Willett, who d 1885 Compton, QUE. She d 1891 Lowell, MA.

F1. Albert Leroy Willett, b 1877 Compton, QUE d 1879

F2. George Leon Willett, b 1881 mar 1911 Lowell, MA, Edytha Young dau of Wm. and Augusta (Scruton) Young. George served in Panama Canal Zone. She d 1955 Tampa, FLA, and he in 1974

G1. Leon Edward Willett, b 1911 Canal Zone, d 1912

G2. Adelaide Edith Willett, b 1913 Panama, mar 1938 Lawrence Fansler Bushong, b 1912 Timberville, VA

H1. Philip Lewis Bushong, b 1943 Canal Zone mar 1965 in New Market, VA Dorothy S. Kite and 2. Lois E. Riggins.

H2. John Alan Bushong, b 1945 mar 1969 Binghamton, NY Carol Smith

F3. Katie Barbara Willett, b 1883 QUE, d 1884 F4. Charles Willett

E5. Julia A. Davis b 1856 Oswego, NY mar Charles A. Colby, res MA.

F1. Sybil Colby F2. Bertha Colby

E6. Charles Dearborn Davis, b 1857 Oswego, NY mar 1884 Anna Maria Dwight, b 1855 Hatfield, MA, dau of Ebenezer and Sarah A. (Strong) Dwight. Charles a tinsmith in Springfield, MA d 1911. and she in 1941. 4 chn: Raymond, Harold, Elmer, and Marion L.

D4. ?Samuel, b 1820 Gilmanton, NH mar Sarah Barnet, d 1907 QUE.

D5. ?John True Lougee, b 1823 mar Alsina Carr, 1823-1898, d 1905.

C11. Daniel, b ca 1795 Exeter, NH mar Sally Kimball, b 1797. He d 1886 and she in 1891. Both bur Smith Meeting House Cem., Gil.
D1. Francis S., b 1842 d 1862 Washington, DC in Army, 12th NH.Vol.
C12. Samuel, b 1797 Exeter, d 1819 Gilmanton, NH
C13. Dearborn, b 1801, mar 1825 Henrietta Wheeler, and d 1881 Somersworth, NH. Chn?
B5. Jesse, b ca 1753 Exeter, NH d 1816 Gilmanton, mar Polly Rollins? or Rawlings?, 5 daus: Lucy, Hannah, Sally, Polly, Elsey.
B6. Molly, b ca 1755 mar Moses Stevens 1783 Gilmanton, NH
B7. Jonathan, b ca 1757 Exeter? mar 1. Haverhill, MA, Elizabeth Mitchell, and 2. Lois ___. Res Fairlee or Thetford, VT 1846
B8. Elsie, Elsey, b ca 1759 Gilmanton, NH
B9. William ,b ca 1871 mar 1788 Sarah Brown
B10. by 2nd wife, Henry, b ca 1763 prob in Gilmanton, mar Sarah Mason res Gilmanton, NH 1810. 10 chn: John, Judith, Henry, Sarah, Benjamin, Thomas, Susan, Samuel, William and Joseph.
B11. Shuah, b ca 1765 Gilmanton, mar John Pittman
B12. Susan, b ca 1767 Exeter, NH B14. Sarah, b ca 1774
B13. Benjamin, b 1772 Gilmanton, mar 1791 Ruth Folsom. He d 1847 VT?
B15. Emerson, b ca 1778, d 1844 Gilmanton, poss fam listed as bur in Crystal Lake Cem., formerly known as Lougees Pond. A Gilman d.y.1818; infant d 1826; Betsey d 1861 age 44; Emerson d 1867 age 63; Lydia d 1868 age 55.
B16. Sarah? (Lancaster's HIST. OF GILMANTON)
A2. Joseph, tailor, b ca 1723 Exeter? mar 1. before 1742 Elizabeth Scribner, and 2. by 1787 Lydia Lamson. Joseph d 1790s, 6 chn
B1. Betty, bp 1747/8 Exeter, NH B4. John, bp 1757
B2. Joseph, bp 1753 B5. Nicholas, bp 1759, d.y.
B3. Simeon, bp 1755 B6. Nicholas again, bp 1762
A3. Anna, b ca 1725, mar 1753 Jonathan Folsom, his 2nd wife, res Brentwood, Exeter, NH.
A4. Moses, b ca 1727 mar Lydia Folsom, ca 1748, served in Louisburg Expedition 1745. He and wife both dead by 1785, more data, puzzling, in WRCIC.
B1. Mehitable, bp 1751 Exeter, NH B3. John, bp 1755 B5. Moses,b 1760
B2. Jonathan F., bp 1753 B4. Noah, with desc in TN named Cooney?
A5. Gilman, a tailor, b 1729 d 1811, mar 1752 Kingston, NH Susannah Mudgett, b 1737, d 1811 Parsonsfield, ME, dau of John and Susan (Scribner) Mudgett, rem to Gilmanton 1763. Uncertain, see sources. 14 chn?
B1. Gilman, b 1753 Exeter, d 1788 Parsonsfield, ME mar 1775 Joanna SMITH, b 1759 d 1831, res Parsonsfield, ME 1778
C1. Susanna, b 1781 mar John BENNETT
C2. Gilman, b 1783 mar Mary Buzzell 1810
D1. Mary, b 1811 mar Augustus Wentworth D3. Ann B., 1815-1840
D2. Joanna, b 1813 mar Samuel Eastman of Cornish, NH, a son
D4. Gilman, b 1817 mar Elmira B. Richardson
E1. Juliett, b 1842 mar Ansel HAWKES E2. Mary A., b 1843 mar
E2. Mary A., b 1843 mar Stephen A. Hussey
E3. Amelia, b 1845 mar Nathaniel Hussey
E4. Delphina, b 1847 mar Dr. Osborn G. Lord
E5. Hugh B., b 1848 mar Annah Eastman, dau of Timothy Eastman.
E6. Louisa R., b 1851 mar 1. Simeon P. Gerrish and 2. Samuel Garland, son of Ira Garland.
E7. David G., b 1858 mar Almira L. Fogg
F1. Arthur Fogg, mar ___
G1. Arthur Townsend, had chn: David, Eleanor and Arthur LOUGEE

D5. Susan B., b 1821 mar D.W.C. Merrill, a son Fred Merrill.
D6. John, b 1823, mar Marshall Peirce of Saco, ME. Marshall?
D7. Albion K.P., b 1827 mar 1. Mary Thurston and 2. Orinda Merrill of Limerick, ME
D8. Clarinda S., b 1829 mar Thomas Brown.
C3. Hugh Bartis, b 1785, rem to Salem, MA?
D1. Delphine D2. Marguerite D3. Aileen D4. Marion
C4. Joanna, b 1788 mar Jonathan Watson
B2. Samuel, b ca 1755/60, prob in Exeter, mar 1779 Sarah Rand, some chn. Was first settler of E. Parsonsfield, ME 1780. Data on chn is unverified
C1. Taylor? b 1784 mar 1. ___Watson, had sons Samuel and Thomas. Mar 2. ___Tibbetts, had sons Greenleaf and Sylvester of Effingham, NH? Sylvester or Greenleaf had large fam including a lawyer and 2 doctors. Taylor d after 1840.
D. or E.? Dr. George E. Lougee of Freedom, NH mar 1827 Sabrina Hayes of Limerick, 2 sons, Hayes and Cyrus.
B3. John, Capt. John?, b 1758 Exeter, NH d 1832 age 74, mar Betsy Smith b 1765.
C1. John, b 1784 mar Anna Parsons, settled in S. Parsonsfield, NH. 9 chn: John P., Abigail M., Charles, d.y., George W., Elizabeth, Caleb, James S. d.y., James F., and Charles.
C2. Samuel b 1787 mar Sally Goodwin, dau of Aaron, b 1795.
C3. Dorothy, b 1788 C4. Simeon, b 1795
C5. Gilman, b 1796 mar dau of James Sanborn, a son John res Parsonsfield
C6. Elizabeth, b 1798 mar Dr. Wilkinson of Tamworth, NH
C7. Sarah, b 1801 mar John Dearborn, son of Francis and d in Dexter, Maine
C8. William R., b 1804 C9. Horatio P., b 1806
C10. Ithiel S., lived and d at E. Parsonsfield, NH, at least 2 sons, John and Abner, also res there.
B4. Susanna, b 1760 Exeter, d.y.
B5. Jonathan b 1761, d 1851 age 90 in Canterbury, NH, Shaker Covenant in 1796. Poss mar Nancy Simpson 1783 at Exeter, was in 1790 Canterbury, NH census.
B6. Susanna living 1807, b 1764 Gilmanton, mar 1788 Peter Dudley
C1. Anna Dudley, b 1789 C3. Susanna Dudley b 1798
C2. Peter Dudley b 1795 C4. Nicholas Gilman Dudley b 1801
B7. Simeon, b 1767 Gilmanton, NH d 1855 Barnstead, NH mar 1. Molly Smith b 1773 in 1794, and 2. Mary/Polly Edgerly 1813 in Barnstead, NH. Mary b 1778.
C1. Susannah mar Joseph Sleeper C2. Mary mar Isaac Joseph
C3. Betsy mar Samuel Woodman
C4. Lydia b 1800 mar Joseph C. Young, b 1800, son of Phineas and Dorothy. Lydia d 1882 and Joseph in 1862.
D1. Francis Young, 1820-1846
D2. Laura Young, b 1839 D3. Jane G. Young b 1840
C5. Simeon Jr, b 1806 mar Mary Tebbetts b 1810, dau of Ephraim and ___Tebbetts. Simeon a shoemaker. Mary d 1879, Simeon 1891
D1. Clara b 1844 D2. John G., 1848-1873 D3. David
C6. Ann, 1808-1837 C7. Gilman, 1815-1842
C8. David, b 1817 mar Betsey McDuffee b 1828. He d 1894, she 1897
D1. Leslie, d 1936
B8. Anna, b 1769, d 1846, mar 1791 David Edgerly, anc. of C. Nicely.
B9. Betty, b ca 1768, mar 1791 Levi Rundlett of Meredith, NH
B10. Levi, b ca 1770, d.y. B11. Joseph b ca 1772, d.y.
B12. Levi again, b ca 1774, d.y.
B13. Molly, b ca 1776 d by 1807, poss mar Capt. Thomas Ross of

Parsonsfield, ME 1799.

B14. Lydia, b ca 1778, poss Shaker Covenant 1796. Poss mar Jonathan Gilman 1807 at Exeter, NH.

A6. Edmund b 1731 mar ca 1754 Hannah Lord, sister of Robert, and dau of Jonathan and Hannah (LIGHT) Lord. D 1807 Loudon, NH

B1. Hanah?, b 1855 Exeter, NH Other chn?

A7. Shuah, b ca 1734, prob in Exeter, NH, poss a Susannah?

A8. Elizabeth, b ca 1737, living 1770. Mar Robert Lord 1757, son of Jonathan and Hannah (LIGHT) Lord, b 1735 Ipswich, MA.

B1. Robert Lord, b 1758, d.y. B3. Hannah Lord, b 1765 B5. Betty Lord
B2. William Lord, b 1760 B4. Robert Lord, b 1768 b 1770

A9. Joanna, b 1745 Exeter, mar 1767 Eliphalet Gilman, res Kensington, NH. She d 1810 Halowell, ME.

LOUVEL, LOVELL in J ca 1150. LOUVEL curr J. LOVELL curr G and J.

LOVELL, LOUELL, Benjamin Berwick, ME 1696. (Noyes) OUTC

LOVELL, Elisha res Newcastle, NH 1720, with wife Mary Loving? of Newcastle, bp Oyster River, NH 1728. (Noyes) OUTC.

LOVELL, John? a passenger on the THREE FRIENDS, wrecked in Casco Bay, ME 1711. (Noyes) OUTC.

LOVELL, John, arrived in Boston 1760s on sloop ADVENTURE from Nfld., a mariner. His name was spelled LOVLEL. (Whitmore) OUTC.

LOW, Thomas from C.I. in MA before 1650.

LOVETT, curr G and J. Not traced.

LOWE, in C.I. Curr G and J.

LOW, John of Fifeshire, Scotland settled in J, mar there 1798 Elizabeth Villeneuve, of Hug? fam, 13 chn. (CIFHS Autumn 1981) Poss the Low bros. of ONT were from this fam. See Q.A. IN CANADA.

LOW, at least 30 of this name had households in MA 1790. Were some from the C.I.? OUTC. Cf LOWE, 31 households, ditto. Note John, E Elias, Joshua and Judith. Lowe from J to Canada 1800s.

LUCAS in J 1274, old in G. Curr G and J. See COHU

LUCAS, many in early New England, none verified as from C.I. See records in NH, MD, CT, VT; Bicknell Gen; Baldwin's SC records, etc. Augustin Lucas was a Hug. to RI.

LUCAS, Leland of Tucson, AZ, said to be from J fam.

LUCAS, John C.V. of Arcadia, CAL, from J fam in the 1800s, Midwest.

LUCAS, Daniel, mar Harriet Mansbandle. See chn of Susan COHU and John LONEY. OUTC.

LUCE, surname of France, C.I. and the south of England. In J 1515, also in G early. In St. Laurens and St. Heliers J 1668, and in St. Peter, St. John and St. Laurens J 1749. LUCE arms: Azure, a crescent argent. LUCE crest: an eagle with wings displayed regardant, holding in dexter claw a sword erect, all proper. LUCE curr G and J. See CIFHS #9.

"It is considered probable that most of the Luce families came to England either directly from France or from the Isle of Jersey." (Third and Last REVISION OF THE AMERICAN DESCENDANTS OF HENRY LUCE OF MARTHA'S VINEYARD, 1640-1978, by Marcia Fletcher McCourt, softbound, copy in Western Reserve Gen. Library, Cleveland, OH)LUCE ON LONG ISLAND, by C.E. Luce, 1979, also in WR Lib. Compiler has rec'd info from desc saying that Henry came from England, others say he came from C.I. Much data on his desc available.

LUCE, Philippe, also known as Philip Lewis, b ca 1817 as Hilliard John Luce in J, d 1892 Miscou, NB, Canada. His father may have been from Normandy, or was native to J. Philip enlisted at 18 in Brit. Navy and mar Martha DOREY of J, 2 chn. She soon died, and his chn were given temporarily to a BISSON. He then settled about 10 yrs. later in Grande Riviere, QUE, and mar 2. Annie Ward, from a fam of NY, settled in Gaspe, the dau of Wm. and ___(Hays) Ward. Philip had his chn brought to Canada, and after his 5th ch was born, the fam res Bonaventure, QUE, and later in Chatham, NB and Miscou Island, NB ca 1880. (GEN.PHILIP LUCE,by T.W. Luce, Box997, Penticton, BC,V2A-7N7) 10 chn, plus 3 d.y. See book.

A1. William, b ca 1854 J mar Ellen Gerret, Bathurst, NB, 9 chn.

A2. Mary, b ca 1857 J mar Frank Scott of New Carlisle, QUE, his 2nd wife, 6 chn, many desc.

A3. Charles Philip, by 2nd wife, b 1864, res Three Rivers, QUE and Bathurst, NB, mar 1886 Marie Ann Vallee, b 1863 Island River, NB, had farm, and lobster fishery, was coastal shipper, customs officer. 13 chn, many desc.

A4. Marie Genevieve, b 1865 rem to US, poss Bangor, ME? where she mar a Mr. Curran.

A5. Elie Jean/John Lewis, b Hamilton, QUE, called John Lewis, b 1867, rem to US early 20s, settled in Rhinelander, WIS, where he operated a greenhouse. Mar ___, had 4 chn, including 2 sons, Hilliard and Leonard, who res NM, a dau in WIS and another dau in Winnipeg, MAN.

A6. Francois/Frank, b 1869 rem to E. Millinocket, ME, but not found

A7. Thomas Wallace LEWIS, b 1870 mar in Carquet, NB, Georgina DeGrace, and 2. in 1911, mar Elizabeth Duguay, and 3. in 1934, Madeleine Saint-Coeur, d 1959 NB. 7 chn by 1st wife, 4 by 2nd and 9 by 3rd.

A8. George, bp 1872 NB, d 1928 Middle River, NB. Mar 1894 Clementine de Silva, 14 chn.

A9. Mary Anne Elizabeth b 1874 d 1920, mar Island River, NB, 1896 Olivier Vallee, dau Rita who mar Ernest Chiasson, had 14 chn.

LUCE, see Ralph RENOUF

LUCE, Alexander from C.I.? to Portsmouth, NH early 1700s. A dau Hannah bp 1736/7, and son John bp 1744. (NEHGS Vol 81) OUTC

LUCE, Capt Edward, master of the MARY, from J and Falmouth, England to Boston 1715. (Whitmore) A Capt. John LUCE had sloop MARY 1729. (A. John Jean, Jersey) (Whitmore)

LUCE, Capt. Joseph, mariner, to Boston 1769 on ship MOLLY from J./

LUCE, see FOLLOWING THE FRONTIER, By Freeman Tilden, NY, 1964; Ed Bailey, Ashland, OR; Boston VR; HIST. OF BARNARD VT; Noyes, CT Marriages and books noted at beginning of LUCE.

LUCE, Donald, b J, rem to Burnaby, BC, mar Pamela DOWNER, dau of Arthur of J. To Canada 1955, 2 sons, Darren and Nigel. (Elaine Hall, Toronto, ONT)

LUCE, Rachel, widow of Edw. LE MESSURIER, who wrote to her bro-in-law, Benj. LE MESSURIER in Salem, MA from J 1677. (NEHGS Vol 31)

LUSCOMBE in G before 1809. Curr G.

LUSHER. Shows up in FIRST SETTLERS OF NEW ENGLAND by John Farmer. An Eleazar was in Dedham, MA 1638. OUTC, but LUSHER is very similar in sound to LACHEUR. See LASHURE and LE LACHEUR.

MABEY, MABILLE in G 1300s. MABEY curr G.
MACE, MASSY, MASSEY, MASSIE, Agnes from C.I., mar ____VALPY, qv in Dover, Me. 1733. MACE in J 1515, curr G.
MACE, Samuel from G? in VA and Carolinas 1600s. OUTC. Note also James MASSEY in VA from G, poss MACE ? Peter MASE in ME 1695. (Noyes) OUTC.
MACDONALD, research curr in C.I. See CIFHS #8
MACHON in J 1340. In St. Martin J 1668, in St. Martin and Grouville,J 1749. In St. Laurens J 1788. MACHON in G 1200s. In St. Saviour G 1777, current.
MACHONS are still involved in travel! John of the RI fams has lived and worked in Argentina, Guam, S.Africa, Cuba, Chile, Nassau, Arabia, and parts of the Mid-East, Latin America, and Europe.
MACHON, in 1806 a large fam consisting of several married bros sailed from G to Prince Edward Island, Canada, a shipload of 73 men, women and chn. They were convoyed part way over by a man-of-war, owing to the conflict between France and England at that time. See Q.A. IN CANADA. (Pat Sinclair, Charlottesville, VA; Mrs. Chester Le Lacheur, PEI; Herbert Machon, Bristol, NH; Leland Nicolle, Murray Harbor, PEI, Heritage Foundation, PEI; Doris Le Lacheur, Burlington, ONT; Elizabeth Graham, London, ONT; Alice Roes, Dorothy, ALTA; Marilyn Cahill, Cherry Hill, NJ; Charles M. Machon, Randolph, MA and Mrs. F.D. Machon, Champaign, ILL) MANY DESCENDANTS TO US.
MACHON, Daniel, b ca 1767 d 1828 PEI, mar Frances Pullem, Pullen, Poulain, Pulham? Not clear if she was English or from G. She was the sister of Mrs. BREHAUT, qv.
A1. Daniel, b ca 1800 G, mar Eliz. TAUDVIN/TOSTEVIN, 1804-1883. Daniel d 1876 PEI. See Q.A. IN CANADA for more on this fam.
B1. Henry, b 1826
B2. Elizabeth, b 1827, mar Alex. Van Iderstine, res Gladstone, PEI,3chn
C1. William, mar Sarah MacLennan C3. Bessie
C2. Peter, mar Lavenia Beare and 2. Christine MARTIN
B3. Mary Ann, mar Henry Sencabaugh, b 1829 PEI, res Guernsey Cove,PEI More data in Calnek and Savary, 8 chn, one of whom, Solomon Sencabaugh, mar Lillian Watson, res Providence, RI
B4. Daniel, b 1833 PEI mar Barbara Sencabaugh
C1. Daniel Charles, b 1872 Prov. RI mar Sarah MacKenzie, b 1884 Sydney, Nova Scotia.
D1. Charles b 1914, mar Jessie Le Brocuy, b 1925
E1. Richard D., mar Barbara Saba, 2 chn: Danielle and Emilie, b Northboro, MA.
E2. Stephen C., b Boston, unmar
E3. William J., unmar E4. Jeannine M., unmar
D2. Edmund K., b 1916, mar Elizabeth Robinson, b Boston, MA.
E1. Robert, has son Alan, b Belmont, MA.
C2. Hattie/Harriet C4. Caroline C6. John
C3. Clara C5. Alexander C7. Henry
B5. John Thomas, b 1837 PEI mar Mary Ann DARBY BECK, b 1847 PEI, d 1927 Prov., RI. C1. Francis d.y.
C2. Charles Vere, b 1870 PEI, mar Euphemia MacKay, res PROV, RI. She d 1913 SASK.
D1. Archibald T., b 1894 Prov., mar Gertrude Smith
E1. Charles Vere, mar, 4 chn, res Darien, CT.
E2. Elizabeth, mar, 1 ch E3. Archie, no issue
D2. John Thomas, b 1897, mar Ethel Ayer, d Kingston, RI
E1.John T. res Cranston, RI. E2. Norman A.
D3. Charles Vere, b 1898, d Prov. 1972, mar Lillian Hunter.
E1. Euphemia, Effie, res Attleboro, MA

D4. Norman Hugh, b 1900 mar Elsie Knowles, res NH
E1. Norman H. Jr., res Bristol, NH? mar Edna ____. Sons Norman, David and Glen
E2. Lolita, mar 1952 Robert W.P. WILLIAMS, res Bristol, NH, sons: Robert, Steven and Bruce Williams
D5. Euphemia/Effie T., b 1902 Prov, RI mar Nelson Hoxsie, res Bristol
E1. Russell Hoxsie, b 1928 mar Mary Ann___, res Martha's Vineyard,MA 5 chn: Deborah, Steven, Pamela, Russell, Christopher Hoxsie.
E2. Donald Hoxsie, mar Silvia Carlson, res Buffalo, NY, 2 chn: Eric and Susan Hoxsie
E3. Joan Hoxsie, mar William Bell, 5 chn: William Jr., David, Donald, Douglas and Cynthia Bell.
D6. Herbert William, b 1911 Victoria, BC, mar Dorothy Howard, res Bristol, NH.
E1. Stephen H., b 1943 Bangor, ME, mar Cely ____, res Phillippines, 2 chn: Virginia and Wm. C. MACHON
E2. Janet D., b Hartford, CT mar 1. Lisle Gilbert, and 2. Richard Foster, res Waitsfield, VT, son Lisle Gilbert b 1969
E3. Emily M., b 1957 Hartford, CT.
D7. Ruth, b 1913, d.y.
C3. William, d.y. C4. Maude Mary, 1875-1960, unmar
C5. Herbert J., mar Margaret Murphy
D1. Herbert Jr., b 1917 Prov., RI res Barrington, RI
C6. Asa, d.y.
C7. Stella Jane, b 1878 Prov., d there 1957, mar Wm. Berry
D1. Hope C. Berry, b 1917 mar Raymond Stockley
E1. Raymond Stockley, Jr, b 1940 E2. Nancy, b 1943
E3. Jane Stockley, mar ___, dau Kristen, res Bristol, ME.
C8. Lillian M., d 1974 Prov. RI, unmar
B6. William, mar Emily Campbell, res Prov., 6 chn: Ethel Marr, Ernest, Bertha, Cecil, Sydney and Percy
B7. Sophie, 1843-1925, mar James LE LACHEUR, qv.
C1. Frederick LE LACHEUR mar Emily Murley
C2. Cyrus LE LACHEUR, mar Lizzie Hooper, res Prov. RI
C3. Lillian LE LACHEUR, mar Will Hugh. C4. Rose mar G. MacDuff.
B8. Mary Jane mar ___Boyce, res Prov.
C1. Daniel Boyce mar Barbara Sensebaugh, res Prov., RI
C2. Alexander Boyce. C3. Harriet Boyce
B9. Charlotte? B10. Abraham? B11. Rachel
A2. Henry, b ca 1800 G, mar Anne LE LACHEUR, 12 chn?
B1. Charles, mar 1. Elizabeth McIntyre and 2. ___Tweedy, 12 chn
B2. Elizabeth, b 1831 mar William CLEMENTS, qv, 3? chn
C1. Albert Clements, mar Jane MacLeod, res Murray Harb., PEI
C2. Cecelia Clements, mar I.J. Kier, res US
C3. Charlotte Clements, mar ___MacMillan
B3. Margaret, b 1833, unmar
B4. Daniel, b 1834, PEI mar Isabel Macleod, res Guernsey Cove, PEI
C1. Reuben, b 1870, mar Belle Hyde
C2. Daniel Walter, b 1871 PEI mar Jane/Jennie Harris who d 1967. He d 1936, bur Glastonbury, CT, 32nd Deg. Mason.
D1. Daniel Walter Jr, mar ____, res Boston and Latin America.
E1. Karen, res Agoura, CAL, works in TV
E2. Marc, mar Christina Frick, res Los Angeles, CAL
C3. Fred Seymour, b 1874 PEI, mar res Hartford, CT
C4. Gower?, engineer in Los Angeles, CAL C5. Minnie, b 1878
C6. Cecelia, b 1883, d 1932, mar James LE LACHEUR?

B5. Frances, b 1836 PEI mar George Harris
C1. Perley Harris mar Barbara MacLeod C3. Nettie Harris Lemon
C2. Harry Harris C4. Lizzie Harris
B6. Henry MACHON b 1837 PEI B7. James, b 1839, rem to Phila., PA
B8. Sarah mar ___DAVEY, res Pictou, Nova Scotia
B9. Charles, b 1842, d 1918, mar 1. Eliz. MacIntosh, 2. Elizabeth Tweedy, 1852-1929, 4 chn by 1st wife, 3 by 2nd.
C1. Benjamin James, 1867-1936
C2. Henry Alexander, 1869-1943, d Dorothy, ALTA, lived 10 yrs. in Boston, MA, where 4 sons were born, mar Ann Donovan.
D1. Charles Henry, b 1898 Boston, d 1976 ALTA, unmar., used MASHON
D2. James Alexander, 1900-1901
D3. Albert Francis, b 1902 Boston, d 1876 Calgary, unmar
D4. William Edward b 1904 Boston, mar Dorothy Brown, chn b ALTA,BC.
E1. Leslie William, b 1941 mar Alice Crawford, 2 daus, Sharmon and Shannon
E2. Louise Ann, mar Leonard B. Erickson, 2 chn: James and Sheri Erickson.
E3. Richard Edw. MASHON, b 1951 mar Carrie Weber, 2 chn: Rae Ann and Cody MASHON.
E4. Edward Kenneth MASHON, b 1954, mar Shirley Mathers
D5. Annie Elizabeth MASHON, b 1906 d 1980 Drumheller, ALTA, mar John Edwin Beck, 7 chn
E1. Grace Gloria Beck, mar Douglas A. Cox, 4 chn
F1. Dwight Wesley Cox, b 1945, mar Helena Rudderham, 2 chn: Richard and Angele Cox.
F2. Bruce A. Cox, b 1946 mar Donna Mae Leinweber, 3 chn: Edward, James and Shelley Cox
F3. Marilyn Faye Cox, b 1948 mar Arthur G. Ramsay, 2 chn: Suzanne and Lance Ramsay.
F4. Valerie Dianne Cox, b 1950, mar Wm. J. McLean, 2 daus, Cynthia and Sheri McLean.
E2. Benjamin Charles Beck, b 1927 mar Alice Faechner, 3 chn: Ruby Randy and Bud Beck
E3. Morris Gene Beck, b 1930, mar Ella MARTIN, 7 chn: Terry, Kathaleen, Robin, Barbara Guidolin, Darrell, Lorna and Darline Beck, 3 with desc.
E4. Alfred James Beck, b 1932 marShirley Gladys Pfall, dau Deborah, poss Deborah Gemell, of Shirley's 1st husband?
E5. Shirley Ann Beck, b 1936, mar Patrick Rowden, 3 chn: Nancy, Susan and David Rowden
E6. Gordon Percy Beck, b 1935.
E7. Viola Frances M. Beck, b 1943 mar Richard A. Pearson, 2 chn: Kelvin and Christine Pearson.
D6. Cecelia Helen MASHON, b 1908 Mossleigh, ALTA, d 1911
D7. Francis Joseph MASHON, b 1910 d 1979 Calgary, ALTA
D8. Hulbert Daniel MASHON, b 1912 Dorothy, ALTA, mar Doris Berwick,
E1. Patricia, b 1951, adopted, mar Francis Roes, 2 sons: Sheldon and Neal Roes.
E2. Carl Clement MASHON, b 1955 mar Sandra L. Gushway
D9. Mary Rose MASHON, b 1914 ALTA, mar James R. Job
E1. Charles Philip Job, b 1947 mar Pamela J. MacDonald, 2 daus: Twyla and Vicki Job
D10. Alice Ellen MASHON, b 1916 mar Christian Roes
E1. Francis C. Roes, mar Patricia A. MASHON, see Hulbert
E2. Andrew J. Roes b 1944 mar Sheena MacDonald, 3 chn: Marissa, Stacey and Christian Roes

E3. John Allen Roes, b 1946 mar Rosalee M. Conroy, 2 sons: Michael John and Trevor J. Roes.
E4. Elizabeth Ann, b 1948 mar James A. Peake, 2 sons: Jason James and Ryan Anthony Peake
D11. Walter Copps MASHON, b 1918 mar Dorothy, ALTA, Mary Van Kerk-Voode
E1. Marlene P. Mashon, b 1950 mar Lloyd Nelson, dau Tyna CarmanNelson
D12. Lillian Theresa MASHON, b 1920, d.y.
C3. Charles Herbert b ca 1871 PEI C5. dau, d.y.
C4. Drusilla Malina, b 1874 C6. Cedric Errol, 1890-1899
C7. Pansey, Elizabeth (Tweedy) Machon, 1892-1963, mar a HAWKINS, qv.
B10. Maria, mar Wm. Howe and res Guernsey Cove, PEI. See Q.A. IN CANADA, by Turk.
C1. Milton Howe mar Ethel BREHAUT, qv.
C2. Blanche Howe mar Fred. LE LACHEUR, qv. C3. Sarah, d.y.
C4. Myrtle Howe, mar Carl Spaulding, res Beverly Hills, CAL
C5. Ella Howe mar Charles Wadey, res Vancouver, BC
C6. Hattie Howe, mar Wm. Brodie, res Los Angeles, CAL
A3. William, b 1801 G, d 1874 PEI, mar 1. Charlotte Reid, b 1804, d1877 PEI, poss Wm. mar 2. Emily Campbell? (Mrs.FD Machon, Champaign,ILL)
B1. William, b 1839 PEI d 1933, mar Margaret Jennings LE LACHEUR, qv, 1847-1908.
C1. Gertrude, b 1873 PEI mar John Herring, res Murray Harbor, PEI
D1. Stanley Herring, d 1936
D2. Harold Herring, b 1934 D3. Margaret Herring, d age 7.
C2. William Le Bert, b 1877, d 1942, mar Elsie Louise Penny, res White Sands, PEI, 1883-1950.
D1. Freeman David, b 1902 PEI d 1978, mar Agnes Alleyne Rowland, b 1902 res Park Ridge, ILL, and Champaign, ILL.
E1. Robert Rowland, b 1930 mar Marilyn Kane 1951, res ILL
F1. Marilee, b 1954, mar John C. Edgar 1977, 2 sons: Todd and Owen J. Edgar.
F2. Kirk Robert b 1957 F3. Melissa b 1961
E2. Gary Freeman, b 1936 mar Donna Matheson 1959, res WISC, 4 sons: Kevin M., Brett J., Jason K., and Jack R.
E3. Barbara Alleyne, b 1939 mar 1959 David P. Hernandey, res Champaign, ILL, 3 chn: Michelle, Lana, David Hernandey.
A4. Elizabeth, 1804-1838, mar John NICOLLE, qv.
A5. Thomas, b 1807 PEI mar Rachel TAUDVIN/TOSTEVIN of G, had 11 chn, some of whom rem to US. See Q.A. IN CANADA, by Turk
B3. John, b 1834 PEI mar Eliz. ROBERTS, qv, and 2. Mary Moore. Most desc to US.
C1. Sarah mar Wm. Glover and res Prov., RI
C2. Thomas mar Mary MacLeod and res Prov., 3 chn: Grace, Mildred and Olive
C3. Joseph, b 1865, d 1966, mar 1. Mary Sooner, 2. Emily Craven, res Prov. RI.
C4. Daniel, mar Janet Marshall, and res Prov., RI
C5. Matilda mar Wm. Byrne and res Stellarton, Nova Scotia
C6. Peter J., b 1872 d 1968, mar Sarah Glover, res Prov., RI
D1. John. H.B. mar Florence Harrison, b 1906 Prov., res Vincennes, IND, a dau d.y. 1931
D2. Joseph, d Prov. 1966 age 101? D3. a son res FLA
D4. son,res FLA D5. dau, res Baltimore, MD
C7. Mary Ellen, mar Albert Stuttard, res Prov., RI
C8. Rebecca, mar Thos. Brooks, res Prov. and Chelmsford, MA
C9. Lauretta, mar David Brooks, res PEI, a son John Brooks

B7. William, b 1841 mar Susan Sensebaugh, res Prov. RI
C1. Elizabeth mar George Jenks, res Prov.
C2. Sarah, mar 1. Dan. MacLeod, 2. Arthur Fiedler, res RI
C3. Bertha, mar Byron Reid, res MICH.
C4. Maria, mar Thomas Jenks, res Prov., RI
C5. Albert, d in MICH. C6. William, mar Ann Browning, res RI
C7. Clarence, mar Abby ____, res Prov., RI
B8. Samuel, mar Emily DAVEY, res Prov., RI
C1. Lydia, mar Leroy MORREL, res Prov., RI
C2. Jane mar Robert MacDuff C4. Hubert, mar Lena MacKay
C3. Rosa May, mar Neil Crawford, res Wood Island.
A6. Nancy Ann, b 1810 PEI mar Matthias HAWKINS, qv of G, some of whose desc. res Boston, MA and Boothbay, ME. See HAWKINS
A7. John, b 1816 PEI mar Mary Buchanan, res Machon Pt., PEI, mar 1838.
B1. Esther, b 1839 called MARCHON. Mar Joseph Thompson, 1833-1909 res Milltown Cross, PEI d 1922, 7 chn. C1. Kezia d.y.
C2. Ann Thompson, mar Will Reynolds, res Murray Harv. then Concord, NH, 5 chn: Charles, Emma, Ralph, Josephine and Matilda Reynolds.
C3. Robert Thompson, 1867-1919, mar Christy Ann MacDonald, 1871-1919
D1. Milton Thompson, 1893-1896 and 3 stilborns
D5. Etta/Pat, b 1909 res Charlottesville, VA, raised by uncle Murdoch F. MacDonald, Bellevue, PEI, taught school in Calgary, ALTA Mar 1935 John T. Sinclair of Lafayette, IND, 3 chn
E1. John Frederick Sinclair, b 1943 lawyer, unmar
E2. Kathleen Isabel Sinclair, b 1946, mar Anthony J. Van Hover, 2 daus: Stephanie, and Angela Van Hover
E3. Joan Leslie Sinclair b 1947 mar Lionel Melville, dau Fritha
C4. John Thompson mar Mary ____, res Winthrop, MA, 3 chn: Edith, Esther (d in teens) and Marion Thompson
C5. Martha Thompson, b 1873 mar 1902 Charles Haughn, res MA, 5 chn: Chester, Joseph, Erminie plus the following:
D4. Robert Haughn, b 1902, twin, d 1975, res Boston. Mar his cousin Mildred Haughn, 4 chn. Mildred remar. A dau d.y.
E2.Donald Haughn E3. William Haughn
E4. Marilyn Haughn, mar Rev. Rich. Farnsworth, res Belvidere, ILL
D5. Helen Haughn, twin, b 1902, raised by aunt, and known as Helen Leonard. Mar Asaph Simeon Himmelman, b 1906 of La Have, Nova Scotia in 1930, res Quincy, MA
E1. Leonard Bracy Himmelman b 1931 mar Harriet Saunders, 2 chn: Emma and Anna
E2. Gerard, mar Dian Hicks, div, and 2. Karen Olsen, div, and 3. Catherine McDaniels, 2 chn by 1st, one by 2nd, one by 3rd. 3 chn: Gerard, Dee Dee and Edward Himmelman.
E3. Selena Ruth Himmelman, b 1933 mar Harold Soederburg, 3 chn: Cathy Wessinger, Eric and Lisa Soederburg
E4. Martha Helen Himmelman, b 1937 mar T. Kirkland Nelson, 3 chn: Rebecca, Geoffrey, Jennifer Nelson
E5. William Robert Himmelman, b 1942 mar Romance ___, and 2. Karen Baker, 4 chn: William Jr., Bruce, Robert & Brian Himmelman
E6. Asaph Simeon Himmelman Jr, b 1947 mar Kristie Johnson, 2 chn: Heidi and Tamara Himmelman
C6. Esther Thompson, unmar d 1947
C7. Priscilla, mar and div, cut off by family!
B2. Mary A., b 1841 PEI d 1929 Boston, unmar
B3. Jane B., b 1848 PEI d 1889, unmar, res Lynn, MA
B4. Emma Jane, b 1852, d 1905 unmar, teacher. A school in Swampscott, MASS was named for her.

B5. John, mar Frances Brooks, had son Ira? and a dau?

MACHON, Josue, Joshua, b 1819 J, mar 1. Rachel BLAMPIED, had son Philip b 1834. Rachel d young and Josue mar 2. Anne QUEREE, b 1854. Josue was son of Josue and Rachel (BLAMPIED) MACHON of J. Ann was dau of Charles and Marie (MACHON) QUEREE. Chn b St. Helier and Trinity, J. Widowed when Josue d age 83 in 1902, Ann brought 8 chn to North Chelmsford, MA. See MA section. (Thomas G. LE MASURIER family chart; Edith Hainsworth, No. Chelmsford, MA)

A1. Philippe, b 1834 J, by 1st wife. A8. Lydia
A2. Joshua Jr., b 1882 Trinity, J, to No. Chelmsford ca 1907, d 1963
A3. Christine, b 1883 d 1924 MA. Mar Thomas J. LE MASURIER, qv.
A4. Eveline, b 1884 J d 1953 MA? Mar Octave L'HERAULT, qv.
A5. Ophelia, b 1885 J, res MA, d 1967
A6. Theophilus, b 1889 J, d 1966 MA, mar Harriet DE CARTERET
A7. Philip, b 1891 J, res NCH, dau Edith mar __Hainsworth.

MACHON, see HAWKINS, LE MARINEL AND NICOLLE

MACHON, Austin, silversmith in Phila. 1759. OUTC. See also MARQUAND, another silver and goldsmith in Phila. 1800s. OUTC.

MACHON, noted in Fremont, CAL, from C.I.?

MACHON, a fam hist compiled by mother of Ray Brooks of PEI, not seen by compiler. She d 1964.

MACHON, John in Essex Co., MA 1679, d there by 1680. OUTC

MACHON, MACCHONE, etc, Hannah, b 1659 Cambridge, MA, dau of John and Deborah (Bush) MACHONE. Prob from C.I. See GAVET

MACHON, John, b 1847 J, fam rem to Norfolk Co., ONT. John res Langton, ND, d in Canada. (Q.A. by Turk)

MACHON, John res Cranberry Twp., Crawford Co., OH 1860. OUTC. Many in Scioto Co., OH, not researched.

MACHON, T.S., res Jefferson Twp., Musk. Co., OH 1860

MACHON, Ann QUEREE, b J, mar in MA John DUMARESQ DE CARTERET early 1900s

MACHON, some research in C.I.? (CIFHS #9)

MACHON, John in Saco, ME ca 1670, another in Exeter 1681. (Noyes)

MACHON, James, b 1848 England or C.I.? served on the USS BROOKLYN during successful attacks on Fort Morgan, rebel gunboats and the ram TENNESSEE in Mobile Bay, ALA 1864. "Stationed in the immediate vicinity of the shell whips, which were twice cleared of men by bursting shells, Machon remained steadfast at his post, and performed his duties in the powder division throughout the furious action", was given Medal of Honor. (USNavy Biog.Dict by Karl Schuon, 1964, NY)

MACKEY, Alan, arrived in Canada 1958 from Alderney Is. Mar Lucille Romain in Ottawa, ONT, 2 chn: Marc and Sean, b Ottawa. Francis MACKEY mar in Ald. Linda Margaret BENFIELD. See Q.A. IN CANADA,LIHOU (Lucille Roy, Malartic, QUE)

MACY, see MACE and MASSEY. MACEY, MACE in J from 1309.

MADDOCKS in J before 1814, not traced by compiler

MAHE, MAHER, MAHIER, MAHY in J 1309, also in G. MAHIER in St. John, J, 1668, also MAHIER dit ALLAIN.

MAHIER, Richard from St. John J, was in Accomack, VA 1720. He mar Mary Savage of a pioneer fam in VA. His will mentions Mary HUES, qv, of Boston, MA, his sisters in J, who were mar to RENOUF and VODEN, qv. He had nephew Richard MAHIER in Boston, and friends Lloyd and Bowdwin. (VIRGINIA GLEANINGS IN ENGLAND, Vol 12, p.83)

MAHER, Richard Jr., d in Boston 1742, left money to parish of St.John,J. Was he the nephew of Richard above?

MAHEUE, John and Steven served in Rev. War, from C.I.? OUTC. Cf MAHU

MAHU in J 1309
MAHEU curr in Pac. Palisades, CAL. OUTC
MAHY, new data in CI COLLECTION.
MAHU in Lawrence Co., OH middle 1800s. OUTC
MAHY in Vale G 1821. See CIFHS #14. See BOUGOURD and ROBERTS
MAHY Anthony LE PATOUREL, from G to PA 1900s
MAHY, Gordelia, nee LE PELLEY, of Catel G, to US. Cf LE PELLEY
MAHY, John and Margaret res MRB, OUTC, but prob from C.I.
A1. Margaret, bp 1772 A2. John, bp 1775 A3. Margaret, bp 1776
MAHY, Joseph mar in Nfld. 1855 Mrs. Julia Butt, widow of Basil Butt of Clown's Cove, Nfld. Joseph b G. (THE COURIER; John Bowes, Brockton,MA
MAHEY, Henry res Portage Co., OH 1860 OUTC
MAHY, Nicolas mar in G, and rem to New Brunswick
A1. Amelia, b 1875, mar Adolphus SARRE, son of Edmund SARRE of G
B1. Dorothy Sarre, mar ___HAMMOND, res Saint John E., New Brunswick.
MAHY, see MEHUY, etc. See also Q.A. IN CANADA by Turk
MAILLARD, old in J, curr in J, also noted in Los Angeles, CAL. Noted too in Meadville, PA, but OUTC
MAIN, old in J as MAIN, MAINE, MAYNE. Many in colonies, poss a few from C.I.?
MAIN, John mar Sarah Collier 1743, MRB, a dau Sarah bp 1746
MAINE, John mar Eliz. PICKETT 1799 MRB, 2 daus: Betsy, bp 1799 and Elizabeth, bp 1801. OUTC
MAIN, Thomas mar Eleanor Coes, poss DE CAUX? 1714 MRB, daus Hannah and Elizabeth bp 1727. OUTC
MAIN, William, mar Ruth BOWDEN, qv, 1788 MRB, 3 chn. OUTC
A1. William, bp 1788 A2. Mary bp 1790 A3. Sarah Rhoads
MAIN, John, b ca 1828 J, d 1872, age 44, bur St. James, Toronto, ONT. Mar Sophia Victoria ___, who mar 2. N.J. LE COCQ, qv. of C.I. She d 1911 Toronto, age 81.
MAIN, Thomas mar Hannah Stiles 1800 MRB. Cf STEELE, STILLE.
A1. Hannah, bp 1801 A4. Sarah L. again, bp 1811
A2. Sarah Laskey, bp 1803, d.y.? A5. Richard Stiles, bp 1814
A3. Thomas, bp 1807 A6. Desire Roundey, bp 1817
MAINDONALD in G 1331, curr and common. Noted in US, see OGIER
MAINDONALD, Albert James, b G? mar Alice Mary GALLIENNE, dau of Thomas, rem to Canada 1907, settled ONT. See GALLIENNE. (Aldo Brochet)
A1. Walter, b 1909 mar, a son Frederick b 1941
A2. Edna May, b 1912 mar ___Dauson. Edna d 1937. A son ?
Dau Lillian adopted by grandparents, mar Gordon Poff
A3. Margaret Dorothy, b 1916 mar ___Gibbons, 3 chn: Gary C. b 1939, Jack D., b 1942 and Jo Anne Raab b 1947
MAINE, in Portsmouth, NH early, poss from C.I.? (Noyes)
MAINGUY, see Q.A. IN CANADA by Turk
MAINWARING, surname of Grt. Britain and C.I. Curr J
MAINWARING, John a Boston mariner mar 1729 Elizabeth Sharp, dau of John of Saco, ME. (Noyes) OUTC
MAINWARING, James of New London, CT mar 1799 Hannah Campbell, OUTC.
MAINWARING, Nathaniel mar Abigail COLLINGS, qv 1731 Boston, MA. OUTC
MAJOR. See also LE MESSURIER and MAUGER. Many fams of this surname in England and C.I. MAUGER can also be German, use CAUTION. M. Denys Munger of Quebec City has researched the many hundreds of variant spellings in this field: MAUGET, MONGET, MAUGE, MUNGER, etc, etc. Some claim origin in J, some in G. and some in England. A few of the English fams. came originally from the C.I. MAUGER dates at least from 1299 in J. Some MAUGERS changed spelling to MAJOR in US and in Canada. MAJOR girls in RI, See CI COLL. (M.Stone,ILL)
(AYLESWORTH GENEALOGY)

MAJOR. "A 17th century pioneer was Richard, son of Richard MAJOR of Hursley Manor, Hampshire, England, desc of John MAUGER of Handois Manor, Jersey, on the border of St. John and St. Lawrence parishes, of the MAUGERS of Normandy and Guernsey. Richard left England with wife and 2 small sons, George and Robert, about the year 1634, 27 years after the settlement of Jamestown, VA. He had a patent on 300 acres of land in Charles River County, 1638", and eventually had 3650 acres, and was a leading tobacco plantation owner. (GUERNSEY WEEKLY PRESS, July 1, 1976) There are now many desc of this fam in America, a good portion of them serving in the Army and Navy, becoming Captains Majors, Lieutenants, Colonels, and so on, including a few women officers. There are severalMajor Majors, and Capt. Majors!

MAJOR, a fam chart by Richard D. Gloor of Palos Verdes, CAL takes the family back to:

LE MESURIER, Michael, d before Feb. 1435 Jersey, mar Guillemme, dau of Jean LE PREVOST

A1. Pierre LE MESURIER, b G

B1. Guillaume LE MESURIER, b Poole, England, mar before 1508 Laurence PERRIN

C1. James LE MESURIER, b Poole, England, alive 1566, mar Edith White

D1. Benjamin LE MESURIER b J.

E1. Leonard LE MESURIER, b St. Lawrence J, mar ___LE GROS

F1. Benjamin LE MESSURIER, b ca 1624 mar Jeanne LE GROS

G1. George MAJEIRE, MAJOR, b 1648. NOTE CHANGES IN SURNAMES

MAJOR, MAJEIRE, George, b 1648 in "St. Lora", prob St. Laurens J, rem to Newbury, MA, and mar 1672 Susanna PARY, PERRY?, b ca 1655, d before 1682 Newbury, MA. Note that George was a LE MESSURIER of J. (ANCESTORS OF GUILFORD S. TINGLEY; Noyes; Coffin; Savage)

A1. Hannah, b 1673 Newbury, MA mar 1692 Richard Goodwin, son of Rich. and Hannah (Jones) Goodwin, 8 chn. Richard b 1669 Glou., MA. See GOODWIN GEN.

B1. Hannah Goodwin, b 1692 mar Thomas Pettingill 1719

B2. George Goodwin, b 1695 mar Mary Gooch 1729

B3. Richard Goodwin, b 1698

B4. Susanna Goodwin, b 1700/01,mar Joseph Russell 1739

B5. Major Goodwin, b ca 1703 d 1791, mar Mary Atkinson 1726

B6. Elizabeth, b ca 1705 mar John Pease 1725

B7. Martha, b ca 1709 mar David Poor 1729

B8. Daniel b 1711 mar Eliz. BISHOP, qv, ca 1734.

A2. George Jr., b 1676 mar 1701 MRB. Jane ___, 5 chn

B1. George MAGER, b 1701 MRB B3. Thomas, b 1705 MRB

B2. Jane, b 1703 MRB B4. William, b 1707 B5. Eleanor, b 1710

A3. Benjamin MAJORY, b 1678 mar 1702 Hannah BALEY, 5 chn. He rem to Arundel, ME, later Cape Porpoise 1720, d 1747

B1. Benjamin Majery, b 1703 Newbury, MA, killed by Indians 1725

B2. Priscilah Majery, b 1704 mar Lt. John Burbank, d 1835, 5 chn

B3. George Majery, b 1707 MRB B4. William, b 1710

B5. Eleanor, b 1712

A4. Susanna Majory, b 1680 Newbury, MA, mar 1. 1697 Lawrence MASURY, qv of Salem, son of Lawrence and Mary (Kibben) MASURY, b 1674 Salem, d before 1710. She mar 2. 1710 John Wester or Vestry, 5 chn. See under MASURY.

A5. Elizabeth MAJOR, b 1682 Newbury, mar (int) 1703 Richard Jackman of Newbury, son of Richard and Eliz. (PALMER) Jackman, b 1684 Newbury.

B1. Mehettable Jackman, b 1705 B2. Richard Jackman, b 1709

MAJOR, see MAUGER

MAJOR, MAUGER, Capt., privateer of Jersey Island 1692

MAJOR, Elizabeth mar Geo. BOUCHER of J? 1727 Boston, MA
MAJOR, Elizabeth mar Philip BENNET of J? 1730 Boston
MAJOR, Elizabeth mar Samuel WHEELER, WHILEUR?, 1751 Boston.
MALHERBE in J 1292. Edward MALHERBE b G, but of a J fam, was adopted by Harry Tanner when the fam came to US early 1900s? (Theda Connell, Pleasant Ridge, MI) See also Fern Malherbe in HEAUME fam, Belgian?
MALET, MALLET, MALLETT, accursed, in J from 1180. In Grouville and St. Martin J 1668; in Grouville, St. Martin and St. Saviour J 1749. Curr G and J.
MALET, see CIFHS #5 and #12.
MALLETT noted in OLD FAMS OF FAIRFIELD, by Jacobus, but OUTC
MALLET, Abigail, mar 1742 Robert Angier of Boston, whose will is dated 1753. 4 chn, OUTC. (GENS AND ESTATES OF CHARLESTOWN, MA)
A1. Abigail Angier, bp 1743 A3. Robert Angier, bp 1751
A2. Sarah Angier, b 1744 A4. Margaret Angier, bp 1757
MALEY, Alice mar John LEWIS 1764 MRB. OUTC
MALEY, many marriages in MRB 1700s, 1800s, but OUTC
MALEY, MALLET?, Daniel, listed in 1790 census with fam of 9.
MALEY, Daniel, mar Annis Pittman 1749 MRB. OUTC
A1. Daniel, bp 1750 MRB A4. Elizabeth, bp 1757
A2. John, bp 1752, d.y.? A5. Sarah, bp 1760
A3. Annis, bp 1755 A6. John, bp 1763
MALEY, Daniel, poss same as above? bp 1750? mar Jane MALZARD, qv, 1774. Daniel d ca 1781. OUTC
A1. Daniel Jr., bp 1775 MRB, poss mar Eliz. Vickery 1801, a son Daniel
A2. Nicholas, bp 1777, d.y.? A3. Jane, bp 1780
A4. Nicholas again, bp 1781, posthumous, may have mar Hannah LE CRAW, 1808 in MRB.
MALEY, Daniel, mar Jane ____, see also above fam.
A1. John, bp 1785 MRB A2. Annis, bp 1790 A4. Thomas Pitman, bp 1798
A3. Polly Bean, bp 1794, poss mar Jos. Dismore Jr., 1822?
MALEY, Daniel mar Eliz. HOOPER, qv, 1720, a widow
A1. William, bp 1723 MRB A2. Eliz., bp 1727 A3. Benjamin, bp 1728
MALEY, Hannah, mar Richard BESOM, BISSON 1814 MRB.
MALEY, John mar Alice Tucker 1744 MRB, 5 chn
A1. Eliz., bp 1745 A4. John, bp 1752, mar? Eliz. Tucker 1773
A2. Alice, bp 1748, did she marry John LEWIS above?
A3. Miriam, bp 1750 A5. Philip, b 1755 mar? 1777 Sarah Frost
MALEY, John mar Mary Reed Twisden 1808 MRB, and 2.? Robert Glidden 1820.
MALLETT, Hosea, fisherman from C.I. in Sagadahoc, ME 1664, master of 4 vessels. In Boston 1678, where dau Eliz. was born. She mar Peter Wooding 1696. (Noyes) OUTC.
See MALEY, MALLEY, MALET, MALLETT in 1790 census, much more data.
MALEY, William mar Mary Girdler 1754 MRB
A1. William, bp 1754 MRB A5. Alice, bp 1762, sev. marriages?
A2. Benja., bp 1756, d.y.? A6. Benjamin again, bp 1765
A3. Daniel, bp 1758 A7. Elizabeth, bp 1767, see many marriages
A4. Mary, bp 1760 in MRB late 1700s.
MALLETT, see PORTER
MALLET, Thomas, bp 1810 Grouville J, mar 1832 Jenny LE BRUN, b 1811, dau of Jean LE BRUN and Marie BINET. Thomas the son of Thomas and Ester (BISSON) MALLET. Thos and Jenny joined the Saints in J 1852, but Thomas d 1853 in St. Heliers J. Jenny left J with a group of Islanders and came to US via ship MARSHFIELD 1854 sto St. Louis, MO. They joined the Wm. Empy Co., leaving the Miss. River in July and arriving at SLCity Oct. 1854. At least 2 daus, poss other chn? (Shirley Rizzuto, Sandy, UT)

A1. Mary Elizabeth, b 1848 J, res SLCity and mar Robert Hamill Porter, qv at age 20. Later res Coalville, UT, at least 7 chn by Porter. More data from source and in SLCity records.
B1. Henry Irvin Porter, b 1870 B4. Annie E. b 1874 Almy, WY
B2. George Edward Porter, b 1871 B5. Rosella F., b 1876
B3. Mary Jane Porter, b 1873 d 1876 B6. Jos. A., 1877-1878
A2. Jane, b J, to UT, mar Wm. Taylor, bro of Pres. Zach. Taylor
MALLET, Elvina, b 1856 J, dau of Capt. MALLETT and Jane LUCAS, rem to UT, mar Francis DE LA MARE, qv, 5 chn
MALLORY, MALOREY, poss a J man who rem to N. Chelmsford, MA 1900?
MALZARD, see MELZARD
MANLEY, Ann Maria, b 1854 St. Heliers, J, mar John BOWDIDGE, qv, d 1939 Salt Lake City. Ann dau of Wm. MANLEY and ___CHEVALIER. MANLEY curr in J. (SLCITY records)
MANNING, James LUSCOMBE, butcher, res G, d 1878, age 68, son of James and Jenny PAIGA MANNING. His nephew, Abner MANNING, res Aurora, ILL late 1800s, had learned the trade from his uncle in G. However, Abner born in Kingsbury, Somerset, Eng. "A cousin told me that Uncle Abner visited the Isle in the 1920s and when he entered the dining room in the hotel everyone stood up, because he so much resembled the Gov. of the Island that everyone thought it was the Governor!" Close intermarriage in the Islands has produced many look-alikes!
MANSELL in St. Peter Port G 1616. Curr G and J.
MANSELL, a C.I. and south of England surname noted in Trumbull, Hamilton, Lucas, Mahoning and Cuyahoga Cos. of OH in the 1800s. OUTC
MANSELL, James, b G, rem to Cleveland, OH ca 1840. A son John T. MANSELL enlisted in Civil War 1861. MANSELLS were farming in North Royalton, OH 1850. (Stone; HIST. OF CUYA. CO., OH by Johnson&Blackmre
MANSEL, Annie, John, James C., Aubrey C., John Leon and Wm. G. are other MANSEL, MANSELLS noted in 1800 and early 1900 Cleveland city directories.
MANSEL noted in NC and PA records also, but OUTC
MARANG, see MOURANT
MARCH, see also MARSH. LA MARCHE and DE LA MARCHE in C.I. by 1200s. MARCH, MARSH sometimes confused. See CIFHS #12. Note Clement MARCH in Noyes, p. 457.
MARCH, Hannah, mar Paul PENDEXTER, qv, b 1737.
MARCH, William, b 1742 mar Thankful PENDEXTER, qv.
MARCHAND, see also LE MARQUAND and MARQUAND. MARCHAND often French, sometimes from C.I.
MARCHANT, LE MARCHANT in J 1304/5. LE MARCHAND in St. Brelade and St. Heliers J 1668. LE MARCHANT in St. Laurens J 1749. MARCHAND, MARCHANT curr J.
MARCHANT found in Fairfield, Tusc., Scioto, Highland and Franklin counties of OH in 1860. OUTC.
MARCHANT, Fred, a grocer from C.I.? to New York, rec'd by Philip Ebert. OUTC. (NY Naturalizations, by Scott)
A number of MARCHANTS noted in CT 1700s, OUTC.
MARETT, MARRETT in J from 1274. In St. Heliers, St. Saviours, St.John, St. Laurens, St. Martin J, and in 1749, these parishes plus Trinity, St. Clement, St. Brelade and Grouville, J. At times common in J. MARETT, MARRIOTT curr G and J. Many variants of spelling in US. DUMARESQ, qv, may have derived from DE MARET, DES MARETS of 1331. See more than 300 pages of data on MARRET, MERRET in SLCity records.
MARETT shield: Argent, three bars gules.
MARRET, fam in Cambridge, MA early 1700s, OUTC. Amos of this fam mar 2. 1732 Ruth Dunster, poss Ruth's dau by another mar.(DUNSTER GEN)

MARETT, Daniel Philip, native of Nfld. d 1852 age 42, son of Daniel MARETT, merchant in Nfld. and nephew of Judge MARETT of the Royal Court, J. Widow and 6 chn survived. (John Bowes, Brockton, MA)
MARRIOTT, Isaac, mar Joyce ____, res Burlington Co., W.Jersey. Joyce d 1695. OUTC. Chn: Isaac, Samuel, Richard, Joyce and Thomas., b 1680s and 1690s.
MARETT, James LAMPRIERE, prob from C.I. fam, mar 1801 QUEBEC CITY, at St. Andrew's Presb. CH, Henriette BOONE. (LOST IN CANADA, Aug.'81)
MARRIOT, John in MRB 1674, from C.I.?
MARETT, John from C.I. to UT 1863 via ship ANTARCTIC. (SLCITY RECORDS)
MARETT, John from C.I. to UT 1855 via ship CHIMBORAZO. Poss John was b St. Laurens J 1810, and mar Rachel SHELTON, b 1814 St. Lawrence,J. Dau Mary Ann b 1836. (Fam records of Eliz. J. DU FRESNE Stevenson)
MARRETT, MERIT, MARETT, MARRIOTT, Nicholas, b 1613, fisherman in Salem, MA 1635, from J? mar Mary Sandin, rem to MRB 1648. (Holmes; Virkus; Essex Coll IV; Savage) OUTC
A1. Martha living 1685, mar ___Owens
A2. Rebecca, mar ___CHINN, living 1685. A3. Mary, helpless in 1685.
A4. John A. A5. James A6. Samuel, in MRB 1669. A7. Nicholas
MARET, Nathaniel, draper, served in Rev. War. (MASS SOLDIERS AND SAILORS) OUTC.
MARETT, MARRET, Nicholas and Eliz. res MRB 1704, had Eliz. bp 1704.
MARRET, Philip and Mary res Boston, MA early, from J?
A1. Daniel, b 1703 A2. Susanna, b 1706 A3. Experience, b 1710.
MARETT, Philip, b 1819 St. Clement J d 1872 Kamas, UT, son of Jedediah M. and Maria Ann (AHIER) MARETT. He mar 1. Esther VOLWAY/SOLWAY? prob in C.I. and 2. Mary LE GRESLEY, qv. Philip and Esther from J 1851 on ship OLYMPUS (SLCITY RECORDS) (Robert F. Gould's EZRA T. CLARK'S ANCESTORS and DESCENDANTS, 1975, Bethesda, MD; Lois Saunders, Boise, ID)
A1. Mary Ann, b 1854 Kearney, NEB, mar 1875 Joseph Warr, d 1918
A2. Ephraim, b 1858 Pleasant Grove, UT mar Cornelia LAMBERT. See Gould book. This fam unverified.
B1. ? Parley Marvel MARETT, mar Mary Mitchell?
C1. George Ephraim, b 1916 Lake Fort, UT, sheriff of DuChesne Co., mar Edythe L. Wimmer, dau of Harold J. and Lucille (Wilcox) Wimmer.
D1. Adele, b 1949 Mesa, AZ
D2. Julie, b 1951 mar Max Forbush, sons Troy and Nathan Forbush
D3. Annette, b 1953 D5. Jeffery Wynn, b 1960
D4. Roger K., b 1955 D6. dau, d.y. 1963
A3. Amelia/Emelia?, b UT mar Emanuel BROWN
MARRETT, Philip. Three generations of this name. The first Philip was b in St. Heliers J 1742, rem to Boston, then returned to J, where he d ca 1760. His son Philip, sea Captain also, rem to Boston and mar Elizabeth Cunningham. Their son Philip, b 1792 Boston, was a noted financier and politician, d 1869. (BIO. DICT. OF JERSEY)
MARET, Richard, from J? served in Rev. War. (MASS SOLDIERS, SAILORS)
MARETT, Stephen, res Hancock, MA 1790 with others. OUTC.
MARRETT, MARRITT, MARITT, MARRIOT, MARYOTT, Thomas to Cambridge, MA before 1638. OUTC. Mrs. J.M. Loring of Portland, OR has worked on this fam. See also DUNSTER GEN; Paige's HIST OF CAMBRIDGE; Farmer's GEN. REGISTER, 1829; MARRETT GEN; HIST OF LEXINGTON, MA; NEHGS, etc.
MARETT, see CIFHS #9. MARETT noted in petition of Quebec City residents 1838 with other C.I. surnames. MARETTE noted in Petit Riviere QUE 1858, from C.I.? (Aldo Brochet, London, ONT)
MARETT, MARRIOT noted in MD 1600s. OUTC. (Skordas)

MARGORY, Joseph served in Rev. War from MA. Prob a MASURY, MAJORY, qv. Also a Jonathan MARGORY.

MARIE, surname of France and C.I. One Capt. MARIE was a privateersman in J 1813/14. (A. John Jean, Jersey)

MARINEL, LE MARINEL in St. John J 1668-1749, curr J. See LE MARINEL.

MARINER, MARRINER, LE MARRINEUR, MARINEL, all appeared in New England early. It means Sailor. Underhill says these New England MARRINERS were Huguenots that settled formerly in England and in Ireland, and were closely associated with the BOWDOINS, known to be Huguenots. Compiler believes that some MARRINERS were LE MARINELS of J, poss from St. John parish, as one MARINER mentions an uncle in J. Thomas MARINER, LE MARINEL? was said to have come from Nfld. to Salem, 1650. At least one MARINER came from Brading, Isle of Wight,England in the early 1700s.

MARINER, Andrew, related to James and Joshua below, was a sadler. Andrew in Portsmouth, NH, 1678-1680, rem to Dover, NH then to Boston ca 1683, where he was a shoemaker. Mar Ruth, dau of George Holland, living in NYork 1703. Chn at Boston 1685-1690. (Noyes) OUTC, but leatherworking was common in J then.

A1. Margaret, b 1685 Boston A3. Priscilla, b 1688 Boston
A2. Ruth, b 1686/7 A4. Andrew, twin, b 1689
A5. George, twin, b 1689, mar Mary GRAY, Newington, NH 1724/5. Taxed in Portsmouth, NH 1725, gone by 1731. In Dover 1739 and kept ferry, in legal trouble 1744. A George served at Louisburg, NS. Note that Mary MURRINER mar Geo. GRAY 1720 Boston. See also GEAR.

MARINER, LE MARINEL?, Isaac, Nathaniel, Charles, Capt. Richard, Andrew, Thomas and Joseph were in the colonies, 1600s, 1700s. OUTC. (MASS SOLDIERS AND SAILORS)

MARINER, MARINEL?, James, mariner, rigger, b ca 1651, witness 1681, in Casco, ME 1686, deposed in Boston 1705, as former master of brigantine DOVER. Deposed 1731 age ca 80 that he had lived in Falmouth 40-50 yrs earlier. Will dated 1732. (Noyes) OUTC.

A1. Elizabeth, mar 1. in Boston 1707 John LACOOTER, prob LE COUTEUR of J? and 2. in 1713 Edward MASTERS, qv, seaman, also of J? No issue by LA COUTEUR?
B1. Edward Masters, b 1714, also John, James and Elizabeth
A2. Adam, brewer in Boston, soap boiler 1742, sold for 15 pds. to Stephen Boutineau of Boston, any claim that he might have to real estate of his uncle John GROVE, ALGROVE? of St. Mary, J. He mar 1. Hannah Nessbye, 2. Rachel Hayward.
B1. Hannah, mar Richard Kent Jr. in Newbury, MA 1734 and in 1774 was only surv. heir of James MARINEL of Falmouth.
A3. Hannah/Johannah, mar 1707 Philip PERREWAY, PIROUET, qv, Hug. from J, 4 chn, res Marblehead, MA 1674.

MARINER, John, b 1644 Gloucester, MA d 1717, mar 1. Elizabeth, 2 daus, and 2. Rachel ____, who d 1723 age ca 76. (Underhill) OUTC. A son John, b ca 1681 d 1748, mar 1. Sarah Sawyer and 2. Mary or May Cobb. Mar 3. in 1737 Martha Turner. At least 9 chn. See records in SLCity.

MARINER, Joshua/Josue from J, sadler and land owner in Boston by 1789. Mar Hannah ___, rem to Falmouth, ME 1715, said to be related to Andrew and James. (LEGRO; Davis; Underhill: NOyes; SLCity records)

A1. Joseph/Josue b 1694 Boston or NYork.
A2. Nathaniel, b 1695 Boston, d.y., as did Wm. and Priscilla.
A5. Edward, b 1702 Boston A 7. Deborah, b 1706.
A6. Hannah, b 1705 A8. Joshua, b 1707 d.y. A9. Josue, b 1709

MARINER, Thomas of Nfld. in Salem, MA 1650. OUTC

MARINER, also noted in Sharon,CT. OUTC.

MARKS in J 1600s. In some cases MARKS and LE MARQUAND were confused.
MARKS, Jane, b 1653 J, to Salem, MA, mar there 1674 John Blethen, Blythen. "Jane Lemarcom, a Jarzey maid" (CR7, Monthly Meeting of Friends) John to America 1659 from England? d 1704, 6 chn. (Helen Herman, Jackson, MI) Jane was prob a LE MARQUAND from Jersey, see.
A1. John Blethen, b 1676 Salem, mar 1701 Mary ___.
A2. Jane, b 1678 Salem. A4. Hannah Blethen
A3. Elizabeth, b 1680 d 1719 Swansea, MA, mar 1704 Isaac Chase
B1. James Chase B3. Isaac Chase B4. Elizabeth Chase
B2. Waitstill Chase B5. William Chase
A5. Sarah, b 1684 Salem. A6. Abigail, b 1686, mar Thomas HIX.
MARKS, Fred and George, from J? to America, settled in Boston area with widowed mother Elizabeth, 1800s. (Dorothy Hampshire, QUEBEC)
MARK, Israel of Grt. Britain, poss of C.I.? mar Eliz. Brawden and/or Hannah MURRY, qv, 1750 in MRB.
MARK, Manuel mar Elizabeth RENEW, qv, 1773 Marblehead, MA. (int)
MARKS, Ann, mar Joseph LAWRENCE, qv, in Boston 1742. (int)
MARLEY, Thomas, Henry and Edward, bros from G, to BC, Canada ca 1911/12. Thomas mar Helen WEBBER of G. (Mary Marley, Duncan, BC & Mesa, AZ.)
MARQUAND, see LE MARQUAND
MARQUAND, LE MARQUAND in G at leastby 1600. In St. Laurens, St. Brelade, St. Peter and St. Ouen J 1668, and in St. Peter and St. Brelade J, 1749. Curr G and J. There is a chart of the family of St. Martin G, in which a David MARQUAND mar Michelle DE LA MARCHE, early 1600s. David had at least 11 chn, and it appears that most if not all of the Ohio MARQUANDS are his descendants. (HIST OF MUSK. CO., OH; Cem. records as in Conner-Eynon books in GCO; Courthouse records, Coshocton, OH; THE GILMAN FAM; MARRIAGES IN COSHOCTON by Miriam Hunter; Mary S. McEwen, SLCity, UT; Carl Marquand, Baltimore, MD; Lenora Marquand, W. Lafayette, OH; Mrs. C.E. Renner, Zanesville, OH; Mrs. Jean Reddick Coshocton, OH; Mrs. Harold Marquand, Muskegon, MI; Mrs. Rodney Sheets Coshocton, OH; Mrs. Gordon Wilde, Los Angeles, CAL; Mrs. Catherine Marquand, Columbus, OH: Wolfe; Hill; Davis; Sarchet; Williams; SLCity records; CIFHS bulletin #15. (See CIFHS #24,and chart at Priaulx Library, Guernsey)
CAUTION: TRIAL CHARTS
MARQUAND, Charles, b ca 1765 G, mar there Rachel LOVIS, or LOVETT? Charles was son of Charles and Elizabeth (GUERIN) MARQUAND of G, had at least 6 chn: Rachel, Sophia, Charles, Peter, John and Solomon. Charles to America, settling fist at Georgetown, DC, where he worked at his trade, and owned property, then rem to Cambridge, OH,but soon left for Monroe Twp., of Musk. Co., OH where he built a log house, cleared a farm, bought property, ran a salt works, had gristmill, sawmill, carding and fulling mills, and a store. In 1836/7 he built a large 2 story brick house, first in this area. (HIST. OF MUSK.CO)
A1. Rachel, poss mar 1812 Thomas OGIER, qv, 3 chn: John, Elizabeth and Thomas OGIER, not traced. See OGIER.
A2. Sophia, poss mar George Bagnall Sr. (Will of Peter M.)
B1. George Bagnall Jr. B2. Johanna Bagnall Johnson
B3. Maria Bagnall mar George Baird. She rec'd land in Cosh. from Peter Marquand, her uncle. Other chn?
C1. Mary Elizabeth Baird, mar George Brownfield
D1. Lettie Brownfield mar Raymond Reddick
E1. Mrs. Jean F. Reddick, res Coshocton, OH
B4. William Bagnall. Bagnall & Retilley was a firm in GCO 1800s. See LE RETILLEY.
A3. Charles E., b ca 1796 G, had wife Eliza B., age 39 in 1850, res Perry Twp., Cosh. Co., OH.

B1. Sarah S., b ca 1833 mar James T. Edwards 1857?
B2. Laura W., b ca 1837 B4. Ruth b ca 1844
B3. Helen V., b ca 1839 B5. Viola b ca 1848
A4. Peter b ca 1796 G, mar Emily ____, b ca 1803 VA. No issue, but will in Book 2., p. 325, Cosh. gives some MARQUAND data, as he willed his estate to various desc of his bros. and sister. Obit of Mrs. Emily MARQUAND, outstanding citizen, who d 1885, is in DEMOCRAT, and DEMOCRAT STANDARD, local papers, Cosh. Library.
In the fam there is a John Downing MARQUAND, son of a Charles MARQUAND, BUT IT IS NOT CLEAR WHICH BRANCH HE BELONGS TO, poss above family?
B1. John Downing b 1822 d 1916, mar Amelia Boyd, 1829-1861, mar 2. Charlotte Thompson.
C1. Charles Absolom, b 1853 OH, d 1934, mar Melissa Ellen Thompson, b 1856, d 1940. (Thos. Marquand, Kendallville, IND)
D1. Effie May mar Burt R. Rutherford. She was b 1878, he in ILL,'77
D2. Abbie Lois, b 1880 mar James Claudius Kizer 1898
E1. Raymond Marquand Kizer b 1900 mar Bertha L. Wright
F1. Richard Wright Kizer b 1927 mar 1951 Nancy Thompson, 2 chn: Timothy Ross Kizer & Marilyn J. Kizer Stengel.
E2. Effie Madge Kizer b 1903 mar 1925 Paul H. Bell, b 1900
E3. James Oliver Kizer, b 1906 mar 1929 Erma K. Smith.
D3. Archie Downing, b 1883 near Endep. KS mar 1911 Bertha Louette Ferguson, b 1888?
E1. Boyd Charles, b 1912 near Redmon, ILL mar Eliz. Davis and 2. June Loyd, b 1919, in 1940. 3 chn: Charles Loyd, b 1941, Jola Luetta, and Arnelia Lynn, b 1955.
E2. John Thomas b 1915, mar Jessie Mae Smith, b 1916
E3. Emily? b 1919
D4. Jessie Emily, b 1886 near Indep., KS
C2. Joseph C5. William, 1858-1859
C3. Melissa Ellen, b near Columbus, OH?
C4. Emily, b 1856 C6. John A., b 1861
A5. John, b G, some data here is uncertain.
B1. George L., res Cambridge, OH?
B2. Lucy, mar ___Johnson, named in Peter's will
B3. Maria, mar ____Seward, 7 chn: John, Charles, Grant, Matilda, Victoria, Isadore and Harriet Seward.
A6. Solomon, b G, worked in his father's mills and store. In 1833 mar Eliza Hanks, dau of Jeremiah and Catherine (Shively) Hanks. Jeremiah a farmer of Irish and Dutch ancestry, and the Shiveleys were Swiss and Welsh. Poss related to Abe. Lincoln's Hanks family? Hanks to OH 1817. Solomon d 1841. (BIO. AND HIST. MEMOIRS OF MUSKINGUM CO., OH, 1892)
B1. Charles, b 1837, farmer, mar at age 23 in 1851 Elizabeth Sutton, dau of Samuel and Eliz. (Slack) Sutton from NJ. (Leonora Marquand, W. Lafayette, OH; Roger W. Marquand, Chagrin Falls, OH)
C1. Henry/Harry Clinton, mar Margaret Sturtz, res Otsego, OH.
D1. Nora E., res Cosh., mar W.J. Reed 1914. Note large diff. in age here, poss an error?
D2. Gertrude Idella, b 1912, mar ?, res OR & FLA, d 1972
D3. Roger, b 1914, res Chagrin Falls, OH mar 1. Grace ___, and 2. Halina Jablonski, b Cleveland, OH
E1. Patricia, b 1945, mar James Meadows, res Wash, DC, son Craig
E2. Joan, b 1955 mar Robert Willse, res PA
E3. Geoffrey, b 1956, mar Sue R.
D4. Earl? of Columbus, OH, uncertain data, mar twice.
E1. Virginia Rupersburg of Newark, OH E2. Roger W. Marquand?

C2. Walter E. mar 1888 Louise Trottman
D1. Clarence, mar 1924 Clara McAllister, res W. Lafayette, OH and Otsego, OH.
E1. Harold M., mar Ruth Arnold, no issue
E2. Mary, mar Russell Garber, 3 chn: Terry, Gary, Cindy Garber
D2. Lester L., b 1893 d 1965, mar 1917 Grace L. MacAllister, res W. Lafayette, OH
E1. Velma, mar Allan Hall
F1. Carol Jean Hall, mar Wm. Owens, attny.
C3. George Ezra, b 1872 d 1936, mar in Sharon, PA, Daisy Jones 1900. Daisy, b 1879 d 1965, fam res Sharon 24 yrs., then rem to Grove City, PA. George a preacher in 1915.
D1. Paul, b 1903 res Silver Springs, MD and Baltimore, mar 1. Helen ___, who d 1975, and 2. Mrs. Peggy Ann ROBERTS, dau Molly Ann.
D2. Harold Peter, b 1909, chemist, mar Emma Gould, 2 sons.
E1. David Laurence, b 1936 mar & div, dau Judith Annette
E2. H. Bruce, b 1943, mar Kirsten Moy, b 1946
C4. Ella M., unmar, res Columbus, OH C5. Annie B., unmar
C6. Miner, b 1867, data unclear, res W. Laf., OH, mar Mary RosaSturtz 1892. Miner d 1947
D1. Carl, at one time a Prof. at OH State, later res Wash., D.C.
D2. Paul?
B2. John William, a miller, b 1839, was last of fam to own the MARQUAND Mills in Muskingum, OH. Mar 1874 Anne Walker, 3 chn. (Jane Marquand, Columbus, OH)
C1. Laura, b 1875 d 1967, mar ___McKinney, res Columbus, OH.
D1. Katherine McKinney, had fam tree, but res where?
C2. Emma, mar ___, res Columbus, OH
C3. William, res Zanesville, OH, mar Eura ___, a dau Elizabeth.

MARQUAND, John, b 1760 G, son of Nicholas and Marguerite (DE LA RUE) MARQUAND, rem to US 1806 on ship ELIZA OF BOSTON. (See Ohio section) Some accounts in GCO and Musk. Co. books. Mar Caroline LANGLOIS, said to be blind, and had d in G. Settled in Adams Mill, OH. 2 sons plus other chn? TRIAL CHART: CAUTION

A1. John M., b 1797 G, d 1880 OH, mar Mary Ann MARQUAND 1819 in GCO.
B1. Emily, mar 1. Beal Waggoner/Wagner, b 1817 GCO, d 1852, son of Joseph and Rebecca (Beal) Wagner. Emily and Beal were mar 1839 Cosh. Co., OH. Chn?
B2. Henry, b 1861 Cosh. OH where he mar Jemima, dau of Lemuel and Jemima(Turker) Richards. Uncertain data
B3. Mary, b 1824, d 1898, mar Mordicai Waggoner, b 1819, d 1885, bro of Beal above, 12 chn
C1. Joseph Wagner, b 1842 C6. Charles M. Wagner
C2. Mary Wagner, 1844-1924 C7. Lydia, b 1853 mar W.W. Greer
C3. Martha Wagner, 1845-1920 C8. Rebecca Wagner, b 1856, d.y.
C4. James Wagner, b 1847 C9. Jane G. Wagner, 1857-1928
C5. William G. Wagner, b 1850
C10. Elizabeth M. Wagner, b 1860, mar Wm. T. Meredith 1891?
C11. Louisa T. Wagner, b 1863 C12. Margaret C. Wagner d 1890
B4. Margaret b 1839 d 1919 mar Wm. Wesley Speck of Trinway, OH 1856. (Virkus 7)
A2. Charles, b ca 1798 G d 1880 OH?, mar Elizabeth Downing of Delaware. (Note John Downing MARQUAND above, but dates are puzzling) Eliz. b 1801, d 1875, res Coshocton, OH, 10 chn.
B1. James, b ca 1838? d 1901? Franklin Twp., Cosh, OH mar Mary E.Cave who d 1907 age 59? James and Milton, his bro, were early postmasters at Conesville, OH.

C1. Carrie? b 1864 mar 1881 Jacob H. Beck, res Conesville, OH.
D1. Sherman Beck D2. James Beck D3. Velma Beck
C2. Alice, mar P.C. Shipps, gardener, res near Cosh., OH
D1. Herman Marquand Shipps, b ca 1887, VP of OH Wesleyan Coll? d 1980 Columbus, OH, age 93.
D2. Flavilla Shipps D4. John Shipps, twin of Ruth below
D3. Fred Shipps D5. Ruth Shipps, mar Paul Rice, res Col., OH.
C3. Elizabeth, b 1872 Franklin Twp., Cosh. Co., OH
C4. poss Edward? b 1868, doctor in Conesville, OH, mar Estelle Millican? Another ch d.y.?
D1. Dr. Edgar? b 1902
C5. R.H., poss Russell?, b 1870 d 1929, res Lafayette, OH, mar 1893 Hattie S. Elliott, 1872-1931, dau of Samuel and Harvilla.
D1. Charles Russell, b 1895, d 1918, mar Pearl ACORD, see ACOURT.
E1. Russell, b 1918 mar Melva Craig, 3 daus
D2. Myrta I., 1897-1921, unmar
D3. Pollard, b 1899 mar Helen Maneely, d 1954
D4. Edith, b 1914 mar Clarence E. Renner
E1. Edward E. Renner, b 1934 E2. Dorothy E. Renner Morrison
E3. Jane E. Renner McFarland, b 1942
D5. Ralph E., b 1902 Lafayette Twp., d 1952, mar Mabel Dreher?
E1. Marilyn J., b 1933 mar ___Elson, a son Michael Elson
C6. Kate E., b 1872 mar 1902 E. Jesse Robinson, farmer in Cosh.Co.
C7. Dr. Bert Allan, of New Phila., OH, mar 1906 Bertha Carr, no issue
C8. Milton Scott, b 1877 , in business in W. Laf. and Warsaw, had meat market. Mar 1906 Mary N. Giffin, res New Castle Twp, d 1938
D1. Merlin, res Cosh. OH
C9. Blanche b 1879 mar 1901 J.V. Smailes of New Moscow, OH,farmer, merchant and postmaster in OH
D1. Hazel Smailes, mar ___Brennan? A son Max Brennan, 1910-1925
D2. Zephiel, mar Hennegar, sons Wm. and Jesse?
C10. Grace A., b 1882 mar 1901 Roland M. Lanning, B&O RR dispatcher at Pitts., PA, 3 chn: Addison, Marian and Mabel Lanning Swank, res Pitts., PA.
B2. Joseph, mar 1868 Mina or Mindwell Adams
C1. Harry, mar _____
D1. Hazel, b 1900 mar ___Moss, res Kalamazoo, MI, d 1979
D2. Joseph D3. Lucille
D4. Edgar, mar Frances Curtis 1929 Cosh., OH D5. Harry
C2. Minwell, b 1872 Va Twp., Cosh.Co., OH prob d.y.
B3. William L., b 1841 Cosh.Co., OH enlisted 1862, served under Gen. Sherman in Atlanta campaign, farmed in VA. Twp., mar 1867 Eliz. Kreider, dau of George and Martha (Cave) Kreider, d 1918 Cosh.Co.
C1. Della, mar 1888 Beal A. Adams of Tusc. Twp., whose first wife was Lewinda Wright
C2. Jay, 1873-1940, mar Elsie Wolford, son Wolford b 1905
C3. Eura, mar Alta Powelson 1905, son William, b 1905
C4. Ward, 1890-1952
B4. Eliza North, had one son, William
B5. Josephus, mar 1863 Jane Adams, sister of Mina above, 5 chn. Josephus killed in train accident 1873.
C1. Emma, d age 19, unmar
C2. Elizabeth mar Perry C. or P.G. Wolfe 1890, 6 chn: Dwight, Grace, Dennis, Robert, Orlando and Lucille Wolfe.
C3. Anna, mar ___Buxton, 3 chn: Rolland, Ruth, Edmund Buxton
C4. Minnie, mar ___Dozer, 2 sons: Donald and Russell Dozer
C5. Wm.T., b 1865 mar Anna Balo, b 1868, 1893, 5 chn.(James Marquand)

D1. Harold McKinley Marquand, b 1893 mar ?
E1. Ethel Maxine, b 1917 mar Charles Stratton, no issue. She mar 2. Samuel Erskine, res Athens, OH?
E2. James William, b 1925 mar Lillian Lee Lewis 1946 in Columbus,OH.
F1. Margaret Marie b 1952 mar Michael Fouts 1975, twins: Heather and Heidi Fouts, b 1981
D2. Lelia Gertrude, b 1898 mar Paul Howland, res Detroit, MI,no issue
D3. Helen I., b 1910 Va.Twp., OH mar Laville Foley, res Chagrin Falls, OH, 2 sons
D4. Lillian Belle, b 1902 mar Charles Beals, who d 1951/2, bDetroit.
A3. Catherine, mar ___SARCHET, qv.
A4. Mary?, b 1844, mar George L. her cousin. She d 1902 in Franklin Twp., Cosh.Co., OH, poss belongs in next generation?
MARQUAND, Elias, b ca 1817 OH?, carpenter, mar Mary E. or Mary G.?, b ca 1821 NJ. An Elias C. mar Eliz. Barkelew in Cosh.Co., OH 1838.
A1. Nancy H., b ca 1840
A2. Mary G., b ca 1843
A3. Charles H., b ca 1845
A4. Theodore, b ca 1847
A5. Harriet L., b ca 1848
A6. Louisa A., b ca 1849
MARQUAND, one fam said to have settled in WISC before 1847. (Guernsey Soc. Bulletin, Spring 1973)
MARQUAND, Judith b 1788 Vale G, d 1860, OH. She was sister of John MARQUAND, b 1760, who settled at Adams Mill, Musk.Co., OH, and dau of Jean and Caroline (LANGLOIS) MARQUAND of G. She mar 1805 Philip LE GRESLEY, qv, prob in G, poss came over as widow? (SLCity records)
MARQUANDS below may be connected with families from either J or G, and appear in Conner-Eynon books about GCO.
Annie M., b 1869 VA Twp., Cosh., dau of B.F. & Jane
Blake mar Mae M. Garrett 1921
Catherine Louise, 1867-1950
Charles mar Clem. D. Madison 1846
Charles E. d age 78 Martinsburg, OH
Charles mar S. Eastinghausen 1847
Charles M. mar Mary A. Hummer 1869
Charles W. mar Susie E. Harmer 1880
Charles E., postmaster New Guilford,OH 1836
Earl R. mar Pearl MacIntyre 1912
Edna Margaret, 1908-1980 Cosh.,OH
Elsie May, 1875-1911
Estella, 1873-1943
Esther Jean, 1932-1972
Elizabeth, 1847-1904
George, b 1811 OH mar Eliz. OGIER, qv, and d 1900 bur Cambridge, OH
Henry C., 1860-1943
James W. d 1859 Cosh.,OH.
James S. d age 63 Conesville, OH.
John A. mar Arminta Kreider 1883
Katherine mar Harrison Glosser
Louisa mar Jonathan Coggins 1838
Margaret mar Wm. M. Cox 1856
Margaret I., b 1866 d 1948 Cosh.
Mary, mar Thomas OGIER, qv.
Mary Amanda 1882-1941 Cosh.Co., OH
Mary Rosella, 1869-1955
Max E., b 1910 d 1925 Jefferson, OH
Martha E., mar James Davison 1843
Minta, Araminta?, mar Garfield Watson 1908. See Krider, Kreider data
Sarah E. mar James T.Edwards 1857
Nora, b 1885, mar Wm. J. Reed. She was the dau of John A. and Minta. (Kreider) MARQUAND.
Stanley, b 1904 Conesville, OH, son of E.W. and Stella Millican MARQUAND.
Thomas, mar Martha Ann Huff 1855
William Edwin, b 1881, d 1956 Cosh.Co., OH
William T., b 1865, d 193-, Coshocton, OH.
MARQUAND. Fam below is part of the Guernsey/Muskingum/Coshocton fams in OH from Guernsey Island. Uncertain which branch they belong to.
MARQUAND, John Thomas of OH, mar ?(James/Terry Marquand, Columbus, OH)
B1. Howard b when? mar who?

C1. Walter, res Gary, IND, 4 sons. C3. George, res Sharpsville,IND.
C2. Earl, res Kokomo, had 2 sons, 2 daus. C5. Mary Ellen, d.y.
C4. Esther, mar Armand Sheetsie?, res near Kokomo, IND.
C6. How rd, mar ?, had son Thomas who mar and had 4 chn: Thomas Allen Michele, Matthew and Michael.

MARQUAND, small town in Missouri. MARQUAND Cem. in Northwest OH.

MARQUAND, Capt. Daniel from G 1732, settled MA, prospered. Mar 1739/40, widow Mary BROWN. At least one son Joseph, who had a large fleet of privateer ships and amassed a fortune. (Margaret Beebe, Center Harbor, NH; THE LATE JOHN MARQUAND, by Stephen Birmingham)

A1. Joseph, shipbuilder b 1748, d 1833 age 79. Mar Rebecca Coffin,res Newburyport, MA.
B1. through B5., daus: Rebecca, Eliz., Mary and Anna d.y. Another Rebecca may have lived to 19 & poss mar Joseph Coffin?
B6. Susanna, b 1789 B7. Charles, 1792-1879
B8. Joseph, b 1793, poss mar Sarah Winslow?
C1. John Phillips, b 1831 d 1900, New York stockbroker & investment banker, mar 1. Laura Wheelwright and 2. Margaret Searles Curzon, 1828-1898, 6 chn
D1. Joseph, 1861-1899 D2. Mollie/Mary, b 1863 D3. Bessie, b 1865
D4. Philip, b 1867 res Concord, Boston and Newburyport, MA. Mar Margaret Fuller of the Buckminster Fuller fam. Lost his fortune in the stockmarket 1907.
E1.? John Phillips, b 1893 d 1960, mar 1. Christina Sedgewick and 2 in 1937 Adelaide F. Hooker. He mar 3. ? This is the well-known author of the best sellers: THE LATE GEORGE APLEY, THE MOTO BOOKS, POINT OF NO RETURN, WOMEN AND THOMAS HARROW, WICKFORD POINT, B.F.'S DAUGHTER, and many magazine stories. 5 chn?
F1. ? F4. Blanche Ferry, b ca 1940
F2. John Jr. b ca 1924, by 1st wife
F3. Christina, b ca 1935? F5. Elon/Lonnie H. Hooker, b 1943
E2. poss other chn?
D5. Russell
D6. Margaret/Greta, mar Herbert Dudley Hale, son of author Edward Everett Hale, 6 chn. She mar 2. John Oakman, a dau
E1. Dudley Hale E2. Russell Hale E3,4,5,6.
E7. Renee Oakman
C2. and C3. several daus of Joseph
A2. poss other chn of Capt. Daniel?

MARQUAND, Henry, b 1737 G, to America 1761, res Fairfield, CT, mar 1.? and 2. 1761, Lucretia Jennings, b 1737, 11 chn. She mar 2. Capt. John Redfield? (HIST. AND GEN. OF OLD FAIRFIELD, Vol 2; OLD BURYING GROUND OF FAIRFIELD, by Kate Perry, 1882; ANDREW WARD GEN; Mildred Beebe, Center Harbor, NH; Virkus #4,5; AMERICAN FAMILIES, from American Hist. Society, New York)

A1. Isaac, b 1766 mar 1796 Mabel PERRY, 1778-1855, dau of Peter PERRY. Isaac d Brooklyn, NY 1838 age 72, a jeweler. 10? chn.
B1. Henry, b 1797 d 1818
B2. Frederick, b 1799, d 1882 mar 1822 Hetty PERRY, who d 1859. A Fred. MARQUAND had a silversmith business, Phila. 1823. There was also a firm of this name in NYCity 1819-1825. Fred. is said to have worked also in this field in Savannah, GA, then rem to NYork, where there was a Marquand firm 1839. Fred was founder of MARQUAND CHAPEL, Yale College, New Haven, CT, & at Princeton, NJ. 11 chn?
B3. Gurden Seymore, b 1801 d 1805 B6. Josiah Penfield, 1809-1879
B4. Lucretia, 1804-1836 B7. Sarah Elizabeth, 1811-1881

B5. Cornelius Paulding-1807-1832
B8. Mary Penfield, 1813-1838, mar Erastus Osborn Tompkins, son of Elihu and Aletta (Osborne) Tompkins, res Brooklyn, NY. He d in Savannah, GA, 1851, a jeweler.
C1. Virginia Marquand Tompkins, who d 1926. Mar 1872 NYCity, Elbert Brinckerhoff Monroe. This fam very active in philanthropic work.
B9. Julia Perry, 1816-1882
B10. Henry Gurdon, b 1819 NYcity mar 1851 Elizabeth Love Allen, 1826-1895. Henry a banker in Wall St., RR director, art collector, d 1902, poss other chn?
C1. Allen, b 1853 NYCity
C2. Mabel, b 1860, d 1896, mar Henry Galbraith Ward? b 1851 NY. Two sons d in WWI, Galbraith and Marquand
C3. Elizabeth Love, b 1862, mar 1884 Harold Godwin. Another Eliz. Love Marquand, b 1891, and still another b 1920 Newburyport, MA.
B11. Hetty Caroline, b 1922
A2. Rachel, mar Nathaniel Penfield 1782 Fairfield, CT, b 1758 d in Rye NY 1810. 3 chn.
B1. Henry Lewis Penfield, bp 1784 poss mar Polly PERRY?
B2. Josiah Penfield, bp 1785 B3. Robert Penfield, bp 1789
A3. Bethia, b ca 1770, d ca 1842 age 72. Mar at Trinity Church, Fairfield, CT Jesse Dimon, bp 1771, d 1822 Augusta, GA, age 52.
A4. poss Frederick?, who worked in NYCity, 1809-1839.

MARQUAND, Francis, b 1861 New Brunswick, d 1915 Pawtucket, RI. Mar Mary Duffy, b 1858 Southbridge, MA, Irish. Res Lincoln, RI, and Fall River, MA. Francis may be related to the LE MARQUAND fams settled in Gaspe early 1800s. Settlements of Marquands were in PEI and Shippegan, NB. A Francis was b J, was in Gaspe 1861 with 3 chn: Mary Catherine, Mary Ann and Francis Elias. (Mildred Beebe, Center Harbor, New Hampshire)
A1. Rena, unmar
A2. James B., b 1886 d 1941. B Lincoln, RI, James mar Annie Faulkner 1901 East Lyme, CT., da of Wm. J. and Frankie Faulkener.
B1. Leo Sheridan, b 1909, d 1979, mar Velva Winona Bray
B2. Merena Elizabeth, b 1910, d 1981, mar Wm. Mitchell and 2. Harold Stevens, 2 plus 1 chn.
B3. Philip Elwood, b 1913, d 1969, mar Lillian Ayers Saunders, 5 chn: Marianne, Janet, Philip, Katherine and Wilma.
B4. Willard Keith, b 1915, d 1978, mar Barbara Phillips 1939, 1? ch: Willard Keith Jr.
B5. Mildred Frances, b 1918, mar Oliver S. Beebe, 5 chn
B6. William Francis, b 1923, B7. Marie Evelyn, b 1926
B8. Sally Ann, b 1929, d.y.
A3. Francis Joseph, b 1898, d 1965 b Fall River, MA, mar Helen Eagleson, a dau Valerie mar Earl W. Stephenson.

MARQUAND, David, from G to Newburyport, MA ca 1729
MARQUAND, Frederick b 1889 Newburyport, MA
MARQUAND, Ichabod, 1699-1759 mar Ruth Staples in MA?
MARQUAND, LE MARQUAND, James of St. Peter J, whose three sons: Ernest Philip, Elias John and Judge Samuel James, are said to have come to America at one time in the 1800s. Judge Samuel James made a fortune in NYCity with the Pullman Co. (Geo. Le Feuvre, Detroit, MI)
MARQUAND, John, b 1910? d 1966 NYCity
MARQUAND, Laura Margaret, b 1857 Brookline, MA
MARQUAND, Mildred, b 1918 Newburyport, MA. See Eliz. Love Marquand.
MARQUAND, Philip, 1736-1816, mar Silence Howard in MA 1757

MARKOON, MARQUAND?, Penelope, mar 1807 in Boston, John BARTON, qv.
MARQUAND, Peter, 1767-1820, mar 1792 Sarah Snell in MA. There was also a Peter in Braintree, MA 1735 with servants.
MARQUIS in G 1300s. Curr G and J. Note that MARKEE is the pron. in French. Therefore some MARKEY, MARKEE may be orig. MARQUIS
MARQUIS, Giles from G to North Bay, ONT ca 1905. Giles Clark MARQUIS mar 1920 in St. Martin G, Lucia? MARTEL, rem to Erie,PA, 1921.
A1.Sidney mar Leonne-Louise Glorel, dau of Peter and Ursule Glorel, 1920, rem 1921 to US. Sidney d 1959, res Erie, PA. Leonne b 1894.
B1. Donald b 1924 Erie, PA mar Clara Louise BETTIS 1946
C1. Donna Marquis, b 1947 mar Jack Fish 1969, who d 1973. Donna res Erie, PA, a son Mark C. Fish, b 1969
C2. Dennis b 1949 mar Patricia Binkley, div 1977, a dau Joey P.
C3. Timothy, b 1955 mar Christina Simos 1980, res Fairview, PA.
C4. Randall J., b 1956 mar Antoinette Rose de Mauri 1979
A2. Giles A3. Walter A4. John, killed in WWII.
MARQUIS noted in OH 1860 census, but OUTC.
MARR, ___, arrived in New England in the 1700s on a JANVRIN ship from Surinam. OUTC
MARR, John, drowned out of schooner FRIENDSHIP bound to the Straits, 1811, from Marblehead, MA. OUTC.
MARRIETTE, MARIETTE in J 1309, 1377, 1399, curr G. See also MARETT.
MARRIETTE, Daniel from G? to GCO early, poss 1810? with chn/Grchn. At least 3 mar into the Waller family. Jesse Waller, b Berkeley Co. VA, rem 1807 from Captina Cr., Belmont Co., to Byesville, OH. He then rem to Noble Co., (then Morgan Co). He is bur Taylor Cem. in Noble Co. Jesse mar Mary Farley, 1760-1841, dau of Thomas and Jane Farley of Ft. Ashby, WVA. MARRIETTE is spelled in various ways in this fam's records, including MEARITTE and MERRIT. The desc may have taken name MERRITT, and the original form entirely lost.
MARRIETTE, Daniel, prob the grandfather of the young people married in GCO in the early 1800s, as Martha, wife of Dan MEARITTE d 1839 age 96. If this is so, then the generation in between is missing from available records. (Henry Waller, MD; Abington, MA records; GEN. OF JACOB JORDAN AND MARY ANN SCHRIVER, by Mrs. Mary Yerian Mainetti, Columbus, OH; Census records; Land records of McConnellsville, OH Court House; Taylor Cem. stones) CAUTION! TRIAL CHARTS.
MARRIETTE, Thomas, b 1791 G d 1855, bur Taylor Cem., Jackson/Noble Co. OH. Mar 1813 in GCO Jane Waller, 1797-1838. Res Noble Co. 1836. (Conner-Eynon books)
A1. James MERRITT, b ca 1817 OH, father born "France", mother in OH, mar Eliz. Jordan, b MD. Elizabeth, 1825-1901. She and James are bur Crooked Tree, OH? James served in Civil War?
B1. Isaac, b ca 1861 res Jackson, Noble Co., OH 1880
B2. Jacob, b ca 1864 B3. Catherine B4. McClelland B5. Phebe
A2. David?, b ca 1820 GCO, poss bro of James above? age 60 in 1880.
MARRIETTE, John mar Polly Waller 1815 GCO, and by 1830 res Morgan/ Noble Co., OH, had at least a son and dau, poss other chn?
MARRIETTE, Elizabeth, b G, mar John Waller in GCO 1813. Eliz. may have been b in G ca 1795.
MARRIETTE, Rachel, b 1813 GCO? 2nd wife of David Waller,1785-1850. David had mar 1. Elizabeth Jordan. Note other Eliz. Jordan above, wife of James. 3 chn by 1st wife, including Mary/Polly, b 1813, bur 1840, mar John Yerian, 1814-1890.
MARRIETTE, MERRITT, David? noted in Wash. Co., and Wayne Co., OH early 1800s. MARRIETT, John res Burlington, MA 1810 Census. OUTC.

MARSH, MARCH? MARSH curr G and J, old in G. Cf also LA MARCHE, DE LA MARCHE of C.I.

MARSH, Elisha in Phila. PA 1872, age ca 40. OUTC. (Quaker Ency)

MARSH, Samuel to SC before 1675, OUTC. (Baldwin)

MARSH. Compiler not certain this fam should be included. There appear to be 2 Marsh fams in early GCO. Moses Marsh is included here because of the fam trad. that he was b in G 1801, and was brought as a small ch to GCO by the SARCHET fam, qv, in 1806. Trad. also says tha that he mar twice and had 6 sons, 3 by each wife. He was a bricklayer, also poss County Recorder, and d of typhoid fever, res Cambridge, OH. He mar 1. Sarah Borton, dau of Reuben and Eliz. (Tedrick) Borton, 1814-1846. Did he mar 2. 1867 Isabella ___? Moses and Sarah sold their land in GCO 1834 to Alex. Cochrane. CAUTION: TRIAL CHART. Note MARSH in Millwood, Cambridge, Jefferson and Oxford Twps. in GCO. See orig. data if possible. (Beverly Shepherd, Cambridge, OH; 1850 census; Mrs. Lorraine Dykman, Seymour, MO)

A1. Elizabeth, b ca 1833 GCO poss mar John Wharton Nov. 1852

A2. John W., b ca 1836

A3. Phebe, b ca 1838, poss mar Edward CARNAL?CORNEL?, Sept. 1852, or mar Charles M. SARCHET? qv, 1857, poss both?

A4. Mary S. or Mary L., b ca 1841

A5. David Clark, b 1843 Millwood Twp., GCO, rem to MO, SD, then settled in ILL. Mar 1873 Amanda Sylvester in St. Louis, MO. He d 1916, prob in Maywood, ILL. Amanda b 1848 PA, d 1910 Cook Co., ILL, bur Oakridge Cem. She the dau of John and Melinda (Everson) Sylvester.

B1. Davanna, b 1873 St. Louis, MO, d before 1915. B2. Erma, 1875-1914

B3. May F., b 1879, mar ca 1895 Frank Warner Johnson, b 1872 Portage, WI, son of Charles A. and Sarah M. (Cooley) Johnson. Frank d 1952 Napierville, ILL. He mar 2. Lillian Walker and by her had 3 daus and 2 sons.

C1. Fern May Johnson, b 1896 mar 1919 Albert P.J. Heitman, and d 1974, Cook Co., ILL, a son Albert Heitman.

C2. Aletha Amanda Johnson, b 1899, mar 1. John Wienacht, and 2. John Englehart. Chn: June and Robert Wienacht.

C3. Leslie Warner Johnson, b 1901 Chicago, ILL mar Elsie Koski, cremated Catalina Island, CAL. A dau Jenette Leslie Johnson.

C4. Erma Louise Johnson, b 1904, mar Leo ___, but d age 19.

C5. Lillian Pearl Johnson, b 1906 Stoutsburg, IND, mar Clarence Wesley Carr.

D1. Lorraine May Carr, b 1931 mar Wilbur Dean Dykman, b 1925 Bates Co. MO, 1950, son of Claus Johnson & Katherine (Meinen) Dykman.

E1. Rebecca Ann Dykman, b 1951 Springfield, MO mar 1970 John A. Smith, sons John and Joel Smith

E2. David Dean Dykman, b 1953 mar Mamie Linda Valdez, a dau April

E3. Daniel Eugene Dykman, b 1954, unmar

E4. Douglas Andrew Dykman, b 1955 KC, MO, mar Vicky Lynn Jones, a son Jess Dykman.

C6. Mabel Ruth Johnson, b 1909 Kersey, IND mar 1. Wm. Leschman & 2. Andrew Muto. 3 chn: Robert & Sandra Leschman & Leroy Muto.

C7. Helen Frances Johnson, b 1911 Wheatfield, IND, mar Henry Andrews, a son Edward Clayton Andrews.

C8. Perlie Edward, mar Loretta Klein, several chn.

B4. Perlie S., b 1884 Pierre, SD, d 1949 unmar

B5. Edward M., b 1886 SD, d in Cleveland, OH

B6. Raymond Clark, b 1888 SD, mar, had at least one dau.

B7. David Wesley, b 1892, mar Jeanette Louise Bixby, d 1955 Maywood, ILL.

MARSH, Abraham, mar Mary Ann BICHARD in GCO early. See BICHARD
MARSH, John R., b 1851 G? or NY?, d 1917, bur Scotch Plains Bapt. Ch-yard in NJ. He was son of John R. Marsh & Josephine. OUTC.
MARSILL, MOURSEL, Richard had supplies at Richmond IS., ME 1643. OUTC, but MORCEL is an old J surname.
MARSTON, said to be corruption of name LE MAISTRE, LE MASTER of C.I. However, no corroboration was found by compiler. See Noyes, Salem, Mass data. See MARSTONS in CABOT fam, and in early POINDEXTER fam.
MARTEL in J 1229. In St. Brelade J 1749 (in VA)
MARTEL in G 1331, still common there, in St. Saviour G 1729, etc.
MARTELL, Mary mar John Cannon 1727 Boston, MA. OUTC.
MARTELL, ___, from G? who said he had a grant for the river at Machias, ME, from Quebec, 1688. MARTEL, see CH.IS.COLLECTION
MARTEL, Nicholas appeared in Guernsey Co., OH early 1800s. He was b ca 1795, prob in G, and d before 1853, when his estate was approved. He mar Judith BLAMPIED, qv, also of G. The heirs of Nicholas were, in 1855: Judith Mattitall, RAchel and David Long, Peter Martel, Mary Ann Allison, Eliza Jane Davis, John Blampied Martel, Mary Ann Martel, John Thomas Martel, Catherine Martel and Judith Martel, the widow. Some Martels in WIS and IA were not located. There is a story that one of the Martel bros. went to Cuba where he owned a large sugar plantation, and raised a family. Richard Van Horn, a desc., states he heard that Leah Pugh Martel was sole heir of a sugar plant. in Cuba but did not claim her inheritance. There is a fine book on this family that covers much more information. Write Mary K. Daniels, P.O. Box 164, Salem, ILL, 62881. (Frances Hale, Ft. Worth, TX; Betty Briggs, Nashville, ILL; David Smallshaw, Cambridge, OH; Maud Ruff, Dallas, TX; Lucille Thompson, Cambridge, OH) THIS CHART HAS
A1 Peter b ca 1823 ERRORS. See new chart in CI COLLECTION.
A2. John Blampied, b ca 1827 OH, a saltmaker in 1850, mar 1. 1849 Nancy Maria SARCHET, qv, dau of David SARCHET, who was son of Thomas, the immigrant. Nancy said to have had 6 chn, poss some d.y. They rem ca 1856 to Wash. Co., ILL where Nancy d 1863. John then mar Leah Pugh, widow of ___GILBERT, who prob d in the Civil War, leaving 3 small chn. Leah was b 1839 in ILL and d 1931 in TX.
B1. Mary Electa b 1851 mar Joshua Bales Pugh, and d in Newport, ARK, quite young, leaving 2 small daus.
C1. Elizabeth Pugh , b 1872 d 1936
C2. Eunice Pugh, b 1876 ILL, d 1959, mar Otto M. Bowen, 1874-1936
D1. Raymond Pugh Bowen D2. Eliz. Morrow D3. Otto M. Bowen
B2. Orion, b 1853, d 1877, bur Mt. Zion Cem., Wash., ILL.
B3. Oscar Shiloh, b 1857, mar 1879 Mary Elnora Hargett, dau of John S.W. Harget and Mary Elnora Reeves. Mary d 1944. Oscar d 1951, Sesser, ILL. He was a farmer, school director, treasurer, tax assessor, highway commissioner, police magistrate, 10 chn.
C1. Wm. Arthur, b 1880, d 1881
C2. Elsie Lou, b 1882, d 1968, bur Du Quoin, ILL mar Major Axum Revelle, 8 chn: Elnora Schurtz, Howard M., Elmer A., Verda Lou Stevison, Eugene, Eunice Ritter, Glenn M. and Evelyn
C3. Edna Mae, b 1884, mar 1909 Springfield, ILL Nova Leon Phillips, 1886-1945, 2 chn.
C4. John frank, 1886-1892, bur Ashley, ILL.
C5. Mary Alice, b 1880, d 1975, mar 1909 Roy A. Gulley, 1887-1945, 8 chn: Marie, Gerald, Mary K. Daniels, Lida Enid Pyle, Ronald Alwyn, Halbert Edison, Maurine Yarbro, & Roy O. Gulley.
C6. Elmer C., b 1891 mar Bertie Bracey, bur Marion, ILL.

C7. Bertha Lee, b 1893 mar 1912 at Pinckneyville, ILL Mathew J. De Lapp,1890-1965,8 chn: Sammy Louise, Georgina, Doris Ann, Wallace, Glen Norman, Perry Marvin, Loris Whelan, David Lee De Lapp.
C8. Nellie F., 1896-1905 C9. Jennie B., b 1899, unmar
C10. Zetta Pauline, b 1904 mar Ralph Oglesby, bur Sesser, ILL
B4. Alva, Alvin?, b 1859 OH, d Gourney, TX
B5. Elmer, b ca 1861 ILL, d Texas of TB.
B6. Charles W., by 2nd wife, mar Mary Hutchens, had barber shop, gen. store, and was once Mayor of Magnolia, ARK. 7 chn: Glen, Elmer, Charles, Ora Strothers of FLA, Mildred Luck of Shreveport, LA, Oscar of FLA and Frank of Magnolia, ARK.
B7. Bert, b Ashley, ILL mar Nanie Mae McAlister, bur Dallas, TX. 4 chn? Louise, Beverly, Mary and Ben.
B8. John C., unmar, d 1956
B9. Rosella/Rose Ellen?, b 1865, mar Henry Elmore, b 1866 ILL, 3 chn: Elisabeth Huddleston, Velma Erisman, Eula Douglas.
B10. William Benjamin, b 1869 Ashley, ILL mar Eva Mae Haddix, b IA. 5 chn: Maurine, Evalyn, Maude, Frances and Ruth.
B11. George, b 1870 ILL, d.y.? B12. Jonathan, b 1873 d 1890 Ft.Worth.
B13. Jennie, b 1875 ILL d 1965, bur Ft. Worth, mar Richard Van Horn, 3 chn,Richard, Faye and Elizabeth ?
A3. Charles, b 1834 GCO d 1867 ILL mar age 26 Emily Hunter, a son Nicholas was b 1861 ILL, mar Eudora Wilson, 4 chn.
A4. Judith mar ___Mattitall, had dau who mar ___Long. (Will)
A5. Mary Ann/Nancy, b ca 1832 mar ___Allison?
A6. Eliza Jane mar John Davis, who bought land from J.B. Martel 1856
A7. Catherine.
MARTEL, Judith b 1815 G, d 1869 GCO, prob relative of Nicholas.
MARTEL, Jane b 1830 G or GCO, prob also a relative, rem first to Balt., MD, then to GCO. She mar there Benj. Trott, 1832-1904, at least 7 chn. (David Smallshaw, Cambridge, OH)
A1. Virginia Trott, b 1861 mar David Cox, 8 chn
A2. Annie Trott, mar Will Hutton, 2 chn
A3. Nannie Trott, mar John Nicholason, 2 chn
A4. Elmer Trott A6. Ida Trott, mar Albro Smith, 1 ch
A5. Elsa/Elza Trott, mar Allie Moseley, 2 chn. A7. Walter Trott
MARTEL, Margaret Charlotte, b G,? said to be of same fam as above. Her chn were heirs of Nicholas the immigrant. She mar David Dull, blacksmith res Kimbolton, GCO. At least 3 chn.(Lucille Thompson, Camb.,OH)
A1. James Dull, b 1830 d 1870? (Mrs.PrestonHale, Fort Worth,TX)
A2. Eliza Jane Dull, b after 1836, d ca age 34. Mar Alfred WEEDON, b ca 1836, d 1925. Eliza d 1871. Cf WEEDON & WHEEDON, G surname. Alfred taught school in GCO until 1868, when they left for Adair Co., then res Crawford Co., both in KS.
B1. David B2. Susan
B3. Lucille L. Marling, b 1894 mar Clyde R. Thompson, 1889-1968, GCO.
C1. John Raymond Thompson, b 1914 mar Thelma Braden, dau
D1. Carol Thompson, b 1943 mar Wayne Fairchild, 2 daus.
C2. Robert G. Thompson, b 1917 mar Ethel Jackson
D1. Jerry L. Thompson b 1944 mar Patricia Dunlap, a ch.
D2. Jon S. Thompson, b 1947 mar Karen Johnson, 2 sons.
A3. Joseph Dull, mentioned in Nich. Martel's will.
A Margaret Dull, 1823-1846 is bur in Old Kimbolton Cem., GCO.
MARTEL, Nicholas and wife Henriette (LE MESURIER) DOREY, with 2 daus came from G to New York 1870, settled a month later in Racine, WIS. (E. Archambault, Oshkosh, WI)
A1. Henriette Eliza

A2. Alice Le Mesurier, mar 1898 Edwin Ongimie Archambault, son Edwin
A3. Cora A4. Frank A5. Ernest A6. Francis
MARTEL, John B., b G, mar Nancy SARCHET, qv and rem to Wash. Co., ILL where she was bur 1863 age 31. She was the dau of David Sarchet, the son of Thomas Sarchet. John B. was 22 in 1850, b GCO?
A1. George, 1843-1854
MARTEL, E.C. of St. Louis, MO was in France WWI, and found his name with a great many MARTELS bur there. (Mary K. Daniels, Salem, ILL)
MARTEL, "Charles, Duke of the Franks, who gained the decisive victory of Poitiers in 732, that checked the power of the Moslems and saved Western Europe from further invasions." (Sarchet Scrapbook)
MARTEL cognac is famous throughout the world. Jean MARTEL, son of Thomas M. and Martha HERAULT, b 1715 St. Brelade J, d 1753. He was first a partner with Jean FIOTT, and established a firm at Bordeaux, France, then Martel had an estab. at Cognac. In 1728 the Bordeaux farm was abandoned and Martel began the firm under his own name. He mar 1. 1726 Jenne Brunet of Cognac, and 2. 1737 Rachel Lallemand. He left a widow of 33 and 7 chn. She carried on the business until her sons were able to take over. Jean and Frederic carried on the business. Rachel d 1787. MARTELS and FIOTTS were close friends in St. Brelade, Jersey for many generations. (Mary Daniels)
MARTIN, common, compiler did not research this name in America. Poss. many Martins from C.I. settled in America. Name is old in G, from the 1100s, and in St. Martin G 1700s. Name in St. Brelade J 1668. Poss some current research. See CIFHS #9.
MARTIN, Sarah mar Sam. BROWN 1796 in MRB. OUTC
MARTIN, Judith of G mar ca 1830 in G John Hillman, 7 chn. At least two came to America. See HILLMAN.
MARTIN, Susanna mar Lewis OGIER 1783 in Charleston, SC. OUTC (Clemons)
MARTIN, Thomas mar Charlotte OGIER 1786 Charleston, SC. (N. and S. CAROLINA MARRIAGE RECORDS)
MARTIN, many in early MRB, many marriages with Channel Islanders. OUTC.
MASSEY, James from G to Maryland 1644. See also MACE. (DAB)
MASSEY, Samuel from G? to Boston 1684 or before. OUTC
MASSEY, John of Salem, had fam of at least 7 chn. OUTC. (Perley II)
MASTER, MASTERS, see also LE MASTER, LE MAITRE, LE MAISTRE. Several to colonies, but all MASTERS are <u>not</u> from C.I. MASTER in J 1607.
MASTERS, 4 fams in Newtown, Roodbury and New Milford, CT by 1790. OUTC Poss some were desc of Capt. Nicholas below.
MASTERS, Capt. Nicholas, b 1688 G, arrived in CT 1720 on his own ship, at Black Rock, d 1756 Woodbury, CT. Mar 1717 Stratford, CT Elizabeth SHELTON, 1693-1758, dau of Daniel Shelton & Eliz. Welles. There is a Masters cem. in Schaghticoke, NY. (Pat Sayler, Cleveland,OH; Pam Hallock, Bothell, WA)
A1. Daniel, b 1718, d.y.
A2. Samuel, farmer, res ca 1790 Schaghticoke, NY, later in Arlington,VT
B1. Elizabeth, mar John BAKER 1771 in Washington, CT.
B2. Sarah, b 1762 Schaghticoke, NY mar 1778 Moses Canfield, b 1757, d 1803, bur Masters Cem., son of Thomas Canfield & Martha Camp.
C1. William Masters Canfield, b 1780, d 1845 Onondaga Co., NY, mar Polly Ann Stoddard, b 1783, d 1872 Auburn, NY
D1. Sally Ann Canfield b 1807 mar Samuel Goetschius
D2. Samuel Sheldon Canfield mar Rachel Goetschius, b 1798 Cortlandtown, West. Co., NY, d 1840 Elbridge, NY, dau of Christian G.& Letty Blauvelt. Samuel mar at least 3 times, and poss 5 times; 1. Rachel, 2. Lucy Ann Palmer, 3. Prusia Jane Stark.
E1. Catharine Canfield b 1822, d 1902, mar 1841 Nelson Riker,

b 1820, d after 1900

F1. George Nelson Riker, b 1842 NY, d 1877 Bay City, MI, mar Glorivina Hoffman

F2. Antoinette Riker, b 1843 NY, mar Delzon or Dalyon Colby, res Tuscola Co., MI.

F3. Alfred Riker, b 1845 Hillsdale, MI d 1885 prob in PA. Mar 1868 Emma Hoffman, 1851-1928

G1. James Alfred Riker, b 1870 PA, d 1949 unmar

G2. Cecelia Iona Riker, b 1872PA, d 1949 Evans, PA, mar 1892 Wallace MERRY, b 1868 NY, d 1951 Buffalo, NY.

H1. Edith Merry, b 1894 Erie Co., NY

H2. Lyman Merry, b 1895 Erie, mar 1. Mary Fitzpatrick, a son Joseph Merry and mar 2. Alberta ____.

H3. Bruce Merry, b 1899 Erie Co.,NY, d 1979 Buffalo, NY, mar 1927 Princess Cordelia Belle Little Harper, 1899-1979

I1. Princess Patricia, b 1929 Lockport, NY, mar 1950 Paul T. Sayler, Jr., b 1928 Cleveland, OH.

J1. Nancy Lee Sayler, b 1951 Cleveland, OH mar 1970 Dennis Bihary, b 1947, 4 chn: Sharon, Keith, Stephen & Diane

J2. Stuart Wm. Sayler, b 1952

J3. Linda Louise Sayler, b 1954 mar 1978 Andrew F. Rerko, III.

J4. John Liston Sayler, b 1956 mar 1979 Merribeth Woike

H4. Clayton Merry, b 1907 mar Rosella Hoffman

H5. Viola Merry, b 1911 mar Allen Guest

G3. Francis John Riker, b 1873 PA, d 1967 Evans Center, NY, unmar

G4. Charles Alonzo Riker, b 1875 PA, d 1951

G5. William Henry Riker, b 1878 PA, d 1969

G6. George Edward Riker, b 1883 PA, d 1936 unmar in Newfane, NY.

G7. Anita May Riker, b 1885 d 1962 Erie Co., NY

F4. Flora Riker, b 1848 Onondaga Co.,NY mar ___GILBERT

F5. Fanny Riker, b 1850 Genessee Co.,NY mar ____Malone

F6. Viola Ella Riker, b 1852 Erie Co.,NY mar 1879 Henry Strevely

F7. Frank Riker, b 1854 NY, mar Sarah E. ____.

F8. Minnie Riker, b 1861 NY, d 1882 Wisner, MI.

E2. Analiza, Ann Eliza Canfield, b 1824 Onondaga,NY d 1889 Byron, MI, mar ca 1842 Platt Gale, JR, b 1822 DutchessCo,NY, d 1884MI.

F1. William M. Gale, b 1843 Elbridge,NY mar Mary ____.

F2. Henrietta Eliz. Gale, b 1847 Elbridge, mar 1867 Hiram Leslie Chipman in Owosso, MI.

G1. Winnifred Chipman, b 1868 Owosso, MI mar 1886 in Bad Axe,MI Henry Franklin Walker. She d 1940 Seattle,WA, bur Bad Axe.

H1. Florence Mildred Walker, b 1888 Lake Odessa, MI, d.y.

H2. Bessie Louise Walker, b 1889 MI mar 1911 Jay George Finkbeiner, d 1946 NYCity.

H3. Morgan Chipman Walker, b 1891 MI, d.y.

H4. Irma Gale Walker, b 1892 MI, d.y.

H5. Guy Harry Walker, b 1894 Unionville, MI mar 1913 Etta May Hance, d 1957 Charlotte, MI.

H6. Henrietta Eliz. Walker, b 1898 mar 1926 Seattle, WA,Edward Villard Mackie. She d 1974, bur Ald. Manor, WA. Edward b 1892 in Alameda, CAL.

I1. Patricia Ann/ Pam Mackie, b 1931 Seattle, WA, mar 1955 Wm. Herbert Hallock, 4 chn

J1. Gregory Wm. Hallock, b 1957 mar 1977 Mildred Nettie Garoutte, a dau Vonita Jennifer Hallock

J2. Douglas Edw. Hallock, b 1959 J3. Janis P. Hallock,b 1960

J4. Bradley Herbert Hallock, b 1962

H7. Winifred Gertrude, called Ann, b 1907 Unionville,MI mar 1931 George Henry Jennings.
G2. Irma Chipman, b 1870 Byron, MI d.y.
G3. Gale Chipman, b 1874 MI res Arlington, VA, mar Robert Morrison and d 1966.
G4. Miner Chipman, b 1882 Bad Axe, MI mar Gertrude Foster, d1956 San Francisco, CAL, bur San Raphael, CAL.
F3. C. Morell Gale, b 1849 Elbridge, NY mar Minda ____.
B3. Polly, mar Noah Gold
B4. Nicholas Shelton, b ca 1757 d 1796 New Milford, CT mar 1. 1781 Hannah Starr, who d 1781 age 21, and 2. Tamar Taylor, dau of Rev. Nathaniel Taylor and Tamar Boardman. 7 in fam in 1790 census.
C1. William Starr, b 1781 d 1804 C3. Charles Shelton, a lawyer
C2. Frederick William, a physician, by 2nd wife
C4. Susan, b 1793 mar 1826 Deacon Judson Blackman, d 1849
B5. Samuel
A3. John b ca 1725 d 1811 Woodbury, CT, mar Dinah __,ca 1725-1810.
B1. Eunice, b 1748 mar Reuben Castle B2. Samuel, b 1750, d.y.
B3. Elizabeth b 1754, mar 1824? David Shelton, b 1741. She d 1827
B4. Lydia, b 1757, d.y.
B5. John, b 1759 mar Huldah ___. He d 1836 Woodbury, CT, prob the fam with 2 men, 3 boys and 3 females in census of 1790.
A4. James, b ca 1731 Fairfield, CT d 1820 Schaghticoke,NY. James mar 1. ___Rogers, and 2. ___TOUCEY, cf TOUZEL. He mar 3. Mrs. Hull, mother of Gen. Wm. Hull, and grmother of Commodore Isaac Hull, of US Frigate CONSTITUTION. James had 5 chn.
B1. James Shelton, mar 1. ___Allen and 2. Mrs. Cronkhite, widow. By 1st wife 7 chn.
B2. Nicholas, mar Sally Phelps of Rupert, VT, 2 chn.
C1. Nicholas Merritt, b 1790 Schaghticoke, NY d 1872 Greenwich,NY, mar Anna T. Thomas of Sandy Hill,NY
D1. Sarah Ann, 1816-1825
D2. John T., mar Mary Eliz. Mowry of Greenwich, Wash.,Co,NY, 1840
E1. Nicholas Merrit Mowry mar 1866 Mary Hervey of Cincy,OH, 2 chn
F1. Blanche Eliz., 1867-1869 F2. Maude, b 1870 mar W.A. Cottrell
E2. Mary Elizabeth, 1845-1854
E3. William, d.y. 1845 E4. Leroy, 1851-1868
C2. Albert Phelps mar Sally Maria Rising of Rupert, VT 1817,4 chn.
D1. Josiah Rising Masters, b 1818 d 1895
D2. Edward Nicholas mar 1850 Alice Le Barnes of Sheffield,MA, rem to Montrose, COL 1890, 8 chn
E1. William Bliss, 1852-1861 E4. Ellen Maria, b 1859 d 1861
E2. Alice Adelaide, b 1854 E5. Edward Bliss, b 1865
E3. Mary Eliz., b 1856 mar Sterling Sherman of Salem, NY
E6. Anna Maria, b 1862 d 1863 E7. John A. b 1867 E8. Albert M.
D3. Marshall Merritt, b 1823 Schaghticoke, NY d 1858, mar Lucy Mary Benjamin of Pittstown, NY 1842, 3 chn
E1. Georgina Maria, b 1844 mar Calvin B. Lockwood of Bkln, NY 1870
E2. Francis Albert, b 1847, member of Marston & Masters in the grocery and provision business, Troy, NY.
F1. Lucy Benjamin, b 1886 d 1890 F2. Harold L., b 1887
E3. Edward Shelton Lockwood b 1849, farmer and coal dealer, rem to Williamsburgh, KS where he was in RR construction and coal mining. Returned to Troy 1880, mar 1. Fanny L. Marston, dau of Perrin M. Marston of Troy, NY, 1877, who d 1887. He mar 2. Martha L. Marston, sister of 1st wife, 1890.
F1. Helen Elizabeth, b 1878 KS, d there 1880

F2. Robert Shelton, b 1880 Troy, NY F3. Perrin M.,b 1892,2nd wife
D4. Anna Maria, b 1831 mar George G. Arnold of Troy, NY 1856
B3. Judge Josiah Masters, mar 1. ___Adams of Litchfield, CT, and 2. Lucy Hull of Derby, CT., 3. Ann Smith of Hamilton, NY. Josiah in Legislature from 1797 to 1802, in Congress from 1806-1810. Judge for 25 yrs. of the County Court, 7 chn.
C1. Josiah
C2. Samuel J., b 1801 d 1883, Middle Falls, Wash.Co.,NY, followed the sea for 46 yrs., 90 voyages to Europe, Asia, Africa and S.A. U.S. consul under Pres. Pierce.
C3. Augustus, 1807-1881 C5. Lanthe C7. Elizabeth/Eliza?
C4. Eunice C6. Louise
B4. Elizabeth, mar 1. James Mallory, 2. Dr. Jabez Hurd, and 3. George Reab. A son George Reab Jr., Capt in US Army, was taken prisoner at Queenston, War of 1812.
B5. Lydia, mar Merritt Clark of Oyster River, 9 chn.
MASTERS, Edward from J? or G? mar Elizabeth MARINER, dau of James MARINER, qv, 1713 in MA? MASTERS a seaman. (Elizabeth had mar first John LE COUTEUR of J) 4 chn: Edward, b 1714, John, James & Elizabeth MASTERS.
MASTERS data in WRCIC. See also Essex Coll, Vol 8, Census & Little's GEN. AND HIST. OF MAINE, p.803. Much data in Salt Lake City.
MASTERS, John mar Deborah Dove, both of Salem, MA 1683 in MRB,MA.OUTC
MASTERS, fam of Somerset Co.,NJ and Wilmington, NC, and several places in OH isbeing researched by Josephine Stapleton, Tulsa, OK and Donna Randall, Xenia, OH. OUTC. NJ.
MASTERS, large number in OH in 1800s, but OUTC. Some said to be from/
MASURY, MAZURY, MAJORY, etc, mangled forms of the Channel Island surnames LE MASURIER, LE MESSURIER, and LE MESURIER. A town in eastern OH is named MASURY. Use much caution in dealing with these surnames as the distorted spellings complicate the situation. The spellings changed from generation to generation. See data under MAJOR.
MAZURY, LE MESSURIER of Salem was from Jersey. (Konig)
CAUTION: TRIAL CHARTS
MASURY, LE MESSURIER, Benjamin of J, b ca 1624, mar Jeanne/Jane LE GROS qv, dau of John and Elizabeth (LE POITERICE) LE GROS, bp 1620. They had sonsLaurence, George, Benjamin, and Martin, all of whom settled in MA. Poss other chn who came, or remained in J? See Jersey record (ANCESTORS OF GUILFORD SOLON TINGLEY)
I. Laurence, b 1646 J, d 1706 Salem, MA, mar 1. 1670 Mary, dau of Arthur Kibben, Kibbee of Salem, who d 1682 Salem. Laurence mar 2. Susanna, widow of ___MAJORE. She may have mar 3.? John Wester or Vestry? See also Laurence below.
A1. Elizabeth b 1671
A2. Mary MARJERY, b 1672 Salem, MA mar Samuel Foster of Salem.
B1. Richard Foster B4. Jonathan Foster B7. Hannah Foster
B2. Mary Foster B5. Bartholomew Foster B8. Timothy Foster,d.y.
B3. Margaret Foster B6. William Foster B9. Timothy again
A3. John, b 1673?
A4. Laurence MAZURE, b 1674 Salem, mar 1697 Susanna, dau of George and Susanna (PARY, PERRY?) MASURY of Newbury, MA, b 1680
B1. James MASURY, MAZURE B3. George
B2. Jane B4. Susanna B5. Benjamin MAZURE
A5. Susannah MARJERY, b 1676 Salem A7, by 2nd wife, Abigail, b 1686
A6. Jane MAZURE, b 1679 Salem, d 1690
A8. Sarah MAJIRY, b 1689 A9. Jane, b 1691
II. George, b 1648 J, bro of above Laurence, to America?

III. Benjamin, b 1650 J, bro of above George and Laurence, d 1695 Salem MA. (Essex Coll, July 1974) Mar 1. 1671 Mary LUCE, sister of Rachel, b ca 1648 J, d 1675 Salem, age 27. Benj. mar 2. 1676 Margaret REW, RUE, DE LA RUE or DE RUE?, also noted as ROWE??, who d 1694 Salem, age 38.

A1. Joseph MAZURE, b 1672 d before 1708, mar 1699 Abigail, dau of John WHITEFOOT, BLAMPIED, qv.

B1. Joseph B2. Abigail B3. Margaret B4. Jane

A2. RAchel b 1673 d 1677 A3. Mary MAZURE, b 1675 Salem, MA

A4. by 2nd wife, Jane MAZURE, b 1677, d 1685

A5. Benj. MAZURE, b 1679 d 1723 at Cape Porpus, ME mar 1701 Rachel___.

B1. Joseph B2. Benjamin B3. Rachel B4. Margaret B5. Jane

A6. Margaret MAZURE, b 1681 d 1682 A7. Margaret again, b 1683

A8. Thomas MAZURE, b 1685, orphan, apprenticed to Wm. Abbott 1696. He mar 1. 1715 Sarah ___, who d 1721. Mar 2. 1723 Mary BLANCH. 4 chn by 1st wife and others by 2econd: Benj., Sarah, Margaret, Thomas, Elizabeth, etc.

IV. MASURY, Martin, b 1652 J d 1709, mar 1675 Sarah LAROKE, qv. (Perley II & III)

A1. Benjamin, b 1676 mar 1701 Hannah Pickworth, at least 5 chn: John, Sarah, Benjamin, b 1703 and Martin and Susanna.

A2. Martin, b 1678 d 1689. A3. Jane, b 1681 d 1691 A4. John, d 1688

A5. John again, b 1688 mar Lucy ___, at least 5 chn: John, Lucy, Mattin, Sarah and others.

A6. Sarah MAZURY, b 1691 A7. Elizabeth b 1693 A8. David, b 1695

A9. Abraham MAZURY, b 1697, d 1729 mar 1726 Eleanor BROWN, who mar 2. Jonathan BODEN, qv, 1729, or John BARTLETT 1734, poss both? A dau Hannah also d 1729?

A10. Richard MAZURY, b 1698 mar Sarah Poole, a widow.

V. Joseph, b 1655 J mar 1. Sarah, widow of Samuel Pickworth, dau of John MARTIN, and 2. Judah or Judith ___, who mar 2. Joshua Joshua Mackmillion in 1715.

A1. Joseph, b 1680 Salem, MA mar 1712 Anne Scadlock of MRB, at least 6 chn: Anna, Sarah, Joseph, Nathaniel, Judith, William, etc.

A2. Abigail, b 1683 A3. Nathaniel b 1686 A4. Benjamin, b 1689

A5. Jane, b 1698, by 2nd wife

A6. Samuel, b 1700 Salem, d before 1752, mar 1726 Jane Dale of Salem, dau of John and Elizabeth Dale, 2 chn: Sarah and Samuel

A7. William, b 1702 Salem, mar 1727 Sarah Powisland, at least 4 chn: William, Joseph, Joseph again and Sarah.

VI. Jane, b ca 1660 J, d 1677, embarked for America, indentured to Philip ENGLISH, qv, and d on the voyage.

MASURY, William, b 1660 J, son of Edward LE MESSURIER of J, mar 1682 Abigail, dau of Joseph and Mary SWASEY, qv, of Salem, b 1661 Salem, MA. (Tingley)

A1. Mary, b 1683 A3. William, b 1687 Salem, d 1690

A2. Joseph, b 1685 d 1728, mar 1719 Mary Harris, who d 1730 Salem. 3 chn? poss others? Mary, Rachel and Joseph.

A4. Abigail, b 1689 Salem, d 1715 mar 1710 John GRAY of Provincetown, MA, son of Robert and Sarah (Grover) GRAY. He mar 2. SusannaJones.

B1. Robert Gray B2. William Gray B3. Abigail Gray

A5. Margaret, b 1691 Salem, mar 1712, (int) Joseph Tapley of Beverly, MA, son of Gilbert and Lydia (Small) Tapley. A son Gilbert Tapley

A6. Edward, b 1693, d 1696 Salem.

MAJORY, John, b 1658 J, d 1728 Salem, called Benjamin his cousin. John a tailor, mar 1690/93 Mary, dau of Thomas and Hannah(Kettle)Larcum, LARCOMBE, qv. of Salem, MA, b ca 1675.

Did he marry 2. Judah ____ of the real estate transactions? See list of MASURYS at end. (LARCUM GEN; NEHGS Vol 31; Perley Vol 3)

A1. John, b 1694 Salem, d before his father. Mar 1714 Keziah, dau of Thomas and Abigail Woodbury of Beverly, MA.

B1. John MASURY, b 1715 Salem, d 1797, mar 1. 1739 Mary BUSH and 2. (int) 1747 Elizabeth WHITEFOOT or BLAMPIED of Salem.

B2. Susannah, mar Francis Benson. (Essex Coll, Vol 3) Other chn?

C1. Thomas Benson, b 1747 Salem d 1790. Mar 1. Hannah DELAND, qv and 2. Abigail Foster. See Fosters in L. MAZURE fam. Thomas a Master Mariner, commanded ships in Rev. War, and was a prisoner on the infamous JERSEY prisonship. Hannah, 1st wife, bp 1727.

B3. William, mar 1742 (int) Mary Dike of Salem, MA.

A2. Benjamin, b 1697 Salem d before 1763. A cooper, admin. father's estate. Mar 1719 Sarah, dau of Stephen and Sarah (Hodge) Archer of Salem. See ARCHER GEN.

B1. Benjamin, b 1720 Salem, d 1764, age 44, peruke maker. Mar 1743 Deliverance, dau of John and Mehitable (Lord) White of Salem, b 1721 Ipswich, MA, d 1798 Salem age 77 of smallpox. See WHITE GEN.

C1. Benjamin, bp 1744 Salem, mar 1764 Sara Welcome

C2. Sarah, bp 1747

C3. Mehitable, bp 1749 Salem, d ca 1798. Mar 1769 David Murphey, who mar 2. Abigail ___. Dau Mehitable bp 1783 Salem.

C4. Stephen MASURY, bp 1751 Salem, d 1782 Salem age 30. Res first in Beverly, MA. Served in Rev. War Co. of Capt. Eben FRANCIS, mar 1774 Elizabeth, dau of Samuel and Sarah (Goodwin) Woodbury of Beverly, b 1751 d 1782 Salem.

D1. John, b 1774 Beverly, MA d 1862. Mar 1. 1793 Susanna KNIGHT, who d before 1798. He mar 2. 1798 Elizabeth, dau of Jonathan and Mary (Patch) Gage of Beverly, b 1770.

E1. Mary Knight Masury, bp 1794 Salem, d 1819 age 25, mar 1812 James Goomunson? of Salem.

E2. by 2nd wife, Nabby Gage Masury, b 1798 Beverly, mar 1824 Benj. Cressy of Beverly, son of Benj. and Abigail (Track? TRACHY?) Cressy, b 1796 Beverly. Cressy d 1862 age 66, 5 chn: Abigail, Eliza, Adeline, Lucy Ellen and Mary Elizabeth Cressy.

E3. Capt. Stephen, b 1800 Beverly d 1874. Mar 1827 Mary Cressy, 1806-1836. Mar 2. 1837 Sophia Ann, dau of Robert and Sophia (LOVITT) Curry of Beverly, 1814-1864. Mar 3. 1866 Sarah, dau of Zebulon and Betsey (Goodridge) Woodbury of Beverly, b 1814, d 1885 age 71. 5 chn

F1. Mary Elizabeth b 1827 F3. Hannah Augusta, b 1834

F2. Harriet Ellen, b 1830 F4. Stephen, b 1836 F5. ?

E4. John, b 1802 Beverly, d 1887, mar 1827 Sally, dau of Isaac and Dorcas (Woodbury) Hull, b 1796 d 1879 Beverly.

F1. Elizabeth Gage, b 1828 F3. John Francis, b 1837, twin

F2. Lucy Jane, b 1830 F4. Sarah Ellen, b 1837, twin

E5. Asa Goodridge Masury, b 1804 Beverly, d 1806

E6. Harriet, b 1805, d 1806. E7. Harriet again, bp 1808

E8. George, bp 1809, -iving in 1849

E9. Samuel, b 1813 Beverly, d 1889, mar 1845 Bridget B., dau of David and Bridget (Barry) Rohan of Beverly, b Cork, IRE. 1824 d Beverly age 78. 3 chn? John, Mary and George, b 1847.

D2. Elizabeth b 1777, d 1858, mar 1798 Josiah Kent of Beverly, son of Jonathan and Sarah (Wales) Kent, b 1775, d 1842 age 67.

E1. Elizabeth/Betsey Kent, b 1799 Beverly, MA.

E2. Sarah Kent, b 1801, living in 1862, mar 1827 John Peirce of Bev. son of John and Eliz. (Pressen) Peirce, 1803-1860,5 chn: John, Mary Ann, Adoniram, Martha and Harriet Masury Peirce.
E3. Josiah Kent, b 1803 Beverly, d 1844, mar 1. 1830 Susannah, dau of Benj. and Sarah (Morse) Patterson of Bev., b 1808 d 1840. Josiah mar 2. 1841 Martha Phillips, who mar 2. Joseph Elliott. 2 chn by 1st wife, Stephen and Sarah Morse Kent, plus 1 ch.
E4. Harriet Kent, b 1805 Bev., mar 1841 John Elliott Jr.
E5. Abigail Kent, b 1807 d 1853, mar 1832 Mark Morse of Manchester, MA, son of David and Lydia Morse, b 1807, d 1876, dau Lydia.
E6. Joanna Parker Kent, b 1809, d ca 1839. Mar 1834 Thomas PEirce, son of John and Eliz. (Pressen) Peirce, 1810-1867. He mar 2. Hannah B. Loring. 2 chn? Stephen and Joanna Peirce.
E7. Mary Kent, b 1811 mar 1834 Wm. Higgins, of Wenham, MA, son of Mary Higgins. Wm. b 1809,4 chn: Mary,John,Tim.& EverettHiggins.
D3. Samuel Woodbury MASURY, b 1779 Beverly, d 1781
D4. Sarah/Sally, MAJORY b 1780, d 1838 Herrick Twp., PA, age 59, mar 1. 1799 Phinehas Clark, div 1823, mar 2. 1823 John S. Niles of Herrick Twp., Susq.,PA, d ca 1847 there.
C5. James Masury, bp 1753 Salem, d.y.
C6. James again, bp 1755 Salem, mar 1771 Mehitable, dau of Robert and Rebecca (Phillips) Allen of Salem, bp 1750 d ca 1790. (See ALLEN GEN and Essex Ant., Vol 3) 8 chn?
C7. Hannah, bp 1756 Salem, d a widow. Mar 1781 Dixey Morgan of Salem, son of Dixey and Lucy Morgan, bp 1752 Salem, d ca 1790
C8. Edward Masury, bp 1761 Salem, MA
B2. Stephen, b 1722 Salem, d 1755, mar 1752 Hannah, dau of Penuel and Hannah (Masters) Townsend, no issue
B3. Sarah, b 1724 Salem, d before 1801. Mar 1747 Isaac Cook III, of Salem, son of Isaac and Martha (Anniball) Cook, bp Salem 1720, living 1783. 5 chn
C1. Isaac Cook, 1749-1751
C2. Sarah Cook, bp 1750/51, mar Joseph Foster of Danvers, MA
C3. Stephen Cook, b 1752 mar 1776 Mary Carriage of MRB.
C4. Benjamin Cook, bp 1754, mar (int) 1778 Elizabeth, widow of Joshua Beckford and dau of ___Webb.
C5. Martha Cook, bp 1758 Salem
B4. Hannah MAJORY, b 1726 d 1813, mar 1758 Sgt. John BATTEN of Salem, son of John and Hannah(Holland)Batten, b 1735 Salem, d there 1781
C1. Mary Batten, mar 1785 Michael Bateman
C2. Aaron Batten, b 1764 Salem d 1791 on brig HENRIETTE of Texel. Mar 1788 Sarah Coffin, a dau Sally Batten
C3. John Batten, b 1765 Salem, living 1781
A3. James Murray?, b 1699/1700 Salem mar ? Lydia Earl 1721
A4. Samuel b 1702 Gloucester, MA dead before 1751, mar 1724 Mary, dau of Richard and Mary (Pike) Woodmansee, b 1704
B1. Sarah, bp 1728 Salem d.y.
B2. Samuel, bp 1729 Salem d before 1770. Mar 1. 1752 Hannah Tuxbury of Salem. Mar 2. 1752 Martha, dau of John and Martha (Willard) Sterns, 5 chn: Richard, Samuel, William, Mary and Margaret.
B3. Joseph, bp 1731 Salem, d before 1771. Mar 1764 Susannah, dau of Joseph and Hannah (Holton) Cressy of Salem, b 1736. She mar 2. James Ford.
C1. Joseph MASURY, bp 1765 C2. James Cressy MASURY
B4. Richard, b 1728 Salem d 1786 age 58. Mar 1754 Sarah BEADLE, qv of Salem. Chn: Richard, Samuel, William, Sarah & Elizabeth.
B5. John, bp 1738 Salem, d.y. B8. John again, bp 1746 Salem.

B6. Sarah, bp 1740 Salem, mar 1767 Daniel Shehane
B7. Margaret, bp 1742, mar John GILES, qv.
A5. Rachel, 1705-1716 A6. Edward, 1708-1720 A7. Mary, bp 1712 Salem.
MAJORY, Eleanor, mar 1730 Jonathan Bowdoin, son of John, 8 chn. (Underhill)
A1. Habijah Bowdoin, bp 1730 MRB
A2. Simpson Bowdoin, bp 1732 MRB, mar 1758 Abigail EFFORD, qv. She was living 1771. He was a shoreman, no issue?
A3. John Bowdoin, bp 1735 MRB, mar 1761 Hannah Swan. He d before 1765 widow surviving. 2 chn: Thomas Swan and Hannah BOWDOIN.
A4. Edmund Bowdoin bp 1737 MRB, mar 1760 Abigail DENNIS, res MRB 1774. 7 chn: Edmund, Abigail, Elizabeth, Benjamin, Dennis, Eleanor and Mary Bowdoin.
A5. Hitchins Bowdoin, bp 1740 MRB, mar 1761 Hannah Chubb. Another record says he mar Sarah ___. A son Hitchins bp 1761. Other chn?
A6. Ambrose Bowdoin, bp 1743 MRB
A7. Jonathan Bowdoin, bp 1745 MRB mar 1768 Lynn, MA, Hannah (Talbot) Lancaster, widow of Henry Lancaster. Jonathan d before 1772 MRB.
B1. Hannah Bowdoin, b ca 1769 MRB mar 1787 in N. Yarmouth John Hayes Mitchell.
B2. a son, b ca 1771 MRB, said to have gone South, mar a wealthy woman, lived on a plantation, kept slaves. No issue?
A8. Joanna Bowdoin, bp 1747 MRB.
MASURY, Joseph, b ?, d 1775 Danvers, MA, mar 1753 Hannah Pritchard, bp 1734, d 1803, dau of John and Martha (Gould) Pritchard. (PEABODY GEN; Sally P. Wagner, Chatsworth, CAL)
A1. Sarah, bp 1755 Topsfield, MA A2. Joseph, bp 1757 A3.Hannah,b1759
A4. Lucy, b 1763 Danvers, MA or Boxford, MA? d Middleton, MA 1806. Mar 1781 Francis, son of Bimsley Peabody. Francis b 1761, d 1842, mar 2. Mrs. Hannah Giddings. Francis served in Rev. War, and was at the Battle of Bunker Hill.
B1. Allen Peabody, b 1781 mar Middleton, MA 1803 Rebekah Hobbs, and 2. Polly/Mary (Patten) Bryant, who d ca 1875. Allen sailed on a privateer ship from Salem in War of 1812, d Bedford, NH 1865.
C1. Almira Peabody, b 1804 mar 1825 Joseph Bushby. C3, ch d.y.
C2. Elizabeth Hobbs Peabody, b 1806 C4. Francis, b 1809
C5. Rebecca Peabody, b 1811 C6. Allen, b 1816
C7. James B. Munroe Peabody, b 1819 Salem
C8. Daniel H. Peabody, b 1820
C9. Mary Jane Peabody, b 1824 Bedford, NH mar Jonathan Warren,d 1886
C10. William Peabody, b 1827 d in CAL.
B2. Warren Peabody, b 1783 mar 1805 Lydia Dale, 1784-1837. Mar 2. 1838 Mrs. Sally LAMON, LEMON, LE MOIGNE?, dau of Joseph & Mary (Carter) Hold, b 1793, d 1870. Warren d 1854 Wenham, MA.
C1. Emma E. Peabody, b 1806 Danvers, mar 1831 Andrew Wyatt, d 1839
C2. Sally Peabody, b 1807, mar 1835 William Porter, d 1840
C3. Mary D. Peabody, b 1809 Middleton, MA mar 1833 Joseph W. Cook, d 1871.
C4. Elbridge Gerry Peabody, b 1810
C5. Lucy M. Peabody, b 1812, mar 1836 Ephraim Parker Dodge, d 1865
C6. Geo. Wash. Peabody, b 1813 C7. Margaret D. Peabody, b 1815, d.y.
C8. Martha Anne Peabody, b 1818 mar 1840 Wm. B. Morgan.
C9. Wm. Peabody, b 1820 mar 1842 in Wenham, MA Anna Dodge Patch, 1820-1861, dau of Abr. & Sally (Dodge) Patch, 6 chn. He mar 2. Mary Ann Danforth, 2 chn. See GEN. for more on this fam.
C10. Edward Warren Peabody, b 1823 C11. Warren August, b 1823,twin
C12. Henry Ansell, b 1827

B3. Lucy Peabody b 1785
B4. Joseph Peabody, b 1787 mar 1812 Abigail Wilkins, b Danvers, MA. He d 1837, 11 chn. See GEN for more data.
B5. John Peabody, b 1789 d 1794
B6. Hannah Peabody, b 1791
B7. Francis Peabody, b 1793 mar at Boxford, MA, Mary, dau of James & Rebecca RUSSELL, b 1792, d 1884 Reading, MA. Francis d 1866. 10 chn, more data available B8. John Peabody, 1794-1796
B9. John Peabody, b 1800, mar 1828 Clarissa Garvin, dau of Jacob and Margaret, b 1808 Londonderry, NH, d Lynn, MA 1872. John d 1885 Lynn, MA. 7 chn, more data available.
B10. Huldah Peabody, b 1798 B11. Susan Peabody
B12. Jesse Peabody, b 1802 mar at Andover, MA 1823 Susan Leach, 1802-1861. Jesse d 1830, Salem, carpenter & musician, 2 chn.
B13. Ruth Peabody, b 1804 mar Eben Wilkins and d 1878

MASURY, Susanna, mar 1728 John BROWN, b 1703 Salem, d 1771, res Boston and Danvers, MA. (Essex Ant., #13)
A1. John Brown, b ca 1730, cordwainer and Yeoman, res Danvers, MA, mar 1. Dorcas Walden of Salem 1755, and 2. Mary Nurse of Lynnfield, MA 1767. He d Danvers 1800 age 69. Mary survived him and d 1839
B1. John Brown, d.y. B2. Nathaniel Brown, d before 1800
B3. Dorcas Brown, mar 1. John Hart of Lynn, MA 1780, 2. John Day,1796, and 3. James Foster after 1800. She was his widow 1829.
B4. Polly/Mary Brown mar Nathaniel Gowing 1789, living 1800
B5. Joseph Brown, b 1768, has desc. B6. Wm. Brown, b 1770
B7. Daniel Brown, b 1772 mar Love Newhall, res Danvers, MA. She d 1844 age 65 and he in 1846 age 74.
B8. Judith Brown mar Henry Parker of Reading 1818, and d before 1829.
B9. Hannah Brown, b 1777, mar ___Foster before 1829.
A2. Isabella Brown, mar John Silver of Salem 1748, was widow 1794
A3. James Brown, b 1736 mar Ruth Buxton of Danvers 1759, d there 1793 age 57. She d 1812 age 74
B1. James Brown, b 1759 d Halifax, NS, a P.O.W. 1781
B2. John Brown, b ca 1761, rem to Nantucket where he d 1837 age 76 leaving a grdau Elizabeth CARTWRIGHT.
B3. Elizabeth Brown, b 1763, mar Dr. Isaac Williams of Salem, 1781. He d 1807, had chn.
B4. Ruth Brown, mar Nathaniel Nurse of Danvers 1782
B5. Susanna Brown, b 1768 mar ___Ingalls, d before 1840, several chn.
B6. Sarah Brown, b 1770, mar Robert Peele.
B7. Samuel Brown, b 1777, res S. Danvers, mar Nancy Twiss (int)1798, living in 1840
B8. Lucinda Brown, b 1780, mar 1. Josiah Austin and 2. her cousin Samuel Brown, 1816. She was his widow 1866
B9. Mary Brown, mar John MARSH, his wife in 1840
A4. Samuel Brown, b 1738, res MRB, mar Mary Gatchell 1767, who d 1816 age 75. He d 1819 age 81.
B1. Mary Brown, bp 1768, d.y.
B2. Samuel Brown, res MRB, mar his cousin Lucinda Brown 1816, and d d ca 1866 age ca 90. She survived him.
B3. Elisha Brown, bp 1777, d.y.
B4. Elisha again, bp 1778
B5. Molly Brown, bp 1780, mar James Toppan Jr. 1801 of Wenham, MA?
A5. William Brown, settled in Antrim, NH before 1773

A6. Margaret Brown, mar Isaac Very Jr. of Salem ca 1775
A7. Judith Brown mar Cornelius Thompson of Mt. Desert Island, ME (int) 1778, his wife in 1785
A8. Susanna Brown, mar Andrew Newhall before 1773 A10. Joseph, d.y.
A9. Hannah Brown mar ___Potter, his widow of Lynn, MA 1773
A11. Elizabeth Brown mar Edmund Rhoades of Danvers, MA, a cordwainer 1769, res there 1785.
A12. Mary Brown of Danvers, MA mar 1. Eleazar Austin of Salem 1772, and 2. Juduthan Upton.
MASURY, MAJORY, Edward res Exeter, ME 1683, a soldier 1695. Mar before 1712 Abiel, widow of Wm. Morgan. One dau known by an earlier wife.
A1. Jean, mar Benjamin Mason, b ca 1696, blacksmith in Strath-Stratton? ME. She d by 1735 and Benj. d 1770. (Noyes) 7 chn: Edward, Benj., Francis, Mary, Catherine, Elizabeth and Jane Mason.
MASURY, Elizabeth mar 1788 Jonthan MILLET, b 1764 Salem, MA, 7 chn. (DRIVER GEN)
A1. Jonathan, b 1791, lost at sea 1821
A2. Charles, b 1793, mar 1. Ruth Driver and 2. Sarah Archer?
A3. William, b 1795, lost at sea A4. Eliza, b 1798
A5. Nathan, b 1800, living in Salem, MA 1886. A6. Joseph, 1802-1868
MASURY, Elizabeth mar Wm. Powsland 1755 MRB
A1. Tabitha Powsland, bp 1756 MRB, d.y.?
A2. Elizabeth Powsland, bp 1761 MRB A4. Wm. Powsland, bp 1768
A3. Tabitha again, bp 1764 MRB. A5. Mary Powsland, bp 1768 MRB.
MASSURY, widow Elizabeth, bp 1782 Salem, MA with 2 chn: Sally, Betsy.
MASURY, MAZURYE, Joseph,"prob from the Channel Islands" (Perley), mar ca 1679 Sarah Pickworth, Salem, MA.
A1. Joseph, b 1680 A2. Abigail A3. Nathaniel b 1686 A4. Benj.,b1689
MASURY, John W., mar Laura A. Carlton, b 1822? Salem in 1844
A1. Francis Carleton, b 1845 A2. John W. Jr., b 1847 Salem, MA.
MASURY, Joseph of Beverly, mar Abigail PAINE, qv, 1767 MRB
A1. Joseph, b 1786 mar poss Polly Friend? res Beverly, MA.
B1. Mary, b 1808 B6. Lydia A., b 1819
B2. Abigail, b 1810 B7. Martha J., b 1821
B3. Joseph b 1813 B8. Augusta F., b 1824
B4. Nathaniel Friend, b 1815 B9. Charlotte, b 1826
B5. James, b 1817 B10. Francis Macomber, b 1828
A2. Lydia, b 1789 Beverly, MA.
MASURY, Samuel and Elizabeth res Salem, MA, 6 chn.
A1. Polly/Mary, bp 1786 A3. Stephen Webb, bp 1795 A5. Benjamin, b / 1797
A2. John, bp 1795 A4. Hannah, bp 1795 A6. Eliza, bp 1805
MASURY, Samuel and Nancy res Salem, MA.
A1. Nancy, bp 1793, poss mar Moses Gage?
A2. Harriet, bp 1795 A4. Richard, bp 1798
A3. Samuel, bp 1797 A5. William Browne, bp 1800
MASURY, MAZURY, Samuel res Salem MA with wife Mary.
A1. John, bp 1738 A2. Sarah, bp 1740 A3. Margaret, bp 1742
MAJORY, MASURY, Wm. mar Sarah Powisland, 1727 MRB
A1. William, bp 1728 A3. Joseph again, bp 1732
A2. Joseph, bp 1730, d.y.? A4. Sarah, bp 1735
MASURY, William, mar Anna ___, res MRB
A1. Anna, bp 1753 A2. Mary, bp 1768
RESEARCHER: Please note that a list of more than a hundred MASURY, etc persons and fams of MA is in WRCIC, Cleveland, OH. Also note that Jean Jacques MAZURIE was b 1764 in Brittany, France and rem to US. The fam settled in Philadelphia, PA. Another MASURE came from

Belgium in the 1800s. See Salt Lake City records. There is more data in FIRST CHURCH IN SALEM, by Pierce & Moody, 1974, and in EIGHTEENTH CENTURY BAPTISMS IN SALEM, MA, by James Emmerton, 1886.

MASURY, Benjamin and Jane, bro and sister from J ca 1700. See letter from Rachel LUCE of J, widow of Edward LE MESSURIER, showing connection between the MASURY and LE MESSURIER surnames of New England and the Channel Islands. (NEHGS Vol.31)

MASURIER, see LE MASURIER, etc.

MATHEWS in St. Lawrence J 1788, curr G and J.

MATHEWS, Jane, b 1823 G, mar Charles BREWER, qv, and rem to Racine, WI on wedding trip 1852. 5 chn. (Leach)

MATTINGLY, in J 1556, 1607. (TINGLEY in J 1556) In St. Clement J 1668, in Grouville and St. Clement J 1749. Note also TINGLEY in America, poss shortened form of MATTINGLEY? Although old in J, it is also a name of Great Britain. Found early in Musk. & Cuy. counties, OH, but OUTC. (MUSK.WILLS by Nellie Raber; Cleveland,OH records)

MATTINGLEY, James and Emma res Beverly, MA. OUTC. See VR of Lynn,MA.

MATTINGLY, John and Sarah of VA, she b ca 1787 and he in 1780, 12 chn. b Breckenridge Co., KY. OUTC.

MAUGER, at least 50 different spelllings of this surname, especially in Canada. Some research by M. Denys Munger of Quebec City. This name is also German. See Q.A. IN CANADA; MONGER GEN by Billie Joe Monger, Elkton, VA; THE MUNGER BOOK by Mary L. Wasz, Santa Ana,CAL.

MAUGER in St. Laurens, St. Mary, St. Brelade, St. Ouen, St. John and Trinity J 1668. In Trinity, St. Ouen, St. Laurens J 1749. MAUGER in G 1300s, settled in St. Martin, Forest and Torteval, G, and in Sark Island 1700s. Curr G and J., common in G.

MAUGER shield, gules, an anchor erect in pale argent, on a chief of the second, three roses of the first. See CIFHS #9.

MAUGER, John Wallace Goodenough, b 1879 East Lynn, Belgrave Rd., St. Sampson, G, son of John Timothy MAUGER, b Nfld. of a G fam, and Emily Louisa Goodenough of G. He was 5th in fam of 7 chn. John and his friend George COOPER left G with two other young men, T.COLLAS and A. ROUSSEL 1897 for London, where he met a Mr. LE COUTEUR and son George LE COUTEUR, who were be their escorts to San Francisco, CAL. In the diary kept by J. Mauger, they explored London, left on the SS. PARIS, arrived in New York 10 days later, and explored New York and Brooklyn, leaving by train for Buffalo. From Buffalo they went to Chicago, Kansas City, Mohave and San Francisco, CAL. John enrolled in the Univ. of CAL. He was a barber, and worked at this trade in CAL. He also worked at a mine where he met and married Hattie Trevithick from Cornwall, in Soulsbyville, a Cornish mining town in CAL. He d 1941 and Hattie in 1964. She was b in CAL 1889. 2 chn. (Mrs. Leland Hague, Modesto, CAL)

A1. Mary Bernice, b 1908 Sonora, CAL mar Ewing Rhodes Stewart, b 1902 Okla. City, OK.

B1. Donald Ewing Stewart, b 1830 Sonora, CAL mar Joanne Rouse, b 1931 Winnetka, ILL.

C1. Pamela, b 1952 mar John Taylor, 2 chn: Portia & Wesley S.Taylor

B2. John, b 1935 mar Suzanne Roetsisoender, b 1941 Everett, WA,3 chn: Erik, Todd and Mark Stewart

A2. Jack Elwyn, b 1912 Sonora, CAL mar Mary Eliz. Foulks, b 1913 Elk Grove, CAL.

B1. Marylyn Jane, b 1938 Sacramento, CAL mar Wm. Bateson McInnes, b 1934 Boston, MA, 3 chn: Kristyn, Geoffrey, Peter McInnis.

B2. Jacklyn Elizabeth b 1941 mar Wm. Edward Linn, b 1936 Portland, OR. 3 chn: Karin, Michael and Brian Linn.

MAUGER, Frederick, b 1886 St. Heliers J, son of Fred. Mauger Sr. and Caroline LE MOTTEE, qv. Fred Jr. mar Ella Cooke 1923 and d 1965 in Gaspe, QUE. Res 1903 in Paspebiac, QUE to work for Charles Robin's firm for free board, plus 3 pounds a month salary! (Evelyn McLellan, Moncton, NB)

MAUGER, Thomas from C.I.? mar Mary ___, res MRB. OUTC

A1. Elizabeth, bp 1724 A3. Sarah, bp 1728, d.y.?

A2. Mary, bp 1726, d.y. A4. Mary again, bp 1730 A5. Sarah, bp 1734

MAUGER, George and Sarah res MRB. OUTC

A1. John, bp 1727 A2. George, b 1730 A3. Sarah, bp 1733

MOGIE, Rowland and Sarah res MRB, prob MAUGER

A1. Frances, b 1741/42 A2. Mary, bp 1745

MAUGER-MAJOR. There is additional data below to add to that on p.429 of QUIET ADVENTURERS IN CANADA, by Turk, which see.

MAUGER, Richard, b 1765 J, mar 1. Polly Flowers and 2. ca 1809 at Paspebiac, QUE, Angelique Loiselle, dau of Robert L. & Anne Elizabeth Roussy, b ca 1796. Richard d 1860 Pabos, QUE age 95. (Stanley Major, Toronto, ONT; Aldo Brochet, London, ONT; Therese Gravel, Montreal,QUE)

A1. Charles, b 18o1 Paspebiac, mar 1833 Anne Travers, dau of James T. and Genevieve Chatterton.

B1. Charles, b 1834 Coxtown, QUE B2. Esther J. B3. Anne

A2. Angelique, b 1812, poss d.y.

A3. Elizabeth, b 1814, mar 1934 Michel Molloy, son of Hugh Mallou or Malloy, and Catherine Devlin.

A4. Susanne, mar 1830 in Paspebiac, QUE, Isaac Roussy, son of Pierre & Genevieve Parise Roussy, (disp.2/2) Susanne d 1885, at least one ch, Robert Roussy, b 1834

A5. Jean, b 1817 A6. Angelique again

A7. Jane, mar 1844 Charles Bourget, son of Charles and Sarah (Beck) Bourget.

A8. Richard, b 1821, mar in Paspebiac, QUE 1842 Charlotte Chatterton, dau of Amasie and Nancy (Huntington) Chatterton.

B1. Anne, b 1844 Hopetown, Gaspe, QUE

B2. Richard, b 1843 mar Pauline ___, b 1845 Hopetown, QUE

C1. Philip, b 1868 C3. Rachel b 1872 C5. Melvind, b 1879

C2. John, b 1870 C4. Charles, b 1876 C6. James b 1880

B3. Amedee Elie or Amice-Elias, b 1845 d 1933 Hopetown, QUE mar 1. Elizabeth WATT and 2. Flora Smith, b 1854, who d 1936. NOTE: THIS BRANCH USES MAJOR.

C1. Henry, b 1871

C2. Robert E., b 1873, mar 1. Roxie McRae, b Hopetown, and 2. Eliz. Huntington. 3 chn b 1st wife, 3 by 2nd.

D1. Harry Wilson MAJOR, b 1899 Hopetown, d 1971 Welland, ONT, mar Olive Alberta Neff, dau of Ezra and Anne (Kinnard) Neff. She was b 1903 Wainfleet, ONT, d 1936 Port Colborne, ONT, 4 chn.

E1. Geraldine Alice MAJOR, b 1922 Niagara Falls, ONT mar Thomas Powell, 7 chn.

F1. Roberta Olive Powell, b 1947 SASK, mar 1971 Charles Thompson, 3 chn: Shannon, Carmen and Gavin Thompson

F2. Elizabeth F. Powell, b 1947/9 Flin Flon, MA, mar 1970 in Calgary, ALTA Alan Kellett, 4 chn: Andrew (by his first wife), Matthew, Stephen and Peter Keelett, and ?

F3. Geraldine F. Powell, b 1951 mar 1971 Randy Tronsgaard, 2 chn: Kirstin and Jordan Tronsgaard.

F4. Barbara J. Powell, b 1953 mar 1975 in Calgary, ALTA.

F5. Thomas Barrett Powell, b 1956 North Bay, ONT.

F6. Brenda Nadine Powell, b 1959 Medicine Hat, ALTA
F7. Scott Nelson Powell, b 1966 Edmonton, ALTA.
E2. Stanley Scott MAJOR, b 1924 Welland, ONT mar 1965 Toronto,ONT Anne Haughton, b 1936 Toronto, 2 chn: Eliz.Ann & Robert Hugh
E3. Joyce Anna MAJOR, b 1926 ONT, mar in Vancouver, BC Peter Spring, b 1931, 3 chn: Bradley, Paul & Janette Spring.
E4. Marjorie O. MAJOR, b 1928 Port Colborne, ONT mar 1947 John Detenshen, b 1925, 2 chn: David and Wendy Detenshen
D2. Scott MAJOR, b 1905 d 1974, mar Eliz. Hutchinson, 1912-1978
E1. Robert Ford Major, b 1931 Niagara Falls, ONT mar 1. Norma Beach, 5 chn and 2. in 1972 Betty Lamond. Chn: Scott, Harry, Donald, Allen and Elaine MAJOR.
E2. Betty Major, b 1934 ONT mar Harold Jacobi 1952, 6 chn: Joanne Terryberry, Brian, Kevin, Harold, Carol Ann & Leslie Jacobi.
E3. Olive Major, b 1942 ONT, mar 1961 John Hudson, b 1939, 3 chn: John, Dianne and Douglas Hudson.
D3. Olive Major mar Waldo ANEZ, AGNES. See Q.A. IN CANADA. 9 chn: Elmer, Cora, Geraldine, Edith, Eileen, Betty, Lindsay, Keith and Marylyn ANEZ.
D4. George, by 2nd wife. D5. Pearl Major D6. Edith Major.
C3. Elizabeth b 1874
C4. Charles Smith MAJOR, b 1888 Hopetown, QUE d 1962, mar Mary Effie Ross, b 1893
D1. Clifford C. MAJOR, b 1914 mar 1934 Dorothy M. Ross
E1. Ruth Le Febvre, b 1939 mar 1959
E2. Kenneth, b 1941 mar 1966
E3. Erma Le F., b 1942
E4. Shirley Lauzon, b 1944
E5. Basil b 1945
E6. Gerald, b 1946 mar 1970
E7. Dora Robinson, b 1947 mar 196-.
E8. Leslie b 1949 mar 1971
E9. Sybil b 1950 mar 1972
E10. Colin Burns, b 1951
E11. Martha, b 1952 mar 1973
E12. Joy, b 1954 mar 1976
E13. Brian, b 1955
E14. Barry, b 195-.
E15. Dean, b 1958
E16. Dianne b 1959
E17. David, b 1961
E18. Pauline, b 1962
D2. Martha MAJOR, b 1916 Hopetown, QUE mar 1938 Allison W. McRae, b 1903 d 1977, and 2. Russel Thompson in 1979
E1. Iva Joan McRae, b 1940 mar 1960
D3. Hubert C. MAJOR, b 1918 Hopetown, QUE mar 1941 Della ANEZ
E1. Charles b 1942 mar 1963
E2. Wayne b 1946 mar 1968
E3. Sheila b 1947
E4. Billy b 1950 mar 1972
E5. Harold b 1952 mar 1973
E6. Earl b 1953
E7. Wilson, b 1955
E8. Darlene, b 1956
E9. Gordon, b 1960
E10. Betty b 1961
E11. Freda b 1962
E12. Marlene, b 1966
D4. Wilson R. Major, b 1920 Hopetown, d 1940 WWII
D5. Lester Major b 1922
D6. Lloyd F. Major, b 1923, mar 1944 Lorna E. Upper
E1. Shirley, b 1945 mar 1964
E2. Joan, b 1946 mar 1964
E3. Eileen, b 1947 mar 1968
E4. Arleen, b 1947, mar 1966
E5. Carol b 1951 mar 1970
E6. Helen b 1956 mar 1977
E7. Kenneth b 1959
E8. Peter b 1964
D7. Alta, b 1925 Hopetown, QUE mar 1946 Michael Konola
E1. Roy Konola, b 1947 E2. Marie Konola, b 1946 mar 1978
E3. Bonnie Konola, b 1951 mar 1972
D8. Dorothy Major, b 1925 mar 1927 Gordon Fair
E1. Clifford G. Fair, b 1952 mar 1976 E2. John W. Fair, b 1954
E3. Marylyn D. Fair, b 1955 mar Kevin D. Knight, dau Sarah Knight

D9. James J. MAJOR, b 1927? Hopetown, QUE mar 1950 Martha E. Reece
E1. James, b 1951 mar 1972 E4. Joanne, b 1964
E2. David b 1953 mar 1973 E5. Tammy b 1967
E3. Darla Major, b 1954 mar 1973
D10. Gladys S. MAJOR, b 1929 mar 1945 Windy Huntington. She d 1968
E1. Donna Huntington, b 1947 mar 1967
E2. Joyce Huntington, b 1948 E6. Joanne Huntington, b 1959
E3. James Huntington, b 1950 E7. Carrie Huntington, b 1963
E4. Roy Huntington, b 1954 E8. Wendy Huntington, b 1964
D11. Guy E. MAJOR, b 1931 mar 1959 Evelyn J. PRINCE b 1940, 3 chn: Cindy, Fay and Mona Major
D12. Ervin Major, b 1933 mar 1962 Hilda R.S. Hayes, b 1938, 2 chn: Karen and Dianne Major
D13. Watson Joan Major b 1935 mar 1960 Robert A. Barr, b 1935, a dau Susan Barr.
D14. Eileen A. Major, b 1937 mar 1957 Colin Kerry b 1939, 2 sons: Kenneth and Timothy Kerr.
C5. Martha Jane Major mar ___Le Tourneau, b 1880, d 1955 New Bruns.
C6. Philip Major
C7. James Major mar Myrtle Huntington and d 1918
D1. Robert V. Major b 1917 mar 1. 1940 Kathleen Wright and 2. in 1960 Donelda Baptist, b 1925 2 chn by 1st wife.
E1. Janette Major b 1941 E2. Dorothy Major b 1945
C8. Cyprian Major, b 1893 d 1973, mar 1. Lydia Carney, 2 chn and 2. Dorothy Ayers, who d 1972
D1. Persey Major, b 1918 D2. Gladys b 1924, d.y. D3. Clifford
D4. Malcolm Major, b 1926 mar 1947 Cora ANEZ/AGNES, b 1925, 2 chn
E1. Larry Major, b 1949 mar Mary Robinson, 2 chn: Larry, Dennis.
E2. Dianne Major, b 1956 mar 1976
D5. Flora b 1925 mar Richard Gorham. D6. Gladys Major d.y.
A9. Sophie MAUGER A10. Marguerite MAUGER, b 1829 Paspebiac, QUE.
A11. Robert MAUGER, b 1933 Paspebiac, mar Sarah McGinnis, age 37 in 1871, English, R.C. Robert a merchant, L'Anse aux Basques,Gaspe.
B1. John George, b ca1860 B2. Robert Richard, b ca 1862
B3. Peter, b ca 1863 mar Marty Brotherton, dau of Wm. and Mary (Flynn) Brotherton.
C1. Bernadette, b 1884 Grand Riviere, QUE
B4. Charles Robert MAUGER, b 1866 Pabos, Gaspe, QUE
B5. Anna, b 1868 B6. Simon Mauger b ca 1870 B
A12. Guillaume Honore William MAUGER, b 1837, d.y.
A13. Florence MAUGER b 1839

MAUGER, Mr. and Mrs. Alfred James, res Racine, WIS 1970s, from G.

MAUGER, Daniel, business man, b Les Villets G, rem to NYCity early 1800s. He took as apprentices GUILLE & ALLES, qv, 1834, who made their fortunes and retired to G, where they promoted a fine library still in use. (G. Soc. Bull, Spring, 1973)

MAIGER, Edward mar Margaret Starr 1738 Boston, MA. MAUGER?

MAUGER, Eva Marie, b 1884 St. Peter Port G, dau of John and Eva Mitchell MAUGER. See PRIAULX

MOGEY, MAUGER?, Frances mar John Smith MULLET, MOLLET?, 1766 MRB, MA.

MOGEE, MAUGER?, Hannah mar Charles FLOWERS of Salem (int) 1832. Is FLOWERS-FLEURY of C.I.? OUTC.

MAUGER, James, mar 1828 Elizabeth LA VALLE in St. Andrews Presb. CH in QUEBEC City, Canada. (Lost In Canada, Aug. 1981) OUTC

MOGE, MAUGER?, Joseph mar Mary NEWELL 1724 MRB or Charlestown, MA. Mrs. 'MUGEY' d 1764. (Wyman)

MAUGE, MAJOR, Mary mar James BALL, 1708 Boston, MA. OUTC.

MAUGER, Miss, related to COUTANCHE of J, rem to Wilmington, DEL 1800s and mar ___Hudson.
MAUGER, P., of J, master of ship CITY OF DERBY built 1775 in RI, owner--LEMPRIERE. (A. John Jean, Jersey)
MAUGER, Samuel, b 1855, son of Jeremiah and Sarah MAUGER, mar 1879 Susan Macklin, Mechling, in Fairfield Co., OH (Dorothy M. Mercy, Falls Church, VA) OUTC
MOGER, Samuel mar Rachel Waterbery 1750/51 MRB.
MOJEY, Sarah mar Jeremiah Hagerty 1757 MRB.
MOUJER, MAUGER?, Thomas mar Mary BLANCHE 1723 MRB
MAUGER, Thomas James, letter from New York to his bro in G. 1861. This letter included in Quarterly Review of G. Soc., Winter, 1957.
MAUGER, many noted in Fairfield and Licking Cos., OH 1860s. OUTC
MAUGER, noted in Boston, MA 1970s. OUTC
MAWNEY, LE MOIGNAN, LE MOINE?, Sarah, b 1600s MRB, poss of J fam? See LE MOIGNAN, LE MAINE in St. Heliers J 1668. MAWNEY, LE MOINE?, Mary, in E. Greenwich, RI 1686. (DAB, Vol 15) OUTC
MAXWELL, Mrs. Ethel b 1890 G, to US. Her sisters rem to Canada. MAXWELL CURR G and J.
MAY, curr G and J
MAY, LE MEE in J early, not researched by compiler.
MAY, William, res Twillingate, Nfld. 1818, poss from J? Some research done by Muriel M. Reed, Essex, MA. OUTC.
MAYER, see also MAHIER. Some English MAYERS claim desc from C.I. MAUGER
MAYER, John Richard, Walter of Saco and Black Pt., ME. (Noyes) OUTC
MANNER, MANIARD in J since 1309. In St. Martin J 1668 and in Grouville J 1749. MAYNARD curr G.
MAYNARD, MANNYARD, Ruth mar Elias Stileman 1667 in NY. (NY Prov.Records)
MAYNARD, John, b 'France' 1816 to NH age 9, cabin boy. Sometimes France given as origin for C.I. persons in America. OUTC.
MAYNARD, Stephen, in Barnard VT 1787. OUTC.(Newton's HIST OF BARNARD)
MAYO, noted in early Col. records. Cf MAHAUT of J, pron. like MAYO
MAYOH, Edward and Robert to Oyster Pt., SC before 1678. Edward was Deputy and Reg. of province, had wife Anne 1683. OUTC
MAHAUT in J 1308, 1668 & 1749 from name of Matilda/Maud.
MAZURY, see MASURY, etc. and LE MESSURIER.
MC Bride, Susan, b ca 1830 St. Heliers J, mar ___HENROID, qv. MCBride curr G and J.
MC CLOCKLIN, see Q.A. IN CANADA by Turk.
MC CLOCKLIN, Louisa age 18 of Usborne, ONT, b J, dau of D.P. McClocklin and Eliz. Phinnemore, mar 1858 in Hibbert, ONT John Williams age 24, of Hibbert, b NYCity, son of Wm. and Nancy Williams. Witness David McClocklin of Usborne. (Huron Co.Mar Reg; Wm. Britnell, Miss., ONT)
MC CRAE, Scottish surname, but one branch of Kintail, settled in G, & there were many marriages with old C.I. fams such as DE SAUMAREZ, DOBREE, BELL, CAREY and CARTERET. Many in this fam served in the Brit. Army in Africa, India, the Crimea and one branch lived in New Zealand. An American branch of the McCrae fam, that of Wm., who rem to America ca 1710, was estab. in or near Newark, DEL. Wm. mar a Creighton, and had a son Rev. James, who had a large fam. (Gerald McCrae, Grt. Falls, MT; HIST OF THE CLAN MCCRAE) Tenth ch of James:
C10. Robert, b 1754 fought on the Loyalist side in the Rev. War, and was a Major in the First American Reg't, or Queen's Rangers, 1782. He was severly wounded in the battle of Brandywine 1777, and rec'd a pension. In 1788 was stationed in G, and d in Paris 1835, bur in Pere La Chaise Cem. He mar 1. Jane COUTART, and 2. in 1804, Sophia LE MESURIER, 1780-1860. She was sister of Gen. Wm. LE MESURIER of

Old Court G, who served in the Peninsular War. Major McCrae had issue by both marriages.
C11. Philip, killed in Rev. War? Mar and had son Philip in OH 1831
C12. Creighton, formerly of NJ. Capt in the 75th Highlanders, India, & served on Loyalist side in Rev.War. Res in G, d in America 1818.
C13. Catherine, mar a MacDonald, res OH 1842, had large family.
MC CULLOUGH, noted in Petition of QUE City residents 1838. (LOST IN CANADA, Aug. 1981) Mc Cullough is old in C.I.
MC KAY, see TRESEDER
MC KINSEY, Archie, a plasterer, res J, rem to IA 1800s. (Brechtel) McKenzie is curr in G.
MEGHER, James Robert Richard Sledin, age 27 of Brampton, ONT, b J, son of James R. and Frances Agnes MEAGHER, mar 1866 Margaret McCaniff of Toronto, ONT b Montreal, at St. Michaels, Toronto.(Church records)
MEHUY, MEHY, MEHYI, HIGH?, all poss MAHY? John from G? and wife Mary in MRB 1700s. OUTC. See MAHY
A1. Margaret, bp 1766, d.y. A2. Margaret again, bp 1772 A3. John,1775
MELLO, see SArah GOSLIN, BUTLER-WOOD Chart. MALLO in J 1340, 1607 and in St. Heliers J 1668.
MELLOWNEY, many in varied forms in the colonies, early in Portsmouth,NH as MAILLONEY, MELONA, MELOON, MILLONY. From St. Heliers, J? where wife of John MELLOWNEY is mentioned in 1749. (NEHGS Vol 82)
MELZARD, as MALZARD in St. John J 1668, 1749. In St. Lawrence J 1800s. Curr G and J. Many named MELZARD in MA early, see VRS, MRB, etc.
MELZARD, George and Mary res MRB. A Mary, wife of George Jr. d 1818. Another Mary, wife of George Jr. d 1825 age 49. (Joy Ann Sweet, Algonquin, ILL) OUTC.
A1. Sally, bp 1794, d.y.? A2. Sally, bp 1796 A3. Mary, bp 1799, d.y.?
A4. Mary Dennis, bp 1801 A6. Hannah Elledge, bp 1806, twin
A5. Betsy Smith, bp 1806, twin A7. George, bp 1809
A8. Rebecca Gowan, bp 1812 MRB, mar 1830 Newton, MA, Thomas Townsend. She d 1887 Mt. Pleasant, IA. Townsend b 1802 Salem d 1882.
B1. Eliza Jane Townsend, b 1835 Newton, MA mar there E.H. Wilson 1855, d Osceola, KS.
B2. Thomas H. Townsend, b 1837 mar Mary M. Wright 1865
B3. George A., 1841-1844
B4. George Francis Townsend, b 1848, d.y.
B5. Emma Eden Townsend, b 1851 Walpole, MA mar 1883 Walter Eugene Keeler, Emma d 1893 Mt. Pleasant, IA
C1. George Townsend Keeler, b 1886 IA, mar 1914 Mabel Piper, d 1934 Cook Co., ILL.
D1. Florence Keeler, b 1916 Chicago, mar Charles Fred. Abel 1936.
D2. Jean Lillian Keeler, b 1918 Chicago, mar Edw. F. Buehlman 1942
D3. Georgia T. Keeler, b 1923, mar Jack Edw. Weidenmiller 1944
E1. Joy Ann Weidenmiller, b 1946 Chicago mar Charles Sweet, 2 chn
E2. Robert Edw. Weidenmiller, b 1949 mar Catherine Carter
C2. Florence Rebecca Keeler, b 1890, d.y.
See MELZARD fams in MA and in WRCIC. of J.
MENSEEN, AMAZEEN noted in early New England.(Noyes) OUTC,poss MESNY?/
MERCER in G 1200s, also a surname of France and England.
MERCER, Ann Elizabeth b G, d 1880 age 76, bur Renforth Bapt.CH cem., Etobicoke Twp., ONT. She was b Ann E. ROSS, dau of Alex. Ross, Royal Engineers, 1767-1820, and wife Dorothy. Ann mar 1821 Levi MERCER.
MERCER. This fam of London, England was connected with Peter PRIAULX, qv of J. MERCER, found in Nfld. was variant spelling of MESSERVY, a J fam. (BATCHELDER GEN; Q.A. IN CANADA) The London Mercers were cousins of the C.I. PRIAULX family.

MERCER. "These Mercers, or perhaps more properly, LE MERCIERS, may have emigrated from France or from the Channel Isles."(NEHGS V 39,50)
MERCHANT, mostly from England to New England 1700s. Poss that a few of these were MARCHANT or MARQUAND of C.I. See PIERCE GEN.
MERCIER, LE MERCIER in J 1234, means haberdasher. Note that some LE MERCIERS were Huguenots.
MERHET, old in J, pron. much like MERRY, qv. Curr J.
MERIT in J 1749. Compiler lacks the years required to differentiate between all the varied forms of these very similar names in New England: MERRY, DE MERRY, DEMERIT, MERIT, MERIOTT, MARRIOTT, etc, etc. See in this book. MERIOTT in J 1607. See Salt Lake City records on these many variants. MERRY CURR in J.
MERITT, MERRITT, see MARRIETTE, a fam in GCO 1800s. (Henry Waller, Abingdon, MA)
MERO, Daniel and Frances, had Martha b 1713 Boston, MA, poss MERHAUT?
MERONG, see MOURANT.
MERROW, noted in New England, was this MERHAUT of J?
MERIT, MERRITT, poss of C.I.? Philip of Boston, who mar Rachel Barnes of Watertown 1731; Samuel, who mar 1733 Mary Bowdoin, living in 1737; Nicholas, who mar Eliz. HILLIERS; Mary MERRY, who mar Abram QUINER, qv, 1743/44; Joseph MERRY, who mar 1659 Eliz., widow of Emanuel HILLiard, who drowned; Nicholas Jr. who mar Anna Girdler 1700/01 MRB; and Nicholas who mar Jane GIFFARD in MRB 1724.
MERRIT, Philip, 2nd husband of Mary (LE GRESLEY) DU HAMEL, who d in UT 1877. She was dau of Philip and Judith (LE MARQUAND) LE GRESLEY.
MERRIT, MERIT, Francis, from J? had sons James and Edward bp 1733 and 1736 in Portsmouth, NH. OUTC. (NEHGS Vol 81)
MERRIT, Philip and Mary had Rachel, b 1713/14 Boston. OUTC.
For some MERIT, MERRIT data see Underhill; FAMOUS FAMS OF MASS, by Mary Crawford, Vol2; MRB VR; Boston VR; DUTCH UNCLES AND NEW ENG.COUSINS.
MERRY, poss some in early colonies should be MERIT, as this name would be pronounced MERRY by French speaking immigrants. See MERIT above. See this name in MRB VRs and records in WRCIC.
MERRY, Daniel from C.I.? mar Judith. Chn in MRB 1722-1726
MERRY, Capt. John, mariner, lost at sea 1798-1800, mar Sarah Davis, b 1762 MA. (YYH, 10-1980; Marilla Bagby, Columbus, OH; REPORT, Fall1980)
A1. Catherine, b 1786 Albany, NY
A2. Harriet, b 1788 NY, d 1835 Trumbull Co., OH mar Theron Plumb, b1783 MA, d 1864 Adams Co., IA, mar 1805. A dau Harriet Plumb Danforth mar Rev. Robert Hunter.
MESSEN in Noyes, poss MESNEY of J? there in 1583, curr G and J.
MESNEY, Peter, b G, to Long Island, NY early 1900s.
MESNEY, Wm. went to sea at 12, and at 18 deserted ship in Hongkong,China He learned the language and by 1882 was Advisor on Foreign Affairs, mar a Chinese woman, by whom he had a son and dau. The dau Mary mar a Briton, F.H. Watson, who lived in CAL 1953. Much more of interest in this man's life. (Balleine's BIO. DICT OF JERSEY)
MESSERVY in J 1309, means ill-treated. In St. Clement, St. Martin, St. Saviour, Grouville and St. Helier J 1668. In St. Clement, St. Martin St. Heliers, Grouville, St. Saviour, Trinity and St. Peter J 1749. Curr G. See THE MESSERVY GENEALOGY, edited by Eva Messerve, who lived in Rutherford, NJ 1960s? There are over 800 Messerves listed, and over 535 collateral surnames. The data below is only a small portion of the very large MESSERVY line in America. See WRCIC for more data, including that of Lady Richmond of New Zealand.
MESSERVY, Gregoire, b 1490 St. Martin J, mar Jeanette ___, 5 chn
Richard, b ca 1511 St. Martin, mar Marie DE GRUCHY, 6 chn

Thomas, b ca 1530 mar 1. Eliz. FALLE and 2. ___LE BASTARD, 4 chn
Thomas, b 1559 Grouville J, mar Eliz. PAYN, 9 chn
Clement, b 1595 Grouville J, mar Susanne PERCHARD, 3 chn
Jean, b 1615 Grouville J mar Marie MACHON, 2 sons: Clement,Jean
Clement, the immigrant, mar 1. Jeanne__& 2. Elizabeth__in ME.

MESSERVY, Clement, b May 1655 Gorey, Grouville, J mar Elizabeth from Welch Cove, Kittery, ME 1675. She d before 1721, as did Clement, in Newington, NH. Clement arrived ca 1670 at Strawberry Banke, later called Portsmouth, NH, was herdsman, took oath of allegiance 1685, fam then rem to Newington. All chn except Aaron changed spelling to MESERVE. (NEHGS Vol 23; Ridlon; Kingsford; Noyes; Balleine B.D.; Stackpole; Earl Meserve, Indep., MO; J.J. Laughlin, Walla Walla,WA; Vicki Weber, Portland, OR; Lillian Mathias, Bethany, ILL; Janet Seitz Eagle River, AK; MESERVE GEN, by Mrs. H. Lewis, Saco, ME, 1970)

A1. John living in 1705, but prob d by 1710
A2. Elizabeth mar Michael Whidden 1694
A3. Clement, b 1678 Portsmouth, NH mar 1702 Eliz. Jones and 2. Mrs. Sarah Stone 1738. 9 chn by 1st wife.
B1. Clement mar Sarah Decker 1726, 8 chn
C1. John, bp 1728 mar 1. Mary Yetty and 2. Sarah Strout, other chn?
D1. John Jr., mar 1797 in Wells, ME, Mary Blaban, dau of Richard and Keziah (Crediford) Blaban. (Town records, Wells, ME; VR of Standish, ME; BLABON FAM IN AMERICA, by Irving Blabon, San Rafael, CAL)
E1. Richard Meservey, b 1797 or 1801? mar Susan Sampson or Susan Williams? poss same person? Res Unity, ME 1813 age 16, from Standish, ME. Richard d 1882. Susan Williams, 1785-1867, was dau of Tim. Williams and Susan GRAY. Other chn?
F1. Susan b 1818 mar Alden B. Grant, 1818-1865. Susan d 1898, chn uncertain, poss: Mary Jane, Elander, Evander (twins), Frances, Susan E., Jessie, Wilbur and Bell Grant.
F2. Timothy M., b 1820, d 1825/6.
F3. Mary Jane, b 1822 d 1875 mar Joseph Blabon 1844, son of Rich. and Sarah (Spear) Blabon. Jos. d 1898,6 chn: Jobn, Addie, Susan, Joseph, Albert and Jennie.(BLABON GEN,by J.Makepeace)
E2. Clement, b 1805 mar 1. Sarah Deering & 2. Olive Edgecombe
E3. John, b 1808 mar Celina W. Wood
C2. Elizabeth, bp 1731 mar 1751 Col. Edmund Phinney
C3. Clement, bp 1733 mar 1757 Mary Wooster
C4. Hannah, bp 1736 C5. Joseph, bp 1738
C6. Margaret, bp 1741 mar Wm. Westcott C7. Benjamin, bp 1744
C8. Nathaniel, bp 1749 mar Rebecca MARTIN (Mrs. Alfred Smith, Houston, TX)
D1. Nathaniel Jr. b 1769 mar Ruth Winslow
E?. Caroline, b 1813 Jefferson, ME mar Wm. MOODY, res Liberty, ME.
F1. William H. Moody, b 1836 mar Abbie S. ___, res Liberty, ME.
F2. Helen Amanda Moody, b 1838 d 1855
F3. Henry Waterman Moody, b 1842 res Lowell, MA.
G1. Jesse Williams Moody, res Somerville, MA
D2. John, b 1770 mar Martha McLain, McClain
E1. John, b 1794 E2. Henry E3. Amos
E4. Elizabeth, b 1797 Appleton, ME d 1887 Bancroft, ME, mar 1828 Daniel Prescott, b 1802, who d 1888 Oakland, CAL. Res Cincy, OH 1842, rem to Bancroft after 1855. At least 2 chn, others? (Lillian Matthias, Bethany, ILL)
F1. Mary Prescott, mar Henry Loomis, 5 chn: Eva, Dora K., Ruth, Bessie and John Loomis
F2. Cyrus S. Prescott, b 1830 ME d 1900 Oakland, CAL.

E5. Phebe. More data on Amy's line below from L. Matthias, WRCIC.
E6. Amy, b 1802 Appleton, ME d Clarington, OH, bur WVA 1842. Mar 1829 John MOODY, b 1798 Landaff, NH son of Jacob and Polly, 3 chn.
F1. John Moody Jr., b Bangor, ME d 1876 New Carthage, LA.
F2. Mary Eviline Moody, b 1829 Bangor, ME d 1903. Mar 1845 Ravenswood, WVA to Zadok S. Thorn, b 1820 Bulltown, WVA, d 1907 Reedy, WVA, 9 chn.
G1. Charles W. Thorn, 1846-1910
G2. Emma F. Thorn, b 1848 mar Jacob Baumgarner, res WVA, 3 chn Harry, Gay and Charles Baumgarner
G3. Arthur B. Thorn, b 1851 mar Edith A. Morris, res WVA
G4. Isabelle Jane Thorn, b 1853 mar Orlando Hardman
G5. Martha Ellen Thorn, b 1856
G6. Mary Ida Thorn, b 1858 mar Alex Cheumont, res WVA
G7. Zadok Elliott Thorn, b 1860 mar Georgia Butcher
G8. Anna Moody Thorn, b 1863 mar George ROBERTS of Eliz., WVA, 6 chn: Leslie, Ralph, Paul, Roger, Walter and Louise Roberts.
G9. Lucy Minerva Thorn, b 1865 mar Henry A. Smith
G10. John W. Thorn, stepson, b 1842 Ravenswood, WVA, d 1905,13 chn.
F3. Lysander H. Moody, b 1831 Marietta, OH d 1876 Bethany, ILL, mar 1. 1855 in Cincy, OH Deb. V. Crossman, b 1835 NYCity, d 1916 in Bethany, ILL, 9 chn.
G1. Thaddeus C. Moody, b 1856 Utopia, OH d 1862
G2. Wm. Henry Moody, b 1858 d 1862
G3. Emma Florence Moody, b 1860 Utopia, d 1892 Kingfisher, OK, mar Edwin A. Renshaw 1879 at Sanner Chapel, ILL. D St. Louis, MO.
H1. Ray Renshaw mar Kate ___, no issue
H2. Charles L. Renshaw, mar 1. Nora Sanders, 3 chn, and 2. Lillie, no issue. Mar 3. Rose Manal, dau Margaret. Charles d 1961
I1. Amy Lee Renshaw, mar Sidney Riel, res Little Rock, ARK
I2. Marie Renshaw mar ___Huess, res OH.
I3. Richard R. Renshaw, b Yukon, OK, d 1963, bur Londell, MO. Mar Lillian Begalabacher, 3 chn.
J1. Robert Edw. Renshaw, b 1934 mar Mary Woods, 3 chn: Robert, Kenneth and Lulia Ann Renshaw, b 1962
J2. Richard Jr., b 1936 mar Jonnie Sue Talor, 4 chn: Constance, Guyus, Veronica and Vicky Renshaw, b 1963
J3. Albert Francis Renshaw, mar 1959 Pat. Hampton, div, son Rodney
I4. Margaret Renshaw, mar ___Gleason, res St. Louis, MO.
H3. John Renshaw, b 1887 Shelby or Macon Co., ILL mar Jennie May Schaefer, div.
I1. Edith Mae Renshaw, b 1908 mar Syl. G. Bucher 1925, 1 ch
J1. Wallace Dale Bucher, 1928-1966, mar Joan Sanlberg, 2 chn
I2. Louise Renshaw, b 1911 d 1971, mar Syl. Kohlenberger, 3 chn: Gerald, Ronald and Diana Lee Kohlenberger.
H4. Estella Renshaw
G4. John Moody, b 1862 Utopia, OH d 1941 Dalton City, ILL mar Emily Brennan, 1866-1949. She is bur Bethany, ILL, 4 chn
H1. Brilla Jane Moody, b 1886 d 1960 Decatur, ILL mar 1908 Otis Blaine Kearney, 1884-1955. Brilla a teacher. 4 chn
I1. John K. Kearney, b 1910 Lovington, ILL mar Irene Lacrone 1940
I2. Emily Eliz. Kearney b 1913 ILL mar 1931 Delenar F. Barnett, b 1909.
J1. Genanne Barnett, b 1932 Decatur, ILL mar Maurice R. Martin, 2 chn: Elizabeth and Jack Martin.
J2. Emily Sue Barnett, b 1938 mar Theo. Kirby, 3 chn: Emily, Theo. C. and Emily Elizabeth Kirby.

I3. Kathryn Lucille Kearney, b 1920 ILL mar 1949 Charles Reed Bloxan, b 1924. Dau Theresa Huffman has son Brian.
I4. Otis Blaine Kearney Jr., b 1926 mar Veree D. Newton, dau Judith.
H2. Edward Moody, b 1890 ILL d 1966, mar 1911 Ethel Mae Humphrey, 1888-1978, bur Bethany, ILL. Edward a farmer, 6 chn.
I1. Jean Irene Moody, b 1911 Moweaqua, ILL mar 1935 Wm. Carl Shelton, 3 chn
J1. David Edward Shelton, b 1943 mar 1967 Kay Ruth Salogga,2 chn: Stephanie Kay and Daniel D. Shelton.
J2. Michael Carl Shelton, b 1945 mar 1965 Constance Sue White,1 ch.
J3. Diane Shelton
I2. Hunter Courtland Moody, b 1913 Dalton City, ILL mar 1937 in PA Dorothy Frances Henry, b 1911 Charles, ILL, 2 chn.
J1. Henri Anne Moody, b 1942 Montreal, QUE mar 1962 Decatur,ILL, Gary J. Burnett, 3 chn: Gary, Jeffry & Sheila Kay Burnett
J2. Hunter Courtland Moody Jr. b 1945 Montreal, mar 1969 Marilee Logan, res Decatur, ILL, dau Melissa Nicole Moody
I3. John Edward Moody, b 1915, d.y.
I4. Edwina Americaus Moody, b 1917 mar 1942 Wm. G. Cazier, res Lake City, ILL, dau Alice J. Cazier, b 1955 mar F. Deffenbaugh
I5. Earl Humphrey Moody, b 1919 Dalton City, mar 1940 Okla.City, OK Kathryn Irene Foley, b 1919. Res Sullivan, ILL, 3 chn. div.
J1. John Edward Moody, b 1942 OK, mar 1969 INDpls, IND Ann Brink,/
J2. Gary Humphrey Moody, b 1944 Montreal, QUE mar 1966 Mary V. Donell, b 1947, 2 chn: Melissa and Michelle Moody
J3. Kay Erline Moody, b 1946 mar 1969 Champaign, ILL, Eduardo Blanco, div, dau Kristen E. Blanco, b 1962 Costa Rica.
I6. Mary Frances Moody b 1921 ILL mar 1941 Wm. Russell Daum, 1920-1944, WWII, 1 ch. Mar 2. Walter E. York, 4 chn.
J1. Marcia L. Daum, b 1944 mar Arthur Sulenski, div, ch Diane L.
J2. Scott Moody York, b 1948
J3. Stephen W. York, b 1951 mar Carol Reeves, ch Heather A. York
J4. Hunter Lee York J5. Sue Ellen York, b 1958
H3. Harriet Blossom Moody, b 1894 ILL, d 1952 Treasure Is., FLA mar 1. 1912, Oliver B. Scott, d 1935, 2 chn. Mar 2. 1949 in ILL, Lawrence Fulton, no issue
I1. Bonnie Jeanne Scott, b 1914 mar 1941 Hubert W. Baker, 2 chn.
J1. Bonnie Jeanne Baker, b 1944 Boston, mar 1965 NElson J. Rowe, 2 chn: Craig and James Rowe
J2. Stuart Flint Baker?
I2. Stuart Bertram Scott, b 1917 mar 1938 Catherine L. Cox.
J1. Oliver B. Scott b 1940 mar Marcella White, 2 chn: Tammy Jane and Stuart B. Scott.
J2. Mary Beth Scott, b 1950 mar 1966 Larry H. Marlowe, 2 chn: Caroline and Scott C. Marlowe.
H4. Bernice Moody, b 1896, d 1901
G5. Mary Eviline Moody, b 1864 Utopia, ILL d 1923, mar 1885 Perry J. Bushert, b 1862 d 1942, 8 chn
H1. Lela V. Bushert, b 1886 d 1964 San Bern., CAL, mar 1909 Daniel Allen Francisco, b 1879 d 1935, 2 chn
I1. Mary Frances Francisco, b 1913 d 1970 Bloomall, PA, bur ILL. Mar 1941 Donald K. Eckfeld, no issue
I2. Ruth Kathryn Francisco, b 1932 mar 1943 Gordon W. Flint, adopted dau Marilyn Kae Flint, b 1965
H2. Nina Lois Bushert, b 1887 ILL d 1979 Bend, OR, mar 1919 Bethany, Webb Wesley Deupree, b 1890, d 1967 CAL, res Bend, OR, 2 chn.
I1. Mary Martha Deupree, b 1920 Mora, MO mar 1944 Robert H. Smith.

I2. Grace Virginia Deupree, b 1924 mar 1943 in FLA, James B.Scott, b 1919 MT, res Bend, OR, 2 chn.
J1. Patricia Ann Scott, b 1947 San.Bern., CAL mar 1969 Henry A. Howe III, b CT, son Scott C. Howe.
J2. James Rudoff
H3. Harold Vaughton Bushert, b 1889 ILL, d 1961. Mar 1909 Iola Luvella Wheeler, 1892-1966, 2 chn
I1. Hillis Vaughton Bushert, b 1910 Bethany, ILL mar 1930 Halden Lionel Jordon, b 1905, 1 ch
J1. Lionel Vaughton Jordon, b 1937 mar 1960 Raylene F. Williams, res Arthur, ILL, 2 chn: James Roos & Curtis Lionel Jordan
I2. Ellen V. Bushert, b 1915 mar 1938 Ray K. Mallison
J1. Sheila? Joyce Mallison, b 1943 mar Roger L. Reed, 2 chn: Charles K. and Teresa Lea Reed, b Tuscola, ILL.
J2. Donald Craig Mallison
H4. Lester Vaughton Bushert, b 1891 mar 1912 Florence Anna Kennedy, res San Diego, CAL, no issue
H5. Grace V. Bushert, b 1892, unmar H6. Ruth V. Bushert
H7. Laurence V. Bushert, b 1896 mar Alice Cole, no issue
H8. Hubert V. Bushert, b 1899 mar 1918 Luella Kennedy, 2 chn
I1. Maurice Kennedy Bushert, b 1923, mar 1. 1942 Grace Maxine Rule, div, 1 ch. Mar 2. 1959 Helen Ann Radcliff, div, 2 chn
J1. Connie Lee Bushert, b 1943, mar 1965 Terry L. Heinz, 2 chn Laura and Wade Heinz
J2. Mary Louella J3. Lisa Christine Bushert
I2. Craig V. Bushert, mar 1943 Betty Eileen Lehman, 10 chn
J1. Craig K. Bushert, b 1944 mar 1961 Linda D. Waggoner, 3 chn: Bruce, Stephen and Mark Bushert
J2. Cheryl Ann Bushert, b 1946, mar 1968 Brent Lee Keebaugh, b 1940 NEB, 2 chn: Tara L. and Shawn A. Keebaugh
J3. Deborah Luella Bushert, b 1947 mar 1965 Jack M. Miller, b WIS, div, 2 chn. She mar 2. Theo. Rohner, chn: Jacquelin and Jessica Miller.
J4. James V. Bushert, b 1949 mar 1974 Maria Juanita Reyes
J5. Gary Dean Bushert, b 1953 J8. Patrick L. Bushert, b 1961
J6. Susan Ruth Bushert, b 1954 J9. John S. Bushert, b 1962
J7. Douglas C. Bushert, b 1958 J10. Teresa E. Bushert, b 1964
G6. Annie Elizabeth Roe Moody, b 1866 New Bellsville, IND, d 1951 mar 1888 Joseph Finley Mathias, b OH, farmer, 10 chn
H1. Chester Leland Mathias, b 1890 d 1970, mar Cecile Lulu Roney,9 ch
I1. Oscar F. Mathias, b 1911mar 1937 Helene Luella Gordon, b 1915
J1. Patricia L. Mathias, b 1944 d.y.
J2. Sandra Sue Mathias, b 1947 mar Kenneth I. Milligan, no issue
J3. Nelda Ann Mathias, b 1953 mar Carl Plotner, dau Michelle
I2. Waldo E. Mathias, b 1913 ILL mar Genevieve L. Taylor, 6 chn
J1. Leland L. Mathias, b 1938 mar Bonnie Ann Haney, 2 chn: Darren Lee and Melanie Ann Mathias
J2. Audrey Lavonne Mathias, b 1940 mar Ronald Lee Stickler, 4 chn: Christopher, Ronald, Michael and Nicole Stickler.
J3. Carol Ann Mathias, b 1942 stillborn
J4. Marvin Owen/Oran Mathias, b 1944 mar Avenell D. Long
J5. Sheila/Shelia? Lynn Mathias, b 1951 mar Maynard E. Forlines, 3 chn: Eric Wayne, Joel and Ross Forlines.
J6. Monte Marlene Mathias, mar 1981 R.D. Schwartz
I3. James Oran Mathias, b 1914 Findlay, ILL mar Mildred M. Cruitt, div, 3 chn.
J1. Gary Oran Mathias, b 1939 mar Kathleen A. Richardson, div,3 chn

Lisa Ann, Renee, and Christine Mathias
J2. James Richard Mathias, b 1943 mar Ruth L. Yenelle, 3 chn: Dawn Marie, James A. and Robert J. Mathias
J3. Linda Lucille Mathias, mar Fred. De Bolt, no issue
I4. Marvin Russell Mathias, b 1916 had son Terry Michael b 1950, who mar twice, 2 chn: Katherine J. and Christopher Mathias
I5. Evelyn Laverna Mathias, b 1918 mar 1940 Denver E. Page.
J1. Robert Carl Page, b 1943 mar Gaylee C. Jensen, 2 chn: Wade Michael and Whitney L. Page
I6. Donald Wayne Mathias, b 1920, d 1944 WWII in Sicily.
I7. Wilma Lorraine Mathias, b 1922 mar 1946 John Wm. Lampert, b CT res Pittsburgh, PA, 3 chn
J1. Deborah L. Lampert, b 1951 COL mar Peter F. Singleton, son Matthew D. Singleton.
J2. John Dudley Lampert, b 1953 mar Brenda Barnett, 2 sons: David (adopted) and Justin Lampert.
J3. Thomas Kent Lampert, b 1958, unmar
I8. Maurice Dean Mathias, b 1924, mar Marceleen M. Spears, res Kenney ILL, 4 chn
J1. Kathy Suanne Mathias, b 1948 ILL mar Rob't Bishop, div and 2. John D. Schobe, 2 chn: Julia Ann and John D. Schobe
J2. Maurice Dean Mathias Jr, b 1947 mar Joyce Lou Miller, 3 chn: Marc Alan, Amy and Alysha M. Mathias
J3. Ronnie Ray Mathias, b 1952 twin, mar 1975 Katherine Sue Morris, 3 chn: Angela, April and Ashley Sue Mathias
J4. Connie Kay Mathias, b 1952, twin, mar Terry Lee Spencer, 2 chn: Amanda Dawn and Dana De Shay Spencer
I9. Helen Emily Mathias, b 1926 mar Richard Reid, 2 chn
J1. Bradley Wayne Reid mar Debbie Dunaway, res Charlotte, NC
J2. Robert Michael Reid
H2. Carl Finley Mathias, b 1891 d 1972 Stanton, CAL, mar 1919 Mildred Maurine Hudson, b 1898 ILL, bur Glendale, CAL, 3 chn
I1. Carlos Loyd Mathias, b 1921 d 1976, mar 1940 Phyllis Wainwright, div, 1 ch: Geoffrey A. Mathias, b 1943
I2. Allen Lane Mathias, b 1922 ILL, killed in action Corsica, WWII, mar Phyllis L. Gibford, dau Diane Lynn mar Dennis Fox,son Donald
I3. Veryle Jeannette Mathias, b 1938 Glendale, CAL mar 1957 Donald Gene Ritter, 2 chn, and 2. Rev. R.J. Eichenberger, res Waucoma,IA
J1. Susan Lyn Ritter, b 1958 mar Jeffery Gozzo 1976
J2. Debbe Lou Ritter, b 1959 Newport Beach, CAL.
H3. Russell Gordon, b 1893 ILL d 1972 Stanton, CAL mar 1935 IdaMartin.
H4. Robert Roland Mathias, b 1895 d 1939 mar 1920 Zion, ILL Altha Vyrl Walker, 5 chn
I1. Robert Minor Mathias, b 1920 d 1980 MD, mar 1942 Frances Lois Hall, 3 chn
J1. Robert M. Mathias Jr., unmar
J2. Donna Aletha Mathias, b 1947 mar James Mason Triplett
J3. Patricia Ann Mathias, b 1948 IND, mar Douglas Wm. Pool, res Indianapolis, IND, 2 chn: Rodney and Russell Pool.
I2. Esther Jeanne Mathias, b 1922 ILL mar 1. Robert A. Hairfield, div, 1 ch, and 2. Grover J. Graven, 2 chn, res Madera, CAL
J1. Robert W. Graven, adopted by Graven, mar La Puente, CAL, Diana Gentry, div, 2 chn: Jennifer and Billy Ray, adopted.
J2. Marjorie Jeanne Graven, b 1946 mar 1. Royce Kite, 1ch, 2. Ron. Shattler, 1 ch, mar 3. Paul M. Aparacio, 1ch, and 4.James Hall. Chn: Robert Kite, Derrick Shattler, Aletha Aparicio.

J3. Sally Lou Graven, b 1954 mar Dirk Lowell Milligan, res CAL, son Jason Dirk Milligan.
I3. Lewis Ray Mathias, 1923-1958, veteran.
I4. Ivan Leonard Mathias b 1924 mar 1947 NJ, Lillian F.(Chiles)Bell
I5. Donald Ernest Mathias, b 1926 PA, mar 1. Wilma J. Tolliver, 1ch and 2. Jeanne Rita (Hedke) Karl, 2 chn
J1. Glenna Dianne Mathias, b 1948 mar 1965 David E. Bush, div 1972, mar 2. John Philip Archer. Chn: Michael T., Tami M., Timothy D. and Tara D. Bush.
J2. Richard J. Mathias b 1963, adopted
H5. Fredora Fern Mathias, b 1896 mar 1914 Ernest Bliss Schwartz, 4 chn
I1. Edwin Kohler Schwartz, b 1914 mar Martha Jane Craig, WWII Vet.
J1. David Craig Schwartz, b 1951 mar Susan A. Robinson, res TX.
I2. Roger Dean Schwartz, b 1918 mar Evelyn Jeanette Pritts, 7 chn
J1. Janet Dean Schwartz, b 1940 mar Alex N. Shealy, 2 chn: Patricia Jane and Alex. N. Shealy III, b Erie, PA
J2. Evelyn Kay Schwartz, b 1941 mar 1960 Henry T. Atkinson, 2 chn: Henry T. and Michael R. Atkinson.
J3. Lou Anne Schwartz, b 1943 mar David R. Banks, 2 chn: Sara E. d.y. and Roger Glen Banks, b 1971
J4. Shirley Marie Schwartz, b 1944 mar Lowell G. Ford, 2 chn: Amy M. and Abby Jean Ford.
J5. Zona Fern Schwartz, b 1948 CAL mar Jerry Alan Spearsl, res St. Louis, MO, 2 chn: Jarrod and Jennifer Spearsl.
J6. John Roger Schwartz, b 1950 mar Marsha D. Taylor, 2 chn: John T. and Rachel J. Schwartz.
J7. Peggy Doreen Schwartz, b 1952 mar Alphonso S. Greco, son Michael
I3. Vernon Eugene Schwartz, b 1920 mar Dorothy Woods Lemore. Vernon a WWII Vet., res Buda, TX, 3 chn
J1. Joseph Lynn (Lemore) Schwartz, b 1941 adopted, mar Deborah Deering, div, 2 chn: Shannon and Sonja Schwartz
J2. Mary Helen (Lemore) Schwartz, b 1942 TX, mar John M. Percifield, 2 chn: John M. and Paul E. Percifield.
J3. Jack E. Schwartz, b 1946 ILL mar Theresa D. Shipp, res Kyle,TX 3 chn: Jason E., Joshua Kyle and Clarie J. Schwartz
I4. Joseph Fred. Schwartz, b 1923, mar Helen Louise Parris, 3 chn
J1. Deborah Ann Schwartz, b 1951
J2. Joseph Michael Schwartz, b 1953 ILL mar Susan Jane Iler, 3 chn: Bliss Allen, Michael D. and Jacob D. Schwartz.
H6. Joseph Lysander Mathias, b 1898 ILL, d 1974, unmar
H7. Hobart Leonard Mathias, b 1902 d1962, Vet. of WWII, unmar
H8. Lois Lorraine Mathias, b 1903, ILL, mar 1929 Earl O. Lippold, a Judge, one son.
I1. Rodney E. Lippold, b 1930 CAL, mar Marjorie L. Johnson, a son Earl Brian Lippold, b 1957
H9. Dorothy Evelyn Mathias, b 1905 mar 1. 1923 Claude Fiddler, 1ch, div, mar 2. 1928 HowardMarion Moore, b 1906 IND, d 1978, 2 chn
I1. Betty Marie Fiddler, b 1924 IND mar 1944 KY, Jesse James Sumpter
J1. James G. Sumpter, b 1946 ILL mar 1972 Linda Joyce Freidoltz, res Eugene, OR, 1 chn: Jaime Lyn Sumpter
J2. Wayne Wiley Sumpter, b 1950 mar Marilyn Struffert, res MO.
I2. Joan Moore, b 1931 ILL mar 1946 Charles O. Baugher, res ILL.
J1. Linda Day Baugher, b 1948 mar 1. CAL, James Cunningham, a son, div, and mar 2. Dennis M. Garrett, a son, res Memphis, TN,2 chn: Christopher W. Cunningham and Chad M. Garrett.

J2. Charlotte Ann Baugher, b 1952 mar 2. Lynn Maxedon, res ILL.
I3. Marian Moore, b 1934 mar 1. George Funderburk, div, 1 ch, and 2. Paul Bolin, and 3. Martin Tomlinson.
J1. Darcel Funderburk, b 1953
G7. Lois Moody, b 1868 ILL d 1939, mar Col. Edward Coombes, b Troy,IND. She was a school superintendant. 4 chn.
H1. Cecil Lysander Coombes, b 1888 ILL d 1975 Ft. Worth, TX, mar 1. Ruby Austin, 1 ch, and 2. Mary E. Wyse, no issue. Cecil was a professional baseball player.
I1. Helen Emily Coombes, b 1908 ILL mar Dallas, TX, Edwin A. Alexander, 2 chn.
J1. Ruby Ann Alexander, b 1925 TX, mar Milton B. Broyles, 2 chn: Melinda A. and Milton A. Broyles
J2. Marilyn Alexander, b 1930 mar 1948 Greenville, TX, James R. Muncy, 3 chn: Emily, James and John Muncy.
H2. Deborah Eliz. Coombes, b 1890 d 1979. Mar 1914 Otto Martin Walk,
I1. Betty Lou Walk, b 1922, adopted, mar Roscoe L. Trexlee, 5 chn: Lowelle, Diane, Deborah, Rebecca, Cheryl Ann.
I2. George Samuel Walk, b 1931 mar Marilyn Joann Newlin, 3 chn
J1. Bruce Alan Walk, b 1954 Olney, ILL mar 1976 Deb.A.Barnett,div.
J2. Bradley Lane Walk, b 1957 mar Laura L. Welsh
J3. Brett Eric Walk, b 1965 Bloomington, ILL
H3. Amy Florence Coombes, b 1892 mar Roy Judson Silver, 2 chn
I1. Jack Almon Silver, b 1920 mar 1944 Marian Eliz. Hanlon, 4 chn
J1. Micki Lee Silver, b 1946 mar 1969 Melton Larson, div.
J2. Patricia Lou Silver, b 1948 mar 1973 Rodger A. Walker, a dau Traci Lee Walker.
J3. Susan Eliz. Silver, b 1953 Delaware, OH
J4. John Judson Silver, b 1955 res Dallas, TX
I2. Mary Lou Silver, b 1924 Decatur, ILL mar 1949 Kewanee, ILL Carl Lee Rhodes, res Bloomington, ILL 2 chn.
J1. Roger Lee Rhodes, b 1952 Portsmouth, VA, mar 1974 Susan Marie Frederick.
J2. David Loren Rhodes, b 1955 mar Connie Rose Hamby, Portland, OR.
H4. Golden Vaughton Coombes, b 1893 Macon Co., ILL mar Jesse Granville Dowers, div and 2. Fred Robertson. 6 chn by Dowers.
I1. James Reginald Dowers, b 1909 mar Crystal Birkhead, res FLA
I2. Elizabeth Enid Dowers, b 1911 ILL mar 1. Otis A. Darling, div, and 2. Dwight R. Flenner, 1 ch
J1. Betty Joyce Darling b 1927 mar Alfed B. Murfee, 2 chn: Pamela and Paul Murfee.
J2. William Otis Darling, b 1929 mar Lois Luzella Loftus, res Princeton, ILL, 6 chn: Sue Diane, William D., Debra C., David J. Daniel M. and Dwight C. Darling.
J3. Dwight Richard Flenner, b 1939, d.y.
I3. Jessie Lucille Dowers mar Harry Bechler, 3 chn, res FLA.
J1. Donald Bechler J2. Robert Bechler J3. Jacquelin Bechler
I4. Richard Wm. Dowers, b 1914 mar Ione G. Wheeler, no issue
I5. Deborah Bernice Dowers, b 1917 mar 1. James Musser, 1 ch, mar 2. John Henry Mudge, no issue.
J1. James P. Musser mar in England Margaret A. Robertson, 2 chn: Tammy Ann and James Patrick Musser.
I6. Dorothy Eloise Dowers b 1919 mar 1. Barney Sebeckis, 1 ch and 2. Ernest P. Giese.
J1. Steven Wm. Sebeckis, b 1949 ILL mar 1. Barbara Weaver, div, 2 chn, and 2. Vicki L. Williams, 1 ch. 3 chn: J. Christine, Amy Lynn, and Jody A. Sebeckis.

G8. Samuel Franklin Moody, b 1871 d 1943 mar 1898 Ethel Eliz. Ward,
H1. Frank Lysander Moody, b 1899 unmar H2. Donald V. Moody, d.y.
G9. Ellen Gertrude Moody, b 1874 mar 1894 Robert M. Shelton,4chnd.y.
H1. Rita Margaret Shelton, b 1895 mar 1917 Herschel B. Wilson
I1. Marjorie Wilson, b 1918 mar 1042 Howard C. Stromquist, 2 chn
J1. Howard Shelton Stromquist, b 1943 Elmhurst, ILL
J2. Kristin Stromquist, b 1946 Champaign, ILL
I2. Robert Byron Wilson, b 1936 Flint, MI mar 1964 in Germany, Heidi Metz. Dau Martina Leah Wilson b 1965 NY.
H2. Zelma Grace Shelton, b 1908 Dalton, ILL mar 1926 Orin Walter Goetz, 3 chn
I1. Rose Marie Goetz, b 1927 mar 1946 James Dale Hammitt, 3 chn
J1. Dana Jean Hammitt, b 1952
J2. Diane Gay Hammitt, b 1955 J3. Randy Lee Hammitt, b 1960
I2. Beverly Nell Goetz, b 1934 mar 1951 Merrill W. Lacy, 2 chn.
J1. Kathryn Lyn Lacy, b 1952 mar Michael F. Haugh
J2. Deborah Ann Lacy, b 1955
I3. Lyle Orin Goetz, b 1946 mar Nellie C. Spencer, 4 chn: Michael, Donald Lee, Rhonda C. and Marilyn Sue Goetz
F4. Jacob Votto Moody, son of John and 2nd wife, Hannah Hines. Jacob was b 1842 Monroe Co., OH d 1917 ILL, mar Julia Anna Forman, b Macon, ILL, 8 chn
G1. John A. Moody, b 1867 OH, d Dover, OK of TB
G2. Charles Warren Moody, b 1868 OH, d 1935, mar Minnie Mae Lacost, bur Mt. Zion, ILL.
H1. Guy Walter Moody, b 1897 d 1967, bur Salem, OR
H2. Mary Grace Moody, b 1902 ILL, mar 1922 Charles Cecil Karch,/2 chn
I1. Elizabeth Mae Karch, b 1923 mar Earl LaMarr Lockett, 2 chn
J1. Sheila Sue Lockett, b 1947, unmar
J2. Gregory K. Lockett, b 1951 mar Lela Byers, 3 chn: Jason, Angela and Adam Lockett, res WIS.
I2. Charles Cecil Karch, b 1925 ILL mar 1947 Lois May Deadman
J1. Deborah C. Karch, b 1949 mar David Lee Diss, 3 chn: Christine Amy Marie and Paul Eugene Diss.
J2. Cleve Eugene Karch, b 1951 ILL mar 1974 Karen Sue Heironymus, 1 ch: Kelly Susanne Karch, b ILL.
G3. Frederick Howard Moody, b 1870
G4. Clarence Ashley Moody, b 1874 mar Lola LaCost 1902, 5 chn
H1. Vivian Moody, b 1916 mar Joseph Riestis, res Belleville, ILL
H2. Lola Ivadean Moody, b 1910 mar 2. ___ Hedges
H3. Lynn Moody, b 1903 bur E. St. Louis, MO.
H4. Clarence Moody, res FLA H5. another ch, bur ND.
G5. Luella May Moody, b 1877 bur Macon, ILL G6. Walter Moody,b1872
G7. Ethel G. Moody, b 1880 mar Dick A. Dance, 4 chn, res MO.
H1. Cecil H2. Clarence H3. Winfred
G8. Melva Myrtle Moody, b 1885 mar 1904 Sherman Elmer Houser,bur SD
H1-5, Albert, ?, Viola, Jacob, Buelah, another ch?
More on the above fam in WRCIC and with researcher Ann Mathias, Bethany, ILL.
E7. Nancy MESSERVY, b 1805 d 1840 mar Isaac Prescott
E8. Charity MESSERVY, b 1806 mar John DAVIS
E9. Deborah MESSERVY, b 1808 mar Samuel Whittier
D3. William MESSERVY, b 1773 mar Damarias Ripley (Vicki Weber,Portland, ORE.)
E1. William, b 1799 mar Elvira Bond
E2. Abraham, 1801-1803 E3. Abraham again, 1804-1825
E4. Thomas, b 1806, mar ?

E5. John, b 1813 ME, mar Mary Sproul, b 1817 ME
F1. Elizabeth, b 1839 ME F2. Susan, b 1840
F3. John Jr., b 1844 Whitefield, ME, d 1896 Portland, OR, mar 1877 Bessie Electa Hower, b 1858 WIS, d 1926
G1. Albert Eugene, b 1878 San Fran., CAL d 1926 Portland, mar 1903 Mary Benson, 1881-1969
H1. Constance Lucille, 1906-1938
H2. Eugene Drexell, 1910-1976, Los Angeles, CAL, mar 1940 Helen Aamun, no issue
H3. Roma Frances, b 1912 Portland, mar 1. 1931 Frank Chape, and 2. 1939 Bill Askim, 3. 1968 Jack Perkins, no issue
H4. Mary Elizabeth b 1919 mar 1. 1942 Calvin Tompkins, and 2. Ernest M. Weber, b 1908, in 1952 (Vicki Weber, Portland, OR)
I1. Michael David Tompkins, b 1943 Portland, mar 1964 Darlene Richmond, 2. Charlotte Ashford 1970, and 3. Rae Hayden. 1 ch by 1st and 2nd wives, and 2 chn by #3. 4 chn: Sean Patrick, Sean Leonard, Terra Sunday and Michele Ellen Tompkins.
I2. Mary K. Elizabeth Tompkins, b 1944 Portland, OR d 1961
I3. Lynda Frances Tompkins, b 1945 d 1959
I4. Larry Albert Weber, b 1953 mar 1978 Vicki Ann Morris
I5. Vicki Ann Weber b 1955 I6. Patti Diane Weber, b 1955
H5. Albert Dallas, b 1923 mar 1942 Leanna Severson, b 1922
I1. Terri Lynn b 1951 mar 1969 John F. Burrows, a son Brian
I2. Corey Gene, b 1959
G2. Emily May MESERVE, b 1882 San.Fran.,CAL, d 1956 Turner, OR, mar Elmer Patterson, no issue
F5. Andrew, b 1846 ME. F6. Willie, b 1859 ME
E6. Hepsibeth, b 1810 E7. Mary, b 1816
E8. Rebecca, b 1819 mar John MERSERVEY
D4. Samuel D5. Betsy, mar Fugas McLain D6. Sally mar Prince Pease
D7. Jennie mar ____MESERVEY
D8. Anne mar ____BUTLER D9. Nancy
B2. Col. Nathaniel mar 1. 1725 Jane Libby, and 2. Mary D. JACKSON. He d 1758
B3. John MESSERVY, b 1708 mar Jemima HUBBARD, qv, b 1712, d 1768. (Mrs. Malcolm Meserve, Wilton, ME)
C1. George, b 1740 Scarboro ME, mar Susanna Staples
D1. Simon, b 1770s?, mar Sally Burnall ca 1805
E1. Charles E., b 1807 Scarboro, mar Eunice Larrabee
F1. Isaac L., b 1853 Scarboro, d 1933 Mechanic Falls, ME, mar Nettie Rose Goos, b 1860, d 1926 Lewiston, ME.
G1. Clarence Windsor, 1891-1968, mar 1918 Gladys R.H. Dunton, b 1925 Bingham, ME.
B4. Daniel, b 1715 mar Mehitable Bragdon 1737/8. He d 1803, 10 chn? (Ann Mathias, Bethany, ILL) Mehitable was dau of Arthur Bragdon.
C6. Gideon, b 1749 mar Elizabeth Fogg, 10 chn
D3. David, b 1783 mar Nancy Bickford, 3 chn
E1. Henry, 1818-1836
E2. Gideon, b 1825 mar Ermaline MOODY, qv, 1854 at Pittston, ME, b 1827 dau of Jeremiah and Annie (McKnight) MOODY, 7 chn
F1. Plumer J., b 1858 mar Emma A. Marson
F2. Abbie A., b 1845 (Janet Seitz, Eagle River, AK)
F3. Alva A., b 1853 F6. William K., b 1864
F4. Ida E., b 1855 F7. Luella
F5. Henry L., b 1863 mar Ada E. Blanchard
E3. Eliza, mar Harris Pulsifer

B5. George, mar Elizabeth Hamm 1737
B6. Peter, mar Sarah LOND, poss DELON, DES LANDES?, qv, 1737
B7. Joseph, living in 1740 B8. Elizabeth mar James Libby 1725
B9. Abigail mar 1727 Samuel Libby, son of Henry. Abigail was poss his first wife? She d 1734, 2 chn d.y. Sam. mar 2. 1739 Mary Jones, who d 1754, 5 chn
A4. Daniel Merry MESSERVY, b 1715 a Saco soldier 1693, mar 1738 Deborah MERROW?, or Deborah Otis Meserve, 7 chn.
B3. Clement, 1716-1800, of Dover, NH, mar _____?
C1. Stephen of Dover, mar Abigail Yeaton
D1. Col. John, 1785-1871, res Rochester, now Milton, NH, mar 1806 Sarah Hayes Clough, 1785-1864. (Virkus 7)
E1. Andrew Jackson, 1815-1895, Somerville, MA, mar Elizabeth PRAY RICKER, qv, b 1815, d 1894
F1. Lizzie Frank, b 1850 d 1937, of Boston and Brookline, MA, mar 1875 Charles Edward Wiggin, 1848-1931, banker of Boston.
G1. Arthur Meserve Wiggin, mar Dorothy M. Taylor, 2 chn
H1. Henry T. Wiggin, b 1922 H2. Jean Wiggin, b 1925
G2. Mary Locke Wiggin, b 1880 mar Charles E. Robinson
B? Elizabeth, mar 1726 Joseph Libby, sailor and fisherman, 2 chn bp.
A5. Tamsen, mar 1. Joseph HAIN or HAM? in MA 1704, & 2. John Tibbets
A6. Aaron, b 1676, mar Susannah Sawyer 1695, res Salem, MA had 2 sons. His widow mar 2. John BATTEN.
See sources for more data.
MESSERVE, Thomas, b ca 1714 New England or J, settled Gloucester, MA. Since there were many in J, perhaps this Thomas was not closely related to those in ME and NH. He mar 1731/2 Elizabeth Foster, b 1714 Gloucester, d ca 1790. She was dau of Samuel and Eliz. Foster, 8 chn (Thomas E. Davis, St. Paul, MN; ANC. & DESC OF JOSIAH MENDUM TARR, by Hugh A. Johnson)
A1. Betty/Betsy, b 1732 Gloucester, mar 1762 Jonathan Hedkins Jr.?
A2. Ellice/Alice b 1734 mar 1765 Amos DAVIS of New Gloucester. She d 1803. Amos b 1741, d 1815 Lewiston, ME.
B1. Amos Davis Jr., b 1769 Glouc., d 1848. Mar Mehitable Wilkins, 1771-1847, dau of David and Molly (Harris) Wilkins of Middleton or Dracut, MA and Lewiston, ME.
C1. Henry Davis, b 1805 Lewiston, ME d 1874. Mar 1831 Olive W. Woodward, b 1808 Lisbon, ME, d 1867 Lewiston, ME.
D1. Albert Smith Davis, b 1834 Lewiston, d 1883 Clifton, Pierce Co., WISC, mar 1866 Eliz. S. Frees, b 1841 Wooster, OH d 1933 MINN.
E1. Charles Ray Davis, b 1875 MN, d 1934. Mar 1907 Nettie Louise Asp, b 1874 WI, d 1963 St. Paul, MN.
F1. Alfred Laurence Davis, b 1915 Golden Valley, MN, mar Barbara Peabody, b 1902, dau of Francis and Barbara(Alstatt) Peabody.
G1. Thomas Eugene Davis, b 1945 NYCity
A3. John MESERVE, b 1737 A6. Ephraim MESERVE, b 1747
A4. Obed or Eben MESERVE, b 1738/9 A7. William, b 1750 Gloucester, MA
A5. Sarah MESERVE, b 1733 A8. Elizabeth, b ca 1753? mar 1767 Michael ✓
Earl C. MESSERVE of Independence, MO, who has done much research (Power✓ on this surname, aided in preparation of above charts.
MESSERVYS are noted in the reduction of the Louisbourg fortress in Cape Breton, Nova Scotia. See also NOTABLES.
Addition data in WEYMOUTH FAM HIST; GELEVLAND GEN; OLD NORTHWEST, Vol 8; Noyes; NEHGS Vol 81; WRCIC, Cleveland, OH.
MESSERVE, Josue, Joshua, b 1807 St. John J, mar 1832 St. Mary J, Jeanne or Jane ROBERT, qv. Josue was son of Edward and Jane (LAURENS) MESSERVY of J. He d 1871 Hooper, UT. Mar 2. Sarah MARKS.

This fam came from J to UT 1843 via ship GOLCONDA. A Jacob also came and there are prob desc in UT of this fam. (Rosalia Watson, Salt Lake City, UT; SLCity files)

A1. Joshua, b 1833 St. Mary J, d 1911. Mar 1. Jane Eliz. COUTANCHE,qv 2. Amelia Brindle, 3. Jane Marten, and 4. Caroline Hansen.

A2. Jeanne, Jane b 1834 St. Helier J, d 1837

A3. Harriet, Henrietta, b 1836 St. Helier J d 1919. Mar 1. Alsen Hamblin 1856, and 2. Robert Dowdie.

A4. John, b 1838 d 1921 mar 1. Mary Jane Whitaker, and 2. Martha Ann Black Hale.

A5. Josephus, or Joseph?, Robert, b 1842 St. John J d 1924. Mar 1. Augusta P. Cook, 2. Laura S. Southworth, 3. Mary Kingsbury 1877.

A6. Jane, b 1844 mar 1859 Amelius W. Hanson

A7. James, b 1846 St. John J, d 1890. Mar Betsy Ann HAMMON 1875

A8. Laurens A9. Elizabeth A10. Jacob, all 3 d.y.

A11. Ann Elizabeth, b 1852 St. Heliers J mar 1868 Amelius Hanson,d1875

MESSERVY, Aaron res Salem, late 1600s. (Essex Coll, Vol 8)

A1. Aaron M., bp 1697 Salem. A2. William bp 1701 A3. Mary, bp 1702

MESERVE, Abigail mar 1727 Samuel Libby. She d 1734, 2 chn d.y.

MESSERVY, Abigail mar 1767 Benj. Bell, both of Salem, MA(Essex Ant,V8)

MESERVEY, Amos, mar Eliz. Caswell 1773 MRB, 3 chn

A1. Eliz., bp 1773 A2. Hannah, bp 1775 A3. Amos, bp 1777

MESSERVY, Anne, in Salem, MA 1790 with fam of 2. (Census)

MESSERVY, Anna, mar 1771 Nathaniel BROWN. (Essex Ant., Vol 13)

A1. Nathaniel Brown A2. Anna Brown A3. Abigail Brown, bp 1797 Salem.

MESSERVE, Ann mar James Nute, b 1712/13 of Dover, NH. He d 1776

MESSERVEY, Benj. drowned at ferry, 1811, age 33, Salem, MA

MESSERVY, Benj. d 1821 age 23 in OH. (OLD NORTHWEST, Vol 8)

MESERVE, Daniel, bro of Col Jonathan above mar Betsy PENDEXTER, 8 chn.

A1. Jonathan, b 1809, dsp
A2. Samuel P., mar Licia Bowell
A3. George, no issue
A4. David mar Sarah Hobbs
A5. John Langdon?, b 1828, d.y.
A6. Eliza P., mar Joseph Emery
A7. Mary D., b 1814 mar J. PENDEXTER
A8. Martha P., b 1821 mar ___Wyman

MESSERVY, Charles, b 1849 J, son of George of Rouge Bouillon, J and CHarlotte Bolt, served in Civil Service, West Indies, d St. Ouens, J 1925. Mar 1875 Emelie DE FAYE, 9 chn. (Balleines's BIO. DICT. OF J)

MESERVE, Charles of Jackson, NH mar Nellie M. Mansfield, dau of Hollis and Abby (BUZZELL) Mansfield of ME. 2 chn. (GARNSEY-GUERNSEY GEN by E.Card, revision by Judith Young-Thayer, 1979)

MESSERVEY, Ephraim, "of Virginia", mar Martha Friend 1804 in Beverly, MA. An Ephraim was b 1747 in Glouc., MA. His widow poss mar 2. John O. Glover 1838 in Beverly. (Anis E. Woodman, Waltham, MA)

A1. Martha, b 1805
A2. Thomas b 1808
A3. Jonathan b 1810
A4. Ephraim, b 1812
A5. Martha Ann, b 1815, mar Wm. F.Davis & d 1887.

MESSUERRE, Francis, son of Peter, bp 1746 in Portsmouth, NH. Sarah bp 1739. (MRB VR)

MESSERVE, MISSERVY, etc., Francis mar Anne CORNEY 1752 MRB. Cf LE CORNU. A Francis mar Abigail___in MRB, had son Francis Kerney b 1782 MRB

A1. George bp 1756 MRB A2. Francis, bp 1758

MESSERVY, Capt. George, a privateersman of J 1756. A George of Jersey was customs collector in Boston, at tea party.(A. J. Jean, Jersey)

MESERVE, George, arrived in Boston 1765 from London, ship THOMAS AND SAM, Capt. Montgomerie.

MESSERVE, Hannah, b ca 1815, mar 1. Nathaniel Foss and 2. Luther Weymouth, 2nd wife, farmer, b 1804 Lyman, ME. (WEYMOUTH FAM HIST)

A1. Mary Foss Weymouth, b 1849 d 1937 res Drayton 1899, mar 1867 Clark Remick Cole, 7 chn: Warren, Wendell, Wallace, Lee, William,Harris

and Helen Cole, who mar Alf. Waterhouse.
MESSERVY, Jane mar George Strong 1761 MRB
MESSERVY, John mar 1715 in MRB Annis Cruff, Craft?
MESSERVE, John mar 1762 Abigail Small, b 1742 Scarboro,ME. John was son of John and Jemima (HUBBARD) MESSERVE of Scarboro. John d 1804, widow Abigail 1830. (Underhill) 7 chn: Joseph, Dorothy, Abigail, John, Benjamin, Samuel Small and Anna.
MESSERVEY, John mar in MA Sarah Hoar of Nfld., 3 chn: Albert, Walter and Reuben.
MESSERVE, John mar Ruth ____, res MRB.
A1. Ruth b 1798 A3. John b 1805 A5. Susan Ireson, b 1811
A2. Mary, b 1802 A4. William, b 1808 A6. Martha, b 1815
MESSERVY, Jonathan mar Hannah Slueman, 1780-1852, res Essex Co., MA. Jon. res Salem, MA 1790, fam of 5. (Census; Essex Coll.#3)
A1. William, b 1780, d 1852, master mariner, empl. by Simon Forrester
MESERVE, Col. Jonathan, b 1772, son of Jonathan and Mary (DAVIS)MESERVE mar 1797 Alice PENDEXTER, 7 chn
A1. Gen. George P. Meserve, 1793-1884 A4.John P., b 1812 mar L.Rogers
A2. Harriet Eastman Meserve A5. Andrew J.b 1815, no issue.A7. Alice
A3. Daniel, b 1801 mar Joanna Meserve.A6. Martha, b1804 mar Capt.J.T.
MESSERVY, Joseph W.H., mar (int) 1834 Sarah Salter Sweet, prob dau or grdau of Sam. SWETT. Capt. Sam had mar Sarah SALTER 1784, res MRB, d 1820, and she in 1816. 7 chn. Sarah b 1815 d 1848 MRB.
MESSERVEY, Kate Louise see p.337 in MORRILL KINDRED, by Smith
MESSERVEY, Capt. Mark, mar Nancy ___res MRB
A1. Michael, bp 1796, d.y.? A7. Nancy again, bp 1810
A2. Philip Haskell, bp 1798 A8. Joseph Hammond, b ca 1812, bp 1816
A3. Nancy, bp 1800, d.y.? A9. Michael Haskell, bp 1815, d.y.
A4. Thomas Hammond, bp 1801 A10. Michael again, bp 1816
A5. Ambrose Haskell, bp 1804 mar Lydia ___res MRB. An Ambrose d 1829 on Grand Banks. Another Ambrose lost at sea from schooner SALUS 1831. Lydia mar 2. Peter HULEN/UNION?, qv.
B1. Ambrose Haskell, b ca 1826 bp 1832 age 6½. An Ambrose H., seaman mar Sarah Ann ___, had son Ambrose b 1849
B2. Lydia, b ca 1830, bp 1832
A6. William, bp 1807 Also poss John Lewis Brown?, 1818-1830?
MESSERVEY, Mark J., mar Grace ___res MRB. Son or nephew of above Capt. Mark?
A1. Nancy Jane, bp 1829 A2. Mark Haskell, bp 1829 at 22 mos.
A3. Philip Ambrose, b 1835 A4. John Lewis Brown. Note other above.
MISSERVY, Mary mar Benj. Ashton 1753 MRB.
MESSERVY, Mary d 1835 age 84 MRB. See also p.518, Noyes,ODIORNE FAM.
MESSERVE, Philip & Lydia res MRB, had adopted dau Eliz. HAILS,d 1842
MESSERVY, Philippe mar 1920 Nfld. Harriet Jacobs, dau of Solomon Jacobs of Halifax, NS. Desc in New England. (Pamela Griffin, Malden, MA)
MESSERVY, Philip from J mar Mary Charder 1727 MRB, 7 chn
A1. Philip bp 1728 MRB A3. Jean, bp 1739 A5. Samuel bp 1744
A2. Mary, bp 1731 A6. John, bp 1746/7 A7. Wm., bp 1750/51
A4. Philip, bp 1742 poss mar Remember ___of MRB.
B1. Philip, bp 1773 B2. Mark, bp 1775 See Capt. Mark above.
MESERVE, Samuel b ca 1780 mar Sarah PENDEXTER, 12 chn. See MESERVE GEN.
MESSERVY, Samuel mar Eliz. BOWDEN in MRB 1768. (Essex Coll, Vol 11)
A1. Samuel bp 1769 poss mar Anna ___, res MRB.
B1. Anna, bp 1791 B2. Samuel, bp 1793 B3. Eliz. Bowden, bp 1795
B4. Jonas Pearce, bp 1799
MISSERVY, Susanna, had dau Abiel, bp 1705 Salem,MA (Essex Coll, Vol 8)

MESSER, MESSERVY? or MERCER, qv, William, mar Mary ___, res MRB.
A1. William, bp 1718,19,d.y. A3. Sarah, bp 1722 A5. Mary, bp 1727,d.y.
A2. Andrew, bp 1720/21 A4. William, bp 1725 A6. Mary again, bp 1732
MESSERVY, William, res MRB, had son John, b 1730. Another Wm. mar Eliz. ___, res MRB, had dau Mary, bp 1749. Wm.res Salem 1790, fam of 5.
MESSERVY, Wm., res Salem, MA.
A1. Abigail, bp 1749 A3. William, bp 1753 A5. Elizabeth, bp 1758
A2. Anna, bp 1740 A4. Hannah, bp 1756 A6. Rebecca, bp 1760
MESSERVE, William, served on ship MARGARET 1800, piked up in Batavia, Dutch E. Indies, brought back to Salem. (Essex Coll, Vol 2)
MESSERVY, Wm. Capt of the GALATEA, owned by Henry GRAY of Boston,MA, 1810. (Essex Coll, Vol 6)
MESSERVY, Wm., fish seller, d 1822 MRB age 72.
By the 1790 census there were many fams of this surname in ME. See Census and other sources. CAUTION: TRIAL CHARTS
MESSERVY. In the 1935 issue of the Soc. Jers. of St. Heliers J are two letters from Daniel Messervy, a captain who sent over to Boston 20 young Channel Islanders in the 1700s. The second letter was from Philip DUMARESQ, who was also involved financially in this business. Seven to ten guineas were asked for each servant, and they could have 'disposed' of one hundred more!
MICHEL in J 1299. In G early. In Grouville and St. Heliers J 1668. Curr G and J. See CIFHS #8.
MICHEL, Ada, from J mar James DE LA HAYE, qv, rem to Lexington, MA 1926 with 4 daus.
MICHEL, Francois, a smith, b ca 1831 J, mar Mary Ann Scott, b ca 1838 Canada, res QUE.
A1. Francis, b ca 1857 A2. Elias, b ca 1859 hill)
MICHALL, Joseph in Kittery, ME 1745, had son Samuel. From J? (Under/
MICHELL, MITCHELL, Richard from J 1665 with CARTERET, qv, to NJ on ship PHILIP. See NJ section.
MICHEL, MICHELL, MITCHELL in ME and NH in 1600s, assoc. with other C.I. fams. OUTC.
MICHEL, fam in Salem, MA 1693, from J? or Hug.? OUTC.(First CH records
MICHEL noted in Boston 1970s, OUTC. See records in UT.
MIDDLETON, MILLETON in J 1617. MIDDLETON in St. Saviour J 1668, and in St. Heliers J 1749. Curr G. The Earl of Middleton res J 1977. There is much info on Middletons in PA.Gen.Soc., Vol2, fams of NJ. See also Quaker Ency. V.#2; Noyes, MRB VR; AMY and DELAND fam records; Troxler; Baldwin.
MIDDLETON in SC before 1680, OUTC. (Baldwin)
MIERE, MYRE in J 1299. MIERE curr J, also old in G.
MILES, old J surname
MILLAIS in J 1309, 1607, 1668 and 1749. The famous painter MILLAIS went to England from J. MILLAIS in St. Martin and St. Saviour J 1668 and 1749.
MILLARD, old and curr in G.
MILLET, prob a Hug surname in C.I. In J 1586 and in Grouville J 1607. Curr J.
MILLET, see PIERCE GEN. and see PUNCHARD. Other MILLET data in Essex Coll., Vol 3; Essex Ant., Vol 10; BICKNELL GEN; Kittery, Glouc. and Falmouth records. Some data in WRCIC.
MILLETT, Benj. and Mary res Salem, MA, OUTC. 6 chn b 1797-1808: Mary, Sarah, Benj., Joseph Hardy, Mary Hardy and Elizabeth.
MILLETT, Clarissa, 2nd wife of John BERTRAM, qv, d 1848. OUTC.
MILLET, Jonathan, mar Eliz. MASURY, poss son of Jonathan & Sarah? bp 1764. A Jonthan d 1795 age 76 in Salem. Another Jonathan

MILLETT mar Sarah PUNCHARD, qv, in late 1700s, MA. See PUNCHARD, and MASURY. See also HARDY name above in Benj. MILLET fam.
A1. Jonathan, bp 1790 Salem A3. William, bp 1795
A2. Charles, bp 1793 A4. Eliza, bp 1798 A6. Joseph Hardy, bp1803
A5. Nathan, bp 1800, mar 1823 Ursula K. Chapman, who d fairly soon. Nathan a tailor and Customs Inspector, poss other chn?
B1. Charles, b 1829 mar Eliz. S. Wright. He was a Master Mariner.
MINCHINTON, Harry, b C.I., d 1969 Toronto, ONT, related to MINCHINTON fam of Gaspe, QUE, and to Pope fam of St. Johns, MI. (Mrs. E. Minchinton, Toronto, ONT)
MITCHELL, see MICHEL
MITCHELL, Mary Jane, b ca 1847 J mar John Halse, rem to Jersey City, NJ. (Carol Wylie, Fallon, NEV)
A1. George Edw. Halse, b 1885 Jersey City, NJ
A2. Mary Halse A4. Emma Halse
A3. John Francis Halse A5. Henry Halse A6. Florence Halse
MITTAN, MITTIN, MITTEN, MITTON, etc, John from J? to NH with CARTERET on ship PHILIP 1665? See NJ section. This may be a Welsh name, as Mittans were in England in 1100s. "My ancestors came from Jersey Is." (Nina Mitten Christenson, Laconia, NH) "Many Mittens in MonmouthCo. NJ in early 1700s, & in Burlington Co,NJ" OUTC. A short chart from Nina Christensen: Thomas Mitten of Susex Co., NJ; Samuel Mitten of Newton, PA; Alva Mittan, b NJ, d ILL; James Mittan, b Lee Co.,ILL, d KS; Oscar Mittan, b Norton, KS, d there; Nina Mittan, b Norton, KS res Gilford, NH.
MOFFET, MAFFETT appears in GCO at time the Channel Islanders were settling there, early 1800s. OUTC. MOFFET curr G and J.
MOGEE, MOJEY, see MAUGER, MAJOR.
MOLLET in St. Saviour, St. Helier and St. Laurens J 1668, and in St. Saviour and St. Laurens J 1749. Old in G, in St. Martins G 1795 and in Vale G 1821. Curr G and J. CIFHS #8,#14. Note also that MULLEY in early New England may have been MOLLET of C.I.
MOLLET, John b 1812 Grouville, J d 1892 BC Canada. Mar Margaret CARTER, b ca 1810 St. Peter Port G, d 1886 BC Canada. John and Margaret sailed from J or G to Gaspe 1862 on 35 ft boat, taking six weeks on voyage. They soon rem to a small farm near London, ONT, until 1871 when they bought a farm in Bruce Co., ONT. In 1884 John, Margaret and son John and his wife, rem to BC, living first at Port Alberni, later on Salt Spring Island, BC. Son Philip and his fam remained in ONT. (Colleen Massabki, Weston, ONT)
I. John C., first son, b 1848 St. Clement J, mar Eliz. LE JEUNE, b1848 St. Saviour J, rem to ONT with parents.
A1. Alexander John, b 1880s ? mar Maud LEE, res BC
B1. Edna b early 1900s? mar J. Fraser, 3 chn with desc: Leslie, Ray and Heather Fraser
B2. Thornton J., d 1916
B3. Florence, mar Al Soderquist, 2 chn with desc: Don and Norman Soderquist.
B4. Leslie? b 1917 mar Mary Bennett, Fulford Harb. BC, 4 chn: Terri Manuck, Ted, Bob and Anna Moncey
A2. Elizabeth Carter, b 1875-1962, mar Joseph Hudson LEE, 1887-1977 of Salt Spring Is., BC.
B1. Ron Hudson Lee, b 1909 mar 1. Gwendoline Stanbridge, d 1946 and 2. Evelyn M. Bennett, b 1918. A son d.y.
C1. Melbourne S. Lee, b 1935 d 1949 C3. Rhona M. b 1948 mar L.Farrow
C2. Lois Lee mar Peter Nadin C4. Elizabeth b 1953
B2. Clifford Le Jeune Lee, b 1912 mar Gladys Townsend, b 1913

C1. Roy Lee b 1936 d 1981 mar Jeanette ____, 3 chn
C2. Patrick Lee, b 1938 mar Marguerite Gear, 3 chn
C3. Sharon Lee b 1945 mar Leonard Voegeli, 2 chn
C4. Colleen Lee b 1947 mar Herman Soule, Sask., SASK, 3 chn
A3. Philip Charles, 1878-1965, mar Lilly Lee 1908 in BC
B1. Kenneth b 1910 mar Ethel CARTER, b 1911 Sidney, BC
C1. Kenneth Jr. b 1937 mar Norma ____, 3 chn
C2. Mary Janice, b 1942, unmar
II. Philip Carter, 2nd son, b 1848 St. Saviour J, d 1940 ONT, mar 1878 Ellen Lorre, b 1860 ONT, d 1925.
A1. Wilfred Philip, b 1879 d 1957, mar Margaret Hatchett, 1888-1971.
B1. Nora, mar Bill Stevens, res Owen Sound, ONT; 3 chn: Allen, Douglas and Barbara Stevens
B2.Ida, mar Patterson, in Tara, ONT, a son George Patterson
B3. Grace, mar Wes. Hemstock, Dobbinton, ONT, 5 chn: Lewis, Colleen, Bill, Henry and Philip Hemstock
B4. Maurice Wilfred, 1907-1972, no issue B5. Arthur J.C.,1910-1973
B6. Bernice, mar Maurice Trelford, Tara, ONT, 6 chn: Jim, Murray, Sharon, Laverne, Roy and Brian Trelford.
A2. James Arthur Carter, b 1882, d 1954 mar 1903 Emma Poucher, who d 1912, 2 chn. He mar 2. 1924 Vida Rogers, had a son. He mar 3. N. Ruth Braybeal, b 1021, WVA, d Toronto, ONT 1962, 2 daus.
B1. Irene, b 1905 d 1939, mar Blake Boyce, no issue
B2. Melford, b 1910 d 1973, mar Adele McEwen, no issue
B3. Philip Alva, b 1925 Windsor, ONT mar Frances Jackson 1946, res Detroit, MI, a son Gregory Dennis MOLLET
B4. Colleen Joyce b 1929 mar Richard Massabki, b 1922, res Weston,ONT 2 chn: Christopher E., b 1967 & Claire Ruth Massabki, b 1970
B5. Betty Ruth, b 1931
A3. Lena/Margaret Gertrude, b 1883 d 1946 mar Frank Allison, 4 chn: Melbourne, Arthur, Douglas and Eleanor/Lila Allison.
A4. Chesley John, b 1888, d 1960 mar 1925 Doris Hearn, res Allenford,/ONT
B1. Fraser, mar Ellen ___,4 chn: Sheridan,Catherine,Claudia,Trent.
A5. Onolee, mar Thomas Burke, div, 2. Jim Feik, res Kitchener,ONT, 2 chn: Lawrence and Sandra Burke.

MOLLET, John, res Boston, MA 1790 with fam of 3, prob from J?

MOLLET, Esme Patricia, b 1918 J, mar John Philip RENOUF,qv, 5 chn, US.

MONAMY, old and common in J, now extinct there but Monamys rem to Australia and Canada.

MONTBRUN. Some SIMON fams in N.A. are desc of this Hug. fam of Switzerland, of Germany 1699, to Haye, France before 1745, and in St. Clement J by middle 1700s. (Noreen Annett, Victoria, BC)

MONTESS, MONTAYE, LE MONTAIS, LE MONTES, etc, etc., qv. Philip Joseph from J, son of Philip LE MONTAIS, MONTAYE & Jeanne TOURGIS, qv, was a captive of the French, "taken at Port Grave, Nfld. 1705". MONTESS was from St. Ouen J. See also LE MONTES. (Noyes, Tanguay, Coleman)

MONTESS, Jane from J in Kittery, ME, mother of Marie Francoise HAMMOND, qv, b 1688, captured by Abenaki Indians 1705. Marie d 1707 QUE, Canada. (Noyes; Tanguay; Coleman)

MOODY, not in lists of old C.I. surnames, but curr G and J. It has been suggested that MOODY is the equivalent of MOTTEE, LE MOTTEE of J Much data available on this surname but none verified as from C.I. However, Clement below was prob from J, as he and another Jerseyman, Clement MESSERVY, were co-owners of land in Scarboro, ME. He mar 1. Sarah Clark, dau of John, said to be from Scotland. He mar 2. Alice ____? (Noyes) See sources: MS OF HERBERT MOODY, Boston Library;

Mrs. Jessie D. Wright, Beloit, WI; First Ch records of Falmouth, ME; JOURNAL OF MAINE HIST. by Sprague; WEYMOUTH FAM HIST; PEABODY GEN; Maine Libraries and VRs. Note that John MOODY, progenitor of most New England Moodys was said to be from Wales. George Moody, said to be from Moulton, England. See MESSERVY for MOODY families.

MOODY, Clement, "poss a Jerseyman" (Noyes) in Exeter, NH 1692. Moody said to be LE MOTTEE, qv. (Lillian Mathias, Bethany, ILL)

A1. Clement an ex-scout in 1712. He or son Clement mar Eliz. Scribner dau of John.

A2. Philip, res Kingston, ME 1725, living there 1747. He and 3 chn were bp 1727, and 4 more in 1735

A3. John, corporal in 1724, mar Abigail, widow 1731, bondsmen being Nicholas and Cart-e Gilman. He was an heir in 1740.

A4. Jonathan, will dated 1731, names wife Joanny, a son Jonathan under age and a dau Sarah. Widow mar 2. at Kingston 1731 Jonathan Wadleigh.

A5. Josiah, mar poss Sarah Scribner, dau of John 1736, both of Brentwood NH 1747.

A6. Elizabeth mar Jeremiah BROWN, who was bp 1702, d ca 1780 Saco, ME, 8 chn.

A7. David, in 1733 the widow Alice was his mother-in-law(stepmother). He mar in Kingston 1733 Mary Gilman, dau of Jacob.

B1. Jane, "admitted to Kingston Ch 1727/8, must have belonged to this fam by birth or marriage." (Noyes)

MOODY, Nicholas from J? at Lamprill River, ME 1679 (Noyes)

MOODY, Philip from J? in Exeter, ME 1684, poss related to Clement?

MOON, Samuel b Cornwall, England, while fishing was wrecked on a small Island with his bro. They were picked up and taken to G. The bro. returned to Cornwall, but Samuel stayed and worked in G., mar Eliz. RABEY, qv, of an old G fam. Samuel d 1836 and his wife survived to age 83. (Racine, WI ALBUM)

A1. Joseph, b 1829 G mar Sophia GILBERT, dau of John GUILBERT, b G. Rem first to London, then sailed to NYork on American ship AMERICAN CONGRESS, and settled in Racine, WIS, 4 chn. Josepha builder, at one time partner of John GALLIEN, qv, and later with M.J.P.Corse & with W.D.Davis. Many old Racine bldgs. were his work, such as Cong. Church, Taylor Orphan Asylum, St. Luke's CH, First National Bank, etc.

B1. Mary Eliz., 1852-1862 A2. Sophia, d.y. A4. John S., d.y.

B3. Ella S. b 1857 mar A. Cary Judd of Racine, WISC 1878.

MOON, several noted including Thomas and Jane who were in MRB middle 1700s, but may have been from Cornwall, England.

MOON, Elizabeth res J, mar 1843 Emanuel Hill (Rose Vincent, Belleville, Michigan)

A1. Rosalia Mary Hill, b 1844 J, to America 1850, landing at New London CT, rem to Rockford, ILL 1854.

A2. Emanuel Hill Jr., b 1847 J? A3. John Moon, b 1849 J?

MORANT, SEE MOURANT.

MORCEL, Frank, b J, mar Angelina LE TELLIER, res Montreal, QUE 1900s. (Maurice Le Tellier, Longueuil, QUE)

MOREAU, old and curr in J.

MOREL, meaning dusky, like a Moor. In J 1331, in St. Clement, St. Saviour, Grouville and St. Martin J 1607, in St. Saviour J 1668. In St. Laurens J 1788. Curr J. See CIFHS #7. Note that this name appears as MORRELL, MORRILL in early New England, but most were from English fams. Write MORRELL FAM ASSOC.,3312 E.Costilla,Littleton,COL.

MOREL, Isaac of MA, Peter of Falmouth, ME & Nick of Boston, from J?

MOREL, Isaac from J was involved during King William's War in New Engl. in a plot to subvert the slaves and Indians, threatening to destroy Haverhill, Amesbury and Newbury. A George Major, Moger, MAUGER was to lead the assault. Other J folk were more loyal. MAJOR & MOREL were apprehended, poss both from J. (Essex Coll, July 1974; MORRELL ASSOC., Vol 2, #2, June 1982)

MORRELL, MURRELL, prob MOREL, Peter from J, seaman, rem to Beverly,MA then bought land in Falmouth, ME from Thomas Mason of Salem ca 1681. Mar 1675 Mary BUTLER of J, also in Salem, MA, who was living 1714. Poss just 2 chn by MORRELL. (Noyes; DUTCH UNCLES & NEW ENGLAND COUSINS, by Clough; GAGE FAM, by Clude Gage; HIST OF KIMBALL FAM, by Morrison; Beverly and Salem VRS; Charts by Betty Wayne King, Lafayette, CAL; National Archives; Salem, NH Town Hist; Sullivan NH Probate records; Cattaraugus Co., NY records; JOHN OF KITTERY, A MORRELL MEMORIAL, typescript, 1936?, Salem, MA)

A1. Sarah, mar 1698 JOhn Ellinwood in Beverly, MA, where a ch was born. A widow, she quitclaimed to Geo. TUCK Jr, 1725, poss nephew.

A2. Mary, mar by 1701 George TUCK, poss TOCQUE of J? Chn b Beverly. In 1734 a TUCK was mariner, and she was surviving ch & heir of Peter MURRELL. Res Falmouth, ME 1734.

B1. Ch, b Beverly, MA?

B2. Mary Tuck, b 1703/4 mar 1719/20 John OBER Jr., b 1699, d 1767, rem to Salem, NH where she d 1768. John was son of first John OBER and Hannah Woodbury. 5 chn

C1. John Ober Jr., b 1720/21 Beverly, MA mar 1743 Anna Thorndike, d 1758.

C2. Mary Ober, b 1723 mar 1745 Oliver Kimball

C3. Elizabeth Ober, b 1724 Beverly mar 1763 Isaac Thorndike

C4. Israel Ober, b 1726 mar 1744 Mary Pittman, 16 chn. See DUTCH UNCLES, etc for much more info on Hulls, Obers & McLaughlins.

By 1790 Morrells in 14 areas in ME, 29 towns in NH. OUTC.

MOREL, Mary in Boston 1677, from J? (NEHGS Vol 31)

MOREL, Peter from J? to GA 1733/4 with wife and 4 chn. (Filby)

MORICE in J 1309-1562. Later poss changed to MORRIS? which is curr in G and J.

MORICE, Daniel Nicholas to Phila, PA 1804 from J? OUTC

MORICE, John to America 1644/1663 (Filby) OUTC

MORICE, Marguerite to LA 1719. (Filby) OUTC

MORIN in J 1236-1607. In St. Saviour and St. Heliers J 1668. MORIN CURR J. None traced in America, but name noted here.

MORRISON, C. of J had a ship named CAMBRAI built in Portsmouth, NH 1865. (A. John Jean of Jersey)

MOSER, MOSSER, MUSSER, John in Lancaster Co., PA 1711 from Switzerland, the Palatinate or from Alsace, to PA. CAUTION! Fam below from G.

MOSER, MOSSER, John b 1800 G, rem to GCO, when? He mar Sarah H. ___, b 1802 G. John d 1877, Sarah 1891. Conflicting records prevent preparation of a verifiable early chart. This is not in C.I. name lists, may poss be of Germanic or Dutch origin like SUNNAFRANK, qv, also from G to GCO. However, MOSER is curr in G. "Name was changed to MOSSER by Mary Jane Mosser, b 1837". (Mrs. Delores Mosser Grant, Cambridge, OH) CAUTION: TRIAL CHART

MOSERs arrived in GCO 1821, 1827, 1834 and 1847 (Mrs. Grant) "In my investigation of the Moser, Mosier fam of Senecaville, I pronounced the name MOSSER. I soon found that older residents pronounced the name MO-ZURE". (Wm.Cale, GCO) Most desc use name MOSSER.

MOSER, MOSSER, John, b 1800 G, rem to GCO after 1839? Wife Sarah H. b 1802 G, d 1891. John d 1877. Order & relationships unverified.

Chn of John and Sarah MOSER, MOSSER, of Guernsey Co., OH.
A1. Nancy, b 1824 G, d 1912 bur Ohio Temple Cem.
A2. Christian, b ca 1832 G, d 1909 age 77. Mar Mary Jane ___,b 1837
B1. John Wesley, b 1858 GCO d 1927. Mar 1. Jane Stewart2 chn, and 2. Maria Adamson, widow of Isaac Tucker, with 5 chn: Nannie, Lincoln, Rebecca, James B. and Lula. Maria & John W. had 7 chn.
C1. Clara, 1878-1965, mar ___Williamson
C2. Jane, 1878-1965?, bur Newport, OH
C3. by Maria, Ora John, b 1886, d 1966, bur Cambr. OH, mar Barbara Hague, 9 chn. Barbara, 1884-at least 1975. Ora John was with the Cambridge Glass Co. for 50 years.
D1. Dallas William
D2. Marjorie Olive Addison
D3. Kathryn Adaline Galliher
D4. Dolores Juanita Grant
D5. Madylon Jane Whitis
D6. Jack Taylor, d 1972 Dayton, OH
D7. Betty June Whitis
D8. John Donald Mosser
D9. Thomas Richard Mosser
C4. Otha Freeman, b 1887, d 1973, mar Mary Early, 1886-1945, bur Cambridge, OH, RC Cem.
C5. Virgil, b 1890 d 1908, bur Wheeling, WVA
C6. Minnie, b 1892, d 1965, mar ___Conlon, d 1965, bur Twinsburg, OH
C7. Cleo Mosser Utterback, 1894-1950, bur Cambridge, OH
C8. Letha, b 1886 mar ___Boots?, d 1970, bur Twinsburg, OH
C9. Floyd Noble Mosser, b 1898
A3. William Wesley, b 1839 G, d 1921 Senecaville, OH, mar Mary A. ___, 1846-1906.
MOSER, John H., 1880-1952, bur Senecaville Cem., Richland Twp., GCO
MOSER, Mary MALLETT, 1874-1938, bur ditto MOSER, Faris V, 1862-1901
MOSER, William G, 1883-1952 bur ditto MOSER, John Conrad, 1847-1903
MOSER, Mathias A., 1856-1890, bur GCO
MOSER, Julia, b 1857, d 1935, poss mar Pinkney L. Walker,1857-1914.
MOSER, Conrad, had 164 acres in Richland Twp., GCO 1840
MOTTEE, LE MOTTEE in J 1541. Simeon LE MOTTAIS in St. Heliers, J 1668. LE MOTTEE, qv, curr J.
MOTTEE, Jacob res Charlestown, SC in 1700s, poss from C.I? He mar 1. Eliz. ___, who d after ca 7 chn. He mar 2. Ann___1763. Bought land from Clement LEMPRIERE, qv, had plantation in Christchurch. Had sons-in-law named Thomas Lynch and John Huger, prob a Hug.
A1. Jacob A5. Charlotte A6. Charles
A2. Abraham. An Abr. was in St. Philip-St. Michael par.SC 1790 with 2 females and 17 slaves.
A3. Francis, and Francis & co. were in same place with 3 men.
A4. Isaac. An Isaac also there with boy, 4 females & 12 slaves, 1790
A7. Martha Dart, with chn and grchn.
A8. Sarah, deceased 1790 but with chn and grchn.
A9. Elizabeth A10. Ann A11. Hannah A12. Mary A13. Martha
MOTTE, Rebecca in St. James Santee Par., Charleston SC 1790, poss widow with son, in possession of 71 slaves. OUTC
MOTTE, William in Camden, Fairfield Co., SC 1790 with fam of 2 men, 5 boys and 3 females. OUTC.
MOTT, Nathaniel, pioneer of Scituate, MA 1643. OUTC.
LE MOTTEE, John from J to MA early 1800s? Son Walter, mar res Weymouth
MOTTE, Daniel from C.I.? to Cambridge, OH 1809. Sarah and Maria S., wife of James, Hugh (1786-1863), Margaret and Daniel all noted in Conner-Eynon Cem. records with no dates. OUTC.
MOTTEE, Mary mar Joseph Cockrell (SARCHET SCRAPBOOK) OUTC.
MOTTE, W.D. d GCO 1800s. OUTC.
MOTTE, Lillie, res GCO 1800s, as did Margaret. (Conner-Eynon) OUTC

MOUILPIED, DE MOUILPIED. This C.I. surname in OH and WI early 1800s, prob from G or J. Curr J.

MOULLIN, DU MOULIN in G 1331, still common there. MOULIN curr J. MOULLIN curr G. Poss some MILL fams originated as MOULIN from C.I. Cf also surname MULLIN. MORE DATA IN CH.IS.COLLECTION.

MOULIN, Charles mar Eliz. Rhodes of MRB 1740 Boston. His widow mar in 1750 Mathew West, Boston, MA.

MOUNTS, MOUNCE, MONTAIS, MONTESS, LE MONTAIS, LE MOUNTS,etc, etc. Many variants of this surname, see

MOUNTS, MOUNCE, Christopher was in Cecil Co., MD early 1700s with wife Martha, poss from C.I.? (Virkus 7)

MOUNTES, James and Sim., both with crew of ship SUCCESS 1685 in ME/NH. (Noyes) Note they were with John HATCH & Philip FALL, qv.

MONTESSE, Jean/Jane, wife of Edmund HAMMONS of Kittery. "A French version of some English name, but what one?" (Noyes) LE MONTAIS?

MONTAWAY, John, poss MONTAIS? living in 1706 with Francis ALLEN of Kittery, ME.

MONTASE, Philippe, in captivity 1710 (Noyes). Evidently captured by Indians in New England.

MORONG, MERONG, MORANT, MURRAIN, MARANG, etc, etc. These may all be variant spellings of MOURANT, in J 1309. In Grouville, St. Saviour, and St. Martin J 1668. In Grouville & St. Saviour J 1749. Curr G and J. MOURANT shield, gules on a chevron argent, three talbots passant sable.

MOURANT, Peter, is said to have started the first greenhouse in G in 1792, now an extremely important part of business there.

MOURAN, MOURANT?, John of Boston mar Sarah Wilson 1600s.

MOURANT, J. and wife, grandau of Wm. and Remember Wilson, sold 2 acres in Charlestown,MA 1700s. (Wyman)

MARANG, Clement, bur 1900 Warner CH Cem. Cochocton, OH. OUTC. More data in Coshocton.

MURRAIN, Ebenezer, in Lenox, MA 1790 with small fam. Jesse ditto. Moses in Pittsfield, MA, 4 fem. in fam, 1790. MOREAN and MURRINE appeared in this census also, Hubbardston & Boston. OUTC.

MERONG, Jonathan and Mary res Salem, MA 1790, chn Thomas & Polly.

MERONG, MORONG, Jonathan and wife Martha? res Salem 1790, 4 chn bp 1800: Martha, Priscilla, Elizabeth and Anna.

MOURANT-GIFFARD, Mr. and Mrs. John res Portland, ME with 2 daus, 1900s. Prob of C.I. fam.

MORONG, John, bp 1767 Salem, MA, son of John.

MORONG, Mary Lamson, dau of Thomas and Mary L., b Woburn, MA 1852

MORANT, Capt. Philip H., res Pepperell, MA mid 1800s, from J. Mourant family?

MORONG, Thomas and Jemima res Salem, MA. Jemima res Salem 1790, with fam of 3.

A1. John, bp 1741 First CH, Salem A2. Benj., bp 1747, other chn?

MORONG, Thomas, bp 1767 Salem, son of Capt. Thomas.

MOYSE curr J. Means Moses? See CIFHS #6.

MOYSE, Mary, dau of Joseph and Hannah, mar Andrew GREELEY, b ca 1617, settled in Salisbury, MA. OUTC.

MUDDLE, Philip was in Portsmouth, NH 1688, in Berwick, ME 1713. (Noyes) Note that this name is very close to the pron. of the C.I. surname LE MUSTEL (silent s). LE MUSTEL in J 1274, 1668, and in 1749 as MUTEL.

MUDGE, see MAUGER

MULLET, see also MOLLET

MULLET, sometimes MOLLET? MOLLET in J 1612 and old in G. In St. Martin G 1795. A Philip MULLET in G 1511 mar ___LENFESTEY.
MULLET, MULLEY, close to pron. of MOLLET. Note that Abr. and Susanna were from J. CAUTION: TRIAL CHARTS.
MULLY, ABRAHAM and Susannah PAIN, both of J mar in MRB 1722/23
MULLET, MOLLET?, Abraham Jr. also called Abram, mar 1762 Rebecca BOIT, qv, from C.I.? Res MRB. She was b ca 1744, d 1819 age 77.(DRIVER G.)
A1. Abraham, bp 1765 An Abr. was in Salem 1790 with fam of 4. (Census)
A2. John, bp 1767 A3. James Pitman, bp 1768 A4. Benj., bp 1770
A5. George, b 1775 MRB d 1836, mar 1804 Hannah Wellman, 1770-1840. George was blind in his later yrs. and was for some time the town crier of Salem, MA.
B1. Hannah, 1805-1883 B3. George Whitefield, b 1809
B2. Mary Kempton, b 1807, d.y. B4. Mary again, 1811-1859
MULLET, Abraham, res MRB, poss son of immigrant Abraham? OUTC.
A1. Benj., bp 1739 A5. Sarah, bp 1748
A2. Hannah, bp 1742 A6. Rachel, bp 1750
A3. Rebecca, bp 1744, mar Clement BARNARD? 1762 MRB. A7. Thomas,bp1752
A4. Benjamin, bp 1746 A8. Elizabeth, bp 1756
MULLET, Thomas, mar Mrs. Abigail RUSSELL 1780 MRB. Thomas soon died. (Betty Lenth, Essex, CT) OUTC. 6 chn. More data in WRCIC & B. Lenth.
MULLET, Thomas and Mary Smith? res MRB. At this same time a Thomas Jr. and Mary HALES, HAILES,qv, res MRB. Poss that Eliz., bp 1744 & Mary bp 1748, poss others also, belonged to the HALES group and not the SMITH group. OUTC. Some marriages with C.I. fams.
A1. Thomas, bp 1740, d.y. A7. Mary, bp 1748
A2. Greenfield HOOPER, bp 1741 A8. Alice, bp 1748/9
A3. John Smith, bp 1743/44, mar Frances ____
B1. Sarah, bp 1769 B2. Rowland MOGEE, qv, bp 1772
A4. Elizabeth, bp 1744 A9. Sarah, bp 1750/51
A5. Elias, bp 1746 A10. Rebecca, bp 1753
A6. Thomas, bp 1746 A11. Mary, bp 1758
MULLETT, see much more in Boston and MRB records.
MULLET, Abigail, d 1829 MRB age 78
MULLEY, MULLET, Elias and Rebecca res MRB, dau Rebecca bp 1745
MULLET, Ephraim, res Charlestown, MA 1790, fam of 8.
MOLEY, MOLLET?, Hannah mar Geo. DEMERITT 1749 Boston, MA.
MULLY, Mary mar 1732 Edward HAMMOND, MRB
MULLET, Sarah mar George MELZARD 1770 MRB.
MUNGER,MAUGER, Nicholas from G? in Guelph, CT 1659. See MAUGER
MUNION, MOIGNAN?, LE MOIGNAN?, qv. MUNION not a C.I. surname but pron. very close to MOIGNAN. See records in WRCIC, etc.
MUNION, LE MOIGNAN?, Clement mar Rachel QUILL 1777 MRB. (int) OUTC.
MUNION, Gabriel, res Essex Co., MA, fam of 2. (1790 Census) SOURCES: Rev. Tim. Goldrick, New Bedford, MA; Alan Teague, Detroit, MI; T.L. McAdam, Warren, MI; Maxwell Emerson, Memphis, TN. Also WRCIC.
MOUNSELL, south of Egnland and Guernsey Is. surname.
MOUNSELL, MOONSELL, MUNSELL, Thomas in Dover, ME 1667. OUTC
MUNSELL, Thomas in New London, CT 1680-1712, when he d. (Noyes) OUTC
MUNSEY, etc. Wm. and Cooper from C.I. or England? res Kittery, ME, 3 chn by 1686. OUTC.
MUNSELL noted in Licking Co., OH 1789,1819. (OLD NORTHWEST, Vol 8)
MURRY in St. Lawrence J 1788. Curr G and J.
MURRY, John mar Hannah Proctor 1746 MRB. OUTC. One John mar Hannah Brimblecomb 1766 MRB. Another John mar Mary Pitman 1774 MRB.
MURREY, Mary mar Joseph M. Laurance 1777 MRB. James mar Sarah Pitman.

MYGOOD, Nicholas, Jerseyman, tavern keeper, seen 1718-1720 at Hampton Falls, NH, mar widow of Capt. John Lane of Winterharbor. The Lanes had 7 plus chn. One Capt. John Mygood b ca 1701 mar 1724 Mary NOWELL of York, ME. Of their 5 chn, 3 sons were Captains in the Rev. War. Capt. John Sr. said to be bur at Crown Pt., NY. MYGOOD not listed by Stevens as old J surname. Poss English fam in J?

NAFTEL, old and common in G. See OUR KIN and GUERIN.

NAFTEL, Abraham, b 1814, son of Caroline COLLINGS and Daniel NAFTEL, mar in G Elizabeth Stonehouse, settled in Canada, had 2 sons and a dau. (OUR KIN)

NAFTEL, Daniel, b 1796 G, d 1872 GCO. To Ohio ca 1807. (Sarchet; Conner-Eynon; census)

A1. Maria, b 1821 d 1857 GCO.

NAFTEL, John, bro of Abraham above, b 1816 G, mar Caroline Slocomb and settled in Canada. (OUR KIN, by Guerin)

NAFTEL, Louise, 1850-1866 res GCO.

NAFTEL, Nicholas of St. Peter Port G, clockmaker, son of Thomas and Eli Eliz. NAFTEL, mar 1789 in Melksham, ENG. Mary Higman.(Quaker Records)

NAFTEL, Thomas from G to OH 1806 with wife and chn, d by 1820.(Sarchet)

NAY. This is not in Stevens J name list. Poss that a Hug fam came from France and settled in J a short time. John of Hampton, NH is said to have come from J. Other Nays came to America from France. See SOME DESC. OF JOHN AND ABIGAIL NAY, by John B. Nay, 1980, of Concord, NH, 03301. Other sources: HIST OF HAMPTON, NH: Dr. Ernest O. Nay, Terre Haute, IND; Hurd; John Herlihy, Silver Spgs., MD.

NEAL, old in G curr G and J. In J 1331. Common in Grt. Britain.

NEALE, Capt. ___, sailed from the C.I. ca 1890 with 30 persons from the Islands to settled in CAL. Other in group were named LE BRUN and DEBENHAM. (Philip Luce, BC, Canada, 1975)

NEAL, Francis of Falmouth may have been from the C.I.?

NEEL in J 1309 form of Nigle. In Grouville, St. Clement, St. Saviour St. Martin and Trinity J 1668. In Grouville, St. Brelade and Trinity J 1749. In St. Lawrence J 1788. Nelson NEEL was a clockmaker in J 1832. NEEL an old Norman French and Viking surname. See CIFHS #3. Curr G and J. NEIL curr J. (Lola Eubank, Ballinger, TX)

NEEL, Elias of Grouville J mar Marie MOURANT, dau of Philip MOURANT, 15 chn. More data compiled by Lola Eubank, Ballinger, TX and Laura J.W. Ford, San Antonio, TX, some in WRCIC.

I. Elias mar Ann LE BAS, several chn, all res J.

A1. Elias, mar Ann Boyd, a son Elias Boyd Neel or Dr. Boyd Louis NEEL, b 1905 London, England res ONT, Canada, well-known musician and conductor.

A2. Samuel Francis, b 1839 J, mar his first cousin Emma Jane NEEL, b 1843 J, dau of Francis and Jane (LE BOUTILLIER) NEEL. 8? chn. This f fam rem to TX ca 1873. Two older daus returned to J after Emma's death, but soon d ca 1882. Samuel mar 2. Mary E. Lay, no issue. Samuel a successful farmer, county agri. agent, etc., d Seguin,TX 1922.

B1. Samuel Francis Jr b 1865 J, mar Margaret Bates, and res Seguin, TX 3 chn: Francis, Gladys and Etha Maxine.

B2. Edith Emma, b 1867 J, d 1942, mar Neill P. Rogers ca 1890 at least 4 chn.

C1. Lillian Rogers, b 1892, d 1963 mar Pleasant Rogers.

D1. Vivian Rogers, mar Bill Orr, had dau Janie Sue Orr

D2. Evelyn Rogers, mar Cyril Wilks, a son Linus Wilks

D3. Joanelle Rogers, mar Fred Gibson a ch.

D4. Mary Beth Rogers mar Lindy Pierce, 3 chn

C2. Myrtle Rogers, b ca 1895 mar Rev. C. Edwin Wilbanks 1921, res Ft. Worth, TX. C3. a dau C4. a dau
D1. CharlesE. Wilbanks Jr. D2. Neill Wilbanks D3. MaryJo McGivern
B3. Florence Eliz., 1869-1882 B5. Annie Maude, b 1871?
B4. Lillian Gertrude, 1870-1882
B6. Isabel Adeline, b 1872 d 1916 mar Samuel Marvin Lillard, b 1871
C1. Winnifred Maude Lillard, b 1896 mar H. Everall Dibrell, res TX
D1. H.E. Dibrell Jr.,b 1917 mar Jane Metzgar.D4. Emma D. Dibrell
D2. Marvin Lillard Dibrell, b 1920 mar Nora Mae Cutter
D3. Robert Wayne Dibrell mar Nellie Catherine Sharper
C2. Virginia Lillard, b 1898 mar Raymond A. Dibrell, b 1895
D1. Virginia L. Dibrell, b 1922 D3. Doris W. Dibrell, b 1930
D2. R.A. Dibrell Jr, b 1928 D4. Margaret J. Dibrell, b 1932
D5. Joseph Marvin Dibrell b 1940, lawyer in Brown Co., TX
C3. Samuel Lillard C4. Edith E. Lillard, d.y. 1901
B7. Frederick, d.y.
II. Philip, b 1815 J, missionary to Southern France, mar in J Frances Ceriziere.
III. Francis, b 1819 J, mar Jane LE BOUTILLIER, 11 chn. Jane d 1866 in J. and Francis mar 2. Mrs. Susannah (Hargreaves) Croskell, widow of Joseph, 1870 in J., no issue.
A1. Emma Jane, b 1843 J, mar her first cousin Samuel Francis NEEL. See family above.
A2. Louisa Maria, b 1844 Alderney Is., d 1891, bur Mt. Enterpirse Cem. near Old Fort Dade, FLA. She came to America later than the others, and mar Rev. Isaac Vernon, no issue.
A3. John Francis, b 1848, d 1874, unmar, bur Seguin, TX
A4. Alfred, b 1850, d 1923 said to have come to Montreal, QUE, lived for a time in Cameron, 35 miles N. of QUE, then worked for a farmer naed Reed, near Peopria, ILL. Alfred mar his first cousin Margaret Emily Fisher, b 1857 J, d 1902, 12 chn.
B1. Elsie Margaret, b 1877, d 1928 mar Harry Beard.
C1. Charles Noble Beard, b 1902, mar Miss Fred. Fitzgerald, a son Charles b 1929
C2. Carrie Beard, b 1904 mar James A. Bellar, and 2. Guy Chester Matthews, 3 chn by each husband.
D1. James A. Bellar Jr., b 1932 D4. Guy C. Matthews Jr, b 1944?
D2. Elsie Fay Bellar, b 1933, mar, has a son
D3. ___Bellar D5. ? D6. ?
B2. Alice Gertrude, b 1879, d 1960, mar 1. Max Herron, 2 chn, and 2. _____Bradford, 3. J.W. Sell, and 4. Ed Crissey
C1. Andrew Sidney Herron, b 1903 mar Elfreda Prell, who d 1945, a dau
C2. Mabel Herron, b 1909, d 1975, mar 1. Wm. B. Mulvey, who d 1964, and 2. Joe Lamb. Adopted dau by Mulvey, mar, has 3 chn.
B3. Mabel Catherine NeeL, b 1883 d 1966, mar Henry Lester. Chn: Bell, Gertrude, Marie and Marguerite Lester.
B4. John, d.y. B6. Fanny, d.y.
B5. Sidney Alfred, b 1885 d 1960, mar 1917 Olivia Marchbanks, b 1895 res Waco, TX.
C1. Odell, b 1919 mar Harold Elliot Jones, 2 chn, both mar 1968: Shirley Ann and Connie Dell Jones
C2. Evelyn Sidney, b 1920 mar James Hallon Sparks, d 1970, had adopted dau, Kay Sparks
C3. Emily Jane, b 1920 mar Edw. James Sherrill, adopted dau Neel S.
C4. Mary Frances, b 1925 mar Howard B. Gross, dau Beverly? d age 10.
B7. William David, b 1890, mar 1914 Lena Rains, b 1891, res Waco,TX.
C1. Mildred, b 1915, mar Wm. F. Todd, div. & 2. James M. Moran.

C2. William Alfred, b 1917 mar 1937 his first cousin ,Florence Estelle Dabney, res Waco, TX. She is also a first cousin to Albert Sherrod and Harold Allen of Austin, TX.
D1. Wm. A. Neel, Jr., b 1938 mar Wanda Sullivan, 2 chn: Donna,Karen
D2. Margery Ann, b 1940 mar 1958 Jerry E. Duncan, 3 chn: Jerry, Jeffrey and Jodie Duncan.
D3. Lana Jane, b 1942 mar 1972 ?
D4. George Brooks, b 1945 mar 1968 Pat Patterson, a son George B.
D5. Elizabeth Diane, b 1954 D6. Debbie Lynn, b 1956
C3. Virginia Lee, b 1918 mar Charles W. Shaw, who da 1967 age 74
D1. Mary Eliz. Shaw, b 1940 mar 1958 Richard Novak, 3 chn: Cathy, Mike and Laurie Novak
D2. Leslie Eldon Shaw, b 1944 mar 1968 Sara L. Oliver.
D3. Frances Ann Shaw, b 1947 mar 1968 Harry Lynch
C4. Dorothy Jane, b 1922 mar 1947 Harold Fred. Fick, 3 chn: Larry, Michael and Morlys Jeanne Fick.
C5. Clovis Owen Neel b 1927 mar Virginia Mayberry 1950, son Cliff.
C6. James Boyd Neel, Master Sgt. with USAir Force, Spain, mar Anita Wimberly, English, 4 chn: Patti, Sherri, Robert, and ?
B8. Madelyn Edith b 1892 d 1975 mar Benj. Clark, 1891-1944.
C1. Alton Benj. Clark, b 1931 mar Helen Gunn Palmer, who had several chn by her first husband.
B9. Margaret Emily, b 1894 mar Chester Cox, 1877-1932. Had chicken farm near Hillsboro, TX. Maggie mar 2. Ed Blackwell and 3. John Rose, res Bruni, TX, no issue
B10. Arthur James, b 1897 mar Zelma Wheeler, 4 chn: Florence, Bonnie Dell Cochran, Billy Ray and Betty Fay, twins.
B11. Helen Florence, b 1899 mar James Harry Cowan, 1893-1946. She mar 2. Karl Klint, who d 1961
C1. James Harry Cowan b 1923, mar Berly Roberts 1946. James killed in airplane collision, 2 chn: Cheryl Damron & Eliz.Furr, twins.
B12. George Francis, b 1902, mar Maude ____, 2. Alice Yondel, and 3. Carrie Bates, 4. Florene ____, no issue.
A5. Emily Sophia, b 1851 J d 1928, mar Levi McCollum 1915, when she was 64. He was killed by gangsters while sitting on his front porch in FLA. She later res New Rochelle, NY.
A6. James Frederick, b 1852 J d 1916, mar Florence Eliz. GAVETT, 1856-1927. Mar and bur in Seguin, TX, where James farmed.
B1. Ida Clara, b 1886 mar Albert Sicincores Allen 1913, who d 1936.
C1. Alberta Allen, b 1915 mar Wm. Curtis Sherrod 1945, res Galveston.
C2. Roland Harold Allen, b 1921 mar Elnora Daniel, res Austin, TX 3 chn: Donna Carol, James Edwin & Wm. Harold Allen, b 1960
B2. Edwin James, b 1896 d 1947, bur Seguin, TX
B3. Velma Florence, b 1892 d 1947, mar Henry Oscar Dabney, bur Waco,TX
C1. Rowena Velma Dabney, b 1915
C2. Florence Estelle Dabney, b 1918, mar William Alfred NEEL, b 1917 in Waco, TX 1937. See fam. under William's chart
C3. Henry Oscar Dabney, Jr., b 1919 mar Martha Ray Jackson, 3 chn: Carolyn Rowena Van Winkle, Terri Jean & H.O. Dabney called Trey
C4. George Kenneth Dabney, b 1921, has ward or adopted son Don Korenek, who mar 1967 Kathleen Lough.
A7. Annie Esther b 1853 J, d 1884, mar John Archibald Franklin Hubbard 1875, 1853-1928.
B1. Lillian Maude Hubbard, 1876-1940, mar 1901 Edwin M. Eubank, 1874-1948.
C1. Carl Edwin Eubank, 1901-1924
C2. Lola Esther Eubank, b 1903, unmar, res Ballinger, TX.

C3. Joseph M. Eubank, b 1906 d 1968, mar Adella Bartlett 1928.
D1. Jo Ann Eubank, b 1929 mar Daniel Daughterty, 3 chn: Daniel, Adella and Joseph Daugherty.
D2. Ruth Gayle Eubank, b 1932 mar Bob I. Vancil 1953, 2 sons: Karl and Paul Vancil.
C4. Thomas Neel Eubank, b1908, mar Margaret E. Danielson, no issue.
B2. Alice Louise Hubbard, b 1878 mar 1898 Thomas Logan Eubank, 1871-1923. Alice d 1930
C1. Charles Hubbard Eubank, b 1899 mar 1. Bessie Baysinger 1919, 2. Gladys Wright in 1930, who d 1975 and Dama Lohman in 1976
D1. Edna Ruby Eubank, b 1921 d ca 1934 KS. D4. Lena G.,b1933,d.y.
D2. Alice Charlotte Eubank, b 1931 mar Earnest F. Garrett, b 1926 in 1948, res Shreveport, LA, 3 chn: Bruce, Marie and Larry Dean Garrett.
D3. Charles H. Eubank Jr., b 1934 mar 1956 Lavelta Lawrence, 4 chn: Wm., John, Joseph and Ruth Eubank.
C2. Claude Duncan Eubank, b 1905 mar 1927 Alger Vernon Bryan who d 1968. D1. Thomas Edw. Eubank, b 1928, d unmar
D2. James Arthur Eubank, b 1931 mar 1959 Christine Allison, 2 chn: Truitt James and Margie Kay Eubank.
B3. Grace Eliz. Hubbard, b 1879 mar 1898 TX, Henry Ashe Wootten, and d 1918. 9 chn.
C1. Willard Freeman Wootten, b 1899 d 1969, mar Ima Peters, no issue
C2. Grace Eliz. Wootten, b 1900, unmar
C3. Ruth Love Wootten b 1902 mar Wm. H. Thomas 1928, res Delta, COL
D1. Laverne Thomas, b 1929 mar Lester Allen Doyle 1947
E1. Lynda Gay Doyle, b 1949 mar Terry E. Brown, 1967. 4 chn: Shannon, Evan, Kimberly and Mistie Brown.
D2. Daniel Allen Doyle, b 1952 res Delta, COL.
C4. Lois Ashe Wootten, b 1904 mar Carlos Olin Lincecum 1928 a son
D1. Larry Gene Lincecum, b 1941 mar Lois Mary Buley 1964 in WISC.
C5. Weta Wootten, b 1906-1909
C6. Hubbard A. Wootten, 1909-1973, mar Connie Mayes, no issue
C7. Frances Marie Wootton, b 1911 mar Fred Coleman, no issue
C8. Henry Wooton, 1914-1980, unmar C9. Dorothy L. Wootton, b 1916.
B4. Arthur F. Hubbard, 1881-1947, mar Janie Sellingsloh, no issue
B5. Paul Edmund Hubbard, b 1896, served in WWI, mar Joyce Hooper.
A8. Maria Laura b 1856 J, first cousin of Sam. Francis NEEL above. Mar William Erwin Wilson. (Records of Laura Lane Wilson Ford, of San Antonio, TX)
B1. William Erwin Wilson, b 1886, poet, d 1966 Brady, TX, unmar
B2. Neel Wilson B4. Herndon Wilson, 1882-1909 B5. Lydia Wilson,d1920
B3. George Wilson, d 1980, mar ___, res Corpus Christie, TX & Conroe.
C1. Laura Jane Wilson, mar Ernest Ford, musician
D1. Melanie D2. ? D3. A son d.y. D4. Adopted son Peter Ford
B6. Grace Eliz. Wilson, mar ___Witt, d 1978, ca 90, several chn.
B7. Clara Wilson, b 1895 mar Brack Simpson of St. Louis, no issue.
A9. Albert Elias Neel, b 1858 d 1909, mar Mary Hargreaves Croskell, his step-sister, 1863-1905, dau of Jos. & Susannah H. Croskell.
B1. Florence Elizabeth, b 1888, mar1902 Charles Cecil Hancock
C1. Albert O. Hancock, b 1903 mar Ethel Louise Prine.
D1. Albert Oreon Hancock, Jr., b 1930 mar 1955 Kathleen Burke,b 1934, a dau Susan Eileen Hancock, b 1957
B2. Joseph C., b 1885 d 1948, mar Ione O'Neill, b 1896. Joseph, b Seguin, TX had music shop in Dallas for many years. Austria.
C1. Dr. Joseph Croskell Neel Jr. b 1917 mar Gertrude Koudella of /
B3. Albert Henry Hargreaves NEEL, b 1892 mar 1919 SArah/Sadie Holmes.

C1. Noel Henry, b 1921 d 1969, mar Virginia Lee McCoy, and 2. Betty, widow with a son. D1. by 2nd wife, Linda NEEL, b 1952
C2. Mary Wanez, b 1922 mar Frank ___, son Pat. C3. Gwendolyn, b 1932
B4. Mary Susannah, b 1895 mar 1917 CHarles Cecil Hollingsworth.
A10. Lydia M.A. b 1859 d 1877, mar Joseph K. Butler, no issue
V. Frederick, artist, d.y.
VI. Mary mar Philip LE FEUVRE, res St. Clement J, 5 chn. A son Gilbert LE FEUVRE of J rem to Seguin, TX late 1800s.
VII. Elizabeth mar James Finnie, res J? VIII, Jane, d.y.
IX. Anne, mar George GAUDIN of J.
X. Emily XI, Margaret, mar David FISHER in J?

NEEL, Amy T., last of her name and fam in J, left the Island 1957 to live in Scotland.

NEEL, Francis Jr. and Sr. were at Casco Bay, NH 1680 from C.I.? OUTC

NEVEU, see LE NEVEU

NEWCOM, old in G but not researched by compiler.

NEVILLE in J 1224, 1607 and old in G. Also English & French surname. Some noted in early New England, and a few mar into C.I. fams such as LE GROW and MOGE. See GENS & ESTATES OF CHARLESTOWN, MA; MRB VR; TINGLEY GEN, Vol 2.

NEWELL, David mar Polly LE CRAW, qv, 1807 MRB. OUTC.

NICHOLS, NICHOLLS, NICOLLS, NICOLLE, NICHOLAS, at least 140 heads of fams in early New England by 1790. Spellings differ greatly, not easy to distinguish between those of Eng. & the NICOLLE fams of C.I.

NICOLLE in J 1309. In St. Heliers, Trinity, Grouville, St. Clement, St. Saviour, St. Peter and St. Martin J 1668. In Trinity, St. Martin and Grouville J 1749. Curr G and J. NICHOLL and NICHOLS are now common in G, but poss from England and Scotland?

NICHOLAS, old in J and G.

NICHOLAS, Edward, mar Hannah Bicknell, b 1837, in MA, dau of Alfred and Eliz. (Austin) Bicknell. 2 sons: Alphonso & George NICHOLAS. (BICKNELL GEN)

NICHOLAS, John, d 1756 in Phila.,PA, from C.I.? OUTC. (Quaker Ency)

NICHOLLS, Abraham and Rebecca, res Boston, MA early. OUTC.

NICHOLLS, Clement of J mar Sarah ROGERS 1714 Boston MA. Dau b 1714

NICHOLS, Eli of Loudon Co., VA, rem to Belmont Co., OH then to Cosh. More data in Will records, Coshocton, OH. OUTC. (Noyes)

NICHOLS, Eli, merchant and ship captain from J at Piscataqua 1682./

NICHOLS, Francis, Capt of Guard for Sir Edmond ANDROS, qv, from G?

NICHOLS, Grace May, b C.I. mar Richard John HERIVEL, qv, res DetroitMI. See VR of Boston, MRB and Newburyport, MA for other NICHOLS fams, a also Noyes, Essex Coll Vol 3; OLD BURYING GROUND OF FAIRFIELD, CT, by Kate Perry 1882; Wyman's CHARLESTOWN, MA.

NICHOLSON in J 1497, curr G and J. However, there were Nicholsons in J who came from Devon, England in early 1800s. CAUTION. NICOLSON, ship builders in J 1800s. (A. John Jean, Jersey)

NICHOLSON, Henry Luscombe, b 1832 St.Heliers J, mar 1853 Matilda Ann Cort, b Hampshire, England d 1894 St. Catharines, ONT. George was son of George T. Nicholson, b 1798 Devon, and Mary Luscombe. Matilda was dau of James and M. (Purkis) Cort. (J.Robt.McAdam, Sacramento)
A1. Wm. Henry Cort Nicholson, b 1854 St. Heliers J, mar 1877 Emilie/ Amelia ALLEZ, b 1856 St. Brelade J, d 1898 St. Catharines,ONT. She was dau of John ALLEZ and Eliz. Esther HELLEUR of St. Brelade,J
B1. William Henry Allez Nicholson, b 1880 St. Brelade J, mar 1903, d 1962 Vancouver, BC

NICOLLE in J 1309. In St. Heliers, Trinity, Grouville, St. Clement, St. Saviour, St. Peter and St. Martin J 1668. In Trinity, St.Martin, and Grouville J 1749, curr G and J. In G the spelling is often modernized to NICHOLS. See CIFHS #4. See PP 442,443,445 in Q.A. IN CANADA by Turk. These additions and corrections by Marilyn Cahill, Cherry Hill, NJ.

NICOLLE, John Thomas, b ca 1795 G, farmer, sailmaker, rem to Guernsey Cove, PEI, Canada, 1806 and d 1856, bur Murray Harb. Cem. Mar 1. Elizabeth MACHON, qv, who d 1863, and 2. Margaret Irving, b 1805, who d 1887.

A1. Margaret, b 1822, mar Thomas S. HENRY, qv. She d 1902, bur Georgetown, PEI.

A2. Mary Ann, b 1824 mar Charles Cupp. A3,4,5 in Canada book.

A6. James Henry, may have been A6. and not A8, and b ca 1833? Elizabeth would then be A8.

A8. Elizabeth b 1839 mar 1. Neil PENNY and 2. James Clark. Eliz. d. 1930, bur Forest Hills, Boston, MA.

B1. Samuel PENNY, b 1867

B2. Elizabeth Catherine Penny, b 1869 PEI mar 1. Bert ___, and 2. James Nathan Taylor. Elizabeth d 1932.

B3. Louise M. Penny, b 1870 PEI, mar 1. ___ROBBINS and 2. N. Howard Thompson. Two chn named ROBBINS. She d 1950.

B4. Isabella Jane Penny, b 1872 PEI, unmar, d 1967

B5. Eliza Mary Penny, b 1873 PEI.

NICOLL, noted in Petition of QUE city residents 1838 with other C.I. surnames. OUTC. (LOST IN CANADA, Aug. 1981)

NICOL noted in Ohio 1860 census. OUTC

NICOL, Elizabeth, dau of Eliz., bp 1696 in Salem, MA (Essex Coll #8)

NICOLLE, Francis from J? noted in Maine Petition 1689. (Noyes)

NICOLLS, Thomas, res MRB 1790 with fam of 8. (Census) OUTC.

NICOLLS, Wm., res MRB 1790 with fam of 6. (Census) OUTC.

NICOLLES below are part of the Guernsey Is. fams settled in PEI early 1800s. See John Thomas above, and Q.A. IN CANADA, by Turk.

NICOLLE, Laura, mar Euben Willard PENNY, b 1872 d 1939, 1st wife. (BECK GEN)

NICOLLE, Laura Cecelia, mar Samuel John BECK, 1898-1978,(BECK GEN)

NICOLLE, Maie W. mar Ezra BECK, b 1884, d 1946, 1st wife. (BECK GEN)

NICHOLS, NICHOLAS, NICOLLS, NICOLLE, etc, at least 28 persons of these surnames in SC in 1790 census. Poss some from C.I.?

NIGHTINGALE, LE ROSSIGNOL, Benj. from France or C.I. to Braintree, MA, res there 1689. Note LE ROSSIGNOL in GUSTIN GEN. LE ROSSIGNOL in St. Ouen J 1607 and 1668. Curr G and J. See also Q.A. IN CANADA.

NOEL in J 1309. In St. Martin J 1668. In St. Mattin and St. Heliers J 1749. Curr J.

NOEL common in northern Europe. NOEL from Holland to America 1736, also from France and England. (THE NOEL TREE by Charles Noel, Mansfield, OH 1979) See CIFHS #9.

NOEL, Asenath, wife of John Moores, res Lisbon Falls, NH from Nfld. John worked in mills at Lisbon ca 1900. Some NOELS in Nfld from C.I.

NOWELL, Capt Peter from Salem, MA in York, ME 1694, mar 1. ca 1698 Sarah Weare, who d 1729 age 53. He mar 2. 1729/30 widow Mary Preble, who d ca 1753. Peter d 1740 age 70, 9 chn. More in Noyes. OUTC.

NOEL, David mar Jane Eliza BUESNEL, b 1865 J, d 1943. David d 1934 in St. Martin J. At least 2 chn came to Canada. (Eric Buesnel, Farnham, Surrey, England) See BUESNEL.

A1. Edmund, 1899-1921 A2. Dora, 1891-1925 A3. David, 1892-1969, res Canada

A4. Renouf, b 1892, twin, res Canada.

NOWELL, NOEL, Philip, a Jerseyman of Salem, MA, lost at sea 1675.(Konig)

NOWEL, Philip and Ann had Sarah, b 1719 Boston, MA.

NOWELL, NOEL, Philip of Trinity J left bros. John and Richard NOWELL in Salisbury MA 1684. (Essex Co. Quarterly Court Records 1684)

NOLAIS, Mrs. ___, of J to US. Her dau mar ___Jones, res Dearborn, MI 1930s.

NOURY in J 1500s. NORE, NOURY, NOURSE noted in MA. OUTC.

NORE, Elizabeth mar 1784 Thomas GRUSH, qv at MRB. She soon d and he mar 2. widow Margaret JACKSON 1785.

NORMAN in J 1309. In Trinity J 1668. In Trinity, St. Laurens and Grouville J 1749. Note that NORMANS from Dorchester, England aleo settled in New England. NORMAN in G 1331, still common there.CurrJ.

NORMAN, Clement and Abigail had Clement in boston 1712

NORMAN, John in Salem 1636, OUTC. (Essex Coll #4)

NORMAN, John b ca 1660 J? mar 1683 Sarah Maverick, res MRB. OUTC. 11 chn b 1684 to 1706 in MRB: Richard, Margaret, Eunice, Moses, John, Sarah, who mar John BROUGHTON 1693, qv, BEnjamin, John, Jonathan and Elizabeth. See also Essex Coll, vol 7.

NORMAN, John and Mary res MRB. OUTC.

A1. Mary, bp 1721 A2. John, posthumous, bp 1725

NORMAN, Mary, widow of Joseph NORMAN, mar at MRB 1691 as 2nd husband Henry HOUPER, qv, son of Robert HOOPER. (HOOPER GEN) OUTC. By 1790 only one Norman fam in MA Census? John in Boston had fam of six.

NORMAN in MD 1600s. OUTC. (Skordas)

NORRICE, Thomas and Elizabeth had dau Eliz. bp 1719 Salem, MA. (Essex Coll, #8) OUTC. NORRIS in J and G 1800s.

NORTHY, NORTHEY. Compiler believes this may be at times in New England the J surname NORTHEAST, in J 1461,1607 and in St. Martin J 1668. NORTHY curr G. See Boston and MRB VR and census.

NORTHEY, John and Mary CROSS, LE CRAW?, res MRB. Poss Joseph below was related to this John.

A1. John, bp 1788 d.y.
A2. Mercy Craw, bp 1791
A3. John again, bp 1793
A4. Deborah Peach, bp 1795
A5. Joseph, bp 1798
A6. Samuel, bp 1801, d.y.?
A7. Hooper, bp 1804
A8. Samuel, bp 1805

NORTHEY, John and Susanna had chn in MRB 1732-1738. OUTC.

See JOURNALS OF ASHLEY BOWEN of MRB for the many ships commanded by Capt. J. NORTHEY in the 1760s and 1770s.

NORTHEY, Joseph mar Mercey LE CRAW 1762 MRB. OUTC.

A1. John, bp 1762
A2. Mercy, bp 1765
A3. Joseph, bp 1770, prob d.y.
A4. Sally Craw, bp 1772
A5. Roger, bp 1774, twin
A6. Joseph, bp 1774, twin
A7. Roger again, bp 1776
A8. Hannah, bp 1778

NORTHY, Samuel, mariner arrived in Boston 1715 on sloop MARTHA(Whitmore)

OBER. Tradition says the OBER fam went from France to Jersey and then to England. OBEAR is very close to the pron. of the French surname AUBERT. (GEN. OF THE OBER FAM, by Katharine P. Loring and May Toomery, Beverly, MA 1941) "AUBERT from Normandy to England to MASS. as OBER." W.O. Clough, Laramie, WY) "George AUBER, AUBERT?, said to have been a French Huguenot, perhaps from Rouen by way of the Isle of Jersey, and his son William, b 1586, married to an Edith MOLLET. Their son John, b 1613, mar Elizabeth BUTCHER, BOUCHER? sired as a first son our Richard OBER, who turned to Massachusetts around 1664, after which time both OBER and OBEAR appear, the latter being pronounced O-BEER still." (DUTCH UNCLES AND NEW ENGLAND COUSINS, by Wilson Ober Clough, Univ. of WY) Richard settled first in Norfolk, then by 1668 to Salem, MA, and next year to Beverly, MA. He mar 1671 Abigail Woodbury, who lived until 1742. See MOLLET.

Richard d 1706 leaving a good sized estate, had 6 sons and 3 daus. Many desc served in Rev. War. (MASS SOLDIERS AND SAILORS) Did all OBERS in America stem from this one fam or were there others who came from the Channel Islands named AUBERT, who became OBER? See also Essex Antiq. vol 8 for OBER-BECKFORD fam.

OBING, see AUBIN

OBERT, Bertram in Christ Ch parish VA with dau Agatha. (Virkus)

OGIER in J 1331, also very early in G. Curr and common in G. OGIER in Vale G 1821. (CIFHS #14)

OGIER, James, b 1795 G son of Henri and Marie (GALLIENNE) OGIER, mar 1816 Castel G, Mary E. MAINDONALD, qv, b 1796 G, dau of Jean and Martha (BLONDEL) MAINDONALD. This name sometimes written McDonald in US. Mary and James may have been from St. Saviour or St. Peter G. James d 1840 Jackson Co., OH. Mary d 1871 Hocking Co., bur Lancaster Co.,OH. James first went to Phila. 1817. Their mar in G was by Rev. N.P. DOBREE of G. 10 chn. (Nova Weller, Columbus, OH; Jean Donner, Spokane, WA; Willa Griffin, Moses Lake, WA; Vermelle Ogier, El Cajon, CAL; Janice Morrow, Welston, OH; Twilla Dillard, Indianola, IA; Ruth Mason, Columbus, OH)

A1. James Jr., b 1817 G or PA d 1842 Vinton Co., OH.

A2. William, b 1818 Phila., PA d 1891 Vinton Co., OH. mar 1837 Westland Twp., GCO Ann Elizabeth Hodges

B1. Rebecca Ann, b 1839 GCO mar 1859 Jackson Co., OH Henry C. ROBBINS

B2. James Harvey, b 1841 OH, d 1919 OH, mar 1863 Anne E. DARBY of Maysville, MO, 8 chn b Vinton & Jackson Cos.

C1. Charles Fillmore, b 1865 d 1940, mar 1887 Ross Co.,OH, Cora B. Chapman. 1964

C2. Della Elizabeth, b 1867 OH d 1947, mar Charles A. Blackstone, d/

C3. Flora Lola, b 1870 Jackson Co. d 1947, mar James ROBBINS 1889.

C4. Herbert Early, b 1873 d 1951, mar 1893 Lottie E. McNeal

C5. Stephen Hilborn, b 1876 Jackson Co., d 1958 St. Cloud, FLA. Mar 1903 Eliza E. CARR, qv, dauof Willard Henry and Mary D. (Campbell) Carr.

D1. a son b 1904, d.y.

D2. Willard Harvey, b 1905 mar 1926 Sylvia Martendill

E1. Betty Arletha, b 1929 mar 1946 John L. Stimmer, Chillicothe,OH

E2. Doris Ilene, b 1932 mar 1948 David W. Lee

D3. Theodore Ray, b 1906 mar 1930 Zella Marie BURR, qv, no issue

D4. a son b 1908 d.y.

D5. Lola Alma, b 1909, d 1981 Columbus, OH mar 1929 Hamden, OH Elmer J. NICHOLS.

D6. Stephen Lincoln, b 1912 Jackson Co., OH mar 1934 Elsie Irene Muncy, b 1917 dau of Jefferson E. and Mary (Hutchison) Muncy.

E1. Janice Faye b 1935 mar 1955 Jimmie D. Morrow.

E2. Melvin Larry, b 1939 Wellston, OH mar 1958 Beverly S. Bobo.

D7. Othello Thomas, b 1914 d 1980 Chillicothe, OH mar 1941 Desta Mae Douglas.

E1. Steven Othello, b 1947 mar 1967 Judith E. Lanman.

C6. Maud Estella, b 1879 d 1955, mar 1900 Silas H. Kinsel

C7. Hudson Holly, b 1882, d 1927, unmar?

C8. Ora Virginia, b 1884 d 1971, mar 1905 John W. Cox

B3. Mary Jane, b 1844 Jackson Co., OH d 1861

B4. Lucinda b 1846 d ca 1863 Hamden, OH, mar 1862 Geo. W. Snyder

B5. John Thomas, b 1849 Vinton Co., OH d 1930 Sarasota, FLA mar 1870 Lida A. Forster, and 2. in 1874 Sarah Cherington, and 3. in 1888 Mary Cherrington; 8 chn by 2nd wife, one by 3rd.

C1. Orson Homer, b 1875 d 1955, mar 1900 Mary E. Brown, 4 chn. She was dau of James and Eliz. (Ralston) Brown of Vinton Co., OH.
D1. Benson mar 1. Mary Helfrich; 2. Jenny Davis, 3. Julie ___.
E1. Robert, b 1925? mar Neva Fisher
E2. Marilyn, mar Dick Morbitzer E3. John mar Barbara ___
D2. Thomas Ralston, b 1904 d 1976 Ross Co., OH mar 1934 Franklin Co., OH Margaret Schmidt, 2 chn.
E1. Thomas Ralston, b 1936 mar Suzanne Thomas
E2. Janice Margaret, b 1944 Columbus, OH, mar Nicholas Miller
D3. Charles Frederick, mar Dorothy Geyser, 2 chn
E1. Charles F. Jr. mar ___Tosh. E2. Thomas mar beverly ___.
D4. Elizabeth mar Edward Reilly.
C2. T. Frank, b 1877 Vinton Co., OH d 1881
C3. William John, b 1879 d 1932 Hamden, OH mar 1904 Lena Vollenwider.
C4. Freddie b 1881, d.y. C5. Blanche, b 1882 d.y. C6. Marian, also
C7. John Thomas Jr. b 1884 d 1937, mar 1908 Norma D. Knopp, a son Robert d.y.
C8. Lida Elenor, b 1886 by 2nd wife, d 1923, mar 1910 N.T. Spiker
C9. Gerald Dwight, b 1891 by 3rd wife, d 1930 Cincy, OH. Mar 1912 Mary ROBBINS, qv.
D1. Dwight, b ca 1913 D2. Fred. b ca 1922
B6. a son, b 1857, d.y.
A3. Thomas, b 1819 Germantown, PA, d.y.
A4. Mary Ann, b 1920 mar 1839 in GCO, William Noble
A5. Sophia, b 1822 GCO mar 1840 William Craig. She d 1840 JacksonCo,OH
A6. Judith, b 1823, mar 1842 Adam Tarr, and 2. in 1845 James H. Leach.
A7. John, 1825-1827
A8. Thomas, b 1827 GCO mar 1847 Nancy Grimes, dau of John and Ellen Grimes. Nancy, b ca 1829, d 1890 Columbus City, Louisa Co., IA.
B1. John, b 1848 OH B2. Mary E., b 1850 OH
B3. William Henry, b 1852 IA, d 1909, mar 1873 Elizabeth A. Duncan, who was b 1855 IA, d 1920, dau of George Bell & Anna(Shaw) Duncan, 3 chn
C1. Minnie Della, b 1874 Wash. Co., IA d 1880
C2. Joanna Pearl, b 1876, d 1912 IA, mar 1900 Joseph Leroy Parsons, b 1876 IA, son of Abr. Hamilton Parsons and Sarah Amanda Duncan. Joseph d 1938 Columbus JCT, IA.(Willa Griffin, Moses Lake,WA)
D1. Laird Le Roy Parsons, b 1901 Wash. Co., IA d 1976, mar 1922 Nita Kemp.
D2. Fred Emerson Parsons, b 1903 IA, mar 1935 Anna Lena Hayes
D3. William Frank Parsons, b 1910 Guymon, TX or OK?, d 1972 Martinez CAL, mar 1936 Rock Island, ILL Harriette Lurene Simmons,b1909 IA, dau of Harry and Vinnie Grace (Bennington) Simmons,2 chn.
E1. Joanna Patricia Parsons, b 1945 Santa Barbara, CAL mar Kent Marvin Decker 1964 in Idaho Falls, ID.
E2. Willa Frances Parsons, b 1947 Coronado, CAL mar 1946 Ronald J. Griffin, Oakland, CAL, son of Lynwood N. & Marian L. (Bule) Griffin, 2 chn: Margaret Elaine,b 1972 & Paul R. Griffin.
C3. Frank Earl, b ca 1882 IA, d 1961 MI? Mar Mae Burke, 2 sons: Chester and Walter.
B4. James F., b 1854 B6. T. Lewyellian, b 1866 mar Margaret ___
B5. Florence, b 1860 mar John Stapp. B7. Leroy b 1869 IA.
A9. John again, b 1829 d 1847 Vinton Co., OH A10. Peter E., b 1830 GCO
A11. Nancy, b 1832 Westland Twp, GCO d 1914 Clearfield, IA, mar 1853 Ephraim ROBBINS, qv. See Large ROBBINS fam, for an Ephraim.
A12. Isaiah M., b 1834, mar 1854 Vinton Co. Emiline Nixon, 8 chn.
B1. James Aunel, b 1855, mar ____1876.

B2. Henry Sanford, b 1857 OH, mar 1886 Zilpha E. Smith res Beaconsfield, IA. 1 ch?
C1. William Earl, b 1889 IA mar 1910 Jessie E. Bohall, dau of Joseph and Dasey (Lamb) Bohall, 8 chn.
D1. Clyde Melvin, b 1911 mar 1945 Catherine Maloney, 3 chn.
E1. Melvin Earl b 1947 Lamoni, IA
E2. Wm. Anthony, b 1949 E3. Malcolm Lee, b 1952 IA
D2. William Everett, b 1913, mar 1934 Corinne Hershner,res Butler,OH
E1. Sue Ann, b 1936 mar ___Black. E2. Gwyenna Lee, b 1938, mar Charles Lifer.
D3. Hazel Marie, b 1918 mar 1940 Earl Stanley
D4. Ethelene May, b 1921 mar 1944 Shellie Scott
D5. Ralph Warren, b 1924 mar 1947 Louise Laird
E1. Ralph James, b 1948 E2. Connie Sue b 1951
D6. Ernest L. Glenn, b 1926 mar 1946 Leona Herfel, 4 daus.
E1. Mary Ann, d 1948 E3. Kay Lou, b 1952, twin
E2. Susan May, b 1950 E4. Karen Lee, b 1952, twin
D7. Jessie Fern, b 1927 mar 1946 Robert Higday
D8. Elbert James, b 1929 mar 1949 Ruth Rush, 4 chn
E1. Elbert James Jr., b 1950 E3. Ricky Lane, b 1956
E2. David Allen E4. Marlene Jo, b 1958
B3. Elizabeth Ellen, b 1859 mar 1877 B5. Josephine b 1864 IA
B4. Mary Katherine, b 1861 Jackson Co.,OH d 1931 Mar 1880 Charles Woodruff
B6. William Calvin, b 1866 Louisa Co.,IA d 1951. Mar ___, 1891
B7. Eva, b 1868 IA, d 1871 B8. Perry Almon, b 1870 IA
A13. Nicholas Pedwin (see POIDEVIN), b 1835 GCO d 1912 Glendale, CAL, mar 1. 1854 Almira Leach and 2. 1894 Susan C. Stealy. Served in Civil War with WVA troops.
B1. James Willis, b 1856 Vinton Co., OH d 1930 Pomona, CAL mar 1881 Jennie Talcott
C1. Clyde C2. Edna mar ___Ellington
C3. Pedwin Willis, b 1897 Brunswick, NEB, d 1945 Pomona, CAL, mar 1920 Bessie K. Fields.
D1. Robert Willis, b 1921 d 1972 San Diego, CAL, mar 1947 Las Vegas, NEV, Vermelle Maberry.
E1. Pamela Carol, b 1948 Pomona, CAL mar 1969 David E. Schmidt.
E2. Kim W., b 1955 San Diego, CAL
D2. Betty Jean, b 1923
C4. Violet
B2. Lewis Chalmer, b 1859 Louisa Co., IA
B3. Mary Juday, b 1862 Wood Co., WVA, d 1894 mar 1882 William E.Tear.
B4. Robert Clayton, b 1864 Parkersburg, WVA mar 1885 Hortense Lillian Coats, 4 chn.
C1.Hazel Lillian, b 1885 Schuyler, NEB C2. Fred, b 1887
C3. Walter Eston, b 1890 C4. Rex Adelbert, b 1893 Wallace, NEB.
B5. Sarah Louisa, b 1868 WVA, mar 1885 William Henry Widemer.
B6. Thomas Franklin, b 1871 WVA mar 1895 Agnes Licty
B7. Isaiah Clarence, b 1874 WVA, mar 1899 Nora Sykes.
C1. James Nicholas, b 1897 Wallace, NEB d 1964, mar 1924 in Wallace Agnes Elizabeth LIGHT.
D1. Ruth Marie b 1924 D3. Norma Jean, b 1939 D4. Nora Ann,b1934
D2. Charles Robert, b 1926 D5. Bill Lee, b 1937 Grainton, NEB.
C2. Leroy, b 1900, d 1901 C6. Edward Clarence, 1910-1956
C3. Ruth Bertha, b 1902, d 1959 C7. Ralph Kenneth, 1912-1957
C4. Lyle, b 1905 C5. Paul Eugene, b 1908 mar Margaret, son Willis.
B8. Nicholas Edwin, b 1877 WVA, mar 1896 Rae, Raie Garman.

OGIER. There are a few puzzles in connection with the OGIERs of Ohio. Several men came to Guernsey Co., OH from Guernsey Island, but some records say the immigrant was born in France. Other records refute this. "on Nancy Ogier Robbins death certificate it states that her father's name is John OGIER, born in France. On her brother Nicholas Ogier's death cert. it says his father's name is William, born in France. In the Ringgold Co., Iowa History, the biography of her bro Isaiah say that his father's name was James Ogier. James, John and at least 2 William Ogiers res in GCO 1820,1830 and 1840, all with chn that could be of comparable age to Nancy and her brothers. Also, all three are listed in the tax records thru 1843. But none are on the 1850 census, and Mary Ogier is head of the house...I have ruled out John just recently through old probate records. My mother has clippings about the activities of all three names taken from a newspaper in Guernsey Co., and found in the Bible of Nancy Ogier Robbins. It would be quite logical to assume that they are all 3 brothers. If so, it appears that Nancy Ogier's father and mother both came from France, born there, but they must have stopped in the Channel Islands on the way, as part of the children of the other families were born in the Channel Islands." (Jean Donner,Spokane,WA) It seems that James, John and William, from Island records, possibly born in Guernsey, but their parents or grandparents may have come from France. Note the fam of John of Baltimore had fam originating in or near Caen, France. Note also that the OGIER fam of Elizabeth M. Hosmer of Camden, ME in HIST OF THE OGIER FAM, 1894, is about a French Ogier fam, settled first in London, England, then in Canada, and finally in Camden, ME.

OGIER, one fled from G after accidentally killing one of the Russian soldiers quartered there by the British govt. In 1828 one Ogier built a fine home, still in good shape, a little modernized, occupying a rise which looks out over a fine 160 acre farm on a most attractive bend in the river near Cambridge, OH. One OGIER brought from G to GCO a fine large cradle said to have been in the family a long time, displayed in 1975 in the Cambridge, OH library. Other Guernsey items are in the local museum there, and in the hands of descendants. Family charts of those below are not yet made by compiler. See sources: Sarchet; Campbell; Wolfe; Williams; Howe; Conner-Eynon books about GCO; Cambridge Library & GCO County records.

OGIER, Catherine, b 1828 GCO d 1882

OGIER, Daniel of G fam, b early 1800s mar Lucinda SARCHET, qv,d 1909

OGIER, Elizabeth, b 1826,8 mar George MARQUAND, qv, d 1891, bur Cambr.

OGIER, Eliza Jane, b 1812 d 1865 Cambridge, OH

OGIER, James from G to GCO ca 1810. Same or another James to GCO 1820

OGIER, Mr. and Mrs. John of Rockdale, Rue des Covins, Castel, G, rem with 2 daus and 4 sons to OH. In that year, 1920, one son Edward returned to G, and res in St. Martin parish, G.

A1. Edward, res G A2. Kathleen mar ___ Jewell, res Barberton, OH.

OGIER, John, orig. stockholder in GCO Bank of Cambridge, OH 1872

OGIER, John, b 1826 G, son of Thomas and Rachel (MARQUAND) OZIER of G, mar in GCO 1848, 1. Catherine Neelands, b 1827, and had son Charles who d.y. Mar 2. Serepta BONNELL, dau of Mary SARCHET, qv. (RECORD)

OGIER, John, b 1817, d 1891 Cambridge, OH.

OGIER, John b 1799 G, in GCO by 1820, d in Cambridge, OH 1872, marMary Ann SHERRARD, 1803-1897, no issue. She was dau of Wm. and Mary (Bogle) Sherrard, b Ireland. (Williams)

OGIER, John Jr. b 1829 GCO, son of Thomas and Mary (MARTIN) OGIER. Thomas was educated in England, b G. John Jr. (Sarchet,#2,p.541)
OGIER, Mrs. Judith over 76 in 1876, res GCO. (Wolfe)
OGIER, Lucinda, 1832-1909, res GCO
OGIER, Margaret, b 1817 d 1892 GCO, poss mar Thomas LE PAGE?, qv.
OGIER, Mary, res Valley Twp., GCO, mar a Thomas LE PAGE.
OGIER, Mary b 1822 GCO mar Daniel F. BICHARD, qv, 1846, d 1872 GCO
OGIER, Mary Alice mar John E. Crosgrove of Cumberland, GCO 1873. A son Charles S. Crosgrove b 1874. (Lee Crosgrove, Dallas, TX)
OGIER, Peter, b 1801 G, d 1883 Cambridge, OH, living there 1876, had a pharmacy there 1860?
OGIER, Thomas b 1776 G mar Rachel MARQUAND, qv, 1812. Poss arrived 1810 in GCO, 8 chn. (Williams)
OGIER, Thomas b 1781 G, d 1850 GCO
OGIER, Thomas res GCO 1820 with fam of 7. A.T.W. OGIER in Cambr.1883
OGIER, Thomas and J.P. Mahaffey owned the Cambridge NEWS in 1882 Changed name of paper to HERALD, publ for 28 years.
OGIER, Thomas had 479 acres in Spencer Twp., GCO 1840. CAUTION: MANY NAMED THOMAS, WILLIAM AND JOHN.
OGIER, William, b G, mar Judith FERBRACHE, qv, GCO 1819, chn.
OGIER, William, b 1821 GCO, son of Wm. OGIER, who came 1806. Wm. Jr. d 1897, mar Eliz. MAHAFFEY 1854, dau of ___Mahaffey and Margaret BLAMPIED, qv.
An OGIER desc in 1975 was Mrs. A.L. King of North of Cambridge, OH, said to be only desc of Wm. Ogier, bro of Thomas, who came in 1807
OGIER, some from G to CAL in the 1920s.
OGIER, Miriam, b Vrangue Manor, G, mar there 1921 Frank LE PATOUREL, qv. rem to West Grove, PA, where they raised Guernsey cattle. A dau Elizabeth mar J. Lewis Powell, 4 chn. See LE PATOUREL
OGIER, Lewis mar Susannah MARTIN 1783 in Charleston, SC (Skordas) Data gathered by compiler on this fam but not certainly from C.I. Poss Hug. with English connections. See more data in WRCIC.
OGIER, John b 1772 St. Sampson G, son of Peter of G, d 1821 Baltimore, MD, mar in G to Mary ___, b 1778, d 1852. (Louise Howard, Balt., MD) This fam said to originate in Caen, France.
A1. John Jr. b 1809 St. Sampson, G d 1880 Balt., mar there 1838 Jane Carruthers, his 3rd wife, b 1819 BALT., d there 1908.
B1. George Wash., b 1845 Balt., d 1917 Col.Spgs., COL. Mar 1873 Isabella Noble Bond, b 1849 d 1908.
C1. Herbert Leakin, b 1881 Balt., d 1973 St. Pete, FLA, mar at Balt. 1907 Elizabeth Raymond Ballard, 1883-1975.
D1. Louise Ballard Ogier Stansbury Howard, b 1912 Balt., MD.
C2. James Wallace, b before Herbert Leakin above.
OLIVER, surname of England and France, curr G and J.
OLIVER, Esther, b 1817 G, d 1888 poss in OH?, mar 1847 (his 2nd wife) William GLENN of PA, 1808-1898, son of John and Nancy Glenn.6 chn. (Ruth Wolfe, San Jose, CAL; Mrs. L.R. Myers, Fullerton, NEB)
A1. Emiline Glenn, b 1848 mar Wm. Long, d 1870
A2. Rachel Ann Glenn, b 1850 mar Louis Wilcox, d 1936
A3. Nancy Jane Glenn, b 1852 mar Friend Joshua Brown
A4. John Thomas Matson Glenn, mar Alice Howard, d 1938
A5. Adnarm Arthur Judson Glenn, mar 1. Mary ___, 4 chn, and 2. Kather= ine Stevenson, 3 chn. Arthur d 1938.
B1. Claud, twin, d.y. B2. Arthur twin? d.y.
B3. Charles M., mar and had several chn. B4. Mabel
B5. Gladys Mary Stevenson Glenn, b 1895 mar 1913 Richard Jepson,3 chn

C1. Richard Louis Jepson, b 1914 mar Lillian Oson, a ch d.y.
C2. Ralph Glenn Jepson C3. Marilyn Mae Jepson, b 1924
A6. Joseph Oliver Glenn, b 1859 d 1929
OLIVIER, old in J 1200, and in G 1300s. In Ald. 1671, curr G. In St. Heliers J 1668. See CIFHS #6. and Fosdick.
OLLIVIER, Peter James, mariner of G to US 1860 age 40, mar ___TORODE, qv, 3 chn. (Alyce Olliver Ryan, Maple Shade, NJ)
OQUENER, Ann, apprentice, from J 1772 to James Cresson of Phila.,PA. Her term was 7 years and the pay was 17 pounds. See also DE STE. CROIX, another apprentice to Phila. (RECORD OF INDENTURES, 1771-1773, by Gibson and Fisher, 1907, Lancaster, PA)
ORANGE, curr J, rare in America. In J 1296,1668,1749, and 1820.
ORNE. "I have material on the ORNE and LE FAVOR, LE FEVRE families of Jersey and Guernsey". (Mrs. Wm. Boyer, Pinellas Park, FLA, 1973, data not seen by compiler.
ORNE, one fam in MA ca 1700 thought to be from C.I. Poss Joshua, res in MRB with wife Elizabeth. See also LE CORNU. OUTC.
A1. Joshua, bp 1707/8 A3. John again A5. Caleb, b 1728
A2. John, b 1721, d.y.? A4. Benjamin, bp 1726
ORNE, see GALE and REVERE fams in MRB and Boston, more data available.
ORVIS, res in Bardwell, Suffolk Co., England 1616, no connection made. (HIST. OF ORVIS FAM IN AMERICA, by F.W. Orvis, 1922)
ORVIS. "In 1847 Wm. Orvis from Isle of Jersey, Capt. of brig RICHARD said the family originally came from Cornwall.". (Dellis Orvis Jr., Seneca, ILL) Research by Mr. Orvis shows there were a few of this surname in the C.I. in the 1700s and 1800s. Curr J.
ORVIS, George, seaman, b ca 1603, thought to have come from C.I. in 1638 to Boston, MA, mar Eliz. CARPENTER, widow of David, in Farmington, CT. (W.G. Orvis, Cardston, ALta, Canada; NEHGS Vol 50)
A1. Elizabeth, b 1644 A4. Samuel b 1653 A7. Ebenezer, b 1659
A2. David, b 1647 A5. Hannah, b 1655 A8. Margaret, b 1661
A3. Mary, b 1650 A6. Roger, b 1657 A9. Mary again, b 1663
ORVIS, Margaret, mar Wm. Goodrich 1706 in Litchfield, CT. (DEMINGS AND THEIR KIN, by Mary F. Tryon, Iowa Falls, IA, 1972
OSBORNE in J 1299,1400,1749. In G 1600s,curr G,J. SEE LATE ADDITIONS.
OSMOND, OSMENT, OSMONT, old in J and in G in1300s.
OUEN, Wm. served in the Rev. war from MA. (MASS SOLDIERS & SAILORS) St. Ouen is a parish in Jersey Island. OWEN curr G and J.
OXLAND, a British surname. OXLAND, Arthur Conrad, b or res Beaumont,J, mar there Phyllis Maud BRIARD, qv, dau of Ernest BRIARD, Capt. R.J.. of Bulwark House, St. Aubin J and of Maud Irene DE GRUCHY, his wife. Arthur settled in Acme near Calgary, ALTA 1912. A little more info. is in WRCIC. (Guy Dixon, Shropshire, England)
A1. Margaret Eleanor, mar C.J. Lawrence, 2 chn, and 2. Dr. R. RUE, son. Mar 3. J.G. Dunbar, a dau.
B1. Eleanor Mary Lawrence, mar Klaus Suborn B3. Robert R. Rue
B2. Robert Julian Lawrence B4. Elizabeth Maud Dunbar.
A2. Victor Conrad, mar Eleanor Evans, farmed the family place.
A3. Robert Guy, mar Arvis Harbour, 2 chn: Deborah Susan, Peter R.Oxland
OZANNE, old and curr, in Vale G 1821. See CIFHS #9, #14.
OZANNE, Palm Sunday, from Hosanna, "save us, we pray". OZANNE shield of G, purple crossed by a gold chevron lying between two gold fleurs -de-lis. On the chevron are 2 red crosses and a helmet. See WRCIC for a short article on trip to G 1952 by Carol Gray Norris.
OZIN, poss from OZANNE?, Thomas from G? fam, b 1746 in Bristol, ME.
OZANNE, Joseph, from St. Sampson G, settled in Westerly, RI, between March 1888 and Nov. 1889. In 1888 Joseph mar Ada PEARCE of St. Peter

Port, G. In RI, he had a variety of businesses, including a ferry service across the river which separates CT from RI, for transporting workers from Westerly to Pawcatuck, CT, to work in the Amer. Thread Co. Joseph was son of James OZANNE, who had a blacksmith in St. Sampson, G, and wife Elizabeth Mary FALLA, qv. They res in Vale parish, in a house named Brierton. The fam trade was ferrier-smith. 4 chn. (Adele Ozanne, Newtown, CT)

OZANNE, see also Q.A. IN CANADA by Turk.

OZANNE, Rev. James of the Great Mill of St. Martin G, b there 1797, d 1872 Somers, WI age 45. Said to have come to America with a shipload of 17 friends and relatives. He was a citizen by 1850, minister, miller and baker. Mar 1. Rachel Ann THOUME, b G, who d 1846, and 2. Mary CARRE, 1819-1906. Rev. James built a large windmill in WI, an octagonal structure 5 stories high, built of heavy hand-hewn timbers and beams. The wheel was made of wood and strips of iron, and the sails were of canvas. He imported the grinding stones from France, and shepherded their long journey across country to WI. (Stone; Ozanne; G.Soc. Bulletin, Spring 1973; Carol Gray Norris, Rapid City, MI; Commem. Bio. Record, Racine, WI; Mrs. Lynn Farnham, Kenosha, WI; Mrs. Thomas F. Smith, Coral Gables, FLA) CAUTION: TRIAL CHART.

A1. James Jr., M.D., b 1825 St. Martin G, poss at Les Blanches?, mar 1851 Maria Fedelia Kellogg.
B1. Rachel A., b 1858 Somers, WI d 1952 NYCity, mar 1884 Myron L. Norris, desc in MI?
B2. Walter Henry, b 1861 d 1888 B3. Gail Austin, 1864-1888
B4. Dr. Irving E., 1865-1945, mar 1903 Marjorie Beers, 4 chn
C1. Bryce K., b 1908 Neenah, WI mar 1935 Dorothy Jane Merten, 4 chn
D1. Judith Carol, b 1939 Chicago, mar 1. Lyon and 2. Santo Pullela
D2. Gerard, b 1941 mar 1965 Linda Ewert
D3. Jacqueline, b 1948 Moline, IL mar Gregory Wille
D4. Steven, b 1952 mar Linda Geisling
C2. Irving, b ?, unmar C3. Lucille, mar Charles Cassell
C4. Robert, b 1914 Neenah, Wi., mar 1938? Frances Barnett Webb
B5. Rev. Herbert Giles, b 1869 mar 1906 Charlotte Magill
B6. James THOUME, b 1863 or 1869? d 1952 WIS, mar 1880 Carrie Jane Barneslai, 2 chn: Roy/James? & Herbert G. who mar ?
A2. Peter, b 1827 d 1905 mar Mary Anne LE MESSURIER, b 1832 G, d 1916, dau of Abraham and Mary (LE PREVOST) LE MESSURIER, qv. Both bur Oakwood Cem., Somers, WI. Peter was town clerk 19 yrs.
B1. dau b 1852 d.y. B3. Lawrence E., b 1864, twin, mar M. Bradley
B2. Pierre Thoume, b ca 1858, unmar B4. Clarence F., 1864-1884, twin
B5. Rose A., b 1866 mar Fred L. Holmes, res South Haven, MI, 5 chn: Bertrand M, Harry R., Fred B., Beatrice R. & Mary L. Holmes.
B6. Charles H. 1870-1877
A3. John B. b 1829 G, bur 1844 Somers, WI A4. Rachel, d.y.
A5. Helena, b 1848 d 1916 Kenosha, WI, mar Hiram A. Hitler
A6. Alfred C., b 1850 G, d 1916, mar 1878 Estelle Hoypradt, 3 chn
B1. Edna, mar Phoenix, AZ Walter S. Wilson
B2. Philo H., b 1881 B3. Alfred Lloyd b 1893
A7. Emma, 1852-1935, unmar
A8. Edward Girard, b 1854 mar 1881 Ida Clemens, 1856-1895, and 2. Minnie Alice Grimshaw, who d 1960.
B1. Edward/Ward Clemons, b 1884 d 1960 mar 1908 Ida Nellie Reed
C1. Paul Reed, b 1908 mar 1. Lucille Rose MACHON?, div and mar 2.Ruth Salsbury, and 3. Mary ___, who later mar Wm. Richardson?
C2. Dalton Robert Reed, b 1912 mar 1938 Lois Marie Smith, 2 chn:

Robert James and Dennis John, of Pontiac, MI, both married.
C3. Ward Jr., b 1916 Racine, mar 1946 Elizabeth Rice, 2 chn
C4. Donald Earl, b 1919 mar 1943 Eldora Marquette, a son Marc
C5. Alice Mae, b 1922 mar Samuel Valeo. A dau Lynn Ida Valeo mar James Di Palma, and C.E. Farnham 2 chn: Michelle, David Di Palma.
B2. Mary Eliza, b 1889 d 1948, unmar

Ozanne, John Blanche, b 1844 St. Martin G, son of Joseph and Rachel (Wilson) Ozanne, rem to US 1859 with his uncle James OZANNE above. John res near Somers, WI, a farmer, mar Almeda Cobb 1875 in Kenosha, WI, dau of Josiah Irving Cobb and Lois Snow Bolton, 5 chn. John d 1919 Miami, FLA, his wife in 1925. See more data in LATE ADDITIONS AND CORRECTIONS. (Dorothy Dewing, Palo Alto, CAL)

OZANNE, Abraham, res Somers, WI, related to above fam. (ALBUM)
A1. Amelia, mar 1891 Emery D. Bush, b ca 1856, son of Levi Bush of WI.

OZANNE, ___, widow of Abraham, to WI 1847, d 1886 age 75. She mar 2. William Graham, who served in the Mexican War, ship carpenter, d ca age 79. See Graham.

OZARD, curr G.

OZARD, Mr. and Mrs. from G. Mr. Ozard d in WI? ca 1948, and Mrs. Ozard nee Julia MARQUIS, d in her 90s. 2 daus b Racine, WI.
A1. Mrs. Le Roy G. Thielen, Racine, WI
A2. Rita MARQUIS, mar George White, has chn.

OZIER, poss OGIER?, Sarah, mar John G. ROW 1833 MRB. OUTC.

OZIER, at least one fam from G to GCO often spelled their name OZIER.

OZIER, John, b 1826 G, son of Thomas and Rachel MARQUAND OZIER of G, mar in GCO Catherine Neelands, had son Charles, who d.y. He mar 2. Serepta BONNELL, dau of Mary SARCHET, qv. (Ohio RECORD)

OZIER, John, also OGIER, b 1809 G, mar Mary Ann SHERRARD, also b G. No Issue. See Nicholas PRIAULX and OGIER. (Williams)

OZOUF in J 1274, and curr in J.

PACK, not in lists of old C.I. surnames. PACKE curr G. Cf PASQUIOU.

PACK, Mary from G? was in GCO, middle 1800s. OUTC. (Conner-Eynon)

PACK, Harriet, b G? mar James WHERRY in GCO 1821. OUTC (Conner-Eynon)

PACK, John, from G? to UT 1852 via ship KENNEBEC. (SLC records)

PASQUET, pron. PACKETT, in J 1607, in St. Martin J 1668 and 1749. Note that this may be the orig. form of colonial PUCKETT, qv.

PACKETT, John of Casco, ME, d before 1640. (Noyes)

PAGE, see LE PAGE

PAGE, John in Salem, MA 1790 with fam of 7, from C.I.? OUTC. (Census)

PAIN, PAYNE in G 1300s. PAYNE in J 1293, means Pagan. PAYN in St. Martin, St. Saviour, Grouville, St. Ouen, St. Clement, St. Saviour and St. Peter J 1668, and 1749, also then in St. Mary J. Most PAINS in early New England may have been from England.

PAINE, Philip, formerly of J, was taxed for milldam in 1707-1712, res Newcastle, NH. Both Philip and John were taxed 1724/5. Mar Christian BALL?, BAAL?, who was rec'd at church 1709. 3 sons, daus also? Philip d 1746. (Noyes)
A1. John, bp 1710 A2. William, bp 1710 A3. Amos, bp 1710 to NY,3 sons

PAIN, Abigail, John and Jonathan were bp 1714 in Salem, MA. From J? (Essex Coll Vol 8)

PAINE, Rachel mar Thomas D. CROSS 1793 MRB, from J?

PAINE, Susanna of J, mar 1722/3 Abraham MOLLET/MULLEY of J? in MRB.

PAINE, Sarah of Glouc.,MA mar Jonathan MOULTON of Hampton, NH, 3 chn.

b 1711-1716. Moulton of Hampton, NH. (Noyes)

PAINE, Samuel, b ca 1663 England or C.I.? d Woodstock, CT. (Cem.Stone) Was he the ancestor of those below?

PAINE, Capt. Daniel mar 1729 (int) Leah SMITH of Barrington, CT, res Woodstock, CT, bur there. Leah d 1790 age 79. OUTC. A dau Sarah d 1757 age 25. Daniel d 1795 age 93.

PAINE, Capt. Amos, res Woodstock, CT, d 1790 age 53, mar Priscilla___. 3 chn d.y. OUTC.

PAINTER, surname of G. PAYNTER of Cornwall, England. See PAINTER in Vol V, Stillwell's MISCELLANY, and ALIENS in NY by Scott, Conway.

PALFREY, in J 1299. Note that several were bp in Salem, MA early.OUTC

PALLOT in J 1299. In St. Saviour, Grouville and St. Clement J 1668, and in Grouville and St. Saviour J 1749. Curr G and J. See CIFHS#9. PALLET in England 1797.

PALLOT, Francis from J? was sued for wages by Capt. Robert Taprill of the pink HOPEWELL 1676 in Portsmouth, NH. OUTC. (Noyes)

PALLOT, Jean, b 1755 J, mar Marguerite ESNOUF of J. Sealed as per Mormon belief to first husband Jean LE VAIN, and to 2nd husband Jean PALLOT, by desc. Waldo LE SUEUR of AZ.

PALLOT, Joseph and Jane res Hampton, NH? and Isles of Shoals? early. From J? (NEHGS Vol66) A son Nathaniel bp 1754 Hampton, NH.

PALLOT, Elizabeth G., from C.I. to UT 1851 via ship OLYMPUS. (SLC)

PALLOT, Mary A.E. from C.I. to UT via ship OLYMPUS. (SLC)

PALMER in J 1309, in G 1300s. Curr G and J, but also a surname of England and France.

PALMER, John of MRB, from J? assoc. with GALE, MERRIT, BUBIER and other C.I. fams. Mar Mary ___, 1652-1734. His heir was Christopher BUBIER in 1728. (DRIVER GEN)

A1. Capt. John administered the estate and d 1741.

A2. Margaret mar Christopher BUBIER, and 2. ___ANDREWS. Margaret bp 1701. See BUBIER.

B1. Joseph Bubier, b 1703/4 d,y.

B2. Christopher BUBIER PALMER, b 1706 d 1786.

PALMER, Thomas, b ca 1850 Braye Bay, ALD, mar Anne GALE, qv, of ALD, ca ca 1870. Rem from ALD to J, then to Alton, ONT; Toronto and Chatham, ONT; and Detroit, MI. Thomas d in Detroit 1884. 5 chn, 1 d.y. (Mildred Chase, Montague, MA)

A1. William, b ca 1872, res Detroit A2. Louise, b ONT, res Detroit.

A3. Ethel, b Toronto, ONt, res Detroit, mar Chase.

A4. Ann, res Detroit.

PAPE, Geo. of Saco, ME 1670. (Noyes) LE PAPE, Pope, old J surname.

PARMALEE, PARMALIN. This Hug. fam said to be from Bursins, near Gilly, Bursinel, Canton de Vaud, Switzerland. Poss in C.I. a short time. (NEHGS Vol 42)

PARCHER, see PERCHARD.

PARCQ, see DU PARCQ, and PARK.

PARELL, PERELL, cf DE LA PERELLE of C.I. Edward, John and Rachel mentioned in EARLY RECORDS OF HAMPSHIRE CO., VA, now WVA, by Clara Sage and Laura Jones, Balt., MD, 1976. OUTC. See PEARL.

PARRETT, see FALLE of Lansingburgh, NY.

PATOUREL, see LE PATOUREL and PATRILL

PATRIARCHE in St. Heliers J 1668 and 1749.

PATRIARCHE, Philip Charles, bro of Wm. Patriarche, d 1882 Burlington, ONT, b J.

PATRIARCHE, Elizabeth Rose, b ca 1842 J, dau of Wm. and Catherine,mar 1868 in C.of E., Toronto, ONT, Geo. H. Greene, 25, of Port Nelson, ONT, son of Rev. G. and Kate Jane Emma.

PATRIARCHE, William Heath, b 1840, The Grove, J, d Cincinnati, OH 1891, age 51. Bur St.Lukes Ang.Cem. Burlington. Mar 1866 Helen Matilda Racey of Milton, ONT, dau of Thomas Racey. Wm. had res in Detroit, MI 1866. (Wm. Britnell, Mississauga, ONT)
PATRIARCHE, William Philip, b J, d 1872, mar Catherine Elanor ___in ONT
PATRIARCHE, Charles, a witness at wedding of Eliz. above, a bro?
PATRILL, see LE PATOUREL
PATRILL, Joseph of G, settled in Ware, MA middle 1700s. He mar Esther ___, 10 chn. Joseph was in hot water often with the law, and suffered many of the tragedies of the poor of those times. He was put up for auction for 5 shillings a week, and his son at 2 shillings. Joseph served in Col. Israel Williams Regt. that went to the relief of Fort William Henry in 1757. In one of the army records the name is given as PATTORELL, and in another record, PATTOUREL. Joseph also served in the French and Indian Wars, and in the Rev. War from Dorchester, MA. The original farm is said to have been in Patrill Hollow in town of West Hardwick. (HIST. OF WARE,MA; Roberta Smith, Pepperell, MA; Christopher Lee, Huntington, NY)
A1. Thomas, b 1753 A4. Josiah, b 1759 A6. Sarah, b 1762
A2. Joseph, b 1754 A5. Ephraim, b 1759? A7.Esther, b 1765
A3. John, b 1756
A8. Isaac, b 1768 Ware, MA, mar there 1797 Sally CAREY, of G? who d 1822. Isaac mar 2.? Eveline ____, 8 chn.
B1. Isaac, b 1799, mar 1825 Sally/Sarah JOCELYN, dau of Abr. and Abigail JOSLYN, qv, Sally d 1870 age 78.
C1. Anna Maria b 1827
C2. Charles Augustine, b 1829 Ware, MA, served in Civil War, d Lowell MA, mar Sarah Enslin McIntyre, b 1828 Boston, d Lowell. 7 chn.
D1. Elbridge Winslow, b 1851 Enfield, MA, d Springfield, MA
D2. Mary Elizabeth, b 1854 Dorchester, MA, d Lowell, MA
D3. Otis, b 1856 d Granby, MA
D4. Cyrus Burnette, b 1860 Springfield, MA, d Otisville, NY
D5. Hattie Georgianna, b 1863 Chicopee, MA, d Fishkill, NY
D6. Oliver Lincoln, b 1866 Granby, MA, d Springfield, MA.
E1. Oliver Lincoln Jr., mar ___
F1. Oliver Lincoln III, 3 sons, 2 in Hartford, CT and Donald in NYCity.
D7. Eva May, b 1874 Palmer, MA, d Northboro, MA.
C3. Clarissa Brakenridge, b 1831 C4. Margaretta Brown, b 1834
B2. Sally, b 1800 B4. Barshiba, b 1804 B6. Eliza b 1808
B3. David, b 1801, d 1804 B5. Esther, b 1806 B7. Tirra Mallivan,b1812
B8. James Brackenridge, b 1814, mar 1836 Lovinia Bosworth, res Hardwick, MA? 8 chn.
C1. George Wilson, b ca 1842 mar Diana Barber of Ware, MA 1864, 1ch. He mar 2.? Lydia M?, who had Lewis W., b 1878. Poss mar 3. Louisa Bosworth before 1851?
D1. Effie G., b 1865 D2. Lewis W., b 1878 Other chn?
C2. Sophia M., b ca 1844, mar Albert Sturtevant 1866
C3. David H., b ca 1845, drowned 1848
C4. Ellen, b ca 1847 mar Augustus D. Blackmer or Blackman, ca 1867, d at Ware, MA 1878
C5. Hannah Julia, b 1849 C7. Charles Elmer, b 1854
C6. James Homer, b 1851 mar Rosina Tourtelotte 1878, b Hardwicke,MA. He mar 2. Grace (Law) Dougherty 1897, he at 46, dau of James and Louise Bosworth of Hardwick.
C8. Joseph Warren, b 1856, mar Emma A. Robinson of Barre, VT 1876.

B9. William Paige, b 1817 Ware, MA, d 1894 Springfield, MA, mar Etta/ Esther Hovey, b Charleston, SC or Erie, PA?, dau of John and Charlotte Hovey.

C1. Henry Ward Beecher Patrell, b 1875 Springfield, MA, theater Mgr? mar 1899 Windsor Locks, CT, Flora Mabel Abbott, b 1877 Springfield, d 1952 Perkinsville, VT, dau of John E. and Addie (Cook) Abbott of VT. Henry d 1918 Leominster, MA, bur Chester, VT.

D1. Fern Lilla b 1900 Chester, VT d 1977 Boston, MA, mar Harold E. Stokes, 1903-1971, son of Edw. and Ethel (Taylor) Stokes of Wilmington, MA.

E1. Roberta Joan Stokes, b 1929 Springfield, CT, res Pepperell,MA.

B10. Sophia Snell, b 1820

B11. Nathan R., b 1831, son of Isaac Patrell Jr. and Eveline___.

A9. Lois, b 1771 A10. Thomas, b 1774.

PATTEN, James. Census of 1850, Holmes Co., Richland Twp., OH, gives his birthplace as Jersey, also his son John's. However, this may have been New Jersey? Catherine Body, Bodie, his wife, was born in Germany 1802 and legend has it they were married in Germany. A James PATTEN was also in Wayne Co., PA 1830. (Donna Golightly, Dexter, IA) PATTEN is curr in G, and see also Q.A. IN CANADA for PETTEN, PATTEN of Nfld., thought to have come from C.I. (J.H. Bowes, Brockton, MA) PATTEN is also found in Essex, England and in the North of England, and in Scotland.

PAYNE, see PAINE. PAYN in Jersey a long time. Shield: argent, three trefoils slipped sable. See CIFHS #6.

PAYNE in MA 1790, at least 21 heads of fam of this surname, some in MRB

PAYN, Amos, mar 1800s? Lydia Clark, dau of Lydia Abbot, b Portsmouth, NH, and Ichabod Clark. (DESC OF GEORGE ABBOT OF ANDOVER, MA, 1906)

PAYN, John and Bethia had Stephen 1712/13 in Boston, from J?

PAYN, Frank, res Ashtabula, OH 1860. OUTC

PAYN, Joshua mar Constance PAIN 1737 in CT. (CT. MARRIAGES) From J?

PAYN, Peter mar Hannah COURSER 1696 Boston, MA. OUTC

PAYN, Wm. and Hannah had Elizabeth b 1710 Boston, MA. OUTC

PAYNE, Rachel mar Francis HUBBARD, HUBERT, qv, 1724, Boston, MA. OUTC.

PAYSANT, PAYSON, etc. "The PAYSANT family of Jersey, of Huguenot origin, who had moved from Normandy to Jersey after the Revocation of the Edict of Nantes in 1685." There are many desc. of this family in America, from the immigrant Louis who lived in J ca 1735 for about 13 years, and then rem to Nova Scotia, Canada. See Q.A. IN CANADA and THE PAYZANT AND ALLIED JESS AND JUHAN FAMILIES IN NORTH AMERICA by Marion M. Paysant, Wollaston, MA 1970.

PEARL, PERREL, PERILL, etc. This name is not definitely DE LA PERELLE OF THE C.I., research in Maryland might open some doors. DE LA PERELLE in J 1528, 1607. In St. John, St. Peter, St. Mary and St. Ouen J 1668, and in St. Ouen, St. John, St. Brelade and St. Peter J 1749. A Capt. De La Perrelle was a noted Jersey privateersman.

PEARL, PERREL, William, b ca 1800 Maryland? d 1863 Sparta, OH. He mar 1828 Nancy Doty, b 1807/8 Mt. Vernon, OH, d 1902 Fulton, OH, bur Sparta, OH, dau of Peter and Susannah M. (Boyle) Doty. 12 chn, mostly b Sparta, OH. (SOME OF THE DESC OF WILLIAM PEARL-PERREL AND NANCY DOTY, by Bernard Pearl, Richmond, MI) See book for much more info. (WRCIC)

PEARL, Benjamin mar Eliz. RICKER, b 1723, MA. Poss DE LA PERELLE?

PEDDLE. "Mariners and Marines, English and French Huguenots, some from South Somerset, England and the Isle of Jersey" to America 1600s on. Some said to be involved in very early ship building and cooperage in New England, Philadelphia and Newfoundland. (Thos.Peddle, Augusta,ME)

Despite research by Mr. Peddle, nothing concrete was located on the connection of this surname with the C.I. It is quite possible that the old J surname PETEL was an earlier form of PEDDLE.

PEDDLE, Anthony, a fisherman in Monhegan, ME 1672, from Nfld. or C.I.? (Noyes)

PEDDLE, George, with consent of his father Joseph, was apprenticed to Joseph MASTER, qv, of Phila., PA, a cooper in 1772. (EMIGRANTS TO PA, 1641-1819, Michael Tepper, Balt., 1975)

PEDRICK, noted in early New England. Has anyone considered PATRIARCHE for the original form of this surname? See PATRIARCHE.

PEDVIN, sometimes a corruption of old C.I. surname LE POIDEVIN.

PELLEY, PELLY, LE PELLEY. Some Channel Islanders of this surname rem to Nfld., Canada, and to US. A LE PELLEY was Lord of Sark Is. 1721.

PELLY, Capt of vessel HORTA, owned by George Forward 1847, of Nfld.

PELLEY, ___, Capt. of vessel CORSAIR in the seal fishery 1853, Nfld. (NEWFOUNDLANDER)

PELLEY, see LE PELLEY.

PELLIER, PELIER, in J 1700s. Cf Thomas PILLAR, who mar 1731 Elizabeth AMEE, qv, of Kittery, ME, dau of John and Sarah AMY, a C.I. fam? Note Note Daniel PELLIER on LE BOUTILLIER chart in WRCIC.

PELLIER, P. of J owned the JACOB HORTON, built in Bridgeport, US,1862, and the RESCUE, built Newburyport, MA 1860. (A.John Jean, Jersey)

PENDEXTER, see POINDEXTER. The PENDEXTERS of early New England are believed to be POINGDESTRES of J, there in 1309, in Grouville, St. Clement, St. Saviour, St. Peter, St. Heliers and St. John J 1668. In Grouville, St. Saviour, St. Heliers and St. John J 1749. In St. Lawrence J 1788. CAUTION: TRIAL CHART.

PENDEXTER, Edward, b ca 1682 Nfld., Jersey or Devon, mar Elizabeth Larrabee, bp No. Ch., Portsmouth, NH 1715, d 1771 age 81, dau of Thomas. (MAINE RECORDER; HIST. AND GEN. OF THE PENDEXTERS, by Ridlon; Stackpole; S.E. Pendexter, E. Orange, NJ; Noyes; Priscilla Gilbert, Indian Harbor Beach, FLA; Marge Reed, Huntington Beach, CAL; MORE OF EARLY CORNISH, by Leola Ellis of King St., Cornish, NH) See old PENDEXTER house in Dover, ME, owned by Mrs. O. Rolinson 1981.

A1. Henry, b early 1700s, parentage not firmly estab. Henry res Biddeford, ME 1727, mar 1727 Deborah Wellfeald, b 1702, dau of Eliab and Rachel (Sibley) Littlefield or Wellfield. In 1728 he bought land in Biddeford. May have come from Portsmouth or Newington, NH and "was of same family as the Pendexters in Bartlett" (Ridlon). He had a large fam, several sons married in Biddeford.

B1. Abiel, b 1729, d.y. B2. Mary, b 1730 mar Robt Cole 1750, of Bid?

B3. Henry, b 1732, mar 1755 Sarah SHEPARD, SHEPERD, settled on farm in Biddeford, where he res until 1774/5 when he sold his land and homestead for a parsonage to the Cong. parish, and rem to Francisborough, now Cornish, NH, with his sons and daus. D 1788. Was pioneer in Cornish, and it is said that he and his fam carried his household goods on hand sleds. He built a cabin on the stream that issues from Grafton's pond, more than a year before moving, made aclearing and planted corn, and "two of his sons lived there alone about 3 months while keeping the bears from the growing crop ...survived to a good old age to relate to desc. the adventures of their pioneer days. " (Ridlon)

C1. Henry, b 1758 mar Polly Watson, 6 chn.

D1. Daniel mar Mercy Weeks 1821 D4. Edmund mar Jane ___

D2. James, mar Sally Hammond D5. Jane mar Henry PENDEXTER 1833

D3. Henry, mar Clarissa Hammond D6. Oliver mar Robt.BRIER, 1832.

C2. Sarah, b 1760 mar James Miles 1782.

C3. Eliab, b 1761 mar Mary Thomas of Biddeford, b ca 1762, d 1846. Res Francisborough/Cornish, NH. Eliab d 1842, 11 chn.
D1. Eliab b ca 1784 entered Army during War of 1812 and d Burl., VT.
D2. Susan b ca 1786 mar Philip Severance
E1. Eliab Severence E2. James Severence E3. Darling Severence
D3. John b ca 1788 mar Sarah Stewart
D4. Lydia b 1785 d 1860, mar Stephen Day
D5. Oliver, b ca 1792 mar Eliza and/or Nancy Bidsford or Bickford. "While visiting the neighborhood where Henry Pendexter and his sons settled..entered a narrow valley...emerged upon a broad farm in the middle of which stood the base of an old-fashioned big chimney surrounded by scattered and decaying timbers from the frame of a dismantled dwelling...beneath the shadow of a great maple we found nine graves, slightly mounded still, only marked with one exception by low rough blocks of granite at the head and feet of those who reposed below. Here were buried Oliver Pendexter, his wife Nancy Bickford and a dau..silence and lonliness of the place were impressive."(Ridlon)
D6. Elder Samuel, b 1795, d 1869, mar Kathrine MORRELL, b ca 1794. Built a log house on the mountainside, some distance from the road, after his homestead burned down. He was a preacher of the Freewill Baptists. He d age 74, and widow in 1876. 6 chn.
E1. Reuben M., mar 1. Martha O. Poor and 2. Sarah Dow, settled ILL.
E2. Catherine, mar Cyrus B. MORRILL, res Cornish, NH, d 1883
E3. Mary, mar J.T. Pike of Cornish
E4. D.W., mar 1. LaDow of Iowa, 2. Eliza Grammond of Detroit, MI, res Ashton, SD, a teacher, lawyer and Judge.
E5. Elmira M., mar D.M. Parsons of Parsonsfield, ME. Elmira a teacher, b ca 1837.
E6. Rev. Samuel, b 1820 Cornish mar 1849 Ruth Wadsworth, dau of Charles and Sarah (Lewis) Wadsworth, b Hiram 1826, d 1875. Sam. mar 2. 1882 Sarah E. Bucknam, b Unadiller, NY 1824. She d 1890. He mar 3. 1893 Sarah E. Jepson, b 1841 Lanc. England, dau of Benj. B. and Alice HARDY. Rev. Samuel was Capt. of Militia,a preacher, selectman, assessor, overseer of the poor, etc. Taught 30 terms of school. Res Shapleigh, ME.
F1. Carrie W., b 1851 d 1873
F2. Charles W., b 1853 mar Mary Dooly of Montana, res BoiseCty, ID
F3. Marshall L. b 1856, d 1881 F4. Moriah? b 1858?
F5. Katie S., b 1858 mar T.S. Bachelder of Waterborough, d 1890
F6. Willis S., 1861-1884
F7. Addie M., b 1863 mar Frank S. NOWELL of Sanford, ME/ d 1886
F8. Lillie A., b 1867 mar Edward H. Emery of Sanfrod, res there.
D7. David, b ca 1797 D8. Sally, b ca 1799 mar Samuel Day
D9. Aurelia, b 1802 d 1835 D11. Mary or Hannah?, b ca 1806.
D10. Almira, b ca 1804 d 1891, mar Edmund Kennard, who d 1881, at 74.
C4. Paul, bp 1764 mar Hannah Whales, dau of John Whales, half-blood Indian, who came from Western Reserve, Ohio. He settled Cornish.
D1. Paul, mar Lydia Haley 1817. D3. William mar Elizabeth MORRILL
D2. Henry, mar 1. Hannah PENDEXTER and 2. Jane PENDEXTER, had issue.
D4. Nathan, b 1797 mar Charlotte MESSERVE, 1799-1882, dau of James and Jane (Mayfield) MESERVE. Nathan d 1872, bur Bridgton, ME.
E1. Joseph H., b 1820 E2. James, b 1824 E3. Harriott b 1829.
E4. William Edward, b 1831 Bridgton, ME mar Julia Onthank, 1831-1895 res Milford, MA. Wm. d 1906.
F1. Eugene Scotto, b 1858 Worcester, MA, mar Cora E. Green, 1861-1935 in 1883, res Portland, ME, d 1946, bur Milford, MA.

G1. Sidney Eugene, b 1885 Portland, mar Julia H. Muller, 1883-1964, res E. Orange, NJ, d 1962, bur Montclair, NJ.
H1. Sidney Eugene, b 1916 E. Orange, NJ mar Eleanor Jane Walter, 1918-1946, 3 chn: Nancy Jane, Robert E. and William Sands Scotto Pendexter.
E5. Nancy, b 1832 E6. Maria, b 1837 E7. Charles, b 1838
E8. Nathan Henry, b 1828? E9. Nathan, d.y.?
D5. Sarah, mar Theodore Stuart, and 2. John PENDEXTER.
C5. Thomas, b 1767, mar Catherine Whales and 2. Mary Sargent 1827. He d 1852, wife in 1868 age 79. Res Cornish and Durham, NH,12chn.
D1. Jonathan, mar Sarah Pendexter
E1. Levi W., d unmar at 44 E4. Noah W. d at New Orleans
E2. Catherine, mar Freedom Berry E5. Charles H. mar Abbie Rhodes
E3. William, d at sea
E6. Gilman B., mar Henrietta PAINE, worked in customs house at Portland, ME.
E7. Edmund W., marAlmira Downs.
D2. Henry mar Sarah Weeks 1830 D7. Annie, mar Ichabod Weeks 1815
D3. Thomas, d.y. D8. Ruth mar Ezra Miles 1824
D4. Thomas again, d in Mex. War. D9. Jerusha, mar Geo. Kennard 1830
D5. Eliza, mar Stephen Fenderson 1815 D10. Sarah
D6. Katherine, mar Nathaniel Parker 1816
D11. George J., b 1828 mar Clara B. Watson, teacher, 1854. She was b 1835. He manufactured clothing at E. Parsonsfield from 1858 to 1870, making uniforms for Union soldiers. 11 chn.
E1. Alma, b 1855 Limerick, ME, mar 1886 Charles H. Hayden at Manchester, MA 2 chn. Poet and teacher, res Haverhill, MA.
E2. Nellie, b 1858 E. Parsonsfield, ME mar C. Franklin DURELL, qv of Oxford, ME, 1882, d 1893 leaving husband and 1 ch.
E3. Bertha, b 1864 mar 1892 Henry Eldridge, res Rochester, NY, a son b 1894.
E4. Ralph, mar Rachel Stephenson of Bangor, ME 1893
E5. Carl, also Hugh, a doctor?, Thomas, J. Watson, Ralph W., Clare and Herman J.
D12. David, mar Eliza PENDEXTER, res Parsonsfield, ME.
C6. Anna, b 1769/79, mar 1792 Noah Weeks, son of Samuel. Noah b 1768 6 chn.
D1. Ichabod Weeks, b 1794 2 sons b Parsonsfield, James and Austin
D2. Henry, b 1797, mar ___PENDEXTER, 2 chn.
E1. Mercy B. Weeks PENDEXTER, mar Moses R. Brackett, res Saco, ME
E2. Edward P., mar Harriet PENDEXTER, res E. Parsonsfield, ME.
D3. Mary, mar David Johnson, and res Garland, ME
D4. James W., a Major, mar Sarah Frye of Limerick, ME, 8 chn. James a Repr. in Legis. 1833. In 1853 rem to MASS, then to MICH, d 1875 age ca 76. Two daus were wives of Isaac Brackett.
C7. Edmund, b 1770, mar 1794 Mary,dau of Daniel Field of Hollis, ME, 1794 and res Cornish, NH where his chn were born.
D1. Noah, mar Judith ALLEY
D2. Oliver, mar Clarissa Johnson, res Naples, Glenburn and Fryeburg, ME.
E1.Almond Rich b 1850 E2. Sumner David, b 1852
E3. George Elliott, b 1855 Fryeburg, ME, d 1939, bur Mapleton, ME. Mar 1880 Mary Ann Judkins, b 1862 Ornville, ME, d 1949, Presque Isle, ME, dau of Andrew and Dolly (Rollins) Judkins, 6 chn. (SLCity records)
F1. Lillian Bell, b 1881 Chapman, ME mar 1901 Geo. McKelvey
F2. George Oliver, b 1882 mar 1903 Sarah Briggs.

F3. Maude May, b 1884 Villard, MN d 1921, mar 1907 Charles Burtt.
F4. Gladys Evelyn, b 1886 Chapman, ME, d 1941, mar E.L. Spinney
F5. Dolly Clarissa, b 1889 mar 1909 Charles Day.
F6. Andrew Judson or Judkins?, b 1894 mar 1935 Chrystal McPherson
E4. Horace b 1860 E5. others?
D3. Annie, mar Henry PENDEXTER, res 1894 with son Edmund in Cornish
D4. Sibbley mar Abigail Johnson D6. Sarah mar Jonathan PENDEXTER
D5. Rachel mar Matthias Ridlon of Sweden, ME.
C8. Hannah, b ca 1771/2 mar George Allard C10. Rachel, bp 1775, mar Nathaniel Day.
C9. Mary/Molly, bp 1774 mar John Kennard
B4. Deborah?, b 1733/4, mar 1759 Samuel Whitten, Biddeford, ME.
B5. Hannah, b 1735, mar 1765 David Sawyer Jr. of Saco, ME, b 1744 Scarboro, ME, d Saco, ME.
C1. Hannah Sawyer, b 1767 d 1843 Saco, ME, mar 1780/81 Daniel Patterson, who d 1817 Saco, ME. (Marge Reed, Huntington Beach, CAL)
D1. Daniel Patterson, b 1782 mar Hannah ___, b 1780, d 1826
E1. Fidelia, b 1811 mar George Whitten 1828 E4. Eliz., 1816-1819
E2. Charles, 1812-1828 E5. Daniel, b 1818
E3. George, b 1815, drowned 1828 E6. Mark, b 1820
D2. Olive Patterson b 1784 D3. David Patterson 1786-1800
D4. Hepzibah Patterson, b 1788
D5. Nathaniel Patterson, b 1790 mar Jane Coates 1814, b 1786, 4 chn.
E1. Seth Patterson, b 1815 E3. Nathaniel Patterson, b 1820
E2. Eliza J. Patterson, b 1817 E4. John Patterson, b 1823
D6. Richard Patterson, b 1792 mar Mehitable ___, b 1801, 4 chn
E1. Solomon G. Patterson, b 1815 E3. Abigail Patterson, b 1818
E2. Harriet G. Patterson, b 1816 E4. Edward Patterson, b 1820
D7. Nahum Patterson, b 1796 Saco, ME, d there 1870, mar 1. before 1828 Dorcas Frost, who d 1832. 2 chn. He mar 2. 1833 Mary Batchelder, widow, b 1800 ME, d 1890 Saco, ME, 4 chn.
E1. Moses F. Patterson, 1828-1833
E2. John R. Patterson, b 1830 mar Margaret Jones
E3. David F. Patterson, b 1834 d 1838
E4. Dorcas F. Patterson, b 1835, mar Obed F. Bickford
E5. Thomas D. Patterson, b 1837 mar Sarah E. Bean, b 1837 Brownfield, ME d 1919 Saco, ME, 7 chn b Saco.
F1. Mary Etta Patterson, b 1856/7 mar 1. ___Lumb, and 2. __Staples
F2. Nathan Willie Patterson, b 1860 F4. Dorcas A. b 1870 mar Ladd.
F3. Charles T. Patterson, b 1865 F5. Herbert A. b 1872
F6. George A. Patterson, b 1876/7 Saco, ME d 1966 Biddeford, mar 1904 Fannie C. Merrill, b 1885/6, d 1912.
G1. Leslie D. Patterson, b 1905 mar Lillian Labonte, d 1977
G2. Alton Patterson, b 1907, d.y.
G3. Millard G. Patterson, b 1909 Saco, ME, mar Marian Brown, b 1909 Saco, res Vista, CAL, 1 ch.
H1. Marjorie Ellen Patterson, b 1935 Biddeford, mar 1953 Bruce Reed, b 1931 Springvale, ME, res Hunt.Beach, CAL, 2 chn: Steven and Lynne Reed Campbell
F7. Maurice E. Patterson, b 1878 d 1881
E6. Alonzo Patterson, b 1839 mar Annie E. Hunter
D8. Edmund Patterson, b 1796, twin to Nahum above.
D9. John Patterson, b 1799 D12. Hanah again, b 1808
D10. David Patterson, b 1802 D13. Elizabeth, b 1810
D11. Hannah Patterson, b 1805 d 1806.
C2. Betty Sawyer, b 1769 mar Richard Berry, Jr.
C3. David Sawyer, b 1771 mar Olive ___.
C4. Sarah Sawyer, b 1774 mar J. Webster

B5. Rachel b 1736 mar Benj. Proctor?
B6. Paul, b 1737, mar Hannah Murch/March 1760
B7. ? B8. Thankful Relief b 1742 mar Wm. Murch/March 1765, Biddeford.
B9. Sibbley, b 1744, mar Mary Joy in Biddeford 1766, or May Joy?
B10. Bathsheba/Barsheba, b 1746 mar 1765 Moses Stevens.
B11. Stephen, b ca 1750, mar Hannah Curtis of Biddeford, ME 1797, at least 2 chn: Mary b 1798 and Rhoda b 1801.
A2. Elizabeth, bp 1715, d unmar
A3. Margaret, bp also in 1715, mar 1729 Geo. SEWARD of Portsmouth, NH. He d ca 1759, 3 sons. Seward a boat builder, poss of J fam?
A4. Mary, bp 1715 also, mar 1738 Richard Tibbetts.
A5. Philip, b 1719-20, bur from St. John's CH, Portsmouth 1799,4? chn.
A6. John, shipwright, bp 1719/20, mar 1738 Alice Miller, dau of Joseph, living in 1765, 6 or more chn.
A7. Alice?, bp 1715? A8. Edward, mar and had 3 or more chn.
PENDEXTER below is undoubtedly part of the other PENDEXTER fam. (Noyes; Ridlon; Stackpole)
PENDEXTER, John, b 1752, mar 1774 Martha Jackson, 1753-1846. He d1835. These two were among the early settlers of Lower Bartlett, NH. Came from Portsmouth, NH in winter of 1775/6. "It has been said that she rode through the woods on an old horse with a featherbed under her for a saddle, and a child in her arms." They built a large house now known as the PENDEXTER MANSION. John held several munic.offices was a carpenter by trade.
A1. Alice, b 1776 mar 1797 Col. Jonathan MESERVE, qv, d 1872
A2. Nancy, b 1778 d unmar 1798 A3. Sally, b 1780 mar Benj. Pitman
A4. Susanna, b 1782 mar Stephen Rodgers, d 1828
A5. John, b 1784 mar Susan Eastman 1806 and d 1840. Susan b 1786, d 1844, dau of Noah and Hannah (Holt) Eastman.
B1. George, b 1808 mar 1839 Ursula, dau of Sam. Cushman of New Glouc., and settled there. He d 1882, wife b New Clouc. 1815.
C1. John, b 1840 Bartlett, NH, d 1841
C2. Sarah Amelia, b 1841 mar 1865 C.W. Dunn of Poland, ME, several daughters.
C3. John Cushman, b 1843 Bartlett, NH mar 1868 Rosa A. Witham, had daus Lillie and Edith.
C4. Rev. Merritt Caldwell, b 1846 mar 1874 Rebecca W. Strout of Poland, ME.
D1. Ursula E., b 1877 Naples, ME D2. Merritt T., b 1882 Cape.Eliz.
C5. George E., b 1848 New Cloucester, unmar
C6. Charles Henry, b 1850 mar 1878 Mary W. La Monde of New York, and d there 1894. Charles was a Judge in NY.
D1. George W., b Auburn, ME, res NYork. D2. Hessie L.
C7. Mary Ella, b 1853 mar J.W. Cole of NY, 1877, d there 1878.
B2. Alice M., b 1812, mar Rev. Henty Butler, who d in ME 1850 age 43. Alice d in Minneapolis, MN 1880 age 68, had large fam.
B3. Hannah E., b 1814, mar Rev. Thomas Hillman. She d at Mechanic Falls 1886, 2 chn.
B4. Susan, b 1816, mar Dr. J.S. Farnum of Brockton, MA
B5. Amelia A., b 1819, mar Haskett D. Eastman of Conway, NH 1844. He was b 1818, rem to Minn. in 1871 where he d. One son.
B6. Daniel E., b 1822, mar Harriot O. Cushman, Daniel the prop. of the Pequawket house in Conway, NH, large family.
B7. Benjamin, b 1824 mar Esther P. Dinsmore, res Mechanic Falls, ME, a son Frank.
B8. Lydia P., b 1827 mar Samuel Shackford of Conway, NH 1848.
A6. Joseph, b 1786 mar Lydia Dinsmore, and d 1855. His wife d 1880 in

Dover, NH.
B1. Solomon D., b 1813 mar his cousin Mary D. MESERVE 1838, and d1868. Kept a summer boarding house in Bartlett.
B2. Eliza D., b 1817 mar Cyrus A. Tasker 1850, owners of FairviewHse.
B3. Martha J., b 1819 d unmar 1886 B6. Mary D. mar Hazen Pitman
B4. Nancy, mar George P. Stilphen 1837 B7. Abigail mar James C.Willey
B5. John, b 1822 mar Malinda Chase, b 1840 Fryburg, prop. of Langdon House, Intervale, NH.
B8. Augusta, b 1834, d unmar 1860
A7. Betsey, b 1789 mar Daniel MESERVE 1804, d 1880.
A8. George, 1790-1797 A9. Martha, b 1792, mar William Stilphen
A10. Samuel b 1794 mar Lydia T., dau of Silas MESERVE and d 1883. She was b 1800 and d 1868.
B1. Silas M., b 1819, mar Lydia D. Hale 1850, d 1883
B2. Betsey M., b 1822 d unmar 1864
B3. Charles C., b 1828 mar Caroline P. Gale 1866, d 1881. He was prop of the PENDEXTER MANSION.
PENDEXTER, see MESSERVY.
PENDEXTER, Almira, b ca 1809 res Cornish, ME 1860, lived with a SMITH family.
A1. Elizabeth b ca 1829 mar Samuel SMITH, b ca 1829
B1. Daniel Smith, b ca 1850
PENDEXTER, Charles, b ca 1840, was 46 in 1886, res Parsonsfield, ME, had wife Julia A., 40 in 1886, and chn. (HIST. OF PARSONSFIELD)
A1. Mary E., b ca 1864 A3. Lizzie C., b ca 1872
A2. Anna M., b ca 1868 A4. Laura N., b ca 1878
PENDEXTER, Charles b ca 1799 Suffolk, MA mar Susan Tilson, b 1803, dau of John and Susan (SIMONDS) Tilson, 6 chn b CHelsea, MA. (SLCITY)
A1. Maria T., b 1837 Chelsea A4. Eliza C., b 1843
A2. France E., b 1840 A5. Charles b 1845
A3. Susan M., b 1841 A6. Kate, b 1848, d.y.?
PENDEXTER, Edward, b 1778 Durham, NH, mar 1803 Mary/Polly Joy, b 1784 dau of Jacob and Hannah (Cram) Joy(SLC records;HIST OF HINGHAM)
A1. Hannah C., b 1803 Durham, NH mar 1826 Stephen P. Chesley
A2. Jacob Joy, b 1803 d 1870, mar MaryT. Fernald
A3. Edward, b 1805, d 1884, mar 1840 Martha C. Stickney
A4. George W., b 1807, d 1890, mar 1. 1836 Ruth C. HAWKES
A5. Martha, b 1809 d 1835
A6. James Monroe b 1815, d 1881 mar 1850 Mary MESERVE, qv.
PENDEXTER, Henry mar Nancy MESERVE, res Bridgeton, ME?
A1. Albron, b 1843 A3. George H. b 1846 A4. Ida Ella, b 1852
A2. Almira, b 1844 A4. Simeon, b 1849
PENDEXTER, Henry mar Jane ___
A1. Hannah, b 1832 Cumberland, ME. A2. Olive Jane b 1834
A3. Nancy H. b 1838
PENDEXTER, Mary, b ca 1800, mar Samuel Nason in Biddeford, ME. (Priscilla Gilbert, Indian Harbor Beach, FLA)
A1. John Nason, b 1826 Biddeford, mar Isabel Swan, b 1839 Halifax,NS.
B1. Albert Nason, b 1858
B2. Mary Elizabeth Nason, b 1863 mar Charles Sumner Carle, b 1859, son of Henry S. Carle and Miranda Hill. Mar 1881 res Portland,ME.
C1. Minnie Alberta Carle, b 1885 d 1961 Kennebunk, ME mar 1907 Wallace R. Record, 1879-1951.
D1. Gladys Ruth Record, b 1910 Saco, ME mar Douglas Irving Pate 1931, b 1909 Saco, son of Thomas and Edith(Allen)Pate.
E1. Priscilla Louise Pate b 1936 mar 1953 Allen Roland Gilbert.

RESEARCHER: See the many PENDEXTERS in NH, ME and MA records, and in the census of 1790. Some records in WRCIC.
PENDEXTER, Drusilla B., mar Wm. B. Glidden of Tuftonborough, NH 1833 in Dover First Ch.
PENDEXTER, Edward, acting ensign, 1862-1865, USN, Callahan List.
PENDEXTER, Edward mar Eliz. Larrabee, b 1690, dau of Thomas, had chn.
PENDEXTER, Elizabeth from J in Machias, ME 1668. (Noyes)
PENDEXTER, George mar in Dover, NH 1808 Nabby Titcomb of Dover,ME.
PENDEXTER Hannah of Francisboro, NH mar Geo. PERRY in Biddeford, ME1785
PENDEXTER, Hannah C. mar Stephen P. Chesley in Madbury, NH 1826
PENDEXTER, Hannah mar Peter SMITH of Wiscasset 1809.
PINDEXTER, Hannah mar Benj. Hichbourne 1801 in Boston, MA.
PENDEXTER, Henry in New England 1666. (Underhill)
PENDEXTER, Henry b ca 1805 mar Sarah ___, b ca 1807, res Cornish, SON.
PENDEXTER, Isaac from St. Heliers J, mariner on a J ship in Newcastle, ME 1698, age 34. (Noyes)
PENDEXTER, James, bro of Job, mar Jane, a sister of Lydia A. MESERVE, who mar Job. PENDEXTER. Lydia b ca 1830 and Jane, were daus of Eben and Elizabeth (Lombard) MESERVE.
PENDEXTER, John M., b ca 1831 res Cornish, ME 1860 with wife Sarah J. and chn. Sarah b ca 1833.
A1. Catherine, b ca 1855 A2. Elvira, b ca 1856 A3. John S., b ca 1869.
PENDEXTER, John mar Sarah MARTYN 1768 Portsmouth, NH (NEHGS Vol 82)
PENDEXTER, Joseph had wife Lydia who d 1880 age 85.
PENDEXTER, Joseph of Cornish, NH mar Hannah J. Cole in Freedom, NH 1858 (1860 census)
A1. Frederick, b 1859 A2. Sarah, b 1860.
PENDEXTER, Lucy poss mar (his 1st wife) Geo. Richardson, b 1763, said to be first white ch b on Mt. Desert Island. (Mt. DESERT, Eben Hamor)
PENDEXTER, Margaret J. mar Richard Kimball 1832 Dover, NH.
PENDEXTER, Mary b ca 1772 res Cornish ME 1860.
A1. Jonathan, b ca 1805 mar Sarah ___. Other chn?
B1. Levi b ca 1826 B2. Edmond, b ca 1846
PENDEXTER, Mary mar 1738 Richard Tibbetts, joiner, son of Henry of Dover, ME and his second wife was Mary Akerman Sampson. (Noyes)
PENDEXTER, Molly mar Jeremiah Goodrich 1786.
PENDEXTER, Samuel mar Lydia Thompson, dau of ___Thompson & Harriet MESERVE.
PENDEXTER, Samuel mar Mary ___, res Boston, MA.
A1. Alexander, b 1779 Boston A2. Mary, b 1785 Boston
PENNELL, PINNELL, PINEL. PINEL in J since ca 1172, in St. John J 1668 and in St. Peter J 1749, in St. Laurens J 1788. "The first PINELS were armourers, makers of high grade armour and coats of mail for the knights of the Crusades." (British Nat. Museum, London, Eng) Some settled in Wales in the Middle Ages. F. Edward Pinnell, of West Ealing of London, England, has gathered a great deal of information on the family. Some PINELS came from Normandy with William the Conqueror in 1066. PINELS appered in very early times in Alsace-Lorraine, and their shield was at the Battle of Poitiers, France in 732, when Charles MARTEL overthrew the Saracens. At least 52 different spellings. Some Pinells are still working in metal, such as PINNELL WIRE PRODUCTS co. of Dallas,TX, in recent times. PINELS are related distantly to the Prince of Monaco, through a marriage of 1-15. (Royal Family Society)
PINELS, PENNELS, PINNELS came from Jersey, Cornwall and Devon to New England, poss also from Wales. Therefore, CAUTION: TRIAL CHARTS.

Since researchers vary in their beliefs as to origin of certain of these families, when using this information go back to the sources. Compiler is not absolutely sure that all of these fams came from the Channel Islands. More data in WRCIC and in records of sourcepersons. (Maine Hist. Soc. Library; Nova Scotia Archives; Libby Logan, Dennison, TX; Bolton; Wheeler; Noyes; PENNELL FAM GEN. by C.P. Phinney; ARMORIAL OF JERSEY; NEHGS Vol 17; PENNELL FAM BULLETINS; Ridlon; Essex Coll; STINCHFIELD FAM by Roger Stinchfield; PENNELL FAM IN BRUNSWICK, ME, MHS, 1916, Portland, ME; Freeman Morgan, Takoma Park, MD; Rev. Charles Sinnett MS; Kenneth Creed, St. Petersburg, FLA; MESSERVE GEN; NEHGS Vols 5,14,17,24,31,63)

PINEL, Philip, mar in J Anne LE MONTAIS, qv, who soon died after two sons were born. He mar 2. Marie LE HARDY, who gave him 2 daus, Marie and Rachel. The sons, Thomas and Clement came to New England, but the daus, so far as is known, stayed in J. The names Thomas and Clement are fairly common among C.I. fams, and other Thomases and other Clements named PENNEL and PINEL apparently arrived in New England. Therefore great care must be taken in crediting persons to their correct groups. CAUTION: TRIAL CHARTS

A1. Clement PENNELL, b 1682 J, prob arrived in Glouc. MA before 1710 with his bro Thomas.

A2. Thomas, b 1684 J, res Gloucester, MA, mar 1. Sarah Cheisemore/Chisholm, b 1694 Newbury, MA, dau of Daniel and Cyprian (Sampson) Chismore. He mar 2. her cousin, Sarah DUREN/DURELL, qv, dau of Moses and Sarah (SAMPSON) DURELL. By second wife poss 3 chn recorded at Glouc., including another Thomas of Biddeford, and Rachel Clay of Biddeford and Buxton (Libby)

B1. Thomas, b ca 1716/7 Gloucester, d ca 1770 Brunswick, ME, mar 1735 Rachel Riggs, b 1717, 3 chn.

C1. John, b 1736 mar Mrs. Harriet Graham, who d 1833. John d ca1820, res Maine. 8 chn.

D1. Hannah, b 1763 d 1840 mar 1781 William Spear Jr, b 1763 Brunswick, ME, rem to New Portland, ME. Wm. 1758-1862, 6 chn.

E1. Betsy Spear, 1790-1829 E4. Mary Spear, 1796-?

E2. Hannah Spear, 1792-1846 E5. James Spear, 1800-1858

E3. Jane Spear, 1794-1838 E6. Sarah Spear, 1804-1849

D2. Mary, b 1767 mar Wm. Mitchell of Harpswell, ME, 3 chn

E1. Hannah Mitchell, no issue

E2. Mehitable Mitchell E3. Mary Mitchell

D3. Lucy, b 1770 mar 1791 Capt. Jesse Holbrook of Harpswell, ME

E1. Abizer Holbrook, b 1792 E4. George Holbrook

E2. John Holbrook, b 1795 had dau who d early, no issue

E3. Jesse Holbrook, b 1797, went North, not traced

D4. John, b 1772, d.y.

D5. Mehitable, b 1775, d 1849 bur Brunswick, ME. Mar 1796 Samuel Ross, 1773-1828, 7 chn

E1. Lucy Ross, 1798-1850 E5. Paulina Ross, 1808-1861

E2. Martha Ross, 1800-1879 E6. Rachel Ross, 1810-1857, unmar

E3. Mary Ross, 1803-1880 plus E7. Samuel Ross, 1816-1873

E4. Barton Ross, 1805-1851

D6. Janet, b 1779, d 1849 mar 1802 John Burk of Lisbon, ME. and 2. Geo. Leavitt, 1786-1842. One ch by 1st, and 7 by 2nd husband.

E1. Barton Burk, res Small Point ME, a dau

E2. Moses Leavitt, b 1810, d 1883, res Great Island ME, mar 1831 his cousin Nancy Leavitt, who d 1875 age ca 63.

E3. William Leavitt, b 1814, twin of Abigail?

E4. Abigail Leavitt, b 1814 d 1838, unmar

E5. John P. b 1818 mar Susan Fisher Preble. See Sinnett papers for more Preble info.
E6. Alice Leavitt, b 1820 mar Abizer York of Brunswick, ME.
E7. Mary Jane Leavitt, b 1824, d 1873 mar Daniel Jones of Lisbon,ME
E8. George Leavitt, b 1832
D7. Margaret Pierpoint, b 1782 d 1827 China, ME mar 1807 Henry CAREY of Brunswick, ME, tailor who came from Hyde Co., NC.
E1. Henry Clark Carey, b 1808 res China, ME
E2. Mary E. Carey, b 1810 d 1870 E3. Dummer Carey, b 1814, d.y.
E4. Joseph Eborn Carey, b1817 China, ME
E5. Hannah P. Carey, 1819-1865 E6. Mary Jane Carey, 1822-1827
C2. Thomas Pennell Jr., b 1739 d 1912 Brunswick, ME age 74, mar Alice Anderson of Freeport, ME. 10 chn.
C3. William, b 1741, lost at sea as a young man, unmar.
C4. Lucy, b 1742, d 1786, mar 1761 William Cotton Jr. of Falmouth, ME who came from Londonderry, NH. Later res New Meadows, Brunswick, ME. He had 2 other wives. He was b 1736 Portsmouth, NH, and mar 2. Joanna Ferrin. 10 chn by Lucy. (NEHGS Vol 58)
D1. Thomas Cotton, b 1762 d 1840, farmer at Pownal, ME, 7 chn
D2. Lucy Cotton, b 1764 mar Nehemiah Allen, res New Gloucester,ME.
D3. William Cotton b 1766 d 1841, 9 chn
D4. Sarah Cotton, b 1768 mar Seth or John Finney/Phinney of Bowdoin, ME, res Lisbon, ME, 4 chn.
D5. Jeremiah Cotton, b 1770, his wife was from Boston, 3 chn.
D6. Martha Cotton, b ca 1772, mar David Flagg, brickmaker of Topsham
D7. Rachel Cotton, b ca 1775, d unmar
D8. John Cotton, 1777-1797, at sea, unmar
D9. Comfort Cotton, b 1779, mar Jotham Chick, no issue.
D10. Rachel again, d.y.
C5. Rachel, b 1745, d 1770/1777, mar 1764 Capt. Joshua Boynton,1 ch.
D1. Theophilus Boynton, b 1764 d 1793 mar Hannah Plummer, who d 1794, age 27, dau of Moses and Esther Plummer.
E1. Harriet Boynton, b 1790 d Boston 1849, mar Benj. Hudson, broker.
C6. Matthew, b 1748 d 1817, caulker, d Portland, ME, mar 1778 Nancy Tukey, see TOCQUE and TUCK. Matthew mar 2. ___Sweetsire, who d ca 1825. CAUTION: Other Matthews of this fam group 1740s in ME &NH.
D1. John, b 1779 d 1854, mar ___, 9 chn
D2. Frances D5. Alice, bp 1783 d before 1803
D3. Nancy, 1780-1812 D6. Josiah, b 1788 d 1794?
D4. Betsy, 1782-1854 D7. Josiah, mar and had 8 chn, d 1866.
C7. Stephen, b 1752 Falmouth, ME d 1822. Mar 1778 Mary Cotton, dau of Thomas and Agnes (Smith) Hinckley Cotton.
D1. Apphia, b 1779 Topsham, ME d 1853 Bowdoin, ME mar 1802 A. Wilson
D2. Joshua, b 1782 d 1861 Machias, ME, mar 1809 Mary E. Edgecombe.
E1. Stephen, b 1811 mar 1836 Mary C. Dinsmore
E2. Aaron Edgecombe, b 1813 Bowdoin, ME d 1847 Machias mar 1834 Arethusa B. Whitney, dau of Ephraim and Mary (Crocker) Whitney.
F1. Isaac E. b 1835 Machias, d 1918 Whitneyville, ME, mar ca 1858 Rebecca Olive DREW, qv, 7 chn. She was dau of Stephen Otis Johnson and Abigail (Getchell) DREW. Isaac a blacksmith and mechanic.
G1. Andrew Foster, b 1861 Whitneyville, ME G3. Edgar O., b 1866
G2. Laura A., b 1863 mar _______ McEachern
G4. Abbie Z., b 1871 ME mar Isaac PENNELL.
H1. Charles M., b 1887 ME, d there 1912
H2. Athelena, b 1889 d 1973 Machias, ME mar Irving FairfaxHarmon
I1. Irving Jr, b 1922 mar Mary PENNELL

I2. Frances Elizabeth Harmon b 1931 mar Carl Vane
H3. Frances Maria PENNELL b 1893 d 1933 Phila., PA, mar1917 Kenneth Everett Creed, son of Joseph C. and Annie L.(Blake) Creed.
I1. Kenneth E. Creed Jr, b 1921 Needham, MA, mar 1943 Margaret Eaton Nyce, b 1921 dau of Robert J. and Flora G.(Stevens) Nyce. 3 chn
J1. Kenneth E. III, b 1949 Charleston, WVA, mar Nancy Gould
J2. Robert J. Creed, b 1951 mar Debra L. Hannah, div
J3. Douglas Blake Creed, b 1954 Bartow, FLA
H4. Anna Katherine, b 1896 Whitneyville, ME d 1980 Lincoln,NC, mar Charles A. Mitchell.
I1. Frances Eliz. Mitchell, b 1926, mar 1946 Horace B. Dellinger, a son Paul Wayne Dellinger b 1948 Boston.
H5. George S., b 1898
G5. Leverett J., b 1874 d 1910 Whitneyville, ME
G6. Frank Michael, b 1876 d ca 1933 mar 1907 Zella B. Albee
G7. Ernest N., b 1882 d ca 1967
F2. Hannah Penniman, b 1836 mar 1857 Asa Kingman Smith
F3. Laura Agnes, b 1838 mar1857 Caleb Smith
F4. William Henry, b 1842 mar 1864 Sarah Wilder
F5. Edgar Oscar, b 1843 mar 1874 Mary Miller
F6. Charles Whails, b 1844 d 1864, in Civil War?
E3. William Eaton, b 1814 d 1868 Machias, ME, mar 1841 Sarah Kelly.
E4. Mary Eliz., b 1823, d 1877 mar 1841 Samuel Longfellow.
E5. Charles Jameson, b 1826 mar 1850 Martha U. Whitney
E6. Sarah Brown, b 1829 d 1863 mar 1848 Shepard M. Ingersoll.
E7. Emeline Hall, b 1838 mar 1863 Charles L. Stratton
D4. Agnes, b 1787 Topsham, ME d 1873 mar Nathaniel Plummer
D5. Thomas Jefferson, b 1790 d 1845 New Portland, ME, mar Rhoda Mellet. Cf MALETT, MALLETT.
D6. Rachel, b 1794 d 1848, mar Isaac Purrington
D7. Hannah, b 1797 d 1858, mar Benj. Thompson
D8. Sarah, b 1800, d 1884 Machias, ME, mar 1820 William Brown.
C8. Sarah, b 1755 mar 1775 Isaac Hinkley of Brunswick, ME b 1751. Or Aaron Hinkley? Desc of this fam.
C9. Hannah, b 1757 Falmouth, d 1825 Lisbon, ME, mar 1776 Thomas Ham of Bowdoin, ME. and 2. ca 1823 widower James Merryman, no issue
C10. Affia Coombs, b 1763 mar David Given or Giffen? 8 chn
C11. Jacob, not traced.
B2. Clement, b ca 1723, d at Stroudwater, ME before 1781, was at Falmouth, ME 1741, a shipwright. Mar 1742 Ruth Riggs, b 1723 Glouc., MA, dau of Jeremiah and Rachel (Haskell) Riggs. She d 1781. More on this family.
C1. Jeremiah, b 1742 d ca 1800, mar 1. ___Gould, and 2. Priscilla Thompson of NH, d Mayfield, ME.
D1. Samuel Gould, b 1789 d 1876 Hartland, ME served on the lakes in 1812 War, mar Sarah Leighton of Falmouth, b 1793, dau of Silas.
E1. Charles Henry, b 1811, went to sea, disappeared.
E2. Betania, b 1813 d 1863 New Vineyard, ME, mar Benj. JORDAN, had chn: Betania, Mary Jane, Silas N., Nelson, Nancy D., Catherine Jordan. More on this fam.
E3. Samuel, b 1815, a seaman, disappeared. E4. Greenleaf, b 1817
E5. Mary, b 1820, mar at Madison, ME 1840 her cousin Samuel Pennell Young, son of Mary Young.
F1. Harriet Hall Young, b 1840 mar 1865 Anthony Cummings

F2. Olive Barrett Young, b 1843 mar 1876 David Devoll of Carthage or Bridgton, ME. Chn: John E. Devoll, b 1863, Mary Abbie, Charles Henry, Lillie Altaria, Harriet May and Melvina Jane Devoll.
F3. Ellen Young, b 1845, d.y. F4. Isabella Young, b 1846, d.y.
F5. Mary Abigail Young, 1847-1864 F6. Iranna, b 1848, d.y.
F7. Augusta Young, b 1851 mar 1870 Paul Weston Kimball ofParkman, ME. Chn: Reuel, Marris, Seth, Rose and Geo. Kimball.
F8. Mary Ann Young, b 1853 mar ___Libby of Wellington, ME
F9. Orpha Young, b 1856 mar ___Frye of Sebago, ME.
F10. Seth Young, b 1859 res Bridgton, ME. F11. Lilly, d.y.
E6. Silas Leighton, b 1824, minister at Palmyra, ME.
E7. Priscilla, 1826-1833 E9. Jason, b 1832
E8. Abigail S. b 1827 mar 1847 Enoch Lincoln Ford, farmer in Mayfield, ME. At least 5 chn.
F1. Charles Melvin Ford, b 1850 res Alpena, MI
F2. Joseph L. Ford, b 1858 F5. Horace Ford, b 1872
F3. Sadie Ford, b 1860 mar 1877 Vielle Stratton, dau Rena Belle
F4. Rowena Ford, b 1864 Hartland, ME d 1870
D2. Jeremiah, b 1790 d 1863 Skowhegan, ME. Mar 1. Eleanor Leighton sister of Sarah Leighton above, and 2. Eliza Merrill, sister of Dolly, who mar Joseph T. PENNELL. 8 chn by 1st, 2 by 2nd wife.
E1. Sumner Pennell, b 1812 Westbrook, ME, truckman in Boston, mar Eunice Carrier of Lyman, ME, dau of Deacon John Carrier.
F1. Mary F. b 1842 mar Geo. W. Aborn of Wakefield, MA, coaldealer had son Geo. P. Aborn, also Arthur S., Willard Grant and Grace Eleanor.
F2. Ida E. Pennell, b 1857 d 1879.
E2. William Lloyd, b 1815 d 1872,engineer in Boston, mar ?
F1. Edward Thomason, b 1839 d 1842
F2. Helen Bernard, b 1842 mar 1863 Joseph BASSETT, agent in Lynn, MA. Had chn: Frank L., Harry Wilbur and Florence Louise Bassett.
F3. Lloyd Waite b 1847 res Brighton, MA mar 1870 Evaline Amelia Otis. Had chn: Grace Leonard and Marion Brooks.
F4. Julia E., b 1849 d 1859
F5. Wiliam Leonard, b 1852 res Uxbridge, MA mar Alice Cornell or Cornwall, had daus Alice L. and Edith B.
F6. Jennie Thompson, b 1855.
E3. Mary Ann, b 1817 mar 1840 Jerome Bonaport Veazie of Boston, a mason, 1818-1867. 4 chn.
F1. Frances M. Veazie, b 1844, mar Geo. M. Vinal of Boston, 2 daus Laura and Mary Gertrude Vinal.
F2. Susan Ellen Veazie, b 1846 mar 1876 Charles WEARE, grocer in Boston, MA. A son Charles Weare b 1876.
F3. Mary Eldon Veazie, b 1848 mar 1874 Francis Hanscom, grocer of Boston.
F4. Laura Matilda Veazie, b 1851 d 1858.
E4. Frances, b1819, d 1847 mar Geo. R. Cooper
F1. Frances E. Cooper, 1847-1865
E5. Emily Jane, b 1822 mar 1845 Morris True, b 1821 N. Yarmouth,ME.
F1. Charles Franklin True, b 1847 res Middleton, OR, served in Civil War. Mar 1871 Luella Van Duran of McMinnville,OR, had chn: Albion, Moses, Emily Estelle True.
E6. David Spear, b 1824, d 1861 unmar E8. Eunice, 1830-1846
E7. Elias Leighton, b 1826 rem to CAL, not traced.

E9. Emma G., mar 1852 Geo. W. PENNELL, her cousin, son of Joseph Thomas Pennell. Geo. a teamster at St. Albans, ME.
F1. Franklin Pierce Pennell, b 1853 joiner at Harmony, ME, mar 1875 Emma Hurd. Daus Camilla and Winifred.
D3. Mary, b ca 1793 Gray, ME, d 1843 mar Samuel Young.
E1. Samuel P. Young, b 1818 mar 1840 Mary PENNELL, dau of Samuel Gould Pennell, qv.
E2. Mary Susan Young, mar ___Shaw of Norridgewock, ME
E3. Ephraim Young, res Lewiston, ME
E4. William Clark Young, b 1826 res Greenville, ME, mar Eliza J. Foss of Kingsbury, ME. No issue 1880
E5. Elander F. Young, res Woodstock,ME E6. John G. Young.
E7. Martha C. Young, res Woodstock, ME
E8. Caroline M. Young, b 1835, mar 1857 Guldin Starbird, farmer of Dover, ME. Prob more data on this fam.
F1. Willard Starbird, b 1859 d,y. F5. Minnie R. Starbird, b 1871
F2. Hannah Inez Starbird, b 1860, mar Charles J. Pope of Dover.
F3. Willard M. Starbird, b 1864
F4. John C. Starbird, b 1866 F6.-F8. 3 chn d.y.
D4. Joseph T., b 1798 Brighton, ME, farmer, mar 1. Dolly Merrill of Cornville, ME, and 2. 1854 Mary Jane Judkins of Kingsbury, ME.
E1. Geo. W., b 1826, mar his cousin Emma G. PENNELL, dau of Jere.
E2. Almeda E3. Andrew E4. Jane
E5. Benjamin J., served in Civil War, then disappeared.
E6. Caroline E7. R. Bradford, killed in Civil War 1864, unmar
E8. Margaret, b 1855 E9. Julia, b 1857 E12. Edwin G, b 1864.
E10. Darius, b 1859 E11. Greenleaf, b 1861, d of TB
C2. Mary/Molly/Polly, b ca 1745 mar 1765 Nathaniel FICKETT, qv, at Cape Eliz., ME. He was son of Thomas and Mary (Moulton)Fickett of Scarboro and Kittery, ME. She mar 2. Geo. Fogg, no issue.
C3. Joseph, b 1747 d 1833, res Gray, ME. Mar 1. Eunice or Charlotte Nash, b 1764 d ca 1788, 8 chn? He mar 2. Hannah Ward, who d 1813 8 chn. Mar 3. Mrs. Bathsheba Bowker, no issue. More data.
C4. Clement, b 1751 d 1835, served in Rev. War. Res Gray, ME. Mar 1784 Esther Kinningham/Cunningham?, 1764-1814, 10 chn. More.
C5. Eunice, b 1752 d 1839, mar John Gould, son of Clement of Westbrook, ME, 8 chn.
D1. Clement Gould, b ca 1775, mar ___.
E1. John Gould, res Livingstone Mills, ME. E2. Miles Gould
D2. Clarissa Gould, b ca 1779 unmar.
D3. Eunice Gould, b 1781 Falmouth, ME d 1868 Gorham, ME, mar Isaac Winship, teamster, libby's Corner, ME.
E1. Isaac Winship, b 1808, blacksmith and farmer of W. Bridgewater ME, mar Drusilla Augusta Lathrup of Leeds, ME. More in record.
D4. Samuel Gould b 1783 d 1848, unmar. Illeg.?
D5. Betsy Gould Pennell? 1785-1850. More data available
D6. Sally Gould Pennell, b 1788 d Steep Falls, ME 1868, mar Hon. Edward Mann of Gorham, ME.
E1. James P. Mann, b 1822, d 1868 New Orleans. Congressman from N.O. Mar 1841 Miriam Frances Johnson of Gorham, ME, had chn: Horace, James and George Mann.
E2. George Mann, b 1822, d 1863, unmar, served with Confed.Army.
E3. Hannah Mann, b 1824 d 1869, res Standish, ME, mar Rev. Peletiah Johnson, b 1818 Buxton, ME, daus Sarah, Adeline, Mary Johnson.
D7. Abby Gould Pennell, b 1791 d 1831 bur Stroudwater, ME, mar Jos. Copps, farmer, bro of Mary Copps who mar Wm. Gould

E1. Abbie Copps, b 1832 mar 1850 John Small of Scarappa, ME, had daus Florietta and Abbie Ann Small.

D8. William Gould Pennell b 1795 mar Mary Copps. Mary b 1801 Lebanon, ME, chn b Westbrook, ME.

E1.Mary Elizabeth Pennell b 1827 mar Joseph P. RICKER, qv.

F1. Charles H. Ricker, b 1849 res Berwick, ME mar 1875 Carrie S. Lunt. A son Percy Leroy Ricker

F2. Geo. C. Ricker, b 1851, res Portland, ME.

F3. Frank F4. Arthur F5. Alice Ricker.

E2. Ellen Sargent, b 1831 d 1874mar Joshua B. Larrabee, no issue

E3. Samuel Copp Pennell, b 1838, d.y. E4. Emeline M, b 1840, unmar

E5. William Nevins, b 1844, res Saint John, NB, Canada, mar Ella A. Hamblett of Deering, ME, son Herbert Everett, b 1868.

C6. Abigail, b 1759 d 1785, mar Zebulon Adams, who d in Rev.War.More

C7. Samuel

C8. Thomas, b 1767 d 1848 Wes brook, ME res Nason's Corner and Deering, ME, mar 1791 Eunice KNIGHT, b 17-- Buxton, ME and 2. 1809, Sally Jones of Standish, ME. 8 chn b Buxton, ME. Sally d 1863 at 81, bur Sacarappa, ME. 3 chn by 1st wife.

D1. Nancy, b 1791 d 1874 mar Levi Starbird of Westbrook, ME, 1784-1865, mechanic.

E1. Eunice Starbird, b 1810 mar 1834 Charles D. Nason, b 1810, trader at Westbrook, ME. Sons Levi and Benj. Nason.

E2. Delia Ann Starbird, b 1814

E3. Catherine Starbird, b 1819, d 1847, mar 1841 Smith Gould

F1. Charles Gould, b 1842, farmer, 3 chn.

F2. Ann Louisa Gould, b 1845 mar 1874 Edward Chapman, farmer. Son Abraham and dau Kate G. Chapman.

F3. Hannah Frances Gould, b 1846 mar 1863 Walter Scott Boynton, b 1841, painter at Haverhille, MA, 6 chn.

F4. Henry Pennell Gould, b 1848, unmar

E4. Levi Russell Starbird, b 1822, Farmer, Stroudwater, ME, mar 1851 Margaret Ann Seal.

F1. Alfred Lewis Starbird, b 1852 mar Alice Ham

F2. Henry Lincoln Starbird, - 1860

E5. Edward D. Starbird, b 1824 res Westbrook, ME, mar Martha Jane Libby.

F1. Frank Levi Starbird, b 1869, twin F4. Starr K. Starbird,b1875

F2. Fred L. Starbird, b 1869,twin. F5. Scott R. Starbird, b 1878

F3. Grace Louisa Starbird, b 1871

E6. Frances Jane Starbird, b 1827 d 1862, mar 1850 Charles JORDAN, res Portland, ME, 2 chn.

F1. Walter Russell Jordan, b 1859 F2. HattieJ.Jordan, b 1861

E7. Harriet L. Starbird, b 1829 res Buxton, ME, mar Dr. Martin Coffin, a son Walter H. Coffin b 1865

D2. Henry, b 1792 Westbrook, ME d 1877 Buxton, ME mar Emma Thombes, b 1794 Buxton, d 1870

E1. Thomas Thombes, b 1821 d 1870, farmer, mar 1853 Sarah E. Rounds

F1. Mary Ellen, b 1854 mar 1875 Nathan FLOOD, no issue

F2. Clara Louise, b 1863

E2. Alexander, b 1826 mar 1848 Sarah G. Berry, d 1873

F1. James W., b 1850 had son Frank, dau Edith Emily

F2. Charles Henry, b 1852, d.y.

F3. Eliza B., b 1854 mar Gilbert DAVIS, farmer of Buxton, ME, had Sarah Mabel and Thomas Henry Davis.

F4. Sarah L., b 1857 mar 1879 Stephen W. Carle of Gorham, ME.

F5. Charles Henry, b 1859 F6. John C. b 1864

F7. Edward Starbird, b 1868
D3. Almira, b 1795 d 1862 unmar
D4. by 2nd wife Sally Jones, Thomas, b 1810, d 1844, unmar
D5. Charles, b 1811, d 1836 Calais, ME.
D6. Jonathan Jones Pennell, called Jones Pennell, b 1813, lumber dealer at Portland, ME, mar Mary Ann Fowler, no issue.
D7. George, b 1815, d 1842, res Boston, unmar.
D8. John Philbrook, b 1819, d 1897, cooper and tinsmith, mar 1852 Mary Augusta Norton, b 1828 N. Madison, CT, dau of Jonathan E. and Eliza (Stone) Norton, desc of Theophilus Eaton.
E1. Geo. E., b 1854, attny, Atlantic, IA, mar 1878 Mary Addie Kidder, b 1855 Bridgewater, ME.
F1. Iva H. b 1879 Atlantic, IA d 1903
F2. Henry Hodgdon, b 1881, res TX.
F3. Zina May, b 1884 mar 1906 Robert H. Ely
F4. Dev. Dell, b 1886, mar 1906 Charles W. Gregory.
E2. Henry Beaumont, b 1858 Westbrook, ME res Portland. In 1884 was member of firm Cook, Everett and Pennell, wholesalers. Mar 1883 Grace Woods Fribley, b 1861 Marion, OH, dau of Jacob and Harriet (Conklin) Fribley. Son Henry Jr. b 1887
E3. Lillian Gertrude, b 1871, unmar
D9. Sophia, b 1821 mar 1848 William Libby Pennell, son of John P.
D10. Ephraim, b 1823, lumber dealer in Sacarappa, ME, mar 1847 Clarinda Small, b 1822 Auburn, ME.
E1. Mary, b 1848 d 1851
E2. Charles Randolph, b 1851 teamster mar 1876 Kate Bragdon of Scarboro, ME, had chn: Irving, Florence and Everett.
E3. Laura Eva, b 1852, mar 1876 Fred Briggs, Deering, ME, a tin sealer. No issue in 1879.
E4. Albert Henry, b 1853, d ca 1890
E5. Clarence, b 1855
E6. Frank Hilton, b 1857
E7. Elmer Ellsworth, b 1861.
B3. Thomas again, unlikely, but poss, b 1720 Glouc.,MA by 2nd wife.
B4. Rachel, b 1721 Glouc., MA mar ___Clay

One early member of the above fam is said to have rem to Kingston,ONT, Canada, but not located by compiler. (Ridlon)

PENNELL, Matthew, b J or Cornwall, mar 1743 in MRB Agnes TREFRY, from Cornwall?7 chn: Matthew, Thomas, Matthew again, Elizabeth Moreau, John, Anis/Agnes, and Rebecca Homer Hopkins. (WRCIC; Libby Logan, Denison, TX; Barrington, Nova Scotia records)

PENWELL, Clement from Devon, England. Cf PENOUIL of J, which sounds like Penwell.

PENWELL, John,mariner in NH, also in York, ME? (Noyes) OUTC.

PENWELL, Peter of Ipswich, mar Phebe Newmarch, b ca 1659, widow, by 1702, when she mar Samuel Chapman, who rem with fam to North Hampton.

PENNY, PENNEY, curr G and J. Common in G. PENNEY, said to be ship owner from G to Nfld. 1700s. Poss from LE PENN, PENNEC of C.I. A large PENNY fam in the BECK GEN, WRCIC. From C.I.? See NICOLLE in Q.A. IN CANADA.

PENNY, P., arrived in Boston 1769 on ship MOLLY from J. (Whitmore) Poss same or another mar Elizabeth Bouve 1785 Boston. Note also Edmund Penny in Boston and Charlestown records. OUTC.

PEPIN, see VAUTIER. PEPINS res St. Peter and St. Ouen J early. Some desc to Switzerland from J. (A. Sweetman, Sask, Canada)

PEPIN, Helier, b J, rem to Gillingham, England ca 1912, then to Woodstock, ONT. A bro or son of this fam is said to have gone to Australia, then to San Francisco, CAL, arrived just after the earthquake. He then rem to Canada.

PERCHARD in J 1309. In St. Martin, Grouville, St. Saviour and Trinity J 1668, and in St. Saviour, Grouville and Trinity J 1749. Curr G and J. One PERCHARD was Sheriff of London 1793, then Lord Mayor of London. See CIFHS #8. Curr PARCHER research: P. Bohanan, Contoocook, NH.

PERCHARD, Clement mar Mary DROIT, LE DROIT? 1732 in King's Chapel, Boston, MA. See LE DROW.

PARCHER, poss an early or variant spelling of PERCHARD? PARCHER of Carolina is thought to be a Hug. surname. OUTC.

PARCHER, Henry, res Portsmouth, NH 1790 with fam of 4.

PARCHER, Elias at Dover, ME 1696, taxed at Greenland 1698. Mar 1708 Grace Allard, who was bp 1715 in Greenland with her chn. (Noyes; Virginia Swartz, Alexandria, MN; WRCIC) OUTC.

A1. George mar 1739 Patience Carroll, in Scarboro, ME 1741.
A2. Deborah, mar 1726 Edmund WEBBER, qv. A4. Eliz, mar 1757 John Fass
A3. Elias, bp 1725 Greenland, NH A5. Sarah, res Hampton, NH 1741

PERKINS in J at least by early 1800s.

PERREE, see PERRY

PERREL, see also PEARL and DE LA PERELLE, some to Canada from C.I. In J 1607-1749, curr J. See Q.A. IN CANADA. Nicholas PEARL, poss Perelle, noted in Noyes. OUTC. DE LA PERELLE was in St. John and St. Mary J 1668, in St. Ouen J 1749.

PERREL, Elizabeth, b 1805 G? to OH, d 1875 OUTC

PERRIL, Enoch, from C.I.? mar Esther Sappington, Pike Co., OH 1817. OUTC

PERREL, Nathaniel, b C.I.? in Pickaway Co., OH 1840 OUTC

PERRIL, Peter, from C.I.? mar Phebe DUPEE in Morrow Co., OH 1848. OUTC

PERRELL, Gideon, mar Sarah Brown of Charlestown at Boston 1788. (WYman)

PERREWAY, PERRIWAY, PERROWAY, all prob PIROUET, a Hug for time settled in J. PIROUET in St. Clement and Grouville J 1668, and in Grouville 1749. PIROUET in St. Saviour J 1850. Curr G and J. See GRAY. See also CIFHS #3,4.

PERREWAY, PIROUET, Philip, b J or France mar Johanna MARINER, LE MARINEL, qv, 1707 Boston, MA. Some rem to Liverpool, NS, Canada. (Underhill)

A1. James, b 1709/10 Boston A3. Abraham again, b 1713 Boston
A2. Abraham, b 1711/12, d.y. A5. John, b 1723, Boston, MA.

PARRAWAY, Abigail mar Cornelius Thompson 1794 MRB

PERRIWAY, James mar Abigail Dickenson 1746 King's Chapel, Boston, MA.

PARAWAY, Mary dau of John and Ruth, bp 1730 MRB.

PARREWAY, Mary mar Charles Holmes 1740 Boston

PERREWAY, Mary mar John Jenkins 1743 Boston

PERREWAY, Mary mar 1713 Sam. Rouso, Boston, MA.

PIROUET, Daniel, b J, mar in Caraquet, NB 1800s? Marie QUEREE of a J fam. (Marcel Poirier, New Richmond, QUE) Marie was dau of Jean-Bapt. QUEREE, and grnddau of Simone QUEREE of J, settled in Caraquet, NB.

PERRIN, in France first, in London, England 1606, poss earlier, old in G, in Vale G 1820. (CIFHS #14) In J 1340, 1524. In St. Martin J 1668, curr in J. CAUTION: TRIAL CHART

PERRIN, Daniel b 1640 J or La Rochelle, France, rem to NJ with the CARTERET group on the ship PHILIP 1665. He then rem to Staten Is., NY where his father Peter PERRINE had already settled. Daniel mar 1. 1666 Marie THOREL, prob b Rouen, France. He mar 2. 1687 Elizabeth ___. No of chn is uncertain. A Daniel PERRIN mar in La Rochelle, France 1620. Tradition says that 3 bros. came to America. Chart not included as this fam is really French. For more info. see WRCIC and sources listed. (DANIEL PERRINE THE HUGUENOT; HIST. OF ELIZ. NJ, by Rev. Hatfield; Wilma Moore, Harrisburg, ILL; Hazel Perrine, Ashland,

ORE; Margaret Jasperson, Galesburg, ILL; Jean Overfield, Lakemore, OH; Walter J. Burnham, Pittsburg, PA; Alice Winesinger, Haddam, KS; Anne Long, Grangeville, ID; Stillwell's MISCELLANY; SOME ANCESTRAL LINES by R.M. Tingley, Rutland, VT 1935; NY,NJ and MA records)

PERRIN, Gladys b 1897 G, mar 1929 in Chicago, ILL Fred. John DE BRODER

PERRIN, Judith from C.I. to UT 1862, via ship ANTARCTICA. (SLCity)

PERRIN, John Sr. mar Ann HUBERT, qv. Roxbury, MA. Anne d 1688. (W.R. Wineinger, Haddam, KS)

PERRIN, John had wife Mary POLLEY, POULET?, bp 1650 Roxbury, MA.OUTC.

PERRY, PERREYE in G 1100s to 1700s, also a Sark Is. surname, and early in England. PERREE in J before 1607, in St. Ouen J 1668, 1749. PERREE often spelled PERRY in America. Some fams rem from the Islands to England and to Canada. See Q.A. IN CANADA, by Turk. Name curr G and J.

PERRY, Bennett, b 1846 J, son of Bennett and Mary (HOOPER) PERRY, d in Waterbury, VT, 1925. Mar Mary Phillips ca 1867 at St. Buryans, Cornwall, England. She was b there 1845 and d 1932 VT. (Joyce Masterpaul, Ithaca, NY; Fam. Bible)

A1. William Harry Bennett, b 1868 Penryn, Cornwall, d 1952 Waterbury. Mar Margaret Scott at Lansingburgh, NY 1889.

B1. Robert, b 1890 d 1939 VT B2. Bertel Thorwaldsen, 1894-1964

B3. Allan Scott, b 1896, d 1947 Franklin, PA.

A2. Annie, b 1870 Concord, NH d 1946 Clearwater, FLA. Mar 1. Fred Willis Mould at Keeseville, NY 1891, and 2. Capt. Benj. F.Fogg 1906 in NYCity.

B1. Willis Perry Mould, b 1892

B2. Charles Edwards Mould, b 1893 at Concord, NH

C1. Joyce Mould, mar Charles Masterpaul, a ch mar ___Turk of Ithaca, NY.

A3. George, b 1872, d.y.

A4. Charles, b 1873, d 1957 Largo, VLA, mar 1. 1908 Julia MOODY and 2. Agnes Gierson in 1923, no issue

A5. Mary, b 1876 Concord, mar 1897 Edward M. Cogswell

B1. Lucille Cogswell, b 1897

A6. Francis, b 1878 NH d in Waterbury, CT 1935

A7. Bennett b 1881 Lansingburgh, NY d Northfield, VT 1952. Mar Stella M. Colson, a dau Nina Rose b 1932

A8. Eliza b 1884 Troy, NY, d there 1887. A9. John, 1887-1920?

PERRY, Harry, bro of Bennett above, b ca 1840s? had a granite firm in Pennacook, NH.

PERREE/PERRY data below is an addition to that on the PERRY FAM in Q.A.IN CANADA, by Turk. The new data comes from Gerald Perry, Cap-aux-Os, Quebec, Canada and J.A. Perry of Okotoks, ALTA, Canada. Other data from Frank Remiggi, Montreal, QUE. See WRCIC.

PERREE/PERRY, John, b J, mariner and partner in various Gaspe ports ca 1800. Mar in J. Partner in Peter Du Val and Co., and founded in Malbaie, Gaspe, QUE with son JOHN PERREE AND SON FISHERY. John Sr. bought the Janvrin Fishery room at Malbaie in 1851 from John LE COUTEUR LA GERCHE of J. (Remiggi

A1. Edward, b J, mar Jane LE BROCK, qv.

B1. John, b 1830 B2. Edward, b 1833 Perce, QUE

A2. Philip, b J ca 1779, d 1874 age 95. Mar Elisabeth Bond res Cap-aux-OS,Gaspe, QUE., 1817-1894.

B1. Elisabeth, b 1814 mar 1832 Daniel ROBERT, qv.

B2. Philippe, b 1816, mar Charlotte Packwood, and 2. in 1855 Marie Dumas.

C1. Marie Melinda, bp 1846 mar 1871 ___Fergusson.

C2. Appolline, bp 1848 mar 1868 ___Chouinard
C3. Georges, b 1845 mar 1878 Celina Boulet, bp 1861, dau of Paul Boulet and Marie Marin? Res Cap des Rosiers, both d 1893.
C4. Joseph, bp 1849 mar 1874 Susanne Fortier of Cap Rosier, dau of Aubain F. and Marguerite STE. CROIX, qv.
C5. John, bp 1852 mar 1883 Jane Whalen, dau of James W.& Julie Bond.
C6. Edouard, bp 1855 mar 1879 Malvina English of Anse Griffon, dau of Martin English and Henriette Whalen.
C7. Narcisse, b 1851
B3. Jane/Genevieve, b 1819, unmar. Had dau Mary b 1853.
B4. Marie, b 1821
B5. John, b 1824, called Jack, mar Sophie Smith, bp 1829 Canada. He d 1894 age 70.
C1. John, b 1848 mar 1871 Sara Poitras, dau of Michel of Mont Louis.
D1. John b 1872 Cap-aux-OS, d 1943 Cap Des Rosiers. Mar 1899 J. Normand.
E1. Delicia, Delcia, b 1901, mar 1930 Arthur Edward PERRY
F1. Reginald Perry, b 1931 mar 1960 A. Cassivi
F2. Maurice, b 1936 mar 1978 G. Gelbert
F3. Jean Paul, b 1938 mar 1961 N. Courdier
E2. Victoire, b 1906 mar 1943 F. Smith
F1. John Smith b 1944 F2. Austin Smith, b 1947
E3. Leontine, b 1907, d.y.
E4. Elise, b 1911, d 1969, mar 1935 Joseph Whalen, 2 daus: Regina Sylvestre and Elise B. Cote, both with chn.
E5. John, b 1915, d 1936 E6. Therese, b 1916 mar M. Smith
E7. Helene, b1917, mar J. Shaw, 4 chn: Hedwige, Irvin, J. Bermance, and Raoul Shaw, all b Gaspe, QUE.
E8. Antoine, mar T. Le Duc, 8 chn.
D2. Nazaire, b 1875 d 1967, mar 1901 Emilia Cassivi.
E1. Lewis, b 1902 mar 1928 Mary Sylvestre, 9 chn: Dorothy Ferguson, Lawrence, Gerty Boufard, Francis, Herbert, James, Doreen Blanchette, Patrick and Henry, all but two having desc.
D3. Vergil, b 1876 killed by lightning age 16
D4. Michael, b 1877 mar 1917 Regina, SASK, Eliz. Haggerty, b 1885 Croy, Scotland, d 1960. Michael d 1966, both bur Moose Jaw, SASK, chn b near Chaplin, SASK.
E1. John, b 1921, Vet WWII, mar 1952 Lucille Mildred Torvik, res Lorburn, SASK, 6 chn: Michael, Kathryn McIntosh, Evelyn Fiske, David, Agnes and Joel W. Perry.
E2. Joseph A., b 1922, Vet WWII, mar 1944 Margaret A. Prehn,res Okotoks, ALTA, 5 chn: Eliz. Shaw, Brian, John E., Robert and Maryanne Perry.
E3. Agnes J., b 1924, mar 1950 Barney Klok, res Vancouver, BC, with 2 chn: Eileen and Thomas Klok.
E4. Edward H., b 1926, mar Dolores Jennings, res Chaplin, SASK, 5 chn: Donna, Bill, Judy, Marion and Gerald.
D5. Agnes, b 1878, d.y. 1968.
D6. Clara, b 1879 mar 1909 Frank PITON, qv, son of John. Clara d/
D7. Josephin, b 1883 mar 1900 S. Cassivi, d 1906
E1. Dolphas Cassivi, b 1901 Cap-auxOs, QUE. E2. Rose, b 1903
D8. Leontine, b 1889 mar L. Fournier, d NB, many chn
D9. Louise, b 1892 mar A. Fournier, d Belldune, NB, many chn.
C2. Philip, b 1853, mar 1876 C. Boulay, d 1927, 4 chn
D1. Mary, b 1880 mar R. Doyle, 2 sons res Boston, MA
D2. Joseph, b 1883 mar 1915 A. Sylvestre, d 1961
E1. Lionel, 1917-1971 E3. Teodore, b 1919, d.y.

E2. Roland, 1918-1946, WWII E4. Elias, 1920, d 1971.
E5. Austin, b 1922, mar 1947 P. NOEL, 8 chn: Nicole Fortin, Yvon Giasson, Lisette Fortin, Jean Mac, Jacques, Sylvie, Chantal, and Francine.
E6. Marie Rose, b 1924, mar 1966 S. Margenian, a ch Stephane.
D3. Israel, b 1885 mar H. Normand, 2 daus Filia Leduc, and Elise Smith.
D4. Jerome, mar Margaret ___
D5. Elisa, b 1890 mar 1920 A. Bernier
E1. Yvonne Bernier, b 1921 mar W. O'Connor, many chn.
E2. George Bernier, b 1923, Vet. WWII, mar C. Fournier, res Fontenelle, QUE
E3. Georgiana Bernier, b 1924 mar C. Fournier, 11 chn: Leopold, Ghisline, Firmin, C. Auguste, Eddy, Gelina, George, Bertrand, Bernadette, Roszaire and Raymond Fournier
E4. Alphonse, b 1925, mar 1949 B. Lacombre, 12 chn: Francois, Francoise, Alphonsine, Paul, Pauldine, Florence, Yvonne, George, Dannille, Celestin, Marie, Stephane
E5. Leo, b 1926 mar 1955 M.R. Fortin, 5 chn: Leonard, Dianne, Fabienne, Jean Eudes, and Etienne.
E6. Emilie, b 1928, mar 3 times, #3 J. Fournier, dau Chantal F.
E7. Elisabeth, b 1931 mar C. Abraham, a dau Mirelle.
D6. Auguste, b 1893 mar ?, at least 2 chn: Romeo and a dau.
C3. Elisabeth, bp 1855, uncertain.
B6. Sophie, mar Alfred Stanley from Fontenelle, Que, d there 1932 age 106, many chn.
B7. Henriette?, b 1829.

"The old Perrys were very big men...my grandfather Nazaire's brother John, the one who mar Josephine Normand, could climb up the mast of a schooner with a barrel of salt pork tied to his feet. His hands were big enough he could cover a pie plate with one hand. My grandfather Nazaire Perry, was no baby either. He once carried a big rock and placed it in the line between his property and his father's property...My grandfather's other brother Michael was supposed to be the strongest one of all. He once struck and killed a horse with his fist, just the one blow. Their mother, Sarah Poitras could load a barrel of salt pork on board of a cart all by herself. I know a barrel was around 400 lbs. She was an awful big and tall person, smoked a clay pipe, and had a big pocket on her apron to keep her tobacco and pipe...Uncle Philly ...sure had good legs and jaws and teeth. He would bite a piece off axe blade, or bite a nail in two. He could walk to Gaspe from Cap-aux-Os twice in the same day, about 20 miles each way...Philippe Perry settled down at Cap des Rosiers." (Gerald Perry, Forillon, Gaspe, QUE)

PERRY. This fam also uses PERREE. George Joseph below had 9 brothers, and at least 3 rem from J to Canada.

PERREE, George Joseph, b 1869 J, rem to Edmonton, ALTA 1908, mar Susan Elizabeth LE MESURIER from C.I. and brought 3 sons and dau to Canada in 1909. (Lenore Law, Lepean, ONT)
A1. George Henry, b 1892, d.y.?
A2. George Herbert, b 1898, mar his cousin Phyllis PERREE, had 1 dau, adopted.
A3. Arthur Oswald, used PERRY, b 1901, drowned 1936, mar 1920 Florence Beatrice Jack.
B1. Lenore Florence, b 1925 mar Herbert James Cunningham Law, b 1946, res Nepean, ONT.
C1. Moira Jeanne, b 1949 mar Georges J.P. Leduc, no issue.

C2. Catherine Anita, b 1954, mar Gordon Ronald McAinsh, 1973, two daus: Molly and Amanda McAinsh.
A4. Royston Edward, b ca 1903 mar Mary Marnier, and drowned 1936
B1. Royston Arthur, b 1937, posthumous. Mary remarried.
A5. Iris Doreen Ina, b ca 1905, mar Harry Fisher, 2 daus. Res BC?
PERREE, Walter, bro of George Joseph above, mar Alice ___.
A1. Walter A2. Phyllis, mar her cousin G.Herbert above.
A3. Irene, mar Dave Sturt
PERREE, Ernest, another bro of George Joseph above, b C.I., rem to Can.
PERREE, Jack, another bro, b C.I., rem to Canada.
PERREE, PERRY, John, b ca 1800 J?, had 4 sons, some rem to Canada. (Michael Perree, Plymouth, England)
A1. Edward, had 2 sons, John, b 1830 and Edward, b 1833
A2. Philip, had 7 chn:
B1. Elizabeth, b 1814 B3. Jane Genevieve, b 1819 J
B2. Philippe, b 1816 J B4. Marie, b 1821 J
B5. John, b 1824 J B6. Sophie b 1826 B7. Henriette, b 1829
PERRY, Francis, from C.I.? in MRB 1631. Francis and Jane res Salem1638 (Essex Coll, Vol 8)
PERRY, Mary b ca 1660 J, to Salem, MA 1677, indentured to Philip ENGLISH, qv. (NEHGS Vol 31)
PERRY, John from J? mar Elizabeth GROSSEE, LE GROS?, qv, in MRB 1724
PERRY, Commodore, desc. from Hug fam which fled to J from France, then rem to England. (Sarchet, Vol 2)
PERRY, a fam from G to GCO early 1800s. Thomas, Maria, and Francis, b 1816, d 1893. (GCO records)
PERRY, fam noted in Fairfield, CT 1700s. Note that MARQUAND fam from G settled in Fairfield, some intermarriage. (OLD BURYING GROUND OF FAIRFIELD, CT, by Kate E. Perry, 1882)
PEVIER, PERVEAR, PREVEAR, PEAVIER, PERVIER, etc, etc. A Hug fam from France to G to Boston, MA ca 1722. Philip PEAVEAR mar 1. ca 1722 Maria or Martha Emmons, b 1696, and 2. Mary W. Swaine, a widow. Fam res Hampton Falls, NH, where Philip d ca 1753. Some data in WRCIC, but not charted here, as this family was really French. (Noyes; Pillsbury Gen; Underhill; Essex Coll Vol 6; Boston VRS; Brown's HIST. OF HAMPTON FALLS, NH; Abby Eastman, Exeter, NH; NEHGS Vol 82; Ted Pevear, Provo,UT; GREELEY GEN; PHILBRICK GEN: Whitmore)
PETEL in St. Brelade J 1668, in St. Heliers J 1749. There is also said to be a Hug. PETEL fam to America. See PEDDLE.
PETEL, John and Rachel res Boston, from C.I. or France? OUTC.
A1. Rachel, b 1703 A2. Susanna, b 1704 A3. Noah, b 1714.
PETEL, John mar Eliz. Kinchin 1746 Boston (int)
PETEL, John mar Elizabeth FALL 1746 Boston
PETEL, John mar Eunice Chamberlin 1733 Boston (int)
PETEL, Rachel mar 1730 in Boston Andrew NICHOLS, both from C.I.?
PETELL, Peter mar Mary Ghent 1739 King's Chapel, Boston.
PETHIC, Charles, b 1859 Alderney, son of Abel and Eliz. Sandercook. The fam was Welsh, but settled in the Islands. Charles d in Lake-Wood, OH 1941. Came to US 1885, mar Pearl Pake. (Richard Brugler, Warren, OH)
A1. Raymond C. A2. Ralph S.
A3. Berenice, mar Frank Peebles, res Fairfield, IA
A4. Dorothy Verne, b 1908 mar 1. Andrew Brooks, and 2. Paul A. Winter of Lakewood, OH and Lake City, FLA.
B1. Jean Elizabeth Brooks, b 1931 Lakewood, OH mar Richard K. Brugler, b 1928 Warren, OH, son of Herman and Mildred M. (Fell) Brugler.
C1. David K. Brugler, b 1953 C2. Diane J. Brugler, b 1955

C3. Eric P. Brugler, b 1957 C4. Kurt E. Brugler, b 1958
PEZET, old in J and in Alderney 1309. Noted in Petition of Quebec City residents 1838, with other C.I. surnames. (LOST IN CANADA, Aug.1981)
PEZET, William mar Maria GRAY 1825 at St. Andrews Presb. Ch, City of Que Quebec, Canada. (LOST IN CANADA, Aug. 1981)
PEZET, Walter and Carrie to US from C.I. ca 1900?. Walter d in Detroit, MI, and Carrie d in a nursing home 1970s at 93, 3 chn: Walter, Marian and Elaine, all living in 1970s. (Richard Herivel, Detroit,MI)
PHALATER, Abraham, "a Jerseyman" met in Maine waters 1660s by John Josslyn, noted for his TWO VOYAGES TO NEW ENGLAND. LE FILIATRE in St. Laurens J 1607, 1668. FILLASTRE curr J. (Noyes)
PHILLIPS, in G 1100s, curr G and J. In Grouville J 1607.
PHILIPPE, PHILIPPS, many in early New England, poss some from C.I.
PHILLIPS, Jane mar Samuel Brimblecome 1765 MRB. OUTC.
PHILLIPS, Nicholas mar Hannah SALTER 1651 Boston, MA. OUTC.
PICKARD. Poss that some of this surname were PICOT of C.I. See Essex Coll., Vols 4,6.
PICKERNELL. Compiler did not find place of origin for PICKERNELL fam of early New England. Poss from C.I.? Note SPIGOURNEL, PIGOURNEL in J 1331, 1461. Also in G 1300s.
PICKERNELL, James bought land in Kittery, ME 1707. At this time there were other C.I. fams in ME and NH. See WRCIC for some data, also see OLD FAMS IN KITTERY, Underhill's SMALL GEN, and MAINE RECORDER.
PICKETT, many in early MA, but not known to compiler if any were definitely from C.I. Note than many mar into C.I. fams. PICOT in J 1299. In St. Martin, and Trinity J 1668, in St. Lawrence J 1788. PIQUET in St. Heliers J 1668. PICOT also noted in Devon and Cornwall. PICOT, Elie was in Nfld. early 1700s. See CIFHS #6 and CIFHS #3. See Pirate section.
PICKETT, D.J. from G to Canada, res Noranda, QUE 1980. (Lucille Roy, Malartic, QUE)
PICKETT, John, mar Eliz. SCIVERY, SYVRET?, qv, 1721 MRB. OUTC.
A1. Elizabeth b 1717! A3. Sylvester, b 1722 A5. Nicholas, bp 1726
A2. Thomas, b 1720 A4. Elizabeth b 1724 A6. John, bp 1728
PICKETT, Nicholas and Jane res MRB, from C.I.? Poss that chn were b elsewhere, J?, and re-bap. in MA?
A1. Elias, bp 1718 A3. John, bp 1718 A5. Nicholas, bp 1718
A2. Elizabeth, bp 1718 A4. Mary, bp 1718 A6. Samuel, bp 1720.
PICKETT, see records in Beverly, MA and Haverhill, MA, etc.
PICKETT, Mary mar Francis SALTER Jr., 1732/33 MRB
PICKETT, Nicholas, res MRB 1790 with fam of 6. See BUBIER, QUINER.
PICKETT, PICOT?, Nicholas from St. Heliers, J? mar 1702 Salem or MRB. Jean or JaneBUBIER, qv. (Essex Inst.)
PICKETT, Tabitha, mar Charles DARBY, qv, 1780 MRB
PICKETT, Wm., mar Abigail MELZARD 1799 MRB.
PICKETT, Capt. William of Newburyport, MA mar 1795 in MRB. Mrs. Rebecca HOOPER.
PICOT GEN in progress in J. PICO is the French pron. of PICOT. It seems likely that these PICOS were either from France or C.I. PICOT in St. Lawrence J 1788.
PICO, Abigail mar Nathaniel Shepard Prentis of Roxbury, MA 1807. OUTC
PICO, Eliz., mar Anthony NOCON? Cf NOYON of C.I. OUTC
PICO, Francis built schooners in J 1700s. (A. John Jean, Jersey)
PICOT, A., on ship TEPIC from the Queen Charlotte Islands, BC to San Francisco, CAL 1852. (RASMUSSEN)
PICOT, Elias and Jane had Elias b 1723 Boston, from J?
PICOT, Joshua and Susanna had son Joshua b 1733 Boston.

PICO, Joshua mar Abigail Howland 1760 Boston. Mar also? Isabella BROWN 1788?

PICOT, PICO, Joshua res Boston 1790 with fam of 8. One Joshua mar 1806 Sarah Callender.

PICO, Lucy, mar James Rob 1760 Boston. OUTC. Same or another Lucy mar 1793 Lem Gardner in Boston.

PICO, Richard Lane mar Hanna Gore 1794 Boston. OUTC.

PIDGEON, see DUMARESQ. PIDGEON curr G and J.

PIKE, old in G, but common in southern England and Cornwall. In J 1800s.

PIKE, Mary, dau of Anthony Pike of G, res Vale House, mar in St. Sampson Church 1832 William Proctor. They rem to England, had several sons and daus. One son, William rem to Canada. A grandson, Douglas Coates, res Winnipeg, MAN, Canada 1970s. Poss other Can. desc.? (Guernsey Soc. Bulletin, Spring 1981)

PIKE/PORKE, Edward, mentioned in Noyes, p. 716.

PIKE, James from C.I. res North Shore in Duplessis Co., QUE early 1900s. He mar Mary TRACHY, qv, of J fam? See TRACHY. (Aldo Brochet, London, ONT)

PILL, John, b 1780 St. Peter Port G, d 1855 Mormon Grove, UT. He was son of John PILL and Marie TOUZEAU of G. Seven members of fam to America 1855 on ship CHIMBORAZO. John mar Eliz. HENRY, qv, 1802. Elizabeth the dau of Thomas and Rachel (LE CHEMINANT) HENRY. (SLCITY Rec)

A1. John, b 1803 St. Peter Port G, mar 1827 Susanne TOURTEL

A2. Elizabeth, b 1805 G, mar 1827 Thomas Colley Stayner.

A3. Thomas Henry, b 1807 G

A4. Henry, b 1810 G, mar Ann or Sarah ___ A5. George, b 1812 G.

A6. William John Ozanne, b 1815 G, mar Ada Alice ___, d 1855

A7. Daniel, 1816-1819

A8. Mary Elizabeth, b 1819 G, mar 1854 John MARETT, qv, d 1891

A9. Caroline, b 1821 G, mar 1858 Augustus Alvin Farnham, qv, d 1894

A10. Adolphus Frederick William, b 1824 G, d 1843

A11. Alfred John James, b 1826 G, mar Marie LE GRESLEY, qv, d 1855

A12. Louisa Sarah, b 1828 G, d 1853

PINCHARD, see PYNCHARD, PUNCHARD.

PINDEXTER, see PENDEXTER.

PINEL in J 1274 from a place near Cherbourg, France. In St. John J, 1668 and in St. Peter J 1749. Curr J. PINEL, see also PENNELL.

PINEL shield, per pale argent and or, an eagle displaying, standing on a billet, raguly azure.

PINEL. Winston PINEL in Jersey has computerized 14 generations of various PINEL persons and fams in J. If you have a PINEL ancestor, request access through the Channel Islands Fam. Hist. Society.

PINEL, Helier and Elizabeth AUBERT of St. John's, J, were mar at St. Clement J. They had at least 4 chn, poss 5: Helier David, b 1813, Thomas d.y. 1814; Elizabeth bp 1814; Philip b 1816 (See below) and Jean/John, 1818-1819. (Arthur PINEL, Hingham, MA)

PINEL, Philippe, b 1816 Trinity or St. John J, mar 1840 Henriette/ Harriet VAUTIER, qv, b 1819, dau of Abraham and Mary Ann(BLAMPIED) VAUTIER. She d 1903. Philippe d 1895.

A1. Mary Ann, b 1841 J, d 1926, res G. Kept postoffice in Vale, G. Had dau Henrietta.

A2. Philippe, b 1842 J, d 1921, rem to US 1875, mar Trephenia, 1846-1917, both bur Quincy, MA.

B1. Emma B., b 1888, mar W.J. Martin from Cornwall. Emma d 1957, and Martin in 1969.

C1. Philip, b 1893, d 1969, mar Marion White who d 1978

D1. Harold B. Martin, 1919-1952

D2. Marjorie Martin, b 1926 mar 1950 Richard H. Belcher
E1. Kenneth B. Belcher, b 1954 E3. Donald H. Belcher, b 1957, twin
E2. David H. Belcher, b 1957, twin.
C2. Mildred Martin, b 1895 d 1980
C3. Wiliam B. Martin, b 1900, mar 1928 Marjorie B. England
D1. Marilyn B. Martin, b 1933 mar 1955 Donald Smith. 4 chn: Jeffrey, Bradley, Christopher and Randall Smith, b 1956-1963.
D2. William J. Martin, b 1936, d 1971, two sons: Wm. and Timothy
A3. Harriet, b 1843 J, later res G, and mar A.J. SEBIRE ca 1866, and 2. ____GALLIENNE, no issue. She d 1930 G. Adopted Peter Gallienne, who mar and had 2 sons and dau in G.
A4. Joshua, b 1845, d.y. in J.
A5. Elizabeth b 1847 J, mar 1873 Thomas Mark HATCHARD in St. Saviour J and d 1925 in England. Hatchard was a tailor of St. Saviour, J.
B1. Gertrude Hatchard, b 1874 d 1969, bur Streatham Cem, London, Eng.
B2. Walter Douglas Hatchard, b 1876 London, d.y .
B3. Frederick Hatchard, b 1878 London, d.y.
B4. Ernest Harry Hatchard, b 1880 London, mar Louise Margaret Nugent, 1883-1960. Ernest d 1954.
C1. Eileen Louise Hatchard, b 1910 mar Wilfred John Ward, res Surrey England. She d 1973.
D1. Ann Eileen Ward, b 1938
D2. John Hatchard Ward, res Cheam, Sutton, England, mar Carol Ranger. Two chn: Nicola Jane and Duncan John Ward.
A6. John, b 1850 J, unmar, res Montreal, purser on ships.
A7. Alfred, b 1852 J, d 1940 Quincy, MA, to Boston 1872, mar 1874 Ellen HUELIN, in G, 2 chn. When she d 1883, he sent for and mar her sister Alice HUELIN of G.
B1. Alfred Philip Jersey, b 1875 d 1942, mar Annie Gifford Peterson, 1874-1959.
C1. Roland Hammond, b 1896 d 1973, mar Mabel Manning, res Wareham, MA and Sarasota, FLA. Has 2 chn.
D1. Roland, mar, with son Toby D2. Leslie, mar and has 2 sons.
C2. Alfred Vernon, b 1898, d 1963 mar Eliz. Lehman, dau Virginia.
C3. Helen Marie, b 1900, mar Dr. Elliot H. Luther
C4. Lawrence Elliot, b 1902, mar Rachel WILLIAMS 1926, b 1904.
C5. Nancy Gifford, b 1904 mar James E. Peckham 1930, res Mystic, CT, a son.
C6. Philip John, b 1906, mar Helene Fernier, res Brookville, ME.
D1. Mark D2. Philip, res Santa Cruz, CAL
C7. Marguerite Alice, b 1907, mar Richard Ericson
C8. Dorothy Quincy, b 1910 mar John Wagner.
C9. Ethel Leigh, b 1910 mar U.S. MacConnell
C10. Robert Troupe, b 1914, mar Thelma Burke 1960
C11. David Lincoln, b 1916, mar 1947 Jeanne Slamin
B2. Gladys, b 1889/90, d 1956, mar ___, has 2 chn, Ruth and Raymond, who res Brookville, ME.
B3. Philip John, called Jack, b 1891, res Quincy, MA and Brookville, ME, d 1979, mar Helene ___, 3 chn: Phyllis Aitken, Jean, Mary.
B4. Joseph Walter, b 1893 d 1979, mar Anna M. Lehmann, who d 1980.
B5. Edgar Leigh, b 1894 res Quincy, MA, mar Margaret Woolaver, 1894-1931. 3 chn: Priscilla, b 1921, Leigh/Lee, b 1923, res Ballston Lake, NY, and Carolyn, b 1928.
A8. Jane, b 1854 G, mar James Renney, and 1936 in G. They had a green-house in Vale parish.
B1. Ethel Renney, adopted
B2. Marie Renney, mar C. Stanway, rem to India, had 3 daus and a son.

A9. Joseph, b 1856 St. Peter Port G, lived in J, mar 1884 Eliza D. Killam, dau of John Killam IV, and Lucy Ann Harris. Eliza called Lida. Joseph was first a cook on a fishing vessel, then rem to Canada 1870, where he later became a Methodist minister and missionary. They res North Kingston, NS and Quebec, settling finally in Ottaw. Joseph d 1932 in Montreal. See Memoirs.

B1. Harriet Louise, b 1885 Montreal, d 1981. Mar 1. George Bunton, 1917 in Beach Hill, ONT 1943. Mar 2. Rev. Lloyd H. Morrison, 1947 who d 1961, no issue.

B2. Gilbert Alfred, b 1887 Montreal, QUE mar Harriet Heath, 1884-1974. Gilbert d 1975, Kemptville, ONT. He was affiliated with A.E. LE PAGE, realtors of C.I. desc. of ONT, and with Royal Bank of Can. They are bur Portland, ONT.

C1. Ruth, b 1922, mar John H. Spaulding, b 1923, res Sarnia, ONT, 2 chn: Sandi and Patricia Spaulding.

C2. Jean, b 1924, mar Lawrence Austin Donoghue, b 1928 Oxford Mills, ONT. 2 chn: John Pinel and Shelane Donoghue.

B3. Ethel Maude, b 1889, supervisor in Prot. School Board, Montreal, res later in Ottawa, ONT. D 1981, bur Montreal.

B4. Reta Mildred, b 1892 d in Brockville, ONT 1957

B5. Florence Lillian Lucy, b 1896 d 1907.

B6. Philip John Killam, b 1898 Montreal, mar 1934 Mary I. A. Fowler, b 1902, res Ottawa, ONT.

C1. John Fowler, b 1940 Montreal, mar Helen Louise McBeath 1967, who was b 1943. Res Kanata, ONT. 4 chn: David, Bruce, Douglas and Shawn, the latter adopted.

A10. Walter Philip, b 1858 G, mar 1877 Elizabeth Wallace Norris, 1860-1940. He d 1938, rem to MA 1873. Eliz. b Aberdeen, Scotland. Fam res Braintree, MA.

B1. Walter Joseph, b 1878 d 1879

B2. Arthur Gordon, b 1880, d 1947 Quincy, MA, mar 1902 Lorn Catherine Forbes, b 1877, d 1952

C1. Lorn Traill, b 1903, d 1974, mar W. Goodwin Tyler

D1. Wayne G. Tyler, b 1939, 2 chn?

C2. Arthur Forbes, b 1906, mar G. Rosalind Otway, b 1911

D1. Bruce Arthur b 1936 mar Cynthia Connell, div, 1969, 2 chn: Bruce and Susan. Bruce mar Terry C., 2 chn, Crystal & Bruce III

D2. Roger Gordon, b 1939, mar1968 Julie Schramm, b 1942, res Westwood, MA, 2 chn: Julie Anne and Denise

C3. Walter William, b 1907, d 1973, mar Dorothy Quincy Morrison,b1907

D1. Walter Morrison, b 1935 mar ?, res Glendale, CAL

D2. Richard William, b 1938, mar Maria Garfogle, Div? res Columbus, OH. 2 sons: Kevin and Christopher

C4. Alexander Wyness, b 1909, d 1967, mar 1938 Elizabeth McMillan, had plumbing and heating business.

D1. Jean Kerr, b 1939 mar Thomas McGrath, 4 chn: Deborah, Wygent, Susan and Sandra McGrath.

D2. Elizabeth b 1941 mar Chester Fiske, 2 sons: Stephen and David Fiske.

D3. Nancy Sandra, b 1943, mar Jerald Bassett, 2 chn: Scott and Sherry Bassett.

B3. Louisa Ann, 1881-1969,mar

B4. Edith Gertrude, 1883-1962, mar

B5. William Everett, b ca 1886

B6. Eleanor Annie, 1887-1969, mar

B7. Alice Evelyn, 1889-1972, mar

B8. Elizabeth Wallace, 1891-1913

B9. Walter Frederick, 1893-1977

B10. Ruth Marion, b 1895, mar 1921

B11. Harriet, 1896-1902

B12. Clarence Sidney, b 1899, d.y.

A11. Louisa, b 1860 G, mar Thomas O'Neill, and d 1944, res G. Thomas d 1921.
B1. Thomas O'Neill, b 1889 St. P. Barrack, J, mar Aileen ___, d Ottawa, ONT.
C1. a dau, mar Meagher, rem to Ottawa, ONT.
C2. Kathleen O'Neill, b 1890 J, d 1972 Surrey, England
C3. Louisa O'Neill, nurse, b 1891 J, d 1965
C4. Bernard O'Neill, b 1900 mar Marian Jarrett, d 1966 J.
D1. Nancy O'Neill, mar Alan Alexander, res Grouville, J
D2. Jill O'Neill, mar Michael Gould, res Grouville, J, 2 chn.
C5. Nora O'Neill, b 1892 J, mar Charles E. Niker, res Surrey,England
D1. Kathleen Niker, b 1927, England
D2. Barbara Niker, b 1929, mar John Clarke, res FLA, 3 chn: Diane, Douglas and Janet, twins.
C6. Jane O'Neill, d.y.

PINEL, Louisa, b J, mar Elias DE LA HAYE, qv, and rem to Lowell, MA, with 2 sons and a dau in 1896.

PINEL, Walter, res Saco, ME 1647, mar Mary Booth. Six chn listed by Ridlon. This PENNELL or PINEL poss from Cornwall, or C.I.

PINEL, Philip, Capt. of the HUNTER, built 1807 Salem, MA, owned by Jerathmiel Peirce.

PINEL, Capt. Charles of J, d near Cyprus in the Medit. in 1735.

PINEL, Peter, arrived in Boston, MA 1769 on ship MOLLY from J, a servant. (Whitmore)

PIPON in J 1331, in St. Peter, St. Brelade, St. Helier, and St. Mary J 1668. In St. Peter, St. Ouen, St. Helier, St. Laurens, St. Brelade, and St. Clement J 1749. Curr J.

PIPON, Thomas, a Jerseyman residing in Dartmouth, England was importing goods from Maryland to England in 1731 for John LE COUTEUR of J. He was bringing in worsted hose from Jersey to England for Nicholas Patriarche, a Jerseyman in England. He brought in rice from South Carolina for a London merchant, staves from Maryland for George LE FEUVRE of Jersey, tobacco from Maryland on a Jersey ship for himself, and he was exporting Carolina rice to Rotterdam, Holland. (A.John Jean)

PIPON, Elie, b ca 1700, son of Philippe PIPON, b 1671. Elie rem to NY ca 1724, and mar there a Blanche Lafonds. (A.S. Pipon, St. Lawrence, Jersey) A son Jean was b 1730. In the book CARTERET AND BRYANT GENEALOGY, by Catharina R. Baetjer, NY, 1887, some descendants are listed but without dates.
A1. Elizabeth? mar ___Bonnel of New Jersey
A2. Hannah, mar Cornelius Bryand, Briand of Hackensack, NJ. 6? chn.

PIPON, Capt. Elias of the Royal Nfld. Reg't, gave permission in 1805 for the marriage of Emanuel MITCHEL to Mary Evans in NS. (NS NEWSLETTER, #29; NS newspapers)

PIPON, Guillaume, William, mar Francoise Muret 1793 Boston.

PIPON, James a Jersey shipowner based in London, England was engaged in the South Carolina trade during the late 1740s and 1750s. (A. John Jean, Jersey)

PIPON, Joshua, ensigne of ship in Pemaquid, ME 1687. (DHSM)

PIPON, ___, from J?, ship master in Salem, MA 1673. (Holmes)

PIPON, Laura Elizabeth b 1825 J? mar Rev. Wm. Braithwaite, res J, had relatives in Montreal, QUE. (Joan Stevens, Jersey)

PIPPOON, PIPON?, Lucretia mar Jabez Winchester, 1783 Boston, MA.

PIPPOON, Mary mar Nicholas PETERS, 1792 Boston, MA.

PIPPON, Mary mar John LEWIS 1781 Boston, MA.

PIPON, Mary, dau of John and Abigail, b Boston, MA 1700s. (NEHGS V100)

PITMAN, English but found in J 1796.(A. John Jean, Jersey)

PITON, see Q.A. IN CANADA by Turk. Some changed name to PEYTON.
PITON, in J 1607, poss Hug? In St. Brelade J 1668, 1749.
PITON, PEYTON, Philippe, b 1772 St. Laurens J, son of Abraham and Susanne (LE BROCQ) PITON. At age 32, single, res Beaumont, QUE,mar Marie Henriette Filion of St. Peter, St. Paul's Bay, dau of Zach. Filion, blacksmith, 1808, Holy Trinity CH, QUE. (Mary Piton, Columbus, OH; Violet Lambley, Vancouver, BC) More data in book.
A1. Marie Sophie, b 1811 QUE A2. Marie Henriette, who d 1812
A3. Philippe, b 1813 Baie St. Paul, QUE, d 1962 St. Roch, QUE, mar 1836 Flore Allard, and 2. Luce Casgrain-Gagnon, b 1824 Canada. Philippe res Quebec City, then rem to Brooklyn, NY, grocer and merchant furrier. 5 chn d.y.: Edmond Noe, Marie Lucy, Jean-Phil., Joseph George, his twin, and Abraham.
B1. Marie Emma Sarah, b1849 QUE, d 1897 Chicago, ILL, mar G. Simard
B4. Honorene, b 1853, d 1920s, mar Joseph Kalotte, res WISC.
B7. Harriet, b 1858 Brooklyn, NY
B9. George, b 1860, d 1918 Chicago, ILL mar Sophie Baliff
B10. Emile George, b 1862 Brooklyn, NY d 1952 Chicago, ILL, mar Margaret Dempsey, b 1868 Ireland, d Chicago 1958.
C1. George Joseph, b 1901 Chicago, mar Catherine Burns
C2. Victor Emile, b 1901, twin, mar Ann Mary Panek, 3 chn: Patrick, Dorothy and Victor L.
C3. Peter Phillip, b 1903 Chicago, ILL mar Mary D. Brady, a dau Margaret b 1946 res Columbus, OH
C4. Theodore Michael, b 1904 d 1960. C5. Marie Lucille, b 1906 Chi.
B11. Lucy
A4. Francois, b 1815 Quebec A7. Jean Taouse, b 1819 A10. Marieb1925
A5. Marie Florence PITHON, b 1816 A8. Etienne, b 1821 A11. Marie,d.y.
A6. Jean Hercule, b 1818,d.y. A9. Caroline, 1822-1824.
PITON, John said to have come from J to Cap-aux-Os, QUE, mar Charlotte PRICE at Little Gaspe, QUE. She from Scotland. (Ida Stanley, Parma, OH) See also G.E. ROBERTS.
A1. James, b 1877, drowned in PEI?
A2. Frank b 1878 mar 1909 Clara PERRY, qv, b 1879 Gaspe, QUE,who d1968
B1. Sarah, b 1910 Cap-aux-Os mar Roland Forgues
C1. Andre Forgues mar Ginette, 2 chn
C2. Monique Forgues mar Wayne King, 3 chn
B2. Wilfred, b 1912, mar 1938 Aurine PERRY, qv.
C1. Bernard, b 1939 mar 1963 Yoaine Roussy, 2 chn: Louise, Andre
C2. Gerard, b 1940, mar 1964 Agnes PERRY, 3 chn: Eric, b Laval, QUE, Danny and Lee Ann.
C3. Georges, b 1942, mar 1966 Jacqueline Mainville, 3 chn: Martin, Annie and Simon
C4. Roger, b 1946 mar 1972 Micheline LaJeunesse, dau Martine, b Mont.
C5. Patricia, b 1947 mar 1967 Claude Desrosiers, 2 chn: Manon and Sonia
C6. Albert, b 1949 mar 1971 Diane Goudreau, 3 chn: Frederick, and twins Stephanie and Karine.
C7. Jean-Charles, b 1952 mar 1972 C. Roy, a son Yannic, b Montreal.
C8. Blandine, b 1953 Gaspe, QUE
C9. Aline, b 1957mar Normand Grenier, a dau Karine Grenier.
B3. Mathilda, b 1913 Cap-aux-Os mar 1934 A. Campeau
C1. Murielle Campeau, b 1941, mar R. Sansterre
B4. Josephine, b 1914, d.y.
B5. Raymond, b 1915 mar 1952 A. PERRY, 3 chn: Linda, Danny andBrenda PERRY
B6. Adeline, b 1916 mar J. Calamatas, 4 chn: Nick, George, Andrew and

Frank Calamatas.
B7. Eileen, b 1918 mar Simon Goldman
A3. Edward, b 1879 mar A. Cassivi 1912
B1. Hilda b 1913 mar A. SIMON, qv. B2. Eveline, b 1914
B3. Stella, b 1915 mar A. Cassivi, 4 chn: Robert, Marlene, Oniel and Florent Cassivi.
B4. Anita, b 1916 mar ____LE RASIGNOLD, poss LE ROSSIGNOL?, b Gaspe.
B5. Hermel, b 1917
A4. John, b 1880 d. unmar. A6. Bella, b 1882
A5. Mildred, b 1881 mar Charles ROBERTS, bro of James ROBERTS, qv.
A7. Alice Jane, b 1886 d 1967, res Gaspe, mar Geo. A. ROBERTS, qv. of Gaspe, 10 chn.
A8. Allan, b 1895 mar 1935 I.M. LANGLOIS and 2. 1937, B. Boulet. Allan d 1972, bur Forillon, Gaspe, QUE
B1. Marina, b 1936 mar 1953 Lucien Normand.
C1. Grant Normand, b 1954 mar 1978 C. Bernier, 2 chn, 1 d.y.
C2. Raoul Normand, b 1956 C5. Micheline Normand, b 1964
C3. Martin Normand, b 1960 mar R.M. Dorion
C4. Monique Normand, b 1964 C6. Mireille Normand, b 1974
B2. Norbert, b 1939
B3. Ernest, b 1942 mar 1969 J. Desbiens, res Sept Isles, QUE, 2 chn: Danny and Cathy
B4. Howard, b 1946 mar 1976 C. Shaw, res Labrador City?, son Jimmy

PLACE. Compiler believes some in early New England may have been DE LA PLACE of Jersey. DE LA PLACE in J 1576, poss Hug? DE LA PLACE in Trinity and St. Martin J 1668, and in Trinity and St. Brelade J 1749.

PLACE, DE LA PLACE?, John with fam at York, ME 1676, farmer. OUTC. (Noyes)

PLACE, John, mariner in Boston 1686, son of Peter, who res Boston, MA 1650. (Noyes) OUTC

PLACE, Sarah mar in Boston 1695 Thomas STEVENS, shipwright, res Charleston, MA. (Noyes)

PLACE, 18 of this surname were heads of fams in NH 1790 (Census) Res Rochester, New Durham, Bartlett, Barnstead, Middleton & Portsmouth.

PLACE, Ebenezer mary Jane PEAVEY. OUTC.

POAKE, POKE, PORKE, LE PORCQ, POCQUET, PASQUET. Several similarly pronounced surnames produced some questionable data in early New England Needs more research. POAKE was a cordwainer in Wells, ME 1731. POQUET a Hug. surname in C.I.? LE PORCQ was the name of a J fam 1772, when Abraham PITON mar Susanne LE PORCQ. LE PORKE in St. Heliers and St. Laurens J 1668.

POCHARD, fam name of G, said to have desc in North America.

POCKET, POQUET, PUCKETT, see above about POKE & POCQUET.

POIDEVIN, old name in C.I. In St. Brelade and St. Peter J 1668. In St. Peter 1749. Curr J. Curr and common in G. See Guernsey Soc. Bull. Spring 1973.

POIDEVIN, PLODVIN, LE POIDEVIN, Nicholas from G to GCO 1807. Mar there Sarah O'Hara. Nicholas was a cousin of James BICHARD, who also came to GCO 1807. Nicholas was the grandfather of the SARCHET who wrote several volumes about the Guernsey Islanders who settled in GCO. 1ch. (WRCIC; Sarchet, Vol 1)
A1. Sarah mar James P. Williams, res Jackson Twp., GCO.

POIDEVIN, ___, wife of John SAYRE, qv, in GCO 1800s.

POINDEXTER, see also PENDEXTER

POINGDESTRE in J 1309. In Grouville, St. Clement, St. Saviour, St.

Peter, St. Heliers, and St. John J 1668. In Grouville, St. Saviour, St. Heliers and St. John J 1749. Curr J.

POINDEXTER, George of Swan Farm, J, sonof Thomas, Seigneur of the Fief es Poingdestre, and of Elizabeth EFFARD, qv, dau of Rev. Nicholas Effard of G and J. George was b ca 1627 J, rem to Virginia ca 1657, had a land grant in Gloucester Co., and 850 acres of land in Williamsburg, later the site of the Virginia capital. George was a vestryman of Bruton Parish, VA, planter, slave holder and ship owner. Said to have imported the first Jersey cattle to America. Mar Susannah ---, poss NICOLLE?, qv, 3 chn. He d ca 1690, and his wife in 1693. Much more data in sources. (POINGDESTRE-POINDEXTER, A NORMAN FAMILY, by John P. Landers, Austin, TX; Mrs. Paul De Voe, Marion, IND; Mrs. Charles Phillips, Woodland Hills, CAL; OUR KIN, by Ackerly, etc; INDIANA HIST. LIBRARY MAGAZINE; VIRGINIA HIST. MAG; EVENING POST of St. Heliers J, 1910; SLCITY records; Rose Johnson, Hickman, KY; Lawton, VHM; BIO. DICT. OF JERSEY by Balleine; Stanard; ELLIS FAM OF VIRGINIA; BACHELDER GEN; OLD NORTHWEST, Vol 8)

A1. George, b ca 1651 mar ___, ca 1672, d 1716
B1. George III, b ca 1673 mar Mary ___, 6 chn.
C1. George IV, mar Susanna Marston. Note MARSTON in CABOT fam, MA. Geo. res Christ's Cross, VA.
D1. George Benskin, mar Frances LIGHTFOOT and 2. ___. 6 chn, poss desc in TN? (See CI COLL B Safford, Darien, CT)
C2. Philip, b 1708 mar/1st Eliz. then Sarah Crymes C3. Jacob mar Sarah ___
C4. Judith, b 1705 C5. John C6. Mary, b 1715
B2. Thomas, b ca 1664 or 1675 Williamsburg, VA, mar Sarah, dau of David Crawford of VA, from Scottish fam. Res St. Pauls Parish, Hanover Co., VA. Thomas d 1753?
C1. Susanna, b 1696 mar ___Snead C2. Elizabeth b 1699, mar ____
C3. Sarah, b 1702
C4. John, b 1703 mar Christian Gorsuch/Gissage. Another source says he mar 1. Christian Vesperman? and 2. Sarah SHELTON, qv.
D1. Thomas, b ca 1733 d 1807? mar Lucy Jones, ca 1733-1816, and 2. Elizabeth Pledge. 10 chn, many desc.
E1. William Pledge, 1766-1844, mar Eliz. Ashburn, Stokes Co., NC, 1795.
F1. Denson Ashburn, 1799-1876, mar Sarah Jones, 1823
G1. Thomas J., 1826-1869, mar Lucy Marler of Surrey Co, NC1847.
H1. John J., 1869-1950, mar 2. Augusta (Martin) Smith, dau of Gilbert Martin of Yadkin Co., NC 1896
I1. Archie Row of Henry Co., IND, mar Inez Houdeshell
J1. Helen b 1921 mar Paul Volney 1943
D2. John, res Campbell Co., VA, 2 daus, Ann Cobbs and Mary Slaughter
D3. William, b ca 1734, mar Margaret ___, 5 chn: Wm., Peter, Charles Joseph and Sally, who mar John Tate 1799.
D4. Capt. Joseph, b 1736 served in Rev. War, rem to Bedford Co., mar Jane Kennerly, or Elizabeth?, res Campbell Co., VA, 11 chn: Samuel, James, Joseph, William (desc in MO), Reuben (rem toSC) Thomas K., John, Louis, Ann, Elizabeth and Richard (went West)
D5. Richard, b ca 1738 d before 1779, 2 daus, Christian and Febey
D6. Frances, mar ___Anderson D8. Sally/Sarah mar ___Triton
D7. Ann, mar ___Slaughter D9. Elizabeth/Betty
B3. Sarah, b ca 1676 mar John Vaughn
B4. Ann, b ca 1677, mar Richard Clough
A2. John, b ca 1652 mar Katherine ___, by 1689, had land on Mill Swamp.
A3. Elizabeth, b ca 1654
A4. Thomas, b ca 1664? mar Sarah Crawford A5. Jacob?

Another POINDEXTER line goes from George, John, Joseph, Samuel, Willis, Edward and Zelpha. (Rose Johnson, Hickman, KY) There are several other POINDEXTER GEN books to cover other lines, not found by compiler. See sources.

POINDEXTER, lawyer in Ann Arbor, MI 1800s. (OLD NORTHWEST, Vol 8)

POINDEXTER, Sarah K., mar 1880 Timothy Simon Batchelder b 1854, son of Ephraim and Hannah (Hanson) B., the second wife. (BACH. GEN)

POINDEXTER, 20 of these noted in OH 1860 census

POINDEXTER in MA 1600s. (Essex Hist. Coll. 1979)

POINDEXTER, Americans named Anderson and Lawton claim Hug. ancestry through POINGDESTRE of Guernsey Island. (Lawton)

POIGNARD, cabinet maker from J said to have settled in Lexington, KY.

POLLEY, cf POULET of Grouville J 1668.

POLLY, POLLEY, John in early New England. Some research done by Alice Wineinger, Haddam, KS and Plyllis Broderson, Charlotte, NC.

POOLE, John in Harbour Breton, Nfld. 1811. Some research in J, see CIFHS #8.

PORKE, see POAKE.LE PORCQ, LE PORKE in several J parishes 1668.

PORTER, not an old C.I. surname. However, marriages with C.I. women in Utah. See SARAH FARR AND HER DESC, #929.273, Mormon records.

PORTER, Robert Hamil, b 1819 New Utica?, NY, son of Wm. or Robert Porter. Prob English, but came to our notice as husband of Sarah Judith LE GEYT, dau of John, who came from England and settled in Hartford, CT. Robert Porter mar 1. Sarah LE GEYT; 2. in Spring 1855 Sarah Farr LE CHEMINANT, widow of Peter LE CHEMINANT, qv.; 3. Eliza or Elizabeth J., poss Mary?, Graham Aug. 1855; 4. Mary Ann WILLIAMS in 1856, b J. He mar 5. Matilda ___, and 6. Mary Eliz. MALLET, b 1848 J, dau of Thomas and Jenny. LE CHEMINANT, WILLIAMS and MALLET were all J surnames, qv. Robert had an interesting life, see records in WRCIC and in sources. (Dorothy Le Geyt, E. Hartland, CT; WRCIC; STALEY FAM. HIST: Dion France, Coalville, UT; Shirley Rizzuto, Sandy, UT; BIOG. OF SARAH LE CHEMINANT by Sarah Johnson and Peter & Sarah F. Le Cheminant; THE 1854 MORMON EMIG. FROM EUROPE TO SLCITY, not seen by compiler, by Wilfred H. Le Cheminant. Some data is uncertain. CAUTION: TRIAL CHART.

A1. Elizabeth A2. Henry A3. Lewis

A4. Joseph A5. Margaret (note another Margaret later)

A6. Harriet Amelia, b 1845 Monroe, ILL, dau of Sarah LE GEYT, mar 1867 William Bailey, 3 chn.

A7. Robert, b ca 1848 Iowa, by Sarah LE GEYT, d.y. A8. another ch?

A9. Edward, b ca 1856, poss by Matilda and previous husband?

A10. Agnes Georgina, b 1856, dau of ___Graham, b 1827 PA, d ca 1863. Her chn were James Hamil, Mary Geneva, and Wm. W. Georgiana mar 1873 Conrad H. Staley, had 18 chn b Upton, UT.(STALEY FAM HIST)

A11. William J., b ca 1857 UT, poss son of Sarah LE GEYT?

A12. Wilmont I., b 1857 UT, son of M.A. Williams, b J, her 1st ch?

A13. James Hamil, b 1858 Skull Valley, UT son of Eliza Graham. Mar Eliz. Starkins Lowe and d 1892?

A14. John Alma, ch of M.A. Williams, b 1859, played with Indian chn in Chalk Creek, UT a child.

A15. Sarah/Sadie, b 1863 dau of Graham or Le Geyt, was taken, after her mother's death, along with William and/or Wilmont, to be raised by Sarah LE CHEMINANT for 10 yrs. then taken by Robert Porter.

A16. Mary Geneva, b ca 1860, poss d.y.? Dau of Eliz. J. Graham

A17. William W. Porter, b ca 1861, son of Eliz. Graham?

A18. David, b 1864, son of Mary Ann Williams of Wyoming.

A19. Mary, b ca 1865, dau of Mary Ann Williams. Mary/Molly b UT or WY mar Byron Nelson 1885, and d 1936 in Coalville, UT

A20. Ephraim, b ca 1864, mother not named, poss son of Matilda? The father, Robert Porter, res this year in Yellow Creek, UT.

A21. Margaret, b ca 1865, also ch of Matilda?

A22. Marie, b ca 1867 A23, Alice, b ca 1868 UT, by Matilda?

A24. Emma/Melissa?, b ca 1869, dau of Mary Ann WILLIAMS, in WY. In 1870 Mary Ann Williams, Eliza Graham and Sarah Farr LE CHEMINANT do not appear in the eensus with Robert Hamil Porter, nor do chn Wilmont J., age 13, John A. age 11, nor Mary Geneva. Emma/ Melissa mar 1885 Stephen D. Wade and d 1936.

A25. Henry Irvin, b 1870, son of Mary Eliz. MALLET, qv, mar 1899 Karen Strom, d 1949

A26. George Edward, b 1871 by MALLET, mar 1. Ida A. Howell, d 1943

A27. Mary Jane, b 1873 d 1876, by MALLET, inCoalville, UT.

A28. Annie Elizabeth, b 1874 dau of MALLET, in Almy, WY, mar 1895 John R. Henstrom, d 1955.

A29. Rose Ella Florence, dau of Mary MALLET, b 1875 Almy, WY, mar 1899 Theo. Hopfenbeck, d 1939

A30. Joseph Amos, b 1877, d.y.

A31. Poss several other chn belong here. Robert Porter res Rawlins, WY 1878, and d that year in Ogden, UT. Mary Ann WILLIAMS Porter, rem to Almy WY 1879, res with son John Alma Porter and his fam. There were 3 young chn in the house.

A32. Other chn b to Matilda?

A33. There is also an Earl Daniel that belongs in this fam, ch of Mary Ann WILLIAMS, year of birth not known to compiler.

See MALLET, WILLIAMS, and LE CHEMINANT.

POTWIN, LE POITEVIN, John, a goldsmith from J? mar in Boston 1721 Mary JACKSON, qv. LE POIDEVIN curr J. (NEHGS Vol 41)

POULAIN, Susanna, b France or J, to NJ with CARTERET in 1665, ship PHILIP. See NJ section. Susanna mar Richard SKINNER, qv. She is said to have been lady's maid to Lady CARTERET in J. POULAIN curr G and J. (Holcombe; Roland Rossiter, Patchogue, NY)

PRAY, south of England surname, also found in C.I. at times. Sometimes may equal DU PRE of J and G. Also Cf DE PREAUX in G 1200s.

PRAY, Quinton, b 1595, rem to Lynn, MA as iron-worker ca 1640, rem to Braintree, MA, and d there 1667. The fam is given in OLD KITTERY AND HER FAMILIES. Several chn mar into C.I. fams. OUTC.

PRAY, John, bp 1753 mar Jane MESIER, poss MESURIER?, qv. He was a sea captain, and d NY 1812. Desc.

PREVOST, PROVOST in J 1309. LE PREVOST in St. Clement and St. Heliers J 1668, 1749. PROVOST curr J. Pronounced LE PRAYVO, LE PROVO.

PREVOST, Brig. Gen. Augustine, S.C. royalist. See Troxlers book; SC Hist. Magazine, Jan. and April 1942; Coulter; Filby; Tingley.

PREVOST noted in Quebec City petition 1838. (LOST IN CANADA, Aug.1981)

PRIAULX, old in J and G. PRIAULX in Vale G 1821 (CIFHS #14) Curr G and J. See also CIFHS #8. One PRIAULX, PREAUX was with William the Conqueror in 1066. Another accompanied King Richard the Lion-Hearted to the Crusades, and saved the King's life.

PRIAULX, Pierre/Peter, 1781-1859 of G, mar 1. Elizabeth MAINDONALD, who d 1817 G; 2. Judith GILBERT, GUILBERT, qv, who d 1829 G; 3. Elizabeth MAHY or MABY. 8 chn, some of whom came to America. (Florence Larrick, Santa Barbara, CAL; Bessie McNiel, Santa Barbara, CAL)

A1. Peter, b 1807 G, d 1875 G, desc, res Le Friquet de Haut, G.

A2. John, b 1808 G, d 1863 or 1868 in US, mar 1837 Elizabeth BAILLEUL, who d 1874. They rem to Jackson Co., IA, near Maquoketa.

B1. Mary Ann, b 1828 OH?, mar Daniel Clark, res Center Point, IA.

C1. Dewitt Clinton Clark, b 1857 d 1928 mar Sally Dower
C2. Leroy Fenamore Clark, b 1858 d 1890 unmar
C3. John Cephas Clark, b 1859 d 1932 mar Martha Gambling, res Terrill IA, a grandson Maurice Clark res La Jolla, CAL
C4. Benj. Franklin Clark, b 1861 d 1945 mar Minnie McVey, res KS. A dau Marie Kling.
C5. James Douglas Clark, b 1862 d 1949, mar Hattie Acres, res Cottage Grove, OR, had at least a son, who mar Elizabeth ___.
C6. Charles Henry Clark, b 1865 d 1903, mar Dora Blackman
C7. Mary Elizabeth/Libby Clark, b 1870 d 1925, mar Andrew Davidson, res Milford, IA, dau Esther Davidson, and other chn?
C8. Smith Edward CLark, b 1871 d 1876
C9. George Wilson Clark, called Wise, b 1874 d 1947, mar Clara Bolton
D1. Hazel Clark, b 1901 mar Arthur Hanson, res Cedar Falls, IA
E1. Jack Hanson, b 1927 mar Lorraine McDowell
F1. Jay Hanson, b 1949 mar Jeanne Wagner, 5 chn: Brent, Brad, Blain Blake, and Lynne Hanson.
F2. Sue Ann Hanson, b 1951 mar Steven Johnson
F3. Kay Hanson, b 1955 mar Greg Johnson, a dau Amanda Johnson
F4. Lee Hanson, b 1958
C10. Susan Estella Clark, b 1877 d 1879
C11. Lucy Ellen/Ella Clark, b 1879 d 1960, mar Clyde McVey, b 1878 d 1968, res Center Point and Vinton, IA.
D1. Fern McVey, b 1904 mar George Carberry, b 1904 Vinton, IA
E1. Kathrine Carberry, b 1943 adopted, mar Elmer Sachs, son Lance.
D2. Clair McVey, b 1906 d 1980, mar Fern Caldwell, 1908-1969, mar 2. Lucille Armstrong.
E1. Leota McVey, b 1927 mar Leo Williams, res Marion, IA, 5 chn: Duane, Diana Ashley, Dixie, Connie and Suzanne Williams.
E2. Jack McVey, b 1930, d 1966, mar Ann Hanzlik, 2 chn, Sheila and Tracy McVey.
E3. Virginia McVey, b 1931 mar John Evans, res Davenport, IA, 3 married chn: John, Karen and James Evans.
D3. Orval McVey, b 1908 mar Lavonne Dake, b 1912, res Vinton, IA
E1. Beverly McVey, b 1937 mar Jack Hodges, res Beatrice, NEB. 3 chn: Jay, Michael and Randall Hodges
E2. Barbara McVey, b 1944 mar Gary Anderson, res Longwood, FLA, 2 chn: Brook and Matthew Anderson.
E3. Janice McVey, b 1945, mar James SARCHETT, qv, res Vinton, IA.
B2. James, name sometimes spelled PREO,PREEO in the West. Mar and wife died soon. A picture in IA shows the father, five sons and a dau, with the wife's picture hanging in background. It seems likely that these three are part of this family.
C1. George Preeo, b 1884 C2. Frank Preeo, 1885-1948
C3. Emma Preeo, b 1887, mar ___ Crawford?
D1. Eula Crawford Person, b 1913 D2. Kathrine Crawford Oddo,1918
B3. John
B4. Eliza, mar Adam Flathers, 5 chn:
C1. Rose Flathers mar Charles Van Doren
C2. Winifred Flathers mar Harvey Bailey
C3. Edward Flathers, no issue
C4. John Flathers, sonRaymond
C5. Emma Flathers mar G. Frary
B5. Nicholas, prob unmar
B6. Peter, mar Lillian Wirst, res IA. These may be their chn:
C1. Oren E. PREO
C2. Lula PREO
C3. John PREO
C4. Nora PREO
C5. Cora PREO.
B7. Joseph, b 1853 d 1931 mar Desire GIFFARD, res Maquokita, IA, 5 chn: William, Flora, Mary, Mabel and Lois.

B8. Daniel, mar Carol Stephens?, d fairly young, fam in CAL?
C1. Duroc Daniel b 1902 C2. Pierre Jean, b 1903
C3. Dora Elizabeth, b 1904
B9. Susan mar Harrison Bobo, 2 chn: Ralph and Flora Bobo
B10. Flora, b 1860, mar Adam Flathers after Eliza above died,no issue
B11. Lucy, b 1863 mar Franklin McNiel, res Center Point, IA, desc. in CAL.
C1. John McNiel b 1893 mar Eleanor Murray, no issue C2. Bessie,unmar
C3. KEnneth McNiel, b 1904, mar Lena McGinnis, res Center Point, IA, 2 chn: Lois and Harold McNiel, unmar.
C4. Clarence McNiel, b 1907, d 1970, mar Doris WILLIAMS, 1917-1966, res Center Point, IA.
D1. Robert McNiel, b 1944 mar Patricia Wood, 2 chn: Kathryn and Christine McNiel, res Lexington, KY.
D2. Nancy McNiel, b 1947 mar James Willert
D3. Dale McNiel b 1948 mar Mary Harvey
D4. Carol McNiel b 1954 mar David Brummer
D5. Opal McNiel b 1956 mar Dennis Ringgenberg, 2 chn: Melissa and Carly Ringgenberg.
A3. Nicholas, b 1809 G, d 1898 GCO, mar Rachel PRIAULX, 1813-1854, settled in Adams Twp., GCO, where he had 80 acres. He was a cabinet maker and wagon maker, d after age 84. 7 chn. Poss the Nich. who was an original stockholder of the National Bank of Cambridge, OH 1863. One Nicholas PRIAULX mar Isabel Sherrard, dau of Wm. and Mary (Bogle) Sherrard, of a fam that went from Ireland to Guernsey then to GCO.
B1. John T., b 1839, mar Elizabeth Sherrard, 4 chn: James, William, Elizabeth and Alice, also Eli.
B2. William H. served in Civil War, mar Sarah Nawsit, res Westland Twp., GCO. Dau Estella May b 1872, other chn?
B3. Mary J. mar James Young of GCO? B5. Louisa mar Johnson Lind
B4. Sarah A., mar Harvey Beard of GCO B6. Amlinda, mar Rob't Ford.
B7. James O. rem to Missouri, mar Elizabeth Sherrard, had dau Elizabeth b 1876.
A4. Mary, b 1815 G, poss d 1817 with mother.
A5. Martha, b 1820 d 1900, mar J. Griffin, who d 1882, res Tasmania, near Australia, where there are desc., visited by F. Larrick.
A6. Rachel, b 1821 G, d 1892, mar 1847 John HEAUME, qv, res GCO, 3 sons, but 2 d.y. desc. Rachel bur Buffalo Cem, GCO.
A7. Thomas, b 1826 d 1905, killed by falling tree in CAL, unmar.
A8. Elizee, Elisha, b 1829, d or was killed during Civil War, served in Iowa infantry. Had farm near Norwich, IA.
B1. Edward? rem to TX ca age 23, poss a fam there? PRIAULX in Houston.
PRIAULX, Eleanor, b 1850 of G fam d 1854 GCO, bur Ford Cem.
PRIAULX, Eliza b G, mar Isaac McIlyar, 1814-1837, GCO.
PRIAULX, Elizabeth b 1824 G? d 1902 Cambridge, OH
PRIAULX, Ernest Blondel, b St. Sampson G, to WIS ca 1910. He the son of John PRIAULX and Marie LANGLOIS, mar Eva Marie MAUGER, dau of John and Eva Mitchell MAUGER, res Racine, WI.(E. Priaulx, Racine,WI)
A1. Ernest B. Jr. mar 1903, 4 chn. See also BLONDEL.
B1. Ernest John B2. John William B3. James Blondel.
PRIAULX, James mar Nancy Smith GCO, a dau Maggie b 1884
PRIAULX, John b 1818 d 1888 GCO, poss served in Civil War?
PRIAULX, Mary, b 1802-1809 G, d Cambridge, OH 1892.
PRIAULX, Rachel b 1821 La Friquet de Haut, Castel, G, dau of Pierre & Judith(GUILBERT) PRIAULX. Rachel to US when only 15, with two older half-brothers, who by then were living in Ohio, and had returned to

Guernsey to marry their sweethearts. The story goes that they were married on the same day in different parishes. It is believed that they brought Rachel and her two younger brothers back to Ohio with them. A brother of Rachel had already emigratedto Australia. One of the younger bros. was killed in the Civil War, and another by a falling tree. Rachel d 1892 and is bur Hartford, OH. She mar John HEAUME, which see for family. (Florence Larrick, Santa Barb.CAL)
PRIAULX, Rachel, 1802-1851, bur GCO
PRIAULX, Reginald, b Le Bourg,Foret, G, rem to Detroit, MI 1920, had 3 sons and 3 daus. Rem to CALIF and NY, also res other places. A Norman PRIAULX res Detroit 1970s.
PRIAULX. "My great grandfather left Guernsey in the mid-1800s and settled in Gaspe, QUE. My grandfather, aprinter, was William Arthur PRIAULX. He migrated to Rochester and Buffalo, NY, then to Pasadena CAL and to ORegon." Son Arthur Wm. res OR. A cousin Edward PRIAULX res OR, and another cousin Percival PRIAULX res CAL mid 1900s. (Allen Priaulx, Honolulu, HAW)
PRIAULX, Sadie, b 1880 GCO, no parents named in record.
PRIAULX, Sara J., b 1843 GCO mar James Baird, res Wills, GCO.(GCO Lib)
A1. Clarinda L. Baird
A2. Wm. K. Baird A3. Alice F. Baird A4. Charles M. Baird.
PRIAULX, Mrs. Sarah mar 1843 James Band in GCO.
PRIAULX, auto dealer in Los Angeles, CAL, name also noted in Toronto, ONT, in IA and in WIS.
PRIAULX, Robert from G, CBS television programmer in recent years.
PRICE in G before 1814. Curr G and J.
PRICE, Edward, res C.I., where son Frederick was b. Fam from England? (Shirley O'Neil, Newport Beach, CAL)
A1. Frederick b G 1800s? A2. William
PRICE, Frederick, b C.I. and Catherine, age 71, res Cap des Rosiers, QUE in 1881. She was Scots Presbyterian. (A.Brochet, London, ONT)
PRIDEAUX, found in C.I. and also in England. See Q.A. IN CANADA.
PRIDEOX, PRIDEAUX, George, a servant to Joseph Dalton 1670s in SC. OUTC. (Baldwin)
PRIDEAUX, Grace from C.I. or England mar Timothy Cumming in MRB 1687. Mary PRIDEAUX mar Jonathan Tewksbury 1717 MRB. Susannah PRIDEAUX mar Timothy Cummings 1701 MRB. OUTC.
PRIDEAUX, Nicholas from J via Barbadoes? or from England? mar Bridget ___, grdau of Rev. John Wilson, desc. (GENS AND ESTATES OF CHARLESTOWN, MA; Wyman) OUTC.
PRINCE, a few res in C.I. 1800s, poss before? Cf PROUINGS of St. Peter and St. Ouen J 1668.
PRINCE, George Harris, and wife Philippa Georgina DE BRODER, qv, from G to Racine, WI. (P. Knudsen, Madison, WI)
A1. Phyllis Maud b 1909 G, mar in Racine 1933 Clarence Henry Knudsen.
PRINCE, Lt. Charles of his Majesty's ship MERCURY, mar Anne LEMPRIERE of a J fam in Christ Church SC 1763. He was from London, England? Census shows that a Charles Prince res in Charleston district, St. Philipps and St. Michael counties with fam of man, boy, 3 females and 1 slave. Another Charles had a fam of 3 in 1790. In still the same area lived a fam headed by Ann Prince, consisting of a man, a boy and 4 females, plus 4 slaves. (Census) There were many Princes living in SC in 96 and Georgetown areas, 13 heads of fams. OUTC.
PROUINGS, of St. Peter and St. Ouen J 1668, in St. Peter 1749.
PROUINGS, Henry from J, shipowner at Kittery, ME 1641. (A. John Jean)
PROULX in Salem, MA 1970s. Very old name in C.I.
PROULX?, PROU, Ellen, b C.I. or France, went to NJ with Carteret on

ship PHILIP, see NJ section.

PROVO, Cf LE PROVOST, pronounced PROVO, in St. Clement and St. Heliers J 1668 and 1749. Curr J. PROVOST also a Dutch surname. (NJ GENESIS)

PROVOST in Salem, MA 1970s. OUTC.

PROVOST noted in Muskingum, Green and Cuya. Counties, OH 1800s. OUTC.

PROVOE, James, a Frenchman or from C.I.? at Pemaquid Fort 1682. He was about 45 in 1684. (Noyes) OUTC.

PROVOST to Maryland 1741 in book 1223, by Coldham, also to CAL. (Rasmussen) OUTC.

PROVOST, Thomas mar 1787 Elizabeth Slason in Stamford-Darien, CT. (CONN. MARRIAGES) OUTC.

PUCKETT, POCKETT, PASQUET?, John from C.I. to Henrico Co., VA 1665. PASQUET, pron. PAHKET, was in St. Martin J 1668. Same or another John POCKETT was headright of John Graves, Eliz. City, VA 1637. One PUCKETT desc believes fam originated in J, as POQUET or PASQUET. John P. had wife Anne and sons John, William and Thomas. See also POAKE. (Pat Dell, Jacksonville, NC; SOME PUCKETTS AND THEIR KIN, by Hester E. Garrett, 1960; PUCKETT GEN, Gladys H. Meier, Brownsville, TX,1955)

PUDEATOR. This name was prob PUDESTOR, PUDDESTER, a Nfld. scrambling of C.I. surname POINGDESTRE, qv. as POINDEXTER.

PUDEATOR, Jacob of Salem MA, mar Ann, widow of Thomas GREENSLADE, qv, of Devon or Somerset, England or poss of J? Jacob d before March 1677. Ann was hanged as a witch 1692. The original papers of this fam were found in the records of the ENGLISH fam. qv. "The name was, as far as I can judge, a Jersey (French) name and seems to have suffered a change in New England." Chn: John, Thomas, Ruth, Samuel, James and Sarah.

PULLING noted in MA 1700s. In Dorset England 1273, but cf POULAIN.

PUNCHARD, PYNCHARD. Origin of this fam may go back to BOUTILLIER/ PINCERNA, two names of one of the great officers of the Duchy of Normandy, who accompanied William the Conqueror to England in 1066. Listed in the Roll Falaise as Hugh Pincerna, his desc. became known as LE BOUTILLIERS and some settled in Trinity Parish, Jersey. The PINCERNA part of the name may have been taken by other descendants. PYNCHARD, PUNCHARDE, PONCHARD and POCHARD are said also to be named from origin in Pontchardon in Normandy, France. (Philip Le Boutillier, Toledo, OH; Reed S. Hall, Denver, COL; records in SLCity) CAUTION: TRIAL CHARTS.

PYNCHARD, PINCHART in J 1461, PYNCHARD in St. Martin J 1528, in J 1607. Jersey appears to be origin of those in early New England. (Pope; Allis; Savage; Perley; Holmes; GLEANINGS; Mary Wislow, Dodge City,KS; Virkus II; NEHGS Vol 11; Essex Coll, Vol 2; Richard B. Dunn, Los Alamos, NM; Essex Ant., Vol 8; Worcester Gen., 1856)

PUNCHARD, William, b ca 1644 J? mar 1669 Abigail Waters, bp 1645 Salem, MA, dau of Richard and Joyce (Plasse) Waters. See also PLACE. Chn b Salem, MA. Note that a Wm. PUNCHARD arrived in Boston on sloop ENDEAVOR from Long Island 1715. (Whitmore) Three ENDEAVORS are ships listed as owned by Jerseymen ca 1760-1770. (A.John Jean,Jersey) (Andover, MA records)

A1. Abigail, b 1670, d.y.? A2. Mary, b 1673 d 1678

A3. William, b 1677 Salem, d 1748. Mar 1. 1703 Hannah BROWN, said to be from J, dau of Eleazar and Sarah (Bulkley) BROWN, or LE BRUN? Wm. mar 2. 1717 Mehitabel PERKINS.

B1. William, b 1704 New Haven, CT.

B2. Abigail, b 1708 CT, d 1774. Mar 1727 Deacon or Capt. Daniel Bradley, 1706-1773 of Hamden, CT, son of Daniel Bradley of New Haven and Sarah BASSETT.

C1. Jabez Bradley, b 1733, d 1793, of Hamden, CT, mar Esther Beach, dau of Moses Beach. Esther d 1794.

D1. Sarah Bradley, b 1760, mar 1781 Elijah Peck

E1. Amerilla Peck, b 1785 mar Asa White

F1. Lura White, b 1808 mar 1830 Harry B. Dickerman

G1. Mary Dickerman, b 1850 mar 1884 Thatcher B. Dunn

H1. Frederick J. Dunn, b 1880? mar 1906 Alice G. Eaton

I1. Richard B. Dunn, b 1912 mar 1938 Margaret P. Myers.

J1. Richard B. Dunn Jr. b 1942 mar 1966 Hedy Mannheimer.

D2. Jabez Bradley Jr. b 1765 d 1917 Lee, MA, rem to Onondaga Co., NY 1794, settled in Northville, Cayuga Co., NY. Mar Esther Bradley, 1765-1850, dau of Eli Bradley.

E1. Walter Goodyear Bradley, 1808-1882, Kings Ferry, NY, mar 1830 Henrietta Todd, 1810-1882.

B3. Hannah, b 1711 mar 1737/8 Hezekiah Beecher.

A4. John, b 1682 mar 1706 Martha LEMON, LE MOINE? of a J fam and 2. Martha HOOPER, qv, dau of Ben HOOPER, cordwainer, who d 1718 and left property to dau Martha and husband John PUNCHARD. Later this estate was sold to James HOOPER, boat builder of J fam? John and Martha res Andover, MA/ and John d ca 1740.

B1. John, b 1708, d 1767, mar 1730 Hannah MARSTON/MARSTIN, who d 1788, Andover? age 77.

C1. John bp 1731 Salem, MA, mar Sarah Bickford, b ca 1733, dau of George and Elizabeth (Butler) Bickford of Salem, living 1761. John may have d soon after 1756? A John in Salem, MA 1790, with fam of 9.

D1. John, mar Keziah Manning 1783 D3. Sarah, bp 1756?

D2. uncertain, Mary? bp 1754, mar Joseph Ellinwood.

C2. William, bp 1733

C3. Benjamin, bp 1735, Port Inspector of Salem, d 1820 age 83. Mar Priscilla Bickford 1757, res Salem. Priscilla was sister of Sarah above, d Lyndeboro, NH 1775. Benj. mar 2. her cousin Rebecca Bickford, dau of John and Eliz. (Hayward) Bickford, 1738-1800. Some chn uncertain.

D1. William, bp 1758 mar 1. Sarah Sprague of Malden, MA 1785, and 2. Sarah Hanover 1795, dau of Benj. of MRB. Res Andover. Wm. a sea Captain, d at sea, bur Martha's Vineyard 1810.

E1. Sarah L. mar Jonathan MILLETT, 5 chn.

F1. William P. Millett, b 1825, an heir of Ben. H. PUNCHARD, d Andover, MA 1868. Mar Martha Marland Gledhill, niece of Mrs. Punchard.

G1. Wm. Henry Millett, b 1841 G3. Eliza Millett, b 1845

G2. Martha P. Millett, b 1843 G4. Frank E. Millett, b 1847

F2. Joseph R. Millett, b 1819, heir of his uncle Ben H. mar Eliz. VALPY, qv, dau of Samuel in 1845, and d 1856.

G1. Henry Millett took name of his step-father, Plato Eames.

G2. Samuel VALPY Millett b 1848 Data uncertain on sons.

F3. Jonathan HARDY MILLETT, d 1840, and son Benj. Hardy Millett mar Lucy S. Clarke.

F4. Amelia Ann, mar J.B. Edwar-s. F5. Sarah, 1822-1839

E2. Mary/Polly, mar Ebenezer Worcester 1804.

E3. Rebecca, b 1798 Salem, by 2nd wife, d Cavendish, VT 1851. Mar 1819 John DARBY, qv. Darby, b 1795 res Salem, MA, rem to Ft. Wayne, IND then to Saginaw, MI. He mar 2. at Cavendish, VT 1853 Mrs. Achsah Cobb, dau of Dr. Nathan Weeks, b Jamaica,VT. 8 chn by Rebecca. (Essex Coll, Vol 2)

F1. Sarah Rebecca DARBY, DERBY, b 1812 Salem, MA d 1857 VT, mar

1846 John L. Whipple, b 1815 Dunbarton, NH, res Boston, MA, 2 chn: G1. Annie Whipple, d.y. G2. Grace Whipple, b 1850 MA.
F2. John Perley Derby, b 1822 Salem F3. Eliz. P. Derby, b 1824
F4. Benj. Punchard Derby, b 1826 Andover, MA
F5. Caroline Derby, b 1828 mar 1859 Geo. A. Lathrop at Saginaw,MI
F6. Martha Punchard Derby, b 1831 mar 1855 Benj. F. Grinnell of NY, b 1829, jeweler, 2 chn.
G1. Florence Grinnell, b 1855 Jersey City, NJ
G2. Clifford Grinnell, b 1860
F7. Maria Derby, b 1834, mar 1859 James Cutler Dunn Parker, Boston
G1. Hamilton Derby Parker
F8. Mary Stone Derby, b 1835, d 1856 Fort Wayne, IND.
E4. Ben Hanover, b 1799 mar Martha Lawton Marland, and before age 18 was employed as bookkeeper by his cousin, Joseph BALLESTIE, BALLESTER, L'ARBALESTIER, qv, of Boston. Had notable career in banking, dry goods, etc. Left large estate, provided for relatives, helped establish Episcopal Ch. and provided funds for a school. More data in Andover, MA. Hist. Soc. No issue but adopted two daus. He d 1850.
D2. Benjamin, 1760-1762 D5. James, bp 1768
D3. Priscilla, bp 1765 D6. Sarah, bp 1769, d.y.
D4. Hannah, bp 1767 D7. Sarah again, bp 1771
C4. James, b 1737 mar 1760 Dorcas Townsend, who d 1777 Lyndeboro, NH James mar late 1777 Elizabeth Sprague of Malden, MA.
D1. John b 1763 Salem, MA d 1857, mar 1783 Keziah MAZURY, qv, d 1846, 11 chn.
E1. Keziah, b 1790 E2. Rev. Geo. b 1806, of BOSTON TRAVELER.
D2. Dorcas/Darkes, bp 1766 D3. Thomas, bp 1771
C5. Samuel, bp 1740 mar 1762 Susanna Bickford, sister of Sarah and Priscilla, b ca 1733, living 1761, and 2. widow Alice Poor 1778. Susanna the dau of Geo. Bickford and Elizabeth BATTER, qv. Poss other chn?
D1. Samuel, bp 1770 D2. Benjamin bp 1770 D3. ? bp 1788
D4. John, b 1791 mar Sarah, dau of Malthus Ward of Haverhill, NH? or MA. Later res Boston, stationer, rem to FLA. D Jax.,FLA 1831. (Essex Coll, Vol 6)
C6. Timothy, b 1744, d 1746 C8. Sarah, bp 1750 mar John CHAMBERLAIN?
C7. Mary?, bp 1747 C9. Hannah, mar Richard Averson 1762
B2. Mary, bp 1711 B4. William, 1715-1724 B5. Abigail, bp 1718
B3. Benjamin, bp 1712, mar Hannah Elles 1739. B6. James, bp 1720
A5. Abigail, bp 1684 A6. Sarah, b 1685
PUNCHARD, Mary Heard, dau of William, mar 1833, his first wife, Dr. Jonathan Fox of Worcester, MA. Res Francestown, NH. She d 1836, he mar 2. 1837, Hannah, dau of John DERBY, qv, in Salem, MA, b 1808, d 1840. Dr. Fox mar 3. 1841 Mary, dau of John BARTON, qv, of Salem, b 1809. (WORCESTER FAMILY, p. 856)
A1., by 1st wife, Mary Helen Fox b 1834, d 1905 Grand Rapids, MI, mar 1855 Rev. George Adams Pollard, b 1830 Hallowell, ME, d 1914. He was a Missionary to Turkey. Rev. Pollard and Mary Helen had 5 chn all b Turkey. (Thea Whipple, Garden Grove, CAL)
B1. ? B2. ? B3. Susie Admas Pollard, b 1861 Turkey
B4. Harry Howard Pollard b 1865 Turkey, mar 1897 Grand Rapids, MI, Kate June Kirkbride, b 1875 Coopersville, MI. He was ordained 1910, res Lignite, ND and Shoshi, WY, a Home Missionary.
C1. Ellen Grace, b New Underwood SD 1912.
PYNCHARD, Abigail, dau of Samuel? bp 1683 MA. OUTC.
PUNCHARD, Benj., res Salem MA 1790 with fam of 5. (Census)

PINCARD, PINCHERT, John and wife Mary, with son John Jr. arrived 1672 in Charlestown, SC, had lot 36. He was elected to the Parliament 1672. OUTC. (Baldwin)
PUNCHARD, John, in 1774 rem to Dunstable then to Lyndeboro, NH and was eyewitness to the treachery of Arnold and the capture of Major Andre. A drummer in Regt. of Col Nichols NH Co. Was journeyman shoemaker in Salem, MA, became town clerk, JP and Judge. (NEHGS Vol 11) John d 1857 age 93.
PUNCHARD, PUSHARD, Lucy of Dresden, MA mar Benj. Parker (int) 1800.
PUNCHARD, Michel from J? see in IMMIGRANTS TO LOUISIANA. OUTC.
PUTNAM, not an old C.I. surname. However: "Steele, Joseph, qv, mar Sarah Putnam, b 28 Nov. 1708 Jersey. She d 1802 Washington, NH." (Rev. Don McAllister, Ann Arbor, MI) Note that other Putnams mar into C.I. fams. Note also that Robert MORRELL's first son was born at the Thomas Putnam place in Falmouth. (Noyes) See MORRELL.
QUARM, Elizabeth and Theresa from C.I. to UT 1866, via ship CAROLINE.
QUARN, Robert and William, from C.I. to UT 1862 via ship ANTARCTIC.
QUARM, origin unknown to compiler. Curr resarch? See CIFHS #5.
QUELENEC, old in J and curr there, from Brittany? See KELENEK.
QUELENEC, Hannah, mar 1719 Samuel Frankling in Boston, as KELENEK.
QUENAULT in J 1528, means a puppy. In St. Martin, Grouville and St. Saviour J 1668, and in Grouville J 1749. Curr J.
QUENAULT, Elizabeth Mary Ann, b St. Peter J, dau of Pierre Samuel QUENAULT, a farmer in St. Peter J. Mar 1893 in Grouville, J, Philippe Helleur BISSON, son of P. John BISSON, b 1866 Gaspe, QUE. They res Gaspe, QUE.
QUERY in Boston 1970s. Poss a QUEREE from C.I.?
QUEREE in St. Lawrence J 1788, in Trinity J 1668 and 1749. Curr J. LE CARRY, LE QUEREE in J 1668, 1749. See MASS SOLDIERS AND SAILORS. Note that QUERY, William of Antrim, Ireland came to NC 1740.
QUEREE, Ann, b 1854 J mar Joshua MACHON, qv, and rem to North Chelmsford, MA ca 1907 and d 1928.
QUEREE, QUERUEE, Simon, b 1700s J, rem to Canada.
A1. Jean Baptiste, mar 1789 in Caraquet, NB Charlotte BRIDEAU, dau of Louis BRIDEAU and Marie Therese THOMAS, whose great grandfather John THOMAS and wife Anna Lara had come from Dover, England. (Marcel Poirier, New Richmond, QUE.
B1. ___, had son David QUERRY, b 1835 Que.
B2. Marie, mar Daniel PIROUET, b J.
QUERIPEL old in G, in St. Peters G 1891. Curr G.
QUERIPEL, William, b 1863 St. Peter du Bois, G, d 1937 Catel, G. Spent 7 years in Australia, visited San Francisco 1880 in the Aust. Navy, loaded wool in Aust. for shipment to CAL, loaded wheat in CAL for Ireland. Retired to farming. Mar at age 28 Mary LE PROVOST, b 1869 G, d there 1961, had lived in Australia, New Jersey and Guernsey, dau of John BONAMY LE PROVOST and Lydia Maria BREHAUT. William and Mary res some time in Adelaide, Aust, but returned by working passage on S.S. TORRENS, where William the son was born at sea 1893. (June Queripel, Shiloh, NJ)
A1. William Torrens LE PROVOST QUERIPEL, b 1893 mar 1920 Groton, CT. Doris M. Douglas, b 1902 Warren, RI, d 1975 Pipersville, PA, bur West Mystic, CT, dau of Otis King Douglas and Jessie G. MacLaren, from Nova Scotia. William d 1970 PA. Was herdsman 50 yrs. with Guernsey cattle, also a shipyard worker during WWII. Res NY,PA,NJ.
B1. Torrens Douglas, 1921-1939 West Mystic, CT.
B2. Warren, b 1923 Morristown, NJ mar Ellen Naomi Parker, b 1927 Gas City, IND. Vet of Navy Air Corps,WWII, dairyman.

C1. Cheryl Ann, b 1947 Bridgeton, NJ mar 1966 PA Robert G. Weigner, 2 chn: Josh Allen and Heather E. Weigner, res PA.
C2. Teri Lee, b 1949 Bridgeton, NJ.
C3. Larry Wayne, b 1952 Doylestown, PA, mar 1972 Kathy Doyne, 2 chn: Jessica E. and Alison Gwen.
C4. Barbara Joyce, b 1955 Doyleston, PA.
B3. Vincent Otis, b 1928 Morristown, NJ, res Shiloh, NJ, mar 1947 June B. Porter, b 1928 NJ, dau of Harold and Laura Hand Porter, 3 chn.
C1. Linda Lou, b 1948 Bridgeton, NJ
C2. Kenneth Wayne, b 1949, mar 1977 Deborah Mick, b 1951, dau Jillian
C3. Ronald Bruce, b 1956, mar 1976 Patricia Manning, b 1956 Manhattan, NY, 3 daus: Christine M., Lisa Jean and Amy Renee.
A2. John, d.y.
A3. Cecil Clifford, b 1896 Beaucamp, Castel, G, d 1917 in France, unmar
A4. John Frederick, b 1897 La Saline, St. Sampson, G, d 1978, res G. Mar 1921 G, Hilda Alice OZANNE, nee DOREY, b 1889 Albecq, Castel, G, dau of Nicholas and Henriette (HAMON) DOREY. A dau.
B1. Hilda May, b 1922 Castel, G, mar 1941 St. Peter Port G, John Nicholas BOUGOURD, b 1908 Castel, son of Daniel N. and Eliz. (OGIER) BOUGOURD.
C1. Betty Hilda Bougourd, b 1941 C3. Ivy May Bougourd, b 1953
C2. Daphne Isabelle Bougourd, b 1947 C4. Vaughn John Bougourd, b1944
C5. Ruth Violet Bougourd, b 1960 Castel, G.
A5. Cecile Elise Mary, b 1900 G, res Short Hills, NJ
A6. Lydia Moriah, or Lydia Maria, b 1901 Castel G, mar in G Robert C. MAHY, St. Peter Port G. He was b 1896, son of Steven and Mary (ROBERTS) MAHY of G. Robert d 1981, 4 chn.
B1. Cecil Robert Mahy, b 1927 G, res Boontown, NJ, served in WWII. Mar 1951 Eliz. Berry, b 1922 Ireland, 3 chn.
C1. Regina L. Mahy, b 1952 C2. Linda Mahy, b 1953
C3. Russel J. Mahy b 1954
B2. Ronald Edward, b 1928 Bernardsville, NJ, Veteran, mar 1950, Dover, NJ Rita Crane, 2 chn: Ronald C. b 1952, Wiliam R, b 1956.
B3. Cecile/Joyce Lena, b 1929 Morris Plains, NJ mar 1959 Flemington, NJ, Frank H. Hults, b 1922. Frank has 3 sons by former marriage. 2 chn: Jeffrey Frederic Hults, b 1962 & David C. 1965-1980.
B4. Gertrude Lydia b 1934 NJ mar 1956 Robert L. Kelly, b 1928 NY. 2 chn: Robert L. and Steven L. Kelly.
A7. Sydney, b 1902 St. Sampson G, d 1965 E. Bridgewater, MA, served in Brit. Navy, later a dairyman, mar 1934 Quincy, MA, Rose Blanche Hirt, b 1908 S. Weymouth, MA.
B1. Elaine Carol, b 1941 NJ mar 1961 MA, Michael Allan Koski, 2 chn: Michael S. and Michele R. Koski.
B2. Mary Christine, b 1943, mar 1975 Philmore Willey Jr, b 1937.
B3. Sydney Edward, b 1948 Salisbury, MD, mar 1980 Boston, Linda LePore, dau of Antonio and Concetta LePore.
A8. Archibald Edward, b 1903 Castel, G, d 1976, bur New Hope, PA. Was in Brit. Army 1917, mar 1929 at Jamaica Plain, MA, Ella Walsh, b 1898 Ireland, d 1966, 3 chn.
B1. Joan Frances M. Jervais, b 1930 Plymouth, MA
B2. William Edward Francis, b 1936 Flushing, NY mar 1960 Doylestown, PA, Beverly Breier, b 1939, no issue. Wm. d 1978 bur Rosemont,NJ
B3. Margaret Nora/Toots, b 1941 Somerville, NJ mar 1961 New Hope, PA, Michael Riordan, b 1939 PA, served in USAF 4 yrs. 2 chn: Sean Michael and Ann Bridget Riordan.
A9. Austin Enright, b 1905 Castel G, mar 1927 Short Hills, NJ Catherine Speers, dau of James and Annie of Ireland, where she was born.

B1. Austin, b 1928 Morristown, NJ served in Army 1951/2, mar Marion Thomas, b 1927 New Rochelle, NY, of Irish fam. No issue.
A10. Lena Queripel, b 1907 Beaucamp, Castel, G, mar 1928 in London, England to John Frederick Fallis, b 1898 London, son of Wm. and Hannah Riley Fallis, 8 chn, most b England: Barbara, David, Peter, John, Richard, Paul Christopher, and Cecil Fallis.
QUERIPEL, Benjamin, farmer b G, age 20 mar 1882 at New Bedford, MA, Annie I. Weymouth, b Bridgton, ME, age 22, dau of Frank Weymouth and Isabell Lowe. (WEYMOUTH FAM HIST)
QUERIPEL, Job, res NJ, where his wife Sarah Ann d 1831 age 19? (Mount Holly NJ Library)
QUERIPEL, Nancy was in Port Elizabeth, NJ church records 1862. From G or from Australia?
QUESNEL, old and curr in G. Old in J.
QUESNEL, Alfred Edward, b 1919 Medford, MA, son of Augustus E. and Catherine A. (Kenny) QUESNEL of Malden, MA, mar Violet Boyde in Medford. She was b 1918 London, England. OUTC.
A1. Linda Ann, b 1947 Medford, MA.
QUINER, COONIER. Compiler understnands that this surname is COIGNARD, COIGNERT of J. Some desc may use COONIER, and a QUEENYARD is noted, which is a little nearer to the sound of the orig. surname. COIGNERT and COIGNARD in J since 1299, in St. Lawrence J 1788. By 1668 their taxes in J were being paid for them by others, which prob. means they had dispersed to England or America, or were renting in town, St. Heliers, J. These various fams may all have been connected in J. CAUTION: TRIAL CHARTS.
A1. Johanna, bp 1743 A3. Mary, bp 1747/8
A2. John, bp 1744, poss the one who res Lynn, MA 1790, fam of 6?
A4. James, bp 1749 MRB
A5. Ester, bp 1753, poss mar John GREEN? 1773 (int)
A6. Abigail, bp 1755, listed under COONIER in MRB VR.
QUINER, Abraham, mar 1769 Elizabeth DOWNE, res MRB. Other chn?
A1. Abraham, bp 1770, poss mar 1792 Susanna Camell? in Manchester, MA. Res Beverly, MA. For CAMELL, prob read CAMPBELL?
B1. Susanna, b 1792, d.y. B5. John Campbell, b 1802 Bev.,MA
B2. Luther, b 1794, prob d at sea 1824 B6. Hannah, b 1805
B3. Joanna, bp 1796 Beverly. B7. Thomas Gilbert, b 1808 or 1818?
B4. Abraham, b 1799 Beverly. B8. Mary Ann, b 1810 Beverly.
B9. Noah, b 1813 mar 1. Mary Abbot 1833 who d ca 1845? He mar 2. at age 33 Eunice Adeline Henderson, 1846, Beverly. Noah a mariner.
C1. Abraham, b 1835, d.y.?
C2. Abraham Kimball, b 1841 Beverly. Other chn?
B10. Susanna again, b 1818
QUINER, Benjamin, b 1781 Beverly, MA mar 1804 Hannah Herrick/Merrick?
A1. Benjamin b 1806 A2. Hannah, b 1808 A3. Priscilla, b 1810, d.y.?
A4. Eleanor, b 1812
A5. Priscilla Eleanor, b 1814 mar 1834 Ephraim G. SYMONDS,of J fam?
A6. John Williams, b 1819 Bev., prob mar Catherine F., res Beverly,MA.
B1. and B2. chn b 1842,43 B4. Ephraim Gardner, b 1847
B3. John William, b 1845, d.y.? B5. John, b 1848
QUINER, Henry Newcomb?, mar Hannah Newell, res MRB 1798, Hannah d 1842.
A1. Hannah Blaney, bp 1798 d 1840?
A2. Susanna Jarvis, bp 1800, note Susanna Jarvis in Nich.Quiner fam.
A3. Lois, b ca 1802, d 1812 A5. Harriet Adoline, bp 1808 MRB
A4. Mary, bp 1805 A6. Eliza Ann?, bp 1811 MRB.
A7. Henry Newcomb, bp 1809, poss mar 1832 Bev.,MA, Mary Ann QUINER??
B1. Laura A., b 1845 Saugus,MA. B2. Ella C., b 1847 Lynn, MA.

QUINER, Capt. John, mar 1812 Susanna Evans, res MRB and 2. Susan Fogg in 1830. Was he the master of schooner REGULATOR at Pt. Petre, WI, 1818? A Susanna, da of Capt. John d 1828 age 37. This may have been a sister of Capt. John, and dau of another Capt. John. Or, Susanna may have been a dau by a previous marriage.
A1. Susan Evans, b 1813 A3. Helen Maria, b 1818, d 1832 age 14
A2. John, b 1816 A4. Joan Abigail, b 1822
A5. Ebenezer Evans, b 1825, mar 1849 Deborah H. ROUNDEY, 24, dau of Benj. and Ruth Roundey.
QUINER, John W. mar Catharine F. Trask 1838 Beverly, MA. 2 chn d.y?
A1. Ephraim Gardner, b 1847 Beverly, MA.
QUINER, John mar Priscilla WILLIAMS 1758 Lynn, MA. A John res Lynn in 1790 with fam of 6.
A1. Samuel Fuller, b 1759 Lynn. A4. Elizabeth b 1766
A2. Susanna, b 1761 A5. Ann, b 1768
A3. John, bp 1763 A6. Lydia, bp 1771 Lynn, MA.
QUINER, Capt. Nicholas, b ca 1749? poss son of Abram and Mary (MERRYqv) QUINER, or an immigrant from C.I.? Nicholas mar 1773 Susannah JARVIS dau of Thomas Jarvis and Mary Newcomb of MRB. (Winnifred Pierce, Ann Arbor, MI)
A1. Susanna Jarvis, bp 1780 MRB A4. Nabby/Abigail, bp 1787, d.y.
A2. Molly/Mary, bp 1783 A5. John , bp 1789
A3. Capt. Thomas, bp 1785 at MRB mar 1809 Jane Miller BIRD, dau of Daniel and Sarah (Blaney) BIRD of MRB.
B1. Jane, b 1810 MRB, mar 1831 Franklin KNIGHT, son of Benj. and Eliz. (Selman) KNIGHT of MRB. See GALLISON for fam.
A6. Nabby again, bp 1791, mar Wm. DENNIS? 1816 MRB.
A7. Esther, bp 1794 MRB, mar John GILLEY 1813. Poss GUILLET of J?
A8. Jane, b 1794 MRB, not verified. A9. Poss a Noah? bp 1799.
QUINER, Capt. Peter, b ca 1752, d 1815 age 63, res MRB. Mar 1776 Elizabeth Nuttin, who d 1827 age 85, poss other chn? A Peter QUININ res 1790 in Gloucester, MA with fam of 2.
A1. Benjamin, and A2. Benjamin, d.y.
A3. Mary, bp 1779 d 1796 age 17, listed under COONIER in MRB VR.
QUINER, Samuel res MRB. mar ?
A1. Stephen, bp 1803 mar 1822 Sally Bartol. Poss other chn?
B1. Stephen, bp 1827 MRB B2. Mary, bp 1839 B3. Wm. Bartoll, bp 1839
QUINER, William and Mary res MRB. Most listed under COONIER in VRs.
A1. Mary, bp 1728/9, bur 1730 MRB
A2. William Coonier, bp 1731 prob mar 1751 Mary KNIGHT? res MRB.
B1. William, bp 1751, d.y.? B4. John, bp 1758
B2. Mary, bp 1753 B5. Samuel, bp 1760, mar Ruth Goodwin? Son John?
B3. Jane, bp 1756 B6. Hannah, bp 1764 B7. William, bp 1767
A3. John, bp 1733/4, COONIER A5. Johanna, bp 1743
A4. Elizabeth, bp 1740 A6. Jane, bp 1756 A7. John, bp 1758 MRB.
See in WRCIC a list of 47 QUINER names in Vrs of Lynn, Beverly, Boston, Brookline, Westford, and Watertown, MA. See other MA towns, also ME and NH records, poss CT? Note varied spellings!! TRIAL CHARTS.
QUINER, William, b 1773 New Haven, CT d 1831 mar 1797? Margaret Doer, at Hartford, CT or poss in Boston? She was b 1773 d 1839 at New Haven, CT. See book for more info. Not known to compiler if this QUINER and the ones in MA are related, but note that Ingall name is in both fams. Margaret later res Milwaukee, WI. (Winnifred Pierce, Ann Arbor, MI; GEN OF THE CARPENTER-QUINNER FAMS by Eliz. C. Eggers, Rochester, MI, 1977; FLINT GEN. QUARTERLY, April, 1971)
A1. to A4, 4 chn b 1798-1803 d.y.
A5. John L., b 1804 d 1826 at New Haven, CT.

A6. Susan E., b 1806 d 1809 A7. Nicholas E., b 1810
A8. Henry Newton, b 1809. Note that there was a Henry Newcomb QUINER b 1809 in MA records. Henry mar 1831 Charlotte W. Tucker at New Haven, CT, 1809-1884, d Rome, WIS. Henry d in a shipwreck on Lake Michigan while chn were small. Widow mar 2. in 1849 Fred M. Holbrook, 1 dau.
B1. Martha M., b 1832 Roxbury, MA d 1836 B6. Eliza Ann, b 1842
B2. Joseph C., b 1834 Cincinnati, OH d 1862 at Shiloh, Civil War.Mar Nancy Frank 1856 at Rome, WIS, 2 sons, Frank and John
B3. Henry C., b 1835 d 1880, mar Polly Ingalls 1859 at Concord, WIS. Polly the dau of Lansford and Laura Ingalls. Chn: Louisa, Lafayette, Thomas H., Charlotte and Albert.
B4. Martha J., b 1837 Richmond, IND.
B5. Caroline L., b 1839 Concord, WIS, mar 1860 Charles P. Ingalls, b 1835 Cuba, NY.
C1. Mary Amelia, b 1865 in WISC.
C2. Laura E. Ingalls, b 1867 Pepin, WIS, d 1957 Mansfield, MO. Mar Almanzo J. Wilder 1885 at DeSmet, SD. He was b 1857 Malone, NY d 1949 age 92. Laura was the famous author of the books from which LITTLE HOUSE ON THE PRAIRIE TV show was constructed. Laura wrote ten books, and was close to 90 when she died.
D1. Rose Wilder, b 1886 DeSmet, SD, d 1968 Danbury, CT, bur Mansfield, MO. She mar Gillette Lane 1909, a son d.y. Div. Rose was also a writer, with 15 books and many magazine articles.
C3. Caroline C. Ingalls, b 1870 KS, d 1946 Rapid City, SD, bur DeSmet, SD, mar David N. Swanzey 1912 at Keystone, SD, no issue, but raised 2 stepchn: Harold and Mary Swanzey. Also a writer.
C4. Charles Frederick, b 1875 MINN.
C5. Grace P. Ingalls, b 1877 Burr Oak, IA, d 1941 Manchester, SD, mar Nathan W. Dow 1901, b 1859, d 1943.
A9. Elisha J., b 1811 New Haven, CT, mar ___? 3 sons: Wm.,George Henry and John. Elisha a printer, res Milwaukee, WIS.
A10. Margaret E., b 1814 New Haven, CT, mar Capt. McGregor, had son Alexander McGregor.
A11. Edwin O., b 1817, printer, wrote HIST OF THE WISC. REGT IN THE CIVIL WAR. Had 6 daus and a son.

QUINN, old in G, curr G and J. Prob an Irish surname.

QUINN, William, chairmaker, b 1806 Grouville, J, son of Robert and Ann, mar Mary Ann Hosking of Devon, England, rem to UT 1856 via ship THORNTON. (SLCity records)
A1. William R., b 1831 St. Heliers J
A2. Mary Ann, b 1833, St. Heliers, mar 1. Wm. C. Dunbar and 2. George Taylor, d 1897.
A3. Harriet, b 1837 J, mar 1. John Hill, d 1878
A4. Elizabeth, b 1839 J mar 1. James V. Stevenson and 2. Graham Douglas, d 1902
A5. George, b 1842 J, mar Elizabeth Wilson, d 1918
A6. Isabella b 1848 A7. Joseph Hyrum, b 1851 St. Heliers J.

QUETTEVILLE, DE QUETTEVILLE. There is apparently no limit to the ways this surname can be spelled: DE CAUTEVILLE, QUETIVEL, KUITFIELD, KITFIELD, QUITTERFIELD, QUEDVILLE, CHETIFIELD, KITVILLE, CODVILLE, etc, etc. The name was in G 1530-1750 from Jersey. In J 1500s, in St. Martin J 1749. (BIO. DICT. OF JERSEY by Balleine, MRB Hist. Society.)

QUITERFIELD, Clement, early settler in Colchester, CT, poss a Hug or from a C.I. fam? He had a home and lot by 1702 and at the time of death in 1723 owned a 42 acre home lot, two 50 acre lots, 4 acres of meadows and other land valued at 412 pounds. He mar Priscilla Collins, dau of Benj. Collins and 2nd wife Elizabeth (Leach) PUTNAM. Priscilla b 1679 Lynn, MA. Desc are known mainly through the female lines of this fam. The widow, Priscilla mar 2. in Colchester, CT, Charles WILLIAMS, ca 1731, and 3. in 1749 Nathaniel Kellogg, whom she survived. She may also have been of a C.I. fam, or an English fam settled for some time in J. (Mrs. Kenneth L. Knight, Clarendon, PA; Frederick Weed, Boston, MA; Dorothy Burnham, W. Hartford, VT; New Haven GEN. MAG, Vol33, No.3; Colchester, CT records; THE AMERICAN GENEALOGIST, 27;212; Sharon, CT records) CAUTION: TRIAL CHARTS! There may be much more data on this fam not found by compiler.

A1. Benjamin, b 1704 Colchester, CT d there 1771, mar 1728 Eunice Kellogg.
B1. Jacob, b 1741 mar Eliz. Kilbourn 1759. He d 1777, she after 1795
C1. Eunice, mar Hugh Stephens
C2. Betty, b 1768 Colchester, d 1861 Pomfret, VT, mar Isaac C. Newton, b 1767 d 1933 Pomfret, VT.
D1. Mary Newton, b 1788 d 1847 Pomfret, mar there 1806 George Chedel b 1780.
E1. Mary Betsey Chedel, b 1807, d 1866 mar Julius Pratt, b 1811, d 1861.
F1. Mary Jane Pratt, b 1841 VT, d 1901. Mar 1863 Woodstock, VT Elba Jillson, b 1841 d 1923
G1. Cora Belle Jillson, 1864-1952, mar 1884 Scott Harrington
H1. Effie Harrington, b 1888, d 1960, mar 1910 at Royalton, VT Wayne Burnham, b 1888, d 1965.
I1. Reginald Burnham, b 1926 Hartford, VT mar Dorothy Douglas
C3. other chn?
B2. Eunice, Unis, b ___, mar 1751 Noah Clark in Fairfield, CT.
C1. Hannah Clark, b ___, mar Simon Cone.
A2. Richard, b 1706, d 1747 Colchester, mar there 1732 Lydia Cripen.
B1. Abner, mar 1755 Esther Dunham of Sharon, CT, rem to Armenia, NY.
B2. Lydia, mar 1. Deacon Ebenezer JACKSON ca 1751, son of Samuel? She mar 2. Stephen Jackson, rem to VT.
C1. Daniel Jackson, b 1751 CT, d 1830 Warren Co., PA. Mar Sylvia or Sybyl White, b Deerfield, NH, d Warren Co., PA.
D1. David Jackson, b NY state, d Warren Co., PA.
E1. James Madison Jackson, b PA, d there
F1. Henry W., had son Harry David who mar Marguerite Jackson Knight of Warren Co., PA.
A3. Elizabeth, b 1709 mar 1728 CT John Douglas, several chn. (AMER. GEN, 27;212)
A4. John, b 1711 res Lanesboro, MA 1771, mar in CT 1733 Elizabeth Kilbourne.
B1. Sarah, mar Jacob Weed and left numerous desc. Note Jacob Weed also under A.1. Benjamin.

KETVILLE, DE QUETTEVILLE, Abraham from J to Essex Co., MA 1600s.(Konig) See Plymouth records for 1850-1860 for other DE QUEDVILLES from J.

DE QUEDVILLE, John, b Quebec, rem to Cambridge, MA and mar ___. DE QUETTEVILLE in Gaspe, QUE 1800s. See Q.A. IN CANADA, also Virkus II.

A1. Mary Frances, b 1860 Cambridge, MA mar 1883 Le Baron Russell Briggs b 1855 Salem, MA, son of Geo. Ware Briggs and Lucia J. Russell, George's second wife.
B1. John De Q. Briggs, b 1885 Cambridge, MA mar 1907 Margaret Floyd Atwater of Helena, MONT, div 1917.
C1. Henrietta Wood Briggs, b 1908 Plymouth, MA
C2. John De Q. Briggs, Jr, b 1911 Duluth, MN, res St. Paul, MN.

B2. Lucia Russell Briggs, b 1887 Cambridge, MA
B3. Le Baron Russell Briggs, Jr, b 1895 mar 1916 Helen ElizabethMason b 1894 Watertown, MA, dau of Charles Francis Mason.
C1. Le Baron Russel Briggs III, b 1921 Bangor, ME.
C2. Robert Mason Briggs, b 1923 Plymouth, MA.

RABEY, surname of G and Cornwall, England. Old in G. See also Q.A. IN CANADA. See CIFHS #6. An early spelling in J was RABET,curr J.
RABE, Ann, b 1781 G? to OH d 1866 GCO. OUTC.
RABEY, David, b G, mar Josephine DU FOUR 1800s, res NY. (Josephine Du Four, Brooklyn, NY)
RABEY, Daniel and Luther, b G, res Brooklyn, NY
RABEY, Elizabeth, mar ___BEST, res G, then rem to US? 2 sons and adau. (Josephine Du Four, Bklyn, NY; Anne Buttle, Worthington, OH)
RABEY, Henry from G? in GCO 1830
RABAY, James arrived in Boston 1760s on sloop ADVENTURE from Nfld., a mariner. Michael also on this ship. (Whitmore)
RABEY, Kathryn of Yarmouth 1637 to New England to stay with her son. (IMMIGRANTS TO AMERICA IN ENGLISH RECORDS by Tepper)
RABE, RABEY?, William, b 1796 G? to OH, d 1876 GCO. OUTC.
RADFORD, Frederick, B Vale, G, rem to Melrose, MA, ca 1913 as coachman and chauffeur. Mar Alice Ann MARRIETTE, qv, 1913. A dau Alice May, b St. Sampson, G, mar ___Simpson. (Alice Simpson, Melrose, MA)
RAIFE, Mr. and Mrs. from G to Racine, WIS 1842 with the OZANNE, qv,Fam.
RAINE, RAINEY, said to be C.I. surname, curr J. (CIFHS bulletin)
RAMIER, fam in Canada, whose name was originally RIMEUR of J. RIMEUR has been extinct in J for some time, means rhymer, reciter.
RAMIER, Pierre, b 1795 St. Brelade J, was placed as an apprentice with Charles Robins firm, 1807 (See Q.A. IN CANADA), by his father Jean RIMEUR and mother Marie PAILLIE. He was sent to Gaspe age 11, and was to work for the company until he was 20. He res at Paspebiac, then at Nouvelle, Gaspe ca 1815, and mar ca 1816 Anne Beebe, 1798-1866, dau of Asa Beebe and Sarah Hall, 9 chn. Peter left the Gaspe area ca 1841, but his fam remained there. He d Grafton, WI 1864. (Cynthia Dow, New Richmond, QUE; Leslie Ramier, Port Daniel, QUE; Joseph Horie, Jr.)
A1. Mary, b 1817 d 1893 mar 1841 Alexander Mann, son of John and Eunice (Hall)Mann, res Shigawake, QUE, at least 7 chn.
B1. Sarah Anne Mann, b 1843 B5. Deborah Mann, b 1853
B2. Eunice Mann, b 1846 B6. Amaliah Mann, b 1855
B3. Wilbert Mann, b 1848 mar 1871 Sarah A. Sullivan
B4. Melinda Mann, b 1850 B7. Caroline Mann, b 1858
A2. Sarah, b 1820, d 1902, mar 1843 David Dow, son of Joseph and Margaret (Miller) Dow. Res Port Daniel, QUE, 11 chn.
B1.James Dow, b 1844, mar 1878 Sarah Enright
B2. Margaret Dow, b 1845 B3. Joseph Dow, b 1848
B4. William Dow, b 1850 d 1938, mar Catherine Hayes
C1. Gavin Dow, b 1882 C4. David Dow mar Ruby ____
C2. Edward Dow, b 1884 d 1977 mar Isabella WILLIAMS
C3. John/Jack Dow, b 1886 mar Sarah Miller, had issue
C5. William Clare Dow, b 1892 d 1971 mar Olive Skene, issue
C6. Leslie, b 1894, unmar C8. Ella Dow, b 1899 mar Caldwell Jacobson
C7. Ernest Dow, b 1897 d 1980, mar Agnes Sweetman, issue
B5. Anne Dow, b 1852, mar 1883 David Beebe
B6. David Dow, b 1854 B9. Sarah Dow, b 1859, mar John LE GALLAIS
B7. Elizabeth Dow, b 1856 B10. Joshua Dow, b 1861
B8. Peter Dow, b 1858 B11. Jane Dow, b 1863 mar Daniel JOURNEAUX.

A3. Judith, b 1822, d 1913, mar 1849 Capt. John SMITH, son of Richard and Isabella (Billingsley) Smith, no issue
A4. John, b 1823, d 1879, mar 1851 Sarah Mann, 1832-1907, dau of Wm. Mann and Barbara Beebe, 8 chn.
B1. Peter William, b 1852
B2. John Thomas, b 1854, d 1940 mar 1888 Charlotte Beebe, 1860-1965
B3. Francis James, b 1856 B6. Margaret Melvina, b 1866
B4. Elias Caldwell, b 1858 B7. Joshua, b 1869
B5. Miriam Jane, b 1860 B8. Herman, b 1872 d 1888
A5. Caroline, b 1827 d 1916, mar 1. 1844 Aeneas Horth, 5 chn. Mar 2. Kenneth McKenzie, no issue
B1. Amaliah Horth, b 1846 B4. James Absolany? Horth, 1866-1870
B2. Ann/Emily Horth, 1848-1872
B3. Peter Philip Horth, b 1862 B5. Margaret Sophia Horth, b 1870
A6. Elizabeth, b 1829 d 1914, mar John MacCallum, res Matapedia, QUE, 8 chn.
A7. William, b 1832 d 1918, mar 1857 Barbara Gillis, b 1832, dau of James and Jane (Forsythe) Gillis, 8 chn.
B1. Jane, b 1858 mar Edward Whittom B7. Mary Cecelia, b 1873, unmar
B2. William Peter, b 1860 mar Jennie Barter of Grand Cascapedia,QUE
B3. James, b 1863 mar Lizzie Dow B8. Bertha, b 1876 mar E.Hayes
B4. Annabella, b 1865 mar Alexander Barter, bro of Jennie above.
B5. Sarah Catherine, b 1870 mar Edward Hayes.
A8. Melinda, b 1835 d 1921 mar 1857 Joseph Horie, b Scotland, son of William and Jane Horie, 10 chn, including:
Peter Malcolm Horie, b 1867 Sabrina Jane Horie b 1871
Elizabeth Horie, b 1869 Joseph Hall Horie, b 1874
A9. Dinah, b 1837 d 1917, mar 1861 John J. Mann, 6 chn including:
Edward William Mann b 1860 Mansell Mann, b 1869
Ann Eliza Mann, b 1867 William Mann, b 1871

RAMSEY, John from J, cordwainer, b ca 1719, volunteer against the West Indies in 1740. (Bolton) Poss a Hug fam in J?

RANDALL, surname of G and of England. A Stephen Randall d 1796 age 91 mar Mary Sawyer, 7 chn. (PARSONSFIELD, ME HIST; SMALL GEN; Noyes)

RAWSTON, RAWSTRON? curr G. One mar a LANGLOIS and rem to Boston, MA ca 1879. This LANGLOIS came from Le Havre, France.

RAY, some in early Boston, MA, OUTC. LE RAY was in J 1548, 1668 and 1749. Curr G and J.

RAYMOND, many in Beverly, MA area early. REMON in J 1331, pron. RAY-MON. In St. Helier and St. Laurens J 1668, and in St. Laurens and St. Peter J 1749. REMON curr J. RAYMOND curr G and J. See REMON.

RAYMOND, Daniel and Abigail res MRB. OUTC.
A1. Sarah, bp 1717 A3. Edward, bp 1721,d.y. A5. William, bp 1726
A2. Abigail, bp 1719 A4. Daniel, bp 1724 A6. Edward again, bp 1728

RAYMOND, Nathaniel and Sarah res MRB, a dau Mary bp 1776. OUTC

RAYMOND, Paul and Margerit res MRB, son Daniel Ward bp 1760. OUTC

RAYMOND, Robert and Eleanor res MRB. OUTC.
A1. Mary bp 1787 A2. Robert bp 1787, but another day.

RAYMOND, Samuel and Eunice res MRB. OUTC.
A1. John, b 1705 A3. Samuel II, b 1715/16
A2. Eunice, bp 1707 A4. Sarah, b 1718 A5. Benjamin, b 1719

RECORD, poss a RICARD of C.I.? RICARD in J by 1528, Hug? RICARD in St. Mary and St. Ouen J 1668, and in St. Ouen and St. Peter J 1749. Cf also RICOU, old in J.

RECORD, John from Weymouth, served in King Philip's War 1676, mar 1677 Mrs. Hannah Burr Hobart, dau of Simon and Hester Burr. 13 chn. More data in sources: Beverly Newton, Pittsfield, ME; Mrs. Howard R.

Wilson, Sharon Springs, KS; HIST OF HINGHAM, MA, Vol 3)
REDAWAY, READAWAY, RIDEOUT, RIDOUET. RIDOUET in Nfld. said to be from C.I. RIDOUET is poss a Hug surname. Compiler could find no origin for James below, but phonetics make it likely that he was from C.I. or France. (Rev. Hammond, Nfld; Rehoboth records)
REDAWAY, James, d 1676 Rehoboth, MA, mar ___?
A1. John, b 1644 mar Mary ___
B1. James, b 1678 mar Joanna, who d 1742/3. James a Captain. 9 chn.
C1. Mary, b 1720, d.y.? C3. Mary again, b 1723/4
C2. Elizabeth, b 1721 C4. Joanna, b 1725
C5. James, b 1728 mar Mehitable ___
D1. Dolly, b 1750 D3. James, b 1754 D5. Comfort, b 1760
D2. Mehitable, b 1752 D4. Joel, b 1757 D6. Preserved, b 1764
C6. Samuel, b 1731 mar Abia ___
D1. Abraham b 1760 D4. Chloe, b 1767 D7. Samuel, b 1775
D2. Martha, b 1762 D5. Ann, b 1770, twin D8. John, b 1779
D3. Lucy, b 1764 D6. Hannah, b 1770, twin
C7. Timothy, b 1733, mar Mary ___
D1. Joanna, b 1757 D3. David b 1762 D5. Elizabeth, b 1766
D2. Timothy, b 1760 D4. Jonthan, b 1764 D6. Mary, b 1768
C8. John, b 1735/6 C9. Samuel, b 1737/8
B2. John, b 1682 d 1718? Wife Mary also d that year
B3. Preserved, b 1684 mar Esther ___. Preserved d 1724/5, or his son?
B4. Martha, b 1687
A2. Mary, b 1646 A4. James, b 1650, d 1684 A6. Lydia, b 1652
A3. Martha, b 1648 A5. Rebecca, b 1651
A6. Sarah?, who mar 1666 Samuel CARPENTER?, qv.
RIDEOUT noted in Weston, VT.
RIDEOUT, RIDOUET?, Violet mar Harold BUTT, qv, b 1903 Nfld. OUTC.
See also RIDGEWAY, RIDGAWAY.
REDFIELD, see WRCIC
REDMAN, Marjorie from G 1920s to New England, mar N. Evans. A dau Audrey Evans. REDMAN curr in G.
REED, READ in J 1528, 1668, 1749. Curr G and J.
REED, Ann, see SEWARD
REED, Eliza from C.I. 1862 to UT, via ship ANTARCTIC. (SLCITY RECORDS)
REGLE, see LE REGLE
REITILLIE, see LE RETILLEY, RETILLEY.
REMON, see RAYMOND. REMOND in J 1331. REYMOND in J 1607. REMON in St. Helier and St. Laurens J 1668, and in St. Laurens and St. Peter J 1749. REMON in St. Lawrence J 1788. REMON in Salem, MA 1970s.
REMON, James and Thomas C. were merchants at Pabos, Gaspe, QUE 1800s, from J. (Geo. Le Feuvre, Detroit, MI) One James mar Alice Jane ANTHOINE from G? had dau Daisy Annette, b 1890, who mar Philip AMY, res Canada 1907. See Q.A. IN CANADA. The younger James REMON, prob b J, rem to Quebec and mar Adele Blais. Poss other chn? (Karen Loftus, Winslow, ME)
A1. Clara, b 1871 J, mar 1885 Ste. Adelaide de Pabos, QUE, Daniel J. De Roche, logger, b 1861, son of Raphael Deraiche and Victoire Cyr. Daniel d 1943 N. Monmouth, ME.
B1. Clara de Roche, b 1884/5 Pabos, QUE d 1969 Monmouth, ME. She mar 1904 Harry Frost.
C1. John H. Frost, b 1905 Monmouth, ME mar Bernice Foster and d 1975.
C2. Frank B. Frost, b 1907 mar Cecelia Cordeiro 1932.
C3. Lawton A. Frost, b 1908 mar 1941 Bernice Poirier, d 1962.
C4. Ada Elvira Frost, b 1914, d.y.

C5. Ruth K. Frost, b 1921 Lewiston ME, mar 1942 Wendell Hartford, b 1913.
D1. Dennis G. Hartford, b 1943 Lewiston, ME mar Montress Smith 1962, dau of Alfred and Elsie (Lovewell) Smith. two chn: Kathleen and Dana Hartford.
D2. Gary W. Hartford, b 1946, mar 1965 Patricia Wallace, b 1948 dau of Ralph Wallace and Angie Dudley, 2 chn: Carlton and George Hartford.
B2. Wilfred De Roche, b 1888 Lewiston, ME d 1943, mar Mabel ___.
B3. Phyllis Mae De Roche, b 1891 d 1979 TX, mar Daniel Hunter
B4. Daniel Joseph De Roche b 1893 d 1969 Waterville, ME. Mar there 1919 Marion Isabelle Toulouse, dau of Edward E. and Celena M. (Giroux) Toulouse.
C1. Phyllis Claire de Roche, b 1920 Waterville, ME mar Herbert E. Aldrich 1946, b 1922, son of Harry and Marguerite (Butler?) Aldrich.
D1. Herbert E. Aldrich II, b 1947 Waterville, ME
D2. James O'Keefe Aldrich, b 1948
C2. Daniel Joseph de Roche, mar 1949 Glenys Goodwin, ME, dau of Albert R. and Maude E. (Merrill) Goodwin, 3 chn.
D1. Karen Phyllis De Roche, b 1950 mar 1970 Robert A. Loftus, 2 chn: Trevor and Traci Loftus.
D2. Cynthia Marion de Roche, b 1954 mar 1978 Laurence J. McCarthy, Vassalboro, ME. A son Ryan Neal McCarthy, b Honolulu.
D3. Patricia Ellen De Roche, b 1957
B5. Margaret De Roche, b 1896 Monmouth, ME d 1971, mar F. Curran
B6. Mae De Roche, b 1897 Monmouth mar Beverly Slauenwhite 1929
B7. Ada de Roche, b 1901, d Monmouth 1908.

REMMON, in Beverly, MA. OUTC. Was this REMON of J?

REMON, see DU FRESNE

RENAULT, RENOULT, Samuel, son of John and Mary, bp 1731 MRB, poss of J fam? RENAULT in J 1274. In St. Martin, Grouville and St. Mary J 1668, and in St. John and St. Mary J 1749, spelled RENAUT. Curr J. Research? see CIFHS #3.

RENAUD in Erie, PA, and RENAULT in Boston, curr. OUTC.

RANOUD, Peter, in Eastchester Co. NY 1790 with fam of 10. Another Peter had fam of 3. Susannah a fam of 2. and Stephen with fam of 2. John with fam of 2 men, 3 boys and 4 females. (Census) OUTC.

RENALDS, John and Ann had Ruth b 1719 Boston, MA. OUTC.

RENOUF. Another C.I. surname with seemingly unlimited spelling variations: RENOUF, RENOFF, RENEW, RENUFF, RENEUF, RENOUGH, RENEFF, RENNO RENO?, RENOW, RENEAUF, etc. Cf also RENAULT, pronounced much like RENO, RENOW.

RENOUF in G 1331, in St. Peter Port G 1870, common in G.

RENOUF in J 1053, in St. Mary, St. Martin, St. Heliers and St. Peter J 1668, plus in parishes of Trinity and St. John J 1749. Curr and common in J. See CIFHS #8. Not all the short entries below are certainly from the C.I. A RENOFF fam came from Alsace-Lorraine to America in middle 1800s.

RENOUF, Mary Ann, b 1842 St. Helier J, dau of Nicholas and Ann Mary (MAUGER) RENOUF, mar 1861 Francis Geo. Kilner, bp 1836 Plymouth, England, res St. Heliers, J. (Edith Thompson, Manhattan, KS) KILNER was a photo-artist of J and Topsham, England.
A1. Francis, b 1862 St. Heliers J, rem to New Zealand
A2. Mary Ann, b 1863 rem to Devon, England
A3. Catherine, b 1864, res Devon A8. Ralph, res Ghana, Africa& Jamaica
A4. Philip, b 1869, res Australia. A9. Elsie, b 1882 St. Heliers, J.

A5. Edmund, b 1869 rem to Kansas City, where he had a restaurant, and later a farm in Pottawatamie, KS.
A6. Florence, b 1873, d 1940 Suffolk, England.
A7. Frederick Arthur, b 1875, d 1974 KS?, a farmer.
RENOUF, Peter. See p. 485, Q.A. IN CANADA. Born J, son of Pierre and Anne LE BRUN, mar 1775 J, apprenticed to someone in Nova Scotia late 1700s. (Jersey Society). Peter, in 1820 had lived 20 yrs. in Cape Breton, NS, the last two at Mabou, where he rec'd a grant of land. (PANS) He was a trader,by 1811 had 8 chn in ARichat, Cape Breton. According to MABOU PIONEER, Book II, rem to Mabou between 1818 and 1821, had the first closed carriage in the area, and fine horses. Signed the 1821 petition to have a Presbyterian minister in Mabou. D before 1842, when his widow sold land. She was Charlotte Sarah ___. (James O. St. Clair, Mabou, NS)
Only known chn:
A1. Maria, b 1804 d after 1871, mar Rev. Wm. Millar, Presb. minister. in Mabou, many desc. See MABOU PIONEERS, II.
A2. David, mar with fam of 4.
A3. Lewis Charles, b 1819, mar Mary Elizabeth ?Young?. A merchant, had at least 6 chn. (1871 census)
B1. Henry, b 1841 B2. Richard b 1846 B3. Allridge, b 1854
B4. Rachel, b 1854, mar John Hawley, son of Isaac and Abigail (Beaton) Hawley. Desc res Mabou.
B5. Mahalla, b 1856, mar Edward Young, 2 chn. B6. David, b 1860
RENIFF, RENEFF, RENEUF, RENOUGH, etc, Philip Sr., served in French and Indian Wars, 1748-1754. His wife Sara d 1773 Rehoboth, MA. (Mrs. Charles Comstock, Belmont, NY) While origin not known to compiler, it seems likely that this was a RENOUF from the C.I. More data in WRCIC and with Mrs. Comstock.
A1. Sarah b 1739 Rehoboth?
A2. Philip, mar Jennie/Jane Darling 1752, at least 3 chn
A3. John and wife Mercy res Cumberland, MA. Note French names Desire and Diademia. Might mean this is a Hug. fam?
B1. Abishaie, b 1755 mar Anna Mowry 1784. He was a Sgt. in Rev. War.
C1. Mowry/Morrey, mar Sally Ball 1806 Holden, MA. She was b 1792. Other chn?
D1. Mary, 1807-1898, mar Wm. Howe 1826 at Whitney Pt., NY. She was b Holden, MA, d Ulysses, PA.
D2. Abisha Ball, 2 desc: Roger B. Reniff in Sterling, NY and Helen WILLIAMS.
D3. Alonzo E., b 1836 NY state, mar Sarah M. Howe 1861 in PA.1ch:
E1. Fred Alonzo, 1866-1936, mar Nettie J. Kohler, 1865-1891
F1. Frank Miles, b 1888 d 1972, mar Idell M. Hollenbeck, 1892-1953. Frank was an only child.
G1. Nettie, b 1908, d 1971 mar Clarence E. Kemp, 1905-1968
G2. Francis A., 1909-1973, mar 1938 Harriet F. Burdick, b 1914
G3. Kathryn Z., b 1918 mar 1936 Ross L. Sturdevant, b 1906
G4. Idell Eunice, b 1923 mar 1945 Robert M. Ellis, b 1915
G5. Olive Matilda b 1925 mar 1942 Charles H. Comstock, b 1921
G6. Neil Herbert, 1930-1980, mar Mavis J. Hooker 1930.
D4. Lewis, b 1821 D5. Lucius, Twin, b 1821
D6. Sally, b 1827 Orange, Steuben Co., NY mar Theodore W. Jolley
E1. Alonzo Jolley, rem West, desc named Iva Vavac,Santa Maria,CAL.
E2. Willard Jolley, res Hannibal, MO? Also Joseph & dau who d.y.
D7. Asa, res Hornby, Steuben Co.,NY. D9. Lucy B, mar Howard ___.
D10. Elisha B., and D11,EPhraim, poss also of this fam.
B2. Charles, b 1757, Sgt. in Rev. War, mar 1. ___, and 2. Almira___

by whom 4 chn: Catherine, Chester, John and Diademia. Diademia mar ___Bortles, desc Esther Wagner, Crown Pt., NY.

B3. John, 1760-1764 B5. Desire, b 1762 B7. George, b 1768

B4. Daniel, b 1762 B6. Diademia, b 1766 B8. Hannah, b 1774

RENOUF, Thomas and Martha, b G, rem to New York. See also Benjamin RENOUF, below.

A1. William, b ca 1781, mar in NY 1804 Hannah Baldwin, b ca 1786 NY City, dau of Benj. and Elizabeth Baldwin of NY. Hannah d 1828. Wm. mar 2. ? in n Y 1830 Phoebe Hull, dau of Joseph and Phoebe Hull? Wm. d 1859 age 78. (Warren Broderick, Lansingburgh, NY; Troy Quaker records) CAUTION: TRIAL CHART

B1. Martha T., b ca 1805 NY? d 1869. Poss b Scipio, NY?

B2. Benjamin B., b 1806

B3. Ann R., b ca 1808 d 1841, age 33 Troy, NY. Mar Peter Simmonds. Peter b Claverack, Ireland?, d 1859.

B4. Mary, b 1810 B6. Samuel, b 1813, d 1814

B5. William, b 1812 B7. Rachel, b 1815 d 1819

B8. Hannah, b 1817, mar John GREEN, b ca 1817, d 1847 age 30. He was the son of Geo. and Mary GREEN, b Saratoga Co.,NY. A son d.y.

B9. Elizabeth, b 1819 B10. Susan, b 1820 B11. John, 1823-1824.

A2. poss a bro of Wm. named Benjamin? See below.

RENOUF, Thomas, b J or France, d ca 1871-1874 in J, mar Jane Mary or Jane K. GOSSELIN, qv, b 1846 J, d 1911 Rochester, NY, bur Mt. Hope Cem. 3? chn. (Margaret Beatty, Rochester, NY) Thomas may have also mar Harriette Lettington? 1846-1907. Thomas was the son of Benj. and and Caroline.

A1. May Jane, b 1865 J, d 1896 Rochester, NY, mar 1894 Peter Vandevate, b 1853 Holland, son of Leonard Vandevate, Sr.

B1. Ada Frances, b 1896 Rochester, d 1948, mar1914 Walter Pressley and 2. Walter Wood. Res Rochester, NY. 4 chn by each husband?

C1. Doris May Pressley, b 1915 Rochester, mar 1938 Harry Earl Johnson, b 1912, 2 chn.

D1. David Earl Johnson, b 1938 D2. Susan Johnson, b 1945

C2. Eleanor Irene Pressley, b 1917 mar Frank Howard Beatty in Long Beach CAL, 1938

C3. Walter Pressley Jr, mar Elizabeth __, chn: Kevin & LauriePressly.

C4. William Nelson Pressley, b 1923 Rochester mar 1942 Margaret Riley, 2 chn: Virginia & Richard A. Pressley, b 1953

C5. Gladys Wood, mar ___NICHOLS C6. Ruth Wood, mar Jeffrey Walsh

C7. Harry/Mickey Wood, mar in Rochester, NY Rosemary ___

C8. Erma Wood, unmar.

A2. William F., b 1871 St. Heliers J, mar 1894 Caroline Klimm Wagner. He d 1926 Rochester. 5 chn: Arthur, Chester, George Klimm, a dau who mar S.A. Meyers and Mary Klimm RENOUF.

RENOUF, Thomas, b 1820 G? mar 1846 Eliza ASTLETT, desc to Canada. (Dorothy Sanders, Cronach, SASK, Canada)

A1. Elizabeth Ann, b 1855, mar 1879 Edward Sanders, son of George. SANDERS of St. Sampson, G. See Sanders.

RENOUF, Amis, arrived in Boston, MA from J 1715 on ship MAY. (Whitmore)

RENOUF, Benjamin, 1807-1878 mar Caroline ___, bur Rochester, NY, 1805-1891.

A1. William?, 1844-1926, mar Harriette Lettington, 1846-1907, bur NY. See also the Thomas above who mar Jane GOSSELIN. Some data on this fam is confused.

RENOUF, Nicholas Bion, b 1822 G, to US 1840s? and d 1874, bur Tarentum PA. Mar Elizabeth Gatewood, 1828-1899, 11 chn. (Don Renouf, Ohio)
A1. John Wesley , mar Annie Eckels, 3 chn: Harry, Charles and Angie Renouf, who was b 1866 d 1894.
A2. Melzena, d 1917, mar John T. McCall, 1841-1919, 2 chn.
B1. Mary McCall B2. Jim McCall
A3. Edward Britton, b 1855 d 1943, mar Eliza Emmeline Eckels 1873 in Blairsville, PA. She was b 1857 d 1934, 5 chn.
B1. Edward Andrew b 1874 Cokesville, PA
B2. Frank Luther Renouf, b Scottsdale, PA 1876, d 1936, mar Mabel Bertha Riblet, b Clarksville, PA 1877, d 1965
C1. James Edward, b 1900 d 1975, bur Ellsworth, OH, mar Janet Demar Truitt, b 1901, Kittaning, PA.
D1. Don Edward Renouf, b 1920 Youngstown, OH, mar Elsie Louise Willison, b 1922 Kellersburg, PA.
E1. Patricia Ann, b 1941 d 1973, mar Don Borlie
F1. David Allen Borlie, b 1964, adopted by Don & Elsie RENOUF.
E2. Cassandra Kay, b 1947 Youngstown, OH mar Rocky Ford, COL Thomas Flower, b Struthers, OH, res Greeley, COL
F1. Adriane Renouf Flower, b 1977 F2. Jason Flower b 1979
D2. John Ola Renouf, b 1922 Youngstown, OH res Austin, TX. Mar Dorothy Dunlap, b Salem, OH.
E1. Michael, mar Evie ___, a ch?
E2. Michele, mar Allen WILLIAMS, 2 chn: Shane and Shawn Williams b Dallas, TX. Michele mar 2. Brian Mahogane, a son Cody Blue Mahagane b Houston, TX.
E3. James, mar Carrie ___, a ch Jori Renouf b Austin, TX 1982
C2. Rose Riblet Renouf, b 1902 Tarentum, PA mar Scott Truitt in Youngstown, OH 1919.
D1. Richard Truitt, b 1921 mar Edith Dierkes
D2. Constance Truitt, mar Jack Standfast
D3. Nancy Truitt mar Nick Hilwa.
B3. William Bion, b 1882 Allsburgh, PA d 1886, drowned.
B4. Emma Pearl b 1888 d 1967, mar Arthur Stoliper 1919
C1. Cecelia Pearl Stoliper, b 1931 Wellsville, OH, mar Dean Dilley, b 1931 Jackson MN.
D1. Margaret Dilley, b 1955 mar Patrick Allen Teal, b 1954 SD.
D2. Mark Arthur Dilley, b 1958 Marion, IND.
D3. Lidia Jane Dilley, b 1962, twin,b in Bolivia, SA.
D4. Licia Jean Dilley, b 1962, twin, ditto
D5. Beka Sue Dilley, b 1967 Pine Ridge
D6. Sarah Beth Dilley, b 1967 res Pine Ridge
A4. Charlotte Renouf mar Luther Dickey, 6 chn: Almedia, Jenny, Nellie, Maude, Bessie and Luther Dickey. Maude and Bessie were twins.
A5. Nicholas Bion, b 1857 d 1935, mar Ruth Hughes, 1863-1945.
B1. Nicholas Bion, b 1884 d 1962
B2. Elizabeth May, mar John A. Seel, 2 sons: John R. and George R.Seel
A6. Thomas William, b 1863 d 1904, mar Ella Dyer.
B1. Grace May b 1890
B2. William Raymond, 1892-1955 mar Neva Hull, a dau Elizabeth Rae Hull
A7. Angelina, 1866-1894 A8. Benjamin, 1869-1897
A9. Almedia, b 1853, d 1921, mar George Parker, 1851-1940
B1. Eddie Parker, 1872-1874 B2. Myrtle
B2. Myrtle Parker, 1875-1957, mar J. Harry Williams, 1871-1948
C1. Marvel Williams
A10. and A11. twins, d.y.

RENOUF, Charles mar Sarah GREEN 1749 Boston, MA (int)
RENEUF, Charles and Sarah, res Boston, a son Clement b 1709
RENEUF, Clement and Elizabeth res Boston, a son Charles b 1726
RENOUF, Edward mar 1772 Rachel BENNETT, both from J? res MRB, mar in Manchester, MA?
A1. Rachel, bp 1773, d.y.? A2. Rachel, bp 1774
RENOUF, Edward, arrived in Boston 1715 on ship MARY from J and Fal-Mouth, England. (Whitmore)
RENOUF, Edward, painter and sculptor, b 1906 res Washington, CT.
RENOUF, Elizabeth, bp 1791 J, d 1849. Husband and chn to UT. Eliz. was dau of Thomas and Rachel (LE MOIGNAN) RENOUF of J. See CADORET.
RENEW, Elizabeth mar Manuel MARK, qv, 1773 Boston.
RENOFF, Elizabeth mar Robert POTELL 1752 Boston, OUTC. Cf BOUTILLIER.
RENOFF, Eliz. mar Benj. May 1753 Boston. Cf LE MAY of J.
RENOUF, Elizabeth mar Robert Harrington 1800 Boston
RENEW, Betsy, mar James Bemiss 1788 Boston. OUTC
RENEW, Elizabeth mar James Mannin 1789 Boston.
RENOUF, Emile, painted a picture called HELPING HAND, A little girl helping her father or grandfather tow a boat, 'which could be in a harbor in one of the Channel Islands.'. (Paul Renoff)
RENOUF, E., curr in TX
RANUFF, Fanny, mar Andrew Harrington 1809 Boston. See Eliz. above.
RENEW, Francis of J?, a sojourner, mar Mary BROWN of Gloucester, dau of Joseph and Mary (Elwell) BROWN, 1700s.
RENO, Francis, res Halfmoon, Albany Co., NY 1790, with fam of 2. OUTC
RENOUF, Harriet Ann, b 1857 St. Sampson G, mar Nicholas FALLA, qv, rem to Holbrook, MA and d 1936. (John Falla, Tenant's Harbor, ME)
RENOUF, Helen M., b 1918 J, to US 1946 as war bride, mar James Juby. Was dau of Arthur and Rosabella Marie (Pierce) RENOUF of St. Saviour Jersey. (Helen Juby, Riverdale, ILL)
A1. John Juby, b 1947 A2. James Juby, b 1950
RENOUF, James and Sarah res MRB.
A1. Sarah, bp 1769 A2. James bp 1772
RENOFF, James res Bridgewater, MA 1790, fam of 5. (Census) OUTC.
RENEUF, John mar Sarah Colman in Charlestown, MA. (Wyman)
A1. Elizabeth mar Wm. Abraham 1745/6.
RENOUF, Kathleen, b St. Sampson G, dau of Ernest John and Helene (ROBIN) RENOUF. Rem to Hamilton, ONT then to Buffalo, NY, mar ___ Souder, 8 chn. Sisters and 2 bros. of Kathleen also rem to Windsor, ONT ca 1900. (K. Souder, Whitesville, NY)
RENEW, Martha mar Samuel B. BROWN 1811 MRB.
RENOW, RENO, Mary mar John Codman 1798 Boston, MA.
RENOUGH, Matthew of MRB mar 1728 Mary Abbot of Salem. (Essex Ant., Vol 2; ABBOT GEN)
RENOUF, Peter mar 1800 Charlotte BEST, both of Pictou dist., NS. (NS NEWSLETTER, Fall 1979)
RENUFF, Philip res Rehoboth, MA 1790, fam of 3. (Census)
RENOUF, Ralph, b 1886 St. Helier J, mar Florence Eugenie LUCE, qv, rem to NYCity 1912, returned to J 1931. A son John, b J, mar Esme P. MOLLET, b 1918 St. Saviour J, and rem to Don Mills, ONT, Canada.
RENEW, Richard, lost at sea from MRB. 1839. Betsy his wife d 1832, 27.
RENOUF, Richard and Elizabeth res MRB.
A1. Richard, bp 1769 A2. Jane, bp 1771
RENEW, Richard and Martha, res MRB. Are A2 and A3 twins?
A1. Patty?, bp 1789 A2. Betsy Brown, bp 1794 A3. Richard, bp 1794
RENEW, Sarah mar Joseph Bariers 1790 MRB.
RENNO, Simeon, res Pawling, Dutchess Co, NY 1790, fam of 9. (Census)

RENEW, Thomas, capt. of ship GOOD INTENT 1767, of MRB. Two ships named GOOD INTENT were owned by Jerseymen in 1700s. (JOURNAL OF ASHLEY BOWEN)

RENOUF, Thomas and Esther, res MRB, at least 4 chn.

A1. Thomas, bp 1735 A3. Mary, bp 1741

A2. James, bp 1739, d.y.? A4. James again, bp 1744

RENOUF, Thomas mar Lydia BODEN, qv, 1760 MRB, a dau Mary bp 1760

RENEW, Thomas of MRB, fisherman and shipmaster, commanded the brig HANNAH 1762, schooner SEAFLOWER 1761-63, and GOOD INTENT, 1766-67; sloop NEWBURY PACKET 1763. Served 1777 in Col Jonathan Glover's 5th Essex Co., Regt of Militia.

RENOUF, a prof. at John Hopkins Univ. in the Chem. Dept. recently.

RENOUF, curr in Baltimore, MD. OUTC.

RESEARCHER: Note that at least 25 RENOUFS of Jersey were listed in JERSEY SAILING SHIPS as seacaptains. (A. John Jean, author, Jersey)

RETILLEY as LE RETILLEY in G middle 1700s and in St. Martin G 1830.

RETILLEY, LE RETILLEY, James Sr., b ca 1788 G (another account says he was b Scotland!). To America 1806, settled Coshocton, OH ca 1850 where he became a Judge, and served on the schoolboard in Roscoe Village, OH. Also res Muskingum Co., OH, and had a salt factory with Geo. Bagnall. They sent the salt to Wooster, OH by canoe and pirogue which soon became unprofitable, so Retilley and Wood rem to Roscoe Village and set up a dry goods store in a log cabin. Wood retired, and the firm became Bagnall and Retilley. There is now a restored historical town called Roscoe Village on the banks of the old Canal. James mar twice, 1. ?, and 2. Elizabeth/Betsey Emerson, 1806-1903, dau of T. Emerson of Keene (NH?). She is bur Granville, OH, desc in Coshocton, Columbus and Granville, OH. Chn below are unverified but appear likely. Poss other chn? (Cosh. Cem. INSCRIPTIONS, by Helen Meredith, 1955; County records; HIST. COLL OF COSHOCTON CO, by Wm. E. Hunt, Cincy, 1-76, supplement dated 1964; OLD NORTHWEST, Vol 8) CAUTION: TRIAL CHART

A1. James, b 1816? d 1892 age 76, mar 1839 Elizabeth Farmer? Another or same mar 1845 M. Eliza Ferguson, Cosh., OH. A Mrs. James L. d 1897 age 54.

A2. Thomas? A Thomas mar Barbara E. Ault 1860 in Cosh., OH.

A3. Rachel?, who mar John Burns 1838. They had a dau who mar Capt. John M. Compton, son of Elisha Compton, of Roscoe, a lawyer.

A4. Barbara Ellen, 1836-1916 A5. Joseph?

A6. William?, who d age 56 in Roscoe Village, OH, a Civil War Vet.

A7. Elizabeth, b 1847 d 1904 Virginia Twp., Cosh., OH.

The following were found in county records in Cosh. OH, named RETILLEY or LE RETILLEY.

Belle, b 1861 Cosh., d 1941

Caroline, mar C.C. Bonnett 1907 Cosh. A Mrs. Carrie LE RETILLEY Bonnett was a member of the Presb. CH in Coshocton, OH 1901.

Clara, d age 22, dau of Thomas Roscoe LE RETILLEY. Ellesworth, Ellesworth, 1861-1939

Edward, b 1852, d 1948, poss mar1880 Ella Blackburn, Cosh. (PresbCh)

Elizabeth, mar Ellsworth Wright 1888 Esther, mar Charles Giffin 1918

Elizabeth mar Tim. Starkey 1859 Etha/Ethel? Martin, 1866-1942

George, father of Roscoe, d Columbus, OH

Helen M. mar Joseph W. Johnston 1919 Coshocton. 1872-1938

Jay L., b 1862 d 1947 Jefferson Twp., Cosh, mar 1896 Nora V. Crown,/

Mrs. James L. d 1897 age 54. Leah L. mar H.C. McConnell 1914 Cosh.

John, d 1838 age 19 Cosh. Mary Ann, dau of James Sr.? d 1850,age 22.

Laura, a pupil in Granville College 1879. Mary F. mar James Crawford.

Thomas, at least 2, poss 3 of this name. One b 1864, d 1909 Roscoe Village. One d age 73. One mar 1889 Ethel M. Martin.
William, d age 56 Roscoe, a Civil War Vet.
REVERE, Paul of the famous Ride, was the son of a Frenchman. This was a Hug. family, some of whom fled to Guernsey Is.
REVERE, Rivoire, Appollos, b Riaucoud, France, was sent to an uncle in Guernsey, from there at age 13 was apprenticed to silversmith John Coney of Boston, MA. He mar Deborah Hichborne, 1704-1777. Paul was the 3rd of 12 chn. His account of the ride is interesting and revealing. Much data available on this fam. See sources. (Taylor; Chamberlain; Douglas; Fosdick; NEHGS Vol 41, etc, etc.)
REYNOLDS, poss some in early New England were RENAULTS of J. Cf Wm. of Saco, ME and Cape Porpoise early 1700s. OUTC. (Noyes)
REYNAL, REYNOLD, RANAULT, RENAULT, Nicholas from J? in Sagadahoc, ME 1665. OUTC. REYNOLD in Grouville J 1528.
RICH. Many in early New England, most from England, but a few from C.I., such as LE RICHE, in Trinity J 1668, 1749. RICH, LE RICHE in J 1304.
LE RICH, Thomas of J? d 1702 Salem, MA
LE RYCHE, Thomas of early Brookfield, MA.
"My grandmother was a Rich, and back in the 1630s the family came from some of the Channel Islands to Cape Cod." (Charles Lee, W.Vancouver)
RICH, Jonathan, from J? mar Phebe Bridges 1727, res MRB. OUTC. See THE AMERICAN BEGINNINGS OF THE RICH FAMILY, by Julia Rich Hogar, Everett, MA, 1969.
A1. Ann, bp 1731 poss mar John Connell 1749
A2. William, bp 1740 A3. John, bp 1742
RICH, Richard and Sarah (ROBERTS) res Dover, ME 1600s. OUTC. (Noyes)
A1. Richard A 2. John A3. Sarah mar 1702 Isaac BAKER
A4. Thomas, b prob at Eastham, MA A5. Samuel b ca 1685
A6. Lydia, living in 1749, mar Samuel Hopkins.
RICHIE, poss LE RICHE?, John in Salem, MA 1790 with fam of 6.(Census)
RICHARDS, curr G and J.
RICHARDSON, see Q.A. IN CANADA and STEVENSON chart. English surname.
RICHARDSON in J 1661, in Grouville, St. Saviour and St. John J 1668, also in 1749.
RICHARDSON, James in Salem, MA 1790 with fam of 6. OUTC. (Census)
RICHARDSON, Francis, from J? to MRB, wife Susannah. OUTC.
A1. Anna, b ca 1699
A2. John, b 1700, rem to Kittery, ME 1722. See Lydia STEVENSON.
A3. Mary, b 1704 A4. William, b 1705 A5. Elizabeth, b ca 1711.
RICHARDSON, see NEHGS Vol 41; MT. DESERT A HISTORY, by Street; BACON AND ALLIED FAMS
RICKARD, Gideon, res NY middle 1800s mar Mary Mansbandle, see COHU, Susan. OUTC. RICKARD a surname of southern England and C.I.
RICHMOND, some curr research in J? See CIFHS #4.
RICKER. This name said to be peculiar to Cornwall. However, some C.I. surnames are very similar, such as RICCAR, RICKERD, RICQUIERT and RICARD. "Whether the two emigrating bros. or only their ancestors were born in Jersey is not known. One of these, George, was a resident of Cocheco, now Dover, NH in 1670, and was taxed then in 1672. The first earnings he could spare appear to have gone to pay for this brother Maturin's passage to America. Both bros. became residents of Dover, where they raised families, and both were killed by Indians 4th June, 1706." (THE ANCESTORS OF THOMAS LOVELL AND MARY ELLEN RICKER, by F.W. Lovell, 1940. See book, and many other sources for info. on this family.

"Large athletic men, endowed with great powers of physical endurance." Note that MATURIN is not a typical C.I. first name, but is more likely to be French. Note also that A.H. Wilson in article about the Rickers in YANKEE MAGAZINE, says that their name was originally VON RYCKEN from Saxony, Germany, and the family settled in Jersey long ago! (April 1973)

Since many books and much data exists on this fam, only a small amount of data will be included here. See sources: NEHGS Vol 5, etc; HIRAM RICKER AND SONS, souvenir program; HALEY GEN; ANCESTORS OF THOMAS LOVELL; RICKER FAM by Bonsall; unpubl MS by Robert Haggett, Lexington, MA; Virginia Ricker, Haverhill, MA; etc, etc.

RICKER, George, b ca 1648 England or J? to Dover, NH ca 1670, mar Elaner Evans ca 1680, 9 chn, d 1706. Eleanor was b 1660 and d ca 1704, dau of John Evans. (Evelyn Wright, San Diego, CAL)

A1. Judith b 1681? mar Thomas Horne 1699, 4 chn. Judith captured by Indians 1696, but was returned. Thomas mar 2. 1720, Esther Hodgdon. (Noyes) at least 4 chn: William Horne, Thomas, Ichabod and George Horne.

A2. John, b 1682 Dover, d there 1771, mar Hannah Garland ca 1715, who was b Dover 1700. 14 chn: Elizabeth, Olive, Judith, Phineas, Nathaniel, Benjamin, Lydia, Benj. again, Paul, Lydia again, Ebenezer, Daniel, John and Hannah, b 1744.

A3. Mary b 1685 mar Wm. Twombley, escaped from Indians, 7 chn.

A4. Maturin, b 1687 mar 1713 Hannah Hunt or Huntress, 11 or 12 chn. She was dau of George Hunt/Huntress and Mary Nutt. (Noyes)

A5. Elizabeth, b 1690, mar 1. Bart. Stevenson/Stimson, b 1683, son of Bart Sr. of Oyster River, Durham, NY. He was killed by Indians 1709. She mar 2. ___Abbot. One ch by STEVENSON and others by Abbot.

A6. Hannah, b 1693, mar Wm. Jones, 3 chn.

A7. Ephraim, b 1696, mar 1. 1720 Dorcas Garland, and 2. Sarah Wentworth, who d 1773. 12 chn, 3 by 1st wife.

A8. Eleanor, b 1699, mar Benj. Stanton, 1 ch.

A9. George, b 1702, mar Jemima Busby. 6 chn: Ephraim, Daniel, a minister, James, Dolly, Betty and Polly.

RICKER, Maturin, came to New England with the aid of his brother George above, said to be from J. A Hug. named MATTHURIN DE VILLENEUVE was in Jersey 1687 from France. (CIFHS Spring 1981) Maturin d 1706 in Dover in the Indian raid. at least 4 chn. (Mrs. K. Rhodes, San Jose, CAL; C. and V. Ricker, Haverhill, MA)

A1. Maturin Jr, mar Lucy Wallingford, had 6 chn. Ason Moses mar Dorcas Ricker b 1727, grdau of George Ricker.

A2. Joseph, mar 1. Eliz. Garland 1720 and 2. in 1761 Mary MAY, LE MAY? qv. Eliz the dau of Jabez and Dorcas Garland. Mary May the dau of Gideon May and Mary Stone in Berwick 1725. 9 chn by 1st wife: Joshua, Noah, Tristum, Jabec, Joseph, etc.

A3. Sarah mar John Wingate, d Dover, NH 1799 age 97, 7 chn.

A4. Noah, taken captive by the Indians at the time his father was killed 1706, educated, and became a Catholic priest in Quebec.

RICKER, Richard in Guernsey 1350. (SOME ANCESTRAL LINES, by Tingley)

RICKER, John Peter, age 30 from Plymouth to America 1776 on EARL OF ERROL. (PASSENGERS TO AMERICA, M. Tepper, 1977)

RICKER, Humphrey and Lucy Wilson of Saco, ME mar 1807. He was b 1786 and she in 1785. Humphrey d 1820. (FIRST BOOK OF TOWN OF PEPPERELL-BORO, 1895) (Doris Smith, Haverhill, MA)

A1. John Berry, b 1808

A2. Richard Tounge?, b 1810 A4. John, b 1816.

A3. Humphrey Weymouth, b 1812, mar Martha HOOKEY, poss LE HUQUET? A dau Mary Ellen b ca 1847 SAco, d 1909, bur Haverhill, ME.

RIDGEWAY, see REDAWAY, RIDOUET.

RIDGEWAY. In Stillwell's MISCELLANY, qv, is a little data on RIDGEWAY which may be a corruption of RIDOUET, a Hug. surname, some members of which family having settled in J.

RIDGAWAY, John mar Elizabeth DE ST. CROIX 1740 Boston. See DE STE. CROIX. OUTC.

A1. Elizabeth, b 1749 Boston. See RIDGWAY FAM, 3 vols, Cong. Library.

RIDGWAY, John res Pemaquid and Charlestown, NH, age ca 32 in 1655, had fishing venture 1651, mar Mary Brackenbury. (Noyes) OUTC.

RILEY, an Irish surname also found in Sark Island 1900s.

RIMER, Sol. and Wm. in GCO early. Was this name RIMEUR of J? See also RAMIER.

RIVE, old in J and current. See CIFHS #4.

RIVE, ___, from J 1928 age 16 on SS ATHENIA, a cattleboat. He brought over a load of J cattle for the B.H. Bull and Sons Co. of Brampton, ONT. Stayed in quarantine with the cattle for a month after arrival. For four months res in NJ with a Mr. and Mrs. Bonnerman, and then rem to Canada for 2 yrs. Mar in Brantford, ONT, Edith McEwan, later taking over Grove Farms. 7 chn. His father was the mgr. of the largest farm in Jersey, owned by J.A. PERREE, who sold cattle to the Bull farm in Ontario. (Dorothy Rive, Niagara-on-the-Lake, ONT)

ROBBINS, ROBINS, ROBIN, ROBAN, etc. in early New England, some from C.I.

ROBBINS in the Islands at least since 1528. ROBIN in St. Peter Port,G 1700s. Curr G and J.

ROBBINS. The large ROBBINS chart(WRCIC)is a TRIAL CHART from many diverse sources. There will be discrepancies. See original sources to validate your data. There were also ROBBINS from England in the colonies and some lines may be confused.

ROBBINS, Nicholas, cordwainer, from G to Cambridge, MA then res Duxbury MA 1638. Prop. of Bridgewater, MA but did not res there. Nicholas gave his son John half of his land at the new plantation and the other half to his daus. He mar Anne ___, b 1620 G?, had at least 5 chn, but some confusion re daus names. See end of this chart. Nicholas' will dated 1650. Blanche Dickover's chart shows that Nich. was born ca 1617 at Theddingworth, Leicester, kngland, res Cambridge MA 1635, said to be son of John ROBBINS and Hester ___. Wife Ann, b ca 1620, poss in C.I. Has anyone researched Church records of G?

Booklet, ROBBINS FAMILY by Henry Robbins?; ROBBINS FAM, MS by Mrs. Richard Bruce Shank; Eugene Robins, Pittsfield, MA; Rev. F.W. Chapman, Rocky Hill, CT; HIST OF BRIDGEWATER, CT; Savage; Pope; HIST. OF DUXBURY, MA; Plymouth, Plympton, and Bridgewater VRs; Carver, MA records; Mrs. A.E. Warren, Hamilton, ONT; Blanche Robbins Dickover, Tenmile, OR; Cambridge Hist. Soc. records; Wm. C. Robbins; NEHGS Vol 4, p. 319; Plymouth Col. records, Vol IV, p.12; LDS records; Yarmouth Nova Scotia Museum Library; Chegobue, NS records; NY GEN. RECORDS, Vol 1; Leaflet, NICHOLAS ROBBINS OF DUXBURY; ROBBINS FAMS by W.R. Robbins; ROBBINS, by M.P. Bunker; GEN OF ROBBINS, RAYMOND AND DURKEE, by G.S. Brown; MEM. OF JAMES ROBBINS, by Estes Howe; HIST. OF WETHERSFIELD, CT, by H.R. Stiles; NOYES-GILMAN ANCESTRY by C.P. Noyes; ROBBINS FAM OF CAPE COD, by H.N. Latey; DESC OF PETER HILL, by S.E. Cushman; FAMILY OF WM. ROBBINS, by F.E. Robbins; RICHARD ROBBINS of CHARLESTOWN AND CAMBRIDGE, by F.L. Wies; DESC OF CHARLES ROBBINS, by B.W. Robbins; leaflets of sev. pages on Nicholas Robbins, Richard Robbins, Robert Robbins and Wm. Robbins; Mrs. F.E. Robbins, W. Newbury, MA.

ROBBINS, Lucy, mar John BEADLE, b 1782, builder of privateer ships. He was son of David, a mariner. Poss both of C.I. fam. See SAMUEL BEADLE FAMILY by Walter Beadle, 1970.

ROBBINS, William, mar Hannah PAINE, res Rindge, NH, at least 1 ch. OUTC, but note that a son mar Sarah STEELE of a J fam. See STEELE. (Thayer Barrowes, SLCity, UT)

A1. Samuel, b 1776 Ringde, NH d 1857, mar 1807 Sarah STEELE, qv, b1781 d 1861. 9 chn.

B1. Mary, b 1807 mar Oliver Wilder

B2. Sabrina, b 1808 d 1874 mar Jason Keith 1831

B3. David A., b 1810 mar 1841 Betsey Coolidge, poss mar 2.?

B4. George W., b 1812 d 1864 mar 1841 Hannah E. Bugbee

B5. Abigail S., b 1814 mar 1859 Uri Day

B6. Ruth, 1816-1819 B7. Rachel P., 1818-1826

B8. Samuel W., b 1820 mar 1847 Mary PAGE.

ROBBINS, ROBINS, John, b 1775 G, d 1840 GCO. The name is spelled both ways in OH for this fam. To Ohio 1807, mar Mary HUBERT, qv, b G, 1787-1845. See HUBERT. John had first res in Wheeling, WVA, rem to Coshocton, OH where he had a salt business. He later rem to Valley Twp., GCO. Had at least 1200 acres of land south of Cambridge, OH. Helped organize the Bethel Methodist Ch. From this small but very active church came many ministers named ROBINS and LE PAGE, from C.I. fams. His will attested to by Edward Heinlein and Peter LANGLOIS, qv. An Elizabeth Carratt is mentioned in the will, record not found (Sarchet; Williams; Hill; Secrest; Robert Wagstaff; GCO records)

A1. Peter D., b 1814 Cosh. OH d 1893, mar 1833 Deborah Maria Thompson, 1816?-1896?, dau of James and Deb. (Sproat) Thompson, Lutherans. 12 chn. Peter served as commissioner in GCO 1852-1857, was at dedication of Courthouse 1883, farmer and wool buyer.

B1. John W., 1834-1887, unmar B2. Mary J, 1836-1850

B3. James T., b 1838 d 1864, served in Civil War.

B4. Madison D., b 1840, d 1899, mar Belle Millhon, res Cambridge,OH. "Shortly after the Civil War, Madison D. and John Robins imported a colony of colored people from the neighborhood of Charleston WVA to work in the Guernsey mines east of Cambridge, OH."(Wolfe)

B5. Harrison, b 1841 d 1918, mar Jemima Moore, and res Eureka, KS, also poss. Baltimore, MD?

B6. Alexander S., b 1844, d 1914, mar ? Some data confusing.

B7. Peter H. or Peter C., b 1846 res Eureka, KS, mar Harriet Cummins. This or another Peter d in prison in Civil War.

B8. Martin Luther, called Luther in some records, 1849-1908, mar Margaret Secrest, 1852-1906. Martin L. d Buffalo Twp., GCO.

C1. Dr. James Emmet, b 1875/1871? GCO mar Martha Maria Laughlin, dau of James and Mary (Secrest) Laughlin. She d 1918, son Herbert.

C2. Elsie E., b Buffalo Twp., GCO mar 1906 Rev. Greer Alvin Foote, b 1873 Pennsville, OH, raised in Sharon, OH.

D1. Margaret Foote, b 1907 D2. G. Alvin Foote, b 1909

C3. Isa Robins, d 1920 mar Arthur Moorehead of Senecaville, OH.

B9. Martha M., b 1851 d 1874 mar Edward Millhon, res Cumberland,OH.

B10. Charles A., b 1857 mar Flora Young, res Eureka, KS

B11. Rose Emma, b 1860 res Cambridge, OH, mar 1. Thomas W. Teener and 2. Henry Moss.

B12. Jessie Florence, b 1862, mar Elijah Neeland, res Cambridge, OH.

A2. Martin E., b 1818 G or GCO mar 1841 Judith HEAUME, qv, who d 1844. 2 chn d.y. Martin mar 2. Catherine Hickle, b 1825, 5 chn. (SPAID GEN; Sarchet Scrapbook)

B1. Eliza Jane, 1845-1901, mar Charles BICHARD, qv, 1843-1922.

See BICHARD for 8 chn.
B2. George Newton B4. Lora M. B5. Rosa G.
B3. Harriet M., mar Robert Wm. Wallace
C1. Ora Wallace, b 1874 mar John T. Vance in GCO.
A3. John T. mar Sarah CORBETT, and rem to Missouri
A4. Thomas James, b 1823 GCO d 1912, mar 1846 Rebecca Fishel of Valley Twp., GCO. At least 6, poss 10 chn?
B1. John H. B2. Mary G.
B3. James W., poss Rev. James?, b 1851 GCO mar 1873 Lottie Johnson, dau of Jesse L. and Charity Jane Johnson. She soon d and he mar 2. 1875, Jennie Hare of Summerfield, OH, 2 chn.
C1. Ora E., mar Rev. Foster G. Anderson of Cleveland, OH.
C2. Homer, res Warren, OH
B4. Eliza M., twin of Charles, b 1854, mar Elmer Keil Frye 1884, who d 1905. Res Pleasant City, OH. (SPAID GEN)
C1. Ethel Frye, b and d 1887 C2. Dwight Frye, b 189-.
C3. Grace Frye, b 1893 mar Harry Millhon, no issue
B5. Charles A., d.y. B6. Thomas F.
A5. Mary, mar Thomas Hammond?
A6. Ezekiel A., b 1826 Valley Twp., mar by Rev. Thomas CORBIT to Sarah Fishel, b VA? 1817. Ezekiel a farmer. 5 chn.
B1. Harrison b 1850, mar Maggie McAlester, had daus Daisy, Olive, Lela, who d 1884 and Irene, who d 1896.
B2. Rachel, d 1873 B4. John F., b 1856
B3. Mary Jane, b 1853 B5. Sarah Rebecca, b 1858
A7. James E., an M.D. A James E. was coroner in GCO 1928
A8. Mary, 1809-1810. A Mary Olimpus is mentioned in Robbin's will.
A9. Martha, 1818-1897? A10. Mary Jane, 1824-1850 These are not
A11. Sarah, 1818-1890? A12. Judith, 1822-1844. verified.
ROBBINS, ROBINS, Carl H., of GCO served in WWI. OUTC.
ROBINS, Rev. James W., in GCO 1800s.
ROBINS, John H. platted town of Kingston, OH 1800s.
ROBINS, Louisa, b G? d 1842 GCO
ROBINS, Margaret E. mar Adam Kempf 1889 Coshocton, OH. OUTC
ROBINS, Mary b 1787 G, d 1845 GCO, prob sister or other relative of immigrant ROBBINS.
ROBINS, Mary MARQUAND, b 1747 G, d 1846 GCO, bur Valley Twp. (CONNER-EYNON). See MARQUAND.
ROBBINS, Thomas mar Sarah Church 1833 GCO. See Church.
ROBINS, Wm. W. served in the Civil War from Cambridge, OH 1861. Mar Mary Moore 1858. OUTC.
ROBBINS, note there are many fams in other Ohio counties such as Athens possibly from C.I. fams to OH. OUTC.
ROBERGE, surname of Alderney Island in the 1800s. William Roberge mar a Miss De Gorgy, res Alderney, 7 chn. At least one to Canada 1900s. This fam connected with LE HURAY, BRAY and LE COCQ fams. qv. (Stephen Le Huray, Middletown, NY)
ROBERGE, Mary mar John LE HURAY, 3 chn, desc in US.
ROBERT and ROBERTS are two distinct surname in the C.I. ROBERT also in G 1300s and in J. ROBERT in St. Mary J 1668, 1749. See Q.A. IN CANADA, by Turk. ROBERT and ROBERTS both curr in G and J. ROBERT at Torteval, G, 1722.
ROBERT, Jeanne/Jane, b 1811 St. Laurens J, d 1894 Teton, ID, dau of John ROBERT and Elizabeth DE LA COUR of J. (SLC RECORDS)
ROBERT, Paul from G to GCO 1807. (Sarchet)
ROBERT, Peter, b G, rem with wife and fam to Racine, WIS 1842. See record of Peter Robert's voyage to America. (WISC.HIST.SOC. ms)

ROBERT, Roy, b 1921 St. Andrews G, mar E. Piniel, rem to Niagara Falls NY 1850. (Eliz. Robert, Niagara Falls, NY)

A1. Joseph, b 1940 Castel G. A2. John b 1944 G.

ROBERT, Nicholas, arrived in Boston from Nfld. 1760s on sloop ADVENTURE, a mariner. (Whitmore) OUTC, but poss from C.I. Nfld. fam.

ROBERTS, see also HILLMAN and MARTIN.

ROBERTS, Thomas John, b 1856 Sibley Back, Cornwall, England, son of Thomas and Elizabeth Jane (WATTS) ROBERTS, mar 1878 St. Sampson G, Rosina Jane Kelly, b 1854 G, dau of Wm. and Eliz. (Hillman) Kelly. Thomas d 1936 San Francisco, CAL and Rosina Jane d Camberwell, London, England 1917. (Carol Elliott, Woodland, CAL)

A1. James Thomas Hillman, b 1880 St. Sampson G, rem to Perth, Australia mar 1. Frances G. Manktelaw, 3 chn, and 2. Eleanor Mabel Sines, b 1900 Bristol, England d 1977 W.Aust. 3 chn: Lillian, Arthur, and Frank Roberts, poss more chn.

A2. Cecil Martin, reg. at birth in G 1883 as John Hillman Martin ROBERTS, later bp Cecil Martin. Cecil mar 1905 Lillian Phoebe Poet and d 1960 San Francisco, CAL. Lilian was dau of James and Sarah Ann (Copley) Poet.

B1. James Cecil Thomas Henry, b 1906 Kennington, England mar Ann T. Berges. He d 1949. She was b 1916 San Francisco, d there 1977, dau of Peter and Marie J. (Brodenauve) Berges.

C1. Martin Peter, b 1937 San Fran., mar 1962 Darline Moresco, 3 chn: James, Sharon and Nancy Jean, b CAL

C2. Lilian Marie, b 1944 SF, mar Louis A. Espinoza, div, son Louis.

B2. Violet Lilian Maud, b 1907 Lambeth, Eng. mar Milton Mecklenburg.

C1. Carol Sue Mecklenburg, b 1932, mar Paul Elliott, 3 chn: Lisa M. Brasfield, David Paul Mecklenburg and Cynthia L. Sharp.

C2. Marcia Marie Mecklenburg, b 1936 mar 1955 Morrison Kai Norton, 3 chn, 1 by 1st wife. 2 chn: Glenn M. and Shelly K. Norton.

C3. Joyce Lilian Mecklenburg, b 1939 SF, mar 1957 John Duncan Hooper 3 chn: Richard, Robin and Craig Hooper

B3. Cecil Edward W. Roberts, b 1908 St. George, London, Eng., d 1909

B4. Henry Charles, 1909-1911

B5. Thomas Early, b 1910 England mar Ethel Ann Casement, 2. Elgiva R Richter and 3. Jean Allison.

C1. William Martin, b 1939 SF, mar 1961 Judith M. Weymouth, 3 chn: Christiane, David and ?

C2. Alison Jean, b 1955, by 3rd wife, mar Robert M. Stanga.

B6. John/Jack RENOUF, b 1912 SF, mar 1. Marie Tuesch, and 2. Louise A. Paldi, 3 chn

C1. Charles Martin, b 1942 SF, mar 1964 Nancy Lee Valentine, div, 4 chn: Brett, Shawn, Kelly and Tracy.

C2. Douglas Edward, b 1944 SF, mar 1965 Donna M. Hill, 3 chn: Dean, Gregory and Jack Robert, b CAL

A3. Willie Henry Martin, b 1884 St. Sampson G, mar Mary Ann HOLMES, 2 sons William and Ronald

A4. Dau, b 1886 stillborn A5. Martin Hillman, b 1887 St. Sampson,G.

A6. Harry Hillman, b 1890 St. Sampson, G, mar Harriet Maud Poet, d1930

ROBERTS, James Adolphus, b ca 1833 G, rem to Gaspe, QUE where he d1915. Mar Jane E. White, b England?, who d1915, age 80, 5 chn. (Ina Stanley, Parma, OH)

A1. Liza A2. Frank, Francis

A3. George Edward, b1880, d1962, mar Alice Jane PITON, qv, b1886, d1967, res Gaspe. 7 chn.

B1. Alice, mar Wilson ROBERTS, 3 chn

B2. Alma, mar Elvin LEGGO, see Q.A. IN CANADA, by Turk, 5 chn
C1. Embert C2. Wesley C3. Cecil C5. Calmus
C4. Ina, mar ___ DEVOUGE, res St. Catherines, ONT
B3. Norman, d age 21
B4. Irene, mar Robert ROWCLIFFE from G. See ROWCLIFFE.
B5. Earl, mar Beatrice LANGLOIS, qv, res Fontenelle, QUE
C1. Iona, mar a second cousin, named LANGLOIS
C2. Dennis, res Calgary, ALTA C5. Syril/Cyril?, res Calgary
C3. Murray C4. Alice C6. Clayton
B6. Hazel, mar Harold LE MASURIER, qv
B7. Audrey, mar Fredrick Morencay, a son, Allen
B8. Ida, b ca 1918, mar Willis Stanley, chn: Gary b1940, Sandra b1950
B9. Graydon, mar Jeanette Fauce, a dau, Barbara
B10. Gwendoline, mar Franklin GAVEY, qv, 5 chn, most reside Calgary, ALTA: Wayne, Cynthia, Phillip, Norman and Lawrence
A4. Mary A5. Charles, mar Mildred, dau of James PITON? See PITON.

ROBERTS, fam in PEI said to be from G ca 1806. See Q.A. IN CANADA; Heritage Foundation in C'Town, PEI. Info below from the BECK GEN. CHART, in WRCIC, by James V. Beck, Okemos, MI. See chart for more info.

ROBERTS, Thomas, in PEI, mar Elizabeth Amma Beck, 1809-1884, dau of Vere Beck and of Elizabeth Sarah Marfleet.
A1. Susan, 1832-1913, mar James Thompson Carmichael, 6 chn: Ida Mary, Ella, Alexander T., Mary Alena, Bessie Maude and Geo. Edgar Carmichael, 2 unmar.
A2. Ann, d.y.?
A3. John, b 1834 PEI, d1920, mar Margaret Mary Lambe, a son, and 2. Teressa L. Gabriel, 10 chn: John Eden, John Freeman, Fenton N., Mary Eliz., Harriet, Charlotte, Aleda, Dianna, James P., Alice Maud, Ethel Grace.
A4. Elizabeth, mar Capt. ___ Baxter, 4 chn: Minnie, Harry, Fred, and Florence Baxter
A5. Margaret, mar William Byrnes, 6 chn: Charles, Lena May, John William, Johnston K., Heber and Harry Byrnes, all married.
A6. Thomas, mar 1. Amelia M. Gabriel, 1 ch, and 2. Nancy Wasson, 8 chn: Thomas H., Emma, Caroline Amelia, Frank, Rebecca, Joseph, Flora and Henry
A7. Samuel
A8. Charlotte, 1844-1939, mar Charles O'Neill, 9 chn: William Eleanor, Walter, Bessie Maud, Frank, Helen, George, Charlotte and David

ROBERTS, Peter, part of the same original Roberts fam from G, mar Martha Lucy Beck in PEI, b 1811, dau of Vere Beck and Eliz. S. Marfleet, more data in Chart, WRCIC.
A1. William, mar 1. Nancy Lambe, 4 chn and 3. Ellen Clark, 8 chn: Peter, Edon, Ida, Florence, Winnie, Clara Maud, Theodore, Walter, Sadie, Flora, Fred and Mary Jane. A2. David, d.y.
A3. James, mar Hannah Catherine Orr, 9 chn: David, Arthur, Albert E., James, Stewart, Frank, Norman, Alfred E., Martha, Harriet & Bertha
A4. Vere, mar Annie Lambe, 2 chn: Eva Gavin and Jessie
A5. Benjamin, mar Rebecca Carey, 12 chn: Minnie, S. Elizabeth, Johnson, Harris, Vere Beck, Edith R., Ida Jane, Grace B., Mabel A., Charles C., Ethel, Mary Edna Hill
A6. Capt. John, 7 chn: Capt. Fred, Capt. Clarence, Ted, Sabra, Ella, Daniel and John
A7. Sarah mar John W. Smith, 3 chn: David, Freeman and Charles A8. June

ROBERTS, Joshua, was in Parsonsfield, ME 1811. He was b 1779 Berwick, ME and mar Abigail HUBBARD, qv. Either, or both, or neither, may be of C.I. ancestry. (HIST OF PARSONSFIELD, ME) He d1855, wife d1863.

A1. Tristam, b 1800, mar Betsy Page, and d 1864, 7 chn
A2. Mark, b 1803, mar Lydia Abbot, and d 1884, 3 chn
A3. Joshua, b 1805, mar Lucy NEAL, d 1882, 7 chn
A4. Hubbard, b 1808, mar Mary Griffin, d 1858, 10 chn
A5. Lewis, b 1810, mar Sarah Weymouth, and d 1858, 10 chn
A6. Joseph, b 1814, d 1878, mar 1. Louisa Howe and 2. Mary J. Cole, 11 chn
A7. John, b 1818, mar Clarissa Cooper, 5 chn, res Dover, NH
A8. Betsy, b 1822, d 1852, mar Abel Jellison, 2 chn
A9. Abby, b 1825, mar Levi Howe, 3 chn

ROBERT, ROBERTS. Many in early New England, poss some from C.I. However, note that Thomas ROBERTS came from Wallaston, England to NH 1623 and was Governor in 1640.

ROBERTS. Many noted in records of Philadelphia, PA, poss some from C.I?

ROBERTS. Large fam in Pontiac, MI from an Ontario C.I. fam. See Q.A. IN CANADA, by Turk.

ROBERTS, Charles, b ca 1818 G, mar Caroline ___, rem to Racine, WI, ca 1860. Poss first settled in OH?

ROBERTS, Jane. See JOSUE MESSERVY, MASS, 1800s.

ROBERTS, Silas Josiah, b C.I., mar 1900 Mary Dithia DE CARTERET qv, MA.

ROBERTS, Edward, from Barbadoes to SC ca 1670. (Baldwin) OUTC.

ROBERTS, Geo. and Sally, res MRB. OUTC, but poss from C.I.
A1. John, b 1814 A2. Hannah Case, b 1816 A3. John again, b 1817

ROBILLIARD, in Torteval, G early, in St. Peter, G 1709. ROBILLIARD in J 1528, 1607, 1668. Curr G.

See Q.A. IN CANADA, by Turk, for large fam settled in ONT and other parts of Canada. Parts of fam reside in MI also. (Marlene Robilliard, Albion, MI)

ROBILLIARD, Joseph and Rose, b G?, rem to Montreal, QUE. (Mrs. Richard Hoey, Encino, CAL)
A1. Arthur, b1820 Montreal, d1889 Poughkeepsie, NY, mar Susan Weaver ca 1845
B1. Edward, b 1862, mar 1. Annie ___, 3 chn. These chn took the surname WEAVER. Edward mar 2. 1887, Lelia B. REED, b 1869, dau of Thomas R. and Elizabeth MUNSELL REED of Manchester, CT
C1. Nellie Weaver C2. Edward Weaver C3. Charlotte Weaver

ROBILLIARD. See DE LA MARE, Edgar NAFTEL.

ROBILLIARD, Peter, b 1832 G, rem to Racine, WI 1848.

ROBILLIARD, James, b 1839 G, rem to Racine, WI 1865.

ROBILLIARD. Noted in Owings Mills, MD, poss from G? Also in Austin, TX, and Boston, MA.

ROBILLIARD. Sail maker in J, middle 1800s. (John Jean, Jersey)

ROBIN, Eugene, b ca 1892 St. Sampson, G, d Tampa, FL 1959. Mar Harriet INGROUILLE, qv, b Lancresse, Vale, G, mar in St. Martin, G 1911, rem to Grimsby, ONT 1914. (Gladys Alexander, Ithaca, NY)
A1. Wilson, b1911 G, res Kings Ferry, NY, mar Florence Briggs 1937, 2chn
B1. Donald, b 1942, mar Lucille Quick, 3 chn
B2. Janet, b 1945, mar Jeffrey Crandall
A2. Gladys, b 1914, res Ithaca, NY, mar Ralph W. Alexander 1937
B1. Ralph W. Alexander, b 1941, mar Janet Bradley, 2 chn
B2. Robin Judith Alexander, b 1943, mar Lindsay Goodloe
B3. Anne Louise Alexander, b 1944, mar Peter Koehler, 2 chn
B4. Nancy Jean Alexander, b 1947 B5. David Wilson, b 1957
A3. Beulah Harriet, b Winona, ONT?, 1915, res Rochester, NY, mar John Janowisc 1939
B1. Judith Janowisc, b 1943, mar William Keys, 2 chn
B2. John Janowisc, b 1945, mar Patricia Autovino, 2 chn

B3. Barbara Janowisc, b 1946, mar Thomas Erdle, 2 chn

ROBIN, Peter Francis, b England, son of Ezekiel ROBIN, master mariner of Grand Clos, Castel, G, rem to Australia, Canada, and later to FLA. Mar Sarah Gibson 1887. He d Mobile, ALA 1929. (Ivy Erwin, Pensacola, FLA)

A1. Victor Francis, res Australia? A2. Elsie, twin, d.y.

A3. Harold, twin, d.y., Australia

A4. Alfred Edwin, b 1889 Brisbane, Aust., d 1950 Prince Rupert, BC, Canada. Mar Clara Nelson, 5 chn, b and res in BC, Canada

A5. Robin Peter, b 1903 Alford, England, mar in Mobile, ALA, Harriet Timbes, 1930, res Port Arthur, TX, 2 chn

B1. Robyna, mar Prescott B2. Harral

A6. Ivy Gibson, b 1908 Manson, MAN, Canada, mar in Mobile, ALA 1928 Winfred Alexander Erwin, 4 chn

B1. Robin Winfred, b 1929, mar B. Jacobs, 4 chn

B2. Dorothy Joan b1931 mar 1956 L. McGlone, res Chula Vista, CA, 3 chn

B3. Patricia Helen, mar L. Wolf, res Gulf Breeze, FLA, 2 chn

ROBIN, Matilda Amy, b 1866 St. Peter Port?, G, to WISC then to Delta, OH 1884. Dau of Daniel and Julia (TOSTEVIN, qv) ROBIN. Daniel was a sea captain. Matilda mar John BLONDEL, qv. ROBIN curr G and J. (Dorothy Harrison, Louisville, KY)

Note other ROBBINS, ROBINS fam from G in Guernsey and Coshocton counties, OH, above. Three similar C.I. surnames are ROBICHON, ROBISSON, and ROBINSON. These are occasionally confused. ROBICHON was in St. Martin, J 1749. ROBISSON in one case later became ROBINSON, curr G and J. ROBIN/PAGE, see CI COLLECTION.

ROBISSON, Timothy, mar Mary Kitchen 1665 in MRB? (Essex Coll.) OUTC. A son, Timothy, b 1667/68.

ROBISSON, William, had a son Timothy b 1644. (Essex Coll, vol 6) OUTC.

ROCK, DE LA ROCQUE, in J 1309. In St. Heliers and Trinity, J 1668. In St. Heliers, St. Peter and St. John, J 1749. See also LAROKE and LARRICK.

ROCK, J. Peter, b 1801/02 in PA, and wife Susanna ___, b 1792, settled ca 1838 in Connensburg, Carroll Co., OH, now Dellroy. Parents not known. Their land was between Monroe Twp. and Rose Twp. in Carroll Co., and they belonged to the United Brethren CH, of which Peter was a trustee. Susanna, b VA?, d 1852. Peter d 1880. Peter mar 2. Lucinda Blake, who d 1859? He mar 3. Mrs. Cassander Buchanan. No certain connection, but Peter and Susanna may have been from C.I. fams. More data available in sources. (Donna Rock, Elyria, OH; WRCIC)

A1. Jacob, b 1824 PA?, mar Hannah Dolvin 1821, dau of Richard and Phebe (Edwards) Dolvin. Hannah d 1852 and Jacob mar 2. Mary GOSSETT, qv, at Malvern, OH?, he d 1898. Some desc res Malvern and Waynesburgh, OH. Nine chn: Matilda Lytle, Peter, Flemming, Oliver, Asberry, Jacob, Mary E., Ferrenda, and Leander.

A2. Josiah, b ca 1826, mar Ferrenda LLOYD, qv, desc res in and around New Harrisburgh and Canton, OH. Josiah d 1902. Seven chn: Randolf, John, Artissy Jane, Waldorf, Hugh, Carolyn Wetzel & Almira.

A3. Henry, b 1828, mar Mary Jane LLOYD, sister of Ferrenda, 2 chn. Henry d 1853, and Mary Jane b 1821, mar 2. John McBeth 1859, his 2nd wife. John had 9 chn by his 1st wife and d 1863. Mary Jane, the widow, settled Perrysville, OH with 2 sons: Alonzo, b 1850, mar Luella Hyatt, and Henry Lee, b ca 1852, mar Martha Carnahan. Both with desc. A4. Arabella, b 1860, mar Thomas Doughterty

NOTE: There were Jersey fams with the surname EDMONDS ALIAS ROCK in J 1607. Also, the Hug surname RACQUE is pron ROCK.

ROCK. Another fam from PA, settled in and around Creston, OH, desc in Wooster and Grafton, OH. Progenitor named Samuel ROCK? OUTC. (Mrs. Darrell Coots, Wooster, OH)

LA ROCQUE. "Family of ancient settlement in Jersey." (NEGHS vol. 31) See LAROKE.

ROCK, John, from C.I.?, in Salem, MA 1686. OUTC.

ROCK, John, from C.I., mar Anne ___, res MRB.

A1. Thomas, bp 1733 A2. Philip, bp 1740 A3. John, bp 1741

ROCK, John GRUSH, of C.I. fam, son of Frederick and Grace ROCK, bp 1744, MRB.

RUCK. It seems likely that some Rucks were Rocks in the colonies, OUTC.

RUCK, Abigail, mar Benj. Wentworth, son of Lt. Gov. John W. of Portsmouth, his 1st wife. (Noyes)

RUCK, James, res Salem, MA. (Essex Coll. Vol. 8) OUTC.

A1. Mary, bp 1717 Salem, MA

RUCK, John and Hannah, res Salem. She d 1660. He mar 2. Sarah Flint, 1661, who d 1672. OUTC. John mar 3. 1672 Mrs. Elizabeth Croade, OUTC. (Essex Coll. Vol 3 and Vol 7) CAUTION: TRIAL CHART.

A1. Eliza, b 1652 A6. Thomas, b 1658 A11. Ruth, b 1673
A2. Hannah, b 1653 A7. Abigail, b 1662 A12. John, b 1675
A3. Sarah, b 1656 A8. Mary, b 1665 A13. Samuel, b 1676
A4. John, b 1655, d.y. A9. Bethia, b 1668
A5. John again, b 1657 A10. Rebecca, b 1671

RUCK, Margaret, mar 1722 Samuel Powsland of Falmouth fam, res Boston. She was his 2nd wife, he was a shipwright, b 1693 Boston. (Noyes) OUTC

RUCK, Samuel, res Salem, MA. (Essex Coll, Vol 8). Two Samuels involved here?, or 2 wives? OUTC.

A1. Elizabeth, bp 1701 Salem A3. Samuel, bp 1705? A5. Martha, bp 1722
A2. Ruth, bp 1703? A4. John, bp 1717

RUCK, John and Hannah, had dau, Mary, 1712 in Boston.

ROGER. In G 1300s, later in Torteval, G. In J 1309-1607. Curr G. No research done by compiler on this fam in America. Note ROUGET, qv, was changed to ROGER in America by one fam.

ROISSIER, ROISSY, Henry, from G to Racine, WIS ca 1855. (Stone) See also ROSIER.

ROMERIL, RUMRILL, etc. ROMERIL in J 1528 and prob before. See quote below about origin.

ROMERIL, in St. Heliers, St. John, Trinity and St. Martin, J 1668. In St. John, St. Saviour, St. Heliers, Trinity and St. Martin, J 1749. Curr G and J. Also in St. Lawrence, J 1788.

ROMERIL shield, argent, a cross indented sable.

ROMERIL, Simeon, son of Jean, who was son of Jacques, was bp 1635 in J, his godfather was Jacques ROMERIL, his grandfather.

ROMERIL, Simon, son of Nicholas ROMRI of St. John, J, son of Simon, and was bp 1641. This may be the ancestor of the Simon RUMRILL who came to Salem, and Enfield, MA in the 1660s/1670s. Note the Rumrey sound of Nicholas' name, which would explain the change to Rumery, RUMRY in some American branches. However, Simeon is also listed in descendant's names. Both Simon and Simeon above res St. John Parish, J. (Marie Louise Backhurst, Grouville, Jersey) See RUMRILL.

ROMERIL. At least 17 different spellings of this name in America, such as ROMERILL, RUMERILL, RUMERY, RUMIEL, RUMILL, RUMLE, RUMRAL, RUMRALL, RUMREL, RUMRIEL, RUMRIL, RUMRY, etc. (MASS SOLDIERS & SAILORS)

"ROMERILLO, a wild medicinal plant of Spain...the family, most probably pirates or seafarers of some kind, came from Spain to the Channel Islands around the year 1400, where they either became shipwrecked, or attempted a landing and were captured, and then allowed to remain."

(Reg. Romeril, Edmonton, Alta., Canada) "In the U.S. we find also ROMERILS, descended without doubt from Matthieu Romeril, originating in St. Laurens or St. Peter, Jersey, who settled in New England before 1685." (Soc. Jers. Bull. #27) The resercher must settle for himself which was his emigrant ancestor. The families below are almost certainly those of Simon's family. However, at the end of this trial chart are a few whose connections are not known to the compiler, and they may be other ROMERILS from Jersey not closely connected with Simon's branch. Note: Not all sources below were seen by the compiler. CAUTION: THESE ARE TRIAL CHARTS.

(HIST. OF ENFIELD, CT; HARTFORD TIMES, Jan. 31, 1942; STILES, POTTER, COOLEY, CLARK, ABBOTT and CHURCHILL GEN; Virkus files not included in the COMPENDIUM; MASS SOLDIERS AND SAILORS; SOC. JERS. BULL. #27, 1902; COLONIAL FAMS OF AMERICA; Salt Lake City Records; CHASE COLL. in Wiscasset, ME Library; FIRST PURITAN SETTLERS, WINDSOR, by Hinman; Pope's PIONEERS OF MASS; SAVAGE; Cutter's NEW ENGLAND FAMILIES #4; LONGMEADOW FAMILIES; D.A.R. Records; CONN. QUARTERLY for Dec. 1896; OUR RUMRILL FAMILY, by Charles L. Rumrill, 1980, booklet; unpublished data in files of NEHGS, Boston, MASS, not seen by compiler; Family Bible records; Army and Navy records; Winifred Holman; Robert G. Steen, Newport Beach, CAL; Graham T. Smallwood, Salt Lake City, UT; Charles L. Rumrill, Pitts-Ford, NY; Donald A. Rumrill, Gloversville, NY; Mrs. Myrtle Avery, Syracuse, NY; Irene Mahan, Holyoke, MASS; Reg. Romeril, Edmonton, Canada; Doris Anderson, Del Mar, CAL; ALVORD GEN; THE LITTLE FAMILY; NYE GEN; LIVERMORE FAMILY; GREELEY GEN; OLDS FAMILY; NEAL FAMILY; REV. WAR RECORDS; HIST. OF NEW IPSWICH, NH, by Chandler; HIST. OF ROYALTON, VT, by Evelyn Lovejoy; SOCIETE JERSIAISE, EXTENTES of 1597,1607,1668,1749.)

See also the ROMERILS in Q.A. IN CANADA, by Turk. One fam res in Washington state.

ROMERIL. Two Romerils appeared in Ohio, Indiana and Kansas in the middle 1800s, from J. Philip's age is a puzzle, as it is different in the two census records, but he was prob b between 1785 and 1795. He mar Elizabeth? ___, poss also b J. Along with Philip and his bro? John, there was a Sarah ROMERIL, b ca 1761 in J, prob the mother of the two men. There were also two females, prob sisters of John and Philip: Easther, b ca 1801 and Elizabeth, b ca 1805, both b J. See John ROMERIL below. (Mildred E. Casper, Kansas City, MO; Census) CAUTION: TRIAL CHARTS.

ROMERIL, John, bro of Philip above?, b 1793 J, was in IND 1850-1860, mar Mary ___, b ca 1804 in PA. Not certain whether John or Philip was father of Jane Elizabeth.

A1. Mary Ann, b ca 1822 OH, or poss in 1824?

A2. Jane Elizabeth, b ca 1822 OH, d ca 1870 in Clinton Co., IND. Mar 1842 James P. Reeves, b ca 1820 Frankfort, KY, at least 7 chn b OH

B1. Heziel Reeves, b ca 1844 OH

B2. Harriet A. Reeves, b ca 1847 OH, mar 1868 William Brown, son of John Brown and Malinda Ludington Doty. Harriet d Augusta, KS, at least 8 chn.

C1. Clara B. Brown, b 1869 IND

C2. Eva Brown, b 1870 Kirklin, IND

C3. Ada Brown, b 1874, mar 1905 John W. Sturgis

C4. Harry Ruferd Brown, b 1877 Kirklin, IND, mar 1902 Olive Pender, 1882-1955, who d Oklahoma

D1. Mildred Elizabeth Brown, b 1913 Alva, OKLA, mar 1935 Flagstaff, AZ, Henry David Casper, b 1907 Isabella, OKLA, no issue

C5. Gazzella/Zella Brown, b 1879 Augusta, KS, mar Charles Koons

C6. Anna Brown, b 1881 KS, mar ___ Sears

C7. William Edward, b1884 Augusta, KS, mar Mamie Lash, who d 1937, San Diego, CAL   C8. Ora, b 1886 KS, d Yellville, ARK
B3. Mary J. Reeves, b ca 1848 OH, mar Alfred RUSSELL and d ca 1921
B4. Sarah E. Reeves, b ca 1850   B7. John L. Reeves, b ca 1858
B5. Hester/Esther?, b ca 1852   B8. Bethaire/Beth Anne?, b ca 1861
B6. Caleb T., b ca 1854   B9. Abraham Reeves, b ca 1865
A3. John W., b 1830 OH   A7. Phillip, b ca 1840 IA
A4. William A., b ca 1832 IA   A8. Catherine, b ca 1842 IA
A5. Fletcher, b ca 1834 IA   A9. Thomas C.?, b ca 1845 IA
A6. Sarah, b ca 1838 IA   A10.Rachel, b ca 1849 IA

ROMERIL, Francis, b 1800 St. John, J, res Grouville, J, mar 1826 St. Helier, J, Marie Ann BILLOT, 1804-1866, dau of Joshua HOTTON. Francis d 1875 J, and Marie d in Bingham Fort, UT. The fam came from J to U.S. via ship CHIMBORAZO 1855, and walked from the Missouri River to SLCity. More info in UT records. Some chn bp St. John and Trinity, J. (Mrs. B. Charlesworth, Ogden, UT; Leona Hansen, Maywood, CAL; Kathryn Westmoreland, SLCity, UT)
A1. Mary, b 1824 St. John, J, mar Richard CORNISH. She d 1888.
A2. John A., b 1826 J, drowned at sea
A3. Francois Thomas, b 1829 J, mar 1. Christina Anderson and 2. Harriet Butchler
A4. George, b 1830 J, mar Patience Swingwood 1861, d 1912
A5. Charles, b 1832 J, d.y.   A6. Mary Ann, b 1834 J, d 1865
A7. Jane Nancy, b1837 Grouville J, mar 1871 George Pierce, d1909 Odgen
A8. Fanny Mary Ann, b1840 Grouville J, mar Charles Singleton 1857, d1903
B1. Florence May Singleton, b1878 UT, d1950, mar John Henry Naisbitt
C1. Kathryn Naisbitt, b1913 UT?, mar Richard H. Westmoreland
A9. Ann, b 1841 J, d.y.
A10. Charles Abraham, b1842 Grouville J, mar 1882 Mary MONTEZ,qv & d1932
A11. Sophia Jane, b 1846 J, mar 1868 Miland Russel, d 1906

ROMERIL, Pierre, Peter, b 1816 St. Laurens J, d 1880 SLCity, UT. Son of Pierre ROMERIL and Rachel MARETT. Mar 1. Ann LE BAS, LE BASS, qv, and 2. Eliz. LE BAS. (SLCity records) Ann was dau of Francis and Mary (DURELL) LE BAS of J. Not known to compiler how many of this fam came to America.
A1. Peter Charles, b1837 St. Helier J d ca 1871 A2. Thomas, bp1842, twin
A3. Henry Prosper, twin, bp1842 St. Helier J
A4. Clara Marguerite, 1845-1852?
A5. Ann Elizabeth, b1850 J, d1857 A7. Henrietta, b 1854 J
A6. Charles Durell, b1852 J, mar 1857 Sarah Bean, d 1929 U.S.?

ROMERIL, Edwin, b St. James, G?, mar 1931, rem to NY 1947, sons. (Linda Romeril, Racine, WI)
A1. Allan, b 1932   A2. Philip, b 1936

ROMERIL, ROMMERY, Elizabeth, wife of Philip LE BLANC, WHITE, qv, of Salem, MA 1720. (Perley)

ROMERIL, George, from J to UT 1851 on ship OLUMPUS.

ROMERIL, ___, from J to U.S. ca 1780, desc settled in Cleveland, OH? Not found by compiler. (Reginald Romeril)

ROMERIL, RUMRILL, Matthieu, from St. Laurens or St. Peter, J to New England before 1685 poss by 1650? (SOC JERS BULL.#27; Reginald Romeril)

RONDEL. In J 1607, fat man. In Trinity, J 1668 & in St. Heliers, J 1749.

RONDEL, Elias of J, served on the LIVELY, a privateer ship taken by the French.

ROSE. In J 1331, in St. Brelade, J 1749. ROSE in G 1300s. Occasionally ROSEs from other places settled temporarily in G and J. In mid-1700s, John ROSE, presbyterian, from Scotland, settled in G and had desc there. (BLAMPIED TYPESCRIPT, in WRCIC) Some research curr in C.I.

See CIFHS #4 and #8. Edmund ROSE in G 1500s.
ROSE. Noted in New England, but no research by compiler.
ROSE, Thomas, in Oyster Pt., 1670s, SC. (Baldwin)
Over 50 Roses are bur in GCO, and there were some marriages with the Guernsey folk settled there. Roses of Guernsey Co., OH are bur in Millwood, Wheeling, Cambridge, Valley, Liberty and Richland townships. Not all are part of the Guernsey family below.
ROSE, John, a Scot, presbyterian, rem from Scotland to G with his wife, where some of their chn were born. They settled in VA ca 1806?, and then rem to OH. CAUTION: Data below is very uncertain. (Christina Rose, San Jose, CAL; Cambridge Library; Dorothy Gullion, Ventura, CA)
A1. Thompson, b G?, in OH 1833
B1. John, b 1798 VA, mar 1824 Jane SHARROCK, dau of Timothy S., an Irishman with an English wife. Timothy served in War of 1812 and had 18 chn. He was son of James.
C1. Timothy mar Katherine Castor of PA Dutch parentage. Timothy killed in Civil War, and legend says it was Quantrell himself who fired the fatal shot. Katherine mar 2. Wm. Van Sickle.
D1. Sarah Jane Rose, b 1855, mar Wm. N. BLAMPIED, qv, 11 chn? See BLAMPIED.
B2. Daniel, to Roscoe, OH ca 1834. Parent said to be from G. Mar 1850 Alcinda Ricketts of VA. (Hill) Six sons: John, Charles F., Marion, William E., A.R., and Walter B.
B3. Dr. Charles Henry Rose, b 1834?, Carroll Co., MD? Father or son mar Harriet BENNETT, qv, of Baltimore, MD, d 1874.
Please note that data in SHARROCK GEN, by Mrs. C.R. Durben and Earl Sharrock of Newcomerstown, OH, in the Cambridge, OH Library, differs in some details from that given here.
ROSE, Thomas, had 80 acres in GCO 1840. (Wolfe) OUTC.
ROSE, Benj. F., from GCO, was a prisoner in the Civil War. He mar Sarah Ann Whaling. (Dorothy Gullion, Ventura, CAL; OHIO RECORDS AND PIONEER FAMS, Vol 7) Benj. said to be son of Benj. and Hannah (Dilley) Rose. OUTC.
ROSE, John, in GCO 1850, age 68, with wife Betsy, both b G? OUTC.
ROSE, George, in GCO, was over 76 in 1876, had 160 acres in GCO. CAUTION: TRIAL CHART below.
ROSE, George W., b 1818 Richland Twp., GCO. His father d when quite young, and his mother remained on the homestead until George W. became of age. He then purchased the homestead from the other heirs, and in 1840 mar Hannah ROBINS, qv, who was b 1817 Belmont Co. and d 1863. George W. mar 2. Elizabeth Barkhurst. 11 chn by 1st wife? OUTC. (Cambridge, OH Library)
A1. Elizabeth, mar J. Garber
A2. Benjamin F.
A3. Eliza, mar Thomas Buchanan
A4. John V.
A5. James
A6. Angeline, who mar William Sayler
A7. Adeline, mar Wesley Nymon
A8. Evaline, mar Jacob Dilley
A9. George W.
A10. Charles
A11. Hannah S.
ROSE. Fam below does not originate in C.I. However, desc mar into several C.I. fams in the Gaspe region in Canada.
ROSE, John, and wife Mary, with their 10 chn, were the first settlers of Roseville, Gaspe, QUE, now called Rosebridge. John Rose's parents were killed in an accident in Scotland, and he and sister Mary were adopted by Sir Isaac BROCK, qv, came to Canada with him, and John served in the British Army until ca 1812. (Mrs. Hazen Stanley, Traverse City, MI; Lynn Cosgrove, Thomatasassa, FLA; Bill Guignion, Windsor, ONT)

A1. John, b 1813, d 1895, bur Roseville, mar Charlotte Simpson
A2. Benjamin, bur Roseville, mar Jane Cunningham from Haldimand, QUE
A3. Charlotte, b 1814, d Roseville, mar David RABEY, see Q.A. IN CANADA
A4. Elias, mar Rachel SIMON, qv, 1857 Gaspe, of a Guernsey fam
B1. Rachel Matilda, 1859-1887, mar John J. GALLIARD/GAILIARD
B2. Elias, 1860-1938, mar Clara Stanley, b 1865
C1. Rachel Matilda/Tillie, 1888-1964, mar Wm. GUIGNION qv 1914, desc
C2. Minnie, d age 8 in Toronto ca 1896
C3. Violet, b 1887, mar John LE LACHEUR, qv. See Q.A. IN CANADA, by Turk. 5 chn: Jean, Freeman, Joyce, Shirley & Keith LE LACHEUR
C4. Iva Sarah, b 1900, mar Alex Gunn, no issue
C5. Irene, b 1903, mar Allan ROBERTS, qv, 5 chn: Allene, Allan, Daniel, Ivy and Carol ROBERTS
C6. Guy, b 1907, mar Ola RABEY, qv, who soon d. He mar 2. Ida RABEY, 3 chn: Gordon, Marilyn and Brenda ROSE
C7. Gordon, d WWI
B3. Sybil, 1863-1942, mar Philip Stanley
B4. Priscilla, 1865-1943, mar Charles Simpson
B5. Melinda, 1868-1943, mar Albert Stanley
B6. Benjamin, 1870-1872
B7. Mary, 1874-1945, mar Abram GUIGNION
B8. Sarah, b1876, mar Edw. LE TOUZEL
B9. Emma Rita, 1879-1955, mar Thomas LE LACHEUR
B10.John Stillman, 1882-1951, mar Julia GUIGNION, qv, mar 2. Clara LE LACHEUR
A5. Harriet, mar Nicholas GUIGNION Sr., qv., res Rosebridge, Gaspe
A6. Rachel, mar Thomas LANGLOIS from G, bur Toronto, ONT
A7. Nicholas, mar ___, res Port Hope, ONT.
A8. Henry, mar Anne ROSE, res Toronto, ONT
A9. Frederick, drowned in the Atlantic, bur at sea, unmar
A10. George, drowned in the Dartmouth River, bur Roseville, QUE, unmar

ROSE, Louise, b Gaspe, QUE?, ca 1830?, mar John Stanley. (Eunice Stanley, Traverse City, MI) For more on others in this large fam group, see GUIGNION.
A1. Lewis, mar Caroline MacKenzie
A2. Arthur Stanley, mar Sarah Adams
A3. Albert Atanley, mar Melinda ROSE
A4. Alvina/Evelina? mar Elias GUIGNION, qv, b 1857
A5. Esther Stanley mar Elias Adams
A6. Clara Stanley mar Elias Rose
A7. Eva Stanley mar William Adams
A8. Edith Stanley, mar Henry Stanley, his 1st wife, and she d in childbirth, a dau. See GUIGNION for more on this fam.

ROSE. A large fam in early New England may be C.I. descendants. See records of Solomon and Sarah (HOOPER) ROSE, and poss son Joseph, bp 1763 Saco, ME, in LIMINGTON, ME records, HISTORY OF CANTON, ME, by D. Huntoon; HOOPER GEN; THE HUNTOON FAM; Marion Rose, So. Boston, MA.

ROSE. Good records contained in ROSE FAM BULLETIN, 1474 Montelegre Dr., San Jose, CAL 95120.

ROSIER, DE ROSIER, ROSSIER, in America are undoubtedly from various origins. There is research curr in America, and at least one book, THE ROSIER-ROSEBUSH FAMILY, by Waldo Emerson Rosebush, about an ONT-NY-MI fam. ROSIER, ROSIERE, was a Hug fam in the Walloon Church, London, England 1581. ROSIER in Sharon, CT, from France?

DE ROSIER, old in J. (Stevens) DE LA ROSIERE in J 1235. See Q.A. IN CAN.

ROSIER, June/Jane?, of J, mar 1827 Joseph Charles DE LOUCHE, qv, in St. Andrews Presb. CH, city of QUEBEC. (LOST IN CANADA, Nov. 1980)

ROSIER, John, a sailmaker in the American Navy 1833-1835. OUTC. (Callahan List)

ROSIER, George Wesley, b 1841, son of Abijah and Dorcas, farmers in or near Baltimore, MD. (Wesley makes it a likely name for a C.I. fam) George d 1929, mar 1867 Caroline Yambert, 1840-1920 in Seneca Co., NY, 4 chn. (Peggy Mershon, Mansfield, OH; CENTENNIAL BIOG. HIST. OF

SENECA Co., p. 471) OUTC. More data in WRCIC.
A1. Sarah Laura, mar 1888 Amos P. Graumlich of Pickaway Co, OH, 3 chn
A2. Annie Lavina, b 1871, mar 1891 J.B. Crumrine and d 1899
A3. Ida May, b 1874, mar Ira J. Montross 1894, 4 chn, 3 sons d.y.
A4. Frank H., b 1882, mar Minnie Freet, 2 chn
ROSIER. Noted in MI and WI. See NEHGS, vol. 41.
ROISSIER. In Grouville and St. Clement, J 1668. In Grouville, St. Martin and St. Heliers, J 1749. None found in America by compiler.
ROSIER, Nathan, b ca 1756 Onondaga Co., NY, 7 chn, many desc, OUTC. (Delores Meisler, Solon, IA)
ROSSIGNOL. See LE ROSSIGNOL. Many in Q.A. IN CANADA, by Turk.
ROSSIGNOL, Josephine, mar 1901 Providence, RI, Leander W. Bicknell, no issue. (BICKNELL GEN.) OUTC.
ROUET, ROWETT. In J 1607, and in St. Saviour, J 1668. None researched in America. One noted in Quebec. See Q.A. IN CANADA, by Turk.
ROUGET, ROUGIER. In St. Peter, G 1698. In St. Ouen, J 1749. Curr G, research curr? CIFHS #12.
ROUGET, James, from G?, mar Judith COHU, qv, 5 chn, res NYCity, 12th ward, 1800s. (Susan George, Phoenix, AZ)
ROUILLARD, Lewis, mar Hannah Parker 1809 Boston, OUTC. ROUILLARD curr G.
ROULAND, ROWLAND, from J to SLCity 1880 with sons, a farmer. (H. Amy, Victoria, BC) See ROWLAND.
ROULAND, William, from C.I.?, bought land in Washington Co., OH ca 1852, from John TORODE. (TORODE records) OUTC. Name also spelled ROWLAND on same page.

"Forefathers of the Roundy family in America came from Ardennes, France, to the Island of Guernsey...to Colonial America...middle 1600s." (A.C.M. Palmer, Sturgis, SASK; Reba Le Fevre, St. George, UT: THE RICHARD WEBBER FAMILY, by Lucy A. Washburn, Medina, OH, 1908) ROUNDY was in London before 1628, and DE RONDE was among the followers of William the Conqueror in 1066. We do not know the length of time in Guernsey so far. It appears that some ROUNDS, ROUND, ROUNDY fams came from the Isle of Wight, England proper, from G, and poss from France directly. See sources: ROUNDY FAM IN AMERICA, by E.E. Roundy, Dedham, MA, 1942; NEHGS, vol. 17; HIST OF BARNARD, VT; Sprague's JOURNAL OF MAINE HISTORY, vol. 4; ROUNDY GEN, by the Capt. George Collins, 1915; Julia Hoyt, Fredonia, AZ; Mrs. Thomas Stevenson, Tampa, FLA; Donald Doliber, Marblehead, MA; Porter Giffard, Dallas, TX; Reba Le Fevre, St. George, UT; Donald L. Jacobus; UTAH GEN AND HIST MAG, Jan. 1938, etc. Jesse Warner, Murray, UT, may have the most data on ROUNDY fams in America.

ROUNDY, Philip, believed to have been b G, d in Salem, MA 1678, poss a Hug? Mar 1. ___, and 2. Anne BUSH, 1671. Note that BUSH was sometimes an anglicized DU BOIS. At least 3 chn.
A1. "Doctor" Robert, a coaster, b ca 1656 Salem, MA, mar Deborah Plumb, 1678 at Beverly, MA, d there 1715. He was prob the son of the 1st wife? (Jesse Warner, Murray, UT)
B1. Elizabeth, b 1679 Beverly, MA
B2. John, b 1681, mar 1. Mary Deland, 1703, div, and mar 2. Elizabeth SAVORY of MRB, 9 chn. See SEVERY and SYVERT.
C1. Robert, b 1704/05 Beverly, mar Elizabeth GREEN 1726 Windham, CT
D1. John, b 1726 Windham, CT, mar 1. 1747 Deborah Johnson, and 2. Mary BASS. See LE BAS, BASS of J. Mar 3. Mrs. ___, and 4. Sarah Harwood.
E1. Uriah, b 1756 Windham, CT, d 1913 Rockingham, VT, mar Lucretia Needham in Windhat, CT
F1. Shadreck, b 1788/89 Rockingham, VT, mar Betsey Quimby 1814, d

1972 Salt Lake City, UT
G1. Lorenzo Wesley, b 1819 Spafford, NY, moved west in 1834, grandfather of Reba Le Fevre
H1. Lorenzo W., mar Priscilla Parish
I1. Samuel H., mar Eugenia E. Taylor
J1. Josephine Roundy, mar Jesse P. Warner
C2. Lydia
C3. Thomas, b 1710 MRB, mar 1. Sarah Stacy 1733, and 2. 1972, Emma Peach Nicholson, 3 chn
D1. Thomas, Jr., bp 1747 MRB, mar 1765 Mary Abbot, 3 chn
E1. Francis Abbot, bp 1766, d 1927, mar Jane Cross 1788
F1. John Hooper, b 1811, d 1865, mar Mary B. Tucker 1835
G1. William LE CRAW, 1850-1927, mar Mary S. SAVORY 1877
H1. Alice Viola, 1878-1924, mar Frank R. Doliber 1902
I1. William Fenton Doliber, b 1903, mar Mary Tucker Harris, 1905-1956
J1. Donald A. Doliber, b1944 mar 1975 Linda Jean Wyzanski b1949
B3. Mary
B4. Deborah
B5. Esther
B6. Benjamin, 1698-1753, mar Charity Stone. (Barbara Stevenson, Tampa, FLA)
C1. John b1726 mar Elizabeth Rea, one of the founders of Blue Hill, ME
D1. Emma, 1762-1852, mar Capt. John Walker
E1. Elizabeth/Betsy Walker, b 1794, d 1847 Brooksville, ME, mar John Roundy Snow, grandson of Mary Roundy, sister of Emma Roundy. Betsy and John R. Snow were second cousins.
F1. Benjamin Snow, b 1817, d 1893 Blue Hill, ME, mar Joann Allen ROBERTS
G1. Anna Maria Snow, 1860-1932, mar Freeman Sparks BRAY
H1. William Harold Bray, b 1890, d 1976 Blue Hill, ME, mar Pauline Elizabeth Mason
I1. Barbara Jane Bray, b 1921 So. Paris, ME, mar Thomas F. Stevenson, Jr.
A2. Mary, b Salem, MA, mar 1695 Thomas WALTER. (Savage)

ROUNDY, Mary, mar 1773 John HOOPER, bp 1752 MRB. One or both prob C.I. descendants. John d before 1811, she in 1824, age 78, 5 chn. (HOOPER GEN) OUTC.
A1. John Hooper, bp 1775, mar Abigail LE CRAW, descendants
A2. Moses Allen Hooper, bp 1777, a son, Joseph, b 1800
A3. Sarah Abbot Hooper, bp 1784, mar 1809 John Johnson
A4. Hannah Hooper, bp 1788, mar 1807 William Clothy, CLOTHIER?
A5. Joseph Abbot Hooper, bp 1790, mar Hannah Thrasher, bp 1791, 6 chn
B1. Joseph Abbot Hooper, bp 1810, d 1853
B2. John Pedrick Hooper, b 1912, mar Lydia, dau of Jos. and Mary ROUNDY, 1816-1889
C1. John Pedrick Hooper, 1835-1853
C2. Sarah Lydia Hooper, b 1837, mar 1859 Edward H. Dixey, Jr.
C3. Mary Elizabeth Hooper, b 1839, mar 1859 Richard Humphrey, Jr.
C4. Joseph Hooper, d.y.
C5. Joseph Hooper again, b 1842
C6. William Micklefield Hooper, bp 1843, desc.
C7. John Hooper, b 1845
C8. George Hooper, II, b1848, desc.
C9. Frank Hooper, b 1851, desc.
C10. Nathaniel, 1853-1865
C11. Carrie Hooper, b 1857, mar 1. 1884, Stephen Leander Hyde, who d 1891. She mar 2. 1905 George Gwinn Hathaway, a banker, res MRB
C12. Annie Hooper, 1859-1862
B3. Hannah Hooper, bp 1817
B4. Moses Hooper, bp1818, d.y.
B5. a ch, d.y.
B6. Hannah Hooper, b1821, mar 1840 John L. ROUNDY, qv, and rem to the west

ROUNDY, Alvin, 1766-1832, son of Samuel and Anne H. ROUNDY, mar Sarah STEELE, qv, dau of Wm. and Hannah, 1769-1839. (Thayer C. Barrowes, Salt Lake City, UT) See STEELE for 9 chn.

See MRB VR for many more ROUNDY fams; a sampling below.

ROUNDY, Elizabeth, mar Ebenezer LE CRAW 1810, MRB.

ROUNDY, John W., mar Mary SWEET, MRB.

A1. Mary K, Roundy, mar 1897 William LE CRAW HOOPER, Jr., son of Wm. L. HOOPER, b 1866 MRB, d 1897

ROUNDEY, Mary, wife of Joseph, and formerly wife of Nicholas QUINER, (See COONIER, QUINER) d 1845, MRB, age 77.

ROUNDS and WEBBER. Are covered in a small booklet published ca 1909 in Medina, OH by the A.I. Root Co., written by Lucy A. Washburn. This fam res first in MA and CT, but many rem to North Central OH, res in Medina, Cleveland, Hinckley, W. Richfield, then to ILL, KS, MO, MI, OR, etc. (WRCIC)

ROUNDS, Joseph, b 1699, blacksmith, res Biddeford, ME 1733, mar Susanna HOMEYARD in Boston. Could HOMEYARD poss be HOMART of J? (Noyes)

ROUSE, Nicholas and ROUSSEL, Philip, were in MA in the 1600s, poss from C.I.? Cf LE ROUX and ROUSE, ROUSSEL of France and C.I. ROUSE, ROUSSEL curr in G. See also RUSSELL. Note ROUSSEL from G to Canada, in Q.A. IN CANADA, by Turk. ROUSSEL from J to New Brunswick, Canada. (LE GRAN CHIPAGAN, by Donat Robichaud)

ROUSSEL, A.E., from C.I. to ONT. (Lillian Dunham, Dundas, ONT.)

ROUSE/ROUSSEL?, of J, Thomas of Portsmouth, NH, mar 1689 Widow Rebecca (Brookings) Pomery as his 2nd wife. A son, Thomas Pomery. Thomas d before 1713. Widow mar 2. 1714, Geo. Alston. By a 1st wife, Rouse had Joanna, who mar Anthony ROWE. (Noyes) OUTC.

ROUSSEL. In Austin, TX 1970s. ROUSELL in Boston 1970. OUTC.

ROUSSEL, John, mar Martha BENOIS, BENAIS?, 1719, Boston. OUTC.

ROUSO, Samuel, to Boston from Nfld. before 1712, a Frenchman (int) mar Mary PERREWAY, qv, 1713, Boston. ROUSO poss spelled orig. ROUSSEAU?

ROWBOTHAM. English surname, but curr in J. There were deaths in Phila., PA 1830s. OUTC.

ROWBOTHAM. Noted in Quebec City along with other C.I. surnames. (LOST IN CANADA, August 1981)

ROWCLIFFE. An English surname, but in J by 1764. Curr G and J.

ROWCLIFFE, George, 1757-1790, merchant, shipowner, ropemaker, in J. (A. John Jean, Jersey)

ROWCLIFFE, William, a lathe worker, and wife, Clara Ann Wilson, res St. Heliers, J middle 1800s. Poss had been mar previously to other persons? Wm. b in Devon. A William was b 1825 in Swimbridge, Devon, poss same? Some, or all, of chn b J? There is a Wm. Rowcliffe curr in G. (Ted Rowcliffe, St. Mary's ONT; Irene Rowcliffe, St. Lambert, QUE)

A1. Walter Keen, b 1857 J, mar Mary Maria CARTER, b 1869, d 1951 Montreal. Mar in J, rem to Canada 1911/12, and d Montreal 1933.

B1. Clarence, d.y.

B2. Percy Sylvan, b ____, d 1927, mar Bertha Newman 1892-1959, 1 dau

C1. Doris Elsie, mar Percy Woodbridge Rhodes, res Montreal 1980

B3. William John, b 1893 J, mar Agnes Clarkson, 1892-1974, 3 chn

C1. Walter Keen, mar Ann Fafard. Walter b 1917, d 1967, 3 chn

D1. Kenneth Thomas, b 1941, mar Joan HARDING, 2 chn: Derek & Jared

D2. Walter Keen, b1944, mar Wanda Bryant, 2 chn: Corbett & Timothy

D3. Nancy Ann Marie, b 1957

C2. Gwendoline Mary, b 1921, mar John FOURNIER, 2 chn

D1. Brian Denton Fournier, mar Laurel MAIN

D2. Gail Mary Fournier, mar David Woodwark
C3. Robert Anthony, mar Cecile Coueney, 2 chn
A2. Robert
B1. Charles Gay, mar Ada Maud LE PATOUREL, who d in Australia in her late 90s. Charles d 1928. Ada lived mostly in G, spoke French.
C1. Robert Gay, b 1905 St. Peter Port, G, mar Irene Violet ROBERTS, b 1908, res St. Lambert, QUE
D1. Lennox Gay Rowcliffe, b 1929, mar Phyllis Graham, no issue. Res Montreal and Victoria, BC, a radio star and columnist.
D2. Shirley Irene, b 1933, mar Gerald Hill of Blenheim, ONT, res Ottawa, ONT.
E1. Mary Louise Hill, b 1956, geologist E3. Alan Robert Hill b1961
E2. Janet Irene Hill, b 1958 E4. Margaret Ann Hill, res Ottawa
D3. Sandra Siane, b 1945, mar Camille Daigle, res Candiac, QUE. Sandra a nurse, 4 chn: Christine, Marc, Nancy & Susan Daigle.
C2. Howard, b G, res there, and d ca 1950, mar ___, 3 chn
C3. A sister, who mar a clergyman, and rem to Australia, 4 chn
B2. Walter Rowcliffe, res Montreal, mar, had grandchn, a son still res Montreal
A3. Albert A4. Arthur A5. Edwin A6. Charles
ROWCLIFFE. See also ROBERTS and LANGLOIS.
ROWCLIFFE, Stephen, a member of a committee in Osceola, WI. OUTC.
ROWCLIFFE, Elizabeth, d 1856, age 52, bur Mount Hope, Osceola, WI, also bur there are Thomas J. and Jennie L. OUTC.
ROWDEN, John, age 36, of Walkerton, ONT, b J, son of John and Elizabeth (CARRY? QUEREE?) ROWDEN mar 1858 in Walkerton, A. Whiteford, age 19, of Lochwinnock, Scotland, dau of Robert Whiteford and Elizabeth Polton, in United Presbyterian Church.
ROWE. Many in ANNALS OF OXFORD, ME, a Cornish surname, but curr G and J.
ROW, Thomas, mar Rachel PEAVEY in Newington, NH 1720 (Noyes) OUTC.
ROWE. Curr G and J, old in G and J, see Q.A. IN CANADA.Not traced US.
ROULAND, ROWLAND, ___, from J to SLCity 1880 with sons, a farmer. (H. Amy, Victoria, BC)
ROWLAND GEN. Not seen by compiler.
ROWLANDS. Said to be in Philadelphia, PA 1830s. OUTC.
ROWLAND, John, age 27, b J, son of John and Nancy Rowland, mar 1859 in Toronto, ONT, Emma George, age 25, b England, dau of Samuel and Ruth George. Witnesses were Robert and Samuel George of Toronto. Baptist. (Britnell, Mississauga, ONT)
ROWLAND, Thomas, age 26, b J, son of John and Mary Rowland, mar 1862 in Toronto, ONT, Mary A. Mullen, age 21, b Toronto, dau of James and Hannah Mullen, Methodist. Witnesses, Augustus Thomas and Caroline Kemp of Toronto.
ROWLAND, Dr. ___, came with CARTERET to NJ 1665 on ship PHILIP. See New Jersey section. ROWLAND also noted in early Salem, MA.
ROWLAND. Noted in Fairfield, CT, where other C.I. fams settled, such as the MARQUANDS from G. OUTC. (OLD BURYING GROUND OF FAIRFIELD, CT, by Kate E. Perry, 1882)
ROWLAND, John, res early 1800s in Marietta, OH. See WILLS OF WASH CO,OH.
ROY. From J to Canada. See Q.A. IN CANADA, by Turk.
ROY, Joseph, b 1686 Scotland, rem to J and mar there?, Ann ___. They rem 1712 to Boston, MA with son John, later res in Woodbridge and Basking Ridge, NJ. (Honeyman; Douglas; Baird; W. Woodward, Canal Winchester, OH; NJ GENESIS, 1956) Other Chn?
A1. John, b 1711 St. Aubin or St. Brelade, J, rem with parents to America, res later in Vealtown, then Bernardsville, now Basking Ridge, NJ, where he d 1780. Mar Margaret Enslee, Inslee, 1735,

Woodbridge, NJ. Wife d 1782.
B1. Rachel, mar Mattias Goble, res Deckertown, NJ
B2. Stephen, res Fredon, NJ
B3. John, mar Margaret Shafer, res Fredon
B4. Inslee
B5. Ann, mar Gershom Goble
ROY. Alias KING, prob LE ROY?, Peter in NH early. (Noyes) OUTC.
RUMRILL. See ROMERIL.
RUMRILL, Simeon or Simon, b 1663 Enfield, CT, son of Simon mar in Enfield 1690 Sarah Fairman, Ferman, dau of John and Elizabeth. A Simon, b 1654, St. John J, was the son of Jean and Marie (BAUDAIN) ROMERIL. Simon of Enfield had first lived in Salem, MA. Were there two Simons, or was one Simeon? Simon or his father served as fence-viewer, constable and tythingman in Enfield, 1700s. One desc says that Simon was son of Thomas. Simon d 1705. (Charles L. Rumrill, Pittsford, NY; Donald Rumrill, Gloversville, NY)
A1. Sarah, b 1691, mar 1711/12 William NICHOLS, poss no issue?, and as widow she mar 2. ca 1718, John Burroughs, 1685-1757, son of John and Hannah of Enfield. (BURROUGHS GEN)
B1. Abner Burroughs, mar Margaret Harper, res Harpersfield, NY? An Abner served in Rev. War.
C1. Roxalana Burroughs, mar Sanford RICHARDSON, other chn?
D1. Harper Richardson, mar Roxana Belknap, other chn?
E1. Paschal Richardson, mar Almina Slafter, other chn?
F1. Charles Judson Richardson, mar Charlotte Elizabeth Wallis
G1. Margaret Richardson, mar Wm. W. Potter
Probably many more descendants in this branch of the family.
A2. Simon, b 1694, d.y.
A3. Simon, also Simeon, b 1696, d by 1757. Mar 2. Mercy Jewel?, dau of Joseph and Mary Jewell. And/or mar Mercy Spaulding in Chelmsford, MA 1722 (int). Poss other chn?
B1. Joseph, b ca 1720, served in Rev. War from Townsend, MA, mar 1749 Lucy STEVENS. At least 2 chn. Joseph d 1799.
C1. Joseph Jr., b ca 1755, served in Rev. War, mar Abigail ___, 1783 Townsend, MA
D1. William, b 1792 Townsend
C2. Peter, served in Rev. War, mar Ruth Parkes, dau of Obadiah and Ruth (STEVENS) Parkes. Rem to Wiscasset, ME after Rev. War. Poss rem to Windsor, VT by 1790 census, where there was also a Henry Rumrill res, with fam of men and boys. Poss Peter had other chn.
D1. William, b 1792
D2. Lucy, b 1794
D3. Peter, b 1796
B2. Aaron, b ca 1735 and B3. David, b 1740, are somewhat doubtful here. A span of 15 years between Joseph and Aaron might be explained, however, by a 2nd wife. Aaron d 1800 Roxbury, MA, served in Rev. War, mar Elizabeth Clapp 1762, who was b 1741 Dorchester, MA.
C1. Thomas, b 1762, mar Abigail RICHARDSON, 1793, who d 1801, and 2. Sarah/Sally (Dudley) Fellows, a widow
D1. Louisa, b 1794, mar John Burton
D2. Mary, b 1795, mar John Watts
D3. Thomas, b 1796, unmar
D4. Joseph, b 1798, mar Mrs. Barlow
E1. Henry J., res Baltimore and Philadelphia
F1. Henry P., a well-known astronomer
D5. Charles, b1800, mar Mary Livermore, dau of John and Rachel (Morse?) Livermore. He d 1837. Res New Bedford, MA?
E1. John Howe?
E2. Lucretia? Archibald, b 1827, mar Geo. T. Smallwood, Sr.
F1. George T. Smallwood, Jr., b 1854, mar Della ___
E3. Abigail Richardson
E4. Rachel, res The Warren, Roxbury, MA 1907

D6. Matilda, b 1801, mar Nathaniel Lawrence
D7. Sarah, b 1804, by 2nd wife, mar Henry Robinson
D8. Elizabeth C., b 1805, mar George Young
D9. Thomas, b 1808, unmar D10. John W.F., b 1811, unmar
D11. William, b 1814, d 1853, mar 1841, Nancy Young, 1820-1900, dau of Lot and Keziah (Pierce) Young. Poss other chn? Res Newton Centre, MA
E1. Ellen, b 1851, d 1933 unmar
E2. Sarah Elizabeth, 1853-1919
E3. Frank, b 1857, living in 1937, had tin box manufacturing firm
E4. William Stanton, b 1861, living in 1937. Mar 1. Ella Frances Thayer, 1853-1897, and 2. 1904, Anne F. Cordingley, b 1856, dau of William of Roxbury, MA
D12. Lucretia?, d.y.
C2. Sarah, b 1764
C3. Samuel, b ca 1765
C4. James Clapp, b 1767
C5. Aaron, b 1770
C6. Alexander, b 1773. This uncertain. Mar Margaret Bliss (Bliss Gen)
D1. James Bliss, mar Rebecca Pierce, a son Augustus b1837, NYCity
D2. Alexander, mar Mary Alvord
E1. Sarah E., b ca 1830?, mar James Stillman, NYCity
B3. David, b 1740 Westford, MA, d 1818 New Ipswich, NH, an early settler there, served in Rev. War in Capt. Stephen Parker's Co., mar 1765 Billerica, MA, Priscilla Cory, Corey, 1745-1814, 15 chn
C1. Simon, b 1767 or 1769 New Ipswich, NH, mar 1. Joanna Kemp 1790, rem to Charlestown, NH, and mar 2. Hannah Perry 1801, poss mar 3. Mary/Polly Holt in 1805, he d 1822, 9 chn. (Donald Rumrill, Gloversville, NY)
D1. Stephen, b 1791 Northfield, VT
D2. Abigail, b 1793
D3. Lois, b 1795
D4. Isaac, b 1797, of Springfield, VT
D5. Rachel, d at age 2
D6. By 2nd wife, Benjamin, b 1800 Charlestown, NH. Descendants were - Peter and Donald of Gloversville. Benj. mar 1. 1825 Mary Garfield and 2. Deborah ___. Benj. d1874 Stratford NY.
E1. Theron Ebenezer, Sr., b 1827 Springfield, VT, d 1902 Utica, NY, mar 1851 Mary H. McDougall, b 1835 New Hampshire, and d 1879, Stratford, NY.
F1. Sarah Alinda, b 1852 Stratford, NY, d 1936 Gloversville, NY, mar 1. Murray Miller and 2. Will Ascott
F2. Elliott M., b 1854
F4. Edwina
F3. Eleanor Jane, b 1856 Stratford, NY, mar 1. James Oathout, mar 2. Joseph Rolly, and 3. Frank Pedrick
G1. George Alfred Oathout, b 1867 Stratford, NY, d 1939, Gloversville, NY. Mar Althea Aletha Rumrill, below.
F5. Theron Ebenezer, Jr., b 1860 Stratford, NY, d 1941 Gloversville, NY, mar Mary Newton
F6. Ellsworth Fessenden, b 1863 Springfield, VT, d . Mar 1889 Gloversville, Lillian M. Clapp, b 1874 Newtonville, NY, who d 1932
G1. Howard William, b 1891 Gloversville, NY, d 1978. Mar 1909 Hattie May Glenar, 1890-1981.
G2. Harold C., b 1897, mar 1916 Emily Mae Abbot, who d 1964
G3. Pearl Elsworth, b 1901, d 1956 Gloversville, NY, mar 1919 Marjorie Teetz, 1900-1980
G4. Elmer Peter, b 1903 Gloversville, NY, d there 1936, mar 1923 Charlotte Emma Anderson, b 1903
H1. Richard Elmer, b 1923, mar 1946 St. Johnsville, NY, 1. Helen

Davis, b 1924, and 2. 1972, Patricia Wilson, b 1928.
H2. Donald Arthur, b 1925, mar 1946 Mary Colleen Rauer, b 1925. Two chn: Donald; Barbara Dahn (son, Curtis).
H3. Marilyn Charlotte, b 1927, mar 1946 Alfred B. Smith, b 1924 Gloversville, NY
H4. Peter, b 1936, mar 1959 Ruth McAllister, b 1937 York, NY
F7. Mary Anna, b 1865, Stratford, NY, mar Charlie Baker
F8. Harriett A., b 1866, d1960 Gloversville, NY, mar Joseph Ormill
F9. Martha E., b 1869, d 1921, mar Clark J. Allen, 1867-1921
F10. Marshall, b 1871 Stratford, NY, d 1938, unmar
F11. Althea Aletha, b 1874 Stratford, NY, d 1964 Gloversville, NY, mar George Alfred Oathout, b 1867, d 1939 Gloversville, NY
F12. Martin, d.y. F13. Joseph, d.y.
E2. Mary, b 1831 Vermont, mar Nathaniel Rockwell 1849
E3. Albert, b 1833 VT, mar Jane E. ___
E4. Almon, b 1835 VT, d 1903 Stratford, NY, mar Eveline Praper, 1830-1915
E5. Alfred, b 1837 VT E6. William, b 1840 VT
D7. Hannah, b 1802 D8. Levi, b 1804
D9. Joseph Perry, b ca 1810?, mar ___, 15 chn? (HIST OF ROYALTON, VT)
E1. ___, b 1848?
E2. Edwin Joseph, b 1850 Claremont, NH, d 1910 Randolph. Mar 1870 in Claremont, Susie Cynthia, dau of Horace Simonds and widow of ___ Newton. She was b 1843 Hartford, d 1894 Royalton. Edwin worked on railroad bridges.
F1. Joseph Clinton, b 1871 Springfield, mar 1901 Marion Emerson, res Royalton, VT
F2. Herbert Clifton, b 1872 Chester, mar Boston, 1892, Alberta Millet, d 1903 Royalton, VT
F3. Harry Leslie, b 1875 Windham, mar 1896 Alice Everett, b 1876, Randolph, VT
F4. Arthur Westley, b 1876 Windham, mar 1895 Revere, MA, Grace Haskell, res Revere
F5. Susie Cordelia, b 1879 Windham, mar 1898 Royalton, VT, Wm., son of Wm. and Jane M. (Griffin) Haskell, res Revere
F6. Flora Ethel, b 1881 Windham, mar 1896 Charlestown, NH, Walter E. Adams, res Charlestown and Framingham, MA
F7. Gertrude May, b 1885, Royalton, d.y.
F8. Eva Lillian, b 1887 Royalton, mar 1905 Edwin Albert KNIGHT of Portland, ME, settled in Winchendon, MA
C2. Joseph, rem to Townsend, MA
C3. David, b ca 1774, d 1861, mar 1. Lydia ___, 1780-1920, and mar 2. ___, 1773-1857. David a farmer near Rindge, NH.
C4. Daniel, b ca 1776, taxed in 1798
C5. Benjamin, b ca 1778, taxed in 1799 and 1800
A4. Ebenezer, b 1701, mar 1725 Sarah Evans of Freetown, d Newport, RI 1743
B1. Sarah, b 1726 B3. Thomas?
B2. Ebenezer, b 1729 B4. poss other chn?
A5. John, b 1704, mar 1728 Abigail Chandler, who d 1772. John d 1770.
B1. John, b 1728, mar Sarah Bliss of Enfield, CT 1762, and d 1809
C1. John C4. Silence C7. Catherine
C2. Sarah C5. Amasa C8. Martha
C3. Elijah C6. Abigail C9. Asahel
B2. Mehitable? B3. Lydia
B4. Nehemiah, b 1733, mar 1758 Alice Parsons, who d 1804. He d 1805. A Nehemiah served in the Rev. War 1777.

C1. Penelope, b 1758, d.y. C3. Alice, twin, b 1759
C2. Penelope, twin, b 1759 C4. Alice again, b 1761
C5. Asa, b 1764, res So. Hadley, MA, mar Rhoda Smith
D1. Susan, b 1798, mar Luther Smith, b Chicopee, MA, res Holyoke, MA
D2. Lucy, b 1802, mar Oton Goodman rem to Bolton, NY near Glens Falls
C6. Susannah, b 1766
C7. Levi, b 1768, res Longmeadow, mar 1792 Elizabeth Bliss, dau of Ebenezer and Sarah Bliss. She d 1816. (COOLEY and BLISS GENS) See end of this chart.
D1. Lorin, Lorrin, b 1793 D4. Chauncey, b 1798
D2. Asa, b 1795 D5. Miranda, b 1801
D3. Betsey, b 1797 D6. Sophia, b 1803
D7. Levi?, b 1812?, named RUMMER, was he also a son? Mar Sarah ___, b 1814, res Dryden, NY 1830-1850. (Doris Anderson, Del Mar, CA)
C8. Susannah, b 1771 C10. Lucy, b 1776
C9. Alexander, b 1773, not verified, see BLISS GEN C11. Ruth? C12. Margaret, b 1781
B5. Simon, b 1743, twin, res Alstead, NH, d Windsor, VT
B6. Henry, b 1743, twin of Simon, mar Mary Simonds of Springfield, MA, res Alstead, NH and Windsor, VT
B7. Ebenezer, b 1745, youngest ch of this fam, mar Eleanor Cooley 1761, dau of Josiah, and 2. Mary Chandler of Longmeadow, MA. Eleanor d 1777. 3 chn. Ebenezer d 1801?, Dryden, NY?
C1. Simon, b 1768, called Simeon Cooley Rumrill?, res Norwich, Chenango, PA 1820s and 1830s. Mar Urbany ___, and d 1825, bur Burlingame Cem. Simeon sold his land in 1835.
D1. William M., b ca 1814, b Sherbourne, Chenango Co., PA, and rem to OH?, mar 1. (?), and 2. Nancy Ann Campbell, 1847, Ashland Co., OH
E1. Jennie, b 1838 NY state, mar Isaac Kunkle, many desc
E2. Henry C., b 1844 Cincinnati, OH, mar, no issue
E3. Laura, b 1846? E6. William E8. Savilla
E4. Charles E7. Phoebe E9. James M., b 1871
E5. Elam Butler, res Indianapolis, IND 1915
D2. George A., d after 1869, mar Minerva ___, ca 1841?, who d 1859
E1. George, b ca 1843, d 1863 Camp Hubbard, LA, serving in Civil War
E2. Mary A., mar ___ Tilles?
E3. Charles Cooley, b 1849 Auburn, NY, d 1925, mar Frances Caroline Starkes, served in Civil War
F1. Charles Cooley, b 1879 in the Chickasaw Nation?, served in ILL Inf., Spanish-American War. Res Chicago, ILL and had son of same name?
F2. A ch, stillborn? F4. (?), dec before 1924
F3. Ethel Frances, b 1883 Gainsville, TX, unmar in 1924, res ARK
F4. George D., b 1891 Gainesville, TX?, served in 131st Regt. WWI. Res Little Rock, ARK. There was a Rumrill Pottery there.
C2. Elam, b 1770 CT, d 1838 Oswego, NY, mar 1796 Easthampton, MA, Electa Clark, b 1773 MA, d 1845. (Civil War Pension files)
D1. Ebenezer, b 1797 D2. Electa, b 1798
D3. Charles Clark, 1807-1847, mar 1830 Almira Fox, who mar 2. ca 1849 Dr. John Stone, and d 1891 Scriba, NY. Dr. Stone was from Brimfield, CT.
E1. Charles Elam, b 1832, mar 1. Elizibeth L. ___, div., and mar 2. Frances E., 3 chn d.y. Served in Civil War and was prisoner.
E2. James A., b 1835 E3. Sarah, b 1837, d.y.
E4. Chauncey Lewis, b 1840, served in NY Inf., Civil War, d 1923 Palmyra, NY. Mar Harriet McComb 1872, b 1848, 2 chn.

F1. Myra, b 1873, mar Samuel McKee Smith
G1. Myron Smith, b 1897
G2. Irving Smith, b 1899, mar Mary Brown ROBERTS, 2 daus
H1. Nancy Smith, mar Claude Philippe, 2 sons: Marc and Richard
H2. Virginia, mar Thomas Adams, res Wilton, CT, 4 chn: Julia, Janet, Claire and Richard Adams
F2. Charles Clark, b 1875, mar Winifred Churchill 1899
G1. Charles Lewis, b 1901, mar 1926 Janice Clark, 2 chn
H1. Janice Winifred, b 1928, mar Geo. Dewire, 3 chn: Steven, Susie and Nancy Dewire
H2. Charles Clark, b 1934, mar 1962 Meriwether Hagerty, 4 chn: Dudley, Richard, Charles and Kathy
E5. George, b 1844
C3. Eleanor, b 1772
C4. Ebenezer, b 1774, d.y., as did Ebenezers b 1775 and 1777
B6. Abigail
B7. Martha
B8. Hannah
B9. Sarah
B10. Lydia
B11. Mehitable

RUMERY, Edward, poss ROMERIL, RUMRILL, qv, mar Sarah DURRELL, qv. Res Saco, ME? NEW DATA, SEE CHANNEL ISLAND COLLECTION!
A1. Jonathan, mar 1754 in Saco, ME, Mary DURRELL
A2. Edward, mar Sarah DURRELL, dau of Moses and Sarah SAMPSON, her 2nd husband. He was b ca 1700. She had mar 1. Thomas PENNELL at Gloucester, MA 1717. Sarah d 1776, age 86.

RUMRELL, Abner, of Boston, mar Abigail Kenrick of Newton, MA 1747 in Boston?

RUMRILL, Abner, mar Sally ___. A dau, Salley, who d 1802, age 19. (CHARLESTOWN ESTATES AND GENS)

RUMRILL, Abner, one from MRB and another from Medford served in Rev. War, one in 1775 and the other in 1777. The same or another served in Dec. 1777. Still another, noted in Cambridge, MA 1777. Poss only one person or two?

RUMERY, Clara A., b 1849, d 1924, mar 1862 Thomas Messerve, son of Simon and Betsy (NASON?) MESSERVE. Poss other chn?
A1. Cora B. Meserve, 1870-1875
A4. Roy F., b 1884, mar Grace I. MESERVE
A2. Minnie Gertrude, b 1874, mar Joseph Cleves, no issue
A3. Clarence E. Meserve, b 1882, mar 1912 Lilla Fogg, b 1882. He d 1929.

RUMRILL, Clement of Portsmouth, NY 1687, prob from J, mar Rebecca (Brookings) Pommery, widow of Thomas Pomeroy, the 2nd of her four husbands. Clement d before 1689, when she mar Thomas ROUSE (ROUSSEL?) of C.I. (Noyes) She was dau of Wm. Brookings of Portsmouth, NH 1652.

RUMRELL, RUMRIL, Ebenezer and Nehemiah in Longmeadow, MA 1790 with fams. (Census)

RUMRALL, Ebenezer, served in Rev. War 1777.

RUMMERY, Edward, in Biddeford, MA before 1728, his widow d 1776, age 86.

RUMRILL, James B. of Springfield, MA, d 1885, obit in NYTimes, 9 April, 1885.

RUMRILL, J.A., V.P. of the Boston and Albany RR Co., wrote in 1891 to Mr. H.J. Rumrill, Camden, NH, that he thought the fam originated in Jersey and Roxbury records of the fam were destroyed by fire. The letter mentions Alexander Rumrill, a bro of the father of J.A., who was 80 years old at that time and had married chn. (WRCIC)

RUMRILL, John of Medford, MA, mar Mary Pierce 1749, rem to Charlestown, MA 1753. Issue.

RUMRILL, John L., b 1795 VT, was age 55 in 1850, Landgrove, VT Census, mar Susanna Chatman/Chatmore/Chetmore, b 1800, at least 4 chn.
A1. Arvilla, b 1833/36 Chester, VT, mar Nathan Sherwin, son of Abner and Lois (Farnum) Sherwin. To Franklin Co., VT ca 1857.

A2. Loveman Luman Rumrill, b 1829 VT, d 1888 Stockton, CA. (HIST OF SAN JOAQUIN CO., CAL, by Mrs. Roy Avery, Syracuse, NY)
A3. Maria, mar Hiram Peck. See PECK GEN.
A4. Julia, b ca 1834, mar ___ Beckwith, who d fairly young, some chn. She d age 40 at home of bro in California.
RUMRELL, John, of Providence, RI, mar Betsy Spurr 1799, Boston.
RUMRELL, Joseph Jr., in Townsend, MA 1790 with fam of 4 females.(Census)
RUMSILL?, Mrs., in Roxbury, 1790, with fam of 5 females. (Census)
RUMRILL, Penelope, mar 1799 George Cooley. Was she dau of Nehemiah? See chart. (COOLEY GEN)
RUMRELL, Mary, mar Boswell Collier 1785 Boston.
RUMRELL, Nabby/Abigail, mar John MILLET 1788 Boston.
RUMRELL, Sarah, mar Peter Youngman 1764 Boston.
RUMERY, Sarah, mar Zachariah WHITE, LE BLANC?, 1678 MA. See ROMERIL and WHITE.
A1. Zachariah White, b 1680
RUMREY, Thomas, of Dorchester, MA, served in Rev. War 1777. (MASS SOLDIERS AND SAILORS)
RUMRIEL, Thomas, a drummer, served in Rev. War 1777-1779. Poss same as Thomas, above?
RUMRIELL, Thomas, in Boston 1790, fam of 3 or 4? (Census)
RUNYON, ROIGNON, etc., etc., a French Hug fam from Poitiers, Poitou, France via Jersey to America. RUNYON, Vincent, left France prob ca 1645, to J (and other places?) then in the 1660s with the CARTERET group via ship PHILIP to Elizabethtown, NJ. "He was a carpenter, doubtless, coming over from Jersey in a second or third importation of laborers." Since this is not a C.I. fam, and since there is a great deal of info available, fam chart is not included. See sources: EARLY GERMANS IN NEW JERSEY, Champers; RUNYON GEN, by R. and A. Runyon, 1955; FIRST SETTLERS OF PISCATAWAY, NY, by O.E. Monette; ANCESTORS AND DESC OF ENOCH M. RUNYON, by Melba M. Aaron, 1975; HISTORY OF WARREN AND ESSEX COUNTIES, NJ, by James Snell, 1881; FIRST SETTLERS OF PASSAIC VALLEY, NJ, by John Littell, 1852; New Jersey Archives; HIST OF PISCAT. TWP, by Walter G. Meuly; PROCEEDINGS, NJ HIST SOC; GEN MAG OF NJ; SOMERSET COUNTY HIST SOC, 8 vols; RUNYON GEN, by Mrs. Stacey Pursell, Newtown, PA; Burke's PRESID. FAMS; HOBBIES magazine, Dec. 1941, coat of arms; REG. OF ANCESTORS, HUG SOC OF NJ, by S.M. Koehler, Bloomfield, NJ, 1956; Mrs. Geri Halstead, Tannersville, PA; H.E. Runyon, Palos Verdes, CAL; Wm. J. Snow, Union City, NJ; WRCIC.
RUSSEL. In J 1340, curr G and J. See also ROUSSEL, curr G.
RUSEL, Henry, to Boston from GB (from C.I.?) before 1720, mar Mary Heath (Bolton). OUTC.
RUSSEL, John, to Boston from GB or C.I.?, before 1713, mar (int).
RUSEL, Noel, mariner, lately of Newcastle, where? in Boston 1699-1701, plus other RUSSELLS. (Noyes) OUTC. Noel may have been from C.I.
RUSSELL, Lewis, mar Abigail (MARTIN) RUSSELL. (G.E. Russell, Middletown, MD)
A1. Robert Martin, b ca 1774 Marblehead, MA, mar MRB 1804. She d 1824, age 68, and Robert d 1829, age 55.
B1. Elizabeth Chambers, bp 1811 MRB
RUSSELL, servant of Philip ENGLISH, qv, poss an indentured man from J, b ca 1647, at Salem, MA 1674, where he mar Elizabeth NOURSE/Nurse 1678. He d 1733. (Genealogy in progress by G.E. Russell, Middletown, MD)
SANGRAY, Abraham, res Boston 1790 with fam of 8 (Census) This is prob STE. CROIX, see below.

STE. CROIX, DE STE. CROIX. This is both an old J surname and a Hug surname. Care must be taken to distinguish whether those in early New England were from C.I. fams or newly come from France to the Channel Islands before removal to America. DE STE. CROIX in J 1214. In St. Heliers, St. Clement, St. Laurens and St. John, J 1668, and in Trinity, St. Heliers and St. Laurens, J 1749 and 1812.

ST. GEORGE, DE ST. GEORGE. In g 1149. In St. John, J 1824.

ST. GEORGE, Thomas Joseph, b 1824 St. John, J, submitted to SLC records by Archie de St. Jeor.

SALMON. In J 1299, in St. Laurens, J 1668. SALMON in St. Peter Du Bois, G 1614, there early. Curr G and J. See LE ROSSIGNOL GEN.

SALTER, Francis, from C.I.?, in MRB with wife Elizabeth 1708. OUTC. Scarce in the Islands now, but has occurred there. OUTC. See SALTER GEN and Essex Coll.

A1. Elizabeth, b 1708
A2. Sarah, b 1710
A3. Mary, b 1715
A4. Abigail, b 1718
A5. John, b 1722
A6. Thomas, b 1725

SALTER, Hannah, mar Nicholas PHILLIPS 1651 Boston. OUTC.

SALTER, Joseph, res MRB 1790 with fam of 2. (Census) SALTER, Jos. Jr., also in MRB 1790 with fam of 5. OUTC.

SALTER, Sarah, mar 1785 Capt. Samuel SWETT, son of Samuel. Res MRB and he d 1820. Note marriages with C.I. fams. She d 1816, 7 chn. (SWETT GEN; DESC OF JOHN S. OF NEWBURY, MA, 1913) See SWETT family.

A1. Samuel SWETT, b 1786, mar 1813 Sarah FREETO, a dau Sarah, bp 1816, mar ___ MESSERVY.
A2. Francis, b 1788
A3. Joseph, 1791-1813
A4. John, b 1794, mar Mary B. Ransdell 1817, d 1824?
A5. Woodbury, b 1979, mar 1820 Sarah G. BESOM (BISSON, qv) and 2. 1824, Mrs. Sarah (Girdler) BROWN.
A6. Benjamin, 1801-1815
A7. Henry, b 1804, mar Elizabeth BROWN 1828

SALTER, William, a carpenter, b J, settled with wife Mary ca 1870s in Osceola, IA. (LE BOUTILLIER GEN)

SALTER. From NC 1737 to Boston. (Essex Coll., vols. 11 and 15)

SALWAY. See SOLWAY.

SAMSON, SAMPSON. Most in early New England from England. SAMSON and SAMPSON in J and G in the 1300s. SAMSON curr J and G. SAMPSON curr J. Curr research? See CIFHS #12.

SAMSON, John and Elizabeth were rec'd 1728 in the Portsmouth, NH CH, poss from C.I.? OUTC.

A1. Rachel, b 1719
A2 John, b 1721
A3. Mary, b 1724
A4. Elizabeth, b 1726 in NH?
A5. Mary, b 1728
A6. Sarah, b 1731

SANDERS. Not known to compiler how long this name has been in G, but at least since 1850, in Vale, G. Curr in G and J. For other Sanders, see NEHGS, vol. 132.

SANDERS, Edward, b 1883 St. Sampson, G, son of Geo. Sanders and Elizabeth Ann RENOUF, qv, mar 1905 Eliza Jane COLE, dau of John and Anna Marie (CHERRY) COLE, b 1880 Bouet, G. Edward and Eliza settled in Canada 1921 at White Bear, SASK, where he worked on a farm for his bro-in-law, Walter DE GRUCHY, qv. A son. They also lived for a time in Kyle, SASK till 1938, then to Coronach, near the Montana border. (Dorothy Sanders, Coronach, SASK; Rev. Peter Simpson, Vale, G)

A1. Edward John, b 1907 G, mar 1931 Dorothy Darline Sorsdahl, b 1907
B1. Janet Elizabeth Sanders, b 1933, mar 1958 Harold John LLOYD, b1933
C1. Mona Norlaine Lloyd, b 1959, mar 1979 Wayne Charles Dulle, b 1955, 1 ch, Brandyn Nicole Dulle
C2. Shauna JoAnne Lloyd, b 1961
C3. Cameron John Lloyd, b 1962
C4. Cara Michelle Lloyd, b 1965
C5. Craig Trevor Lloyd, b 1970

B2. Donald Walter Sanders, b 1938, mar 1. Donna Tucker, a dau, and mar 2. 1978 Beverly Fehr. One ch, Lisa Darlene Sanders, b 1971.

SAUNDERS, Samuel, on sloop ELIZABETH AND MARY, from Nfld. to Boston 1715. (Whitmore) OUTC.

SARCHET. Believed to have settled in G ca 1066 from France. (Guernsey records)

SARCHET. The charts below are tentative, constructed from data acquired from various sources, some unverified. Much more info in hands of desc and in a looseleaf booklet put together by Col. Kenneth Sarchet, Indian Harbour Beach, FLA. In the past 50 years a scrapbook was held by various members of the fam, and added to as info came in. This is truly an interested fam, with a wealth of information, although much is still unclassified. CAUTION: TRIAL CHARTS. See original sources where possible, and books, some of which are in the Western Reserve Gen. Soc. Library, and Main Library, Cleveland, OH.

SARCHET. A fam formerly of the Island of G, said by some to be variant of the French surname DE SOUCHET, of DU SOUCHET, not verified. US tradition has it that Thomas, of a zealous RC fam in France, obtained during his minority, a French Bible, which he persisted in reading against the protests of his father, mother, and the parish priest, who threatened the sanctions of the Church. Through fear he fled from his home to the Island of Jersey, and then to Guernsey, where he assumed the name SARCHET. This was ca 1670. He mar and had one son. The son married and had two sons, Thomas and Peter, who became the heads of two large fams in Guernsey. Thomas, Peter, John and Nicholas were the sons of Thomas, and Peter was the only son of Peter. These five men all emigrated to Guernsey Co., OH in 1807.

Thomas, the elder son of Thomas, b 1750 G, succeeded to the patrimonial estate, the old Sarchet house, a stone structure, with 14 acres of land? He grew veg. and fruit for the market at St. Peter Port, and was also a carter or drayman of the town. He had sons David, Peter, Thomas and Moses. Most of the Sarchets of OH are his descendants.

Thomas, b 1770, was a very outstanding character, and the leader of the group from Guernsey. He was involved in all facets of life in GCO. After the arrival in Cambridge 1807, Thomas wrote the Baltimore Annual Conference of the M.E. Church asking for a preacher. A Rev. James Watts was finally sent, a circuit rider. The congregation first met at the Sarchet house, in Cambridge, then in the Court House, and later in the Masonic Bldg. Their church was built in 1833.

Thomas wanted to navigate Wills Creek, so in 1826 he constructed a boat 70 feet long and 18 feet wide, with a water depth of 3 feet. The sides were boarded up to a height of 8 feet, and the roof placed over 40 feet of the boat. He called his vessel ELIZA OF GUERNSEY. It left Cambridge 1826 with a cargo of wheat, flour and salt, crewed by Capt. R.G.M. Patterson, Thomas, and his sons. In two days they were in Zanesville. Later attempts to use the creek commercially were hampered by the winding course, the accumulation of driftwood, and the low stage of water at many times of the year.

Thomas went by horseback to Putnam's nursery in Marietta, OH and brought back fruit tree cuttings and slips. He also went by horseback to Pittsburgh, and brought back supplies, which he sold. For more info see sources. (GCO COLL. OF HIST. SKETCHES AND FAM HISTORIES, by GCO Gen. Soc; MARTEL GEN, by Mark K. Daniel, Salem, ILL; SARCHET GEN, by Col. Kenneth Sarchet, Indian Harbour Beach, FLA; Conner-Eynon; Howe; Wolfe; Williams; SARCHET SCRAPBOOK; SARCHET HIST. OF GCO, Record; Bessie Sarchet, Byesville, OH; Dan Sarchet, New Carlisle, OH; Beverly Shepherd, Cambridge, OH; Alice Behner, Dover, OH; Shirley Spencer,

Phoenix, AZ; Census; Joyce Huckaby, Darien, CT; Clara Bossuet, Golden, COL; Al Fulton, Canton, OH; Bernard R. Sarchet, Rolla, MO; Hannah Amos, Cambridge, OH; Margaret Brady, Riverside, CAL)

SARCHET, Peter, b G 1798 (son of Peter Sarchet of G) and his son Peter, rem to Cambridge, OH 1818. (Col. Kenneth Sarchet, Ind.Harb.Beach, FLA)
A1. Rachel, mar D.H. Longmin, res New Orleans
A2. Elizabeth, mar William McCrindall
A3. Catherine, mar Francis Donsouchet or DE SOUCHET, qv, a Frenchman from Napoleon's army?
A4. Peter, mar Catherine TOUZEAU, settled Charleston, ILL, later rem to TX, then to COLO. Poss other chn than these three.
B1. Theophilus Touzeau Sarchet, b 1812, mar Hanna Jane Wiers, b 1821
C1. Nancy Catherine, b 1844
C2. Francis Marion, b 1846
C3. William Fletcher, b 1848
C4. Sarah Malinda, b 1849
C5. Matilda Jane, b 1851
C6. Benj. Thomas, b 1853
C7. John TOUZEAU, b 1855
C8. Mary Anetta, b 1857
C9. Peter Harrison, b 1859
C10. Eliz. Anne, b 1861
C11. Sherman Grant, b 1863, mar Lucy Grace ROBERTS, b 1868
D1. Claude Sarchet, b 1891, d 1957, unmar
D2. Willard, mar ___, no issue
D3. Blanche, b 1898, mar ___ Brandon
D4. Beatrice, b 1898, twin, mar Floyd Dunnam
B2. Peter Jr., b ca 1810
B3. Matilda, chose Catherine Sarchet as her guardian, as did her bros when the father d 1823. (GCO Common Pleas Court)

SARCHET, Thomas, b ca 1750 G, mar Mary DE LISLE of G, rem to GCO 1807, see Ohio section in this book, had 8 chn, d 1837.
A1. Thomas, b 1770 St. Sampson, G, mar Anne/Nancy BICHARD, dau of James and Esther (GALLIENNE) BICHARD of La Quartie, G 1789. Four sons and 4 daus, all b G. Thomas was the leader of the group that arrived in Guernsey Co., OH 1807.
B1. Thomas, b 1790 G, mar in GCO 1809 Catharine MARQUAND, qv. He was prob the one who had 260 acres in Cambridge Twp., GCO, 1840.
C1. Solomon Marquand, b 1811, mar May Ann Wilson 1832, d 1906. He rem to Charleston, ILL 1857, and then to Iowa. Seven sons and 6 daus. He d 1906, she d 1892.
D1. Thomas Wilson
D2. Solomon Bichard
D3. Charles Wesley
D4. Josiah Clark
D5. Edward J., b 1853, mar Philene Miller
E1. Milo Bichard, mar Una F. McVey
F1. Algie Marquand, 1883-1952, mar Magdalena Maldaner, 9 chn. They rem to Sask, Sask, Canada 1912, and later to BC Canada 1941. See Q.A. IN CANADA for 9 chn.
D6. George
D7. Reason Addy
D8. Cecelia, 1833/34. There is a stone in Cambridge Cem?
D9. Elizabeth, b 1839, mar Wash. L. Baumgarner
D10. Catherine Marquand, b 1843, d 1920, mar John M. McStay
D11. Lucinda, b 1847, mar George Rector
D12. Martha, b 1843, d.y.
D13. Elnora, d.y.
C2. Thomas Y., b 1819, mar Sacrissa Barkhurst, a son and 5 daus, res near Akron, OH
C3. Charles M., d 1868, mar Phoebe MARSH, qv
D1. Moses Marsh, d 1922, mar Elizabeth Reilly, 4 chn
E1. Phoebe Agnes Hattinburger
D2. Thomas Ulysses, b 1860, mar Minniet Newton 1892, 5 sons & 2 daus
D3. William Kristy, mar Hattie Slaysor and 2. Ella Hudson, 4 sons and 2 daus

D4. Katheryn Marquin (MARQUAND?), mar G.R. Hodson
D5. Sara Florence, mar E.C. Webb D6. Emma Alice, mar William Cooper
C4. Mary Ann?, mar ___ Entz?
C6. Martha Ann? C6. Matilda
C7. Marie, Mary L.?, b 1848, mar Ludlow Bonnell, or Lloyd Bonnell?, unclear. She poss mar in 1884 John OZIER? OGIER? (RECORD)
C8. Lucinda, b 1832, mar Daniel OGIER, qv, d 1909
C9. Catharine F., mar Josiah Clark
B2. Nancy Ann, b 1793 G, mar Capt. Cyrus P. Beatty 1811, 7 chn. Capt. Beatty owned the Guernsey TIMES, 1825/27, was a teacher, served as Capt. of the Militia in War of 1812, and was first postmaster at Cambridge, Oh. He was the son of John of VA. His heirs had 240 acres in GCO 1840. (Wolfe)
C1. John A. Beatty, mar 1. Priscilla Biggs and 2. Cecelia FLOOD. Sev chn?
D1. Cyrus P. Beatty, res Moberly, MO
C2. Thomas M. Beatty
C3. Zaccheus Beatty, mar Margaret Fesler, res Galesburg, ILL
C4. Moses Beatty
C5. Nancy Beatty, mar William D. Noble, sev chn?
D1. Ella Noble, mar ___ Jefferson
E1. Rev. Charles Jefferson of NYCity
C6. Ellen Beatty, mar John K. Fesler, res KS C7. Rachel
B3. David, b 1797 G, had 160 acres in GCO 1840, Liberty Twp. He was over 76 in 1876. Served in the 15th OH Vol. Inf. Civil War. Had salt well on his property near Cambridge, OH and in 1870 had a gas well which gave a constant supply for many years, but was not utilized. He mar 1. Hester/Hetty Hill, 1820 Cambridge, OH, who soon died, had dau Nancy Marie. David mar 2. 1830 Sarah BRITON, bur BElls Cem., Cambr.OH, dau Margaret E., b 1833 who mar 1851 Thomas BICHARD. David mar 3. 1835 Jemima DeHart, no issue? and mar 4. 1840 Mary TORODE, 1823-1888. See TORODE and BICHARD. More data, WRCIC. (Margaret Brady, Riverside, CAL)
C1. Nancy Marie, mar 1849 John MARTEL, see MARTEL.
C2. Margaret E., b 1833, mar 1851 Thomas T. BICHARD,Qv, 2 chn: David Bichard b ca 1853 and Lizzie L. Bichard b ca 1859.
C3. Mary E. SARCHET, b ca 1842 mar 1864 Judson Lingenfelter, 4 chn
D1. Minnie Lingenfelter, b ca 1866 D3. Albert L. b ca 1875
D2. Inez Lingenfelter, b ca 1867 D4. Allice L. b ca 1878
C4. Simon Peter, b 1843, d 1877, mar 1865 Sarah E. BRITTON
D1. Mary E., 1866-1883
D2. Howard F., b 1868 d 1949 mar 1896 Bell Eaton, 1878-1927
E1. Wm. C. Sarchet, mar Laura Danly. He was b 1896
E2. Ralph Howard b 1909, mar 1. Kathlene Calvert, b 1914
F1. Paul Richard, b 1931 mar Shirley Braniger, dau Deborah b 1953
F2. James Austin, b 1935 mar Golde L. Alexander, 3 daus: Jacqueline, adopted, Rebecca K. and Shirley Jean.
F3. Laura E., b 1933 mar Earl Weber, b 1932
F4. Rebecca Jayne, b 1938 mar Santiago Rodriguez
F5. Judith Ann, b 1940 mar Benard D. Camp
F6. WAnda Sarchet, adopted by Dorothy Mast. Wanda b 1943
F7. Linda L. b 1946 F8. Randolph Scott, b 1949
E3. Paul Sarchet, mar Pauline Danly, 3 chn
F1. Ann Laura, mar ___Bell F2. June E. mar Mr. Beatenhead
F3. Sandra Jean Sarchet
D3. Margaret mar 1889 Al Hammersly

D4. David Sarchet, b 1872 d 1960, mar 1895 Laura Gaumer, b 1878
E1. Virgil Dwight, b 1897 mar 1920 Hazel Ava Martin
F1. Dale Virgil Sarchet, b 1923
F2. Millie Joan, b 1926 mar 1. Wm. Viens 1946, and 2. Irwin Brown
F3. Laura Marie, b 1929 mar Wm. Olin 1947
F4. David Henry, b 1931 mar Joyce E. Bateman, 2 chn: Scott D. and Shawn D. Sarchet
E2. Pearl Violet Sarchet, b 1899 mar Jay O. Fuller
E3. Ralph Charles, b 1901 mar 1. Goldie Alice Roash 1923 and 2. Rosa Baker, 1933
F1. Victor Eugene b 1924 mar 1. Adres Pearl Tipping 1944 and 2. Betty Keller 1947.
G1. Larry Dean b 1948 G2. Richard Lee b 1950
F2. Wayne Charles, b 1926 mar Arvilla Heaton 1946
G1. Dennis Wayne, b 1926 D2. Michael, b 1949 D3. Rodney C.1954
F3. Dorothy D., b 1927 mar 1946 Howard King
F4. Virginia Alice, b 1929 mar Baren H. Munyon
E4. Melville Carl, b 1903 mar Bernice E. Drummond 1926
F1. Wm. David, b 1934 F2. Jean Yvonne b 1936
F3. Frederick Walter, b 1939
E5. Maud Laura b 1905 mar Earl Brotamarkle
E6. Raymond Victor, b 1908 mar Mildred M. Hockley 1932
F1. Linda Joanne, b 1932 F3. Robert A., b 1935
F2. Nancy Rae, b 1934 F4. James Lee b 1936 F5. Coral Ann,1938
E7. John Reginald, b 1914, mar Eileen K. Duncan, no issue
D5. Charles M., b 1875 mar Maud Wilson, 1884-1906, 3 chn
E1. Ray mar Hazel Milligan, 5 chn: David, Curtis, Raymond, Joan and Martha J. Sarchet
E2. Hazel Sarchet mar Francis Harboldt E3. Lucille mar Fred Bittner
C5. Rachel E. mar John Hetherington 1863
C6. Fletcher Bishard Sarchet, b 1849 d 1925, mar 1866 Nancy Evaline Bell, b 1847 d 1915, bur Bells Cem., Cambridge, OH.
D1. Elizabeth Jane, b 1866 d 1944 mar 1886 Moses K. Sarchet, b 1861 d 1945. See chn under Moses Klingman.
D2. Perry, b 1869 d 1959 mar 1893 Laura Alexander, and 2. Bessie (Mayberry) Henis.
E1. Merle b 1896 mar 1. Fred Waller and 2. Bert LE PAGE
D3. John b ca 1872, d.y.
D4. Harvey Leonard, b 1880 d 1944, mar Cordy B. Lanning, 1889-1958
E1. Thelma, b 1907 mar Sheldon Young
E2. Clarence, b 1909 mar Kathleen Stiles, dau Donna Ann Morgan
E3. Paul R., b 1911 mar Clara Brill, a son Paul Robert
E4. Harvey, b 1914, mar Mary Whitcraft, no issue
E5. Mary Eliz., b 1921 mar Oliver Wm. Misel
E6. Ruth, b 1923 mar Orton C. Misel
E7. Max, b 1928 mar Laurell Williams, 4 chn: Richard, David, Connie and Christine Sarchet
E8. John W., b 1935 mar Linda Gunn, 3 daus, Melanie, Charlotte and Tina Sarchet
D5. Mary Ellen, b 1874 mar Fred Foltz, dau Vera mar Russell Miller.
D6. Emma M., b 1882 mar Albert BRITTON
D7. Nettie b 1884 d 1957, mar 1. Marion "Cory" Stage & 2. F. Smith
C7. David Tingle b 1854 d 1929, mar 1873 Martha H. Newburn, 1854-1945.
D1. Melvin Erwin, b 1874 d 1947 mar Frances Davis, 1876-1955
E1. Dr. Harry E. Sarchet, b 1897 mar Nell Holden

F1. Harry G. mar Virginia Hoffman, a son Gordon Hoffman Sarchet
E2. Dr. John David b 1899 mar Dorothy Rice, 2 chn
F1. Joan, mar Dr. John F. Brackmann, Jr.
F2. Marilyn mar Richard H. Davis.
D2. Oscar, b 1877 d 1947 mar Sadie O'Doud, 4 chn
E1. Raymond, mar Edna Landman, 2 chn: Mamie and Sally Janis
E2. Rolland, mar Pauline Kirkbride, 2 chn: Jackie, d.y. and Paul L. mar Kay Trishler. Paul was b 1937
E3. Russell mar Mary Sigman and 2. Bernice Hickman, no issue.
E4. Hazel mar Carl Kieser
D3. Myrtle b 1881 d 1937 mar James Warner
E1. Wm. AlbertSarchet mar Dorothy E. Whitcraft, a son William Jr.
E2. Ral;h Sarchet
D4. Joseph M, b 1886 mar 1. May Johnson and 2. Zana Margaret Allen 1947.
E1. Joseph M. b 1918 E2. Sara Jane, b 1923 mar James Warden
D5. Winifred, b 1890 mar 1. Davenport Racy and 2. Willis B. Shepherd, 1954.
D6. Charles G. b 1892 d 1935, mar Hannah Clark
E1. Charles C. mar Edith Mattevi, 2 chn: Linda K. & Joyal Sarchet
C8. Alpheus Torode b 1859 mar 1887 Emma Ross, b 1869
D1. David Ross b 1888 mar Gertrude Guthridge, b 1893
E1. Bernard b 1913 mar Freda McMullan, b 1912, 4 chn
F1. Carol Belle, b 1938, d.y. F3. Lester Lee, b 1945 d 1952
F2. June Eloise mar 1959 Charles Long F4. Wm. Lee, b 1946
D2. Carl T., b 1889 mar Anna Ross, 2 sons.
E1. Orville A.
E2. Melvin R., mar Lucille Ford, dau Shirley Jean
D3. Warren M., mar ___Gill, no issue
D4. Watt Robert, b 1894 mar Merele Marlatt, b 1896
E1. Waldo Emerson, b 1919 mar Fay Cash, a son Rodger b 1948
E2. Wilmer Vernon, mar Lillian Holderman, 4 chn
F1. Jack Wayne, b 1942 F3. Sandra Sue, b 1946
F2. Garry Vernon F4. Brenda Kathleen
D5. Olive M., b 1896 mar Brooks Miller
D6. Mary F., no record
D7. Fred P. mar Geneva Nelson, a son Harold E. Sarchet
C9. Elmer C. b 1861 mar 1891 Nellie Huff, b 1873
D1. Clara b 1892 mar Harold Burt
D2. Bessie b 1895, unmar D3. Helen M., b 1899 mar Albert B. Davis
D4. William R., b 1906 mar Eileen Gersell, 3 chn: Richard, Susan and Mary Christine Sarchet
D5. Bernard R., b 1917 mar Lena V. Fisher 1941, b 1917.
E1. Rene b 1942 E2. Dawne b 1947 E3. Melanie b 1951
D6. Richard D., d.y.
D7. Mary Francis mar Ray Phillips
B4. Peter B., b 1800 G, had 160 acres in Cambridge Twp. 1840. His home was one of the stops on the Underground Railway, to aid escaped slaves. He mar 1. Catherine Holler, 2. Martha M Culley, and 3. Mary Mitchell. He d in ILL.
C1. Thomas C2. Joseph H.
C3. John Miller, d 1861, mar Sarah E. Thomas 1857, had son and dau.
D1. Theodore Henson, 1860-1955, , mar Rose M. Glascock 1880, res Indianaola, IA, d there age 94, had 13 chn: Jacob F., Bert H. Harry Thomas, John M., Orlin Dewitt, George Lester, Foster, Nora Mae Houghtaling, Sarah E. Halterman, Anna B. Brown, Olive J. Hunget, Iolas N. Boothe & Crena Raw Steward.

D2. Mary E., b 1858 mar ___Marlatt
C4. Cyrus Beatty mar Edith Skelton C5. George M.
D1. Horace Lincoln, b 1860 mar Emma Swain. His 3 chn were adopted by J.D. Tate when Emma died quite young. Horace mar 2. Georgie Etta Dotson, 1864-1940.
E1. Harrison E2. Minnie Zoe Crawford E3. Amy Zela Sherman
B5. Moses, b 1802/3, d 1890, the last of the Island-born to d in GCO. He was an outstanding man in Cambridge, assistant clerk of courts, at age 16-24, clerk of courts for 14 years, township clerk,trustee Mayor of Cambridge 2 terms, M.P. 12 years, a contractor and stockholder of the Central Ohio Railway. He mar Martha BICHARD, qv, 1805-1887. In 1887 they had 28 grandchn. (Sarchet, Vol 1) Moses d 1890. 5 sons, 2 daus. Martha was the dau of James Bichard and Rachel DE LA RUE.
C1. Cyrus Parkinson Beatty Sarchet, 1828-1913, mar Margaret Malvina Moore, dau of Andrew Moore. He and his father, Moses, owned and published the Guernsey TIMES, 1855/6. Cyrus a farmer for 40 yrs. Elected Col. of the 3rd Regt. in GCO.
D1. Frank M., d.y.
D2. Andrew M. mar Grace Boetcher, and 2. Dolly Edward, ch d.y.
D3. Inez L., mar Cyrus F. Wilson, 2 chn: Maude and Ralph Wilson
D4. Martha Blanche, mar Theodore Deselm, 2 chn: Margaret & Martha Deselm.
C2. Thomas, 1835-1903, Mayor of Cambridge, OH, mar 1856 Sarah Klingman, 1836-1919
D1. William Jacob Sarchet, 1857-1923, mar Agnes Bell 1881 and 2. Mary Marrow.
E1. Edgar T. Sarchet, b 1884 d 1955, mar 1. Pearl Gregg and 2. Mary Miller.
F1. Juliane, by 1st wife, mar Glen H. Burt
F2. Mary Louise, by 2nd wife mar Wm. H. Davis
E2. Jessie mar Walter McKee E3. Wilma mar Martin Medley
E4. Sarah Edith, b 1891 mar W. Cappas E5. Fay mar Carl Frost
D2. Dora A., b 1859 d 1939 mar 1891 John Anker
E1. Grace Sarchet Anker b 1886 mar 1. Fred Claggett and 2. SamWillis
D3. Moses Klingman, b 1861 d 1945, mar 1886 Eliz. Jane Sarchet, 1866 to 1944. 6 chn, a son Thomas d.y.
E1. Rex Emmet, 1888-1964 mar 1. Mary Dunning, 3 chn and 2. Clara Morrison
F1. William Brennan, b 1908 mar 1934 Lulu Rae Lyons, 7 chn: Mary L. Clementz, Charles W., Violet Jean, Edith I., Ellen Maxine, Sharon Darlene, and Linda Mae, b 1952. (Edith & Ellen-twins)
F2. Lillian (Toots), mar Charles Jenkins F3. Lucille, unmar
E2. Raymond Rolfe, b 1891 mar Lena O. Braden, who d 1980,7 chn
F1. Harold Milton, 1914-1981, mar Martha E. Evans, 2 chn: Harold and Linda Gail Sarchet
F2. Dorothy, b ? mar John Schoger, 2 chn: Gard & Hugh Schoger
F3. Florence J. mar Harold Frye
F4. Raymond B, unmar F6. Kathryn Ann, mar DonaldWilson
F5. Barbara, mar James Reagle F7. Carolyn mar Gene Paulson
E3. Harold Frederick, b 1895 mar Molly I. Simmons, b 1901 Texas.
F1. Edith Margaret, b 1921 Vigo Park, mar M.T. Cruce 1944,4 chn
G1. Paul Theron Cruce, b 1947 mar Linet McClure
G2. Cynthia Elaine Cruce, b 1949
G3. Tana Marilyn Cruce, b 1952 mar 1977 John C. Robison, 2 sons
G4. Kennan Lynn, b 1954 mar 1974 Oleta D. Tanner, 2 chn
F2. Thomas Jr., b 1923, d.y.

F3. Elizabeth Sue, b 1925 Tulia, TX, mar 1950 Charles Skelton
F4. Harold Lloyd, b 1927, mar 1950 Hazel Shell, 2 chn: Michael, b 1951 and Deborah, b 1961
F5. Robert Lee, b 1929, mar 1950 Daisy B. Shelley, 4 chn: Robert, Harold, Barry and Kelly, b 1951-1962
F6. Donald Dean, b 1931, mar 1948 Fay LaNelle Smith, 4 chn: Donald, Kim, Kerry and Karmyn Sue, b 1949-1957
F7. Charles Raymond, b 1934, mar Mary Anne Hill, a son Kenneth A.
F8. Jerry Wayne, b 1943 Tulia, TX, mar 1965 Elta J. Clanton, 2 sons: John F. and Paul Wayne, b 1966-1971, TX
E4. Charles Edwin, b 1902, E. Cambridge, OH, mar Mildred E., 1923, dau of Fred F. and Lillian (Morris) Persons
F1. James K., mar ?, 4 chn: Dennis, Patricia, and Charles, plus ?
F2. Janet Sue, mar ___ Reed, 2 chn: Marcy L. Gaines & Mark Reed
E5. Ada, mar John MAFFETT, qv E6. Charles mar Mildred Eliz.Persons
D4. Joseph White, b 1863, d 1903, mar Sarah MARSH, qv, b 1868, 2 chn: Roya A. and Mildred, who mar Graham Gracey
D5. George Henry, b 1864, d 1936, mar Margaret N. MARSH, qv, 1865-1953, res Detroit, MI 1913, had 5 sons and 5 daus
D6. Charles F., 1868-1933, mar Sarah Moore, no issue D7. John B.
D8. Dean Thomas, b 1873, d 1939, mar Dollie McDowell 1896, 2 chn. Donald and Vesta, who mar James Meyers
D9. Mary Edith, 1876-1954, mar Michael J. Costello, 1876-1943
D10. Lot Boyce, 1879-1898 D11. Thomas, b 1866, d.y.
C3. James B., 1837-1914, mar Elizabeth A. Cook, 1842-1927, 4 chn. A James Sarchet was in OH Nat. Guard 1876, poss not this one?
D1. Albert C., 1862-1943, mar Bessie Young, b 1870, at least 2 chn, William A. and James R., 1916-1943, WWII
D2. James, b 1863, mar Sally White 1896
D3. Ernest W., mar Katherine S. D5. Lillie?
D4. Clarence B., 1868-1939, mar Georgie Wyncoop, 1870-1938, 5 chn
C4. Charles J., b 1840, d 1870 unmar
C5. John Henry, b 1843, mar Emma Davis, had 3 daus who d.y. He served in the Civil War, had music store in Cambridge, sang and entertained, was leader of a band, and wrote political and other songs.
C6. Rachel M.
C7. Nancy B., mar Joseph W. White, 1822-1892, 3 daus
D1. Mary Scott White, res Evanston, ILL
D2. Martha Campbell, res Cambridge, OH
C8. Harriet Josephine, mar James M. Carson 1852, 2 chn
B6. Rachel, b 1805 G, mar John F. Beatty, son of Col. Z.A. Beatty
C1. Zaccheus A. Beatty C5. Harriet A. Beatty, of Millersburg, OH
C2. Anna M. Beatty C6. Ellen A. Beatty, res Indiana
C3. Sarah K. Beatty C7. Margaret M. Beatty, res Toledo, OH
C4. Margery L. Beatty C8. Cecelia F. Beatty
A2. Judith, b 1774 G, mar Daniel FERBRACHE, qv
A3. John, b ca 1775 G, mar Judith FALAISE, to GCO 1806, 10 chn. John d 1861 G. Most of his chn b G, and part of the fam said to have rem to Phila., PA and ONT. He was a ship blacksmith, maker of chains and anchors, advocate of free trade, and a representative of the Iron Masters Union of Phila., PA in the middle 1800s. His report was bitterly assailed by Henry Clay as coming from a "dirty-handed smuggler of the Island of Guernsey." His report was sustained by Albert Galliten. He raised 2 sons & 6 daus. About 1850 they res Penna, then Canada, some living in the London, ONT and Toronto areas.

B1. John M., mar Margaret Wilson
B2. Joseph, mar Juliet Dick
B3. Moses, d.y.
B4. Albin Alfred, d.y.
B7. Marie Falaise, mar Abraham S. See
B8. Sophia, mar Joseph Masters
B9. Eliza, mar Joseph Withers
B10. Ann, mar Peyton B.W. Cooke
B5. Harriett, mar Gideon Cornell and 2. Benjamin Tillinghast
B6. Helen, mar Caleb Coggeshall

A4. Peter, b ca 1778 G, mar 1. Rachel GIBEAUT, GIBAUT, qv, and 2. in 1821 mar Martha LE PAGE, qv. To GCO 1818, d 1859 on way to G, 5chn.
B1. David, 1822-1892, mar Mary Ann Sigman, dau of Luke and Margaret (Arbuckle) Sigman. She was b 1825, d 1902, 5 sons and a dau. A David served in Civil War.
C1. David D., 1850-1910, mar Ella Beymer, dau Rachel mar Albert B. Weirough
C2. Hosea B., 1846-1920, mar Hannah Jane Bailey, 1855-1915, had 2 sons and 4 daus
D1. Henry B., 1884-1886
D2. Everett, mar Elizabeth Caldwell and 2. Mary C. Smith, no issue
D3. Roxie
D4. Susie, mar Ephraim Forshay
D5. Elizabeth, mar Robert Wiley
D6. Anna
C3. Alexander, 1855-1931, mar Ann Beymer and 2. Mary Lawrence,no issue
C4. Roswell, 1852-1906, no issue
C5. James McIlyar, d 1925, mar Kate Beymer, who d 1935, 4 sons, 2 daus
D1. Charles, mar Emma Meyers and 2. May O'Connor, no issue
D2. Earl W., d ca 1971, mar Anna Daum, 2. Ruth Swissgable, and 3. Gertrude Rudy, 4 chn: Paul M., Leroy, Dorothy Mackinaw, Margaret Valenta
D3. Alexander, 1894-1958, mar Forest Hazel Henderson, 1896-1957, and 2. Edna Heeney, 3 sons: John W., Gary J., and James Alexander
D4. Fletcher
C6. Maggie/Margaret?, mar John BONNELL
B2. Peter J., b 1820?, d 1890, mar Jane Wallace, poss and/or Catherine Wallis? Settled near Brazil, IND, 5 sons and 2 daus.
C1. Thomas, d 1912, mar Elizabeth Salida, 3 sons and 1 dau
D1. Bert, 1867-1954, no issue
D2. Elmer, mar Eliz. Galligher
D3. Charles Henry, b 1857, mar Ella Mae Beasley, 1864-1909, in 1883
C2. Peter, unmar
C3. Robert, 1835-1914, mar Margaret Willoughby, 1836-1883, in 1855, had 6 sons and 3 daus
D1. Noah, b 1856, unmar
D2. Simon b1858, mar Effie Hull, a son John
D3. Albert Lincoln, 1860-1931, mar Rose LUCAS 1887, 7 chn
D4. Joseph B., b 1862, mar Dove Moreland, 2 sons and 3 daus
D5. Robert J., b 1864, mar Emma Brown, 4 daus
D6. Edgar M., b 1868, d 1894, unmar
D7. Ella, b 1866, d.y.
D8. Mary, 1870-1895, mar Marion Frazier
D9. Jessie Ann, 1872-1928, mar Charles Piker
C4. Samuel, mar Elizabeth Roberts, had 6 daus
C5. Nathaniel, 1876-1955, mar Emma Rice, who d 1932
D1. Frank, mar Mary Bennett, had son Frank Jr., and 3 daus
D2. Mamie, mar Peter Christman
D3. Gertrude, mar ___ Metz
D4. Kate, mar Fred Lynch
D5. Harriett, mar Wm. Patrick
C6. Harriett, mar ___ Bradley
C7. Lorene, mar Geo. Hursher
B3. Nancy, res Kansas
B4. Sophia, poss d unmar?
B5. Rachel, mar Thomas LE PAGE, qv, b J, his first wife

A5. Nicholas, said to be youngest of Sarchet bros, b ca 1780?, G, mar 1810 Catharine PRICE, d 1864 GCO. He had 120 acres in Cambridge Twp., 1840. (Wolfe)
B1. Nicholas, Jr., mar Margaret Mathers, a son.

C1. Rev. Albert L., res Jefferson, IA, b1856, d 1929, mar Emma F. George, 3 chn
D1. Dr. Hugo N., b 1887, mar Ruth Larman, a son Albert who d 1957
D2. Albert, poss mar and had dau
D3. Helen Cooke, a teacher in Minneapolis, MN?
B2. Joseph, mar, had son
C1. John Wesley, mar Ellen Bell, had a son and 3 daus
D1. Edward E., 1878-1940, mar Fannie Lake, 1872-1941, 2 daus
E1. Lucille Behrendt E2. Blanche
D2. Mary, mar George Bonnell D4. Eva, mar John Barthelow
D3. Martha Blanche, mar ___ Van Vankenbrugh
B3. (?)Malinda A., 1817-1861
B4. (?)Sarah, 1821-1894, mar John H. Tigner
A6. Mary, mar Daniel BICHARD, qv. Had son, Daniel BICHARD, qv.
A7. Judith?, mar Daniel FERBRACHE, qv.
A8. Nancy, mar Peter PRIAULX, qv. Both d in G.
A9. Elizabeth, mar 1. Capt. Morgan of the British Navy, who d at Nova Scotia. She mar 2. John OGIER in England, where she d. She was the grandmother of the John P. OGIER of Cambridge, OH.
SARCHETS named Cemantha, Ellon, Pamelia, etc., not fitted into fam charts, but see SARCHET GEN, by Col. Kenneth Sarchet of Florida.
SARCHET, Harriet, mar Gideon Cornel, his 2nd wife. She is unplaced. (CORNEL ASSOC., H. Dexter, Fenton, MI)
SARCHET, Margaret, b G, mar ___ Talbott 1811, GCO.
SARCHET, Rachel, b G, mar Benj. T. Bell 1821, GCO.
SARCHET, Adam, b G, to GCO.
There is a Sarchet fam cem 4 miles north of Cambridge, OH, between old U.S. #21 and Wills Creek. Much more info available in the Sarchet files of desc and researchers.
SARCHET. Bur in these and other cem in Guernsey Co., OH (GCO); Bird's Run, Methodist Cem; Kimbolton, Liberty Twp.; Zion, Westland Twp.; Bell's Cem, Wheeling Twp., GCO; etc.
SARRE. In J 1274. In St. Martin, St. Heliers, St. John, J 1668. In St. John, J 1749. SARRE in G 1100s. In Torteval, G 1683 and in the 1700s. In St. Peter, G 1723. Curr G & J. Research? See CIFHS #8.
SARRE, Adolphus, b 1876 St. Peter Port, G, cabinet maker, son of James Edmund and Judith (MAHY) SARRE, settled in Hamilton, ONT ca 1908. He mar Amelia Emma MAHY, dau of Nicholas. She was b 1876, d 1935. Adolphus d 1968. Amelia had 2 sisters in G, Maud AUSTIN and Alice LE RUEZ, qv. (Dorothy Hammond, Saint John, NB, Canada)
A1. Violet Daphne Minnie, 1911-1963, mar Donald Ferguson, no issue.
A2. Dorothy Vera Hamling, b 1921, mar 1. George Hannah, 2 chn, and 2. Elmer Atkins HAMMOND, 6 chn
B1. Dorothy Ann Hannah, b 1940, mar Douglas MacKenzie, res Saint John, NB, 3 chn: Donald Wm., Deborah and David A. Mackenzie, b 1963
B2. George Hannah, b 1942, mar Helen Beatty, res Saint John, 3 chn: Dorothy Albert, Barbara and George Hannah
B3. Marily Jane Hammond, b 1943, mar Murray Beyea, no issue, res Rothsay, NB
B4. Howard Neil Hammond, b 1946, mar Gail McHarg, res NB, a son, Howard Neil Hammond
B5. John Leveret Hammond, b 1947, mar Heather Roxborough, res Sussex, NB, 4 chn: Heather, Dorothy, John L. and Katherine
B6. Eleanor Lorraine Hammond, mar Edmond Vanier, res Saint John, NB, 2 chn: Denise and Tanya Vanier
B7. Margaret Ethel Hammond, b 1955, mar Beverley Beyea, res Saint John, a son, Jason A. Beyea.

B8. Robert Earle Hammond, b 1958, unmar

SARRE, LE SARRE, LE SERRE. See SAYRE and SEARS. See Q.A. IN CANADA.

SARRE, Lewis, mar Mary Ann Clark in middle 1800s in GCO, from G?

LE SERE, Kitchen, Hulbert and Cora in Coshocton, OH 1800s. OUTC.

SARRE. Curr Lowell, MA. OUTC.

SAUL. Found in one list of Hug surnames, not listed by Stevens.

SAUL. A puzzling surname. Cf SOULE, SEWALL, similar in sound. Capt. Thomas Saul, below, was Secretary of the East India Marine Society in 1846, now the Peabody Museum of Salem, MA. His portrait there was painted in Antwerp, Belgium. He sailed in 1801 to the Fiji Islands. (Eleanor Conary, Bethel, ME) Curr research in America and Europe.

SAUL, Joseph, b 1751, where?, said to be from C.I., served in Rev. War when he was a sailor on ship SALEM PACKET, age 29 in 1780, five feet, 4 in. tall, complexion light, res Salem, MA. Mar 1775 in Salem, 1. Elizabeth Heather and 2. 1787 Mary Stanley. He d 1825.

A1. Joseph, bp 1775 Salem, MA A2. Betsy, bp 1777 A4. Thomas, bp 1781

A3. Betty, bp 1779, mar Nathaniel Reeves A5. dau, bp 1784

A6. Capt. Thomas, by Mary Stanley, 1787-1875, mar 1812 Sally FOYE, qv, 1787-1875, Capt. Thomas res Salem, MA

B1. Sarah, b 1813 Salem, d 1816 B2. Thomas B4. William Henry

B3. Joseph, b ca 1815, d 1881 Boston, MA, mar 1842 Eliza Winn, who d 1907, dau of Joseph R. Winn and Hannah Dove

C1. William Henry

B5. James B. Saul, barber, b 1830 Salem, d 1906, mar 1852 Martha Ellen Smith, 1832-1885, dau of Thomas Smith and Martha Ann Marciea

C1. James H. Saul, b ca 1853 Salem, d 1930 Bertram Home, Salem, MA. Mar 1875 Adeline Marie Teste, separated. She was b 1858, d 1930, dau of John B. Teste and Esther A. Phippen. Teste a cabinetmaker, b Marblehead, MA.

D1. Ernest Test, b 1875 Salem, d ca 1964, unmar

D2. Mary Ada, b 1877 Salem, mar 1906 Harry R. Wither

D3. Claribell V., b 1879 Salem, d 1944, mar 1907 Charles H. Lendall

C2. Martha M. Saul, b ca 1856 Salem, d 1914, mar 1880 William Joseph Lee, b ca 1857, son of Joseph Lee and Mary A. Huddell. He d 1937. Poss other chn.

D1. Olive W. Lee, b ca 1882 Salem d1947, mar 1901 Frank L. Hamilton, fireman

C3. Walter Saul, b ca 1859 Lynn, MA, d 1921 Salem. Mar Hattie, Harriet N. Prescott, b 1863 Danvers, MA, or Peabody, and d 1891 Salem, dau of Harrison Newell Prescott and Maria or Myra J. Thomas. He mar 2. 1894 Georgietta Moore, 1869-1936, dau of John B. Moore and Sarah E. ___. He was a roofer and clerk.

D1. Mabel Jane, b 1885 Salem, d 1916 unmar

C4. Elmeretta, b ca 1862 Lynn, MA, mar 1882 George A. Lawrence

C5. Frank F., b 1866 Salem, d 1885, unmar

A7. Mary, bp 1789 Salem A9. Joseph bp 1795 Salem d1831 mar Nancy HARVEY

A8. John, bp 1791 A10. John, bp 1797

A11. Mary, bp 1801, d 1921, mar 1820 Samuel ALLEN

A12. Sarah, bp 1805 Salem, d there 1847, mar 1828 William A. Ropes

SAUL, John. OUTC. (Linda Czarny, Denver, CO) See source for more data.

A1. John, b 1793 GA?, d 1864 TX, mar Dicy Netherlin, b 1798 MI d1861 TX

B1. James, b 1832 TX, mar 1852 Hannah Randolph, and d 1912 Hutto, TX. Hannah was b 1835 AL, d 1914 Stephenville, TX, dau of John Randolph, b 1793 and Frances Cooper.

SAUL, John, mar 1824 Salem, MA, Martha FOYE, qv, dau of Wm. and Elizabeth (MASURY) FOYE, qv.

SAUL, Joseph, in Salem, MA 1790 with fam of 4. (Census)

SAUMAREZ. In J 1274, curr G. De SAUSMAREZ in G 1200s. Note different spelling. Many famous Navy men of this surname from the Islands.
SAUMAREZ, Sir Thomas, b 1760 G, with the British Army in the American Rev. War. Was taken prisoner at the surrender in Yorktown, Oct. 1781, d 1845 G. See also DUMARESQ. There is a Saumarez fam in Burke's Peerage on one line.
SAUVAGE. In J 1300s. SAUVAGE and SAVAGE curr G and J. There is a SAUVAGE fam noted in JAMES COX AND HIS DESCENDANTS, by Chattie Cox, Sutherland, NEB 1967. OUTC.
SAUVARIN. Old G surname, curr G. SAUVARY in Vale, G 1821. (CIFHS #14)
SAVAGE, Penrose Ann, b 1824 St. Heliers, J, d 1906 Toronto, ONT, bur St. James Cem there. She mar Col. George Frederick MacDonald of the 16th Regt., Bedfordshires, b 1823 Ceylon, India, d 1897. A dau Edith Maria Aletta MacDonald b 1863, d 1884 Toronto. This fam may be connected to the MARRIOTT fam.
SAVARY, Mary, from C.I.?, bound to Abraham Wilde 4 years, was in MD 1684. See SYVRET. SAUVARY curr C. Note that SAVORY, Wm., of Essex Co. MA 1600s, was from Wiltshire, England.
SAVARY, Mary, wife of Richard MAHIER, qv, of J, in Boston, MA and Accomack, VA early 1700s.
SAVIDENT. Old in G, in St. Saviours, G 1892. Curr G.
SAVIDENT, James, b 1880 Mielles, Vale, G, son of James E. and Lucy (LE MAITRE) SAVIDENT, rem to Victoria, BC 1912, then to San Mateo, CAL. James mar Eliza Jane TOSTEVIN, qv. (J. Savident, San Maeto, CAL)
A1. James, b 1900 Vale, G, to CAL 1924 from BC, mar ___ Craven
B1. Winifred, b 1924 Victoria, BC, mar ___ Moigar, res San Maeto, CAL
B2. Verna M., b 1930, mar Beaumont?, res Redwood City, CAL
B3. James H., b 1933 San Francisco, CAL, res Campbell, CAL
A2. Ernest P., b 1901 G, to Powell River, BC
A3. Arthur J., b 1902 G, d 1965 Canada
SAVIDENT. This name noted in credits of OLIVER TWIST, a movie, 1982.
SAYRE. Another puzzling surname in OH. While a John SAYRE is called "an eccentric Guernseyman" in GCO records, SAYRE is not ordinarily a C.I. surname. It is poss that he was really SERRE, pron much like SAYRE. He mar Mary PEODVIRO, which is prob POIDEVIN. another Guernsey surname. However, SAYER is also found in G. The SAYRE data of GCO was collected but compiler was unable to distinguish fams in the time allotted. Just a few of the many SAYRES of GCO are included below. Please see sources and WRCIC.
SAYRE, Samuel, mar Mary SHARROCK, qv, 1828 GCO. (Sarchet Scrapbook; Conner-Eynon) OUTC.
SAYRE. Most of this surname in OH are thought to be desc of Daniel of Salem, MA, from origin in Bedfordshire, England. (THE SAYRE FAM, by Banta, 1901)
SAYRE. See in these counties in OH, 1860: Guernsey, Hamilton, Butler, Lawrence, Licking, Shelby, Huron, Wash., Gallia, Geauga, Scioto, Champaign, Perry and Union.
SEYRE, SEARE, Michel, Micah?, noted in NEW WORLD IMMIGRANTS, vol. 1, by Tepper. OUTC.
SCELLE. In J as SERLE 1274-1644. See also SEARLE, SERLE, cf SEALE, SEALLY, etc.
SCELLEUR, SEELLEUR. In J 1749, the LEAPER. See LE SCELLEUR in Q.A. IN CANADA, by Turk.
SCOBOL. Not a C.I. surname, however, Ann SCOBOL arrived in Boston, MA 1769 on ship MOLLY, from J, a servant. (Whitmore)
SCOTT. Curr G and J. L'ESCOT an old name in C.I. SCOTT old in G. See Q.A. IN CANADA.

SCOTT, Thomas Rogers, from G to VA ca 1910, but d soon after 1930. (David O. Le Conte, St. Peter Port, G)

SEALE, "Lineage traced back to middle 1600s in south central England, and these Seales are a branch of the Seales of the Isle of Jersey." (THE CARTERET FAMILY, NC GEN, Fall-Winter 1970)

SEALE fam of Southampton, England in 1644 was closely connected with several C.I. fams and may have originated in the Islands. Peter PRIAULX, qv, mar dau of Peter SEALE early 1600s. CEELEY in Isles of Shoals came from Stoke-in-Teignhead, England.

SEALE. "These ancient ancestral connections with the CARTERETS of the Isle of Jersey, being a descendant of the SEALES, and prob also of the CARTERETS." (W.P. Johnson, Raleigh, NC)

SEALE, SEELE. From J to southern England, to the Carolinas 1700s. (Johnson) SEALE was in St. Brelade, J 1668. See PRIAULX, NEHGS, vol. 47, for poss connection with PRIAULX of G.

SEALE. In J 1528-1749. SEALLEY curr G.

SEAL, Mary, res MRB, MA, mar Joseph BOIT, qv, 1766, at least 2 chn, twins, Joseph and Mary bp 1767. OUTC.

SEARLE. In J 1274 and later. Curr J and G. Of the many SEARLES in early New England, apparently only one is said to be from J. Others below may also be from J.

SEARLE, John, b ca 1657 J, d in MRB 1699, mar Mary Pedrick, b 1661, 3 chn. (MHS; Konig)

SEARLE, John and Abigail, res MRB. OUTC. A son John Angier b 1772.

SEARLE, Joseph and Deliverance, res MRB, 4 chn. OUTC.

A1. Joseph, bp 1738, prob d.y.

A2. Joseph, bp 1740/41, twin

A3. Miriam, bp 1740/41, twin

A4. Mary, bp 1734

SEARLE, Richard and Rachel, res MRB, a son Joseph bp 1757. OUTC.

SEARLE, Thomas and Miriam, res MRB, a dau Elizabeth bp 1713. OUTC.

SEARLES, John, in Salem, MA 1790 with fam of 7. (Census) OUTC.

SEARLE, Mary, wife of John SEARLE of MRB, "calls Richard Girdler a Jersey rogue." (NEHGS, vol. 39)

SEARLE, Philip, and wife Hannah, charted by M. Drisco, Boothbay Harb., ME, in WRCIC, but origin of this fam is not certain. Poss that he came from J middle 1600s?

SEARLE. There is an unpublished hist. of the Searl fam compiled by Wm. H. Searle of Elyria, OH, and the SEARLE GEN by C.H. Searle of Topeka, KS, 1925. See also POMROY FAM.

SEARS. "No connection between the English Sears fams, and the one that settled in MA." "The early settlers of Marblehead were many of them from the Channel Islands...the fam of Sarres has been established there for several centuries, and is still represented in Guernsey under the names of Sarres and Serres." (NEHGS, vol. 44, p. 417) Sears was in the Plymouth colony 1633. Richard SARES rem to MRB by 1637. He called Antony THACKER his bro, poss bro-in-law?, then living in MRB. THACKER is an English surname, but was in J in the 1600s.

SEARS. "Mr. May suggests that SARES, SEARS, may have been from one of the Channel Islands." A John SARRE was in St. John Parish, J 1607.

SEARS, Willard, mar Sarah ROBBINS, b 1752 Plympton, MA. Sarah the dau of Eleazar, qv.

SEARS. See NY GEN RECORD, vol. 32.

SEBIREL, LESBIREL, LE SEBIREL, SEBIRE, LISBRILL, etc., etc., SEBIRE in J 1299. A clockmaker of this name in J 1832. LESBIREL in Grouville, St. John and St. Peter, J 1668 and 1749. LESBIREL curr G and J. One form, SEBIRE, is old in G. Curr research? See CIFHS #6 and #9.

LESBIRD, LESBIREL?, Thomas, of J, sold land at Salem, MA 1744 to Capt. John BALCOMB, qv.

LISTRIL, LESBIREL, John, from J to Salem, MA.

LISTRIL, prob LESBIREL, Mary, of J, wrote to her husband from J 1743 and mentioned, "John BEEDLE, your mother and grandmother, sisters and brothers desire to be remembered to you." (SAMUEL BEADLE FAM)

SEBREE, John, b ca 1750, d 1780, served in Battery of York, Rev. War. Mar ca 1770 Mildred Johnson in Orange or Culpepper, VA. (C.B. Huff, Cincinnati, OH)

SEBRELL, Joseph, son of Joseph and Rebecca (Jones) Sebrell, b 1796 Sussex Co., VA, mar Mary Shinn. OUTC.

SEBRELE, Nathaniel, res Surry, VA, noted in the list of James Kee and Samuel Cocke. (Men in one house, with 5 other buildings, in 1784) Another notation in 1782 shows 10 whites and 12 blacks with Nathaniel spelled SEBRELL, also in Surrey, VA. Others, spelled SEBREE, res Northumberland Co. in St. Stephen's Parish, Orange Co., mostly all white groups, in fams of 4 to 11 persons. See lists of Wm. Downing, Kenner Dralle, John Heath, Wm. Nutt, Thomas Barbour, James Kee, and Samuel COCKE.

LE SEBIREL, John, taken by the French in the 1700s on a Jersey ship.

LISBRILL, Sarah, d 1831 at the poorhouse (in Salem?) age 63, dau of Daniel LISBRILL.

SIBRILL, Henry, b Nov. 1818 (stone), d 1857, bur Meeks CH Cem, Hammond Twp., Spencer Co., IND, 1st husband of Elizabeth Bunner, mar 1846 Brown Co., OH. Henry and Elizabeth had chn, and as of 1900 there were still desc in Spencer Co., IND. In 1840, in OH Census, 2 fams. (Melody Warner, Reston, VA) Poss chn of Henry and Elizabeth?

A1. Frederick, res in Franklin Twp., Brown Co., OH 1840, spelled SIBREL

A2. Henry, res Green Twp., Ross Co., OH

SIBRELL, Frederick and John, res Mason Co., VA 1920.

SIBRELL, Frederick, George John, and Owen res Mason Co., VA 1830.

See early records, 1700s, SIBREL, LESBIREL in GUERNSEY QUARTERLY REVIEW, Spring, 1958.

SEELEY, SEALY, SELLEY, CILLEY, etc. This is an English surname. However, Capt. Robert SEELEY came with the CARTERET group via ship PHILIP in 1665 from Jersey. SEALE, SEELE, were in St. Aubin, J 1668. SEELEY and LE SEELLEUR curr J.

SELLEY, John, mar 1700 in Boston Sarah GORY. Was her name GOUREY of J? OUTC.

SEELEY, Wm., was in Isles of Shoals, ME 1653. (Noyes) Note that other C.I. surnames were also present in these Islands. OUTC.

SEGUIN, SEGGIN, Charles, came from J with CARTARET to NJ on ship, PHILIP 1665. Prob. French.

SELLEW, SLEW, SLUCE, etc., appeared in the colonies and were mostly from England. However, note that J surname SELOUS is pron SELLEW. "English soldier Philip SLOW, in 1650 mar a Jersey girl and settled in the Island. The fam name became jersified into SELOUS, and from them descended SELOUS the Painter, and SELOUS the Mighty Hunter." (BAILWICK OF JERSEY, by G.R. Balleine) SELOUS the Hunter wrote at least one book about big game hunting, and the SELOUS GAME PRESERVE in Eastern Africa, one of the world's largest, is said to be a memorial to him. "Containing..elephant, rhino, buffalo, hippo, crocodile, lions, leopards, 350 species of birds and more than 2000 varieties of plants...Unique in size, state of naturalness and variety of genetic and ecological resources." (SAND RIVERS, Peter Matthiessen, NY, 1981, and other books) Frederick Courtenay SELOUS, naturalist, elephant hunter and explores,...white hunter for Theodore Roosevelt, Capt. in the 25th Royal Fusiliers, d of a wound in the British advance to the Rufiji 1917.

SELOUS, SLOUS. Curr research in J, see CIFHS #5 and #12. Poss SELOUS in J by 1607?

SLUCE, Lawrence, master of the HOPEWELL, noted 1681, from NY to Pemaquid. (Noyes) OUTC.

SENNETT, SINNATT. Old in J.

SENNIT, John, mar 1755 Mary BELSHI, prob BAILHACHE of Manchester, MA. Poss both Mary and John from J.

SINNOTT, SYNOTT. Noted in Petition of Quebec City residents 1838, with other C.I. surnames. (LOST IN CANADA, August 1981)

SEVRET, SEIVRY, SEVERY, SYVRET. "...the name SIVRET, SEVRIT, SEVERIT from the Channel Islands...in Massachusetts...being anglicized to SAVORY or SAVARY...My grandfather has nearly five pages of Marblehead records of the Church in Marblehead, which clearly show the gradual change in the name." "...Savary, Thomas, from Hanington in Wiltshire, England...to Plymouth Colony before 1684." CAUTION IS NEEDED WITH THIS SURNAME. "The SYVRET coat of arms is also the arms of Oliver Cromwell!" (Judge A.W. Savary, Nova Scotia)

"The first American progenitor of this family...settled about 1629 by immigrants from the Islands of Jersey and Guernsey in Marblehead." First appears in the records as SEVRIT. "An Englishman, unversed in the French language, hearing a French-speaking man pronounce the name SIVERT/SYVRET and desiring to write it down would be almost sure to write it Scivery or Severy. Either of these two...would be an Englishman convey very nearly, and with about equal effect the name as it would be pronounced by a Frenchman...the letter 'T' at the end is not sounded as it is in English...at Marblehead and Wenham we find the name connected contemporaneously with the Christian names Thomas, Andrew, Peter, James and John; and soon afterwards we meet at Marblehead, Clement, Gregory, and Philip, redolent of the Channel Islands and France; and the more Puritan and Biblically associated names Jonathan, David and Solomon, still common in the family, appeared simitaneously in branches widely separated for generations. Among the soldiers in King Philip's War were Edward and John Severy of Marblehead, and others of the name, and the family contributed a remarkable number to all the wars in which the colonies and the United States were engaged." (GEN.)

CAUTION! Great care must be taken to distinguish between SEVERY, etc., and SAVORY. At least one SAVORY, William, came from Wiltshire, England to Essex Co., MA in the 1630s.

SEVERY, SEAVERY, SEVERIT, SEAVERIT, etc., etc. Many of this surname in MA 1790s Census. There is little doubt that some of these fams were descended from C.I. settlers, and the original form of the surname was SYVRET. See records in Westminster, Petersham, Boston, Roxbury, Sterling, Dorchester, Northborough, Bridgewater, Taunton, Cambridge, Shelburne, Medway, Newton, Partridgefield, Kingston, Sutton, Warwick, Ward and Marblehead, MA. Caution is needed, as some of the fams came directly from England, and were not Channel Islanders.

"My grandfather was born in St. Aubin, J 1849. He was a shipmaster in the Merchant Marine. He came to live with my father in NY while I was very young, ca 1910. He d 1918. ...My paternal great grandmother's maiden name was ESNOUF." (Charles F. Syvret, Denver, COL) Charles is related distantly to Richard Syvret (curr) in J.

Marguerite Syvret, of the Societe Jersiaise, St. Heliers, J wrote in 1976: "I was most interested to read your book...The names of Syvrets settled at Portsmouth, NH and in Marblehead are identifiable in the registers of St. Ouens Parish in J with members of our branch and others living at St. Ouen in the 1600s. All the Christian names you mention appear in that century. The John who died at Wenham, MA in 1742 in his 98th year would seem to be Jean fils Jean bp at St. Ouen in April 1644...The Syvrets mentioned in JERRI JADIS (a book about Gaspe QUE Channel Islanders) are not members of our branch of the family."

SEVRIT, SEVERY, SYVRET, John, b ca 1644 Jersey, son of Jean? of St. Ouen, J, d in Wenham, MA in his 98th year. He had at least 4 chn, b MA. His wife d 1737. See SYVRET; NEHGS, vol. 41; GEN. RECORD OF THE SAVERY-SEVERY FAMILY, Boston 1893. John was poss a carpenter, as he built a coffin and dug a grave for a MRB resident, John Harris, in 1680. (NEHGS, vols. 41,77,81; Q.A. IN CANADA; GEN. AND BIO. RECORD OF THE SAVARY FAMILY, and of THE SEVERY FAMILY, by Judge A.W. Savary, Annapolis Royal, Nova Scotia, and Lydia Savary, E. Wareham, MA, Boston 1893; James B. Severy, Col. Springs, COL; Ann Alexander, Brunswick, ME)

A1. John, b prob before 1683, mar prob Martha Parlow, dau of Thomas P. She d, age 85, in 1768, in Wenham, MA.

B1. John, b 1706, d.y.

B2. John, b 1707, mar 1729 Mary ___, dau of Jonathan ___, whose mother was ___ Stewart. He d 1778 in his 72nd yr. He did not mention all his fam in his will, so most may have predeceased him or d.y. John, b 1735, and Lydia, who mar ___ Tinkham, may have provided the only desc we know of. Bur Middleboro, MA, 8 chn given, 1 with desc.

C1. Martha, b 1731, d before 1743 C2. Mary, 1733-1794, unmar (stone)

C3. John, b 1735, mar 1764 Thankful Cobb, d Middleboro, MA 1770. His widow mar David Bates 1774.

D1. Daniel b 1764 mar 1794 Huldah Soule, d1836, his widow d1853 age 78

E1. John, 1795-1796

E2. Daniel, b1797 of Middleboro, MA, mar 1. 1824 Elizabeth Vaughan, who d 1825, and 2. 1832 Lydia Morton. Daniel d 1869.

F1. Elizabeth, b1825, by 1st wife F2. Priscilla Morton b1833 d.y.

F3. Daniel, b1839, mar Rosetta Y. Wood of New Bedford, MA, no issue

E3. Huldah, b1798 E4. William, 1800-1821 E5. Lydia, b1801

E6. Peregrine White Savery, b1803, mar Mary Drew Cobb, res Savory farm in Middleboro, d 1881, she d 1881, age 76

F1. Mary Drew, b 1835, mar 1871 Nathan B. Maxim

G1. Ernest Maxim, d.y. G2. Phoebe A. Maxim, b 1875

F2. Phoebe Ann, b 1837, d unmar 1870

F3. Luther Wright, b 1839, mar 1881 Alice I. Churchill, dau of James and Rebecca (Carver) Churchill. He d 1886.

F4. Albert T., b 1842, mar 1865 Maria S. Waleman, dau of James and Rebecca Waleman. She was b 1844, res Middletown.

G1. Trueman C., b 1865 G2. Horace H., b 1867, d.y.

G3. Charles A., b 1868, mar 1881 Boston, Nina J. Falline

E7. Sarah Briggs, b 1805 E8. Betsy, b 1812

E9. George Simmons, b 1816, mar 1847 Rhoda J. Churchill

E10. and E11. Prob other chn, no data

D2. Nehemiah, b 1769, d 1846, age 78. Mar 1. 1793 Sarah Cornish, and 2. 1806 Deborah Swife. Res north part of Plymouth, MA. Wife d 1847, age 75.

E1. Thomas, b 1796, mar 1821 Penelope, dau of John Swift. Thomas d 1856. She d 1876, age 75.

F1. Everett Williams, b 1822, unmar

F2. Albert Allen, b 1824, mar 1846 Elizabeth, dau of James and Elizabeth (Thomas) Shurtliffe of Carver, MA

G1. Chester Forest, b 1848, mar 1975 Ella E.F. Snow of Canton, MA dau of Russell & Amelia Atwood Snow, Chester res Taunton, MA.
G2. Elizabeth A., b 1853
G3. Agnes T., b 1856, mar 1875 Elbridge Holloway, son of Benjamin and Harriet (Cole) Holloway of Middleboro, MA
H1. Lillie Bernard Holloway b1875 H2. Eva Agnes Holloway b1877
H3. Wendell Elbridge Holloway, b 1878
G4. Laura Ann, b 1862
F3. Harriet Richmond b1830 mar __Howland F4. Eliza Jane, b 1835
E2. Nehemiah, b 1797, mar 1841 Phoebe, dau of Wm. Stephens. She d 1876, age 63. He d 1877.
F1. Nehemiah Lewis, b 1842, mar Weltha(?) E. Cobb
G1. Charles Lewis, b 1868
F2. Sarah C., b 1843, mar 1874 Edward J. Thompson
F3. Esther S., b 1847, mar 1871 Alex. J. Bartlett
F4. Irene F., b 1848, mar 1869 Wm. F. Petersill?
F5. Mary S., 1850-1856 F7. James E., b 1854
F6. John, 1852-1853 F8. Emmeline, b 1855, d.y.
E3. Winsor, or Windsor, b 1801, mar 1836 Fannie (Smith) Savery, widow of Thomas Savery (who was son of Thomas S.) Winsor d1874.
F1. Winsor Thomas, b 1845, mar 1865 Abigail F. Cobb
G1. Robert Winsor, b 1871
F2. Sarah Cornish b1848, mar 1866 Elisha T. Nelson, son Elisha d.y.
E4. Betsy E5. Mary E6. Sally E7. by 2nd wife, Cordelia
E8. Louisa, mar David H. Holmes, 11 chn
E9. Deborah E10. Marcy E11. a son
C4. Perez, b 1737 C5. Nehemiah, b 1740 C6. Martha, b 1743
C7. Joanna, b 1747 C8. Lydia, b 1747, mar ___ Tinkham
B3. Thomas, mar Mary Williams 1738. Bought land at Hebron, Connecticut 1753 and rem there with his fam, d at Hebron, 1761
C1. Martha, b 1738 C2. Lucia, b 1740 C3. Solomon, 1742-1747
C4. Joseph, b 1744, res Tolland, CT, and his desc spell name SAVORY
D1. Ira, b 1776, Tollard, CT, mar 1802 at Hebron, Lovina or Lavinia Richardson. Rem to Onondago Co., NY until 1818, then to Steuben Co., NY. Died 1842, and his widow d 1864, age 83.
E1. Willard, d at Buffalo, NY, unmar E2. William, d.y.
E3. Walter C. Savory, b 1808 Marcellus, NY, mar Minerva BAKER of Mill Creek, PA, b 1818. Res Beaver Dam, Schuyler Co., NY.
F1. Susan Savory, b Port Creek, Chemung Co., NY F2. George
F3. Ira, b 1843, Hornby, NY, mar 1866 Cynthia A. Sickles of Orange, Schuyler Co., NY F4. Emma F. F5. Annie
E4. Warren W., b 1812, mar ca 1843 Fidelia Perigo, res Elgin and Joliet, ILL and later in MO, 5 chn
F1. Mary E., b ca 1845, mar Geo. C. Grant
F2. Hattie C., b ca 1846, mar John Bonham
F3. Willard W. F4. Walter, b ca 1854 F5. Lula B., b ca 1864
E5. Willis J., b ca 1816
E6. Harriet Savory, mar Thomas Quigley, d 1846, 6 chn
E7. William, mar Lucy Holmes, d 1850, 4 chn
E8. Mary Ann, b 1817, mar Asaph Cole, res Havana, Cuba?
F1. Melina Cole b1836 F2. Harlem Cole b1837 F3. Ira Cole b1839
E9. Wilbur W. Savory, b Catlin, Steuben Co., NY. Mar 1. Rachel BAKER, who d 1852. Mar 2. 1858 Delphine Laurette, b 1840, dau of Reuel Cogswell and Eliza Mead. (See Cogswell Gen.)
F1. Fidelia, 1841-1851 F3. Charles, b 1846
F2. Frank, 1843-1869, served with Sherman in GA F4. Mary Ann, b 1848

F5. Cornelia, b 1851, mar James Whitford
G1. Dillie Whitford G2. Celia Whitford
E10. Fidelia, mar John W. Cuffman, no issue
E11. Washington P. Savary, b 1822, mar 1843 Sarah Cuffman of Dryden, NY, b 1818, res Kendall Sta., Chemung Co., NY
F1. Francis A., b 1847, mar A.C. Place, dau Blanche M., b 1871
F2. Marvin L., b 1850, mar 1882 Lillian B. Littlehale
G1. Edwin Victor
F3. Andra O., b 1854, mar 1870 B.F. Mead, native of Port Dover, Ontario, Canada
G1. Myrtie B. Mead, b1871, d.y. G3. Mary E. Mead, b 1876
G2. Wm. A. Mead, b 1873 G4. Frank Mead, b 1878
C5. Alpha D. Mead, b 1880 Buffalo, NY
F4. Rosealtha D., b 1856, mar 1871 Wm. H. Christian, b 1848
G1. Lowell V. Christian, b 1873 G3. Grace, b 1878
G2. Maude E. Christian, b 1875 G4. Lillian, b 1871
E12. Willard, mar Melissa E. Dailey, no issue
D2. Backus, who is said to have been a leather dealer, and d on a second visit to Spain ca 1804
C5. Sarah, b 1746
C6. Solomon, b 1749, res Hebron, CT, d ca 1874, had 3 daus
D1. Sally, mar Aaron Bills D3. Betsy Savory
D2. Clarissa, mar S. House
C7. Thomas, b 1751 C8. Mary, b1753
C9. John, 1756-1804, no issue found C10. Hiram, b 1761
B4. Elizabeth, and possibly other daus
A2. Joseph, b 1690, mar 1. Mary Crocker of Topsfield, MA, who soon d. He mar 2. Sarah Stockwell, and d 1761, about age 71. His widow d 1770, age 81. They res Sutton, MA ca 1728 and later.
B1. Joseph, b 1714, mar Susannah Stockwell who d 1762, age 53. Res Sutton, MA, now Millbury, MA. Joseph d 1800.
C1. Mary, 1735-1758 C3. Hannah, b 1740, d.y.
C2. Susanna, b 1737 C4. Hannah again, b 1741
C5. Joseph, b 1744, mar Rebecca ___
D1. Joseph Emerson Severy, b 1767, mar Miriam Stone, res Auburn, d 1829. Widow d 1846, age 84.
E1. Stephen Savary, b 1791, mar (int 1816) Daphne Hall, b 1800. He d 1868, and his widow d in 1883.
F1. Nancy, b 1817, mar S. BAKER, 3 sons, 1 d.y.
G1. Henry Baker G2. George Baker
F2. Louisa, b 1820, mar 1844 George Darling
G1. Jacob W. Darling, b 1844 G3. Jerone A. Darling, b 1848
G2. Eugene Darling, b 1846 G4. Ruth M. Darling, 1850-1876
F3. Miriam Stone, b 1823, mar 1842 Sanford A. Inman of Burrillville, R.I., d 1859
F4. Stephen Augustus Savary, b 1825, mar 1. Mary Eddy, and 2. Georgie Case, res W. Millbury, MA
G1. Wendell S. Savary, b 1870
F5. Joseph Emerson Savary, b 1827, mar 1882 Lydia J., dau of Jonathan Ross, of Effington, NH, widow of Benj. Stillings. Res Palmyra, NY, was in CA during and after the Gold Rush and later res Boston in RR business, no issue. F6. John, b 1832
C6. Eunice, b 1747, mar 1772 Samuel Merriman
C7. David, b 1750, Sutton, MA, res Warwick and Northfield. Mar 1. Sylvia ___, who d 1786 and 2. at Northfield, Lydia Barber of Warwick, MA
D1. Mary, b 1777, Warwick, MA D2. Susanna, b 1780, Warwick, MA

D3. Silvia, b 1782, Warwick, MA D4. Lydia, b 1784
D5. Sally, b 1786. Poss other chn.
C8. Jonathan, b 1754 Sutton, MA, res Warwick, served in Rev. War. Died 1810, age 63. Mar ___.
D1. Jonathan, b 1780, res Prospect, now Searsport, ME ca 1800, and d there 1863. Mar ca 1808 Widow Mary (Towle) Piper of Searsport, who was b 1781 Laconia, NH and d 1854.
E1. Maria, 1814-1888, mar 1835 Capt. Elisha Lamphier.
E2. Sarah A., b 1819 or 1821, mar 1848 John Towle
E3. Jonathan M., b 1824, mar 1854 Olivia Sleeper, d 1891
F1. Mary G., b 1855 F2. Frederick M., b1857, mar 1879 Etta Piper
F3. Edwin L., b 1861, mar 1882 Caddie Mason
G1. Maude E., b 1885 G2. Hervey H., b 1889
F4. Jane?, b 1863, mar 1885 Elden Harriman
G1. Olivia Harriman, b 1887
D2. Elisha, b 1783, d 1843, "age 60"
D3. David, b 1785, res Barre, VT, mar 1. Mary or Polly Smith, who d 1843, age 50, 2. Zilpah CASWELL of ME, and 3. Widow Asenath (Pratt) Claflin of Plainfield, VT. He d 1871, age on stone 86 years. Thirteen chn, 3 by second wife.
E1. David, bp 1815, mar ___
F1. William P. Savory, res Manchester, VA
E2. Mary, mar Isaiah Kilgore, res Independence, KS
E3. Jonathan, b 1818, mar 1848 Westfield, MA, Almeda C. Morrison, res Colon, MI
F1. Ida S., 1850-1853 F2. Belle J., b 1852
F3. David W., b 1854, mar Frank? Spreague of Cedar Springs, MI
G1. Vertie M. G2. John O. G3. Jennie C. G4. Leona
F4. Charles P., b 1867 or 1857? F5. Flora M., b 1860 or 1870?
E4. Samuel, d.y. E5. William, d.y. E6. Joseph, d.y.
E7. Oliver A., b 1824, res Manchester, Chesterfield Co., VA
F1. Orvis W., b 1851 F2. Edgar A., b 1853 F3. Sarah L., b 1856
F4. Ida B., 1858-1864 F7. Walter Lee, b 1866
F5. Winfield C., 1861-1869 F8. Nolan C., b 1867
F6. Mary Frances, b 1864 F9. Ethel F., b 1872
E8. Sarah E9. Lorinda
E10. George W., b 1839, mar Flora Blanche, res Williamstown VT, 5chn
F1. Leslie G., b 1869 F2. Willie L., 1872-1876
F3. Mabel T., b 1876 F4. Mary B., b 1879 F5. Vernon B., b 1882
D4. Joseph, b ca 1786, d 1810, age 24
D5. Ephraim, b 1795, mar 1824 Mary Ellis. Served in War of 1812, res Warwick, MA, then settled at Clarendon Spgs., VT 1835. His wife d 1872, and he d 1874. Ten chn, 3 with desc given.
E1. Nancy L., 1824-1890, unmar E2. Mary E., b 1825, unmar
E3. Harriet U., b 1827, mar Lyman Taylor
E4. Lucy A., b 1828, mar 1. 1853 Charles Ellis and 2. Lucian Winslow
E5. Aaron A., b 1829, res Clarendon Spgs., VT until 1859, when he rem to Topeka, KS, but returned to VT. Mar 1861 Almira P. Cheney. Served in Civil War, settled Proctor, VT, where he d 1892. Wife d Danby, VT 1889, 3 chn.
F1. Helen C., 1866-1867 F3. Martha A., b 1871
F2. Franklin A., b 1868, res Centre Rutland, VT, mar 1891 Harriet M. Gee
E6. Sarah J., b 1831, mar 1869 John Kershaw
E7. William Jonathan, b 1833, mar 1859 Margaret A. Harrison, res Cuttingsville, VT

F1. Nancy E., b 1861, mar 1877 Levi J. Taylor
F2. Jennie B., b 1863, mar 1887 Winslow R. Eddy
F3. Lillie M., 1865-1866 F7. Emma C., b 1873
F4. Belle C., b 1867 F8. Bertha B., 1877-1879
F5. William H., b 1869 F9. Harrison B., b 1883
F6. Martha L., b 1871
E8. George W. Savery, b 1835, mar 1860 Diana L. Pratt, res Wallingford, VT, 4 chn
F1. Mary M., b 1861, mar 1886 Sheridan E. Congdon
G1. Harold W. Congdon, b 1889
F2. John H., b 1863, mar 1882 Emma L. Patterson
G1. George H., b 1886 G2. John H., b?, res Cambridge, NY
F3. Herbert G., b 1865, res Wallingford, VT
F4. Luella L., 1867-1870
E9. John H., b 1837, killed at Yorktown, VA in Civil War, 1862
E10. Martha E., 1841-1885, mar 1873 Charles E. Jennings
F1. Frank B. Jennings, b 1874
B2. Sarah, b 1715, mar 1741 James How, rem to Warwick, d there 1801
B3. John, 1720-1729 B4. Mary, b 1724/25, d 1729
B5. John again, b ca 1730, res Auburn, MA, then Lancaster, where he d. Mar 1750 Hannah, dau of Edward Holman, and d 1812.
C1. Sarah, b ca 1751
C2. John, b 1752, mar 1779 Phoebe Kendall. Served in Rev. War, res Lancaster, MA, d 1834, ca age 82, at house of Windsor Brainard.
D1. Edward, b 1780. Poss other chn. In 1813 Windsor Brainard mar Miss Phoebe Severy at Lancaster, poss sister of Edward.
C3. Hannah, b 1753, d.y. C4. Hannah, b 1754 C5. Rebecca, b 1755
C6. Edward, b 1757, accidentally shot himself 1799
C7. Thomas, b 1759, mar 1780 Lucretia Kendall, settled first at Auburn, MA, then in VT, d 1847. Wife d 1840, age 76.
D1. Judith, b 1781 D2. Lucretia, b 1783 D3. Phoebe, b 1785
D4. Harvey, b 1789, mar Lydia Whitney of Westminster, d 1878. She d 1871.
E1. Phoebe, b 1810, mar 1849 Lyman Cotton
E2. Jehiel, b 1811, mar 1853 Eliza Field, and d 1870
F1. Frank B., b 1854 F3. Martha, 1858-1862
F2. Maggie E., b 1856
E3. Betsy, b 1813, mar 1837 George Raymond, d 1887
F1. C.S. Raymond, res Omaha, NB
E4. Kendall, b 1816, mar Phoebe Graves
F1. Walter, res Warren, VT. Poss other chn.
E5. Alvira E6. Celinda, b 1820, mar Leonard Percival
E7. William, b 1822, mar 1847 Eliza Wetmore
F1. Orrel, b 1848, mar 1. 1869 Lydia Shedd, who d 1881 and 2. 1881 Ida M. Churchill. Three chn, 1 by first wife.
G1. Emma O., b 1876 G2. Walter, b 1882 G3. Ralph, b 1886
F2. Leslie, b 1850, mar 1874 Olive Gilbert
G1. Myrtle, b 1877 G2. Harold, b 1885
F3. Maria, b 1851, mar 1869 N.S. Capen
F4. George, b 1853, mar 1876 Aggie BAKER
G1. Lewis W., b 1877 G3. Elva G., b 1885
G2. Bessie F., b 1881 G4. Hazel, b 1888
F5. Joseph, b 1855 F6. Ida, b 1857, mar 1879 Ford Capen
F7. Judson, b 1859, mar 1855 Linnie Wheeler
F8. Eva, b 1861, mar 1879 Herbert BAKER F10. Harry, 1864-1865
F9. Addie, b 1863, mar 1888 Thomas W. Wood F11. William, b 1866
F12. Bertha, b 1870, mar 1886 Lewis Mason

E8. Mary, b 1824, mar Orrell Towne 1845
E9. Diana, b 1826, mar Charles Frilley
E10. Amos, b 1829, mar 1861 Lucy E. Howard
F1. Eugene W., b 1862, d.y. F3. Carrie H., b 1870
F2. Laura K.J., b 1865, mar Joseph St. John
D5. William, b 1802, mar Polly Tuttle who d 1858. He d 1864.
E1. Eliza Ann, b 1823, mar Peter J.M. Powell, d 1881
E2. Charlotte, b 1826, mar Joel Newton
E3. William Franklin, b 1834, mar 1853 Fanny R. Kingsley, d 1885
F1. Ernest A., b 1854, mar 1880 Cora M. Thomas, who d 1886 and 2. Hattie M. Sawyer. Son Fred by 1st wife, b 1884, d.y.
F2. Florence E., b 1857, mar Frank H. Welch
F3. Charles E., b 1861, mar 1887 Edith M. Parker, res Brandon, VT
F4. Chet K., b 1869, mar 1891 Mary J. Parker
G1. Marjorie A., b 1892
C8. Solomon, b 1761 C10. Judith, b 1768
C9. Lucy, b 1765 C11. Joshua, b 1771
B6. Benjamin, b 1731 at Sutton, mar 1756 Widow Elizabeth Harwood, d in the French War 1758
C1. Reuben, b ca 1757, in 1771 his uncle Jacob was appointed his guardian. Res Hardwicke then Uxbridge, MA. Mar Lucy ___.
D1. Marshall, b 1779, res Wellington, mar Chloe ___
E1. Elias, b 1803, mar, some chn b Union, CT, some in Chaplin. Res Warren, MA. Poss 2 wives? Poss other chn?
F1. Eunice Emeline, b 1825, mar ___ Studley of Warren, MA
F2. William Clark, 1829-1930
F3. Martha, b 1846, mar ___ Southworth
F4. Elvira, mar Freeman Severy, son of Levi
F5. Henry, d as young man
D2. Herman or Heman, b 1782 Uxbridge, MA, res Union, CT, mar Jemima ___. Name and date of death uncertain.
E1. Levi, b 1804, mar Sophia ___
F1. Harriet, b 1829 F3. Freeman, mar Elvira, dau of Elias Severy
F2. Betsy, mar ___ Sheldon F4. Miranda F5. George
E2. Elijah, b 1806, farmer, mar Polly Lilley, d Union, CT 1875
F1. Fidelia, b 1829, res Union, CT F2. Fanny, 1831-1878
F3. Lucy, b 1835, d in the West, leaving a family
F4. Polly, b 1839, mar and d Brimfield, MA, leaving 3 daus
F5. Elisha, b 1842, res Waterbury, CT, mar 1863 Emily SNOW, b W. Woodstock
G1. Ernest Elisha, b 1870 Lebanon, CT, res Pennington, NJ
G2. Clarence Lucius, b 1883 Waterbury, CT
E3. Lucy, b 1808, mar ___ CORBIN, res with son Windsor Corbin at Dudley, MA. a dau, Mrs. Silvia Marsh, res Webster, MA
E4. Harriet, b1810, d.y. E5. Reuben, b1812 E6. Fanny, b1816, d.y.
D3. Rosanna, b 1784 D4. Elizabeth, b 1787
D5. George Carroll, b 1790. Mar (int 1811) Chloe Wood, Uxbridge.
B7. Jacob, b 1735, Sutton, MA, mar 1756 Abigail, dau of Joseph Rhodes of MRB, who was b 1733, d 1815. Res on farm at Sutton, but was active in town affairs, such as tax collector, recruiter for Rev. War, settled estates, etc. Jacob d 1826, age nearly 91. (Data from James B. Severy, Colorado Springs, CO)
C1. Mary, b1757, d without issue 1854 C2. Jacob b1758, d1780 Rev. War
C3. Ruth, b 1760, mar Henry King, d Dixfield, ME 1858
D1. Henry King D2. Asenath King
C4. Sarah, b 1762, mar Phineas Goodnough, d at Newton, near Boston, age 85

D1. Jacob Goodnough D2. Phineas Goodnough

C5. Joseph Rhodes, b 1764, mar Eunice Fitts of Oxford 1789. She is said to have been part Indian, "a woman of large physique and fabulous strength." He d Douglas, MA, age 85.

D1. Benjamin, 1791-1844, no issue

D2. Amos, b 1792, mar his cousin Abigail, dau of Moody Severy, d 1837

D3. Judah, b1794, mar Huldah Griffin, poss res Jackson, PA (Lakeview)

E1. Roxanna, mar ___ Avery (Poss spelled name SAVORY)

E2. Gerogiana, mar ___ Avery, a brother

E3. Diantha, mar George Himer, 3 chn

E4. Edward, mar Sarah Jilson, 2 chn

D4. Clarissa, b 1795, mar Abraham Tourtelotte

E1. Amos Tourtelotte E2. Stephen Tourtelotte

D5. Lydia, b 1797, mar M. Cutting, 2 chn. She d 1850?

D6. Cynthia, b 1799

D7. Libra, 1803-1868, mar Sarah Warren

E1. Mary E2. Abigail

D8. Diantha, 1805-1806

C6. Moody, b1765, mar 1793 Judith, dau of Solomon Holman of Petersham res Sutton, MA. She d 1840, age 76, and he d 1848.

D1. Jacob, b 1795 Sutton, MA, mar 1. 1819 Rebecca Stevens of Charlton, MA, settled Dixfield, ME. She d 1832, and he mar 2. 1832 Mary Walker of Milton, ME, he d Mt. Vernon, ME 1877. Four chn by each wife.

E1. Dexter, b 1820 E. Dixfield, ME, rem to Leland, ILL, a stock raiser, at Victor, De Kalb Co. Mar 1848 Susan C. Hanson, b 1821 Barnstead, Ontario?

F1. Amos Henry, b 1851, mar.

G1. Frank Dexter, b 1878

F2. Charles Allen, b 1856, mar.

G1. Edna M. G2. Bessie M. G3. Fern

E2. Satira, b 1822, mar Henry J. Dakin of Jay, ME, settled Millbury, MA, d 1871, no issue

E3. Hiram, b 1826, mar Jane E. Wallace of ILL, res Aurora, ILL, no issue.

E4. John Moody, b 1829, mar Sarah Hubbard of Dixfield, settled Sandwich, ILL. A dau, Frances E.

E5. by 2nd wife, Charles Harrison, 1838-1839

E6. Charles Henry, b 1840, mar 1862 Anna C. Morse of Dixfield, settled Mt. Vernon, ME

F1. Fred W., b 1864 F2. Lena W., b 1867 F3. Morris H.

E7. Frances Helena, b 1842, mar Valorous White of Jay, ME

E8. Marshall Harrison, b 1845, mar 1868 Clara A. Eastman of Danforth, ILL, settled Gilman, ILL

F1. Cora Belle, b 1869

D2. Abigail, b 1786, mar 1827 Amos Severy, res Millbury, no issue

D3. Willard, b 1798, mar Rhoda Hewett of Sutton

E1. Harriet Maria, b 1825

E2. Freeman

E3. Adeline

E4. Willard, d 1855

D4. Moody, 1800-1803 D5. Sally, 1801-1872, mar Hiel Day 1844

D6. Moody Holman, 1803-1874, mar 1843 Charlotte FORBUSH of Weshona, no issue

D7. Solomon, b 1805, mar 1830 Mary B. Knapp, d 1886, widow d 1890

E1. Francis Solomon, b 1846, d.y.

C7. Thomas, 1767-1793

C8. Asa, b 1769, mar 1801 Hannah Walker of Wilton, ME, who d 1820, age 48. He mar 2. Mehitable Fitts, settled Dixfield, d 1859. Seven chn, two by second wife.

D1. Abigail, b 1802, mar 1823 Joshua Blake, who d 1867

E1. Hannah S. Blake, b 1824, mar 1845 Charles MARSTON, who d 1863. She res Farmington, ME.
D2. Asa, 1804-1810
D3. Moody, 1806-1813
D4. Willis, b 1809, mar 1834 Hester Ann Blake of Phillips, ME in 1868. Res Farmington, MI from 1863, she d 1881, he d in 1873.
E1. James, b 1840, mar 1866 Emma A. Bass of Boston, MA, who d 1892. Had medical degree, but became a judge in Colorado Spgs., CO.
F1. Lena P., b 1867, d.y.
F2. John William, 1871-1874
F3. Emma Genevieve, b 1873
D5. Hannah, b 1814, mar John H. Wait, res Canton, ME
E1. Hannah Abigail Wait, 1848-1863
D6. Harriet, b1823 by 2nd wife, mar Amos H. Blake, d1849, no issue
D7. Asa, 1824-1845
C9. Aaron, b Sutton 1770/71, mar 1. Phoebe Tucker of Hebron, who d 1815, age 36. Mar 2. Hannah Morse of Dixfield, who d 1862, age 66, Aaron d 1860. Twelve chn; 4 by second wife.
D1. Aaron, b 1801, mar 1. at Dixfield 1823 Hannah Eustis, b Chelsea, MA 1802, d 1833. Mar 2. at Wilton 1833 Anna Colburn, b Tamworth, NH 1811, d Dixfield 1885, he d 1863. Twelve chn; 5 by 1st wife.
E1. Leonora, 1824-1844
E2. Minerva, b 1825
E3. Orlando, b 1827
E4. Byron, b 1830, d.y.
E5. Mary, b 1831
E6. Wallace F., b 1835
E7. Ransom, 1837-1855, d Stratford, NH
E8. Charles A., b 1839
E9. Wm. H., b 1841
E10. Leonora, 1843-1876 mar in Boston, ___
E11. Clarence, H., b 1845, mar 1867 Carthage, ME, Mahala Tucker
E12. Lucy A., b 1848, mar 1864 John Casey, d 1874
D2. Phoebe, 1803-1884, mar 1824 Nathan Holt
E1. Harriet Ann Holt, b 1827
E2. Phoebe Holt, b 1829, mar 1853 Jesse Blanchard
E3. Lucy Isabella, b 1830, mar 1868 Harrison Lake
E4. Abiel, 1832-1846
E5. Aaron Severy, b 1836, mar Lucetta Smith
E6. Farrington, 1845-1846
D3. Charlotte, b 1805 Dixfield, d 1892, mar 1827 Rev. Waldron Morse, Jr., 1803-1878
E1. Roxana Morse, 1828-1896, mar Daniel Safford
E2. Lucy Ann, 1829-1849
E3. Miriam Morse, b 1831, mar Gilbert Allen 1851
F1. Eben Allen, b 1865, mar Fannie Bean
G1. Philip Bean Allen, b 1898, mar Alexandria MacLean
H1. Jean Allen, b 1923, mar Elroy Doughty
I1. Ann Doughty, b 1944, mar 1963 Bernard Alexander
E4. Hannah Morse, b 1833, mar Ira Russell of Lewiston, ME
E5. Silas Curtis Morse, b 1835, mar 1. Abbie Maxwell and 2. Luly Casey, postmaster at S. Carthage, ME
E6. Lorena, b 1837, mar ___ Dwinall
E7. Philona, b 1943?, mar ___ Potter, d 1864
E8. Abbie C., b 1848, res Carthage, ME
D4. Polly, b 1807, mar 1837 Herman Holt, and d 1887. He d 1868. Res Weld, ME
E1. Hannah E. Holt, 1839-1864
E2. Annie D., b 1843, mar 1868 Frank P. Baker
F1. Frank H. Baker, b 1869
F2. Fred H. Baker, b 1873, d.y.
D5. Silas Severy, b 1808 Dixfield, d 1885, Monson, MA, mar 1. 1832 Lucinda M. Walker of Wilton, ME, who d 1835, mar 2. Betsy P. Gould, who d 1856, mar 3. 1857 Clara Holt, who d a widow 1886. Seven chn, 1 by 1st wife.

E1. Melissa, b 1834, mar 1. 1852 George G.B. Adams, who d 1865. She mar 2. 1870 Harvey Kenney, no issue. Chn all mar.
F1. Edgar Silas Adams, d.y.
F2. Walter S. Adams, b 1855
F3. Ida Jessie Adams, b 1857
F4. Lester W. Adams, b 1859
F5. Nellie A. Adams, b 1861
E2. Benjamin Franklin, by 2nd wife, b 1839, mar 1860 Fanny E. CROSS
F1. George Lester, b 1862
F2. Mary Betsy, b 1867
F3. James Enoch, b 1885
E3. George Mellin, b 1842, mar 1866 Martha M. Pease, res Monson, MA
F1. William Gould, b 1867
F2. Edith Louise, b 1869
F3. Frank Edwin, b 1871
F4. Arthur Mellin, b 1878
E4. Elizabeth Ann, b 1846, d 1874
E5. Julia Gould, b 1848, mar 1880 William Wallace Gleason
F1. Frank Hubbard Gleason, b 1881, res Cheyenne, NY
E6. Everett Holt, by 3rd wife, b 1859, res Lynn, MA
E7. Clara Belle, 1864-1886
D6. Rufus, 1810-1890, mar 1. Mary Jackson, who d 1863, and 2 Mrs. Emmeline B. Kendall, who d 1876
D7. Alden, 1812-1814
D8. John T., b 1814 Dixfield, ME, mar Mary P. Gould of Wilton, ME. Res Dixfield, but d Springfield, MA 1887, she d 1865. He was deputy sheriff, selectman, etc. Two daus d.y.
E1. Emery F., b 1843, res Boston, mar, a dau
E2. James E., b 1845, mar 1870 Mary L. Newman of Bangor, ME, res Springfield, MA. No issue given.
E3. Helen J., b 1847, mar Isaac Hancock, res Boston, MA, 2 sons
E4. Lucy A., b 1849, mar W.H. Boulter, res West Buxton, ME. Two sons and 1 dau living.
E5. John E., b 1852
D9. Charles, by 2nd wife, 1818-1834
D10. Clarinda P., 1820-1892, mar 1840 Frederic P. Butterfield of Wilton, ME
E1. Celestia L. Butterfield, d 1863
E2. Clara Butterfield, 1845-1848
E3. Frederic H. Butterfield, b 1850, mar 1874 Nanna M. Rollins of Hopkinton, NH. Fred. supervisor of music, New Bedford, MA.
F1. Walter H. Butterfield, b 1875
F2. Geo. Butterfield, b 1886
E4. Gideon P. Butterfield, b 1852, mar 1874 Mable J. Smith of Dixfield, ME and was postmaster there
F1. Celestia M., b 1875
F2. Charles A. Butterfield, b1876
F3. Lillian Butterfield, b 1880
F4. Ethel Butterfield, b 1881
F5. Fred, b 1885, d.y.
E5. Clara E. Butterfield, b1856
E6. Edith A. Butterfield, b1860
D11. Alden B., b 1823, mar Rosella Richmond, d 1883, 2 chn
D12. Cyrus M., b 1831 Dixfield, ME, mar 1857 Delona Eastman of Canton, ME, who d 1878. He settled Danforth, ILL, and later in Glenada, ORE
E1. Ernest, b 1859, attorney, Chicago, ILL
E2. Walter, 1861-1865
E3. Lettie Butterfield, b 1865
E4. Drew, b 1868
E5. Delona, b 1873
C10. Archibald, b 1773 Sutton, ME, mar 1805 Olive Holman of Petersham, b 1784, res Dixfield, ME. He d 1856, she d 1882.
D1. Willard, 1805-1870, mar 1. Sarah Reed and 2. Joanna Hiscock.
E1. Eben
E2. Leonard
D2. Moses Holman, 1807-1810
D3. Jones, b 1808, d.y.
D4. Sallie, 1809-1840
D5. Betsey, b 1812
D6. Anna, b 1815, mar Daniel Stimson of Weston, MA

E1. Daniel Munroe Stimson E2. Marshall O. Stimson
E3. Susan Anna Stimson, mar, res Auburndale, MA
D7. Joel, 1817-1841 D9. Harrison, b 1821, d.y.
D8. Daniel, 1819-1886
D10. Moses, b 1823, mar Margaret J. Baxter of Boston, MA. Moses a realtor, res Stockton, CA. Other chn d.y.
E1. Fred Albert E2. Frank Warren E3. Annie L. E4. Will
D11. Solomon, b 1825, mar 1850 Carrie P. Babb, res Boston, MA
E1. Elmer, 1852-1872 E3. Henry F., 1855-1858
E2. Clarence E., 1853-1867
E4. Leon F., b 1860, mar 1888 Georgie Annie Hixson of Boston, MA
F1. Vera, b 1889, d.y. F2. Leila Perrin, b 1891
E5. Lillian V., b 1861
E6. Melvin L., b 1863, mar 1884 Mina Howard
F1. Enid May, b 1887 F2. a son, b 1890
D12. Warren, b 1827 D13. Matilda, b 1829, unmar
D14. Lucinda, b 1831, mar 1854 Henry P. Newton of Boston, MA, b 1829, d 1886
E1. Lilla Eva Newton, 1855-1856
E2. Olive M. Newton, b 1860, mar, res Buffalo, NY
E3. Lucia Viola Newton, 1862-1863 E4. George H., b 1867, d.y.
C11. Samuel, b 1775, mar Mercy Tucker of Dixfield, ME
D1. Lydia D2. Phoebe, mar ___ Cook, settled Norridgewock, ME
D3. Jonas, mar Rebecca Green of Wilton, 2 chn: Zilpha and Asa
D4. Galen, mar Mary Green of Wilton, and settled Dixfield, ME
E1. Mary E2. Amanda E3. Belle E4. Alonzo E5. Nathan E6. Laman
D5. Ruth D6. Shepherd, unmar
D7. Naomi, mar Ransom Green of Wilton, settled Carthage, ME, dau Amanda
D8. Amanda, mar Rev. David Allen, settled at Wilton
E1. Mary Allen E2. Mercy Allen
C12. Lydia, 1777-1792
B8. Thomas, b 1737, d in the French War, 1759. The will of a Thomas Severy of Sutton was proved 1759.
A3. Mary ?, who mar Jonathan Moulton
A4. James, who d ca 1722/23, at about age 21, unmar

Also given in the Syvret Genealogy, pp. 224-227 are many persons of the Scivery, Severy, Savory, Seavory, etc. surnames, which are not included in the charts, but at least some of them belong to the C.I. fams. The following are included here, as they seemed to have mar into other C.I. fams. Please see the Genealogy for many other names.

SEAVERY, SEVERIT, SCIVERY, etc. CAUTION: TRIAL CHARTS.

SEVERY, Andrew and Mary, res MRB
A1. Martha, b 1683 A2. Mary, b 1685 A3. Daniel, b 1693
A4. Andrew, b 1695, mar Mary Pittman, res MRB
B1. Andrew, bp 1724 B3. Mary, bp 1728
B2. Nicholas, bp 1726 B4. Pheebe, bp 1730
A5. Gregory, twin, b 1697 A7. Elizabeth, b 1699 A9. a dau, b 1707
A6. Phoebe, twin, b 1697 A8. a dau, b 1704

SCIVERY, Clement, mar Hannah Dodd, res 1758 MRB
A1. Peter, bp 1759 A2. Clement, bp 1761, d.y.
A3. Clement again, bp 1763, mar Sarah FREETO, qv, 1787, res MRB, there in 1790 with fam of 3
B1. Clement, bp 1787, mar Martha Doliber 1808
C1. Francis Doliber, bp 1808
B2. Sarah, bp 1791 B4. Hannah, bp 1797 B6. Mary, bp 1803
B3. Peter, bp 1794 B5. John Walpee (VALPY, qv) bp 1800

SEIVRE, Deliverance, res MRB, had ch Hannah, bp 1704.
SAVORY, Elizabeth, mar 1708 John ROUNDY in MRB. See ROUNDY.
SEIVRY, Elizabeth, had a number of chn in MRB ca 1700, 1st 5chn bp1699
A1. Deborah A4. Elizabeth
A2. Deliverance A5. Thomas
A3. Elenor A6. Mary, bp1701. Did she mar Henry Darling Jr., 1719?
SAVERY, Gregory of MRB, mar Mary Allen 1725, Gloucester, MA
A1. Mary, bp 1726 A3. Martha, b 1731 A5. Daniel, b 1742
A2. Phoebe, b 1729 A4. Peter, b 1734, poss mar Ann Glover 1755?
SAVERY, Hannah, mar Michael CORBETT 1791, MRB.
SEVERET, Harrison H., mar Dorcas McBride, b 1822 OH, d 1905. (OH. GEN. SOC. BULL., 1968)
SIVRET, James, from J, mar Catharine McNeil at Boston 1797, who d 1805. James d 1806, age 35, in Boston, MA. (TINGLEY GEN.)
A1. James WILLIAMS Sivret, b 1798 A3. Katharine Louisa, 1801-1802
A2. Charles MALLET? Sivret, 1800-1802
SIVRET, James above had bros: Philip and George, and a sister, Elizabeth. Not known to compiler if they res U.S. or J.
SAVERY, John, mar 1708 Hannah GROE (LE GROS?) in MRB.
SEAVERY, Joseph, b 1767?, mar Sarah Bradshaw of MRB 1798, he d 1840.
A1. Sarah, bp 1798
A2. Benjamin, 1801-1837, mar 1827 Rebecca HAMMOND, qv, res MRB
B1. Benjamin, bp 1830 B3. Rebecca Jane, bp 1835, d age 8
B2. Joseph, bp 1834 B4. John HAMMOND, bp 1837
A3. Joseph, bp 1803, d 1875, age 71? A5. John, bp 1807
A4. William, bp 1805 A6. Peter, bp 1811
SEAVERY, Joseph, mar Mary D. WHITE 1829 MRB. Was she the Mary who d 1876 at age 70?
A1. William Green, bp 1832, twin? A4. Elias White, bp 1837
A2. Joseph Franklin, bp 1832, twin? A5. Mary Greeley, bp 1842, "very sick"
A3. Elizabeth Devereux, bp 1835
SEVERY, Joseph, a cordwainer, mar Mary ___, same as Joseph above?
A1. Benjamin T., b 1844
SEVERETT, SYVRET, Capt. Philip of J, mar Joanna, widow of ___ Jose, no issue. Joanna retired to J, d 1691, Philip d 1689 Portsmouth ?, NH. (Noyes)
SEVERY, Peter, mar Mary Tucker?, 1767, MRB.
A1. Mary, bp 1768 A2. Sarah Eliz., bp 1770 A3. ch, bp 1782
SEVERY, Peter, mar 1836 Mary SIMONDS?, res MRB.
A1. Benjamin, 1841-1845 A3. a dau, b 1845
A2. Peter, b 1843 A4. Joseph, b 1847
SEVEREY, Samuel, mar 1728 Mary ANDREWS, MRB.
A1. Philip, bp 1729 A4. Elizabeth, bp 1731, poss mar John CASWELL, 1767, MRB?
A2. William, bp 1729 A5. Mary D., bp 1733
A3. Thomas, bp 1729 A6. Michael?, bp 1731
SEVERY, Thomas and Sarah, res MRB, was he son of Samuel, bp 1727?
A1. Sarah, bp 1753 A2. Thomas, bp 1756 A3. Sarah, bp 1758
SEVERY, Thomas and Elizabeth, res MRB.
A1. Mary, b 1704 A2. Hannah, b 1705 A3. Samuel, b 1707
SAVORY, William and Lydia, res Andover, MA. OUTC.
A1. Mary, b 1759 A2. Jenny, b 1760, mar 1782?, Caesar Freeman
SEVERY, Wm. and Ruth, res Oxford, MA.
A1. Freeman, b 1827 A2. Adeline, b 1829 A3. Willard

A small sample of the many Severy, etc. persons in MRB in 1700s and 1800s follows. See VRS and WRCIC for more data, also MASS libraries.
SEVERY, Elizabeth, mar John PICKETT, qv, both of MRB, 1721.

SEVERY, Sarah, mar W.D. HAMMOND of MRB 1821.
SEAVERY, Elizabeth, mar John CASWELL, qv, 1767, MRB.
SEAVERY, Susannah, mar Richard GROSS, qv, 1719, MRB.
SEVERY, Hannah, mar Michael CORBETT, 1791, MRB.
SCIVERY, John, mar Eliz. FABINS, both of MRB, 1732.
SEVERY, Mary, mar John WEBER, 1758, MRB. See WEBBER.
SIVERET, Mathew, d 1745 MRB, from J.
SEVERY, Nicholas, res MRB 1790 with fam of 3. (Census)
SEWARD, in Grouville, J 1749, early in Castel, G. Noted in early colonies, but OUTC.
SEWARD, Philip, a J privateer capt. 1756/57. A fam in NH had C.I. connections.
SEWARD, William, of J, was Sheriff of Southampton, England 1628.
SEWARD, Ebenezer, from C.I.?, in Portsmouth, NH with wife ___. (Noyes) OUTC.
A1. Ebenezer, bp 1738 A3. Benj., bp 1741/2
A2. Samuel, bp 1739/40 A4. Thomas, bp 1746
SEWARD, Elizabeth, mar in Portsmouth, NH 1726/27, Geo. Huntress, son of George. (Noyes) OUTC.
SEWARD, Manuel and Mary, res MRB. Poss Eliz. below as 2nd wife? OUTC.
A1. Manuel, bp 1790 A2. Betsy, bp 1797 A3. John, bp1802, posthumous
SEWARD, George, in Portsmouth, NY 1729, mar Margaret PENDEXTER, qv. He d 1759, a boat builder.
SEWARD, Henry, mar 1780 Susanna BATTEN, widow of Josiah BEADLE, mariner, who d 1775. Susanna d 1817, age 78. (BEADLE FAM)
SEWARD, John, to Boston from GB before 1716, poss from C.I.?, mar Anna REED 1716 (int). (NEHGS, vol. 28; Bolton) OUTC.
SEWELL. Curr in J, noted in colonies.
SEWELL, Stephen, mar ___? OUTC. (Essex Coll, vols 2,3) TRIAL CHART.
A1. Michell, eldest son mar 1. 1729 Mary CABOT, qv, and 2. Eliz. PRICE 1743 A2. Margaret, b 1687. Other chn?
SHARP. In G 1600s, an English surname.
SHARP, ___, one of three kidnapped boys taken from J or G to New London, CT, late 1600s. See also BISHOP and BISSON. SHARP curr G and J. See FALLEY, another kidnapped boy.
SHARP, John, arrived in Boston on ship MARBLEHEAD from Holland. (Whitmore)
SHARPE, John, mar Ann ROLLAND 1806 Boston. Other Sharps in Boston. OUTC
SHARP, James, mar Dorcas SEELY 1696 Boston, OUTC. See HIST OF BARNARD VT.
SHARROCK. This fam assoc with Guernsey Island fams in GCO. OUTC.
SHARROCK, Mary, mar Samuel SAYRE, from G?, 1828 in Guernsey Co., OH.
SHAYER. From St. Peter Port, G to NY and CA before 1874. Cf SOHIER. SHAYER curr G. One man in fam mar Emma HACKER. Henry SHAYER rem to San Francisco, CA. A girl and boy rem to Eastern U.S. Another bro settled San Jose, CA. (Danette Barksdale, San Mateo, CA)
SHELTON. Curr G. Occurs often in connection with C.I. fams. Not researched.
SHELTON, Rachel, b ca 1814 St. Laurens, J, mar John MARETT, qv, a dau Mary Ann, b MA?
SHELTON, Elizabeth, 1693-1758, mar 1717 Stratford, CT, Capt. Nicholas MASTERS, b 1688 G, d 1756 Woodbury, CT. She was dau of Daniel Shelton and Elizabeth Welles. OUTC.
SHEPHERD, SHEPPARD. Curr G and J. Several from G to North America.
SHEPHERD. Noted in Salem, MA 1790. OUTC.
SHEPHERD, Dr. J.S., from G, rem ca 1860 to Racine, WI, then to Placerville, CA.
SHEPHERD, Laura M., from G?, mar James Flick in WI 1875. Cf FLOHIC, a

G surname.

SHEPHERD, Geo. F., from G to Racine, WI, mar Martha V. FLEURE in G 1856. Geo. d of wounds rec'd in US Civil War 1865, no issue. There is a reel of film in WI State HIST. ARCHIVES, at Madison, WI, which contains about a hundred pcs. of info on the life of Geo. and his wife, who came from G and settled in WI. (Mrs. Harry Friestad, Stevens Point, WI)

SHERRARD. This is apparently a Hug fam from France, settled in Ireland. Wm. SHERRARD, Sr., b Ireland 1788, son of parents also b Ireland, Co. Derry, mar Mary Bogle, b 1792, in Ireland. They emigrated to G where several chn were born. They rem 1824 to Adams Twp., Guernsey Co., OH. Wm. d 1862 and his wife several years earlier, 9 chn. (Williams; Cambridge Library; Conner-Eynon)

A1. Mary Ann, b 1809 G, mar John OGIER, qv.

A2. Isabel, mar Nicholas PRIAULX, qv.

A3. William, b 1826, d.y.

A4. Anna, b 1831, d 1905, not verified

A5. Sarah Jane, b 1832, d 1852, not verified

SHERRARD, James, b 1789 G, d GCO 1876.

SHERRARD, Elizabeth, mar John T. PRIAULX, qv.

SHERRARD. Others in GCO, not verified as desc of William's fam.

SHOOSMITH. In J 1704-1796, one a Privateer captain. (A. John Jean, Jer.)

SHORT. Curr in G and J, old in G.

SHORT, C.F. and wife, from G to CA 1900s. (Guernsey PRESS, 1966)

SHORT. From G to Canada. (L.F. Guy, Orono, ONT)

SILK. Ship owners of J, 1800s. (A. John Jean, Jersey)

SILVESTER. In J 1299, curr G and J.

SILVESTER, Honore arrived in Boston 1760s on sloop, ADVENTURE, from Nfld., a mariner. (Whitmore) OUTC.

SYLVESTER, SILVESTER. Noted in colonies, poss 1 or 2 from the C.I.?

SIMON. In G 1331. SIMON in Grouville and St. Clement, J 1668. In Grouville, St. Peter and St. Clement, J 1749. Curr G and J. Curr research? See CIFHS #8.

SIMON, Arthur ALLEZ, b 1861 G, son of Abraham Simon, b 1818 G, and Elizabeth ALLEZ BLONDEL. Abraham was a son of Abraham and Judith (DUMARESQ) SIMON. Ancestry of this fam charted by contributor. (Capt. George Shepherd, Mercer Island, WA)

A1. Juanita, b ca 1895 G. She mar ___ BARTO.

B1. Thomas Barto

C1. Bruce Barto, mar Sandra Shepherd, dau of George S. and Mary Hannah Shepherd

D1. Jeremy Barto, b 1979 Anchorage, Alaska

SIMON, George, b 1845 St. Brelade, J, mar there 1872 Louisa BERTRAM, qv, dau of Amice BERTRAM and Elizabeth LE NEVEU. George was son of Charles, b 1804, and Anne Elizabeth (LE VESLET) SIMON. Rem to BC ca 1890, stopped first in Santa Cruz, CA. Bur 1938 Victoria, BC. Louisa b 1849, d 1926, bur Vancouver, BC. (Noreen Annett, Victoria, BC)

A1. George Sydney, b 1873 St. Heliers, J, mar 1904 Martha Florence Raines

A2. Julius Bertram, b 1876, mar 1907 Catherine Hendrika Funke

A3. Lewis Reginald, b 1878, mar 1913 Ida Eliza Raines, d 1964

A4. Francois Ralph, b1882 St. Peter, J mar Mary Laurel Simmons or Simon?

A5. Gerald Lionel, b 1883 St. Peter, J, mar 1911 Bertha Augusta Fackler. He d 1940.

A6. Louise Marie Simon, b 1889, d.y.

A7. Louise Margaret Simon, b 1889, twin, d.y.

SIMON, James, res Guernsey Co., OH 1820. Census shows 6 males and 6 females in fam. OUTC.

SIMON, John, b G, rem to Fulton Co., OH, near Delta, mid 1800s. "My grandfather made a quick decision to emigrate...1885. SIMON was a distant cousin of my grandmother's...was asked by a Guernsey man to stop off in OH and give some silver spoons, an inheritance, to a John Simon living in Fulton Co., OH. My grandfather gave his promise." A dau Abby, unmar. (Dorothy Harrison, Louisville, KY)

SIMON and BOURGAIZE. Two Guernsey men settled in Gaspe. (Leona Roy, Montreal, QUE)

SIMON, Nicholas, of G, rec'd by William COHU?, and Henry QUERIPEL, 1833 NYCity. (NY NATURALIZATIONS, by Scott)

SIMON, Rachel, mar Elias ROSE in Gaspe, QUE. See ROSE.

SIMON, Simon Peter, b 1792 G, d Indian Cove, Gaspe, QUE 1878, mar Margaret LE MESURIER, 1790-1841. Desc of this fam. (Shirley O'Neil, Newport Beach, CA)

A1. William P. Simon

SIMON, Sophie, wife of John LANGLOIS qv, from G to Racine WI 1856, sons.

SIMONET, Capt. of the ship UNION, which traded between Jersey Island and VA 1783.

SINCROSS, SINECROSS, either DE STE. CROIX or STE. CROIX of C.I. DE STE. CROIX in G 1200s. ST. CROIX in J 1214, from a place in Cotentin, Normandy. In J 1668 and 1749.

SIGNCROSS, Elizabeth, mar 1767 Ebenezer Graves, in MRB.

SINCROSS, Elizabeth, res MRB, a dau Elizabeth bp 1728.

SIGNCROSS, George, mar 1761 MRB, Deborah Sandin.

SIGNCROSS, Joseph, mar Elizabeth Collier 1727, res MRB, and mar 2. Sarah LA CROIX of J? or G?, 1732.

A1. Joseph, bp 1730 A3. Michael, son of Jos. & Sarah, d 1736 MRB
A2. George, bp 1733 A4. Sarah, bp 1740/41 A5. Elizabeth, bp 1744
A6. Hannah, bp 1747, mar 1766 John HOOPER, qv, bp MRB 1744. John was a fisherman, and d before 1772, when his widow was appointed to admin. the estate. (HOOPER GEN.)
B1. George Signcross HOOPER, bp 1766 B2. John HOOPER, bp 1768
B3. Hannah Hooper, bp 1770, mar 1790 Joseph GREGORY, poss from J?
C1. John Hooper Gregory, bp 1793
C2. Joseph Gregory, bp 1793
C3. Thomas Gregory, bp 1793
C4. Ambrose Martin Gregory, bp 1799
C5. Hannah Gregory, bp 1802, mar Nathaniel Brimblecomb, Jr.
C6. Mary Ellis Gregory, bp 1805

SIGNCROSS, Sarah, mar Francis CANNEL 1760 MRB. Note that CANNET was in J 1607.

SINNETT, SENNETT. Old in J. Also SINNATT.

SINNIT, John, mar 1755 Mary BELSHI, BAILHACHE?, of Mancester, MA. Poss that both came from C.I.

SENNET, James, in Blandford, MA 1790, with fam of 4. (Census)

SENNET, William, in Manchester, MA 1790, with fam of 4. (Census)

SINNOTT, SYNOTT. Noted in petition of QUE City residents 1838. (LOST IN CANADA, August 1981) This list included many C.I. surnames.

SIVRET, see SEVERY, and SYVRET. SIVRET in St. Lawrence, J 1788.

SKINNER. Curr G and J. SKELTON, chart in CI COLLECTION.

Compiler has gathered some SKINNER-RUSH data in the hope that as time went on the situation would clarify. This has not happened. The fam is so large, and there are so many confusing links, that the compiler is not even sure this fam should be included in the book! Consider these facts:

1. There were at least two, not one, fams of Skinners in early New Jersey, and it is difficult to be sure that the right one is being charted.
2. SKINNER is not in itself an old C.I. surname, insofar as the compiler was able to discover. There may be more info in the Islands. Two

origins are possible:

a. The fam is English, but owing to allegiance to the Royal Family during the Interregnum, close association was held with the Carterets and the Islands, during which time privateering was engaged in.

b. The fam may be LE CUIROT, which means SKINNER. LE CUIROT is just mentioned in Stevens' LIST OF OLD JERSEY SURNAMES, with no dates given.

3. "Piracy was known in the islands from time immemorial. Pirates, and privateers on the verge of piracy, named Wake, Baudains, SKINNER, Smith, Blaize, Picquet, Amy and so on were fiercely driven back to the Channel Islands by British forces in 1645." (ENGLISH SEA POWER IN THE EARLY TUDOR PERIODS, by Fowler, and GOLDEN AGE OF PIRACY, by Rankin) We see here that SKINNER was a known privateer, and that he was connected with the Channel Islands. Whether this was the same one, or of the same fam, as the one brought to Elizabethtown, NJ by Carteret, there is no record. We do know that the CARTERET fam was deeply involved in returning the King of England to his throne, and to harassing the ships of the Interregnum anywhere and everywhere. Perhaps erstwhile privateers may have found it most expedient to remove themselves and fams from the continuing wrath of the British Government against these bold Islanders.

4. One researcher, Roland Rossiter, says that Richard Skinner was Lord Carteret's valet, and Susanna POULAIN, his wife, was Lady Carteret's personal maid. This is difficult to equate with a decade spent in depradations against the British government! All we really know is that they did come to America, in a Carteret ship, PHILIP, in 1665.

CAUTION: TRIAL CHART. See sources and WRCIC.

(Hatfield; Monette; DAR PATRIOT INDEX; Holcomb; RUSH GEN: RUSH AND SKINNER FAMS OF LOWER TURKEYFOOT pamphlet; SKINNER GEN, by L.G. Holcomb, not seen by compiler; SALT LAKE CITY RECORDS; Nathalie Averett, Mesa, AZ; Ethel Albin, Sabetha, KS; Becky Skinner, Alexandria, IND; Sylvester Rush; Rosalee Hartinger; Harry S. Rush, Fargo, ND; Corrine Diller, Houston, TX; Louise Wyly, Col. Spgs., COL; Sharon Leon, Spokane, WA; Mrs. Amy Wise, Columbus, OH; Roland Rossiter, Harrison, ARK; Joni Wolfson, Seneca Falls, NY)

SKINNER, Richard, b Isle of Wight or J? or England?, said to be Lord Carteret's valet in J. From J 1665 on ship PHILIP with Carteret to Elizabethtown, NJ. See NJ Section. Res later in Woodbridge, NJ, mar 1666 Susannah POULAIN, qv. Four? chn: John, Richard, Francis, b 1672?, mar 1702?, and Ann, b 1675, rec'd into CH at Woodbridge, NJ 1708. Poss unmar?

A1. John, b 1667 England?, d 1725, mar Ann ___? (Mary Burt, Ks. City

B1. John, mar Elizabeth Cutter, dau of Major Richard Cutter and Mary Pike, from Newcastle-on-Tyne, England, at least 4 chn

C1. Ann C2. Hannah C3. Esther, mar Daniel MARSH C4. Elizabeth

B2. Daniel B4. Benjamin B6. Mary

B3. Richard B5. Ann B7. Catte/Catherine

A2. Deacon Richard, b 1664/1667/1670?, mar Ann Wright, dau of Robert, mar 2. Sarah Moore, dau of Mathew Moore, Jr. and Sarah Parker Moore. CAUTION: Wives not verified.

B1. Mathew, b 1697 Woodbridge, NJ B2. Sarah, b 1700 Woodbridge, NJ

B3. Jonathan, b 1703 Woodbridge, NJ

B4. Rachel?, not verified, mar Oliver Drake

C1. Mary Drake 1734-1805 mar Samuel SKINNER sone of Nathaniel & Elizb.

C2. George Drake, b 1735, d 1825 Harrison Co., VA, mar 1761 Susannah Collier, 1743-1823.

D1. Agnes Drake, b 1769 NJ, d 1853 VA, mar 1785 Isaac Shinn, 1760-1844

D2. James Drake
D3. Catherine Drake
D4. Rachel Drake
D5. Hannah Drake
D6. John Drake

D7. Mary Drake, b 1764 NJ, d 1856 Perry Co., OH, mar Bedford Co., PA Samuel SKINNER, b ca 1756, d 1825 Perry Co., OH, son of Reuben and Sarah (Higgins) SKINNER. (More research on this family being done by Ethel Albin.)

C3. Josepha Drake

C4. Oliver Drake, b 1745, mar Frankie SKINNER, dau of Nathaniel and Elizabeth (King?) SKINNER

D1. Jonathan Drake
D2. Hannah Drake
D3. David Drake

B5. Richard?

B6. Rev. Nathaniel, b 1706 Woodbridge, NJ, d 1801 Turkeyfoot Twp., Somerset Co., PA. Mar Elizabeth King, Elizabeth Harned, or Elizabeth (King) Harned? Nathaniel rem ca 1774 from Woodbridge to Somerset Co., PA with some 20 other fams. He took with him sons Samuel, Reuben, Richard, Robert and James. Mr. Rossiter gives him other chn such as John, Franky, etc. Richard, one son, rem toward Philadelphia. John rem elsewhere. The daus, Franky, Rachel and two others, also came to Turkeyfoot, PA.

C1. Samuel Sr., b 1728 or 1734 Woodbridge, NJ, mar Mary Drake Sr., dau of ___ Drake, and aunt to the other Mary Drake, below. Mary was b 1734 and d 1805, 9 chn? Rossiter lists chn as: John, Catharine, Matilda, Nathaniel, William, Phebe, and Samuel, who was b 1757, d 1840. (Ethel Albin, Sabetta, KS)

D1. John
D2. Catharine Matilda
D3. Nathaniel
D4. William
D5. Phebe

D6. Samuel Jr., b 1755/57, mar 1781 Bedford Co., PA, Agnes Critchfield, b 1757/60, NJ, d 1830 New Lexington, OH.

E1. Rachel, b 1781 Lower Turkeyfoot, PA, d 1876, mar 1799 Nathaniel Rush. See RUSH GEN and Lower Turkeyfoot booklet. This was only one of <u>many</u> Rush-Skinner marriages. Nine chn.

E2. James, 1783-1834, mar Hannah ___, desc res Circleville, OH

E3. John S., b 1785, mar Catherine

E4. Agnes, 1789-1844, mar Isaiah Rush, 1809, 10 chn. See RUSH GEN and WRCIC.

E5. Susie, b 1790, mar Jonathan Colburn, desc in Fairfield Co., OH

E6. Catherine Matilda, 1794-1884, mar Joseph Lanning, who d 1883

F1. David M. Vanburen Lanning, b 1836, d 1903 Logan, OH, mar 1856 Mary Eleanor Powell, b 1839 Perry Co., OH, d 1915, Hawk, Vinton Co., OH

G1. Joseph Leander Lanning, b 1864, mar 1886 Rebecca Jane Bailey, 1856-1940, res Dawson, NEBR

H1. Clara Jane Lanning, b 1893 Kit, Jay Co., IND, d 1973. Mar 1912 Ira Marion Albin, 1889-1976, res Humboldt, NEBR

E7. Samuel Skinner, b 1797, had son Samuel who mar Matilda Rush, a cousin, b 1815

E8. Cornelius (?), b 1801

E9. Polly Skinner, 1808-1891, mar 1828 James Brooks, 7 sons, 3 daus

C2. Reuben, b ca 1736, mar Sarah Higgins, 1739?-1832, bur Hopewell, Perry Co., OH. Sarah left for OH in 1817. He d 1814. One researcher feels Reuben may have been the son of Cortland Skinner, not Nathaniel Skinner.

D1. Mary, b 1761, NJ, d 1826 Ursina, PA (Turkeyfoot), mar 1778 Jacob W. Rush, 1755-1850, son of Wm. Rush and Elizabeth Ream. Jacob mar 2. Ann McNeil. All chn by Mary. See Rush Gen and Turkeyfoot booklet for more on this family.

D2. Nathaniel, b ca 1766, mar Elizabeth? ___, b ca 1765, d 1790. Stone in Jersey Churchyard, PA. He mar 2. Hannah King, bur Bealsville, Belmont Co., OH. Hannah the dau of Philip King, from a Belgian fam.

E1. Amy, b 1786, d 1851, mar Samuel D. Rush, 1788-1871. Both bur Baptish Church yard, New Lexington, OH. He was the son of Stephen and Mary Rush. He bought in Perry Co., OH while res in Fayette Co., PA, 1819, a section of land. When will was probated he had another wife named Priscilla, whom he mar previous to March 17, 1856. See this large fam in Rush data, WRCIC. 12 chn.

E2. Sarah, 1788-1847, mar John Immel, Imel, 1789-1871. According to Mrs. Amy Rugg Wise of Columbus, OH, they are both bur in the Hazelton Cem, Perry Co., OH. In 1836 John Imel acquired the SW section of Saltlick Twp., Perry Co., OH, which in 1862 passed to Samuel Travis. He mar 2. Rosanna ___, who was 40 in the 1850 Census. At that time, two teenagers were living with him, Lydia and Daniel Henderson, and also a Mary E. Helley, age 3, born OH. Seven chn. See WRCIC.

E3. Samuel B., 1789-1853, mar 1817 Elizabeth Hazelton, 1793-1867, dau of John Hazelton, Rev. War Vet. Samuel and Eliz. bur Hazelton Cem, ca 7 miles from New Lexington, above McCuneville, PA. Ten chn. See WRCIC.

E4. Philip, b 1793, d ca 1852, mar Hannah Coon, 1800-1883. Philip was son of 2nd wife, Hannah King. See 8 chn in WRCIC. (Becky Skinner's line.)

E5. Nancy, b 1795, mar George Steward

E6. Mary Phoebe, b 1797, d unmar

E7. Jacob, b 1802, mar Rachel Seals, d Washington Court House, OH.

E8. James K., b 1804, d 1898, mar Elizabeth Jump, 1807-1876, bur Baptish Church Yard, New Lexington, OH, with 3 infant chn. Ten chn. See WRCIC.

E9. Rachel Skinner, 1806-1875, mar 1826 Henry Moore, who d 1891. Seven chn b 1827 to 1844.

E10. Catharine, 1809-1896, mar 1832 Lemuel Moore, 1813-1895. Three chn, desc in Brison Co., IND.

E11. Rhoda, b 1811, mar Utter Moore

E12. Lavinia, 1813-1853, mar Solomon Seal 1836, 1814-1853, 5 chn

E13. William Ohio, 1816-1898, mar Rachel Seal, cousin of Jacob's wife. Rachel d 1885. Eleven chn. See WRCIC.

E14. Charlotte, b 1818, mar David Watson and d Mt. Ephraims, OH

D3. Rev. James, mar 1. Mary, and 2. Eve ___, bur Baptish Church yard, New Lexington, OH. Nine chn.

E1. Mary, 1791-1876, mar John Hyatt, 1790-1850, bur Jersey Church yard, Somerset Co., PA

E2. Sarah, mar Rev. James J. Mitchell

E3. Highly, 1802-1834, mar Wm. Davis, who later mar Highly's sister Rachel, after 1834.

E4. Rachel, mar after 1834, Wm. Davis

E5. Ann, mar Andrew Segar of NY, rem to Adams Co., ILL

F1. Samuel Segar (Harry M. Hyatt, NY City)

E6. Nathaniel, known as Big Nathaniel Skinner, poss the one bur at Bristol, Perry Co., OH

E7. a son, b between 1790 and 1800

E8. Lydia, 1805-1836, mar Isaac BENNET, bur Baptist CH at New Lexington, OH, next to James and wife Mary. Land records indicate there may have been a son, Jonas BENNET.
E9. James?, poss the son of 2nd wife Eve, was in Fayette Co. 1814
D4. Joseph, b ca 1771, d 1798, bur Jersey CHyard, Somerset Co., PA. Chn raised by Joseph's sister, Mrs. Thomas King, who rem to Perry Co., OH ca 1817.
E1. Reuben, b 1793 E2. Hannah, b 1795
D5. Nancy Ann, 1773-1867, mar Thomas King, 1774-1839. No issue, but helped care for 11-12 chn aiding them through school and helping them to get a start in OH. (HIST OF FAIRFIELD AND PERRY COS. MO) Also prob raised the 2 chn of her bro Joseph, who d as a young man. (Mrs. Stella Joyce, De Soto, MO, has copies of the King Bible which gives info from Wm. Harrison Skinner, Bethany, MO)
D6. Samuel, 1778-1863, mar Mary Rush, 1782-1862, rem to PA, bur near New Lexington, OH, later res with a dau in Monmouth, ILL, where they are bur. (Wm. Harrison Skinner, Bethany, MO: Sarah Smith Miller, Seneca, MO)
E1. Henry, mar 1. Adaline Hart, mar 2. ?, and 3. ?
E2. Phebe, 1811-1877, mar 1854 Eli Smith, 1817-1879, both bur Smith Cem, Wroth Co., MO
E3. Jesse Skinner, 1813-1849, mar 1. Esther Talmy Smith, 1816-1845, and 2. ? Jesse and Esther bur New Lexington, OH.
E4. Samuel, 1815-1885, soldier in Mexican War, bur New Lexington OH
E5. Julia Ann, 1818-1853, mar 1847 Eli Smith, 1817-1879, a bro of Esther Talmy Smith above. Julia his 2nd wife, bur New Lexington.
E6. Alva, b 1818, twin?, mar Mary B. Stewart, 1816-1855, res and d New Lexington, OH
E7. Mary Skinner, mar James Law, rem to Monmouth, ILL
E8. Nellie, mar Jonathan Reynolds, a son, single, deranged
E9. Nancy, mar ___ Spencer, sons Ralph and Olson Spencer
E10. Sarah, mar ___ Ross, rem to Monmouth, ILL
E11. Milvilla, b ca 1826, poss unmar in 1850, res Pike Twp., Perry Co., OH E11. Caroline
D7. Phoebe, mar Samuel Hall, who d 1830, a son Joel Hall, 1808-1825
D8. Richard, b ca 1755-1884, d between 1837-1850, Perry Co., OH. Res Fayette Co., PA, Straitsville, OH, d Perry Co., OH before 1841. He mar 1. ?, and 2. after 1820, Rachel Skinner Rush, 1781-1876, widow of Nathaniel Rush, and dau of Samuel Skinner and Mary Drake. She d in Atchison Co., MO.
E1. Thomas Skinner, b ca 1798/1800, d after 1853 in Wapello, IA, mar Elizabeth ___. 4 chn: Rebecca, Samuel, Wm. and Thomas.
E2. Aaron, b ca 1802, d after 1861, bur Bristol, OH, mar Rebecca Ketchum, b 1803, sister of Mary Ketchum, wife of Rev. Reuben Skinner. Reuben said to have been a cousin of Aaron. Fam listed 1850 in Perry Co., OH.
F1. Malinda, b 1823, mar James Hoy, 1817-1900
G1. Alcinda Hoy, 1845-1905, mar John Diller III, 1843-1912, to KS 1870s
H1. John Wm. Diller, 1875-1943, mar Catherine Campbell 1882-1957
I1. John Cleo Diller, b 1917, mar Florence Bentley, b 1920
J1. John Allen Diller, b 1954, mar Corinne Lynn Hanna, b 1954, res Houston, TX
F2.-F8. Alcinda, Richard, Jacob, Harvey, Mary A., Fanny, Sarah E.
F9. Althea?
E3. Richard Jr., mentioned in Deed to lot in Straitsville, OH. Mar 1. ?, mar 2. after 1820, before 1837, Rachel Skinner Rush,

1781-1876, widow of Nathaniel Rush and dau of Samuel Skinner and Mary Drake.

E4. and E5. daus?

D9. Reuben Jr., b ca 1784-94, emigrated to Perry Co., OH with bros, mar Mary Ketchum, b ca 1784, d before 1874. Reuben d 1874. Rem to Salt Lick, Perry Co., OH where they built a log cabin, with no floor except the earth. Later they split puncheons from poplar trees and laid a floor in the cabin. Rem to another log house and then built a hewed log home and barn on the township road which ran through their farm, living there until they d. Reuben was a Baptish preacher at New Lexington, OH, the CH being built in 1847. Reuben also worked as a doctor, undertaker and lawyer! Their crops were corn, wheat, buckwheat, flax, tobacco and truck garden crops. They raised sheep, ducks and geese, spun wool and flax, and made their own clothing. Cooking was done at an open fireplace. The hearth had a stone foundation and the top of the chimney was made of mud and sticks. Reuben lived to 81 yrs. and Mary, 76, bur at New Lexington, OH. (Compiler regrets that source of this data cannot be pinpointed, but thank you!)

E1. Frances, mar Richard Parsons, bur near Portland, IND, 2 chn, Josiah and Stephen Skinner Parsons

E2. Nancy, mar Rudolph Kocher, b ca 1822 PA, bur near Lithopolis, OH, no issue

E3. Andrew, b ca 1826 OH, d after 1889, unmar, bur near Portland IND

E4. Jacob, b ca 1828, mar Sarah/Sally Paxton, 3 chn, bur Lithopolis, OH. Chn: Wm., Amanda and Mary Lizzie.

E5. Lemuel, b 1830 OH, d 1894, mar 1854 Matilda Brooks, 1831-1902, dau of James Brooks and Polly SKINNER. Bur Whipstown, OH. Lemuel in Civil War. Chn: Andrew, Useba, James, Thomas & Ezra.

E6. Martha A., b ca 1833 OH, mar Richard CAIN, bur Whipstown, OH

E7. Reuben, b ca 1836 OH, mar Margaret Donelly E8. Joseph, d.y.

C3. Robert, b 1738 Woodbridge, NJ, d 1823, mar Mary Willetts

C4. James? and a Richard? C5 ?

C6. John, b ca 1740, d 1832, mar Rebecca, poss R. Todd?, who d 1824. He rem from NJ to Somerset Co., PA, then to Perry Co., OH. Both bur Hopewell CHyard. Either John or his son John voted in Perry Co., OH 1817, did road work, and was a blacksmith in Somerset, OH 1820-1825. The Jersey CH in PA granted a letter of dismissal to OH.

D1. Robert, b 1772/23, d 1856, mar Elizabeth Spencer, 1776-1850, res near Hopewell CH. Eliz dau of James Spencer, who was one of the earliest settlers in Lower Turkeyfoot Twp., Somerset Co., PA, ca 1764. James was a Rev. War soldier and is bur Hopewell CHyard. It is prob that Robert Skinner was b in NJ, went to Maryland with his father, then to Lower Turkeyfoot Twp., PA. About 1809 rem to Perry Co., OH. In 1816 he was in Reading Twp., Perry Co.

E1. Rebecca, b 1797, mar Jerry Bartholomew, 5 chn, see WRCIC.

E2. Rhoda, b 1799, mar John Fickle or Fickel, 11 chn, see WRCIC.

E3. Olive, 1802-1898, mar 1825 James McClure, 1798-1859

E4. Mary, 1807-1846, unmar

E5. William H., 1809-1850, mar Matilda Debolt, bur Perry Co., OH

E6. Eleanor, 1812-1851, mar Wm. Yost, 2 chn: John and Martha Yost

E7. John, 1816-1899, mar Rachel Johnson, b 1818?, d 1905, bur Perry Co., OH

E8. Rhahamah, called Amy, 1819-1886, mar another William Yost

E9. Rachel, mar ___ Bartholomew

D2. William, 1776-1856, mar ca 1800 Mary ___, 1793-1868, in 1806 they were living in Thorn Twp., Perry Co., OH, bur Hopewell Baptist Church yard.

E1. William T., 1821-1885, mar Catharine Olinger, 1831-1911

E2. George

E3. Phoebe, 1827-1892, mar Noah Funderberg, 1827-1905, both bur Hopewell

E4. Smith G., mar Belinda ___ E5. Sarah Ann, mar ___ Keyes

E6. Catharine, mar William WALTERS, lived and d in IND

E7. Jane, mar Oben Dick, res New Lexington, OH. She d by 1868.

E8. Reuel, mar Mary ___, a son, Steward Skinner E9. Asa

D3. Cornelius, res Hopewell Twp., Perry Co., OH 1817

D4. John D5. Elizabeth, mar ___ GREEN D6. Rebecca, mar ___ Bard?

D7. George, mar before 1800, and listed with one dau in the Census of 1800, in Somerset Co., PA, in Perry Co., OH 1817

D8. Ellen, mar ___ Trout or Trent

D9. Jane, 1793-1826, mar Col. Samuel Goodin

E1. Nancy Goodin, mar 1830 John Backer. Mrs. Emma Hickman, res Newark, OH ca 1885 was a desc. Some confusion about the chn of Jane's fam.

E2. ? Rebecca Goodin, 1813-1868, mar Jehu B. Jones, 1814-1900, res near Somerset, OH, 4 chn: David, George, Mary & Fidelia Jones

E3. Julia Goodin, unmar

D10. Nancy, mar ___ Goodin? or Gordon? D11. Rhoda, mar ___ Black

D12. Frances, b 1796 PA, d after 1870, last ch. Mar 1. Isaac Sellers and 2. Jacob Rutledge, b ca 1805, d after 1870. Res Perry Co., OH till 1864, then rem to Sharpsburg, Taylor Co., IA. Res there 1870, Marshall Twp., with dau Frances M., b 1845 IA.

E1. Rebecca Sellers, mar ___ Smith, had chn Asa and Frances

E2. John Rutledge, b 1835?, mar Mary Carlisle, rem to Taylor Co IA

E3. William Rutledge, b 1836 OH, mar Louise Biggs, b 1835 OH, rem to IA

E4. Elizabeth Rutledge, b 1831 OH, d unmar Taylor Co., IA

E5. Abraham Rutledge, b 1865 Taylor Co., IA

E6. Frances M. Rutledge, b 1845 IA, d after 1870

D13. Poss also a son named James?

C7. Frankie?, b 1742, mar 1770 Oliver Drake, b 1745, son of Oliver and Rachel (SKINNER) Drake, 3 chn: Jonathan, Hannah & David Drake

C8. Other chn?

A3. Frances A4. Ann

SKINNER, Eli. This Skinner has been researched by Louise Wyly, Col. Spgs., COL; Sharon Leon, Spokane, WA; and Ethel Albin, Sabetha, KS. At time of publication, proof was still lacking that Eli was a desc of Richard Skinner. It is still poss that he was another Skinner from the Channel Islands, or a C.I. fam, and that he headed for Perry Co., OH, knowing that there were Skinners settled there. Eli was a fairly common name in the C.I. in 1700s. Although there is a question on his ancestry, Eli is included here.

SKINNER, Eli, b prob ca 1810-1820, where?, mar 1837 Perry Co., OH, Emeline/Emma Allen (Milla?), b ca 1819 VA. Her mother lived to be 105/106, and her sister may have been Nancy Rush. Emma d age 86, Baptist. Emma mar 2. Reuben Spurgeon, whose mother may have been a Corder or Carder. 4 chn, (Ethel Albin, Sabetha, KS; Louise Wyly, COL; Sharon Leon, Spokane, WA)

A1. Sarah Catherine, b 1838 Perry Co., OH, d 1937 Belfry, Carbon Co., MT. She mar 1864 James McIntyre, 6 chn. James bur Honey Grove Cem, near Grant City, Worth Co., MO. He may have been b Delaware.

B1. Eunice, b 1865 Grant City, MO, d 1968, mar 1894 Wesley WALTER, bur Belfry, Carbon Co., MT. (Eunice McIntyre)
B2. Eli, b Grant City, MO, d 1955. Mar Flora SKINNER, who d 1951 Columbus, MT. (Eli McIntyre)
B3. Idaleen, b Grant City, called "Kit"?, mar Ross Roudebush
B4. Thomas, b Grant City, d.y. (Thomas McIntyre)
B5. James, mar Audrey Elliot B6. Percival, d 1915, unmar
A2. Mary or Margaret, b before 1840?, mar 1865 Perry Co., OH, Samuel Lanning. A son, William Lanning, res Columbus, OH 1940s. Joseph Leander Lanning, res Dawson, NEB, corresponded with Nellie (Cramer) Woolsey of CAL, poss another desc, in 1930s.
A3. Richard A., b 1841 near Straitsville, Perry Co., OH, took middle initial "A" during the Civil War to keep records clear. He d 1931 near Bridgeport, NEB, bur Redington, NEB. Mar 1868 Amy Steith Powell, b 1847 Perry Co., OH, d 1928 near Redington, dau of Moses and Enora (Barnes) Powell. This fam Seventh Day Adventist. Richard a stockman, served in Civil War, 9 chn.
B1. Noah Darlington, 1869-1928, mar 1911 Clara Mae Sickles; he was called DARLEY
B2. Jennie Tempest, b 1870 Straitsville, Perry Co., OH, d 1959. She bur Scotts Bluff, NEB, mar Samuel M. Kelly.
B3. Emma Enory?, 1873-1962, mar Arthur Hermann. She was called "Nora."
B4. Edward Louise, b 1874 Grant City, MO, d 1938, unmar
B5. Laura Belle, b 1876 Redding, IA, called "Belle," d 1957, mar Arthur F. Burnett 1904, 4 chn
B6. Margaret Matilda, b 1880 Grant City, MO, d 1973, mar Charles Spencer Hutchinson
B7. Sarah Eunice Alvaretta, b 1883 Grant City, d 1965, called "Eunice," mar 1900 Bern C. Hutchinson.
B8. Bessie Maude, 1885-1981. She mar 1905 Omer William Smith.
B9. Oca Ona, called "Ona," b 1888 Freeport, NEB, d 1973, mar 1905 Harry Bartling, 2 chn
A4. Eli Morris, b 1845 near Straitsville, OH, d 1925 Glenrock, Converse Co., WY. Mar 1867 Mary Eve Buchman, b 1846 Perry Co., OH, who d 1928 Glenrock, WY. She may have been dau of Jacob? Buchman, pron BUFFMAN. Eight chn.
B1. Flora, Flaura Annie, b 1868 McCuneville, Perry Co., OH, d 1951 Columbus, MT, bur Custer, MT, she mar her 1st cousin Eli McIntyre.
B2. Laura Etta, b 1870 OH, d 1950 Excelsior Springs, Clay Co., MO, mar William Ridge
B3. George Morris, b 1872 OH, d 1961 Columbus, MT, bur Custer, Yellowstone, MT. Mar Mary Miller McNally, no issue.
B4. William Sherman, b 1874 OH, d 1940 Glenrock, WY, mar Rose Masterson
B5. Charles Richard, b 1876 OH, d 1937 Glenrock, mar Cora Hannah Goff
B6. Mary Roseanna, b 1880 McCuneville, OH, d 1979?, mar 1. James Masterson, and 2. Clifford Goff
B7. Olive Grace, b 1883 OH, d 1907 Glenrock, WY, mar John Miller
B8. Lewis Frederick, b 1889 Redington, NEB, d 1975 Thermopolis, WY, mar Eliz. Benjamin.

More data on this fam in OH and elsewhere, in WRCIC, submitted by Sharon Leon, Spokane, WA. More data also in the hands of Marion Jennings of Vassar, MI on desc of a Margaret SKINNER, dau of Richard. OUTC.

SMITH, Susanna, poss a LE FEUVRE?, of J, said to be from Jersey, was mar to David DAVIS, also called DAVISSON, in Lubberland, ME 1688. Davis was apprenticed to John Lang of Portsmouth, NH by court order

1678, and was assigned by Lang to Stephen Jones of Durham, for the trade of cooper. He was killed by Indians 1696. His widow Susan Smith Davis, mar 2. James Durgin in 1697. At least 3 chn by Davis and six by Durgin, poss others? By the 1790 Census, there were 41 Durgin fams in NH. Not all of these were desc of this particular fam. CAUTION: TRIAL CHART. (HIST. OF DURHAM, NH, by Stackpole; Noyes; OLD FAMS OF KITTERY; Elaine Adjutant, Ossipee, NH)

A1. David Davis, mar 1717 Elizabeth Thomas, dau of James and Mary SMITH Thomas. Settled at Packers Falls, and David built a garrison house. Elizabeth was bp 1719 with oldest dau. David was ca 49, 1736, 5 chn.
B1. Hannah, bp 1719 B2. Lydia, bp 1721
B3. Elizabeth, bp 1720, mar Eben Crommett and 2. Joseph DREW. See DREW.
B4. James, bp 1729, mar Elizabeth Durgin 1753
B5. David Davis, bp 1729, mar Elizabeth Crommett, dau of Joshua and Elizabeth (Kenniston) Cormmett. David d 1799. Chn b in the garrison house were:
C1. Mary, b 1750, mar Wentworth Chesley of Newmarket, NH?
C2. Martha Davis, mar Jonathan Stevens, Jr. of Lee, NH?
C3. David Davis, III, bp 1760, mar Hannah Gerrish 1792. David a Rev. soldier, d 1835. Hannah d 1866.
D1. Joseph Davis, b 1793 D2. Timothy G. Davis, 1795-1825
D3. David Davis, IV, b 1799, mar Mrs. Eunice (MESERVE) DEMERITT, widow of Isaac. She was dau of Col. Vincent and Hannah (Crommett) MESERVE, b 1805, d 1880. David d 1882. He served in War of 1812 in Capt. Wm. Wiggins Co., 25th Regt., stationed at Portsmouth, NH.
E1. Timothy Gerrish Davis, b 1827, mar Mary Bartlett, d 1893
E2. Eben MESSERVE Davis, b 1831, mar 1. Martha Bryant and 2. Frances Ann Gove of E. Boston, MA
F1. Edward Davis F3. David Davis F5. Charles Davis
F2. Martha Davis F4. Justina Davis
E3. George Washington Davis, b 1833, mar Hannah HARVEY, d 1901
F1. Wilfred Davis F3. Lewis David F5. Arthur Davis
F2. Allie Davis F4. Guy Davis F6. Bertha Davis
E4. Emmeline Frances Davis, b 1841, mar Jacob Langmaid
D4. Charles Davis, b 1804 D5. Alonzo Davis, b 1807
D6. Jeremiah S. Davis, b 1810
D7. George O. Davis, b 1814, mar ___ Gerrish

A2. Abigail Davis, mar James Goodwin

A3. Elizabeth Davis, bp 1719, last ch of 1st husband, Davis

A4. Francis Durgin, mar Susan DURRELL, dau of Joseph & Rebecca (Admas) Durrell of Durham, NH. First ch of 2nd husband, Durgin.
B1. Rebecca, mar 1758 Calib Smart
B2. Elijah, 1739-1818, mar Ione Davis of Dover, NH, rem to Newmarket, then to Thornton, NH in 1792
B3. Lydia, mar 1763 Samuel Gill
B4. Francis, 1743-1827, d in Tamworth, NH, mar Sally Renie, and 2. Charlotte Wiggin B5. Susanna, b 1745, mar Jude Bean 1763
B6. Louel?, 1749-1752 B8. Benning, 1753-1758
B7. Deborah, 1752-1753 B9. Temperance, 1757-1758

A5. William Durgin, b 1705, mar Margaret Crommett, dau of John and Mary Crommett, who was b 1715
B1. Dorothy, b 1736, mar Joseph Willey 1758 B3. Sarah, b 1742, mar John Footman
B2. Mary, b 1738, mar 1759 Benjamin Willey
B4. William, 1747-1804, mar Sarah Footman
B5. Truesworthy Davis Durgin, 1754-1812, was a Rev. soldier, unmar

A6. Jonathan Durgin, 1709-1768, mar Judith Edgerly, dau of Samuel and

Elizabeth (Tuttle) Edgerly of Durham, NH
B1. Elizabeth Durgin, b 1732, mar James DAVIS of Lee,
B2. Judith Durgin, 1735-1737 B4. Jonathan, 1740-1757
B3. Judith, again, b 1737, mar Jeremiah Taylor of New Durham, NH
B5. David, b 1743, mar Thankful Chesley 1770. Res Middleton, NH. He mar 2. Eunice ___. B6. John Durgin, b 1745
B7. Eleanor Durgin, b 1748, mar John York of Middleton,
B8. Samuel Durgin, b 1751, mar Mary DAVIS of Lee, res Northwood, NH
B9. Nathaniel Durgin, b 1753, d 1812 Eaton, NH, mar Betsy Hartford of Dover. Res Middleton and New Durham, NH before moving to Eaton.
A7. James Durgin, mar Dorothy Edgerly, and 2. Hannah Kent in 1753
B1. Susanna Durgin, b 1727 B4. Henry Durgin, mar Ann Tibbetts
B2. Samuel Durgin, b 1729, mar Mary Mow 1758 B5. Thomas Durgin bp 1750
B3. James Durgin, mar Margaret Smith B6. Dorothy Durgin bp 1754
A8. Truesworthy Durgin, 1717-1787, mar Mary Durrell, who d 1800
B1. Truesworthy Durgin, b 1741, mar Elizabeth DREW
B2. Joseph Durgin, 1743-1823, mar 1. Patience DURRELL and 2. Betsy Edgerly
B3. Ebenezer Durgin, 1745-1797, mar Lydia DREW B4. Samuel, 1747-1749
B5. Daniel Durgin, 1749-1824, mar Ana Smart 1775
B6. James Durgin, b 1751, mar Mary DREW
B7. Zebulon Durgin, b 1754, mar Lettuce Stillson
A9. Susanna Durgin, bp 1722, was the 2nd wife of James Goodwin. His 1st wife was her half sister, Abigail Davis, dau of Davis and Susan (Smith) Davis.

SMITH, John, settled in Portsmouth, NH 1631. Was he the ancestor of Susan who mar Davis and Durgin above? (Noyes)

SMITH, Capt. David, 1742-1822, eldest son of Davis Smith and 1st wife Sara Hamlin, dau of Moses Godfrey and Martha Collins. Capt. David mar Elizabeth GODFREY, both b Chatham, MA. Capt. David spent 20 years in Barrington, NS during the Rev. War. The chn were b there, but returned to U.S. David's father was a grantee at Barrington, NS, had bros Elkanah, Jonathan and Solomon Smith. Capt. David's father was a sea trader between New England, SC and the West Indies. He was finally captured by two British privateers when he was carrying not one, but two sets of papers, poss French papers and Guernsey Island letters of marque. He showed the wrong papers! (NEHGS, vol. 133)

SMITH, Fred, from G to Watertown, NY, also a bro Eldred? (Lady McKie, Ottawa, ONT)

Note SMITH PAPERS, a bulletin from Sims Pub., P.O. Box 9576, Sacramento, CAL.

SNOW. Is an English surname. However, in the 1600s William Snow, an Englishman, mar prob in Jersey, Rachel GIBAUT of Jersey. Margaret and Abraham GIBAUT were the godparents. Nine chn. the SNOW-GIBAUT fam was related or close to the following old Jersey fams: REMON, AHIER, BENEST, BAILHACHE, LE CRAS, MESSERVY, RICHARDSON and DUMARESQ. Most of these fams are represented in Nfld. and in early New England. The SNOW fam res in St. Lawrence, Jersey. (FRON SNOW TO SNOW, by James Snow, Brooklyn, NY; WRCIC)

SNOW, John of Nfld. and his wife Jeanne, had a dau Sarah, b St. Aubin, J 1737.

SNOW, Abraham, b Nfld., d St. Lawrence, J, bur 1730.

SNOW, William, son of Jean Snow, and bro of Abraham, also of Nfld., d at St. Brelade, J and was bur St. Lawrence, J 1730. "Probably the whole family was connected with the fishing trade." (Marie-Louise Backhurst, Jersey) It is believed that the fam was represented in

Nfld. by 1699-1705. "I am sure that all the numerous Snows in Conception Bay had a common origin in the John who was a planter at Kelly's Island in 1708. (Keith Matthews, St. John's, Nfld.)

Since a number of Snows were definitely associated with the New World, it seems likely that some of those in early New England may have come from Jersey, also. Care must be used however, as other Snows came to America directly from England, such as Nicholas, who was on the LITTLE JAMES 1623, with the Leyden Group. (Tepper) A Capt. Snow of Nfld. or Jersey took 9 prize ships between 1744-1745. (JERSEY IN THE 18th AND 19th CENTURIES, by A.C. Saunders) William SNOW, a privateersman in 1704 was from Jersey. He was a bro-in-law of John MAUGIER, qv, another privateersman, with a letter of mark issued in 1692.

SNOW. Only those with a C.I. connection have been included here.

SNOW, Joseph W., a shoe manufacturer, mar Mary SNOW of Mary QUINER, qv, 1827 MRB. See COONIER and QUINER.

A1. Joseph W. Jr., b 1828, mar 1848 Eliza Jane Sweetland, dau of John and Eliza, MRB.

SNOW, Richard D., mariner and cordwainer, mar Sally Q. (QUINER?) Foss, 1840, MRB. OUTC.

A1. Joseph, b 1843, d.y.? A2. Richard, b 1845 A3. Joseph again, b1849

SNOW, Mary, mar William N. QUINER 1836 MRB. See QUINER, COONIER.

The above fams appear to be at least part Channel Islanders. Other couples in MRB, James and Susan, James H. and Hannah Breed, Robert and Robert and Sally, Samuel and Elizabeth, Samuel and Mary, Samuel and Hannah PICKET, PICOT?, Thomas and Lydia, may also be from C.I. fams.

SNOW, Thomas II, trader, and Mary CROSS, mar 1823, res MRB. See CROSS.

A1. Hannah PICKET, bp 1824 A3. Franklin, b 1830 A5. Clinton, b 1843
A2. Thomas, b 1828 A4. Edward, b 1833

SNOW, William, master of a Jersey ship 1776-1778, CHARMING BETSY, built in Newbury, MA. (A. John Jean, Jersey)

The SNOW fam below is believed by descendants and by researcher in Jersey to be from the SNOW fam settled in Jersey in the 1600s.

SNOW, Edward of Coley's Point, Bay Roberts, Nfld., son of either John of Port De Grave, Nfld. 1760s, or of a Thomas SNOW. Edward mar 1785 in Nfld. Some data uncertain, some missing. Order of chn uncertain. (James Snow, Brooklyn, NY)

A1. Edward Jr., 1786-1851. Mar 1812 Jane Gallagher of Harbour Grace, Nfld.

B1. William, b 1815 Bareneed, Nfld., mar Catherine Mandeville at Bareneed. Wm. was Protestant but converted to R.C. age 20. He mar 2. 1861 Rebecca Maher, Meagher. Chn by 1st wife?

C1. Thomas, b 1862 St. John's, Nfld., lost on 1st voyage to sea

C2. James, b 1863 St. John's, d 1927, mar Bridget Hogan, b Nfld., dau of Patrick and Bridget (FOLLET) Hogan. Rem to NY, d 1909. James mar 2. Mary Flaherty 1910 in NY. She d 1930.

D1. Mary, b St. John's, Nfld., d 1977, mar Michael Esposito, an Italian, in Brooklyn, NY, 3 chn

E1. Joseph Esposito, b 1920? E3. James Esposito, d 1960s
E2. Dorothy Espositi, d 1930s

D2. Loretta, b St. John's, Nfld., mar Raymond Escorcia of Cuba, in Brooklyn, NY

E1. Anita Escorcia E2. Dolores Escorcia E3. Raymond Escorcia

D3. Estelle, b Nfld., mar Del Healy, Brooklyn, res Hollis, NY

E1. Gerald Healy

D4. James Gerald, b 1901 St. John's, Nfld., mar Catherine McEldowney, Brooklyn, NY, 4 chn

E1. James, b 1930 Brooklyn, mar Joan McPadden 1955, 4 chn
F1. James Gerard, b 1956
F2. Martin Patrick, b 1960
F3. Mary Catherine, b 1963
F4. John Peter, b 1967
E2. Robert, b 1933 Brooklyn, mar Marianne McNally 1960
F1. Robert, b 1962
F2. Mary Patricia, b 1963
F3. Barbara, b 1965
F4. Kathleen, b 1967
E3. Ann, b 1934 Brooklyn, mar John Wall 1957, Brooklyn, 5 chn
F1. Regina Wall, b 1958
F2. Richard Wall, b 1960
F3. Deidre Wall, b 1963
F4. Denise Wall, b 1964
F5. Kenneth Wall, b 1968
E4. Kathleen, b 1941 Brooklyn, mar Eugene Kalbacker 1970, 3 chn
F1. Brian Kalbacker, b 1971
F2. Neil Kalbacker, b 1974, twin
F3. Kathleen Kalbacker, b 1974, twin
D5. John Alexander, b 1905 St. John's, Nfld., mar Guadelupe Gonzalez, Mexico City. Res Mexico City about 10 years.
E1. John
E2. Josephine
D6. by 2nd wife, Mary Flaherty, Thomas, b 1911 Brooklyn, mar Anna Clark, Bronx, NY, d 1960s. Three chn.
E1. Annmarie, d 1960s
E2. Thomas
E3. Donald

SNOW, James: "My grandfather, James Snow, born in St. John's, Nfld., 1862 and d 1927 in Brooklyn...experience as a crew member on at least one of Admiral Robert Peary's polar expeditions...only clue...is a piece of meteorite which my grandfather brought back from a voyage captained by a man named BARTLETT...Admiral Peary made a voyage to the Northwest coast of Greenland around 1895 on a ship captained by Sam Bartlett...This voyage found and brought to New York a meteorite which is now in the Hayden Planetarium...my grandfather was also a sealer, and my father has Eskimo fish lines carved from seal and walrus teeth which my grandfather acquired on his voyages...my ancestors probably emigrated from Jersey in 1705-1708...there was at least one other Snow in Nfld. before 1700 in addition to my John Snow."

SOHIER. Records of this fam go back to Antenor, King of the Cimerians, in the Middle East in 443 BC! (WRCIC) "Sohiers were ship captains and musicians of brass instruments." (Mrs. Raymond Brown, St. Cloud, MN)

SOHIER. To J from France poss in the 1500s. SOHIER in St. Martin, J 1607. In St. Heliers, J 1668, and in St. Martin and St. Heliers, J 1749. Edw. belowwas son of Edw. & Rachel (STEEL) SOHIER.

SOHIER, Edward III, b 1724 St. Martin, J, rem to Boston, MA ca 1750, mar Susanne Brimmer, grandau of Andre Sigourney & Mary Germain, a Hug fam from La Rochelle, France. Res Oxford, MA, then Boston, MA in 1668. Edward & Susanne mar ca 1758. (W.A. Van Saun, Mahanoy City, PA; Edward Boseley, Rockport, MA; COLONIAL FAMS OF AMERICA, vol. III; CLEVELAND GENS, vol. 2, p. 1615)
A1. Martin Brimmer, b 1760, killed in action in St. Clair's army.
A2. Edward Sohier IV, b 1762 Boston, MA, mar Mary Davies, dau of Wm. Davies, d 1793. There were other chn according to the Census.
B1. William Davies, b 1787 Boston, a lawyer, d Cohasset, MA 1868. Mar 1809 Elizabeth Amory Dexter, b 1787, dau of Dr. Andrew or Dr. Aaron Dexter?, and Rebecca Amory.
C1. Edward Dexter, 1810-1888, mar 1836 Hannah Louisa Amory, dau of Thomas C.
D1. Joseph Foster, b 1836, mar 1860 Letitia B. Watson, a dau Louisa
D2. Hannah Louisa, b 1837, mar 1864 Theo. Metcalfe, 9 chn
E1. Theodore Tracy Metcalfe, 1865-1869
E2. through E7. These chn d.y. or fairly young, prob unmar
E8. Julia T., b 1875

E9. Theodore Metcalfe, b 1879, mar 1906 Ellen Florence Watson, 6 chn
F1. John Tracy Metcalfe, b 1906
F2. Edward Sohier Metcalfe, b 1907
F3. Louisa Sohier Metcalfe, b 1909
F4. Theodore Metcalfe, b 1911
D3. Susanna Prescott, b 1839, mar 1869 Channing Clapp, no issue
D4. Merlin, 1840-1848
D5. Mary Davies, b 1842
D6. George Deyler, b 1845, mar 1876 Sarah S. Pratt
E1. Louis Amory, b 1877
E2. Mary Davies, b 1878
E3. Walter, b 1880, mar 1912 Henrietta Stuart of Sacramento, CAL
E4. Emily Linzee, b 1882, mar 1908 Fred A. Bosley, b 1881
F1. Edward S. Bosley, b 1909
F2. Elizabeth Brimmer Bosley, b 1911
E5. Jane Foster, b 1885, d.y.
F6. Fred Marlin, b 1888
E7. Jeannette Foster, b 1895
D7. Elizabeth Dexter
D8. Emily Linzee, b 1850
D9. Sarah Ineers, b 1862, d 1872
C2. Joseph Foster, 1811-1817
C3. Mary Davies, b 1817, mar 1845 Waldo Higginson
C4. William, b 1822 Boston, d 1894, mar 1846 Susanna Cabot Lowell, dau of John A.
D1. Elizabeth Putnam, b 1847
D2. Alice de Vermandois, b 1850, mar 1878 Eliot C. Clarke, son of Rev. James Freeman Clarke
E1. Susan Lwell Clarke, b 1879
E2. James Clarke, b 1881, d.y.
E3. Anne? Clarke, 1883-1911
E4. Elizabeth Lowell Clarke, b 1887, mar 1908 Charles Eliot Ware Jr.
E5. James Freeman Clarke, b 1889
D3. William Davies, b 1858, mar 1880 Edith Alden
E1. Eleanor, b 1884
E3. William Davies Jr., b 1889
E2. Alice de Vermandois, b 1886, mar 1910 Herbert Branwell Shaw
C5. Elizabeth Brimmer, b 1823 Boston, MA, mar 1848 Dr. Henry Bryant. See Vol. 2, COLONIAL FAMS OF AMERICA.
C6. Geo. Brimmer, b 1832, d 1877 in Paris, France
A3. John Baker, 1767-1801, no issue

SOHIER, John, a ship captain, lost at sea ca 1851.

SOHIER, George, a sea captain, rem to NY 1866, last heard of in Syracuse, NY.

In addition, there were two more Sohiers, one named Peter, that were known of by Mrs. Raymond Brown of St. Cloud, MN, in the 1800s. See LE BRUN, BROWN.

SOHIER. Name of a street in Beverly, MA.

SOHIER, David, mar Mary Olden or Holden 1795, Boston, MA.

SOHIER, Mary, mar Joseph Foster 1796, Boston. These two may have been chn of Edward SOHIER IV, in the above chart.

SOLWAY. Connected with the MARETT fam of UT, qv. Note that SOLWAY is curr in G, but not an old C.I. surname. Cf SOLBE, which is being researched in the Islands. See CIFHS #3. Eva M.R. Solway of Cardston, ALTA, Canada, collected data for 948 gen. charts, some through a Mr. Pepperell of Jersey Island. There is a reel of her work in Salt Lake City, UT (not seen by compiler).

SOPER, Mary Ann, from C.I. to UT 1851, via ship OLYMPUS. SOPER curr J. (SLC RECORDS)

SOREL. Being researched in the Islands. See CIFHS #9. Not in Stevens List.

SPENCER. In St. Lawrence, J 1788, prob from Grt. Britain.

SPRAGUE. In J 1668-1749, prob from Grt. Britain.

SPRAGUE. See Jane Morse in LE MARCUM chart. Note name also in

GARNSEY-GUERNSEY GEN.
SPRATT. Curr G and J, but not old in the Islands. One fam poss to Canada from C.I. (L.F. Guy, Orono, ONT)
SQUIRE. In G 1600s, from Grt. Britain. Some to Nfld., with desc in New England, see Q.A. IN CANADA. (Susan Squires, Newburyport, MA)
STANLEY. Curr G and J. Note STANDLEY in early MRB. OUTC.
STANLEY. Not from the C.I. However, this fam has a great number of marriages with C.I. fams in Gaspe, QUE and other places in the Maritimes; therefore, fam is included. See ROSE & GUIGNION. (Eunice Stanley, Mesa, AZ)
STANLEY, John, 1839-1914, mar Louise ROSE?, 1842-1917, res Quebec
A1. Albert, mar Melinda ROSE
A2. Nellie, mar Moses GUIGNION, qv. See GUIGNION. Eight chn.
A3. Louis, Lewis, mar Caroline Anne MacKenzie, had chn: Mabel, Milton, Clifton, Bert, Ada, Carrie, Hazen and Willis
A4. Eva, mar William Adams, had 10? chn
A5. Arthur, mar Sarah Adams, had 10 chn: Mamie, Maynard, Nellie, Jessie, Kingsley, Bessie, Edison, Clara, Greta and Gladys
A6. Elvina, mar Elias GUIGNION, 11 chn. See GUIGNION.
A7. Clara, mar Elias ROSE, had 6 chn: Violet, Gordon, Ivy, Irene and Guy. See ROSE.
STANLEY, Henry, res Gaspe, mar Edith Stanley? who d on the birth of Edith Jr. He mar 2. Esther or Emmeline Stanley, sister of Edith Sr.
A1. Edith Jr.
A2. Henry Stanley Jr.
A3. Allan
A4. Delie
A5. William
A6. Laura
STARCK. In J 1292 and curr in J. Not researched by compiler.
STARR. See DE JEAN, DE JERSEY.
STAYNER. See PILL.
STE. CROIX. See DE STE. CROIX. SINECROSS and CROSS.
STEAD. Curr in G and J.
STEAD. This name has been associated with Channel Islanders, but is not in Stevens List.
STEAD, Walter Benj. Vere, eldest son of David Stead of Silver Ings., Yorkshire and Mary Jane Belcher of Dublin. Walter was b at Bungeeltap, Victoria Colony 1849, and ordained in 1873, when he mar at St. Peter Port, G, Margaret Heineken, dau of John OZANNE, MD. (NOTES AND GLEANINGS, COS. of Devon and Cornwall, by Cotton and Dallas, England, 1890,92)
A1. Havilland Chepmell Stead, b 1875 A2. Redmond Morres Stead, b 1878
STEEL, STILL. In J 1532, from France? Note that it also was in Suffolk and Yorks, England and in Ayrshire, Berwickshire and Dunfriesshire, Scotland. CAUTION: TRIAL CHART.
STEELE, Joseph, b 1706 J, mar 1731 Middleton, MA, Susannah KNIGHT, dau of Joseph. See CI COLL for more data.
One report says Joseph rem 1760 to Halifax, NS, and d there 1764. Another says he d 1788 Mt. Vernon, NH.
Correction from Mrs. Strath, Melrose, MA. (SLC Records; Thayer Burrowes, SLCity, UT; Rev. Don McAllister, Ann Arbor, MI: STEELE FAM, by Daniel Steele Durrie, Albany, NY, 1862, not seen by compiler; HIST. OF FRANCETOWN, NH, p. 598; HIST. OF WEARE, NH, p. 803; SARGENTS FAM HISTORY; Gladys Steele Lund, Barrington, NH; Grace Davis, Woodland, WA)
A1. Sarah, b ca 1733 J?, mar 1. Lynch? and 2. Elias Hassell
A2. John, b 1735 J, bp 1738 Middleton, MA, d 1821 Ashburnham, MA, mar Elizabeth ___, b ca 1743, 8 chn. He mar 1791 Mehitable Knowland.
B1. Jane, b 1760 Amherst, NH, mar 1782 Adonijah Houghton, and d 1843
B2. John, b 1762 Amherst

B3. Elizabeth, b 1764 Wilton, NH, d 1845, mar Church Tabor
B4. David, b 1766 Wilton, NH
B5. Sarah/Sally, b 1768 Wilton, NH, mar 1789 Jonathan Flanders
A3. Joseph, b ca 1735 J, or 1738 Middleton, MA, d 1821 Ashbournham, MA. He mar 1. Elizabeth ___, b ca 1743, res Amherst, NH, and 2. in 1791 Mehitable Knowland, 8 chn.
B1. Anna, b 1768 Amherst, NH, mar 1783 John McAllister, b 1739 on the ocean from Ireland, son of Richard and of Ann Miller. Res later in Rochester, VT.
C1. John W. McAllister, b 1784 Antrim, NH
C2. Daniel McAllister, b 1786 New Boston, NH
C3. Jesse McAllister, b ca 1787 Antrim, NH
C4. Elizabeth McAllister, b 1788
C5. Isaac McAllister, b ca 1790
C6. David McAllister, b ca 1792
C7. Anna McAllister, b ca 1798
C8. Fannie McAllister, b ca 1800
C9. Nancy, b ca 1802
C10. William McAllister, b 1811
B2. Frances, b 1775 Amherst, NH
B3. Betty/Elizabeth, b 1777
B4. Fanny, b 1780
B5. Polly, b 1781, d.y.
B6. Joseph, b 1782 Amherst
B7. Polly again, b 1785 Amherst
B8. Isaac, b ca 1787 Amherst
A4. William, b 1739 Middleton, MA, d 1810. Mar Hannah ___, 1738-1812, res Wash. and Amherst, NH.
B1. Jane, b ca 1760, mar 1780 William White, b ca 1758 Windsor, VT, son of Archibald White
C1. Hannah White, b 1784 Windsor
C2. William White, b 1786
C3. James White, b 1789
C4. Polly White, b 1791
C5. Sarah White, b 1795
C6. Ira White, b 1797
C7. Emily White, b 1803
B2. Joseph, b 1762 Amherst, NH, mar 1784 Margaret Thayer, b 1757 Braintree, MA, dau of Noah & Margaret (Harmon) Thayer, 12 chn
C1. Margaret, b 1785 Washington, NH, d.y.
C2. Tamer T., 1786-1843, mar 1802 Timothy Scott, 10 chn. He was b ca 1764 Lempster, NH.
D1. Hannah Scott, b 1804 Lempster, NH
D2. Mica, b 1806 Marlow, NH
D3. Doratha, b 1809 Lempster, NH
D4. Jane W. Scott, b 1811
D5. Bera, b 1816
D6. John Scott, b 1818
D7. Timothy Scott, b 1820
D8. Joseph Scott, b 1822, d.y.
D9. Joseph Scott, b 1824
D10. Harvey M. Scott, b 1827
C3. Nancy Steel, 1788-1812
C4. Hannah Steele, twin, 1780-1813
C5. Peggy Steel, twin, 1780-1798
C6. Zachariah M.G. Steele, b 1791, d.y.
C7. Thayer, b ca 1792, d.y.
C8. Levi, b 1793
C9. Zachariah, b ca 1794
C10. Thayer, b 1795
C11. Sally, 1797-1800
C12. Margaret, 1799-1844, mar 1817 Nathaniel F. Lull, b 1793 Wash., NH, d 1881, son of David Lull. Mar 2. Martha Leslie 1845. One ch by Margaret.
D1. Nathaniel A. Lull, b 1827, Unity, NH, mar 1847 Caroline C. Hathorn
E1. Ellen S. Lull, b 1849 Unity, NH, d 1854
E2. Edgar A. Lull, 1851-1882
E3. Frank E. Lull, b 1853
E4. Charles A. Lull, b 1855
E5. Ellen A. Lull, 1857-1864
E6. Allen E. Lull, 1858-1863
B3. Robert, b ca 1765, mar Patience, poss a widow?, 2 chn, res Wash., NH
C1. Samuel, b 1787, Wash., NH
C2. Robert, b 1789, Wash., NH
B4. Debora, b 1766, Wash., NH
B5. James, b ca 1768 Wash., NH, mar 1. Mrs. Patience ___, 1766-1791, mar 2. Sarah McMillen, b ca 1772 Wash., NH, 6 chn.

C1. James, 1790-1814 C4. Henry, 1798-1815 C6. son, b 1802, d.y.
C2. dau, b 1794, d.y. C5. Patience, b 1800 C7. Harvey, b 1803
C3. Elias, b 1796
B6. Sarah, b 1769 Washl, NH. Another record says Amherst, NH, d 1839, mar Samuel ROUNDY, b 1766 Lempster, NH, son of Samuel & Ann (Huntington) Roundy. Nine chn? Did she mar 2. Alvin Roundy, b 1766, d 1832, son of Sam & Anne H. Roundy? See ROUNDY.
C1. Edith Roundy, b 1787 Lempster, NH, d 1825
C2. James Roundy, 1789-1873 C4. Katura Roundy, b 1793
C3. Asahael Roundy, b 1791 C5. Mehitable Roundy, b 1794
C6. Ashbel Roundy, b 1796, mar 1871 Lucretia Nott
C7. Alvin Roundy, 1798-1856, mar 1823 Anna Ellingwood, and 2.?, desc.
C8. Sally or Sarah Roundy, b 1800 C9. Jane Roundy, 1802-1879
B7. Nancy, b ca 1770 B8. William, b ca 1774 B9. Samuel, b ca 1776
A5. Rachel S., b 1740 Middleton, MA, d 1830. Mar John McMillen, b 1741, or New Boston, NH. She d age 90 Lyman, NH and he d there 1835, age 94, 11 chn.
B1. Sarah McMillen, 1767-1826, mar 1787 Robert Cochran, b 1763, son of James & Christina (Aiken) Cochran. Sarah b in Salem, MA.
C1. Levi Cochran, b 1788 New Boston, NH, d 1874, mar 1820 Mary Boyd Cochran.
C2. Jonathan Cochran, b 1789, mar 1812 Susan Cochran
C3. David Cochran, 1791-1884, mar 1817 Betsey E. Huntington
C4. Rebecca Cochran, 1794-1818
C5. Ira Cochran, 1797-1851, mar 1825 Nancy Patterson
C6. Luther Cochran, 1799-1800
C7. Jane C. Cochran, 1801-1865, mar 1. Ebenezer Smith
C8. Achsah Cochran, 1803-1890
C9. Silas Cochran, 1805-1883, mar 1829, 1. Mary E. Trefethen
C10. Annis Campbell Cochran, 1808-1887, mar 1828 Amos Wood Tewksbury
B2. Alexander McMillen, b ca 1769
B3. Mary McMillen, 1770-1856, mar 1786 James McMillen
B4. Samuel McMillen, b ca 1772
B5. Nancy McMillen, b ca 1774
B6. Daniel McMillen, b 1775
B7. Henry McMillen, 1776-1796
B8. Hannah McMillen, b 1778, mar 1805, 1. Zenas Whiting
B9. Joseph McMillen, 1780-1842, mar 1808 Abigail Gordon of Bath, NH
C1. Albert Millen, 1810-1888, b Lyman, NH, mar 1830 Harriet Eastman NOTE CHANGE IN NAME.
C2. Phineas Millen, b ca 1812 Lyman, NH
C3. Abigail Millen, 1814-1893, mar Andrew Gordon
C4. Rachel Millen, b ca 1816
C5. Henry Millen, b 1822, mar 1. Syrihia Wallace
B10. Catherine McMillen, b ca 1782, mar ___ Pike
B11. Rachel McMillen, b 1786 New Boston, NH?, d 1848, mar 1806 Lyman Hoskins, 1784-1862, son of Elkanah & Mindwell Barney Hoskins.
C1. Lyman Hoskins, b 1807 Littleton, NH, d 1889, mar 1836 Bethany Bartlett
C2. Mindwell Hoskins, b 1809 Lyman, NH, d 1882, mar 1830 Jedediah Buffum
C3. William Hoskins, b 1812
C4. Fidelia Hoskins, b 1814, mar 1835 Hiram Clough
C5. John M. Hoskins, 1816-1869, mar Susan F. Page
C6. Rachel M. Hoskins, b 1820
C7. Salmon Hoskins, 1822-1889, mar Jemima A. Bowman
C8. Isabondia B. Hoskins, b 1824, mar Joel Clough
C9. Nehemiah Hoskins, b 1827, mar Mary C. ___
A6. Susannah, b 1741, J?
A7. Mary, b ca 1743 Middleton, mar John McMillen b ca 1767 of New Boston

B1. John McMillen
B2. William McMillen
B3. James McMillen
B4. Ellise McMillen
B5. Robert McMillen
B6. Daniel McMillen
B7. Elizabeth McMillen
B8. Mary McMillen
B9. David McMillen
B10. Sarah McMillen
B11. Ananias McMillen

A8. Susan, b 1745 J, mar Daniel Greenough

A9. Jane, Jennie, b ca 1746 Middleton, MA, mar Angus or Ananias? McAllister, b ca 1740 Ireland, son of John McAllister. He mar 2. Jane Ordway, 3 sons: Joshua, Samuel, Peter.

B1. Daniel McAllister, b ca 1763 Les Lovell, ME, mar Sarah Russell of Dunharton, NH & 2. Lucy Whiting, b ca 1783
C1. Zaccheus McAllister, b1788
C2. Mary McAllister, b 1790
C3. John W. McAllister
C4. James McAllister, b 1794
C5. Daniel McAllister, b 1796
C6. Sarah McAllister, b 1798
C7. Jeremiah McAllister, b 1800
C8. Peter McAllister, b 1801
C9. Olive, b 1808, by Lucy Whiting, 2nd wife

B2. Joseph McAllister, b ca 1765, mar Sarah ___, res Lovell, ME
C1. Joseph McAllister, b1787, mar Sarah Bryant
C2. Isaac McAllister, b1789, mar Sarah Heath
C3. Benjamin, b1791, mar Charlotte Hobbs
C4. John, b 1794, d.y.
C5. John again, b 1795
C6. Sarah, b 1797
C7. Samuel, b 1800, mar Lydia Fogg
C8. Betsy, b 1802
C9. Daniel, b 1804
C10. Asa, b 1806

B3. Asa McAllister, b 1767

B4. Mary McAllister, b 1768, mar 1790 Daniel Harper, b ca 1764, of Lovell, ME. He d 1839.
C1. Sarah Harper, b 1792 Lovell, ME
C2. Andrew Harper, b 1794, mar Eliza Sawyer in Pomeroy, OH, rem to Adams Co., IL. Rem later by covered wagon to Oregon in 1847.
D1. Clarissa, b Adams Co., IL, mar Hamilton Walter Lacky
E1. Sarah Isabelle/Belle, mar Columbia Lancaster Klady, settled in Lewis River Valley, near Woodland, WA
F1. May Klady, mar Jesse Jacob Guild
G1. Grace Guild, b 1901, mar Fred M. Davis, res Woodland, WA
H1. Flo. M. Davis, b 1923
H2. Robert D. Davis, b 1925
H3. Gene R. Davis, b 1926
H4. Osa May, b 1928 WA
C3. Charlotte Harper, b ca 1796
C4. Daniel A. Harper, b ca 1798
C5. Anna Harper, b 1800
C6. Abigail G. Harper, b ca1802
C7. Amy Harper, b 1804
C9. Elizabeth Harper, b 1807
C10. Ezekiel Harper, b 1809
C11. Greenlief S. Harper, b 1811
C12. Greeley D. Harper, b 1813
C13. Temple Harper, b 1816

B5. George McAllister, b ca 1770, mar Alice Kilgore, poss other chn?
C1. Moses McAllister, b 1795
C2. Hannah D. McAllister, b ca 1798
C3. Phebe McAllister, b 1804

B6. Sarah McAllister, b ca 1772, mar James Dustin, b 1768 Hanover, ME, son of Jesse & Elizabeth (Swan) Dustin
C1. Fanny Dustin, b 1795 Bethel, ME
C2. Peregrine Dustin, b 1800 Bethel, ME

B7. Zacheus McAllister, b 1774, mar Tryphena Heald
B8. Jerry McAllister, b ca 1776
B9. John McAllister, b ca 1778
B10. Isaac McAllister, b ca 1780
B11. Anna McAllister, b ca 1781, mar David McKeen
B12. David McAllister, b ca 1782, mar Betsey Butters, b 1785, dau of Abel Butters & Esther. He mar 2. Judith Campbell, b ca 1787, of Lovell, ME.

C1. Sarah McAllister, b 1806 Lovell, ME C2. Esther McAllister b 1808
C3. by 2nd wife, Betsey B. McAllister, b 1811, of Lovell, ME
C4. Alexander C. McAllister, b 1813 C10. Lurison Y. McAllister b1823
C5. Jane Steele McAllister, b 1815 C11. Jacob B. McAllister, b1825
C6. Anna C. McAllister, b 1816 C12. David C. McAllister, b1827
C7. Lovisa McAllister, b 1818, twin C13. Lovice McAllister, b 1830
C8. Sephrona McAllister, b 1818 twin C14. Eliza B. McAllister, b1833
C9. Alvira, b 1821, Lovell, ME
B13. Benjamin McAllister, b 1784
A10. James, 1748-1807, mar 1772 Susanna (Putnam) KNIGHT, a widow, b1753 Middleton, MA, d 1845 Stoneham, MA. James d 1807 Stoneham, 11 chn at least, 8 of whom mar. James may have mar before 1772, as a James b 1771 Antrim, NH is said to be son of James. See this fam in LATE ADDITIONS.
B1. Samuel, b 1773 Stoneham, MA, d unmar age ca 55
B2. Susannah, b 1775, d age 14
B3. Sarah, b 1778, mar Calvin RICHARDSON of Woburn, 1777-1866, son of Jeduthun & Mary Wright Richardson. Mar 1800, 10 chn.
C1. Calvin Richardson, b 1801 Woburn, MA, d 1863. Mar 1825 Mary Eliz. Wade
C2. Sarah Richardson, b 1804 Woburn, MA, mar 1826 Samuel Bartlet White
C3. Samuel Steele Richardson, 1806-1869, mar 1. 1832 Lydia Abigail Meade
C4. Eliza Richardson, 1808-1893, mar 1845 Luke Fowle
C5. Susan Richardson, b 1810, mar 1831 Frederick Flint
C6. Charlotte Richardson, 1812-1827
C7. Mary Richardson, b 1814, mar 1833 Luther Richardson Vining
C8. Fanny Richardson, b 1816, mar 1840 Timothy W. Meade
C9. John Richardson, b 1818 C10. Abigail Richardson, b 1820
B4. John, b 1780 Winchendon, MA, a shoemaker, mar 1808 Betsy Crosby, 1786-1866, of Midford, b ca 1782. John d 1861, res Milford, Rindge, NH and Reading, MA.
C1. Elizabeth W., b 1814 Milford, d 1882, mar 1840 Dana Parker, 1805-1892, son of Amos & Betsey (Taylor) Parker
D1. Milton Dane, b 1845 D2. Galen Adelphia, b 1847
C2. Fanny Steele, b 1817 Rindge, NH, mar 1839 Henry F. Parker
C3. John Steele, b 1819 Woburn, MA, mar 1840 Fidelia Kingman, b ca 1821 Reading, MA
D1. John Henry, b 1841 Reading, MA D3. Martin Edward, 1845-1873
D2. George Francis, b 1843 Reading D4. Sophronia Ella, b 1851 Reading
C4. Samuel Steele, b 1823 Reading, MA, mar 1848 Martha Hackett of Brookfield, NH
C5. Josiah C., b 1825 Reading, mar 1. ___, and 2. Caroline Goldsmith, Irish, a widow, 1869, who was b 1826 Roxbury, MA, d 1901 Medford, MA. Josiah d 1865 Charlestown, MA. Other chn?
D1. Herbert, b 1863 Charlestown, MA, mar Ada Tourtellotte 1887, Dudley, MA, b 1859 Dudley, and d 1939 Somerville, MA. Herbert d 1943 Detroit, MI.
E1. Sumner, b 1888 Medford, MA, mar Loretta Quinn of Boston, MA at Detroit, MI. He d there 1959.
F1. Robert, b 1921 Detroit, mar ___ of Ferndale, MI at Tokyo, Japan, then res St. Louis, MO.
C6. Poss other chn?
B5. Mary, b 1783, Stoneham, MA, d 1860, mar James Wade, b 1784 Woburn, MA, son of Ebenezer & Elizabeth Wade. Four chn.
C1. Mary Elizabeth, b 1807 Woburn, MA, d 1872, mar 1825 Calvin Richardson, son of Sarah Steele & Calvin Richardson, qv.

C2. James Wade, b 1808 Woburn, MA, d 1824
C3. William Wade, 1809-1832 C4. Oliver Wade, 1813-1851, mar Eleanor.
B6. Lucy, b 1785, d.y.
B7. Capt. James, b 1787, mar 1811 Betsy Pierce, res Stoneham, MA, a trader. Betsy b 1790 Stoneham, MA, dau of Ephraim & Abigail (Porter) Pierce.
C1. Elizabeth P., b 1812 Stoneham, MA, mar 1832 Loea or Lora Parker, a carpenter, b 1809 Stoneham, MA, son of Loea & Anna (Bancroft) Parker. He mar 2. 1850 Adeline Emerson.
D1. Eliza Ann Parker, b 1834 Reading, MA
D2. Maria Parker, b 1835 D3. Clarissa Parker, 1838-1839
D4. Julia Parker, b 1842 D5. Gillman Loae Parker, b 1847
C2. James, b 1815 Stoneham, MA, mar 1838 Mary Kittridge of Woburn, MA. He was a shoemaker. She was b ca 1817.
D1. Marietta, b 1839 Stoneham, MA D3. Frank, b 1846
D2. James III, b 1841 D4. Maria Louise, 1848-1849
C3. John, b 1817, mar Ann Wiley, b 1823 Stoneham, 47 yrs. in 1870
D1. Clara Maria, b 1845 Stoneham, MA
D2. Mary Ellen, b 1848 D4. Frederick, b 1853
D3. John, b 1850 D5. Arthur, b 1855
D6. Walter, b 1858 Stoneham, MA, mar 1886 Hillsborough, NH Julia D. Campbell, b 1860 Henniker, NH, dau of John C. & Julia D. (Butler) Campbell.
E1. Clifford C., b 1869 Hillsborough, NH
E2. Ruth, b 1887 E4. Rachel H., b 1893
E3. Philip, b 1891 E5. Julia D., b 1896
D7. Emma A., b 1860
D8. Edith L., b 1863 Stoneham, MA, mar James Harvey Jones, b 1860, Hillsborough, NH. He d 1913, son of Ebenezer & Malvina (Shedd) Jones.
E1. Clara L. Jones, b 1888 E4. Eben P. Jones, b 1897
E2. Jeanette E. Jones, b 1890 E5. Arthur J. Jones, b 1901
E3. Edna S. Jones, b 1892
B8. Betsy/Elizabeth, b 1788, Winchendon, MA, mar Ebenezer Ryder of Goffstown, NH, b 1786 Dunbarton, NH, son of Ebenezer & Abigail (Shaw) Ryder. He had mar 1. Rachel Leach in 1808.
C1. Susan Ryder, b 1829 Goffstown, NH, mar 1852 Harrison Weber
B9. Levi, b 1790
B10. Fanny, b 1792 Woburn, MA, mar Asa Merrill of Milford, NY, 7 chn
C1. Fanny Merrill, b 1821 Milford, NH
C2. Susan Merrill, b 1823, mar Dr. Joseph Mansfield. He had mar 1. Mary Wiley 1845. Mar Susan M. Merrill 1857. Four chn by 1st wife, 1 by Susan.
D1. Jessie F. Mansfield, b 1863 Wakefield, MA
C3. Nathan Merrill, b 1825
C4. Calvin Merrill, b 1827, mar 1857 Lizzie N. Wheeler, b 1831, dau of Daniel & Martha G. (Aiken) Wheeler
D1. John C. Merrill, b 1859 Milford, NH D3. Arthur W. Merrill, b1868
D2. Hattie Elizabeth Merrill, b 1863 D4. Walter Brooks Merrill, b1873
C5. Henry Merrill, b 1829, mar 1855 Mary Fletcherb 1833 Amherst, NH, dau of Sewall & Rheny (Mace) Fletcher. Res Washington, NH.
D1. Delia B. Merrill, b 1856 Milford, NH D3. Frank Henry, b 1866
D2. Mary Rhoda Merrill, b 1860 Milford D4. Clara Ellen, b 1875
C6. Harriet Merrill, b 1831 C8. Rhoda M. Merrill, b 1836
C7. Mary E. Merrill, b 1834
A11. Samuel, b 1751 J, mar Rachel Putnam, b ca 1753 of Haverhill, MA. He d Rindge, NH 1811, ca age 60. Eleven chn.

B1. Daniel, b ca 1775, res Strykersville, NY, d 1852 Arcade, NY, mar Ann ___, b ca 1777 Londonderry, NH, 2 chn
C1. James Steele, b1786 Londonderry C2. David, b 1787 Hollis, NH
B2. William, b 1777, d ca 1823 Plattsburg, NY, mar 1. Susannah Barrett, b 1779 Dublin, NH, 6 chn, and 2. Alvira Hamblin, 3 chn, b ca 1792 Plattsburg, NY. Susanna was dau of Jeremiah & Sarah.
C1. William B. Steele, b 1798 Weberville, MI
C2. Sintha B. Steele, b 1800 Boston, MA
C3. Susan B., b 1802 Boston, MA C5. Almon B., b 1808 Boston, MA
C4. Mariah B., b 1804 Boston, MA C6. Roswell B., b 1810
C7. by 2nd wife, Mary Ann Hamblin, b 1818 Plattsburg, NY
C8. Chester H., b 1820
C9. Samuel Hamblin, b 1822 Plattsburg, NY, d 1892 Goshen, UT, mar Elvira Salome Thayer, b 1826 NY, dau of Sabin & Lovina (Kingsbury) Thayer, 4 chn.
D1. Mary Anne, b 1842 Nauvoo, IL D3. Samuel Chester, b 1847 Mt. Pisgah, IA
D2. Lovina, b 1844 Hancock, IL
D4. Albert Almond, b 1848 Mt. Pisgah, IA
B3. James, b 1779, res Rindge, NH 1834
B4. Sarah, b ca 1781, mar Samuel ROBBINS, res Rindge, NH
C1. Mary Robbins, b 1807 Rindge, NH, d 1843. Mar 1841 Oliver Wilder who may have mar 2. 1845 Calista Kidder, a dau Mary, b 1846
C2. Sabrina Robbins, 1808-1874, mar 1831 Jason Keith
C3. David A. Robbins, b 1810 Rindge, NH, mar 1844 1. Betsy Coolidge 1841, b 1821 Gardner, MA, 2 chn, and mar 2. Louisa Stone 1844, 3 chn
D1. Mary S. Robbins, b 1841 Rindge, NH
D2. Betsy C. Robbins, b 1843 D4. Harlan S. Robbins, b 1848
D3. Ostram A. Robbins, b 1845 D5. Warren A. Robbins, b 1850
C4. George W. Robbins, 1812-1864, mar 1841 Hannah E. Bugbee
C5. Abigail S. Robbins, b 1814, mar 1859 Uri Day
C6. Ruthy Robbins, 1816-1819 C7. Rachel P. Robbins, 1818-1826
C8. Samuel W. Robbins, b 1820, mar 1847 Mary Page
B5. Samuel, b 1785 Winchendon, MA, school teacher in Albany, NY, mar Elizabeth Buttrick
B6. Rachel, b ca 1788 Winchendon, MA B8. a son, d.y. 1792
B7. Abigail, b 1790, mar Asa Hyde, b 1776 Winchendon, MA, son of Ezra & Eliz. Hyde. Abigail d 1831. A son William B. Hyde d.y. 1829.
B8. Susan, b 1794, mar Luke Bemis, b 1788 Winchendon, MA, son of Jason and Mercy (Piper) Bemis. He mar 2. 1843 Susan Goddard, when Susan died. Ten chn. A Bemis fam in DUNSTER GEN.
C1. Sarah Elvira Bemis, b 1814 Royalston, MA, d 1864, mar 1843 Eri Shephardson
D1. John Shepardson, b 1843 Royalston, d 1864
D2. Daniel Shepardson, 1845-1908, mar 1876 Emma Wylie
D3. Susan Steele Shepardson, 1849-1934, mar 1878 Luther E. Stewart, b ca 1853 Royalston, d 1914
E1. Eri S. Stewart, b 1887 Royalston, MA
D4. Edmund Cincinnatus Shepardson, 1847-1910, mar 1874 Emma L. Turner
D5. Luke B. Shepardson, b 1851, mar Ellen L. Tandy, b 1850, dau of Rev. Lorenzo Tandy & Lucy T. Stowell, 5 chn
E1. Florence E. Shepardson, b 1876 Royalston, MA
E2. John Shepardson, b 1877 E4. Carl W. Shepardson, b 1885
E3. Bertha M. Shepardson, b 1879 E5. Lucy Shepardson, b 1889
D6. Delia M. Shepardson, b 1853, mar 1872 A.B. Wood, 1st husband?
C2. Christine Bemis, b 1817 Bull Hill, NY, d 1860, mar Wm. Peckham
C3. William S. Bemis, b 1819 Brutus, NY, mar 1845 Julia Haskins

C4. Susan Amanda Bemis, 1822-1825
C5. Samuel Atwood Bemis, b 1824 Royalston, MA, d 1905, mar Huldah Green Stevens, b ca 1828 Guilford, ME
D1. Roger Wm. Bemis, b 1851 Parkman, ME, mar Nellie M. Coller, b ca 1853 Athol, MA, dau of L.S. Coller, 3 chn
E1. Charles B. Bemis, b ca 1873 Athaol, MA
D2. Leonard A. Bemis, b ca 1875 E3. Muriel L. Bemis, b ca 1877
C6. Susan Amanda Bemis again, b 1827 Warwick, MA, mar 1846 Nathan Smith, b ca 1817, 4 chn b Royalston,? MA
D1. Leander A. Smith, b 1848 D3. Julia A. Smith, b 1852
D2. Louton B. Smith, b 1851 D4. Mary C. Smith, b 1854
C7. Mary Berintha Bemis, b 1829 Royalston, MA, mar 1849 Quincy Adams Shepardson, b 1826, son of Jonathan & Nancy (Joseph) Shepardson. He mar 2. Eunice ___.
D1. Ida C. Shepardson, b 1856 Royalston, MA
C8. Luke Emil Bemin, 1832-1886, mar 1857 Mary Caroline Shepardson, 1837-1906, dau of Jonathan & Nancy Shepardson
D1. Emil H. Bemis, b 1858, mar Ada C. Bartlett, dau of Rev. E.M. Bartlett, 2 sons: Charleton and Edwin.
D2. Carrie M. Bemis, 1860-1862 D4. Mary Ella Bemis, b 1877
D3. George A. Bemis, b 1862
B10. Esther, b 1796, mar Cyrus GROUT, qv, b 1796 Winchendon, MA, d 1862, son of Isaac & Phebe or Sally (Stearns) Grout. Mar 1823.
C1. Abigail E. Grout, bp Winchenden, MA, d 1903, mar Lyman Borden
C2. Esther Augusta Grout, bp 1828, d 1895, mar (int) 1848 Hansen Wheeler
C3. Cyrus A. Grout, 1829-1852 C5. Joseph Lee Grout, 1834-1883
C4. Rachel Marie Grout, 1832-1895, mar John Sweetser
C6. Mary P. Grout, b 1838, mar 1863 Foster Barzilla Whitcomb, desc.
C7. John Grout, b ca 1841, d 1845 C8. Helen E. Grout, b 1844
B11. Elvira, b ca 1800
A12. Hannah, b 1753 Middleton, MA

Since Steeles and Stilles came to New England from Renfrewshire, Scotland, from Sussex, England, and from other parts of Grt. Britain, the compiler is not sure that the STEELE charts below should be included here. More research needed. See also James, in LATE ADDITIONS.

STEELE, Francis of Exeter, NH, 1694, working at Newcastle Fort. His heirs mentioned in 1740, will dated 1718. It seems poss that Francis may have come from J. Mar Elizabeth ___. (Noyes) OUTC.
A1. Clement, often a J first name, mar 1721/22 Joanna Avery, living in 1757
A2. John, mar Dorothy Rollins, dau of Benjamin Rollins, 1736
A3. Henry, accused by Mercy Taylor in 1734

STEELE, Jane of Castine, ME, mar 1813 Nathaniel Dyer, son of Benj. Nathaniel d 1881, age 93. (Underhill, vol. III) OUTC.

STEELE, John, a Chandler will witness 1775 in or near Casco Bay, ME. (Underhill, vol. 3)

STEELE, John, mar Jane ___.
A1. Sarah, b 1768 Wilton, NH, mar Jonathan Flanders, b 1768 Candia, NH, son of Thomas Flanders & Betsey STEVENS. OUTC.
B1. Betty, b 1790 Antrim, NH B2. Thomas, b 1792

STEEL, John and Mary, res Boston, MA. A dau Rachel b 1726. Note that a Rachel Steele was the mother of Edward SOHIER in Jersey. See Edward SOHIER.

STILL. This fam uncertain. His father may have been Benjamin. See STEEL, STILLE.

STILL, Ebenezer, b 1766 MA, son of Benjamin? Ebenezer a bootmaker, (many from C.I.), mar Susanna Preston, b 1775 Windsor, MA, d 1858 Macedon, NY. Ebenezer d 1848 Macedon, 10 chn. (Joy Lehman, Novato, CAL) Calvin and Diadema may be Hug. first names. OUTC.

A1. Abigail/Anna, b 1792 MA, d 1848 Leroy, NY, mar Ezekiel D. Jewett
A2. Susanna, b 1794 MA, d 1866 NY, mar Joseph H. Reeves
A3. Danforth, 1797-1872, mar Hannah Aldrich
A4. Ebenezer, 1798-1861, mar 1818 Malinda Robinson, in NY State
A5. Calvin, b 1800, mar 1818 Palmira, NY, Deborah Shippy
A6. Diadema, b 1802 NY, poss d.y.?
A7. Norton, b 1804, d 1882 Barry Co., MI, mar Eunice HAMMOND
A8. Arnold, b 1805, d 1876 Otoe Co., NEBR, mar 1830 Wayne Co., NY, Sarah May Gould
A9. Samantha, b 1807 NY, d 1833
A10. Nelson, b 1809 NY A11. Kellogg, b 1809 NY
A12. Rosannah, b 1813 NY, d 1843
A13. Sarah/Sally, b 1815, mar 1. Charles W. Reed and 2. ___ Shultz
A14. Willard, b 1818 NY, d 1853 NY

STEPHENS and STEVENS. Old in G. STEPHENS in J 1156 as ESTIENNE. Curr G and J. STEVENS, ESTIENNE, was a privateer in G 1692.

STEVENS, Joseph, a miller in Jersey, d 1890 St. Mary's, Hampshire, South Hayling, England, age 77, the youngest son of John and Mary Stevens of Jersey.

STEVENS. From J to Winnipeg, 1900s. (Joan Stevens, Jersey) Also others from J to Canada.

STEVENS, William, from Jersey, built a ship at Salem, MA for BAILHACHE 1661. (A. John Jean, Jersey)

STEVENSON, John, b J, settled in Salem-Canada, Lyndeborough, NH before 1764. Mar Abigail SHEPHERD of Amherst, NH. (STEPHENSON GEN. by Donovan and Woodward; Joy Richardson, Bedford, NH)

A1. John Jr., b 1767, mar Mary/May Hildreth of Amherst. She d 1845, 6 chn. John d 1847.
A2. Abigail, b 1769, d Lyndeborough, NY, age 65, unmar
A3. Lydia, b 1772, mar 1. 1789 John RICHARDSON, and poss mar 2. ___ DAVIS. Unverified.
B1. John Richardson, poss d before 1847
B2. Hartwell Richardson, rem to Wilington, MA, mar 1833 Rachel Parker
C1. Abby Richardson, mar ___ Young, poss sev. chn? A son John U. Young
B3. Moses Richardson, b 1797 ME?, or Lyme, NH, mar Hannah Runsford Gibbs, b 1799 Tolland/Granville, MA. She was dau of Benj. & Charlotte Gibbs. Hannah d age 76 in 1775 (Fam Bible) Moses d Sandisfield, MA age 81, res Tolland and Montville, MA. At one time the fam res OH where son Levi "left his mother" to enter Civil War.
C1. John Hartwell Richardson, b 1826/27, mar 1855 Mary E. Merrill, age 22, of Sandisfield, MA, dau of Orville Merrill. She d 1856, and John mar 2. 1857 Lucy Clark Deming, age 30 of Otis, MA, dau of James Clark.
D1. William Richardson, b 1856 D4. Edmund Richardson, b 1862
D2. Franklin Richardson, b 1858 D5. May E. Richardson, 1864-1950
D3. George Richardson, b 1860
C2. George Richardson, 1828-1872, poss a lawyer in Denver, Colorado?
C3. Charles N. Richardson, b 1835 Tolland, age 29, mar 1865 Lucelia M. Richardson, poss dau of Lewis Tyrell, b Montville,? MA, res New Boston,? MA, 3 chn b Sandisfield, MA, poss other chn?
D1. Henry E., b 1867 D2. Bertha, b 1870, d.y. D3. Mary, b 1872
C4. William P., b 1837, res Easthampton, MA, d 1911, married
C5. Levi Jack, b 1833 Hampden Co., MA, mar Lucinda A. HUBBARD, b 1840, dau of John H. and Lucinda (Adams) Hubbard of Sandisfield.

Levi served in Ohio Volunteers in Civil War. D 1917, bur Waterbury, CT, where Lucinda d 1926.

D1. Murtella Amelia Richardson, b 1860, d.y.

D2. a son, d.y.

D3. Mary?/Lottie May Richardson, 1870-1950, d unmar

D4. Allan Harvey Richardson, b 1872 Montville, MA, mar 1918 Myra Gertrude Reed, dau of Edw. A. and Mildred (Andress) Reed. Res Searsdale, Poughkeepsie, NY, Manchester, Lakeville & Wilton, CT.

E1. Nancy

E2. Allan Jr., mar 1947 Joy Gregory Keeler, dau of Samuel of Wilton, CT, res Bedford, NH, 2 sons, Daniel and Seth Richardson

D5. Demurest or DeMorris, b 1875, d.y.

C6. Moses? Richardson

C7. Abigail Richardson

C8. Henry Richardson, b 1843

B4. Abigail Richardson, b 1802 Litchfield, NH or Lyndeboro, ME? (Vinton's RICHARDSON MEMORIAL). Abigail d unmar age 65. Jonathan Stevenson was executor.

A4. Sarah Stevenson, b 1778, mar Supply Wilson of New Ipswich, d 1866

A5. William Stevenson, 1780-1830

A6. Lucy Stevenson, 1782-1814

STEVENSON. Several to early Boston, OUTC. John mar Deborah MARTYN 1720 Boston and John mar Elizabeth SQUIRE of Portsmouth, NH 1716. OUTC.

STEWART, Peter of Perthshire, Scotland, rem to NY from Guernsey, a mason age 40 in 1827. (NY NATURALIZATIONS, by M. Scott)

STOCALL. In J 1553. In St. Heliers and St. Saviour, J 1668 and 1749. Stockell noted in colonies but OUTC. (Nutmegger, 15-1, 1982)

STOCKERD. In J 1607, STOCKER is old in St. Peter Port, G. Charles Wm. STOCKER in G 1824. Note Ebenezer of MA mar Sarah Marshall 1674, 9 chn. OUTC. (Essex Coll. 3; NEHGS, vol. 17)

STOCKER, Nancy, b ca 1786, mar Jothan Cook, b 1804. She d 1841 Boston, MA. OUTC. (2nd Boat, Feb. 1981)

STOCKER, Eliz. of Portsmouth, NH, mar James OBER, 5 daus. Sam. in Portsmouth 1673 (Noyes) OUTC.

STODDARD. Not a C.I. surname, but curr in G as STODDART. John Stoddard of Scotland, rem to England and mar Mary ___ of the Channel Islands. (NEHGS, vol. 41) He had 4 chn, b Hurst Castle, Hampshire, England, 1758-1770. Desc to America?

STONEBRIDGE. Not old in the Islands, but curr in both G and J.

STONELAKE. English name, curr G.

STONELAKE, ___, a ship builder from England settled in G 1700s. See HUXTER. Elizabeth Stonelake mar William HUXTER, qv, in G ca 1860. Rem to Elizabeth, NJ ca 1862. (Kimberlee Perkins, Woodland, CAL)

STRONG. See CARRE. STRONG is curr in J.

SUNNAFRANK. See Record of trip to CAL Gold Rush, in Personal Accounts.

SUNNAFRANK. Not a C.I. surname, prob Dutch or German. Desc say John was b 1777 in Guernsey, rem to Loudon Co., VA, where he lived until 1804 and then rem to Cambridge, Guernsey Co., OH, later to Adams Twp., GCO. Another correspondant gives this info: "My Sonnefranks were of Dutch origin...A Dutch lady told me that the name was probably Zonnefrank, son of Frank." We know from old records in the Islands that there was a lot of business done between Holland and Jersey, at least as far back as the 1600s. Compiler would suspect that the immigrant John, or his father in G, was a sailor, and the fam spent some time in G before coming to America.

Note that there was another Sonefrank fam in OH, res Bath Twp., Allen Co., OH 1850. It is doubtful that these two fams were closely connected, but there may be a distant relationship in Europe. (Jeanne Garner, Oroville, WA; Charles Dickey, Richardson, TX)

SUNNAFRANK, John, b 1777 G, arrived in Cambridge, OH ca 1804/05, stayed

11 years and then settled in Adams Twp., on the Pike, res there till death in 1850. His wife d 1852, Elizabeth ___. (Conner-Eynon; Williams; Helen Sunnafrank, Cambridge, OH; Barbara Wilson, Redwood City, CAL; Mae Rott, Reno, NEV; GCO Library; Mrs. James Sunnafrank, Napa, CAL; Alma MacLachlan, Redwood City, CAL) CAUTION: TRIAL CHART.

A1. Jacob, b 1801 VA, d 1887/89 OH, mar 1823 Margaret, 1803-1877, dau of Solomon Adams. Jacob owned 569 acres in GCO.
B1. Absolom, b 1824, mar Adeline ___, rem to Napa, CAL with his bro John, but returned to OH. Another account says not.
B2. Lavinia Ann, b 1826, mar 1853 Lewis BONNELL, 1822-1892. She d 1893 GCO. In the 1860s, a Lewis T. Bonnell was County Coronor in GCO. (Wolfe) Poss other chn?
C1. Louisa Bonnell, 1853-1876 C4. Theodore Bonnell, 1860-1891
C2. Lemuel Bonnell, 1856-1883 C5. Emma Bonnell, 1866-1887
C3. George Bonnell, 1858-1893
B3. Elizabeth Jane, b 1828, mar James Patterson
B4. John A., b 1830, mar Ada Borton. Was he the John who went to CAL with bro Absolom? Ada must have d fairly young, as he mar in CAL a widow, ___ Willis, and settled first in Eldorado Co. near Georgetown, and later in Georgetown, CAL. Chn by Ada?
C1. James Willis C3. Carrie (2nd wife)
C2. Catherine Willis (2nd wife) C4. Eli (2nd wife)
C5. Levi, a farmer at Napa, CAL, d age 52 in San Francisco, CAL. Mar Sylvia Rutherford, had 5 daus and 2 sons. All but one ch b Pope Valley, CAL. May b St. Helena.
D1. Wilhelmina Alma Sunnafrank, b __, mar William Lockhart MacLachlan
D2. Irene D3. Winnifred D4. Catherine
D5. May, b 1896, mar ___ Rott, a Shell Oil man b ca 1890, res Reno NV
D6. James Budd, d 1960s?, bur Napa, CAL
E1. May, res San Anselmo, CAL, mar L.D. McKinnon? of Kelseyville CAL
E2. Wilfred James, only grandson of Levi, res Napa, CAL, mar Ruth __
F1. Michael F2. Timothy F3. Catherine
C6. Frank, had a dau Addie. Was he the one whose desc was named Bill Breedlove and res Georgetown, CAL? Bill d 1960s/70s. (Mae Rott, Reno, NV)
C7. Marion, had dau Virginia C8. Addie, d.y.
B5. Solomon, b 1833, mar Esther McPeak, 1830-1872?, and res GCO
C1. John A.
C2. William A., 1859-1944, mar 1883 Sarah Catherine Moorhead, 1854-1918, 5 chn: Clyde, Wilmer, Herschel, Bessie and Hazel.
C3. through C9. Ulysses, Mary A., Sarah, Jacob, Bertha, Lavinia and Esther.
B6. Sarah Lyda?, b 1838, d 1839?
B7. Levi Joshua, b 1840, mar Lucy M. Wheeler, 1845-1898. Chn uncertain.
C1. Alvira C2. Albert C3. Maggie, 1864-1882 C4. Jacob Ellsworth?
A2. John, b 1805, mar 1830 Margery Beaham, b 1810. John d 1890.
B1. Adeline, mar Joseph White 1856, 2 chn: Maggie and Willie White
B2. Elizabeth, mar John Algeo? 1853, 3 chn: Mary, John & Laura Algeo
A3. Margaret?, 1806-1877 A5. Mary, mar Joseph Boyd 1833
A4. Lavinia, 1809-1835, mar John Annett 1826 GCO

These Sunnafranks of Guernsey Co., OH were undoubtedly of the same group as the chart above:

Anna Eliz., 1830-1872, bur Adams Twp., GCO.

Elizabeth, 1799-1832, thought to be sister of first John, mar Arthur ANNET 1823, GCO.

Frances, b 1789 G, mar John or Jacob Darnhefer. She d 1816 GCO, thought to be another sister of the first John.

Jacob, had 160 acres in Adams Twp., GCO middle 1800s. A Jacob mar Mary E. Bonnel.
Jane, 1846-1881.
John, b 1798 VA, d 1851 OH, had a lot in Cambridge, OH.
John, 1831-1907, bur Wills Twp., GCO. He had a delegate, Wm. M. Rabe, go to CAL for him.
John, 1805-1890.
Levi Johnson, 1864-1874.
Lucinda S., 1860-1942, mar Samuel H. Devore, 1857-1914, bur Kimbolton, GCO.
Margaret, 1806-1877.
Margaret, b 1774 G, d 1851 GCO, mar Samuel Jackson, said to be sister of John, b 1777.
Margery, b 1810.
Mary Forbes, 1872-1898, bur Enon Cem, Jackson Twp., GCO.
Michael J. Sunnafrank, and W.J. Sunnafrank, res Napa, CAL 1973.
Solomon, a charter member of the Cambridge-CAL Mining Co 1849, went to CAL.
Solomon, 1864-1876, bur Adams Twp., GCO.
SUTHERN. Noted in Guernsey Militia 1750. Not researched by compiler.
SUTHERLAND. Curr in G and J, but not an old Island surname.
SUTTON. Curr J.
SUTTON, Henry, youngest son of Lt. Charles Thomas Sutton, R.D., d at Caraquet 1869, age 30. This was possibly a Sutton fam from the C.I.
SWADDEN. This form of SWARTON appeared in early New England. Philip SWADDEN/SWARTON "first known resident at the mouth of the Piscataqua River...who had been a servant to Robert SEELEY, qv, in MA, until freed by the court in 1631." Said to be b ca 1600. SWETTON, SWETT, SWANTON, SWARTON, noted in PLACE NAMES OF DEVON. A Philip SWADDEN res in Wiltshire, England 1619. (Noyes) A SWADDEN/SWARTON was at Muscongus in 1653. (Noyes) No wife or chn noted in records. This is not an old C.I. surname. Several accounts say that John Swarton/Swanton was from Jersey, therefore this fam is included. However, it is poss that Swarton lived in Jersey for a time, then came to America on a Jersey ship, but was originally from England?
SWARTON, SWANTON, John, from J, had served in Flanders under Charles II. Was a tailor in Beverly, MA, mar 1671 Johanna HIBBARD (See HUBBARD), b 1651, d after 1702. She was dau of Robert Hibbard and Joanna Luff, Love? John was killed by Indians in 1689 in the raid on North Yarmouth, and his wife and chn taken captive. The wife was returned in 1695 and wrote of the capture and life in Canada. See APPENDIX TO COTTOM MATHER'S HUMILIATIONS FOLLOWED WITH DELIVERANCES, 1697; NEW ENGLAND CAPTIVES CARRIED TO CANADA BETWEEN 1677 AND 1760; Records of Robert Pilon, Dearborn, MI; OLD TIMES IN NORTH YARMOUTH; Beverly VR: DHSM; Louise Swanton, Newton, MA; NEHGS, vol. 11)
A1. Margaret?, d 1674 Beverly, MA
A2. Samuel, bp 1674, killed before captives reached Norridgewock on way to Canada 1689. An interesting sidelight is the fact that in 1773 an Indian named Swanton was noted as living in Bakerstown, ME. He may have been a grandson of the Swanton-Swarton son who was thought to have died, but may have been raised by the Indians, instead.
A3. Mary, bp 1675, kidnapped by the Indians, and married in Canada, John LAHAY, Irishman?, in 1697, 12 chn. She d ca 1749. Lived in Quebec as Marie-Madeline Souard.
B1. Jean? LA HAYE, mar S. Gautier
C1. Jean-Baptiste Lahaye, mar Louise Cousineau
D1. Angelique Lahaye, mar Thomas Pilon

E1. Thomas Pilon, mar Josephine Levesque
F1. Francis Xavier Pilon, mar Delphine Waters
G1. John Edward Pilon, mar Stella Jarmey
H1. Thomas Bernard Pilon
A4. John, bp 1677 Beverly, MA, mar 1702 Abigail ___kins, prob d soon after.
A5. Abigail, mar 1708 Edward Belshar. Could Edward have been a BAILHACHE, BELASH?
A6. Jasper, bp 1685. He was captured, and redeemed with his mother 1695.

SWARTON, Joshua, said to have been taken by the Indians at Casco Bay, ME, and returned 1695. It is uncertain if he was another person, or perhaps same as Jasper, or a relative.

SWANTON, William, mar Rachel BROWN 1738 Boston, MA (int). OUTC.

SWASEY. Not an old C.I. surname. However, John SWASEY was said to be from Jersey and res Salem, MA middle 1600s. He was close to Philip ENGLISH, a Jerseyman, and they were said to have laid out English St. in Salem, with Swasey's sons. John had at least 7 chn. Another John SWASEY came from England 1632 with two sons, John and Joseph, Quakers. They rem from Salem, MA to Southold, NY. (Boston Transcript, Dec. 1930) No doubt other Swaseys came to America fron England. (Perley, III; Swasey; DRIVER GEN)

A1. Joseph, b 1653, res Salem, MA. Was he the father of Stephen, bp 1670? and Elizabeth, bp 1684?
A2. Elizabeth, b 1655, mar John BLAMPIED, WHITEFOOT, LIGHTFOOT?, a mariner 1680, in Kittery, ME 1684. He mar 2. 1692 Elizabeth Fortune. Two chn by Eliz.?, plus 3/4 recorded in Salem, including John, bp 1696 who mar Mary Elkins. (Noyes)
A3. Mary, b 1659, mar Thomas Mascoll?
A4. Abigail, b 1661, mar Wm. MASURY, qv.
A5. Samuel, b 1664, mar AMMI AIRES, poss AHIER, qv., 1710 Boston, MA. (Essex Coll., bol. 8)
B1. Anna, bp 1716 Salem, MA B2. Nathaniel, bp 1718 Salem, MA
B3. Ammi, bp 1720 Salem, mar John Webb, bp 1712, who d 1779 Boston, MA. John Webb mar 2. Sarah Driver BRAY. (DRIVER GEN)
B4. Joseph, bp 1723 Salem, poss the Joseph who mar Susanna ___, res MRB?
C1. Mary, bp 1772 C2. Abigail, bp 1774
A6. John, b 1666, mar 1695 Salem, MA, Christian GREY, nee LEGRO? of J fam? John was a sea captain for the firm of Philip ENGLISH, qv.
A7. Stephen, b 1669, mar Esther ___, had sev chn
B1. John, b 1694, mar Sarah Archer
B2. Hannah, b 1702, mar John ENGLISH, son of Philip ENGLISH, qv.

See MARBLEHEAD, MA Vital Records for other SWASEYS and SWAZEYS.

SWETT. This is not an old C.I. surname. Other Swett fams in New England are said to have come from Trayne, England and were also in Oxton, Devon, England. (Little) The Devon fam had a coat of arms and a crest. It is not known if the Swetts from G were related to the English fam. One record says that John of Newbury was from Norfolk, England, in Salem by 1636, and was a grantee in 1642, one of the original 91.

There are still unanswered questions. CAUTION: TRIAL CHART. See sources for more info. (Dow's HIST OF HAMPTON, NH; Little's GEN AND FAM HIST OF THE STATE OF MAINE, vols. 2 & 3; Noyes; Dearborn; SWASEY GEN; Stackpole; Hinchman; NEHGS, vol. 6; Forrester's SWETT-ALLEN AND ALLIED FAMS, 1980; Essex Coll; SWETT GEN, DESC OF JOHN S. OF NEWBURY, MA, Lewiston, ME, 1913?; MAINE RECORDER; HOOPER GEN; Marblehead VR; HIST OF PARSONFIELD, ME;TYLER GEN, vol. 1; Sturgis Library in Barnstable, MA; Virkus, vols. 5 & 7; Francena Hunt, E. Wareham, MA;

Mrs. J. Forrester, Concord, MA: Bev. Haughton, Lexington, KY; Rick Buckingham, Harper's Ferry, W VA; Mementos of the Swett Fam, by John W. Thornton, 1851; Louise McClellan, Topeka, KS)

SWETT, John, b 1580 or 1590 G, d 1651 MA, mar 1. Sarah ___ and 2. Phebe ___, who d 1665. Res Newburyport, MA. While this fam was charted by compiler, only part of the info is included here. See WRCIC.

A1. John Jr., b ca 1603 England or G?, mar Mercy Rouse and 2. Jane Hodges. This son is not included in some charts. Reason unknown to compiler. Two chn.

A2. Stephen, b ca 1624, cordwainer, res Newbury, MA, mar 1647 Hannah Merrill, dau of John & Elizabeth, 1633-1662. Stephen mar 2. in 1663 Rebecca SMITH, qv, dau of Thomas.

A3. Capt. Benjamin, b ca 1626/29 in G?, settled in Wellfleet, MA by 1670. Mar 1647 Hester or Esther WEARE, dau of Nathaniel of Newbury, MA. She mar 2. 1678 Stephen Greenleaf of Newbury. Benj. res Hampton, NH, prominent citizen, notable in King Philip's War. Killed by Indians at Black Point, ME. His sons were also prominent men in NH, 11 chn. See Dow's HIST. OF HAMPTON, NH.

A4. Joseph, b ca 1630, mar 1. 1651 Elizabeth TAYLOR and 2. Mrs. Mary Buttolph. Res Newbury, MA until 1650 then Haverhill and later Boston, MA.

A5. Sarah, d 1650 A6. Elizabeth? A7. Moses? A8. Other chn?

SWEET, Noah, said to be from G 1670, settled in Truro, MA. (Hinchman)

A1. Benjamin

A2. Moses?, 1661-1731, mar 1687 Mary Hussey, chn. Much work done on this fam by John N. Simpson of Morgantown, W VA 1933; Elbridge Alvah Goodhue, Sr., b Williamsburg, MA 1897; Louise Holland McLellan, of Woodlawn Ave., Topeka, KS 1933.

SYLVESTER. Early in G, and curr in J. See SILVESTER.

SYLVESTER, Juliette, b 1831 Freeport, mar John Whitney 1853, of Putney, VT. (Underhill) OUTC.

SYMONDS. Many in early New England, but compiler could not find any verified as from C.I.

SYMONS. Curr G and J. SIMON in J 1668 and 1749, curr G and J. SYMONDS, curr research in C.I.? See CIFHS #9.

SYMONDS, Daniel, mar Rebecca ___, res MRB.

A1. George Rounday, bp 1799, mar Eliza J. Cruff 1829, MRB

A2. Daniel, bp 1800

A3. Thomas, bp 1802

A4. Rebeckah, bp 1804

A5. Benjamin, bp 1807

A6. Richard Elkins, bp 1809, mar Rebecca ___?

A7. Elizabeth Dennis, bp 1813, age 6 mos.

A8. Mary Hales, bp 1817, age 5 mos.

SYMONDS. See the many records in Essex Coll; DEMMINGS AND THEIR KIN, by Mary F. Tryon, Iowa Falls, IA, 1972; Salem, MA Records; Census; and in Exeter, York and Oyster River areas. (Noyes)

SYVRET. See SEVERET, SEVERY, SAVARY. SYVRET is thought to be the original form of some surnames in New England and the Maritimes, spelled in various ways, such as SEVERY, etc. (GEN RECORD OF THE SAVERY-SEVERY FAMILY, Boston, MA, 1893)

SYVRET. In J 1607. In St. Heliers, St. Mary, Grouville, and St. Ouen, J 1668, and in St. Mary, St. Ouen and St. Martin, J 1749. In St. Lawrence, J 1788. Arms: Sable a lion rampant or.

SYVRET, Capt. Philip, b J, in Portsmouth, NH 1671, gave all his estate in America to wife Joanna, who was the widow of Jose. His will gave his estate in J to his bro Thomas. (Noyes)

SYVRET, SEVERY, Peter, from J to Wenham, MA, a wife Mary, and a dau Mary b 1684. Estate of Peter admin. by bro Thomas in 1685, and that of Andrew SEVORE by widow Mary in 1715. (NEHGS, vol. 54)

SYVRET, Amelia, fron J to North Chelmsford, MA 1800s, mar Walter LE MARINEL, qv.
SZUSHAY, Stephen, b 1867 GCO? or G? or France?, d 1920, bur Mt. Zion, Jackson Twp., GCO. Cem with Susanna, 1872-1930, and Daniel Jr., 1905-1930. See DU SOUCHET and SARCHET.
TANNER. Old in J, in Trinity & St. Saviour, J 1668 & 1749. Curr J.
TARDIF. Did this name appear in New England as TIDY and TARDY? Rachel below is the only person specified in old records as from Jersey, and the surname TIDY is very close to the pron of the surname TARDIF. Therefore, compiler believes the fams below may be TARDIF from J or G in early New England.
TARDIF. Surname of France, the Channel Islands and French Canada. TARDIVEL was more usual in J. TARDIF in G 1300s and 1750, also curr in G. Research? See CIFHS #11.
TARDIF, Alexander, b G, mar Amy LE NORY, rem to U.S. with dau Vera after wife's death, 1900s?, when Vera was 6. Vera returned to G at age 18. Alexander remar, res Haskell Place, NJ. By 2nd wife, 3 sons, one named Howard, res NJ? Vera mar a FALLA, (Howard Falla, Agincourt, ONT)
TARDY, Elizabeth, in Athens Co., OH, 1860. OUTC.
TARDY, Eunice, dau of Capt. John TARDY of Halifax, NS, Canada, mar Benjamin Pitman of Yarmouth, NS, 1789, at Chebogue, Yarmouth Co., NS. At the same place and by the same minister, Mary TARDY and Nehemial Porter were mar in 1776. "We could not trace a family of this name in Halifax, but as a Mariner he could have been moving around." (Alice A. Wetmore, Yarmouth, NS, Canada) OUTC, but likely to be a C.I. fam.
TIDY, Robert, poss TARDIF of C.I.?, res Kittery, ME 1670s, mar Sarah Libby, whose mother was Abigail MESSERVE, qv, and father was Samuel Libby. (LIBBY FAM, by Charles T. Libby, Portland, ME, 1882; Noyes; Underhill; OLD FAMS OF KITTERY) OUTC.
A1. John Tidy, b ca 1683, mar ca 1712 Hannah, dau of John MORRELL of Kittery, ME. John d 1766. At least 6 chn. John had 100 acres in 1720 on east side of Nonsuch River.
B1. Sarah, b 1714, mar Benj. Stacey, b 1704, res Kittery, ME? (OLD KITTERY & HER FAMS)
C1. Hannah Stacey, mar 1769 Joseph Furbish, 1735-1808, res Berwick, ME. Joseph mar 2. Sarah Ferguson. Joseph was son of Joseph and Elizabeth (Meads) Furbish. At least 2 chn by Hannah.
D1. Stephen Furbish, b 1770, mar Catharine Hill
D2. Sarah, b ca 1772, mar 1795 John Furbish of Lebanon, ME, son of Richard & Jane (McCrillis) Furbish, 1771-1822. Sarah d 1840, 8 chn
D3. John Furbish, b ca 1773, mar Polly White of NH, no issue
C2. Lydia Stacey, mar 1773 David Furbish, 3 chn
D1. Betsey Furbish, mar Jotham Lord 1800
D2. Hannah Furbish, mar Eliakim Staples 1807
D3. Lois Furbish, mar Nathaniel Stacey 1803
B2. Edah, b 1716, mar ___ Emery
B3. Hannah, b 1718, d ca 1799, unmar
B4. Robert, b 1720, no issue
B5. Meribah, b 1722, no issue
B6. John, 1724-1749, unmar
A2. Hannah, mar 1. John Ford 1706, a son John Ford. She mar 2. Daniel Withum of Kittery, ME, son of Peter.
A3. Elizabeth, mar 1708/09 John Witham, 8 chn
B1. Elizabeth Wittam/Witham
B2. John Wittam
B3. Zebulon Wittam
B4. Eleazar Wittam
B5. Gideon Wittam
B6. James Wittam
B7. Nathaniel Wittam
B8. Katherine Witham

A4. Mary, mar 1710/11 George Brawn, son of George?, res York, ME. Mary, widowed, with 5 chn of 1st mar, four under 7 yrs., mar 2. Thomas Penny of Wells, ME 1732. OUTC.

TARDIF. Curr Boston, MA, poss from French Canada?

TARDIF, William, a house carpenter, naturalized 1832 NYCity. (NY NATURALIZATIONS, by Scott)

TAYLER. Prob English surname in J. Curr G.

TAYLER, Josias, d in J 1811, had served in the Compagnie des Invalides.

A1. Josias, a son?, joined the 3rd Regt. of the Buffs in England, a foot regt. No record of birth found in J. Res in Canada after War of 1812, in which he saw service. Settled in the Military Settlement at Perth in Lanark Co., ONT. (Mrs. J.L. Knox, Vancouver, BC, Canada)

TAYLER, Mr. & Mrs. Cyrus, from Ruette Braye, G, rem in 1920 to Canada. He was the son of Richard Charles TAYLER. She was Alice DOREY, qv, age 87 in 1966. One dau was b in G, the other in J? or England? The fam rem to SLCity, UT, where Cyrus was a landscape gardener for the Board of Educ. They retired to Orlando, FL. Two bros? settled in SLCity, UT, and 3 other bros? settled in Canada. The two daus of this fam are mar and have chn, one res in FL and the other in CAL.

TAYLER, TYLER, John, from J in ship PHILIP, 1665, with Carteret to NJ. Both TAYLER and TYLER curr in C.I.

TAYLOR. Noted in Sark 1900s. TAYLOR old in G, in J 1299, curr G and J.

TAYLOR, John Antony, b 1933, bro-in-law of Roy KELLING, qv, mar Anne Elizabeth TAYLOR, not related, b 1938. Mar 1956 and rem to Toronto, ONT. Two chn: Suzette and Anthony.

TAYLOR, Percival Walter DE PUTRON, qv, b 1891 G, served as observer in Royal Flying Corps, WWI, rem to Canada early 1920s, mar a Canadian, farmed in Sooke, Vancouver Island, BC. He was a noted water color artist, d 1979. At least 2 chn: Robert and Fiona.

TAYLOR, J., of J, owned the HOWARD, built in Portsmouth, NH, middle 1800s. (A. John Jean, Jersey)

TAYLOR, Samuel Medhurst, b England or G, mar there 1802 Susannah HEADLEY, HEDLEY, dau of Brian HEADLY, b 1734 G, son of William, and Brian's wife Susannah BISSON/BUISSON, dau of Nicolas & Elizabeth (HENRY) BUISSON. Mar in Vale, G. (Florence Monter, Cincinnati, OH)

A1. Charles Tyler Taylor, b 1804 G, mar 1834 Louisville, KY Catherine Cooper, dau of Wm. Cooper, who emigrated 1799 from Tyrone, Ireland, and wife Margaret Robinson of PENN? Catherine b 1812 OH, d there 1902. Charles d 1870.

B1. Margaret Susannah, b 1850 Louisville, KY, mar 1881 there Samuel Henry Cooper, b 1843 OH, d 1918 Cincinnati, OH. Margaret d 1929 Cincinnati, OH.

C1. Catherine Henrietta Cooper, b 1884 Louisville, KY, d 1952 Cincinnati, OH. She mar 1907 William F. Stoecklin, Jr.

D1. Florence S. Stoecklin, b OH, mar E. Wm. Monter, res Cin., OH

B2. Henrietta Bisson Taylor, b 1806 G B4. Edward Bisson, b 1808 G

B3. Maria Taylor, b 1807 G

Note that Susannah BISSON/BUISSON above may have been a DES LANDES descendant, as the grandfather was called in one record, Nicolas BUISSON DES LANDES.

TEAGUE, William, b ca 1813 St. Helier, J, son of Wm. & Sara (Carne) Teague of Cornwall, England. This Teague may have been connected with an Army company stationed in the Island. (A. Teague, Detroit, MI)

TENNY. In G 1600s. See COLQUITT GEN.

TERRY. Curr G. See COLQUITT GEN.

TEWKESBURY. Spelled many different ways, noted in early MA records, some marriages with C.I. fams, such as PAINE, GRUSHEE, MAIN, PRIDEAUX, etc. TEWKESBURY said to be from Kent, England?

THACHER. English surname. However, one fam settled in J and mar into prominent Island fams such as DE STE. CROIX, MARTIN, LE GALLAIS, INGOUVILLE, RENOUF and LE BOUTILLIER. Most THACHER fams in America prob from Salisbury, Somerset and Sarum, England. The Jersey THACHER fam was associated with the Newfoundland fisheries.

THELLAND. Poss from THALLAND, a Scottish fam in Fife, in Auchterruil 1574, in Burntisland, Scotland 1612 and 1644, and in Dowhill 1698. As THELLEN?, in U.S. and QUE. See also Jean LE BRUN. This is not common in the C.I., curr in J, and listed in STEVENS book of old Jersey surnames. Some rem to Nfld. (Lucille Roy, Malartic, QUE)

THELLAND, Francois, b 1799 St. Peter, J, son of Wm. & Esther (LUCE) THELLAND, mar Angelique Defoy 1823 Newville, QUE. Angelique b 1807 St. Jean Baptiste, Connacona, Portneuf, QUE, dau of Pierre Defoy & Angelique Ouvard dit Laperriere. Francois d 1881 at Mont Carmel, Valmont, QUE, and Angelique d 1887, 6 chn. See LUCE in Q.A. IN CANADA.

A1. Esther, b 1824 Newville, QUE near Quebec City, d 1827
A2. Francois, b 1826 Newville, d.y.
A3. Francois again, b 1828, mar Louise Cloutier 1853 St. Raymond, QUE, dau of Prisque & Josephte Dufresne (Francois) Cloutier. Francois d 1890 at Mont Carmel, QUE and Louise in 1895. Eleven chn.
B1. Francois Xavier, b 1854 St. Raymond, QUE, mar 1874 Hedwidge Beaudoin at Vincennes, QUE B2. Marie Louise, b 1855, d.y.
B3. Elizabeth, b 1856 St. Raymond, Portneuf, QUE, mar 1875 Georges Levasseur in Mont Carmel. Georges b 1849, d 1931, age 82. Elizabeth d 1938, age 81, in Shawinigan, QUE.
C1. Georges LEVASSEUR
C2. Elizabeth Levasseur
C3. Joseph Levasseur
C4. Victor Levasseur
C5. Louise Levasseur
C6. Gedeon Levasseur
C7. Omer Levasseur
C8. Alfred Levasseur
C9. Marie-Anne Levasseur
C10. Aurelie Levasseur
C11. Ephrem Levasseur
C12. Clothilde Levasseur
C13. Marie-Blanche Levasseur
B4. Prisque, 1858-1859 B5. Eliza, b 1859 St. Maurice, QUE, d.y.
B6. Jean Baptiste, b 1860 St. Maurice, mar Josephine Therreault 1882, Mont Carmel, Valmont, QUE, dau of Rene & Lucie (Pothier) Therreault. Josephine d 1913, Shawinigan-South, and Jean d 1944, age 84, Notre Dame de la Presentation, Shawinigan-South, QUE.
C1. Arthur, b 1901 Mont Carmel, mar Bernadette Leclerc 1924 in Villemontel, Abitibi, QUE, dau of Joseph & Aldea (Houle) Leclerc. She d 1962, age 60, in St. Joseph Vald'OR, Abitibi, QUE, and Arthur d 1971, age 70. Four chn.
D1. Lucille, b 1926 Landrienne, Abitibi, QUE, mar Raymond Roy 1945, b 1916 St. Isidore, Dorchester, QUE, son of Joseph & Marie-Anne (Morin) Roy.

E1. Pierrette Roy, b 1946 St. Marc de Figuery, Abitibi, QUE, mar Pierre Colbert 1968 in Malartic, Abitibi, QUE, no issue.
E2. Lise Roy, b 1947, mar Michel Lemire 1969 in Malartic, Abitibi, no issue.
E3. Jacqueline Roy, b 1951 Abitibi, unmar
E4. Yvan Roy, b 1963 Evain, Abitibi
B7. Marie, b 1862 St. Marucie, mar Leon Desilets 1883 at Mont Carmel. He d 1891, age 36, she mar 2. Narcisse Lacerte 1892, Mont Carmel.
B8. Eugene, b 1864 Mont Carmel, Valmont, QUE, mar Caroline Loranger 1885

B9. Josephine, b 1866 Mont Carmel, mar Georges Beaumier 1887
B10. Louise, 1868-1870
B11. Joseph, b 1871 Mont Carmel, mar Marie LeVasseur 1891, who d 1900, age 27. Joseph mar 2. Mary Rheault 1900, who d 1913, age 36. Joseph mar 3. Emma Bourque 1917 at Notre Dame de la Presentation, Shawinigan-South, QUE.

A4, Elizabeth, b 1830 Newville, QUE, d 1866, age 35, mar 1851 Charles Morand at St. Raymond, Portneuf, QUE, 6 chn.
B1. Elizabeth Morand, b 1853 St. Raymond, QUE
B2. Julie Angelique Morand, b1855
B3. Charles Morand, b 1858 St. Raymond, Portneuf, QUE
B4. Georgine Morand, b 1861 St. Maurice, QUE
B5. Francois Morand, b 1864, QUE
B6. Rosalie Morand, b 1866 Mont Carmel, QUE

A5. Jean, b 1832 Neuville, QUE, mar 1854 Malvina Petit at St. Raymond, Portneuf, QUE. Jean d 1915, age 82, and Malvina d 1904, age 72, at Lowell, MA. Thirteen chn.
B1. Jean, b 1855 St. Raymond, d 1859
B2. a ch, d.y. 1857
B3. Celina, b 1858 at St. Maurice, QUE, d.y.
B4. Jean, b 1859, d.y.
B5. Victoire, 1860-1865
B6. Napoleon-Paul, b 1862 St. Maurice, mar 1882 at Lowell, MA, Olivine Beaudry, who d 1949 at Montcalm, QUE. Desc named THELLEN res Montreal, QUE.
B7. Jean, b 1864 Mont Carmel, QUE, mar Delia Archambault 1883 at Lowell, MA. Delia d 1904, and Jean mar 2. Eliza Cardin 1905. Jean d 1922 in Lowell, MA, Eliza Cardin d 1934. Although Jean and Delia had 13 chn, none had descendants!
B8. Joseph, b 1866, mar Mathilda Leblanc, 10 chn b Lowell, MA. Joseph d 1922, and Matilda 1928 in Lowell, MA. Of 10 chn, two had desc: Albany and Edmour THELLEN. Res U.S.
B9. Victoria, 1868-1873
B10. Alphonse, b 1869 QUE, mar Rebecca St. Arnaud at Berlin, NH, Three chn, but no desc left.
B11. Leothilde, b 1871, mar Pierre Caron, rem to Ottawa, ONT.
B12. Edwidge, b 1873 Mont Carmel, mar M. Daigle at Lowell, MA
B13. a ch, d.y. 1878

A6. Olympe, 1834-1845

THOMAS. In J 1331, curr G and J. THOMASSE also old in J.

THOMAS, TOMAS, John, of Jersey, mar Hannah THOMAS? in Portsmouth, NH 1718. Hannah poss b 1697, dau of Roger Thomas. (Noyes)

THOMAS, ___, from J to North Chelmsford, MA ca 1870/1880.

THOMAS, William, res Cape Porpoise, ME, 1680, mar Mary BARRETT. (Noyes) OUTC.

THOREAU. See NOTABLES.

THOREAU. In J 1150, curr J. A CAL THOREAU fam was not found by compiler.

THOREAU, Jean, b St. Helier, J ca 1754, son of Philip & Marie (LE GALLAIS) THOREAU. He was a privateer, and was wrecked near the MA coast where he then settled in 1773 as a cooper in Boston, MA. He mar 1. 1781?, and 2. Rebecca Kettel, Ketil?, he d age 47, leaving a large estate. Poss no desc of this fam, as many d unmar.
A1. Charles
A2. John, the father of Henry David THOREAU, the famous naturalist and author
A3. Jane A4. Maria A5. Louisa A6. Sally or Betsy?

THOREAU, Philip, from J to America 1870, mar Ann TOUET of J, had 2 sons, Philip and Wm. with desc in CAL. (GUILLET GEN) This fam from France to Surrey, England to J middle 1700s.

THOREAU, Philip, b J, a stone mason, rem to Osceola, IA, where the LE BOUTILLIER-BUTLER fam of J had also settled (Brechtel in

LE BOUTILLIER GEN)

THOREAU, Pierre Thomas, mar Sophie HUBERT, 3 chn. He d after 1868.

A1. Sophie, b 1856 A2. Julia, b 1857

A3. Alfred Thomas, from J to Canada, then to NYCity, assoc with Oxford Press, where he was working in 1896. (GUILLET GEN)

THOREAU, Philippe, b 1770 J. Edward John THOREAU of this fam b 1815, mar 1836 Sophie Catherine LERRIER in J. Their son Philip Edward emigrated to New Zealand in 1878. He had spent his youth in Canada in the employ of the Hudson Bay Co. He d 1920, age 75, leaving 5? chn in New Zealand?

THOREL, Maria, to Elizabethtown, NJ on ship PHILIP 1655 with the CARTERET group, qv. Mar Daniel PERRIN. Maria poss from Rouen, France. (Lawton; Perrine)

THORNE. Curr G and J, but none researched by compiler.

THOUME. In Torteval, G 1786, curr and common in G. See CIFHS, vol. 11.

THOMY, Helier, arrived in Boston 1763 on brig ROYAL CHARLOTTE, from Havana, Cuba. Was he a Channel Islander?

THOUME. Some noted in C.I. charts. See Index.

THOUMINE. Curr G, name noted in Chicago, ILL and in MA. Could this have the same origin at TOULMIN?

THOUMINE, ___, res G?, mar Dorcas Fannie Jessup, b 1854 G, rem to Bronx, NY, where she d 1922. Mr. Thoumine was b in London, England of G fam?, d 1886 G. (George Godden, Hartford, CT)

A1. Augustus, b 1885

A2. Florence, b 1886 G, rem to NY, d Bronx, NY 1962, no issue

A3. Dorcas Caroline, b 1882 G, res Bronx, NY 1907, d there 1948

TOULMIN. A J surname from the 1600s? Poss Huguenot? "Origin of the name is apparently Slovenian--there is still a well-known cheese-producing town, north of Trieste, called Tolmin, in a disputed area near the Yugoslav-Italian border." The fams were Unitarian as "early as the 17th century, and my understanding is that they moved North, first to Holland, later to France, before turning up in England." (Stephen Toulmin, University of Chicago)

TOUMINE, THOUMINE?, Lucas, b G, age 36, from G, a shoemaker, with wife Pamela, b Yonkers, NY, age 34, in NY 1828. (NY NATURALIZATIONS, by Scott) Ages in 1828.

A1. Edward, b NYCity, age 13

A2. Clarissa, b Yonkers, age 11

A3. John, b NYCity, age 8

A4. Harriet, b NYCity, age 6

A5. Sarah, b NYCity, age 2

TICKELL. Noted in colonies, one in J 1646 was a Royalist privateersman. (A. John Jean, Jersey)

TIDY. See TARDIF.

TILLEY. In J 1299, and later in J, however, none traced in colonies by compiler.

TINGLEY. Old name in J. See also MATTINGLEY.

TIRELL. In G 1600s, curr J. TYRELL in J 1528. Many noted in early New England, but none traced to C.I. Cf THURELL, THURILL, etc., in early records, also. TURELL, Joseph mar Ruth BUBIER, qv, in MRB 1809. See also BICKNELL GEN.

TISSIER. Said to be Hug name in C.I. See Q.A. IN CANADA. This name also as TESSIER?

TEXIER. The weaver, poss Hug surname that appeared in J? See page 352, LE GRESLEY fam.

TISSUE. Not listed by Stevens as an old J surname, although TISSON is listed. It is probable that the TISSUE fams below are Hug fams, but appear to have come from Jersey where so many Hug fams settled temporaarily. More research needed. Not known to compiler if William below, b ca 1750, and John, b ca 1751, were related, but it seems likely. Note that William lived in the Turkeyfoot, PA area, where the Skinners also lived. See SKINNER.

TISSUE data from SOCIETE JERSIAISE Annual Bulletin of 1927: Peter Tisseau, age about 56, and Louise Remigeau, his wife, age about 57, of Pousange Esvesche of Luson, in Poitou, France, were in Jersey in 1728 and abjured at that time.

TISSUE, William, b ca 1750, in J?, d 1819. By 1772 res in Elk Lick Twp., Bedford Co., PA, where he served as J.P. and was Capt. in the county Militia. By 1798 res in the Turkeyfoot, PA (later Confluence) area with his 2nd wife and fam. He mar 1. Mary Hendrickson, and 2. Huldah Rush, b ca 1750, d 1820/30, poss dau of Wm. & Elizabeth (Ream) Rush. She is not mentioned, however, in the RUSH FAM OF THE APPLACHIANS, or the RUSH GEN., by Sylvester Rush. She may be the dau of a bro of Wm. or poss of Peter. Cf Jacob Rush, son of Wm. & Elizabeth (Ream) Rush, mar Mary SKINNER, qv, also other intermarriages in these two fams. Two chn by 1st wife. William's grandson Ross owned the land in Fayette Co., PA where the FALLINGWATER house is located. He is bur Turkeyfoot Baptist Cem. (John Witt, E. Liverpool, OH: Sharon Ridge, Anchorage, AK; Jack Tissue, Ferndale, MD; WRCIC)

A1. James A3. by 2nd wife, Elizabeth A5. Sebastian
A2. John A4. William
A6. Edward, b 1789 Confluence, PA. Poss more chn.
B1 Hulda. No proof on this. A Huldah Tissue mar Jacob R. White, who d 1855, age 39. She was b 1834, d 1914, res New Lexington, OH, bur Baptist CH. (SKINNER FAMS IN UPPER TURKEYFOOT, PA)
B2. Isaac, b 1832, Allen Co., OH, mar Lucy Bywater, b 1840 Springport, NY, d 1929 N. Muskegon, MI
C1. Clyde Tissue, b 1881 Crockery, MI, d 1932 Everett, WA, mar 1901 Lulu Thusa? Brown, 1882-1970, dau of Fremont & Della (Wright) Brown
D1. Fremont Leroy, b 1902 Nunica, MI, changed name to John Charles Tichue 1928, d 1952 Seattle, WA, mar 1929 Kelso, WA, Edith N. Matthews
E1. Joyce Edith, b 1930 San Francisco, CAL, mar 1950 Seattle, WA, James Guy Klumb
E2. Gary Dean, b 1949 Seattle, WA, mar 1979 Maureen ___
D2. Marguerite MaDella, b 1911, mar 1964 1. William Koerber, 2. Thomas Island, and 3. Arnold C. Solberg
D3. Irene Glayds, b 1916 Grand Rapids, MI, mar 1932 Mt. Vernon, WA, Cyrus Donald Boring, b 1912 Anacortes, WA, son of Cyrus A. and Carrie A. (Moore) Boring.
E1. Donald Clark Boring, b 1933 Everett, WA, mar 1957 Shirley May Peck, b 1939, 3 chn
E2. Sharon Irene Boring, b 1943 Everett, WA, mar 1960 Anchorage, AK, Joseph John Ridge, b 1939, Anaconda, MT, son of Joseph Patrick and Florence B. (Boehler) Ridge
F1. Joseph Donald Ridge, b 1961 Everett, WA, mar 1980 Coeur D'Alene, ID, Kimberly Jo Kennedy, b 1961 Seattle, WA
G1. Brandon Joseph Ridge, b 1980 Everett, WA
F2. Robert Clyde Ridge, b 1962 Reno, NV
F3. Patrick William Ridge, b 1964 Everett, WA
D4. Maxine Virginia, b 1918, d ca 1923
D5. Clyde Arnold, b 1921, d 1972 Tacoma, WA, mar Barbara Hill
D6. Kathleen Zeda, b 1924, mar 1. Walter Ratje, and 2. Donald Rogers
D7. Ruth Maxine, b 1930, mar Kenneth White
A7. Jane Silbaugh A8. Jacob A9. Isaac A10. Thankful Stull

TESHEW, John, b 1751?, "came from Isle of Jersey," d 1838 Marblehead, MA, mar 1771 Hannah MARTIN, bp 1751, d 1843 of MRB. John served in Co. 9 of Capt. John Glover, and Col. John Glover's 21st Regt. of Foot. He was also a sailor with Capt. Samuel TUCKER in 1776, and Capt. John Fish, brig MASSACHUSETTS 1777. At least 4 chn. (Donald Doliber, MRB, MA)

A1. Hannah, bp 1766, by another wife? Poss d.y. A2. Hannah bp1772 d.y.
A3. Hannah again, bp 1778, mar Thomas Kemp 1803 in MRB
A4. Nabby, Abigail, bp 1780, d 1851 MRB, mar Thomas WIDGER TUCKER 1803 MRB. Thomas b 1771, d 1870. Ten chn.
B1. Capt. Thomas Tucker Jr., b 1804 MRB, d ca 1840 at sea on schooner HERMIONE, mar 1832 Betsey Oliver
B2. William Tucker, b 1806, d 1885 MRB, mar Hannah A. BOWDEN 1832
B3. Abigail Brandy Tucker, b 1808, d 1813 MRB
B4. Hannah Martin Tucker, 1810-1812
B5. Hannah Martin Tucker again, b 1812, mar Philip B. Tucker 1834
B6. Mary Grandy Tucker, b 1815, d 1910 MRB, mar Joseph Graves 1835 MRB
B7. George Tucker, b 1818, d 1821 MRB
B8. Mary Widger Tucker, bp 1822, d 1825
B9. Sally Rhoades Tucker, b 1823, d 1907 MRB, mar Samuel Bowden Gardner 1858 MRB
B10. Mary Widger Tucker, b 1825 MRB, d 1898 MRB, mar 1848 John C. Harris, b 1817, d 1881 MRB
C1. John Charles Harris, b 1857 MRB, d 1918 MRB, mar Eliza Chapman Graves 1880, she was b 1860, d 1938 MRB
D1. John Edward Harris, b 1884 MRB, d 1951 Rumney Depot, NH, mar 1903 MRB, Annie Alice Evans, b 1884, d 1967 MRB
E1. Carl Edward Harris, b 1904, d 1920 MRB
E2. Mary Tucker Harris, b 1905 MRB, d 1956 Salem, MA, mar William Felton Doliber 1928 MRB, who was b 1903 MRB
F1. William Felton Doliber Jr., b 1932, mar Caroline L. Boynton 1953 in New Brunswick, NJ, 3 sons and a dau
F2. John Harris Doliber, b 1936 MRB, mar 1978 Karen Young, of Yoke Pond, ME
F3. David Allen Doliber, b 1944, mar 1970 Mary Ann Thornton of Richford, VT
F4. Donald Arthur Doliber, b 1944, mar 1975 Linda Jean Wyzanski in MRB. A son, Donald A. Jr., b 1976 MRB.
E3. John Edward Harris, b 1908 MRB, mar Stella K. Haines 1938, no issue
E4. Myrtle Graves Harris, b 1909, d 1950 MRB, mar Elmer Gray 1940, 3 sons
E5. Elizabeth Phillips Harris, 1910-1911
E6. Gertrude Harris, mar Joseph Berube
C2. Edward Adams Harris, 1861-1931, mar Henrietta V. ___
C3. Abba Tucker Harris, d 1938, mar Leonard Clay Rolins 1877

TISHEO, TISSUE, TISSAU?, etc., John, res MRB, mar 1782 Mrs. Sarah Roads Lear. Not known to compiler if this was the same John as above. A widow of a John TISHEO d MRB 1843, age 84. A John Tisheo d MRB 1838, age 87. (Fosdick, etc.)

A1. John, bp 1784, mar Mrs. Ann HINES 1801, MRB
A2. George, bp 1785, d 1814 at sea. Mar Mary Stone? She mar 2. James Bredeen 1818. Note many Georges in Marblehead, MA records.
B1. Mary Hudson, bp 1815, age 3, mar Thomas ROUNDEY 1833, qv.

A3. Samuel, bp 1787, d 1831, mar Sally Valentine 1818
A4. Peter, bp 1789 d.y. A6. Sally bp 1795, mar John D. Dennis Jr., 1818
A5. Philip, bp 1791 A7. Peter, bp 1796

TISHEO, Peter, mar Hannah ___, res MRB.
A1. Mary, bp 1770
A2. Peter, bp 1773, d.y.
A3. Philip, bp 1775, mar Mrs. Mary Andrews, 1803 MRB
A4. Peter, bp 1777
A5. Molly/Mary?, bp 1780

TISHEO, TISHEW, etc., Abigail, mar Thomas Tucker 1803.

TISHO, etc., George, mar 1. Hannah Cox? (int) 1774 MRB, and poss 2. Hannah Bruce, 1776 MRB, a widow. A dau Hannah was bp 1777. Same or another George mar widow Hannah BROWNE 1776 MRB.

TISSUE, Hannah, mar 1784?

TISHEO, Mrs. Hannah, mar Lewis RUSSELL 1783 MRB.

TISHOE, etc., Hannah, mar Michael Power 1784 MRB. Same or another mar Samuel CALLEY 1800 MRB.

TISHEO, John, mar Hannah Wood 1763 MRB, a dau Hannah bp 1766.

TISHEO, Peter, mar Mrs. Mary Andrews 1802 MRB. See same wife for Philip TISHEO above!

TOADVINE, TODVIN. See TOSTEVIN. Interior "s" is silent.

TOCQUE. In J 1479, in St. Ouen, J 1749. TOCQUE curr J. TUCK curr G. Poss same as TOCQUE?

TOMS, John, from J 1870s to North Chelmsford, MA. TOMS curr G and J.

TOMS, Maria, see Alfred BRAKE. TOMS a G surname, but also Scottish? In Boston, MA 1970s. OUTC.

TOMKINS. In St. Saviour, J 1749, as TANKIN in St. Saviour 1668. No research by compiler on fams in America.

TORODE. Ancient Norse-Viking surname from Thorvaldr. Trudeau is said to be a French variant. TOROLD in England in 1300s. TORODE in J 1299-1607. Sir Winston Churchill had a TORODE in his ancestry. Curr G, in Catel, G 1821. Some to Australia. Curr research? See CIFHS #6.

TORODE, Alfred, b 1860s G, mar Mary DOREY of G. Rem ca 1920s to St. Catharines, ONT with his fam, where he farmed and then had a greenhouse, with a florist shop in downtown St. Catharines. Alfred d age 81 in 1940s. (Frank Torode, Huntington Beach, CAL)
A1. Clifford, mar Amelia OSBORNE 1923, b Coventry, England
B1. Frank Alfred, b 1923, mar Yolande Gagne, b 1933, 3 chn
C1. Linda, b 1956
C2. Michael, b 1958
C3. Susan, b 1964
A2. William/Bill, mar Maida ___. Wm. d before he was 60. Maida res St. Catharines, ONT.
A3. Thomas, res Detroit, MI 1981
A4. Una
A5. Sylvia
A6. Flora
A7. A son who became a railroad station master in Toronto, descendants.

TORODE, Peter, b G, had at least 2 sons, John and Peter, who came to OH 1807. Poss that some TORODES res in ILL early? (Mrs. John Bunner, Kansas City, KS; Jacqueline Beck, Ramona, CAL; Stone; Sarchet; Conner-Eynon; Frank Torode, Huntington Beach, CAL) In 1850, some Torodes and Browns lived near Marietta, OH and apparently rem from there to IA ca 1854. (SOME ERRORS IN THESE CHARTS, CHECK ORIGINALS)
A1. Peter, b G, mar Hannah Burt in GCO 1821. Peter a Vet. of War of 1812? He d ca 1824.
B1. Mary, 1822-1888, mar 1840 David SARCHET, qv, his 4th wife?, 7 chn b GCO. (Stone) This fam res ILL. See David SARCHET.
A2. John Wesley?, b G, mar 1. Asenath Burt 1820 GCO, dau of Luther & Mary Burt. He mar 2. Sarah Lanam, b 1817, of Morgan Co., OH, living in 1900 in IA with dau. Two chn by 1st wife, 3 by 2nd, poss others?
B1. Elizabeth, b 1822, mar 1844 William Lyons in Morgan Co., OH. Lyons had 5 chn by previous wife: John A., b 1831, Wm., b 1833, Albert, b 1835, Hannah A., b 1837, and Catherine, b 1841.
C6. Cyrus N. Lyons, b 1845
C7. Elizabeth J. Lyons, b 1846
C8. Mary A. Lyons, b 1849
C9. James Lyons

C10. David Lyons, b 1857
B2. Peter, b 1825 GCO, was in IA 1854, d 1913 in Des Moines, IA. Mar 1846 Catherine Brown, b 1829 OH, d 1894 Des Moines, dau of Alex. Brown and Sarah Maple.
C1. John Wesley, b 1847 Newport, OH, d 1937 Durant, OK. He mar 1. 1884 Mary Ellen Hill, dau of Jack & Susan (Thompson) Hill, and 2. 1907 Mandana Brundage De Cook. Nine chn by 1st wife. Mary Ellen bur Red Rock Cem., MO, in Boone Co. A son Harry Peter b 1880, d.y.
D2. Willard Arthur/Bill, b 1882, d 1953 Durant, IA, mar Della Wyatt, div., 2 chn. Bill is bur Bryan, OK.
E1. Mary Ellen, b 1911, mar Sam E. NICHOLAS, dau Donna b 1941
E2. John Warren, b 1915 Harrisburg, MO, mar 1939 Mary Rosetta Jones, 4 chn: Larry Willard, Linda Kay, Della Mae and:
F4. Roxanna Ellen, b 1955 St. Louis, MO, mar 2. J.P. Rybak 1978
D3. Earl, b 1884 Dexter, IA, d 1953 Lisbon, MO, mar Gladys G. BUTLER, 3 chn
E1. Imogene Eleanor, b 1919, mar 1. H. Hadley, 2. Wm. Creber and 3. John L. Bunner
F1. Mary K. Hadley, mar Earl F. Ross, 2 chn: Tracy & Heather
E2. Douglas, b 1922 MO, mar Esther Mae Gurnea, 2 chn
F1. Donna Jean Torode, b 1957, mar James Baker
F2. Patricia Ann, b 1959
E3. Doris Mae, b 1928, mar William C. Moulder 1950
F1. Nancy Lynne Moulder, b 1951 MO, Mar John McComas
F2. Susan Clarice Moulder, b 1958 Mt. Clemens, MI
D4. Frank Marion, b 1887, d 1961 Durant, OK, mar Arlena
E1. Betty Ruth, mar, res TX, had dau Pam
D5. John Warren/Dick, b 1886, res 1910 Boone Co., MO, mar Mary Ellen ___, d OK? Served in Civil War.
D6. Ruth Hazel, b 1892 Des Moines, IA, d 1978 Independence, MO, mar 1909 Joe Wilcox in Boone Co., MO, 4 chn
E1. Edith Mae Wilcox, b 1913, mar 1. F.M. Hamilton, div., mar 2. David Black
F1. Marjorie H., b 1932, mar Charles BonnEastridge, 7 chn
F2. Buddy Mirl Hamilton, b 1936, mar Patsy Sue Jones, 7 chn
F3. Bobby Don Hamilton, b 1939, mar Beverly Jane Wyatt, 2 chn
F4. David Earl Black
E2. Louise Chrestine Wilcox, b 1915, mar 2. Gerald Saferite
E3. Wilford Wilcox, b 1919, mar Glenda Abel, 2 chn, 5 grandchn
E4. Herman Lee Wilcox, b 1921, mar Vena Frost, no issue
D7. Kate/Catherine?, b ca 1900, d 1917/18, Durant, OK, mar Samuel Head
E1. Gladys Beatrice Head
D8. and D9. twins who d.y.?
C2. Amanda Welthan, or Welthan Amanda, b 1849 Marietta, OH, d 1925 Mediapolis, IA, bur Kossuth, IA. She mar there John Harper 1870, 10 chn. John was b 1821 Ross Co., OH, d 1909 IA, son of Joab and Lydia (Jones) Harper. John a teacher and farmer. He had mar 1. Emily Harper and 2. Rebecca Jane Hizer.
D1. Mary Amanda Harper, b 1871 Des Moines, IA, mar John K. Garland, res Harrisburg, PA
D2. Katherine Victoria Harper, b 1873 Des Moines, a dressmaker
D3. Edna Leona Harper, b 1875 Des Moines, a nurse at Scranton, PA, d 1970. She mar Nelson C. Storks.
D4. Charles Field Harper, b 1878 Northfield, IA, mar 1907 Lincoln, NB, Janneva Ella Sutton. Charles d 1970 Escondido, CAL, bur Ramona, CAL. Janneva was dau of Moses E. Sutton & Ella

Reifschnider, 5 chn.

E1. Virginia June Harper, b 1908 Council Bluffs, IA, mar 1926 Marion Joseph Hodgson in Ramona, CAL

F1. Marion E. Hodgson, b 1929 F2. June Hodgson, b 1931

E2. Elizabeth Amanda Harper, b 1911 IA, mar Frank Wm. Beck 1932 in Santa Ana, CAL

F1. Charles Darrell Beck, b 1933 F2. Frank Warren Beck, b 1941

E3. Warren Percy Harper, b 1914 Holtville, CAL, mar Ruth Louise Wolf. Warren d 1940 Ramona, CAL. Sons Alfred Lewis and Alfred Harper.

E4. Edna Audrey Harper, b 1916 Hotville, CAL, mar 1933 Yuma, AZ, Arthur Freeman Alford

F1. Judith Dian Alford, b 1935

F2. Arthur Freeman Alford, b 1937

F3. David Stanley Alford, b 1947, d.y.

E5. Janneva Pamela Harper, b 1924 Ramona, CAL, mar 1942 Glenn E. Matthew

F1. Terry Glenn Matthew

F2. Daniel Matthew

F3. Warren Charles Matthew

D5. Robert Hall, b 1880 Des Moines, IA, d ca 1969

D6. William Franklin, b 1883 Des Moines, IA, studied pharmacy in Harrisburg, PA

D7. Nellie, b 1885, a teacher, d 1975 Burlington, IA

D8. Edith Audrey, b 1887 Des Moines, IA

D9. Louise, b 1890 D10. Marjorie Elaine, b 1892 Des Moines, IA

C3. Sarah Virginia, b 1851, mar ___ Purcell

C4. William Alexander, 1853-1933, mar 1883 Jaun Davilla Hamilton, 4 chn

D1. Anna, d.y.

D2. Clyde, b1887 IA, no issue

D3. Jessie Adeline, b1889 IA, mar Arthur Weiderricht

D4. Bertha Ina, b 1894, mar Harley McCulley, 3 chn

E1. Richard Wm. McCulley, b 1918, mar Ruth Huddle, res IA

E2. Jean Joan McCulley, b 1920, d.y.

E3. Raymond C. McCulley, b 1923, mar Phyllis Dudgeon, 2 chn

D5. Martha Irene, b 1900, mar Clarence Deam, 3 chn

E1. Betty Marie Deam, b 1923, mar Arlington Brockway, 2 chn

E2. Donna Roberta Deam, b 1926, mar Charles E. Schmied, 3 chn

E3. William Burt Deam, b 1930, mar Yvonne Howard, 2 chn

C5. Mary Asenaith, called "Sis," b 1856, mar 1877 William Jolliffe, Madison Co., IA

C6. Peter Finley, b 1858 Des Moines, d 1923 Lee, IA, bur Glendale, IA. Mar Dorothy Snellbacker, bur Glendale Cem, IA, 3 chn

D1. Chester C. Torode, b 1886, d ca age 3 D2. Bruce, 1890-1917

D3. Ralph Rizen, b 1895, Des Moines, IA, mar 1. Minnie Elizabeth Dyer and 2. Ellen?

E1. Roy Rizen, b 1926, mar Marilyn Crane, 5 chn: Stephen, Christine, Michael, Brian and Gregory, has grandchn.

C7. Francis Lincoln, b 1860 IA, d 1947 Des Moines, IA, mar Drusilla Baker, 2 chn

D1. Francis Oliver, 1903-1950, unmar

D2. Elmer Byron, 1905-1978, mar 1931 Leatha Merle Neagle, dau Marilyn

C8. Ida Catherine, b 1864, called "Kate," mar ___ Thomsen, d 1941

C9. Charles Luther, b 1867 IA, d 1940 C10. Harry/Hal Marshall b1872 IA

B3. Asenath, b 1838 (by 2nd wife)

B4. Francis M./Frank?, b 1843, mar Charity ___, b 1848 PA, 4 chn?

C1. Rodney, b 1871 IA

C2. Blanch, b 1874

C3. Allice, b 1875 IA

C4. Jay, b 1877 IA

B5. Rachel M., b 1849 OH, mar ___ Smith, 3 chn b IA. In Poweshick Co., Brooklyn, IA 1900.
C1. Katie Smith, b1872 C2. James Smith, b1877 C3. Frank Smith, b1879

TORODE, James, prob the bro of John and Peter, b late 1700s in St. Peter Port, G, where he had lot #1634, came to U.S., enlisted in U.S. Army, settled in GCO. Mar Cartret ___, had at least 3 sons, and poss daus, too? Will made 1812. Thomas SARCHET, an in-law, was executor of will. See David SARCHET. (Jacqueline Beck, Ramona, CAL; GCO Records and Wills; Imogene Bunner, Kansas City, KS)

TORODE, John A., built a saw mill on Salt Creek, ILL ca 1845, where the Graue Mill was later. He built the first dam, and used the water power to saw rough lumber from logs. About 1850 he sold the mill to Fred Graue and opened a stone quarry 3 miles north of Fullersburg on York Rd., now Oak Brook. John Torode set aside a small piece of land for the Torode Cem., the first one in the area; many settlers bur there. It became overgrown, records were lost, and eventually the stones were moved to a special plot in the Butler Cem. The entire area of the Old Torode Cem. is now part of the Oak Brook Shopping Center. (George E. Ruchty, Historian for the local Hist. Soc. at Hinsdale, ILL)

TORODE, Nicholas, son of John, came from G 1820 and settled in Monroe Co., OH. Nicholas was from De Bourg, G, had wife and 2 sons upon arrival in America. Mar 2.? Charlotte Glass 1833. Desc. in ILL. (Knox Co. History, 1881, ILL)

A1. Peter
A2. Charles
A3. Philander, b 1824, Monroe Co., OH
B1. John A., b 1861 Du Page Co., ILL, attended Wheaton College, Wheaton, ILL, mar Minnie Amelia Rodgers, dau of Francis and Mary Rodgers, b Downers Grove, ILL 1867
C1. Vivian, b 1886? C2. Edith Minnie, b 1893 C3. Mildred, b 1901

TORODE, Hannah, poss sister or widow of first Peter in GCO, came to OH and mar 1827 Stephen Reed. Married by Daniel HUBERT, qv, J.P. in GCO.

TORODE, Ella Louise, from G, mar Julee Pierre LE GRAND in ONT 1900s. (Mrs. Duke, Mississauga, ONT)

TORQUET, Paul, b ca 1827 G, res Canada, then rem to San Francisco, CAL, mar, no issue. Was a prop. of Vulcan Foundry there in 1864, when he d. (CAL ARCHIVES; Maxine Turquette, Champaign, ILL)

TORREY. See Jane HAVILLAND. Some TORREY fams in America may be desc of Capt. Wm. Torrey of England and Jane HAVILLAND of an old Guernsey fam. See Underhill and TORREY FAMS OF AMERICA, by Fred Torrey, Lakehurst, NJ, 1924.

TOSTEVIN. Old in J. In St. Andrews, G 1757, poss in Vale Parish? Also noted in Torteval, G. Curr G and J. Sometimes pron TODEVIN.

TOSTEVIN, John, b 1793 G, poss in Vale?, also poss son of Jacques T. & Rachel. John mar Martha LE PREVOST, qv, of G, and rem by ship DARLING To Phila., PA. Martha was 62 at her death in 1856. They res NYCity; Salem, IA; Coldwater, MI; Jersey City, NJ, and poss in CAL? (Fam Letters; Quaker Ency.; Margaret Ramsden, Carson City, NV) A Thomas and a David Tostevin were with them in NYCity, and poss relatives of John?

A1. Martha, b 1820/1825, mar George Davies, res where?
B1. Martha, d.y.
B2. Alitha?, d.y.
B3. Emma, mar Cady Thomas
B4. Charles, mar Felice or Delia ___
B5. George, unmar
B6. Clarence
B7. Bertha, mar Paul Frederick Sutpen, res where?
C1. Ruth Sutphen
C2. Helen Sutphen
C3. Dorothy Sutphen
C4. Walter or Wallace? res Cleveland, OH 1903

A2. John, mar Mary ___, no issue
A3. Alfred, b ___, mar Rachel ___?
B1. Mary Elizabeth, d.y. B2. Katherine mar Joseph Gordon Huntington
B3. Annie, mar ? B4. Ida B5. Alfred B6. Cordelia, mar Edwin Losey
A4. Rachel, b 1825 St. Peter Port, G, at Des Landes Grandes mar George Underhill. Later, she prob mar 2. George Alexander and had 8 chn?
B1. Susan B2. Emma B3. George Henry -Were these Underhills?
B4. Frank Alexander, mar Kate Pickney
B5. Ida Alexander, b 1852 Brooklyn, NY, d 1946 Easton, PA, mar Wm. John Leddell, b 1845 Ralston, Morris Co., NJ, mar 1880, d 1916 Summit, NJ.
C1. William Alexander Leddell, b 1883 Ralston, NJ, mar 1907 Mary E. Otterson, b 1881 Goochland Co., VA. He d 1941 Wickenburg, AZ.
D1. Margaret Leddell, mar P.H. Ransden, res Carson City, NV
C2. Elizabeth Le Provost Leddell, mar ___ Holmes, issue?
B6. Rachel Ella Alexander, mar Edwin Anderson
B7. Martha Alexander, d.y. B8. Theodore Alexander, d.y.
A5. Peter, b ___, mar 1. Mary Shafter, and 2. Margaret Hawkes/Hankes?, res Salem, IA 1847
B1. William Rushforce, mar Nettie Bomboy
B2. Henry, mar Ida ___, 1 ch B4. Martha, mar George HAWKINS
B3. Peter, mar ___ B5. Mary, mar Samuel Figgis?
B6. by 2nd wife, Margaret, b ___, mar Louis Lewey, 2 chn
C1. Samuel Lewey C2. Alfred Lewey
TOSTEVIN. The following brothers and sisters from Vale, G to Canada and the U.S. early 1900s. (James E. Savident, San Mateo, CAL)
A1. Peter, b 1883 G, to New Zealand, d 1967
A2. Jack, b 1884, to NH, a stone mason, mar, 1 dau, he d 1974
A3. William, b 1885 G, to New Zealand, d 1973
A4. Ada, b 1886, to Victoria, BC, Canada, mar ___ Hancock, a dau
A5. Arthur, b 1887, to Milford, NH 1912, mar Jane Hyslop, b 1899, a son d.y.
A6. Ethel, b 1888, mar ___ Marshall, rem to Victoria, BC 1917, a son and a dau
A7. Harry, b 1889, to Milford, NH, mar, 1 dau, he d 1973
A8. Reta, b 1900, to Victoria, BC 1917, then to San Leandro, CAL. Mar ___ DOREY, qv. Living in 1973.
A9. Clifford, b 1901 G, to Victoria BC, mar Lillian MAY
TOSTEVIN, Eliza Jane, b 1882 Le Maison de Bas, Vale, G, mar James SAVIDENT See Q.A. IN CANADA, by Turk.
TOSTEVIN, John, rem from G to Racine, WI ca 1850.
TOSTEVIN, George LEMPRIERE, from G to Racine, WI 1860s. (E. Fred Tostevin, Duarte, CAL)
A1. Geo. Henry, mar ___. A son Clarence had Wm. who d.y. and Clara Louise
B1. Clarence B2. Edna Jane B3. Glen, d.y. B4. E. Fred
TOSTEVIN, Nicholas, from G?, mar Anne LE VALLEE, from G?, 1826, in St. Andrews Presby. CH in Quebec City, QUE.
TOSTEVIN, James P., b 1825 G, mar Julia BURGESS, qv, 1858, settled Racine, WI ca 1860. Five chn including Edward A., b 1864 and Walter J., b 1867. (RACINE HISTORY)
TOSTEVIN, Margaret, b G, mar Peter LE RAY, qv, rem to Racine, WI ca 1860?, 2 chn.
TOSTEVIN, Elizabeth, b G, mar ___ Mutter, rem to Racine, WI.
TOUET. In J 1309, In St. Peter, J 1749.
TOUET, Ann, b J, mar Philip THOREAU, qv, rem to US 1870, desc in CAL.

TOUET. Several to Gaspe and to BC Canada. See Q.A. IN CANADA, by Turk.
TOULMIN. See THOUMINE.
TOURGEE. See also CARPENTER. CAUTION: TRIAL CHARTS. Ongoing research by Borsching, etc.
TOURGIS, TOURGEE. A fam of this name left France 1685, stopped in Guernsey for some time and then settled in Kingston, RI in the late 1600s. What makes it difficult to distinguish between various TOURGIS fams in America is the fact that the name was in J by 1299, from the Danish THORKIL. Also in Grouville, St. Ouen and St. Peter, J 1668, and in St. Ouen and St. Mary, J 1749. Compiler does not know if some of the TOURGIS fams in America may be desc from Jersey immigrants. It seems clear that most of those in early Rhode Island were Hugs. from France to Guernsey to America. Note that some of the TOURGIS in Jersey were called TOURGIS, alias CARPENTER, and CARPENTERS did appear in RI, CT and MA at about the same time. (BAIRD; Potter; Robert Borsching, Honeoye Falls, NY; Theron Smith, Ft. Worth, TX; RI Hist. Tract #5, by Potter)(Nancy T.Mauro,PO Box 116,Oldsmar,FL,33557
TOURGEE, TOURGIS, Peter, and his bros, came directly from Guernsey about the time of the French settlement in Narragansett, 1686.(Baird) Peter had 3 sons: Peter, John and Philip.
TOURGEE, Peter, Jr., from G to No. Kingston, RI, mar 1.? and 2. in 1722 Mary Smith, dau of William & Abigail SMITH, qv. (VR of Arnold, RI; Baird; RI Census of 1774; Potter's FRENCH SETTLEMENT IN RI, 1686; Mrs. Virginia Chappell, Mrs. Violet Rettell and Mrs. Nancy E. Mauro) CAUTION: TRIAL CHART.

A1. Thomas, b 1722 No. Kingstown, RI   A2. Philip, b 1724
A3. Elizabeth, b 1728, d before 1776
A4. Abigail or Marcy?, b 1730, one of these mar 1753 Benjamin Diamond
A5. Peter, Jr., b 1733/34, mar 1755, 2nd wife, Bridget Hill
A6. John, 1735-1812, mar 1761 Priscilla SMITH, who d 1814. Some desc of this fam.
B1. Smith TOURGEE, b ca 1764/65, d prob by 1820, mar 1782 Elizabeth ___, his 2nd wife, b between 1770-1780. The 1st wife may have been ___ SMITH. Smith may have been the son of either John or Peter TOURGEE. (CENSUS, Stonington & Exeter, CT; Death Certf. of Mary Perkins and Rebecca Crandall)
C1. ?, b ca 1783, W. Greenwich or N. Kingstown, RI
C2. ?, b ca 1785, ditto   C3. ?, b ca 1787, ditto
C4. Mary, b ca 1789, d by 1845, mar 1823 in Exeter, 2nd wife, Rhodes Wilcox Perkins
C5. Rebecca, b 1793, Richmond?, d 1870 Coventry, RI, mar 1813 Rowland Crandall
C6. Ann/Nancy, b ca 1799 W. Greenwich or Exeter, d by 1823, mar ca 1813 Exeter, his 1st wife, Rhodes Wilcox Perkins. See Mary, C4.
C7. Benjamin, b ca 1802 Exeter, d Stonington, CT by 1850, mar ca 1838 Lucinda ___
C8. ___, b ca 1806   C10. ___, b ca 1812, Exeter, CT
C9. William R., b ca 1808 Exeter, mar ca 1830 Mary ___, poss BROWN?
B2. Peter, b ca 1764, d by 1809, mar by 1790 Mary ___
B3. Thomas, b ca 1766
B4, Prudence, b ca 1768, mar 1783 William Hunt   B5. Mary, b ca 1770
B6. Philip? Uncertain if he belongs here in the chart. B 1772? North Kingstown, RI, mar ca 1798 Margaret/Peggy Northup, b 1782, d 1844 N. Kingstown. "Philip was prob the son of John & Priscilla Smith Tourgee." Peggy was dau of Zebulon Northup Sr. of N. Kingstown & Mary COLE. Philip d 1852 Exeter, RI. Another record says Peggy's name was SNOW. Could this have been her 2nd husband? 14 chn?

(VR Arnold & Beaman, RI; Census, 1800-1850; Bible records of Mrs. Virginia Chappell; Death Cert. of Eliza Thomas; Theron Smith, Ft. Worth, TX)

C1. Mary, b 1799, mar Benj. Rogers
C3. James b1803, d 1884 N. Kingston
C2. William N., 1801-1864, mar Sarah C. Reynolds
C4. Eliza Snow, b ca 1804, d 1884, mar Jeremiah Thomas
C5. Thomas, b ca 1807, d 1884 N. Kingston, mar 1. Martha A. Greene, and 2. Freelove A. Stedman
C6. Philip, 1808-1810 C7. Amasa, b ca 1809, d 1872, mar Phebe Adams
C8. Henry S., b 1811, d 1895 N. Kingston, mar 1848 Elizabeth Congdon
C9. Lucy, b 1813 C10. Herrington M., b 1815, d 1874 N. Kingston
C11. Zebulon, b 1818 C13. Sarah, b ca 1822?
C12. Margaret/Peggy, b 1820 C14. Dorcas Ann, 1824-1904

B7. Benejah, b 1775, d 1842 N. Kingston, RI, mar ca 1796 Phoebe Tennant

B8. Jeremiah, 1779-1867. Prob other chn?

C1. Ebenezer, b 1809 Warwick, RI, d 1878, father of Prof. Eben TOURGEE of the Boston, MA Conservatory of Music

B9. John, Jr.?

A7. Mary, b 1739, mar Benjamin Whitford

TOURGEE, Philip, b 1738, son of ?, mar 1772 South Kingstown, RI, Desire TOURGEE, his cousin, who was b 1752. Desire had a bro William. Their father, and the father of Philip, were bros. Philip d 1826 Greenfield, Saratoga Co., NY. He served in the Amer. Rev. War in Capt. Thurbers? Co., Col. Church's Regt. of RI Regulars, and in other groups, fighting in several battles. He was discharged at West Point, NY, then res Greenfield, resuming his trade of shoemaker. In 1818 he applied for and was granted a Rev. pension of $8 a month, which continued to his death in 1826. His widow lived with her son Stiles or Giles, and also at her son Thomas' home. She was in the poorhouse for a short time, and was then taken in by a Mr. Conrad Fults. Later palsied, she res in the poorhouse in Herkimer, and then with a Mr. Joseph Bump in Galway, NY at about age 84, apparently a never-say-die type of woman!

B1. Valentine, b 1773, rem to OH

C1. Valentine, Jr., b 1814, rem to Lee, MA, mar 1836 Louisa Emma Winegar, who d 1843, a desc of Edward Doty of the Mayflower. She was of a German fam. They rem to Williamsfield, Ashtabula Co., OH. He mar 2. Rowena SNOW ca 1845, a dau b ca 1848. They lived 1847 in Kingsville, OH, where Valentine d 1889, 2 other chn d.y.

D1. Albion Winegar, b 1838, fought in the Civil War and lost an eye. He was a prolific writer of poems, political articles and novels. He mar 1863 Columbus, OH Emma L. Kilbourne, rem 1865 to Greensboro, NC and was elected judge there. He wrote TOINETTE, which became a well-known work, with much sympathy for the southern colored people. This resulted in a fierce and continuing display of antipathy from the whites of the area, especially those connected to the Klu Klux Klan. He was later a consul to Bordeaux, France, where he d 1905. Eleven thousand of his papers are in the Chatauqua Co., NY historical files at Westfield, NY. There is a microfilm of his works and several books at the Kent State Univ. Library, Kent, OH. They had a dau, no name found.

B2. William, b 1775 B4. Sally, b 1780 (These 3 died before 1837)
B3. George, b 1777 B5. Thomas, b 1784

B6. Stiles/Giles?, b 1788, mar 1809 Providence, Saratoga Co., NY, d 1853 Little Falls, Herkimer Co., NY, Mary PERRY, dau of Henry & Ann (Casplance?) Perry. She was b 1784 and d 1837 Broadalbin, NY.

Stiles/Giles served in War of 1812.

C1. Henry L. TORGEE PERRY, 1810/1812 , adopted by his maternal grandparents and took their surname, Perry. He mar 1. 1841 Elizabeth Casler, 9 chn, and 2. Elizabeth McKinney, and 3. Hannah Pratt. Elizabeth Casler b 1825, d 1859.

D1. William Henry PERRY, b 1845, d 1918 at Little Falls, NY. He mar 1864 Jane Anne Flansburgh, b 1840 New Hartford, Oneida Co., NY, who d1925 Danube, Herk.Co., NY, bur Church St. Cem, Little Falls, NY

E1. Mina Perry, b 1864, mar Ralph Austin E2. Edw. Perry, b1866

E3. Henry Perry, b 1869, mar Lillian Pennally?

E4. Delia Perry, b 1872

E5. Clara Perry, b 1874, mar 1893 William ROULETTE, and d 1964

F1. Wayne Roulette, b 1892, mar Josephine PITON, and d 1960

F2. Hazel Roulette, b 1894, mar Ralph Stewart

F3. Cornelia Roulette, b 1896, mar Richard Frederick Borsching, and d 1923, has desc

G1. Robert Richard Borsching G3. Albert Perry Brosching

G2. William Joseph Borsching G4. Barbara Ann Borsching

F4. Carrie Roulette, b 1900, unmar

F5. Perry Roulette, b 1906, mar Emily Kamasis

E6. Eliza Perry, b 1876, mar Charles Dygert

E7. Edith Perry, b 1878 E8. Hugh Perry, b 1882

E9. William Perry, Jr., b 1884, mar Verna Moss, and d 1956

D2. Charles G. (TOURGEE) PERRY, b 1865, poss other chn b between 1845-1865?

C2. George W. or George T. TOURGEE, b 1821 Little Falls, NY, mar 1843 Janette/Janet McKercher. Also, as George W.?, d 1911, bur Union Hill Cem., Broadalbin, NY. Janet d 1900.

D1. Catherina A.

D2. Mary A. TOURGEE, b 1844, mar James STEELE, qv, d 1905, chn: James E. Steele, Harper Steele, Samuel Steele, Mattie Steele, Cora Steele, Lillie Steele, Lucie? Steele, Clary Steele and Etta Steele.

C3. William B. TOURGEE, 1823/25, d unmar 1847 Jalapa, MEX. with U.S. Army

C4. Jacob H., b ca 1828, res Chillicothe, OH 1911

C5. Betsey, mar, res near Rochester, NY 1876

C6. Lillie, mar and res near Rochester, NY 1876

C7. Anne, mar in Detroit, MI 1876, William Switz

TOURGEE, William, one of at least 2 chn (see sister Desire above, wife of Philip), prob b N. Kingston, RI ca 1740 or earlier, chn of ___ TOURGEE, from G to America late 1600s or early 1700s. William mar Sarah Billington.

TOURGEE, Grizzel, mar Picus Auston, prob in N. Kingstown, RI? (BICKNELL GEN)

A1. Elizabeth Austin, b 1776 N. Kingstown, RI, mar 1793 Jesse Bicknell, b1770, Attleboro, MA. Jesses was son of Japhet & Molly (CARPENTER) Bicknell, a wheelwright, res at Hammond's Mills.

B1. Polly Bicknell, b 1794 B3. Japhet Bicknell, b 1797

B2. William Bicknell, b 1796 B4. Benjamin Bicknell, b 1799

B5. Jesse Bicknell, b 1802, mar Susanna TOURGEE, b 1803 N. Kingstown, RI. Ten chn: Thomas, Nehemiah, Mumford, Elizabeth, who mar David CARPENTER, Ann, who mar Albro Kingsley, Jesse, Andrew, John H., Alfred, and Susan Bicknell, who mar George Warren.

B6. Hosea Bicknell, b 1804

B7. John Bicknell, b 1806, mar Mary Staff 1840 and d Mobile, ALA

B8. Elizabeth, b 1809 mar Jabez C. Gardner 1828
B9. Varnum Bicknell, b 1812 B10. Alfred Bicknell, b 1815

TOURGIS, see Q.A. IN CANADA for ONT fams, also see PEABODY GEN.

TOUR, poss at times changed to TOWER?

TOUR, Joshua and Jerusha, in Rehoboth, MA early. Did he mar 2. Huldah? before 1760, or was Huldah wife of Joshua's son Joshua? OUTC.

A1. Sarah, b 1731/32 A3. Jerusha, b 1741
A2. James, b 1733 A4. Deborah, twin, b 1741

TOUR, Joshua and Huldah res Rehoboth, MA. OUTC

A1. Joshua, b 1761 A2. Hulda, b 1761 A3. Ezra b 1769

TOURTEL, curr and old in G, see John PILL

TOUSSAINT, curr in G, also in Alderney. See Q.A. IN CANADA, and COHU.

TOUZEAU, curr G. See Peter SARCHET

TOUZEAU, Alice, Anna J. a widow; Edwin P., a painter; Harold U. a pressman; and Ralph W., a clerk; all res Cleveland, OH 1901. OUTC

TOUZEL, in St. Clement J 1607 and 1668. Curr J.

TOUZEL, Frances, mar Thomas GALLISON 1795 in MRB.

TOUZEL, George of Manchester or MRB, mar Lucy Allen at Manchester, MA 1772. She was b Manchester 1751, dau of Jacob. (Essex Antiq., Vol 2) Names spelled TOUGIL, etc.

TOUZEL, John, from J, mar Susanna, dau of Philip ENGLISH, qv, in MA 1700. Was John a goldsmith? He was a mariner, sailed for Wm. and Sam. BROWNE of Salem, MA. (Essex Coll, Vol 1)

TOUZEL, John res MRB, a son John, bp 1727

TUZELL, Lucy, res MRB 1790 with fam of 3 females. (Census)

TOUZEL, TOUSEL, Susanna, mar John HATHORNE. (DRIVER GEN)

A1. Susanna Hathorne, mar 1772 at Hampton, MA, Sam. Ingersoll, son of John and Sarah (Bray) Ingersol. Sam. d 1804 age 66.

B1. Ebenezer Ingersol, d 1804 age 23. Other chn?

TOUZELL, TOWSER, TOZZER, Capt. William mar (her 1st husband), Abigail Metcalf, b ca 1734, d before 1787, res Danvers, MA, no issue. (DRIVER GEN)

TOWER, BEnj. and Deborah res REhoboth, MA, a dau Patience b 1702. OUTC

TOWERS, Jean from St. Martin G to CAL 1959. TOWERS curr J.

TOY, Frederick N., age 38 of Toronto, ONT, b G, son of Daniel and Eliza Toye, mar 1866 in Toronto, ONT, Annie C. Daniels, age 25, of Yorkville, ONT, dau of Francis and Susannah Daniels. (Primitive Meth. CH records) Witnesses Benj. R. Toye of Toronto & Dennis Daniels of Yorkville, ONT.

TRACHY, DE TRACEI, in J 1135. TRACHIE in J 1607 in St. Lawrence J. 1788. Many similar surnames in early New England, but OUTC. TRACHY curr G and J. See NEHGS Vol 11.

TRACIE, TRACHY?, in MRB; Capt. Wm. Tracie and wife Sarah had 5 chn in Salem, MA late 1600s. OUTC.

TRACHY, Carole May, dau of Eric Charles TRACHY, b G, settled in Weymouth, Dorset, England. She was b 1939, mar Lawrence DE LA HAYE, qv, and rem to Victoria, BC, Canada, 2 chn.

TRACHY, Mary from C.I. res North Shore in Duplessis Co., QUE (formerly Charlevois and Saguenay Counties) Mar James PIKE, from C.I.? (Aldo Brochet, London, ONT)

A1. Caroline Pike, mar John LE TEMPLIER, in Blanc Sablon 1915. See LE TEMPLIER in Q.A. IN CANADA.

A2. Theresa Pike, mar Geo. CABOT. See CABOT in Q.A. IN CANADA.

TRESEDER, Richard Doughty, b 1813 Devonport, England mar 1833 Elizabeth McKay. Richard d 1881 Salt Lake City, UT. Ten of their 13 chn

were born

St. Heliers, J. Parents and at least 8 chn went from J to UT 1855 via ship CHIMBORAZO. TRESEDER curr J. (SLC) Chn: Charles, Richard, George, Emma, Phoebe Eads, Charlotte Smith, Eliz. Chandler, Maud Mary Neeley, Moroni, Emily and Francis.

TROUTEAUD, Eugene Elias, b 1850 G, d 1902 US?, mar Emma Eliza Hancock, 4 chn. TROUTEAUD curr G. (Wilfred & Brenda Burgess, Jamestown, RI)

A1. Eugene, d in G A3. Henry, res Detroit, MI

A2. Edward, rem to Detroit, MI and Buffalo, NY

B1. Edna, b G, mar Carl Fultz, res Detroit, MI

A3. Christine Emma Louise, b 1876 G, mar Frank BIRD, qv, and d in G 1955. See BIRD for chn.

TUPPER. A privateering fam of England and Guernsey.

TUPPER, Thomas, son of Henry of Chichester, Sussex, England, rem from England to Guernsey in 1592, had many desc. Some of fam settled in St. Peter parish. Early 1600s Thomas was making voyages to New England and to the West Indies, and settled first in Cape Ann, and later in Cape Cod, MA. He d 1676, age 98. Thousands of desc in Canada and the US. Many Tuppers bur in St. Peter, G, along with LE MARCHANTS, LE MESURIERS and CAREYS. A greyhound on the crest. (Sev. books by the TUPPER ASSOC.)

TUPPER, Ferdinand BROCK, b G, rem to Nova Scotia 1816. (Mrs. Robert E. Emerson, Kaneohe, Hawaii)

TOURNEUR. Old and curr in J.

TURNER. Curr G and J and common in Grt. Britain.

TURNER, Charles Patten, b G?, before 1825, mar there Caroline HALE, to NY ca 1858 with wife and several chn. (Kenneth H. Colvin, Holden, MA) Chn: Lorena, Wallace, Charles Edwin, b ca 1842 G, Clara Ann Colvin, Ellen, Thomas, William J., Caroline Mattesen, Fred, Robert, Eva Taylor Lee. CAUTION: DATA UNCERTAIN. (WRCIC)

TURPIN. Surname of southern England and C.I.

TURPIN. Two bros b St. Martin, G, ca 1900, rem to US. (Guernsey STAR, 1966)

TURQUETTE. See TORQUET. Poss a Hug fam?

TUZO, TUSSEAU. Does not appear in compiler's records of old C.I. surnames. However, this fam is included because of the many marriages with Channel Islanders in Gaspe, QUE.

Some very interesting data on this fam line is in WRCIC. A Tuzo, said to be from the West Indies, settled in Gaspe and most of the desc mar into C.I. fams. Not known to compiler where the connection with the Islands was made, but doubtless through the settlement of the Hug fam TUSSEAU. Mrs. Francis TUZO of Campbellton, New Brunswick, Canada, contributes the following.

TUSSEAU? fam, fled France after the St. Bart. massacre and settled in England as a sailmaker. He later went to Jamestown, VA before 1620, then rem to Bermuda where they had plantations, and prob mar into several Spanish fams. Some graves there, and slaves with the same surname.

TUZO. Coming into prominence (in Bermuda) towards the latter end of the 1700s. "...Thomas B. rem to QUE, and went into business there, a partner in the firm of Richard Wood and Co. Tuzos lived on St. David's Island in the West Indies, and a Thomas S. was a member of the House in Bermuda. (H.G. Middleton, Bermuda Hist. Monuments Trust, Hamilton, Bermuda) Mt. Tuzo in the Rockies is named after Henrietta Tuzo, who made the first ascent and was a keen climber, and charter member of the Canadian Alpine Club. (Letitia Echlin)

TUZO. Some b Port of Spain, Trinidad, late 1830s. One b Staten Island, NY 1872. This interesting fam deserves a genealogy.

TUZO. Data below corrects and adds to the info in Q.A. IN CANADA, by Turk, qv, p. 528-529.

TUZO, Joseph Stowe, b 1792 Bermuda?, son of Thomas and Alice Tuzo, mar 1816 in Bermuda, Mary Eve, 1793-1852, dau of Francis and Sarah Ann Eve of Bermuda. They settled in Perce, Gaspe, QUE. She was first postmaster at Perce, 6 plus chn. (Mrs. Francis Tuzo, Campbellton NB, CAN.)

A1. Joseph Eve, b 1825 Malbaie, Gaspe, QUE, mar 1850 QUE City, Louisa Languedoc, dau of Joseph L. & Eliza Boyle, 1825-1914, of QUE. Joseph was gaoler, postmaster and civic official in Perce, d there 1890.

B1. James Thomas, b 1852, mar ca 1875, Edith May LE BRUN, 2nd dau of Frank LE BRUN, qv. She was b 1868, d 1938?

C1. Lillian Edith, b 1890, mar Claude Johnson, res Ottawa, ONT, 1916

D1. Gifford DE CARTERET Johnson, mar Alice ___, from Scotland

E1. Heather, mar Donald Mould, had son and dau

E2. Terry, mar David Hall, div. E3. Ivan

D2. Revell Tuzo Johnson, mar Ruth Lowe

E1. Scott Johnson E3. Graham Johnson E5. Lisa Johnson

E2. Anne Johnson E4. David Johnson

C2. Reginald James, 1891-1964, res Ottawa, ONT, mar Irene LE MARQUAND, qv, from Pabos Mills, Gaspe, in 1927. Two sons.

D1. Kenneth, mar twice, 2 sons and a dau with first wife

D2. James Eliza, mar Rochelle ___, a son and a dau

C3. Muriel Louisa, b 1894, mar Lyndon LE MARQUAND from Pabos Mills, Gaspe, 1923

D1. Lionel LE MARQUAND D2. Ralph LE MARQUAND D3. Samuel LE MARQUAND

C4. Ralph Edward, b 1899, res Shippegan, NB, worked for W.S. Loggie there. Mar Hazel Irene Dower of Chatahm, NB 1924.

D1. Allan James, mar Thelma Drusilla Connors, 2 daus, Pamela and Stephanie

D2. Errol, d at age 33, mar Esther Connors, a son, Allison

C5. Francis Charles, b 1900, res Campbellton, NB, mar Mary Isabella Keith 1935

D1. Margaret Edith, b 1938, mar Dwight Morrow Dower, div. 1979, a son, Peter Dwight Dower, b 1966

D2. Robert Francis, b 1945, mar 1968 Paulette Dorothy Pickard, ch: Keith Kristin, b 1979.

C6. Florence May, b 1902, mar J. McCarthy, res Sept. Isles, QUE, no issue

C7. Nelson DE CARTERET, b 1906, res Riverbend, QUE, mar Marie GAUVIN of St. Hyacinth, QUE, no issue

C8. Harold Clifford, b 1910, mar Jeanette Moskowitz of NY 1947 no iss.

C9. Eileen Susan, b 1907, mar Harold R. LE GRESLEY of Paspebiac, QUE 1936.

D1. Edith Florence, b 1938, unmar

D2. John LE GRESLEY, mar ___ White, dau and son

B2. Alice Louisa, b 1854, d 1947 or 1955?, mar 1875 at Cape Cove, Gaspe, Francis GIBAUT, qv, 1844-1921, bur St. Pauls, Perce, QUE, 7 chn

B3. Eliza Henrietta, b ca 1856 Perce, d 1955, age 99

B4. Elias George, 1858-1935, civil servant in the Gaspe area

B5. Henry/Harry, 1860-1915, bur Perce

B6. Julia VIBERT, b ca 1862, d 1934, mar Clifford NICOLLE DE QUETEVILLE, qv, rem to Poughkeepsie, NY, a dau.

B7. Eva, 1865-1947, mar Philip SYVRET HAMON, b1848 J? res Montreal

B8. Drusilla Dill, b ca 1867, d 1917, mar DUMARESQ VALPY of Perce, his second wife.

B9. Were there other chn named Maria, Laura, and John, who may have d.y.? (Census 1861)

A2. Francis Eve, b 1828, L'Anse au Beaufils

A3. John Darrell, b 1830

A4. Henry Francis, drowned 1843, age ca 23

A5. Thomas, res Annapolis Valley, NS, mar, no issue

A6. Alice, mar ___ Watson, res Bermuda

A7. John D., b 1831, d 1878 Magdalen Islands, QUE. Mar Maria Languedoc, b 1834 Gaspe. His chn returned to live in Gaspe Basin. He was gaoler and deputy sheriff in the Magdalen Is. 1871. Note also that JANVRIN and HOOPER were C.I. assoc. with the Magdalen Islands, St. Pierre and Miquelon.

URANN. This was the surname of Elizabeth, wife of Thomas BEEDE, qv, son of the immigrant, Eli BEEDE. It has been suggested that the "U" was originally a "V" and the surname was VERRIN, of Jersey. VERRIN in J 1331, would be pron VRAN by someone speaking English. (Muriel Gilham, Keyport, WA)

NOTE: Old Jersey surnames beginning with a "U" appear to be mostly British, such as Underwood, Upton, Urquhart, Usher, Udall, Utley, Unwin, and Upson. One very old J surname, L'Utlagh, the Outlaw, appeared in Grt. Britain in the English form.

VADIN. See VAUDIN. The fam below orginally spelled the name VODIN, change spelling in the 1700s.

VADEN. This fam descended from early settlers in VA, may possibly be of C.I. origin. Tradition implies a stay in England before coming to America, and the fam may be Hug. Abram, Marice, Isaak and John had headrights under a 1200 acre grant to Wm. Drummond in James City County, VA before 1662. Variants in spelling include VADEN, VODIN, VAUDEN, VAIDEN, VARDEN, VADIN, VOEDEN, VAIDING, VADING, etc. For moreinfo, see FROM THE CHICKAHOMINY TO THE CANEY FORK, by Anis and John Vaden and Edmond and Emmogene V. Bevelheimer, Nashville, TN 1979.

VAGG, Edward Langrish, from Elsecroft, St. Peter Port, G, rem to America ca 1890. A dau Esther b G, mar ___ Meeres. Some of Edward's bros and sisters also came to America, see below.

VAGG, William, from G to San Francisco, CAL, mar twice, with a shipping firm in CAL.

VAGG, Richard, Henry, Esther (who mar Arnold Heicke), Annie, and Margaret, all said to have come to America from G ca 1890-1910? (Esther Meeres, Jersey City, NJ)

VAGUE. Curr G, poss came from LE VACQUES? in G in the 1300s? Cf Vera Vague of motion pictures. OUTC.

VAILIANCOURT. See DE CARTERET. French, but poss occurred in J?

VALLOT, VALLOTE, VALOTT, LE VALLOT, LE ROUS dit LE VALLOT, in J 1453.

VALLOTE, Claude, b 1649 France or J?, d 1693 Middlesex, VA, from J to NJ 1665 on ship PHILIP, with Philip CARTERET. See NJ section in this book. Claude mar Ann Jenkinsen, dau of Dorothy Jenkinson of Cumberland, England. (Bana Aldridge, San Jacinto, CAL)

A1. Katherine, mar Sam. Batchelder

A2. Ann, b 1693, d before 1748, mar 1708 Stokely Towles

VALLOT. Fam of Nicholas VARLAT from Amsterdam, Holland to NJ. (NJ GENESIS, 1956)

VALPIED. Old and curr in G.

VALPY. In J 1309. In St. Saviour, St. John and St. Martin, J 1668. In St. Saviour, St. John, St. Heliers and St. Martin, J 1749. Some were shipbuilders in J. (A. John Jean, Jersey)

VALPY. "The Valpys are of Italian origin, and the name was originally VOLPI. The family settled at Lucca, Italy before the memory of man, and its members have filled the highest offices, ecclesiastical and civil, in the cities of Lucca, Florence and Como. A branch of the family came to Normandy from their Italian expedition under Roger, son of Tancred. Thence they crossed over to Jersey..." Jeremie Valpy was a Hug Minister in G 1597. (Perley; Fosdick; Marblehead VR; Mary H. MacDonald, Farmington, ME; Cutter's GEN FAMS OF BOSTON AND EASTERN MASS, Vol. 3, 1908)

VALPY. Several fams from the Islands and poss from France came to early North America. Undoubtedly there were others than those noted here.

1. Andrew, to Gaspe 1800s, may have had bros Edward and Dumaresq. See Q.A. IN CANADA, by Turk.
2. Capt. John, to Nova Scotia in the 1770s?, mar Sarah Crocker. See below. Is it poss that this fam was a U.E.L. fam, and not directly from the Islands or France?
3. ___ Valpy, of MA, has desc that were told the immigrant ancestor came from Guernsey Island. This fam had desc in Lynn, MA.
4. Benjamin, from G or J fam?, left New England and settled in Nova Scotia in the 1700s. (Joseph H. Valpey, Detroit, MI, in a letter written in 1903)
5. Others from the Islands to North America? Such as Benjamin, below?

NOTE: See HIST OF THE VALPEY FAM, by Marion Valpy, 1963, not seen by compiler; Cutter's Fams of Boston & Eastern MA, 1908; researchers-Mary MacDonald, Farmington, ME & Francilia Naegele, Yarmouth, N.S.

VALPY, Abraham, mar 1728 Elizabeth Fowles, d 1750, Marblehead, MA?
A1. John, mar 1755, Mary MASURY, qv, who d 1797?, age 62
B1. Sarah, mar 1. James Cully or Creilly?, and 2. John Johnson who d 1808
B2. Margaret, bp 1765 B3. John, bp 1771
A2. Abraham, Jr., b 1735, mar 1761 Lydia Clough, b 1736, who d 1801, age 66. Did she mar 2. John Williams, in MRB 1781?
A3. Benjamin, d 1783, mar 1761 Hannah BERRY. Did he mar 1756 Abigail Pitman in MRB?
B1. Abigail, bp 1757 B2. Elizabeth, bp 1761
A4. Elizabeth, mar 1751 Daniel Darling. A dau, Elizabeth Darling, mar Thomas Talbot.
A5. Richard, b 1735. Were Abraham and Richard twins? Richard d 1799, mar 1756 Hannah Ives, who d 1784. He mar 2. 1788 Margaret Batchelder Hinckly, 1744-1816, she d at age 72.
B1. Abraham, b 1765, d 1799 or 1848?, mar 1788 Elizabeth Abbott, who d 1833, age 67, res Salem, MA
C1. Abraham, bp 1789
C2. Stephen Abbott, bp 1791, poss d on ship MARGARET from Naples 1810?
C3. Samuel Stephens, bp 1795, mar Elizabeth Abbott
D1. Elizabeth M., mar Jos. R. MILLETT, son of Jonathan, 1845, Andover, MA
D2. Samuel George, 1810-1863, mar Sarah Elizabeth H__, 6 chn
E1. George B. E2. Ezra Holt, mar 1870 Mary Adelaide Mayberry
E3. Frederick Samuel, mar ___?
F1. Frederick Louis, mar Bertha Brierly, and 2. Lillian ___
G1. Richard Sanborn, mar Addy ___
H1. Richard, mar Evelyn Ossinger
I1. Richard I2. Scott I3. Douglas I4. Jonathan
H2. James Rounds, mar Nancy Norris, 3 chn, including Down and Todd Norris
G2. Theodore Samuel, b 1910, d 197_, mar Dorthea P. Rines
H1. Theodore Samuel, Jr., b 1932, mar Marion Rich, 5 chn:

Theo Jr., Susan, Sandra, John, and Jessica
H2. Robert Wesley, b 1935, mar 1961 Alice Putney, b 1939, 3 sons: Robert, Edward, and Donald
G3. and G4. twin daus by second wife
F2. Harold, mar Florence ___
G1. Eleanor, mar William Warren, res Daytona Beach, FLA
F3. Jennie, unmar
E4. Edith Hilton E5. Charles Abraham, d as young man
E6. Sarah Elizabeth, mar Joseph Gage, 2 sons and a dau
C4. George, bp 1797 C6. Dorcas, bp 1805, twin? C8. Mary, bp 1808
C5. Simon, bp 1800 C7. Elizabeth, bp 1805, twin?
B2. Samuel, 1782-1792
B3. Richard, d 1799, mar 1781 Susanna Backer of MRB, b 1758. She d 1798 or 1800, age 40.
C1. Joseph, bp 1785 C2. Hannah, bp 1787, d 1798, age 10 C3. a dau
B4. Joseph, 1769-1842, mar 1791 Mehitable MURRY, MURRAY, d 1834, age 70. Was Joseph a prizemaster Captain in 1812? Poss Capt. of the Becket ship HOPE of Salem in 1794. (Essex Coll., vols. 2 and 8)
C1. George, bp 1778, d.y. C2. Richard, bp 1779, d.y.? Other chn?
C3. Joseph, b 1792, d 1816 at sea on ship MIDAS near Canton, China? Mar Abby F.? There seems to be a generation missing here, and poss other data.
D. _______________?
E1. Eliza E., b 1847 E2. Abba Frances, b 1849
C4. Samuel, 1794-1813
C5. Mehitable, 1796-1799. Poss another Mehitable bp 1802?
C6. George, b 1798, d 1825 at sea, on ship CORAL?
C7. Richard, 1799-1876, mar 1820 Mary Ann Emerton of Lynn, MA
D1. Mary Eliza, b 1820 D5. Samuel Burn, poss BYRNE?
D2. Joseph Hedges, b 1823 D6. John Henry, b 1831, d.y.
D3. Mehitable Murrey, b 1825 D7. Almira Eliz., b 1833, d.y.
D4. George Augustus, b 1827
C8. Mehitable again, b 1802?, mar John Pratt in Salem, MA
D1. Henry John Pratt D2. Sarah Ellen Pratt
B5. George, d 1804, mar 1803 Dorcas Abbott, Andover, MA. She mar 2. Joseph Sibley, res MA. Had a son George Valpy?, bp 1801. (OLD FAMS OF SALISBURY, Vol. 3)
B6. Hannah, mar Simon Byrne of Ireland
B7. Elizibeth, mar Daniel Gates or Orford, NH B9. Sarah, unmar
B8. Mary, mar ___ BARTLETT of Orford, NY, and/or ___ MARTIN?

VALPY. Two bros came from France (or C.I.?), John and Calvin. Calvin settled in Nova Scotia ca 1810?, mar ___, had at leas one dau. (Mrs. C.V. Marshall, Quincy, MA)
A1. Emaline, mar James Prosser, 8 chn. Some desc to MA.
B1. Bethia Prosser, mar John Marshall, had 4 chn
C1. James Marshall C2. Ernest Marshall C3. Rena Marshall
C4. Calvin V. Marshall, mar Helen Graham, 2 chn: John Graham and Claire Adele Marshall

VALPY, John, the bro of Calvin, above, went to CAL at the time of the Gold Rush in 1849 and settled there. Desc were found there ca 1930. (Mrs. C.V. Marshall, Quincy, MA)

VALPY, Capt. John, b ca 1773 J? or New England?, mar ca 1795 Yarmouth, NS, Sarah Crocker, b 1774, dau of Daniel Crocker, a UEL, formerly of Plymouth, MA. Capt. John mar 2. Abigail ROBERTS, qv. Capt. Valpy d 1807 when his ship, a brigantine, was wrecked on Mud Islands, off the coast of N.S. Monument in Chebogue, N.S. Sarah d 1865, bur Kemptville, N.S. (Francilia Nagle, Yarmouth, NS; Mary MacDonald,

Farmington, ME; THE CHURCHILL FAM; CROWELL GEN; CROCKER GEN)

Mrs. MacDonald believes Capt. John may have been the son of John and Mary (MASURY) VALPY of Salem, MA. Capt. John d 1807, when his brigantine, THE HIBERNIA, was wrecked on the Mud Islands, off the coast of Nova Scotia. A legend implies he was washed up nearly dead, finished off by two men and a boy tending sheep, and the gold on his person was taken.

A1. Abigail, b 1792, mar Nathaniel Churchill, son of Ephraim C., 9 chn. She d 1871.

B1. Eleanor Churchill, b 1819, mar 1840 Nathaniel Travis, in Yarmouth, Nova Scotia. She d 1896.

C1. Nathaniel Travis, 1841-1842

C2. Nathaniel Travis, b 1843, mar Harriet Ring, Yarmouth, N.S., 1863

C3. Abner A. Travis, b 1844 C6. James H. Travis, b 1849

C4. Elkanah Travis, b 1846, mar Elizabeth Randall, Yarmouth, 1868

C5. Daniel R. Travis, b 1846, twin, killed in NV mine 1880

C7. Alice A. Travis, b 1849, twin, mar William Reid, Yarmouth, 1872

C8. Abigail C.H. Travis, b 1851, mar Fred R.S. Mildon, Yarmouth, 1873

C9. Delight C. Travis, b 1854, mar David Greenlaw, E. Boston, MA 1880

C10. Sabina J. Travis, b 1859, mar Wm. S. Mildon, Eastport, 1884

C11. Sarah A. Travis, b 1861, mar Edgar E. Patten, Great Falls NH 1893

C12. Letitia W. Travis, b 1861, twin

B2. Nathaniel Churchill, b 1821, mar 1. Lydia Ann Crosby 1846; mar 2. Sarah C. Hatfield, 1850, and 3. Mrs. Rebecca (___) Cushing 1884. Res Yarmouth, N.S.

C1. chn by 2nd wife, all b Yarmouth, N.S.: Emmeline W., b 1852, mar Dr. C.M. Tolles, Claremont, NH

C2. William A. Churchill, 1859-1863 C3. Alice Churchill, 1860-1861

C4. William Edgar Churchill, b 1854, mar Sadie McCaskey

B3. Sarah Churchill, b 1823, mar John Sargent Harding 1844. He was b Barrington, NS 1819, d Winthrop, MA while visiting in 1896. Mar Kemptville, NS. She d 1888 Pubnico Head, NS and bur there.

C1. Sarah Abigail Harding, b 1845, mar Nathaniel Sims of Plymouth, NS. She d 1929, Needham, MA, bur Winthrop, MA. A son, Staley Sims, was unmar, and 2 daus d.y.

C2. Arabella Hunter Harding, b 1848, mar Robert N. Crowell, and rem West.

C3. John William Harding, b 1851, mar Alma V. Tedford, a dau

D1. Iris Lillian, b 1888, d 1977 Yarmouth, NS, mar Hanford Chapman

E1. Iris Lillian Chapman, mar Andrew Porter, 4 chn

C4. Iris Lillian Harding, 1853-1877, mar Whitfield Crowell

C5. Hiawatha Montressa Harding, b 1856, called "Bub" or "Bob" and sometimes "Robert," mar 1. Alva Perry 1883 at Charlestown, MA, b 1858 Carlton, NS, d 1902, Winthrop, MA, 1 ch. Mar 2. Harriet Evelyn (Goudy) Perry, sister-in-law of 1st wife, 1903. She d Needham, MA, no issue, and "Bob" mar 3. Sarah E. Nangle, also her 3rd mar. No issue. She d 1949, Needham, MA.

D1. Frank Cushman Harding, b 1884 E. Boston, MA, mar 1907 W. Medford, MA, Elizabeth Gracia Titus. He d 1953 Yarmouth, ME, and she d 1980 Portland, ME, 2 chn

E1. Frances Gracia Harding, b 1908 Roslindale, MA, mar 1944, Alna, ME, Clinton T. Loveitt, who d 1949 S. Portland, ME, no issue

E2. Mary Johnston Harding, b 1916 Needham, MA, mar 1937 Alna, ME, Gregory Dole MacDonald, who d 1969 Farmington, ME, 2 chn

F1. Johnston Gregory MacDonald, b 1941 Boothbay Harv., ME, mar 1973 Wilton, ME, Sandra Helene (Shillady) Mockler, widow with 2 adopted chn. A son, Greg. Donald.

F2. William Harding MacDonald, b 1945 Boothbay Harv., ME, mar 1967 at Vienna, ME, Glenice Elizabeth Bean, 2 chn: William & Mary.
C6. Elizabeth Hatfield Harding, 1858-1887, unmar
B4. Elizabeth Churchill, 1825-1895, mar 1854 William J. Hatfield
C1. Fred Hatfield, b 1850, mar Annie S. Wyman 1885
C2. Fannie C. Hatfield, b 1861 Plymouth, NS?, mar Charles J. Crogg, 1885
B5. Delight Churchill, b 1827, mar 1. Douglas Thorpe 1857, 2. James Cushing
B6. Abner Churchill, 1829-1848, d Liverpool, England
B7. Benjamin Churchill, 1831-1889
B8. Abbie Churchill, b 1832, mar E.W. Darling of MA 1862
B9. Fannie Churchill, b 1835, unmar, d 1890 Portland, OR
A2. Hannah, b 1797, mar Geo. T. Hunter, son of Sheriff George Hunter
A3. Benjamin, b 1802 A4. Capt. John, b 1804, mar ___ MacLaren
A5. Capt. Calvin, b 1806, mar Elizabeth Gardiner, dau of Capt. Reuben G. Gardiner. Capt. Calvin sailed to San Francisco, CAL via Straits of Magellan, 1850.
A6. Sarah, b 1808, mar John Horton, son of Wm. Horton of NS
VALPY, George, mar Dorothy Currier, 1732, Isles of Shoals, ME, poss other chn? (NEHGS, vol. 66)
A1. Mary, bp 1733/34 A3. Sarah again, bp 1739 A5. Nannay, bp 1754
A2. Sarah, bp 1735 A4. Elizabeth, bp 1742
VOLPY, John, mar Agnes MACE, qv, 1733 Isles of Shoals, ME.(NEHGS, vl.66)
A1. Andres, bp 1734, d.y.? A3. Andrew again, bp 1744
A2. Joanna, bp 1741 A4. John, bp 1750
VALPY, Joseph, mar Susanna VOUDEY, poss VAUDIN?, qv, 1772, Isles of Shoals, ME.
A1. Lydia, bp 1773
VALPY, Thomas, mar 1727, Hepzibah RAY, who d 1760 MA.
A1. Rachel, mar Wm. Trafford 1784, poss 1764?
A2. John, mar 1764 Abigail GROSS, or GROVES, qv.
VALPY, Thomas and Rachel res MRB. A dau, Rachel, bp 1764, MRB.
TALPY. Compiler thinks VALPY is meant in this chart. Richard Talpy mar Elizabeth CARTER ca 1733, res Isles of Shoals, ME. (NEHGS, vol. 66)
A1. Elizabeth, bp 1736 A5. Henry, bp 1746 A7. Joanna, bp 1750
A2. Mary, bp 1738 A6. Ruth, bp 1748 A8. Thomas, bp 1754
A3. John, bp 1740/41
A4. Sarah, bp 1744/45. Did she mar Edward Perkins and res Isles of Shoals? Unverified.
B1. George WALPEY Perkins, bp 1767
VALPY, Dupre Andrew, b 1863 Jersey?, d 1932. Rem to BC? Mar 1. Jane DUMARESQ, qv, who d 1900. Mar 2. Charlotte S. Moe, who d 1947 BC? This fam is recorded back to Collas VALPY of Jersey in early 1500s. (ARMORIAL OF JERSEY, by J. Bertrand Payne) Dupre Andrew or his chn rem from J to BC. (David C. Valpy, West Vancouver, BC, Canada)
A1. Ina DUMARESQ, 1898-1976, mar Alfred Miller
A2. Margaret Jane, b 1900, mar Thomas LE BRETON
A3. by 2nd mar, Charles Dupre, 1907-1963, mar Vivian Walkem, 1902-1977
B1. David Charles, b 1936, mar Marguerite Martimer, b 1936, 2 chn
C1. David Randall, b 1960 C2. Kathrun Lynne, b 1961
B2. Michael Grenville, b 1942, mar Amanda Ferguson, b 1944, a dau, Leslie Amanda, b 1973
A4. Mildred Muir, 1912-1974, mar Angus Sweeting
A5. Gordon Francis, b 1916, d.y.
VALPY, WALPEY, VALPEE, etc., etc. Those listed below res mostly in New England, some in Nova Scotia. Most believed to be of C.I. desc.

Abraham, res Salem, MA 1790 with fam of three. (Census)
Benjamin, mar 1773 in MRB, Mrs. Hannah SIMMONDS. (MRB Records, by G. Brown) Res Chebogue, NS?
Benjamin, mar Mrs. Anna Merrifield,1781 MRB (int) A Mrs. Anne Mar Tobias Johns 1783 MRB.
Betsey, mar Thomas WEBBER 1786 MRB.
Daniel, mar Mary BURGAYS, poss BOURGAIZE?, qv, 1746 Boston, MA (int).
Daniel G.A., mar Eliza Ann Stephens 1844 Andover, MA.
Elizabeth, mar John Lilly 1790 MRB.
Elizabeth, mar 1779 Paul Gowen, in Chebogue, NS, or in MRB? (Rev. Jonathan Scott Records, pastor at Chebogue, NS)
Elizabeth, mar 1765 Thomas RICHARDS. (G. Brown Records)
Elizabeth, dau of Joseph and Mary, bp 1768 MRB.
Elizabeth, mar Nathaniel MILLET of Ipswich, MA in Salem, MA 1828.
Elizabeth, mar Wm. Cunningham 1802 MRB. She d 1843.
Eliza, mar James Crookall 1795 MA (int).
John, mar Mary FREETO, qv, 1794 MRB.
John, mar Abigail GROVES, GROSS, 1764 Salem, MA.
John, mar Sarah RENOLPH, poss RENOUF?, 1731 Charlestown?, MA. (TINGLEY GEN)
John, mar 1760 Mary LE CRAW, qv, MRB. John was poss the one who d at the poorhouse 1837, age 79. Mary, the widow, d 1844, age 89.
Capt. John VALPY, lost at sea 1807, poss son of Benj. and Hannah? (Rev. J. Scott Records)
John and Mary ___, res MRB, had son John, bp 1731 MRB.
Lydia, widow, mar John WILLIAMS 1781. See Abraham and Lydia above.
Lydia, mar Robert Maxwell 1782.
Margaret, mar George Gregorson 1804 Salem, MA.
Mary, mar John RUSSELL 1779 MRB (int). A Mary had fam of 5 in MRB 1790. (Census)
Mary, mar Thomas Lee 1773 MRB (int).
Mary, mar John A. Kimball of Ipswich, MA, 1832.
Matilda, mar Edward B. Lane 1836 Salem, MA.
Nancy, mar Joseph Rankins, Salem, MA, 1795.
Peggy, dau of Widow Mary, was bp 1789 Salem, MA. Note Margaret above.
Richard, in Salem, MA with fam of 6 in 1790. (Census)
Richard, mar Susanna MILLET, qv, 1805 Salem, MA.
Samuel and Lydia Lester mar 1757 MRB, dau Abigail bp 1758.
Samuel G., mar Sarah C. Hole, 1840 Andover, MA (int). Note that HOLE and HOYLE are sometimes the same. Hoyle in St. Clement, J 1800s.
Sally, mar Mickel Britt 1798 Salem, MA. Poss Sally d 1820, age 43?
Sarah, mar James Creilly 1788 Salem, MA.
Susan, mar John Austin of Boston, MA 1820 (int).
Thomas, mar Rachel CHINN, res MRB, mar 1756.
VAN COURT. Pieter was in London 1619 with the Weavers Company, prob a Hug. fam from Holland. Note also that the SUNNAFRANK fam in this book may have also been from Holland to G.
VAN COURT, Elias, b 1691 St. Andrew, G, son of Thomas Vancourt and wife ___ Woercker, Dutch Hugs settled in G. Elias mar 1. ___, of G?, and 2. 1726, Ann COOPER. Elias, a cordwainer, d 1750 NJ. (Monnette; Mrs. A. Hunt Wheeler, Dundee, NY; Mrs. Warren Steepel, La Canada, CAL; Norma Kuhn, Bakersfield, CAL; Littell's FIRST SETTLERS OF PASSAIC VALLEY; SAYRE FAMILY, by Banta; Goodspeed's MEMOIRS OF MISSISSIPPI; WILLETT GEN, by Bookstover; Somerset Co. Hist. Quarterly, vol. 3, 1914; NJ Archives; HIST. OF UNION AND MID. COUNTIES, by Clayton; HIST. OF MIDDLESEX CO., NJ, by Pickersgill; HIST OF MONMOUTH CO.)
A1. Thomas, b 1717 A2. Elias, b 1719, mar Mary Kelley

A3. Moses, b 1720 A5. Daniel, b 1724 A8. Thomas, b 1729
A4. Jane, b 1722, d.y.? A6. Agnes, Egnes, b 1726
A7. Jeane/Jane, b 1727, mar 1745 Richard RUNYON, qv, 7 chn
A9. Samuel, b 1730, twin, mar 1753 Mary SAYRE, desc of Thomas of Southampton, LI, NY, 9 chn
A10. Ann, b 1730, twin, mar 1749 Benj. RUNYON, qv
A11. Alvine? Abram?, b 1732, poss twins again?
A12. John or Thomas, b 1734 A13. Elizabeth, b 1735
A14. Michael, b 1739, mar Elizabeth BROWN, who d ca 1814. He d 1815.
B1. Elizabeth, b 1787, d 1851?, mar 1804 John Swegles, 1786-1852, 7 chn
B2. Elias, b 1789, d ca 1830, mar ca 1814 Phoebe WILLIAMS, who soon d. He mar 2. Phoebe Hazzard, who d 1825, 5 chn.
B3. Thomas Brown, b 1781?, d 1866, mar 1813 Maria Dean, b 1794, res Peoria, ILL
C1. Elizabeth B., b 1814, d 1899?, mar 1838 Richard McNair, res Mt. Norris, NY, no issue
C2. Sarah, 1816-1868, unmar
C3. Thomas Millard, 1818-1891, mar 1843 Elizabeth Kimball, b 1821, 4 chn
C4. Benjamin Potter, 1820-1868, mar 1844 Hannah White Stetson, 1823-1913, res St. Louis, MO?
D1. Marion Marie, 1846-1916, mar 1872 Moses Rumsey, res St. Louis
E1. Marion Rumsey, b 1873, mar D. Blyson? Delavan, res NYCity?
F1. Elma Delavan
E2. Elma Rusmey, b 1874, mar Pierre Cartier, res NYCity?
F1. Marion Cartier
E3. Lee Moses Rumsey, b 1876, mar May Hasbrouck, res NYCity?
F1. Margaret Rumsey F2. Lee Moses Runsey, Jr.
E4. Bernice Queen Rumsey, b 1879, mar Erwin Hilts, res St. Louis?
F1. Erwin Hilts, Jr.
D2. Ellen Amy, b 1848, mar 1871 Albert E.F. White, b 1844, res Detroit, MI
E1. Edna Estelle White, b 1874, mar 1897 Ezra Squier Tipple, b 1861, res Madison, NJ
D3. Kitty Edna, 1852-1918, unmar
D4. Benjamin Potter, II, b 1855, mar 1887 Minnie Hamilton MacDonald, b 1856, d 1908 Detroit, MI
E1. Gladys, b 1886, mar 1912 James David Hobson, b 1884, res Missoula, MT
E2. Albert Eugene, b 1892, mar 1917 Miriam Vail, b 1895, res Pasadena, CAL
F1. Albert Eugene, Jr., b 1920
E3. Benjamin Potter III, b 1896, mar 1921 Margaret Cabell Brown, b 1900, res Detroit, MI
D5. Carrie, b 1859, mar 1876 Andrew Warren, 1852-1900. She mar 2. in 1901, Frederick A. Wann, res Los Angeles, CAL
E1. Andrew Warren, Jr., 1876-1916, unmar in Los Angeles, CAL
E2. Carrie Fay Warren, b 1882, mar 1917 Milo D. Eames, b 1875, res Los Angeles, no issue
E3. Van Court Warren, b 1887, mar 1919 Eva Marjorie Richardson, b 1896, Los Angeles, CAL
F1. Jean Marjorie Fay Warren, b 1920
D6. Jessie, b 1862, mar 1887 Herman Robert Stoepel, 1869-1911, res Detroit, MI?
E1. Warren V.C. Stoepel, b 1888, mar 1913 Katharine A. Adams, b 1890 Los Angeles, CAL?
F1. Francis A. Stoepel, b 1915

F2. Warren V.C. Stoepel, 1920-1928 F3. Catherine, b L.A., CAL?
E2. Herman Robert Stoepel, Jr., b 1891, mar 1921 Helen Rohnert, b 1898 Detroit, MI
C5. William, 1822-1840, unmar C7. Hannah M., 1827-1845, unmar
C6. Catherine Edna, b 1825, d 1854? unmar C8. Matthias P., 1828-1830
C9. Caroline A., 1833-1870, mar 1860 Samuel Dorr of Neponset, ILL? 2 chn C10. John M., 1834-1869, unmar
C11. Helen Marion, b 1836, mar 1856 A.L. Snyder, Trumansburg, NY 6chn
B4. Mary, 1797-1849, mar 1814 David Kimball, 1796-1840, 7 chn
B5. Samuel, 1799-1824, mar 1821 Mary Boyd, 2 chn
B6. Sarah?, 1802-1873, mar 1826 Geo. De Clinton Wood, b 1806, d 1856 Mecklenburg, NY, 6 chn? B7. Susan, d.y.

VANDEL, Elias, was in J 1770; St. Lawrence, J, 1788. Poss another Dutch Huguenot?

VARDON. Included in Stevens' List of Old Jersey surnames. VARDON noted in St. Lawrence, J 1788, curr J. See BELFORD family.

VARDON, Carol, mar Lloyd A. LE MESURIER early 1900s. See LE MESURIER.

VARDON, Henry William, b 1870 Grouville, J, was a famous golfer who won both the American and British Open Championships in this sport, plus other important tournaments.

VARDEN. Noted in Hamilton Co., OH 1860. OUTC.

VARDON, Lilly, b J?, res Doon, ONT, on the Grand River. James T. HUBER (was this Mennonite, or a variant of HUBERT of J?), mar Lilly late 1800s. He was a glue manufacturer. (BIOG. HIST. OF EARLY SETTLERS AND THEIR DESC IN WATERLOO, ONT, CANADA, by Ezra Eby, 1896, Supplement by Joseph Snyder 1931) Robertsons in Guelph, ONT have a VARDON connection.
A1. Ethel Lillian Huber A3. Viola Vardon Huber A5. Homer Vardon Huber
A2. Morris Jerome Huber A4. James Clayton Huber, d 1892

VARE. Not known to compiler, and not in Stevens' book of names. Three possibilities, LE VAR, old name in J; VERE, pron VARE in French, old in J; and WEARE.

VARE, Augustus, from J mid 1800s. Mar Abigail Stites of old New England fam. His sons, George, Edwin and William, worked on their father's farm and left school in their early teens. George became a produce merchant, and with his bros then formed a powerful political machine, and owned contracting companies. They had such power that they were named the "Dukes of South Philly." William was a delegate to many of the national conventions in the years between 1908 and 1928, and was national committeeman 1934. He was b 1867 and d in 1934. (D.A.B.)

VARNEY. From Vernai, a parish in Normandy. VARNEY listed as old Jersey surname by Stevens.

VARNEY, Benjamin, mar in Boston, MA 1706 Sarah TIDEY, see TARDIF. Benj. was the son of Peter of Dover, ME. He may have mar 2. Martha Tibbetts who mar before 1747, ___ Whitehouse. (Noyes)

VASSELIN. Old in J.

VASSELIN, VASLIN. Fam or persons from J to N. Chelmsford, MA ca 1870s?

VASSELIN, Charles, res Waltham, MA ca 1900?, mar Raymonde ALEXANDRE, qv, from a Jersey-Canadian fam. (Q.A. IN CANADA; Estelle de Grace, Athol, MA)

VAUDIN, as WAUDYN in J 1309. Poss Hug came later to J? VAUDIN in St. Brelade, Trinity, and St. Ouen, J 1668. In Trinity, St. Brelade, and St. Saviour, J 1749. Curr G and J.

VADEN, VODIN, VODEN, VAUDEN, VAIDEN, VARDEN, VADIN, VOEDEN, VADING, etc. are a few of the variant spellings of this surname. See VADEN.

VAUDIN. In St. Heliers, J 1292. In Sark Island 1700s. "A branch of the fam has been settled for centuries in Guernsey." (AN ARMORIAL OF JERSEY) Seal: two eagles displayed one above the other, with a sun-in-splendor between. Three etoiles of seven points surround the lower eagle. On the border of the seal appears the motto: Pour Ma Libertay-Pour Ma Patree. P.V.D. 1564. This old fam is connected by marriage to dozens of the other old J fams, such as DE GRUCHY, LE BOUTILLIER, LE BRUN, BISSON, PIROUET, SOHIER, etc.

VAUDIN, VODIN, VOUDEN. Sometimes BOODY? (Noyes) John, b J, to Salem, MA ca 1674, mar 1669 ___ Waters, 3 chn. Poss John and his bro Moses below were chn of Philip of La Houguette, St. Heliers, J.

VAUDIN, VOWDEN, Moses, bro of John, b J, to MA, mar Mary ORMES/ORNE?, ca 1665, d before 1716. (Perley 3; Holmes; Joyce Hicha, Phoenix, AZ; Essex Coll. II) VAUDIN, more in CI COLL.--N.DeCarteret,CAL.

A1. Mary, b 1677, mar Richard PALMER

A2. Elizabeth, b 1679, mar John Presson 1714

VODEN, Abigail, mar Othniel Beal 1714, Boston, MA.

VOUDY, Elias, int to wed Olive Banks of York, ME 1830. (NEGHS, vol. 118)

VODEN, Jane, mar Lazurus HUBBERT, HUBERT?, 1702, Boston, MA.

VODEN, Philip, mar Abigail Kemball 1692 Boston, MA (Clemens). Poss dau of Thomas K. She mar 2. in 1698, Isaac JARVIS.

VODEN, Ruth, pub to mar John BENNETT in Kittery, ME 1728.(OLD KIT FAMS)

VOUDY, Matthew, a widower, mar 1737 Lydia Currier, res Isles of Shoals, ME. (NEGHS, vol. 166) Matthew had 2 chn by his first mar to Sarah __, Mary b 1730 and Elias b 1731.

A3. Edward, bp 1738/39

A4. Sarah, bp 1742, poss mar 1761 Edw. Currier in Isles of Shoals, ME

A5. Dorothy, bp 1744

A6. Betty, bp 1746

A7. Susannah, bp 1749, d.y.?

A8. Joanna, bp 1750

A9. Jonathan, bp 1753

VOUDEY, Edward, mar Sarah ___, res Isles of Shoals, ME.

A1. Molly, bp 1761 A2. Sarah, bp 1763 A3. Edward, bp 1769

VOUDEY, Elias and Sarah, res Isles of Shoals, a ch bp 1772. (NEHGS, vol. 66) Poss this was the Elias b to Matthew and Sarah in 1731.

VODEN. Below are all from John Caverly, Placida, FLA, OUTC.

VODEN, Frances, res Dinwiddie Co., VA 1810

VODEN, Henry, res Army Lands, VA 1801

VODEN, Henry, res Woodford Co., KY 1790

VODEN, Henry, res Fayette Co., KY 1789

VODEN, Henry, res Ross Co., OH 1810

VODEN, Milly, res Boone Co., KY 1800

VODEN, Peter, res Dinwiddie Co., VA 1810

VODEN, William, res Boone Co., KY 1800

VODEN, William, res Woodford Co., KY 1790

VADEN, William, Jr., b ca 1767 VA, mar 2. Hanna Johns, ca 1807 in Smith Co., TN. OUTC. (CAR-DEL SCRIBE, November 1982)

VAUDIN. The fam below has had their ancestry traced back very far into England and the C.I. Charles Vaudin's line goes back to Ranulfus DE VAULDIN, living in 1260 in St. Heliers, Jersey. His wife, Eliza Gordon Macalister's line goes back to King Edward II of England. She is "descended in at least 70 different ways from King Edward II, King Edward IV of England, King Henry VII of England, and wife Elizabeth of York, from King James V of Scotland" and many other famous persons of English history. (INTERNATIONAL SOCIETY OF DESC OF WODEN IN NORTH AMERICA, trace ancestry to Woden, who lived ca 76 BC; Brian Young, Alderwood Manor, WA)

VAUDIN, Edward Henry Osborne, b 1865 Val Plaisant, St. Heliers, J, son of Eliza Gordon Macalister and Charles VAUDIN, a Medical Inspector General in J. Edward mar 1891 in St. Heliers, J, Ellen McCreight, b 1855 Galway, Ireland, a widow. He d 1921 Victoria, BC, Canada. She d there also in 1936. The Pearson line below descends from King Edward III of England. (Brian Young, Alderwood Manor, WA)

A1. Doris Eileen, b 1892 St. Heliers, J, mar 1917 Victoria, BC, Charles Peter Leslie Pearson, b 1892

B1. Peter Campbell Pearson, b 1918 Victoria, BC, mar 1940 Bettina Rosemary Clara Healy, b 1919 Toronto, ONT

C1. Richard John Pearson, b 1945 Kelowna, BC, Canada, rem to US 1963

C2. Rosemary Ann Pearson, b 1941 Victoria, BC, mar G. Howard Montgomery?

A2. Nancy, mar ___ Armythe, res North Vancouver, BC.

A3. ___, mar V. Percival of Kelowna, BC

VAUQUELLIN, Robert, native of Caen, France, lower Normandy, and wife, were with CARTERET on ship PHILIP that sailed from J to Elizabethtown, NJ 1655. VAUQUELLIN was called Sieur des Prairies, or del Prairie. From 1675 to 1681 he used signature RO. VAUQUELLIN. In 1678 rem to Woodbridge, NJ, had patent for 175 acres in 1669, later had additional 900 acres. His wife, Jeanne of Woodbridge, had inventory of his estate in 1698. (NJ GENESIS)

A1. Anne, b J, mar Capt. James BOLLEN, BALLEINE, qv, b J

B1. Mary BULLEN, b J middle 1600s, mar Peter Stout, b 1654 NJ. See NJ section in this book. (Perrine; Hatfield; STOUT & ALLIED FAMS)

VAUTIER. In J 1274, a form of "Walter." In St. Martin, Grouville, St. Brelade and St. Ouen, J 1668. In St. Ouen, J 1749. In St. Lawrence, J 1788. Curr J. See also CARTERET. A George VAUTIER built a 792 ton ship in J in the 1800s.

VAUTIER, Capt. John, b 1829, sailed the Atlantic, fam in QUE? From St. Peter Parish, J. One grandmother was a PEPIN.

VAUTIER, Hedley, b 1900, cousin of Adele VAUTIER, grandmother of A. HERIVEL of Sask., Canada.

VAWTER, VAUTIER. From C.I.? Name appears in early VA records. OUTC.

VAUTIER, Geoffrey, b ca 1925 England, son of Arthur VAUTIER of J, and Florence Swan of England, rem to Seattle, WA. He was an engineer. They were related to the GUNTON, qv, fam of ONT. (G. Vautier, Seattle)

A1. Wenda, b 1954 A2. Yvonne, b 1957

VAUTIER, Philip Henry, b La Place, St. Peter, J, fifth ch of Charles P. and Alice Maude (CABOT) VAUTIER. Mar 1925 Olive May SYVRET, and they were grocers in J. Five chn. (Elaine Hall, Toronto, ONT)

A1. Simonne, b 1927, res Jersey

A2. Emile John, b 1929, called "Mel," rem to Canada ca 1952 and mar Joanne Fell 1956. Two chn. Div ca 1974. Mel drowned 1977 in Lake Ontario.

B1. Wayne Charles, b 1959 B2. Paul Kevin, b 1962

A3. Elaine, b 1931, mar 1966 Henry A. Hall of England, 2 chn. Elaine to Canada 1964.

B1. Allison, b 1969 B2. Sarah Elizabeth, b 1973

A4. Germaine, b 1936, res Australia A5. Dionne b 1938, res Switzerland

VAVASOUR, LE VAVASSEUR, Thomas from C.I.?, in Boston, MA early 1700s. LE VAVASSEUR dit DUREL in St. Heliers, J 1668. OUTC. Note that VAVASSEUR and VAVASOUR were also in England. VAWSER, Henry, mar Ann BULLEN in London 1743. Poss both from J fams.

VENTEMAN, John and Eliz., res Boston, 3 chn b 1700-1706. Could this be VENEMENT of J? OUTC.

VERRIN, in J 1331. See URANN.

VERTEE, VERTY, see AVERTY. VERTEE is apparently a spelling variant of AVERTY, a J surname. AVERTY in St. Clement, Grouville and Trinity, J 1668, and in St. Clement and Grouville, J 1749. This name becomes VERTEE in New England.

VERTY, Elizabeth, widow of John, d 1823 MRB. Had dau with illeg. ch that d 1810.

VERTEE, John, b ca 1755 J, mar 1770 Elizabeth WIDGER, qv, of MRB. She was b 1748, d 1823. John served in Rev. War, described as Private, age 26 in 1781, dark complexioned, dark hair, occupation mariner,4chn.

VERTE, Mary, mar John Crandall in MA. (DRIVER GEN.) OUTC.

A1. Hannah Crandall, b 1816, d 1874 Cincinnati, OH, mar ___ Leach, and 2. in 1846, Michael Driver Barnes, b 1806, res Quincy, MA 1885.

B1. William Peele, d.y.

B2. Mary Elizabeth Barnes, b 1849, mar 1869 Geo. Egbert Thomas, res Melrose, MA, 2 chn

C1. Ada Isabelle Thomas, b 1875

VIRTY, Mary, mar Peter Trefrey 1811 MRB (int).

VERTY, Nancy, mar Joseph HOMAN 1814 MRB.

VERTY, AVERTY, Susannah, a Jersey maid at Mr. Martyns 1672. (Noyes)

VESCONTE. See LE VESCONTE.

VIBERT. In J 1299. In St. Peter, J 1668. In St. Peter, St. Brelade and St. Ouen, J 1749.

VIBERT. Early in Vale, G. Curr J.

VIBBARD, Chauncey, b Galway, NY 1811, desc of John VIBERT of J. After beginning his career clerking and bookkeeping, he became chief clerk in the Utica and Schenectady Railroad. By 1849 he was superintendant and a big stockholder. His changes, improvements and consolidations resulted in the great line known as the New York Central Railroad. In later life he helped develop railways in the southern United States and in Central and South America.

Chauncey mar Mary A. Vedder of Milton, NY and d in Macon, GA 1891, leaving a dau and 2 sons. Chauncey was prob a desc of the John VIBERT below.

VIBBER, John and Sarah, res MRB or Salem, MA in 1680s. This name is prob VIBERT of the C.I. "Poss the ones who testified at the infamous witch trials...second marriage for both...who also had a dau Mercy, bp at Wenham First CH 1685, and an infant in a crib." (Ruth Vibber, Jonesport, ME) GEN in progress, looseleaf book, THE VIBBER FAM OF MONTVILLE, CT FROM 1711 TO THE PRESENT DAY, A ROUGH OUTLINE, by Ruth S. Vibber, John Vibber and Pat Vibert; Mrs. Ruth Vibber, Jonesport, ME. Much more info in book. See also James BIBBER, and BISHOP data. (Much intermarriage) Old records spell name VIBER and VEBER. This fam may have been from Sark. John the immigrant may have d 1714 in Hartford, CT. CAUTION: TRIAL CHART. (Ruth Vibber, Jonesport, ME)

A1. Mercy, bp Wenham First CH, 1685 A2. another ch "in a crib"

A3. John, b 1689 Salem, MA?, d ca 1770. Mar 1. 1711 Johanna WILLIAMS, ca 1685-1754. He mar 2. 1754 Miriam (Hurlburt) BAKER. At least 9chn.

B1. James, b 1708, d 1806, mar ___ (Charles Vibberts, Columbus, OH)

C1. Jessie, 1759-1830, of Hockanum, CT

D1. Alvin, 1801-1855, of Hackanum, CT

E1. Lester Albert, 1829-1908, res New Britain, CT

F1. Dana Lester, 1873-1941, res New Britain, CT

G1. Charles Dana, b 1900, res New Britain, CT

B2. Johanna, b 1712/13, mar 1. 1737/38 George Hill, 8 chn, and 2. 1766 Jason Allen, no issue

C1. Charlot Hill, 1739-1752 C2. George Hill, 1740-1752

C3. Joanna, b 1742, mar Atwell Chapel

C4. William Hill, b 1745, mar 1. Ruth Forsyth, and 2. Eunice ___, d before 1792

C5. Jonathan Hill, b 1747, mar Charlotte Fox

C6. Mary, mar Brintnal Fox

C7. Samuel Hill, b 1751, mar Martha Comstock

C8. Anna Hill, b 1752, mar Samuel Fox
B3. John, b 1714/15, mar 1737 Amy Copp, 5 chn
C1. Catherine, 1738-1770, mar Ransford Comstock, 4 chn
C2. John, b 1740 C3. Anna, b 1742 C4. Obedience, 1748-1752
B4. Mercy, b 1715/16, mar Abraham Harden/Harding, desc? Mar 2.? Timothy BISHOP of Eleazar's family, qv.
B5. William, b 1716/17, d ca 1745, mar ca 1740 Ann Leffingwell, 2 chn, desc.
C1. Thomas Vibber, b ca 1740, mar Mercy Fitch and 2. ? Alethan Vibber, had chn Ann, Daniel, Lemuel, William, John, Mercy, and Sarah, b 1769.
C2. Sarah, mar 1761 Thomas Crocker
D1. William Crocker, b 1761
D2. Ann Crocker, b 1764
D3. Thomas Crocker, b 1766
D4. Sarah Crocker, b 1769
D5. Oliver Crocker, b 1772
D6. Phoebe Crocker, b 1774
D7. Huldah Crocker, b 1777
D8. Daniel Wolcott Crocker, b 1781
D9. William Loring Crocker, b 1785
B6. Nathaniel, b 1720, d ca 1773, mar Desire BROWN, 5 chn & many desc.
C1. Aliphal, b 1746 C2. Nathaniel 1748-1825, mar Mehitable Fox, 6chn
C3. Amy, b 1750, mar Jehial Rogers, many desc C4. Fanny, b 1750?
C5. William, 1753-1831, many desc.
B7. Thomas, 1722-1739 B8. Sarah, 1725-1726
B9. Margaret, b 1726 No. Parish, New London, CT, mar John Comstock. (See HIST. AND GEN. OF THE COMSTOCK FAM IN AMERICA, by John A. Comstock, Los Angeles, CAL, 1949) (Wanda Kozlowski, Silver Creek, NY)
C1. Alexander Comstock, mar Elizabeth Willis, who d 1832
D1. Lyman Comstock, res Mayville, NY, mar Harriet BALL, b 1810
E1. Lyman Comstock, Jr., b 1833, res Mayville, NY, mar 1856 Esther Ann Haight, 1837-1916. Lyman d 1909 Carroll, NY and Esther in Frewsburg, NY.
F1. Minnie Comstock, 1868-1929, mar Frank Sisson b1859 Fredonia NY
G1. Clyde Leslie Sisson, b 1903 Frewsburg, NY, d 1976 Jamestown, NY, mar Orpha Hamilton, b 1904 Celeron, NY, mar 1923
H1. Lois Esther Sisson, b 1935 NY, mar 1952 Richard Wm. Freeman, b 1933 Ellington, NY
I1. Wanda Ann Freeman, b 1953, mar 1975 David Leonard Kozlowski. Two chn: Jacob and Jennifer.
B10. Anna, b 1729, mar John Champlin.
SEE VIBBER BOOK FOR MORE INFORMATION.
VIBERT, John and Susannah, res Salem, MA. (Emmerton) A dau Polly bp1782.
VIBERT, Matthew and Sarah, res Boston, MA, a dau Sarah b 1706.
VIBERT, Philip VIBURT Kennedy, b 1748, Boston, MA.
WIBIRD, prob VIBERT?, Richard, mar 1701 Elizabeth Dew, his 2nd wife, and widow of the Hon. Wm. Redford of Portsmouth, NH. (Noyes)
WIBIRD, Thomas, mar Mary MALLET 1752 Boston, MA. Jos. WIBERD of J mar Mary Hedge of Southampton, England in 1725. (CIFHS #15)
VEBBER, William, a farmer of Vermont mar Agnes Lavora Bancroft, dau of Agnes L. MacDonald and Burton Bancroft. (Bicknell Gen.)
A1. Ernest E. Vebber, b 1872 A2. Laura I. Vebber, b 1877
VICK, VICQ, John and Nancy, from C.I. to UT 1855, via ship CHIMBORZO. (SLCity Records)
VICQ. In J 1607, 1668 and 1749.
VICKERY, VICKARY, VICKREY, etc. Many in New England, poss most from Grt. Britain. However, VICARIE is old and curr in J. Many were in MRB where many Channel Islanders settled. See MRB VR; NEHGS Vol. 67; Noyes; WEYMOUTH FAM HIST; Boston Records and Census of 1790 in MA.

Since Eli was a common first name in the Islands, poss he was from an Island fam, and is therefore included here. OUTC.

VICKERE, Eli, res MRB 1790 with fam of 3. Was he the one who served on ship ARGO in 1792 and the privateer ship THORN in 1780? (JOURNALS OF ASHLEY BOWEN)

VIDAMOUR. In G 1331, in St. Peter, G 1728, still common in G. Curr in J. Some research? See CIFHS #5.

VIEL, VIELE. In J 1299, 1528. In St. Peter, J 1668, 1749.

VIELE, Samuel, in Huron Co., OH 1860. VIELE, Hermon in Summit Co., OH 1860. (Census) OUTC.

VIEL, Geo. and wife Sophia, b C.I., res Paspebiac, QUE 1881, 2 chn.

A1. Sophie Isabel, b ca 1867 A2. Geo. Amice, b ca 1872

VILLENEUVE, Capt. G., traded in 1750 on the snow UNITY, between St. Aubin, J and Maryland. (A. John Jean, Jersey) The VILLENEUVES were apparently a Hug fam which came to J 1687. One Villeneuve was a Jersey privateersman.

VINCENT. In J 1331, in St. Peter, J 1749. Early in Forest Parish, G. Curr J. See CIFHS #3. Capt. Jean VINCENT of St. Aubin, J was trading with Virginia in 1737 on the brigantine RACHEL. (A. John Jean, Jersey) Note that there were Hug Vincents also in America early.

VINCENT, John Richard, b ca 1842 J?, shipwright, mar Emma Eliza Smart, b ca 1848 London, England. Poss John Richard was son of Jean Auguste Frederic Vincent and Jane Rachel MOURANT, but not verified. (Violet Coderre-Smith, Hampstead, QUE)

A1. John Auguste Mourant Winter, b 1869?, d 1924, Col. in US Marines, mar Clara, poss 3 daus

A2. Emma Eliza, 1870-1931?, mar Frank Richards, Pvt. Sec'y to Sir Refus Buller. Chn: Richard, Frank, Ernest, Vincent, Marjorie, Victor and Ivy Richards.

A3. Jeannette Maud 1875-1959, mar George Matchett Fox, 1869-1948, metallurgist.

B1. John Jackson, 1906-1934 B4. Marie Louise, 1914-1936

B2. Jeannette Maud, b 1907, mar Alfred Bailey, no issue

B3. Violet Vincent Coderre, b 1911, mar Robert Samuel Smith, d 1969, no issue

A4. Ernest, b 1877, d 1915?, mar Marie Duckworth, no issue

VINCHELEZ. In J 1299. This is an early form of Winchell, usually noted in southern England. In J also in 1607. Note WISHALL in early America and similar variants. No research done by compiler.

VIRGEE. Poss DU VERGEE, in J 1309.

VIRGEE, John & Hannah res MRB. Note Cornish 2nd name for Mary. OUTC.

A1. Elizabeth, bp 1761 A4. Joshua, bp 1769, d.y.?

A2. Hannah, bp1764, d.y.? A5. Joshua again, bp 1771

A3. Hannah again, bp1767 A6. Mary Trefry, bp 1774

VIRGEE, John, mar Hepzibah ___, res MRB, a son John bp 1742.

VIRGEE, William and Ruth res MRB, a son William bp 1769.

VERGE. A fam in Queen's Co., Nova Scotia, said to have originated in the C.I. Poss this fam also derives from DU VERGEE, see above. (Robert Kirkpatrick, De Bary, FLA)

VISCOUNT, Capt. Philip, mar Dorcas BARRETT 1715, res Boston and Charlestown, MA. Died 1769, age 75. Will mentioned wife, James, and Mary. Note strong resemblance of this name to LE VESCONTE, qv of J. OUTC.

A1. Philip, b1716 A4. John, bp1723/24, d.y. A5. Elizabeth, bp1726

A2. James. A James mar Abigail STOCKER 1740 King's Chapel, Boston, MA.

A3. Mary, b 1722?, mar W. RANDALL.

VIVIAN, VYVIAN. A surname of Grt. Britain and of J. In J 1309. In St. Laurens, St. Mary and St. Heliers, J 1668 and 1749. Research? CIFHS#5.

VIVION, John, at Richmond Island, ME? 1635. OUTC.
VOLWAY, Esther. See Philip MARRETT. Poss SOLWAY, qv, which is curr G.
VRIN, and URIN. Found in early New England. Cf VOURIN & VERRIN. See also URANN. (Noyes)
WAGENER. An old note from a parish registry of Guernsey reads: "Capt. Andrew Wagner or WAGGENER, was related to the fam of Charles MARQUAND, and I believe his desc were out in Ohio." There were many Marquands and Wageners marriages in Coshocton Co., OH in the 1800s, but no connections were made with Guernsey. However, a Capt. Andrew Wagner, Waggener was a sponsor to MARQUAND-LE NORMAND chn in St. Peter Port, Guernsey in about the 1760s.
WAKELEY, William & Mary from C.I. to UT 1863 via ship ANTARCTIC. WAKELEY is English, but curr G and J.
WALKE, Thomas, from J to Barbadoes, then to VA 1662. Desc in Chillicothe, OH. This is said to be a Hug fam. WALKE in J 1500s. (DAB)
WALKER. In J 1803. (A. John Jean, Jersey)
WALKER, Mary Jane, from C.I. to UT 1852 via ship KENNEBEC. WALKER curr G and J.
WALKER, Jane, from C.I. to UT 1855, via ship CHIMBORAZO.
WALLER. Surname of south of England and of the C.I. Curr G and J. A WALLER fam lived in GCO in the early 1800s, and three marriages were shown with Channel Islanders. However, these Wallers may or may not have been from the Islands. (Conner-Eynon)
WALLER, Jane W., mar Thomas MARRIETTE, qv, 1813 GCO. This name becomes, later in OH, MERRITT.
WALLER, Mary, mar John MARRIETTE 1815 GCO.
WALLER, John, mar Elizabeth MARRIETTE 1814 GCO.
WALPY. See VALPY
WALTER. In J 1292, WALTER, WALTERS, curr G and J.
WALTER. In J early, but poss WALTERS is later, from England? Traced by Guppy in Devon, Monmouthshire, Staffordshire and South Wales, England. (Seary)
WALTERS, Charles John, b 1842 J, mar Esther Jane DE LA MARE, qv, 1873. To UT mid 1800s. Charles d 1919. (SLC Records; UTAH GEN. MAG, Vol.24)
A1. Mary Jane, b 1875 UT, mar George Phillips, b 1874, son of Leonard W. & Harriet E. (Norton) Phillips. Chn b SLC.
B1. Cleone Esther Phillips, b 1897, mar 1. Eldon A. Grant, b 1896, 2 chn, and 2. Ambrose Young Higham, b 1898, 5 chn.
C1. Lavon Esther Grant, b 1917
C2. Mary Helen Grant, b 1919
C3. Ida Virginia Higham, b 1922
C4. Darlene Martha Higham, b 1924
C5. Gladys Arvilla Higham 1926-1927
C6. Shirley Esther Higham, b 1927
C7. Gloria Higham, b 1930
B2. Charles Royal Phillips, b 1899
B3. George Leonard Phillips, b 1900, mar 1918 Mildred English, b 1900
C1. Judie Phillip Phillips, b 1919
C2. Bobby Phillips, b 1921
B4. Walter Joseph Phillips, b 1902, mar 1927 Muriel G. Lomax, b 1903
B5. Mary Gladys Phillips, b 1905, mar 1921 Faraibee Johnson, 1 ch
C1. Mary Marjorie Johnson, b 1922
B6. La Mar Allison Phillips, b 1907, mar 1927 Ellen Irene Hanson, b 1910, 1 ch: La Mar Allison Phillips, b 1930.
A2. Emily Elizabeth Walters, b 1883, mar Alexander Wilson, b 1883, son of William & Susan (Wallace) Wilson. All chn b SLC.
B1. Charles W. Wilson, b 1909
B2. Earl Alexander Wilson, b 1913
B3. Esther Bernice Wilson, b 1916
B4. Emily Ruth Wilson, b 1920
B5. Ross E. Wilson, b 1922
A3. Florence Mar Walters, b 1886 Tooele, UT, mar Frank E. Cragin, b 1884 SLC, res Los Angeles, CAL

B1. Orline Mar Cragin, 1910-1917, d Los Angeles, CAL
B2. Vivian Frances Cragin, b 1911 B4. Carroll Florence Cragin, b 1922
B3. Maxine Evelyn Cragin, b 1919
A4. Kate Ella Walters, b 1888, mar 1909 Tooele, UT, Walter B. Scott
B1. Charles Walter Scott, b 1909 SLC, d.y.
B2. Ralph Scott, b 1915 B4. Francis Edward Scott, b 1920
B3. Alice Lorene Scott, b 1917 B5. John Floyd Scott, b 1922
A5. There are thought to be 2 other chn; names not found by compiler.

WALTERS, William Henry, b 1840 St. Helier, J, d 1933 Portland, ORE, son of Asa W. & Sara Jane Wescott. Mar Martha Morgan, b ca 1856 MO. William rem from J to UT 1862, ship ANTARCTICA.
A1. William Henry, b 1878 Austin, NV, d 1891
A2. Elizabeth Ann, b 1880, mar Samuel Wilkins
A3. George Washington, 1882-1919, mar Dora LAYNE. See LAISNE pron LAYNE.
A4. Frederick James, b 1884 Austin, NV, d 1968. Mar 1906 Chrissie Mahoney
A5. Matilda Jane, Mattie, b 1885, mar George Ross
A6. Charles Royal, 1888-1927, mar 1910 Georgia Inez Mahoney

WALTERS, William, b C.I.?, mar Nancy FERBRACHE, qv, b 1809 GCO, dau of Daniel & Judith (SARCHET) FERBRACHE. See SARCHET & FERBRACHE. (Williams)
A1. Judith Ann A2. David F., b 1825, mar Mary PATTERSON, 5 chn
A3. John F. A4. John F., again? A5. William W. A6. Hannah M.

WARNER, WARREN, and WARRINER. All old in J. Not researched in America by compiler.

WARREN, Anna R., b G, dau of George WARREN and Philipin JAMES, both poss b Wales? Anna is thought to have one bro and eleven sisters, and d late 1800s. Bur Quaker Valley Cem., Riverton, KS. Mar Robert A. (Alexander?) LEWIS, desc. (Edna Grubbs, Sarasota, FLA)
A1. Warren Charles LEWIS, b 1867 IND. A5. Ruby May Lewis, b 1875
A2. Newton A. Lewis, b 1871 A6. Melvin G. Lewis, b 1876 KS
A3. Walter D. Lewis, b 1872 A7. Isabelle R. Lewis, b 1879
A4. Myrta Laura Lewis, b 1874 IND A8. Rose E. Lewis, b 1881 KS

WAY, Aaron, thought to be from G, settled in Salem, MA 1674. OUTC.

WEBB and WEBBER. Curr G and J. WEBB was in G early. WEBBER in Grouville, J 1749. Many WEBBERS in early New England, poss some from J.

WEBBER, John, from J? to MA before 1675. OUTC.

WEBBER, Thomas, of MRB, mar Betsy VALPY, qv, 1786. OUTC.

WEBBER, Elizabeth, from J to NH 1700s. Her fam sent ___ LE GALLAIS from J to NH to try to convince her to return home. She refused, so LE GALLAIS mar her and remained in New England. They had a son, but LE GALLAIS soon d. She mar 2. ___ Corliss. See LE GALLAIS for son and desc. (David Le Gallee, Park Drive, Parma, OH)

WEBBER, John, was in Boston 1745, subscribed that year for a new set of bells for Christ Church, one of a group of Channel Islanders such as David LE GALLAIS, Capt. John BEADLE, Edward DUMARESQ, and Robert Lightfoot.

WEBBER, Thomas Henry & Helen, had a son Marley Webber, who went from G to Canada 1911/12. (Mrs. Mary Marley, Duncan, BC and Mesa, AZ)

WEEDON, George, age 29, of Hamilton, ONT, b J, son of Stephen & Mary Weedon, mar 1866 in Hamilton Episcopal CH Elizabeth Teeple, age 23, of Waterdown Village, twp. of Nelson, ONT, dau of Eli & Margaret Teeple. Cf WHEADON.

WESTAWAY, John, b ca 1850 J, rem to South America, then to NYCity, and retired to J. (Guillet)

WESTAWAY. Noted in Charlottetown, PEI Records, poss from J? However, WESTAWAY is prob a Grt. Britain surname.

WESTLAKE, John Thomas, res in G 1890s. This is also a British name.
WHEADON. curr G.
WHEADON. A fam from Illminster, southern England, settled in St. Peter Port, G 1700s or 1800s?
WHEADON, Percy, b 1881 G, rem to Western Canada ca 1900 with friend, Walter BIRD, and homesteaded for 10 years. He returned to G, mar Hilda BECKET, and brought her to Seattle, WA.
A1. Jack, b 1945, has greenhouse in Kirkland, WA A2. Kenneth A3. Nora
WHEADON, Thomas, b ca 1885 G, rem to Auburn, CAL, mar Margaret ROLLANDS.
A1. Rolland, a wheat farmer in Sask.
A2. Ruth, mar ___ Jorgenson, res Peace River, BC
WHEADON, Lloyd H., b St. Peter Port, G 1900, mar Amanda MAHY, b 1894 G, dau of Ernest John MAHY & Marie Louise MARQUIS. Lloyd settled first in Oregon City, OR, and was a dairyman in 1923. He later rem to San Luis Obispo, CAL. Had bros Albert, Wm., Percy, Rall and Thomas, who settled in Canada ca 1904.
WHEDEN, Charles, mar 1725 Miriam LE CRAS of MRB. See LE CRAS.
WHITE, LE BLANCQ. In J 1292. In St. Mary & St. Ouen, J 1668, in St. Peter & St. Mary, J 1749.
WHITE, Philip, Zachariah, John, and Abraham, res in MA before 1700. They are thought by some to be LE BLANC of J. (Konig) Zachariah res Salem, MA and soon became WHITE. (Perley, Vol. II; Essex Inst. Hist. Coll., 1974, p. 180)
WHITE, John, b before 1700 in C.I.?, mar Sarah Leonard in Shrewsbury, NJ. Poss some connection with the CARTERET group in Elizabethtown, NJ? (Eric White, Pasadena, TX)
WHITE, LE BLANC, Philip, son of James LE BLANCQ and Catherine LE BROCQ, qv, b 1697 St. Ouen, J, rem to Salem, MA before 1720. Mar Elizabeth ROMERIL, qv, 1720. Had bro, John LE BLANC, b 1700 St. Ouen, J, his heir. Prob no issue. (Essex Inst. Hist. Coll,. Vol. 5; Perley III)
WHITE. Some in US said to be desc of a G fam, including a White in Racine, WIS.
WHITEFOOT. Many in New England early. However, some were from England, and not from the Islands. Those from the Islands would be BLANCPIEDS, sometimes spelled BLAMPIED, BLANPIED, etc. This was translated in America to WHITEFOOT, BAREFOOT, etc. (Perley; Swasey; Noyes)
WHITEFOOT, LIGHTFOOT, BLAMPIED, John, a seaman, b J, son of Nicholas BLAMPIED of St. Mary, J. Res Salem, MA 1678, mar Elizabeth SWASEY, qv, built house on land of her father, corner of Walnut and Derby Streets Salem, MA. (Perley; Noyes)
A1. Joseph, b 1683, a shipwright, mar Elizabeth SKINNER 1706, d 1772/73
B1. Joseph B2. John B3. Samuel B4. Mary
A2. Samuel, b 1685, a mariner, mar Mary JERMAN, 1712, and d 1732. Mary d 1790, age 103.
A3. Margaret, b 1690/91 A4. Sarah
WHITEFOOT, Ebenezer and wife, res Salem, MA. (Emmerton)
A1. Ebenezer, bp 1763 A3. Elizabeth, bp 1767
A2. John, bp 1765 A4. Hannah, bp 1770
WHITEFOOT, Ebenezer, poss son of above, mar Sarah ___, res Salem, MA, had son John bp 1786.
WHITEFOOT, Robert of Newcastle, taxed 1720, killed in accident. (Noyes)
WHITEFOOT, Hannah, poss dau of John and Hannah, bp 1750 MRB.
WIDGER. A surname of the southern coast of England. Widgers, believes Thurlow Widger, "...fished and traded...but family tradition says they plied their trade off the Channel Islands." Widger is not recorded as an old name of the Islands. However, an ancient map of England gives WIHTGARA as a name for the Isle of Wight, a very likely origin

for the surname. A Widger was Commissioner of the Channel Islands in 1274. In any case, they were early seafarers and may have been settled, as fishermen, on Spruce Pt., Maine, before records began for that part of the world. Peter, James, John, and poss William are thought to be the immigrants. James is thought to have settled at Spruce Point, then called Newagen, ca 1618, which might make him the earliest C.I. settler in Maine!

While some data and charts were gathered by compiler, and some marriages took place between the Widgers and Channel Islanders in early New England, it is not thought that the C.I. connection is strong enough to justify including all data, so a small portion will be included here. See WRCIC. (All below from Jane Widger, Rochester, NY)

WIDGER, James, at Widgins, Widgors, Spruce Point, also called Newagen.

WIDGER, James, son of John, son of James, b at Sachedehoc. (Kennebec River area) 1626.

WIDGER, William, b Monhegan 1647.

WIDGER, James, mar Mary Phipps, dau of James Phipps, b Bristol, England 1612, prob the aunt of Sir Wm. Phipps.

WIDGER, John, prob son of James & Mary, b at Pemaquid 1660.

WIDGER, Peter, with 17 other residents of Monhegan, petitioned for some king of govt. in 1672. At this same date is the birth of another Peter Widger in Monhegan.

WIDGER, James & Mary, fled from Indian raids in 1676 and went with others to Salem and Boston, MA, but returned before 1689, when they again left due to Indian raids. Res Boston, MA.

WIDGER, John & Bethia (Sweet/Swett), fled to MRB in late 1600s, had 3 sons: John, b 1686; James, b 1689; and William. John & Bethia had at least 12 chn.

It is poss that the records of Thurlow Stanley Widger of Wellesley, MA are available in a library somewhere. Descendants might make an effort to see that this work is brought up to date and combined with more recent research in a genealogy.

WIDGER, Elizabeth, mar John VERTEE, prob AVERTY of J. John b ca 1751, d after 1790 in MA.

WIE, Magdalaine, arrived in Boston, MA 1769 on ship MOLLY from J, a servant. (Whitmore) This is not a C.I. surname, prob German or Dutch?

WILCOCKE. In G 1600s. WILCOCKE, WILCOX not researched in America by compiler. See COLQUITT.

WILLIAMS. Old in G, curr G and J. GUILLAUME means WILLIAM, was in St. Heliers, J and St. Mary, J 1668, and also 1749. It is quite likely that some GUILLAUMES arriving in America changed name to Williams. See also GUILLIAUME, GILLAM.

WILLIAMS, Mary Ann, b 1831 St. Heliers, J, d 1911 Hamsford, WY, dau of Wm. and Sarah. Mary Ann apparently went to England from J and entered service there. She is said to have been a maid to Queen Victoria, and was converted to the Saint's religion in England. She left 1855 on the ship CHIMBORAZO for Philadelphia, PA, age 24, unmar. A Sarah and David Williams were also on the ship, poss her mother and brother? This group crossed the plains in the 6th company of emigrants, Capt. Charles A. Harper, arriving in SLCity Oct. 1855. Mary Ann mar Robert H. Porter, qv, 1856. They experienced very hard times for a few years. It is said they had 8 chn, including Irvin, Alma, Earl, Mary and Emma. See Porter. Robert d 1878 in Ogden, UT, but Mary Ann was still living in Coalville, UT at this time. She rem to Almy, WY 1879 to live with her son Alma and his fam. In 1885 she moved to Evanston, WY and lived with her dau Emma Wade, where she d 1911, bur Kemmerer Cem.

(Shirley Rizzuto, Sandy, UT)
A1. Wilmont I. Porter, b 1857 SLCity, d 1919
A2. John Alma Porter, b 1859 SLCity, mar 1880 Emma Nelson, who d 1944 Lava Hot Springs, UT?
A3. David Porter, b ca 1864 Unita Co., WY
A4. Molly/Mary Porter, b ca 1865 UT or WY, mar Byron Nelson and d 1936
A5. Emma/Melissa? Porter, b 1869 Evanston, WY, mar 1885 Steven D. Wade, and d 1936
A6. Earl Daniel Porter, b Coalville, UT, d age 66, unmar

WILLIS. Curr G and J, but not in old surname lists of G and J. Variant of WILLIAM.

WILLIS, Thomas, in Talbot Co., MD late 1600s, said to be Irish, but from J. Poss crewman on J ship? Jersey vessels were carrying tobacco and rice from VA and the Carolinas in the 1600s to Jersey and to England. (A. John Jean, Jersey) (Thelma Jenney, Danvers, MA)
A1. Thomas, had Thomas, Richard and John.
B1. Richard, res Dorchester, VA at ROADLEY near Dawson, had Richard, John and Frances
B2. John, res Dorchester Co., Wantage, near Cambridge, d ca 1712
C1. John, b ?, d 1760, rem to Preston, MD to WILLIS REGULATION?, had John Richard, John, Joshua, etc.
C2. Joshua, b ?, d 1805, was half bro of John above. Eleven chn.
D1. Peter, b ?, d 1840, had John Francis, Elizabeth, Margaret, Maria
E1. John F. (Fiske?) Francis, b 1812, had Thomas, Josephine, Charles R., Mary and Ann
F1. Josephine, b ?, had Caroline A., Ida, Florence, Allice, and sons Charles A., Louis B., Archie B., Percy J., and Edward Rowan
G1. Caroline, had Kenneth, Philip, Thelma, Sydne, and Dudley

WINTER. In J early, but none researched by compiler in America. John was in Kittery, ME 1639. (OLD KIT. FAMS) WINTER in G 1700s.

WINTER. A fam from G said to have desc in US. (Alice Ryan, Maple Shade, NJ)

WINTERFLOOD. Curr in G, not traced to America.

WISHALL, WITCHELE. Many variant spellings of this name in early New England. Cf southern England and C.I. surname VYCELES, WINCELEYS, sometimes WINCHELL.

WINSEY, WINCY. See DOREY.

WOLFREY. Prob from Devon to J, not in Stevens List of Old Jersey Surnames.

WOLFREY, Charles, res St. Heliers, J, a chairmaker, with wife Mary. (Kathleen Killeen, Richmond Hills, NY)
A1. George, b 1835 St. Helier, J
A2. William Henry, b 1838 St. Heliers, J, mar 1859 Mary HACKING, b 1841 St. Heliers, J, dau of John Thomas and Sarah HACKING. Sent to US by his employers in London ca 1887.
B1. William Henry, b 1860 St. Heliers, J
B2. Charles James, a lamp manufacturer, b 1863 St. Heliers, J, mar ca 1883 Lydia Eyres. He d 1940 Brooklyn, NY, age 78, bur Evergreen Cem. Lydia d 1950 Brooklyn, age 88, dau of John & Frances (Davis) Eyres.
C1. Charles, b 1885 NY, mar Carrie Murphy 1907. He d 1965; she, 1959.
C2. Frances, b ca 1890, mar Chester Stiles, who d 1975
C3. Harold Frederick, b 1895, mar 1917 Mabel Knapp, who d 1964. He d 1940. Mabel was b 1896 Brooklyn, NY, dau of Walter Scott & Tillie Stelling Crawford Knapp.
D1. Maybelle, b 1919 Bklyn., mar 1938 Joseph Warner, and d 1968

D2. Dorothy Ruth, b 1921, mar 1941 John B. Killeen, son of Michael J. or Ireland and NY, and of Mary E. Dineen

E1. Marjorie M. Killeen, b 1947 Brooklyn, mar Jonathan W. Ruczaj 1969

E2. Kathleen Killeen, b 1952 Brooklyn

A3. Laura Mary Wolfreys, b 1865 A4. Albert Ernest Wolfreys, b 1866

In addition to the above fam, there lived within a couple of blocks of them, several others in 1898. (City Directory) William, William, and Joseph Wolfrey. OUTC.

WOLSTENHOLME. Noted in both UT and in C.I., none traced. This is not an old C.I. surname.

WOOD. In G 1750. Either from England as Wood, or from France as DU BOIS, and changed to Wood in G.

WOLLEY, WOOLLEY, James, from England or G 1668 to NJ, mar into Le Fetra fam, and res in Shrewsbury, NJ. Had Indian lands at Manisquan 1685. There were also John WOOLLEY and William WOLLEY. "James WOLLEY and the Gov. of NY, Edmond ANDROS, 1678, came from the Island of Guernsey." (Marion C. Mizenko, Levittown, PA) Compiler suspects that WOLLEY is the Channel Island pronunciation of the surname WALLIS, in J 1442, in G 1359. See also Larcom data.

WOOTTEN, Edwin and James, rem from Brixham, England and are thought to have settled in J. Poss the source of surnames spelled in many ways, such as Wooden, Wotton, etc., etc., etc.

WOODEN, Benjamin and Mary, res Salem, MA (Emmerton) (Sue Chartier, Banning, CAL) OUTC.

A1. Mary, bp 1745 A2. Elizabeth, bp 1749

Note that some Woottens came to MA from Totness, Devon, England.

YOUNG. At times, a translation of French and C.I. surname LE JEUNE, which was in several J parishes 1607 and later. Curr G & J as YOUNG.

YOUNG, Josias Richard, b 1819 St. Peter Port, G, d 1892 Fairfield, UT. Son of John William & Elizabeth Jane (TAYLOR) YOUNG, mar Elizabeth Esther CANIVET, qv. This fam poss came on ship CHIMBORAZO 1855. YOUNG curr G and J. (SLC)

A1. William John, b 1844 J, mar 1870 Zelpha Rebecca Archer, d 1903

A3. Elizabeth Jane, b 1845 J, d 1939, mar 1860 George E. Coleman

A3. Susan Oliver, b 1847, mar Henry GILBERT

A4. Louisa Sarah, b 1849 St. Peter Port, G, d 1921, mar 1867 Edwin Butler

A5. Brigham, Joseph, b 1851 St. Peter Port, G, d 1855

A6. Josias Richard, b 1851, twin?, d 1935, mar 1872 Agnes Jane PARK

A7. Andrew Henry, b 1854 St. Peter Port, G, d 1924, mar 1. Maggie Lewis and mar 2. J. Van Volkenburg

A8. Maria Ellen or Helen?, b 1857 Provo, UT, d 1927, mar 1878, Roman Siepert?

A9. Charlotte Ann, b 1859 Provo, UT, d 1929, mar 1875 Francis J. BUSH, mar 2. John ARCHER, and mar 3. James H. Fillmore

A10. Eliza A., b 1860 Fairfield, UT, mar ca 1878 James D. Holland and 2. William CLEMENTS

A11. Annie, b 1863 Fairfield, UT, d 1919, mar 1884 Andrew F. PARK

A12. Frederick Gilbert, b 1865 Fairfield, UT, d 1879

A13. George Edwin, b 1868 Fairfield, UT, d 1900, mar 1890 Anna Sabey

YOUNG. Another person or fam to US from J? (Kathleen Killeen, Richmond Hill, NY)

YOUNG, LE JEUNE, John, from J?, mar Elizabeth LE BRETTON, qv, Salem, MA 1713. (Noyes) OUTC.

YOUNG, Lucq LE JEUNE, from J to St. Kitts. BWI, also known as Lucq Young. (Ghirelli)

YOUNG & WRIGHT, ship building firm of J 1865. (A. John Jean, Jersey)
WRIGHT, curr G and J.
WRIGHT, a fam from G appeared in the CEnsus of Morrison Twp., Muskoka, ONT, Canada in 1881. Since there were no older persons listed, possibly the parents had both died. (Gary French, Elmvale, ONT)

A1. Robert b ca 1859 G
A2. Ebenezer, b ca 1855 ALD
A3. Walter, b ca 1865 ONT
A4. Mary, b ca 1868 ONT
A5. David, b ca 1870
A6. Agnes?, b ca 1871
A7. Ann, b ca 1873
A8. Thomas, b ca 1875 ONT.

WRIGHT, William Henry, b 1838 J? rem to PA, formerly served in US Navy. (Freda Babbitt, Langhorne, PA)

THE HUGUENOT, by Sir J.E. Millais, of an old Jersey family. A Major Lempriere, Jerseyman, was the male model. Picture from Sir J.E. MILLAIS, by J. Eadie Reid, London, Eng.,1909.

MARTELLO TOWER, JERSEY
Several in the Islands, built during the Napoleonic wars. (Clive Holland)

CONSTITUTION STEPS, ST. PETER PORT, GUERNSEY
The town of St. Peter Port, built upon hillsides has many steeply climbing streets.(C. Holland)

LATE ADDITIONS

More data on this AUBIN family in Ch.Is.Collection, 1992.
AUBIN, Philip, of St. Saviour, J, mar Eliz. de STE. CROIX, b ca 1824 J, rem to Toronto, ONT 1860s, where part of fam remains. Others in fam rem to BC, Canada. (Linda Bouzane, Gander, Nfld.)

A1. Philip OBEN, b 1856 St. Saviour, J, mar Florence Edith Brand in Toronto 1882, dau of John Grant
 B1. Albert Roy Oben, a lawyer
A2. John Oben, rem to Long Beach, CAL
A3. Frank Oben, res Toronto, ONT, desc.
A4. Catherine Jane AUBIN, OBEN, b 1858 J, mar John SCOTT in Toronto? and rem to Nebraska, then to Vancouver, BC ca 1885. Desc.
A5. a dau, mar Peter DUBOIS of J?, res Burnaby, BC, Canada

BLANCHE, Marguerite, b J, 1848-1911, mar Townsend DREW, qv, whose origin is not verified as Jersey, although the fam sometimes spelled the name DE RUE, qv. (Dorothy Kaiser, Danville, CAL; THE DREWS OF SUSSEX COUNTY, N.J.)

BICHARD:
See pages 101-102, chn of James BICHARD and Rachel DE LA RUE. (Margaret Brady, Riverside, CAL)

A1. Daniel
A2. James, b ca 1800, mar 1821 Martha LE PAGE of G.
 B1. Thomas, b 1824, mar 1848 Mary Ann Buzzard, 1828-1904
  C1. Serena Catherine, 1849-1935, mar 1872 Friend Isaac Maffett, 1852-1910
   D1. John Thomas Maffett, mar Elizabeth McConnell
   D2. Mary Norwood Maffett, mar Glen Wilson
   D3. Ivy Luretta Maffett, mar August Collart
   D4. Elsie Winnifred Maffett, mar Charles Vance
   D5. Annse May Maffett, mar Thomas McManaway
   D6. Friend Isaac Maffett, mar Marie ___
   D7. Alva Kurtz Maffett, d.y.
  C2. Joseph, 1852-1937, mar 1879 Clara Bonnell, 1855-1917
   D1. Charles, b 1880
   D2. David, b 1881
   D3. Pearl, b 1883
   D4. Catherine, b 1886
   D5. James, b 1888
   D6. Olive/Polly, b 1890
   D7. Jessie, 1892-1942
   D8. Ruth, 1894-1943
   D9. Mary, b 1897
  C3. Martha, b 1861, unmar
  C4. Mary Ann, b 1864, mar 1888 W.L. Stiles
  C5. Rosy Bichard, b 1867
  C6. Jesse Thomas, 1869-1942
 B7. Charles J. BICHARD, p. 102, b 1843, mar 1868 Eliza Jane ROBINS, qv, 1845-1901. A Charles served in the Civil War. (Wolfe)
  C1. Wilbur James, b 1870, mar Eliza Maneilly, who d 1948. A James William mar Eliz. Fletcher. Was he a son also?
  C2. Ulysses Grant Bishard, called Grant, 1871-1960. Mar Alma Wagstaff, a son Elmer?
  C3. a dau, d.y.
  C4. Homer Lee, mar Carrie ___, poss 2 daus, Jennie and Louise?
  C5. Anna Bell Bishard, 1877-1938, mar Wm. H. Wagstaff, 9 sons. See pages 102 and 103.
  C6. Eliza Maud Bishard, 1880-1942, mar Joe Shackle, Shackles, 3 chn
  C7. and C8. John and Charles, d.y.
  C9. Minnie Christa Bishard, 1889-1979, mar James Oliver Clark

BREHAUT. See Q.A. IN CANADA and also see BREHAUT, page 128.

BREHAUT, Henry, 1767-1845, from G to PEI 1806 with wife Eliz. Pulham,

and other G fams. (Sally Lomas, Toronto, ONT; Elaine Marney, Hampton, NH)
A1. Henry II, 1792-1883, mar Frances Thorne, 1800-1889?
B1. Thomas Smith, 1821-1905, mar 1849 Janet Clow, 1826-1877, from Scotland, and 2. 1878, Mary Bell, 1841-1892
C1. Benj. Clow, b 1850 C3. Lemuel, 1854-1861
C2. Mary Jane Irving, b 1852
C4. Eliza Sarah, 1856 mar Lorin Southard, no issue
C5. Henry Alexander, 1859 mar Margaret, no issue
C6. Frances Thorne, b 1861, mar ___ Horton, no issue
C7. James William, 1866-1928, mar Annabell HAWKINS, qv, 1859-1943
D1. Wilfred HAWKINS, 1895-1958, mar Olive Payne, 1900-1981
E1. Mary Charlotte, b 1920, mar Richard Treat, b 1920
F1. Richard Jr., b 1948, mar Catherine Lloyd, div. 1978, 3 chn: Margaret, Richard III, and Doris Marie
F2. Mary Ellen, b 1950, d.y. F3. Donald b 1952 mar Anne Ziegler
E2. Wilfred Jr., b 1923, mar Gloria Gillis 1944
F1. Gloria Jill, b 1947, mar Douglas Carlisle, div., son Benj. She mar 2. 1976, Robert Stone.
F2. Joy Linda, b 1950, mar 1965 Daniel Burrows, div., 2 chn: Daniel and Shannon Burrows, and mar 2. Alan Krajec
D2. Ellerton James, b 1897, mar Catherine Farrell, b 1902
E1. Elaine, b 1927, mar 1954 Hubert Marney Jr., b 1929, 2 chn
F1. Susan, b 1956, mar 1975 Roswell Galvin III, b 1954, 2 chn: Valerie and Matthew Galvin
F2. Mary Catherine, b 1958, mar Wm. Standen III
C8. by 2nd wife, Herbert George, 1879-1950, mar 1903 Isabella Derby, 1882-1952
D1. Thomas Whitney, 1906-1977, mar 1930 Eliz. MacPhee, 1910-1978
E1. Isobel, b 1932, mar 1953 Ernest Vaile, b 1928
5 chn: Elizabeth, who mar Kevin Mosher, Mildred, Thomas, David, and Kenneth
E2. Lorin MacPhee, b 1937?, mar 1963 Shirley Harris, 3 chn: Lorin, Lori and Scott
E3. John, b 1945, mar 1965 Sandra Stewart, 3 chn: Linda, John and Marion
B2. Henry, b 1823, mar Maria MACHON, b 1831, qv.
C1. Charlotte, mar Andrew Miller C3. Priscilla
C2. Frances, mar John Hill
C4. Peter, 1870-1954, mar Eliz. Ferguson, 1875-1945, 4 sons: Roy Clarence, Cecil Henry, E. Bert, and Leonard
C5. Bessie, mar James Reid
B3. Sarah, b 1825
B4. Daniel, 1827-1908, mar Elizabeth MACHON, 1830-1909, 3 chn: Albert, Lucy, and Maria
B5. Charles T., b 1829, mar Charlotte MACHON, b 1833
B6. William John, 1831-1866, mar Eliz. Brooks, 1835-1922, 5 chn: Artemus, Hadley or Hedley, Ada Frances, George Herbert and Catherine Lama, who mar Fred. Church and had son Frederick Jr.
B7. Anne, b 1833 B8. Marie, 1837-1874, mar John HAWKINS, 1839-1923
B9. ? B10. George, 1845-1936, mar Margaret MacKinnon, 1854-1919, 6 chn: Ernest, John, Cora, Lester, Alder, and Hammond
A2. Daniel, 1795-1857, mar Isabella Bell

BROACH, BROCHE, poss BROCHET?, Peter, b 1815 G, d 1900 Ohio?, became a citizen 1834, res Plymouth Twp., Richland Co., OH, had lot in West Windsor, OH 1841 where he opened a shop and made boots and shoes for 66 years. Some of this surname are buried in Windsor-Woodhouse Cem.

Peter mar 1842 Lydia Ann Delenbaugh, 1821-1895, had 7 chn. (HIST. OF RICHLAND CO., OH; Doris Miller, Mansfield, OH)

A1. James, b 1843, unmar
A3. William, b 1849, unmar
A2. Mary, b 1845, unmar
A4. Peter, b 1851, mar Christina Pettit, b Hampshire Co., VA, dau of Thomas
A5. Harriet Augusta, b 1854, d Windsor, OH at age 84
B1. Joseph Broach, 1878-1942, mar 1903 Nancy May Conley, 1872-1941, 4 chn. Joseph worked for Westinghouse Corp. Nancy May was dau of Martha Hagerman and Benj. Conley, grgrgrdau of Sarah Holmes and Samuel Osburn, pioneers of Richland Co., OH. One dau d.y.
C1. Rhea Vivian, b 1903, mar Carl Alexander, who d 1973, 12 chn, 3d.y.
D1. Lila Mae, 1921-1973, mar Omar "Buss" Backensto 1941, 2 sons: Ronald and Kenneth, res Windsor, OH. Lila bur Mt. Olive Cem.
D2. Iva, b 1923, mar Charles Backensto, bro of Omar, 1945, res Pavonia, 2 chn: Charles and Kathy Backensto
D3. Carl/Joe
D4. Franke
D5. Edward
D6. Charles, res near Bellefontaine, OH
D7. Dwight, res AZ D8. Ruth mar Robert Stayrock, res Wash.Ct.House OH
C2. Viron Broach, 1906-1967, mar Cora Lambert 1928, 3 chn
D1. Dorothy, b 1929, mar Kenneth Oyler 1950, 2 chn: Joyce and Keith
D2. Richard, b 1930, mar Mary Banks 1952, 3 chn: Cynthia, Terry and Tammy
D3. Roger, b 1942, mar Ruth Swain 1964, 2 chn: Karen and Douglas
C3. Lian, b 1907
C4. Orrel Carey Broach, b 1911, mar Florence Mae Etzwiler 1933, 2 chn
D1. Doris Eilene, b 1933, mar Charles Edwin Miller 1952, a jeweler
E1. Debra Lynn, b 1954, has 2 chn: Jeremy and Lisa Hughes
E2. Michael Carey, b 1961, res NYCity
D2. Gerald Gene Broach, b 1946, mar Debra Woodall 1971, 2 chn: Travis Carey and Monica Ann
A6. Fremont, b 1858
A7. Elmer, b 1861, married

DREW. Much research done on DREW fam of Maine by Irene Nelson, Port Wing, WIS, and others, but not all are classified and charted. (Irene Nelson, Port Wing, WIS)

DREW, Francis, "came in 1648," to Dover, NH, d 1694 Dover, slain by Indians, wife and small son left on trail and died.

DREW, Francis, 1682-1717, son of Sarah Field and John DREW.

DREW, Francis, b 1712, mar 1. Mary Hicks, and 2. Sarah ___

DREW, Francis, b 1746, son of above.

DREW, Francis, b 1727, son of Francis & Lydia of Oyster River.

DREW, Charles, Portsmouth, NH, from St. "Sover" (St. Saviour) Jersey before 1738. There is a Drew fam in Stanstead, QUE from ME. John b 1724, d 1819, was the original settler there and his 3 Loyalist sons settled there. However, some suggestion that this Drew goes back to the Pilgrim era.

DREW, Gilbert, 1732-1812, has been researched by several descs, but his origin has not been proved. However, several of his chn spelled their name DE RUE, therefore, he may have been a Channel Islander. A desc. Townsend E. DREW, (Ezra, Townsend, Samuel, Gilbert) 1844-1920, mar Marguerite BLANCHE, b 1848 J, d 1911. (Dorothy Kaiser, Danville, CAL; THE DREWS OF SUSSEX CO., NJ)

FOY. A Foy fam of Richland Co., OH has been researched by Wilma Gleason, Sacramento, CAL. Origin unproved. John FOY was b 1793 Richland Co., and his son John mar Catherine Markley 1856. Some desc to Galion, OH.

OSBORNE, Sir James, b J, rem to NJ, then to Chesterfield, NY in late 1700s? Sir James was said to be a "belted Earl." Record uncertain on this fam. There were two Elias Osborns, a father and son. These two men fought in the Rev. War, as did Sir James and his seven sons, in the Continental Army. One Elias was a cabinetmaker. Sir James Osborn d Chesterville, NY. (Louise Gibson, Almond, NY: STORIES OF THE CANISTEO VALLEY)

A1. John James A3. David A5. Benjamin
A2. Peter A4. George
A6. Elias, b NJ, mar Jemima COURTER, COERTEN, COURTIER, from a Dutch fam, and lived to be 112. Her parents were Peter & Hannah. Peter d ca 1825 in Vernon Twp., Sussex Co., NJ, bur Cameron, NY.
B1. David C. B2. Peter F.
B3. Esther Ann, d 1873, mar Rev. Jacob Stuart
B4. Eliza Jane, b 1808 NJ or 1811?, d 1873, mar Rev. Wm. Knapp
C1. Harriet Knapp, b 1838, d 1923 Andover, NY, mar Charles Cheesman, 1843-1928
D1. Ethel Oriel Cheesman, 1877-1955, mar Aug. Burrows Cook, 1878-1961, bur Andover, NY
E1. Louise Cook, b 1908, mar Jay Gibson, b 1909
F1. Rev. Robt. Gibson, b 1943 Rochester, NY, mar Joy Hearn of Waycross, GA 1941, 2 chn: Catherine Ruth and Meredith Joy
F2. Carol Rae Gibson, b 1945, mar John Dentinger, div., 2 chn: Marta and Emma

OZANNE, John BLANCHE, b 1844 St. Martin, G, son of Joseph & Rachel (Wilson) OZANNE, rem to US 1859 with his uncle, James OZANNE. John res near Somers, WI, a farmer, mar Almeda Cobb 1875 in Kenosha, WI, dau of Josiah Irving Cobb and Lois Snow Bolton, 5 chn. John d 1919 Miami, FLA, his wife d 1925. (Dorothy Dewing, Palo Alto, CAL)
A1. Mary Bolton, by Almeda's 1st husband, mar Ira Tower, a son
A2. Blanche, b 1876, mar ___ Tower, one adopted dau
A3. Eva A., b 1878, mar Harley Core, no issue
A4. Chester I., b 1881, mar Martha Wilson, a dau
B1. Jeannette, b ca 1900, d 1981 Cora Gables, FLA, mar Thos. Smith
A5. Albert Edward, b 1887 Kenosha, WI, d 1967 Miami, FLA, mar 1910 Cornelia B. Royce, who d 1972 in Costa Rica
B1. John Arthur, b 1913 Coconut Grove, FLA, unmar
B2. Dorothy Mae, b 1930 FLA, mar 1953 William Robert Dewing, b 1927 Missoula, MT, 3 chn
C1. Elizabeth Mae Dewing, b 1955 Inglewood, CAL, mar 1976 in Palo Alto, CAL, Mark Blomenkamp, chn
C2. John William Dwing, b 1956 CAL C3. Bruce Douglas Dewing, b 1957

OZIERS, Frederick and Nelson, res Richland Co., OH. Nelson and John b Union Co., PA ca 1823, sons of Stephen OZIER. Not verified as from C.I. fam. (pp. 780-781, HIST. OF RICHLAND CO., OH, by A.A. Graham, 1880)

ROMERIL. Data from Mildred Casper, Kansas City, MO.

ROMERIL, Mary A., mar Henry Jenkins, Shelby Co., IN 1853

ROMRIL, Emmaline Harriet, mar Wm. W. Power 1845, in Indiana.

ROMERIL, John, appraised estate of Overton Jenkins in Shelby Co.IN 1855

ROMERIL, John, witnessed Will of Peter CROSS in Shelby Co., IN, 1846.

ROMERIL, RUMRIL, Elizabeth, div. Fletcher Rumril 1865 in IN. Fletcher mar Abby Keith 1867.
A1. ?Nora A., b Shelby Co., IN, mar John A. Roberts, b ca 1867, son of Simeon P. & Lucy A. (Materback) ROBERTS, res Fairland, IN. Nora was dau of Fletcher Romeril and Abi Keith.

ROMERIL, Sarah, was an officer in the GAR Ladies Aux., in Shelby Co., IN, 1860s.

ROMERIL, John W. of Switzerland Co., IN was a private in the Civil War.

SARCHET, Ada Margaret, dau of Moses Klingman Sarchet and Elizabeth Jane, was b 1900 and d 1978. See pages 571-572. Ada mar 1921 John Kenneth MAFFETT, 1901-1975. (Mrs. Edith Cruce, Lubbock, TX; Margaret Brady, Riverside, CAL)

F1. Kenneth Robert Maffett, 1922-1973, unmar
F2. Richard Lawrence Maffet, b 1926, mar 1954 Laverne Rouse
F3. John Russell Maffett, b 1931, mar 1959 Joanne Cashbaugh, 3 chn?: Jamie, James and Jackie Maffett
F4. Margaret Ann Maffett, b 1933, mar 1955 Russell D. Brady, b 1934, 3 chn: Sally Ann Brady, mar Michael Kent Walters, Mary Eliz. Brady, and Kathleen Patricia Brady
F5. Harold Thomas Maffett, b 1934, mar Delores Newton, 2 chn: Donna Marie and John Thomas Maffett
E6. Charles Edwin Sarchet, b 1902, mar 1924 Mildred Eliz. Persons, b 1905
F1. James Klingman Sarchet, b 1926, mar 1947 Marian Keefer, b1927
G1. Dennis James Sarchet, mar Linda Cagnon, 2 chn: Dennis James and Christine Lynn
G2. Patricia Ann, b 1951
G3. Charles Reed, b 1955, mar 1978 Loraine Joseph, b 1956, ch Bradley Charles Sarchet
F2. Janet Sue, b 1936, mar 1954 Richard Reed, 2 chn: Marcy Lynn Reed, mar John Gaines, and 2. Mark Lynn Reed, b 1956

SARCHET. See page 572 of Sarchet family: (dau of Thomas and Sarah K.)

D9. Mary Edith Sarchet, 1876-1954, mar 1902 Michael James Costello, 1875-1943
E1. Marian Costello, b 1904, unmar
E2. Catherine Costello, mar Albert Stock and 2. Wm. Brandes, d 1961
E3. Helen Costello, 1907-1982, unmar
E4. Rose Costello, 1909-1972, mar Leslie Woods and 2. Jos. Rafferty
E5. Michael James Costello Jr., 1916-1964, mar Isabelle Tulip
D10. Lot Boyce, 1879-1898, unmar

STEELE, James, said to be son of James, but does not fit into large STEELE chart. James b 1771 Antrim, NH, mar Anna Cram, b 1763 Weare, NH, d 1845, dau of Jedidiah Cram and Abigail Hooks. This James poss by an earlier wife of James, A10., on page 610, see. (Ann Alexander, Brunswick, ME)

C1. Daniel, b ca 1788
C2. Abigail, b ca 1790. An Abigail Steele mar 1733 Joseph Foster of Dorchester, MA and Topsham, ME
C3. James, b ca 1792
C4. Samuel, b ca 1794
C5. Lydia, b 1796 Antrim, NH, mar 1813 Moses Sargent, living in 1880
C6. Sally, b ca 1798
C7. Jacob C., b 1800 Warren , VT, mar 1826 Mehitable Greggs
C8. Phineas
C9. Nancy
C10. Israel
C11. Louise

LE CAIN, LE QUESNE. Much research done on this family by many, including Richard LE CAIN of Bridgewater, NS, who has charted the probable ancestors back to ca 1550 in Jersey. See Q.A. IN CANADA and WRCIC.

PARCHER, poss PERCHARD? Records of NH show Edmund & Deborah (PARCHER) WEBBER with land in Plymouth, NH 1741. Also an Elias, George, Henry, Margaret, Samuel and Hannah of NH early. OUTC. (Priscilla P. Bo-Hanan, Contoocook, NH)

BIBLIOGRAPHY

ABBOT, ____, DESC. OF GEORGE ABBOT SR. OF ANDOVER, MA, 1906
ALBUM, PORTRAIT AND BIOG. ALBUM OF RACINE & KENOSHA COUNTIES, WISC., Chicago, ILL, 1892
ALLIS, Marguerite, CONNECTICUT RIVER, NYCity, 1939
ANDREWS, Charles, Ed., NARRATIVES OF THE INSURRECTIONS, NYCity 1915
ANDREWS, Charles, FATHERS OF NEW ENGLAND, CHRON. OF AMERICA SERIES, Cambridge, MA, 1919
ARMORIAL OF JERSEY
ARMOUR, Charles A. and Thomas Lackey, SAILING SHIPS OF THE MARITIMES
BACON, Col. Wm. P., ANCESTRY OF DANIEL JAMES SEELY, Yale, 1858
BAETJER, Catherina, CARTERET AND BRYANT GENEALOGY, NYCity, 1887
BAILYN, Bernard, THE NEW ENGLAND MERCHANT IN THE 17th CENTURY
BAIRD, ____, HISTORY OF THE HUGUENOT EMIGRATION TO AMERICA
BALCOME, Frank W., BALCOMBE FAMILY, Peabody, MA, 1942
BALDWIN, Agnes, FIRST SETTLERS OF SOUTH CAROLINA,1670,1680, Columbia, SC, 1969
BALITSON, T. ATLANTIC YACHTSMEN, Periodical, article May, 1972, Somerville, MA.
BALLEINE, G.R., BIOGRAPHICAL DICTIONARY OF JERSEY, London & NYork,1945
BANCROFT, Hubert H., HISTORY OF CALIFORNIA, Baltimore, 1964
BANKS, ___TOPOGRAPHICAL DICT. OF ENGLISH EMIGRANTS TO NEW ENGLAND, 1620-1650.
BARDSLEY, Charles W., DICTIONARY OF ENGLISH AND WELSH SURNAMES, Balt., MD, 1968
BEEDE FAMILY, a film, Salt Lake City, UT.
BELL, Charles, HISTORY OF EXETER, NH, Exeter, 1888
BESSOM, Frank L., GUIDE TO OLD BURYING HILL, Marblehead, MA, 1914
BILLIAS, George A., GENERAL JOHN GLOVER AND HIS MARBLEHEAD MARINERS, Excerpt from book, in American HERITAGE, Feb. 1960, NYCity.
BLAKE, Almira, BLAKE AND TORREY GENEALOGY, Boston, MA, 1916
BOLTON, Ethel S., IMMIGRANTS TO NEW ENGLAND, Salem, MA, 1931
BOND, Henry, HISTORY OF WATERTOWN, NYCity, 1855
BONLEY, Charles, BRIEF SKETCHES OF THE PIONEER SETTLERS OF NEW ENGLAND, Barre, VT,1964
BRIGGS, L.Vernon, THE CABOT FAMILY, 1928
BRONSON, Henry, THE HISTORY OF WATERBURY, CT, Waterbury, 1858
BUNKER, Mary, LONG ISLAND GENEALOGIES, Albany, NY, 1895
BURKE, ___, PRESIDENTIAL FAMILIES OF THE USA, London, England, 1975
BURRAGE, Henry S., Ed., EARLY ENGLISH VOYAGES, CHIEFLY OUT OF HACKLUYT, NYCity, 1932
CALLAHAN, Edw. W., Ed., LIST OF OFFICERS OF THE NAVY AND MARINE CORPS, U.S., New York, 1901.
CALNEK, Wm. A., A HISTORY OF ANNAPOLIS, Toronto, ONT, 1897
CARLETON, Hon. Hiram, GENEALOGICAL AND FAMILY HISTORY OF THE STATE OF VERMONT, New York, 1903
CARSE, Robert, THE SEAFARERS, New York, 1964
CARSE, Robert, THE AGE OF PIRACY, New York, 1957
CARTER, Kate B., OUR PIONEER HERITAGE, Vol. 9, Salt Lake City, UT.
CHADWICK, St. John, NEWFOUNDLAND, ISLAND INTO PROVINCE, Cambridge, MA, 1967
CHAMBERLAIN, John, THE ENTERPRISING AMERICANS, Evanston, ILL, 1961

CLEMENS, Wm. M., GENEALOGY, a periodical ca 1917, 1918, NYCity
CLEMENS, Wm., AMERICAN MARRIAGE RECORDS BEFORE 1699, Pompton Lakes, NJ, 1926
CLEMENT, Percival, CLEMENT GENEALOGY, Phila., PA, 1927
CLEMENT, Percival W., ANCESTORS AND DESC. OF ROBERT CLEMENTS, 1927
COFFIN, Robert, KENNEBEC, CRADLE OF AMERICANS, NYCity, 1937
COLEMAN, Emma Lewis, NEW ENGLAND CAPTIVES CARRIED TO CANADA, Portland, Maine, 1925
CONNER-EYNON, Records of Guernsey Co., OH, Marriages, Land and Cemetery books by Margaret Conner and Nola Eynon, ca 1963
COOKE, ___, THE DRIVER FAMILY
COTTON, Wm. and James Dallas, NOTES AND GLEANINGS, of Devon Co., England 1890,1892.
COX, __James COX AND HIS DESCENDANTS, Sutherland, NEB, 1967
CRIDSEY, Donald Barr, THE AMERICAN PRIVATEERS, NYCity, 1962
CROSS, Ilian, JOHN FRANCIS CROSS, Oakland, CAL, 1933
CUTTER, W.R., NEW ENGLAND FAMILIES, several vols., NY 1913, also his MASS. GENEALOGIES
DAVIS, Geo. W., JOHN GROW OF IPSWICH, Washington, DC, 1913
DAY, Edward Warren, ONE THOUSAND YEARS OF HUBBARD HISTORY.
DEARBORN, N.J., et al., HISTORY OF PARSONSFIELD, ME, Portland, ME,1888
DONOVAN, D. and Woodward J., HISTORY OF LYNDSBOROUGH, NH, 1906
DOW, Joseph, HISTORY OF THE TOWN OF HAMPTON, Summersworth, NH, 1970.
DOWNEY, Fairfax, LOUISBOURG, KEY TO A CONTINENT, ENGLEWOOD CLIFFS, NJ 1965
EMMERTON, James EIGHTEENTH CENTURY BAPTISMS IN SALEM, MA, Salem, 1886
ESSEX COLLECTIONS and ESSEX ANTIQUITIES, from Essex Institute, Salem, MASS, many years of issues
FARMER, John, A GENEALOGICAL REGISTER OF THE FIRST SETTLERS OF NEW ENGLAND, Lancaster, MA, 1829
FILBY, P.W. and Mary Meyer, PASSENGER AND IMMIGRATIONS LISTS INDEX, Detroit, MI, 1981
FISKE, John, BEGINNINGS OF NEW ENGLAND, Boston, MA, 1917
FOSDICK, see HUGUENOT BIBLIOGRAPHY
GILROY, Marion, LOYALISTS AND LAND SETTLEMENTS IN NOVA SCOTIA, Halifax, Nova Scotia, Canada, 1937
GHIRELLI, Michael, EMIGRANTS FROM ENGLAND TO AMERICA, 1682-1692
GOLDTHWAIT, Wm. Johnson, and Mary Lydia Pitman, GENEALOGICAL NOTES OF MARBLEHEAD, MASS.
GOSSE, Philip, PIRATES WHO'S WHO, London, England, 1924
GOSSE, Philip, HISTORY OF PIRACY, NYCity, 1934, and other books.
GUSTIN, Capt. Joseph, GENEALOGY OF THE GUSTIN FAMILY ca 1895.
HATFIELD, Rev. Edwin F., HISTORY OF ELIZABETH, NJ, NYCity, 1855
HAWTHORNE, Nathaniel, AMERICAN NOTEBOOKS
HENDERSON, Helen W., A LOITERER IN NEW ENGLAND, NYCity, 1919
HINCHMAN, Lydia, EARLY SETTLERS OF NANTUCKET, Phila., PA, 1901
HIRSH, Arthur, HUGUENOTS OF COLONIAL SOUTH CAROLINA, Durham, NC
HOLBROOK, Steward, THE YANKEE EXODUS, NYCity, 1950
HOLCOMBE, L.G., SKINNER GENEALOGY
HOLMES, Frank, DIRECTORY OF THE ANCESTRAL HEADS OF N.E. FAMILIES, 1620-1700, NYCity, 1923
HONEYMAN, A. Van Doren., Ed., NORTHWESTERN NEW JERSEY, A HISTORY, NYCity, 1927
HOYT, David W., OLD FAMILIES OF SALISBURY AND AMESBURY, Ma, Prov., R.I. 1916
HORN, W.F., THE HORN PAPERS
HOSKINS, W.G., OLD DEVON, re commerce of Devon, England, 1500s, 1600s.

HOWE, Henry, HISTORICAL COLLECTIONS OF OHIO, Vols. 1 & 2, Ohio, 1896
HOWE, C.D., NEWFOUNDLAND, AN INTRODUCTION TO CANADA'S NEWEST PROVINCE, Ottawa, ONT, 1950
HOSMER, Geo. L., AN HIST. SKETCH OF THE TOWN OF DEER ISLE, ME, Boston, MA, 1905
HUNTER, Miriam, MARRIAGES IN COSHOCTON CO., OH, 1967
HURD, Charles Edwin, GEN. AND HIST. OF REPRESENTATIVE CITIZENS OF MASS, Boston, MA, 1902
HURD, D. Hamilton, HISTORY OF ROCKINGHAM, Phila., PA, 1882
JACKSON, Shirley, THE WITCHCRAFT OF SALEM VILLAGE, NYCity, 1956
JAMIESON, John, PRIVATEERING AND PIRACY IN THE COLONIAL PERIOD, NYCity, 1923
JEAN, A. John, JERSEY SAILING SHIPS, England, 1982
JOHNSON, W.P., Ed., NORTH CAROLINA HIST. REVIEW, Raleigh, NC, 1970, Fall and Winter Issue.
JOHNSON, B.F., MAKERS OF AMERICA, Vol 4, Washington, DC, 1922
KEMPTON, E.E., OUR NEW ENGLAND HADLEY AND ALLIED FAMILIES, 1979
KING, Marquis F., ANNALS OF OXFORD, ME, 1903
KING, Marquis F., FIRST CHURCH IN FALMOUTH, ME, Portland, 1898
KONIG, David Thomas, LAW AND SOCIETY IN PURITAN MASS., Univ. of NC Press, 1981
LAMB, Harold, NEW FOUND WORLD, NYCity, 1966
LEACH, E.W., HISTORY OF THE FIRST METHODIST EPISCOPAL CHURCH, Racine, WISC, 1912
LEE, Thomas Amory, GALLISONS OF MARBLEHEAD, MA, Essex Inst. Hist. Collections, 1922
LEESON, M.A., SETTLEMENT AND PROGRESS OF STARK CO., ILL, 1887
LEETE, Frederick Deland, THE DELAND FAM. IN AMERICA, Deland, FLA,1943
LIBBY, Charles T., LIBBY FAMILY, Portland, ME, 1882
LEMASTER, Howard M., GANO FAMILY HISTORY, Waggoner, ILL.
LITTLE, ___, GENS AND FAMS OF THE STATE OF MAINE
LUCE, Philip of Vancouver, BC, Canada, unpublished writings & speeches
MCKENZIE, Geo.,COLONIAL FAMS. OF AMERICA, Vol. 3, 1912
MCNULTY, Capt. R.R., Ed., AMERICANS WHO HAVE CONTRIBUTED TO THE HIST. AND TRADITIONS OF THE US MERCHANT MARINE, King's Pt., NY, 1943
MADDOX, Joseph T. and Mary Carter, FORTY THOUSAND EARLY GEORGIA MARRIAGES, 1976
MARBLEHEAD HIST. SOCIETY, OLD MARBLEHEAD SEA CAPTAINS AND THE SHIPS IN WHICH THEY SAILED, 1915
MATTHEWS, John, COMPLETE AMERICAN ARMOURY AND BLUE BOOK, NYork, 1965
MEREDITH, Helen, COSHOCTON CEMETERY INSCRIPTIONS, Vols 1 and 2, in one book, 1955
MITCHELL, Edwin V., IT'S AN OLD CAPE COD CUSTOM, New York, 1949
MONNETTE, Orra E., FIRST SETTLERS OF PISCATAWAY AND WOODBRIDGE, NJ,1930
MONSON, S.E., MARITIME HIST. OF MASS., Boston, MA, 1941
MOORE, Caroline, several vols of abstracts of wills of SOUTH CAROLINA, Columbia, SC, 1960s, 1970s.
MORRISON, Samuel Eliot, EUROPEAN DISCOVERY OF AMERICA, Boston, MA, 1971
MORSE, Wm. Inglis, GRAVESTONES OF ACADIE, London, 1929
MURRAY, Nicholas, NOTES, HIST. AND BIOG., Elizabethtown, NJ, 1884
NELSON, Wm., NEW JERSEY MARRIAGE RECORDS, 1665, Paterson, NJ, 1900
NOYES, Sybil, with Charles Libby and Walter Davis, GEN. DICT. OF MAINE AND NEW HAMPSHIRE, Portland, ME, 1928,1939
NUTE, Grace, CAESARS OF THE WILDERNESS, NYCity, 1943
OLIVIER, Reginald L., YOUR ANCIENT CANADIAN FAMILY TIES, Sanford, ME, 1972

OSGOOD, Charles C., and H.M. Batchelder, HISTORICAL SKETCHES OF SALEM, Salem, MA, 1879
OWEN, HISTORY OF THE OWENS FAMILY IN AMERICA, 1922
OZANNE, Minnie A.G., HISTORY LEADING UP TO THE ESTABLISHMENT OF THE TOWN OF SOMERS, WISC, Kenosha, WI, 1948
SOUTH CAROLINA HIST. SOCIETY, Collections of, Vol 5, 1897
SNOW, Edward R., PIRATES AND BUCCANEERS OF THE ATLANTIC COAST, Boston, MA,1944
SNOW, Edward R., TALES OF SEA AND SHORE, Boston, MA, 1966, & other books
STACKPOLE, Everett S., DESC. OF JOHN SWETT OF NEWBURY, MA, Lewiston, ME, 1912?
STACKPOLE, Everett S., HISTORY OF KITTERY, ME, and OLD FAMS. OF KITTERY 1903
STANARD, W.G., SOME EMIGRANTS TO VIRGINIA, Baltimore, MD, 1972
STARKEY, Marion, THE DEVIL IN MASSACHUSETTS, Garden City, NY, 1961
STARR, Burgess Pratt, HISTORY OF THE STARR FAMILY, Hartford, CT, 1879
STEGNER, Wallace, THE GATHERING OF ZION, NYCity
STEVENS, Wilbur, PIONEERS ON MAINE RIVERS, Portland, ME, 1930
STEWARD, George R., NAMES ON THE LAND, Cambridge, MA, 1958
STICK, DAvid, OUTER BANKS OF NORTH CAROLINA, Chapel Hill, NC, 1958
STILLWELL, GEN. AND HIST. MESCELLANY
STONE, Fanny S., RACINE, BELLE CITY OF THE LAKES, 1916, Chicago, ILL.
STREET, George E., MT. DESERT, A HISTORY, Cambrige, MA, 1926
SWASEY, B.F., SWASEY GENEALOGY, Cleveland, OH, 1910
SWETT, R.A. and SS Forrester, SWETT-ALLEN and ALLIED FAMILIES, Concord, MA, 1978
SYVRET, Marguerite, JERSEY SETTLERS IN GASPE, leaflet, THE MUSEUM, St. Heliers, Jersey, C.I.
TALCOTT, GENEALOGICAL NOTES OF NEW ENGLAND FAMS.
TANGUAY, Cyprian , A TRAVERS LES REGISTRES, Montreal, QUE, Canada,1886
TAYLOR, Emerson, PAUL REVERE, NYCity, 1930
TEPPER, Michael, EMIGRANTS TO PENNSYLVANIA, Baltimore, MD, 1975
THWAITES, Reuben G., THE COLONIES, 1492-1750, NYCity, 1901
TINGLEY, Raymon Meyers, of Herrick Center, PA, SOME ANCESTRAL LINES, Rutland, VT, 1935 and ANCESTORS OF GUILFORD SOLON TINGLEY, VT, 1935.
TROXLER, Georgia C.W., MIGRATION OF CAROLINA AND GEORGIA LOYALISTS TO NOVA SCOTIA AND NEW BRUNSWICK, Chapel Hill, NC, 1974
TROW, Charles E., OLD SHIP MASTERS OF SALEM, NYCity, 1905
UNDERHILL, Lora, DESC. OF EDWARD SMALL OF NEW ENGLAND, Cambridge,MA1934
UTAH GEN. MAGAZINE, sev. issues re DE LA MARE and WALTERS, see
VALPY, A.J., BIOG. DICT. OF LIVING AUTHORS, London, England, 1816
WALDEN, Blanche L., PIONEER FAMS. OF THE MIDWEST, Ann ARbor, MI, 1939
WALLIS, Helen, CARTERET'S VOYAGE AROUND THE WORLD, Cambridge, England, Hackluyt Soc., 1963
WASZ, Mary L., THE MUNGER BOOK, noted in Santa Ana, CAL
WENTWORTH, J., WENTWORTH GENEALOGY, Boston, MA, 1878
WEYMOUTH, Ruth E., WEYMOUTH FAM HISTORY, Provo, UT, 1978
WHEELER, George A., HIST. OF BRUNSWICK, TOPHAM AND HARPSWELL, ME, Boston, MA, 1878
WHITMORE, W.H., PORT ARRIVALS AND IMMIGRANTS, Boston, 1715, 1716, and/ 1762-1769
WHITTEMORE, Henry, GENEALOGICAL GUIDE TO THE EARLY SETTLERS OF AMERICA Baltimore, MD, 1967
WICKHAM, Gertrude, PIONEER FAMS. OF CLEVELAND, OH, Vol 1, 1914
WILLIAMS, T.F., HOUSEHOLD GUIDE AND INSTRUCTOR AND HIST. OF GUERNSEY COUNTY, OHIO, Cleveland, OH, 1882
WYMAN, Thomas B., GENS. AND ESTATES OF CHARLESTOWN, MA, 1629-1818, Boston, MA, 1879

WOLFE, Wm., STORIES OF GUERNSEY CO., OHIO, Cambridge, OH, 1943, and repr reprint 1975
YOUNG-THAYER, Judith L., GARNSEY-GUERNSEY GENEALOGY, new edition, Baltimore, MD, 1979

BIBLIOGRAPHY: CHANNEL ISLANDS

There are, according to Ian Monins of Jersey, several thousand books referring to and about the Channel Islands. Very few are easily available in the United States, but some may be ordered from the bookstores and societies of the Islands. See list at end of this section. Some books may be available through the bookstores of Toronto, ONT and Vancouver, BC, Canada. The list below is minimal. Excellent maps are also available.

ANSTEAD, David T. and Robert G. Latham, THE CHANNEL ISLANDS, revised an and edited by E. Toulmin Nicolle, London, England, 1929
ARMORIAL OF JERSEY
BALLEINE, G.R., THE BAILIWICK OF JERSEY, London, England, 1951
BICKNELL, E.E., THE CHANNEL ISLANDS, London, 1910
BALLEINE, G.R., A BIOGRAPHICAL DICTIONARY OF JERSEY, London and New York, 1945
BERRY, Wm., HISTORY OF THE ISLAND OF GUERNSEY, London, 1815
BRETT, C.E.B., BUILDINGS IN THE TOWN AND PARISH OF ST. PETERPORT, Guernsey, 1975
CAMPBELL, Alfred S., PORTRAIT OF SARNIA, Annapolis, MD, 1960, also GOLDEN GUERNSEY
CERUTTI, James and James Amos, BRITAIN'S 'FRENCH' CHANNEL ISLANDS, National Geographic Magazine, May, 1971
DE SELINCOURT, A., THE CHANNEL SHORE, London, 1953
DEWAR, Stephen, WITCHCRAFT AND THE EVIL EYE IN GUERNSEY, St. Peterport Guernsey, 1970, booklet
DUNCAN, Jonathan, HISTORY OF GUERNSEY, London, England, 1841
ELLIOT, Blanche B., JERSEY, AN ISLE OF ROMANCE, New York, 1923
FLEURE, H.J., GUERNSEY, A SOCIAL STUDY, article in John Ryland's Library Bull., Manchester, England, Vol 26, 1941
GUERIN, BAsil, THE NORMAN ISLES, Oxford, England, 1948
HARGREAVES, R., THE NARROW SEAS, London, 1959
HAWKES, Ken., SARK, London, 1977
HOLLAND, Cleve, THINGS SEEN IN THE CHANNEL ISLANDS, London, 1929
HOOKE, Wilfred D., THE CHANNEL ISLANDS, London, 1953
JEAN, A. John, JERSEY SAILING SHIPS, Sussex, England, 1982
JEE, Nigel, THE LANDSCAPE OF THE CHANNEL ISLANDS, 1982
JOHNSTON, Davie D., THE CHANNEL ISLANDS; AN ARCHAEOLOGICAL GUIDE, 1981
L'AMY, J.H., JERSEY FOLK LORE, Jersey, 1927
LE FEUVRE, George, JERRI JADIS, Jersey, 1973, in the Jersey language.
LE HURAY, C.P., THE BAILLIWICK OF GUERNSEY, revised and edited by J.C.T. Uttley, 1969
LEMPRIERE, Raoul, CUSTOMS, CEREMONIES AND TRADITIONS OF THE CHANNEL ISLANDS, London, England, 1976
LEMPRIERE, Raoul, HISTORY OF THE CHANNEL ISLANDS, London, 1974, good!
LEMPRIERE, Raoul, PORTRAIT OF THE CHANNEL ISLANDS, London, 1975
LE SUEUR, Frances, A NATURAL HISTORY OF JERSEY, 1976
LOCKLEY, R.M., CHARM OF THE CHANNEL ISLANDS, London, England, 1950
MAIS, S.P.B., THE CHANNEL ISLANDS, London, 1953
MARR, L. James, A HISTORY OF GUERNSEY, 1982

MAYNE, Richard, and Joan Stevens, JERSEY THROUGH THE LENS, fascinating old pictures of Jersey Island people and places. London, 1975
MOLLET, Ralph, A CHRONOLOGY OF JERSEY, Soc. Jersiaise reprint with additions. Original by E.T. Nicolle, 1892
ROBINSON, G.W.S., GUERNSEY, N. Pomfret, Vermont, 1977
RYBOT, N.F.L., and E.F. Carey, HERALDRY IN GUERNSEY, part Four, reprint of the Guernsey Soc., 1928
PAYNE, J.B., ARMORIAL OF JERSEY, Jersey, 1860.
SAUNDERS, A.C., JERSEY IN THE 18TH AND 19TH CENTURIES, plus other books about the 16th and 17th centuries also. Jersey, 1930.
SHEBBEARE, John, AN AUTHENTIC NARRATIVE OF THE OPPRESSIONS OF THE ISLANDERS OF JERSEy, London, England, 1771. (Copy in Main Library, Cleveland, OH, gift of a Capt. E. Fiott)
TUPPER, Ferdinand Brock, HISTORY OF GUERNSEY AND ITS BAILIWICK, Guernsey, 1854.
UTTLEY, J.C.T., see LE HURAY above.
WARING, Geo. E., OLD JERSEY, A FARMER's VACATION, travel in Europe, including Jersey Island, Scribner's Magazine, Boston, 1876.
WARNER, Richard, COLLECTIONS FOR THE HISTORY OF HAMPSHIRE, printed late 1700s, 5 vols. in one very large book. (Cleveland Library)
WARREN, J.P., THE GUILLE-ALLES LIBRARY AND MUSEUM, Guernsey
WIMBUSH, Henry B., co-author with CAREY, of THE CHANNEL ISLANDS, London, England, 1904.

MISCELLANY ABOUT THE ISLANDS

BULLETINS of the Channel Island Societies
SOCIETE JERSIAISE, The Museum, Pier Rd., St. Heliers, Jersey
SOCIETE GUERNSAISE, Guille-Alles Library and Museum, St. Peter Port
THE GUERNSEY SOCIETY, Over-Seas House, Park Place, London, England
THE JERSEY SOCIETY IN LONDON, still current?
THE LITERARY REPOSITORY, Mont Durand, St. Peter Port, Guernsey
BUTTONS, Lts., 21 Smith St., St. Peter Port Guernsey, current books.
HILGROVE BOOKS, 22B Hilgrove St., St. Heliers, Jersey, current and old books
CURRENT TRAVEL INFORMATION, with colorful pamphlets and maps, from Tourist Bureaus both in England and the Channel Islands, and sometimes available in New York City.
BULLETINS of the CHANNEL ISLANDS FAMILY HISTORY SOCIETY, P.O. Box 507, St. Helier, Jersey, Ch.Is., Gr.Britain.

SOME CHANNEL ISLAND FICTION

BROSTER, D.K., SIR ISEMBRAS AT THE FORK
EDWARDS, Gerald, EBENEZER LE PAGE, New York, 1981. "Both my wife and I were greatly intrigued by it, as we knew Gerald Edwards, the author. He was my closest friend when I left Guernsey in 1919, and I remember him saying that he hoped to write a book some day. A great many people whom we knew when we were young are mentioned by name; and her family, Bird, is spoken about at least twice. My father,'Burgess, the chemist' is also spoken of; while Clarrie Bellot, the cobbler, was a mutual friend. There are also a great many references to familiar places. The book, however, is not autobiographical. How sorry I am that Gerald has passed on." W. De L. Burgess, Jamestown, RI)
FERGUSON, John, DEATH COMES TO PERIGORD
FLETCHER, Inglis, LUSTY WIND FOR THE CAROLINAS. (Huguenot families)
GOUDGE, Elizabeth, GREEN DOLPHIN STREET and ISLAND MAGIC. GREEN DOLPHIN STREET became a motion picture.
HUGO, Victor, TOILERS OF THE SEA

KAYE-SMITH, Sheila, THE GEORGE AND THE CROWN, about Sark Island
MANNIN, Ethel, CHILDREN OF THE EARTH
MACKENZIE, Compton, FAIRY GOLD
OXENHAM, John, four romances
PARKER, Sir Gilbert, A LADDER OF SWORDS and BATTLE OF THE STRONG
PILGRIM, David, GRAND DESIGN
REYNOLDS, Mrs. Baillie, SPELL OF SARNIA
ROBIN, Miss Eva GALLIENNE, several tales, some children's stories.
STRETTON, Hesba, THE DOCTOR'S DILEMMA
TICKEL, Jerrard, PORTRAIT OF VENUS. This also was made into a motion picture. VENUS was a special Jersey cow.

SOME HUGUENOT SOURCES

AGNEW, David C. PROTESTANT EXILES FROM FRANCE IN THE REIGN OF LOUIS FOURTEENTH, London, England 1874
AGNEW, DAvid C., HUGUENOT REFUGEES AND THEIR DESCENDANTS IN GREAT BRITAIN AND IRELAND, 3 vols, Edinburgh, Scotland, 1871-1874
ARCHIVES NATIONAL DU QUEBEC, Report of 1970, Tome 48, which lists many Protestants who removed to Canada.
BAIRD, C.W., HISTORY OF HUGUENOT EMIGRANTS TO AMERICA, 1954
COOPER, Wm. Durant, LIST OF FOREIGN PROTESTANTS AND ALIENS RESIDING IN ENGLAND, 1618-1688, Westminister, England, 1857
DE FAYE, W.E., HUGUENOTS IN THE CHANNEL ISLANDS, Hug. Soc. Preceedings London, England, Vol. 19, 1954
DOUGLAS, Donald, THE HUGUENOT, NYCity, 1954
FOSDICK, Lucien J., FRENCH BLOOD IN AMERICA, NYCity, 1906
FOX, Frank B., TWO HUGUENOT FAMILIES, DE BLOIS AND LUCAS, Cambridge,MA, 1949
GODFRAY, H.M., EARLY PROTESTANT REFUGEES IN THE CHANNEL ISLANDS, Jersey Soc. Bulletin for 1927
HIRSCH, Arthur, HUGUENOTS OF COLONIAL SOUTH CAROLINA, Durham, NC,1929
HUGUENOT SOC. PROCEEDINGS, London, England, Vols. 1, 1885 and 21,1965
KOEHLER, Sara M., REGISTER OF ANCESTORS, Hug. Soc. of NJ, Bloomfield, NJ, 1956
LAWTON, Mrs. James, FAMILY NAMES OF HUGUENOTS, 1901, 1973
LOUGHREY, Amry Ellen, FRANCE AND RHODE ISLAND, 1686-1800, New York,1944
REAMAN, G. Elmore, THE TRAIL OF THE HUGUENOTS, Toronto, ONT, 1963
ROCHE, O.T.A., THE DAYS OF THE UPRIGHT, NYCity, 1965
SMILES, Samuel, THE HUGUENOTS, THEIR SETTLEMENTS, CHURCHES AND INDUSTRIES IN ENGLAND AND IRELAND, London, England, 1881

SURNAME INDEX

The reader should note that Channel Island surnames included in this book constitute only a portion of the many surnames found in the Islands over the centuries. More are noted in current Jersey and Guernsey telephone books. THE CATALOGUE OF JERSEY FAMILY NAMES, by Charles Stevens, 1970, contains the oldest Jersey names up to about the first quarter of this century, nearly 2000 surnames. Mr. Stevens has a very interesting article about Channel Island surnames in the bulletin of the CHANNEL ISLAND FAMILY HISTORY SOCIETY, No. 17, Winter 1982, 1983.

Lacking in this index are the names of contributors, which are noted in parentheses in the main portion of the book.

In regard to Mc and Mac surnames, some in this book have not been differenciated; the reader will have to check on the pages indicated.

READER! Please note that indexed names can occur two or more times on one page.

Surnames in this index preceded by an asterisk (*) mean that one or more of that name in this book will have a Canadian connection. Others not marked may also have lines to Canada.

FOLLET-226,316,603

Heredity is that marvelous concept that allows you to share the blame!

www.ingramcontent.com/pod-product-compliance
Lightning Source LLC
Chambersburg PA
CBHW072057040426
42334CB00040B/1290

* 9 7 8 1 5 5 6 1 3 6 1 8 4 *